WHAT DO CHILDREN AND YOUNG ADULTS

READ NEXT?

A Reader's Guide to
Fiction and Nonfiction
for Children
and Young Adults

ISSN 1540-5060

WHAT DO CHILDREN AND YOUNG ADULTS

READ NEXT?

A Reader's Guide to Fiction and Nonfiction for Children and Young Adults

BETTY CARTER
PAM SPENCER HOLLEY

GALE
CENGAGE Learning

Detroit • New York • San Francisco • New Haven, Conn • Waterville, Maine • London

What Do Children and Young Adults Read Next? 2009-2011

Project Editors: Dana Ferguson, Michelle Kazensky

Editorial: Matthew Derda and Reed Kalso

Composition and Electronic Prepress: Gary Leach, Evi Seoud

Manufacturing: Rita Wimberley

For product information and technology assistance, contact us at
Gale Customer Support, 1-800-877-4253.
For permission to use material from this text or product,
submit all requests online at **www.cengage.com/permissions.**
Further permissions questions can be emailed to
permissionrequest@cengage.com

While every effort has been made to ensure the reliability of the information presented in this publication, Gale, a part of Cengage Learning, does not guarantee the accuracy of the data contained herein. Gale accepts no payment for listing; and inclusion in the publication of any organization, agency, institution, publication, service, or individual does not imply endorsement of the editors or publisher. Errors brought to the attention of the publisher and verified to the satisfaction of the publisher will be corrected in future editions.

Gale
27500 Drake Rd.
Farmington Hills, MI, 48331-3535

LIBRARY OF CONGRESS CONTROL NUMBER 2002214329
ISBN-13: 978-1-4144-9039-7
ISBN-10: 1-4144-9039-9

ISSN: 1540-5060

Printed in Mexico
1 2 3 4 5 6 7 16 15 14 13 12

Contents

Introduction

Thousands of books aimed at children and young adults are published each year, and with that number growing every year, parents and their children often wonder, "What do I read next?" *What Do Children and Young Adults Read Next? 2009-2011* is a reader's advisory tool designed to match readers from preschool through high school with books that reflect their interests and concerns. It guides both reluctant and avid readers to new authors and new titles for further reading. *What Do Children and Young Adults Read Next? 2009-2011* allows readers quick and easy access to specific information on recent titles, both fiction and nonfiction. In addition, each entry provides alternate reading selections, giving children, parents and librarians the answer to the frequently-asked question: "What do I read next?"

Highlights

- Compiled by Betty Carter and Pam Spencer Holley, both experts in the field of juvenile and young adult literature.

- Overview essays describe a retrospective of trends and events in young peoples' literature over the last three years.

- "Other books you might like" included in each entry, leads to the exploration of additional authors or titles.

- Ten indexes help locate specific titles or offer suggestions for reading in favorite time periods or geographic locales, about special subjects or characters, or for a particular award winner.

- All authors and titles listed in entries under "Other books by the author" and "Other books you might like" are indexed, allowing easy access to thousands of books recommended for further reading.

Details on 1,200 Titles

What Do Children and Young Adults Read Next? 2009-2011 contains entries for 1,200 books published between 2009-2011 aimed at young readers. Titles have been selected on the basis of their currency, appeal to readers, and literary merit. The entries are listed alphabetically by author. Books by authors with more than one entry are then subarranged by title. The following information is provided where applicable:

- **Author or editor's name:** Co-authors, co-editors, translators illustrators, and photographers are also listed where applicable.

- **Book title.**

- **Name of publisher, publication date, and place of publication.**

- **Series name.**

- **Age Range:** Indicates the age levels for which the title is best suited.

- **Subject(s):** Gives the subject matter covered by the title.

- **Major character(s):** Names and brief descriptions of the characters featured in the title.

- **Time period(s):** Tells when the story takes place.

- **Locale(s):** Tells where the story takes place.

- **What the book is about:** A brief plot summary.

- **Where it's reviewed:** Citations to reviews of the book, including the source of the review, date of the source, and the page on which the review appears. Included are reviews from sources such as *Booklist* and *Publishers Weekly*.

- **Other books by the author:** Titles and publication dates of other books the author has written, useful for those wanting to read more by a particular author.

- **Other books you might like:** Titles by other authors

written on a similar theme or in a similar style. These titles further the reader's exploration of the genre.

Indexes Answer Readers' Questions

The ten indexes in *What Do Children and Young Adults Read Next? 2009-2011* used separately or in conjunction with each other, create many pathways to the featured titles, answering general questions or locating specific titles. For example:

"Are there any new titles in the Diary of a Wimpy Kid series?"

The SERIES INDEX lists entries by the name of the series of which they are a part.

"I would like to read a book that has won an award recently."

The AWARDS INDEX lists awards given in the field of children and young adult literature.

"Do you know of any young adult stories set during the 18th century?"

The TIME PERIOD INDEX is a chronological listing of the time settings in which the main entry titles take place.

"I'm looking for a story set in an alternate universe."

The GEOGRAPHIC INDEX lists titles by their locale. This can help readers pinpoint an area in which they may have a particular interest, such as their hometown, another country, or even space.

"My daughter needs a book about life in the military"

The SUBJECT INDEX is an alphabetical listing of all the subjects covered by the main entry titles. Topics include such things as fiction genres (e.g. Fantasy, Ghost Stories, Amateur Detective Stories), life and relationships (e.g. Self-Perception, Friendship, School Life), and subjects of interest to today's children and young adults (e.g. Sports, Clothes, Vampires).

"Do you have any books with a character whose name is the same as mine?"

The CHARACTER NAME INDEX lists the major characters named in the entries. This can help readers who remember some information about a book, but not an author or title.

"What books are available that feature ducks?"

The CHARACTER DESCRIPTION INDEX identifies the major characters by occupation (e.g. Beekeeper, Police Officer) or persona (e.g. Toy, Dog).

"Which picture books are illustrated by Jerry Pinkney?"

The ILLUSTRATOR INDEX is an alphabetical listing of the illustrators of the main entry titles.

"What has Donna Jo Napoli written recently?"

The AUTHOR INDEX contains the names of all authors featured in the entries and those listed under "Other books you might like."

"I want to read a book that's similar to the Harry Potter books."

The TITLE INDEX includes all main entry titles and all titles recommended under "Other books by the author" and "Other books you might like" in one alphabetical listing. Thus a reader can find a specific title, new or old, then go to that entry to find out what new titles are similar.

The indexes can also be used to narrow down or broaden choices. A reader interested in stories set in England during World War II would consult the SUBJECT, and GEOGRAPHIC indexes to see which titles appear in both. Someone interested in detective stories set during the 1930s could compare titles in the TIME PERIOD and CHARACTER DESCRIPTION indexes. And with the AUTHOR and TITLE indexes, which include all books listed under "Other books by the author" and "Other books you might like," it is easy to compile an extensive list of titles for further reading, not only with the titles recommended in a main entry, but also by seeing other titles to which the main entry or its recommended titles are similar.

About the Contributors

Betty Carter (Children): Betty is a former New Orleans, Louisiana reading teacher; Houston, Texas school librarian; and Texas Woman's University professor of children's and young adult literature. She's been a member of the Newbery Committee, which annually selects the most distinguished book in children's literature and the Sibert Committee, which annually selects the most outstanding informational book in children's literature. She's also been a juror and chair of the Boston Globe-Horn Book Award and is a past coordinator of the Texas Bluebonnet Committee which oversees the selection and use of an annual reading list of books read by over 2,000 school children in Texas. With Richard Abrahamson, Betty co-authored, *Nonfiction for Young Adults: from Delight to Wisdom*. She presently works as a reviewer for *The Horn Book Magazine*.

Pam Spencer Holley (Young Adults): Pam, coordinator and author of *What Do Young Adults Read Next?*, volumes 1-6, and retired coordinator of library services for the Fairfax County Public schools in Virginia, is a recognized expert in young adult literature. Elected to the Margaret A. Edwards Award Committee by the Young Adult Library Services Association of the American Library Association, she also served on their Alex Award Task Force, a committee that annually selects the top adult books for young adults. She chaired the 2004 Michael L. Printz Award Committee which selects the finest book for young adults, based solely on literary quality, as well as the 2009 Odyssey Award that annually selects the best audiobook for children or young adults. She is a past-president of the Young Adult Library Services Association, a division of the American Library Association, and remains active in that division. She served as a past chair of the column "Adult Books for Young Adults" for *School Library Journal*, authored the audiobooks column "Audiobooks, It Is!" for *Voice of Youth Advocates*, better known as *VOYA*, and currently reviews audiobooks for *Booklist* magazine. She's listed in *Who's Who in America*, as well as *Who's Who among American Women*. Currently she serves as the chair of the Board of Trustees for the Eastern Shore of Virginia Public Library and is secretary of their Library Foundation. Recently she edited *Quick and Popular Reads for Teens* [ALA Editions, 2009] and co-wrote *Annotated Books Lists for Every Teen Reader* [Neal-Schuman, 2010].

Also Available Online

The entries in this book can also be found online in Gale's *Books & Authors* database. This electronic product encompasses over 172,700 books, including genre fiction, mainstream fiction, and nonfiction. All the books included in the online version are hand-picked by librarians or other experts, award winners, or appear on bestseller lists. The user-friendly functionality allows users to refine their search-ing by using several criteria, while making it easy to identify similar titles for further research and reading. *Books & Authors* is updated with new information weekly. For more information about *Books & Authors*, please visit Gale online at gale.cengage.com.

Suggestions Are Welcome

The editors welcome any comments and suggestions for enhancing and improving *What Do Children and Young Adults Read Next? 2009-2011* Please address correspondence to the Editors, *What Do Children and Young Adults Read Next? 2009-2011*, at the following address:

Gale Group
27500 Drake Rd.
Farmington Hills, MI 48331-3535
Phone: 248-699-GALE
Toll-free: 800-347-GALE
Fax: 248-699-8054

Children's Fiction Highlights in Children's Literature: 2009 to 2011
by
Betty Carter

To paraphrase Mark Twain, the death of children's literature has been greatly exaggerated. Its demise centers around two discussions: the decline of picture book sales and the emergence of digital technology. Despite these trends, there are several bright notes on the children's publishing scene that we'll discuss below.

Let's go back twenty years to the last big heyday in children's publishing. In *Minders of Make-Believe: Idealists, Entrepreneurs and the Shaping of American Children's Culture*, author Leonard S. Marcus writes: "During the 1990s, children's book publishing became the fastest-growing area of the American publishing industry. In 1994 an estimated five thousand titles were published, more than double the number of a decade earlier. The sheer magnitude of the sector's latest growth spurt thrust the field into the media spotlight as never before. Children's literature was becoming impossible to ignore" (2008, pp. 303-304).

Historically, growth in publishing is cylindrical, and this trend of the 1990s was not sustained throughout the first decade of the 21st century. Bookstores (particularly independent children's ones) were hard hit by the recession; even large brick and mortar stores, such as Borders, were not immune. Still, blockbuster children's titles, beginning most notably with the Harry Potter books (harbingers not only of sales but also of content and length), but also including offerings such as the *Diary of a Wimpy Kid*, often outsold adult titles. During this time libraries enjoyed a renaissance, but often their budgets were cut, thereby impacting sales. Publishers responded by reducing the number of titles they released. In 2012, Jean Feiwel, senior vice president and publisher director of Macmillan Children's Book Group, notes, "The size of the publishers' lists has come down" (Roback, 2012).

And those pared-down lists have changed. Not only are fewer picture books being published, but the new offerings are not necessarily the books adults fondly remember from their own childhoods. Many are splashier, have a stronger role for illustrations, and are shorter. Addressing the latter point on a November 2, 2011, post on the blog "Read Roger" (http://www.hbook.com/blogs/

readroger), Linda Crotta Brennan writes: "When I started in this business twenty plus years ago, the average length of a picture book was 1200 words. And it was common to have picture books of over 1500 words…Jennifer Laughran, agent at the Andrea Brown Literary recently wrote on her blog that 300-550 words is the 'sweet spot' for picture books."

About the same time, Anita Silvey brought up the same point, indicating that backlist picture books were outselling frontlist titles, and suggests that perhaps length (and the subsequent lure of repeated readings) may contribute to the situation (Silvey, 2008). In addition, Silvey posits that these shorter books appeal to younger children, and that parents of youngsters in grades one through three may naturally turn to chapter books for those wishing a longer story. This conclusion is in direct contrast to a controversial *New York Times* article (Bosman, 2010) that suggests parents purchasing chapter books for their primary grade youngsters are pushing their children to read at an earlier age due to testing pressures in the schools.

Still, veteran publisher and editor Nancy Paulsen proudly declared in 2012: "The picture book is alive and well" (Roback 2012). Couple that optimism with "The Sign on Sendak's Door," a proclamation by authors and illustrators who believe in the magic of both picture books and children's literature. Their plea for books that are "fresh, honest, piquant, and beautiful" must be met with gatekeepers who honor the same. As Roger Sutton, Editor In Chief of the *Horn Book Magazine*, comments: "But we—librarians, teachers, parents—have to do our part. We may pride ourselves on our ability to find for a young reader 'another one just like it!' but if we stop there we've left the job half done. If we want artists and writers to take risks, and publishers to do the same, we have to read, and promote reading, with the same spirit" (Sutton 2011).

That spirit may be inspiring adult gatekeepers to purchase and recommend comic books for young readers (Gutierrez 2009). Now a staple in young adult collections, the 21st century has not only seen comics enjoy popularity but also critical acclaim for kindergarten, primary, and middle grade kids. The best of these combine the familiar illustrations from picture books (remember, picture books are a youngster's first introduction to books) with different kinds of narration, giving readers both something old and something new.

In a number of ways, comics, or graphic novels, work particularly well for beginning readers. The illustrations carry the trajectory of the story for those who may not know all the words (or for those who want to retell a story they've just heard—a solid step towards becoming independent readers) and the conversation balloons and text boxes divide the reading process into small segments.

In 2008 the Geisel Award committee, a group within the American Library Association charged with annually selecting "the most distinguished American book for beginning readers published in English in the United States during the previous year" ((Thedor Seuss) Geisel Award, 2012) smartly recognized and honored these points. That year, *There Is a Bird on Your Head!* (Willems 2007), one of the initial books by Mo Willems in the Elephant and Piggie series, received the coveted award. Here two disparate friends, perky Piggie and glum Gerald the elephant, must deal with birds nesting on Gerald's head. Naturally Piggie thinks this situation is full of wonder and surprise; Gerald's not so sure. The entire text is composed of color-coded speech balloons, letting young readers know who is saying what and thus easing their reading process. In addition, font size varies, indicating the intensity of tone from a whisper to a shout creating a feature that aids beginning readers in becoming more animated as they encounter words and sentences. These irrepressible heroes and winning format have appeared on the Geisel list three more times, again receiving the award in 2009 for *Are You Ready to Play Outside?* (Willems 2008), and as honor citations in 2011 for *We Are in a Book!* (Willems 2010) and in 2012 for *I Broke My Trunk!* (Willems 2011).

Genius though he is, Williams is not the only graphic novelist receiving acclaim within this genre for beginning readers. Eleanor Davis's *Stinky* (Davis 2008) received a Geisel Honor citation in 2009. In a smart role reversal, Davis introduces a swamp monster afraid of children and Stinky's point of view (eating cake is repulsive but feasting on pickled onions a gourmet treat) affords a clever twist within a humorous story. Brother and sister, Benny and Penny, appearing in their second graphic novel, *Benny and Penny and the Big No-No!* (Hayes 2010), also nabbed a Giesel honor citation in 2011.

Often graphic novels for middle-grade readers are relegated to reluctant readers and not considered "really reading" by parents and teachers. Dismiss this idea. The best books in this format offer characteristics that greatly influence both tone and readability. Graphic novels for middle graders tend not to be daunting, but this characteristic is one among many that leads to their success. First of all they must have a good story, and the

two that have received the greatest critical acclaim in the past couple of years do.

Raina Telgemier (who was previously best known for adapting Ann Martin's The Baby-sitter's Club series into graphic novels) invites readers into her own life, beginning with a fall in the sixth grade that results in major dental surgery, braces, embarrassing headgear, false teeth, and implants. *Smile* continues her saga through high school. The humorous illustrations ameliorate the agonizing dental procedures and allow those universal crises of pre-adolescence and adolescence with mean girls, family, and school to emerge within a very personal story. *Smile* deservingly received an honor citation from the 2010 Boston Globe Horn Book Award Committee (Boston Globe Horn Book, 2012.)

Matt Phelan, winner of the Scott O'Dell Award for Historical Fiction (Scott O'Dell Award 2012) for *The Storm in the Barn* (2009), uses illustrations in his graphic novel to provide much of the historical setting of the Dust Bowl. Although there is much historical fiction published for middle grade readers, it fails to reach readers because often children view these books as just another history lesson. Such is not the case with *The Storm in the Barn*.

A failed attempt to get a comic strip started in 2004 propelled Jeff Kinney to pen an interesting merger between comic strip and episodic novel on the website Funbrain (2012). The conglomerate of these online creations became the basis for the first three books in the Wimpy Kid series in which self-depreciating Greg Heffley tells readers, in direct address, his comical ups and downs in middle school. His diary (a name he rejects, claiming that he's not going to write "Dear Diary," but will keep a journal) is a faux replication complete with lined paper, hand-lettered text, and a generous amount of black and white cartoon art. Imitators followed, such as Rachel Renee Russell in her three-book (so far) Dork Diary (2009) series aimed at girls.

Following a different path, syndicated comic strip creator Lincoln Peirce brought his main character, Nate, to hardcover fame, beginning with *Big Nate: In a Class by Himself* (2010.) When asked how he decides to include illustrations, Peirce responds: "Sometimes it's very obvious, because the text will indicate very clearly that a drawing, or series of drawings, is needed in a certain spot. I always try to err on the side of providing more rather than fewer visuals. I try to put myself in a 10-year-old reader's shoes: Would I rather read about Nate hitting someone in the face with a pie, or see a picture of it? In a lot of cases, I know exactly where I want to place the drawings from the moment I write the text" (Sutton 2010.) This combination of text and illustrations has its roots in both picturestory books and comic strips, and for those kids who have trouble 'getting a picture in my mind of what the author's saying' may prove an extra boost.

How popular are these novels in cartoon format? According to Jason Wells, Executive Director, Publicity and

Marketing for Abrams Books for Young Readers, the first printing of *Diary of a Wimpy Kid* in 2007 was 20,000 copies. By the time the seventh book in the series, *Diary of a Wimpy Kid: Cabin Fever*, came out in 2011, the print run increased to six million copies (Wells, 2011).

Which brings us to another point: Books in series are a huge part of children's reading. This trend is not new. Series ranging from the Horatio Alger Books to the Boxcar Children, and including Elsie Dinsmore, the Hardy Boys, Nancy Drew, and Sweet Valley High, have existed for well over a century. These books in series are most often termed sub-literature, but many fine, multi-layered books exist in series: Phillip Pullman's His Dark Materials, C. S. Lewis's The Chronicles of Narnia, and Nancy Springer's Enola Holmes Mysteries.

Roger Sutton traces the latest burst of series books to the popularity of Harry Potter (Sutton, 2010). In 2010 Sutton examined the books reviewed (all children's and young adult books from publishers listed in Literary Marketplace) in *The Horn Book Magazine*'s sister publication, *The Horn Book Guide*. The numbers are astounding. In 1998 *The Horn Book Guide* reviewed 175 fiction books in series. By 2010 that number had jumped to 520, or in Sutton's words, "a whopping 40% of all fiction reviewed" (Sutton, 2010). The bulk of those series books were fantasy; fiction as a published form almost doubled, increasing from 18% of all books reviewed in *The Horn Book Guide* in 1998 to 33% in 2010.

As an interesting note, it is in the area of children's nonfiction that currently appears to represent the most change in the past few years. In the lead article for an issue of *The Horn Book Magazine* devoted exclusively to nonfiction, Kathleen Isaacs (Isaacs 2011) posits that design, subject matter, documentation, and presentation, from narrative nonfiction to dual (employing both story narrative and exposition) story lines to poetry, have all ushered in a golden age of nonfiction. (Barbara Bader puts these comments in historical perspective in a later *Horn Book* article, "Nonfiction: What's Really New and Different—and What Isn't" (Bader 2011).

Kicking up quite a stir, author and editor Marc Aronson brings another view about nonfiction to the table: that nonfiction writers "set out to discover new knowledge" (Aronson 2011, p. 57) rather than "translate" from existing sources for children. Perhaps, but nonfiction is not a zero sum game. There are speculators, such as Aronson; and translators; and authors, such as Russell Freedman, who do both (Freedman, 2011). The result is fine books with distinct points of view, such Freedman's *Lafayette and the American Revolution* or Kadir Nelson's *Heart and Soul: The Story of America and African Americans*. Strong books, with strong points of view, speak to strong readers with inquiring minds. Who could hope for more?

The second big question in today's children's literature is: What is the role of digital publishing? The answer is: We don't know. At the moment, electronic formats are trickling down. First there are adult crossover titles, such as *The Hunger Games* (Collins 2008) that are being downloaded and supposedly read by adults and young adults. Then middle-grade readers may imitate their elders by reading related electronic book versions such as *Gregor the Overlander* (Collins 2003) by the same authors their older siblings or parents are reading.

But what about younger children? For many, the book shelf is just an extension of the toy shelf and portable applications such as *Curious George's Dictionary* (2009) can provide much diversion when sitting in traffic about twenty minutes after nap time should begin. Here, a forward-thinking adult can pass a well-loaded portable electronic device to the fussy toddler and enjoy a small respite. But for now, real reading, that time when adults and young children share picture books, seems to come through "dead tree" books (Richtel and Bosman 2011). There is no way to know what the future will hold, a dilemma that publishers and permissions departments share. For now, to repeat Nancy Paulsen's optimistic statement, "The picture book format is alive and well" (Roback 2012).

This essay began with Leonard S. Marcus's description of the publishing boon in the 1990s. Beyond publishing figures, one of the sources of evidence he gave for this spurt was the reintroduction of Children's Books in the National Book Awards (Marcus 2008). Let's end with another optimistic note from the first decade of the 21st century. In 2008, the Children's Book Council and the Library of Congress Center for the Book created a National Ambassador for Young People's Literature to "raise the awareness for the importance of young people's literature as it relates to lifelong literacy, education and the development and betterment of the lives of young people" (National Ambassador for Young People's Literature, 2012). Since then, authors Jon Scieszka and Katherine Paterson, have served their two-year terms with distinction. The present Ambassador, Walter Dean Myers, simply states a strong vision for the future: "Reading is not optional" (National Ambassador for Young People 2012).

Authors in Memoriam

2009

Esther Hautzig, best known for her fictionalized memoir, *The Endless Steppe*, but also recognized as a translator, died on November 1.

Beth Krush, who illustrated the 1957 Newbery Award Book, *Miracles on Maple Hill*, died at the age of 90.

Karla Kuskin, distinguished as an author and illustrator, died at the age of 77.

Blair Lent, who received the 1973 Randolph Caldecott Medal for illustrating *The Funny Little Woman*, died at the age of 80.

Eden Ross Lipson, *New York Times Book Review*

Children's Editor and author of *Applesauce Season*, died at the age of 66.

Milton Meltzer, the author of more than one hundred nonfiction books and 2001 recipient of the Laura Ingalls Wilder Medal, died at the age of 94.

2010

Lucille Clifton, a former poet laureate of Maryland and recipient of the Coretta Scott King Award in 1984 for *Everett Anderson's Good-bye*, was 73 when she died.

Eleanor Coerr, best known for *Sadako and the Thousand Cranes*, written in 1977 and adapted in 1993 with illustrations by Ed Young, was 88 when she died.

Sid Fleischman, screenwriter, magician, and children's book author who received the Newbery Medal for *The Whipping Boy* in 1987, died in California, at the age of 90.

Stuart Hample, who created children's books, plays, and cartoons as Stoo Hample, died in New York City New York City at the age of 84.

Eva Ibbotson, born in Australia, received the Nestle Smarties Prize Gold Medallion 2001 for *Journey to the River Sea* in 2001 and died at her home in England at the age of 85.

Patricia Lauber, most remembered as an author of more than 125 nonfiction books, including the 1987 Newbery Honor, *Volcano: The Eruption and Healing of Mount St. Helens*, died at the age of 86.

William Mayne, who received the Carnegie Medal in 1957 for *A Grass Rope*, died in England when he was 82.

Ruth Park, whose book *Playing Beatie Bow* was honored as the 1981 Children's Book of the Year in Australia, died in Sydney at the age of 93.

John Schoenherr, illustrator of *Owl Moon* and recipient of the 1987 Caldecott Award, died at the age of 74.

Joan Steiner, who used found objects to create Look-Alikes series, died at her home in Claverack, New York on September 8.

Patricia Wrightson, an author of fantasy and recipient of the Hans Christian Aandersen Award in 1986, died in her native Australia at the age of 88.

2011

Florence Parry Heide, author of more than one hundred books and best known for *The Shrinking of Treehorn*, died at the age of 92.

Russell Hoban, best known as the author of the Frances Books (*Bedtime for Frances*, for example) died at the age of 86.

Brian Jacques, author of the Redwall Series, died in his native England at the age of 71.

Dick King-Smith, author of *Babe: The Gallant Pig* as well as many other children's books, was 88 when he died.

Steven Kroll, who wrote more than ninety books for children, including *Pooch on the Loose and Barbarians*, was 69 when he died in New York.

Georgess McHargue, author of 35 children's books such as *Stoneflight* and *The Beasts of Never*, died at the age of seventy.

Janet Schulman, pioneering editor and author of the critically acclaimed *Pale Male: Citizen Hawk of New York*, died in New York City at the age of 77.

William Sleator, best known for writing young adult books but remember by children for the chilling *Among the Dolls*, died at the age of 66.

George Edward Stanley, who wrote a number of books for children and young adults and received the 2010 Oklahoma Center of the Book Award for *Night Fires*, died at the age of 68.

Simms Taback, author of the 2000 Caldecott Award Book *Joseph had a Little Overcoat*, died at the age of 79.

Often children's books are in production when their authors die, such as Sid Fleischman's *Sir Charlie Chaplin, the Funniest Man in the World*; Janet Schulman's *Ten Easter Egg Hunters*; and Diana Wynne Jones's *Earwig and the Witch*. Occasionally, an author's estate will hire other writers to continue a successful series, as is the case for Gertrude Chandler Warner's Boxcar Series (*The Clue in the Recycling Bin*, the 136th entry in the series and published 32 years after her death in 1979, for example.)

In other cases, older manuscripts and little known publications are found and published. *The Bippolo Seed and Other Lost Stories* by Dr. Seuss is one such example. Seuss scholar Charles Cohen examined *Redbook Magazine* from 1950-1951 and found seven stories never published outside the magazine, which he reintroduces to young readers. Yes, there are a few anachronisms ("'Good gracious!' I gasped. 'How the news gets around!/And steak so expensive! A dollar a pound!'", p. 52) but the familiar rhyme schemes and newly colorized illustrations feel right at home for fans of the good doctor.

Leave it to "Katherine the Great" (as Kathleen Horning refers to her in a February 2010 issue of *School Library Journal*) Paterson and her husband, John, to uncover a true gem in the children's literature archives. The two took Eden Philllpott's 1910 modern fantasy, *The Flint Heart*, and a hundred years later abridged it for today's readers. The story, following a traditional and satisfying structure of two children facing three trials to conquer evil, receives a light and pared down narration that contrasts to Phillpott's wordy and didactic one. John Rocco's illustrations help create an inviting design. This is a book that not only looks beautiful but also reads well. And sometimes a deceased author's archives yield strong offerings. Such is the case with the late Shel Silverstein's *Every Thing On It*, published posthumously in 2011. The bittersweet first poem ("Although I can not see your face/As you flip through these poems awhile", p. 9) opens a book with all the energy and humor, both in the loose illustrations and short poems, that children have come to expect from this beloved poet.

Books into Movies

Beloved children's books are often the raw materials for movies, especially those aimed at a family audience. Typically such films come from novels, but according to Rachel Deal in a 2009 *Publishers Weekly* article, the recent success of translating picture books into film (See *Where the Wild Things Are* and *Cloudy with a Chance of Meatballs* below—but omit *Mars Needs Moms*, which did not enjoy commercial success) has led to numerous options for future films based on picture books. She mentions Dr. Seuss's *The Lorax*, which will reach the big screen in 2012, but others, such as David Small's *Fenwick's Suit*, have been optioned but not yet produced. As Deal concludes, some agents are leery about mucking around with classics, but are still on the lookout for possibilities, and "if you can tease a story out of it, nothing may be off limits" (Deal, 2009, p. 6).

In a January 29, 2012, post on his blog "Collecting Children's Books", Peter D. Sieruta noted an unusual characteristic of the 2012 Academy Award nominees. For the first time, two films based on children's/young adult books (*Hugo* and *War Horse*) were also nominated for "Best Picture." Few such films have reached this honor (and Sierruta lists those that have), but never before have two films based on children's/young adult books been nominated in a single year.

Capitalizing on the popularity of the movie, authors and publishers will produce books that either capture the new, adapted story or concentrate on the making of the film. Such books are indicated below. *The Hugo Movie Companion* by Brian Selznick is the best all-around making-of-the-movie-book for children and the gold standard against which others should be judged.

From 2009 through 2011 the following movies were adapted from, or loosely based on, children's books.

2009

Cloudy with a Chance of Meatballs, an animated film with voice work by Bill Hader, Anna Faris, Neil Patrick Harris, and James Caan, bears only a slight resemblance to beloved picture book classic written by Judi Barrett, illustrated by Ron Barrett, and originally published in 1978. Movie tie-in: Deutsch, Stacia and Rhody Cohan. (2009) *Cloudy with a Chance of Meatballs Junior Novelization*. New York: Simon & Schuster.

Coraline, starring Dakota Fanning as the titular Corlaine, is based on the book (and subsequent graphic novel) of the same name by Neil Gaiman. Movie Tie-in: Jones, Stephen. (2009) *Coraline: A Visual Companion*. New York: It Books.

The Fantastic Mr. Fox, adapted from the 1970 Roald Dahl novel of the same name, is animated and features the voices of George Clooney, Meryl Streep, Jason Schwartzman, and Bill Murray.

Inkheart, starring Brendon Fraser (as Mortimer Fokhart), Paul Bettany, Helen Mirren, and Andy Serkis. The movie is based on Cornelia Funke's book of the same name, published in the United States in 2003.

Race to Witch Mountain, starring Dwayne Johnson, Anna Sophia Potts, and Alexander Ludwig is based on the 1968 novel, *Escape to Witch Mountain* by Alexander Key. This live-action movie is the second such production, the first premiering in 1975. Movie Tie-in: Ponti, James. (2009) *Race to Witch Mountain: The Junior Novel*. New York: Disney.

Where The Wild Things Are, adapted from Maruice Sendak's 1963 Caldecott book of the same name, stars Max Records as the main character, also named Max. The movie combines live action with computer-generated images. Movie Tie-in: Bersche Barb. (2009) *Where The Wild Things Are: The Movie Storybook*. New York: HarperCollins.

2010

Alice in Wonderland, the first fantasy written entirely for children's enjoyment, receives the Tim Burton treatment in this live action/computer animated film starring Johnny Depp, Mia Wiskowska, Helen Bonham Carter, and Anne Hathaway. The film received Academy Awards for Best Art Direction and Best Costume Design.

Curious George 2: Follow That Monkey! is based on the popular and beloved Curious George books by Margaret and H. A. Rey. The animated, musical film was not released in theaters, but is available on DVD. Frank Welker provides the voice for Curious George.

Diary of a Wimpy Kid, based on the first book in the Wimpy Kid series by Jeff Kinney, stars Zachary Gordon as Greg Heffley. He reprises that role in the sequel, *Diary of a Wimpy Kid 2* released in 2011. Movie Tie-in: Kinney, Jeff. (2011) *The Wimpy Kid Movie Diary*. New York: Amulet.

How to Train Your Dragon, a 3D computer animated movie, was nominated for an Academy Award in the category of Best Animated Film. It is based on the 2003 novel, *How to Train Your Dragon*. A sequel is projected for release in 2013.

Legend of the Guardians: The Owls of Ga'Hoole, based on the Legend of the Guardians series written by Kathryn Lasky, is an animated film with voice work by, among others, Helen Mirren, Sam Neil, and Geoffrey Rush.

Nanny McPhee Returns is a sequel to *Nanny McPhee* released in 2005. The latter is based on the first of the Nurse Matilda Books (by Christianna Brand and illustrated by Edward Ardizonne) while *Nanny McPhee Returns* is based on the second in the trilogy. Emma Thompson wrote the screenplay and stars and Nanny McPhee. Movie Tie-in: Thompson, Emma. (2010) *Nanny McPhee Returns*. New York: Bloomsbury.

Ramona and Beezus, based on the eight Ramona novels (beginning with Beezus and Ramona first published in 1955) by Beverly Cleary, stars Joey L. King as Ramona Quimby and Selena Gomez as her big sister Ramona.

Shrek Forever: The Final Chapter serves as a prequel to *Shrek*, which was based on the book of the same title by William Steig. The movie is computer animated (as have been the others in the series) and Shrek is voiced by Mike Myers, Donkey by Eddie Murphy, and Princess Fiona by Cameron Diaz. Movie Tie-in: Alexander, Lauren. (2010) *Shrek Forever: The Novel*. New York: Little Brown.

The Voyage of the Dawn Treader is the third movie in the Chronicles of Narnia series (following *The Lion, the Witch and the Wardrobe* and *Prince Caspian*), and based on the third book in the literary series of the same title, written by C. S. Lewis in 1950. The movie was produced in 3D as well as a more widely available 2D format.

2011

The Adventures of Tintin is based on the comic book series that was published for approximately 45 years and written by the Belgian author Herge, a pen name for Georges Remi. Jamie Bell stars as the intrepid reporter Tintin. The movie has been nominated for an Academy Award for Best Original Score. Movie Tie-in: Irvine, Alexander. (2011) *The Adventures of Tintin: A Novel*. New York: Little Brown.

Hugo, a 3D film based on the 2008 Caldecott Medal Winner, *The Invention of Hugo Cabret* by Brian Selznick, is directed by Martin Scorsese. Asa Butterfield stars as Hugo. The movie has been nominated by the Academy Awards for Best Picture. Movie Tie-in: Selznick, Brian. (2011) *The Hugo Movie Companion*. New York: Scholastic.

Judy Moody and the Not Bummer Summer is an original story based on characters created in the Judy Moody and Stink books by Megan McDonald. This live action movie stars Jordana Beatty as third grader Judy. Movie Tie-ins: MaDonald, Megan. (2011) *Judy Moody and the Not Bummer Summer*. Cambridge, Candlewick. McDonald, Megan. (2011) *Judy Moody Goes to Hollywood*. Cambridge: Candlewick.

Mars Needs Moms is a motion captured animation movie based on the book of the same name by Berkley Breathed. Seth Green stars as Milo and Joan Cusak as his mother captured by Martians.

Mr. Popper's Penguins is a live action movie starring Jim Carrey and Angela Landsbury. It is loosely, very loosely, based on the 1939 Newbery Honor book of the same name and written by Richard Atwater.

Professional Resources

A number of books for adults interested in children and their literature have been published in the past three years. Bibliographic information for the best of these is found below:

Baxter, Kathleen A., and Marcia Agnes Kochel. (2010) *Gotcha Again for Guys! More Nonfiction Books to Get Boys Excited about Reading*. Santa Barbara, California: Libraries Unlimited.

Bird, Elizabeth. (2009) *Children's Literature Gems: Choosing and Using Them in Your Library Career*. Chicago: American Library Association.

Hamilton, Virginia. (2010) *Virginia Hamilton: Speeches, Essays, and Conversations*. New York: Blue Sky/Scholastic.

Horning, Kathleen T. (2010) *From Cover to Cover: Evaluating and Reviewing Children's Books*. New York: HarperCollins.

Juster, Norton. (2011) *The Annotated Phantom Tollbooth*. Illustrated by Jules Feiffer; annotated by Leonard S. Marcus. New York: Knopf.

Maguire, Gregory. (2009) *Making Mischief: A Maurice Sendak Appreciation*. New York: Morrow/HarperCollins.

McClosky, Jane (2011) *Robert McCloskey: A Private Life in Words and Pictures*. Kittery Point, Me.: Seapoint.

McClure, Wendy. (2011) *The Wilder Life: My Adventures in the Lost World of Little House on the Prairie*. New York: Riverhead.

The Newbery and Caldecott Awards: A Guide to the Medal and Honor Books. (2011) Chicago: American Library Association.

Reid, Rob. (2009) *Rob Reid's Read-Alouds: Selections for Children and Teens*. Chicago: American Library Association.

Reid, Rob. (2010) *Reid's Read-Alouds 2: Modern-Day Classics from C. S. Lewis to Lemony Snicket*. Chicago: American Library Association.

Sims, Michael. (2011) *The Story of Charlotte's Web: E. B. White's Eccentric Life in Nature and the Birth of An American Classic*. New York: Walker.

Sutton, Roger, and Martha V. Parravano. (2010) *A Family of Readers: The Book Lover's Guide to Children's and Young Adult Literature*. Cambridge, Mass.: Candlewick.

Wolf, Shelby A.; Karen Coats; Patricia Encisco; and Christie A. Jenkins. (2011) *Handbook of Research on Children's and Young Adult Literature*. New York: Routledge.

Works Cited

American Library Association. Association for Library Service for Children. (Thedor Seuss) Geisel Award. (http://www.ala.org/alsc/awardsgrants/bookmedia/geiselaward).

Bader, Barbara. "Nonficiton: What's Really New and What Isn't." *The Horn Book Magazine*, November/December 2011.

Bosman, Julie. "Picture Books no Longer a Staple for Children." New York Times, October 7, 2010. (http://www.nytimes.com).

Carter, Betty. "Interview with Jason Well." 2011.

Deal, Rachel. "Hollywood Takes a Close Look at Picture Books." *Publishers Weekly*, November 16, 2009.

Freedman, Russell. "Letters to the Editor." *The Horn Book Magazine*, May/June 2011.

Gutierrez, Peter. "Good & Plenty." *School Library Journal*, September 2009.

The Horn Book. Boston Globe Horn Book Award. (http://archive.hbook.com/bghb).

Horning, Kathleen T. "Katherine the Great." *School Library Journal*, February 2010.

Isaacs, Kathleen T. "The Facts of the Matter: Children's Nonfiction, From Then to Now." *The Horn Book Magazine*, March/April 2011.

Library of Congress. National Ambassador for Literature for Young People. "Reading is not optional." (http://read.gov/cfb/ambassador).

Marcus, Leonard S.. *Minders of Make-Believe: Idealists, Entrepreneurs and the Shaping of American Children's Culture*. Boston: Houghton Mifflin, 2008

Richtel, Matt and Julie Bosman. (2011) "For Their Children, Many E-Book Fans Insist on Paper." *The New York Times*, November 20, 2011. (http://www.nytimes.com).

Roback, Diane. (2012) "Four Industry Veterans Lay Out Advice at SCBWI." *Publishers Weekly*, February 2, 2012. (http://www.publishersweekly.com).

Silvey, Anita. "Make Way for Picture Books." *School Library Journal*, November 1, 2011.

Scott O'Dell. Scott O'Dell Award. (http://www.scottodell.com).

Sieruta, Peter D. (2012) "A Brunch with Lots of Links." Collecting Children's Books. January 29, 2012. (http://collectingchildrensbooks.blogspot.com).

Sutton, Roger. "Five Questions for Lincoln Peirce." *The Horn Book*, November 2010. (www.hbook.com).

———. "The Sign on Sendak's Door." Read Roger, November 1, 2011. (www.hbook.com).

———. "What Hath Harry Wrought?" (Paper presented as the 2010 Ezra Jack Keats Lecture, Hattiesburg, Mississippi, April 7, 2010).

Children's Titles

1

DAVID A. ADLER
EDWARD MILLER, Illustrator

Money Madness

(New York: Holiday House, 2009)

Story type: Young Readers
Subject(s): Money; History; Learning

Age range(s): 5 - 8+

Summary: In *Money Madness*, author David A. Adler begins to introduce the tricky subject of currency, commerce, and basic finance to young readers. He provides a brief history of currency and explains early systems of bartering and using rocks and feathers before currency was developed. Readers are then introduced to our current forms of currency, including cash, checks, credit cards, and digital payments. Inflation and the value of money are also discussed. Accompanying the text are photos of bills and coins, as well as several pages depicting foreign currency.

Where it's reviewed:
Booklist, April 1, 2009, page 38
Horn Book Magazine, May/June 2009, page 317
Publishers Weekly, January 19, 2009, page 59
School Library Journal, May 2009, page 92

Other books by the same author:
Mystery Math: A First Book of Algebra, 2011
Fractions, Decimals and Percents, 2010
Time Zones, 2010
You Can, Toucan, Math: Word Problem-Solving Fun, 2006

Other books you might like:
Stuart J. Murphy, *Less than Zero*, 2003
Elizabeth Keeler Robinson, *Making Cents: The Nuts and Bolts of Money and a Whole Lot More!*, 2008
David M. Schwartz, *How Much Is a Million?*, 1985
Judith Viorst, *Alexander, Who Used to Be Rich Last Sunday*, 1978

2

ARNOLD ADOFF
R. GREGORY CHRISTIE, Illustrator

Roots and Blues: A Celebration

(New York: Clarion Books, 2011)

Story type: Collection
Subject(s): Poetry; Short stories; African Americans

Age range(s): 9 - 12+

Summary: In this collection of poetry and short prose pieces, children's author Arnold Adoff gives a lesson about the history of blues music and African American culture. The poems in the collection trace African American history back to the time of slavery. The poems express the sounds the slaves heard and the songs they sang. The poems also describe how the blues evolved from the music of slaves into music performed on stage and on the radio. As the poems and prose pieces follow the history of the blues, they give a colorful history of African Americans. The poetry and pose in this collection are accompanied by illustrations by R. Gregory Christie.

Where it's reviewed:
Booklist, February 15, 2011, page 69
Bulletin of the Center for Children's Books, January 2011, page 222
Horn Book Guide, Fall 2011, page 463
Publishers Weekly, November 29, 2010, page 48
School Library Journal, February 2011, page 122

Other books by the same author:
The Basket Counts, 2000
Street Music: City Poems, 1995

Other books you might like:
Julius Lester, *The Blues Singers: Ten Who Rocked the World*, 2001
J. Patrick Lewis, *Black Cat Bone: The Life of Blues Legend Robert Johnson*, 2006
Walter Dean Myers, *Blues Journey*, 2003

3

JON AGEE, Author/Illustrator

Orangutan Tongs: Poems to Tangle Your Tongue

(New York: Disney/Hyperion Books, 2009)

Story type: Collection; Young Readers
Subject(s): Poetry; Rhyme; Humor

Age range(s): 7 - 10+

Summary: *Orangutan Tongs: Poems to Tangle Your Tongue* is a collection of humorous rhymes and tongue-twisters for young readers from author and illustrator Jon Agee. The book contains 34 poems with clever, tricky, and funny plays on words that will trip up any tongue. Agee's vivid, colorful illustrations accompany the rhymes in *Orangutan Tongs*, making the book engaging and captivating for young audiences. The poems vary in level of difficulty, but each piece contains at least one tricky phrase or rhyme. The poems in this collection include "Cranky Oyster" and "Orangutan Tongs." Agee is also the author of *The Retired Kid, Milo's Hat Trick,* and *Who Ordered the Jumbo Shrimp?.*

Where it's reviewed:
Bulletin of the Center for Children's Books, April 2009, page 311
Horn Book Magazine, March/April 2009, page 207
School Library Journal, March 2009, page 131

Other books by the same author:
Smart Feller, Fart Smeller and Other Spoonerisms, 2006
Palindromania!, 2002
Elvis Lives! And Other Anagrams, 2000
Go Hang A Salami! I'm a Lasagna Hog and Other Palindromes, 1991

Other books you might like:
Calef Brown, *Hallowilloween: Nefarious Silliness from Calef Brown*, 2010
Brian P. Cleary, *Six Sheep Sip Thick Shakes: And Other Tricky Tongue Twisters*, 2011
Edward Lear, *The Duck and the Kangaroo*, 2009
Jack Prelutsky, *Be Glad Your Nose Is on Your Face: And Other Poems: Some of the Best of Jack Prelutsky*, 2008
Shel Silverstein, *A Light in the Attic: Special Edition*, 2009

4

ALIKI, Author/Illustrator

Push Button

(New York: Greenwillow Books, 2010)

Subject(s): Children; Toys; Books and reading

Age range(s): 2 - 5+
Time period(s): 21st century; 2010s

Summary: Aliki's *Push Button* charts the experiences of a young boy who loves to push buttons. He spends his days pushing any button he can find, from the clasp of an umbrella to the television set and toaster. When his finger gets sore, the digit is bandaged, and the boy must find some different pastimes.

Where it's reviewed:
Booklist, February 15, 2010, page 77
Horn Book Magazine, July/August 2010, page 84
School Library Journal, April 2010, page 119

Other books by the same author:
Quiet in the Garden, 2009
Ah, Music!, 2003
All by Myself, 2001
Hello! Goodbye!, 1996
I'm Growing, 1991

Other books you might like:
Leonid Gore, *The Wonderful Book*, 2010
David McPhail, *Fix-It*, 1984
Ida Pearle, *A Child's Day: An Alphabet of Play*, 2008
Antoinette Portis, *Not a Box*, 2006
Carmen Tafolla, *What Can You Do with a Rebozo?*, 2008

5

ELANNA ALLEN, Author/Illustrator

Itsy Mitsy Runs Away

(New York: Atheneum Books for Young Readers, 2011)

Story type: Young Readers
Subject(s): Children; Family life; Humor

Age range(s): 5 - 7+
Major character(s): Itsy Mitsy, Girl, Daughter; Dad, Father (of Itsy Mitsy)

Summary: In this picture story from author and illustrator Elanna Allen, Itsy Mitsy is *done* with bedtime. Mitsy, a tiny girl in bright green pajamas, has decided to pack up and move to a place where bedtimes don't exist. As she starts to pack, however, she realizes that running away won't be as easy as she first thought. Her helpful dad keeps reminding her of things she should pack—her stuffed dinosaur, a snack, and her dog. Before long, Mitsy has packed everything, including her house, her yard, and even her dad. Mitsy is finally ready to run away to a place without bedtimes. All that packing sure does make a little girl tired, though.

Where it's reviewed:
Booklist, June 1, 2011, page 96
Horn Book Guide, Fall 2011, page 292
Publishers Weekly, March 21, 2011, page 73
School Library Journal, May 2011, page 71

Other books you might like:
Barbro Lindgren, *Benny's Had Enough!*, 1999
John Segal, *Far Far Away*, 2009
Judy Sierra, *The Sleepy Little Alphabet: A Bedtime Story from Alphabet Town*, 2009
Mathilde Stein, *The Child Cruncher*, 2008

Shelley Moore Thomas, *Good Night, Good Knight*, 2000

6

ZOE B. ALLEY
R.W. ALLEY, Illustrator

There's a Princess in the Palace: Five Classic Tales

(New York: Roaring Brook Press, 2010)

Subject(s): Fairy tales; Royalty; Humor

Age range(s): 6 - 9+

Summary: Author Zoe B. Alley reimagines a series of fairy tales centering on princesses. *There's a Princess in the Palace: Five Classic Tales* includes the legendary stories of Sleeping Beauty, Cinderella, the princess and the pea, Snow White, and the princess and the frog. Each tale is retold with humor and whimsical wordplay, following the princesses on their respective adventures through the worlds of love, family, and identity. *There's a Princess in the Palace* contains illustrations by R.W. Alley.

Where it's reviewed:
Booklist, August 1, 2010, page 51
Horn Book Magazine, September/October 2010, page 102
Publishers Weekly, August 23, 2010, page 46
School Library Journal, September 2010, page 178

Other books by the same author:
There's a Wolf at the Door, 2010

Other books you might like:
Babette Cole, *Prince Cinders*, 1987
Paul Fleischman, *Glass Slipper, Gold Sandal: A Worldwide Cinderella*, 2007
Ellen Jackson, *Cinder Edna*, 1994
Lois Lowry, *The Birthday Ball*, 2010
John Steptoe, *Mufaro's Beautiful Daughters: An African Tale*, 1987

7

JULIA ALVAREZ

Return to Sender

(New York: Knopf Books for Young Readers, 2009)

Subject(s): Family relations; Friendship; Illegal immigrants

Age range(s): 9 - 11+

Major character(s): Tyler, Farmer, Narrator, 13-Year-Old, Student—Middle School; Mari, 13-Year-Old, Student—Middle School, Migrant Worker, Friend (of Tyler), Farmer

Time period(s): 21st century; 2000s

Locale(s): Vermont, United States

Summary: In *Return to Sender*, Tyler's family lives on a farm in Vermont. Recently hurt in a bad accident with a tractor, Tyler's father can no longer help his family keep the farm running smoothly. Desperate for help with the farm work, Tyler's family decides to hire a Mexican family that isn't properly documented. Both families have a lot at stake, but they realize that they need each other. Meanwhile, Tyler becomes interested in Mari, one of the daughters of the immigrant family. Mari has strong ties to her Mexican roots, but she also appreciates her American setting. Tyler and Mari want to be friends, but they are afraid of what everyone will think. They also continue to hope that the farm will be saved and that Mari's illegal immigrant family will not be discovered.

Where it's reviewed:
Bulletin of the Center for Children's Books, February 2009, page 96
Horn Book Guide, Fall 2009, page 362
School Library Journal, February 2009, page 96

Other books by the same author:
Before We Were Free, 2002

Awards the book has won:
Americas Book Award, 2010
Pura Belpre Award: Author Award, 2010

Other books you might like:
Fran Leeper Buss, *Journey of the Sparrows*, 1991
Ann Jaramillo, *La Linea: A Novel*, 2006
Francisco Jimenez, *Breaking Through*, 2001
Ben Mikaelsen, *Sparrow Hawk Red*, 1993
Pam Munoz Ryan, *Esperanza Rising*, 2000

8

GEORGE ANCONA

Ole Flamenco

(New York: Lee & Low Books, 2010)

Subject(s): Dance; Art; History

Age range(s): 9 - 12+
Locale(s): Santa Fe, New Mexico

Summary: Photo essayist and author George Ancona provides young readers with an introduction to the elegance of the flamenco in this book. Ancona begins by taking his audience on a visual journey through the history of the flamenco from its birth in Ancient Rome to its use in the Middle East, in Africa, and in Europe. Ancona also illustrates how the flamenco reflects the powerful emotions of its Roman inventors. In the second half of the book, Ancona shifts his attention to a dance company in Santa Fe, New Mexico, as they prepare for a performance celebrating Spanish culture that will feature the flamenco. He captures the dancers as they practice, and he shows readers the intricacies of the dance.

Where it's reviewed:
Booklist, December 1, 2010, page 41
Bulletin of the Center for Children's Books, January 2011, page 223
Horn Book Magazine, January/February 2011, page 107
School Library Journal, January 2011, page 86

Other books by the same author:
Capoeria: Game! Dance! Martial Art!, 2007

Murals: Walls that Sing, 2003
El pinatero/The Pinata Maker, 1994

Other books you might like:
Li Cunxin, *Dancing to Freedom: The True Story of Mao's Last Dancer*, 2008
Jan Greenberg, *Ballet for Martha: Making Appalachian Spring*, 2010
Susanna Reich, *Jose! Born to Dance: The Story of Jose Limon*, 2005
Siena Cherson Siegel, *To Dance: A Ballerina's Graphic Novel*, 2006

9

TOM ANGLEBERGER

The Strange Case of Origami Yoda
(New York: Amulet Books, 2010)

Subject(s): Middle schools; Interpersonal relations; Social conditions
Age range(s): 9 - 12+
Major character(s): Tommy, 6th Grader; Dwight, Classmate (of Tommy); Harvey, Friend (of Tommy); Sara, Classmate (of Tommy)
Time period(s): 21st century; 2010s
Locale(s): United States

Summary: In *The Strange Case of Origami Yoda* by Tom Angleberger, a group of middle-school students encounters an eerily accurate fortune-telling finger puppet. Tommy and his friend Harvey are accustomed to classmate Dwight's oddball ways. But when Dwight takes to wearing an origami Yoda finger puppet that dispatches advice, Tommy and Harvey begin to think that the paper toy may have true psychic ability. With a big school dance approaching, Tommy hopes for a date with new student, Sara, but considers consulting Dwight and his origami Yoda first. Instructions for making an origami Yoda are included in the book. First novel.

Where it's reviewed:
Booklist, May 1, 2010, page 55
Bulletin of the Center for Children's Books, June 2010, page 417
Horn Book Guide, Fall 2010, page 329
New York Times Book Review, June 6, 2010, page 24
School Library Journal, May 2010, page 25

Other books by the same author:
Darth Paper Strikes Back, 2011

Awards the book has won:
Book Sense Book of the Year Award: Children's Book, 2011
Texas Bluebonnet Award, 2012

Other books you might like:
A.C.E. Bauer, *Come Fall*, 2010
Maureen Fergus, *Exploits of a Reluctant (but Extremely Goodlooking) Hero*, 2007
Jordan Sonnenblick, *Dodger and Me*, 2008
Kristin Clark Venuti, *Leaving the Bellweathers*, 2009

10

KATHI APPELT

Keeper
(New York: Atheneum Books for Young Readers, 2010)

Subject(s): Sailing; Mermaids; Mother-daughter relations
Age range(s): 9 - 12+
Major character(s): Keeper, Girl, 10-Year-Old, Daughter (of Meggie Marie); Meggie Marie, Mythical Creature (mermaid), Mother (of Keeper); Signe, Guardian (of Keeper); Dogie, Military Personnel (soldier, former)
Time period(s): 21st century; 2010s
Locale(s): Gulf of Mexico, At Sea; Texas, United States

Summary: In the novel *Keeper* by Kathi Appelt, the ten-year-old title character goes to sea to find her mermaid mother. Though Keeper lives on the Texas coast with her guardian, Signe, she is drawn to the waters of the gulf where her mother, Meggie Marie, has swum with the other mermaids for the past seven years. With Keeper in her boat as she heads out on the night of the blue moon are her dog named BD and a seagull named Captain. As she heads to the sandbar where the mermaids will meet under the moon, Keeper faces the dangers of the tides and her own doubts about her quest. Appelt is also the author of *The Underneath*.

Where it's reviewed:
Booklist, June 1, 2010, page 73
Horn Book Magazine, September/October 2010, page 71
Publishers Weekly, May 3, 2010, page 52
School Library Journal, July 2010, page 56

Other books you might like:
Neil Gaiman, *The Graveyard Book*, 2008
Patricia MacLachlan, *Sarah, Plain and Tall*, 1985
K.A. Nuzum, *The Leanin' Dog*, 2008
Susan Patron, *The Higher Power of Lucky*, 2006

11

TEDD ARNOLD, Author/Illustrator

I Spy Fly Guy
(New York: Scholastic, 2009)

Subject(s): Insects; Pets; Humor
Age range(s): 3 - 7+
Major character(s): Buzz, Child; Fly Guy, Fly

Summary: In *I Spy Fly Guy* by Tedd Arnold, a boy goes to great lengths to find the pet fly he loses during a game of hide-and-seek. Though Buzz's fly, Fly Guy, usually chooses the garbage can as his favorite hiding spot without incident, the ill-timed arrival of the trash collectors ends their latest game abruptly. Desperate to locate his insect buddy, Buzz convinces his father to take him to the local landfill. Buzz finds lots of flies there, of course, but they are all indistinguishable from Fly Guy. Eventually, Fly Guy reveals that he was not hiding in a garbage can but on Buzz's hat.

Where it's reviewed:
Horn Book Guide, Spring 2010, page 53

School Library Journal, December 2009, page 77

Other books by the same author:
Buzz Boy and Fly Guy, 2010
Hooray for Fly Guy, 2008
Shoo, Fly Guy, 2006
Super Fly Guy, 2006
Hi, Fly Guy!, 2005

Other books you might like:
Dayle Ann Dodds, *Where's Pup?*, 2003
Cari Meister, *Tiny's Bath*, 1998
Lori Ries, *Aggie and Ben: Three Stories*, 2006
Pat Thomson, *Drat That Fat Cat!*, 2003

12

MARC ARONSON

Trapped: How the World Rescued 33 Miners from 2,000 Feet below the Chilean Desert

(New York: Atheneum Books for Young Readers, 2011)

Subject(s): Mining; Rescue work; Survival

Age range(s): 10 - 13+

Summary: Author Marc Aronson presents a detailed account of the amazing rescue of 33 miners from a Chilean copper mine in 2010. Writing for a middle grade audience, the author covers the event that held the world spellbound for two months from the perspective of the trapped miners and their rescuers and provides fascinating information on Chile's geological history and the mining industry. As the narrative describes the courage of the men struggling for survival 2,000 feet below the earth, and the efforts of the drillers, engineers, scientists, and well-wishers from around the world who worked and prayed for the miners' rescue, an inspiring story of human strength and cooperation emerges. Photographs and diagrams enhance the text. A list of titles for suggested reading encourages readers to investigate the topic further.

Where it's reviewed:
Booklist, September, 1 2011, page 103
Horn Book Magazine, September/October 2011, page 109
Publishers Weekly, June, 13 2011, page 51
School Library Journal, August 2011, page 127

Other books by the same author:
If Stones Could Speak: Poems for Children and Their Parents, 2010
The World Made New: Why the Age of Exploration Happened and How It Changed History, 2007

Other books you might like:
Susan Campbell Bartoletti, *Growing Up in Coal Country*, 1996
Josh Berk, *The Dark Days of Hamburger Halpin*, 2010
Sandra Markle, *Rescues!*, 2006

13

LINDA ASHMAN
CHRISTINE DAVENIER, Illustrator

Samantha on a Roll

(New York: Farrar, Straus and Giroux, 2011)

Story type: Young Readers
Subject(s): Roller skating; Children; Adventure

Age range(s): 2 - 7+
Major character(s): Samantha, Girl, Child, Skater

Summary: A young girl faces a thrilling adventure in this picture book for young readers by author Linda Ashman with illustrations by Christine Davenier. Young Samantha is so excited about her new roller skates that she just can't wait any longer to try them out. Despite the fact that her mom told her to wait, Samantha straps the skates on as soon as her mom is distracted by a phone call. After skating down the hallway, Samantha decides to put her skates to work in the great outdoors. Her adventure starts out simple enough, until she skates to the top of Hawthorne Hill and begins rolling downhill at high speeds, wreaking havoc on the town below!

Other books by the same author:
No Dogs Allowed, 2011
M Is For Mischief: An A to Z of Naughty Children, 2008
Just Another Morning, 2004
Babies on the Go, 2003
Can You Make a Piggy Giggle?, 2002

14

ATINUKE
LAUREN TOBIA, Illustrator

Anna Hibiscus

(London: Walker Books, 2010)

Series: Anna Hibiscus Series. Book 1
Subject(s): Africa; Africans; Children

Age range(s): 6 - 8+
Major character(s): Anna Hibiscus, Child
Time period(s): 21st century; 2000s
Locale(s): Nigeria

Summary: This story, written for children, takes place in Nigeria. A young girl called Anna Hibiscus lives in a home with her entire family, all of whom are very wealthy, including grandparents, aunts, uncles, and cousins, and she enjoys her life in a Nigerian city. She does fun things such as playing games with her cousins, planning parties, swimming in the ocean, and selling oranges. Anna wishes for one thing to be different in her life, however; she wants to see snow. Illustrations by Lauren Tobia accompany the text. Other books in the series include *Hooray for Anna Hibiscus* and *Good Luck, Anna Hibiscus!*

Other books by the same author:
Anna Hibiscus' Song, 2011
Have Fun, Anna Hibiscus!, 2011

Hooray for Anna Hibiscus!, 2011
Good Luck, Anna Hibiscus!, 2010
Hooray for Anna Hibiscus!, 2010

Other books you might like:
Judy Blume, *Soupy Saturdays with the Pain and the Great One*, 2007
Anne Fine, *The Jamie and Angus Stories*, 2002
Sara Pennypacker, *Clementine*, 2006
Sara Pennypacker, *Clementine's Letter*, 2008
Julie Sternberg, *Like Pickle Juice on a Cookie*, 2011

15

AVI
GREG RUTH, Illustrator

City of Orphans
(New York: Atheneum Books, 2011)

Subject(s): Detective fiction; Mystery fiction; Family life

Age range(s): 10 - 13+

Major character(s): Maks Geless, Newspaper Carrier, Brother (of Emma), Detective—Amateur; Emma Geless, Sister (of Maks), Crime Suspect; Bartleby Donck, Lawyer; Willa, Streetperson

Time period(s): 19th century; 1890s (1893)

Locale(s): New York, New York

Summary: In this young adult novel by Avi, Maks Geless is a 13-year-old boy whose family has just immigrated to 19th century New York City. By day, Maks earns meager wages working as a newspaper boy; by night, he navigates the streets of New York, trying to avoid the members of the Plug Ugly Gang as he attempts to break his sister Emma from the city jail. Emma has been imprisoned for pilfering a watch at the Waldorf Astoria, and Maks is determined to prove her innocent. With the help of a tough homeless girl named Willa and an enigmatic attorney named Bartleby Donck, Maks embarks on an investigation to discover who really stole the watch. With only four days until Emma's trial, can boy detective Maks and his friends come up with enough evidence to keep his sister free?

Where it's reviewed:
Booklist, August 2011, page 43
Horn Book Magazine, September/October 2011, page 82
New York Times Book Review, November 13, 2011, page 33
Publishers Weekly, August 22, 2011, page 64
School Library Journal, August 2011, page 94

Other books by the same author:
The Traitor's Gate, 2007
The True Confessions of Charlotte Doyle, 1990
The History of Helpless Harry, 1980
Emily Upham's Revenge, 1978

Other books you might like:
Raymond Bial, *Tenement: Immigrant Life on the Lower East Side*, 2003
Russell Freedman, *Immigrant Kids*, 1995
Karen Hesse, *Brooklyn Bridge*, 2008
Deborah Hopkinson, *Shutting out the Sky: Life in the*

Tenements of New York 1880-1924, 2003
Gail Carson Levine, *Dave at Night*, 1999

16

JIM AYLESWORTH
BARBARA MCCLINTOCK, Illustrator

The Mitten
(New York: Scholastic, 2009)

Story type: Young Readers
Subject(s): Animals; Folklore; Human-animal relationships

Age range(s): 4 - 7+
Time period(s): 21st century; 2000s

Summary: Based on a classic Ukranian folktale, Jim Aylesworth's *The Mitten* tells the story of a group of forest animals who enjoy the warmth and solace provided by a single mitten. Accidentally left behind by a little boy, the mitten captures the hearts and imaginations of a variety of animals, who fill it up in order to stay warm. *The Mitten* includes illustrations by Barbara McClintock.

Where it's reviewed:
Booklist, November 1, 2009, page 31
Horn Book Magazine, November/December 2009, page 690
Publishers Weekly, October 19, 2009, page 50
School Library Journal, December 2009, page 95

Other books by the same author:
Goldilocks and the Three Bears, 2003
The Tale of Tricky Fox, 2001
Aunt Pitty's Piggy, 1999
The Gingerbread Man, 1998

Other books you might like:
Jan Brett, *The Mitten: An Old Ukranian Folk Tale*, 1989
Jan Brett, *The Three Snow Bears*, 2007
Don Freeman, *Corduroy*, 1968
Steven Kellogg, *The Missing Mitten Mystery*, 2000
Alvin Tresselt, *The Mitten*, 1964

17

JIM AYLESWORTH
BARBARA MCCLINTOCK, Illustrator

Our Abe Lincoln
(New York: Scholastic Press, 2009)

Subject(s): Plays; Poetry; Presidents (Government)

Age range(s): 5 - 8+
Major character(s): Abraham Lincoln, Historical Figure, Political Figure (President of the United States)
Time period(s): 21st century
Locale(s): United States

Summary: A group of contemporary youngsters (from a multicultural classroom) are putting on a play about the life of our sixteenth president. Each act is a single verse adapted from an old campaign song, "Our Abe Lincoln," and sung to the tune of "The Old Grey Mare." The first act, for example, has the following script: "Babe Abe Lincoln was born in the wilderness/Born in the wilderness/Born in the wilderness//Babe Abe Lincoln was born in the wilderness/Many long years ago." Each double-page spread covers one incident in Lincoln's life through a single verse and an illustration of the children acting out the incident. The natural repetition of words and phrases, and the expected rhythm of the song, creates a picture book biography that even beginning readers may tackle on their own.

Where it's reviewed:
Bulletin of the Center for Children's Books, January 2009, page 186
Horn Book Magazine, May/June 2009, page 319
Publishers Weekly, January 12, 2009, page paghe 46
School Library Journal, December 2008, page 108

Other books by the same author:
Folks In the Valley: A Pennsylvania Dutch ABC, 1992

Other books you might like:
Amy Cohn, *Abraham Lincoln*, 2002
Deborah Hopkinson, *Abe Lincoln Crosses a Creek: A Tall, Thin Tale (Introducing His Forgotten Frontier Friend)*, 2008
Doreen Rappaport, *Abe's Honest Words: The Life of Abraham Lincoln*, 2008
Anne Rockwell, *Presidents' Day*, 2008
Sarah L. Thomson, *What Lincoln Said*, 2008

18

JULIANNA BAGGOTT

The Prince of Fenway Park
(New York: HarperCollins, 2009)

Subject(s): Monsters; Baseball; Racism

Age range(s): 9 - 13+
Major character(s): Oscar Egg, 12-Year-Old; Malachi Egg, Father (of Oscar Egg); The Bobs, Mythical Creature
Time period(s): 21st century; 2000s (2004)
Locale(s): Boston, Massachusetts

Summary: In Julianna Baggott's *The Prince of Fenway Park*, Oscar Egg is a 12-year-old who believes that he is cursed—just like the Red Sox. His adoptive mother has just sent him to live with his strange, sickly father, Malachi, who lives in the tunnels below Fenway Park. There Oscar discovers that the curse on the Red Sox is real, placed on the team by a half-elven fan who was angry at baseball. Since that time, an entire society of mythical creatures has been living in Fenway Park, cursed to stay there forever. Among them are a banshee in the outfield, a pooka in the Green Monster, and a two-headed sportscaster named The Bobs. Some of the creatures don't want the curse broken, either. Oscar and his father travel across time to assemble an ultimate All-Star team of good-guy baseball players including Ted Williams, Jackie Robinson, Willy Mays, and Babe Ruth. That team plays a secret game against a team of all-time baseball baddies to lift the curse from the Red Sox and restore some dignity to the game of baseball.

Where it's reviewed:
Booklist, May 15, 2009, page 56
Horn Book Guide, Fall 2009, page 363
School Library Journal, May 2009, page 100

Other books by the same author:
The Ever Breath, 2009

Other books you might like:
Suzanne Collins, *Gregor the Overlander*, 2003
Lynn Curlee, *Ballpark: The Story of America's Baseball Fields*, 2005
Donald Hall, *When Willard Met Babe Ruth*, 1996
Kadir Nelson, *We Are The Ship: The Story of Negro League Baseball*, 2008
Gary Soto, *Baseball in April and Other Stories*, 1990

19

JEANNIE BAKER, Author/Illustrator
JEANNIE BAKER, Illustrator

Mirror
(Somerville, Massachusetts: Candlewick Press, 2010)

Subject(s): Family life; Cultural identity; International relations

Age range(s): 5 - 8+

Summary: In *Mirror*, illustrator Jeannie Baker shows young readers how similar families can be, even if they are located on opposite sides of the world. Baker presents readers with illustrations of a family in Morocco and another family in Australia. Each family wakes up, eats breakfast, and gets ready to start their day. They each go shopping, too. One family visits a shopping center, the other a marketplace. Baker places pictures of the families side by side throughout the pages of this wordless picture book so readers can draw their own conclusions about similarities and differences between the families.

Where it's reviewed:
Booklist, February 15, 2010, page 77
Bulletin of the Center for Children's Books, January 2011, page 225
Horn Book Magazine, January/February 2010, page 76
New York Times Book Review, November 7, 2010, page 33
School Library Journal, January 2010, page 69

Other books by the same author:
Home, 2004
Window, 1991
Where the Forest Meets the Sea, 1988

Awards the book has won:
Australian Children's Book of the Year Awards: Picture Book, 2011

Other books you might like:
Edith Baer, *This Is the Way We Go to School*, 1948
Lee Bennett Hopkins, *Amazing Faces*, 2010
Mary D. Lankford, *Hopscotch Around the World*, 1992
Ann Morris, *Houses and Homes*, 1992
Marilyn Singer, *Mirror, Mirror: A Book of Reversible Verse*, 2010

20

KEITH BAKER, Author/Illustrator

LMNO Peas

(New York: Beach Lane Books, 2010)

Subject(s): Rhyme; Occupations; Food

Age range(s): 3 - 7+
Time period(s): 21st century; 2010s

Summary: Green peas are the stars of author and illustrator, Keith Baker's *LMNO Peas*. Each page of this volume is emblazoned with a different letter of the alphabet, and every letter features a different occupation performed by each of 26 tiny green peas.

Where it's reviewed:
Booklist, February 2, 2010, page 50
Horn Book Magazine, March/April 2010, page 43
Publishers Weekly, March 22, 2010, page 67
School Library Journal, March 2010, page 113

Other books by the same author:
Quack and Count, 1999

Other books you might like:
Ann Jonas, *Aardvarks, Disembark!*, 1994
Judy Sierra, *The Sleepy Little Alphabet: A Bedtime Story from Alphabet Town*, 2009
Al Yankovic, *When I Grow Up*, 2011

21

MOLLY BANG
PENNY CHISHOLM, Author/Illustrator

Living Sunlight: How Plants Bring the Earth to Life

(New York: Blue Sky Press, 2009)

Story type: Young Readers
Subject(s): Science; Animals; Biology

Age range(s): 7 - 10+

Summary: In *Living Sunlight: How Plants Bring the Earth to Life*, authors Molly Bang and Penny Chisholm explain the process of photosynthesis to young readers. Accompanied by Bang's illustrations, this volume is narrated by the mighty, friendly sun as he details the links between photosynthesis, animal breathing, and the whole process of life on Earth.

Where it's reviewed:
Booklist, December 1, 2008, page 67
Bulletin of the Center for Children's Books, April 2009, page 313
Horn Book Magazine, May/June 2009, page 32
New York Times Book Review, April 12, 2009, page 15
School Library Journal, February 2009, page 89

Other books by the same author:
My Light, 2004
Common Ground: The Water, Earth, and Air We Share, 1997

Other books you might like:
G. Brian Karas, *On Earth*, 2005
Robert E. Wells, *Why Do Elephants Need the Sun?*, 2010

22

MAC BARNETT
ADAM REX, Illustrator

The Case of the Case of Mistaken Identity

(New York: Simon & Schuster Books for Young Readers, 2009)

Series: Brixton Brothers Series. Book 1
Subject(s): Libraries; Espionage; Detective fiction

Age range(s): 9 - 12+
Major character(s): Steve Brixton, 12-Year-Old, Detective—Amateur; Mr. E., Spy
Time period(s): 21st century; 2000s

Summary: *The Case of the Case of Mistaken Identity* is the first installment of Mac Barnett's Brixton Brothers mystery series. On the surface, book lover Steve Brixton appears to be your average 12-year-old, but in reality he longs to be a master detective. Soon, he wonders if maybe he should have picked another lifelong dream when he gets involved in a caper with undercover secret agents acting as librarians and a villain known only as Mr. E. Now Steve must seek out a lost fortune, uncover Mr. E's true identity, and, worst of all, finish his social studies report before time runs out.

Where it's reviewed:
Booklist, October 15, 2009, page 63
Bulletin of the Center for Children's Books, January 2010, page 184
Horn Book Guide, Spring 2010, page 62
School Library Journal, March 2010, page 151

Other books by the same author:
It Happened on a Train, 2011
The Ghostwriter Secret, 2010

Other books you might like:
M.T. Anderson, *Jasper Dash and the Flame-Pits of Delaware*, 2009
Carl Hiaasen, *Hoot*, 2002
Richard Peck, *Here Lies the Librarian*, 2006
Brandon Sanderson, *Alcatraz Versus the Evil Librarians*, 2007

23

KELLY BARNHILL

The Mostly True Story of Jack

(New York: Little, Brown Books for Young Readers, 2011)

Story type: Magic Conflict
Subject(s): Suspense; Supernatural; Magic

Age range(s): 10 - 14+
Major character(s): Jack, Boy, Nephew (of Mabel and

Clive); Wendy, 14-Year-Old, Twin (of Frankie), Friend (of Jack); Frankie, 14-Year-Old, Twin (of Wendy), Friend (of Jack); Anders, Psychic, Friend (of Jack); Clayton Avery, Bully; Mabel, Aunt (of Jack), Spouse (of Clive); Clive, Uncle (of Jack), Spouse (of Mabel)

Time period(s): 21st century; 2010s
Locale(s): Hazelwood, Iowa

Summary: In author Kelly Barnhill's first novel, Jack finds himself in Hazelwood, Iowa, home of eccentric Aunt Mabel and Uncle Clive, after his parents decide to divorce. A solitary individual, Jack has always felt somewhat invisible, so he is surprised when he quickly makes friends with psychically endowed Anders and twins Wendy and Frankie. He's even more bewildered when the town bully, Clayton Avery, beats him up. Worse, he learns that Clayton's evil father, who has a stronghold on the town, wants him dead. Jack realizes something is amiss in Hazelwood, and he's curious as to why everyone is suddenly so interested in him—as if they somehow expected his arrival. As danger and suspense mount, Jack will come to rely on his new friends to help him solve the mystery.

Where it's reviewed:
Booklist, August 1, 2011, page 44
Publishers Weekly, June 27, 2011, page 158
School Library Journal, September 2011, page 144
Voice of Youth Advocates, August 2011, page 284

Other books you might like:
Ingrid Law, *Savvy*, 2008
Kate Milford, *The Boneshaker*, 2010
Sally Nicholls, *Season of Secrets*, 2011

24

SUSAN CAMPBELL BARTOLETTI
HOLLY MEADE, Illustrator

Naamah and the Ark at Night

(Boston: Candlewick Press, 2011)

Story type: Young Readers
Subject(s): Bible stories; Animals; Singing

Age range(s): 3 - 7+
Major character(s): Naamah, Spouse (of Noah), Singer, Biblical Figure; Noah, Spouse (of Naamah), Biblical Figure

Summary: Noah, his wife Naamah, and their children worked together to build an ark and collect many different animals. As the rain falls outside for forty days and forty nights, Naamah decides to make the night more peaceful by singing. Naamah, whose name means "great singer," sings a lullaby to the animals and her family members on the ark. They all fall asleep peacefully thanks to Naamah's beautiful song. This children's book is written by Susan Campbell Bartoletti and illustrated by Holly Meade.

Where it's reviewed:
Booklist, November 1, 2011, page 60
Horn Book Magazine, July/August 2011, page 123
Publishers Weekly, June 27, 2011, page 266
School Library Journal, July 2011, page 82

Other books you might like:
Ruth Eitzen, *Tara's Flight*, 2008
Mem Fox, *Time for Bed*, 1993
Peter Spier, *Noah's Ark*, 1977
Jane Yolen, *Switching On the Moon: A Very First Book of Bedtime Poems*, 2010

25

CHRIS BARTON
TOM LICHTENHELD, Illustrator

Shark vs. Train

(New York: Little, Brown Books for Young Readers, 2010)

Subject(s): Sharks; Trains; Toys

Age range(s): 2 - 5+

Summary: Who will win in the ultimate showdown: a shark or a train? A young boy tackles that very question in *Shark vs. Train* when he takes his toy shark out of the toybox, only to see that his friend has chosen a toy train from the very same box. Together the boys come up with unique ways to test the muster of their respective toys; contests include high diving, staying silent in the library, and the best Halloween costume. Which toy will come out on top? Author Chris Barton and illustrator Tom Lichtenheld humorously portray a plucky duo of boys and their overactive imaginations.

Where it's reviewed:
Bulletin of the Center for Children's Books, May 2010, page 370
Horn Book Magazine, July/August 2010, page 85
New York Times Book Review, July 18, 2010, page 15
School Library Journal, April 2010, page 120

Other books you might like:
Lucy Cousins, *I'm the Best*, 2010
Richard Egielski, *Captain Sky Blue*, 2010
Kate McMullan, *I'm Big*, 2010
Bob Shea, *Dinosaur vs. Bedtime*, 2008
Janet Stevens, *The Tortoise and the Hare: An Aesop Fable*, 1984

26

CHRIS BARTON
TONY PERSIANI, Illustrator

The Day-Glo Brothers: The True Story of Bob and Joe Switzer's Bright Ideas and Brand-New Colors

(Watertown, Massachusetts: Charlesbridge, 2009)

Subject(s): Inventions; Brothers; Painting (Art)

Age range(s): 9 - 11+
Time period(s): 20th century
Locale(s): United States

Summary: In the 1930s, an aspiring magician and his brother came up with a new idea that changed the way people viewed color: the invention of neon. Chris Barton's *The Day-Glo Brothers: The True Story of Bob and Joe Switzer's Bright Ideas and Brand-New Colors* chronicles the story of these two siblings as they use their intellect and creativity to craft paints that glow in the dark. Accompanied by Tony Persiani's illustrations, this volume sheds light on the benefits of the Switzers' invention, from the use of neon in the Second World War to its role in art and popular culture.

Where it's reviewed:
Booklist, June 1 2009, page 85
Horn Book Guide, Spring 2010, page 168
New York Times Book Review, December 20, 2009, page 12
School Library Journal, August 2009, page 118

Other books by the same author:
Can I See Your ID? True Stories of False Identities, 2011

Other books you might like:
David Almond, *My Dad's a Birdman*, 2008
Robert Crowther, *Robert Crowther's Amazing Pop-Up House of Inventions*, 2006
David Macaulay, *The New Way Things Work*, 1998
Joyce Sidman, *Eureka!: Poems about Inventors*, 2002

27

NORA RALEIGH BASKIN

Anything but Typical

(New York: Simon & Schuster Books for Young Readers, 2009)

Story type: Young Readers
Subject(s): Mental disorders; Children; Writing

Age range(s): 12 - 14+
Major character(s): Jason Blake, 6th Grader, Autistic
Time period(s): 21st century; 2000s
Locale(s): United States

Summary: Jason Blake is a sixth grader who has been diagnosed with autistic spectrum disorder. He has dealt with teasing and bullying his whole life from those he calls "neurotypicals," and though he is on the high-functioning end of the autistic spectrum, he finds it extremely difficult to communicate with others face-to-face. Jason has a loving and supportive family, who encourage him in every way they can and discover that he is a gifted creative writer. Jason begins to participate in an online group called Storyboard, where he posts stories and develops a close friendship with a girl. When his parents decide to take him to a group meeting for Storyboard, Jason is horrified to realize that he will interact with his friend face-to-face. He has no choice but to deal with his life and his interactions the only way he knows how.

Where it's reviewed:
Booklist, February 1, 2009, page 40
Bulletin of the Center for Children's Books, April, 2009, page 313

Horn Book Magazine, May/June 2009, page 289
Publishers Weekly, February 9, 2009, page 49
School Library Journal, March 2009, page 141

Other books by the same author:
The Summer Before Boys, 2011
All We Know of Love, 2008
What Every Girl (Except Me) Knows, 2001

Other books you might like:
Gennifer Choldenko, *Al Capone Does My Shirts*, 2004
Suzanne Crowley, *The Very Ordered Existence of Merilee Marvelous*, 2007
Siobhan Dowd, *The London Eye Mystery*, 2008
Kathryn Erskine, *Mockingbird*, 2011
Cynthia Lord, *Rules*, 2006

28

HESTER BASS
E.B. LEWIS, Illustrator

The Secret World of Walter Anderson

(Somerville, Massachusetts: Candlewick Press, 2009)

Subject(s): Biographies; Art; Artists

Age range(s): 7 - 9+

Summary: In children's book *The Secret World of Walter Anderson*, author Hester Bass tells the story of the watercolor artist who, in 1947, took a rowboat into the Gulf of Mexico and headed for Horn Island, where he proceeded to live without company, electricity, or running water. Bass reveals how the artist sought escape from modern conveniences and disturbances in order to concentrate on the offerings of nature and on creating his art. Anderson is now well-known for a series of detailed watercolors he created during his time on Horn Island. Bass invites young readers into the world of this eccentric artist, and shows children both how Anderson lived and the pieces he created.

Where it's reviewed:
Booklist, August 2009, page 65
Horn Book Guide, Spring 2010, page 155
School Library Journal, September 2009, page 138

Awards the book has won:
Orbis Pictus Award for Outstanding Nonfiction for Children, 2010
Other books you might like:
Jacqueline Davies, *The Boy Who Drew Birds: A Story of John James Audubon*, 2004
Lita Judge, *Yellowstone Moran: Painting the American West*, 2009
Rachel Victoria Rodriguez, *Through Georgia's Eyes*, 2006

29

EMILY BEARN
NICK PRICE, Illustrator

Tumtum and Nutmeg: Adventures beyond Nutmouse Hall

(New York: Little, Brown Book for Young Readers, 2008)

Subject(s): Children; Family relations; Fantasy

Age range(s): 9 - 11+

Major character(s): Tumtum, Mouse, Guardian (of Arthur and Lucy), Spouse (of Nutmeg); Nutmeg, Mouse, Spouse (of Tumtum), Guardian (of Arthur and Lucy); Arthur Mildew, Impoverished, Brother (of Lucy), Child, Friend (of Tumtum and Nutmeg); Lucy Mildew, Friend (of Tumtum and Nutmeg), Child, Impoverished, Sister (of Arthur)

Time period(s): 21st century; 2000s

Locale(s): Rose Cottage, Fictional Location

Summary: Two mice try to protect a pair of poor children in *Tumtum and Nutmeg: Adventures Beyond Nutmouse Hall*. Tumtum and Nutmeg are mice who live in a rundown closet in Rose Cottage. They live in peace and harmony with the other woodland creatures that live around the cottage. When Arthur, Lucy, and their father move into the cottage, Tumtum and Nutmeg watch with intense curiosity. On the father's small income, the family attempts to fix up the dilapidated house. This action begins a series of events that soon threatens the safety of Arthur and Lucy. The mice like their two new friends so much that they will stop at nothing to try to ensure the children's safety.

Where it's reviewed:
Booklist, April 15, 2009, page 44
Bulletin of the Center for Children's Books, June 2009, page 393
Horn Book Guide, Fall 2010, page 363
Publishers Weekly, April 6, 2009, page 47
School Library Journal, May 2009, page 70

Other books by the same author:
Tumtum and Nutmeg: The Rose Cottage Tales, 2010

Other books you might like:
Elise Broach, *Masterpiece*, 2008
Kate DiCamillo, *The Tale of Despereaux: Being the Story of a Mouse, a Princess, Some Soup, and a Spool of Thread*, 2003
Kenneth Grahame, *The Wind in the Willows*, 1908
Lynne Jonell, *Emmy and the Incredible Shrinking Rat*, 2007
Mary Norton, *The Borrowers*, 1953

30

CECE BELL, Author/Illustrator

Itty Bitty

(Somerville, Massachusetts: Candlewick Press, 2009)

Subject(s): Dogs; Housing; Identity

Age range(s): 3 - 6+

Major character(s): Itty Bitty, Dog

Time period(s): 21st century; 2000s

Summary: Author/illustrator Cece Bell's *Itty Bitty* tells the story of a little dog with big hopes. Itty Bitty stumbles upon a huge bone, which he proceeds to transform into his very own house. But after carving and chewing and nibbling the bone into a residence, he realizes he has no furniture small enough to fit inside. His trip to the local home furnishings store proves unhelpful... until he is directed toward the "Teeny-Weeny Department." Soon Itty Bitty has all the goods he needs to make his house a home.

Where it's reviewed:
Booklist, July 1, 2009, page 71
Horn Book Guide, Fall 2009, page 320
Publishers Weekly, June 1, 2009, page 122
School Library Journal, September 2009, page 115

Other books by the same author:
Bee Wigged, 2008

Other books you might like:
John Burningham, *It's a Secret!*, 2009
Michael Foreman, *The Littlest Dinosaur*, 2008
Bob Graham, *Dimity Dumpty: The Story of Humpty's Little Sister*, 2007
Cari Meister, *When Tiny Was Tiny*, 1999

31

PETER BENTLY
HELEN OXENBURY, Illustrator

King Jack and the Dragon

(New York: Dial Books, 2011)

Story type: Young Readers

Subject(s): Dragons; Magic; Adventure

Age range(s): 3 - 5+

Major character(s): Unnamed Character, Boy ("King Jack")

Summary: Peter Bently creates a magical world for children, accompanied by Helen Oxenbury's illustrations. Near bedtime, a few small children use their imaginations to play a game of make-believe. One of the children takes the lead as King Jack, while the others help him build a castle and fight off dragons and other creatures. As the other children get sleepy, they go to bed, while King Jack continues to play by himself. After he finds himself alone and in the dark, he tries to be brave because after all, he is the king. He then decides that the dark scares him, and that he doesn't want to be king anymore.

Where it's reviewed:
Booklist, September 2011, page 126
Horn Book Magazine, November/December 2011, page 78
Publishers Weekly, May 16, 2011, page 69

Other books by the same author:
Shark in the Dark, 2009
A Lark in the Ark, 2008

Other books you might like:
Kevin Henkes, *My Garden*, 2010
Suzy Lee, *Shadow*, 2010
Antoinette Portis, *Not a Box*, 2006
Jean Reidy, *Light Up the Night*, 2011
Katie Van Camp, *CookieBot! A Harry and Horsie Adventure*, 2011

32

CARIN BERGER, Author/Illustrator

OK Go

(New York: Greenwillow Books, 2009)

Subject(s): Natural resource conservation; Recycling; Trees (Plants)

Age range(s): 4 - 8+

Summary: *OK Go* is a picture book for children illustrated with collages made from recycled materials. The book begins with a group of cars driving through a clean world with a bright blue sky. Eventually, the sky darkens around them and the people driving the cars realize that changes need to be made. The book encourages kids to make small changes and "live green" by reducing, reusing, and recycling, giving specific suggestions and ideas that even young children can do.

Where it's reviewed:
Booklist, June 1, 2009, page 76
Horn Book Guide, Fall 2009, page 321
New York Times Book Review, November 8, 2009, page 24
School Library Journal, April 2009, page 100

Other books by the same author:
The Green Mother Goose, 2011

Other books you might like:
Marc Brown, *Arthur Turns Green*, 2011
Peter Brown, *The Curious Garden*, 2009
Judy Sierra, *Ballyhoo Bay*, 2009
Melanie Walsh, *10 Things I Can Do To Help My World!: Fun and Easy Eco Tips*, 2008

33

ERIC BERLIN

The Potato Chip Puzzles: The Puzzling World of Winston Breen

(New York: G.P. Putnam's Sons, 2009)

Subject(s): Games; Mystery; Friendship

Age range(s): 9 - 12+

Major character(s): Winston Breen, Student; Jake, Student; Mal, Student; Mr. Garvey, Teacher

Time period(s): 21st century; 2000s

Summary: In *The Potato Chip Puzzles: The Puzzling World of Winston Breen* by Eric Berlin, the sequel to *The Puzzling World of Winston Breen*, Winston and his gang attend a day-long puzzle competition sponsored by a potato chip company. With a cutthroat teacher intent on winning, the team faces their most challenging bout of puzzles yet. But they face stiff competition from the other schools, and a fellow player is using some underhanded tactics to nab the $50,000 prize. Can Winston stop the cheater before it's too late? Blending mystery, suspense, and interactive games, *The Potato Chip Puzzles* brims with puzzles for readers to solve along with the characters.

Where it's reviewed:
Booklist, May 1, 2009, page 40
Horn Book Guide, Fall 2009, page 364
School Library Journal, August 2009, page 98

Other books by the same author:
The Puzzling World of Winston Breen, 2007

Other books you might like:
Benedict Carey, *The Unknowns: A Mystery*, 2009
Jody Feldman, *The Gollywhopper Games*, 2008
Rick Riordan, *The 39 Clues: The Maze of Bones*, 2008
Trenton Lee Stewart, *The Mysterious Benedict Society*, 2007

34

BRIAN BIGGS, Author/Illustrator

Everything Goes: On Land

(New York: Balzer + Bray, 2011)

Series: Everything Goes Series. Book 1
Story type: Young Readers
Subject(s): Transportation; Travel; Learning

Age range(s): 3 - 7+
Major character(s): Henry, Boy

Summary: Illustrator Brian Biggs takes his first turn as both author and illustrator in this interactive children's book about all things that go. The first in the Everything Goes series, this volume focuses on vehicles that travel on land. Henry and his dad visit a bustling city filled with vehicles such as cars, buses, subways, bikes, trains, and even ice cream trucks, and they learn about counting along the way.

Where it's reviewed:
Horn Book Magazine, November/December 2011, page 79
Publishers Weekly, August 1, 2011, page 46
School Library Journal, November 2011, page 79

Other books you might like:
Byron Barton, *My Car*, 2001
Anita Ganeri, *Things that Go*, 2010
William Low, *Machines Go to Work*, 2009
Richard Scarry, *Richard Scarry's Cars and Trucks and Things That Go*, 1974
Peter Stein, *Cars Galore*, 2011

35

JEANNE BIRDSALL
MATT PHELAN, Illustrator

Flora's Very Windy Day

(New York: Clarion Books, 2010)

Subject(s): Fantasy; Weather; Sibling rivalry

Age range(s): 5 - 8+

Major character(s): Flora, Girl, Child, Sister (of Crispin); Crispin, Boy, Child, Brother (of Flora)

Time period(s): 21st century; 2010s

Summary: *Flora's Very Windy Day* is an imaginative picture book for young readers. It's quite a surprise for Flora and her annoying little brother, Crispin, when a strong and mighty wind carries them up into the sky. The siblings blow to and fro, meeting a variety of interesting characters along the way. Their chance encounters open up a very exciting opportunity for Flora: the opportunity to get rid of Crispin for good. A dragonfly, a sparrow, and even the man in the moon, each express an interest in taking the little boy, but Flora can't seem to decide. Surely, her reluctance can't be because she actually wants to keep Crispin for herself, can it? *Flora's Very Windy Day* is filled with whimsical illustrations from Matt Phelan.

Where it's reviewed:
Booklist, July 2010, page 62
Bulletin of the Center for Children's Books, October 2010, page 62
Horn Book Guide, Spring 2011, page 18
Publishers Weekly, July 12, 2010, page 62
School Library Journal, Jul 2010, page 55

Other books you might like:
Judy Blume, *Soupy Saturdays with the Pain and the Great One*, 2007
Vicki Cobb, *I Face the Wind*, 2003
Shutta Crum, *Thunder-Boomer!*, 2009
Ted Kooser, *Bag in the Wind*, 2010
Tim Wynne-Jones, *The Boat in the Tree*, 2007

36

TOM BIRDSEYE

Storm Mountain

(New York: Holiday House, 2010)

Subject(s): Cousins; Mountaineering; Adventure

Age range(s): 9 - 12+

Major character(s): Cat, Girl, 13-Year-Old, Cousin (of Ty); Ty, Boy, 13-Year-Old, Cousin (of Cat)

Time period(s): 21st century; 2010s

Locale(s): Cascade Mountains, Washington

Summary: In the novel *Storm Mountain* by Tom Birdseye, two cousins embark on a dangerous adventure to honor the memories of their fathers. Cat and Ty, both 13, are the children of legendary mountaineers who died scaling the peaks of the Cascade Mountains. They live at the foot of the range, aware of the power of the mountains but awed by their majesty. When the teenagers are left unsupervised for a few days, Ty tries to convince Cat to join him on an expedition into the mountains to scatter their fathers' ashes. Cat refuses but ends up following Ty when he strikes out alone. The ill-conceived plan is soon complicated by a violent snowstorm and the cousins' adventure becomes a fight for survival.

Where it's reviewed:
Booklist, December 1, 2010, page 61
Horn Book Guide, Spring 2011, page 65
School Library Journal, December 2010, page 100

Other books by the same author:
A Tough Nut to Crack, 2006

Other books you might like:
Kathryn Lasky, *John Muir: America's First Environmentalist*, 2006
Louise Moeri, *The Devil in Ol' Rosie*, 2001
P.J. Petersen, *Wild River*, 2009
Sherry Shahan, *Death Mountain*, 2005
Roland Smith, *Peak*, 2007

37

NIC BISHOP

Nic Bishop: Lizards

(New York: Scholastic, 2010)

Subject(s): Reptiles; Photography; Animals

Age range(s): 4 - 8+

Summary: *Nic Bishop Lizards* is a collection of fascinating facts and detailed photography about lizards for young readers from Sibert Honor photographer Nic Bishop. The book, designed for elementary age children, educates readers about the lives of lizards. Colorful and vivid full-page photography gives children a closer glimpse at the reptiles in their natural habitats. Accompanying the images are a series of scientific and fun facts about the appearance of lizards, their eating habits, and their life cycles. *Nic Bishop Lizards* offers interesting information on a variety of lizards, including the tiny dwarf gecko, the thorny devil, bearded-dragon hatchlings, and the basilisk.

Where it's reviewed:
Booklist, December 12, 2010, page 49
Bulletin of the Center for Children's Books, November 2010, page 120
Horn Book Magazine, November/December 2010, page 112
School Library Journal, October 2010, page 97
Science Books & Film, January 2011, page 22

Other books by the same author:
Nic Bishop Marsupials, 2009
Nick Bishop: Butterflies and Moths, 2009
Nic Bishop Frogs, 2008
Nic Bishop Spiders, 2007

Awards the book has won:
Blue Ribbon Awards: Non-fiction, 2010

Other books you might like:
Carmen Bredeson, *Fun Facts About Lizards*, 2009
Jason Glaser, *Horned Lizards*, 2006
Melissa Stewart, *Salamander or Lizard? How Do You Know?*, 2011

38

NIC BISHOP

Nic Bishop: Butterflies and Moths
(New York: Scholastic Inc., 2009)

Subject(s): Insects; Photography; Science

Age range(s): 5 - 9+

Summary: In this photographic essay, author and nature photographer Nic Bishop introduces young readers to the differences between those colorful flying insects: butterflies and moths. Full-color photos and descriptive text explain the distinct variations between the two insects— and the characteristics that butterflies and moths share with one another. Bishop also provides young readers with information about caterpillars and the processes by which these creatures turn into either butterflies or moths. This book includes more than 15 photographs of butterflies and moths, a glossary of definitions, and an index to help readers navigate the text.

Where it's reviewed:
Booklist, June 1-15 2009, page 65
Bulletin of the Center for Children's Books, May 2009, page 535
Horn Book Magazine, July/August 2009, page 438
School Library Journal, June 2009, page 104
Science Books & Film, January 2009, page 31

Other books by the same author:
Nic Bishop Lizards, 2010
Nic Bishop Marsupials, 2009
Nic Bishop Frogs, 2008
Nic Bishop Spiders, 2007

Other books you might like:
Margarita Engle, *Summer Birds: The Butterflies of Maria Merian*, 2010
Avis Harley, *The Monarch's Progress: Poems With Wings*, 2008
Irene Kelly, *It's a Butterfly's Life*, 2007
Alan Madison, *Velma Gratch and the Way Cool Butterfly*, 2007
Antoine O Flatharta, *Hurry and the Monarch*, 2005

39

MICHAEL IAN BLACK
KEVIN HAWKES, Illustrator

A Pig Parade Is a Terrible Idea
(New York: Simon & Schuster Books for Young Readers, 2010)

Subject(s): Animals; Humor; Special events

Age range(s): 4 - 7+

Summary: *A Pig Parade Is a Terrible Idea* is a picture book for young readers, written by actor and comedian Michael Ian Black and illustrated by Kevin Hawkes. Even though a pig parade sounds like a great idea in this humorous book, in reality, it could not be a worse one. The pigs in the book don't like to march, refuse to put on their parade uniforms, ignore the floats when they are walking, and want to play terrible music, among many other reasons a pig parade is a terrible idea.

Where it's reviewed:
Booklist, August 2010, page 55
Horn Book Guide, Spring 2011, page 19
New York Times Book Review, November 7, 2010, page 34
Publishers Weekly, August 9, 2010, page 49
School Library Journal, December 2010, page 78

Other books by the same author:
Chicken Cheeks, 2009
The Purple Kangaroo, 2009

Other books you might like:
Jennifer Armstrong, *Once upon a Banana*, 2006
Mac Barnett, *Oh No!: Or How My Science Project Destroyed the World*, 2010
Ian Falconer, *Olivia Goes to Venice*, 2010
Elizabeth Cody Kimmel, *The Top Job*, 2007

40

SOPHIE BLACKALL, Author/Illustrator

Are You Awake?
(New York: Henry Holt and Co., 2011)

Story type: Young Readers
Subject(s): Sleep; Children; Family

Age range(s): 3 - 6+
Major character(s): Edward, Child, Son; Mom, Mother (Edward's mother)

Summary: "Why aren't you awake?" asks young Edward of his mother in this picture book by author and illustrator Sophie Blackall. "Because I'm asleep," mother responds. This early-morning exchange forms the basis of Blackall's story, which follows Edward as he curiously questions his sleepy mother while he waits for his dad to return home from his job as a pilot. Edward's questions continue as the sun begins to rise and the new day dawns. By the time the story ends and Dad arrives home, Mom is finally awake and Edward is asleep.

Where it's reviewed:
Booklist, May 1, 2011, page 17
Horn Book Magazine, July/August 2011, page 124
Publishers Weekly, March 21, 2011, page 72
School Library Journal, June 2011, page 77

Other books by the same author:
Edwin Speaks Up, 2011

Other books you might like:
Bonny Becker, *A Bedtime for Bear*, 2010
Roz Chast, *Too Busy Marco*, 2010
Russell Hoban, *Bedtime for Frances*, 1960

Kate Lum, *What! Cried Granny: An Almost Bedtime Story*, 1999

Shelley Moore Thomas, *Good Night, Good Knight*, 2000

41

TOMEK BOGACKI, Author/Illustrator

The Champion of Children: The Story of Janusz Korczak

(New York: Farrar Straus Giroux, 2009)

Subject(s): Biographies; Jews; Polish history
Age range(s): 6 - 9+
Time period(s): 19th century-20th century; 1870s-1940s
Locale(s): Poland
Summary: In *The Champion of Children: The Story of Janusz Korczak*, author Tomek Bogacki relates the inspiring story of the Polish doctor, author, and humanitarian who devoted his life to the welfare of Warsaw's poorest children. In 1912, Korczak established an orphanage for Jewish children that would empower its residents by giving them a voice in the organization's governance. After years of success, the orphanage was driven to the city's ghetto by Hitler's growing influence in Poland. Even under the desperate conditions imposed by Nazi rule, Janusz Korczak remained dedicated to his cause, finally losing his life at Treblinka with the beloved children of his orphanage.

Where it's reviewed:
Booklist, October 1, 2009, page 39
Bulletin of the Center for Children's Books, December 2009, page 146
Horn Book Magazine, January/February 2009, page 99
School Library Journal, December 2009, page 137

Other books by the same author:
Monkeys and Dog Days, 2008
The Turtle and the Hippopotamus, 2002
Circus Girl, 2001
Five Creatures, 2001
My First Garden, 2000

Other books you might like:
Deborah Durland DeSaix, *The Grand Mosque of Paris: A Story of How Muslims Rescued Jews During the Holocaust*, 2009
Malka Drucker, *Portraits of Jewish-American Heroes*, 2008
Richard Michelson, *A Is for Abraham: A Jewish Family Alphabet*, 2008
Susan Goldman Rubin, *Irena Sendler and the Children of the Warsaw Ghetto*, 2011

42

TONYA BOLDEN

Finding Family

(New York: Bloomsbury USA Children's Books, 2010)

Subject(s): Orphans; Grandfathers; Family history
Age range(s): 9 - 12+

Major character(s): Delana, 12-Year-Old, Orphan; Tilly, Aunt (of Delana); Grandfather, Grandfather (of Delana)
Time period(s): 20th century; 1900-1910 (1905)
Locale(s): Charleston, West Virginia

Summary: Inspired by antique photographs Tonya Bolden found throughout the years, *Finding Family* follows twelve-year-old Delana as she searches for a family she knows only through stories. When she was younger, Delana lost her parents and went to live with her great Aunt Tilly and her quiet grandfather. Aunt Tilly would often tell Delana about members of her family and their odd accomplishments, while her grandfather rarely said a word. When Aunt Tilly dies, Delana is left to wonder which parts of Tilly's stories were fact and which were fantastic fiction. She sets out to find the answers, unaware that the answers are actually closer than she originally thought.

Where it's reviewed:
Booklist, September 1, 2010, page 96
Bulletin of the Center for Children's Books, October 2010, page 64
Horn Book Guide, Spring 2011, page 65
School Library Journal, September 2010, page 146

Other books by the same author:
Tell All the Children Our Story: Memories and Momentos of Being Young and Black in America, 2002
A Book of African-American Women: 150 Crusaders, Creators and Uplifters, 1997

Other books you might like:
Patricia Reilly Giff, *Storyteller*, 2010
Debbie Levy, *Year of Goodbyes: A True Story of Friendship, Family, and Farewells*, 2010
Patricia C. McKissack, *Away West: Scraps of Time*, 2006
Walter Dean Myers, *Brown Angels: An Album of Pictures and Verse*, 1993
Dan Waddell, *Who Do You Think You Are?: Be a Family Tree Detective*, 2011

43

REBECCA BOND, Author/Illustrator

In the Belly of an Ox: The Unexpected Photographic Adventures of Richard and Cherry Kearton

(Boston: Houghton Mifflin Books for Children, 2009)

Subject(s): Biographies; Photography; Wildlife

Age range(s): 6 - 9+
Time period(s): 19th century
Locale(s): England

Summary: *In the Belly of an Ox: The Unexpected Photographic Adventures of Richard and Cherry Kearton* by Rebecca Bond describes the innovative methods of two naturalists in the late 19th century. Fascinated with the wildlife of their boyhood Yorkshire home, the Kearton brothers revolutionized the way man observed and recorded wild birds in their habitats by devising methods of camouflage that allowed them close access to their subjects. Their "hides" included tree trunks, rocks, and, as the title reveals, the hollow belly of an artificial ox. In 1895, the Keartons published the world's first nature book illustrated with photographs.

Where it's reviewed:
Booklist, October 1, 2009, page 48
Horn Book Magazine, January/February 2010, page 100
School Library Journal, October 2009, page 109

Other books by the same author:
Bravo Maurice, 2010

Other books you might like:
Jacqueline Davies, *The Boy Who Drew Birds: A Story of John James Audubon*, 2004
Kathryn Lasky, *John Muir: America's First Environmentalist*, 2006
Deborah Kogan Ray, *The Flower Hunter: William Bartram, America's First Naturalist*, 2004
Peter Sis, *The Tree of Life: A Book Depicting the Life of Charles Darwin, Naturalist, Geologist & Thinker*, 2003

44

ELLEN BOORAEM

Small Persons with Wings

(New York: Dial Books for Young Readers, 2011)

Subject(s): Fantasy; Fairies; Family

Age range(s): 10 - 12+
Major character(s): Mellie Turpin, 13-Year-Old; Fidius, Mythical Creature (fairy); Inepta, Mythical Creature (fairy); Durindana, Mythical Creature (fairy); Timmo, Neighbor (of Mellie)
Time period(s): 21st century; 2010s
Locale(s): Baker's Village, New England

Summary: In this young adult novel by Ellen Booraem, Mellie Turpin and her parents move into an old inn left to them by Mellie's grandfather. There Mellie, now 13, becomes reacquainted with the fairy folk that she remembers from her childhood. In kindergarten she had a fairy friend named Fidius, but Mellie has since replaced her juvenile fantasies with realistic pursuits such as math and science. But when Mellie learns from the Parvi (the politically correct term for fairies) that she and the rest of the Turpin family members are fairy guardians who possess a magic artifact, she is drawn into an enchanting world of spells and adventure. As she searches for the missing moonstone, Mellie forges a friendship with the human boy next door.

Where it's reviewed:
Booklist, January 1, 2011, page 108
Horn Book Magazine, March/April 2011, page 112
Publishers Weekly, November 29, 2010, page 50
School Library Journal, January 2011, page 100

Other books by the same author:
The Unnameables, 2008

Other books you might like:
Michelle Harrison, *13 Treasures*, 2010
Diana Wynne Jones, *Howl's Moving Castle*, 1986
Laura Amy Schlitz, *The Night Fairy*, 2010
Kate Thompson, *The New Policeman*, 2005
Catherynne M. Valente, *The Girl Who Circumnavigated Fairyland in a Ship of Her Own Making*, 2011

45

KIMBERLY BRUBAKER BRADLEY

Jefferson's Sons: A Founding Father's Secret Children

(New York: Dial Books, 2011)

Story type: Historical; Young Adult
Subject(s): Slavery; History; Presidents (Government)

Age range(s): 10 - 14+
Major character(s): Thomas Jefferson, Lover (of Sally), Father (of Beverly and Madison), Historical Figure, Government Official (president of the United States); Sally Hemings, Slave, Lover (of Thomas Jefferson), Mother (of Beverly and Madison); Beverly, Slave, Son (of Sally and Thomas Jefferson), Brother (of Madison); Madison, Brother (of Beverly), Slave, Son (of Sally and Thomas Jefferson); Peter Fossett, Slave, Young Man
Time period(s): 18th century-19th century; 1740s-1820s (1743-1826)
Locale(s): Charlottesville, Virginia

Summary: Kimberly Brubaker Bradley puts a fictional spin on the lives of President Thomas Jefferson's slaves. Sally Hemings lives as the president's slave and secret lover on his Monticello plantation with her children—fathered by Jefferson—and many other slaves. Although they have a special status as Jefferson's children, Sally doesn't let her children forget that they are slaves. She focuses on finding freedom for them. The book follows three points of view: Sally's son, Beverly; Sally's son, Madison; and a slave boy named Peter Fossett. Beverly is light-skinned and can pass for a white man. When he turns 21, he will have to decide whether he wants to be free, even if it means deserting his black family forever. Madison is dark-skinned and cannot pass as white, so he must deal with the harsh reality of being a slave for the rest of his life. Peter is a slave whose loses his entire family when they are sold after Jefferson's death.

Where it's reviewed:
Booklist, September 15, 2011, page 63
Horn Book Magazine, January/February 2012, page 84
School Library Journal, October 2011, page 131

Other books you might like:
Tonya Bolden, *Finding Family*, 2010
Christopher Paul Curtis, *Elijah of Buxton*, 2007
Cheryl Harness, *Thomas Jefferson*, 2004
Kadir Nelson, *Heart and Soul: The Story of America and African Americans*, 2011

46

GAYLE BRANDEIS

My Life with the Lincolns

(New York: Henry Holt and Co., 2010)

Subject(s): Family; United States; Civil rights

Age range(s): 10 - 13+

Major character(s): Mina Edelman, Girl, 12-Year-Old, Reincarnated Person (Willie Lincoln); Albert Baruch Edelman, Father (of Mina), Reincarnated Person (Abraham Lincoln)

Time period(s): 20th century; 1960s (1966)

Locale(s): Chicago, Illinois

Summary: What would you do if you thought your family was the reincarnation of a famous, historic family? In *My Life with the Lincolns*, 12-year-old Mina believes that her family is the reincarnation of the Lincolns, living in the United States during the 1960s. After discovering this, Mina becomes convinced that her family will suffer the same misfortunes that Abraham Lincoln's family did, and she's determined to stop them all from occurring. However, Mina's goal proves difficult as her family becomes more involved in the civil rights movement. Can Mina find a way to save her family from a future of death and insanity?

Where it's reviewed:
Booklist, February 15, 2010, page 78
Bulletin of the Center for Children's Books, July/August 2010, page 472
Horn Book Guide, Fall 2010, page 331
Publishers Weekly, January 25, 2010, page 120
School Library Journal, March 2010, page 152

Other books you might like:
Russell Freedman, *Lincoln: A Photobiography*, 1987
Patricia C. McKissack, *A Friendship for Today*, 2007
Elizabeth Partridge, *Marching for Freedom: Walk Together, Children, and Don't You Grow Weary*, 2009
Gary D. Schmidt, *The Wednesday Wars*, 2007
Deborah Wiles, *Countdown*, 2010

47

ELISE BROACH
ANTONIO JAVIER CAPARO, Illustrator

Missing on Superstition Mountain

(New York: Henry Holt, 2011)

Series: Missing on Superstition Mountain Series. Book 1

Story type: Mystery; Series

Subject(s): Mystery; Detective fiction; Brothers

Age range(s): 9 - 11+

Major character(s): Henry Barker, 10-Year-Old, Brother (of Simon and Jack); Simon Barker, 11-Year-Old, Brother (of Henry and Jack); Jack Barker, 6-Year-Old, Brother (of Henry and Simon); Delilah, 10-Year-Old, Neighbor (of Barker brothers)

Time period(s): 21st century; 2010s

Locale(s): Arizona, United States

Summary: In this first novel in the Missing on Superstition Mountain Series by Elise Broach, the Barker family has moved from the exciting city of Chicago to a tiny town in Arizona. There 11-year-old Simon, 10-year-old Henry, and six-year-old Jack anticipate a dull summer until their wandering pet cat leads them into a dangerous mystery. When Josie the cat strays, the boys' search takes them to Superstition Mountain—a location that had been deemed off-limits by their parents. As Simon, Henry, and Jack look for Josie, they find a trio of human skulls. With help from their new neighbor Delilah, the boys investigate the mystery and dig up clues that include an abandoned gold mine and spooky local legends.

Where it's reviewed:
Booklist, May 1, 2011, page 46
Bulletin of the Center for Children's Books, June 2011, page 458
Horn Book Magazine, July/August 2011, page 141
School Library Journal, July 2011, page 93

Other books by the same author:
Masterpiece, 2008
Shakespeare's Secret, 2005

Other books you might like:
Blue Balliett, *Chasing Vermeer*, 2004
Andrew Clements, *We the Children*, 2010
Steve Cotler, *Cheesie Mack Is Not a Genius or Anything*, 2011
Cynthia DeFelice, *The Light on Hogback Hill*, 1993
Troy Howell, *The Dragon of Cripple Creek*, 2011

48

DON BROWN

America Is under Attack: September 11, 2001: The Day the Towers Fell

(New York: Roaring Brook Press, 2011)

Series: Actual Times Series. Book 4

Subject(s): Terrorism; History; Social sciences

Age range(s): 8 - 10+

Summary: In *America Is Under Attack: September 11, 2001: The Day the Towers Fell*, author and illustrator Don Brown presents a frank account of the country's worst terrorist attacks for elementary-age readers. Brown tells the story of the tragic day in simple text and watercolor illustrations that express the emotions experienced by witnesses, first responders, and the American public. Written especially for children born after 9/11, and those who were just babies when the attacks took place, *America Is Under Attack* balances honest reporting with sensitivity to the frightening nature of the subject matter. This volume is the fourth book in the Actual Times series.

Where it's reviewed:
Booklist, September 1, 2011, page 93

Horn Book Magazine, November/December 2011, page 123
School Library Journal, September 2011, page 134

Other books by the same author:
Gold! Gold from the American River, 2011
A Wizard from the Start: The Incredible Boyhood and Amazing Inventions of Thomas Edison, 2010
All Stations! Distress!: April 15, 1912: The Day the Titanic Sank, 2008
Let It Begin Here!: April 19, 1775: The Day the American Revolution Began, 2008
Kid Blink Beats the World, 2004

Other books you might like:
Carmen Agra Deedy, *14 Cows for America*, 2009
Mordicai Gerstein, *The Man Who Walked between the Towers*, 2003
Mara Miller, *Terrorist Attacks: Disaster and Survival*, 2005

49

MONICA BROWN
SARA PALACIOS, Illustrator

Marisol McDonald Doesn't Match/Marisol McDonald no combina

(San Francisco, California: Children's Book Press, 2011)

Story type: Young Readers
Subject(s): Cultural identity; Self perception; Racially mixed people

Age range(s): 5 - 7+
Major character(s): Marisol McDonald, Girl (mixed race)

Summary: Everyone says Marisol McDonald doesn't match. But she doesn't see things this way. Plucky Marisol likes pairing polka dots with stripes, sports with make believe, and peanut butter and jelly with tortillas. These things are just what make this red-headed, brown-skinned girl one of a kind. The mixed-heritage child even comes up against her teacher for her seemingly contrary preferences—Marisol combines print and cursive when she writes her name—but in the end, even the teacher tells Marisol that she is unique and special. This bilingual story is enhanced with lively acrylic illustrations.

Where it's reviewed:
Publishers Weekly, September 5, 2011, page 49

Other books by the same author:
Waiting for Biblioburro, 2011
Chavela and the Magic Bubble, 2010
Butterflies on Carmen Street/Mariposas en la Calle Carmen, 2007

Other books you might like:
Alma Flor Ada, *I Love Saturdays Y Domingos*, 2002
Pat Mora, *Gracias Thanks*, 2009
Nicola Winstanley, *Cinnamon Baby*, 2011

50

PETER BROWN

The Curious Garden

(New York: Little, Brown Books for Young Readers, 2009)

Subject(s): Ecology; Trees (Plants); Gardens

Age range(s): 3 - 7+
Major character(s): Liam, Child, Gardener
Time period(s): 21st century; 2000s

Summary: *The Curious Garden* is a magical tale for young readers from author Peter Brown. One day, a young boy named Liam sets out to explore the aged and dingy city he calls home. While on his journey, he is surprised to discover a small garden, struggling to survive, in the midst of the bustling metropolis. Seeing the pitiful plants gives Liam an idea: he'll do what he can to help them grow! He never imagines that his kind act will lead to chaos. As the plants begin to flourish and thrive, they slowly spread, taking over the city bit by bit. Everything in the city is gradually changed as the garden expands until eventually the whole city has been transformed into magical and lush greenery.

Where it's reviewed:
Booklist, May 15, 2009, page 44
New York Times Book Review, May 10, 2009, page 14
Publishers Weekly, March 23, 2009, page 58
School Library Journal, April 2009, page 101

Other books by the same author:
Flight of the Dodo, 2005

Other books you might like:
DyAnne DiSalvo-Ryan, *City Green*, 1994
Michael Foreman, *A Child's Garden: A Story of Hope*, 2009
Bob Graham, *How to Heal A Broken Wing*, 2008
Sarah Stewart, *The Gardener*, 1997

51

ANTHONY BROWNE, Author/Illustrator

Me and You

(New York: Farrar, Straus and Giroux, 2010)

Subject(s): Bears; Fairy tales; Adventure

Age range(s): 4 - 8+
Major character(s): Baby Bear, Narrator
Time period(s): 21st century; 2010s

Summary: Author/illustrator Anthony Browne's *Me and You* is a modern reworking of the legendary fairy tale *Goldilocks and the Three Bears*. Set in a major metropolitan city, this volume finds a girl losing her way and ending up in the home of a family of bears. She eats their food and sleeps in their beds until the family comes back home and is shocked at the appearance of this stranger in their midst. The girl runs home to her mother, learning hard lessons about family, culture, and friendship.

Where it's reviewed:
Booklist, September 15, 2010, page 69
Bulletin of the Center for Children's Books, October 2010, page 65
Horn Book Magazine, November/December 2010, page 72
Publishers Weekly, October 11, 2010, page 43
School Library Journal, November 2010, page 90

Other books you might like:
John Burningham, *Time to Get out of the Bath, Shirley*, 1978
Bob Graham, *April and Esme: Tooth Fairies*, 2010
Dr. Seuss, *And to Think That I Saw It on Mulberry Street*, 1937

52

ASHLEY BRYAN
BILL MCGUINNESS, Photographer

Ashley Bryan: Words to My Life's Song

(New York: Atheneum Books for Young Readers, 2009)

Subject(s): Photography; Art; Autobiographies

Age range(s): 8 - 10+

Summary: *Ashley Bryan: Words to My Life's Song* is an autobiography written by Ashley Bryan with photographs by Bill McGuinness. In a scrapbook-type format of text and photographs, Bryan discusses his life, beginning with his parents who were born in Antigua and moved to New York with him and his five siblings. They inspired his lifelong love of art and writing, so much so that he even kept his art supplies in his gas mask when he was a soldier during World War II. Bryan then discusses his current home and lifestyle on a small island in Maine, where he keeps his studio and frequently walks along the beach looking for objects to use in his art. Bryan is also interested in foreign cultures, literature, and teaching others.

Where it's reviewed:
Booklist, December 15, 2009, page 51
Bulletin of the Center for Children's Books, January 2009, page 190
Horn Book Magazine, January/February 2009, page 109
School Library Journal, February 2009, page 115

Other books by the same author:
All Things Bright and Beautiful, 2010
A Beautiful Blackbird, 2003
What a Wonderful World, 1995
All Night All Day, 1991

Awards the book has won:
Golden Kite Awards: Nonfiction, 2010

Other books you might like:
Jen Bryant, *A River of Words: The Story of William Carlos Williams*, 2008
Langston Hughes, *My People*, 2009
Tony Medina, *I and I: Bob Marley*, 2009

53

LESLIE BULION
LESLIE EVANS, Illustrator

At the Sea Floor Cafe: Odd Ocean Critter Poems

(Atlanta: Peachtree Publishers, 2011)

Subject(s): Poetry; Oceanography; Animals

Age range(s): 9 - 12+

Summary: In this collection of poems by Leslie Bulion, with illustrations by Leslie Evans, strange and interesting sea creatures come to life through a variety of poetic devices, such as rhyming poems, haikus, and other forms of verse. Much of the ocean remains a mystery, but in this volume, readers gain a clearer understanding of animals like bottlenose dolphins, snapping shrimp, and violet snails. Containing 18 poems in all, the volume provides additional information in prose to further describe each animal. Several pages are devoted to explaining how to recreate the various forms of poetry employed throughout the book. Includes a glossary.

Where it's reviewed:
Horn Book Guide, Fall 2011, page 463
Publishers Weekly, February 14, 2011, page 55
School Library Journal, April 2011, page 190

Other books by the same author:
Uncharted Waters, 2009
Hey There Stink Bug, 2008

Other books you might like:
Chris Barton, *The Day-Glo Brothers: The True Story of Bob and Joe Switzer's Bright Ideas and Brand-New Colors*, 2009
Jennifer Berne, *Manfish*, 2008
Sylvia Earle, *Sea Critters*, 2000
David McLimans, *Gone Fishing*, 2008
Joyce Sidman, *Ubiquitous: Celebrating Nature's Survivors*, 2010

54

RAND BURKERT
NANCY EKHOLM BURKERT, Illustrator

Mouse and Lion

(New York: Scholastic, 2011)

Story type: Young Readers
Subject(s): Fables; Animals; Learning

Age range(s): 5 - 8+

Major character(s): Mouse, Friend (of Lion); Lion, Friend (of Mouse)

Summary: Illustrator Nancy Ekholm Burkert teams up with her son, Rand Burkert, to retell one of Aesop's classic tales. A small mouse trips over a sleeping lion, waking the beast from a long slumber. The terrified mouse apologizes to the lion and pleads for mercy. The mouse promises to help the lion if the large cat should ever need assistance. The lion takes pity on the mouse and lets him go. Later, the lion finds himself trapped in a hunter's net and in desperate need of the mouse's help. Nancy Ekholm Burkert is the illustrator of classic books such as *James and the Giant Peach* and *Snow-White and the Seven Dwarfs*. This is Rand Burkert's first book.

Where it's reviewed:
Booklist, December 1, 2011, page 51
Horn Book Magazine, November 2011, page 120
Publishers Weekly, August 22, 2011, page 62
Publishers Weekly, August 27, 2011, page 62
School Library Journal, August 2011, page 70

Other books you might like:
Kees Moerbeek, *Aesop's Fables: A Pop-Up Book of Classic Tales*, 2011
Jerry Pinkney, *Aesop's Fables*, 2000
Ed Young, *Seven Blind Mice*, 1992

55

JOHN BURNINGHAM, Author/Illustrator

It's a Secret!

(New York: Walker Books, 2009)

Subject(s): Animals; Entertaining; Adventure

Age range(s): 4 - 7+
Major character(s): Marie-Elaine, Child; Malcolm, Cat
Time period(s): 21st century; 2000s
Locale(s): United States

Summary: In *It's a Secret!* by John Burningham, Marie-Elaine, an inquisitive young girl, wonders what tires her cat Malcolm so much at night that he must sleep each day away. When she catches the cat on his way out, obviously dressed for a night on the town, Marie-Elaine accompanies him on his evening prowl. Magically making herself small and vowing to secrecy, Marie-Elaine makes the feline social circuit with Malcolm. Their outrageous adventures, captured in the artist's lively illustrations, take the pair from a rooftop gala to a royal feline feast, then safely back home where Marie-Elaine takes a much-needed catnap.

Where it's reviewed:
Booklist, June 1-15, 2009, page 65
Bulletin of the Center for Children's Books, September 2009, page 8
Horn Book Guide, Fall 2010, page 322
New York Times Book Review, December 6, 2009, page 52
School Library Journal, June 2009, page 80

Other books by the same author:
Time to Get Out of the Bath, Shirley, 1998
Hey! Get Off the Train, 1994

Other books you might like:
Cece Bell, *Itty Bitty*, 2009
Kevin Henkes, *Kitten's First Full Moon*, 2004
Ursula K. LeGuin, *Cat Dreams*, 2009
Ian Schoenherr, *Cat and Mouse*, 2008
Johanna Wright, *The Secret Circus*, 2009

56

JOHN BURNINGHAM
HELEN OXENBURY, Illustrator

There's Going to Be a Baby

(Somerville, Massachusetts: Candlewick Press, 2010)

Subject(s): Family; Brothers; Sisters

Age range(s): 2 - 7+

Summary: In *There's Going to be a Baby*, a small child finds out that he is going to be a big brother. Throughout the day, the boy asks his mother questions about the baby's name and what the baby will do when he or she grows up. The boy imagines his new brother or sister as a chef and then as a superhero. He looks forward to playing games with his sibling and secretly hopes the new baby is a boy. He anticipates the baby's arrival, but questions whether the sibling is really necessary. John Burningham and Helen Oxenbury are award-winning authors and illustrators, respectively.

Where it's reviewed:
Booklist, November 1, 2010, page 53
Bulletin of the Center for Children's Books, January 2011, page 229
Horn Book Guide, Spring 2011, page 5
Publishers Weekly, September 13, 2010, page 4
School Library Journal, October 2010, page 81

Other books by the same author:
The Magic Bed, 2007
Would You Rather, 1978
Mr. Gumpy's Outing, 1971

Other books you might like:
Kathi Appelt, *Brand-New Baby Blues*, 2010
Ezra Jack Keats, *Peter's Chair*, 1967
Sarah Sullivan, *Once Upon a Baby Brother*, 2010
Jacqueline Woodson, *Pecan Pie Baby*, 2010

57

LOREE GRIFFIN BURNS
ELLEN HARASIMOWICZ, Photographer

The Hive Detectives: Chronicle of a Honey Bee Catastrophe

(Boston: Houghton Mifflin Books for Children, 2010)

Subject(s): Bees; Science; Insects

Age range(s): 9 - 13+

Summary: In *The Hive Detectives: Chronicle of a Honey Bee Catastrophe*, author Loree Griffin Burns describes the phenomenon of Colony Collapse Disorder (CCD) in this accessible book for young readers. Burns introduces beekeeper Dave Hackenberg, who discovered in 2006 that his 3000 Florida hives had suddenly lost 20 million bees. When other apiarists reported similar incidents, a group of scientists was dispatched to explore the problem. Burns explains the investigative process that followed, providing information about the bees' physiology and its role in the environment and agriculture in the process. Photographs by Ellen Harasimowicz show bees and beekeepers at work.

Where it's reviewed:
Booklist, May 1, 2010, page 84
Bulletin of the Center for Children's Books, May 2010, page 372
Horn Book Magazine, May/June, 2010, page 104
School Library Journal, June 2010, page 123
Science Books & Film, August 2010, page 214

Other books by the same author:
Citizen Scientist: Be Part of Scientific Discovery From Your Own Backyard, 2012
Tracking Trash: Flotsam, Jetsam, and the Science of Ocean Motion, 2007

Other books you might like:
Jay Hosler, *Clan Apis*, 2000
Charles Micucci, *The Life and Times of the Honeybee*, 1995
C.C. Payne, *Something to Sing About*, 2008
Banning Repplier, *Letters from the Hive: An Intimate History of Bees, Honey, and Humankind*, 2006

58

CHRIS BUTTERWORTH
LUCIA GAGGIOTTI, Illustrator

How Did That Get In My Lunchbox?: The Story of Food
(Somerville, Massachusetts: Candlewick Press, 2011)

Subject(s): Food; Agriculture; Nutrition

Age range(s): 5 - 8+

Summary: Author Chris Butterworth and illustrator Lucia Gaggiotti examine the typical contents of a child's lunchbox and explain where food comes from in this picture book for young readers. Butterworth and Gaggiotti describe how wheat becomes flour, flour becomes dough, and dough becomes the bread in a sandwich. They also detail the source—and yummy flavors—of cheese, fruits and vegetables, and even chocolate. Complete with tips on healthy eating and an overview of the basic food groups, this book will teach young readers how farms, dairies, and factories make the foods they eat every day.

Where it's reviewed:
Booklist, April 15, 2011, page 50
Horn Book Magazine, March/April 2011, page 136
Publishers Weekly, January 31, 2011, page 47
School Library Journal, April 2011, page 157

Other books by the same author:
Sea Horse: The Shyest Fish in the Sea, 2006

Other books you might like:
Susan E. Goodman, *All in Just One Cookie*, 2006
Joan Holub, *The Garden That We Grew*, 2001
April Pulley Sayre, *Rah, Rah Radishes!: A Vegetable Chant*, 2011
Janet Stevens, *Tops and Bottoms*, 1995
Lauren Thompson, *The Apple Pie That Papa Baked*, 2007

59

SARAH C. CAMPBELL
RICHARD P. CAMPBELL, Photographer

Growing Patterns: Fibonacci Numbers in Nature
(Honesdale, Pennsylvania: Boyds Mills Press, 2010)

Subject(s): Science; Mathematics; Nature

Age range(s): 7 - 9+

Summary: This volume by Sarah C. Campbell and Richard P. Campbell introduces Fibonacci numbers and gives examples of how these numbers show up in nature. The Fibonacci sequence is created by adding the first number in the sequence to the next number to make a third number. The book shows how the Fibonacci numbers are seen in many different formations in nature, including seashells, pineapples, and sunflowers. The book includes photographs of the natural items, and it includes text explaining the images or inviting readers to discover how the Fibonacci sequence relates to the images.

Where it's reviewed:
Booklist, March 15, 2010, page 40
Bulletin of the Center for Children's Books, May 2010, page 373
Horn Book Magazine, May/June 2010, page 104
Publishers Weekly, February 22, 2010, page 64
Science Books & Film, August 2010, page 207

Other books by the same author:
Wolfsnail: A Backyard Predator, 2008

Other books you might like:
Joseph D' Agnese, *Blockhead: The Life of Fibonacci*, 2010
Nancy Farmer, *Clever Ali*, 2006
Betsy Franco, *Mathematickles*, 2002

60

CLAY CARMICHAEL

Wild Things
(Honesdale, Pennsylvania: Front Street, 2009)

Subject(s): Family; Trust (Psychology); Orphans

Age range(s): 10 - 12+

Major character(s): Zoe, 11-Year-Old, Orphan; Henry, Uncle (of Zoe), Artist, Doctor; Mr. C'mere, Cat

Time period(s): 21st century; 2000s

Locale(s): North Carolina, United States

Summary: In *Wild Things*, author Clay Carmichael spins a tale of family, trust, and second chances that focuses on a young orphan named Zoe and the uncle who takes her in. Eleven-year-old Zoe finds it next to impossible to trust adults, who seem to leave her behind with surprising ease. She is far from thrilled about being shipped to the backwoods of North Carolina to live with her sculptor/doctor uncle, Henry. Soon, however, Zoe and Henry forge a unique bond, discovering the wild world around them—and the even wilder frontiers of the human heart.

Where it's reviewed:
Booklist, April 15, 2009, page 395
Bulletin of the Center for Children's Books, June 2009, page 395

Awards the book has won:
AAUW Award, 2009

Other books you might like:
Ann M. Martin, *A Corner of the Universe*, 2002
Marilyn Taylor McDowell, *Carolina Harmony*, 2009
Renee Watson, *What Momma Left Me*, 2010

61

MARY KAY CARSON
TOM UHLMAN, Photographer
The Bat Scientists
(Boston: Houghton Mifflin Books for Children, 2011)

Subject(s): Animals; Bats (Animals); Science
Age range(s): 10 - 14+
Summary: This book describes bats and the scientists who try to keep them safe. Bats are flying mammals that usually sleep during the day and hunt for food at night. They live in different places all around the world, often in colonies with millions of members. Although some people are afraid of bats, they are actually helpful to humans because they pollinate plants and eat pests that bother humans, such as mosquitoes. Even though bats are helpful to humans, many types of bats are in danger. Bats around the world are dying because their habitats are being destroyed and because a dangerous disease, called white-nose syndrome, is spreading to many different bat colonies. Scientists are trying to keep bats' homes safe, and they are trying to find a cure for white-nose syndrome so that more bats can survive.

Where it's reviewed:
Booklist, October 15, 2010, page 50
Horn Book Magazine, Nov/Dec 2010, page 113

Other books by the same author:
Emi and the Rhino Scientist, 2007

Other books you might like:
Toney Allman, *From Bat Sonar to Cranes for the Blind*, 2006
Deborah Chase Gibson, *Bats and Their Homes*, 1999
Sophie Lockwood, *Bats*, 2008
Kim Williams, *Stokes Beginning Guide to Bats*, 2002

62

MARK CASSINO
JON NELSON, Co-Author
NORA AOYAGI, Illustrator
The Story of Snow: The Science of Winter's Wonder
(San Francisco: Chronicle Books, 2009)

Subject(s): Weather; Science; Photography
Age range(s): 5 - 8+

Summary: In *The Story of Snow: The Science of Winter's Wonder*, author and photographer Mark Cassino and teacher Jon Nelson offer young readers a detailed introduction to the world of snow. This volume explains what snow is, how it is formed, and what makes snow crystals so unique and varied. Accompanied by in-depth photographs, *The Story of Snow* is a one-of-a-kind celebration of winter's most beautiful gift. First book.

Where it's reviewed:
Booklist, December 1, 2009, page 57
Bulletin of the Center for Children's Books, December 2009, page 143
Horn Book Magazine, January/February 2010, page 107
School Library Journal, November 2009, page 93
Science Books & Film, November 2009, page 250

Awards the book has won:
Blue Ribbon Awards: Non-fiction, 2008

Other books you might like:
Jim Aylesworth, *The Mitten*, 2009
Carol Fenner, *Snowed in with Grandmother Silk*, 2003
Douglas Florian, *Winter Eyes: Poems and Paintings*, 1999
Jacqueline Briggs Martin, *Snowflake Bentley*, 1998
Neil Waldman, *The Snowflake: A Water Cycle Story*, 2003

63

P. W. CATANESE
Happenstance Found
(New York: Aladdin, 2009)

Series: Books of Umber Series. Book 1
Subject(s): Adventure; Fantasy; Identity
Age range(s): 9 - 12+
Major character(s): Happenstance "Hap", Adventurer, Amnesiac, Supernatural Being; Lord Umber, Adventurer, Inventor; The Creep, Villain
Time period(s): Indeterminate

Summary: In P.W. Catanese's *Happenstance Found*, the first entry in the Books of Umber series, a boy awakens in an underground cave in a strange new world and realizes that he has no recollection of his past. The boy eventually meets an adventurer, Lord Umber, who decides to call him Happenstance ("Hap" for short). Hap joins Lord Umber and his two sidekicks on their journey. As they travel, Lord Umber grows curious about the unique traits that Hap displays, such as his ability to see in the dark and leap to great heights. Hap also discovers that someone—or something—is following him. As Hap and his new pals try to learn more his past, they face many adventures and dangers and uncover some surprising secrets about Lord Umber as well.

Where it's reviewed:
Booklist, April 1 2009, page 31
Bulletin of the Center for Children's Books, March 2009, page 278
Horn Book Magazine, January/February 2009, page 89
Publishers Weekly, January 5, 2009, page 51
School Library Journal, May 2009, page 101

Other books by the same author:
The End of Time, 2011
Dragon Games, 2010

Other books you might like:
Patrick Carman, *Atherton: The House of Power*, 2007
Suzanne Collins, *Gregor the Overlander*, 2003
Brandon Mull, *Fablehaven*, 2006
Obert Skye, *Leven Thumps and the Gateway to Foo*, 2005

64

ANDREW CHAIKIN
ALAN BEAN, Illustrator

Mission Control, This Is Apollo: The Story of the First Voyages to the Moon

(New York: Penguin Group, 2009)

Subject(s): Space flight; Space exploration; United States history

Age range(s): 8 - 12+

Summary: This fully illustrated volume celebrates the life-changing mission of Apollo 11—the first spacecraft to land on the moon—and the subsequent moon-bound journeys of the United States space program. In *Mission Control, This Is Apollo: The Story of the First Voyages to the Moon*, author Andrew Chaikin chronicles the program's initial treks to the moon, from Apollo 1, which was plagued by a devastating fire, through the triumphs of Apollo 17. Artist and former astronaut Alan Bean provides a wealth of vibrant illustrations. *Mission Control, This Is Apollo* includes a listing of recommended movies, books, and Web sites, a full bibliography, and an index.

Where it's reviewed:
Booklist, May 1, 2009, page 80
Horn Book Magazine, July/August 2009, page 438
School Library Journal, May 2009, page 121
Science Books & Film, October 2009, page 221

Other books by the same author:
Voices From the Moon: Apollo Astronauts Describe Their Lunar Experiences, 2009
Space: A History of Space Exploration in Photos, 2004
A Man on the Moon: They Voyages of the Apollo Astronauts, 1999
Apollo: An Eyewitness Account by Astronaut/Explorer Artist/Moonwalker, 1998

Other books you might like:
Alan Dyer, *Mission to the Moon*, 2009
Brian Floca, *Moonshot: The Flight of Apollo 11*, 2009
Bea Uusma Schyffert, *The Man Who Went to the Far Side of the Moon: The Story of Apollo 11 Astronaut Michael Collins*, 2003
Jerry Stone, *One Small Step: Celebrating the First Men on the Moon*, 2009
Catherine Thimmesh, *Team Moon: How 400,000 People Landed Apollo 11 on the Moon*, 2006

65

EMMA CHICHESTER-CLARK, Author/Illustrator

Goldilocks and the Three Bears

(Somerville, Massachusetts: Candlewick Press, 2010)

Subject(s): Bears; Fairy tales; Housing

Age range(s): 2 - 6+

Major character(s): Goldilocks, Child, Girl; Mama Bear, Bear; Papa Bear, Bear; Baby Bear, Bear

Summary: *Goldilocks and the Three Bears* is a humorous and entertaining picture book for young readers from author and illustrator Emma Chichester-Clark. While the three bears are away, Goldilocks will play! Goldilocks is a young girl looking for a simple meal and an afternoon of relaxation when she stumbles upon the cottage belonging to the three bears. After trying out Papa Bear, Mama Bear, and Baby Bear's lunch, chairs, and beds, Goldilocks discovers the one that's just right for her—before the bears discover her! Filled with acrylic and pencil illustrations, this version of the popular story offers more detail about the bears' reaction to their uninvited guest.

Where it's reviewed:
Booklist, December 1, 2010, page 46
Bulletin of the Center for Children's Books, February 2010, page 240
Horn Book Guide, Fall 2010, page 400
School Library Journal, February 2010, page 80

Other books by the same author:
Pied Piper of Hamlin, 2011
Hansel and Gretel, 2008
Little Miss Muffet's Count-Along Surprise, 1997
Thumbelina, 1996
The Frog Princess, 1995

Awards the book has won:
Blue Ribbon Awards: Picture Books, 2010

Other books you might like:
Anthony Browne, *Me and You*, 2010
Mary Ann Hoberman, *You Read to Me, I'll Read to You: Very Short Fairy Tales to Read Together*, 2004
James Marshall, *Goldilocks and the Three Bears*, 1988

66

JASON CHIN, Author/Illustrator

Coral Reefs

(New York: Roaring Brook Press, 2011)

Subject(s): Islands; Natural resources; Oceanography

Age range(s): 5 - 8+

Summary: In this picture book, author and illustrator Jason Chin introduces young readers to coral reefs. When a young girl visits the library, she chooses a book about coral reefs that transforms the library setting into an ocean floor. There, she views the majesty of coral reefs and learns about their importance and why they exist. Along the way, the young girl also encounters the flora and fauna that coexist in sea their home. Chin uses brightly colored illustrations to depict the sea life that surrounds the girl as she swims among the intricate coral formations. Jason Chin is also the author of *Redwoods*.

Where it's reviewed:
Booklist, August 2011, page 40
Horn Book Magazine, September/October 2011, page 110
Publishers Weekly, September 19, 2011, page 60
School Library Journal, October 2011, page 40

Other books by the same author:
Redwoods, 2009

Other books you might like:
Sylvia Earle, *Coral Reefs*, 2003
Julia Sarcone-Roach, *Subway Story*, 2011
Niki Walker, *Life in the Coral Reef*, 1996

67

JASON CHIN

Redwoods

(New York: Flash Point, 2009)

Subject(s): Trees (Plants); Science; Adventure

Age range(s): 5 - 8+
Time period(s): 21st century; 2000s
Locale(s): California, United States

Summary: A little boy happens upon a book about redwood trees as he waits for the subway. Once he boards the train, he becomes engrossed in the volume, learning all about the towering trees and their fascinating history. As he reads the stories of the redwoods, the boy is surprised to find the pages of the book coming to life all around him. From ancient Rome to modern-day California, *Redwoods* blends accessible scientific information and childlike whimsy to tell of an imaginative boy's adventure to the tops of the tallest trees on Earth. Author Jason Chin provides the volume's illustrations.

Where it's reviewed:
Booklist, April 1, 2009, page 39
Horn Book Magazine, May/June 2009, page 321
Publishers Weekly, March 9, 2009, page 49
School Library Journal, May 2009, page 72

Other books by the same author:
Coral Reefs, 2011

Other books you might like:
Timothee de Fombelle, *Toby Alone*, 2009
Debbie S. Miller, *Are Trees Alive?*, 2002
Claire A. Nivola, *Planting the Trees of Kenya: The Story of Wangari Maathai*, 2008
Richard C. Vogt, *Rain Forests*, 2009

68

GENNIFER CHOLDENKO

No Passengers beyond This Point

(New York: Dial Books, 2011)

Subject(s): Alternative worlds; Brothers and sisters; Adventure

Age range(s): 10 - 12+
Major character(s): Finn, 12-Year-Old, Brother (of India and Mouse); India, 14-Year-Old, Sister (of Finn and Mouse); Mouse, 6-Year-Old, Sister (of Finn and India)
Time period(s): 21st century; 2010s
Locale(s): Colorado, United States

Summary: In Gennifer Choldenko's *No Passengers Beyond This Point*, Finn, India, and Mouse are young siblings who lose their home and are in no way prepared for the time-bending adventure that awaits. En route to stay with a relative, they somehow land in an alternate reality, where the entire world is different. And in this strange place, the citizens seem intent on keeping the children right where they are. But forces of evil seem to be roiling just below the surface, and when the kids' new home is destroyed, their battle for survival and their hopes for return become the ultimate fight of their lives.

Where it's reviewed:
Booklist, February 1, 2011, page 80
Bulletin of the Center for Children's Books, January 2011, page 230
Horn Book Magazine, January/February 2011, page 90
School Library Journal, February 2011, page 104
Voice of Youth Advocates, April 2011, page 77

Other books by the same author:
If a Tree Falls at Lunch Period, 2007
Al Capone Does My Shirts, 2006
Al Capone Shines My Shoes, 2004
Notes from a Liar and Her Dog, 2001

Other books you might like:
Natalie Babbitt, *Tuck Everlasting*, 1975
Margaret Peterson Haddix, *Found*, 2008
Rebecca Stead, *When You Reach Me*, 2009
Gabrielle Zevin, *Elsewhere*, 2005

69

BONNIE CHRISTENSEN, Author/Illustrator

Fabulous!: A Portrait of Andy Warhol

(New York: Henry Holt and Co., 2011)

Subject(s): Biographies; Art; Painting (Art)

Age range(s): 8 - 11+

Summary: Author and illustrator Bonnie Christensen shares the life story of artist and pop culture icon Andy Warhol in this book for young readers. Christensen begins Warhol's story in 1930s Pittsburgh, Pennsylvania, where Warhol spent his childhood sketching pictures and reading comic books. She then explains Warhol's rise to fame, describing the obstacles he overcame to achieve success. Christensen ends at the pinnacle of Warhol's career in the 1960s, when he seamlessly blended the worlds of commercial and fine art. Through a combination of prose, oil painting, and collage, Christensen reveals the life of an art legend.

Where it's reviewed:
Booklist, June 1, 2011, page 78
Horn Book Magazine, July/August 2011, page 169
School Library Journal, May 2011, page 95

Other books by the same author:
Django: World's Greatest Jazz Guitarist, 2009
The Daring Nellie Bly: America's Star Reporter, 2003
Woody Guthrie: Poet of the People, 2001

Other books you might like:
Jan Greenberg, *Action Jackson*, 2002
Jon Scieszka, *Seen Art?*, 2005
James Warhola, *Uncle Andy's Cats*, 2009
James Warhola, *Uncle Andy's: A Faabbbulous Visit with Andy Warhol*, March 10, 2003
Natasha Wing, *An Eye for Color: The Story of Josef Albers*, 2008

70

BONNIE CHRISTENSEN, Author/Illustrator

Django: World's Greatest Jazz Guitarist

(New York: Roaring Brook Press, 2009)

Story type: Young Readers
Subject(s): Biographies; Jazz; Music

Summary: *Django: World's Greatest Jazz Guitarist*, by Bonnie Christensen, is an illustrated biography of legendary jazz musician Django Reinhardt. Born in Belgium to a Romany clan, Reinhardt learned to play violin and guitar at a very young age. He spent much of his young life playing in his gypsy caravan until he made his way to France after his father left him. There, he quickly gained a local reputation and was booked in clubs around Paris. When a tragic fire left him with a handicapped hand, he worked around his disability to play jazz music once again. Here, Christensen tells a story suited for young readers about an artistic musician who played a major role in the Jazz era.

Where it's reviewed:
Booklist, November 1, 2009, page 139
Bulletin of the Center for Children's Books, January 2010, page 190
Horn Book Guide, Spring 2010, page 169
School Library Journal, September 2009, page 139

Other books by the same author:
Fabulous!: A Portrait of Andy Warhol, 2011
The Daring Nellie Bly: America's Star Reporter, 2009
Woody Guthrie: Poet of the People, 2001

Other books you might like:
Bonnie Christensen, *Woody Guthrie: Poet of the People*, 2001

Walter Dean Myers, *Jazz*, 2006
Levi Pinfold, *The Django*, 2010
Sarah Sullivan, *Passing the Music Down*, 2011

71

NATHAN CLEMENT, Author/Illustrator

Job Site

(Honesdale, Pennsylvania: Boyds Mills Press, 2011)

Story type: Young Readers
Subject(s): Construction; Machinery; Work environment

Age range(s): 3 - 6+
Major character(s): Boss, Construction Worker (boss)

Summary: A construction site filled with big, heavy machines provides the backdrop for this picture story by author and illustrator Nathan Clement. Bright, digital illustrations accompany the text and show each machine carrying out a task as directed by Boss. Whether leveling a pile of rock, digging a hole, or lifting a big stone, the machines follow Boss's orders to get the job done. Among the many machines are a bulldozer, an excavator, a dump truck, and a crane. Alternating perspectives allow readers to see the construction site from various angles, and the completed project—revealed at the end of the book—is one kids can appreciate.

Where it's reviewed:
Horn Book Guide, Fall 2011, page 294
Publishers Weekly, January 24, 2011, page 148
School Library Journal, May 2011, page 74

Other books by the same author:
Drive, 2008

Other books you might like:
Tana Hoban, *Construction Zone*, 1997
William Low, *Machines Go to Work*, 2009
Lynn Meltzer, *The Construction Crew*, 2011
June Sobel, *B Is for Bulldozer: A Construction ABC*, 2003
Sally Sutton, *Roadwork*, 2008

72

ANDREW CLEMENTS
ADAM STOWER, Illustrator

We the Children

(New York: Atheneum Books for Young Readers, 2010)

Series: Benjamin Pratt and Keepers of the School Series. Book 1
Subject(s): Schools; Mystery; Sailing

Age range(s): 9 - 11+
Major character(s): Benjamin "Ben" Pratt, 6th Grader, Detective—Amateur; Jill, Friend (of Ben)
Time period(s): 21st century; 2010s
Locale(s): New England, United States

Summary: *We the Children* is the first novel in Andrew Clements's Benjamin Pratt and Keepers of the School series. This volume introduces sixth grader Benjamin

Pratt, who is shocked to learn that his school is slated for demolition at the hands of a powerful corporation. Determined to save the historic building, Benjamin teams up with his friend Jill, and they attempt to rally the community. But Ben has a secret weapon. The school janitor, moments before his death, handed Ben a mysterious coin—a coin that just might have the power to alter the fate of the entire school. *We the Children* contains illustrations by Adam Stower.

Where it's reviewed:
Bulletin of the Center for Children's Books, May 2010, page 375
Horn Book Magazine, May/June 2010, page 78
School Library Journal, May 2010, page 107

Other books by the same author:
The Whites of Their Eyes, 2012
Troublemaker, 2011
Fear Itself, 2010
Extra Credit, 2009
Frindle, 1996

Other books you might like:
Blue Balliett, *Chasing Vermeer*, 2004
Simon Cheshire, *The Curse of the Ancient Mask and Other Case Files*, 2011
Jody Feldman, *The Seventh Level*, 2010
Lynne Jonell, *Emmy and the Incredible Shrinking Rat*, 2007
Louis Sachar, *Holes*, 1998

73

BROCK COLE, Author/Illustrator

The Money We'll Save

(New York: Farrar, Straus and Giroux, 2011)

Story type: Holiday Themes; Humor
Subject(s): Turkeys; Christmas; Holidays

Age range(s): 5 - 8+
Major character(s): Pa, Father; Ma, Mother; Alfred, Bird (turkey)
Time period(s): 19th century
Locale(s): New York, United States

Summary: In 19th-century New York, Pa decides to get a head start on Christmas dinner preparations. He brings home a tiny turkey and tells Ma that if they keep the turkey in a box by the stove and feed it table scraps, it will be nice and plump in time for Christmas. Pa adds, "Think of the money we'll save!" The turkey, whom the family names Alfred, soon outgrows his box and wreaks havoc on the tiny apartment. Alfred wrinkles Ma's clothes and eats the baby's food. One day he escapes and Pa and the children must hunt him down and bring him back. Unable to keep him in the kitchen any longer, Pa suggests giving Alfred his own bedroom. As Christmas approaches, Alfred is as big as can be and the family must make a difficult decision—one that will leave them all satisfied after Christmas dinner.

Where it's reviewed:
Booklist, December 1, 2011, page 67

Horn Book Magazine, November/December 2011, page 67
Publishers Weekly, September 26, 2011, page 71
School Library Journal, October 2011, page 57

Other books by the same author:
Good Enough to Eat, 2007
Larky Mavis, 2001
Buttons, 2000

Other books you might like:
Candace Fleming, *Clever Jack Takes the Cake*, 2010
Polly Horvath, *The Pepins and Their Problems*, 2004
Tanya Landman, *Mary's Penny*, 2010
Isaac Bashevis Singer, *The Fools of Chelm and Their History*, 1973
Jeanne Steig, *Fleas!*, 2008

74

HENRY COLE, Author/Illustrator

A Nest for Celeste: A Story about Art, Inspiration, and the Meaning of Home

(New York: Katherine Tegen Books, 2010)

Story type: Historical
Subject(s): Human-animal relationships; Animals; Artists

Age range(s): 9 - 11+
Major character(s): Celeste, Mouse; John James Audubon, Naturalist, Historical Figure; Joseph Mason, Artist, Apprentice (to Audubon); Cornelius, Bird (thrush); Lafayette, Bird (osprey)
Time period(s): 19th century; 1820s (1821)
Locale(s): New Orleans, Louisiana

Summary: In this novel for children and young adults by author and illustrator Henry Cole, the famed naturalist John James Audubon and his apprentice, Joseph Mason, have come to Louisiana's Oakley Plantation to study the wildlife there. Living in the plantation house is a mouse named Celeste, who weaves baskets and does her best to avoid the plantation's rats and cats. When Celeste finds safe haven beneath the floor of Joseph's room, the boy and mouse become friends. Joseph is working hard to draw suitable backgrounds for Audubon's depictions of the local birds; Celeste is struggling to find a permanent home. As Celeste interacts with the humans and wildlife at the plantation, she learns difficult lessons about man's treatment of animals and her own place in the world.

Where it's reviewed:
Booklist, February 15, 2010, page 78
Horn Book Guide, Fall 2010, page 333
Publishers Weekly, February 8, 2010, page 50
School Library Journal, March 2010, page 116

Other books by the same author:
Sojourner Truth's Step-Stomp Stride, 2009
Boycott Blues: How Rosa Parks Inspired a Nation, 2008
Let It Shine: Stories of Black Women Freedom Fighters, 2000

Hold Fast to Dreams, 1995
Dear Benjamin Banneker, 1994

Other books you might like:
Jennifer Armstrong, *Audubon: Painter of Birds in the Wild Frontier*, 2003
Elise Broach, *Masterpiece*, 2008
Jacqueline Davies, *The Boy Who Drew Birds: A Story of John James Audubon*, 2004
Carmen Agra Deedy, *The Cheshire Cheese Cat: A Dickens of a Tale*, 2011
William Wise, *Christopher Mouse: The Tale of a Small Traveler*, 2004

75

CAROLYN COMAN
ROB SHEPPERSON, Illustrator

The Memory Bank

(New York: Arthur A. Levine, 2010)

Subject(s): Child abuse; Parent-child relations; Memory

Age range(s): 8 - 11+

Major character(s): Hope Scroggins, Sister (of Honey); Honey Scroggins, Sister (of Hope)

Summary: *The Memory Bank* focuses on Hope Scroggins, a young girl whose sister, Honey, has been abandoned on the side of the road by their parents at the beginning of the novel. Soon, Hope finds herself at a place called the Memory Bank, a mysterious place where everything that anyone has ever dreamed or remembered is filed away. Although she is at first intrigued by the Memory Bank's efficiency and order, she soon learns that the Memory Bank is less innocuous than she had originally believed. Meanwhile, Honey joins a band of children known as the Clean Slate Gang, who want to bring the Memory Bank to its knees in order to free the world of its oppression.

Where it's reviewed:
Booklist, November 1, 2010, page 52
Bulletin of the Center for Children's Books, December 2010, page 177
Horn Book Guide, Spring 2011, page 67
School Library Journal, December 2010, page 106

Other books by the same author:
Sneaking Suspicions, 2007
The Big House, 2004

Other books you might like:
Lyn Gardner, *Into the Woods*, 2006
Adam Gidwitz, *A Tale Dark and Grimm*, 2010
Lois Lowry, *Gossamer*, 2006
Elaine Scott, *All About Sleep from A to ZZZ*, 2009
Anne Ursu, *Breadcrumbs*, 2011

76

YING CHANG COMPESTINE
SEBASTIA SERRA, Illustrator

The Runaway Wok

(New York: Dutton Children's Books, 2011)

Story type: Young Readers
Subject(s): Chinese (Asian people)

Age range(s): 5 - 8+
Major character(s): Ming, Boy, Impoverished
Locale(s): China

Summary: Ming's family needs food to eat for the Chinese New Year, so Ming is tasked with going to the market to trade his family's last egg for some rice. When Ming arrives at the market, he sees a man selling an old, rusty wok. When Ming sees that the wok is magical and can sing, he trades his last egg for the pot. When Ming returns home with the seemingly worthless object, his parents are angry. However, when the wok begins to sing, Ming's family also sees its worth. The magical wok runs away to visit the wealthy Zhang family, for whom Ming's family works. The wok tricks the greedy Zhang family members into giving it food, toys, and money—all of which the wok gives to Ming, his family, and their friends.

Where it's reviewed:
Booklist, January 1, 2011, page 114
Horn Book Guide, Fall 2011, page 311
Publishers Weekly, November 29, 2010, page 49
School Library Journal, February 2011, page 76

Other books by the same author:
Boy Dumplings, 2009
D Is for Dragon Dance, 2005
The Runaway Rice Cake, 2001

Other books you might like:
Karen Chinn, *Sam and the Lucky Money*, 1995
Virginia Haviland, *The Talking Pot: A Danish Folktale*, 1990
Grace Lin, *Dim Sum for Everyone!*, 2001

77

JANE LESLIE CONLY

Murder Afloat

(New York: Hyperion Books, 2010)

Subject(s): Adventure; Sailing; Kidnapping

Age range(s): 10 - 13+
Major character(s): Benjamin Franklin Orville, Boy, Kidnap Victim, 14-Year-Old
Time period(s): 19th century; 1880s
Locale(s): Baltimore, Maryland

Summary: In *Murder Afloat*, young Benjamin Orville lives a life most people only dream of; he gets everything his heart desires, he has loving family, and he's even won the attention of a cute neighbor. Benjamin leads a blessed life, so he's caught completely unaware one afternoon when he is kidnapped and dragged aboard an oyster ship. Benjamin's life takes a complete turn. His pleas to return home fall on deaf ears, and he's forced to do hard labor while he's starved for food. Yet despite his misery, Benjamin learns to appreciate his new life. Now, he wonders if he'll ever want to return to land.

Where it's reviewed:
Booklist, December 1, 2010, page 61
Bulletin of the Center for Children's Books, November 2010, page 124
Horn Book Magazine, November/December 2010, page 87
School Library Journal, March 2011, page 158

Other books by the same author:
In the Night, on Lanvale Street, 2005

Other books you might like:
Deborah Hopkinson, *Into the Firestorm: A Novel of San Francisco, 1906*, 2006
Iain Lawrence, *The Convicts: The Curse of the Jolly Stone Trilogy*, 2005
L.A. Meyer, *Bloody Jack: Being an Account of the Curious Adventures of Mary "Jacky" Faber, Ship's Boy*, 2002
Andrea Warren, *Orphan Train Rider: One Boy's True Story*, 1996
Elvira Woodruff, *Fearless*, 2007

78

LESLIE CONNOR

Crunch

(New York: Katherine Tegen Books, 2010)

Subject(s): Self reliance; Coming of age; Brothers and sisters
Age range(s): 10 - 12+
Major character(s): Dewey Marriss, 14-Year-Old; Lil Marriss, 18-Year-Old, Sister (of Dewey)
Time period(s): 21st century; 2010s
Locale(s): United States

Summary: Leslie Connor's *Crunch* follows 14-year-old Dewey Marriss and his attempts to run the family business while his parents are unexpectedly stranded. When a gas shortage stops Dewey's parents' vacation in its tracks, the elder Marrisses are marooned near the Canadian border. This chain of events forces Dewey and his older sister, Lil, to operate the family-owned bicycle repair shop and keep up with the chores on the family farm on their own. Suddenly Dewey's life takes on new purpose and meaning as he learns the challenges and rewards of responsibility.

Where it's reviewed:
Bulletin of the Center for Children's Books, June 2010, page 425
Horn Book Magazine, July/August 2010, page 102
School Library Journal, May 2010, page 107

Other books by the same author:
Waiting for Normal, 2008

Other books you might like:
Sue Corbett, *The Last Newspaper Boy in America*, 2009

Lynne Rae Perkins, *As Easy as Falling off the Face of the Earth*, 2010
Susan Beth Pfeffer, *Life as We Knew It*, 2006

79

KATE COOMBS

The Runaway Dragon

(New York: Farrar, Straus and Giroux, 2009)

Story type: Fantasy
Subject(s): Dragons; Prisoners; Giants

Age range(s): 10 - 13+
Major character(s): Meg, 16-Year-Old (princess), Adventurer; Laddy, Runaway, Dragon (of Meg); Dilly, Friend (of Meg); Cam, Gardener (assistant), Friend (of Meg); Lex, Young Man, Wizard, Friend (of Meg); Nort, Guard, Friend (of Meg); Bain, Outlaw; Spinach, Girl

Summary: Princess Meg has been neglecting her pet dragon, Laddy. Sick of being cooped up, he takes flight and runs away from home. The 16-year-old princess sets off through the enchanted forest in pursuit. She takes along her pals Dilly, the lady-in-waiting; Cam, the assistant gardener; Lex, a youthful wizard; and Nort, a guardsman, as well as some of her parents' guards. Though this daring princess won't give a second glance to preening princes who come to call, an encounter with a bandit named Bain certainly makes an impression. The group encounters a girl giant, an evil witch, and other obstacles on its journey. Meg also rescues Spinach, a girl with incredibly long hair, from a tower and adds her to the dragon search team.

Where it's reviewed:
Booklist, September 1, 2009, page 86
Horn Book Magazine, September/October 2009, page 556
School Library Journal, September 2009, page 154

Other books by the same author:
The Runaway Princess, 2006

Other books you might like:
Jessica Day George, *Dragon Slippers*, 2007
Catherine Gilbert Murdock, *Princess Ben: Being a Wholly Truthful Account of Her Various Discoveries and Misadventures, Recounted to the Best of Her Recollection, in Four Parts*, 2008
Nancy McKenzie, *Guinevere's Gift*, 2008
Patricia C. Wrede, *Dealing with Dragons*, 1990

80

ELISHA COOPER, Author/Illustrator

Beaver Is Lost

(New York: Schwartz and Wade Books, 2010)

Subject(s): Beavers; Adventure; Family
Age range(s): 3 - 7+
Major character(s): Beaver, Beaver
Time period(s): 21st century; 2010s

Summary: Told with no words, this volume chronicles the adventures of a young beaver who becomes lost and ends up on the mean streets of a big city. Determined to find his way home, Beaver runs into a dog, an artificial alligator, a family of beavers at the city zoo, and much more as he attempts to navigate the city streets. An instinctual decision to trail a mouse leads him to a body of water, which eventually carries him home to his waiting, worried family. *Beaver Is Lost* is told through Elisha Cooper's illustrations.

Where it's reviewed:
Booklist, June 1, 2010, page 90
Bulletin of the Center for Children's Books, June 2010, page 425
Horn Book Magazine, July/August 2010, page 88
Publishers Weekly, May 17, 2010, page 47
School Library Journal, June 2010, page 66

Other books by the same author:
Bear Dreams, 2006
A Good Night Walk, 2005
Magic Thinks Big, 2004

Other books you might like:
Dan Andreasen, *The Treasure Bath*, 2009
Emily Gravett, *Meerkat Mail*, 2007
Margaret Hall, *Beavers*, 2004
Antoinette Portis, *A Penguin Story*, 2009
Jane Simmons, *Come Along, Daisy!*, 1998

81

ELISHA COOPER, Author/Illustrator

Farm

(New York: Orchard Books, 2010)

Subject(s): Rural life; Animals; Family

Age range(s): 4 - 8+

Summary: *Farm* is an educational picture book about rural life from award-winning author and illustrator, Elisha Cooper. The book teaches children about life on a farm throughout every season of the year. *Farm* follows the daily adventures of a family and group of animals that reside at the farm. The children must do chores every morning, seeds must be planted in the spring, and crops are harvested every fall. The farm is home to countless animals, including cows, chickens, cats, and a dog. Complemented by beautiful watercolor illustrations from Cooper, *Farm* reveals the lifestyle, creatures, and activities associated with rural living.

Where it's reviewed:
Booklist, February 1 2010, page 49
Bulletin of the Center for Children's Books, June 2010, page 416
Horn Book Magazine, May/June 2009, page 63
Publishers Weekly, February 15, 2010, page 128
School Library Journal, March 2010, page 116

Other books by the same author:
Beach, 2006
Building, 1999
Ballpark, 1998

Awards the book has won:
Blue Ribbon Awards: Picture Books, 2010

Other books you might like:
David Elliott, *On the Farm*, 2008
Arthur Geisert, *Country Road ABC: An Illustrated Journey Through America's Farmland*, 2010
Jon Katz, *Meet the Dogs of Bedlam Farm*, 2011
Mary Lyn Ray, *Christmas Farm*, 2008

82

ILENE COOPER

Angel in My Pocket

(New York: Feiwel and Friends, 2011)

Story type: Light Fantasy
Subject(s): Interpersonal relations; Grief; Friendship

Age range(s): 10 - 12+
Major character(s): Bette, 7th Grader, Sister (of Barbra); Barbra, Student—College, Sister (of Bette); Vivi Minkus, 7th Grader, Twin (of Andy); Andy Minkus, 7th Grader, Twin (of Vivi); Joe, 7th Grader, Bully (of Andy); Gabby, Woman, Neighbor (of Bette)
Time period(s): 21st century; 2010s
Locale(s): Chicago, Illinois

Summary: An angel coin in a pile of loose change turns out to be a magical talisman capable of changing lives in this novel by Ilene Cooper. Seventh-grade student Bette has been through a lot. Her mother passed away two years ago, and her sister, Barbra, just moved away to attend college. Bette has had trouble dealing with all this loss, but after discovering a strange angel coin one day, things in her life start to improve. After meeting Gabby, a kind new neighbor in her Chicago apartment building, Bette starts to overcome her grief and move on. Meanwhile, the angel coin makes its way into the hands of three of Bette's classmates, who also experience positive changes in their lives. Somehow—whether through luck, fate, or magic—the four very different children form an unlikely bond and develop newfound confidence.

Where it's reviewed:
Booklist, February 15, 2011, page 74
Bulletin of the Center for Children's Books, May 2011, page 410
Publishers Weekly, January 24, 2011, page 153
School Library Journal, March 2011, page 158
Voice of Youth Advocates, June 2011, page 160

Other books by the same author:
Sam I Am, 2004

Other books you might like:
Deirdre Baker, *Becca at Sea*, 2007
Katie Pickard Fawcett, *To Come and Go Like Magic*, 2010
Lindsey Leavitt, *Princess for Hire*, 2010
Pat Murphy, *The Wild Girls*, 2007

83

SUE CORBETT

The Last Newspaper Boy in America

(New York: Dutton Juvenile, 2009)

Subject(s): Newspapers; Friendship; Family

Age range(s): 9 - 12+
Major character(s): Wilson "Wil" David, 12-Year-Old
Time period(s): 21st century; 2000s
Locale(s): Steele, Pennsylvania

Summary: Wilson "Wil" David has looked forward to turning 12 for a long time. He's been looking forward to this birthday for so long because it's a tradition in his family that when a boy turns 12 he gets his own newspaper route. Wil is disappointed when the big newspaper company decides to stop delivering the paper to Wil's hometown of Steele, Pennsylvania. Wil isn't afraid of the company, however, and he begins a campaign to keep the paper in town. With the help of his brother and his neighbor, Wil hopes to save the town's newspaper—but he might do even more. *The Last Newspaper Boy in America* is a novel written by Sue Corbett, who is also the author of *Free Baseball*.

Where it's reviewed:
Booklist, August 1, 2009, page 69
Bulletin of the Center for Children's Books, November 2009, page 106
Horn Book Guide, Spring 2010, page 66
Publishers Weekly, July 27, 2009, page 63
School Library Journal, October 2009, page 124

Other books by the same author:
Free Baseball, 2008

Other books you might like:
A.C.E. Bauer, *No Castles Here*, 2007
Andrew Clements, *The Landry News*, 1999
Lois Duncan, *News for Dogs*, 2009
Liza Ketchum, *Newsgirl*, 2009
Michael Winerip, *Adam Canfield of the Slash*, 2005

84

FRANK COTTRELL BOYCE

Cosmic

(Walden Pond Press, New York: Harper, 2010)

Subject(s): Adventure; Space exploration; Humor

Age range(s): 9 - 12+
Major character(s): Liam, 12-Year-Old
Time period(s): 21st century; 2010s
Locale(s): United Kingdom

Summary: Frank Cottrell Boyce's *Cosmic* chronicles the space-traveling adventures of 12-year-old Liam, an adolescent who looks much older than he actually is. Constantly mistaken for an adult, Liam utilizes his mature looks to finagle his way onto a rocket ship transporting average citizens into space. But this undertaking is far more perilous—and humorous—than Liam had counted on. He soon joins forces with his fellow passengers to make his way through the unknown frontiers of outer space in hopes of finding his way back home.

Where it's reviewed:
Booklist, November 15, 2010, page 36
Bulletin of the Center for Children's Books, February 2010, page 231
Horn Book Magazine, March/April 2010, page 52
New York Times Book Review, January 17, 2010, page 13
School Library Journal, February 2010, page 105

Other books by the same author:
Framed, 2006
Millions, 2004

Other books you might like:
Michael J. Daley, *Shanghaied to the Moon*, 2007
Donna Gephart, *How to Survive Middle School*, 2010
David Klass, *Stuck on Earth*, 2010
Geraldine McCaughrean, *The Death-Defying Pepper Roux*, 2010
Rodman Philbrick, *The Mostly True Adventures of Homer P. Figg*, 2009

85

FRANK COTTRELL BOYCE
CARL HUNTER, Photographer
CLARE HENEY, Photographer

The Un-Forgotten Coat

(Somerville, Massachusetts: Candlewick Press, 2011)

Story type: Young Readers
Subject(s): Immigrants; Emigration and immigration; Children

Age range(s): 8 - 12+
Major character(s): Julie, 6th Grader, Friend (of Chingis and Nergui); Chingis, Brother (of Nergui), 6th Grader, Friend (of Julie); Nergui, Friend (of Julie), Brother (of Chingis), 6th Grader
Locale(s): Bootle, England

Summary: Two new students from Mongolia arrive in Julie's sixth-grade class in Bottle, England. The brothers, Chingis and Nergui, immediately designate Julie as their "Good Guide." She happily takes on this role, showing them around the school and telling them everything they need to know about life in Britain. As she grows closer to the boys, Julie finds herself learning from them and wondering about their home life. The mystery surrounding the boys deepens when they tell her that a demon is pursuing them. Author Frank Cottrell Boyce writes the story from grown-up Julie's perspective. She begins writing down memories of her two friends after an unclaimed coat is found at her former school. The photographs found inside the coat's pockets make Julie wonder what happened to Chingis and Nergui.

Where it's reviewed:
Booklist, September 1, 2011, page 122
Publishers Weekly, August 22, 2011, page 64

School Library Journal, November 2011, page 113

Other books by the same author:
Cosmic, 2010
Millions, 2004

Other books you might like:
Tony Abbott, *Firegirl*, 2006
Katherine Applegate, *Home of the Brave*, 2007
Ted Lewin, *Horse Song*, 2008
Jenny Lombard, *Drita, My Homegirl*, 2006

86

PHILIPPE COUDRAY, Author/Illustrator
LEIGH STEIN, Translator

Benjamin Bear in Fuzzy Thinking
(New York: Toon Books, 2011)

Story type: Young Readers
Subject(s): Bears; Problem solving; Comic books
Age range(s): 4 - 8+
Major character(s): Benjamin Bear, Bear
Summary: This comic book for young readers was originally published in French but has been translated to English. Written by Philippe Coudray, the book focuses on a fuzzy bear with an interesting sense of logic. Each story takes place within the confines of a single page. Benjamin Bear and his friends find themselves in all sorts of interesting scenarios. In one story, Benjamin and his bunny rabbit friend prepare to sleep under the stars. Benjamin is dressed warmly, wearing a T-shirt and a sweater. Unfortunately, rabbit doesn't have a sweater. Not to worry. Benjamin Bear solves the problem: The last frame shows the bunny asleep on Benjamin Bear's belly, using the sweater—which Benjamin is still wearing—as a cozy blanket. Young readers will enjoy seeing the interesting ways in which Benjamin Bear solves problems.

Where it's reviewed:
Booklist, October 15, 2011, page 36
Horn Book Magazine, November/December 2011, p. 97, page 97
Publishers Weekly, September 5, 2011, page 51
School Library Journal, November 2011, page 152

Other books you might like:
Peggy Parish, *Amelia Bedelia Goes Camping*, 1985
Agnes Rosenstiehl, *Silly Lilly and the Four Seasons*, 2008
Shel Silverstein, *Runny Babbit: A Billy Sook*, 2005
Art Spiegelman, *Jack and the Box*, 2008
Mo Willems, *Happy Pig Day!*, 2011

87

AUDREY COULOUMBIS
JULIA DANOS, Illustrator

Lexie
(New York: Random House, 2011)

Story type: Contemporary - Mainstream
Subject(s): Divorce; Family life; Vacations

Age range(s): 9 - 11+
Major character(s): Lexie, 10-Year-Old, Child of Divorced Parents; Mom, Mother (of Lexie); Daddy, Father (of Lexie); Vicky, Girlfriend (of Daddy), Mother (of Ben and Harris); Ben, Teenager, Son (of Vicky), Brother (of Harris); Harris, 3-Year-Old, Son (of Vicky), Brother (of Ben)
Time period(s): 21st century; 2010s
Locale(s): New Jersey, United States

Summary: In this novel, Newbery Honor-winning author Audrey Couloumbis tackles a tough issue that many children must face—the aftermath of divorce—from the perspective of a ten-year-old girl. Lexie used to love traveling to the shore with her parents in the summer. This is the first summer since her parents' divorce, however, and it feels strange to go to her favorite vacation destination without her mom. Worse, Lexie learns on the way to the beach house that her father's new girlfriend, Vicky, and her sons, teenage Ben and preschooler Harris, will be joining them for the week. How can Lexie enjoy her vacation with people she doesn't even know? As Lexie struggles to establish her place in her father's new life, she learns that growing up is hard to do—and that things may not be as bad as they first seem. The text is accompanied by black-and-white illustrations by Julia Danos.

Where it's reviewed:
Booklist, July 1, 2011, page 60
Bulletin of the Center for Children's Books, June 2011, page 462
Horn Book Magazine, July/August 2011, page 146
School Library Journal, July 2011, page 64

Other books by the same author:
Jake, 2010
Getting Near to Baby, 1999

Other books you might like:
Julia Alvarez, *How Tia Lola Saved the Summer*, 2011
Anne Fine, *Step by Wicked Step*, 1996
Stephanie Greene, *The Lucky Ones*, 2008
Kevin Henkes, *Junonia*, 2011

88

AUDREY COULOUMBIS

Jake
(New York: Random House, 2010)

Subject(s): Grandfathers; Accidents; Single parent family
Age range(s): 9 - 12+
Major character(s): Jake, 10-Year-Old; Granddad, Grandfather (of Jake)
Time period(s): 21st century; 2010s
Locale(s): Baltimore, Maryland

Summary: Audrey Couloumbis's *Jake* centers on the surprising bond that develops between a 10-year-old boy and the aloof grandfather who cares for him. Jake's mother suffers a mishap just before Christmas and breaks her leg, forcing her to ask the boy's grandfather to help look after him. Jake hasn't had much of a relationship with Granddad ever since the youngster's father died a few years prior. But the more time they spend together, the more Jake penetrates the icy barrier around the old man, and the two form a deep connection neither of them expected.

Where it's reviewed:
Booklist, September 1, 2010, page 105
Bulletin of the Center for Children's Books, December 2010, page 169
Horn Book Guide, Spring 2011, page 67
Publishers Weekly, August 30, 2010, page 53
School Library Journal, October 2010, page 70

Other books by the same author:
Lexie, 2011
The Misadventures of Maude March: Or Trouble Rides a Fast Horse, 2005
Say Yes, 2002
Getting Near to Baby, 2001

Awards the book has won:
Blue Ribbon Awards: Fiction, 2010

Other books you might like:
Beverly Cleary, *Dear Mr. Henshaw*, 1983
Rosanne Parry, *Heart of a Shepherd*, 2009

89

AUDREY COULOUMBIS
AKILA COULOUMBIS, Co-Author

War Games

(New York: Random House, 2009)

Subject(s): World War II, 1939-1945; Wars; Friendship
Age range(s): 10 - 13+
Major character(s): Petros, 12-Year-Old, Brother (of Zola); Zola, Brother (of Petros)
Time period(s): 20th century; 1940s
Locale(s): Greece

Summary: Although World War II used to seem like some type of faraway nightmare to Petros and his brother Zola, the war comes close to home when the Germans invade Greece. After the Germans invade, it seems as though all the families—including his own—in Petros's small town begin keeping secrets. Life changes in other ways, too. The Germans occupy the town, and a German commandant comes to stay. To pass their time, Petros, Zola, and their friends play war-like games that not only are fun for the boys, but also train them to be fighters. As the dangers of war draw ever closer, Petros and his friends and family will be forced to make difficult decisions and fight for what they believe in. *War Games* is written by Audrey Couloumbis and Akila Couloumbis and is based on Akila Couloumbis's own experiences during World War II.

Where it's reviewed:
Booklist, October 1, 2009, page 38
Bulletin of the Center for Children's Books, January 2010, page 191
Horn Book Guide, Spring 2010, page 66
New York Times Book Review, January 17, 2010, page 13
School Library Journal, October 2009, page 124

Other books by the same author:
Love Me Tender, 2008
The Misadventures of Maude March, or, Trouble Rides a Fast Horse, 2005
Summer's End, 2005

Other books you might like:
Nina Bawden, *The Real Plato Jones*, 1993
Kimberly Brubaker Bradley, *For Freedom: The Story of a French Spy*, 2003
Bjarne B. Reuter, *The Boys from St. Petri*, 1994
Michael O. Tunnell, *Brothers in Valor: A Story of Resistance*, 2001

90

LUCY COUSINS, Author/Illustrator

Yummy: Eight Favorite Fairy Tales

(Somerville, Massachusetts: Candlewick Press, 2009)

Subject(s): Folklore; Fairy tales; Short stories
Age range(s): 5 - 8+

Summary: In *Yummy: Eight Favorite Fairy Tales*, author and illustrator Lucy Cousins presents eight short retellings of time-honored folk tales, complete with her own vibrant illustrations. Among the stories in this volume are "The Three Little Pigs," "Little Red Riding Hood," "The Little Red Hen," "The Three Bill Goats Gruff," "Goldilocks and the Three Bears," "Henny Penny," "The Musicians of Bremen," and "The Enormous Turnip." Cousins doesn't shy away from the gory details of the original stories—for example, she depicts the beheading of the villainous wolf in "Little Red Riding Hood" and the death-by-boiling of the wolf in "The Three Little Pigs." The classic stories, nonetheless, are appropriate for—and will surely please—young readers.

Where it's reviewed:
Booklist, October 15 2009, page 51
Horn Book Guide, Spring 2010, page 128
New York Times Book Review, November 8, 2009, page 20
School Library Journal, September 2009, page 139

Other books you might like:
Rebecca Emberley, *Chicken Little*, 2009
Emily Gravett, *Spells*, 2009
Charlotte Huck, *Princess Furball*, 1989
David Wiesner, *The Three Pigs*, 2001
Paul O. Zelinsky, *Rapunzel*, 1997

91

LUCY COUSINS, Author/Illustrator

I'm the Best

(Somerville, Massachusetts: Candlewick Press, 2010)

Subject(s): Friendship; Dogs; Animals
Age range(s): 2 - 6+

Major character(s): Dog, Dog; Goose, Goose; Donkey, Donkey; Ladybug, Insect (ladybug); Mole, Mole

Summary: Lucy Cousins's *I'm the Best* centers on Dog, a self-assured pooch who is incessantly bragging about how superior he is to all his animal friends. But Donkey, Goose, Ladybug, and the whole gang are tired of Dog's bluster, and they set out to teach him a lesson he'll never forget. Cousins also provides the illustrations to this volume.

Where it's reviewed:
Booklist, May 1, 2010, page 85
Horn Book Guide, Fall 2010, page 278
School Library Journal, May 2010, page 80

Other books by the same author:
Maisy's Amazing Big Book of Learning, 2011
Maisy's Amazing Big Book of Words, 2007

Other books you might like:
Anna Alter, *Disappearing Desmond*, 2010
Bob Shea, *Big Plans*, 2008
Kevin Sherry, *I'm the Biggest Thing in the Ocean*, 2007
Carol Thompson, *I Like You the Best*, 2011

92

DOREEN CRONIN
KEVIN CORNELL, Illustrator

The Trouble with Chickens

(New York: Laura Geringer Books, 2011)

Story type: Mystery; Young Readers
Subject(s): Mystery; Animals; Dogs

Age range(s): 7 - 9+
Major character(s): J.J. Tully, Dog, Detective—Private; Sugar, Chicken; Dirt, Chicken

Summary: J.J. Tully is a dog who is used to adventure. He used to be a search-and-rescue dog, but lately he has been taking it easy. One day, two small chickens named Dirt and Sugar show up. It seems that the chickens' siblings have gone missing, and they, along with their mother, want J.J. to search for them. Although J.J. is not very keen on the idea of searching for a bunch of lost chickens, his payment (a cheeseburger) is just tempting enough to entice him to take the job. J.J. will have to investigate every angle of the mystery if he wants to find the lost chickens. This mystery story for young readers is written by Doreen Cronin and illustrated by Kevin Cornell.

Where it's reviewed:
Bulletin of the Center for Children's Books, March 2011, page 325
Horn Book Magazine, March/April 2011, page 113
School Library Journal, February 2011, page 78

Other books you might like:
Polly Horvath, *Mr. and Mrs. Bunny—Detectives Extraordinaire!*, 2012
Margie Palatini, *The Web Files*, 2001
Suzanne Selfors, *Smells Like Dog*, 2010

93

LAUREL CROZA
MATT JAMES, Illustrator

I Know Here

(Toronto: Groundwood Books, 2010)

Subject(s): Fear; Rural life; Nature

Age range(s): 3 - 6+
Time period(s): 21st century; 2010s
Locale(s): Toronto, Ontario; Saskatchewan, Canada

Summary: Laurel Croza's *I Know Here* charts a young girl's life-changing experiences as she prepares to relocate with her family. The girl feels safe and secure in her northern Saskatchewan home until her family announces that they are moving to Toronto. She envisions what life will be like in the big city and quells her fears by holding tight to the memories of her beloved country home. *I Know Here* contains illustrations by Matt James and is the first title from Croza. First novel.

Where it's reviewed:
Booklist, May 15, 2010, page 82
Horn Book Magazine, May/June 2010, page 65
New York Times Book Review, May 16, 2010, page 17
School Library Journal, October 2010, page 82

Awards the book has won:
Boston Globe - Horn Book Awards: Illustrator or Picture Books, 2010

Other books you might like:
Katherine Applegate, *The Buffalo Storm*, 2007
Libby Gleeson, *Half a World Away*, 2007
Marjorie Weinman Sharmat, *Gila Monsters Meet You at the Airport*, 1980
Mark Siegel, *Moving House*, 2011
Jane Yolen, *Elsie's Bird*, 2010

94

SHUTTA CRUM
CAROL THOMPSON, Illustrator

Thunder-Boomer!

(New York: Clarion Books, 2009)

Subject(s): Rural life; Weather; Family

Age range(s): 5 - 8+
Time period(s): 21st century; 2000s

Summary: In *Thunder-Boomer!*, author Shutta Crum presents a story-length poem chronicling the adventures of a family caught in a rainstorm. On a sweltering afternoon, the family is trying to stay cool on their farm when they notice murky clouds overtaking the sky. They know that rain is imminent and the family retreats indoors. Soon the rain is falling, and along with it comes howling winds and hammering hail. But out of this melee comes a very surprising guest: a drenched kitten looking for a home. The family rallies around the new arrival, learning that special gifts sometimes pop up in the most unlikely of circumstances. *Thunder-Boomer!* contains illustrations by Carol Thompson.

Where it's reviewed:
Booklist, July 1 2009, page 70
Bulletin of the Center for Children's Books, September 2009, page 12
Horn Book Magazine, July/August 2009, page 406
School Library Journal, June 2009, page 80

Other books you might like:
Jeanne Birdsall, *Flora's Very Windy Day*, 2010
Cynthia Cotten, *Rain Play*, 2008
Karen Hesse, *Come On, Rain!*, 1999
George Ella Lyon, *Come a Tide*, 1990
Robert McCloskey, *Time of Wonder*, 1957

95

SHUTTA CRUM
PATRICE BARTON, Illustrator

Mine!

(New York: Alfred A. Knopf, 2011)

Story type: Young Readers
Subject(s): Children; Learning; Human behavior
Age range(s): 2 - 6+
Summary: Many children love their toys, and some can be quite protective of them. In this children's picture book, developed by Shutta Crum, two children and a dog have to find a way to share a pile of toys. The children use only one word: "Mine!" The dog can only bark. The three still manage to convey their wants and then negotiate. In the end, they learn to share—and that makes playtime all the more fun. This story is illustrated with the digitized pencil drawings of Patrice Barton. Shutta Crum is also the author of *Thunder-Boomer* and *All on a Sleepy Night*.

Where it's reviewed:
Booklist, July 1, 2011, page 65
Bulletin of the Center for Children's Books, July/August 2011, page 507
Horn Book Guide, Fall 2011, page 295
Publishers Weekly, April 18 2011, page 50
School Library Journal, June 2011, page 78

Other books by the same author:
Thunder Boomer, 2009
A Family for Old Mill Farm, 2007

Other books you might like:
Samantha Berger, *Martha Doesn't Share*, 2010
Margaret Chodos-Irvine, *Best Best Friends*, 2006
Kevin Henkes, *Sheila Rae's Peppermint Stick*, 2001
Barbro Lindgren, *Benny and the Binky*, 2002

96

SHUTTA CRUM
LEE WILDISH, Illustrator

Thomas and the Dragon Queen

(New York: Knopf Books for Young Readers, 2010)

Subject(s): History; Dragons; Knights
Age range(s): 8 - 10+

Major character(s): Thomas, 12-Year-Old, Knight; Eleanor, Royalty (princess)
Time period(s): 4th century-15th century

Summary: In Shutta Crum's *Thomas and the Dragon Queen*, twelve-year-old Thomas has always dreamed of knighthood. The only problem is that he's too tiny. No one has ever taken him seriously as a squire—until now. Thomas is the only squire left in the village when Princess Eleanor is kidnapped by the Dragon Queen; therefore, the King asks Thomas to risk his life for his daughter and bring her back. Thomas knows that if he can defeat not only the Dragon Queen, but also the many monsters along the way, he will finally gain the respect of the kingdom and perhaps even be granted knighthood. Thomas vows to bring back Princess Eleanor, despite the fact that the odds are truly against him.

Where it's reviewed:
Booklist, July 1, 2010, page 61
Bulletin of the Center for Children's Books, September 2010, page 12
Horn Book Magazine, July/August 2010, page 104
Publishers Weekly, June 21, 2010, page 46
School Library Journal, August 2010, page 72

Other books you might like:
Tony Davis, *Roland Wright: Future Knight*, 2007
Cornelia Funke, *Dragon Rider*, 2004
Kate Klimo, *Dragon Keepers No. 1: The Dragon in the Sock Drawer*, 2008
Christopher Maynard, *Days of the Knights: A Tale of Castles and Battles*, 1998
Gerald Morris, *The Adventures of Sir Givret the Short*, 2008

97

KAREN CUSHMAN

Alchemy and Meggy Swann

(New York: Clarion Books, 2010)

Subject(s): Father-daughter relations; Murder; Physically disabled persons

Age range(s): 10 - 12+
Major character(s): Meggy Swann, 13-Year-Old, Handicapped; Roger Oldham, Apprentice (of Meggy's father)
Time period(s): 16th century-17th century; 1550s-1600s
Locale(s): London, England

Summary: Set in Elizabethan-era London, Karen Cushman's *Alchemy and Meggy Swann* tells the story of a young girl looking to reconnect with the father she has never known. Meggy Swann and her pet goose move to London, hoping to find a new home with the girl's estranged father. Meggy's alchemist father, however, has no time for the child—who he was hoping would be a son. Now, Meggy is left to her own devices in a city she despises. Crippled and alone, she stumbles upon a mystery involving several men who purchased arsenic from her father. Determined to find the truth, Meggy hits the streets of London and investigates.

Where it's reviewed:
Booklist, March 1, 2010, page 72
Bulletin of the Center for Children's Books, May 2010, page 376
Horn Book Magazine, May/June 2010, page 79
Publishers Weekly, March 29, 2010, page 59
School Library Journal, April 2010, page 152

Other books by the same author:
The Midwife's Apprentice, 1995
Cathrine Called Birdy, 1994

Other books you might like:
Susan Cooper, *King of Shadows*, 1999
Frances Hardinge, *Fly by Night*, 2006
Michael Scott, *The Alchemyst: The Secrets of the Immortal Nicholas Flamel*, 2007

98

KURT CYRUS, Author/Illustrator

The Voyage of Turtle Rex
(Boston: Harcourt Children's Books, 2011)

Story type: Young Readers
Subject(s): Animals; Turtles; Science

Age range(s): 5 - 8+
Major character(s): Unnamed Character, Turtle

Summary: In this book for young readers, author and illustrator Kurt Cyrus shares the story of a young turtle's adventure in the sea. When an ancient sea turtle is born, it must pass from the relative safety of the beach into the ocean, which is filled with many dangerous creatures. The young sea turtle finds a place to hide once she reaches the sea. Although she is small at first, the turtle soon grows into a large animal. When the turtle grows up, she no longer has to hide. One day, she will go back to the beach to lay her own eggs.

Where it's reviewed:
Horn Book Guide, Fall 2011, page 311
New York Times Book Review, April 10, 2011, page 17
School Library Journal, May 2011, page 74

Other books by the same author:
Big Rig Bugs, 2010
Tadpole Rex, 2008

Other books you might like:
Nicola Davies, *One Tiny Turtle*, 2001
Steve Jenkins, *Prehistoric Actual Size*, 2005
April Pulley Sayre, *Turtle, Turtle, Watch Out!*, 2010
Stephen R. Swinburne, *Turtle Tide: The Ways of Sea Turtles*, 2005

99

JEF CZEKAJ, Author/Illustrator

A Call for a New Alphabet
(Watertown, Massachusetts: Charlesbridge, 2011)

Story type: Young Readers
Subject(s): Writing; Humor; Dreams

Age range(s): 6 - 8+
Summary: The letter X is tired of always appearing at the end of the alphabet. He doesn't like that he is one of the last letters to be read in alphabet books, and he thinks people mostly overlook him. To change his place in the alphabet, X talks to the other letters living in the Alphabet City. He convinces the other letters that they should change the order of the alphabet. Although the other 25 letters go along with X's plan, X changes his mind when he has a strange dream about his new place in the alphabet lineup.

Where it's reviewed:
Booklist, February 2, 2011, page 80
Horn Book Magazine, May/June 2011, page 71
Publishers Weekly, January 10, 2011, page 50
School Library Journal, March 2011, page 120

Other books by the same author:
Cat Secrets, 2011

Other books you might like:
Mary Elting, *Q Is for Duck*, 1980
Neil Gaiman, *The Dangerous Alphabet*, 2008
Alethea Kontis, *Alpha Oops!: The Day Z Went First*, 2006
Susan Meddaugh, *Martha Speaks*, 1992

100

CATHLEEN DALY
STEPHEN MICHAEL KING, Illustrator

Prudence Wants a Pet
(New York: Roaring Brook Press, 2011)

Story type: Young Readers
Subject(s): Pets; Imagination; Problem solving

Age range(s): 3 - 7+
Major character(s): Prudence, Girl

Summary: Prudence has a problem. She wants a pet, and both her mother and father have said no to her requests. Pets are noisy, messy, expensive, and too much work, they tell Prudence. So the little girl adopts a series of unusual, readily available pets: Branch, who lives on the porch but trips Dad eight times before being sent to the wood pile; Twig, who meets his end in the wash; Formal Footwear, a dress shoe that conveniently provides its name on its label; and others. Prudence even adopts her baby brother as a pet, to disastrous results. Prudence's parents finally find a solution to her problem. The watercolor and pen-and-ink illustrations provide much of the story's humor, as little Prudence beguilingly interacts with her "pets" and parents.

Where it's reviewed:
Booklist, June 1, 2011, page 97
Bulletin of the Center for Children's Books, September 2011, page 65
Horn Book Magazine, July/August 2011, page 126
Publishers Weekly, May 9, 2011, page 50
School Library Journal, May 2011, page 74

Other books you might like:
Tedd Arnold, *Hi, Fly Guy!*, 2005

Peter Brown, *Children Make Terrible Pets*, 2009
Steven Kellogg, *Can I Keep Him?*, 1971
Laura Joy Rennert, *Buying, Training & Caring for Your Dinosaur*, 2009

101

JACQUELINE DAVIES
S.D. SCHINDLER, Illustrator

Tricking the Tallyman

(New York: Knopf Books for Young Readers, 2009)

Subject(s): Tricksters; United States history; Humor

Age range(s): 7 - 10+
Major character(s): Phineus Bump, Worker (Tallyman); Mrs. Pepper, Trickster
Time period(s): 18th century; 1790s (1790)
Locale(s): Tunbridge, Vermont

Summary: *Tricking the Tallyman*, written by Jacqueline Davies and illustrated by S.D. Schindler, takes place in the small town of Tunbridge, Vermont, in 1790. Phineus Bump, the tallyman, has come to take the first United States census and just wants to do his job and go home. The people of the town are afraid, however, that if they are counted accurately their taxes will be increased, they won't have fair representation in government, or they will be drafted into the military. The townspeople, especially Mrs. Pepper, have an idea—they will trick Phineus and make it impossible for him to take an accurate count. Phineus needs to help the townspeople understand the real reason for the census so that he can get an accurate count.

Where it's reviewed:
Booklist, February 15, 2009, page 88
Bulletin of the Center for Children's Books, July/August 2009, page 439
Horn Book Magazine, May/June 2009, page 280
School Library Journal, March 2009, page 108

Other books you might like:
Teresa Bateman, *Keeper of Soles*, 2006
Lynne Cheney, *We the People: The Story of Our Constitution*, 2008
Jean Fritz, *Shh! We're Writing the Constitution*, 1987
Lane Smith, *John, Paul, George and Ben*, 2006

102

NICOLA DAVIES
NEAL LAYTON, Illustrator

Just the Right Size: Why Big Animals Are Big and Little Animals Are Little

(Somerville, Massachusetts: Candlewick Press, 2011)

Subject(s): Animals; Science; Nature

Age range(s): 9 - 12+

Summary: This illustrated book teaches young readers about physics, biology, science, nature, and natural selection by explaining how and why various animal species develop the way they do. Author Nicola Davies describes why some of the smallest animals and insects—like birds, mice, or ants—are capable of feats not possible for humans and other larger animals. The author uses mathematical equations and explanations of scientific properties, yet discusses these topics in an easy-to-understand voice. Illustrations by Neal Layton accompany the text. Davies is also the author of *Poop,Extreme Animals*, and *What's Eating You?*, all of which were also illustrated by Layton.

Where it's reviewed:
Booklist, August 1 2009, page 64
Bulletin of the Center for Children's Books, September 2009, page 13
Horn Book Magazine, September 2009, page 580
School Library Journal, August 2009, page 120
Science Books & Film, November 2009, page 252

Other books by the same author:
Talk Talk Squawk: A Human's Guide to Animal Communication, 2011
What's Eating You? Parasistes—the Inside Story, 2007
Extreme Animals: The Toughest Creatures on Earth, 2006
Poop: A Natural History of the Unmentionable, 2004

Other books you might like:
Ben Hillman, *How Big Is It? A BIG Book All About Bigness*, 2007
Steve Jenkins, *Actual Size*, 2004
John Schwartz, *Short: Walking Tall When You're Not Tall at All*, 2010

103

ELEANOR DAVIS, Author/Illustrator

The Secret Science Alliance and the Copycat Crook

(New York: Bloomsbury USA Children's Books, 2009)

Subject(s): Science; Friendship; Criminals

Age range(s): 9 - 12+
Major character(s): Julian Calendar, 11-Year-Old, Friend (Ben and Greta), Scientist; Ben, Friend (of Greta and Julian), Scientist; Greta, Friend (of Julian and Ben), Scientist
Time period(s): 21st century; 2000s

Summary: When Julian Calendar transfers to a new school, he wants to fit in with the rest of the kids, but he doesn't quite know how to do it. Julian is a science whiz, and when he meets Greta and Ben—two kids with similar interests in science—he knows he's found good friends. Julian, Greta, and Ben form the Secret Science Alliance, and they use a secret lair as their hideout. The friends make plans for all types of amazing inventions, such as glue bombs and nighttime goggles. When the Secret Science Alliance learns about an evil scientist's plot, they will have to use all of their creations and knowhow to stop him. *The Secret Science Alliance and the Copycat Crook* is a graphic novel by Eleanor Davis.

Where it's reviewed:
Booklist, July 1, 2009, page 63
Horn Book Guide, Spring 2010, page 67

Other books by the same author:
Stinky, 2008

Other books you might like:
Otis Frampton, *Oddly Normal: Volume One*, 2006
Saul Griffith, *Howtoons: The Possibilities are Endless!*, 2008
Dan Gutman, *The Homework Machine*, 2006
Madeleine L'Engle, *A Wrinkle in Time*, 1962
Trenton Lee Stewart, *The Mysterious Benedict Society*, 2007

104

MATT DE LA PENA
KADIR NELSON, Illustrator

A Nation's Hope: The Story of Boxing Legend Joe Louis

(New York: Dial Books, 2011)

Subject(s): Sports; Boxing; History

Age range(s): 6 - 8+

Summary: This book by author Matt de la Pena and illustrator Kadir Nelson shares the true story of a boxing match that helped bring together Americans of all different backgrounds. In 1938 Word War II was just over the horizon, and the Nazis held power in Germany. That year, African American boxer Joe Louis fought German boxer Max Schmeling. The winner of the fight would be named the best heavyweight boxer in the world. Louis and Schmeling had met in the ring before, and Schmeling won their first fight. This time, however, Louis was determined to win the fight for himself, his family, and his country.

Where it's reviewed:
Booklist, February 1, 2011, page 72
Bulletin of the Center for Children's Books, January 2011, page 232
Horn Book Magazine, January/February 2011, page 109
Publishers Weekly, November 1, 2010, page 41
School Library Journal, February 2011, page 41

Awards the book has won:
Michigan Notable Books Award, 2012

Other books you might like:
David A. Adler, *Joe Louis: America's Fighter*, 2005
Ted Lewin, *At Gleason's Gym*, 2007
Andrea Davis Pinkney, *Bird in a Box*, 2011
Charles R. Smith Jr., *Black Jack: The Ballad of Jack Johnson*, 2010
Jonah Winter, *Muhammad Ali*, 2008

105

CARMEN AGRA DEEDY
RANDALL WRIGHT, Co-Author
BARRY MOSER, Illustrator

The Cheshire Cheese Cat: A Dickens of a Tale

(Atlanta, Georgia: Peachtree Publishers, 2011)

Story type: Historical
Subject(s): Felidae; Animals; Writers

Age range(s): 10 - 13+
Major character(s): Skilley, Cat, Friend (of Pip); Pip, Mouse, Friend (of Skilley); Charles Dickens, Writer, Historical Figure; Pinch, Cat; Maldwyn, Raven
Time period(s): 19th century
Locale(s): London, England

Summary: Skilley the cat thinks it's smooth sailing once he lands a plush job as a mouser at a popular pub called Ye Olde Cheshire Cheese. However, one of the tavern's frequenters, Charles Dickens, who is working on a new novel, notices something is amiss at Cheshire Cheese after Skilley is hired. His suspicions are confirmed when a mouse named Pip discovers Skilley's dirty secret: Skilley hates the taste of mice and prefers to munch on cheese. Instead of catching the mice, he agrees to free them in exchange for cheese. After Pip makes this discovery, he makes a pact with Skilley. Pip won't reveal Skilley's secret if Skilley protects his friend Maldwyn, an injured raven, from the stray cat Pinch. As the saga unfolds, it seems Skilley and Pip aren't the only ones harboring secrets.

Where it's reviewed:
New York Times Book Review, November 13, 2011, page 37
Publishers Weekly, September 5, 2011, page 48
School Library Journal, September 2011, page 150

Other books by the same author:
14 Cows for America, 2011

Other books you might like:
Elise Broach, *Masterpiece*, 2008
Michael Hoeye, *Time Stops for No Mouse*, 2000
Robert Lawson, *Ben and Me*, 1939
Peter Vennema, *Charles Dickens: The Man Who Had Great Expectations*, 1993

106

CYNTHIA DEFELICE

Signal

(New York: Farrar, Straus and Giroux, 2009)

Subject(s): Friendship; Parent-child relations; Child abuse

Age range(s): 10 - 13+
Major character(s): Owen McGuire, 12-Year-Old, Friend (of Cam); Cam, Friend (of Owen)
Locale(s): New York, United States

Summary: After his mother died, Owen McGuire and his workaholic father move from Buffalo to the country around New York's Finger Lakes. Owen is lonely in his new home and has only his dog to keep him company. But, when Owen meets a young girl named Cam, he finds a new companion. Cam is a green-eyed girl with a mysterious background. She tells Owen that she is alien, and she wants to send a signal to her home planet so that her parents will come back and find her. Although Owen doesn't know what to make of his new friend, he agrees to help her. *Signal* is a novel by Cynthia DeFelice.

Where it's reviewed:
Booklist, August 1, 2009, page 72
Bulletin of the Center for Children's Books, December 2009, page 149
Horn Book Magazine, November/December 2009, page 666
Publishers Weekly, September 29, 2009, page 65
School Library Journal, November 2009, page 102

Other books by the same author:
Nowhere to Call Home, 1999
Weasel, 1991

Other books you might like:
Frances O'Roark Dowell, *Chicken Boy*, 2005
Michelle D. Kwasney, *Itch*, 2008
Nan Marino, *Neil Armstrong Is My Uncle and Other Lies Muscle Man McGinty Told Me*, 2009
Ruth White, *Tadpole*, 2003
Tim Wynne-Jones, *Rex Zero and the End of the World*, 2007

107

BARRY DENENBERG

Titanic Sinks!

(New York: Viking Juvenile, 2011)

Subject(s): Ships; Shipwrecks; Disasters
Age range(s): 9 - 13+
Time period(s): 20th century; 1910s (1912)
Locale(s): *Titanic*, At Sea

Summary: On April 15, 1912, the *Titanic* ocean liner—which was thought to be unsinkable—sunk in the Atlantic Ocean after its hull was punctured by an iceberg. In this book, author Barry Denenberg commemorates the 100th anniversary of the ship's sinking by bringing the ship's story to life. The book includes facts about the ship, its passengers and crew, and its voyage. It also contains fictional accounts of the events surrounding the ship's sinking, including the voyage the survivors made on lifeboats after the ship had sunk. Denenberg uses imaginary news bulletins, headlines, and more to tell the *Titanic*'s story from the ship's building to the survivors' harrowing journey to safety.

Where it's reviewed:
Booklist, October 15, 2011, page 44
Publishers Weekly, October 17, 2011, page 70
School Library Journal, November 2011, page 146

Other books by the same author:
Lincoln Shot: A President's Life Remembered, 2008

Other books you might like:
Robert D. Ballard, *The Discovery of the Titanic*, 1987
Deborah Hopkinson, *Titanic: Voices from the Disaster*, 2012
Walter Lord, *A Night to Remember*, 1955
Allan Wolf, *The Watch That Ends the Night: Voices from the Titanic*, 2011

108

SHARON PHILLIPS DENSLOW
CATHIE FELSTEAD, Illustrator

Big Wolf and Little Wolf

(New York: Enchanted Lion Books, 2009)

Subject(s): Animals/Wolves; Bedtime; Parent and Child
Age range(s): 5 - 7+
Major character(s): Little Wolf, Wolf; Big Wolf, Wolf, Father; Mama Wolf, Mother, Wolf
Locale(s): Earth

Summary: Before Little Wolf goes to bed he asks Big Wolf to sing a song and then another. Little Wolf has a song to sing for Big Wolf too, but while singing he hears something moving in the bushes nearby and becomes afraid. When Mama Wolf appears singing her own song Little Wolf is relieved and joins Big Wolf in chasing Mama Wolf. Before he sleeps Little Wolf requests one more song from Mama Wolf and she sings a soothing wolf good night. (32 pages)

Where it's reviewed:
Booklist, June 1, 2009, page 62
Horn Book Guide, Fall 2010, page 322
School Library Journal, August 2009, page 72

Other books by the same author:
Big Wolf and Little Wolf: Such a Beautiful Orange, 2011
Big Wolf and Little Wolf: The Leaf That Wouldn't Fall, 2009

Other books you might like:
Bonny Becker, *A Visitor for Bear*, 2008
Nadine Brun-Cosme, *Big Wolf and Little Wolf: The Little Leaf That Wouldn't Fall*, 2009
Ruth Huddleston, *Time for Bed*, 1994
Mei Matsuoka, *Footprints in the Snow*, 2008
Mo Willems, *City Dog, Country Frog*, 2010

109

KAREN GRAY RUELLE, Author/Illustrator
DEBORAH DURLAND DESAIX, Author/Illustrator

The Grand Mosque of Paris: A Story of How Muslims Rescued Jews During the Holocaust

(New York: Holiday House, 2009)

Subject(s): World War II, 1939-1945; Holocaust, 1933-1945; Jewish history

Age range(s): 8 - 11+
Time period(s): 20th century; 1940s
Locale(s): Paris, France

Summary: In *The Grand Mosque of Paris: A Story of How Muslims Saved Jews During the Holocaust*, Karen Gray Ruelle and Deborah Durland DeSaix relate a little-known story of bravery and loyalty from World War II. During the Nazi occupation of Paris, when Jews lived in fear of detention or deportation, most French citizens were reluctant to intervene, worried for their own safety. But the Muslims who congregated at the city's Grand Mosque offered the immense gathering place as a haven for Jewish men, women, and children. The richly illustrated book features a glossary, bibliography, and list of related books and films.

Where it's reviewed:
Booklist, November 15 2009, page 45
Bulletin of the Center for Children's Books, November 2009, page 126
Horn Book Guide, Spring 2010, page 180
Publishers Weekly, September 7 2009, page 46
School Library Journal, October 2009, page 152

Other books by the same author:
Hidden on the Mountain: Stories of Children Sheltered in Le Chambon, 2007

Other books you might like:
Tomek Bogacki, *The Champion of Children: The Story of Janusz Korczak*, 2009
Jo Hoestlandt, *Star of Fear, Star of Hope*, 1995
David Macaulay, *Mosque*, 2003
Christos Nicola, *The Secret of Priest's Grotto: A Holocaust Survival Story*, 2007

110

BARRY DEUTSCH, Author/Illustrator

Hereville: How Mirka Got Her Sword

(New York: Amulet Books, 2010)

Subject(s): Jews; Dragons; Adventure

Age range(s): 8 - 12+
Major character(s): Mirka, 11-Year-Old
Time period(s): 21st century; 2010s
Locale(s): Hereville, Fictional Location

Summary: In the Orthodox Jewish community of Hereville, 11-year-old Mirka is an adventurous little girl with a keen interest in slaying dragons. The only problem is that no dragons live in Hereville. There are, however, a series of other interesting events to keep Mirka occupied. Barry Deutsch's *Hereville: How Mirka Got Her Sword* follows Mirka on her adventures through the town, where she encounters bullies, a witch, and a very vociferous pig.

Where it's reviewed:
Booklist, October 15, 2010, page 41
Horn Book Guide, Spring 2011, page 69
Publishers Weekly, August 2, 2010, page 48
School Library Journal, November 2010, page 144

Awards the book has won:
Sydney Taylor Children's Book Awards, 2011

Other books you might like:
Joanna Cole, *Bony-Legs*, 1983
Shannon Hale, *Rapunzel's Revenge*, 2008
Kazu Kibuishi, *Amulet: The Cloud Searchers*, 2010
Steve Sheinkin, *Rabbi Harvey vs. The Wisdom Kid: A Graphic Novel of Dueling Jewish Folktales in the Wild West*, 2010

111

KATE DICAMILLO
ALISON MCGHEE, Co-Author
TONY FUCILE, Illustrator

Bink and Gollie

(Somerville, Massachusetts: Candlewick Press, 2010)

Subject(s): Friendship; Humor; Adventure

Age range(s): 5 - 7+
Major character(s): Bink, Girl; Gollie, Girl, Friend (of Bink)
Time period(s): 21st century; 2010s
Locale(s): United States

Summary: In *Bink and Gollie* by Kate DiCamillo and Alison McGhee, two girls share a special friendship based on adventure, fun, and roller skating. Bink—short and blond—and Gollie—tall and brown-haired—spend their days hanging out in their amazing tree house, eating peanut butter and pancakes, and skating their way into new escapades. In this book, illustrated by Tony Fucile, the friends travel to the Andes Mountains, get into a tricky situation with ridiculously brilliant socks, and deal with a fishy new pal, keeping their friendship and sense of humor along the way.

Where it's reviewed:
Booklist, September 15, 2010, page 68
New York Times Book Review, November 7, 2010, page 21
Publishers Weekly, August 9, 2010, page 52
School Library Journal, August 9, 2010, page 74

Other books by the same author:
Mercy Watson Princess In Disguise, 2007
Mercy Watson Fights Crime, 2006
Mercy Watson Goes For a Ride, 2006
Mercy Watson Thinks Like a Pig, 2006
Mercy Watson to the Rescue, 2005

Other books you might like:
James Howe, *Houndsley and Catina*, 2006
Grace Lin, *Ling and Ting: Not Exactly the Same!*, 2010
Megan McDonald, *Judy Moody & Stink: The Mad, Mad, Mad, Mad Treasure Hunt*, 2009
Lucy Nolan, *On the Road*, 2004
Sara Pennypacker, *The Talented Clementine*, 2007

112

KATE DiCAMILLO
YOKO TANAKA, Illustrator

The Magician's Elephant

(Somerville, Massachusetts: Candlewick Press, 2009)

Subject(s): Orphans; Magic; Elephants

Age range(s): 9 - 12+

Major character(s): Peter Augustus Duchene, 10-Year-Old, Orphan

Summary: In *The Magician's Elephant* by Kate DiCamillo, Peter Augustus Duchene has led a hard life in his brief existence. At the age of 10, he is an orphan on the hunt for a sister he barely remembers. When he sees a booth for a fortune teller at the local fair, he decides to try his luck there. The fortune teller explains that he will find his sister, but only if he follows the elephant. Peter has no idea what the fortune means. Later that night during a magician's performance, a botched trick leads to the miraculous appearance of an elephant that seems to have come from thin air. Peter follows the elephant to his future.

Where it's reviewed:
Booklist, July 2009, page 63
Bulletin of the Center for Children's Books, November 2009, page 108
Horn Book Magazine, September 2009, page 57
New York Times Book Review, December 6 2009, page 46
School Library Journal, August 2009, page 102

Other books by the same author:
The Tiger Rising, 2001

Awards the book has won:
Minnesota Book Awards, 2010

Other books you might like:
Tim Binding, *Sylvie and the Songman*, 2009
Ted Lewin, *Balarama: A Royal Elephant*, 2009
Mal Peet, *Cloud Tea Monkeys*, 2010
Lauren St. John, *The White Giraffe*, 2007

113

GAIL DONOVAN
JANET PEDERSEN, Illustrator

In Memory of Gorfman T. Frog

(New York: Dutton Children's Books, 2009)

Story type: Contemporary
Subject(s): Frogs; Schools; Individualism

Age range(s): 8 - 10+

Major character(s): Josh Hewitt, 5th Grader; Ms. O'Reilly, Teacher

Time period(s): 21st century; 2000s

Locale(s): United States

Summary: In this children's novel by Gail Donovan, Josh Hewitt is an exuberant boy whose antics get him in plenty of trouble at home and school. After finding a five-legged frog in a pond, Josh shows the unusual amphibian to his fifth-grade classmates and teacher, Ms. O'Reilly. The children's reaction is nothing short of pandemonium, but when Ms. O'Reilly calms the kids down, they learn that the frog's deformity may have been caused by pollution. While Josh investigates his findings, the frog dies and the school principal takes the tiny body. Josh devises a plan to get the deceased frog to a scientist and, in the process, prompts his family, friends, and classmates to see him in a new light.

Where it's reviewed:
Booklist, February 15, 2009, page 90
Bulletin of the Center for Children's Books, May 2009, page 358
Horn Book Guide, Fall 2009, page 368
School Library Journal, April 2009, page 132

Other books by the same author:
What's Bugging Bailey Blecker?, 2011

Other books you might like:
William Bee, *Beware of the Frog*, 2008
Andrew Clements, *Frindle*, 1996
Barbara O'Connor, *The Fantastic Secret of Owen Jester*, 2010
Gary Paulsen, *Mudshark*, 2009
Angie Sage, *Frognapped*, 2007

114

SANDY DONOVAN
JOHN CHRISTOPH, Illustrator
JAMES CHRISTOPH, Illustrator

Pingpong Perry Experiences How a Book Is Made

(Minneapolis, Minnesota: Picture Window Books, 2010)

Subject(s): Books; Publishing industry; Storytelling

Age range(s): 6 - 8+

Major character(s): Pingpong Perry, Child, Writer
Time period(s): 21st century; 2010s

Summary: *Pingpong Perry Experiences How a Book Is Made* is an educational book for young readers from author Sandy Donovan. Pingpong Perry teaches kids about the path a book takes from its original idea to publication. When Pingpong Perry has a question about ping-pong players, he scours the library looking for information. When he comes up empty-handed, he decides to write his own book about professional ping-pong players. Along the way, Pingpong Perry educates readers on how a creative idea can evolve into a tangible book found in the library. The book is filled with colorful illustrations by James Christophe.

Where it's reviewed:
Booklist, April 1, 2010, page 74
Horn Book Guide, Fall 2010, page 387

Other books by the same author:
Bob the Alien Discovers the Dewey Decimal System, 2010
Bored Bella Learns about Fiction and Nonfiction, 2010
Karl and Carolina Uncover Parts of a Book, 2010

Other books you might like:
Aliki, *How a Book Is Made*, 1986
Toni Buzzeo, *No T. Rex in the Library*, 2010
Michelle Knudsen, *Library Lion*, 2006
Ian Schoenherr, *Read It, Don't Eat It!*, 2009

115

FRANCES O'ROARK DOWELL

Falling In

(New York: Atheneum Books for Young Readers, 2010)

Subject(s): Fantasy; Alternative worlds; Witches

Age range(s): 9 - 12+
Major character(s): Isabelle Bean, 6th Grader, Outcast
Time period(s): 21st century; 2010s
Locale(s): United States

Summary: *Falling In* is a fantasy novel for young readers from bestselling author, Frances O'Roark Dowell. Isabelle Bean has always been a bit different from her sixth-grade counterparts, preferring vintage clothing to the latest trends, possessing an uncanny ability to irritate all of her teachers, and hearing a constant buzzing in her ears. Her misfit status goes to new levels when, during a trip to the school nurse, she enters a portal into an alternate world. Unfortunately, the land she stumbles into is filled with terrified children who, after one look at Isabelle's unusual outfit, mistake her to be the witch they loathe. When Isabelle makes the shocking discovery of the witch's true identity, she must do all she can to get the villagers to change their minds about the misunderstood woman.

Where it's reviewed:
Booklist, January 1, 2010, page 80
Bulletin of the Center for Children's Books, April 2010, page 333
Horn Book Guide, Fall 2010, page 336
Publishers Weekly, February 8, 2010, page 51
School Library Journal, April 2010, page 154

Other books by the same author:
Chicken Boy, 2005
Where I'd Like to Be, 2003

Other books you might like:
Marion Dane Bauer, *The Blue Ghost*, 2005
Francesca Lia Block, *House of Dolls*, 2010
Clara Gillow Clark, *Secrets of Greymoor*, 2009
Pam Conrad, *Stonewords: A Ghost Story*, 1990
Sid Fleischman, *The 13th Floor: A Ghost Story*, 1995

116

FRANCES O'ROARK DOWELL

The Kind of Friends We Used to Be

(New York: Atheneum Books for Young Readers, 2009)

Subject(s): Adolescence; Friendship; Feuds

Age range(s): 9 - 12+
Major character(s): Marilyn, 7th Grader, Cheerleader; Kate, 7th Grader, Songwriter, Musician (guitar player)
Time period(s): 21st century; 2000s
Locale(s): United States

Summary: *The Kind of Friends We Used to Be* by Frances O'Roark Dowell is a novel for young adult readers. The sequel to *The Secret Language of Girls*, this book follows the strained relationship between former best friends Marilyn and Kate. Despite their big falling out last year, the two girls long to be friends again. Neither one, however, is sure how to go about mending their broken relationship. It doesn't help that seventh grade seems to be pulling the girls into opposite worlds. Marilyn is a bubbly cheerleader now, and Kate is showing interest in playing guitar and writing songs. The story switches between Marilyn and Kate's perspectives, allowing readers to gain insight into the thoughts, fears, and desires of each girl as she tries to repair her friendship.

Where it's reviewed:
Booklist, March 1, 2009, page 46
Bulletin of the Center for Children's Books, May 2009, page 359
Horn Book Guide, Fall 2009, page 368
School Library Journal, March 2009, page 143

Other books by the same author:
The Secret Language of Girls, 2004

Awards the book has won:
Blue Ribbon Awards: Fiction, 2009

Other books you might like:
Brenda A. Ferber, *Jemma Hartman, Camper Extraordinaire*, 2009
Susan Patron, *Lucky Breaks*, 2009
Lynne Rae Perkins, *All Alone in the Universe*, 1999
Tricia Springstubb, *What Happened on Fox Street*, 2010

117

DENISE DOYEN
BARRY MOSER, Illustrator

Once Upon a Twice

(New York: Random House, 2009)

Subject(s): Animals; Adventure; Rhyme

Age range(s): 5 - 8+
Major character(s): Jam Boy, Child

Summary: Written by Denise Doyen and illustrated by Barry Moser, *Once Upon a Twice* is a picture book for children. In the book, a group of children led by Jam Boy play in the nighttime woods. The children receive a warning from a mouse, however, that much danger hides in the dark. Jam Boy asserts that he is not afraid and goes to sit by the dark pond, which has a snake slowly sliding across it and is lit only by fireflies. After a splash, Jam Boy seems to disappear. The book ends with a positive resolution, and much of the text is written in rhyme, making this a good choice to read aloud.

Where it's reviewed:
Booklist, January 1, 2009, page 68
Horn Book Guide, Spring 2010, page 22
Publishers Weekly, August 10, 2009, page 54
School Library Journal, August 2009, page 74

Other books you might like:
Jim Arnosky, *Babies in the Bayou*, 2007
Mini Grey, *Egg Drop*, 2009
Brenda Z. Guiberson, *Spoonbill Swamp*, 1992
Jerry Pinkney, *The Lion and the Mouse*, 2009

118

SHARON M. DRAPER

Out of My Mind

(New York: Atheneum Books, 2010)

Subject(s): Cerebral palsy; Communications; Interpersonal relations

Age range(s): 10 - 12+
Major character(s): Melody, 11-Year-Old
Time period(s): 21st century; 2010s
Locale(s): United States

Summary: In *Out of My Mind* by Sharon Draper, an 11-year-old girl with cerebral palsy struggles to communicate with the outside world where her parents, classmates, and teachers underestimate her intelligence. Melody has spent her life confined to a wheelchair, unable to walk, speak, or control her arm movements. While those around her presume that she is handicapped mentally as well as physically, Melody is actually extremely bright despite her inability to participate in discussions or express herself in writing. A device that can translate information that Melody inputs into audible speech finally gives her the freedom she has wanted for so long.

Where it's reviewed:
Booklist, January 1, 2010, page 81
Bulletin of the Center for Children's Books, March 2010, page 282
Horn Book Magazine, March/April 2010, page 53
School Library Journal, March 2010, page 156
Voice of Youth Advocates, August 2010, page 245

Other books by the same author:
Double Dutch, 2002

Awards the book has won:
Josette Frank Award, 2011

Other books you might like:
Tony Abbott, *Firegirl*, 2006
E.L. Konigsburg, *The View from Saturday*, 1996
Karon Luddy, *Spelldown*, 2007
Tracie Vaughn Zimmer, *Reaching for Sun*, 2007

119

ALLAN DRUMMOND

Energy Island: How One Community Harnessed the Wind and Changed Their World

(New York: Farrar, Straus, and Giroux, 2011)

Subject(s): Ecology; Natural resource conservation; Energy conservation

Age range(s): 5 - 8+

Summary: In *Energy Island: How One Community Harnessed the Wind and Changed the World*, author Allan Drummond describes to young readers how an island in Denmark stopped their dependence on fossil fuels through wind power. In 1997, the island of Samso won a competition hosted by the Danish government to have all of its energy resources switched to renewable energy. In addition to wind power, residents also began driving electric cars and using solar energy and, as a result, were able to reduce the island's carbon emissions by 140 percent. In this book, Drummond chronicles how the island began using renewable energy solutions to change the residents' lives.

Where it's reviewed:
Booklist, March 1, 2011, page 54
Horn Book Guide, Fall 2011, page 415
Publishers Weekly, January 17, 2011, page 48
School Library Journal, March 2011, page 142

Other books by the same author:
Tin Lizzie, 2008
The Flyers, 2003

Other books you might like:
Vicki Cobb, *I Face the Wind*, 2003
Joanna Cole, *The Magic School Bus and the Climate Challenge*, 2010
Bruce McMillan, *How the Ladies Stopped the Wind*, 2007

120

CHRIS DUFFY, Editor

Nursery Rhyme Comics: 50 Timeless Rhymes from 50 Celebrated Cartoonists

(New York: First Second, 2011)

Story type: Collection
Subject(s): Rhyme; Fables; Tall tales

Age range(s): 3 - 7+

Summary: Nursery rhymes have been popular with children for hundreds of years. In this book, editor Chris Duffy and 50 well-known cartoonists join forces to ensure that old-fashioned rhymes don't get stale. These cartoonists add some humorous comic characters to illustrate the action in the well-loved rhymes. The artists include Roz Chast, Nick Bruel, Gene Yang, Patrick Mc-

Donnell, Richard Thompson, Gilbert Hernandez, and others. The many classic rhymes they bring to life include "London Bridge Is Falling Down," "Pop Goes the Weasel," "Three Little Kittens," and "There Was a Crooked Man." This book includes an introduction by Leonard S. Marcus.

Where it's reviewed:
Booklist, November 15, 2011, page 42
Publishers Weekly, August 1, 2011, page 51
School Library Journal, September 2011, page 189

Other books you might like:
Philippe Coudray, *Benjamin Bear in Fuzzy Thinking*, 2011
Regis Faller, *The Adventures of Polo*, 2006
Jack Prelutsky, *The New Kid on the Block: Poems*, 1984
Robert Sabuda, *The Movable Mother Goose*, 1999
Shel Silverstein, *A Light in the Attic*, 1981

121

ANNIKA DUNKLEE
MATTHEW FORSYTHE, Illustrator

My Name Is Elizabeth!

(Toronto, Ontario, Canada: Kids Can Press, 2011)

Story type: Humor
Subject(s): Humor; Children; Anger

Age range(s): 3 - 7+
Major character(s): Elizabeth, Girl, Child

Summary: A feisty young girl struggles with the nicknames she's been given in this humorous picture book by author Annika Dunklee. Young Elizabeth simply adores her name. It's nine letters long and so much fun to say. Unfortunately, the folks in her town don't seem to recognize the importance of calling her by her full moniker. Instead, they insist on shortening it to unpleasant nicknames like Lizzy, Beth, Liz, or Betsy. As everyone continues to get her name wrong, Elizabeth grows more and more frustrated, until she finally lets her anger be heard by all. This witty tale is complemented by retro illustrations from artist Matthew Forsythe.

122

JOAN DUNNING, Author/Illustrator

Seabird in the Forest: The Mystery of the Marbled Murrelet

(Honesdale, Pennsylvania: Boyds Mills Press, 2011)

Subject(s): Birds; Nature; Trees (Plants)

Summary: In this nonfiction work for young readers, author and illustrator Joan Dunning describes the life of the marbled murrelet, a type of seabird. Dunning explains that marbled murrelets mate for life and begins her account with a pair of the birds traveling inland from the Pacific Ocean to the tall redwood trees of the Pacific Northwest, where they build a nest and raise one baby each year. Dunning provides plenty of information about the murrelets' habitat in sidebars that accompany the story and illustrations of the birds. Dunning concludes by describing the baby murrelet's first journey to its ocean home.

Where it's reviewed:
Booklist, April 15, 2011, page 51
Publishers Weekly, April 4, 2011, page 14
School Library Journal, May 2011, page 95

Other books by the same author:
Secrets of the Nest, 1994

Other books you might like:
Roxie Munro, *Hatch!*, 2011
Deborah Ruddell, *Today at the Bluebird Cafe: A Branchful of Birds*, 2007
Janet Schulman, *Pale Male*, 2008
Cybele Young, *Ten Birds*, 2011
Ed Young, *Hook*, 2009

123

HALLIE DURAND
CHRISTINE DAVENIER, Illustrator

Dessert First

(New York: Atheneum Books for Young Readers, 2009)

Subject(s): Cooking; Family life; Restaurants

Age range(s): 8 - 10+
Major character(s): Dessert Schneider, 8-Year-Old; Mummy, Mother (of Dessert); Daddy, Father (of Dessert); Wolfgang, Brother (of Dessert); Mushy, Brother (of Dessert)
Time period(s): 21st century; 2000s
Locale(s): United States

Summary: In *Dessert First* by Hallie Duran, eight-year-old Dessert Schneider's uncontrollable sweet tooth gets her into a deliciously funny mess at her family's French restaurant. Encouraged by her teacher, Mrs. Howdy Doody, to express her individuality, Dessert incorporates a maraschino cherry into her signature and persuades her parents to serve dessert first. But when Dessert disobeys Mummy and consumes all of the Double-Decker Chocolate Bars in the Fondue Paris cooler, she must find a way to atone for her offense. In a supremely selfless act, Dessert offers her services at the restaurant and even gives up sweets—temporarily. Illustrations by Christine Davenier capture Dessert's wit and energy.

Where it's reviewed:
Bulletin of the Center for Children's Books, September 2009, page 16
Horn Book Guide, Fall 2009, page 368
Publishers Weekly, May 4, 2009, page 50
School Library Journal, July 2009, page 62

Other books you might like:
Rozanne Gold, *Kids Cook 1-2-3: Recipes for Young Chefs Using Only 3 Ingredients*, 2006
Charise Mericle Harper, *Just Grace*, 2007
Alison McGhee, *Julia Gillian (and the Art of Knowing)*, 2008

Sara Pennypacker, *Clementine*, 2006
Eileen Spinelli, *The Dancing Pancake*, 2010

124

LOIS EHLERT, Author/Illustrator

RRRalph

(New York: Beach Lane Books, 2011)

Story type: Humor; Young Readers
Subject(s): Dogs; Humor; Human-animal relationships
Age range(s): 3 - 5+
Major character(s): Ralph, Dog; Unnamed Character, Narrator

Summary: Ralph is a talking dog. Just ask him his name, and he'll tell you—"RRRALPH / RALPH." But Ralph knows other words, too. A distant howl, according to Ralph, belongs to a "WOLF." And the stuff on that nearby tree? Ralph says it's "BARK / BARK / BARK." Throughout this story by Lois Ehlert, the narrator proves that Ralph can talk. The narrator asks Ralph all kinds of questions, and Ralph seems to have all the answers. Ehlert's simple text is accompanied by images created from found objects including soda can tabs, buttons, tree bark, and more.

Where it's reviewed:
Booklist, February 15, 2011, page 69
Bulletin of the Center for Children's Books, June 2011, page 466
Horn Book Magazine, May/June 2011, page 74
Publishers Weekly, March 21, 2011, page 72
School Library Journal, May 2011, page 75

Other books by the same author:
Boo to You!, 2009
Wag a Tail, 2007
Top Cat, 1998
Nuts to You, 1993
Feathers for Lunch, 1990

Other books you might like:
Eric Carle, *The Very Quiet Cricket*, 1990
Denise Fleming, *The Cow Who Clucked*, 2006
Anita Lobel, *Hello, Day!*, 2008
Alice Schertle, *Little Blue Truck*, 2008

125

DAVID ELLIOTT
HOLLY MEADE, Illustrator

In the Wild

(Somerville, Massachusetts: Candlewick Press, 2010)

Subject(s): Poetry; Animals
Age range(s): 5 - 8+

Summary: *In the Wild* by David Elliott presents a collection of lively animal poems for young readers. Elliott's energetic verses convey the unique physical traits and locomotion of each featured mammal—14 in all—from the lion's majestic presence on the savannah to the elephant's powerful grace to the giraffe's lofty splendor. The poet carefully considers buffalos, orangutans, zebras, pandas, and polar bears in brief poems that convey powerful themes of biodiversity and nature conservation in engaging, memorable language. Holly Meade's watercolor-enhanced woodblock illustrations capture the diversity of Elliott's menagerie and the beauty of each animal's habitat.

Where it's reviewed:
Booklist, July 1, 2010, page 66
Horn Book Magazine, September/October 2010, page 104
School Library Journal, July 2010, page 73

Other books by the same author:
On the Farm, 2008

Other books you might like:
Francisco X Alarcon, *Animal Poems of the Iguazu/Animalario del Iguazu*, 2008
Julie Hofstrand Larious, *Yellow Elephant: A Bright Bestiary*
Martin Jenkins, *Can We Save the Tiger?*, 2011
Laurie Krebs, *We All Went on Safari: A Counting Journey through Tanzania*, 2003
Simms Taback, *Simms Taback's Safari Animals*, 2008

126

DEBORAH ELLIS

No Ordinary Day

(Toronto: Groundwood Books, 2011)

Subject(s): Indians (Asian people); Diseases; Disadvantaged persons
Age range(s): 10 - 14+
Major character(s): Valli, Girl; Dr. Indra, Doctor
Time period(s): 21st century; 2010s
Locale(s): Jharia, India; Kolkata, India

Summary: This novel by author Deborah Ellis focuses on a young Indian girl named Valli. Living with her aunt and cousins in Jharia, India, a small coal-mining town, Valli is a fiercely independent girl who has lived her entire life in the impoverished slums without complaint. Mostly undisturbed by many of the things that typically terrify other children, Valli has one fear: the diseased lepers who live across the railroad tracks. Eventually, Valli learns that her aunt, the woman who raised her, is actually no relation to her at all; the woman was paid by Valli's mother to adopt her unwanted child. Angered by this news, Valli strikes out on her own and leaves Jharia, visiting a number of different locations before finally arriving in Kolkata. Once there, she meets a local doctor and learns that she has contracted leprosy. Crushed by the realization that her worst nightmare has come true, Valli rejects all offers of help and resigns herself to her unhappy fate.

Where it's reviewed:
Horn Book Magazine, November 20 2011, page 99
Publishers Weekly, July 11 2011, page 58
School Library Journal, September 2011, page 150

Other books by the same author:
No Safe Place, 2010
Sacred Leaf, 2007
The Heaven Shop, 2004
Mud City, 2003
The Breadwinner, 2000

Other books you might like:
Lisa Cindrich, *In the Shadow of the Pali: A Story of the Hawaiian Leper Colony*, 2002
Chitra Banerjee Divakaruni, *The Conch Bearer*, 2003
Julia Durango, *The Walls of Cartagena*, 2008
Monika Schroder, *Saraswati's Way*, 2010
Kashmira Sheth, *Boys Without Names*, 2010

127

SUSAN MIDDLETON ELYA
MELISSA SWEET, Illustrator

Rubia and the Three Osos
(New York: Hyperion, 2010)

Subject(s): Fairy tales; Bears; Forgiveness
Age range(s): 4 - 8+
Major character(s): Rubia, Girl

Summary: *Rubia and the Three Osos*, by author Susan Middleton Elya, is a retelling of the classic fairy tale, *Goldilocks and the Three Bears*. Rubia takes Goldilocks's place this time, however, as she arrives at the bears' house and sits in three chairs, samples three bowls of porridge, and sleeps in three beds. Elya adds a twist to the storyline, however: Rubia returns to apologize to the bears. The author peppers Spanish words in with English to help young readers become acquainted with new languages. This book is illustrated by Melissa Sweet. Elya is also the author of *Say Hola to Spanish* and *Bebe Goes Shopping*.

Where it's reviewed:
Horn Book Guide, Spring 2010, page 135
Publishers Weekly, October 25, 2010, page 46

Other books by the same author:
Fairy Trails, 2005

Other books you might like:
Jim Aylesworth, *Goldilocks and the Three Bears*, 2003
Anthony Browne, *Me and You*, 2010
Lisa Campbell Ernst, *Goldilocks Returns*, 2000
Steven Guarnaccia, *Goldilocks and the Three Bears: A Tale Moderne*, 2000
James Marshall, *Goldilocks and the Three Bears*, 1988

128

SUSAN MIDDLETON ELYA
ELISABETH SCHLOSSBERG, Illustrator

Adios, Tricycle
(New York: G.P. Putnam's Sons, 2009)

Subject(s): Bicycles; Children; Money
Age range(s): 3 - 7+

Major character(s): Unnamed Character, Pig

Summary: In Susan Middleton Elya's *Adios, Tricycle*, a young piglet has outgrown his tricycle, but is not ready to give it up just yet. Many people at his mother's yard sale show interest in buying the tricycle, but the little piglet will not sell it. As the day comes to a close, a little boy, who is the perfect size for the tricycle, wants to buy it. The little piglet knows that now is the right time to say good-bye to his beloved trike. He is surprised when he learns that the money from the yard sale will go toward buying him a new bike. *Adios, Tricycle* is written in Spanish and English and is illustrated by Elisabeth Schlossberg.

Where it's reviewed:
Booklist, June 1, 2009, page 60
Horn BookGuide, Fall 2009, page 310
School Library Journal, August 2009, page 74

Other books by the same author:
Oh No, Gotta Go, 2003
Eight Animals Bake a Cake, 2002
Say Hola to Spanish, 1996

Other books you might like:
Ilene Cooper, *Jake's Best Thumb*, 2008
Kevin Henkes, *Owen*, 1993
Juan Felipe Herrera, *Grandma and Me at the Flea, Los Meros Meros Remateros*, 2002
Alison McGhee, *Bye-Bye, Crib*, 2008
Mo Willems, *Knuffle Bunny Free: An Unexpected Diversion*, 2010

129

REBECCA EMBERLEY, Author/Illustrator
ED EMBERLEY, Author/Illustrator

Chicken Little
(New York: Roaring Brook Press, 2009)

Subject(s): Folklore; Chickens; Animals
Age range(s): 4 - 8+
Major character(s): Chicken Little, Chicken; Henny Penny, Hen; Lucky Ducky, Duck; Loosey Goosey, Goose

Summary: In *Chicken Little*, author Rebecca Emberley and her father, illustrator Ed Emberley, update the classic story with amusing language and vivid artwork. The story begins with the excitable Chicken Little being struck by an acorn, which he interprets as the start of a sky collapse. As he races around frantically, alerting his fowl friends Henny Penny, Lucky Ducky, and Loosey Goosey of the impending disaster, his antics are punctuated with comical "Bonks," "Eeps," and "Awks." Throughout, a sarcastic narrator pokes fun at the birds' self-induced predicament. Fortunately, Chicken Little and company gather their wits when an overly friendly fox offers them shelter within his jaws.

Where it's reviewed:
Bulletin of the Center for Children's Books, May 2009, page 360
Horn Book Magazine, May/June 2009, page 312
Publishers Weekly, January 19, 2009, page 58
School Library Journal, May 2009, page 76

Other books by the same author:
The Red Hen, 2010

Other books you might like:
Lucy Cousins, *Yummy: Eight Favorite Fairy Tales*, 2009
Barry Downard, *The Race of the Century*, 2008
Valeri Gorbachev, *Dragon Is Coming!*, 2009
Margie Palatini, *Earthquack!*, 2002
Jon Scieszka, *The Stinky Cheese Man and Other Fairly Stupid Tales*, 1992

130

MARGARITA ENGLE
JULIE PASCHKIS, Illustrator

Summer Birds: The Butterflies of Maria Merian

(New York: Henry Holt and Co., 2010)

Subject(s): Insects; Science; Good and evil

Age range(s): 5 - 8+

Summary: In *Summer Birds: The Butterflies of Maria Merian*, Margarita Engle tells the story of a young Maria Merian. At the age of 13, Merian defied hundreds of years of beliefs and traditions when she refused to believe that insects were evil beings that rose from the mud of the earth. After watching a caterpillar spin a cocoon and emerge as a beautiful butterfly, Merian knew for sure that everyone else was wrong. She captured this phenomenon and many others with paintings and sketches and soon showed the world what she had learned. In the 1600s, few wanted to believe her and instead labeled her a witch. Years later, she would find scientific research to support her theories.

Where it's reviewed:
Booklist, March 15, 2010, page 43
Bulletin of the Center for Children's Books, June 2010, page 43
Horn Book Guide, Fall 2010, page 412
School Library Journal, July 2010, page 74

Other books you might like:
Nic Bishop, *Nic Bishop Frogs*, 2008
Nic Bishop, *Nic Bishop: Butterflies and Moths*, 2009
Deborah Hopkinson, *The Humblebee Hunter*, 2010
Alan Madison, *Velma Gratch and the Way Cool Butterfly*, 2007
Antoine O Flatharta, *Hurry and the Monarch*, 2005

131

KAREN ENGLISH
LAURA FREEMAN, Illustrator

Nikki and Deja: Birthday Blues

(New York: Clarion Books, 2009)

Subject(s): Birthdays; Adolescence; Friendship
Age range(s): 8 - 10+
Major character(s): Nikki, 3rd Grader, Student—Elementary School, Friend (to Deja); Deja, 3rd Grader, Student—Elementary School, Friend (to Nikki)
Time period(s): 21st century; 2000s
Locale(s): United States

Summary: *Nikki and Deja: Birthday Blues* is a humorous, entertaining, and fun book for young readers from author Karen English. This story is the second book to follow the adventures of Nikki and Deja: third graders and best friends. Deja's long-anticipated birthday is almost here, but it arrives with its own share of trouble. Auntie Dee has to leave on an emergency business trip right before the big day, leaving Deja in the care of her neighbor, an old lady who cooks terrible food and doesn't own a color television! As if that's not bad enough, Deja's newest enemy, Antonia, is trying to destroy Deja's special day. Could things get any worse? Nikki and Deja need to devise a plan to save Deja's birthday, and they need to come up with one fast!

Where it's reviewed:
Bulletin of the Center for Children's Books, April 2009, page 319
Horn Book Guide, Fall 2009, page 358
School Library Journal, January 2009, page 74

Other books by the same author:
Nikki and Deja: Election Madness, 2011
Nikki and Deja: The Newsy Newsletter, 2010
Nikki and Deja, 2007

Other books you might like:
Sharon M. Draper, *Sassy: Little Sister is Not My Name*, 2009
Fredrick McKissack, *Tippy Lemmey*, 2003
Sara Pennypacker, *Clementine's Letter*, 2008
Chris Van Allsburg, *Probuditi!*, 2006
Stephanie Watson, *Elvis and Olive*, 2008

132

ADAM JAY EPSTEIN
ANDREW JACOBSON, Co-Author
BOBBY CHIU, Illustrator

The Familiars

(New York: Harper, 2010)

Series: Familiars Series. Book 1
Subject(s): Domestic cats; Magic; Wizards

Age range(s): 9 - 11+
Major character(s): Aldwyn, Cat; Gilbert, Frog; Skylar, Bird (blue jay); Jack, Wizard
Time period(s): 21st century; 2010s
Locale(s): Vastia, Fictional Location

Summary: Aldwyn is a spunky, streetwise alley cat who, while on the run from a merciless vigilante, claims he is an enchanted animal helper, or familiar. His fib gains him the trust of Jack, a young sorcerer still learning the ropes. Aldwyn, clumsy tree frog Gilbert, and brainy blue jay Skylar become Jack's familiars, helping him save the realm from the machinations of a sinister queen. *The Familiars* is the first installment in a series by Adam Jay Epstein and Andrew Jacobson. First book.

Where it's reviewed:
Booklist, June 1, 2010, page 67
Bulletin of the Center for Children's Books, October
  2010, page 73
Horn Book Guide, Spring 2011, page 69
Publishers Weekly, August 9, 2010, page 52
School Library Journal, August 2010, page 98

Other books by the same author:
Secrets of the Crown, 2011

Other books you might like:
Kelly Barnhill, *The Mostly True Story of Jack*, 2011
Sarah Prineas, *The Magic Thief*, 2008
Rick Riordan, *The Red Pyramid*, 2010
Jacqueline West, *The Shadows*, 2010

133

KATHRYN ERSKINE

Mockingbird

(New York: Philomel Books, 2010)

Subject(s): Schools; Death; Family life

Age range(s): 9 - 11+

Major character(s): Caitlin, 10-Year-Old; Mrs. Brook,
  Counselor (to Caitlin)

Time period(s): 21st century; 2010s

Locale(s): United States

Summary: In *Mockingbird* by Kathryn Erskine, a 10-year-
old girl with Asperger's syndrome tries to cope with the
death of her brother. Caitlin, who had already lost her
mother, relied on her older brother, Devon, to help her
make her way in a world that she often found
bewildering. When Devon was killed in a school shooting, Caitlin was left alone with her father, who is now
dealing with a double dose of grief. With the help of a
school counselor, her love of art, and a deepening
relationship with her father, Caitlin begins to heal and to
deal with the daily disorder she encounters.

Where it's reviewed:
Booklist, February 15, 2010, page 78
Bulletin of the Center for Children's Books, May 2010,
  page 377
Horn Book Magazine, March/April 2010, page 54
Publishers Weekly, March 8, 2010, page 57
School Library Journal, April 2010, page 154

Other books by the same author:
The Absolute Value of Mike, 2011

Awards the book has won:
National Book Awards: Young People's Literature, 2010

Other books you might like:
Suzanne Crowley, *The Very Ordered Existence of
  Merilee Marvelous*, 2007
Siobhan Dowd, *The London Eye Mystery*, 2008
Lisa Graff, *Umbrella Summer*, 2009
Barbara Park, *Mick Harte Was Here*, 1995
Lauren Tarshis, *Emma-Jean Lazarus Fell out of a Tree*,
  2007

134

SHANE W. EVANS

Underground: Finding the Light to Freedom

(New York: Roaring Brook Press, 2011)

Story type: Historical - Antebellum American South;
  Young Readers

Subject(s): Slavery; Underground Railroad (Slave escape
  network); Family

Age range(s): 5 - 7+

Summary: This picture book tells the story of a group of
slaves who wish to be free. One night, the slaves escape
from their owners and begin their journey on the
Underground Railroad. They crawl most of the way,
keeping their bodies close to the ground. They walk
through the darkness barefoot. They watch for lanterns
that indicate friends are close and will let them stay the
night. They also watch for signs that slave catchers are
nearby. They are determined to reach the other side of
the Railroad, where freedom waits for them. Author and
illustrator Shane W. Evans crafts the slaves' story for
young readers through his dark illustrations and a
minimal amount of text. This book received the American
Library Association's 2012 Coretta Scott King illustrator
award.

Where it's reviewed:
Bulletin of the Center for Children's Books, February
  2011, page 276
Horn Book Magazine, January/February 2011, page 111
Publishers Weekly, November 29 2010, page 47
School Library Journal, January 2011, page 88

Other books by the same author:
We March, 2012

Awards the book has won:
Coretta Scott King Book Award: Illustrator Award, 2012

Other books you might like:
Ellen Levine, *Henry's Freedom Box: A True Story from
  the Underground Railroad*, 2007
Doreen Rappaport, *Freedom River*, 2000
Joseph Slate, *I Want to Be Free*, 2009
Carole Boston Weatherford, *Moses: When Harriet
  Tubman Led Her People to Freedom*, 2006

135

KATE FEIFFER
DIANE GOODE, Illustrator

My Mom Is Trying to Ruin My Life

(New York: Simon & Schuster Books for Young Readers, 2009)

Story type: Young Readers

Subject(s): Mother-daughter relations; Father-daughter
  relations; Humor

Age range(s): 5 - 8+

Major character(s): Emma, Narrator, Girl

Summary: Author Kate Feiffer and illustrator Diane Goode share the story of a young girl's annoyance with her overprotective parents in this humorous picture book. Emma knows that her mother performs some worthwhile functions, like baking cookies and bandaging wounds. But the narrator is fed up with her parents' embarrassing behaviors, which include telling dumb jokes and kissing her in front of her friends. Emma thinks about how different her life would be if her mother and father were arrested for their parental misdeeds—no more pestering to do homework and no rules about what time to go to bed. Emma soon realizes that she still needs her parents, however, and she begins to understand that they are not trying to ruin her life after all.

Where it's reviewed:
Booklist, March 15, 2009, page 66
Horn Book Guide, Fall 2009, page 327
Publishers Weekly, December 1, 2008, page 45
School Library Journal, May 2009, page 76

Other books by the same author:
My Side of the Car, 2011
President Pennybaker, 2008
Double Pink, 2005

Other books you might like:
Cornelia Funke, *Pirate Girl*, 2005
Bob Graham, *April and Esme: Tooth Fairies*, 2010
Marty Kelley, *Twelve Terrible Things*, 2008
Susan Kuklin, *Families*, 2006
Judith Viorst, *Lulu and the Brontosaurus*, 2010

136

JODY FELDMAN

The Seventh Level

(New York: Greenwillow Books, 2010)

Subject(s): High schools; Students; Friendship

Age range(s): 9 - 11+

Major character(s): Travis Raines, 7th Grader, Classmate, Student—Middle School

Time period(s): 21st century; 2010s

Summary: In Jody Feldman's *The Seventh Level*, Travis Raines has always wondered about The Legend, the secret group of students who control all school events. He knows that people in the club are identified as being Legendaries, but he doesn't personally know any of them. In fact, no one knows who is in The Legend. No one knows anything about The Legend until they are invited to join. One day, Travis finds an envelope in his locker that appears to be from The Legend. Although he's not sure if it's real, he decides to complete the challenges listed in the invitation anyway. He must complete seven levels of intricate and mind-bending puzzles and games before he, too, can become Legendary. When he finishes the challenges, he must decide if being part of The Legend is worth the time and effort or if he's happy being a normal student.

Where it's reviewed:
Booklist, May 1, 2010, page 53
Horn Book Guide, Fall 2010, page 338
School Library Journal, October 2010, page 114
Voice of Youth Advocates, August 2010, page 246

Other books by the same author:
The Gollywhopper Games, 2009

Other books you might like:
Blue Balliett, *Chasing Vermeer*, 2004
Eric Berlin, *The Puzzling World of Winston Breen*, 2007
Benedict Carey, *The Unknowns: A Mystery*, 2009
Dan Gutman, *Mission Unstoppable*, 2011
E.L. Konigsburg, *The View from Saturday*, 1996

137

VALORIE FISHER, Author/Illustrator

Everything I Need to Know before I'm Five

(New York: Random House, 2011)

Story type: Young Readers
Subject(s): Learning; Children; Storytelling

Age range(s): 2 - 5+

Summary: In this children's picture story, author Valorie Fisher provides young readers with educational tools to help them learn integral skills before they enter school. By looking at the book's bright colors, large numbers, cute illustrations, and pictures of familiar objects, children can learn the skills they will need in kindergarten. Topics include counting to 20, identifying basic colors, learning the alphabet, identifying shapes, and naming all four seasons. Fisher is also the author of *When Ruby Tried to Grow Candy, How High Can a Dinosaur Count?*, and *Ellsworth's Extraordinary Electric Ears*.

Where it's reviewed:
Booklist, July 1, 2011, page 64
Horn Book Magazine, July/August 2011, page 127
Publishers Weekly, May 30, 2011, page 67
School Library Journal, July 2011, page 65

Other books by the same author:
The Fantastic 5 & 10cent Store, 2010
How High Can a Dinosaur Count?, 2006
My Big Sister, 2003
My Big Brother, 2002

Other books you might like:
Simon Basher, *ABC Kids*, 2011
Ina Cumpiano, *Quinito, Day and Night/Quinito, dia y noche*, 2008
Paul Giganti, *Each Orange Had 8 Slices: A Counting Book*, 1992
Tana Hoban, *26 Letters and 99 Cents*, 1987
Laura Vaccaro Seeger, *Black? White! Day? Night!: A Book of Opposites*, 2006

138

PAUL FLEISCHMAN
DAVID ROBERTS, Illustrator

The Dunderheads

(Somerville, Massachusetts: Candlewick Press, 2009)

Subject(s): Teachers; Theft; Adventure

Age range(s): 9 - 11+

Major character(s): Miss Breakbone, Teacher; Junkyard, Student; Wheels, Student; Pencil, Student; Spider, Student; Einstein, Student

Time period(s): 21st century; 2000s

Locale(s): United States

Summary: Miss Breakbone is the meanest teacher in school. She even despises the children in her class, calling them dunderheads. But one day, Miss Breakbone does the unthinkable: she takes away a cat statue belonging to a student named Junkyard. Junkyard and his classmates, however, are not about to let their teacher get away with it. Teaming up with Einstein, the school nerd, Junkyard and his pals hatch a plan to retrieve the statue, but their rogue act will require all their courage. In order to get back the precious item, they will have to break into Miss Breakbone's scary—and possibly haunted—house. Paul Fleischman's *The Dunderheads* contains illustrations by David Roberts.

Where it's reviewed:
Booklist, June 1, 2009, page 53
Bulletin of the Center for Children's Books, July/August 2009, page 41
Horn Book Magazine, July/August 2009, page 421
Publishers Weekly, page 53, page May 18, 2009
School Library Journal, June 2009, page 84

Awards the book has won:
Pen Center USA West Literary Awards: Children's Literature, 2010

Other books you might like:
Andrew Clements, *Frindle*, 1996
Lois Lowry, *The Willoughbys*, 2008
Phyllis Reynolds Naylor, *Roxie and the Hooligans*, 2006
Patricia Polacco, *Junkyard Wonders*, 2010

139

SID FLEISCHMAN

Sir Charlie Chaplin: The Funniest Man in the World

(New York: Greenwillow Books, 2010)

Subject(s): Actors; Movie industry; Biographies

Age range(s): 10 - 15+

Summary: *Sir Charlie Chaplin: The Funniest Man in the World* is a comprehensive biography for young readers from bestselling author, Sid Fleischman. Born into poverty in England, Charlie Chaplin first took the stage at five years old and never looked back. Chaplin went on to become one of Hollywood's biggest stars and most famous comedians. The actor was a legendary film star whose physical comedy earned him rave reviews and many admirers. In *Sir Charlie Chaplin*, Fleischman educates children about the actor's difficult childhood, his foray into acting, his long and successful career, and his escape from the public eye.

Where it's reviewed:
Booklist, June 1, 2010, page 99
Bulletin of the Center for Children's Books, July/August, 2010, page 480
Horn Book Guide, Fall 2010, page 441
Publishers Weekly, May 24, 2010, page 55
School Library Journal, June 2010, page 27

Other books by the same author:
The Trouble Begins at 8: A Life of Mark Twain in the Wild, Wild West, 2008
Escape!: The Story of the Great Houdini, 2006
The Abracadabra Kid: A Writer's Life, 1996

Other books you might like:
Judy L. Hasday, *Extraordinary People in the Movies*, 2003
Clay Nichols, *Filmmaking for Teens: Pulling Off Your Shorts*, 2005
Rosemary Wells, *On the Blue Comet*, 2010

140

CANDACE FLEMING
G. BRIAN KARAS, Illustrator

Clever Jack Takes the Cake

(New York: Schwartz and Wade Books, 2010)

Subject(s): Fairy tales; Food; Birthdays

Age range(s): 5 - 8+

Major character(s): Jack, Child

Time period(s): 21st century; 2010s

Summary: The creative team of author Candace Fleming and illustrator G. Brian Karas present the story of a boy who wants to bring the princess a worthy birthday gift. *Clever Jack Takes the Cake* finds Jack baking a special cake just for the princess, but when he sets off through the forest to deliver the sweet treat, it is methodically destroyed. Crows, bears, and trolls are just a few of the creatures who each do their best to ruin the cake, and when Jack shows up at the palace, all he can present to the princess is the adventurous story of the cake's travels.

Where it's reviewed:
Booklist, July 1, 2010, page 62
Bulletin of the Center for Children's Books, October 2010, page 74
Horn Book Guide, Spring 2011, page 27
Publishers Weekly, July 19, 2010, page 127
School Library Journal, July 2010, page 59

Other books by the same author:
Imogene's Last Stand, 2009
Gator Gumbo, 2004

A Big Cheese for the White House: The True Tale of a Tremendous Cheddar, 1999

Westward Ho, Carlotta, 1998

Other books you might like:

Norton Juster, *The Odious Ogre*, 2010

Tanya Landman, *Mary's Penny*, 2010

Simms Taback, *Joseph Had a Little Overcoat*, 1999

Margaret Willey, *Clever Beatrice: An Upper Peninsula Conte*, 2001

Karma Wilson, *Whopper Cake*, 2007

141

CANDACE FLEMING
NANCY CARPENTER, Illustrator

Imogene's Last Stand

(New York: Schwartz and Wade, 2009)

Subject(s): United States history; Community relations; Children

Age range(s): 6 - 9+

Major character(s): Imogene, Child, Historian

Summary: In Candace Fleming's *Imogene's Last Stand*, Imogene is a little girl who has loved history from the time she could speak. The first words she spoke were quoted from the Declaration of Independence, and her first art project was a historically accurate map of the Oregon Trail created with finger paints. When the mayor of her town decides to demolish the site of the town's historical society, Imogene is up in arms. The town wants to build a factory there, but Imogene has other ideas. She tries to explain the importance of history to her fellow citizens. The story is filled with historical quotes, and an index provides biographical information on important historical figures cited throughout the text. Nancy Carpenter supplies the illustrations for this lively tale.

Where it's reviewed:

Bulletin of the Center for Children's Books, November 2009, page 110

Horn Book Magazine, November/December 2009, page 652

School Library Journal, October 2009, page 90

Other books by the same author:

A Big Cheese for the White House: The True Tale of a Tremendous Cheddar, 1999

Westward Ho, Carlotta, 1998

Other books you might like:

Kelly DiPucchio, *Grace for President*, 2008

Belinda Hollyer, *She's All That!: Poems about Girls*, 2006

Doreen Rappaport, *Eleanor, Quiet No More*, 2009

Lane Smith, *John, Paul, George and Ben*, 2006

Linda Arms White, *I Could Do That! : Esther Morris Gets Women the Vote*, 2005

142

CANDACE FLEMING
RAY FENWICK, Illustrator

The Great and Only Barnum: The Tremendous, Stupendous Life of Showman P.T. Barnum

(New York: Schwartz & Wade Books, 2009)

Subject(s): Biographies; Circuses; Popular culture

Age range(s): 10 - 14+

Summary: Candace Fleming explores the life of the man behind "The Greatest Show on Earth" in *The Great and Only Barnum: The Tremendous, Stupendous Life of Showman P.T. Barnum*. Early in life, Phineas Taylor Barnum was described as a jokester who hated manual labor. He was credited for inventing aquariums and was famous for his American Museum and circuses. He had many successes and failures, struggling with money, alcohol, and marriage. He kept his public circus master persona separate from his private life as a religious man who dedicated much money to helping those less fortunate. Fleming also describes the human oddities in his museum—tiny Tom Thumb, the bearded woman, skeleton man, and conjoined twins Chang and Eng. Sidebars, photographs, posters, and illustrations by Ray Fenwick accompany the text.

Where it's reviewed:

Booklist, June 1-15, 2009, page 87

Bulletin of the Center for Children's Books, October 2009, page 64

Horn Book Magazine, September 2009, page 581

New York Times Book Review, December 6 2009, page 48

School Library Journal, September 2009, page 181

Other books by the same author:

Amelia Lost: The Life and Disappearance of Amelia Earhart, 2011

Other books you might like:

Jill Esbaum, *To the Big Top*, 2008

Sid Fleischman, *Escape!: The Story of the Great Houdini*, 2006

Margaret Mahy, *Maddigan's Fantasia*, 2007

Elaine Scott, *Secrets of the Cirque Medrano*, 2008

George Sullivan, *Tom Thumb: The Remarkable True Story of a Man in Minature*, 2011

143

DENISE FLEMING, Author/Illustrator

Sleepy, Oh So Sleepy

(New York: Henry Holt, 2010)

Subject(s): Sleep; Infants; Animals

Age range(s): 1 - 4+

Summary: In *Sleepy, Oh So Sleepy* by Denise Fleming, a drowsy menagerie of baby animals comforts little readers at bedtime. In Fleming's rhythmic tale, a variety of animal parents—anteaters, pandas, orangutans, penguins, and others—lull their children with the soothing refrain, "Sleepy, oh so sleepy." As each baby falls asleep, another mother seeks out her tired child—"Where's my sleepy baby?"—until the last pages reveal a human infant, awaiting his turn to be hushed into slumber. Fleming's rich pulp-painting illustrations capture the calming scenes of heavy-lidded animal babies familiar and exotic in their natural habitats.

Where it's reviewed:
Booklist, June 1, 2010, page 69
Bulletin of the Center for Children's Books, September 2010, page 3
Horn Book Magazine, July/August 2010, page 88

Other books by the same author:
The Everything Book, 2000
Time to Sleep, 1997
Barnyard Banter, 1994

Awards the book has won:
Blue Ribbon Awards: Picture Books, 2010

Other books you might like:
Lucy Cousins, *Maisy Goes to Bed*, 2010
Karen Katz, *Princess Baby Night-Night*, 2009
Jean Monrad, *How Many Kisses Good Night?*, 2010
Diane Muldrow, *Somewhere So Sleepy*, 2010
Beatrix Potter, *Peter Rabbit Sleepy Time*, 2010

144

CANDACE FLEMMING

Amelia Lost: The Life and Disappearance of Amelia Earhart
(New York: Schwartz & Wade Books, 2011)

Subject(s): Aviation; Accidents; Missing persons
Age range(s): 9 - 13+

Summary: In this biography for young readers, author Candace Flemming tells the story of one of aviation's most famous women: Amelia Earhart. Earhart was famous around the world before she ever took to the sky for her final flight. However, when news broke that Earhart was missing, her fame grew even more. In this volume, Flemming tells the story of Earhart's final flight, her mysterious disappearance, and the ensuing search. She also tells about Earheart's early life, the beginning of her aviation career, and the flying skills that made her famous. This volume includes black-and-white photographs, maps, informative sidebars, primary documents, and other information.

Where it's reviewed:
Booklist, December 1, 2010, page 41
Bulletin of the Center for Children's Books, March 2011, page 327
Horn Book Magazine, March/April 2011, page 138
School Library Journal, March 2011, page 179

Other books by the same author:
The Great and Only Barnum: The Tremendous, Stupendous Life of Showman P.T. Barnum, 2009

Our Eleanor: A Scrapbook Look at Eleanor Roosevelt's Remarkable Life, 2005
Ben Franklin's Almanac: Being a True Account of the Good Gentleman's Life, 2003
The Lincolns: A Scrapbook Look at Abraham and Mary, 2003

Other books you might like:
Michael Ferrari, *Born to Fly*, 2009
Tanya Lee Stone, *Almost Astronauts: 13 Women Who Dared to Dream*, 2009
Sarah Stewart Taylor, *Amelia Earhart: This Broad Ocean*, 2010

145

BRIAN FLOCA, Author/Illustrator

Moonshot: The Flight of Apollo 11
(New York: Atheneum Books for Young Readers, 2009)

Subject(s): Space flight; Science; Space exploration
Age range(s): 7 - 10+
Time period(s): 20th century; 1960s (1969)

Summary: In *Moonshot: The Flight of Apollo 11*, Brian Floca recreates the excitement of the historic 1969 moon landing. The work begins with a poetic reflection on the moon itself, floating high and mysterious above Earth. The preparations of the three astronauts and mission control are shown, and the rocket itself, "a tower of fire," is also displayed. Soon the three astronauts are strapped into the rocket and blast into space at unbelievable speeds. In space, the *Columbia* and *Eagle* vehicles both launch and successfully dock together. The astronauts pilot the crafts toward the moon, ultimately disengaging the *Eagle* and setting it down upon the surface of the moon. Then the astronauts put on their spacesuits and set foot on the moon's surface. Floca's illustrations demonstrate both the powerful science needed to make this historic feat possible and the subdued awe felt by those involved.

Where it's reviewed:
Booklist, February 15 2009, page 80
Bulletin of the Center for Children's Books, July/August 2009, page 436
Horn Book Magazine, May/June 2009, page 32
New York Times Book Review, September 13, 2009, page 17
School Library Journal, March 2009, page 134

Other books by the same author:
Lightship, 2007

Awards the book has won:
Blue Ribbon Awards: Non-fiction, 2008

Other books you might like:
Buzz Aldrin, *Look to the Stars*, 2009
Andrew Chaikin, *Mission Control, This Is Apollo: The Story of the First Voyages to the Moon*, 2009
Mark Haddon, *Footprints on the Moon*, 2009
Jack Prelutsky, *The Swamps of Sleethe: Poems from Beyond the Solar System*, 2009

Jerry Stone, *One Small Step: Celebrating the First Men on the Moon*, 2009

146

DOUGLAS FLORIAN, Author/Illustrator

Dinothesaurus

(New York: Simon & Schuster, 2009)

Subject(s): Poetry; Dinosaurs

Age range(s): 7 - 10+

Time period(s): Indeterminate Past

Summary: Combining verbal wit and solid scientific information, Florian takes readers back to the Triassic, Jurassic, and Cretaceous Periods and the age of dinosaurs. He describes eighteen different species such as Pterosaurs ("The pterrifying pterosaurs/Flew ptours the ptime of dinosaurs"); Ankylosaurus ("Tough as tanks and hard as nails."); and Triceratops ("Born with three great horns in place,/Triceratops was in your face.") Mixed media art decorate each poem, giving young readers much to contemplate among the drawings, collages, and rubber stamps. A "Glossarysaurus," with additional information about each poem, a list of dinosaur museums and fossil sites, and suggestions for further reading complete the book.

Other books you might like:

Elaine Marie Alphin, *Dinosaur Hunter*, 2003

Barbara Kerley, *The Dinosaurs of Waterhouse Hawkins: An Illuminating History of Mr. Waterhouse Hawkins, Artist and Lecturer*, 2001

Kathleen V. Kudlinski, *Boy, Were We Wrong about Dinosaurs!*, 2005

Deborah Kogan Ray, *Dinosaur Mountain: Digging into the Jurassic Age*, 2010

Matthew Reinhart, *Encyclopedia Prehistorica: Dinosaurs*, 2005

147

GREG FOLEY, Author/Illustrator

Willoughby and the Lion

(New York: HarperCollins, 2009)

Subject(s): Friendship; Wishes; Magic

Age range(s): 4 - 8+

Major character(s): Willoughby Smith, Child; The Lion, Lion

Time period(s): Indeterminate

Summary: Willoughby Smith and his parents have just moved to a new home—a place the young boy greatly dislikes. While brushing his teeth one day, he peers out a window and he sees a lion perched on a rock in his backyard. Willoughby confronts the lion, who offers him ten wishes. These wishes come with a caveat—one of Willoughby's "must be the most wonderful thing of all," or the lion will be stuck on the rock forever. Willoughby starts wishing for anything and everything his heart desires. As his wishes begin to dwindle, Willoughby realizes that the lion has given him everything he could possibly want. For his last wish, Willoughby must figure out a way to give back to this kind creature.

Where it's reviewed:

Booklist, January 1, 2009, page 96

Horn Book Guide, Fall 2009, page 327

Publishers Weekly, January 5, 2009, page 49

School Library Journal, February 2009, page 74

Other books by the same author:

Willoughby and the Moon, 2010

Thank You Bear, 2007

Other books you might like:

James Daugherty, *Andy and the Lion*, 1938

Henrik Drescher, *McFig & McFly: A Tale of Jealousy, Revenge, and Death (with a Happy Ending)*, 2008

Rachel Isadora, *The Fisherman and His Wife*

Jerry Pinkney, *The Lion and the Mouse*, 2009

William Steig, *Sylvester and the Magic Pebble*, 1969

148

MEM FOX
STEVE JENKINS, Illustrator

Hello Baby!

(New York: Beach Lane Books, 2009)

Subject(s): Rhyme; Animals; Infants

Age range(s): 2 - 5+

Time period(s): 21st century; 2000s

Summary: *Hello Baby!* is an exciting, read-aloud book for young children, told through whimsical rhyme by Mem Fox and bright illustrations by Steve Jenkins. The toddler at the heart of the story comes in contact with a variety of baby animals, including a lion, an owl, a monkey, a warthog, an elephant, and a zebra. And as the infant learns about each of these animals, a valuable lesson is learned about one's own specialness and importance in the world.

Where it's reviewed:

Booklist, May 15, 2009, page 46

Bulletin of the Center for Children's Books, September 2009, page 17

Horn Book Guide, Fall 2010, page 310

School Library Journal, April 2009, page 104

Other books by the same author:

Ten Little Fingers and Ten Little Toes, 2008

Time for Bed, 1993

Other books you might like:

Eve Bunting, *Hurry! Hurry!*, 2007

Lesley Wynne Pechter, *Alligator Bear Crab: A Baby's ABC*, 2011

Tony Ross, *Three Little Kittens and Other Favorite Nursery Rhymes*, 2009

Simms Taback, *Simms Taback's Safari Animals*, 2008

149

BETSY FRANCO
STEFANO VITALE, Illustrator

Pond Circle

(New York: Margaret K. McElderry Books, 2009)

Subject(s): Animals; Nature; Biology

Age range(s): 5 - 8+
Major character(s): Anna, Child, Animal Lover
Time period(s): 21st century; 2000s
Locale(s): United States

Summary: *Pond Circle* is a picture book for young readers by author Betsy Franco and illustrator Stefano Vitale. The story, which is told in rhythmic prose, follows a young girl named Anna as she observes the exciting and interesting creatures that live behind her house. Anna witnesses a number of wild animals in their natural habitats, and she gets a firsthand look at the ecological cycle of life. She sees a fishing fly insect eat the pond's algae before it is eaten by a beetle. She also witnesses the roles of the frogs, snakes, owls, skunks, raccoons and coyotes in the backyard habitat. A special section at the end of the book includes additional facts about each of the animals featured in the book.

Where it's reviewed:
Booklist, June 1, 2009, page 76
Horn Book Magazine, July/August 2009, page 407
Publishers Weekly, June 22, 2009, page 45
School Library Journal, May 2009, page 78

Other books by the same author:
Birdsongs, 2007
Bees, Snails and Peacock Tails, 2006

Other books you might like:
Vivian French, *Growing Frogs*, 2000
Heather Lynn Miller, *This Is Your Life Cycle*, 2008
Wendy Pfeffer, *From Tadpole to Frog*, 1994
Joyce Sidman, *Song of the Water Boatman and Other Pond Poems*, 2005

150

MARLA FRAZEE, Author/Illustrator

The Boss Baby

(New York: Beach Lane Books, 2010)

Subject(s): Humor; Children; Infants

Age range(s): 3 - 6+
Major character(s): Boss Baby, Baby

Summary: *The Boss Baby* is a picture book for children, written and illustrated by Marla Frazee. In the book, Boss Baby is a demanding baby who is shown wearing a suit and tie and a displeased expression; he keeps his parents busy all day and all night with his demands, until they finally get too tired and stop responding. He then realizes that a few magic words can make a big difference. This book is intended for families with a new baby, where older children may be struggling with loss of attention.

Where it's reviewed:
Booklist, July 1, 2010, page 65
Bulletin of the Center for Children's Books, September 2010, page 17
Horn Book Magazine, July/August 2010, page 90
Publishers Weekly, July 5, 2010, page 41
School Library Journal, July 2010, page 59

Other books by the same author:
Walk On! A Guide for Babies of All Ages, 2006
Hush, Little Baby: A Folk Song With Pictures, 1999

Other books you might like:
Jeanne Birdsall, *Flora's Very Windy Day*, 2010
Marla Frazee, *Walk On! A Guide for Babies of All Ages*, 2006
Simon James, *Baby Brains: The Smartest Baby in the Whole World*, 2004
Bob Shea, *Big Plans*, 2008
Mo Willems, *Knuffle Bunny: A Cautionary Tale*, 2004

151

RUSSELL FREEDMAN

Lafayette and the American Revolution

(New York: Holiday House, 2010)

Subject(s): Biographies; American Revolution, 1775-1783; History

Age range(s): 10 - 14+
Time period(s): 18th century; 1770s

Summary: In *Lafayette and the American Revolution*, author Russell Freedman presents a biography of Gilbert de Lafayette for middle-school students. When Marquis de Lafayette, a French nobleman, was just 19, he left his wife, child, and country to join the Continental Army. Though he was an untested soldier, Lafayette demonstrated his value to General George Washington and garnered increasingly important assignments. After the war, Lafayette restored his French citizenship but soon found himself at odds again with the king when he called for political reform. Caught between two countries, Gilbert de Lafayette finally decided that he truly was an American at heart.

Where it's reviewed:
Booklist, August 2010, page 54
Bulletin of the Center for Children's Books, November 2010, page 128
Horn Book Magazine, November/December 2010, page 114
Publishers Weekly, August 16, 2010, page 55
School Library Journal, September 2010, page 172

Other books by the same author:
Washington At Valley Forge, 2008

Other books you might like:
Laurie Halse Anderson, *Forge*, 2010
Stuart Murray, *American Revolution*, 2002
Rosalyn Schanzer, *George vs. George: The American*

Revolution as Seen from Both Sides, 2004
Steve Sheinkin, *King George: What Was His Problem?: The Whole Hilarious Story of the Revolution*, 2008
Steve Sheinkin, *The Notorious Benedict Arnold*, 2010

152

VIVIAN FRENCH
JESSICA AHLBERG, Illustrator

Yucky Worms

(New York: Walker Children's Books, 2009)

Subject(s): Worms (Animals); Intergenerational relations; Gardening

Age range(s): 4 - 8+

Summary: *Yucky Worms* by Vivian French is a book for young readers about the helpfulness of worms. When a young boy sees his grandmother pull a worm from her garden, he declares that it is yucky and should be discarded. The grandmother takes this opportunity to teach her grandson about the benefits of having worms in the garden, and the many things worms can do to take care of the soil. Through colorful illustrations and humorous captions, the author—along with illustrator Jessica Ahlberg—teaches young readers all about worms: what they eat, where they live, and how they help us grow fruits and vegetables.

Where it's reviewed:
Booklist, May 1, 2010, page 94
Bulletin of the Center for Children's Books, June 2010, page 431
Horn Book Guide, Fall 2010, page 412
School Library Journal, June 2010, page 70
Science Books & Film, December 2010, page 324

Other books by the same author:
T Rex, 2004
Growing Frogs, 2000
Whale Journey, 1998

Other books you might like:
Caroline Arnold, *Wiggle and Waggle*, 2007
Carol Brendler, *Winnie Finn, Worm Farmer*, 2009
Doreen Cronin, *Diary of a Worm*, 2003
Cris Peterson, *Seed, Soil, Sun: Earth's Recipe for Food*, 2010
Wendy Pfeffer, *Wiggling Worms At Work*, 2004

153

TONY FUCILE, Author/Illustrator

Let's Do Nothing!

(Somerville, Massachusetts: Candlewick Press, 2009)

Subject(s): Imagination; Games; Children

Age range(s): 5 - 8+
Major character(s): Frankie, Child, Brother (of Sal); Sal, Child, Brother (of Frankie)

Summary: Feature-film animator Tony Fucile makes his debut in the world of children's books in *Let's Do Nothing*. Sal and Frankie have done everything—played every sport imaginable, read every comic book, and baked tons of cookies. They're at a loss for something new to do, until Sal suggests doing nothing: that is, sitting perfectly still for 10 seconds. But young Frankie's imagination ruins the game. When they try to be statues, Frankie imagines a flock of pigeons around him and shoos them away. When they pretend to be giant redwoods, Frankie imagines a dog taking care of business. And when they try to be the Empire State Building, Frankie envisions King Kong climbing up and stealing his glasses. Frustrated, Sal is about ready to give up—until Frankie thinks of a new idea. Fucile's cartoonish illustrations complete the madcap feel of the text.

Where it's reviewed:
Booklist, July 1, 2009, page 66
Bulletin of the Center for Children's Books, July/August 2009, page 442
Horn Book Guide, Fall 2009, page 328
School Library Journal, July 2009, page 63

Other books you might like:
Jon Agee, *The Retired Kid*, 2009
Marla Frazee, *A Couple of Boys Have the Best Week Ever*, 2008
Dr. Seuss, *The Cat in the Hat*, 1957

154

NEIL GAIMAN

Odd and the Frost Giants

(New York: HarperCollins, 2008)

Subject(s): Mythology; Animals; Adolescence

Age range(s): 8 - 11+
Major character(s): Odd, Child
Time period(s): 21st century; 2000s
Locale(s): Asgard, Norway

Summary: In *Odd and the Frost Giants*, Neil Gaiman tells a dark story about an interesting boy named Odd. When Odd's father dies, his mother marries an evil stepfather with children of his own. Odd's new stepfather doesn't have time for the young boy. After an unusually lengthy winter, Odd decides to leave his home and live in the jungle. Odd stumbles upon some animals in trouble and helps them. He discovers that the animals he helps are not average woodland creatures; they are gods who have been transformed into animals through magic. Odd joins the animals on their quest to turn themselves back into gods. The characters meet many dangers along the way, and eventually, Odd must face his own problems when he comes home to his family.

Where it's reviewed:
Booklist, July 1, 2009, page 61
Bulletin of the Center for Children's Books, February 2010, page 246
Horn Book Magazine, Nov/Dec 2009, page 672
School Library Journal, October 2009, page 126

Other books by the same author:
Instructions, 2010
The Dangerous Alphabet, 2008
The Wolves in the Walls, 2003
Coraline, 2002

Awards the book has won:
Blue Ribbon Awards: Fiction, 2010

Other books you might like:
Bruce Coville, *Thor's Wedding Day*, 2005
Nancy Farmer, *The Sea of Trolls*, 2004
Lise Lunge-Larsen, *The Adventures of Thor the Thunder God*, 2007
Sally Nicholls, *Season of Secrets*, 2011

155

SUSAN GAL, Author/Illustrator

Night Lights

(New York: Knopf Books for Young Readers, 2009)

Subject(s): Learning; Children

Age range(s): 4 - 7+

Summary: One summer evening, a young girl observes the many different places from which people get light. When the girl goes for a bike ride, she uses a headlight to help her see her path. At home, a porch light, a reading light, and a night light help the young girl see. Even when the girl goes to bed, she notices moon light streaming into her room from her window. *Night Lights* is a storybook written by Susan Gal.

Where it's reviewed:
Booklist, December 1, 2009, page 51
Horn Book Guide, Spring 2010, page 7
New York Times Book Review, February 14, 2010, page 15
School Library Journal, November 2009, page 78

Other books by the same author:
Please Take Me For A Walk, 2010

Other books you might like:
Kate Banks, *And If the Moon Could Talk*, 1998
John Coy, *Night Driving*, 1996
Joan Bransfield Graham, *Flicker Flash*, 1999
Il Sung Na, *A Book of Sleep*, 2009
Susan Marie Swanson, *The House in the Night*, 2008

156

CHRIS GALL, Author/Illustrator

Dinotrux

(New York: Little, Brown Young Readers, 2009)

Subject(s): Dinosaurs; Automobiles; Fantasy

Age range(s): 3 - 6+
Time period(s): Indeterminate Past

Summary: In *Dinotrux*, author and illustrator Chris Gall turns the familiar world of dinosaurs on its head when he introduces kids to a fictional ancient species: the Dinotrux. The Dinotrux were half-truck, half-dinosaur, with names like Craneosaurus, Garbageadon, and Tyrannosaurus Trux. When the Dinotrux are faced with severe changes in the weather, some head south while others rust and stop forever. Gall also provides a look at the modern trucks that "evolved" from the Dinotrux.

Where it's reviewed:
Booklist, July 1, 2009, page 65
Bulletin of the Center for Children's Books, September 2009, page 20
Horn Book Magazine, September/October 2009, page 541
New York Times Book Review, November 8 2009, page 24
School Library Journal, June 2009, page 86

Other books by the same author:
Dear Fish, 2006

Other books you might like:
William Low, *Machines Go to Work*, 2009
Deb Lund, *Monsters on Machines*, 2008
Margaret Mayo, *Stomp, Dinosaur, Stomp*, 2010
Kate McMullan, *I'm Big*, 2010
Andrea Zimmerman, *Trashy Town*, 1999

157

JACK GANTOS

Dead End in Norvelt

(New York: Farrar Straus Giroux, 2011)

Subject(s): Coming of age; Conduct of life; Old age
Age range(s): 10 - 13+
Major character(s): Jack Gantos, 12-Year-Old; Miss Volker, Writer (obituaries)
Time period(s): 20th century; 1960s (1962)
Locale(s): Norvelt, Pennsylvania

Summary: In this young adult novel, author Jack Gantos names the 12-year-old main character after himself and sets the story in his boyhood hometown of Norvelt, Pennsylvania. Despite these autobiographical touches, however, this coming-of-age tale is a work of original, insightful, and funny fiction. When a harsh grounding derails Jack's plans for the summer of '62, the boy must spend his days typing obituaries of the local deceased under the direction of elderly Miss Volker. As he deals with the details of death, Jack also faces a range of strange occurrences, including a visit from Hell's Angels, encounters with the town's past, and his own frequent, messy nosebleeds.

Where it's reviewed:
Booklist, August 2011, page 49
Horn Book Magazine, September/October 2011, page 85
Publishers Weekly, July 25, 2011, page 54
School Library Journal, September 2011, page 154

Other books by the same author:
Jack's Black Book, 1997
Heads or Tails: Stories From the Sixth Grade, 1994
Joey Pigza Series, 1998-

Awards the book has won:
Newbery Medal, 2012

Other books you might like:

Georgia Bragg, *How They Croaked: The Awful Ends of the Awfully Famous*, 2011

Russell Freedman, *Eleanor Roosevelt: A Life of Discovery*, 1993

Gary D. Schmidt, *Lizzie Bright and the Buckminster Boy*, 2004

Tim Wynne-Jones, *Rex Zero and the End of the World*, 2007

158

SALLY GARDNER

The Silver Blade

(New York: Dial Books, 2009)

Subject(s): Romances (Fiction); History; Magic

Age range(s): 14 - 18+

Major character(s): Yann, Gypsy; Sido, Noblewoman; Count Kalliovski, Villain

Time period(s): 18th century; 1790s (1794)

Locale(s): France

Summary: *The Silver Blade* by Sally Gardner is the sequel to *The Red Necklace*. This novel for children and young adults is set during the French Revolution in 1794. In the previous novel, Yann, a young gypsy, was able to help his love Sido, a noblewoman, escape to England. In this book, Yann goes back to France to help people escape the Revolution alive. In addition, Yann and Sido plan to marry, but when Sido's guardian refuses the marriage and Sido is kidnapped, Yann must again face Count Kalliovski to rescue his bride and help save France.

Where it's reviewed:

Booklist, August 1, 2009, page 61

Horn Book Magazine, September/October 2009, page 559

School Library Journal, November 2009, page 106

Other books by the same author:

The Red Necklace: A Story of the French Revolution, 2008

I, Coriander, 2007

Other books you might like:

Kimberly Brubaker Bradley, *The Lacemaker and the Princess*, 2007

Charles Dickens, *A Tale of Two Cities: Graphic Classics*, 2008

Marie Rutkoski, *The Cabinet of Wonders: The Kronos Chronicles: Book I*, 2008

159

ARTHUR GEISERT, Author/Illustrator

Ice

(New York: Enchanted Lion Books, 2011)

Story type: Young Readers

Subject(s): Adventure; Imagination; Islands

Age range(s): 5 - 8+

Summary: In this wordless picture story, author and illustrator Arthur Geisert spins a tale of island-dwelling pigs who are suffering under the heat of the blazing sun. With the water supply running low, the pigs meet to discuss their problem and to develop a solution. The pigs finally decide that their best option is to find an iceberg and haul it home to replenish their water supply and provide some much-needed refreshment. Detailed etchings show the pigs' determination and inventiveness as they embark on a journey aboard their balloon-powered boat. Will the pigs make it back home safely with the ice in tow, or will their plan fail?

Where it's reviewed:

Booklist, April 15, 2011, page 130

Bulletin of the Center for Children's Books, May 2011, page 405

Horn Book Guide, Fall 2011, page 314

Publishers Weekly, February 21, 2011, page 130

School Library Journal, May 2011, page 76

Other books by the same author:

Country Road ABC: An Illustrated Journey through America's Farmland, 2010

Hogwash, 2008

Oops, 2006

Pigaroons, 2004

The Giant Book of String, 2002

Other books you might like:

Jon Agee, *Terrific*, 2005

Jeannie Baker, *Home*, 2004

Istvan Banyai, *The Other Side*, 2005

Elisha Cooper, *Beaver Is Lost*, 2010

David Wiesner, *Sector 7*, 1999

160

KRISTINE O'CONNELL GEORGE
NANCY CARPENTER, Illustrator

Emma Dilemma: Big Sister Poems

(New York: Clarion Books, 2011)

Subject(s): Poetry; Sisters; Humor

Age range(s): 5 - 8+

Major character(s): Jessica, 4th Grader; Emma, 3-Year-Old, Sister (of Jessica)

Summary: In *Emma Dilemma: Big Sister Poems*, Kristine O'Connell George uses a collection of poems to examine the unique relationship of fourth-grader Jessica with her little sister, three-year-old Emma. In "Stuff Grownups Say," "Role Model," "Soccer Game," "Emma's Hand," "Emma Dilemma," and other poems, George conveys the complexities, joys, and challenges of sibling relationships. While Jessica understands her duties as big sister, she sometimes wonders what Emma's responsibilities are. But while Jessica can find her little sister extremely annoying, sisterly love prevails and the two eventually settle into their respective family roles. Illustrations by Nancy Carpenter harmonize with George's poem story.

Where it's reviewed:

Booklist, May 15, 2011, page 44

Bulletin of the Center for Children's Books, January 2011, page 235

Horn Book Magazine, January/February 2011, page 104

School Library Journal, February 2011, page 96

Other books by the same author:

Fold Me a Poem, 2005

Hummingbird Nest: A Journal of Poems, 2004

Little Dog and Duncan, 2002

Toasting Marshmallows: Camping Poems, 2001

Little Dog Poems, 1999

Other books you might like:

Bob Graham, *April and Esme: Tooth Fairies*, 2010

Rukhsana Khan, *Big Red Lollipop*, 2010

Grace Lin, *Ling and Ting: Not Exactly the Same!*, 2010

Alan Madison, *Velma Gratch and the Way Cool Butterfly*, 2007

Vera B. Williams, *Amber Was Brave, Essie Was Smart: The Story of Amber and Essie Told Here in Poems and Pictures*, 2001

161

MORDICAI GERSTEIN, Author/Illustrator

A Book

(New York: Roaring Brook Press, 2009)

Subject(s): Storytelling; Family; Humor

Age range(s): 6 - 9+

Summary: *A Book*, by Mordicai Gerstein, is the tale of a young girl trying to find her story. This unconventional picture book tells about the family that lives inside of the actual work. The mother, father, son, and daughter sleep when the book is closed. When it is open, they participate in their own stories—being firefighters, astronauts, and circus performers; however, the youngest relative, the girl, doesn't have a tale. The entire narrative is about how she tries to find something that fits. Readers follow her into different scenarios, including adventures, mysteries, and histories as she explores each setting. Finally, in the end, she realizes where she belongs, and makes the perfect decision.

Where it's reviewed:

Booklist, May 2009, page 60

Bulletin of the Center for Children's Books, July-August 2009, page 443

Horn Book Magazine, May/June 2009, page 281

School Library Journal, May 2009, page 78

Other books by the same author:

The Absolutely Awful Alphabet, 1999

Other books you might like:

Eileen Christelow, *What Do Authors Do?*, 1995

Barbara Lehman, *The Red Book*, 2004

Lane Smith, *It's a Book*, 2010

Bob Staake, *Look! A Book!: A Zany Seek-and-Find Adventure*, 2010

Mo Willems, *We Are in a Book!*, 2010

162

ADAM GIDWITZ

A Tale Dark and Grimm

(New York: Dutton, 2010)

Subject(s): Fairy tales; Fantasy; Folklore

Age range(s): 9 - 12+

Major character(s): Hansel, Child; Gretel, Sister (of Hansel)

Summary: In *A Tale Dark and Grimm* by Adam Gidwitz, the fairy tales of the Grimm brothers inspire new adventures for famed siblings, Hansel and Gretel. As the brother and sister make their way through their darkly enchanting forest and beyond, they meet human characters both good and evil, as well as magical and menacing beings. These new adventures of Hansel and Gretel stay true to the dark mood of the Grimm tales, with the book's narrator interrupting the action intermittently to alert readers of upcoming mayhem and terror. A generous dose of appropriately black humor balances the book's fright factor. First novel.

Where it's reviewed:

Bulletin of the Center for Children's Books, December 2010, page 185

Horn Book Magazine, Jan/Feb 2010, page 93

New York Times Book Review, November 7, 2010, page 26

Publishers Weekly, October 18, 2010, page 50

School Library Journal, November 2010, page 114

Other books you might like:

Carolyn Coman, *The Memory Bank*, 2010

Vivian French, *The Robe of Skulls*, 2008

Lois Lowry, *The Willoughbys*, 2008

Donna Jo Napoli, *The Magic Circle*, 1993

Lemony Snicket, *The Bad Beginning*, 1999

163

MARK GONYEA, Author/Illustrator

A Book about Color: A Clear and Simple Guide for Young Artists

(New York: Henry Holt and Co., 2010)

Subject(s): Art; Painting (Art); Drawing

Age range(s): 6 - 9+

Summary: In *A Book About Color: A Clear and Simple Guide for Young Artists*, author Mark Gonyea introduces young, aspiring artists to the color wheel. Gonyea uses basic descriptions to explain color theory. Six houses on his imaginary Color Street depict primary and secondary colors and demonstrate the role that complementary and analogous colors play together. This book is ideal for children ages 9 to 12. Gonyea is also the author of *A Book About Design: Complicated Doesn't Make It Good* and *Another Book About Design: Complicated Doesn't Make It Bad*. He is also a cartoonist and graphic designer.

Where it's reviewed:
Booklist, February 15, 2010, page 72
Horn Book Magazine, May/June 2010, page 107
Publishers Weekly, March 22, 2010, page 69
School Library Journal, March 2010, page 139

Other books by the same author:
Another Book about Design: Complicated Doesn't Make It Bad, 2007
A Book about Design: Complicated Doesn't Make It Good, 2005

Other books you might like:
Molly Bang, *Picture This: How Pictures Work*, 2000
Menena Cottin, *The Black Book of Colors*, 2008
Mark Gonyea, *A Book about Design: Complicated Doesn't Make It Good*, 2005
Joyce Sidman, *Red Sings from Treetops: A Year in Colors*, 2009
Natasha Wing, *An Eye for Color: The Story of Josef Albers*, 2008

164

CARTER GOODRICH, Author/Illustrator

Say Hello to Zorro!

(New York: Simon & Schuster Books for Young Readers, 2011)

Subject(s): Dogs; Friendship; Pets

Age range(s): 4 - 8+
Major character(s): Mr. Bud, Dog; Zorro, Dog
Time period(s): 21st century; 2010s

Summary: *Say Hello to Zorro!* is a humorous and entertaining picture book for young readers from author and illustrator Carter Goodrich. Mister Bud is a creature of habit. In the furry canine's world, there is a time and place for every activity. Everything from napping to eating to throwing a fit is scheduled perfectly into his calendar, but things are thrown out of whack when a new dog arrives on the scene. Zorro is energetic and bossy and, at first glance, Mister Bud wants nothing to do with him. Soon, the two dogs realize they have a lot more in common than they thought—like a penchant for napping and general distaste for the cat—and become fast friends.

Where it's reviewed:
Bulletin of the Center for Children's Books, March 2011, page 329
Horn Book Guide, Fall 2011, page 315
Publishers Weekly, January 17, 2011, page 47
School Library Journal, March 2011, page 122

Other books by the same author:
Zorro Gets an Outfit, 2012
The Hermit Crab, 2009
A Creature Was Stirring, 2006

Other books you might like:
Peggy Rathmann, *Officer Buckle and Gloria*, 1995
Lori Ries, *Aggie and Ben: Three Stories*, 2006
Eric Rohmann, *My Friend Rabbit*, 2002

165

ROBBIN GOURLEY, Author/Illustrator

First Garden: The White House Garden and How It Grew

(New York: Clarion Books, 2011)

Subject(s): Gardening; Cooking; Nature

Age range(s): 6 - 9+

Summary: The grounds of the White House, where presidents and their families live, are always changing. Thomas Jefferson grew fruit trees there. Eleanor Roosevelt planted a World War II victory garden. In this volume, author and illustrator Robbin Gourley focuses on the White House kitchen garden, which was created under the direction of First Lady Michelle Obama as part of her campaign to raise awareness about childhood obesity and to promote living a healthy lifestyle. Often called the First Garden, the White House kitchen garden provides food for both the Obama family and for a nearby homeless shelter. Gourley describes the team that helped plant the garden, which included children from nearby schools, White House chefs, and others. At the end of the book, Gourley provides tips on gardening, choosing healthier foods to eat, and cooking with locally grown fruits and vegetables. Includes recipes.

Where it's reviewed:
Booklist, April 15, 2011, page 52
Horn Book Guide, Fall 2011, page 449
School Library Journal, June 2011, page 103

Other books by the same author:
Bring Me Some Apples and I'll Make You a Pie: A Story about Edna Lewis, 2008

Other books you might like:
Joan Holub, *The Garden That We Grew*, 2001
Deborah Hopkinson, *First Family*, 2009
Lela Nargi, *The Honeybee Man*, 2011
Sarah Stewart, *The Gardener*, 1997

166

ROBBIN GOURLEY, Author/Illustrator

Bring Me Some Apples and I'll Make You a Pie: A Story about Edna Lewis

(New York: Clarion Books, 2009)

Subject(s): Food; Biographies; African Americans

Age range(s): 5 - 8+

Summary: *Bring Me Some Apples and I'll Make You a Pie: A Story about Edna Lewis* is a biography by author and illustrator Robbin Gourley. In this book, Gourley recounts the childhood and career of Enda Lewis, who was a prominent female African American chef. Lewis was one of the first African American females to hold such a position. She was also important in her field because she promoted the use of whole foods and organic fruits and vegetables for cooking. Along with discussing Lewis's childhood and career, this biography also talks about her methods of planting, harvesting, and using fresh fruits and vegetables in her booking. *Bring Me Some Apples and I'll Make You a Pie* also contains five recipes that are geared toward children.

Where it's reviewed:
Booklist, February 1, 2009, page 46
Bulletin of the Center for Children's Books, January 2009, page 198
Publishers Weekly, December 1, 2008, page 46
School Library Journal, February 2009, page 76

Other books by the same author:
First Garden: The White House Garden and How It Grew, 2011

Other books you might like:
Deborah Hopkinson, *Fannie in the Kitchen: The Whole Story from Soup to Nuts of How Fannie Farmer Invented Recipes with Precise Measurements*, 2001
Eden Ross Lipson, *Applesauce Season*, 2009
Mary Quattlebaum, *The Hungry Ghost of Rue Orleans*, 2011
Ken Robbins, *Food For Thought: The Stories Behind the Things We Eat*, 2009
Gaylia Taylor, *George Crum and the Saratoga Chip*, 2006

167

LISA GRAFF

Umbrella Summer

(New York: HarperCollins, 2009)

Subject(s): Grief; Fear; Death

Age range(s): 9 - 12+
Major character(s): Annie Richards, 10-Year-Old
Time period(s): 21st century; 2000s
Locale(s): United States

Summary: *Umbrella Summer* is a novel for older children and young adults from author Lisa Graff. For 10-year old Annie Richards, life has always been simple and worry free—that is, until her older brother, Jared, suddenly dies and leaves the Richards family in a world of grief. As Annie's parents cope with the tragedy in their own ways, Annie suddenly grows very fearful and anxious. Desperate to prevent anything bad from ever happening again, Annie avoids almost everything and everyone in an effort to keep herself safe. It takes the arrival of a new elderly neighbor, who is dealing with grief of her own, to help Annie find the healing and hope that she so desperately needs.

Where it's reviewed:
Booklist, August 1, 2009, page 72
Bulletin of the Center for Children's Books, July/August 2009, page 445
Horn Book Magazine, July/August 2009, page 424
School Library Journal, June 2009, page 126

Other books by the same author:
Sophie Simon Solves Them All, 2010

The Life and Crimes of Bernetta Wallflower, 2008
The Truth About Georgie, 2006

Other books you might like:
Katherine Hannigan, *Ida B.: . . . and Her Plans to Maximize Fun, Avoid Disaster, and (Possibly) Save the World*, 2004
Sally Nicholls, *Ways To Live Forever*, 2008
Barbara Park, *Mick Harte Was Here*, 1995
Katherine Paterson, *Bridge to Terabithia*, 1977
Lauren Tarshis, *Emma-Jean Lazarus Fell out of a Tree*, 2007

168

BOB GRAHAM, Author/Illustrator

April and Esme: Tooth Fairies

(Somerville, Massachusetts: Candlewick Press, 2010)

Subject(s): Fantasy; Fairies; Sisters

Age range(s): 4 - 8+
Major character(s): April Underhill, 7-Year-Old, Mythical Creature (fairy); Esme Underhill, 6-Year-Old, Mythical Creature (fairy), Sister (of April); Daniel Dangerfield, Boy

Summary: In *April and Esme, Tooth Fairies*, two modern-day tooth fairies accept their first mission and leave their enchanted home beneath a tree stump armed with a shiny coin and their cell phones. Seven-year-old April Underhill and little sister, Esme assure their anxious parents that they'll text if they run into trouble as they set out to recover Daniel Dangerfield's lost tooth. Though the young fairies are briefly distracted by Daniel's grandmother's dentures, and are almost seen by humans, they successfully collect the tooth and leave the coin for Daniel. Charming illustrations complement the sweet story.

Where it's reviewed:
Bulletin of the Center for Children's Books, November 2010, page 131
Horn Book Magazine, September/October 2010, page 59
Publishers Weekly, September 9, 2010, page 63
School Library Journal, September 10, 2010, page 80

Other books by the same author:
"The Trouble With Dogs . . . " Said Dad, 2007
"Let's Get a Pup!" Said Kate, 2001

Awards the book has won:
Blue Ribbon Awards: Picture Books, 2010

Other books you might like:
Kate Banks, *Monkeys and Dog Days*, 2008
Barbara Bottner, *Pish and Posh Wish for Fairy Wings*, 2006
Eloise Greenfield, *Brothers and Sisters: Family Poems*, 2008
Kevin Henkes, *Chrysanthemum*, 1991

169

BLEXBOLEX BLEXBOLEX, Author/Illustrator
BERNARD GRANGER, Author/Illustrator
CLAUDIA BEDRICK, Translator

Seasons

(New York: Enchanted Lion Books, 2010)

Subject(s): Seasons; Learning; Imagination

Age range(s): 5 - 7+

Summary: In *Seasons* by Blexbolex, a landscape is depicted in each of the four seasons, sometimes more than once. More than illustrating simple concepts, however, this book encourages the reader to make connections between what is depicted in the different seasons. Some of the connections include "leaf/caterpillar" and "firefly/shooting star." It is up to the reader to determine the connection by using his or her imagination. Slow changes may be seen in the illustrations as the months and seasons pass. Some are caused by nature, such as weather events, whereas others are caused by human behavior, such as leaving items behind on the grass after a picnic. The abstract concepts make it easier for children to get creative when learning about the seasons and the passage of time.

Where it's reviewed:
Horn Book Magazine, July/August 2010, page 86
New York Times Book Review, October 17, 2010, page 17
School Library Journal, July 2010, page 55

Other books by the same author:
People, 2011

Other books you might like:
Mitsumasa Anno, *Anno's Counting Book*, 1975
Kevin Henkes, *Old Bear*, 2008
G. Brian Karas, *The Village Garage*, 2010
Il Sung Na, *Snow Rabbit, Spring Rabbit: A Book of Changing Seasons*, 2011
Mo Willems, *City Dog, Country Frog*, 2010

170

MICHAEL GRANT

The Call

(New York: HarperCollins, 2010)

Series: Magnificent 12 Series. Book 1
Subject(s): Fantasy; Alternative worlds; Phobias

Age range(s): 9 - 12+

Major character(s): Mack MacAvoy, Teenager; Jarrah, Teenager; The Pale Queen, Villain, Mother (of Ereskigal); Ereskigal, Daughter (of The Pale Queen), Villain

Summary: *The Call* is the first installment of The Magnificent 12 series by Michael Grant. The series centers on an alien dictator known as the Pale Queen and a group of 12 teenagers who are the only ones with the power to protect the planet. In this book, readers are introduced to Mack, the first of the teenagers who is summoned to work against the Pale Queen. Unfortunately Mack has a ton of phobias, but he must face those fears in order to travel to Australia to retrieve the second Magnificent, Jarrah. Will Mack get to Jarrah before the Pale Queen and her evil daughter Ereskigal stop him in his tracks?

Where it's reviewed:
Booklist, November 15, 2010, page 36
Bulletin of the Center for Children's Books, October 2010, page 76
Horn Book Guide, Spring 2011, page 72
Publishers Weekly, August 23, 2010, page 50

Other books by the same author:
The Magnificent 12: The Trap, 2011

Other books you might like:
P. D. Baccalario, *Ring of Fire*, 2009
Margaret Peterson Haddix, *Found*, 2008
Rick Riordan, *The Red Pyramid*, 2010
David Wisniewski, *Golem*, 1996

171

ALAN GRATZ

The Brooklyn Nine: A Novel in Nine Innings

(New York: Dial Books, 2009)

Subject(s): Baseball; Family history; Immigrants

Age range(s): 9 - 12+
Major character(s): Felix Schneider, Father (of Louis Schneider); Louis Schneider, Son (of Felix Schneider); Walter Snider, Father (of Kat Snider); Kat Snider, Mother (of Jimmy Flint); Jimmy Flint, Father (of Michael Flint); Michael Flint, Son (of Jimmy Flint)
Time period(s): 19th century-21st century
Locale(s): Grand Rapids, Michigan; New York, New York

Summary: In *The Brooklyn Nine: A Novel in Nine Innings*, Alan Gratz follows one family's passion for baseball over the course of nine generations. The story begins with German immigrant Felix Schneider, who uses his speed on both the baseball field and in his job as a courier for his uncle. Felix's son, Louis, fights in the Civil War for the Union, but feels sympathy toward a Confederate soldier when their shared love of the game is revealed. Later, the descendants of Felix and Louis change their name to Snider, but the love of baseball continues. Walter Snider is a batboy for the Brooklyn Superbas, and he battles racism in the game by securing a tryout for Negro League star "Cyclone" Joe Williams. In the 1940s, Kat Snider leaves Brooklyn to play for the Grand Rapids Chicks in the All-American Girls Baseball League. In the 1980s, her grandson, Michael Flint, pitches a perfect game during Little League.

Where it's reviewed:
Booklist, February 1, 2009, page 245
Bulletin of the Center for Children's Books, April 2009, page 322
Horn Book Magazine, March/April 2011, page 194

Publishers Weekly, March 16, 2009, page 62
School Library Journal, March 2009, page 253

Other books by the same author:
Samurai Shortstop, 2006

Other books you might like:
Julianna Baggott, *The Prince of Fenway Park*, 2009
James Charlton, *Hey Batta Batta Swing!: The Wild Old Days of Baseball*, 2007
Kadir Nelson, *We Are The Ship: The Story of Negro League Baseball*, 2008
Linda Sue Park, *Keeping Score*, 2008

172

EMILY GRAVETT, Author/Illustrator

Blue Chameleon

(London: Macmillan Children's, 2011)

Story type: Young Readers
Subject(s): Loneliness; Friendship; Art

Age range(s): 3 - 6+
Major character(s): Chameleon, Reptile

Summary: In this picture story by author and illustrator Emily Gravett, Chameleon is blue; he's blue in color because, well, he's a chameleon and he can be whatever color he wants to be. But Chameleon is also blue in mood, because he is all alone and desperately wants to find a friend. Chameleon tries to make friends with whatever he can find, including a banana, a cockatoo, and even a "stripy" sock, all while changing colors and patterns in an attempt to fit in. Despite his efforts, though, Chameleon just can't seem to find someone to talk to. Will Chameleon ever find a companion, or will his search for friendship go on forever?

Where it's reviewed:
Booklist, March 15, 2011, page 63
Horn Book Magazine, March/April 2011, page 102
Publishers Weekly, January 31, 2011, page 46
School Library Journal, March 2011, page 124

Other books by the same author:
Monkey and Me, 2008
Orange Pear Apple Bear, 2007

Other books you might like:
Eric Carle, *The Mixed-Up Chameleon*, 1984
Leo Lionni, *A Color of His Own*, 2006
Ellen Stoll Walsh, *Mouse Paint*, 1989

173

EMILY GRAVETT, Author/Illustrator

The Odd Egg

(New York: Simon & Schuster, 2009)

Subject(s): Animals; Conformity; Parenthood

Age range(s): 3 - 7+
Major character(s): Duck, Duck

Summary: In English author Emily Gravett's *The Odd Egg*, a character named Duck begins to notice that all of the birds have eggs—all of the birds except Duck that is. Duck is unable to create an egg of his own, but one day, Duck finds an egg. Duck is very happy, but the other birds think Duck's egg looks funny. Duck admits his egg is different from the other eggs, but he defends his egg, and when the egg hatches, everyone, even Duck, is surprised. The book features artistic pages that allow young readers to flip open sections of the egg so that they can experience its hatching and the surprise of what is inside the egg.

Where it's reviewed:
Booklist, January 1, 2009, page 92
Bulletin of the Center for Children's Books, January 2009, page 199
New York Times Book Review, November 8, 2009, page 23
Publishers Weekly, October 27, 2009, page 53
School Library Journal, January 2009, page 76

Other books by the same author:
Blue Chameleon, 2011
The Rabbit Problem, 2010
Spells, 2009
Orange Pear Apple Bear, 2007
Wolves, 2006

Other books you might like:
Dianna Hutts Aston, *An Egg Is Quiet*, 2006
Anthony Browne, *Little Beauty*, 2008
Michelle Knudsen, *Argus*, 2011
Laura Vaccaro Seeger, *First the Egg*, 2007
Alex T. Smith, *Foxy and the Egg*, 2011

174

JAN GREENBERG
SANDRA JORDAN, Co-Author
BRIAN FLOCA, Illustrator

Ballet for Martha: Making Appalachian Spring

(New York: Flash Point, 2010)

Subject(s): Ballet; Dance; United States history

Age range(s): 9 - 12+
Time period(s): 20th century
Locale(s): United States

Summary: Authors Jan Greenberg and Sandra Jordan provide an inside peek at the brilliant collaboration that came together to make choreographer Martha Graham's "Appalachian Spring" one of the most singular and unforgettable ballets in American history. Graham, composer Aaron Copeland, and set designer Isamu Noguchi work together to craft the ballet that would become a landmark cultural event, eventually premiering it to universal acclaim in 1944. Accompanied by Brian Floca's illustrations *Ballet for Martha: Making Appalachian Spring* includes a listing of resources and notes on the text.

Where it's reviewed:
Booklist, July 1, 2010, page 58
Horn Book Magazine, July/August 2010, page 132
Publishers Weekly, November 8, 2010, page 31
School Library Journal, August 2010, page 119

Other books by the same author:
Christo and Jean-Claude: Through the Gates and Beyond, 2008
Action Jackson, 2002
Chuck Close Up Close, 1998

Other books you might like:
Russell Freedman, *Martha Graham: A Dancer's Life*, 1998
Robert Levine, *The Story of the Orchestra: Listen While You Learn about the Instruments, the Music, and the Composers Who Wrote the Music*, 2001
Leda Schubert, *Ballet of the Elephants*, 2006
Siena Cherson Siegel, *To Dance: A Ballerina's Graphic Novel*, 2006

175

STEPHANIE GREENE

Happy Birthday, Sophie Hartley
(New York: Clarion Books, 2010)

Subject(s): Birthdays; Children; Monkeys

Age range(s): 8 - 10+
Major character(s): Sophie Hartley, 9-Year-Old
Time period(s): 21st century; 2010s
Locale(s): United States

Summary: *Happy Birthday, Sophie Hartley* is a humorous novel for young readers from author Stephanie Green. As Sophie Hartley's 10th birthday approaches, she feels lost in the chaos of what's going on with her older siblings. Her parents are paying too much attention to her 16-year-old brother and the car he's planning to get and her 13-year-old sister, who is about to move into her own room. As Sophie anticipates her double-digit birthday, the gift she wants more than anything is a pet gorilla. Desperate to get attention, Sophie begins telling her classmates that she'll soon have a gorilla. As her birthday draws near, Sophie starts to feel pressured to produce a gorilla or be deemed a liar.

Where it's reviewed:
Horn Book Magazine, July/August 2010, page 105
School Library Journal, July 2010, page 60

Other books by the same author:
Sophie Hartley on Strike, 2006
Queen Sophie Hartley, 2005
Owen Foote Mighty Scientist, 2004
Owen Foote, Money Man, 2003
Owen Foote, Super Spy, 2001

Other books you might like:
Kevin Henkes, *The Birthday Room*, 1999
Kimberly Willis Holt, *Piper Reed Gets a Job*, 2009
Johanna Hurwitz, *Birthday Surprises: Ten Great Stories to Unwrap*, 1995
Lois Lowry, *The Birthday Ball*, 2010

176

STEPHANIE GREENE
STEPHANIE ROTH SISSON, Illustrator

Princess Posey and the First Grade Parade
(New York: G.P. Putnam's Sons, 2010)

Subject(s): Fear; Schools; Teachers

Age range(s): 5 - 7+
Major character(s): Posey, Girl, 1st Grader; Nick, Neighbor (of Posey); Tyler, Neighbor (of Posey)
Time period(s): 21st century; 2010s
Locale(s): United States

Summary: In the chapter book *Princess Posey and the First Grade Parade* by Stephanie Greene, a little girl deals with the anxieties of the first day of first grade. Posey knows that the new school year will bring changes. She'll have to leave her tutu at home when her mother drives her and drops her at school where she'll face the horrors of the blue hallway. (Older boys Tyler and Nick have told Posey about snakes and monsters that live at school.) In the classroom, Posey is pleased to find a teacher who is sympathetic to her new class's concerns. When the teacher encourages her students to wear their favorite outfits to school, Posey helps to organize a first-grade parade.

Where it's reviewed:
Booklist, July 2010, page 67
Bulletin of the Center for Children's Books, June 2010, page 433
Horn Book Magazine, July/August 2010, page 106
Publishers Weekly, May 3, 2010, page 50
School Library Journal, June 2010, page 72

Other books by the same author:
Princess Posey and the Next-Door Dog, 2011
Princess Posey and the Perfect Present, 2011

Other books you might like:
Jenny Han, *Clara Lee and the Apple Pie Dream*, 2011
Megan McDonald, *Judy Moody*, 2000
Kate McMullan, *Pearl and Wagner: Three Secrets*, 2004
Robert Quackenbush, *First Grade Jitters*, 2010
Erica Silverman, *Cowgirl Kate and Cocoa: School Days*, 2007

177

ELOISE GREENFIELD
JAN SPIVEY GILCHRIST, Illustrator

The Great Migration: Journey to the North
(New York: Amistad, 2011)

Subject(s): Poetry; African Americans; History

Age range(s): 6 - 8+

Summary: Poet Eloise Greenfield and artist Jan Spivey Gilchrist share the story of the Great Migration in this picture book for young readers. Greenfield uses free verse poems to recount the historic movement of one million African Americans as they escaped the oppression of the South for a new start in the North in the 1910s and '20s. The collection conveys the range of emotions—joy, fear, relief, apprehension—that the travelers carried on their northbound trains. The subject is a personal one for the book's creators. Greenfield was part of the Great Migration as a baby; Gilchrist's parents met in Chicago after leaving the troubled South.

Where it's reviewed:
Booklist, February 1, 2010, page 72
Bulletin of the Center for Children's Books, February 2011, page 267
Horn Book Magazine, February 2011, page 105
School Library Journal, April 2011, page 160

Other books by the same author:
Paul Robeson, 2009
How They Got Over: African Americans and the Call of the Sea, 2003
Rosa Parks, 1995

Other books you might like:
Alan Govenar, *Stompin' at the Savoy: The Story of Norma Miller*, 2006
Jacob Lawrence, *The Great Migration: An American Story*, 1993
Patricia C. McKissack, *A Song for Harlem*, 2007
Walter Dean Meyers, *Harlem*

██**178**██

LISA GREENWALD

My Life in Pink and Green

(New York: Amulet Books, 2009)

Subject(s): Family; Ecology; Mother-daughter relations
Age range(s): 10 - 13+
Major character(s): Lucy Desberg, 12-Year-Old
Time period(s): 21st century; 2000s
Locale(s): Connecticut, United States

Summary: Lisa Greenwald's *My Life in Pink and Green* tells the story of 12-year-old Lucy Desberg, an inventive girl who helps run her family's pharmacy. When she learns the business is in danger of shutting down, Lucy springs into action. She pulls in new business by doing makeovers and dispensing beauty advice, but the pharmacy needs more money to stay in the game. Lucy then draws on what she learns as a member of her school's Earth Club. In transforming the family business into an environmentally conscious, earth-friendly environment, Lucy finds something she never expected: herself. First novel.

Where it's reviewed:
Booklist, February 15, 2009, page 92
Publishers Weekly, January 12, 2009, page 48
School Library Journal, April 2009, page 134

Other books by the same author:
Reel Life Starring Us, 2011

Sweet Treats and Secret Crushes, 2010

Other books you might like:
Laura Bowers, *Beauty Shop for Rent: Fully Equipped, Inquire Within*, 2007
Lisa Papademetriou, *How to Be a Girly Girl in Just Ten Days*, 2007
Jill Wolfson, *Home, and Other Big, Fat Lies*, 2006

██**179**██

MINI GREY, Author/Illustrator

Three by the Sea

(New York: Alfred A. Knopf, 2010)

Story type: Contemporary
Subject(s): Animals; Friendship; Working conditions

Age range(s): 4 - 7+
Major character(s): Dog, Dog, Gardener; Cat, Cat, Housekeeper; Mouse, Cook, Mouse; The Stranger, Fox

Summary: This book for young readers by Mini Grey tells the story of three animals that live together in a bungalow by the beach. These animals are Dog, Cat, and Mouse, and on the surface it seems like they have a well-balanced plan for running their household. Dog tends the garden, Cat does the cleaning, and Mouse prepares the food. One day, a fox appears at the three friends' door. This fox, the Stranger, points out some flaws in their plan: Dog plays all day, Cat takes too many catnaps, and Mouse isn't a great chef. The friends have to reevaluate their tasks and find new ways to divide the work so everyone benefits.

Where it's reviewed:
Booklist, February 1, 2011, page 83
Horn Book Magazine, March/April 2011, page 102
Publishers Weekly, February 28, 2011, page 57
School Library Journal, April 2011, page 144

Other books by the same author:
Ginger Bear, 2007
The Adventures of the Dish and the Spoon, 2006
Traction Man Is Here!, 2005
The Very Smart Pea and the Princess-to-Be, 2003

Other books you might like:
Jon Agee, *Terrific*, 2005
Emily Gravett, *Meerkat Mail*, 2007
Laura Vaccaro Seeger, *Dog and Bear: Two Friends, Three Stories*, 2007

██**180**██

NIKKI GRIMES
R. GREGORY CHRISTIE, Illustrator

Make Way for Dyamonde Daniel

(New York: G.P. Putnam's Sons, 2009)

Series: Dyamonde Daniel Series. Book 1
Subject(s): Friendship; African Americans; Schools

Age range(s): 7 - 9+
Major character(s): Dyamonde Daniel, 9-Year-Old, Child of Divorced Parents; Free, Classmate (of Dyamonde)
Time period(s): 21st century; 2000s
Locale(s): New York, New York

Summary: In *Make Way for Dyamonde Daniel*, author Nikki Grimes introduces a new series featuring a feisty title character with a heart of gold. After her parents' divorce, third grade student Dyamonde Daniel moves to a new neighborhood in New York City. Now Dyamonde is the new girl in school, but she isn't about to let that stop her from making a splash. With her brazen personality and effervescent charms, Dyamonde wins over her classmates—all except for another new student, a dour-faced boy named Free. It seems nothing can penetrate Free's sadness, but Dyamonde is determined to make him her friend.

Where it's reviewed:
Bulletin of the Center for Children's Books, September 2009, page 21
Horn Book Guide, Fall 2009, page 359
School Library Journal, July 2009, page 64

Other books by the same author:
Almost Zero: A Dyamonde Daniel Book, 2010
Rich: A Dyamonde Daniel Book, 2009

Other books you might like:
Sharon M. Draper, *Sassy: Little Sister is Not My Name*, 2009
Karen English, *Nikki and Deja*, 2008
Sharon G. Flake, *The Broken Bike Boy and the Queen of 33rd Street*, 2007
Jenny Lombard, *Drita, My Homegirl*, 2006
Jacqui Robbins, *Two of a Kind*, 2009

181

BRENDA Z. GUIBERSON

Disasters: Natural and Man-Made Catastrophes through the Centuries
(New York: Henry Holt and Co., 2010)

Subject(s): Disasters; Natural disasters; History

Age range(s): 9 - 12+

Summary: In *Disasters: Natural and Man-Made Catastrophes Through the Centuries*, author Brenda Z. Guiberson presents an age-appropriate look at various natural and manmade disasters throughout time. Guiberson profiles such events as the smallpox epidemic, the Great Chicago Fire, the sinking of the Titanic, the Great Depression, and Hurricane Katrina. This volume includes photos, drawings, a bibliography, and an index.

Where it's reviewed:
Booklist, March 15, 2010, page 36
Horn Book Magazine, July/August 2010, page 134
School Library Journal, June 2010, page 130
Voice of Youth Advocates, August 2010, page 278

Other books by the same author:
Earth: Feeling the Heat, 2010

Other books you might like:
Hugh Brewster, *Inside the Titanic*, 1997
Jim Murphy, *The Great Fire*, 1995
Jewell Parker Rhodes, *Ninth Ward*, 2010
Laurence Yep, *The Earth Dragon Awakes: The San Francisco Earthquake of 1906*, 2006

182

BRENDA Z. GUIBERSON

Earth: Feeling the Heat
(New York: Henry Holt and Co., 2010)

Subject(s): Environmental history; Science; Ecology

Age range(s): 6 - 8+

Summary: In *Earth: Feeling the Heat*, author Brenda Z. Guiberson introduces young readers to the concept of global climate change and the impact that the phenomenon could have on the Earth. The author describes how the changing climate could affect various species, including the Arctic polar bear, the orangutan, many species of fish and fowl, and even humans. Tips and lessons are also given on how each person can work toward the preservation of the planet to help lessen the effects of climate change. Illustrations by Chad Wallace help round out the book's message. Guiberson is also the author of *Into the Sea*, *Life in the Boreal Forest*, and *Rain, Rain, Rain Forest*.

Where it's reviewed:
Booklist, November 1, 2009, page 49-50
Horn Book Guide, Fall 2010, page 397
School Library Journal, March 2010, page 140

Other books by the same author:
Life in the Boreal Forest, 2009
Ice Bears, 2008
Rain, Rain, Rain Forest, 2004
Into the Sea, 1996

Other books you might like:
Joanna Cole, *The Magic School Bus and the Climate Challenge*, 2010
Nancy Smiler Levinson, *North Pole, South Pole*, 2003
Seymour Simon, *Global Warming*, 2010

183

DAN GUTMAN

Mission Unstoppable
(New York: Harper, 2011)

Series: Genius Files Series. Book 1
Story type: Adventure; Series
Subject(s): Adventure; Brothers and sisters; Twins

Age range(s): 9 - 12+

Major character(s): Coke McDonald, Genius, 12-Year-Old, Brother (of Pepsi), Twin (of Pepsi), Son (of Mom and Dad); Pepsi McDonald, 12-Year-Old, Sister (of Coke), Twin (of Coke), Daughter (of Mom and Dad), Genius; Dad, Father (of Coke and Pepsi), Spouse (of

Mom), Professor; Mom, Mother (of Coke and Pepsi), Spouse (of Dad)
Time period(s): 21st century; 2010s
Locale(s): United States

Summary: Author Dan Gutman launches his Genius Files series for young readers with this adventure novel featuring 12-year-old twins Coke and Pepsi. Just a week before their 13th birthday, Coke and his twin sister, Pepsi, embark on an RV tour of the country with their parents. But this won't be an ordinary family adventure: The twins are members of The Genius Files—an antiterrorism organization made up of super-smart kids. As the McDonalds make their way to significant US landmarks like a candy museum, an enormous ball of string, and a SPAM factory, Coke and Pepsi dodge villains and avoid such perils as poison darts, burning buildings, and deadly sandpits. Gutman supplements the book with photos, illustrations, and Internet map references.

Where it's reviewed:
Booklist, December 1, 2010, page 59
Bulletin of the Center for Children's Books, April 2011, page 373
Publishers Weekly, December 13, 2010, page 58
School Library Journal, March 2011, page 162

Other books by the same author:
The Genius Files: Never Say Genius, 2012
Nightmare at the Book Fair, 2008
The Homework Machine, 2006
The Million Dollar Kick, 2001

Other books you might like:
Blue Balliett, *Chasing Vermeer*, 2004
Benedict Carey, *The Unknowns: A Mystery*, 2009
Rick Riordan, *The Red Pyramid*, 2010
David Stahler Jr., *Truesight*, 2004

184

DEAN HACOHEN
SHERRY SCHARSCHMIDT, Illustrator

Tuck Me In
(Somerville, Massachusetts: Candlewick Press, 2010)

Story type: Young Readers
Subject(s): Animals; Sleep

Age range(s): 2 - 5+

Summary: In this children's book by Dean Hacohen, different types of baby animals need to be tucked in before they can go to sleep. As night draws near, baby animals prepare to sleep, but they have to be tucked in first. The book features a pig, a moose, a peacock, a hedgehog, and other baby animals that need to go to bed. The book includes illustrations by Sherry Scharschmidt.

Where it's reviewed:
Horn Book Guide, Spring 2011, page 8
Publishers Weekly, September 23, 2010, page 48
School Library Journal, August 2010, page 76

Other books you might like:
Phillis Gershator, *Moo Moo Brown Cow! Have You Any Milk?*, 2011

Alex Lamb, *Tell Me the Day Backwards*, 2011
Emma Quay, *Good Night, Sleep Tight: A Book about Bedtime*, 2011

185

MARGARET PETERSON HADDIX

Sent
(New York: Simon & Schuster, 2009)

Series: Missing Series. Book 2
Subject(s): Fantasy; Time travel; History

Age range(s): 10 - 13+
Major character(s): Chip, 13-Year-Old; Alex, Brother (of Chip); Jonah, 13-Year-Old; Katherine, Sister (of Jonah)
Time period(s): 15th century; 1480s (1483)
Locale(s): England

Summary: *Sent* is a novel for young readers by Margaret Peterson Haddix. It's the second book in The Missing series. At the end of the first novel, it was revealed that 13-year-old Chip and his younger brother, Alex, are really brothers Edward and Richard, the King of England and the Duke of York, respectively. They were kidnapped from the 15th century and brought to the present day. When time traveler JB chooses to send them back to the 15th century, their friend Jonah and Jonah's sister Katherine grab their arms and also end up back in time, where they do not belong. All realize that they need to save Chip and Alex from certain death without altering history too much, while also finding a way to get Jonah and Katherine back to the present.

Where it's reviewed:
Booklist, August 1, 2009, page 60
Horn Book Guide, Spring 2010, page 71
School Library Journal, October 2009, page 126

Other books by the same author:
Torn, 2011
Sabotaged, 2010
Found, 2008
Double Identity, 2005
Among the Hidden, 1998

Other books you might like:
Ted Bell, *Nick of Time*, 2008
Susan Cooper, *King of Shadows*, 1999
Ali Sparkes, *Frozen in Time*, 2011
Rebecca Stead, *When You Reach Me*, 2009

186

MARY DOWNING HAHN

The Ghost of Crutchfield Hall
(New York: Clarion Books, 2010)

Subject(s): Ghosts; Orphans; Horror

Age range(s): 9 - 12+
Major character(s): Florence Crutchfield, 12-Year-Old, Orphan; Sophia Crutchfield, Spirit

Time period(s): 19th century
Locale(s): England

Summary: *The Ghost of Crutchfield Hall* is a chilling ghost story for young readers from author Mary Downing Hahn. After spending seven years in a London orphanage, 12-year old Florence is anxious to move in with her friendly great-uncle and his austere wife at Crutchfield Hall. Unfortunately, life at Crutchfield Hall is nothing like young Florence dreamed it would be. The house is dark, gloomy, and filled with sickness. Not to mention, the ghost of Florence's cousin, Sophia, is on the loose with a devious plan. It's not long before Sophia gains control over Florence in hopes of using the young orphan to fulfill her murderous deeds. Terrified of Sophia's intentions, Florence desperately tries to break free from the ghost's spell and warn the others before it's too late.

Where it's reviewed:
Booklist, October 1, 2010, page 90
Bulletin of the Center for Children's Books, October 2010, page 77
Horn Book Magazine, Sept/Oct 2010, page 79
School Library Journal, August 2010, page 101

Other books by the same author:
Closed for the Season, 2010
All the Lovely Bad Ones, 2009
The Old Willis Place, 1994
The Doll in the Garden, 1989
Wait Till Helen Comes, 1986

Other books you might like:
Avi, *The Seer of Shadows*, 2008
Amber Benson, *Among the Ghosts*, 2010
Chris Grabenstein, *The Crossroads*, 2008
Jane Kelley, *The Girl behind the Glass*, 2011

187

SHANNON HALE
DEAN HALE, Co-Author
NATHAN HALE, Illustrator

Calamity Jack

(New York: Bloomsbury USA Children's Books, 2010)

Subject(s): Adventure; Folklore; Fairy tales

Age range(s): 9 - 13+
Major character(s): Jack, Young Man; Rapunzel, Young Woman; Blunderboar, Monster (giant); Pru, Sidekick (pixie); Freddie Sparksmith, Journalist
Time period(s): Indeterminate Past
Locale(s): Shyport, Fictional Location

Summary: *Calamity Jack* is a graphic novel written by Dean and Shannon Hale and illustrated by Nathan Hale. Based on well-known fairy tales, *Calamity Jack* is the sequel to *Rapunzel's Revenge*. In the book, Jack and Rapunzel return to the fictional town of Shyport in the American West to find that Jack's mother is being held captive by the giant Blunderboar, who is now running the city. They decide to join their old friends, Pru, a pixie, and Freddie Sparksmith, a journalist, to take Shyport back from Blunderboar and rescue Jack's mother.

Where it's reviewed:
Booklist, October 1, 2009, page 41
Horn Book Guide, Fall 2010, page 340
Publishers Weekly, January 4, 2010, page 49
School Library Journal, January 2010, page 128

Other books by the same author:
Rapunzel's Revenge, 2008

Other books you might like:
George O'Connor, *Zeus: King of the Gods*, 2010
Aaron Renier, *The Unsinkable Walker Bean*, 2010
Joann Sfar, *Klezmer: Tales of the Wild East*, 2006
Bill Willingham, *Jack of Fables, Vol. 1: The (Nearly) Great Escape*, 2006

188

MICHAEL HALL, Author/Illustrator

Perfect Square

(New York: Greenwillow Books, 2011)

Story type: Young Readers
Subject(s): Art; Imagination

Age range(s): 3 - 5+

Summary: A perfect square with "four matching corners and four equal sides" turns lemons into lemonade in this picture story by author and illustrator Michael Hall. In the course of a week, the perfect square is cut, torn, pierced with holes, and wrinkled, but no matter what happens, the square finds a way to reinvent itself and find happiness. Each turn of the page shows how the pieces of the square from the previous day's destruction have been retooled into a new shape.

Where it's reviewed:
Booklist, April 15, 2011, page 53
Horn Book Magazine, March/April 2011, page 103
Publishers Weekly, February 7, 2011, page 55
School Library Journal, April 2011, page 144

Other books by the same author:
My Heart Is Like a Zoo, 2010

Other books you might like:
Eric Carle, *The Very Hungry Caterpillar*, 1969
Suse MacDonald, *Alphabatics*, 1986
Ellen Stoll Walsh, *Mouse Shapes*, 2007

189

JENNY HAN
JULIA KUO, Illustrator

Clara Lee and the Apple Pie Dream

(New York: Little, Brown Books for Young Readers, 2011)

Subject(s): Schools; Grandfathers; Korean Americans

Age range(s): 6 - 8+
Major character(s): Clara Lee, Granddaughter, Student—Elementary School, 3rd Grader; Grandfather, Grandfather (of Clara)
Time period(s): 21st century; 2010s

Summary: In Jenny Han's *Clara Lee and the Apple Pie Dream*, Korean-American Clara Lee desperately wants to win the title of Little Miss Apple Pie and ride on the float during the town's apple festival. She's afraid of public speaking, though, and to enter the contest, she must write and then read a speech. Just before she's ready to enter, Clara has a terrifying dream. Her Grandfather tells her that according to Korean tradition, bad dreams bring good luck. Can Clara count on good luck to come her way and help her get ready for the contest? Will she win the title of Little Miss Apple Pie?

Where it's reviewed:
Booklist, December 1, 2010, page 59
Bulletin of the Center for Children's Books, January 2011, page 236
Horn Book Magazine, March/April 2011, page 118
Publishers Weekly, November 15, 2010, page 58
School Library Journal, February 2011, page 81

Other books you might like:
Stephanie Barden, *Cinderella Smith*, 2011
Judy Blume, *Soupy Saturdays with the Pain and the Great One*, 2007
Louise Borden, *The John Hancock Club*, 2007
Suzy Kline, *Song Lee in Room 2B*, 1993
Lenore Look, *Ruby Lu, Brave and True*, 2004

190

AVIS HARLEY
DEBORAH NOYES, Photographer

African Acrostics: A Word in Edgeways

(Somerville, Massachusetts: Candlewick Press, 2009)

Subject(s): Poetry; Africa; Animals

Age range(s): 9 - 12+

Summary: Children's poet Avis Harley introduces young readers to the animals of Africa and the wonders of acrostic poems in this unique book. Acrostics are poems in which the first letter of each line spells out a word when read from top to bottom. Harley explains acrostic poetry in an introduction—which is itself an acrostic—then uses the form to celebrate crocodiles, elephants, lions, and other wild African beasts. Some of the poems are basic acrostics; others are double acrostics, multiple acrostics, and cross acrostics. Illustrated with color photographs by Deborah Noyes, this poetry collection also includes information about the featured animals and a note from the photographer about her travels in Africa.

Where it's reviewed:
Booklist, July 1, 2009, page 58
Bulletin of the Center for Children's Books, September 2009, page 22
Horn Book Magazine, September/October 2009, page 578
School Library Journal, June 2009, page 143

Other books by the same author:
The Monarch's Progress: Poems With Wings, 2008

Sea Stars: Saltwater Poems, 2006

Other books you might like:
Robert Bateman, *Safari*, 1998
David Elliott, *In the Wild*, 2010
Steven Schnur, *Winter: An Alphabet Acrostic*, 2002
Joyce Sidman, *Ubiquitous: Celebrating Nature's Survivors*, 2010

191

CHARISE MERICLE HARPER

Just Grace Goes Green

(Boston: Houghton Mifflin Books for Children, 2009)

Series: Just Grace Series. Book 4
Story type: Series; Young Readers
Subject(s): Friendship; Recycling; Schools

Age range(s): 6 - 8+
Major character(s): Grace "Just Grace" Stewart, 3rd Grader, Friend (of Mimi); Mimi, 3rd Grader, Friend (of Grace); Miss Lois, Teacher
Time period(s): 21st century; 2000s
Locale(s): United States

Summary: In this fourth novel for young readers in Charise Mericle Harper's Just Grace Series, third grader Grace Stewart embarks on a quest to protect the environment. When her teacher, Miss Lois, instructs the class to come up with ideas for "going green," Grace and her friend Mimi take on the topic of conserving plastic bottles. While other classmates work on projects focused on saving energy and water, Grace and Mimi learn and share shocking information about plastic's impact on the earth. Meanwhile, Grace also helps Mimi deal with a delicate issue at home when a visiting relative commandeers one of Mimi's favorite plush toys.

Where it's reviewed:
Booklist, February 15, 2009, page 92
Horn Book Magazine, March/April 2009, page 196
Publishers Weekly, March 16, 2009, page 63
School Library Journal, March 2009, page 114

Other books by the same author:
Just Grace and the Double Surprise, 2011
Just Grace and the Terrible Tutu, 2010
Just Grace and the Snack Attack, 2009
Just Grace Walks the Dog, 2008
Still Just Grace, 2007

Other books you might like:
Sheila Greenwald, *Watch Out World: Rosey Cole Is Going Green*, 2010
Dan Gutman, *Recycle This Book: 100 Top Children's Authors Tell You How to Go Green*, 2009
Ted Kooser, *Bag in the Wind*, 2010
Kathy Ross, *Earth-Friendly Crafts: Clever Ways to Reuse Everyday Items*, 2011

192

JESSICA HARPER
JON BERKELEY, Illustrator

Underpants On My Head

(New York: G. P. Putnam's Sons, 2009)

Series: Uh-Oh, Cleo Series. Book 2
Subject(s): Brothers and sisters; Sibling rivalry; Vacations

Age range(s): 6 - 8+
Major character(s): Cleo Small, Sister (of Jenna), 8-Year-Old, Narrator; Jenna Small, Sister (of Cleo)
Time period(s): 21st century; 2000s
Locale(s): Colorado, United States

Summary: *Underpants on My Head* is part of the Uh-Oh, Cleo series by Jessica Harper. In eight-year-old Cleo's latest adventure, her six brothers and sisters travel to Colorado for summer vacation. After a quick trip to her grandmother's house, Cleo, her parents, and her two older sisters decide to take a hike up a mountain. Cleo is surprised when she discovers that even in the summertime, it snows at the top of a mountain. The family finds themselves in trouble when a harsh snowstorm blows through. In order to stay warm, they get creative and use their underpants as hats.

Where it's reviewed:
Booklist, February 1, 2009, page 44
Bulletin of the Center for Children's Books, February 2009, page 240
Horn Book Magazine, March/April 2009, page 196
School Library Journal, March 2009, page 114

Other books by the same author:
I Barfed On Mrs. Kelly, 2010
Uh-oh, Cleo, 2008

Other books you might like:
Beverly Cleary, *Ramona Quimby, Age 8*, 1981
Carol Fenner, *Snowed in with Grandmother Silk*, 2003
Charise Mericle Harper, *Just Grace*, 2007
Kimberly Willis Holt, *Piper Reed, Navy Brat*, 2007
Katy Kelly, *Lucy Rose: Here's the Thing About Me*, 2004

193

ROBIE H. HARRIS
NADINE BERNARD WESTCOTT, Illustrator

Who Has What?: All about Girls' Bodies and Boys' Bodies

(Somerville, Massachusetts: Candlewick Press, 2011)

Subject(s): Anatomy; Biology; Children

Age range(s): 4 - 7+
Major character(s): Gus, Brother (of Nellie), Boy; Nellie, Girl, Sister (of Gus)

Summary: In this educational introduction to the concept of gender, author Robie H. Harris offers a simple guide for curious young readers all about those "special parts" that make girls and boys different. Gus and his sister Nellie just love a day at the beach. While they have many things in common, they also know that there are some important differences between them. While the two are changing into their bathing suits in separate dressing areas, Harris introduces readers to the body parts that make Gus a boy and Nellie a girl. Though he avoids any references to sexuality or the reproductive process, Harris clearly points out the key male and female parts using their correct biological names.

Where it's reviewed:
Booklist, September 1, 2011, page 103
Publishers Weekly, July 25, 2011, page 49
School Library Journal, October 2011, page 126

Other books by the same author:
It's Not the Stork!: A Book about Girls, Boys, Babies, Bodies, Families and Friends, 2006

Other books you might like:
Laurie Krasny Brown, *What's the Big Secret?: Talking about Sex with Girls and Boys*, 1997
Shannon Riggs, *Not in Room 204*, 2007
Gail Saltz, *Amazing You!: Getting Smart about Your Private Parts*, 2005

194

MICHELLE HARRISON

13 Treasures

(New York: Little, Brown and Company, 2010)

Subject(s): Fantasy; Fairies; Mystery

Age range(s): 10 - 13+
Major character(s): Tanya, 13-Year-Old
Time period(s): 21st century; 2010s
Locale(s): England

Summary: *13 Treasures* is a mysterious fantasy novel for children and young adults from debut author, Michelle Harrison. Tanya is a 13-year old girl with an exceptional gift. All of her life, she's been able to see fairies in another realm, but the fairies that grace her visions are evil and mischievous. After a lifetime of taking the fall for the fairies' pranks, Tanya is sent away by her mother to live with her grandmother at Elvesden Manor, an isolated country home in a strange part of Essex. During her stay, Tanya finds herself pulled into a 50-year old mystery involving a young girl who vanished in Hangman's Wood, a haunted stretch of forest. First novel.

Where it's reviewed:
Bulletin of the Center for Children's Books, September 2010, page 22
Horn Book Guide, Fall 2010, page 340
Publishers Weekly, March 8, 2010, page 56
School Library Journal, April 2010, page 158

Other books by the same author:
13 Curses, 2011

Other books you might like:
Cornelia Funke, *Reckless*, 2010
Katherine Langrish, *The Shadow Hunt*
Kate Thompson, *The New Policeman*, 2005

195

BEN HATKE, Author/Illustrator

Zita the Spacegirl

(New York: First Second, 2011)

Story type: Adventure; Alternate World
Subject(s): Space exploration; Courage; Extraterrestrial life
Age range(s): 8 - 12+
Major character(s): Zita, Girl, Friend (of Joseph), Heroine; Joseph, Boy, Friend (of Zita), Captive
Locale(s): Planet—Imaginary

Summary: In this graphic novel for children by author and illustrator Ben Hatke, Zita and her friend Joseph discover a mysterious red button that appears to have crash-landed on Earth. Zita can't resist the urge to press the button, and in the blink of an eye, aliens abduct Joseph and take him to their home planet. But Zita's not one to let things go without a fight, and she quickly follows. Navigating the strange new planet, Zita meets some interesting characters—a mouse that she rides like a horse, an enormous blob creature, robots, and even another human traveler. Zita and her pals encounter a number of obstacles along the way, but Zita remains determined to save her friend. Hatke's illustrations depict the zany world and crazy creatures that Zita meets during her journey.

Where it's reviewed:
Booklist, December 15, 2010, page 37
Horn Book Guide, Fall 2011, page 356
School Library Journal, January 2011, page 132
Teacher Librarian, February 2011, page 23

Other books you might like:
L. Frank Baum, *The Wonderful Wizard of Oz*, 1900
Barry Deutsch, *Hereville: How Mirka Got Her Sword*, 2010
Kazu Kibuishi, *The Stonekeeper*, 2008
Dan Santat, *Sidekicks*, 2011
Kean Soo, *Jellaby*, 2008

196

GEOFFREY HAYES, Author/Illustrator

Benny and Penny in the Big No-No!

(New York: RAW Junior, 2008)

Subject(s): Animals; Friendship; Cartoons
Age range(s): 5 - 8+
Major character(s): Benny, Mouse, Child, Brother (of Penny); Penny, Mouse, Child, Sister (of Benny); Melina, Child, Animal, Neighbor (of Benny and Penny)
Time period(s): 21st century; 2000s
Locale(s): United States

Summary: Benny and Penny's Mom lets them in on the big news: a new kid has moved in next door. But Benny and Penny but they haven't seen this new neighbor.

When Benny's pail goes missing, they sneak over the fence to see if the new kid has taken it. A mud fight and a quick escape ensues, but when they return with the "recovered" bucket, they find Benny's bucket in the sandbox where they left it. Can Benny and Penny make it up to their new neighbor? Warm panel illustrations introduce early readers to comic book formatting.

Where it's reviewed:
Booklist, March 1, 2009, page 66
Publishers Weekly, May 18, 2009, page 54
School Library Journal, May 2009, page 131

Other books by the same author:
Patrick in a Teddy Bear's Picnic and Other Stories, 2011
Benny and Penny in the Toy Breaker, 2010
Alligator and His Uncle Tooth, 1977
Bear by Himself, 1976

Other books you might like:
Frank Cammuso, *Otto's Orange Day*, 2008
James Kochalka, *Johnny Boo: The Best Little Ghost In The World*, 2008
Jay Lynch, *Mo and Jo: Fighting Together Forever*, 2008
Agnes Rosenstiehl, *Silly Lilly and the Four Seasons*, 2008
Mo Willems, *Don't Let the Pigeon Drive the Bus!*, 2003

197

JOHN HENDRIX, Author/Illustrator

John Brown: His Fight for Freedom

(New York: Abrams Books for Young Readers, 2009)

Subject(s): Biographies; Abolitionists; Slavery
Age range(s): 9 - 12+
Time period(s): 19th century; 1850s

Summary: John Hendrix's *John Brown: His Fight for Freedom* is an illustrated biography about the life of an abolitionist for older children and young adults. The book discusses the life of white abolitionist John Brown, whose fierce passion to end slavery ultimately led to his own end. His most renowned action occurred in Harpers Ferry, Virginia, where he and his followers attempted to raid a U.S. arsenal to arm slaves with weapons and begin a revolt. Though ultimately unsuccessful—the military, under the direction of Robert E. Lee, stopped the raid—the event shed light on the important issue of ending slavery. Hendrix describes Brown's actions—both good and bad—and his words alongside his own vivid pen-and-ink illustrations.

Where it's reviewed:
Booklist, October 15 2009, page 50
Bulletin of the Center for Children's Books, December 2009, page 156
Horn Book Magazine, November/December 20, page 693
Publishers Weekly, October 19 2009, page 53
School Library Journal, November 2009, page 132

Other books by the same author:
Nurse, Soldier, Spy: The Story of Sarah Edmonds, a Civil War Hero, 2011
Abe Lincoln Crosses a Creek: A Tall, Thin Tale (Introducing His Forgotten Frontier Friend), 2008
*How to Save Your Tail: *if You Are a Rat Nabbed by Cats Who Really Like Stories about Magic Spoons, Wolves with Snout-warts, Big, Hairy Chimney Trolls . . . and Cookies, Too*, 2007
The Giant Rat of Sumatra: Or Pirates Galore, 2005

Other books you might like:
Janet Halfmann, *Seven Miles to Freedom: The Robert Smalls Story*, 2008
Doreen Rappaport, *Freedom River*, 2000
Anne Rockwell, *Only Passing Through: The Story of Sojourner Truth*, 2000
Carole Boston Weatherford, *Moses: When Harriet Tubman Led Her People to Freedom*, 2006

198

KEVIN HENKES

My Garden

(New York: Greenwillow Books, 2010)

Subject(s): Gardening; Imagination; Mother-daughter relations

Age range(s): 3 - 6+

Summary: In Kevin Henkes' *My Garden*, a small child helps her mother tend to a garden of tomatoes, lettuce, and carrots. After the parent and child pull weeds and water the plants, the young girl imagines what it would be like to have her own garden. In her garden, flowers change color and shape, tomatoes grow so big that she can hide behind them, and the rabbits that inhabit the garden are made of chocolate. Instead of carrots in the ground, the little girl also chooses to grow jelly beans in a bush. The young child's imagination grows as easily as the jelly bean and seashell plants in Henkes' illustrated tale.

Where it's reviewed:
Booklist, January 1, 2010, page 98
Bulletin of the Center for Children's Books, April 2010, page 337
School Library Journal, March 2010, page 119

Other books by the same author:
Little White Rabbit, 2011
Old Bear, 2008
A Good Day, 2007
Kitten's First Full Moon, 2004

Other books you might like:
Elise Broach, *When Dinosaurs Came with Everything*, 2007
Lois Ehlert, *Growing Vegetable Soup*, 1987
Mary Ann Hoberman, *Whose Garden Is It?*, 2004
Thatcher Hurd, *The Weaver*, 2010
Ruth Krauss, *The Carrot Seed*, 1945

199

KEVIN HENKES, Author/Illustrator

Little White Rabbit

(New York: Greenwillow Books, 2011)

Story type: Contemporary
Subject(s): Animals; Children; Rabbits

Age range(s): 2 - 5+
Major character(s): Rabbit, Rabbit (with a big imagination)

Summary: In this picture book for very young readers, Kevin Henkes presents a tale of a little white rabbit that sets out looking for adventure. Although the bunny lives in a pretty plain yard, he finds all the adventure he's looking for in his own imagination. The rabbit imagines being as tall as a tree, as green as the grass, and much more. Each of the rabbit's flights of fantasy is illustrated by Henkes. This book is intended for preschool children aged two and up.

Where it's reviewed:
Booklist, November 15, 2010, page 50
Horn Book Magazine, January/February 2011, page 79
Publishers Weekly, December 13, 2010, page 55
School Library Journal, February 2011, page 81

Other books by the same author:
My Garden, 2010
Old Bear, 2008
A Good Day, 2007
Kitten's First Full Moon, 2004

Other books you might like:
Eve Bunting, *Tweak Tweak*, 2011
Greg Gormley, *Dog in Boots*, 2011
Wong Herbert Yee, *Tracks in the Snow*, 2003

200

KEVIN HENKES

Junonia

(New York: HarperCollins, 2011)

Subject(s): Beaches; Vacations; Family

Age range(s): 9 - 12+
Major character(s): Alice Rice, 10-Year-Old
Locale(s): Sanibel Island, Florida

Summary: Alice Rice is excited to spend her birthday on vacation at Sanibel Island, Florida. Alice imagines this year's birthday celebration to be the best ever: she thinks about seeing the people she has become accustomed to meeting every year and is certain this will be the year she finds a colorful Junonia shell along the beach. Yet when she arrives, she finds some of the people who usually vacation at the same time as her family have not come to the beach this year, and some new people have come as well. Will Alice be able to deal with these changes, or will her tenth birthday party be ruined?

Where it's reviewed:
Booklist, March 1, 2011, page 48

Bulletin of the Center for Children's Books, June 2011, page 472

Horn Book Magazine, May/June 2011, page 92

Publishers Weekly, April 11, 2011, page 52

School Library Journal, June 2011, page 119

Other books by the same author:
Bird Lake Moon, 2008
Olive's Ocean, 2003
The Birthday Room, 1999
Sun & Spoon, 1997
Words of Stone, 1992

Other books you might like:
Deirdre Baker, *Becca at Sea*, 2007
Audrey Couloumbis, *Lexie*, 2011
Jennifer L. Holm, *Turtle in Paradise*, 2010
Eileen Spinelli, *The Dancing Pancake*, 2010
Winston Williams, *Florida's Fabulous Seashells And Other Seashore Life*, 1988

201

KEVIN HENKES
LAURA DRONZEK, Illustrator

Birds

(New York: HarperCollins, 2009)

Subject(s): Birds; Children; Animals

Age range(s): 3 - 6+

Summary: In *Birds*, a little girl enjoys looking out her window at all of the beautiful birds that fly by each day. The book emphasizes the different colors and shapes of various types of birds. Author Kevin Henkes and illustrator Laura Dronzek show young readers how to enjoy the different birds that reappear in the spring. Even if they can't be seen, birds still provide beautiful music for families to enjoy. The little girl notices some similarities between herself and the birds she sees outside her window. She imagines what birds might be thinking, and notices how the birds change the landscape in dynamic ways.

Where it's reviewed:
Booklist, January 1 2009, page 76
Bulletin of the Center for Children's Books, April 2009, page 323
Horn Book Magazine, March/April 2009, page 182
New York Times Book Review, May 10 2009, page 17
School Library Journal, February 2009, page 76

Other books by the same author:
Little White Rabbit, 2011
My Garden, 2010

Other books you might like:
Dianna Hutts Aston, *An Egg Is Quiet*, 2006
Lois Ehlert, *Color Zoo*, 1989
Emily Gravett, *Orange Pear Apple Bear*, 2006
Ellen Stoll Walsh, *Mouse Paint*, 1989

202

AMY HEST
ANITA JERAM, Illustrator

Little Chick

(Somerville, Massachusetts: Candlewick Press, 2009)

Subject(s): Learning; Family

Age range(s): 3 - 6+
Major character(s): Little Chick, Chicken

Summary: Little Chick is sometimes impatient about things she wants. During a series of three adventures, Little Chick learns that everyone needs to be patient sometimes. When Little Chick plants a carrot, she expects that the plant will quickly grow to be very large; however, she learns that some things take time. Little Chick has another lesson in patience when she learns to fly a kite. With her Old Auntie's help, Little Chick also learns that (no matter how far she stretches) she cannot pull a star from the sky and put it in her pocket. *Little Chick* is written by Amy Hest and illustrated by Anita Jeram.

Where it's reviewed:
Bulletin of the Center for Children's Books, May 2009, page 364
Horn Book Guide, Fall 2010, page 312
School Library Journal, May 2009, page 70

Other books by the same author:
You Can Do It Sam, 2003
Make the Team, Baby Duck, 2002
Baby Duck and the New Eyeglasses, 1996

Other books you might like:
Suzanne Bloom, *A Splendid Friend, Indeed*, 2005
Ruth Krauss, *The Carrot Seed*, 1945
Layn Marlow, *Hurry Up and Slow Down*, 2009
Cynthia Rylant, *Brownie and Pearl Step Out*, 2010
Martin Waddell, *Hi, Harry!: The Moving Story of How One Slow Tortoise Slowly Made a Friend*, 2003

203

CARL HIAASEN

Scat

(New York: Alfred A. Knopf, 2009)

Subject(s): Teachers; Missing persons; Mystery fiction

Age range(s): 10 - 13+
Major character(s): Mrs. Bunny Starch, Teacher (biology, of Nick, Marta, and Duane); Marta Gonzalez, Classmate (of Nick and Duane); Duane "Smoke" Scrod Jr., Classmate (of Nick and Marta); Nick Waters, Classmate (of Marta and Duane); Drake McBride, Businessman (president of Red Diamond Energy Company), Con Artist; Jimmy Lee Bayliss, Con Artist, Manager (project, of Red Diamond Energy Company); Twilly Spree, Wealthy, Environmentalist
Time period(s): 21st century
Locale(s): Florida Everglades, Florida

Summary: Hiaasen's latest begins innocently enough with a school field trip to the Florida Everglades. Nick and Marta's class evacuate because of a wildfire, and soon realize that everyone is accounted for except Mrs. Starch, their science teacher. Days go by and there's no word from her, just a feeble excuse that she's away on family business. Neither Nick nor Marta buys this and they soon discover that supposed bad boy, Duane the Dweeb, aka Smoke, is also suspicious. Their hunt leads them deep into the Everglades as the trio comes across a crooked drilling deal; an eccentric millionaire; and the scat from a Florida panther, the most illusive and endangered species living in the Everglades. Added to their mission to find Mrs. Starch, protect the panther, and thwart the drilling, is Nick's uncertainty about his father's deployment to Iraq. Hiaasen gives readers another full dose of his own brand of humor and quirky characters, a thoughtful consideration of the costs of protecting wildlife, and a dandy mystery.

Where it's reviewed:
Booklist, November 1, 2009, page 41
Bulletin of the Center for Children's Books, February 2009, page 242
Horn Book Magazine, January/February 2009, page 94
Publishers Weekly, October 27, 2009, page 55
School Library Journal, January 2009, page 104

Other books by the same author:
Flush, 2005
Hoot, 2002

Other books you might like:
Jim Arnosky, *Wild Tracks*, 2008
Cynthia DeFelice, *Lostman's River*, 1994
Richard W. Jennings, *Stink City*, 2006
Rosanne Parry, *Heart of a Shepherd*, 2009

204

LABAN CARRICK HILL
BRYAN COLLIER, Illustrator

Dave the Potter, Artist, Poet, Slave

(New York: Little, Brown and Company, 2010)

Subject(s): Slavery; Art; Poetry

Age range(s): 7 - 10+
Time period(s): 19th century
Locale(s): South Carolina, United States

Summary: Though his life remains shrouded in mystery, the man known only as Dave the Potter has captured the hearts of millions with the astounding works of art he left behind. This volume presents a speculative account of Dave's story: his life as a slave, his passion for pottery, poetry, and all art forms, and his thoughtful approach to his craft. Laban Carrick Hill's *Dave the Potter, Artist, Poet, Slave* includes illustrations by Bryan Collier.

Where it's reviewed:
Booklist, November 1, 2010, page 58
Horn Book Guide, Spring 2011, page 69
New York Times Book Review, November 7, 2010, page 30
School Library Journal, August 2010, page 90

Awards the book has won:
Carter G. Woodson Book Award: Elementary, 2011
Coretta Scott King Book Award: Illustrator Award, 2011

Other books you might like:
Nancy Andrews-Goebel, *The Pot That Juan Built*, 2002
Ellen Levine, *Henry's Freedom Box: A True Story from the Underground Railroad*, 2007
Margot Theis Raven, *Circle Unbroken*, 2004
Jacqueline Woodson, *Show Way*, 2005

205

MARY ANN HOBERMAN

Strawberry Hill

(New York: Little, Brown and Company, 2009)

Subject(s): Rural life; Friendship; Great Depression, 1929-1934

Age range(s): 8 - 10+
Major character(s): Allie Sherman, 10-Year-Old; Martha, Friend (of Allie); Mimi, Friend (of Allie)
Time period(s): 20th century; 1920s
Locale(s): Stamford, Connecticut

Summary: Set in Depression Era New England, Mary Ann Hoberman's *Strawberry Hill* is the story of 10-year-old Allie Sherman and her struggles to fit in at a new school. When her family relocates from a house in the city to a farm in the country, Allie is determined to find her niche in this strange new place. She meets two girls her age, Martha and Mimi, but is soon forced to learn some tough lessons about friendship and acceptance. Yet through it all, young Allie is optimistic that she will find her place and a best friend to call her own.

Where it's reviewed:
Booklist, June 1, 2009, page 66
Bulletin of the Center for Children's Books, October 2009, page 66
Horn Book Guide, Spring 2010, page 72
School Library Journal, July 2009, page 64

Other books you might like:
Jeanne Birdsall, *The Penderwicks: A Summer Tale of Four Sisters, Two Rabbits, and a Very Interesting Boy*, 2005
Karen Hesse, *Brooklyn Bridge*, 2008
Wendy Mass, *11 Birthdays*, 2009
Sydney Taylor, *All-of-a-Kind Family*, 1951

206

JENNIFER L. HOLM

Turtle in Paradise

(New York: Random House, 2010)

Subject(s): Family; Adventure; Great Depression, 1929-1934

Age range(s): 9 - 11+
Major character(s): Turtle, 11-Year-Old, Granddaughter (of Nana); Nana Philly, Grandmother (of Turtle)
Time period(s): 20th century; 1930s (1935)
Locale(s): Key West, Florida

Summary: In *Turtle in Paradise*, Newbery-winning author Jennifer L. Holm charts the escapades of an 11-year-old girl who finds a new life in Key West, Florida. It is 1935, and the Great Depression is in full force. Turtle's mother is fortunate enough to land a job as a live-in maid, but she must send Turtle to live with family in Florida. There, Turtle must adapt to an entirely different way of life with her grandmother and rambunctious cousins. Adventure and self-discovery await young Turtle as she enters this new phase of childhood in the paradise of Key West.

Where it's reviewed:
Booklist, April 15, 2010, page 60
Bulletin of the Center for Children's Books, May 2010, page 380
Horn Book Magazine, May/June 2010, page 81
Publishers Weekly, May 3, 2010, page 52

Other books by the same author:
Penny From Heaven, 2006

Awards the book has won:
Golden Kite Awards: Fiction, 2011

Other books you might like:
Judy Blume, *Starring Sally J. Freedman as Herself*, 1977
Russell Freedman, *Children of the Great Depression*, 2005
Marian Hale, *The Truth about Sparrows*, 2004
Matt Phelan, *The Storm in the Barn*, 2009

207

JENNIFER L. HOLM

The Trouble with May Amelia

(New York: Atheneum Books for Young Readers, 2011)

Subject(s): Family; Father-daughter relations; Agriculture
Age range(s): 9 - 12+
Major character(s): May Amelia Jackson, 13-Year-Old
Time period(s): 20th century; 1900s (1900)
Locale(s): Washington, United States

Summary: May Amelia is a 13-year-old living on a farm in Washington State with her parents and her brothers. Her father, a Finnish immigrant, complains that girls aren't as useful as boys around the farm. May Amelia does not feel the same way, however, and she keeps trying to earn his respect. When someone comes to the farm to inquire about buying it from the family, May Amelia acts as the interpreter for her foreign parents. Can May Amelia prove to her father and the rest of her family that she has important skills, too? This novel is a follow-up to Jennifer L. Holm's *Our only May Amelia*.

Where it's reviewed:
Booklist, March 1, 2011, page 61
Bulletin of the Center for Children's Books, May 2011, page 420

Horn Book Magazine, May/June 2010, page 94
Publishers Weekly, March 7, 2011, page 64
School Library Journal, April 2011, page 174

Other books by the same author:
Turtle in Paradise, 2010
Penny from Heaven, 2006
Our Only May Amelia, 1999

Other books you might like:
Mary Jane Auch, *One-Handed Catch*, 2006
William Durbin, *Song of Sampo Lake*, 2002
Richard Peck, *Fair Weather*, 2001
Matt Phelan, *The Storm in the Barn*, 2009

208

JENNIFER L. HOLM, Author/Illustrator
MATTHEW HOLM, Author/Illustrator

Squish: Super Amoeba

(New York: Random House, 2011)

Series: Squish Series. Book 1
Story type: Fantasy
Subject(s): Schools; Bullying; Cheating

Age range(s): 6 - 10+
Major character(s): Squish, Student—Elementary School (amoeba); Pod, Student—Elementary School (amoeba), Friend (of Squish and Peggy); Peggy, Student—Elementary School (paramecium), Friend (of Squish and Pod); Lynwood, Student—Elementary School, Bully

Summary: Jennifer L. Holm and Matthew Holm launch a new series of graphic novels for children with this volume. The series focuses on Squish, an amoeba whose microscopic world closely resembles our own. Squish enjoys reading comic books and dining on snack cakes, and he faces many of the same dilemmas that ordinary kids face—school bullies, mean principals, and even detention. Late to school one too many times, Squish and his pals, nerdy Pod and perpetually happy Peggy, land in detention with school bully Lynwood. Lynwood wants Squish to help him cheat on an upcoming test and threatens to eat Peggy if Squish refuses to help him. Faced with an impossible decision, Squish wonders how his favorite comic book character, Super Amoeba, would handle the situation.

Where it's reviewed:
Booklist, March 15, 2011, page 42
Horn Book Guide, Fall 2011, page 357
New York Times Book Review, May 15, 2011, page 21
Publishers Weekly, April 4, 2011, page 55

Other books by the same author:
Babymouse: Mad Scientist, 2011
Brave New Pond, 2011
Babymouse: Queen of the World, 2005

Other books you might like:
Jarrett J. Krosoczka, *Lunch Lady and the Cyborg Substitute*, 2009
Stephen McCranie, *Mal and Chad: The Biggest, Bestest Time Ever!*, 2011

Scott Morse, *Magic Pickle*, 2008
Ashley Spires, *Binky the Space Cat*, 2009
Michael Townsend, *Kit Feeny: On the Move*, 2009

209

SARA LEWIS HOLMES

Operation Yes

(New York: Arthur A. Levine Books, 2009)

Subject(s): Teachers; Acting; Military bases

Age range(s): 10 - 13+
Major character(s): Miss Loupe, Teacher
Time period(s): 21st century; 2000s
Locale(s): United States

Summary: In Sara Lewis Holmes's *Operation Yes*, Miss Loupe is a new teacher who has just accepted her first teaching position at a school on a military base. The students in her sixth grade class are baffled by the unorthodox Miss Loupe, who teaches through improvisational theater and acting lessons. But when Miss Loupe's brother goes missing while serving in Afghanistan, her students come to her rescue and help her process her feelings utilizing the theatrical methods she has taught them.

Where it's reviewed:
Booklist, September 15, 2009, page 60
Horn Book Magazine, Nov/Dec 2009, page 676
Publishers Weekly, August 17, 2009, page 63
School Library Journal, November 2009, page 110

Other books by the same author:
Letters from Rapunzel, 2007

Other books you might like:
Frances O'Roark Dowell, *Shooting the Moon*, 2008
Barbara Kerley, *Greetings from Planet Earth*, 2007
Rosanne Parry, *Heart of a Shepherd*, 2009
Gary D. Schmidt, *The Wednesday Wars*, 2007

210

KIMBERLY WILLIS HOLT
CHRISTINE DAVENIER, Illustrator

Piper Reed, Campfire Girl

(New York: Henry Holt and Co., 2011)

Series: Piper Reed Series. Book 4
Story type: Contemporary - Mainstream
Subject(s): Camping; Family; Halloween

Age range(s): 8 - 10+
Major character(s): Piper Reed, 5th Grader; Stanley, 5th Grader
Time period(s): 21st century; 2010s
Locale(s): Pensacola, Florida

Summary: In the fourth outing in author Kimberly Willis Holt's Piper Reed series, Piper Reed is thrilled about her family's upcoming camping trip with other Navy families—until she learns that it will interfere with Halloween! Is there any way she can bring Halloween fun to the campsite? To make matters worse, Piper discovers that Stanley—the irritating new boy in class who is also a member of the Gypsy Club for "navy brats"— is going on the camping trip, too. When Stanley ends up in an embarrassing situation, however, Piper decides to find a way to help him regain confidence. Holt's text is accompanied by illustrations by Christine Davenier.

Where it's reviewed:
Booklist, January 1, 2011, page 106
Horn Book Guide, Spring 2011, page 73

Other books by the same author:
Piper Reed Gets a Job, 2009
Piper Reed the Great Gypsy, 2008
Piper Reed Navy Brat, 2007

Other books you might like:
Ruth McNally Barshaw, *Ellie McDoodle: Have Pen, Will Travel*, 2007
Meg Cabot, *Allie Finkle's Rules for Girls*, 2008
Wendelin Van Draanen, *Sammy Keyes and the Night of Skulls*, 2011

211

PHILLIP M. HOOSE

Claudette Colvin: Twice Toward Justice

(New York: Melanie Kroupa Books, 2009)

Subject(s): African Americans; Segregation; Civil rights movements

Age range(s): 11 - 16+
Locale(s): Montgomery, Alabama

Summary: In *Claudette Colvin: Twice Toward Justice*, author Jim Hoose provides an in-depth look at the life and accomplishments of the little-known civil rights activist. Claudette Colvin was just 15 years old when, in 1955 Alabama, she refused to give up her seat to a white passenger on a city bus. This was nine months before Rosa Parks would make history for doing the same thing, but Colvin's bold actions were met with widespread dismissal. Colvin, however, did not give up the fight. She soon took part in a revolutionary case that challenged Jim Crow laws and forever shook the foundations of the segregated American South.

Where it's reviewed:
Booklist, February 1 2009, page 49
Bulletin of the Center for Children's Books, February 2009, page 243
Horn Book Magazine, March/April 2009, page 212
New York Times Book Review, May 10, 2009, page 14
School Library Journal, February 2009, page 120

Other books by the same author:
We Were There, Too!: Young People in U.S. History, 2001

Awards the book has won:
Blue Ribbon Awards: Non-fiction, 2008
National Book Awards: Young People's Literature, 2009
Carter G. Woodson Book Award: Secondary, 2010

Jane Addams Children's Book Award, 2010

Other books you might like:
David A. Adler, *Heroes For Civil Rights*, 2010
Russell Freedman, *Freedom Walkers: The Story of the Montgomery Bus Boycott*, 2006
Diane McWhorter, *A Dream of Freedom: The Civil Rights Movement from 1954 to 1968*, 2004
Andrea Davis Pinkney, *Boycott Blues: How Rosa Parks Inspired a Nation*, 2008
Ntozake Shange, *We Troubled the Waters*, 2009

212

DEBORAH HOPKINSON
CARSON ELLIS, Illustrator

Stagecoach Sal

(New York: Disney Hyperion Books, 2009)

Subject(s): Stagecoach travel; Frontier life; Criminals

Age range(s): 6 - 9+
Major character(s): Sally "Sal", Child, Driver (of a stagecoach); Poetic Pete, Outlaw
Time period(s): 19th century
Locale(s): West Coast, United States

Summary: Deborah Hopkinson's picture story *Stagecoach Sal* is a tall tale based on a true story. In the book, which is set in the 19th-century American West, Sal often rides with her dad in his stagecoach, where she entertains passengers with her singing. An unfortunate accident renders her dad unable to conduct a mail run one day, however, so Sal sets out alone to do it for him. And sure enough—her mother's worst fears come true. Sal runs into the notorious outlaw Poetic Pete, who wows his victims with rhyming verse as he steals from them. Sal, however, is not about to let Pete pull one over on her. She's got a plan to deal with this criminal—and it might just work! *Stagecoach Sal* features artwork by Carson Ellis.

Where it's reviewed:
Horn Book Guide, Spring 2010, page 29
Publishers Weekly, August 2009, page 53
School Library Journal, September 2009, page 125

Other books by the same author:
Apples to Oregon: Being the (Slightly) True Narrative of How a Brave Pioneer Father Brought Apples, Peaches, Pears, Plums, Grapes, and Cherries (and Children) Across the Plains, 2004
A Packet of Seeds, 2004
Fannie in the Kitchen: The Whole Story From Soup to Nuts of How Fannie Farmer Invented Recipes with Precise Measurements, 2001

Other books you might like:
Eleanor Coerr, *Buffalo Bill and the Pony Express*, 1995
Deborah Hopkinson, *Home on the Range: John A. Lomax and His Cowboy Songs*, 2009
Diane Stanley, *Saving Sweetness*, 1996
Kate Thompson, *Highway Robbery*, 2009

213

JAMES HOWE
RANDY CECIL, Illustrator

Brontorina

(Somerville, Massachusetts: Candlewick Press, 2010)

Subject(s): Dinosaurs; Ballet; Dance

Age range(s): 4 - 8+
Major character(s): Madame Lucille, Teacher (dance); Brontorina, Dinosaur
Time period(s): 21st century; 2010s
Locale(s): United States

Summary: In *Brontorina* by James Howe, illustrated by Randy Cecil, a young dinosaur doesn't let her size get in the way of her ballerina dreams. Brontorina wants to be a dancer, but she doesn't own a pair of ballet shoes and she can't even fit inside the local dance studio without cracking the ceiling. Though Madame Lucille is sympathetic to her prospective student's situation, she sees no easy solution. As Randy Cecil's charming illustrations reveal, Madame Lucille's Academy of Dance is revolutionized when classes move outside. Now there is plenty of headroom for joyous Brontorina, who has even found a male partner—a dancing triceratops—strong enough to lift her into the air.

Where it's reviewed:
Booklist, May 15, 2010, page 40
Horn Book Guide, Spring 2011, page 31
Publishers Weekly, July 5, 2010, page 41
School Library Journal, July 2010, page 61

Other books by the same author:
Horace and Morris Say Cheese (Which Makes Delores Sneeze), 2008
Horace and Morris Join the Chorus (But What About Delores?), 2002
Horace and Morris but Mostly Delores, 1999

Other books you might like:
Steve Jenkins, *Prehistoric Actual Size*, 2005
Anne McEvoy, *Betsy B. Little*, 2008
Marisabina Russo, *A Very Big Bunny*, 2010
Mo Willems, *Elephants Cannot Dance*, 2009

214

LANGSTON HUGHES
E.B. LEWIS, Illustrator

The Negro Speaks of Rivers

(New York: Hyperion Books, 2009)

Subject(s): Poetry; African Americans

Age range(s): 5 - 8+

Summary: *The Negro Speaks of Rivers* is a republication of Harlem Renaissance poet Langston Hughes' original work, which was first published in 1941. This poem compares the history of African Americans to several rivers, including the Congo, the Euphrates, the Nile, and the Mississippi. Artist E. B. Lewis depicts the subject matter to complement Hughes' verse. Lewis' watercolor illustrations make the meaning of this classic poem accessible to young readers.

Where it's reviewed:
Booklist, November 15, 2008, page 45
Horn Book Guide, Fall 2009, page 465
Publishers Weekly, November 17, 2009, page 58
School Library Journal, February 2009, page 120

Other books by the same author:
My People, 2009
Poetry For Young People, 2006

Other books you might like:
Michelle Cook, *Our Children Can Soar: A Celebration of Rosa, Barack, and the Pioneers of Change*, 2009
Langston Hughes, *My People*, 2009
Walter Dean Myers, *Looking Like Me*, 2009
Kadir Nelson, *He's Got the Whole World in His Hands*, 2005

215

LANGSTON HUGHES
CHARLES R. SMITH JR., Photographer

My People

(New York: Atheneum Books for Young Readers, 2009)

Subject(s): African Americans; Poetry; Children

Age range(s): 4 - 9+

Summary: In *My People*, photographer Charles Smith Jr. pairs Langston Hughes's famous poem of the same name with his photographs. The poem is a celebration of African Americans and this book has a similar goal. Smith has broken the short poem into small chunks of two or three words to a page and has then added his own photographs of African Americans of all ages and sizes to illustrate the poem and its meaning. At the end, Smith shares the steps he took to make the book and discusses the creative process he used to approach the project. Young readers and those new to poetry will appreciate the visual aids to help them interpret the text.

Where it's reviewed:
Booklist, February 1 2009, page 56
Horn Book Guide, Fall 2009, page 464
School Library Journal, February 2009, page 92

Other books by the same author:
The Negro Speaks of Rivers, 2009
Poetry For Young People, 2006

Awards the book has won:
Coretta Scott King Book Award: Illustrator Award, 2010

Other books you might like:
Ashley Bryan, *Let It Shine : Three Favorite Spirituals*, 2007
Floyd Cooper, *Coming Home: From the Life of Langston Hughes*, 1994
Dinah Johnson, *Hair Dance!*, 2007
Willie Perdomo, *Visiting Langston*, 2003
Joyce Carol Thomas, *The Blacker the Berry*, 2008

216

SHIRLEY HUGHES, Author/Illustrator

Don't Want to Go!

(London: Bodley Head, 2010)

Story type: Young Readers
Subject(s): Family; Children; Psychology

Age range(s): 3 - 5+
Major character(s): Lily, Child (toddler); Mum, Mother (of Lily); Dad, Father (of Lily); Melanie, Friend (of Mum and Dad), Mother (of Sam and Jack); Sam, Baby, Son (of Melanie), Brother (of Jack); Jack, Son (of Melanie), Brother (of Sam)

Summary: Author and illustrator Shirley Hughes follows stubborn toddler Lily as she reluctantly spends the day at a neighbor's house. With Mum sick and Dad needed at work, Lily must leave the familiar surroundings of home to spend the day with family friend Melanie. Although Lily is adamant that she doesn't want to go, she gradually warms up to Melanie's calm demeanor. When she first arrives at Melanie's, Lily hides under a table. As the day progresses, however, she begins to enjoy Melanie's fun activities and interacts with baby Sam, his brother Jack, and the family dog. By the time Dad arrives, Lily doesn't want to go home.

Where it's reviewed:
Bulletin of the Center for Children's Books, November 2010, page 134
Horn Book Magazine, Nov/Dec 2010, page 74
Publishers Weekly, September 27, 2010, page 56
School Library Journal, November 2010, page 72

Other books by the same author:
Olly and Me 123, 2009
Rhymes for Annie Rose, 2006
Olly and Me, 2004
Annie Rose Is My Little Sister, 2003
Alfie and the Birthday Surprise, 1998

Other books you might like:
Mo Willems, *Knuffle Bunny: A Cautionary Tale*, 2004

217

SHIRLEY HUGHES, Author/Illustrator

The Christmas Eve Ghost

(Somerville, Massachusetts: Candlewick Press, 2010)

Subject(s): Holidays; Ghosts; Christmas

Age range(s): 6 - 9+
Major character(s): Bronwen, Child, Sister (of Dylan); Dylan, Child, Brother (of Bronwen); Mam, Seamstress, Mother (of Bronwen and Dylan), Widow(er)
Time period(s): 20th century; 1930s
Locale(s): Liverpool, England

Summary: *The Christmas Eve Ghost* is an uplifting holiday picture book for young readers from award-winning author and illustrator, Shirley Hughes. Life is tough for young Bronwen and Dylan in Liverpool in the early 20th century. Their widowed mom works long hours as a seamstress and launderer to provide for the family. Mam tells spooky stories about ghosts and goblins to the children and warns them about the religious neighbors, the O'Rileys. One day, while Mam is at work, Bronwen and Dylan hear a scary sound that sends them running to the neighbors, where they discover a wonderful blessing for the whole family.

Where it's reviewed:
Booklist, November 1, 2010, page 75
Horn Book Magazine, Nov/Dec 2010, page 63
School Library Journal, October 2010, page 72

Other books you might like:
Kate DiCamillo, *Great Joy*, 2007
Karen Hesse, *Spuds*, 2008
Eric A. Kimmel, *The Spider's Gift: A Ukrainian Christmas Story*, 2010
Katie Smith Milway, *One Hen: How One Small Loan Made a Big Difference*, 2008
Jeanette Winter, *Nasreen's Secret School: A True Story from Afghanistan*, 2009

218

PATRICIA INTRIAGO, Author/Illustrator

Dot

(New York: Farrar, Straus and Giroux, 2011)

Story type: Young Readers
Subject(s): Humor; Rhyme

Age range(s): 3 - 6+

Summary: Graphic designer Patricia Intriago enters the field of children's books with this simply illustrated volume. A few lines indicate "fast dot" is indeed a speedy fellow, while "slow dot" lags behind. On other pages, dots themselves are altered. A "loud" dot, for example, is missing a large wedge, the gap resembling a wide-open mouth. A few photographs, such as one of a Dalmatian, add visual interest. Much of the book is in black and white. The simple rhyming text grows progressively thoughtful until it's time to give the dots a rest.

Where it's reviewed:
Bulletin of the Center for Children's Books, October 2011, page 85
Horn Book Magazine, September/October 2011, page 67
Publishers Weekly, July 18, 2011, page 149
School Library Journal, August 2011, page 76

Other books you might like:
Keith Baker, *No Two Alike*, 2011
Valorie Fisher, *Everything I Need to Know before I'm Five*, 2011
Ginger F. Guy, *Perros! Perros! Dogs! Dogs!*, 2006
Dr. Seuss, *The Foot Book: Dr. Seuss's Wacky Book of Opposites*, 1968
Salina Yoon, *Opposnakes: A Lift-the-Flap Book About Opposites*, 2009

219

ANNE ISAACS
PAUL O. ZELINSKY, Illustrator

Dust Devil

(New York: Schwartz & Wade Books, 2010)

Subject(s): Folklore; Horses; Human-animal relationships
Age range(s): 5 - 8+
Major character(s): Swamp Angel, Woodsman (woman); Dust Devil, Horse; Backward Bart, Outlaw
Time period(s): 19th century
Locale(s): Montana, United States

Summary: *Dust Angel*, an imaginative and adventurous picture book for young readers, is the follow-up to the Caldecott Honor-winning *Swamp Angel* from author Anne Isaacs. Swamp Angel, a brave and powerful wood-swoman, has outgrown the state of Tennessee, so she travels west in search of a more spacious place. She settles in Montana, a large land filled with breathtaking prairies and strong storms. It doesn't take long for Swamp Angel to find a pal in the form of a horse named Dust Devil. When a wicked outlaw named Backward Bart starts wreaking havoc on the prairie, Swamp Angel and Dust Devil must join forces to thwart the villain.

Where it's reviewed:
Horn Book Magazine, November/December 2010, page 74
New York Times Book Review, October 17, 2010, page 16
Publishers Weekly, August 9, 2010, page 52
School Library Journal, September 2010, page 126

Other books by the same author:
Swamp Angel, 1994

Other books you might like:
Steven Kellogg, *Sally Ann Thunder Ann Whirlwind Crockett: A Tall Tale*, 1995
Jerdine Nolen, *Thunder Rose*, 2003
Phyllis Root, *Paula Bunyan*, 2009
Robert D. San Souci, *Cut from the Same Cloth: American Women of Myth, Legend, and Tall Tale*, 1993

220

JENNIFER RICHARD JACOBSON
ABBY CARTER, Illustrator

Andy Shane and the Barn Sale Mystery

(Somerville, Massachusetts: Candlewick Press, 2009)

Series: Andy Shane Series. Book 5
Subject(s): Detective fiction; Friendship; Gifts
Age range(s): 5 - 8+
Major character(s): Andy Shane, Child, Detective—Amateur; Dolores Starbuckle, Friend (of Andy); Granny Webb, Grandmother (of Andy)
Time period(s): 21st century; 2000s
Locale(s): United States

Summary: *Andy Shane and the Barn Sale Mystery*, the fifth book in Jennifer Richard Jacobson's Andy Shane series, finds the child sleuth on the hunt for his grandmother's beloved binoculars. When Andy finds a binocular case he knows would be an ideal birthday gift for his grandmother, he joins forces with his friend Dolores and holds a barn sale in order to raise the necessary funds. But in the chaos of the sale, the binoculars are sold. Now Andy and Dolores must track down the missing binoculars in time for Granny Webb's birthday. This volume includes illustrations by Abby Carter.

Where it's reviewed:
Horn Book Guide, Spring 2010, page 59
School Library Journal, September 2009, page 85

Other books by the same author:
Andy Shane Hero At Last, 2010
Andy Shane and the Queen of Egypt, 2008
Andy Shane is NOT In Love, 2008
Andy Shane and the Pumpkin Trick, 2006
Andy Shane and the Very Bossy Dolores Starbuckle, 2005

Other books you might like:
Jon Agee, *Nothing*, 2007
Joe Cepeda, *The Swing*, 2006
O. Henry, *The Gift of the Magi*, 1997
Jeanne Steig, *Fleas!*, 2008

221

PAUL B. JANECZKO, Editor
CHRIS RASCHKA, Illustrator

A Foot In the Mouth

(Somerville, Massachussets: Candlewick Press, 2009)

Subject(s): Poetry

Age range(s): 10 - 14+

Summary: Here are thirty-eight poems all selected for their sounds. Some contain sounds one speaker may make; others are for two or three readers or even a full chorus. Janeczko also includes limericks, list poems, and even a selection from Macbeth. But what these poems all have in common is sound: sounds of readers, sounds in the rhythms and rhymes, and sounds of nonsense words. "Squirrel and Acorn" by Beverly McLoughland showcases a squirrel's conversation with itself; "Us Two" by A. A. Milne covers a conversation with Christopher Robin and Pooh; and Sandra Cisneros's "Good Hot Dogs" brings readers the sounds of eating — in both Spanish and English. Raschka's impressionistic watercolors are vibrant, capturing the mood of each poem.

Where it's reviewed:
Booklist, February 15, 2009, page 80
Bulletin of the Center for Children's Books, February 2009, page 243
Horn Book Magazine, March/April 2009, page 209
Publishers Weekly, January 5, 2009, page 50
School Library Journal, March 2009, page 164

Other books you might like:
Bernice E. Cullinan, *A Jar of Tiny Stars: Poems by*

NCTE Award-Winning Poets, 1996
Paul Fleischman, *Joyful Noise: Poems for Two Voices*, 1988
J. Patrick Lewis, *Arithme-Tickle: An Even Number of Odd Riddle Rhymes*, 2002
Jack Prelutsky, *The Dragons Are Singing Tonight*, 1993

222

MINA JAVAHERBIN
A.G. FORD, Illustrator

Goal!

(Somerville, Massachusetts: Candlewick Press, 2010)

Subject(s): Soccer; Friendship; Bullying

Age range(s): 7 - 9+
Major character(s): Ajani, Boy, Soccer Player
Time period(s): 21st century; 2010s
Locale(s): South Africa

Summary: In the picture story *Goal!* by Mina Javaherbin, the game of soccer provides a source of self-esteem for a group of poor boys in South Africa. Ajani and his friends love to play soccer, despite the threats of violence in the streets of the neighborhood. When Ajani wins a federation-size soccer ball at school, the boys are further inspired to improve their game. But their game attracts the attention of a band of bullies, who threaten the younger boys. A smart maneuver by Ajani conceals the new ball from the thugs, but the danger of everyday life in the neighborhood remains. Illustrations by A.G. Ford capture the energy of the boys' game. First book.

Where it's reviewed:
Booklist, March 1, 2010, page 77
Horn Book Guide, Fall 2010, page 302
Publishers Weekly, March 15, 2010, page 52
School Library Journal, February 2010, page 88

Other books by the same author:
The Secret Message, 2010

Other books you might like:
Lesa Cline-Ransome, *Young Pele: Soccer's First Star*, 2007
Gail Gibbons, *My Soccer Book*, 2000
Clive Gifford, *The Kingfisher Soccer Encyclopedia*, 2006
Rachel Isadora, *At the Crossroads*, 1991
Rich Wallace, *Kickers Book 1: The Ball Hogs*, 2010

223

MARTIN JENKINS
VICKY WHITE, Illustrator

Can We Save the Tiger?

(Somerville, Massachusetts: Candlewick Press, 2011)

Subject(s): Animals; Endangered species; Wildlife conservation

Age range(s): 5 - 8+

Summary: This nonfiction work for young readers provides a detailed look at some of Earth's most beautiful creatures—all of which are in danger of disappearing forever. Author Martin Jenkins and illustrator Vicky White introduce readers to tigers, ground iguanas, white-rumped vultures, and other animals whose fates are closely linked to human activities that upset the balance of the natural world. Jenkins explains how people can both hurt and help threatened animals and uses the uplifting story of the American bison—which bounced back from the brink of extinction—to show that change is possible. Jenkins maintains a kid-friendly tone throughout the book, and White's illustrations capture each animal in impeccable detail. Jenkins and White also collaborated on the book *Ape*.

Where it's reviewed:
Horn Book Magazine, May/June 2011, page 115
Publishers Weekly, January 3, 2011, page 50
School Library Journal, March 2011, page 143

Other books by the same author:
Ape, 2007
The Emperor's Egg, 1999

Other books you might like:
Frances Barry, *Let's Save the Animals: A Flip the Flap Book*, 2010
Nick Dowson, *Tracks of a Panda*, 2007
Jean Craighead George, *The Wolves Are Back*, 2008
Kathryn Lasky, *Interrupted Journey: Saving Endangered Sea Turtles*, 2001
Patrick McDonnell, *Me . . . Jane*, 2011

224

STEVE JENKINS, Author/Illustrator

Bones: Skeletons and How They Work

(New York: Scholastic, 2010)

Subject(s): Biology; Anatomy; Animals

Age range(s): 7 - 10+

Summary: Author Steve Jenkins guides young readers through a fun and exciting exploration of bones. Jenkins introduces inquiring young minds to just about every type of bone in the human body, including the bones of the skull, hands, feet, ribs, vertebrae, and more. In addition, Jenkins provides images and illustrations that compare human bones to their counterparts in other animal species such as snakes, elephants, whales, and even dinosaurs. Jenkins doesn't stop after describing the bones themselves, however. He also covers other bone-related topics such as skeletal symmetry, joints, the science of movement, and other bony trivia.

Where it's reviewed:
Bulletin of the Center for Children's Books, September 2010, page 25
Horn Book Magazine, July/August 2010, page 135
Romantic Times, July 2010, page 102
Science Books & Film, November 2010, page 299

Other books by the same author:
Dogs and Cats, 2007
Living Color, 2007
Prehistoric Actual Size, 2005
Actual Size, 2004
Life on Earth: The Story of Evolution, 2002

Other books you might like:
Cynthia DeFelice, *The Dancing Skeleton*, 1989
Kelly Milner Halls, *Dinosaur Mummies: Beyond Bare-Bones Fossils*, 2003
Donna M. Jackson, *The Bone Detectives: How Forensic Anthropologists Solve Crimes and Uncover Mysteries of the Dead*, 1996
Seymour Simon, *Bones: Our Skeleton System*, 1998
Charlotte Wilcox, *Mummies, Bones and Body Parts*, 2000

225

STEVE JENKINS, Author/Illustrator

Down, Down, Down: A Journey to the Bottom of the Sea

(Boston, Massachusetts: Houghton Mifflin Harcourt, 2009)

Subject(s): Oceanography; Octopuses; Sharks

Age range(s): 7 - 10+

Summary: In *Down, Down, Down: A Journey to the Bottom of the Sea*, Steve Jenkins leads readers on a voyage to the bottom of the earth's oceans. Jenkins utilizes detailed cut-paper illustrations to render the many strange creatures that live in the oceans and provides facts about each of them. He begins above the ocean, noting some of the birds that fly above the seas and some of the animals that can leap out of the water. From there, he slowly descends into the waters, describing the different types of creatures found at each level of the sea. Sharks, jellyfish, octopuses, whales, filter feeders, and many other types of animals are explored. A sidebar on each page keeps track of how deep into the ocean the animals on each page are and the colors of the papers Jenkins uses for his illustrations get darker and darker in turn. Endnotes give further information about the many sea creatures in the depths of the ocean.

Where it's reviewed:
Booklist, April 1 2009, page 35
Bulletin of the Center for Children's Books, July/August 2009, page 431
Horn Book Magazine, May/June 2009, page 325
New York Times Book Review, May 10, 2009, page 16
School Library Journal, April 2009, page 149

Other books by the same author:
Sisters and Brothers: Sibling Relationships in the Animal World, 2008
Almost Gone: the World's Rarest Animals, 2006
What Do You Do With A Tail Like This?, 2003
Hottest, Coldest, Highest, Deepest, 1998
Biggest Strongest and Fastest, 1995

Other books you might like:
Jennifer Berne, *Manfish*, 2008

Leslie Bulion, *At the Sea Floor Cafe: Odd Ocean Critter Poems*, 2011
Sneed B. Collard, *The Deep-Sea Floor*, 2003

226

TONY JOHNSTON
YUYI MORALES, Illustrator

My Abuelita

(Boston: Houghton Mifflin Harcourt, 2009)

Story type: Young Readers
Subject(s): Grandparents; Intergenerational relations; Grandmothers

Age range(s): 3 - 7+

Summary: In this children's book, author Tony Johnston tells the story of a young boy and the daily routine he shares with his grandmother. The boy and his grandmother share a Mexican heritage, and the author describes their cultural identity through their various tasks and customs. Along the way, the boy reveals that his grandmother, his *abuelita*, has some very important work ahead of her—and she needs certain items in order to complete this work. But what exactly is this job that is so important? Spanish words are included with English definitions to help young readers identify objects in both languages. This book is illustrated by Yuyi Morales.

Where it's reviewed:
Booklist, August 1, 2009, page 80
Horn Book Guide, Spring 2010, page 30
Publishers Weekly, August 31, 2009, page 55
School Library Journal, August 2009, page 78

Other books by the same author:
Day of the Dead, 1997
The Quilt Story, 1985

Other books you might like:
Arthur Dorros, *Abuela*, 1991
Lucia M. Gonzalez, *The Storyteller's Candle/La velita de los cuentos*, 2008
Ginger Foglesong Guy, *My Grandma/Mii Abuelita*, 2001
Juan Felipe Herrera, *Grandma and Me at the Flea, Los Meros Meros Remateros*, 2002
Gary Soto, *Too Many Tamales*, 1993

227

TONY JOHNSTON
STACY INNERST, Illustrator

Levi Strauss Gets a Bright Idea: A Fairly Fabricated Story of a Pair of Pants

(Boston: Houghton Children's Books, 2011)

Subject(s): United States history; Biographies; Clothing

Age range(s): 5 - 8+

Summary: Author Tony Johnston weaves a tall-tale account of Levi Strauss's invention of blue jeans in this picture story for young readers. Based on the limited information available about Strauss, Johnston's humorous account follows the New York tailor as he arrives in California, where gold fever has attracted men from all over the country, in 1853. Unfortunately, many of those men are mining in tattered pants, in their underwear, or in the nude. Traditional trousers are no match for the rugged conditions of the West. But Levi Strauss has an ingenious plan to remedy the pants problem. Using tent canvas and his tailoring expertise, Strauss creates blue jeans—a durable clothing item for gold miners that becomes a part of American history and culture. Stacy Innerst enhances Johnston's tale with acrylic on denim illustrations.

Where it's reviewed:
Booklist, September 15, 2011, page 70
Publishers Weekly, July 18, 2011, page 151
School Library Journal, August 2011, page 77

Other books by the same author:
The Cowboy and the Black Eyed Pea, 1996
Alice Nizzy Nazzy, 1995
The Soup Bone, 1992

Other books you might like:
Laurie Winn Carlson, *Boss of the Plains: The Hat That Won the West*, 1998
Sid Fleischman, *By the Great Horn Spoon!*, 1963
John Frank, *The Toughest Cowboy: Or How the Wild West Was Tamed*, 2004
James Rumford, *Don't Touch My Hat*, 2007

228

LYNNE JONELL

The Secret of Zoom

(New York: Henry Holt, 2009)

Subject(s): Adventure; Orphans; Fantasy
Age range(s): 9 - 12+
Major character(s): Christina, 10-Year-Old; Dr. Adnoid, Father (of Christina), Scientist; Beth Adnoid, Mother (of Christina), Scientist (geologist); Lenny Loompski, Villain
Time period(s): 21st century; 2000s
Locale(s): Starkian Mountains, Earth

Summary: In *The Secret of Zoom* by Lynne Jonell, 10-year-old Christina lives in a huge stone house near the Starkian Mountain Ridge and the dark forest that holds Loompski Labs and the Loompski Orphan Home. The lab is where Christina's father, Dr. Adnoid, works—and where her mother allegedly died in an explosion. The orphanage is off-limits to Christina. When she befriends one of the orphans, a boy named Taft, she learns of a hidden tunnel used to transport the children to the mines where they dig for zoom—an explosive new fuel. As Christina works to expose Lenny Loompski's wicked scheme she also discovers the truth about her mother's disappearance.

Where it's reviewed:
Booklist, June 1, 2009, page 57

Bulletin of the Center for Children's Books, December 2009, page 158

Horn Book Guide, Spring 2010, page 73

School Library Journal, November 2009, page 112

Other books by the same author:

Emmy and the Incredible Shrinking Rat, 2007

Other books you might like:

Glenn Dakin, *The Society of Unrelenting Vigilance*, 2009

Victoria Forester, *The Girl Who Could Fly*, 2008

Gordon Korman, *The Emperor's Code: The 39 Clues, Book 8*, 2010

Tim Lott, *Fearless*, 2007

Trenton Lee Stewart, *The Mysterious Benedict Society*, 2007

229

CARRIE JONES
MARK OLDROYD, Illustrator

Sarah Emma Edmonds Was a Great Pretender: The True Story of a Civil War Spy

(Minneapolis, Minnesota: Carolrhoda Books, 2011)

Subject(s): Biographies; Spies; Wars

Age range(s): 6 - 9+

Summary: This biography by author Carrie Jones and illustrator Mark Oldroyd tells the story of a woman who spent most of her life pretending to be someone else. Sarah Emma Edmonds grew up in Canada, but she came to the United States at the start of the Civil War. Sarah wanted to be in on the action of the Civil War rather than on the sidelines. She pretended to be a man named Frank Thompson so she could serve as a nurse in the war. When the Union Army needed someone to act as a spy, Sarah decided that she wanted to take on the challenge. She soon began disguising herself as many different people, including an African American slave and an Irish peddler. Sarah was very brave and put herself in a number of dangerous situations so she could help the Union cause.

Where it's reviewed:

Booklist, April 15, 2011, page 48

Bulletin of the Center for Children's Books, May 2011, page 424

Horn Book Magazine, July/August 2011, page 170

School Library Journal, April 2011, page 161

Other books you might like:

Marissa Moss, *Nurse, Soldier, Spy: The Story of Sarah Edmonds, a Civil War Hero*, 2011

Patricia Polacco, *Pink and Say*, 1994

Anita Silvey, *I'll Pass For Your Comrade: Women Soldiers in the Civil War*, 2008

230

MARCIA THORNTON JONES
C.B. DECKER, Illustrator

Ratfink

(New York: Dutton Children's Books, 2010)

Subject(s): Conduct of life; Grandfathers; Old age

Age range(s): 9 - 11+

Major character(s): Logan Malone, 10-Year-Old; Grandpa, Grandfather (of Logan); Emily Scott, Classmate (of Logan); Malik, Friend (of Logan)

Time period(s): 21st century; 2010s

Locale(s): United States

Summary: In *Ratfink* by Marci Thornton Jones, a ten-year-old boy faces new challenges when his aging grandfather moves in with his family. Logan Malone's school career has been less than successful so far, but he hopes to make fifth grade a turning point. The unpredictable behavior of his grandfather, who has Alzheimer's disease, complicates Logan's social life—especially when an awkward photo Grandpa takes of Logan ends up in the hands of mean girl, Emily. The only way Emily will keep the picture under wraps is if Logan rats on his friend Malik and reveals some damaging information he's been hiding.

Where it's reviewed:

Booklist, December 15. 2010, page 39

Horn Book Guide, Fall 2010, page 343

School Library Journal, February 2010, page 114

Other books you might like:

Sharon Creech, *Heartbeat*, 2004

Betsy Duffey, *Utterly Yours, Booker Jones*, 1995

Barbara O'Connor, *The Fantastic Secret of Owen Jester*, 2010

Barbara Park, *The Graduation of Jake Moon*, 2000

231

BARBARA JOOSSE
JAN JUTTE, Illustrator

Sleepover at Gramma's House

(New York: Philomel Books, 2010)

Subject(s): Grandmothers; Sleep; Children

Age range(s): 4 - 7+

Major character(s): Granddaughter, Granddaughter, Child; Gramma, Grandmother, Artist

Time period(s): 21st century; 2010s

Locale(s): United States

Summary: *Sleepover at Gramma's House* is a fun and lively picture book for young readers from author Barbara Joosse. The story follows the exciting adventure of spending a night with grandmother. There is a lot to do before Granddaughter can head over to Gramma's house, like packing her suitcase and saying goodbye to her family. Once she arrives at Gramma's house, Granddaughter has a fun-filled day of dancing, painting, and partying before it's time for bed. Filled with vivid and colorful illustrations by Jan Jutte, *Sleepover at Gramma's House* is a charming story for children to prepare them for a night away from home.

Where it's reviewed:
Booklist, May 1, 2010, page 85
Bulletin of the Center for Children's Books, June 2010, page 439
Horn Book Guixs, Fall 2010, page 283
Publishers Weekly, April 26, 2010, page 105
School Library Journal, October 2010, page 81

Other books by the same author:
In the Night Garden, 2008
Grandma Calls Me Beautiful, 2006
Ghost Wings, 2001

Other books you might like:
Maya Ajmera, *Our Grandparents: A Global Album*, 2010
Kelly Bennett, *Your Daddy Was Just Like You*, 2010
Mary Ann Hoberman, *I'm Going to Grandma's*, 2007
Kate Lum, *What! Cried Granny: An Almost Bedtime Story*, 1999
Bernard Waber, *Ira Sleeps Over*, 1972

232

LITA JUDGE, Author/Illustrator

Red Sled

(New York: Atheneum Books for Young Readers, 2011)

Story type: Young Readers
Subject(s): Adventure; Winter; Friendship

Age range(s): 3 - 7+

Summary: A child returns home after a day of winter play and leaves a red sled outside for the night. As the forest grows dark, the animals venture out. Soon a bear swipes the red sled and sets off on a run. A rabbit goes along for the ride. In no time at all the sled is swooshing along carrying the bear, rabbit, and a moose. Some young raccoons and other creatures hop on as the sled races by. The minimal text consists entirely of sounds, including "Ssssssffft" and "Whoa!" Author and illustrator Lita Judge brings the action to life with vivid watercolor illustrations.

Where it's reviewed:
Publishers Weekly, October 17, 2011, page 66
School Library Journal, October 2011, page 110

Other books by the same author:
Strange Creatures: The Story of Walter Rothschild and His Museum, 2011
Pennies for Elephants, 2009

Other books you might like:
Jim Aylesworth, *The Mitten*, 2009
Kim Norman, *Ten on the Sled*, 2010
Cynthia Rylant, *Snow*, 2008
Komako Sakai, *The Snow Day*, 2009

233

MAVIS JUKES

The New Kid

(New York: Alfred A. Knopf, 2011)

Story type: Young Readers
Subject(s): Travel; Schools; Friendship

Age range(s): 7 - 9+
Major character(s): Carson Blum, Friend (of Weston), 8-Year-Old; Weston Walker, Friend (of Carson)
Time period(s): 21st century; 2010s
Locale(s): El Cerrito, California

Summary: Eight-year-old Carson Blum moves with his father, an attorney, to El Cerrito, California. He is reluctant to leave behind his life in Pasadena—his grandparents, private school, and two best friends. At his new public school, Carson struggles to make new friends and adjust to his surroundings. Things get easier when he develops a kinship with the class pet, Mr. Nibblenose the rat. When Mr. Nibblenose disappears, Carson searches for him. Along the way, he discovers the culprit to the missing lunch mystery and finds a friend in his classmate Weston Walker—even though Weston likes to tell tall tales and gets in trouble at school. Carson finds that his new home and school may not be so bad after all.

Where it's reviewed:
Booklist, December 15, 2011, page 57
Horn Book Magazine, January/February 2012, page 93
Publishers Weekly, October 17, 2011, page 68
School Library Journal, December 2011, page 86

Other books by the same author:
Smoke, 2009
The Guy Book: An Owner's Manual (Maintenance, Safety, and Operating Instructions for Teens), 2002
It's a Girl Thing: How to Stay Healthy, Safe and in Charge, 1996
Blackberries in the Dark, 1994
Like Jake and Me, 1987

Other books you might like:
Kate Banks, *Howie Bowles, Secret Agent*, 1999
Betsy Duffey, *Hey, New Kid!*, 1996
Maggie Lewis, *Morgy Makes His Move*, 1999
Lincoln Peirce, *Big Nate: In a Class by Himself*, 2010
Jack Prelutsky, *The New Kid on the Block: Poems*, 1984

234

SUZANNE TRIPP JURMAIN
LARRY DAY, Illustrator

Worst of Friends: Thomas Jefferson, John Adams, and the True Story of an American Feud

(New York: Dutton Children's Books, 2011)

Subject(s): History; Politics; Presidents (Government)
Age range(s): 6 - 9+

Summary: Suzanne Tripp Jurmain shares the story of the friendship and the rivalry between two of America's Founding Fathers. John Adams and Thomas Jefferson were very good friends, but they also had very different ideas about how the new country should be run. Jurmain explains to young readers that Adams and Jefferson had differences of opinion about many different subjects. They even started America's first political parties to help gain support for their respective beliefs. The book notes that the two men stopped speaking for a number of years because of their differences. Because of their friendship, however, they eventually reconciled. Larry Day provided illustrations for this volume.

Where it's reviewed:
Booklist, December 1, 2011, page 51
Publishers Weekly, October 24, 2011, page 53
School Library Journal, November 2011, page 100

Other books by the same author:
George Did It, 2006

Other books you might like:
David A. Adler, *A Picture Book of John and Abigail Adams*, 2010
Dennis Brindell Fradin, *Duel!: Burr and Hamilton's Deadly War of Words*, 2008
James Giblin, *Thomas Jefferson: A Picture Book Biography*, 1994
Barbara Kerley, *Those Rebels, John and Tom*, 2012

235

NORTON JUSTER
G. BRIAN KARAS, Illustrator

Neville

(New York: Schwartz & Wade Books, 2011)

Story type: Young Readers
Subject(s): Friendship; Children; Neighborhoods

Age range(s): 5 - 8+

Summary: Caldecott winner Norton Juster, author of the beloved children's book *The Phantom Tollbooth*, teams up with award-winning illustrator G. Brian Karas in this humorous picture book for young readers. A boy is devastated when he has to move to a new town with his family. He's feeling rather lonely, not knowing a single kid in the neighborhood, so his mother encourages him to take a walk. While exploring the block, the boy discovers a rather unconventional way of meeting the neighborhood kids and earning their friendship. His bizarre activities are chronicled with whimsical and colorful illustrations from Karas.

Where it's reviewed:
Booklist, October 15, 2011, page 44
Horn Book Magazine, September/October 2011, page 68
Publishers Weekly, August 15, 2011, page 70
School Library Journal, September 2011, page 123

Other books by the same author:
The Odious Ogre, 2010
Sourpuss and Sweetie Pie, 2008
The Hello Goodbye Window, 2005

Other books you might like:
Maggie Lewis, *Morgy Makes His Move*, 1999
Marjorie Weinman Sharmat, *Gila Monsters Meet You at the Airport*, 1980
Mark Siegel, *Moving House*, 2011
Judith Viorst, *Alexander, Who's Not (Do You Hear Me? I Mean It!) Going to Move*, 1995

236

KIMIKO KAJIKAWA
ED YOUNG, Illustrator

Tsunami!

(New York: Philomel Books, 2009)

Subject(s): Natural disasters; Folklore; Japanese (Asian people)

Age range(s): 4 - 7+
Major character(s): Ojisan, Wealthy, Farmer
Locale(s): Japan

Summary: Kimiko Kajikawa's *Tsunami!* chronicles the lifesaving adventures of Ojisan, a rich farmer in the Japanese countryside. One day while tending his fields, Ojisan looks out across the mountains to the sea, where he is horrified to see a tidal wave forming. Determined to help the villagers and lead everyone to safety, he sacrifices his own welfare (and income) and sets his rice paddies on fire. This alerts the villagers to the impending catastrophe, and Ojisan's heroics do not go overlooked. *Tsunami!* includes illustrations by Ed Young.

Where it's reviewed:
Bulletin of the Center for Children's Books, January 2009, page 205
Horn Book Magazine, March/April 2009, page 182
School Library Journal, January 2009, page 76

Awards the book has won:
Aesop Prize: Accolade List, 2009

Other books you might like:
Demi, *The Magic Pillow*, 2008
Craig Hatkoff, *Owen & Mzee: The True Story of a Remarkable Friendship*, 2006
Ann Morris, *Tsunami: Helping Each Other*, 2005
Mari C. Schuh, *Tsunamis*, 2010
Jeanette Winter, *Mama: A True Story in Which a Baby Hippo Loses His Mama During a Tsunami, but Finds a New Home, and a New Mama*, 2006

237

BRUCE ERIC KAPLAN, Author/Illustrator

Monsters Eat Whiny Children

(New York: Simon & Schuster, 2010)

Subject(s): Humor; Children; Monsters

Age range(s): 3 - 6+

Summary: In *Monsters Eat Whiny Children*, written and illustrated by Bruce Eric Kaplan, a group of monsters has captured the whiniest children they can find, but they cannot decide how to prepare them. They can't make a whiny child salad because they are out of paprika; they spill the flour for their whiny child cake; and can't get the grill lit to make whiny child burgers. Only after they finally decide what to make do they notice that the whiny children have escaped.

Where it's reviewed:
Booklist, August 1, 2010, page 60
Horn Book Guide, Spring 2011, page 32
Publishers Weekly, July 5, 2010, page 42
School Library Journal, September 2010, page 27

Other books you might like:
Hilaire Belloc, *Jim, Who Ran Away from His Nurse, and Was Eaten by a Lion*, 2010
A.W. Flaherty, *The Luck of the Loch Ness Monster: A Tale of Picky Eating*, 2007
Jenny Offill, *17 Things I'm Not Allowed to Do Anymore*, 2007

238

G. BRIAN KARAS, Author/Illustrator

The Village Garage

(New York: Henry Holt and Co., 2010)

Subject(s): Seasons; Urban life; Weather

Age range(s): 3 - 7+
Time period(s): 21st century; 2010s

Summary: G. Brian Karas's *The Village Garage* highlights the goings-on at a small local garage throughout a single year. With the changing of the seasons, the responsibilities of those who work at the garage change, and they band together to take care of the town's residents. In summer, there is a Fourth of July celebration in which the garage workers take part. In the fall, they rid the town of pesky leaves. Winter finds them removing snow from roads, while spring entails clearing the roads once more of dirt and the remnants of winter. Karas's illustrations accompany this volume.

Where it's reviewed:
Bulletin of the Center for Children's Books, July-August 2010, page 486
Horn Book Magazine, July/August 2010, page 91
School Library Journal, June 2010, page 76

Other books by the same author:
The Windy Day, 1998

Other books you might like:
Janet Lord, *Albert the Fix-It Man*, 2008
William Low, *Machines Go to Work*, 2009
Joyce Sidman, *Red Sings from Treetops: A Year in Colors*, 2009

239

JACQUELINE KELLY

The Evolution of Calpurnia Tate

(New York: Henry Holt, 2009)

Subject(s): Coming of age; Nature; Biology

Age range(s): 9 - 12+
Major character(s): Calpurnia Virginia Tate, 12-Year-Old, Naturalist
Time period(s): 19th century; 1890s (1899)
Locale(s): Texas, United States

Summary: In *The Evolution of Calpurnia Tate* by Jacqueline Kelly, a coming-of-age novel set in Texas at the turn of the century, 12-year-old Calpurnia Tate bucks the traditional role of a young woman and instead develops a keen interest in the natural world. Her outdoor explorations bring her closer to her crotchety grandfather, who is a distinguished naturalist. The two investigate different kinds of grasshoppers and even happen upon a previously undiscovered variety of legume, which they endeavor to get acknowledged by scientific authorities. Against the backdrop of her nature-fueled adventures, Calpurnia confronts the challenges of adolescence as she grows up with her six brothers in rural America. First novel.

Where it's reviewed:
Booklist, May 1 2009, page 80
Bulletin of the Center for Children's Books, July/August 2009, page 448
Horn Book Magazine, September/October 2009, page 565
School Library Journal, May 2009, page 110

Awards the book has won:
Blue Ribbon Awards: Fiction, 2009
Off the Cuff Awards, 2009
Josette Frank Award, 2010

Other books you might like:
Jen Bryant, *Ringside 1925: Views from the Scopes Trial*, 2008
Alice B. McGinty, *Darwin*, 2009
Gary D. Schmidt, *Lizzie Bright and the Buckminster Boy*, 2004
Catherine Thimmesh, *The Sky's the Limit: Stories of Discovery by Women and Girls*, 2002
Rosemary Wells, *Red Moon at Sharpsburg*, 2007

240

KATY KELLY
GILLIAN JOHNSON, Illustrator

Melonhead

(New York: Delacorte Press, 2009)

Subject(s): Inventions; Inventors; Humor

Age range(s): 8 - 10+
Major character(s): Adam "Melonhead" Melon, Inventor; Sam, Friend; Lucy Rose, Friend
Time period(s): 21st century; 2000s

Locale(s): Washington, District of Columbia

Summary: In Katy Kelly's *Melonhead*, Adam Melon, christened Melonhead by his pal Lucy Rose, is a world-class inventor—or so he likes to think. Melonhead loves coming up with new creations and experimenting with new ideas—with little regard for the disasters he leaves in his wake. But when it is announced that his class will be taking part in the school's science fair, he is elated. This is Melonhead's chance to show the world what an innovative inventor he is. Together with his friend Sam, he investigates all the nooks and crannies of Washington, D.C., trying to accumulate enough spare parts to put together the most awe-inspiring invention the school science fair has ever seen.

Where it's reviewed:
Bulletin of the Center for Children's Books, April 2009, page 327
Horn Book Guide, Fall 2009, page 374
School Library Journal, March 2009, page 118

Other books by the same author:
Melonhead and the Undercover Operation, 2011
Melonhead and the Big Stink, 2010
Lucy Rose: Working Myself to Pieces and Bits, 2007

Other books you might like:
Frances O'Roark Dowell, *Phineas L. MacGuire Erupts!: The First Experiment*, 2006
Jessica Scott Kerrin, *Martin Bridge: Out of Orbit!*, 2007
Megan McDonald, *Stink: The Incredible Shrinking Kid*, 2005
Graham Salisbury, *Calvin Coconut: Trouble Magnet*, 2009
Barbara Seuling, *Robert and the Great Pepperoni*, 2001

241

SHEILA M. KELLY
SHELLEY ROTNER, Author/Illustrator

Shades of People

(New York: Holiday House, 2009)

Subject(s): Social sciences

Age range(s): 5 - 8+

Summary: In *Shades of People*, authors Shelley Rotner and Sheila Kelly use simple text and photographs to demonstrate the range of human skin colors. Written for preschoolers and young elementary-age children, this engaging book depicts dozens of happy children with obviously different shades of skin tone, hair types, and facial structures. While the pictures reveal the unique nature of each person's physical appearance, the text reinforces the concept that skin is just a covering for the body that doesn't determine a person's inner qualities. Rather than focusing on race colors, *Shades of People* celebrates the countless skin tones that humans wear.

Where it's reviewed:
Booklist, August 1 2009, page 82
Horn Book Guide, Spring 2010, page 120

School Library Journal, September 2009, page 132

Other books by the same author:
Lots of Feelings, 2003
Lots of Dads, 1997
Lots of Moms, 1996
Faces, 1994

Other books you might like:
Rebecca Baines, *Your Skin Holds You In*, 2008
Nina Crews, *The Neighborhood Mother Goose*, 2004
Lee Bennett Hopkins, *Amazing Faces*, 2010
Grace Lin, *The Ugly Vegetables*, 1999

242

BARBARA KERLEY
EDWIN FOTHERINGHAM, Illustrator

The Extraordinary Mark Twain (According to Susy)

(New York: Scholastic, 2010)

Subject(s): Writers; Father-daughter relations; Humor

Age range(s): 7 - 10+

Summary: The daughter of Mark Twain narrates this fictionalized biography of her famous father. Barbara Kerley's *The Extraordinary Mark Twain (According To Susy)* finds 13-year-old Susy convinced that public perceptions of her father are inaccurate. He is not the consummate jokester everyone thinks him to be, but a wise and loving father who has imparted many valuable life lessons to his daughter. Through a journal she faithfully keeps, Susy presents an intimate look at the man behind the literary legend. This volume includes illustrations by Edwin Fotheringham.

Where it's reviewed:
Booklist, December 1, 2009, page 44
Horn Book Magazine, January/February 2010, page 101
New York Times Book Review, May 16, 2010, page 115
Publishers Weekly, December 14, 2009, page 59
School Library Journal, January 2010, page 76

Other books by the same author:
Walt Whitman: Words for America, 2004

Other books you might like:
Robert Burleigh, *The Adventures of Mark Twain by Huckleberry Finn*, 2011
Sid Fleischman, *The Trouble Begins at 8: A Life of Mark Twain in the Wild, Wild West*, 2008
Deborah Hopkinson, *Abe Lincoln Crosses a Creek: A Tall, Thin Tale (Introducing His Forgotten Frontier Friend)*, 2008
Kathryn Lasky, *A Brilliant Streak: The Making of Mark Twain*, 1998
Patricia MacLachlan, *Word After Word After Word*, 2010

243

LIZA KETCHUM

Newsgirl

(New York: Viking, 2009)

Subject(s): California Gold Rush, 1849; Newspapers; Friendship

Age range(s): 10 - 13+

Major character(s): Amelia Forrester, 12-Year-Old; Patrick, Friend (of Amelia), Orphan

Time period(s): 19th century; 1850s (1851)

Locale(s): San Francisco, California

Summary: Liza Ketchum's *Newgirl* is set in San Francisco in 1851, where 12-year-old Amelia Forrester has just arrived with her mother and her mother's best friend. While the adults set out to become working professionals in a world dominated by men, Amelia decides to sell newspapers. Her efforts, however, are met with failure. Nonplussed, Amelia disguises herself as a boy and, with her new friend Patrick, goes in search of a news story. Their quest leads them into a dangerous situation, but Amelia knows that the circumstances may just make for the biggest news story of the day.

Where it's reviewed:
Booklist, September 15, 2009, page 61
Horn Book Guide, Spring 2010, page 74
School Library Journal, September 2009, page 163

Other books by the same author:
The Gold Rush, 1996

Other books you might like:
Ann Bausum, *Muckrackers: How Ida Turbell, Upton Sinclair, and Lincoln Steffens Helped Expose Scandal, Inspire Reform, and Invent Investigative Journalism*, 2007
Karen Cushman, *The Ballad of Lucy Whipple*, 1996
Pat Derby, *Away to the Goldfields!*, 2004
Deborah Hopkinson, *Into the Firestorm: A Novel of San Francisco, 1906*, 2006
Tod Olson, *How to Get Rich in the California Gold Rush: An Adventurer's Guide to the Fabulous Riches Discovered in 1848*, 2008

244

RUKHSANA KHAN
SOPHIE BLACKALL, Illustrator

Big Red Lollipop

(New York: Viking, 2010)

Subject(s): Sisters; Birthdays; Conduct of life

Age range(s): 4 - 8+

Major character(s): Rubina, Sister (of Sana), Daughter (of Ami); Sana, Daughter (of Ami), Sister (of Rubina); Ami, Mother (of Rubina and Sana)

Time period(s): 21st century; 2010s

Summary: Rubina has just been invited to her first-ever birthday party. There's just one problem. Rubina's mother, Ami, insists that Rubina take her younger sister Sana to the party with her. The older daughter reluctantly agrees, but when Sana misbehaves at the festivities, Rubina is not invited to another party for a long while. Sana herself eventually receives an invitation to a birthday party, and while Ami insists again that the two girls go together, Rubina tries to convince her otherwise. Rukhsana Khan's *Big Red Lollipop* includes illustrations by Sophie Blackall.

Where it's reviewed:
Booklist, February 1, 2010, page 44
Horn Book Guide, Fall 2010, page 303
Publishers Weekly, March 1, 2010, page 49
School Library Journal, March 2010, page 120

Other books by the same author:
Silly Chicken, 2005

Awards the book has won:
Charlotte Zolotow Award, 2011
Golden Kite Awards: Picture Book Text, 2011

Other books you might like:
Kate Banks, *Monkeys and Dog Days*, 2008
Jeanne Birdsall, *Flora's Very Windy Day*, 2010
Jennifer LaRue Huget, *Thanks a LOT, Emily Post!*, 2009

245

SUSAN KIM
LAURENCE KLAVAN, Co-Author
PASCAL DIZIN, Illustrator

City of Spies

(New York: First Second, 2010)

Subject(s): Spies; World War II, 1939-1945; Adventure

Age range(s): 9 - 13+

Major character(s): Evelyn, Artist (comic book artist); Tony, Friend (of Evelyn)

Time period(s): 20th century; 1940s (1942)

Locale(s): New York, New York

Summary: In *City of Spies*, authors Susan Kim and Lawrence Klavan team up with illustrator Pascal Dizin to offer an original young adult spy story set in World War II-era New York City. Young Evelyn, a budding comic book artist, is sent to Manhattan to live with her aunt. There she meets her neighbor, Tony, and the two strike up a friendship. They soon set out to eradicate Nazi spies from the city's boroughs, but a questionable tip leads them squarely into a web of danger and deceit.

Where it's reviewed:
Booklist, March 15, 2010, page 60
Publishers Weekly, April 5, 2010, page 64
School Library Journal, May 2010, page 141

Other books by the same author:
Brain Camp, 2010

Other books you might like:
Herge, *The Crab with the Golden Claws*, 1974
Carla Jablonski, *Resistance*, 2010
Aaron Renier, *The Unsinkable Walker Bean*, 2010
J. Torres, *Alison Dare: Little Miss Adventures*, 2002

246

ELIZABETH CODY KIMMEL

The Reinvention of Moxie Roosevelt

(New York: Dial Books for Young Readers, 2010)

Subject(s): Identity; Self esteem; Boarding schools

Age range(s): 10 - 13+

Major character(s): Moxie Roosevelt Kipper, 13-Year-Old, Musician (pianist)

Time period(s): 21st century; 2010s

Locale(s): United States

Summary: *The Reinvention of Moxie Roosevelt* is a humorous novel for children and young adults from author Elizabeth Cody Kimmel. Thirteen-year old Moxie Roosevelt Kipper has spent her entire existence as an unnoticed, unremarkable girl. When she earns a music scholarship to Eaton Academy, an elite boarding school for girls, she's ready to start fresh in every way possible. Eager to take on a new identity, Moxie weighs her options as to the type of girl she wants to be. Keeping a journal of her progress, Moxie tries her hand at being an outspoken activist, an athletic sports junkie, a too-cool-for-school type, and a bohemian princess, but soon discovers that keeping a secret identity is far too much work and not that much fun.

Where it's reviewed:
Booklist, June 1, 2010, page 76
Bulletin of the Center for Children's Books, June 2010, page 441
Horn Book Guide, Fall 2010, page 344
School Library Journal, July 2010, page 91

Other books by the same author:
Spin the Bottle, 2008
Mary Ingalls on Her Own (Little House), 2007
Lily B. on the Brink of Paris, 2006
Lily B. on the Brink of Cool, 2003

Other books you might like:
Lindsey Leavitt, *Princess for Hire*, 2010
Robin Palmer, *Yours Truly, Lucy B. Parker: Girl vs. Superstar*, 2010
Janette Rallison, *It's a Mall World After All*, 2006
Gina Willner-Pardo, *The Hard Kind of Promise*, 2010

247

KEN KIMURA
YASURARI MURAKAMI, Illustrator

999 Tadpoles

(New York: NorthSouth, 2011)

Story type: Young Readers
Subject(s): Animals; Frogs; Family

Age range(s): 4 - 7+

Summary: Mother and father frog have a large family with 999 tadpoles. In fact, the family is so large that the small pond they live in no longer has enough room for everyone. Mother and father frog decide it's time for their big family to move to the big pond nearby. Although the big pond isn't that far away, the trip between the small pond and the big pond will be dangerous. Many different predators—including a hawk and a snake—are lurking about. Will the tadpoles and their parents make it safely to the big pond before something bad happens? This volume, written by Ken Kimura and illustrated by Yasurari Murakami, was first published in Japan in 2003.

Where it's reviewed:
Booklist, July 1, 2011, page 52
Horn Book Magazine, July/August 2011, page 130
New York Times Book Review, June 19, 2011, page 17
Publishers Weekly, April 11, 2011, page 49
School Library Journal, June 2011, page 88

Other books you might like:
Nic Bishop, *Nic Bishop Frogs*, 2008
Joy Cowley, *Red-Eyed Tree Frog*, 1999
Jean-Luc Fromental, *365 Penguins*, 2006
Ann Hassett, *Too Many Frogs!*, 2011

248

JEFF KINNEY

Diary of a Wimpy Kid: Cabin Fever

(New York: Amulet Books, 2011)

Series: Diary of a Wimpy Kid Series. Book 6
Subject(s): Adolescent interpersonal relations; Family; Weather

Age range(s): 9 - 12+

Major character(s): Greg Heffley, Son (of Susan and Frank), Brother (of Manny and Roderick); Roderick Heffley, Son (of Susan and Frank), Brother (of Greg and Manny); Manny Heffley, Brother (of Greg and Roderick), Son (of Susan and Frank); Susan Heffley, Mother (of Manny, Greg, and Roderick), Spouse (of Frank); Frank Heffley, Father (of Manny, Greg, and Roderick), Spouse (of Susan)

Summary: In the sixth book in Jeff Kinney's popular series, Greg Heffley is stuck inside with his entire family during the worst snowstorm he has ever seen. That means he not only has to put up with his parents' constant worrying about the weather, but also with Manny's whining and Rodrick's meanness. Worst of all, as the snow outside falls harder and harder with no sign of letting up, Greg finds himself dealing with a major case of claustrophobia. Will the Heffleys finally find relief before cabin fever sets in?

Other books by the same author:
Diary of a Wimpy Kid: Dog Days, 2009
Diary of a Wimpy Kid: Last Straw, 2009
Diary of a Wimpy Kid: Roderick Rules, 2008
Diary of a Wimpy Kid: Greg Heffley's Journal, 2007

Other books you might like:
Lincoln Peirce, *Big Nate: In a Class by Himself*, 2010
Janet Tashjian, *My Life as a Book*, 2010

249

MATTHEW KIRBY

The Clockwork Three

(New York: Scholastic, 2010)

Subject(s): Friendship; Adventure; Adolescent interpersonal relations

Age range(s): 10 - 13+

Major character(s): Giuseppe, Musician; Frederick, Apprentice (to a clockmaker); Hannah, Hotel Worker (maid)

Time period(s): 19th century

Locale(s): United States

Summary: The lives of three youths in the 19th century are fatefully linked in Matthew J. Kirby's *The Clockwork Three*. The orphan, Giuseppe plays his violin on the streets in order to get by, while Frederick works as an apprentice to an established clockmaker. Hannah is also trying to make ends meet, toiling as a hotel maid to bring money home to her family. Each one of these youngsters is sent on a treasure-hunting voyage that brings them together—and changes them forever. First novel.

Where it's reviewed:
Booklist, October 15, 2010, page 63
Bulletin of the Center for Children's Books, December 2010, page 192
Horn Book Guide, Spring 2011, page 75
School Library Journal, November 2010, page 119
Voice of Youth Advocates, February 2011, page 571

Other books by the same author:
Icefall, 2011

Other books you might like:
Karen Hesse, *Brooklyn Bridge*, 2008
Brian Selznick, *The Invention of Hugo Cabret: A Novel in Words and Pictures*, 2007
Matthew Skelton, *The Story of Cirrus Flux*, 2010

250

DAVID KLASS

Stuck on Earth

(New York: Farrar, Straus and Giroux, 2010)

Subject(s): Extraterrestrial life; Bullying; High schools

Age range(s): 9 - 12+

Major character(s): Tom Filber, 14-Year-Old, Bullied Child; Ketchvar III, Alien

Time period(s): 21st century; 2010s

Locale(s): New Jersey, United States

Summary: David Klass's *Stuck on Earth* charts the adventures of an extraterrestrial who occupies the mind of a bullied teenager. Ketchvar III comes to Earth with a huge mission: to decide whether the human race should be destroyed. To gain insight into the workings of humanity, he infiltrates the brain of geeky 14-year-old Tom Filber. As he sees the world through Tom's eyes, the alien becomes entangled in the day-to-day life of an American teenager, forcing him to learn firsthand the trials and tribulations of being human.

Where it's reviewed:
Booklist, December 15. 2009, page 36
Bulletin of the Center for Children's Books, April 2010, page 341
Horn Book Magazine, March/April 2010, page 60
New York Times Book Review, July 18. 2010, page 15
School Library Journal, February 2011, page 112

Other books you might like:
Adam Rex, *The True Meaning of Smekday*, 2007
Jordan Sonnenblick, *Dodger and Me*, 2008
Mark Teague, *The Doom Machine*, 2009
Sylvia Waugh, *Space Race*, 2000

251

JON KLASSEN, Author/Illustrator

I Want My Hat Back

(Somerville, Massachusetts: Candlewick Press, 2011)

Story type: Young Readers
Subject(s): Clothing; Bears; Animals

Age range(s): 5 - 8+

Summary: A bear has lost his hat, and he is determined to find it in this picture story by author and illustrator Jon Klassen. The bear begins searching for his hat, and he asks all the animals he sees if they have his hat. Although none of the animals has the bear's hat, a deer gives the bear a clue as to where his hat might be.

Where it's reviewed:
Booklist, November 1, 2011, page 77
Horn Book Magazine, November/December 2011, page 83
Publishers Weekly, July 4, 2011, page 63
School Library Journal, August 2011, page 78

Other books you might like:
William Bee, *Beware of the Frog*, 2008
P.D. Eastman, *Go, Dog. Go!*, 1961
Emily Gravett, *Wolves*, 2005
Oliver Jeffers, *The Incredible Book Eating Boy*, 2006
Jon Scieszka, *The True Story of the 3 Little Pigs*, 1989

252

KATE KLISE
M. SARAH KLISE, Illustrator

Stand Straight, Ella Kate

(New York: Dial Books, 2010)

Subject(s): Giants; United States history; Self confidence

Age range(s): 5 - 8+

Major character(s): Ella Kate Ewing, Teenager (who is 8 feet tall)

Time period(s): 19th century; 1870-1890 (1872-1890)

Locale(s): Missouri, United States

Summary: In *Stand Straight, Ella Kate*, Kate Klise tells the story of Ella Kate, a real-life giant from Missouri. When she was eight years old, Ella Kate realized she didn't fit under her desk at school as well as the other students. Her peers made jokes about her abnormal height, so as Ella continued to grow, she attempted to hide her tallness by slouching. When she reached the height of eight feet around her 17th birthday, Ella decided she should no longer be ashamed of her height and embraced it instead. In this picture book, which is based on a true story, young readers learn that it's okay to be different.

Where it's reviewed:
Booklist, June 1, 2010, page 100
Horn Book Guide, Fall 2010, page 441
New York Times Book Review, May 16, 2010, page 16
Publishers Weekly, April 26, 2010, page 107
School Library Journal, June 2010, page 76

Other books by the same author:
Little Rabbit and the Meanest Mother on Earth, 2010
Little Rabbit and the Night Mare, 2008
Imagine Harry, 2007
Why Do You Cry? Not a Sob Story, 2006

Other books you might like:
Dan Andreasen, *The Giant of Seville: A "Tall" Tale Based on a True Story*, 2006
Dick King-Smith, *The Twin Giants*, 2008
Kathleen Krull, *Wilma Unlimited: How Wilma Rudolph Became the World's Fastest Woman*, 1996
Deborah Kogan Ray, *Down the Colorado: John Wesley Powell, the One-Armed Explorer*, 2007

253

KATE KLISE

Grounded

(New York: Feiwel & Friends, 2010)

Subject(s): Grief; Family; Mystery

Age range(s): 9 - 12+

Major character(s): Daralynn Oakland, 12-Year-Old; Clem Monroe, Con Artist; Josie, Aunt (of Daralynn)

Time period(s): 20th century; 1970s

Locale(s): Digginsville, Missouri

Summary: Kate Klise's *Grounded* takes place in 1970s Missouri, where 12-year-old Daralynn Oakland is struggling to come to terms with the deaths of her father and two siblings in a plane crash. She was supposed to be with them that fateful day but was grounded for sneaking out without permission. Now Daralynn must deal with her overwhelming guilt as she attempts to move forward with her life. When her aunt gets involved with a mysterious stranger, Daralynn finds an outlet for her pent-up feelings and investigates the charming Clem Monroe—and discovers that he is a con artist of the highest caliber. In a letter to her deceased family members, she relays the story of what happens when she takes on Clem and sets out to save her small hometown.

Where it's reviewed:
Booklist, October 15, 2010, page 53

Bulletin of the Center for Children's Books, January 1, 2010, page 221
Horn Book Magazine, Nov/Dec 2010, page 93
Publishers Weekly, October 25, 2010, page 49
School Library Journal, February 2011, page 112

Other books by the same author:
Far from Normal, 2006
Deliver Us from Normal, 2005

Awards the book has won:
Blue Ribbon Awards: Fiction, 2010

Other books you might like:
Andrea Cheng, *Where Do You Stay?*, 2011
Kathryn Erskine, *Mockingbird*, 2010
Clare Vanderpool, *Moon over Manifest*, 2010
Deborah Wiles, *Each Little Bird That Sings*, 2005

254

KATE KLISE
M. SARAH KLISE, Illustrator

Dying to Meet You

(Boston: Harcourt, 2009)

Series: 43 Old Cemetery Road Series. Book 1
Subject(s): Writers; Haunted houses; Ghosts

Age range(s): 9 - 12+
Major character(s): Ignatius B. Grumply, Writer; Seymour, 11-Year-Old; Shadow, Cat; Olive, Spirit
Time period(s): 21st century; 2000s

Summary: In *Dying to Meet You*, sisters Kate Klise and M. Sarah Klise spin an entertaining tale of a crotchety old man and the strangers he encounters living in his house. When author Ignatius B. Grumply moves into a dilapidated old mansion, he just wants to work on his next book in peace. But those plans are thrown by the wayside when he discovers he has three uninvited house guests: an 11-year-old named Seymour, a cat called Shadow, and an anxious ghost named Olive. Can this ragtag group of strangers learn to get along—or is the big old house just not big enough for the lot of them?

Where it's reviewed:
Booklist, April 1, 2009, page 36
Bulletin of the Center for Children's Books, July-August 2009, page 449
Horn Book Magazine, May/June 2009, page 299
Publishers Weekly, April 13 2009, page 49
School Library Journal, May 2009, page 112

Other books by the same author:
Till Death Do Us Bark, 2011
Over My Dead Body, 2009

Other books you might like:
Sally Grindley, *Dear Max*, 2006
Chris Mould, *The Wooden Mile*, 2008
Dan Poblocki, *The Stone Child*, 2009
Helen Stringer, *Spellbinder*, 2009
Kristin Clark Venuti, *Leaving the Bellweathers*, 2009

255

JEFFREY KLUGER

Freedom Stone

(New York: Philomel Books, 2011)

Subject(s): Time travel; Slavery; Freedom

Age range(s): 10 - 12+

Major character(s): Lillie, 14-Year-Old, Slave, Sister (of Plato); Plato, 6-Year-Old, Slave, Brother (of Lillie); Bett, Aged Person, Slave (with magical powers)

Time period(s): 19th century; 1860s (1863)

Locale(s): Vicksburg, Mississippi; South Carolina, United States

Summary: In this young adult novel, author Jeffrey Kluger combines history and fantasy to spin a tale of a teenage slave determined to free her family. Lillie's family is trapped in the bonds of slavery. Her father agrees to fight for the Confederacy during the Civil War in exchange for his family's freedom. After his death during the Battle of Vicksburg, however, Lillie's master refuses to free the family, claiming that Lillie's father was a thief. In the meantime, Lillie learns that her master may sell her six-year-old brother, Plato, at auction. Determined to prove her father's innocence, keep her family intact, and gain freedom, Lillie enlists the help of Bett, a slave who bakes magical bread, and undertakes a difficult journey into the past to discover the truth about the events surrounding her father's death.

Where it's reviewed:
Booklist, February 1, 2011, page 72
Bulletin of the Center for Children's Books, February 2011, page 282
Publishers Weekly, November 29, 2011, page 50
School Library Journal, June 2011, page 122

Other books you might like:
Patricia Polacco, *January's Sparrow*, 2009

256

HILARY KNIGHT, Author/Illustrator
STEVEN KROLL, Co-Author

Nina in That Makes Me Mad!

(New York: Toon Books, 2011)

Story type: Young Readers
Subject(s): Anger; Children; Comic books

Age range(s): 4 - 8+
Major character(s): Nina, Girl

Summary: In this book for young readers, author and illustrator Hilary Knight brings to life the plight of Nina, who is not shy about expressing what makes her angry. Based on a text by Steven Kroll, the book features two-page spreads in a comic book format. On the left, Nina clearly states her frustration: "When you get mad at me and I didn't do it...that makes me mad!" On the right, Knight highlights an example of Nina's frustration—in this case, getting blamed for splashing water all over the bathroom when it was really Tony's fault. A helpful guide included in the book explains how to read comics with kids.

Where it's reviewed:
Booklist, October 15, 2011, page 37
School Library Journal, November 2011, page 152

Other books by the same author:
The Circus Is Coming, 2007
A Christmas Stocking Story, 2003
Where's Wallace?, 2000
A Firefly in a Fir Tree, 1994

Other books you might like:
Molly Bang, *When Sophie Gets Angry — Really, Really Angry. . .*, 1999
Jon Klassen, *I Want My Hat Back*, 2011
Mercer Mayer, *I Was So Mad*, 1983
Judith Viorst, *Alexander and the Terrible, Horrible, No Good, Very Bad Day*, 1972
Mo Willems, *The Pigeon Has Feelings, Too!*, 2005

257

ALETHEA KONTIS
BOB KOLAR, Illustrator

Alpha Oops!: H Is for Halloween

(Somerville, Massachusetts: Candlewick Press, 2010)

Subject(s): Halloween; Holidays; Humor

Age range(s): 5 - 8+

Summary: In *Alpha Oops! H Is for Halloween*, the letters of the alphabet rearrange themselves for a silly, scary holiday tribute. H comes first, of course, with the other letters following randomly, each dressed as a favorite Halloween character. In this mixed-up alphabet book, illustrated by Bob Kolar, B is for Boo, P is for pirate, O is for ogre, Y is for yeti, Z is for zombie, K is for kraken, N is for nightmare, U is for undead, and V is for vampire, while X has trouble deciding what he should be. As the book progresses, the letters arrange themselves in proper order along the bottom of the page.

Where it's reviewed:
Booklist, July 2010, page 64
Horn Book Guide, Spring 2011, page 34
New York Times Book Review, October 17, 2010, page 17
School Library Journal, August 2010, page 78

Other books by the same author:
Alpha Oops!: The Day Z Went First, 2006

Other books you might like:
Jef Czekaj, *A Call for a New Alphabet*, 2011
Maira Kalman, *What Pete Ate from A-Z: Where We Explore the English Alphabet (in Its Entirety) in Which a Certain Dog Devours a Myriad of Items Which He Should Not*, 2001
Alison McGhee, *Only a Witch Can Fly*, 2009
Judy Sierra, *The House That Drac Built*, 1995
Caroline Stutson, *By the Light of the Halloween Moon*, 1993

258

JIM KRIEG

Griff Carver, Hallway Patrol

(New York: Razorbill, 2010)

Subject(s): Humor; Middle schools; Crime

Age range(s): 9 - 12+

Major character(s): Griff Carver, Student—Middle School, 7th Grader (hall monitor)

Time period(s): 21st century; 2010s

Locale(s): United States

Summary: *Griff Carver, Hallway Patrol* is a humorous novel for young readers. The story, which reads like a purposefully overdramatic police procedural, is about Griff Carver, newly appointed hallway monitor at Rampart Middle School. Griff takes his job and badge a bit too seriously and isn't afraid to bust troublemakers, regardless of the cost to himself. When it becomes evident that an undercover crime ring is creating counterfeit hall passes, Griff is determined to get to the bottom of it, even if it means busting Marcus "The Smile" Volger, one of the coolest kids in school. First novel.

Where it's reviewed:
Booklist, May 1, 2010, page 53
Bulletin of the Center for Children's Books, June 2010, page 442
Horn Book Magazine, May/June 2010, page 85
Publishers Weekly, March 29, 2010, page 59
School Library Journal, March 2010, page 160

Other books you might like:
Josh Berk, *The Dark Days of Hamburger Halpin*, 2010
Carl Deuker, *Payback Time*, 2010
James Leck, *The Adventures of Jack Lime*, 2010
Chris Rylander, *The Fourth Stall*, 2011
Richard Sala, *Cat Burglar Black*, 2009

259

UMA KRISHNASWAMI
ABIGAIL HALPIN, Illustrator

The Grand Plan to Fix Everything

(New York: Atheneum Books for Young Readers, 2011)

Story type: Young Readers

Subject(s): Movies; Movie industry; Indians (Asian people)

Age range(s): 9 - 13+

Major character(s): Dini, Friend (of Maddie), 11-Year-Old; Maddie, Friend (of Dini)

Time period(s): 21st century; 2010s

Locale(s): Swapnagiri, India; Maryland, United States

Summary: Dini's family may be from India, but she has known suburban Maryland as home for her entire life. When Dini's mother is offered a job in India, however, Dini learns that she and her family will be moving to Swapnagiri, an Indian village, for a few years. Dini is sad to leave her best friend Maddie, but she is also excited because she might be able to meet her favorite Bollywood star, Dolly Singh. Life in Swapnagiri isn't exactly like life in Maryland, but Dini finds that her new home is actually a great place to live. She keeps in touch with Maddie through telephone calls and Internet chats. With any luck, Dini will make the most of her time in India, and she might even get to meet her favorite movie star.

Where it's reviewed:
Booklist, September 1, 2011, page 119
Publishers Weekly, April 20, 2011, page 52
School Library Journal, May 2011, page 116

Other books by the same author:
Shower of Gold: Girls and Women in the Stories of India, 1999

Other books you might like:
Anjali Banerjee, *Seaglass Summer*, 2010
Narinder Dhami, *Bindi Babes*, 2004
Amy Ignatow, *The Popularity Papers: Research for the Social Improvement and General Betterment of Lydia Goldblatt and Julie Graham-Chang*, 2010
Wendelin Van Draanen, *Sammy Keyes and the Hollywood Mummy*, 2001

260

JARRETT J. KROSOCZKA

Lunch Lady and the League of Librarians

(New York: Alfred A. Knopf, 2009)

Series: Lunch Lady Series. Book 2

Subject(s): Books and reading; Libraries; Schools

Age range(s): 7 - 10+

Major character(s): Lunch Lady, Worker (lunch lady), Heroine (superhero); Terrence, Child; Hector, Child; Dee, Child

Time period(s): 21st century; 2000s

Locale(s): United States

Summary: The crime-fighting Lunch Lady of author and illustrator Jarrett Krosoczka's graphic novel series returns for another zany adventure in *Lunch Lady and the League of Librarians*. The school's librarians are normally a cheerful bunch, but lately they've become distant and mysterious. The members of the Breakfast Bunch—Dee, Terrence, and Hector—soon learn about the impending arrival of a shipment of video games, which the librarians are intent on wiping out. When all hope of saving the shipment seems lost, the children turn to Lunch Lady for help. Now, it's up to Lunch Lady to take on the librarians and save the video games from destruction.

Where it's reviewed:
Horn Book Guide, Spring 2010, page 75
School Library Journal, September 2009, page 188

Other books by the same author:
Lunch Lady and the Field Trip Fiasco, 2011
Lunch Lady and the Bake Sale Bandit, 2010
Lunch Lady and the Summer Camp Shakedown, 2010

Lunch Lady and the Author Visit Vendetta, 2009
Lunch Lady and the Cyborg Substitute, 2009

Other books you might like:
Frank Cammuso, *Knights of the Lunch Table: The Dodgeball Chronicles*, 2008
Jimmy Gownley, *Amelia Rules!: The Whole World's Crazy*, 2003
Scott Morse, *Magic Pickle*, 2008
Trenton Lee Stewart, *The Mysterious Benedict Society*, 2007

261

KATHLEEN KRULL
GREG COUCH, Illustrator

The Boy Who Invented TV: The Story of Philo Farnsworth

(New York: Alfred A. Knopf, 2009)

Subject(s): Inventors; Television; Science

Age range(s): 8 - 10+
Time period(s): 20th century
Locale(s): Idaho, United States

Summary: In *The Boy Who Invented TV: The Story of Philo Farnsworth*, author Kathleen Krull and illustrator Greg Couch team up to bring young readers the story of the brilliant young man who invented television. Through sparkling prose and vivid illustrations, this volume charts the genius of Philo Farnsworth, an Idaho farm boy who saw in the potato fields a way to transmit images through the atmosphere. Just a few years later, he would develop his vision into the worldwide phenomena of television and become an indelible part of American history. *The Boy Who Invented TV* was chosen as a Junior Library Guild selection and contains a listing of bibliographical references.

Where it's reviewed:
Booklist, June 1, 2009, page 84
Bulletin of the Center for Children's Books, November 2009, page 115
Horn Book Guide, Spring 2010, page 172
School Library Journal, September 2009, page 144

Other books by the same author:
The Road to Oz, 2008
The Boy on Fairfield Street, 2004
They Saw the Future: Oracles, Psychics, Great Thinkers and Pretty Good Guessers, 1999

Other books you might like:
Marfe Ferguson Delano, *Inventing the Future: A Photobiography of Thomas Alva Edison*, 2002
Lee Bennett Hopkins, *Incredible Inventions*, 2009
Marc McCutcheon, *The Kid Who Named Pluto: And the Stories of Other Extraordinary Young People in Science*, 2004
Wendie Old, *To Fly: The Story of the Wright Brothers*, 2002
Steven Otfinoski, *Television*, 2007

262

KATHLEEN KRULL
BORIS KULIKOV, Illustrator

Albert Einstein

(New York: Viking, 2009)

Subject(s): Biographies; Science; History

Age range(s): 9 - 13+

Summary: *Albert Einstein* is a biography for young readers that focuses on Einstein's early life. The author explains the difficulties Einstein had in school and in his dealings with authority figures. No one believed he would amount to much due to his issues in school. Although he earned good grades, he often gave his teachers trouble and was very absentminded. This didn't change much throughout his life, even after he became a parent. Krull then explains Einstein's theories and contributions to science, using images and examples to make them easier to understand. She then completes the text with a chapter about what makes his work so significant and how modern scientists still work with experiments based on Einstein's theories.

Where it's reviewed:
Booklist, September 1, 2009, page 79
Bulletin of the Center for Children's Books, January 2010, page 203
Horn Book Magazine, November/December 2009, page 203
School Library Journal, October 2009, page 147

Other books by the same author:
Charles Darwin, 2010
Marie Curie, 2007
Isaac Newton, 2006
Sigmund Freud, 2006
Leonardo daVinci, 2005

Other books you might like:
Don Brown, *Odd Boy Out: Young Albert Einstein*, 2004
Marfe Ferguson Delano, *Genius: A Photobiography of Albert Einstein*, 2005
Ellen Klages, *The Green Glass Sea*, 2006

263

KATHLEEN KRULL
ROBERT BYRD, Illustrator

Kubla Khan: The Emperor of Everything

(New York: Viking, 2010)

Subject(s): Royalty; Dictators; Mongol Empire, 1206-1502

Age range(s): 8 - 11+
Time period(s): 13th century
Locale(s): China

Summary: *Kubla Khan: The Emperor of Everything* by author Kathleen Krull is a young adult biography about Kubla Khan, the fifth emperor of the Mongol Empire. Khan ruled from 1260 until 1294; during this time, he set up the Yuan Dynasty and became Emperor of China. In this book, the author explores the early years of the ruler-to-be, as he hunts for rabbits with his grandfather, the infamous Genghis Khan, and fulfills the destiny of his heritage. This book is illustrated by Robert Byrd. Krull is also the author of *The Boy Who Invented TV: The Story of Philo Farnsworth* and *Harvesting Hope: The Story of Cesar Chavez.*

Where it's reviewed:
Booklist, July 1, 2010, page 54
Bulletin of the Center for Children's Books, November 2010, page 137
Horn Book Magazine, Nov/Dec 2010, page 115
School Library Journal, October 2010, page 100

Other books by the same author:
A Boy Named FDR: How Franklin D. Roosevelt Grew Up to Change America, 2010
The Brothers Kennedy: John, Robert, Edward, 2010
The Boy Who Invented TV: The Story of Philo Farnsworth, 2009
Pocahontas: Princess of the New World, 2007
The Boy on Fairfield Street, 2004

Other books you might like:
Demi, *Genghis Khan*, 2009
Russell Freedman, *The Adventures of Marco Polo*, 2006
Ted Lewin, *Horse Song*, 2008

264

LAURA MCGEE KVASNOSKY, Author/Illustrator

Zelda and Ivy: Keeping Secrets
(Somerville, Massachusetts: Candlewick Press, 2009)

Story type: Humor; Young Readers
Subject(s): Foxes; Family; Sisters

Age range(s): 7 - 9+
Major character(s): Zelda, Fox, Sister (older, of Ivy); Ivy, Fox, Sister (younger, of Zelda); Eugene, Fox, Neighbor (of Zelda and Ivy)

Summary: In this book for young readers, Zelda has a secret to share. She knows that her younger sister, Ivy, can't keep a secret, so she decides to tell her next-door neighbor Eugene. It seems Eugene can't keep a secret either, and before long, the cat is out of the bag. In the meantime, Zelda tries to pull off the perfect April Fool's Day prank on Ivy, but young Ivy outsmarts her older sibling with each outlandish gag. Author and illustrator Laura McGee Kvasnosky is the 2007 winner of the Theodor Seuss Geisel Award.

Where it's reviewed:
Bulletin of the Center for Children's Books, June 2009, page 406
Horn Book Guide, Fall 2009, page 355
School Library Journal, April 2009, page 110

Other books by the same author:
Zelda and Ivy: The Big Picture, 2010
Zelda and Ivy: The Runaways, 2006
Zelda and Ivy: One Christmas, 2000
Zelda and Ivy and the Boy Next Door, 1999

Zelda and Ivy, 1998

Other books you might like:
Monika Bang-Campbell, *Little Rat Makes Music*, 2007
Jennifer Richard Jacobson, *Andy Shane and the Queen of Egypt*, 2008
Kate McMullan, *Pearl and Wagner: One Funny Day*, 2009
Sara Pennypacker, *The Talented Clementine*, 2007

265

LEO LANDRY, Author/Illustrator

Grin and Bear It
(Watertown, Massachusetts: Charlesbridge, 2011)

Story type: Humor; Young Readers
Subject(s): Humor; Comedians; Friendship

Age range(s): 6 - 8+
Major character(s): Bear, Friend (of Emmy), Bear (comedian); Emmy, Bird (hummingbird), Friend (of Bear)

Summary: In this short, illustrated chapter book by Leo Landry, young readers will learn an important lesson about achieving their goals. Bear has a dream: He wants to be a comedian and make his friends laugh. Unfortunately, Bear suffers from a bad case of stage fright. After spending time practicing his hilarious jokes in front of a mirror, he invites friends to watch him perform onstage. With all eyes on him, the worst happens: Bear botches his jokes and flees in embarrassment. Luckily for Bear, a humorous hummingbird finds Bear's jokes, and she may just have a solution to his problem.

Where it's reviewed:
Booklist, July 1, 2011, page 65
Horn Book Magazine, September/October 2011, page 89
Publishers Weekly, May 23, 2011, page 43
School Library Journal, July 2011, page 70

Other books you might like:
Marc T. Brown, *Spooky Riddles*, 1983
Wong Herbert Lee, *Mouse and Mole, Fine Feathered Friends*, 2009
Marco Maestro, *What Do You Hear When Cows Sing?: And Other Silly Riddles*, 1994
Kate McMullan, *Pearl and Wagner: One Funny Day*, 2009

266

ALEX LATIMER, Author/Illustrator

The Boy Who Cried Ninja
(Atlanta, Georgia: Peachtree, 2011)

Story type: Young Readers
Subject(s): Honesty; Children; Storytelling

Age range(s): 4 - 8+
Major character(s): Tim, Boy

Summary: Tim has a problem. No one believes him, even when he is telling the truth. Tim saw a ninja eat the last piece of cake, but when he told his parents about it, they didn't believe him. No one believed his stories about the time-traveling monkey or the sunburned crocodile, either. Tim is determined to prove to his family that he's actually telling the truth, and he comes up with an ingenious plan to do it. Will Tim's family finally believe his far-out tales? This picture story is by author and illustrator Alex Latimer.

Where it's reviewed:
Booklist, April 1, 2011, page 71
Horn Book Guide, Fall 2011, page 319
Publishers Weekly, February 7, 2011, page 55
School Library Journal, March 2011, page 128

Other books you might like:
Simon James, *Dear Mr. Blueberry*, 1991
J. C. Phillipps, *Wink: The Ninja Who Wanted to Be Noticed*, 2009
John Rocco, *Wolf! Wolf!*, 2007
Judy Sierra, *Tell the Truth, B. B. Wolf*, 2010

267

IAIN LAWRENCE

The Giant Slayer

(New York: Delacorte Books, 2009)

Subject(s): Diseases; Children; Imagination

Age range(s): 9 - 12+

Major character(s): Laurie Valentine, 11-Year-Old, Friend (of Dickie); Dickie, Friend (of Laurie); Carolyn, 14-Year-Old; Chip, Orphan

Time period(s): 20th century; 1950s (1955)

Summary: When Laurie Valentine's friend Dickie is hospitalized with polio, she has only one mission: to cheer him up by telling him one of her imaginative stories. At the hospital, Laurie forms a bond with Dickie and the other sick children as she tells them stories about a boy named Jimmy, a giant slayer. Will Laurie's storytelling give the children the strength to get well and overcome the odds against them, just like Jimmy the Giant Slayer? *The Giant Slayer* is a children's novel by Iain Lawrence.

Where it's reviewed:
Booklist, November 1 2009, page 46
Bulletin of the Center for Children's Books, January 2010, page 205
Horn Book Guide, Spring 2010, page 76
Publishers Weekly, November 16, 2009, page 54

Other books by the same author:
Lord of the Nutcracker Men, 2001

Other books you might like:
Susan Cooper, *Victory*, 2006
Peg Kehret, *Small Steps: The Year I Got Polio*, 1996
Kathryn Lasky, *Chasing Orion*, 2010
Jean-Claude Mourlevat, *The Pull of the Ocean*, 2006
Louis Sachar, *Holes*, 1998

268

SUZY LEE, Author/Illustrator

Shadow

(San Francisco: Chronicle Books, 2010)

Subject(s): Imagination; Learning; Children

Age range(s): 3 - 6+

Summary: *Shadow* is a picture book created by Suzy Lee and is nearly devoid of text. In the story, a young girl discovers she can create shapes using her hands in the shadow cast by a lightbulb. She gets more imaginative as she continues her play, eventually imagining a forest filled with many different creatures, including a wolf who chases the others. She makes use of ordinary objects in her home to create all kinds of different images. The book is intended to be read both horizontally and vertically, with the top page representing the walls and ceiling in a room, and the bottom page representing the floor. It ends with the young girl's mother calling her for dinner, though the shadow shapes play on in the background.

Where it's reviewed:
Horn Book Guide, Spring 2011, page 10
New York Times Book Review, Novembe 7, 2010, page 33
Publishers Weekly, September 20, 2010, page 62
School Library Journal, November 2010, page 76

Other books by the same author:
Wave, 2008

Other books you might like:
Ann Jonas, *Round Trip*, 1983
Kazuno Kohara, *Ghosts in the House!*, 2008
Peter McCarty, *Jeremy Draws a Monster*, 2009
Herve Tullet, *Press Here*, 2011

269

WONG HERBERT LEE, Author/Illustrator

Mouse and Mole, Fine Feathered Friends

(Boston: Houghton Mifflin Books for Children, 2009)

Subject(s): Animals; Birds; Spring

Age range(s): 5 - 8+

Major character(s): Mouse, Mouse; Mole, Mole

Summary: In *Mouse and Mole, Fine Feathered Friends* by Wong Herbert Yee, two friends learn about birds and cooperation on a bird-watching expedition. When Mouse and Mole set out to observe the local bird population, they are surprised by how easily frightened their fine-feathered friends are. Before they can sketch the cardinal, goldfinch, and blue jay, the skittish birds fly away. Mouse and Mole hatch a plan to disguise themselves as birds by rolling in glue and feathers, and then create an oversized nest in which to hide. Throughout the endeavor, Mouse and Mole offer one another support and encouragement.

Where it's reviewed:
Booklist, September 15, 2009, page 60
Horn Book Guide, Spring 2010, page 55
School Library Journal, February 2, 2010, page 98

Other books by the same author:
Mouse and Mole: A Winter Wonderland, 2010
A Brand New Day With Mouse and Mole, 2008
Abracadabra! Magic With Mouse and Mole, 2007
Upstairs Mouse, Downstairs Mole, 2005

Other books you might like:
Carin Berger, *Forever Friends*, 2010
Leo Landry, *Grin and Bear It*, 2011
Cynthia Rylant, *Annie and Snowball and the Cozy Nest*, 2009
Jon Scieszka, *Cowboy & Octopus*, 2007

270

BARBARA LEHMAN, Author/Illustrator

The Secret Box

(Boston, Massachusetts: Houghton Mifflin Books for Children, 2011)

Story type: Fantasy; Young Readers
Subject(s): Time travel; Adventure; Magic

Age range(s): 5 - 8+
Time period(s): Multiple Time Periods

Summary: Barbara Lehman's wordless adventure begins with a boy wearing old-fashioned clothing hiding a box in his dormitory at a boarding school. The subsequent pages show a group of boys in modern clothing finding a box in the same school dormitory. The boys open the box and discover old photographs of a boy, other documents, and a map showing the Seahorse Pier. They follow the map to the Seahorse Pier and travel through a tunnel to a boardwalk amusement park filled with numerous children, including the boy from the photograph—the same boy featured in the beginning of the book. The last pages of the book show more children finding a box and setting off on the same path to the boardwalk, perpetuating the same adventure cycle.

Where it's reviewed:
Booklist, February 1 2011, page 83
Bulletin of the Center for Children's Books, March 2011, page 334
Horn Book Magazine, July/August 2011, page 131
Publishers Weekly, January 3, 2011, page 50
School Library Journal, May 2011, page 82

Other books by the same author:
Trainstop, 2008
Rainstorm, 2007
Museum Trip, 2006
The Red Book, 2004

Other books you might like:
Istvan Banyai, *Zoom*, 1995
Paul Fleischman, *Sidewalk Circus*, 2004
David Wiesner, *Flotsam*, 2006

271

HELEN LESTER
LYNN MUNSINGER, Illustrator

Tacky Goes to Camp

(Boston, Massachusetts: Houghton Mifflin Books for Children, 2009)

Subject(s): Camps (Recreation); Bears; Penguins
Age range(s): 5 - 8+
Major character(s): Tacky, Penguin
Time period(s): 21st century; 2000s

Summary: Tacky the Penguin returns for another adventure in Helen Lester's *Tacky Goes to Camp*. It's summertime, and Tacky and his penguin pals are off to Camp Whoopi-haha for a season of fun and games in the great outdoors. The birds enjoy the abundance of activities waiting for them: line dancing and jumping on rocks to playing Capture the Ice Cube. When the sun goes down and the campfire is raging, Tacky and his friends try to outdo one another with frightening ghost stories. They have no idea, however, that one of these stories is about to come true. This volume contains illustrations by Lynn Munsinger.

Where it's reviewed:
Booklist, April 1, 2009, page 46
Horn Book Magazine, May/June 2009, page 283
Publishers Weekly, May 18, 2009, page 54
School Library Journal, April 2009, page 110

Other books by the same author:
Tacky and the Winter Games, 2005
Tacky In Trouble, 2005
Tacky and the Emperor, 2002
Tacky the Penguin, 1998
Three Cheers for Tacky, 1996

Other books you might like:
Diane de Groat, *Gilbert, the Surfer Dude*, 2009
Denise Fleming, *Buster Goes to Cowboy Camp*, 2008
Marla Frazee, *A Couple of Boys Have the Best Week Ever*, 2008
Bill Martin, *The Ghost-Eye Tree*, 1985
Chris Van Allsburg, *Probuditi!*, 2006

272

ARTHUR A. LEVINE
JULIAN HECTOR, Illustrator

Monday Is One Day

(New York: Scholastic Press, 2011)

Story type: Young Readers
Subject(s): Parent-child relations; Working mothers; Family life

Age range(s): 3 - 6+

Summary: This picture book for young readers by author Arthur A. Levine and illustrator Julian focuses on a town filled with children who have working parents. The book encourages readers to count the days of the workweek. Though the parents and children in the book look forward to the weekend—when they can spend two whole days together—each workday unveils special moments when parents and children can share time together. Hector's illustrations create a diverse cast of characters (black and white, young and old, gay and straight) who live in a town that includes urban, suburban, and rural areas, so all children will be able to relate to the book's message.

Where it's reviewed:
Booklist, February 1, 2011, page 69
Horn Book Guide, Fall 2011, page 299
Publishers Weekly, February 2, 2011, page 54
School Library Journal, April 2011, page 147

Other books by the same author:
Pearl Moscowitz's Last Stand, 1995

Other books you might like:
Eric Carle, *Today Is Monday*, 1993
Trish Cooke, *So Much*, 1994
Rachel Isadora, *Yo, Jo!*, 2007
Todd Parr, *The Family Book*, 2003
Dan Yaccarino, *Every Friday*, 2007

273

KRISTIN LEVINE

The Best Bad Luck I Ever Had

(New York: G.P. Putnam's Sons, 2009)

Subject(s): Racism; Segregation; Murder

Age range(s): 11 - 14+
Major character(s): Harry "Dit" Sims, Friend (of Emma Walker); Emma Walker, Friend (of Harry "Dit" Sims)
Time period(s): 20th century; 1910s
Locale(s): Moundville, Alabama

Summary: In Kristin Levine's *The Best Bad Luck I Ever Had*, 12-year-old Harry "Dit" Sims hopes that the new postmaster's arrival to his Moundville, Alabama, home will also bring a young boy for him to play with. But when the new postmaster turns out to be black and his child turns out to be a girl, Dit is thrown for a loop. The year is 1917, and racist attitudes threaten to tear Moundville apart. Still, Dit and Emma, the postmaster's daughter, become friends. Emma is bookish and clever, but knows nothing about throwing a ball or climbing trees; Dit is able to teach her these things, while Emma slowly begins to change his perspectives on the world around them. Meanwhile, Dit helps the local doctor care for patients during the 1918 influenza epidemic and worries as his father sits on shotgun vigil to protect his neighbors from nightriders. When Emma and Dit witness the self-defense killing of the alcoholic, abusive sheriff by a local black barber, they must make a stand for justice and equality in their small town. First novel.

Where it's reviewed:
Booklist, November 15, 2008, page 59
Bulletin of the Center for Children's Books, April 2009, page 328
Horn Book Magazine, May/June 2009, page 301
Publishers Weekly, December 15, 2009, page 55

School Library Journal, January 2009, page 108

Other books by the same author:
Lions of Little Rock, 2012

Other books you might like:
Shana Burg, *A Thousand Never Evers*, 2008
Chris Crowe, *Getting Away with Murder: The True Story of the Emmett Till Case*, 2003
Kimberly Newton Fusco, *The Wonder of Charlie Anne*, 2010
Tony Johnston, *Bone by Bone by Bone*, 2007

274

TED LEWIN, Author/Illustrator
BETSY LEWIN, Author/Illustrator

Balarama: A Royal Elephant

(New York: Lee and Low Books, 2009)

Subject(s): Indian history; Culture; Elephants

Age range(s): 8 - 10+

Summary: *Balarama: A Royal Elephant* is an illustrated travel book for young readers by Ted and Betsy Lewin. The Lewins describe their vacation to the southern region of India. In the royal city of Mysore, the people celebrate the festival of Dasara. The ten-day celebration commemorates the victory of Rama versus Ravana. It culminates in a huge procession through the streets of Mysore, where an idol in the form of the goddess Chamundeshwari sits atop an extravagant elephant seat, called an Ambaari. The Lewins are introduced to the elephant named Balarama. The story recounts the meeting and the rest of their cultural discoveries.

Where it's reviewed:
Booklist, November 15, 2009, page 36
Horn Book Magazine, January/February 2010, page 102
Publishers Weekly, September 7, 2009, page 46
School Library Journal, September 2009, page 144

Other books by the same author:
Horse Song, 2008
The World's Greatest Elephant, 2006
Elephant Quest, 2000

Other books you might like:
Ralph Helfer, *The World's Greatest Elephant*, 2006
Jody Morgan, *Elephant Rescue: Changing the Future for Endangered Wildlife*, 2004
Leda Schubert, *Ballet of the Elephants*, 2006
Tracie Vaughn Zimmer, *Cousins of Clouds: Elephant Poems*, 2011

275

GILL LEWIS
YUTA ONODA, Illustrator

Wild Wings

(New York: Atheneum Books, 2011)

Story type: Young Adult; Young Readers
Subject(s): Birds; Friendship; Scotland

Age range(s): 10 - 12+
Major character(s): Iona McNair, 11-Year-Old, Friend (of Callum); Callum, 11-Year-Old, Friend (of Iona)
Time period(s): 21st century; 2010s
Locale(s): Gambia, The; Scotland

Summary: An endangered bird connects a small town in Scotland to a West African village. Iona McNair, an eccentric 11-year-old, moves in with her grandfather on his Scottish farm. At first she has trouble making new friends. One day she finds an osprey nest on the farm. She names the endangered bird Iris and keeps it a secret. After Iona develops a friendship with a classmate, Callum, she tells him about the bird. He helps Iona keep the osprey safe until it injures its wing on a fishing wire. They enlist the help of a bird expert, who bandages Iris's wing and puts a tracking device on the bird. When the bird flies south for the winter, Iona and Callum track Iris until they lose the signal. Determined to find Iris, Callum connects with a girl living in Gambia through e-mail. She helps him track down the location of the osprey.

Where it's reviewed:
Booklist, March 1, 2011, page 54
Horn Book Guide, Fall 2011, page 361
Publishers Weekly, March 14, 2011, page 74
School Library Journal, May 2011, page 116

Other books you might like:
Jim Arnosky, *Thunder Birds: Nature's Flying Predators*, 2011
Carl Hiaasen, *Hoot*, 2002
Katherine Paterson, *Bridge to Terabithia*, 1977

276

YU LI-QIONG
ZHU CHENG-LIANG, Illustrator

A New Year's Reunion

(Somerville, Massachusetts: Candlewick Press, 2011)

Story type: Young Readers
Subject(s): Family life; Father-daughter relations; Chinese (Asian people)

Age range(s): 5 - 8+
Major character(s): Maomao, Girl (Chinese); Papa, Worker, Father (of Maomao)
Time period(s): 21st century; 2000s
Locale(s): China

Summary: Little Maomao lives on mainland China with her mother. Her father, like many Chinese parents, works far away and comes home only to celebrate the New Year. To Maomao, though, Papa seems like a stranger. She is distressed by his beard and his return after so long. The girl and her father slowly become reacquainted as they make sticky rice balls and help prepare for the New Year's celebration. They listen to the sounds of firecrackers and watch a dragon dance in the street. Maomao finds that she and her father do have a lot in common, and she is glad that he could home for the New Year. This picture book was first published in 2008 in Taiwan.

Other books you might like:
Karen Chinn, *Sam and the Lucky Money*, 1995

Ying Chang Compestine, *The Runaway Rice Cake*, 2001
Nina Simonds, *Moonbeams, Dumplings and Dragon Boats: A Treasury of Chinese Holiday Tales, Activities, and Recipes*, 2002
Janet S. Wong, *This Next New Year*, 2000

277

TOM LICHTENHELD, Author/Illustrator

E-mergency!

(San Francisco: Chronicle Books, 2011)

Story type: Young Readers
Subject(s): Humor; Storytelling; Learning

Age range(s): 4 - 7+

Summary: In this children's picture story by Tom Lichtenheld, the author creates a world in which the letters of the alphabet take on anthropomorphic characteristics. A tragedy has occurred in the alphabet, and the letter E has tumbled down the steps. While E recovers in the hospital, it is up to one of the other 25 letters to step up and do double duty. Yet which letter is best suited for the job and able to take on the responsibility of being E? Lichtenheld uses onomatopoeia and identifiable characteristics of various letters to describe each alphabetical character's personality. For example, the letter Z is too lazy, Y is too inquisitive, and P is too incontinent to fill in for E. When O volunteers to take E's place, the day is saved—that is, as long as everyone can remember when O is acting as E.

Where it's reviewed:
Booklist, December 1, 2011, page 51
New York Times Book Review, November 13, 2011, page 36
Publishers Weekly, October 10, 2011, page 55

Other books you might like:
Jef Czekaj, *A Call for a New Alphabet*, 2011
Stephen T. Johnson, *Alphabet City*, 1996
Ann Jonas, *Aardvarks, Disembark!*, 1994
Maira Kalman, *What Pete Ate from A-Z: Where We Explore the English Alphabet (in Its Entirety) in Which a Certain Dog Devours a Myriad of Items Which He Should Not*, 2001
Mike Lester, *A Is for Salad*, 2000

278

TOM LICHTENHELD, Author/Illustrator

Bridget's Beret

(New York: Henry Holt, 2010)

Subject(s): Art; Children; Artists

Age range(s): 5 - 8+
Major character(s): Bridget, Child, Artist
Time period(s): 21st century; 2010s

Summary: *Bridget's Beret* is an uplifting picture book for young readers, written and illustrated by Tom Lichtenheld. Bridget is a young aspiring artist who enjoys spending long hours drawing pictures of her beautiful surroundings. The most important instrument for her artwork is Bridget's black beret, similar to the one she's spotted on famous artists around the world. When a strong wind blows Bridget's beret away, she's desperate to track it down. A dedicated search for the beret is fruitless and Bridget fears that she'll never be able to overcome her creative slump without her prized hat. Filled with vivid watercolor illustrations, *Bridget's Beret* is an inspiring story about creativity, art, and commitment.

Where it's reviewed:
Booklist, February 5, 2010, page 76
Bulletin of the Center for Children's Books, May 2010, page 386
Horn Book Guide, Fall 2010, page 305

Other books by the same author:
Cloudette, 2011

Other books you might like:
Will Hillenbrand, *Louie!*, 2009
Shelley Jackson, *Mimi's Dada Catifesto*, 2010
Angela Johnson, *Lily Brown's Paintings*, 2007
Peter H. Reynolds, *The Dot*, 2003

279

STEVE LIGHT, Author/Illustrator

The Christmas Giant

(Somerville, Massachusetts: Candlewick Press, 2010)

Subject(s): Christmas; Giants; Friendship

Age range(s): 3 - 6+

Major character(s): Humphrey, Human (giant), Designer (wrapping paper); Leetree, Human (elf), Designer (wrapping paper)

Time period(s): Indeterminate

Locale(s): Christmastown, Fictional Location

Summary: *The Christmas Giant* is a picture book for young readers from author and illustrator, Steve Light. Humphrey is a giant who works for Santa Claus. Along with his best friend, the elf named Leetree, Humphrey designs Christmas wrapping paper for Santa. This year, Santa gives Humphrey and Leetree a very special assignment: grow a Christmas tree. The pair works together to grow the most wonderful tree of all, but when they set off to deliver it, they encounter a challenge they never expected. Leetree and Humphrey must work together to come up with a way to avert disaster and save Christmas.

Where it's reviewed:
Booklist, October 15, 2010, page 54
Horn Book Magazine, November/December 2010, page 65
School Library Journal, October 2010, page 74

Other books by the same author:
The Shoemaker Extraordinaire, 2003
Puss in Boots, 2002

Other books you might like:
Julia Donaldson, *The Spiffiest Giant in Town*, 2003
Mark Gonyea, *A Wish for Elves*, 2010

Mary Lyn Ray, *Christmas Farm*, 2008
Jan Wahl, *The Golden Christmas Tree*, 1988

280

GRACE LIN, Author/Illustrator

Ling and Ting: Not Exactly the Same!

(New York: Little, Brown and Company, 2010)

Subject(s): Twins; Chinese Americans; Identity

Age range(s): 4 - 7+

Major character(s): Ling, Twin (of Ting); Ting, Twin (of Ling)

Locale(s): United States

Summary: Grace Lin's *Ling and Ting: Not Exactly the Same!* is comprised of six short stories centering on a set of Chinese-American twins. From all outward appearances, Ling and Ting are identical in every way. However, as these tales illustrate, the siblings have their own unique personality, interests, and opinions. From hairstyles to cooking, Ling and Ting take young readers into their world and show the many ways they are different from one another. *Ling and Ting* includes illustrations by the author.

Where it's reviewed:
Booklist, May 1, 2010, page 85
Bulletin of the Center for Children's Books, July-August 2010, page 490
Horn Book Magazine, July/August 2010, page 113
Publishers Weekly, June 21, 2010, page 46
School Library Journal, July 2010, page 64

Other books by the same author:
The Year of the Rat, 2008
The Year of the Dog, 2005

Other books you might like:
Kate Banks, *Monkeys and Dog Days*, 2008
Jennifer Richard Jacobson, *Andy Shane and the Barn Sale Mystery*, 2009
Laura McGee Kvasnosky, *Zelda and Ivy: The Big Picture*, 2010

281

GRACE LIN, Author/Illustrator

Where the Mountain Meets the Moon

(New York: Little, Brown Books for Young Readers, 2009)

Subject(s): Folklore; Chinese history; Dragons

Age range(s): 8 - 11+

Major character(s): Minli, Child, Daughter, Friend, Traveler

Locale(s): Fruitless Mountain, Fictional Location

Summary: Minli wants a better life for her family, but the only way to get it is to track down the Old Man in the Moon. In *Where the Mountain Meets the Moon*, author

Grace Lin combines Chinese folktales with original fiction to tell the story of a little girl who would travel to the ends of the earth to secure a solid future for her loved ones. After leaving the small hut she shares with her family, Minli begins a journey, which she hopes will end with answers to life's biggest questions. On the way, she receives help from talking goldfish, magical dragons, and even a Chinese king. With the stories her father told her as a small child serving as a guide, Minli and her new friends attempt to track down the Old Man in the Moon. The text is accompanied by hand-drawn, full-color illustrations by Lin.

Where it's reviewed:
Booklist, May 1 2009, page 81
Bulletin of the Center for Children's Books, September 2009, page 29
Horn Book Magazine, September/October 2009, page 566
School Library Journal, July 2009, page 87

Awards the book has won:
Josette Frank Award, 2010
Mythopoeic Fantasy Awards: Children's, 2010
Beehive Awards: Children's Book, 2011

Other books you might like:
Susan Cooper, *The Magician's Boy*, 2006
Kate DiCamillo, *The Magician's Elephant*, 2009
Lyn Gardner, *Into the Woods*, 2006
Jean Merrill, *The Superlative Horse: A Tale of Ancient China*, 1961
Eric Shanower, *The Wonderful Wizard of Oz*, 2009

282

RENATA LIWSKA, Author/Illustrator

Red Wagon
(New York: Philomel Books, 2011)

Story type: Young Readers
Subject(s): Imagination; Friendship; Foxes

Age range(s): 3 - 5+
Major character(s): Lucy, Fox, Child

Summary: All Lucy wants to do is play with her new red wagon. Unfortunately, her mother sends her to the market to pick up some vegetables. Lucy is resistant to the idea of doing chores; nevertheless, she begins her journey. Along the way, she picks up a few friends. They pass through a rain storm before reaching the market, where they buy vegetables. Then, they return home. Author and illustrator Renata Liwska keeps the text in this picture book simple and straightforward, but her illustrations reveal a much more exciting adventure for Lucy and her friends. Her little red wagon becomes a boat, a covered wagon, a circus train, and a spaceship. When Lucy returns home, chore completed, her mother gives her permission to play. However, Lucy is so tired that all she can do is curl up and take a nap!

Where it's reviewed:
Booklist, February 15, 2011, page 68
Horn Book Magazine, January/February 2011, page 79
Publishers Weekly, December 20, 2010, page 51
School Library Journal, February 2011, page 86

Other books by the same author:
Little Panda, 2008

Other books you might like:
Aliki, *Push Button*, 2010
Alexandra Day, *Carl's Summer Vacation*, 2008
Will Hillenbrand, *Down by the Station*, 1999
Antoinette Portis, *Not a Box*, 2006

283

ANITA LOBEL, Author/Illustrator

Nini Lost and Found
(New York: Alfred A. Knopf, 2010)

Subject(s): Domestic cats; Adventure; Animals

Age range(s): 4 - 8+
Major character(s): Nini, Cat
Time period(s): 21st century; 2010s

Summary: In *Nini Lost and Found*, award-winning author/illustrator Anita Lobel follows the escapades of a curious tabby cat named Nini and the excitement—and terror—she discovers in the outdoors. When Nini finds herself standing before an open front door, she just can't refuse the opportunity to explore what lies beyond. She has no idea, however, of both the thrill and danger that await her on the other side of that door. At first, it all seems like fun and games, but as darkness blankets the area and scarier animals come out to cavort, Nini begins to miss her cozy home.

Where it's reviewed:
Booklist, August 2010, page 55
Horn Book Magazine, Nov/Dec 2010, page 77
New York Times Book Review, October 17, 2010, page 17
School Library Journal, September 2010, page 130

Other books by the same author:
Nini Here and There, 2007

Other books you might like:
Laura Godwin, *One Moon, Two Cats*, 2011
Betsy Lewin, *Where Is Tippy Toes?*, 2010
Eric Litwin, *Pete the Cat: I Love My White Shoes*, 2010
Viviane Schwarz, *There Are Cats in This Book*, 2008
Mo Willems, *Knuffle Bunny: A Cautionary Tale*, 2004

284

LOREN LONG, Author/Illustrator

Otis
(New York: Philomel Books, 2009)

Subject(s): Agriculture; Friendship; Machinery

Age range(s): 4 - 7+
Major character(s): Otis, Worker (tractor)

Summary: *Otis*, written and illustrated by Loren Long, is a picture book for young readers. Otis is a friendly tractor who lives on a farm and enjoys working with the farmer every day. He is friends with a young calf. They sit side-by-side in the barn every night and play in the fields every day. After the farmer buys a new, bigger tractor for the farm, he puts Otis out behind the barn. A lonely Otis sits there until one day when the calf becomes stuck in the mud pond. Otis is the only one who can help pull his friend out of the mud.

Where it's reviewed:
Booklist, September 1 2009, page 102
Horn Book Guide, Spring 2010, page 33
Publishers Weekly, August 17 2009, page 60
School Library Journal, September 2009, page 128

Other books by the same author:
Otis and the Tornado, 2011

Other books you might like:
Virginia Lee Burton, *Mike Mulligan and His Steam Shovel*, 1939
Kersten Hamilton, *Red Truck*, 2008
Maira Kalman, *Fireboat: The Heroic Adventures of the John J. Harvey*, 2002
Watty Piper, *The Little Engine That Could*, 1978
Robin Pulver, *Axle Annie*, 1999

285

LENORE LOOK
LEUYEN PHAM, Illustrator

Alvin Ho: Allergic to Camping, Hiking, and Other Natural Disasters

(New York: Schwartz & Wade, 2009)

Series: Alvin Ho Series. Book 2
Subject(s): Camping

Age range(s): 7 - 9+
Major character(s): Alvin Ho, Child
Time period(s): 21st century; 2000s

Summary: *Alvin Ho: Allergic to Camping, Hiking, and Other Natural Disasters* is the second installment of the series about the boy who is afraid of just about everything. If you can name it, Alvin Ho is allergic to it. And this time, his allergies are causing him serious anxiety about an upcoming camping trip with his father. But he is able to go on the trip—and he even has a good time, learning camping tricks from his uncle and having a few adventures of his own. *Allergic to Camping, Hiking, and Other Natural Disasters* is the second book in the Alvin Ho series.

Where it's reviewed:
Bulletin of the Center for Children's Books, September 2009, page 30
Horn Book Magazine, September/October 2009, page 567
School Library Journal, July 2009, page 66

Other books by the same author:
Alvin Ho: Allergic to Dead Bodies, Funerals, and Other Fatal Circumstances, 2011
Alvin Ho: Allergic to Birthday Parties, Science Projects and Other Man-Made Catastrophes, 2010
Alvin Ho: Allergic to Girls, School and Other Scary Things, 2008

Other books you might like:
Judy Blume, *Tales of a Fourth Grade Nothing*, 1972
Claudia Mills, *Being Teddy Roosevelt: A Boy, a President, and a Plan*, 2007
Graham Salisbury, *Calvin Coconut: Trouble Magnet*, 2009
Rachel Vail, *Justin Case: School, Drool, and Other Daily Disasters*, 2010
Lisa Yee, *Bobby the Brave (Sometimes)*, 2010

286

CYNTHIA LORD

Touch Blue

(New York: Scholastic, 2010)

Subject(s): Foster home care; Foster children; Islands

Age range(s): 9 - 11+
Major character(s): Tess Brooks, 11-Year-Old; Aaron, Foster Child
Time period(s): 21st century; 2010s
Locale(s): Bethsaida Island, Maine

Summary: In *Touch Blue*, author Cynthia Lord tells the story of resourceful 11-year-old Tess Brooks, who lives on an idyllic island off the coast of Maine. The island has a quaint one-room schoolhouse where Tess attends classes, but the authorities want to close the school because of the island's rapidly-decreasing student population. In order to bolster the number of students at the school, Tess and her family take in a troubled foster child named Aaron, who plays the trumpet—and changes young Tess's life forever. *Touch Blue* was a 2010 Newbery Honor book.

Where it's reviewed:
Bulletin of the Center for Children's Books, September 2010, page 28
Horn Book Magazine, Nov/Dec 2010, page 94
Publishers Weekly, August 9, 2010, page 53
School Library Journal, September 2010, page 157

Other books by the same author:
Happy Birthday Hamster, 2011
Hot Rod Hamster, 2010
Rules, 2006

Other books you might like:
A.C.E. Bauer, *Come Fall*, 2010
Christopher Paul Curtis, *Bud, Not Buddy*, 1999
Katherine Paterson, *The Great Gilly Hopkins*, 1978
Richard Peck, *The Teacher's Funeral: A Comedy in Three Parts*, 2004
Cynthia Voigt, *Homecoming*, 1981

287

WILLIAM LOW, Author/Illustrator

Machines Go to Work

(New York: Henry Holt and Co., 2009)

Subject(s): Machinery; Children; Trains

Age range(s): 2 - 5+

Summary: Author and illustrator William Low provides toddlers with an up-close look at the exciting world of machinery. *Machines Go To Work* presents detailed illustrations and information on a variety of equipment. Some of the pieces covered in this volume include a helicopter, a cement mixer, a backhoe, a tugboat, a train, and a truck. The accompanying text mimics the sound each machine makes, inspiring children to recreate each machine's unique music. *Machines Go To Work* includes a large fold-out illustration featuring a large train.

Where it's reviewed:
Booklist, March 15, 2009, page 64
Horn Book Magazine, July/August 2009, page 409
School Library Journal, May 2009, page 82

Other books you might like:
Kersten Hamilton, *Red Truck*, 2008
G. Brian Karas, *The Village Garage*, 2010
Jonathan London, *I'm a Truck Driver*, 2010
Sally Sutton, *Roadwork*, 2008

288

LOIS LOWRY
BAGRAM IBATOULLINE, Illustrator

Crow Call

(New York: Scholastic Press, 2009)

Subject(s): Father-daughter relations; Hunting; Love

Age range(s): 7 - 10+

Major character(s): Liz, 9-Year-Old, Daughter; Daddy, Father (of Liz)

Time period(s): 20th century; 1940s

Locale(s): Pennsylvania, United States

Summary: In Lois Lowry's *Crow Call*, a nine-year-old girl tries to reconnect with her father, who has been off fighting in World War II for so long that he's basically a stranger. Together, Liz and her father walk through the Pennsylvania countryside on a crisp fall day. Liz's father allows his daughter to eat cherry pie for breakfast, buys her a plaid hunting shirt many sizes too big (she must have it), and lets her operate the crow call that will make his prey flock to him. It becomes clear, however, that the "hunt" is less about the crows (her father never fires his gun, and Liz expresses her fears about the point of their excursion) and more about forming a special bond with each other. *Crow Call*, which features illustrations by Bagram Ibatoulline, is based on experiences from Lowry's own life.

Where it's reviewed:
Booklist, October 15 2009, page 50
Bulletin of the Center for Children's Books, January 2010, page 369
Horn Book Guide, Spring 2010, page 33
Publishers Weekly, September 28 2009, page 64
School Library Journal, October 2009, page 98

Other books you might like:
Robert J. Blake, *Swift*, 2007
Nicola Davies, *White Owl, Barn Owl*, 2007
Bob Graham, *How to Heal A Broken Wing*, 2008
Karen Hesse, *Sable*, 1994
Jerry Spinelli, *Wringer*, 1997

289

LOIS LOWRY
ERIC ROHMANN, Illustrator

Bless This Mouse

(Boston: Houghton Mifflin Books for Children, 2011)

Story type: Young Readers
Subject(s): Animals; Survival; House mouse

Age range(s): 9 - 11+
Major character(s): Hildegarde, Mouse; Father Murphy, Religious; Ignatius, Mouse

Summary: Hildegarde, the Mistress of Mice, is the leader of a group of church mice living at Saint Bartholomew's. With the terrifying annual Blessing of the Animals—which always brings with it a bevy of cats—quickly approaching, Hildegarde's mouse community is faced with an even bigger problem: The Great X. While the mice are usually careful to avoid being seen, several recent sightings have forced Father Murphy to summon the dreaded Great X (mouse terminology for exterminator). Seeking to save her fellow mice, Hildegarde must lead them to a mysterious place known only as Outdoors. Will they be able to make it back to the safety of the church before the feline invasion begins?

Where it's reviewed:
Booklist, March 1, 2011, page 60
Bulletin of the Center for Children's Books, April 2011, page 382
Publishers Weekly, January 17, 2011, page 49

Other books by the same author:
The Birthday Ball, 2010
Gooney Bird Greene, 2002
Stay!: Keeper's Story, 1997

Other books you might like:
Avi, *Poppy*, 1995
Dick King-Smith, *A Mouse Called Wolf*, 1997
Cynthia Voigt, *Young Fredle*, 2011
Frances Weller, *The Day the Animals Came: A Story of Saint Francis Day*, 2003

290

MIKE LUPICA

Hero

(New York: Philomel Books, 2010)

Subject(s): Fathers; Death; Magic

Age range(s): 9 - 13+

Major character(s): Zach Harriman, 14-Year-Old; Kate, Girlfriend (of Zach); Mr. Herbert, Aged Person

Time period(s): 21st century; 2010s

Locale(s): United States

Summary: In *Hero*, Mike Lupica tells the story of Zach Harriman, a 14-year-old boy facing a dangerous investigation and a life-changing decision. After his government-agent father is killed, Zach looks into his death and makes a shocking discovery: his dad had special magical powers. What's more is that Zach has seemingly inherited these abilities. Now the teen must decide whether to just let himself be a kid—or follow in his father's footsteps to use his power for the good of the world...and jeopardize his safety.

Where it's reviewed:
Booklist, October 1, 2010, page 86
Bulletin of the Center for Children's Books, December 2010, page 195
Horn Book Guide, Spring 2011, page 76
School Library Journal, December 2010, page 118
Voice of Youth Advocates, February 2011, page 572

Other books by the same author:
The Batboy, 2010
Million-Dollar Throw, 2010
The Big Field, 2009
Safe at Home, 2009
Miracle on 49th Street, 2007

Other books you might like:
Patrick Carman, *Thirteen Days to Midnight*, 2010
Martine Leavitt, *Heck Superhero*, 2004
Barry Lyga, *Archvillain*, 2010
Gary D. Schmidt, *First Boy*, 2005
Roland Smith, *Independence Hall: I, Q*, 2008

291

GEORGE ELLA LYON
KATHERINE TILLOTSON, Illustrator

All the Water in the World

(New York: Atheneum, 2011)

Subject(s): Science; Nature; Natural resource conservation

Age range(s): 5 - 8+

Summary: This nonfiction picture book explores how vital water is in the world's diverse environments. Author George Ella Lyon tells the story of water in rhythmic prose that evokes the sound and movement of water through rainfall, ocean waves, a spraying garden hose, and a trickling faucet. Illustrator Katherine Tillotson uses lively digital images to convey the sensual appeal and awesome power of water as Earth's most important life-sustaining resource. The book's thoughtful combination of text and pictures introduces readers to scientific concepts such as evaporation, condensation, precipitation, drought, and natural resource conservation.

Where it's reviewed:
Booklist, March 15, 2011, page 52
Bulletin of the Center for Children's Books, April 2011, page 382
Horn Book Magazine, May/June 2011, page 113
Science Books & Film, May 2011, page 98

Other books by the same author:
My Friend the Starfinder, 2008
Mother to Tigers, 2003
Dreamplace, 1993
ABCedar, 1989

Other books you might like:
Karen Hesse, *Come On, Rain!*, 1999
G. Brian Karas, *Atlantic*, 2002
Walter Wick, *A Drop of Water: A Book of Science and Wonder*, 1997

292

GRACE MACCARONE
CHRISTINE DAVENIER, Illustrator

Miss Lina's Ballerinas

(New York: Feiwel and Friends, 2010)

Subject(s): Dance; Ballet; Rhyme

Age range(s): 5 - 8+

Major character(s): Miss Lina, Dancer, Teacher; Regina, Dancer, Student; Christina, Dancer, Student; Edwina, Student, Dancer; Sabrina, Dancer, Student; Justina, Dancer, Student; Katrina, Dancer, Student; Bettina, Dancer, Student; Marina, Dancer, Student; Nina, Dancer, Student

Time period(s): 21st century; 2010s

Locale(s): Messina, Italy

Summary: *Miss Lina's Ballerinas* is a humorous and clever picture book for young readers from author Grace Maccarone and illustrator Christine Davenier. In a quaint Italian town of Messina, Miss Lina teaches eight children, with rhyming names, in the ways of ballet. The children line up in "four lines of two" and dance to and fro throughout the Sicilian town. Things quickly go awry for the students of Miss Lina's ballet class when a ninth student named Regina arrives and joins the group. Suddenly, their perfect order is disrupted and they can't seem to find their fluidity again. Told in rhyming text and complemented with pink illustrations, *Miss Lina's Ballerinas* is a comical tale of dance, friendship, and change.

Where it's reviewed:
Booklist, November 1, 2010, page 60
Entertainment Weekly, Spring 2011, page 37
School Library Journal, December 2010, page 84

Other books by the same author:
Miss Lina's Ballerinas and the Prince, 2011

Other books you might like:

Alyssa Satin Capucilli, *My First Ballet Class*, 2011

Anna Kemp, *Dogs Don't Do Ballet*, 2010

Matthew McElligott, *The Lion's Share: A Tale of Halving Cake and Eating It, Too*, 2009

Linda Skeers, *Tutus Aren't My Style*, 2010

293

PATRICIA MACLACHLAN

AMY JUNE BATES, Illustrator

Waiting for the Magic

(New York: Atheneum Books for Young Readers, 2011)

Story type: Contemporary - Fantasy

Subject(s): Family; Family life; Dogs

Age range(s): 8 - 10+

Major character(s): William, 5th Grader, Brother (of Elinor); Elinor, 4-Year-Old, Sister (of William); Mama, Mother (of William and Elinor), Spouse (of Papa); Papa, Father (of William and Elinor), Spouse (of Mama), Teacher (of literature), Writer; Bryn, Dog; Bitty, Dog; Neo, Dog; Grace, Dog; Lula, Cat; Nicholas, Baby, Brother (of William and Elinor)

Time period(s): 21st century; 2010s

Summary: A broken family learns to mend itself and grow stronger through the help of some wise canine and feline friends in this novel for children and young adults by Patricia MacLachlan. After Papa walks out, William accompanies Mama and his little sister, Elinor, to the local animal shelter to pick out a pet. One pet becomes five as the family returns home with four dogs and a cat. The new pets help to fill the void created by Papa's absence—especially when William and Elinor realize they can hear the dogs talking to each other. Mama's big announcement and Papa's return change the dynamic of the household once again—for the better this time—and the family's bond grows stronger. MacLachlan blends fantasy with reality in this story about family, love, and, of course, pets. Illustrations by Amy June Bates accompany the text.

Where it's reviewed:

Booklist, August 1, 2011, page 50

Publishers Weekly, July 4, 2011, page 65

School Library Journal, October 10, 2011, page 112

Other books by the same author:

The True Gift: A Christmas Story, 2009

More Perfect Than the Moon, 2004

Baby, 1995

Journey, 1991

Sarah, Plain and Tall, 1985

Other books you might like:

Joy Cowley, *Chicken Feathers*, 2008

Kate DiCamillo, *Because of Winn-Dixie*, 2000

Eileen Spinelli, *The Dancing Pancake*, 2010

294

KEKLA MAGOON

Camo Girl

(New York: Simon and Schuster, 2011)

Subject(s): Race relations; Racially mixed people; Fantasy

Age range(s): 10 - 14+

Major character(s): Ellie, 6th Grader, Friend (of Z); Z, 6th Grader, Friend (of Ellie); Bailey, 6th Grader

Time period(s): 21st century; 2010s

Locale(s): Nevada, United States

Summary: In this young adult novel, author Kekla Magoon tells the story of an adolescent girl of mixed race who must circumnavigate the pitfalls of friendship and popularity at her middle school. Ellie's only friend in sixth grade is a boy named Z. He is the only one who does not tease Ellie about her mixed race or the skin disorder that afflicts her face. Ellie relies on the fantasy world that Z has created in his imagination to get them through their days at school. Another common bond they share is the loss of their fathers, which also helps Ellie relate to the new boy at school, Bailey. Bailey's father is a war veteran who suffers from post-traumatic stress disorder and has left his family. Ellie feels drawn to popular Bailey, the only other person in town of African American heritage. Yet in order to maintain her friendship with Bailey, Ellie must forgo her relationship with Z. Can Ellie make the right choice, or will her need to belong supersede her friendships?

Where it's reviewed:

Booklist, February 2011, page 74

Bulletin of the Center for Children's Books, March 2011, page 337

Publishers Weekly, December 6, 2010, page 48

School Library Journal, January 2011, page 112

Other books you might like:

Martine Leavitt, *Heck Superhero*, 2004

Cynthia Lord, *Rules*, 2006

Rebecca Stead, *When You Reach Me*, 2009

Jacqueline Woodson, *Feathers*, 2007

295

MARGARET MAHY

POLLY DUNBAR, Illustrator

Bubble Trouble

(London: Frances Lincoln Children's Books, 2008)

Story type: Young Readers

Subject(s): Storytelling; Children; Brothers and sisters

Age range(s): 3 - 6+

Major character(s): Mabel, Girl

Summary: In this children's picture story by author Margaret Mahy, a little girl named Mabel loves to blow bubbles. One day while bubble-blowing, Mabel blows a bubble so big it envelopes her baby brother and sends him floating up into the air. As everyone around Mabel attempts to figure out how to catch the baby and bring him back to the ground, someone has the bright idea of shooting the bubble with a slingshot, causing it to pop. Now who will catch Mabel's baby brother and keep him safe? Mahy's lyrical text and colorful pictures by Polly Dunbar bring the story to life.

Where it's reviewed:
Booklist, April 15 2009, page 46
Bulletin of the Center for Children's Books, May 2009, page 369
Horn Book Magazine, May/June 2009, page 284
School Library Journal, May 2009, page 83

Other books by the same author:
A Summery Sunday Morning, 1998
17 Kings and 42 Elephants, 1987

Other books you might like:
Allan Ahlberg, *The Baby in the Hat*, 2008
Mem Fox, *A Particular Cow*, 2006
Alice Schertle, *Little Blue Truck*, 2008
Audrey Wood, *King Bidgood's in the Bathtub*, 1985

296

CHARLES C. MANN

Before Columbus: The Americas of 1491

(New York: Vintage, 2009)

Subject(s): History; United States history; Native Americans

Age range(s): 10 - 14+
Time period(s): 15th century; 1490s (1491)

Summary: In *Before Columbus: The Americas of 1491*, author Charles C. Mann presents a history of the Americas. Mann talks about the Native Americans who lived undisturbed in the area before European explorers came. Mann says that although many people believe these Native Americans had little impact on the surroundings, they actually had a huge influence on the world as we know it. Furthermore, Mann describes some of the farming and cultural practices of the Native Americans. Throughout the book, Mann uses artifacts and other ancient evidence to support his claims. *Before Columbus* is a book for young adults that accompanies Mann's *1491: New Revelations of the Americans before Columbus*, a book intended for an adult audience.

Where it's reviewed:
Booklist, September 1, 2009, page 92
Horn Book Guide, Spring 2010, page 178
School Library Journal, September 2009, page 183

Other books you might like:
Marc Aronson, *The World Made New: Why the Age of Exploration Happened and How It Changed History*, 2007
Laurence Bergreen, *Columbus: The Four Voyages*, 2011
Michael Dorris, *Morning Girl*, 1992
Russell Freedman, *Who Was First?: Discovering the Americas*, 2007

297

FANI MARCEAU
JOELLE JOLIVET, Illustrator

Panorama: A Foldout Book

(New York: Abrams Books for Young Readers, 2009)

Subject(s): Nature; Ecology; Geography

Age range(s): 5 - 10+

Summary: Author and teacher Fani Marceau and illustrator Joelle Jolivet have teamed up to bring young armchair travelers an all-encompassing look at the natural splendor and ecological beauty of the modern world. The pages of *Panorama: A Foldout Book* open up to reveal a single panoramic vista of the earth's natural majesty. Through one-of-a-kind illustrations and concise text, readers are taken on a voyage from Iceland and India to Scotland and Central America. Presenting ocean scenes, mountain ranges, towns and villages, and wildlife habitats, *Panorama* is a unique volume that celebrates the diversity and grandeur of all the natural world has to offer.

Where it's reviewed:
Booklist, March 1, 2009, page 45
Horn Book Magazine, July/August 2009, page 410
Publishers Weekly, April 6, 2009, page 48

Other books you might like:
Lindsay Barrett George, *Around the World: Who's Been Here*, 1999
Ann Jonas, *Round Trip*, 1983
David McLimans, *Gone Wild: An Endangered Animal Alphabet*, 2006

298

LEONARD S. MARCUS, Editor

Funny Business: Conversations with Writers of Comedy

(Somerville, Massachusetts: Candlewick Press, 2009)

Subject(s): Biographies; Authorship; Literature

Age range(s): 11 - 14+

Summary: In *Funny Business: Conversations with Writers of Comedy*, Leonard S. Marcus interviews and provides insight into the lives of some of the best-known children's authors of all time. The list includes Judy Blume, author of *Tales of a Fourth Grade Nothing* and *Superfudge* as well as young adult novels such as *Tiger Eyes* and *Forever*; Beverly Cleary, author of the Ramona Quimby series; and Louis Sachar, author of *Holes* and the Wayside School series. Other notable authors to whom Marcus speaks include Sharon Creech, Norton Juster, and Hilary McKay. All of the authors share insight into their childhood as well as their process of writing for a young audience in a way that speaks to children without preaching.

Where it's reviewed:
Booklist, October 15, 2009, page 42
Horn Book Magazine, November/December 2009, page 696

School Library Journal, November 2009, page 134

Other books by the same author:
A Caldecott Celebration: Six Artists Share Their Paths to the Caldecott Medal, 2008
Pass It Down: Five Picture-Book Families Make Their Mark, 2006
World in the Word: Conversations With Writers of Fantasy, 2006
Ways of Telling: Fourteen Interviews With Masters of the Art of the Picture Book, 2002

Other books you might like:
Judy Blume, *Tales of a Fourth Grade Nothing*, 1972
Norton Juster, *The Phantom Tollbooth: Special 35th Anniversary Edition*, 1961
Hilary McKay, *Dog Friday*, 1995
Louis Sachar, *Holes*, 1998
Jon Scieszka, *Guys Read: Funny Business*, 2010

299

NAN MARINO

Neil Armstrong Is My Uncle and Other Lies Muscle Man McGinty Told Me

(New York: Roaring Brook Press, 2009)

Subject(s): Bullying; Friendship; Family

Age range(s): 9 - 12+
Major character(s): Tammy, 10-Year-Old; Douglas, Neighbor
Time period(s): 20th century; 1960s (1969)
Locale(s): New York, New York; Massapequa Park

Summary: *Neil Armstrong Is My Uncle & Other Lies Muscle Man McGinty Told Me* is the debut novel from author Nan Marino. In 1969, 10-year-old Tammy is living in Massapequa Park, Long Island, New York, with her distant parents. While her brother is off fighting in Vietnam, Tammy struggles to come to terms with her feelings of alienation and loneliness. She finds an outlet for her despair in Douglas, a new arrival in the neighborhood who lives with a foster family. She picks on him mercilessly, making fun of his outrageous tall tales and scrawny appearance. But beneath her bullying, Tammy is attempting to find some genuine connection and meaning in the ever-changing world of America in the late 60s. First novel.

Where it's reviewed:
Booklist, April 15, 2009, page 54
Bulletin of the Center for Children's Books, July/August 2009, page 450
Horn Book Guide, Spring 2010, page 77
Journal of Adolescent and Adul, November 2009, page 266
School Library Journal, June 2009, page 130

Other books you might like:
Tony Abbott, *Firegirl*, 2006
A.C.E. Bauer, *Come Fall*, 2010
Frances O'Roark Dowell, *Shooting the Moon*, 2008

Barbara Kerley, *Greetings from Planet Earth*, 2007
Stephanie Watson, *Elvis and Olive*, 2008

300

SANDRA MARKLE
ALAN MARKS, Illustrator

Hip-Pocket Papa

(Watertown, Massachusetts: Charlesbridge, 2010)

Subject(s): Amphibians; Frogs; Fathers

Age range(s): 5 - 8+

Summary: The hip-pocket frog of Australia has some unorthodox child care habits. Though the male and female frogs take turns watching over the eggs, the father takes on a new role once the little amphibians hatch. The minuscule tadpoles wriggle right up their father's hind legs. Then they hide in little pockets on his legs. The male frog keeps the hatchlings safe through the dry season, when he has trouble finding food. He has about 30 days to find a creek, where the developing little frogs can leave the safety of their father's pockets to set out on their own. The pen, pencil, and watercolor illustrations give children an up close view of the frogs, which could easily sit on a thumbnail, and their tiny offspring.

Where it's reviewed:
Horn Book Guide, Fall 2010, page 414
School Library Journal, March 2010, page 142

Other books by the same author:
Finding Home, 2008
Little Lost Bat, 2006
A Mother's Journey, 2005

Other books you might like:
Nic Bishop, *Nic Bishop Frogs*, 2008
Joy Cowley, *Red-Eyed Tree Frog*, 1999
Brenda Z. Guiberson, *Rain, Rain, Rain Forest*, 2004
Marilyn Singer, *Tough Beginnings: How Baby Animals Survive*, 2001
David Wiesner, *Tuesday*, 1991

301

ALBERT MARRIN

Years of Dust: The Story of the Dust Bowl

(New York: Dutton Children's Books, 2009)

Subject(s): Ecology; United States history; Great Depression, 1929-1934

Age range(s): 10 - 14+

Summary: In *Years of Dust: The Story of the Dust Bowl*, Albert Marrin gives young readers a historical and ecological background on the disaster known as the Dust Bowl, which took place in the 1930s in the Great Plains region of the United States. Marrin argues that this was not entirely a natural disaster, but the effect of industry and other human impacts on the environment, coupled with droughts, a plague of locusts, other natural factors, and the effects of the Great Depression. Marrin asserts that such tragedies can be prevented, and highlights places around the world where there is a possible danger of reoccurrence due to excessive farming. Historical photographs accompany the text.

Where it's reviewed:
Booklist, August 2009, page 68
Bulletin of the Center for Children's Books, October 2009, page 74
Horn Book Guide, Spring 2010, page 182
New York Times Book Review, November 8 2009, page 18
School Library Journal, August 2009, page 124

Other books by the same author:
Flesh and Blood So Cheap; The Triangle Fire and Its Legacy, 2011

Other books you might like:
Karen Hesse, *Out of the Dust*, 1997
Matt Phelan, *The Storm in the Barn*, 2009
Catherine Reef, *John Steinbeck*, 1996
Martin W. Sandler, *The Dust Bowl Through the Lens: How Photography Revealed and Helped Remedy a National Disaster*, 2009
Jerry Stanley, *Children of the Dust Bowl: The True Story of the School at Weedpatch Camp*, 1992

302

CAROLYN MARSDEN

Take Me with You
(Somerville, Massachusetts: Candlewick Press, 2010)

Subject(s): Adoption; Friendship; Identity
Age range(s): 9 - 12+
Major character(s): Susanna, 11-Year-Old, Orphan; Pina, 11-Year-Old, Orphan
Time period(s): 20th century; 1950s
Locale(s): Naples, Italy

Summary: *Take Me with You* is a heartfelt historical novel for young readers and young adults about friendship, identity, and adoption from author Carolyn Marsden. Set a decade after World War II, the story follows the friendship of Pina and Susanna, two orphan girls being raised by nuns at the Istituto di Gesu Bambino in Naples. The girls grew up together after being abandoned during the war and now, at age 11, they still cling to the hope of adoption but are terrified at the thought of being apart. When prospective parents begin visiting the home, both girls are fearful they won't be selected. Pina suspects her bad behavior will prevent her from being adopted, while Susanna is certain her dark skin will deter prospective parents from taking her home.

Where it's reviewed:
Booklist, January 1, 2010, page 82
Bulletin of the Center for Children's Books, April 2010, page 346
Horn Book Guide, Fall 2010, page 347
Publishers Weekly, February 22, 2010, page 68
School Library Journal, March 2010, page 164

Other books by the same author:
Sahwira: An African Friendship, 2009
Bird Springs, 2007
The Jade Dragon, 2006
Moon Runner, 2005
Silk Umbrellas, 2004

Other books you might like:
Nikki Grimes, *The Road to Paris*, 2006
L.S. Matthews, *Lexi*, 2008
Jacqueline Woodson, *Peace, Locomotion*, 2009

303

RUEBEN MARTINEZ
RAUL COLON, Illustrator

Once upon a Time: Traditional Latin American Tales/Habia una vez: Cuentos tradicionales latinoamericanos
(New York: Rayo, 2010)

Story type: Ethnic; Multicultural
Subject(s): Fairy tales; Fables; Hispanic Americans
Age range(s): 6 - 9+

Summary: Presented by author Rueben Martinez and illustrator Raul Colon, this collection of classic Latin American fairy tales features side-by-side English and Spanish translations for the benefit of both single-language and bilingual readers. Among the traditional tales included in the collection are "Wedding Rooster," "The Flower of Lirolay," "The Tlacuache and the Coyote," "The Mother of the Jungle," "Pedro Urdemales and the Giant," "The King and the Riddle," and others. In addition to the original text of the stories and Colon's accompanying illustrations, Martinez includes information on the historical origins and literary importance of each tale.

Where it's reviewed:
Booklist, February 15, 2010, page 73
Horn Book Guide, Fall 2010, page 401
School Library Journal, December 2009, page 103

Other books you might like:
Lulu Delacre, *Golden Tales: Myths, Legends, and Folklore from Latin America*, 2002
Lucia M. Gonzalez, *Senor Cat's Romance and Other Favorite Stories from Latin America*, 1997
Joe Hayes, *La Llorona / The Weeping Woman*, 2006

304

MARGARET H. MASON
FLOYD COOPER, Illustrator

These Hands
(Boston: Houghton Mifflin Harcourt, 2011)

Story type: Young Readers
Subject(s): Children; African Americans; Working conditions

Age range(s): 5 - 8+

Major character(s): Joseph, Child, Grandson (of Unnamed Character); Unnamed Character, Grandfather (of Joseph), Narrator

Summary: A grandfather tells his grandson, Joseph, about everything he can do with his hands. He can tie a knot, throw a baseball, play the piano, and tie his shoes. But there were also things that his grandfather could not do with his hands. While working at the Wonder Bread factory in the 1950s and 1960s, his grandfather used his hands to load trucks, fix machines, and sweep floors. His bosses, however, did not allow him to make bread or touch dough because they feared that white people would not eat bread made by African Americans. So he used his hands for other things. He carried protest signs and signed petitions, which helped enable all hands to make bread in the future.

Where it's reviewed:
Booklist, February 1, 2011, page 75
Horn Book Guide, Fall 2011, page 321
Publishers Weekly, January 31, 2011, page 48
School Library Journal, March 2011, page 130

Other books by the same author:
Inside All, 2008

Other books you might like:
Michael S. Bandy, *White Water*, 2011
Lois Ehlert, *Hands*, 1997
Andrea Davis Pinkney, *Sit-In: How Four Friends Stood Up by Sitting Down*, 2010
Calvin Alexander Ramsey, *Ruth and the Green Book*, 2010
Aaron Reynolds, *Back of the Bus*, 2010

■305■

WENDY MASS

Finally

(New York: Scholastic, 2010)

Subject(s): Adolescent interpersonal relations; Birthdays; Family

Age range(s): 10 - 13+

Major character(s): Rory Swenson, 12-Year-Old; Jake Harrison, Actor

Time period(s): 21st century; 2010s

Locale(s): United States

Summary: Wendy Mass's *Finally* follows the adventures of Rory Swenson, who has been waiting with baited breath to at last turn 12 years old. Sheltered by her overly concerned parents, Rory compiles a list of things she wants to accomplish now that she's turned 12 and her parents are loosening their restrictive rules. But Rory has no idea just how thoroughly the big 1-2 will change every aspect of her life, and her relationship with a famous movie star is just the tip of the iceberg. *Finally* is the sequel to *11 Birthdays*.

Where it's reviewed:
Booklist, February 1, 2010, page 42
Horn Book Guide, Fall 2010, page 348
Publishers Weekly, February 1, 2010, page 47

School Library Journal, July 2010, page 47

Other books by the same author:
13 Gifts, 2011
11 Birthdays, 2010
Jeremy Fink and the Meaning of Life, 2006

Other books you might like:
Jennifer L. Holm, *Middle School Is Worse than Meatloaf: A Year Told through Stuff*, 2007
Diana Lopez, *Confetti Girl*, 2009
Cynthia Lord, *Rules*, 2006
Raina Telgemeier, *Smile*, 2010

■306■

TRUUS MATTI
NANCY FOREST-FLIER, Translator

Departure Time

(South Hampton, New Hampshire: Namelos, 2010)

Subject(s): Fantasy; Death; Family relations

Age range(s): 10 - 14+

Major character(s): Mouse, 11-Year-Old, Girl

Summary: In this novel by Truus Matti, translated from the Dutch by Nancy Forest-Flier, an 11-year-old girl named Mouse is lost in a strange land where nothing seems familiar. Wandering aimlessly, she enters an old, rundown hotel operated by a fox, who doubles as the hotel's chef, and a rat, who is in charge of maintenance. Also at the hotel is another young girl who wistfully plays a piano. Mouse learns that the girl recently lost her father, a musician, in an accident that might have been avoided if he had come home to celebrate her birthday. As the two tales unfold, it becomes increasingly clear that the girls' separate stories are more closely related than either realizes.

Where it's reviewed:
Booklist, June 1, 2010, page 66
Bulletin of the Center for Children's Books, October 2010, page 84
Horn Book Magazine, Nov/Dec 2009, page 96
Publishers Weekly, August 2, 2010, page 46
School Library Journal, August 2010, page 108

Other books you might like:
David Almond, *Skellig*, 1999
Kate Klise, *Grounded*, 2010
Jean-Claude Mourlevat, *The Pull of the Ocean*, 2006
Linda Newbery, *Lost Boy*, 2007

■307■

SALLEY MAVOR, Author/Illustrator

Pocketful of Posies: A Treasury of Nursery Rhymes

(Boston: Houghton Mifflin, 2010)

Story type: Collection; Young Readers
Subject(s): Poetry; Short stories

Age range(s): 3 - 7+

Summary: In this collection of classic children's nursery rhymes, illustrator Salley Mavor uses cloth to depict the well-known stories. Each of the rhymes in the book is accompanied by one of Mavor's illustrations. The illustrations are made mostly from fabric, but they also include everyday materials like acorns, beads, and seashells. This volume includes the stories of famous characters such as Jack and Jill, Little Miss Muffett, Jack Sprat, and Simple Simon.

Where it's reviewed:
Horn Book Magazine, Nov/Dec 2010, page 110
Publishers Weekly, August 9, 2010, page 50
School Library Journal, September 2010, page 138

Other books by the same author:
Jack and Jill, 2006
Wee Willie Winkie, 2006
Hey Diddle Diddle, 2005
Mary Had a Little Lamb, 2000

Awards the book has won:
Boston Globe - Horn Book Awards: Illustrator or Picture Books, 2011
Golden Kite Awards: Illustration, 2011

Other books you might like:
Lucy Cousins, *Lucy Cousins' Book of Nursery Rhymes*, 1999
Nina Crews, *The Neighborhood Mother Goose*, 2004
Leo Dillon, *Mother Goose: Numbers on the Loose*, 2007
Iona Opie, *My Very First Mother Goose*, 1996
Andrew Fusek Peters, *Here's a Little Poem: A Very First Book of Poetry*, 2007

308

MEGHAN MCCARTHY, Author/Illustrator

The Incredible Life of Balto

(New York: Alfred A. Knopf, 2011)

Subject(s): Dogs; Animals; Biographies

Age range(s): 4 - 7+

Summary: This book by author and illustrator Meghan McCarthy profiles the life of the famous sled dog Balto. Balto became famous for leading a pack of dogs during an emergency in 1925. That year, an epidemic of diphtheria hit Nome, Alaska, and the town needed medicine and supplies to fight the disease. Balto led the team of dogs that delivered the much-needed medicine to the town. After that daring adventure, Balto and his owner enjoyed fame and fortune. People even erected a statue of Balto to honor his bravery. However, Balto's luck changed when he was sold to a vaudeville act. The owners of the act did not treat Balto well. When schoolchildren learned about Balto's living conditions, they donated pennies to buy him from his owners. Eventually Balto—the famous and brave dog—was taken to a local zoo.

Where it's reviewed:
Booklist, July 1, 2011, page 50

Bulletin of the Center for Children's Books, July/August 2011, page 530
Publishers Weekly, May 23, 2011, page 43
School Library Journal, June 2011, page 57

Other books by the same author:
Pop: The Accidental Invention of Bubble Gum, 2010
Seabiscuit: The Wonder Horse, 2008
City Hawk: The Story of Pale Male, 2007

Other books you might like:
Robert J. Blake, *Togo*, 2002
Debbie S. Miller, *The Great Serum Race: Blazing the Iditarod Trail*, 2002
Gary Paulsen, *Dogteam*, 1993

309

MEGHAN MCCARTHY, Author/Illustrator

Pop! The Invention of Bubble Gum

(New York: Simon and Schuster Books for Young Readers, 2010)

Subject(s): Inventors; Inventors; Food

Age range(s): 4 - 8+
Time period(s): 20th century; 1920s

Summary: Whether blowing bubbles or chewing its sugary sweetness, bubble gum has captured the taste buds and imaginations of children for decades. In *Pop! The Invention of Bubble Gum*, author and illustrator, Meghan McCarthy profiles the inventor of bubble gum, Walter Diemer, an accountant who begins a series of experiments that lead to the creation of the eponymous sweet.

Where it's reviewed:
Bulletin of the Center for Children's Books, June 2010, page 445
Horn Book Magazine, May/June 2010, page 166
New York Times Book Review, August 15, 2010, page 13
School Library Journal, May 2010, page 98

Other books by the same author:
The Incredible Life of Balto, 2011
Strong Man: The Story of Charles Atlas, 2007

Other books you might like:
Gene Barretta, *Now & Ben: The Modern Inventions of Benjamin Franklin*, 2006
Monica Brown, *Chavela and the Magic Bubble*, 2010
Joe Hayes, *The Gum Chewing Rattler*, 2008
Stu Smith, *The Bubble Gum Kid*, 2006

310

PETER MCCARTY, Author/Illustrator

Henry in Love

(New York: Balzer + Bray, 2010)

Subject(s): Children; Friendship; Animals

Age range(s): 4 - 7+

Major character(s): Henry, Cat; Chloe, Rabbit

Summary: *Henry in Love* is a picture story for young readers, written and illustrated by Peter McCarty. In the story, Henry, a cat, walks to school with his friends. Once there, he sees Chloe, the rabbit he has a crush on. He is thrilled when the teacher reassigns their seats so he is sitting right next to her. He tries to impress her by chasing her around the playground and doing a somersault, but then Chloe does a much better cartwheel. Later on, at snack time, Chloe finally talks to Henry and asks what he has to eat. He shows her the perfect blueberry muffin his mother made, which he has been saving since lunch, and she simply says, "Thank you!" and takes it from him. Though Henry is disappointed he won't get to eat his blueberry muffin, he is excited to finally be friends with Chloe.

Where it's reviewed:
Booklist, December 1, 2009, page 50
Bulletin of the Center for Children's Books, March 2010, page 295
Horn Book Guide, Fall 2010, page 307
New York Times Book Review, February 14, 2010, page 14
School Library Journal, January 2010, page 77

Other books by the same author:
Jeremy Draws a Monster, 2009
Fabian Escapes, 2007
Hondo and Fabian, 2007

Other books you might like:
Margaret Chodos-Irvine, *Best Best Friends*, 2006
Kevin Henkes, *A Good Day*, 2007
John Langstaff, *Frog Went A-Courtin'*, 1955
Sarah Weeks, *Woof: A Love Story*, 2009

311

GERALDINE MCCAUGHREAN

The Death-Defying Pepper Roux

(New York: Harper, 2010)

Subject(s): Adventure; Survival; Fate

Age range(s): 9 - 12+
Major character(s): Pepper Roux, 14-Year-Old, Adventurer
Time period(s): 20th century
Locale(s): France

Summary: Award-winning author Geraldine McCaughrean chronicles the adventures of French teen Pepper Roux, who was informed by his mean aunt that he would die on his 14th birthday. *The Death-Defying Pepper Roux* follows the Pepper as he flees his home on his 14th birthday in the hope of outwitting the dark prophesy. He ends up embarking on a series of adventures, taking jobs as a ship captain, a Foreign Legion member, and a writer, all of which alter the course of his life—and his long-foretold destiny.

Where it's reviewed:
Booklist, November 1, 2010, page 34
Bulletin of the Center for Children's Books, April 2010, page 346
Horn Book Magazine, January/February 2010, page 88

Publishers Weekly, December 7, 2010, page 49
School Library Journal, January 2010, page 108

Other books by the same author:
The Glorious Adventures of the Sunshine Queen, 2010
The White Darkness, 2007
The Kite Rider, 2002
The Stones are Hatching, 1999

Other books you might like:
Ted Bell, *Nick of Time*, 2008
Ellen Booraem, *The Unnameables*, 2008
Eoin McNamee, *The Navigator*, 2006
N.D. Wilson, *Leepike Ridge*, 2007

312

GERALDINE MCCAUGHREAN

The Glorious Adventures of the Sunshine Queen

(New York: HarperCollins, 2010)

Story type: Historical; Young Readers
Subject(s): Adventure; History; Boats

Age range(s): 10 - 13+
Major character(s): Cissy, 12-Year-Old, Friend (of Kookie and Miss Loucien), Student (of Miss May March), Student (former, of Miss Loucien); Kookie, Student ((former) of Miss Loucien), 12-Year-Old, Friend (of Cissy), Student (of Miss May March); Miss Loucien, Teacher ((former) of Cissy and Kookie), Actress; Miss May March, Teacher (of Cissy and Kookie)
Time period(s): 19th century; 1890s
Locale(s): Oklahoma, United States

Summary: Geraldine McCaughrean revisits the characters of Cissy and Kookie from *Stop the Train!* in this follow-up. Cissy misses her former teacher, Miss Loucien, who gave up teaching to pursue a career as a traveling actress with the Bright Lights Theatre Company. To make matters worse, the grocery store Cissy's family owned was destroyed in a freak accident. When a diphtheria outbreak spreads across town, Cissy, her friend Kookie, and new teacher Miss May March must evacuate. They find refuge aboard Bright Lights' steamship, the *Sunshine Queen*. Soon, the girls find themselves on an adventure on the Missouri River, enduring catastrophes and brushes with death along the way.

Where it's reviewed:
Bulletin of the Center for Children's Books, July/August 2011, page 530
Horn Book Magazine, May/June 2011, page 97
School Library Journal, July 2011, page 102

Other books by the same author:
Stop the Train!, 2003

Other books you might like:
Audrey Couloumbis, *The Misadventures of Maude March, Or, Trouble Rides a Fast Horse*, 2005
Sid Fleischman, *The Trouble Begins at 8: A Life of Mark Twain in the Wild, Wild West*, 2008
Dianne E. Gray, *Tomorrow, the River*, 2006
Joseph Helgerson, *Crows and Cards*, 2009

313

GEORGE MCCLEMENTS, Author/Illustrator

Dinosaur Woods: Can Seven Clever Critters Save Their Forest Home?

(New York: Beach Lane Books, 2009)

Subject(s): Endangered species; Animals; Dinosaurs

Age range(s): 4 - 8+
Major character(s): Rojo, Fox
Time period(s): 21st century; 2000s

Summary: In *Dinosaur Woods: Can Seven Clever Critters Save Their Forest Home?*, author and illustrator George McClements tells the story of a group of animal friends who band together to save their habitat from destruction. When Rojo the fox learns the Plas-Tic Tree Company is going to demolish the forest and put up a factory, he is outraged. With his friends at his side, Rojo comes up with a plan: erect a huge dinosaur made from found objects and scare away the developers. Their plan draws attention, but it isn't long before the world discovers the dinosaur isn't real. Luckily, the attention sheds new light on the plight of Rojo and his friends, and they may not have to leave their beloved forest after all.

Where it's reviewed:
Booklist, May 1, 2009, page 85
Horn Book Guide, Fall 2009, page 336
Publishers Weekly, May 25, 2009, page 56
School Library Journal, June 2009, page 94

Other books by the same author:
Ridin' Dinos with Buck Bronco, 2007

Other books you might like:
Eve Bunting, *Our Library*, 2008
Greg Foley, *Willoughby and the Lion*, 2009
Kate Lum, *What! Cried Granny: An Almost Bedtime Story*, 1999
Nicholas Oldland, *Big Bear Hug*, 2009

314

PATRICK MCDONNELL, Author/Illustrator

Me . . . Jane

(New York: Little, Brown and Company, 2011)

Story type: Historical; Young Readers
Subject(s): Biographies; Africa; Nature

Age range(s): 4 - 7+
Major character(s): Jane Goodall, Child; Jubilee, Toy (stuffed animal), Chimpanzee
Time period(s): 20th century; 1930s-1940s
Locale(s): England

Summary: Author and illustrator Patrick McDonnell shares the fictionalized biography of Jane Goodall in this picture story. Goodall, who studied chimpanzees in Africa for more than four decades, is a world-renowned conservationist and animal rights activist. McDonnell plucks bits and pieces from Goodall's autobiography to spin this tale of a young Jane. Born and raised in England, Jane dreams about one day living in Africa and working with animals. In one scene—Jane, who is curious about the natural world—and her treasured stuffed chimpanzee, Jubilee, sneak into the chicken coop to learn about the origins of eggs. In another, Jane imagines herself swinging through the jungles of Africa like Tarzan. The book includes a message from Goodall and biographical information about her numerous achievements.

Where it's reviewed:
Booklist, March 15, 2011, page 53
Bulletin of the Center for Children's Books, April 2011, page 384
Horn Book Magazine, March/April 2011, page 140
New York Times Book Review, May 15, 2011, page 20
School Library Journal, April 2011, page 148

Other books by the same author:
South, 2008

Awards the book has won:
Charlotte Zolotow Award, 2012

Other books you might like:
Cindy Bickel, *Chimp Math: Learning about Time from a Baby Chimp*, 2002
Michele Coxon, *Termites on a Stick: A Chimp Learns How to Use a Tool*, 2008
Jeanette Winter, *The Watcher: Jane Goodall's Life with the Chimps*, 2011

315

MARILYN TAYLOR MCDOWELL

Carolina Harmony

(New York: Delacorte Press, 2009)

Subject(s): Runaways; Orphans; Rural life

Age range(s): 9 - 11+
Major character(s): Carolina, 10-Year-Old, Runaway; Ray Harmony, Farmer; Miss Latah, Spouse (of Mr. Ray); Auntie Shen, Grandmother (of Carolina, surrogate); Russell, Foster Child
Time period(s): 20th century; 1960s (1964)
Locale(s): Blue Ridge Mountains, North Carolina

Summary: In *Carolina Harmony* by Marilyn Taylor McDowell, 10-year-old Carolina has been bouncing from foster home to foster home since her Auntie Shen died. Taken in by the elderly woman when Carolina's parents and brother were killed in a car crash, the young girl is once again without a family—and unhappy with the arrangements available to her in the Blue Ridge Mountains in 1964. But when she makes her way to Harmony Farm, and the welcoming arms of Mr. Ray and Miss Latah, Carolina seems to have found a home. The arrival of Russell, another runaway, brings about a tragedy that changes everything for Carolina and the Harmonys.

Where it's reviewed:
Booklist, February 1, 2009, page 40
Horn Book Guide, Fall 2009, page 377
School Library Journal, August 2009, page 109

Other books you might like:
Frances O'Roark Dowell, *Where I'd Like to Be*, 2003

Kimberly Newton Fusco, *The Wonder of Charlie Anne*, 2010

Ann Haywood Leal, *Also Known as Harper*, 2009

Margaret McMullan, *When I Crossed No-Bob*, 2007

Ruth White, *Belle Prater's Boy*, 1996

316

MATTHEW MCELLIGOTT, Author/Illustrator

Even Monsters Need Haircuts

(New York: Walker & Company, 2010)

Subject(s): Monsters; Humor; Storytelling

Age range(s): 4 - 8+

Major character(s): Unnamed Character, Boy, Hairdresser (barber)

Summary: *Even Monsters Need Haircuts* is a picture story by Matthew McElligott. In it, the author tells a humorous story about a boy who moonlights as a barber. A young boy watches his father every day as he makes his living as a barber. But once a month, late at night, after everyone else has gone to bed and the clock has struck midnight, the young boy opens up the shop by himself to cut the hair of some very unusual clients. Frankenstein's monster is one of his regular customers, as is Cyclops, Medusa, and the Wolfman. Then one night, a new client enters the shop. It's a human, and the boy doesn't know what to do. After cutting monsters' hair for so long, will he be able to cut the hair of a person?

Where it's reviewed:
Booklist, August 1, 2010, page 59
Horn Book Guide, Spring 2011, page 38
Publishers Weekly, July 5, 2010, page 42
School Library Journal, September 2010, page 130

Other books by the same author:
Absolutely Not, 2004

Other books you might like:
Thomas Docherty, *Big Scary Monster*, 2010
Helen Ketteman, *Goodnight, Little Monster*, 2010
Roxanne Heide Pierce, *Always Listen to Your Mother*, 2010
Mathilde Stein, *The Child Cruncher*, 2008

317

ALISON MCGHEE
DRAZEN KOZJAN, Illustrator

Julia Gillian (and the Quest for Joy)

(New York: Scholastic Press, 2009)

Subject(s): Schools; Friendship; Family life

Age range(s): 8 - 10+

Major character(s): Julia Gillian, 10-Year-Old; Bonwit Keller, Friend; Mr. Mixler, Teacher

Time period(s): 21st century; 2000s

Locale(s): Minneapolis, Minnesota

Summary: Julia Gillian is a 10-year-old student struggling with growing up. Her best friend in the world, Bonwit Keller, is hiding something from her, leaving her feeling alienated and alone. Meanwhile, the school lunch lady, whom Julia adores, is no longer working at the school; in her place is a mean old man who frightens young Julia. Julia isn't faring well with her trumpet lessons, either, but something her music teacher tells her sticks in her mind. Mr. Mixler advises her to "look for the joy," but poor Julia is sure having a tough time finding it. Alison McGhee's *Julia Gillian (and the Quest for Joy)* is the sequel to *Julia Gillian (and the Art of Knowing)*.

Where it's reviewed:
Horn Book Magazine, May/June 2009, page 302
Publishers Weekly, April 13, 2009, page 50
School Library Journal, July 200, page 88

Other books by the same author:
Julia Gillian (and the Dream of the Dog), 2011
Julia Gillian (and the Art of Knowing), 2008

Other books you might like:
Jeanne Birdsall, *The Penderwicks: A Summer Tale of Four Sisters, Two Rabbits, and a Very Interesting Boy*, 2005
Hallie Durand, *Dessert First*, 2009
Peggy Gifford, *Moxy Maxwell Does Not Love Practicing the Piano: But She Does Love Being in Recitals*, 2009
Lisa Glatt, *Abigail Iris: The One and Only*, 2009
Lois Lowry, *Anastasia Krupnik*, 1979

318

LESLIE MCGUIRK, Author/Illustrator

If Rocks Could Sing: A Discovered Alphabet

(Berkeley, California: Tricycle Press, 2011)

Story type: Young Readers
Subject(s): Education; Reading; Nature

Age range(s): 3 - 6+

Summary: Leslie McGuirk has collected 26 quirky stones that greatly resemble the letters of the alphabet, and she presents her collection in this book for young readers. The author's book of letters includes tableaus illustrating the use of the letter. "D is for dog," for example, is accompanied by a rock resembling a dog, wearing a dog collar and tethered to a colorful doghouse. On the "C is for couch potato" page, a lumpy rock figure reclines on a luxurious chaise lounger. Other pages include weathered stones that bear remarkable resemblance to faces conveying various emotions. In addition to the letters and photo illustrations, the entire stone alphabet is included on the end pages.

Where it's reviewed:
Booklist, May 1, 2011, page 93
Horn Book Guide, Fall 2011, page 300
Publishers Weekly, March 14, 2011, page 70
School Library Journal, May 2011, page 83

Other books by the same author:
Tucker's Spooky Halloween, 2007
Snail Boy, 2003

Other books you might like:
Kate Banks, *A Gift from the Sea*, 2001
Simon Basher, *Basher: ABC Kids*, 2011
Stephen T. Johnson, *Alphabet City*, 1996

319

PATRICIA C. MCKISSACK
LEO DILLON, Illustrator
DIANE DILLON, Illustrator

Never Forgotten

(New York: Schwartz & Wade Books, 2011)

Story type: Historical; Young Readers
Subject(s): Slavery; Father-son relations; Single parent family
Age range(s): 9 - 12+
Major character(s): Dinga, Blacksmith, Father (of Musafa); Musafa "Moses", Slave (blacksmith's apprentice), Son (of Dinga); Mother Earth, Guardian (of Musafa); Fire, Guardian (of Musafa); Water, Guardian (of Musafa); Wind, Guardian (of Musafa)
Time period(s): 18th century
Locale(s): Mali; Charleston, South Carolina
Summary: Dinga, a Mende blacksmith in Mali, West Africa, loses his wife when she dies in childbirth. Dinga decides to raise his newborn son himself. He calls upon the elements—Mother Earth, Fire, Water, and Wind—to help him. Young Musafa grows up to become his father's apprentice. Then one day slave traders capture the boy and take him away. Dinga asks the elements to help him find his son. Many years later Wind brings news of Musafa to his father. The boy, now named Moses, has become an apprentice to a blacksmith in Charleston, South Carolina, and will soon be freed by his owner. Patricia C. McKissack relates this story in verse. Leo and Diane Dillon illustrate the characters with thick black lines, reminiscent of woodcut engravings. The elements are depicted in soft watercolors.

Where it's reviewed:
Booklist, August 1, 2011, page 201
Horn Book Magazine, September/October 2011, page 72
Publishers Weekly, August 8, 2011, page 44
School Library Journal, September 2011, page 162

Other books by the same author:
Dear America: A Picture of Freedom, 2011
Days of Jubilee, 2003
Nzingi Warrior Queen of Matamba, Angola Africa 1595, 2000
The Dark Thirty: Southern Tales of the Supernatural, 1992
Mirandy and Brother Wind, 1988

Other books you might like:
Baba Wague Diakite, *A Gift from Childhood: Memories of an African Boyhood*, 2010
Tom Feelings, *The Middle Passage: White Ships/Black Cargo*, 1995

Virginia Hamilton, *Her Stories: African American Folktales, Fairy Tales, and True Tales*, 1995
Laban Carrick Hill, *Dave the Potter, Artist, Poet, Slave*, 2010

320

LISA MCMANN

The Unwanteds

(New York: Simon and Schuster, 2011)

Subject(s): Twins; Children; Coming of age
Age range(s): 10 - 13+
Major character(s): Alex, Twin (of Aaron); Aaron, Twin (of Alex)
Summary: A dark annual tradition has come to pass in the land of Quill. During this ritual, every adolescent is determined to be Wanted, Necessary, or Unwanted. Those who are Wanted will be given the best education and military training; those who are Necessary will keep the land running and working smoothly. Those who are Unwanted are uncertain of their fate but believe they will be exterminated. Aaron and Alex are twin brothers who are separated in an extraordinary turn of fate: Aaron is Wanted while Alex is Unwanted. Alex gets lucky, however. He will go to the magical land of ArtimE, where he will be trained in the gifts of magic. Yet the link between twins is powerful enough to bridge the gap between the world of Quill and the magical land of ArtimE. When Aaron learns that his brother fared far better than he, he sets in motion a plan for vengeance that could destroy ArtimE forever.

Where it's reviewed:
Bulletin of the Center for Children's Books, October 2011, page 94
Publishers Weekly, July 18, 2011, page 154
School Library Journal, August 2011, page 111

Other books you might like:
Paul Bajoria, *The God of Mischief*, 2007
Margaret Peterson Haddix, *Shadow Children Series*, 1998
Robert Newman, *The Boy Who Could Fly*, 1967
Garth Nix, *Shade's Children*, 1997
John Stephens, *The Emerald Atlas*, 2011

321

KATE MCMULLAN
R.W. ALLEY, Illustrator

Pearl and Wagner: One Funny Day

(New York: Dial Books, 2009)

Subject(s): Animals; Schools; Humor
Age range(s): 5 - 7+
Major character(s): Wagner, Mouse, Friend (of Pearl); Pearl, Rabbit, Friend (of Wagner); Bud, Pig, Classmate (of Pearl and Wagner); Henry, Frog, Classmate (of Pearl and Wagner)

Summary: Wagner (the mouse) and best friend, Pearl (the rabbit), aren't quite on the same wave length this particular day. First of all, it's April 1, and Wagner doesn't seem to be able to "get" April Fool's Day. There are a lot of jokes going around the school and he's taking them literally (he thinks he has an overdue library book and that the cafeteria is serving bug juice.) But it's not a joke when Pearl decides to dance with Bud, the pig. Wagner feels left out, but, with lots of cleverness, he winds up getting the last laugh. This beginning reader has plenty of pen, ink, and watercolor illustrations to keep the plot moving right along and three short chapters to provide stopping and starting points.

Where it's reviewed:
Booklist, November 15 2009, page 51
Bulletin of the Center for Children's Books, June 2009, page 412
Horn Book Guide, March-April 2009, page 199
School Library Journal, March 2oo9, page 122

Other books by the same author:
Pearl and Wagner: Four Eyes, 2010
Pearl and Wagner: Three Secrets, 2004
Pearl and Wagner: Two Good Friends, 2003

Other books you might like:
Jennifer Richard Jacobson, *Andy Shane and the Very Bossy Dolores Starbuckle*, 2005
Laura McGee Kvasnosky, *Zelda and Ivy: Keeping Secrets*, 2009
Arnold Lobel, *Frog and Toad Are Friends*, 1970

`322`

COLIN MCNAUGHTON
EMMA CHICHESTER CLARK, Illustrator

Not Last Night but the Night Before

(Somerville, Massachusetts: Candlewick Press, 2009)

Subject(s): Birthdays; Animals

Age range(s): 5 - 8+

Summary: When a young boy hears a knock at his door, he answers it to find a parade of storybook characters who want to come inside. First, the young boy lets in three black cats. Then, he lets in the man in the moon, Little Miss Muffet, Goldilocks, Jack and Jill, the three little pigs, Little Bo-Peep, and others. All of the young boy's guests are carrying packages. When all the guests have arrived, they sing the young boy a funny version of the Birthday Song. *Not Last Night but the Night Before* is written by Colin McNaughton and illustrated by Emma Chichester Clark.

Where it's reviewed:
Bulletin of the Center for Children's Books, November 2009, page 119
Horn Book Magazine, November/December 2009, page 656
New York Times Book Review, December 6, 2009, page 52
School Library Journal, October 2009, page 98

Other books by the same author:
Once Upon an Ordinary School Day, 2005

Other books you might like:
Janet Ahlberg, *The Jolly Postman, Or, Other People's Letters*, 1986
Bonny Becker, *A Birthday for Bear*, 2009
Joe Kulka, *Wolf's Coming!*, 2007
Ian Schoenherr, *Pip and Squeak*, 2007
Melanie Watt, *Scaredy Squirrel Has a Birthday Party*, 2011

`323`

HOLLY MEADE, Author/Illustrator

If I Never Forever Endeavor

(Somerville, Massachusetts: Candlewick Press, 2011)

Story type: Young Readers
Subject(s): Birds; Courage; Adventure

Age range(s): 3 - 5+

Summary: A young bird faces a big decision and the possibility of a great adventure in this endearing picture book for young readers, written and illustrated by Caldecott Honoree Holly Meade. A young fledgling considers the world from the safety of his warm nest. Are his new wings working? Should he give them a try? As he ponders the possibilities, he is overcome with fear and doubt. If his wings don't work, he faces danger, failure, and humiliation. But if he's able to take flight, wonderful adventures and beauty await him. Filled with bold, colorful illustrations, this picture book offers support and hope to readers in need of a little courage.

Where it's reviewed:
Booklist, April 15, 2011, page 52
Bulletin of the Center for Children's Books, May 2011, page 432
New York Times Book Review, June 5, 2011, page 27
Publishers Weekly, February 28, 2011, page 56
School Library Journal, May 2011, page 84

Other books by the same author:
Inside, Inside, Inside, 2005

Other books you might like:
Ursula Dubosarsky, *The Terrible Plop*, 2009
Edel Rodriguez, *Sergio Makes a Splash*, 2008
Eric Rohmann, *A Kitten Tale*, 2008

`324`

PAUL MEISEL, Author/Illustrator

See Me Run

(New York: Holiday House, 2011)

Story type: Young Readers
Subject(s): Dogs; Adventure; Imagination

Age range(s): 4 - 6+
Major character(s): Unnamed Character, Dog (narrator)

Summary: Pups romp and run in a dog park in this picture book by Paul Meisel. Told from a dog's point of view, the tale for early readers follows the frolicking dogs across the grass and through the mud. The running and chasing temporarily gives way to some time spent digging. The dogs' excavation uncovers some giant bones. More running is in store for the digging pooches as a huge dinosaur skeleton rises from the ground and chases the dogs around the park. Meisel's simple, repetitive text complements the action of the wide-eyed dogs in the illustrations.

Where it's reviewed:
School Library Journal, November 2011, page 79

Other books you might like:
Dayle Ann Dodds, *Where's Pup?*, 2003
P.D. Eastman, *Go, Dog. Go!*, 1961
Cari Meister, *Tiny's Bath*, 1998

325

COLIN MELOY
CARSON ELLIS, Illustrator

Wildwood

(New York: Balzer & Bray, 2011)

Subject(s): Birds; Trees (Plants); Magic

Age range(s): 9 - 12+

Major character(s): Prue McKeel, Sister, Friend (of Curtis); Curtis, Friend (of Prue)

Locale(s): Portland, Oregon

Summary: When Prue McKeel's infant brother is stolen by a flock of crows, it's up to her to find out where they took him. Prue tracks the birds to a section of Portland, Oregon, from which no one has ever returned—a heavily wooded area known as Impassable Wilderness. As Prue and her intrepid friend Curtis venture deeper into the forest, they find a hidden land called Wildwood filled with unknown creatures, dangers, and an Evil Queen who has Prue's little brother in her clutches. Now Prue and Curtis are ready for the fight of their lives, but are they ready to have their own reality turned upside down? This book is illustrated by Carson Ellis.

Where it's reviewed:
Booklist, July 1, 2011, page 53
New York Times Book Review, September 18, 2011, page 20
Publishers Weekly, July 18, 2011, page 154
Voice of Youth Advocates, September 2011, page 292

Other books you might like:
Kelly Barnhill, *The Mostly True Story of Jack*, 2011
Jon Berkeley, *The Hidden Boy*, 2010
Madeleine L'Engle, *A Wrinkle in Time*, 1962
C.S. Lewis, *The Lion, the Witch and the Wardrobe*, 1950

326

SEBASTIAN MESCHENMOSER, Author/Illustrator

Waiting for Winter

(Tulsa, Oklahoma: Kane Miller, 2009)

Subject(s): Winter; Animals; Nature

Age range(s): 4 - 7+

Major character(s): Deer, Deer; Hedgehog, Hedgehog; Squirrel, Squirrel; Bear, Bear

Summary: In *Waiting for Winter* by Sebastian Meschenmoser, a group of forest animals anticipates the season's first snow. While Deer has seen snow before, little Squirrel, Hedgehog, and sleepy Bear, are unfamiliar with the concept. As the excitable squirrel waits impatiently for the first flakes to fall, he and his friends wrongly envision the forest floor covered in empty cans, old toothbrushes, and white socks. When the real snow finally falls, the animals are amazed at its beauty and attempt to build their first snowman. Colored pencil illustrations capture the wonder of the simple tale.

Where it's reviewed:
Booklist, November 11, 2009, page 55
Horn Book Guide, Spring 2010, page 35
New York Times Book Review, November 8, 2009, page 22
School Library Journal, September 2009, page 129

Other books you might like:
Susan Blackaby, *Brownie and Groundhog and the February Fox*, 2010
Bernette Ford, *First Snow*, 2005
Leonid Gore, *Danny's First Snow*, 2007
Eric Rohmann, *A Kitten Tale*, 2008

327

KATE MESSNER
CHRISTOPHER SILAS NEAL, Illustrator

Over and Under the Snow

(San Francisco: Chronicle Books, 2011)

Story type: Young Readers
Subject(s): Animals; Nature; Winter

Age range(s): 5 - 8+

Major character(s): Unnamed Character, Girl, Daughter; Father, Father (of girl)

Summary: A father and daughter cross a winter landscape. As they ski through the forest, the man tells his daughter of the activity unseen in winter. Beneath the snow, shrews and squirrels scurry through tunnels and deer mice snuggle down in nests of fur and feathers. The girl sees a fox pounce and dig hurriedly through the snow to catch its prey. Other creatures, including bullfrogs and bumblebee queens, await spring in their hidden dens. The father and daughter are joined by the girl's mother for a bonfire. They roast hot dogs and drink hot cocoa before returning to their warm home for the night. The girl's dreams are filled with all she has seen and learned about wildlife in winter. The author includes additional information at the back of the book about the animals mentioned in the text.

Other books by the same author:
Sea Monster's First Day, 2011

Other books you might like:
Lindsay Barrett George, *In the Snow: Who's Been Here?*, 1999
Ellen Obed, *Who Would Like a Christmas Tree? A Tree for All Seasons*, 2009
Janet Stevens, *Tops and Bottoms*, 1995

328

MENNO METSELAAR
RUUD VAN DER ROL, Co-Author
ARNOLD J. POMERANS, Translator

Anne Frank: Her Life in Words and Pictures

(New York: Roaring Brook Press, 2009)

Subject(s): Holocaust, 1933-1945; Jews; Biographies
Age range(s): 10 - 14+
Summary: In *Anne Frank: Her Life in Words and Pictures*, authors Menno Metselaar and Ruud van der Rol, in association with the Anne Frank House, have assembled a scrapbook of the family's photographs that bring to life Anne's powerful diary entries. From the time that the Frank family hid themselves away in an Amsterdam apartment in 1942 to the date of their capture two years later, young Anne recorded the details of their confinement, as well as her own very personal feelings, in a diary. The photos from family and school events emphasize the horror of the Holocaust through their innocence and universality. Translated from the Dutch by Arnold J. Pomerans.

Where it's reviewed:
Booklist, November 1 2009, page 34
Horn Book Magazine, January/February 2010, page 103
New York Times Book Review, March 14 2010, page 14
School Library Journal, October 2009, page 149

Other books you might like:
Barry Denenberg, *Shadow Life: A Portrait of Anne Frank and Her Family*, 2005
Anne Frank, *Anne Frank: The Diary of a Young Girl*, 1947
Alison Leslie Gold, *Anne Frank Remembered: The Story of the Woman Who Helped to Hide the Frank Family*, 1987
Mirjam Pressler, *Anne Frank: A Hidden Life*, 2000

329

RICHARD MICHELSON
R.G. ROTH, Illustrator

Busing Brewster

(New York: Alfred A. Knopf, 2010)

Subject(s): Schools; Race relations; African Americans
Age range(s): 6 - 8+

Major character(s): Brewster, 1st Grader; Bryan, Brother (of Brewster); Mama, Mother (of Brewster and Bryan); Miss O'Grady, Librarian
Time period(s): 20th century; 1970s (1974)
Locale(s): Boston, Massachusetts

Summary: In *Busing Brewster* by Richard Michelson, two African-American brothers face the challenges of attending a white school in 1974 Boston. When first-grader Brewster and his brother, Bryan learn that they are to be bused from their black neighborhood to attend a new school, their mother tries to convince them of the increased opportunities they will have. Brian remains skeptical, while Brewster tries to keep an open mind. When the bus arrives to a jeering crowd of white parents, and the brothers end up in detention on their first day, Brewster's hopeful spirit sags. The school librarian who monitors detention offers much-needed support.

Where it's reviewed:
Booklist, March 15, 2010, page 46
Horn Book Guide, Fall 2010, page 18
New York Times Book Review, November 7, 2010, page 18
Publishers Weekly, March 29, 2010, page 59
School Library Journal, June 2010, page 80

Other books by the same author:
Lipman Pike: America's First Home Run King, 2011
As Good as Anybody: Martin Luther King and Abraham Joshua Heschel's Amazing March toward Freedom, 2008
Happy Feet: The Savoy Ballroom, Lindy Hoppers and Me, 2005

Other books you might like:
Fredrick McKissack, *Goin' Someplace Special*, 2001
Doreen Rappaport, *This School Is Not White!: A True Story of the Civil Rights Movement*, 2005
Aaron Reynolds, *Back of the Bus*, 2010

330

LYDIA MILLET

The Fires Beneath the Sea

(Easthampton, Massachusetts: Big Mouth House, 2011)

Series: Dissenters Series. Book 1
Story type: Fantasy; Series
Subject(s): Fantasy; Ghosts; Missing persons

Age range(s): 10 - 14+
Major character(s): Cara, Sister (of Jackson & Max), Child; Max, Brother (of Cara & Jackson), Child; Jackson, Brother (of Cara & Max), Genius, Child
Time period(s): 21st century; 2010s
Locale(s): Cape Cod, Massachusetts

Summary: This suspenseful fantasy novel for young readers is the first installment in the Dissenters Series from award-winning author Lydia Millet. Cara's scientist mother has vanished and no one in the family is willing to embrace the reality of the situation. Her father won't talk about it, her older brother Max is drowning out his problems with music, and her younger brother Jackson is consumed with his collection of creepy-crawlies from the beach. When a mysterious ghost appears in the family's Cape Cod home, Cara begins to fear that there's much more to her mom's mysterious disappearance than her father is letting on. Determined to uncover the truth about their mother and the ghosts haunting the island, the three siblings embark on a dangerous adventure that leads them across the Cape and down to the bottom of the ocean.

Where it's reviewed:
School Library Journal, August 2011, page 112

Other books you might like:
Kelly Barnhill, *The Mostly True Story of Jack*, 2011
Mark Kurlansky, *World Without Fish: How Could We Let This Happen?*, 2011
Blake Nelson, *They Came from Below*, 2007
Anne Ursu, *The Siren Song*, 2007

331

CLAUDIA MILLS
HEATHER HARMS MAIONE, Illustrator

How Oliver Olson Changed the World

(New York: Farrar, Straus and Giroux, 2009)

Subject(s): Science; Family; Friendship
Age range(s): 7 - 9+
Major character(s): Oliver Olson, 3rd Grader; Crystal, Classmate
Time period(s): 21st century; 2000s
Summary: Third-grade student Oliver Olson would love to attend his class's forthcoming space-themed sleepover, but he knows that his parents will never allow it. His protective mom and dad are leery of letting their son do anything by himself, and surely a sleepover will be out of the question. But his science partner, Crystal, has a few ideas to help her friend find his voice and communicate his feelings to his parents. Can Oliver heed Crystal's lessons and confront his overly cautious mother and father in time for the much-anticipated sleepover? *How Oliver Olson Changed the World* contains text by Claudia Mills and bright illustrations by Heather Maione.

Where it's reviewed:
Booklist, February 15 2009, page 82
Bulletin of the Center for Children's Books, April 2009, page 309
Horn Book Magazine, March/April 2011, page 201
School Library Journal, March 2009, page 123

Other books by the same author:
Mason Dixon: Pet Disasters, 2011
Being Teddy Roosevelt: A Boy, a President, and a Plan, 2007
7 X 9 = Trouble, 2002

Awards the book has won:
Blue Ribbon Awards: Fiction, 2009

Other books you might like:
Douglas Florian, *Comets, Stars, the Moon, and Mars: Space Poems and Paintings*, 2007
Lisa Graff, *The Thing about Georgie*, 2006

Jessica Scott Kerrin, *Martin Bridge: Out of Orbit!*, 2007
Louis Sachar, *Marvin Redpost: Super Fast, Out of Control!*, 2000

332

SY MONTGOMERY
NIC BISHOP, Photographer

Kakapo Rescue: Saving the World's Strangest Parrot

(Boston, Massachusetts: Houghton Mifflin Books for Children, 2010)

Subject(s): Birds; Endangered species; Research

Age range(s): 9 - 13+
Locale(s): New Zealand

Summary: *Kakapo Rescue: Saving the World's Strangest Parrot* is an educational guide to the endangered species for children and young adults from author Sy Montgomery. The Kakapo Parrot, a large, flightless bird native to New Zealand's Codfish Island, is rapidly facing extinction. With only 91 Kakapo parrots remaining on the planet, the men and women at New Zealand's National Kakapo Recovery Team are working hard to revive the population of these breathtaking and unusual birds. Sy Montgomery and photographer Nic Bishop spent ten days with the recovery team at an island refuge documenting their research and conservation efforts and tracking the various parrots in their care.

Where it's reviewed:
Bulletin of the Center for Children's Books, June 2010, page 438
Horn Book Magazine, July/August 2010, page 136
School Library Journal, June 2010, page 134
Science Books & Film, September 2010, page 241

Other books by the same author:
Saving the Ghost of the Mountain: An Expedition Among Snow Leopards in Mongolia, 2009
The Tarantula Scientist, 2004
The Snake Scientist, 1999

Awards the book has won:
Blue Ribbon Awards: Non-fiction, 2010

Other books you might like:
Kelly Milner Halls, *Saving the Baghdad Zoo*, 2010
Stephen R. Swinburne, *Once a Wolf: How Wildlife Biologists Fought to Bring Back the Gray Wolf*, 1999
Pamela S. Turner, *Gorilla Doctors: Saving Endangered Great Apes*, 2005

333

PAT MORA
JOHN PARRA, Illustrator

Gracias Thanks

(New York: Lee & Low, 2009)

Subject(s): Hispanic Americans; Family; Values (Philosophy)

Age range(s): 3 - 6+
Major character(s): Unnamed Character, Child
Time period(s): 21st century; 2000s
Locale(s): United States

Summary: In *Gracias Thanks* by Pat Mora, a young boy expresses gratitude for his life's simple joys in the languages of his multiracial family—English and Spanish. The boy finds delight and reason for celebration in his day's smallest details, from a close encounter with a ladybug to a safely distant encounter with bees. John Parra's lively acrylic illustrations follow the boy's adventures as he reads a friend's book, catches a fish, and listens to his uncle play the guitar. As the boy gives thanks for the last gift of his day, the lullaby song of a cricket, he invites young readers to join his practice of gratefulness.

Where it's reviewed:
Booklist, November 1 2009, page 35
Horn Book Magazine, January/February 2009, page 77
School Library Journal, December 2009, page 103

Other books by the same author:
The Desert Is My Mother/El desierto es mi madre, 1994
Pablo's Tree, 1994

Awards the book has won:
Golden Kite Awards: Illustration, 2010

Other books you might like:
Amada Irma Perez, *My Very Own Room*, 2000
Shelley Rotner, *Feeling Thankful*, 2000
Liz Garton Scanlon, *All the World*, 2009

334

PAT MORA
RAFAEL LOPEZ, Illustrator

Book Fiesta!: Celebrate Children's Day/Book Day; Celebremos El dia de los ninos/El dia de los libros

(New York: HarperCollins, 2009)

Subject(s): Children; Special events; Books and reading
Age range(s): 3 - 7+
Locale(s): United States

Summary: In *Book Fiesta!: Celebrate Children's Day/ Book Day; Celebremos El dia de los ninos/El dia de los libros*, a bilingual picture book written by Pat Mora and illustrated by Rafael Lopez, children celebrate Children's Day/Book Day. The children read books in different languages, visit the library with friends, and listen to their family members tell stories. These events emphasize the importance of recognizing and celebrating differences in language, culture, and each other. Each page is written in both English and Spanish. The book includes a letter from the author about the celebration of Children's Day/Book Day in the United States, traditionally celebrated in Mexico on April 30. Such celebrations are now found in various places such as museums, schools, libraries, and community centers. Suggestions for ways to celebrate Children's Day/Book Day are also included. A percentage of the profits from the book will

be donated to programs that improve children's literacy.

Where it's reviewed:
Booklist, January 1 2009, page 90
Horn Book Guide, Fall 2010, page 338
School Library Journal, February 2009, page 93

Other books by the same author:
Tomas and the Library Lady, 1997

Awards the book has won:
Pura Belpre Award: Illustrator Award, 2010

Other books you might like:
Denys Cazet, *Will You Read to Me?*, 2007
Anna McQuinn, *Lola Loves Stories*, 2010
Ian Schoenherr, *Read It, Don't Eat It!*, 2009
Judy Sierra, *Wild about Books*, 2004
Louise Yates, *Dog Loves Books*, 2010

335

BRANDON MULL

A World without Heroes

(New York: Simon and Schuster, 2011)

Series: Beyonders Series. Book 1
Subject(s): Spacetime; Time travel; Revolutions
Age range(s): 9 - 12+
Major character(s): Jason, 14-Year-Old; Rachel, Teenager; Maldor, Ruler (of Lyrian)
Locale(s): Lyrian, Alternate Universe

Summary: *A World Without Heroes* is the first installment from author Brandon Mull's fantasy series Beyonders. In this book readers are introduced to Jason and Rachel, two teenagers who are sucked from the real world into an alternate universe. Set down in a dark land called Lyrian, the teens must figure out how to get back to their reality. Soon Jason and Rachel learn that they must reveal a secret word designed to conquer Maldor, Lyrian's sinister ruler, in order to return home. As the two teens search for each syllable of the mysterious word, they must fight unimaginable obstacles along the way.

Where it's reviewed:
Booklist, February 15, 2011, page 75
Bulletin of the Center for Children's Books, March 2011, page 339
Publishers Weekly, January 31, 2011, page 50
School Library Journal, March 2011, page 166
Voice of Youth Advocates, August 2011, page 294

Other books by the same author:
Keys to the Demon Prison, 2010
Secrets of the Dragon Sanctuary, 2009
Rise of the Evening Star, 2007
Fablehaven, 2006

Other books you might like:
Cornelia Funke, *Reckless*, 2010
Mike Lupica, *Hero*, 2010
Emily Rodda, *The Key to Rondo*, 2008
John Stephens, *The Emerald Atlas*, 2011
Jonathan Stroud, *The Ring of Solomon*, 2010

336

ROXIE MUNRO, Author/Illustrator

Go! Go! Go!: More Than 70 Flaps to Uncover & Discover!

(New York: Sterling, 2009)

Subject(s): Art; Transportation; Children

Age range(s): 4 - 8+

Summary: This interactive volume introduces young readers to the ways various people, animals, and objects get from point A to point B. *Go! Go! Go!: More Than 70 Flaps to Uncover & Discover!* contains durable flaps that lift up to reveal a series of findings that will both educate and entertain children. Readers witness balloons soaring through the skies, horses galloping gleefully around a path, racing cars zipping around a racetrack, firefighters sliding down poles and fighting flames, a submarine plummeting to the depths of the ocean, and much more. Author Roxie Munro provides the illustrations to this inventive volume geared toward readers ages four and up.

Where it's reviewed:
Bulletin of the Center for Children's Books, Januaary 2010, page 221
Horn Book Magazine, July/August 2009, page 412
School Library Journal, June 2009, page 96

Other books by the same author:
Circus: Over 50 Flaps Plus Seek-And-Find, 2006
Doors, 2004

Other books you might like:
Robert Burleigh, *Clang! Clang! Beep! Beep!: Listen to the City*, 2009
P.D. Eastman, *Go, Dog. Go!*, 1961
Kersten Hamilton, *Red Truck*, 2008
Peter Stein, *Cars Galore*, 2011
Frank Viva, *Along a Long Road*, 2011

337

JIM MURPHY

Truce: The Day the Soldiers Stopped Fighting

(New York: Scholastic Press, 2009)

Subject(s): World War I, 1914-1918; Christmas; Wars

Age range(s): 10 - 14+
Time period(s): 20th century; 1910s (1914)
Locale(s): Belgium

Summary: In *Truce: The Day the Soldiers Stopped Fighting*, award-winning author Jim Murphy relates the story of World War I's Christmas miracle, when British and German troops that had been battling on the Western front observed an unofficial cease-fire on December 25, 1914. While war raged across Europe, the men stationed near Ypres, Belgium, suddenly refused to fight in defiance of their commanders' orders. Some even took part in impromptu Christmas celebrations with their enemies. Written especially for young readers, *Truce* chronicles the remarkable events of the day while also illustrating the absurdity of war and the resilience of the human spirit.

Where it's reviewed:
Booklist, October 15 2009, page 51
Bulletin of the Center for Children's Books, December 2009, page 162
Horn Book Magazine, November/December 2009, page 647
Publishers Weekly, October 26 2009, page 59
School Library Journal, November 2009, page 134

Other books by the same author:
Blizzard: The Storm That Changed America, 2000
The Great Fire, 1995

Awards the book has won:
Blue Ribbon Awards: Non-fiction, 2008

Other books you might like:
John McCutcheon, *Christmas in the Trenches*, 2006
Michael Morpurgo, *War Horse*, 1982
Jenny Moss, *Winnie's War*, 2009
Marcia Williams, *Archie's War*, 2007

338

SALLY MURPHY
HEATHER POTTER, Illustrator

Pearl verses the World

(Somerville, Massachusetts: Candlewick Press, 2011)

Story type: Contemporary; Young Readers
Subject(s): Poetry; Writing; Schools

Age range(s): 8 - 10+
Major character(s): Pearl, Student (of Mr. Bruff), Writer (of poetry), Daughter, Granddaughter; Mr. Bruff, Teacher (of Pearl)
Time period(s): 21st century; 2010s

Summary: Pearl feels like she just doesn't fit in at school. Some of the kids pick on her, and her teacher makes her feel like an outcast. Mr. Bruff tells Pearl that poetry should rhyme, but Pearl can't seem to write rhyming poetry. Pearl likes to spend most of her time at home, where she lives with her mother and grandmother. Her grandmother suffers from dementia, however, so Pearl's mom is always busy. Her mom even says that they might have to move grandma into a nursing home. Then, a tragedy strikes Pearl's family, and she will have to find her own voice so she can deal with her pain. This novel for young readers is written by Sally Murphy and illustrated by Heather Potter.

Where it's reviewed:
Horn Book Magazine, September/October 2011, page 93
School Library Journal, September 2011, page 126

Other books you might like:
Katherine Hannigan, *Emmaline and the Bunny*, 2009
Amy Heist, *Remembering Mrs. Rossi*, 2007
Laura Amy Schlitz, *The Night Fairy*, 2010
James Stevenson, *Mr. Hacker*, 1990

`339`

ALISON MURRAY, Author/Illustrator

Apple Pie ABC

(New York: Hyperion Books, 2011)

Story type: Young Readers
Subject(s): Reading; Dogs

Age range(s): 3 - 6+

Summary: Alison Murray uses the alphabet to entertain and educate young readers in this picture book. In the book a precocious young puppy desperately wants to eat a piece of fresh apple pie. When the puppy sees his owner place the delicious, steaming-hot pie on the kitchen table, he tries everything he can think of to get a bite of it. Murray describes the playful pup's attempts to sink his teeth into the pie using all the letters of the alphabet. Will the hungry pup get a taste of the pie somewhere between A and Z?

Where it's reviewed:
Bulletin of the Center for Children's Books, June 2011, page 481
Horn Book Magazine, July/August 2011, page 134
Publishers Weekly, March 14, 2011, page 70
School Library Journal, July 2011, page 73

Other books you might like:
Robbin Gourley, *Bring Me Some Apples and I'll Make You a Pie: A Story about Edna Lewis*, 2009
Anita Lobel, *On Market Street*, 1981
Anne Rockwell, *Apples and Pumpkins*, 1989
Gennady Spirin, *A Apple Pie*, 2005
Lauren Thompson, *The Apple Pie That Papa Baked*, 2007

`340`

LAURA MURRAY
MIKE LOWERY, Illustrator

The Gingerbread Man Loose in the School

(New York: G.P. Putnam's Sons, 2011)

Story type: Young Readers
Subject(s): Cooking; Food; Schools

Age range(s): 4 - 7+
Major character(s): The Gingerbread Man, Object (cookie)

Summary: In this freshly baked take on the traditional tale, a gingerbread man navigates his way through school hallways in search of the students who baked him and then left him behind to attend recess. In his search for the children, the gingerbread man meets the art teacher, the physical education teacher, the principal, and the school nurse, who tends to his injured toe. A poster in the back pocket of the book provides a recipe that students can use to bake their very own gingerbread man cookies and other fun activities to engage students. Author Laura Murray provides the book's rhyming narrative, and Mike Lowery provides the illustrations.

Where it's reviewed:
Booklist, August 1, 2011, page 53
Horn Book Magazine, September/Octobert 2011, page 73
School Library Journal, August 2011, page 81

Other books you might like:
Ying Chang Compestine, *The Runaway Rice Cake*, 2001
Dotti Enderle, *The Library Gingerbread Man*, 2010
Lisa Campbell Ernst, *The Gingerbread Girl Goes Animal Crackers*, 2006
Ann Hassett, *Can't Catch Me*, 2006
Naomi Howland, *The Matzah Man*, 2002

`341`

WALTER DEAN MYERS
CHRISTOPHER MYERS, Illustrator

We Are America: A Tribute from the Heart

(New York: HarperCollins, 2011)

Subject(s): History; United States; Poetry

Age range(s): 8 - 11+

Summary: *We Are America: A Tribute from the Heart* is a picture book for young readers celebrating the history of the United States from best-selling author Walter Dean Myers and Caldecott Honor illustrator Christopher Myers. The book pays homage to America's rich and complex history, invaluable freedom, and long line of heroic leaders. *We Are America* is written in lyrical free verse and includes a slew of allusions to the nation's remarkable history and icons, from Abraham Lincoln to Jimi Hendrix. Artist Christopher Myers complements the text with beautiful and colorful layered-text illustrations done in a panoramic style.

Where it's reviewed:
Booklist, May 1, 2011, page 75
Horn Book Guide, Fall 2011, page 464
New York Times Book Review, July 17, 2011, page 13
Publishers Weekly, March 21, 2011, page 76
School Library Journal, May 2011, page 135

Other books by the same author:
Looking Like Me, 2009
Harlem, 1997
Brown Angels: An Album of Pictures and Verse, 1993

Other books you might like:
Lynne Cheney, *America: A Patriotic Primer*, 2002
Linda Glaser, *Emma's Poem: The Voice of the Statue of Liberty*, 2010
Lee Bennett Hopkins, *America at War*, 2008
Lee Bennett Hopkins, *Hand in Hand: An American History through Poetry*, 1994

342

WALTER DEAN MYERS
CHRISTOPHER MYERS, Illustrator

Looking Like Me
(New York: Egmont USA, 2009)

Subject(s): Individualism; Family life; African Americans

Age range(s): 7 - 10+

Major character(s): Jeremy, Child

Time period(s): 21st century; 2000s

Locale(s): New York, New York

Summary: In Walter Dean Myers's *Looking Like Me,* a young boy named Jeremy ventures out into his Harlem neighborhood to revel in the varied facets of his identity. Told in rhythmic rap verse and illustrated with vibrant collages, Jeremy's quest reveals his roles as son, brother, dancer, writer, runner, and dreamer. As Jeremy greets family members, teachers, and passersby with a celebratory fist-bump and an "I am BAM," he invites young readers to explore their own inner selves and discover the wonders of individuality. Father and son team Walter Dean Myers and Christopher Myers collaborated previously on *Harlem.*

Where it's reviewed:
Booklist, October 15, 2009, page 50
Bulletin of the Center for Children's Books, December 2009, page 163
Horn Book Magazine, November/December 2009, Page 656
Publishers Weekly, October 5, 2009, page 47
School Library Journal, November 2009, page 96

Other books by the same author:
We Are America: A Tribute From the Heart, 2011
Harlem, 1997
Brown Angels: An Album of Pictures and Verse, 1993

Other books you might like:
Molly Bang, *All of Me: A Book of Thanks,* 2009
Bryan Collier, *Uptown,* 2000
Carolivia Herron, *Nappy Hair,* 1997
Vaunda Micheaux Nelson, *Who Will I Be, Lord?,* 2009
James Rumford, *Silent Music,* 2008

343

LAUREN MYRACLE

Luv Ya Bunches
(New York: Amulet Books, 2009)

Series: Flower Power Series. Book 1

Story type: Humor

Subject(s): Friendship; Technology; Schools

Age range(s): 10 - 12+

Major character(s): Katie-Rose, 5th Grader, Filmmaker (amateur); Camilla "Milla", 5th Grader; Yasaman, 5th Grader; Violet, 5th Grader, Student (new); Modessa, 5th Grader

Time period(s): 21st century; 2010s

Summary: Tweens navigate the social circles surrounding a tyrannical queen bee in this series from Lauren Myracle. Katie-Rose, Milla, Yasaman, and Violet seem to have nothing in common at first. Katie-Rose is a lonely girl who devotes herself to making films. Milla, who has two moms, is part of the popular crowd. Yasaman, a Muslim, is super savvy with technology and has designed an online social site. Violet, the new girl, is lost and struggling. Yet when queen bee Modessa tells a lie, these four very different girls work together to clear Katie-Rose of theft accusations. Texting, chat rooms, and storytelling combine to create the world of these fifth-grade girls and move the story along.

Where it's reviewed:
Booklist, September 15, 2009, page 58
Horn Book Guide, Spring 2010, page 78
Publishers Weekly, October 5, 2009, page 50
School Library Journal, November 2009, page 116

Other books by the same author:
Violet in Bloom, 2010

Other books you might like:
Meg Cabot, *Best Friends and Drama Queens,* 2009
Amy Ignatow, *The Popularity Papers: Research for the Social Improvement and General Betterment of Lydia Goldblatt and Julie Graham-Chang,* 2010
Wendy Mass, *11 Birthdays,* 2009
Rachel Renee Russell, *Dork Diaries: Tales from a Not-So-Fabulous Life,* 2009

344

LAUREN MYRACLE

Ten
(New York: Dutton, 2011)

Series: Winnie Years Series. Book 5

Story type: Series; Young Adult

Subject(s): Friendship; Family; Coming of age

Age range(s): 8 - 10+

Major character(s): Winnie Perry, 10-Year-Old, 5th Grader, Sister (of Sandra and Ty), Friend (of Amanda), Bullied Child (by Mindy); Amanda, 5th Grader, Friend (of Winnie); Mindy, 5th Grader, Bully (of Mindy); Sandra, Sister (of Winnie and Ty); Ty, 3-Year-Old, Brother (of Winnie and Sandra)

Time period(s): 21st century; 2000s

Summary: The fifth book and prequel to Lauren Myracle's Winnie Years series goes back in time to revisit Winnie Perry as she turns ten years old and enters fifth grade—her last year of elementary school. Winnie is an eccentric girl, secure with herself, even as she faces self-doubts throughout the book. In addition to dealing with a three-year-old brother, Ty, and older sister, Sandra, at home, Winnie finds that turning ten is a big deal and begins a journal on her birthday. She discovers that fifth grade has its ups and downs such as noticing boys, fighting with friends, and surviving bullies. Winnie's best friend, Amanda, starts hanging around boys and makes less time for Winnie, who decides she is not ready for boys just yet. Winnie has other problems—namely a bully, Mindy. Myracle continues Winnie's adventures in *Eleven,*

Twelve, Thirteen, and Thirteen Plus One.

Where it's reviewed:
Booklist, June 1, 2011, page 92
Horn Book Guide, Fall 2011, page 63
School Library Journal, September 2011, page 162

Other books by the same author:
Thirteen Plus One, 2010
Thirteen, 2008
Twelve, 2007
Eleven, 2004

Other books you might like:
Marion Dane Bauer, The Double Digit Club, 2004
Barbara Dee, Solving Zoe, 2010
Frances O'Roark Dowell, The Secret Language of Girls, 2004
Wendy Mass, 11 Birthdays, 2009

345

LELA NARGI
KYRSTEN BROOKER, Illustrator

The Honeybee Man
(New York: Schwartz & Wade Books, 2011)

Story type: Young Readers
Subject(s): Bees; Gardens; Agriculture

Age range(s): 5 - 8+
Major character(s): Fred, Man (elderly), Beekeeper
Locale(s): New York, New York

Summary: Fred lives in Brooklyn, New York, with a dog and a cat. He also shares his house with three other families, but they don't live inside. They live in three bee houses on the roof of Fred's home. A queen bee lives in each house with her drones and worker bees. All the worker bees are sisters. Fred visits them on the roof all summer and into the fall. He greets the bees fondly and imagines all the places they travel as they gather nectar. In the fall, Fred carefully removes some of the honey the bees have made, bottling the golden liquid for sale and to give as gifts. Author Lela Nargi includes facts about beekeepers, honey, and honeybees, and she explains that two beekeepers, or apiarists, in Brooklyn were the inspiration for her story. Kyrsten Brooker's illustrations include diagrams of bees, flowers, and hives to supplement the story.

Where it's reviewed:
Booklist, March 15, 2011, page 63
Horn Book Magazine, March/April 2011, page 105
Publishers Weekly, January 31, 2011, page 49
School Library Journal, March 2011, page 130

Other books you might like:
Joanna Cole, The Magic School Bus: Inside a Beehive, 1996
Bobbie Kalman, The Life Cycle of a Honeybee, 2004
Cristina Kessler, The Best Beekeeper of Lalibela: A Tale from Africa, 2006
Charles Micucci, The Life and Times of the Honeybee, 1995

Shelley Rotner, The Buzz on Bees: Why Are They Disappearing?, 2010

346

PHYLLIS REYNOLDS NAYLOR
ROSS COLLINS, Illustrator

Emily's Fortune
(New York: Delacorte Press, 2010)

Subject(s): Orphans; Voyages and travels; Inheritance and succession

Age range(s): 9 - 11+
Major character(s): Emily Wiggins, 8-Year-Old, Orphan, Niece (of Victor); Jackson, Orphan; Victor, Uncle (of Emily)
Time period(s): 19th century
Locale(s): American West, United States

Summary: In Emily's Fortune, award-winning author Phyllis Reynolds Naylor tells the story of a shy eight-year-old girl who embarks on the adventure of her young life in the Wild West. After Emily Wiggins's parents suddenly die, the little girl is put on a train bound for the West, where she is to live with distant family. But a band of child thieves—hired by Emily's cruel uncle—is on her trail, hoping to place Emily with her dastardly uncle and thereby collecting a hefty profit. She soon crosses paths with another orphan named Jackson, and the two set out to elude the child-catchers and outsmart the inheritance-seeking Uncle Victor. Emily's Fortune includes illustrations by Ross Collins.

Where it's reviewed:
Horn Book Guide, Fall 2010, page 349
School Library Journal, June 2010, page 80

Other books by the same author:
Roxie and the Hooligans, 2006

Other books you might like:
Carolyn Coman, The Big House, 2004
Audrey Couloumbis, The Misadventures of Maude March, Or, Trouble Rides a Fast Horse, 2005
Sid Fleischman, The Ghost in the Noonday Sun, 1965

347

PHYLLIS REYNOLDS NAYLOR

Faith, Hope, and Ivy June
(New York: Delacorte Press, 2009)

Story type: Young Readers
Subject(s): Friendship; Family sagas; Diaries

Age range(s): 9 - 12+
Major character(s): Ivy June Moseley, 7th Grader; Catherine Combs, 7th Grader
Time period(s): 21st century; 2000s
Locale(s): Kentucky, United States

Summary: In Faith, Hope, and Ivy June, prolific children's author Phyllis Reynolds Naylor explores the relationship between two very different girls who come together at a pivotal time in their adolescence. Ivy June and Catherine are taking part in a student exchange program, through which the two girls share their seemingly dissimilar lives with one another: living together, going to school together, and navigating the uneasy waters of young adulthood. Though they come from different worlds, Ivy June and Catherine soon discover that they have a lot in common, and their friendship becomes a beacon of strength and support for both girls.

Where it's reviewed:
Booklist, May 15, 2009, page 42
Bulletin of the Center for Children's Books, September 2009, page 33
Horn Book Magazine, September/October 2009, page 569
Publishers Weekly, June 15, 2009, page 49
School Library Journal, September 2009, page 168

Other books by the same author:
Who Won the War?, 2006
Alice the Brave, 1995
All But Alice, 1992
Shiloh, 1991
Alice in Rapture, Sort Of, 1989

Other books you might like:
Kristin Levine, *The Best Bad Luck I Ever Had*, 2009
Marilyn Taylor McDowell, *Carolina Harmony*, 2009
Margaret McMullan, *When I Crossed No-Bob*, 2007
Ruth White, *Little Audrey*, 2008
Ruth White, *Way Down Deep*, 2007

348

KADIR NELSON, Author/Illustrator

Heart and Soul: The Story of America and African Americans

(New York: Balzer & Bray, 2011)

Subject(s): African Americans; Blacks; American Reconstruction, 1865-1877

Age range(s): 9 - 12+

Summary: In this picture book, author Kadir Nelson portrays the African American experience through a character called Everywoman. Everywoman follows details the early history of African Americans as they reached US soil on slave ships prior to the American Civil War. The character proceeds to tell the story of how African Americans fought and worked endlessly to gain basic civil right. The story focuses on various points of African American history, including the aftermath of the Civil War, the effects of Jim Crow laws, and the influence of the mid-20th century civil rights movement. Nelson is the author of *We are the Ship: The Story of Negro League Baseball*.

Where it's reviewed:
Booklist, August 1, 2011, page 44
Horn Book Magazine, November/December 2011, page 125
Publishers Weekly, June 20, 2011, page 53
School Library Journal, September 2011, page 184

Other books by the same author:
Change Has Come: An Artist Celebrates Our American Spirit, 2009
We Are the Ship: The Story of Negro League Baseball, 2008

Awards the book has won:
Coretta Scott King Book Award: Author Award, 2012

Other books you might like:
Ruby Bridges, *Through My Eyes*, 1999
Laban Carrick Hill, *Dave the Potter, Artist, Poet, Slave*, 2010
Walter Dean Meyers, *Harlem*
Andrea Davis Pinkney, *Bird in a Box*, 2011
Anne Rockwell, *Only Passing Through: The Story of Sojourner Truth*, 2000

349

MARILYN NELSON
TIMOTHY BASIL ERING, Illustrator

Snook Alone

(Somerville, Massachusetts: Candlewick Press, 2010)

Subject(s): Friendship; Human-animal relationships; Wilderness survival

Age range(s): 6 - 9+
Major character(s): Abba Jacob, Religious (monk), Human; Snook, Dog, Animal (pet of Abba)
Time period(s): 21st century

Summary: *Snook Alone* is a heartwarming picture book for young readers from award-winning poet, Marilyn Nelson. Abba Jacob, a dedicated monk, lives on an isolated island with his rat terrier, Snook. A faithful companion, Snook accompanies Abba throughout his daily tasks and activities, which include gardening, plumbing, and prayer. The pair is inseparable until a horrible storm forces them apart. All alone in the foreign wilderness, Snook must learn to survive without his companion. Will the two friends ever be reunited? Filled with beautiful paintings by Timothy Basil Ering, *Snook Alone* is a moving tale of friendship, hope, and survival.

Where it's reviewed:
Booklist, June 1, 2010, page 69
Bulletin of the Center for Children's Books, October 2010, page 87
Horn Book Magazine, January/February 2010, page 80
Publishers Weekly, August 30, 2010, page 49

Awards the book has won:
Blue Ribbon Awards: Fiction, 2010

Other books you might like:
Robyn Belton, *Herbert: The Brave Sea Dog*, 2008
Joan Hiatt Harlow, *Thunder from the Sea*, 2004
Robert Kraske, *Marooned: The Strange But True Adventure of Alexander Selkirk, the Real Robinson Crusoe*, 2005
Pamela S. Turner, *Hachiko: The True Story of a Loyal Dog*, 2004

350

VAUNDA MICHEAUX NELSON
SEAN QUALLS, Illustrator

Who Will I Be, Lord?

(New York: Random House, 2009)

Subject(s): Family history; African Americans; Values
(Philosophy)

Age range(s): 4 - 7+

Summary: In *Who Will I Be, Lord?*, written by Vaunda
Micheaux Nelson and illustrated by Sean Qualls, a young
African American girl considers her family tree and her
ancestors, wondering what type of person she will turn
out to be. In her family tree are many interesting people
with good values, including a mailman who enjoyed
playing the banjo and a jazz musician who worked as a
cook. Believing family is the most important thing in the
world, the young girl hopes to grow to be just like her
ancestors.

Where it's reviewed:
Booklist, November 15, 2009, page 47
Horn Book Magazine, November/December 2009,
page 657
School Library Journal, October 2009, page 100

Other books by the same author:
Insectlopedia, 2002
Mammalabila, 2000
In the Swim, 1997
On the Wing, 1996
Beast Feast: Poems, 1994

Other books you might like:
Toni Morrison, *Little Cloud and Lady Wind*, 2010
Walter Dean Myers, *Looking Like Me*, 2009
Marilyn Nelson, *Beautiful Ballerina*, 2009
Liz Garton Scanlon, *All the World*, 2009

351

VAUNDA MICHEAUX NELSON
R. GREGORY CHRISTIE, Illustrator

Bad News for Outlaws: The Remarkable Life of Bass Reeves Deputy U.S. Marshal

(New York: Minneapolis, Minnesota, 2009)

Subject(s): Law; Americana; United States history

Age range(s): 8 - 10+

Summary: *Bad News for Outlaws: The Remarkable Life of
Bass Reeves Deputy U.S. Marshal* is the story of Bass
Reeves, one of the most successful U.S. Marshals in
American Western history. This volume shows how
Reeves broke through racial barriers and prejudices to
become one of the most trusted lawmen of his time.

Where it's reviewed:
Booklist, October 1 2009, page 39
Bulletin of the Center for Children's Books, January
2010, page 210

Horn Book Magazine, November/December 2009, page
698
Publishers Weekly, November 2 2009, page 52
School Library Journal, November 2009, page 134

Awards the book has won:
Carter G. Woodson Book Award: Elementary, 2010
Coretta Scott King Book Award: Author Award, 2010

Other books you might like:
Julius Lester, *Black Cowboy, Wild Horses: A True Story*,
1998
Morgan Monceaux, *My Heroes, My People: African
Americans and Native Americans in the West*, 1999
Jerdine Nolen, *Big Jabe*, 2000
Gary Paulsen, *The Legend of Bass Reeves: Being the
True and Fictional Account of the Most Valiant
Marshal in the West*, 2006
Gaylia Taylor, *George Crum and the Saratoga Chip*,
2006

352

MARY NETHERY
KIRBY LARSON, Co-Author
BRIAN DENNIS, Co-Author

Nubs: The True Story of a Mutt, a Marine, & a Miracle

(New York: Little, Brown Book for Young Readers, 2009)

Subject(s): Dogs; Wars; Military life

Age range(s): 5 - 9+

Summary: Marine Major Brian Dennis was fighting in
Iraq in 2007 when he came across a wild, earless dog.
The dog, which Dennis named Nubs, became attached to
the marine and tried to follow him when he left the base.
A few months after Nubs befriended Dennis, Dennis and
his fellow troops relocated to an area 70 miles away.
Nubs completed the long, dangerous journey to reunite
with Dennis. Marine policies do not allow troops to keep
pets in war zones, so Dennis had to get Nubs out of Iraq
for everyone's safety. Dennis raised money and used the
funds to send Nubs home to San Diego, California.
Eventually, Nubs and Dennis were reunited in the United
States. *Nubs: The True Story of a Mutt, a Marine, & a
Miracle* is written by Major Brian Dennis, Kirby Larson,
and Mary Nethery.

Where it's reviewed:
Booklist, October 1, 2009, page 42
Horn Book Guide, Spring 2010, page 146
Publishers Weekly, November 9, 2009, page 45
School Library Journal, December 2009, page 97

Awards the book has won:
Christopher Awards: Books for Young People, 2010
Christopher Awards: Books for Young People, 2011

Other books you might like:
Raymond Bial, *Rescuing Rover: Saving America's
Dogs*, 2011
Amy Hest, *The Dog Who Belonged to No One*, 2008
Mona Kerby, *Owney, the Mail Pouch Pooch*, 2008
Haven Kimmel, *Orville: A Dog Story*, 2003

353

ROBERT NEUBECKER, Author/Illustrator

Wow! Ocean!

(New York: Hyperion Books, 2011)

Story type: Young Readers
Subject(s): Animals; Imagination; Adventure

Age range(s): 3 - 6+
Major character(s): Izzy, Girl

Summary: Izzy loves adventure, and in this picture book by author and illustrator Robert Neubecker, she finds a new adventure while visiting the beach with her family. Izzy and her sister are amazed by the sandy beach and tidal pools where they find many interesting creatures. Izzy is even more excited about the ocean, and she and her sister see sharks, whales, and anemones while they dive deep into the blue water. They even enjoy a tea party on the ocean floor! Neubecker has created a number of other books featuring Izzy, including *Wow! City!* and *Wow! School!*

Where it's reviewed:
Horn Book Magazine, July/August 2011, page 135
Publishers Weekly, March 21, 2011, page 74
School Library Journal, July 2011, page 73

Other books by the same author:
Wow! School!, 2007
Wow! America!, 2006
Wow! City!, 2004

Other books you might like:
Elisha Cooper, *Beach*, 2006
Nicola Davies, *Surprising Sharks*, 2003
Pam Munoz Ryan, *Hello Ocean*, 2001
Dan Yaccarino, *The Fantastic Undersea Life of Jacques Cousteau*, 2009
Charlotte Zolotow, *The Seashore Book*, 1992

354

LINDA NEWBERY
CATHERINE RAYNER, Illustrator

Posy

(New York: Atheneum Books for Young Readers, 2009)

Subject(s): Domestic cats; Rhyme; Human-animal relationships

Age range(s): 3 - 6+
Major character(s): Posy, Cat
Time period(s): 21st century; 2000s

Summary: Linda Newbery's *Posy* is the tale of a charming kitten who finds herself in a string of adventurous and comic situations. She loves to play with yarn, steal crayons, snare insects, stare into the mirror, and snuggle up with her owner. Young readers are invited to follow Posy on her daily shenanigans as she discovers the world around her. Told in rhyming verse, this volume contains illustrations by Catherine Rayner.

Where it's reviewed:
Booklist, February 15 2009, page 87
Bulletin of the Center for Children's Books, February 2009, page 251
Horn Book Guide, Fall 2009, page 314
School Library Journal, January 2009, page 82

Other books you might like:
Elisha Cooper, *Magic Thinks Big*, 2004
Kevin Henkes, *Kitten's First Full Moon*, 2004
Ezra Jack Keats, *Hi, Cat!*, 1970
Cynthia Rylant, *Brownie and Pearl Step Out*, 2010
Viviane Schwarz, *There Are Cats in This Book*, 2008

355

JEFF NEWMAN

The Boys

(New York: Simon & Schuster Books for Young Readers, 2010)

Subject(s): Children; Childhood; Baseball
Age range(s): 6 - 9+

Summary: In *The Boys* by Jeff Newman, a small boy moves to a new neighborhood and must overcome his shyness if he wishes to be noticed by the other boys his age. He goes to the baseball diamond, ready to play ball, but is disappointed when the other boys ignore him. He sits on the side of the diamond with a few older men, whose kind and encouraging words later help the boy build courage and approach the other players. In this wordless picture book, illustrated by Newman, the new kid learns what he must do to fit in with the others and earn a place on the baseball team.

Where it's reviewed:
Booklist, December 15, 2010, page 43
Bulletin of the Center for Children's Books, April 2010, page 348
Horn Book Guide, Fall 2010, page 309
Publishers Weekly, January 1, 2010, page 47
School Library Journal, January 2010, page 80

Other books by the same author:
Hippo! No, Rhino!, 2006
Reginald, 2003

Awards the book has won:
Blue Ribbon Awards: Picture Books, 2010

Other books you might like:
Anna Alter, *Disappearing Desmond*, 2010
Barbara Lehman, *Rainstorm*, 2007
Jack Norworth, *Take Me Out to the Ballgame*, 1993
Willy Welch, *Playing Right Field*, 1995

356

LESLEA NEWMAN
CAROL THOMPSON, Illustrator

Mommy, Mama and Me

(Berkeley, California: Tricycle Press, 2009)

Subject(s): Family; Homosexuality; Parenthood
Age range(s): 3 - 6+

Major character(s): Unnamed Character, Baby, Narrator; Mommy, Mother (of baby); Mama, Mother (of baby)

Summary: In the board book *Mommy, Mama and Me* by Leslea Newman, a toddler enjoys a day out with his two mothers. Engaging illustrations by Carol Thompson depict the happy baby and his lesbian parents as they get dressed, play together, and visit the local park where Mommy rides the merry-go-round and Mama takes the child down the slide. Back at home, both mothers bathe their baby and tuck him in bed with a comforting kiss. Newman's other books include *Daddy, Papa and Me* and *Heather Has Two Mommies*.

Where it's reviewed:
Horn Book Magazine, May/June 2009, page 285
Publishers Weekly, April 13, 2009, page 48
School Library Journal, November 2009, page 85

Other books by the same author:
Daddy, Papa and Me, 2009
Heather Has Two Mommies, 1999

Other books you might like:
Rebecca Kai Dotlich, *Mama Loves*, 2004
J.D. Lester, *Mommy Calls Me Monkeypants*, 2009
Kate Spohn, *Mommies!*, 2008
Joyce Wan, *We Belong Together*, 2011
Rosemary Wells, *Love*, 2009

357

SALLY NICHOLLS

Season of Secrets
(New York: Arthur A. Levine Books, 2011)

Story type: Young Readers
Subject(s): Family; Grief; Sisters

Age range(s): 10 - 13+
Major character(s): Molly, Sister (of Hannah), Student; Hannah, Sister (of Molly)
Time period(s): 21st century; 2010s
Locale(s): England

Summary: Molly's mother has just died, and her father has sent her and her older sister, Hannah, to live with their grandparents. Hannah's way of dealing with the grief is to be angry most of the time. Molly, however, is different from her sister. She becomes withdrawn, and she begins seeing a vision of a man whose face and hair look as though they are covered in sticks and leaves. When Molly sees the man's face carved in a local church, she decides to investigate further. That's when her teacher tells her about the Oak King, the Holly King, and the battle they wage against each other. Are Molly's visions occurring because of her grief, or are they real?

Where it's reviewed:
Booklist, December 15, 2010, page 55
Bulletin of the Center for Children's Books, February 2011, page 288
Horn Book Magazine, January/February 2011, page 98
Publishers Weekly, November 1, 2010, page 44
School Library Journal, February 2011, page 116

Other books by the same author:
Ways to Live Forever, 2008

Other books you might like:
Sally Pomme Clayton, *Persephone*, 2009
K.L. Going, *The Garden of Eve*, 2007
Merrie Haskell, *The Princess Curse*, 2011
Rebecca Stead, *When You Reach Me*, 2009

358

CLAIRE A. NIVOLA, Author/Illustrator

Orani: My Father's Village
(New York: Farrar Straus Giroux, 2011)

Subject(s): Family; Family history; Islands
Age range(s): 6 - 9+

Summary: Claire A. Nivola recounts childhood memories of spending time in the Sardinian village where her father grew up in this book for young adults. Nivola's father grew up in the village of Orani in Sardinia, an island in the Mediterranean, and Nivola's family often visited the village during the summer while she was growing up. Nivola's aunts, uncles, and cousins still lived in the town, and the book describes the town and some of Nivola's experiences in it. The book explains that Nivola and her family traveled from New York to Orani by boat. While in the village, Nivola drank water straight from a well, wandered around the town, and picked and ate fresh fruit. The town of Orani was much different from her hometown, but she savored and enjoyed the different culture and lifestyle.

Where it's reviewed:
Horn Book Magazine, September/October 2011, page 112
New York Times Book Review, July 17, 2011, page 12
Publishers Weekly, May 16, 2011, page 69
School Library Journal, June 2011, page 106

Other books by the same author:
Planting the Trees of Kenya: The Story of Wangari Maathai, 2008

Other books you might like:
Jeannie Baker, *Mirror*, 2010
Laurel Croza, *I Know Here*, 2010
Allen Say, *Grandfather's Journey*, 1993
Uri Shulevitz, *How I Learned Geography*, 2008

359

DENNIS NOLAN, Author/Illustrator

Sea of Dreams
(New York: Roaring Brook Press, 2011)

Story type: Young Readers
Subject(s): Sea stories; Ships; Imagination

Age range(s): 3 - 6+
Major character(s): Unnamed Character, Girl

Summary: In this picture story, author and illustrator Dennis Nolan tells a fantastical story about a young girl's sandcastle. At the beginning of the book, a young girl is playing in the sand at the beach. She creates a beautiful castle, but she must leave it behind when she goes home in the evening. When the girl goes home, the ocean's waves move closer to the sandcastle. Suddenly, a light comes on in one of the castle windows and small faces appear at its windows. Then a small ship sails in to rescue the people stuck in the castle. Although one of the boat's passengers is nearly lost, they all finally make it shore. In the book's next scene, the little girl is again at the beach building a sandcastle. When she leaves, a small light turns in a window of the castle, presumably so the adventure can begin again.

Where it's reviewed:
Booklist, March, 15 2011, page 44
Horn Book Magazine, September/October 2011, page 74
Publishers Weekly, August 8, 2011, page 44

Other books by the same author:
The Skywriter, 2008
Shadow of the Dinosaurs, 2001
Androcles and the Lion, 1997
The Castle Builder, 1993
Dinosaur Dream, 1990

Other books you might like:
Arthur Geisert, *Ice*, 2011
Barbara Lehman, *Rainstorm*, 2007
Bill Thomson, *Chalk*, 2010
David Wiesner, *Flotsam*, 2006

360

AMY NOVESKY
DAVID DIAZ, Illustrator

Me, Frida
(New York: Abrams Books for Young Readers, 2010)

Story type: Young Readers
Subject(s): Biographies; Art; Painting (Art)

Age range(s): 7 - 9+

Major character(s): Frida Kahlo, Spouse (of Diego), Artist (painter), Immigrant (from Mexico); Diego Rivera, Spouse (of Frida), Immigrant (from Mexico), Artist (painter)
Time period(s): 20th century; 1930s
Locale(s): San Francisco, California

Summary: In this semi-fictional biographical story by author Amy Novesky and illustrator David Diaz, readers learn about the life of famous painter Frida Kahlo. Frida had just begun painting when she moved to the United States with her husband, famous artist Diego Rivera, in 1930. Frida left her home country of Mexico to move to San Francisco, California, with Rivera. When Frida first moved to the United States, she worried that she would be lonely because she had never left Mexico before. However, over time Frida grew to love the city, and she was inspired by her new home to become a painter. Eventually Frida became one of the most famous painters of the 20th century.

Where it's reviewed:
Booklist, November 1, 2010, page 60
Horn Book Guide, Spring 2011, page 270
Publishers Weekly, October 4, 2010, page 46

School Library Journal, December 2010, page 60

Other books you might like:
Carmen T. Bernier-Grand, *Frida: Viva la Vida! Long Live Life!*, 2007
Campbell Geeslin, *Clara & Senor Frog*, 2007
Angela Johnson, *Lily Brown's Paintings*, 2007
Jonah Winter, *Diego*, 1991
Jonah Winter, *Frida*, 2002

361

NAOMI SHIHAB NYE

Time You Let Me In: 25 Poets under 25
(New York: Greenwillow Books, 2010)

Subject(s): Poetry; Writers; Adolescence

Age range(s): 14 - 18+

Summary: In *Time You Let Me In: 25 Poets under 25*, poet Naomi Shihab Nye guides readers through a collection of verse giving voice to a new generation of poets. Nye's journey through the world of youth poetry includes wholly original takes on growing up, family relationships, bonds with friends, and the social pressures young people face. The pieces in this volume also explore the mysteries and delights of everyday life, as well as the experiences of young immigrant poets. Poets contributing to *Time You Let Me In* include Nicole Guenther, Chase Berggrun, Lauren Espinoza, Emma Shaw Crane, and Jonah Ogles.

Where it's reviewed:
Booklist, January 1, 2010, page 58
Horn Book Magazine, May/June 2010, page 100
Publishers Weekly, March 22, 2010, page 72
Voice of Youth Advocates, August 2010, page 279

Other books by the same author:
The Space between Our Footsteps: Poems and Paintings from the Middle East, 1998
The Tree Is Older Than You Are: A Bilingual Gathering of Poems and Stories from Mexico with Paintings by Mexican Artists, 1995
This Same Sky: A Collection of Poems from around the World, 1992

Awards the book has won:
Blue Ribbon Awards: Non-fiction, 2010

Other books you might like:
Kathi Appelt, *Poems from Homeroom: A Writer's Place to Start*, 2010
Neil Astley, *Staying Alive: Real Poems for Unreal Times*, 2002
Robert Pinsky, *Essential Pleasures: A New Anthology of Poems to Read Aloud*, 2009

362

TAO NYEU, Author/Illustrator

Bunny Days

(New York: Dial Books for Young Readers, 2010)

Subject(s): Friendship; Animals; Short stories

Age range(s): 2 - 5+

Summary: *Bunny Days* by author and illustrator Tao Nyeu includes three short stories for young readers. In all the stories, six bunnies live next to two goats and a big bear. Although all the animals like each other, the goats accidentally cause many problems for the bunnies. The bunnies, knowing that the bear is very handy, always run to him for help. Thanks to the goats, the bunnies find themselves covered in mud and sucked into a vacuum cleaner. It's up to Bear to help the bunnies get out of these situations. Tao Nyeu is also the author of the book *Wonder Bear*.

Where it's reviewed:
Booklist, January 1, 2010, page 90
Bulletin of the Center for Children's Books, February 2010, page 257
New York Times Book Review, March 14, 2010, page 15
Publishers Weekly, December 14, 2009, page 57
School Library Journal, December 2009, page 88

Other books by the same author:
Wonder Bear, 2008

Awards the book has won:
Blue Ribbon Awards: Picture Books, 2010

Other books you might like:
Suzanne Bloom, *A Splendid Friend, Indeed*, 2005
James Marshall, *George and Martha*, 1972
Candance Ryan, *Ribbit Rabbit*, 2011

363

PATRICK O'BRIEN, Author/Illustrator

You Are the First Kid on Mars

(New York: G.P. Putnam's Sons, 2009)

Subject(s): Space exploration; Space flight; Mars (Planet)

Age range(s): 9 - 12+
Locale(s): Mars, Outer Space

Summary: Patrick O'Brien takes the reader on a space flight to Mars in *You Are the First Kid on Mars*, using digital art to illustrate what life would be like on an exploration to the planet. The book clearly describes what would go on during a four-month flight on a nuclear thermal rocket to Mars, and what would happen once you arrived and were staying in a habitat with other scientists and engineers. The author imagines the type of technology that would be used, including orbital stations, transport rockets, and landing modules, along with robots that would explore the surface of the planet. Scientific facts about space travel and geology are included throughout the text.

Where it's reviewed:
Booklist, May 1, 2009, page 81
Bulletin of the Center for Children's Books, September 2009, page 33
Publishers Weekly, May 11, 2009, page 51
School Library Journal, July 2009, page 73
Science Books & Film, October 2009, page 22

Other books by the same author:
Fantastic Fighters: One Hundred Years of Flying on the Edge, 2003
The Hindenburg, 2000

Other books you might like:
Douglas Florian, *Comets, Stars, the Moon, and Mars: Space Poems and Paintings*, 2007
Elaine Scott, *Mars and the Search For Life*, 2008
Alexandra Siy, *Cars on Mars: Roving the Red Planet*.

364

JAY O'CALLAHAN
WILL MOSES, Illustrator

Raspberries!

(New York: Philomel Books, 2009)

Subject(s): Food; Friendship; Fables

Age range(s): 4 - 7+
Major character(s): Simon, Baker; Sally, Friend (of Simon)

Summary: Jay O'Callahan's *Raspberries!* is the inspiring tale of Simon, a talented baker who runs into a streak of bad luck. After a robbery and a lightning storm, poor Simon has nothing left in the world. But one of his old bakery customers, Sally, comes to his aid by giving him some raspberries. The raspberries are delicious, and Simon scatters them in his fields. Soon there are raspberries everywhere, and people are coming from miles around to enjoy them. This volume contains illustrations by Will Moses.

Where it's reviewed:
Booklist, September 1, 2009, page 102
Horn Book Guide, Spring 2010, page 37
Publishers Weekly, September 21, 2009, page 55
School Library Journal, September 2009, page 130

Other books you might like:
Deborah Hopkinson, *Apples to Oregon: Being the (Slightly) True Narrative of How a Brave Pioneer Father Brought Apples, Peaches, Pears, Plums, Grapes, and Cherries (and Children) Across the Plains*, 2004
Jeanne Steig, *Fleas!*, 2008
Gaylia Taylor, *George Crum and the Saratoga Chip*, 2006

365

BARBARA O'CONNOR

The Small Adventure of Popeye and Elvis

(New York: Farrar, Straus, and Giroux, 2009)

Subject(s): Southern United States; Adventure; Friendship

Age range(s): 8 - 11+

Major character(s): Popeye, Child; Elvis Jewell, Child, Rebel

Time period(s): 21st century; 2000s

Locale(s): Fayette, South Carolina

Summary: *The Small Adventure of Popeye and Elvis* is a novel for young readers from author Barbara O'Connor. Popeye thinks that life in Fayette, South Carolina, is nothing but dull. There's never any excitement or adventure until some strange visitors come to town and Popeye's world is turned upside down. When a motor home belonging to the Jewell family gets stuck in the mud, the five unruly Jewell children, along with their parents, decide to stay in Fayette for a while. Popeye befriends Elvis, a rebellious and wild child, and it isn't long until the pair stumbles upon an adventure. When they discover a series of small boats containing secret messages floating down the creek, the boys set out to solve this strange mystery and find a little excitement in their small southern town.

Where it's reviewed:
Booklist, September 1 2009, page 93
Bulletin of the Center for Children's Books, December 2009, page 164
Horn Book Magazine, January/February 2010, Page 90
School Library Journal, September 2009, page 169

Other books by the same author:
The Fantastic Secret of Owen Jester, 2010

Other books you might like:
David Almond, *The Boy Who Climbed Into the Moon*, 2010
Betty G. Birney, *The Seven Wonders of Sassafras Springs*, 2005
Kimberly Willis Holt, *When Zachary Beaver Came to Town*, 1999
Don Lemna, *When the Sergeant Came Marching Home*, 2008
Richard Peck, *A Year Down Yonder*, 2000

366

BARBARA O'CONNOR

The Fantastic Secret of Owen Jester

(New York: Farrar, Straus and Giroux, 2010)

Subject(s): Frogs; Submarines; Friendship

Age range(s): 9 - 12+

Major character(s): Owen Jester, 12-Year-Old, Friend, Neighbor (of Viola); Viola, Neighbor (of Owen); Tooley Graham, Frog

Time period(s): 21st century; 2010s

Locale(s): Carter, Georgia

Summary: In Barbara O'Connor's *The Fantastic Secret of Owen Jester*, Owen Jester discovers a large bullfrog and takes it home with him to his grandfather's house in Carter, Georgia. He sees the frog as a sign: This summer is going to be the best one yet. Although it starts out this way, Owen soon realizes that Tooley Graham—the frog—is not healthy. He wonders if keeping him in an aquarium in his room is a good idea, or if he should return him to the wild. While he worries for Tooley's health, he makes a second discovery: In the middle of the night, a train carrying a submarine experiences technical difficulties and the submarine falls off the track. No one seems to notice, except Owen. He shares the secret with his friends and they make plans to learn to drive the sub and take it out to sea. Only one thing stands in their way, however: Viola, Owen's nosy neighbor. Can Owen and his friends go through with their plans now that Viola knows? Or will she tell Owen's grandfather what the boys are doing and ruin their summer for good?

Where it's reviewed:
Booklist, September 15, 2010, page 67
Bulletin of the Center for Children's Books, October 2010, page 59
Horn Book Magazine, November/December 2010, page 100
Publishers Weekly, August 23, 2010, page 49
School Library Journal, October 2010, page 124

Other books by the same author:
The Small Adventure of Popeye and Elvis, 2009

Other books you might like:
Marcia Thornton Jones, *Ratfink*, 2010
Susan Patron, *The Higher Power of Lucky*, 2006
Richard Peck, *A Long Way from Chicago: A Novel in Stories*, 1998
Pamela S. Turner, *The Frog Scientist*, 2009

367

JANE O'CONNOR
ROBIN PREISS GLASSER, Illustrator

Fancy Nancy and the Mermaid Ballet

(New York: HarperCollins, 2012)

Series: Fancy Nancy Series. Book 45
Story type: Series; Young Readers
Subject(s): Childhood; Friendship; Ballet

Age range(s): 4 - 8+

Major character(s): Fancy Nancy, Girl; Bree, Girl, Friend (of Fancy Nancy)

Time period(s): 21st century; 2010s

Locale(s): United States

Summary: Fancy Nancy is back in another installment of the popular picture book series from Jane O'Connor and Robin Preiss Glasser. In this picture book, Fancy Nancy is very excited and getting ready for what she is sure will be a starring role in the mermaid ballet. When casting time comes, though, Nancy is assigned the role of a tree, and is very disappointed by such a boring choice. She starts to wonder, though, if she could perhaps make the tree fancy and fun with the help of her best friend, Bree, who has been given the role of an oyster. When the starring role of mermaid opens up again, Nancy knows who is the best choice for the part.

Where it's reviewed:
New York Times Book Review, February 26, 2012, page 26L

Other books by the same author:
Fancy Nancy and the Too Loose Tooth, 2012
Fancy Nancy: Tea for Two, 2012
Fancy Nancy and the Mean Girl, 2011
Fancy Nancy: Hair Dos and Hair Don'ts, 2011
Fancy Nancy: Stellar Stargazer!, 2011

Other books you might like:
Carmelo D'Amico, *Ella Sets the Stage*, 2006
Victoria Kann, *Pinkalicious: Pinkie Promise*, 2011
James Mayhew, *Ella Bella Ballerina and Swan Lake*, 2011
Jenne Simon, *Lalaloopsy: The Ballet Recital*, 2012
Marilyn Singer, *Tallulah's Tutu*, 2011

368

KEVIN O'MALLEY, Author/Illustrator

Animal Crackers Fly the Coop
(New York: Walker and Company, 2010)

Subject(s): Comedians; Comedy; Adventure

Age range(s): 4 - 8+
Major character(s): Hen, Hen
Time period(s): 21st century; 2010s

Summary: In *Animal Crackers Fly the Coop*, author/illustrator Kevin O'Malley tells the story of a group of animals who set out on an epic adventure to open their very own comedy club. Based on a legendary fairy tale by the Grimm brothers, this volume follows Hen and her pals as they try to realize their dreams of being comedians—with hilarious results.

Where it's reviewed:
Booklist, February 15, 2010, page 79
Horn Book Magazine, March/April 2010, page 48
School Library Journal, February 2010, page 91

Other books by the same author:
Gimme Cracked Corn & I Will Share, 2007

Other books you might like:
Pamela Duncan Edwards, *Four Famished Foxes and Fosdyke*, 1995
Jan Huling, *Ol' Bloo's Boogie-Woogie Band and Blues Ensemble*, 2010
Leo Landry, *Grin and Bear It*, 2011
Kevin O'Malley, *Gimme Cracked Corn & I Will Share*, 2007
Margie Palatini, *Lousy Rotten Stinkin' Grapes*, 2009

369

LAUREN OLIVER
KEI ACEDERA, Illustrator

Liesl and Po
(New York: HarperCollins, 2011)

Story type: Adventure
Subject(s): Magic; Ghosts; Orphans

Age range(s): 9 - 11+
Major character(s): Liesl, Orphan, Abuse Victim, Friend (of Po), 11-Year-Old, Prisoner; Po, Supernatural Being (ghost), Friend (of Liesl); Will, Apprentice

Summary: Bestselling author Lauren Oliver weaves a fantastical tale of magic, friendship, and adventure in this novel for young readers. Liesl is a lonely girl, sentenced by her evil stepmother to a life of solitude in the dark and tiny attic with only her memories and the visiting mice to keep her company. Her life is turned around, though, when she encounters Po, a ghost from the Other Side. Po is lonely too, living an isolated existence without any memories of his previous life. The two are grateful to have found a friendship and devise a plan to break free from the attic to embark on an important mission. But their plans go terribly awry when the apothecary's apprentice accidentally mixes up a delivery and presents Liesl and Po with a box full of magic.

Where it's reviewed:
Booklist, September 2011, page 120
Publishers Weekly, August 29, 2011, page 66
School Library Journal, November 2011, page 135

Other books by the same author:
Pandemonium, 2012
Delirium, 2011
Before I Fall, 2010

Other books you might like:
Neil Gaiman, *The Graveyard Book*, 2008
Mary Downing Hahn, *Closed for the Season*, 2009
Kate Klise, *Grounded*, 2010
Sally Murphy, *Pearl verses the World*, 2011

370

TOD OLSON
SCOTT ALLRED, Illustrator
GREGORY PROCH, Illustrator

How to Get Rich on a Texas Cattle Drive
(Washington, D.C.: National Geographic, 2010)

Subject(s): United States history; Cattle drives; Frontier life

Age range(s): 8 - 12+
Time period(s): 19th century
Locale(s): United States

Summary: In *How To Get Rich on A Texas Cattle Drive: In Which I Tell the Honest Truth about Rampaging*

Rustlers, Stampeding Steers and Other Fateful Hazards on the Wild Chisholm Trail, author Tod Olson describes life on a 19th-century cattle drive as seen through the eyes of fictitious cowhand A.J. Larken. Challenges on the trail include stampedes, angry landowners, Indian attacks, and grueling work. Illustrated with photographs, maps, and period-style art, this informative and engaging book gives young readers a firsthand look at Larken's roping-and-riding lifestyle as he makes his way through Texas, Oklahoma, and Kansas.

Where it's reviewed:
Booklist, May 1, 2010, page 80
Horn Book Guide, Fall 2010, page 451
School Library Journal, June 2010, page 136

Other books by the same author:
How to Get Rich on the Oregon Trail, 2009
How to Get Rich in the California Gold Rush: An Adventurer's Guide to the Fabulous Riches Discovered in 1848, 2008

Other books you might like:
Raymond Bial, *Cow Towns*, 2004
Russell Freedman, *In the Days of the Vaqueros: America's First True Cowboys*, 2001
Loretta Ichord, *Skillet Bread, Sourdough, and Vinegar Pie: Cooking in Pioneer Days*, 2003
Vaunda Micheaux Nelson, *Bad News for Outlaws: The Remarkable Life of Bass Reeves Deputy U.S. Marshal*, 2009
Jerry Stanley, *Cowboys and Longhorns: A Portrait of the Long Drive*, 2003

371

KENNETH OPPEL
LOU FANCHER, Illustrator
STEVE JOHNSON, Illustrator

The King's Taster

(New York: HarperCollins, 2009)

Subject(s): Dogs; Royalty; Food

Age range(s): 5 - 8+

Major character(s): Max, Dog; The King, Royalty; Cook, Cook

Time period(s): 21st century; 2000s

Summary: Kenneth Oppel's *The King's Taster* follows the exploits of Max the dog, the official taster of the King's food. Though Max gets to sample all the pleasures of the royal kitchen, the young king is not satisfied. He wants nothing to do with the elaborate meals the cook prepares. The King's fussiness causes Max and the cook to travel the world in search of foods that will please the finicky royal figure. But nothing seems to appease him. Then one night, Max discovers the King's love of candy and junk food. When the cook threatens to tell the King's mother about these unsavory eating habits, the youthful ruler decides it's time to start eating the delicious meals the kitchen prepares—much to Max's delight. *The King's Taster* contains illustrations by Lou Fancher and Steve Johnson.

Where it's reviewed:
Booklist, March 15, 2009, page 61
Horn Book Magazine, July/August 2009, page 413
Publishers Weekly, June 22, 2009, page 43
School Library Journal, June 2009, page 97

Other books by the same author:
Peg and the Whale, 2000

Other books you might like:
Dayle Ann Dodds, *The Prince Won't Go to Bed!*, 2007
A.W. Flaherty, *The Luck of the Loch Ness Monster: A Tale of Picky Eating*, 2007
Helen Lester, *Tacky Goes to Camp*, 2009
Gaylia Taylor, *George Crum and the Saratoga Chip*, 2006

372

ROBIN PAGE
STEVE JENKINS, Co-Author

How to Clean a Hippopotamus: A Look at Unusual Animal Partnerships

(Boston: Houghton Mifflin, 2010)

Subject(s): Science; Animals; Human-animal relationships

Age range(s): 6 - 9+

Summary: This book discusses some of the symbiotic relationships found in nature. Symbiotic relationships are those that help both of the organisms in the relationship. In the book, some of nature's most interesting and unusual symbiotic relationships are discussed. Many of the relationships involve one of the organisms getting a "free" meal from the other organism. However, other relationships focus on other benefits. The book even features a symbiotic relationship that humans enjoy. This book, by Robin Page and Steve Jenkins, includes a section with notes about some of the featured animals.

Where it's reviewed:
Booklist, March 15, 2010, page 42
Bulletin of the Center for Children's Books, June 2010, page 438
Horn Book Guide, Fall 2010, page 409
Science Books & Film, December 2010, page 322

Other books by the same author:
Sisters and Brothers: Sibling Relationships in the Animal World, 2008

Other books you might like:
Jose Aruego, *Weird Friends: Unlikely Allies in the Animal Kingdom*, 2002
Kathy Darling, *There's a Zoo on You*, 2000
Dr. Paula Kahumba, *Owen and Mzee: The Language of Friendship*, 2006

373

MARGIE PALATINI
BARRY MOSER, Illustrator

Lousy Rotten Stinkin' Grapes

(New York: Simon & Schuster, 2009)

Subject(s): Fables

Age range(s): 5 - 8+

Major character(s): Fox, Fox; Bear, Bear; Porcupine, Porcupine; Possum, Opossum; Beaver, Beaver

Summary: In *Lousy Rotten Stinkin' Grapes* children's author Margie Palatini takes the classic Aesop's Fable "The Fox and the Grapes" and adds a modern twist. Fox knows he can reach the grapes on a high vine with just a little bit of planning; he is, after all, as sly as a fox, because he is one. He involves various creatures of the forest in his plot, including Bear, Porcupine, and Possum, but doesn't want to hear their input—instead, he asks that they leave the thinking to him. Will Fox learn a lesson about teamwork, or will he give up in haste without ever reaching the grapes? This book is illustrated by Barry Moser.

Where it's reviewed:
Booklist, June 1, 2009, page 75
Horn Book Guide, Spring 2010, page 38
Publishers Weekly, July 27, 2009, page 62

Other books by the same author:
Earthquack!, 2005
Three Silly Billies, 2005
Bad Boys, 2003

Other books you might like:
Arnold Lobel, *Fables*, 1980
Jerry Pinkney, *Aesop's Fables*, 2000
Eric Rohmann, *My Friend Rabbit*, 2002

374

COLEEN MURTAGH PARATORE

Sunny Holiday

(New York: Scholastic Press, 2009)

Subject(s): Urban life; Holidays; Friendship

Age range(s): 8 - 11+

Major character(s): Sunny, 4th Grader; Jazzy, Friend (of Sunny)

Time period(s): 21st century; 2000s

Locale(s): Riverton, New York

Summary: *Sunny Holiday* is a novel for young readers by Coleen Murtagh Paratore. Sunny is only in fourth grade, but she must deal with the difficulty of living in a run-down apartment complex in the inner city, while her father is in prison and her mother works during the day and takes classes at night. She and her best friend Jazzy are trying to create a new holiday, Kids' Day, for the empty month from January to February. When the mayor comes to visit Sunny's apartment building, however, she plans to tell him about her idea but instead discusses all the things around the area that need improvement, such as cleaning up the river and finishing the park that was started. Sunny learns that success comes only from hard work, and through her challenges, remains optimistic throughout the book.

Where it's reviewed:
Booklist, January 1, 2009, page 84
Horn Book Guide, Fall 2009, page 82
School Library Journal, February 2009, page 82

Other books by the same author:
Sweet and Sunny, 2010

Other books you might like:
Karen English, *Nikki and Deja*, 2008
Jenny Lombard, *Drita, My Homegirl*, 2006
Patricia C. McKissack, *A Song for Harlem*, 2007
Jacqueline Woodson, *Locomotion*, 2003

375

LINDA SUE PARK

A Long Walk to Water: Based on a True Story

(Boston: Clarion Books, 2010)

Subject(s): Refugees; Survival; Civil war

Age range(s): 9 - 12+

Major character(s): Salva, 11-Year-Old, Refugee; Nya, Refugee

Time period(s): 20th century-21st century; 1990s-2000s

Locale(s): Ethiopia; Kenya; Sudan; United States

Summary: In *A Long Walk to Water: Based on a True Story* by Linda Sue Park, an African boy and girl separated by time and place are united by shared hardship. In 1985, when Salva Dut is only 11, an attack by rebels on his school in the Sudan changes his life forever. He starts running—through Africa's harsh landscape, across dangerous waters, to a difficult life in a refugee camp. He is eventually adopted by an American family. In 2008, a young girl named Nya faces different challenges in Sudan as her family tries to maintain a supply of usable water. Her hope lies in Salva's return to Africa.

Where it's reviewed:
Booklist, September 1, 2010, page 97
Bulletin of the Center for Children's Books, December 2010, page 201
Horn Book Magazine, January/February 2010, page 98
School Library Journal, October 2010, page 123
Voice of Youth Advocates, December 2010, page 458

Other books by the same author:
The Firekeeper's Son, 2003
A Single Shard, 2001
The Kite Fighter, 2000

Awards the book has won:
Jane Addams Children's Book Award, 2011

Other books you might like:
Katherine Applegate, *Home of the Brave*, 2007
Rochelle Strauss, *One Well: The Story of Water on Earth*, 2007

Mary Williams, *Brothers in Hope: The Story of the Lost Boys of Sudan*, 2005

376

LINDA SUE PARK
BAGRAM IBATOULLINE, Illustrator

The Third Gift

(New York: Clarion Books, 2011)

Story type: Religious; Young Readers
Subject(s): Father-son relations; Deserts; Agriculture

Age range(s): 5 - 8+
Major character(s): Unnamed Character, Father, Merchant (myrrh gatherer and seller); Boy, Son (of the merchant)

Summary: A boy and his father walk long distances every day through the Arab desert, carrying water and a basket. The boy watches as his father carefully examines each spiny, knotted tree to decide if it's the right tree at the right time. When all conditions are right, the man harvests tear-shaped drops of sap. These tears are myrrh, an ancient spice used in medicines and at funerals. The boy's father sells the tears in the marketplace. One day, three strangers arrive at the market. The men, who are dressed in fine, beautifully colored robes, carry gifts of gold and frankincense they are taking to a baby. The travelers buy tears of myrrh from the boy's father before heading on their way. Author Linda Sue Park allows the reader to see the significance of the gatherers' work and the travelers' purchase, though the boy and his father have no idea they have harvested gifts for the Christ child.

Where it's reviewed:
Booklist, October 15, 2011, page 96
Publishers Weekly, September 26, 2011, page 72
School Library Journal, October 2011, page 96

Other books by the same author:
The Firekeeper's Son, 2004

Other books you might like:
Gian-Carlo Menotti, *Amahl and the Night Visitors*, 1986
Michael Morpurgo, *On Angel Wings*, 2007
Susan Summers, *The Greatest Gift: The Story of the Other Wise Man*, 2000

377

ROSANNE PARRY

Heart of a Shepherd

(New York: Random House, 2009)

Subject(s): Father-son relations; Ranch life; Wars

Age range(s): 10 - 12+
Major character(s): Ignatius "Brother" Alderman, 12-Year-Old; Grandpa, Guardian (of Brother), Grandfather (of Brother)
Time period(s): 21st century; (2000s)
Locale(s): Oregon, United States

Summary: Ignatius "Brother" Alderman lives with his father on a ranch in Oregon. When the military calls up his father's army reserve unit, 12-year-old Brother finds himself taking care of the ranch while his father fights in the war in Iraq. Unsure of how he will keep the ranch going in between his schoolwork, Brother gets help from his grandfather. As Brother struggles to deal with the pain of missing his father, he comes to understand what it takes to be a man. *Heart of a Shepherd* follows Brother on a journey of self discovery, as he struggles to understand the responsibilities of ranch life, the struggle of soldiers, and his relationships with the men in his family.

Where it's reviewed:
Booklist, February 15 2009, Page 82
Bulletin of the Center for Children's Books, February 2009, page 251
Horn Book Magazine, May/June 2009, page 304
School Library Journal, March 2009, page 150

Other books you might like:
Deborah Ellis, *Off to War: Voices of Soldiers' Children*, 2008
Dean Hughes, *Missing in Action*, 2010
Louise Moeri, *The Devil in Ol' Rosie*, 2001
Mary Ann Rodman, *Jimmy's Stars*, 2008
Diane Stanley, *Saving Sky*, 2010

378

ELIZABETH PARTRIDGE

Marching for Freedom: Walk Together, Children, and Don't You Grow Weary

(New York: Viking, 2009)

Subject(s): African Americans; Racism; Civil rights

Age range(s): 10 - 15+
Time period(s): 20th century; 1960s (1965)
Locale(s): Alabama, United States

Summary: In March of 1965, men, women, and children led by civil rights activist Dr. Martin Luther Jr. marched from Selma, Alabama, to the state capital in Montgomery to protest voter discrimination. In *Marching for Freedom: Walk Together, Children, and Don't You Grow Weary*, author Elizabeth Partridge documents the events surrounding the march, paying particular attention to the children who participated in the march. All of the marchers faced violence, with children as young as eight and ten tossed in jail alongside the adult protesters. Though the marchers faced a lot of challenges, passage of the Voting Rights Act later that year made their efforts worthwhile.

Where it's reviewed:
Booklist, August 2009, page 67
Bulletin of the Center for Children's Books, January 2010, page 211
Horn Book Magazine, November/December 2009, page 699
New York Times Book Review, January 17, 2010, page 12

School Library Journal, October 2009, page 150

Awards the book has won:
Los Angeles Times Book Award: Young Adult Fiction, 2009
Blue Ribbon Awards: Non-fiction, 2010
Boston Globe - Horn Book Awards: Nonfiction, 2010
Jane Addams Children's Book Award, 2010

Other books you might like:
Shana Burg, *A Thousand Never Evers*, 2008
Ellen Levine, *Freedom's Children: Young Civil Rights Activists Tell Their Own Stories*, 1993
Marshall Poe, *Little Rock Nine*, 2009
Ntozake Shange, *We Troubled the Waters*, 2009

379

KATHERINE PATERSON
PAMELA DALTON, Illustrator

Brother Sun, Sister Moon

(San Francisco: Chronicle Books, 2011)

Subject(s): Nature; Prayer; Religion

Age range(s): 5 - 8+

Summary: In this picture book for young readers, author Katherine Paterson offers a fresh take on Saint Francis of Assisi's "Praise Song of the Creatures," also known as "The Canticle of the Sun," originally penned in 1224 AD. Using Saint Francis's hymn as inspiration, Paterson thanks God for his creations, from animals to nature. Illustrated by Pamela Dalton, the volume contains 19th-century Pennsylvania Dutch cut-paper images of children, birds, animals, trees, vines, flowers, and branches. Paterson received two Newbery Medals, two National Book Awards, and was named the National Ambassador for Young People's Literature in 2010.

Where it's reviewed:
Booklist, August 2011, page 43
Publishers Weekly, May 9, 2011, page 52
School Library Journal, July 2011, page 85

Other books by the same author:
The Light of the World: The Life of Jesus for Children, 2008
The Angel and the Donkey, 1996

Other books you might like:
Tomie dePaola, *Francis, the Poor Man of Assisi*, 1982
Richard Egielski, *Saint Francis and the Wolf*, 2005
Rachel Field, *Prayer for a Child*, 1944

380

KATHERINE PATERSON
JOHN PATERSON, Co-Author
JOHN ROCCO, Illustrator

The Flint Heart

(Somerville, Massachusetts: Candlewick Press, 2011)

Story type: Fantasy; Magic Conflict
Subject(s): Magic; Fairy tales; Fantasy

Age range(s): 8 - 11+
Major character(s): Charles, Brother (of Unity); Unity, Sister (of Charles); Zagabog, Mythical Creature

Summary: Award-winning author Katherine Paterson, along with John Paterson and illustrator John Rocco, offers young readers a modern retelling of Eden Phillpotts's 1910 fairy tale with this fantastical novel of magic and adventure. The tale begins in the Stone Age, with a motivated tribesman commissioning the creation of a talisman that will harden his heart and allow him to rise in power in his tribe. The tribe's shaman complies, despite his reservations, and the Flint Heart ultimately destroys the entire tribe. When the Flint Heart resurfaces after thousands of years, a generous farmer, an innocent fairy, and a domestic badger are put at risk. If Charles and his sister, Unity, want to save the humans, animals, and fairy creatures, they must consult Zagabog, the wisest creature in the universe, for a way to destroy the talisman for good.

Where it's reviewed:
Booklist, September 1, 2011, page 119
Horn Book Magazine, September/October 2011, page 94
New York Times Book Review, September 18, 2011, page 21
Publishers Weekly, July 18, 2011, page 153

Other books you might like:
Bruce Coville, *The Evil Elves*, 2004
Berlie Doherty, *The Goblin Baby*, 2009
Neil Gaiman, *The Graveyard Book*, 2008
Edith Nesbit, *Jack and the Beanstalk*, 2006
Anne Ursu, *Breadcrumbs*, 2011

381

LESLIE PATRICELLI, Author/Illustrator

Higher! Higher!

(Somerville, Massachusetts: Candlewick Press, 2009)

Subject(s): Father-daughter relations; Adventure; Recreation

Age range(s): 2 - 5+

Summary: Told in spare language and vibrant illustrations, *Higher! Higher!* is the story of an unnamed little girl who is being pushed in a swing by her doting dad. She begs him to push her higher, and she is thrilled at the sights she sees from her ever-increasing vantage point. First, she imagines she is viewing the world as a giraffe must see it. Then she feels as if she's on the top of mountain, followed by a lookout from an airplane. Finally, the girl dreams she is so high up that she encounters an alien. *Higher! Higher!* contains illustrations by author Leslie Patricelli.

Where it's reviewed:
Booklist, February 15 2009, page 80
Horn Book Magazine, March/April 2009, Page 183
School Library Journal, February 2009, page 82

Other books by the same author:
Be Quiet Mike, 2011
Potty, 2010
Tubby, 2010

Baby Happy Baby Sad, 2008
Yummy Yucky, 2003

Other books you might like:
Kevin Henkes, *A Good Day*, 2007
Satomi Ichikawa, *Come Fly with Me*, 2008
Karen Roosa, *Pippa at the Parade*, 2009
Cynthia Rylant, *All in a Day*, 2009
David Ezra Stein, *Pouch!*, 2009

382

GARY PAULSEN

Woods Runner

(New York: Wendy Lamb Books, 2010)

Subject(s): History; American Revolution, 1775-1783; Family

Age range(s): 9 - 12+
Major character(s): Samuel, 13-Year-Old, Son (of kidnapped parents)
Time period(s): 18th century; 1770s-1780s
Locale(s): Pennsylvania, United States

Summary: In Gary Paulson's *Woods Runner*, 13-year-old Samuel returns home from a hike in the woods surrounding his town to find that his settlement has been destroyed. Houses have been burned down, people have been murdered, and his parents are missing. Samuel, who has always felt a deep connection to the earth, uses the woods as protection while he follows the trail left by the Iroquois who stole his family. In their Pennsylvania settlement, Samuel's family and their neighbors were far from the Revolution. Now, Samuel must head straight into the war and the British-controlled territories to rescue his parents.

Where it's reviewed:
Booklist, January 1, 2010, page 72
Bulletin of the Center for Children's Books, March 2010, page 301
Horn Book Magazine, March/April 2010, page 66
New York Times Book Review, February 14, 2010, page 15
School Library Journal, February 2010, page 122

Other books by the same author:
Hatchet, 1999
Soldier's Heart, 1998
The Rifle, 1995
The Winter Room, 1989
Tracker, 1984

Other books you might like:
Avi, *The Fighting Ground*, 1984
James Lincoln Collier, *My Brother Sam Is Dead*, 1974
Laurie Halse Anderson, *Chains*, 2008
Elizabeth George Speare, *The Sign of the Beaver*, 1983

383

RICHARD PECK
KELLY MURPHY, Illustrator

Secrets at Sea

(New York: Dial Books for Young Readers, 2011)

Story type: Adventure; Young Readers
Subject(s): Ships; Animals; Travel

Age range(s): 8 - 12+
Major character(s): Helena, Mouse, Sister (of Louise, Beatrice, and Lamont); Louise, Mouse, Sister (of Helena, Beatrice, and Lamont); Beatrice, Mouse, Sister (of Helena, Louise, and Lamont); Lamont, Mouse, Brother (of Helena, Louise, and Beatrice); Olive Cranston, Young Woman
Locale(s): At Sea; England; United States

Summary: Helena and her siblings—Louise, Beatrice, and Lamont—are mice who live in the Cranston family's home. Helena and her family stay warm and are well fed in the home. When they learn that the Cranstons will be traveling on a boat to England, however, the mice decide to join the human family on their trip. Even though mice are generally afraid of water, Helena helps her siblings get past their fear and board the boat. Once she is on the ship, Helena encounters a number of other mice and a one-eyed cat. If Helena wants her family's trip to be a success, she will have to keep herself and her siblings away from the cat and out of trouble with the other mice and the humans. This novel for young readers is written by Richard Peck and illustrated by Kelly Murphy.

Where it's reviewed:
Booklist, September 1, 2001, page 122
Horn Book Magazine, September/October 2011, page 96
Publishers Weekly, August 22, 2011, page 64
School Library Journal, September 2011, page 127

Other books you might like:
Emily Bearn, *Tumtum and Nutmeg: Adventures beyond Nutmouse Hall*, 2008
Henry Cole, *A Nest for Celeste: A Story about Art, Inspiration, and the Meaning of Home*, 2010
Carmen Agra Deedy, *The Cheshire Cheese Cat: A Dickens of a Tale*, 2011
Kate DiCamillo, *The Tale of Despereaux: Being the Story of a Mouse, a Princess, Some Soup, and a Spool of Thread*, 2003

384

RICHARD PECK

A Season of Gifts

(New York: Dial Books for Young Readers, 2009)

Subject(s): Christmas; Neighborhoods; Humor

Age range(s): 10 - 13+
Major character(s): Grandma Dowdel, Neighbor (of the Barnhardts); Bob Barnhardt, 10-Year-Old
Time period(s): 20th century; 1950s (1958)
Locale(s): Illinois, United States

Summary: In *A Season of Gifts*, award-winning author Richard Peck continues the adventures of spirited Grandma Dowdel, first begun in *A Year Down Yonder* and *A Long Way from Chicago*. It is 1958, and Grandma Dowdel has new neighbors in the Barnhardts, a preacher and his family. Ten-year-old Bob Barnhardt is bullied by the other kids in town, and Grandma Dowdel takes a special liking to the youngster. As Christmas approaches, she decides to shower the whole family with some very special gifts.

Where it's reviewed:
Booklist, August 1 2009, page 68
Bulletin of the Center for Children's Books, December 2009, page 64
Horn Book Magazine, September/October 2009, page 573
School Library Journal, October 2009, page 134

Other books by the same author:
A Year Down Yonder, 2002
A Long Way From Chicago, 1998

Other books you might like:
Gennifer Choldenko, *Al Capone Does My Shirts*, 2004
Dan Gutman, *The Christmas Genie*, 2009
Barbara O'Connor, *The Small Adventure of Popeye and Elvis*, 2009
Richard Peck, *A Long Way from Chicago: A Novel in Stories*, 1998
Barbara Robinson, *The Best Christmas Pageant Ever*, 1972

385

LINCOLN PEIRCE, Author/Illustrator

Big Nate: In a Class by Himself

(New York: HarperCollins, 2010)

Subject(s): Schools; Children; Imagination

Age range(s): 9 - 12+
Major character(s): Nate, Student—Elementary School; Mrs. Godfrey, Teacher
Time period(s): 21st century; 2010s

Summary: With a mix of narration and illustration, Lincoln Pierce's *Big Nate: In a Class by Himself* tells the story of Nate, a young boy who believes the world is his for the taking. After receiving a message in a fortune cookie that told him he would have a successful and amazing life, Nate began to see the world from a different point of view. Nate truly believes he is awesome; he will get everything he wants in life, and then some. For now, however, he must make it through elementary school. This proves to be more of a challenge than he thought when he angers one of his teachers and attempts to stand up to his principal.

Where it's reviewed:
Booklist, March 1, 2010, page 70
Bulletin of the Center for Children's Books, May 2010, page 393
Horn Book Magazine, July/August 2010, page 118
School Library Journal, April 2010, page 166

Other books by the same author:
Big Nate On a Roll, 2011
Big Nate Out Loud, 2011
Big Nate From the Top, 2010
Big Nate Strikes Again, 2010

Other books you might like:
Jon Scieszka, *Spaceheadz*, 2010
Alan Silberberg, *Milo: Sticky Notes and Brain Freeze*, 2010
Trudi Truett, *Secrets of a Lab Rat: No Girls Allowed (Dogs Okay)*, 2009
Rachel Vail, *Justin Case: School, Drool, and Other Daily Disasters*, 2010
Lisa Yee, *Bobby the Brave (Sometimes)*, 2010

386

LYNNE RAE PERKINS

As Easy as Falling off the Face of the Earth

(New York: Greenwillow Books, 2010)

Subject(s): Adventure; Accidents; Voyages and travels

Age range(s): 10 - 14+
Major character(s): Ry, Teenager
Time period(s): 21st century; 2010s
Locale(s): Montana, United States

Summary: Newbery Medal-winning author Lynne Rae Perkins chronicles the fantastic journey of a courageous teenager in *As Easy as Falling Off the Face of the Earth*. Ry is stuck in the middle of no-man's-land after the train he was traveling on lurches away without him. Forced to make his way back to civilization, Ry must endure a series of hilarious challenges and obstacles. He soon realizes he will have to rely on the power of sheer good luck to get him home again.

Where it's reviewed:
Booklist, April 15, 2010, page 45
Bulletin of the Center for Children's Books, May 2010, page 393
Horn Book Magazine, May/June 2010, page 88
New York Times Book Review, June 6, 2010, page 25
School Library Journal, July 2010, page 95

Other books by the same author:
Criss Cross, 2005
All Alone in the Universe, 1999

Other books you might like:
Joan Bauer, *Rules of the Road*, 1998
Libba Bray, *Going Bovine*, 2009
Judith Clarke, *One Whole and Perfect Day*, 2007
John Green, *An Abundance of Katherines*, 2006
Walter Dean Myers, *Somewhere in the Darkness*, 1992

387

MATT PHELAN, Author/Illustrator

The Storm in the Barn

(Somerville, Massachusetts: Candlewick Press, 2009)

Subject(s): Droughts; Rural life; Weather

Age range(s): 9 - 13+
Major character(s): Jack Clark, 11-Year-Old
Time period(s): 20th century; 1930s (1937)
Locale(s): Kansas, United States

Summary: Matt Phelan's *The Storm in the Barn* is a graphic novel for children that centers on one boy's courageous adventure during the Dust Bowl of 1937. Eleven-year-old Jack Clark is a Kansas farm boy dealing with the typical trials and tribulations of a kid his age. But Jack's life takes an unexpected turn when he encounters a shadowy form in the family barn. This specter, it turns out, is pure rain. Now, in order to survive the drought that is ravaging the country, Jack will have to harness his strength and confront the forces of nature with all the wit, skill, and intelligence he possess.

Where it's reviewed:
Booklist, August 2009, page 68
Bulletin of the Center for Children's Books, December 2009, page 18
Horn Book Magazine, Nov/Dec 2009, page 683
New York Times Book Review, November 8, 2009, page 18
School Library Journal, September 2009, page 190

Other books by the same author:
Around the World, 2011

Awards the book has won:
Scott O'Dell Historical Fiction Award, 2010

Other books you might like:
L. Frank Baum, *The Wonderful Wizard of Oz*, 1900
Karen Hesse, *Out of the Dust*, 1997
Shaun Tan, *The Arrival*, 2007
Rob Vollmar, *The Castaways*, 2007

388

MATT PHELAN, Author/Illustrator

Around the World

(Somerville, Massachusetts: Candlewick Press, 2011)

Story type: Historical
Subject(s): History; Biographies; Voyages and travels

Age range(s): 9 - 13+
Major character(s): Thomas Stevens, Historical Figure, Adventurer, Traveler; Nellie Bly, Historical Figure, Journalist, Adventurer, Traveler; Joshua Slocum, Sailor, Adventurer, Traveler
Time period(s): 19th century

Summary: In this graphic novel for children and young adults, author and illustrator Matt Phelan recounts the tales of three very different world travelers. After the publication of Jules Verne's *Around the World in Eighty*

Days, adventurers from all walks of life planned their own circumnavigations of the globe in the late 19th century. Featured here are bicyclist Thomas Stevens, who crosses America on two wheels, and then decides to continue his journey by ship; journalist Nellie Bly, who documents her trek with news reports dispatched along the way; and Joshua Slocum, a former sea captain, who circles the world in a 36-foot wooden boat named the *Spray*.

Where it's reviewed:
Booklist, September 15, 2011, page 55
Horn Book Magazine, November/December 2011, page 109
Publishers Weekly, August 1, 2011, page 51
School Library Journal, September 2011, page 190

Other books by the same author:
The Storm in the Barn, 2009

Other books you might like:
Gary L. Blackwood, *Around the World in 100 Days*, 2010
Bonnie Christensen, *The Daring Nellie Bly: America's Star Reporter*, 2003
Brian Selznick, *The Invention of Hugo Cabret: A Novel in Words and Pictures*, 2007
Chris Van Allsburg, *Queen of the Falls*, 2011

389

RODMAN PHILBRICK

The Mostly True Adventures of Homer P. Figg

(New York: Scholastic Press, 2009)

Subject(s): Brothers; Orphans; United States Civil War, 1861-1865

Age range(s): 10 - 13+
Major character(s): Homer P. Figg, Orphan; Harold Figg, Brother (older, of Homer); Squinton Leach, Uncle (of Homer and Harold); Jebediah Brewster, Business-man (owner of Brewster Mines), Quaker (helps fugitive slaves escape to Canada); Webster B. Willow, Religious (Methodist clergyman), Guardian (temporary, for Homer P. Figg); Kate Nibbly, Con Artist (lovely young woman); Fenton J. Fleabottom, Con Artist, Professor, Spy
Time period(s): 19th century; 1860s (1863)
Locale(s): United States

Summary: The setting for this story is 1863, right in the middle of the U.S. Civil War. Homer and Harold Figg are orphans, living with their mean, skinflint of an uncle, Squinton Leach. Leach sells Harold to the Union Army in order to take his own place, but Harold is underage. Homer is, not surprisingly, furious at this miscarriage of justice, and runs away from home to find Harold and spring him from his forced conscription. His journeys give him ample opportunity of encounter all manner of men, from the upstanding (Jebediah Brewster) to the naive (Reverand Webster B. Willow) to charming grifters (Kate Nibbly, Professor Fenton J. Fleabottom). But

Homer holds his own, as he relates in his own humorous voice. Where his humor and wits fail him, however, is in Gettysburg, Pennsylvania where he finally finds Harold. And it appears Harold doesn't want to be saved. Here's an adventure tale that captures the flavor of the Civil War without shying away from its horrors but without dwelling on them either.

Where it's reviewed:
Booklist, January 1 2009, page 84
Bulletin of the Center for Children's Books, January 2009, page 116
Horn Book Magazine, January/February 2009, page 100
Journal of Adolescent & Adult, October 2010, Page 157
School Library Journal, January 2009, page 116

Awards the book has won:
Mitten Award (Michigan Library Association's Children's Services Division), 2009

Other books you might like:
James Lincoln Collier, *My Brother Sam Is Dead*, 1974
Joseph Helgerson, *Crows and Cards*, 2009
Michael Hemphill, *Stonewall Hinkleman and the Battle of Bull Run*, 2009
Jim Murphy, *The Boys' War: Confederate and Union Soldiers Talk about the Civil War*, 1990
Jim Murphy, *The Long Road to Gettysburg*, 1992

390

ANDREA DAVIS PINKNEY
BRIAN PINKNEY, Illustrator

Sojourner Truth's Step-Stomp Stride

(New York: Hyperion Books, 2009)

Subject(s): Race relations; Slavery; Feminism

Age range(s): 5 - 8+

Summary: Written by Andrea Davis Pinkney and illustrated by Brian Pinkney, *Sojourner Truth's Step-Stomp Stride* provides a pictorial of one of the most famous feminists and anti-slavery activists in United States history. Illustrations and prose depict Truth's life in the South as a slave as well as her escape to the North to work as a housekeeper. The author shares some of Truth's greatest speeches, in particular her "Ain't I A Woman?" speech given during a feminism rally in Akron, Ohio. An appendix includes historical portraits of Truth.

Where it's reviewed:
Horn Book Magazine, January/February 2009, page 105
New York Times Book Review, March 14, 2010, page 15
School Library Journal, December 2009, page 99

Other books by the same author:
Boycott Blues: How Rosa Parks Inspired a Nation, 2008
Let It Shine: Stories of Black Women Freedom Fighters, 2000

Awards the book has won:
Jane Addams Children's Book Award, 2010

Other books you might like:
Catherine Clinton, *When Harriet Met Sourjourner*, 2008
Alice McGill, *Way Up and over Everything*, 2008
Jerdine Nolen, *Big Jabe*, 2000
Anne Rockwell, *Only Passing Through: The Story of Sojourner Truth*, 2000
Joseph Slate, *I Want to Be Free*, 2009

391

ANDREA DAVIS PINKNEY
BRIAN PINKNEY, Illustrator

Sit-In: How Four Friends Stood Up by Sitting Down

(New York: Little, Brown Books for Young Readers, 2010)

Subject(s): Civil rights; History; Racism

Age range(s): 4 - 8+
Time period(s): 20th century; 1960s (1960)
Locale(s): Greensboro, North Carolina

Summary: *Sit-In: How Four Friends Stood Up by Sitting Down* is a nonfiction book for children, written by Andrea Davis Pinkney and illustrated by Brian Pinkney. The book depicts an event during the civil rights movement in 1960 in Greensboro, North Carolina. Four African American college students went to a Woolworth's lunch counter and sat peacefully in an attempt to integrate the eatery, ordering doughnuts and coffee. The book is written in rhyming verse and uses the food as a metaphor for integration. A time line of the civil rights movement is included at the end as well as additional information about the sit-in at the lunch counter.

Where it's reviewed:
Booklist, February 1, 2010, page 60
Bulletin of the Center for Children's Books, May 2010, page 394
Horn Book Guide, Fall 2010, page 393
School Library Journal, April 2010, page 148

Other books by the same author:
Sojourner Truth's Step-Stomp Stride, 2009
Boycott Blues: How Rosa Parks Inspired a Nation, 2008
Hold Fast to Dreams, 1995
Dear Benjamin Banneker, 1994

Awards the book has won:
Carter G. Woodson Book Award: Elementary, 2011

Other books you might like:
Shane W. Evans, *We March*, 2012
Andrea Davis Pinkney, *Boycott Blues: How Rosa Parks Inspired a Nation*, 2008
Doreen Rappaport, *Martin's Big Words: The Life of Dr. Martin Luther King, Jr.*, 2001
Carole Boston Weatherford, *Freedom on the Menu: The Greensboro Sit-Ins*, 2004

392

ANDREA DAVIS PINKNEY
SEAN QUALLS, Illustrator

Bird in a Box

(New York: Little, Brown and Company, 2011)

Story type: Historical
Subject(s): Childhood; Dreams; Great Depression, 1929-1934
Age range(s): 9 - 12+
Major character(s): Hibernia, 12-Year-Old, Friend (of Willie and Otis); Willie, Friend (of Hibernia and Otis), 13-Year-Old; Otis, 12-Year-Old, Orphan, Friend (of Hibernia and Willie); Joe Louis, Historical Figure, Boxer
Time period(s): 20th century; 1930s
Locale(s): New York, United States
Summary: This novel by Andrea Davis tells the story of kids from a small town in upstate New York who look up to legendary box Joe Louis. Hibernia, the 12-year-old daughter of a local minister, dreams of becoming a great jazz singer just like mother, who left the family when Hibernia was young. Thirteen-year-old Willie also has big dreams—he wants to become a professional boxer—but his hopes are dashed when his father abuses him and burns his hands. Otis is a 12-year-old orphan who still enjoys the riddles his parents taught him when he was younger. Although Hibernia, Willie, and Otis all have challenging lives, they find comfort in watching the fights of their hero, boxer Joe Louis. Together the friends follow Joe's career as he attempts to become the heavyweight boxing champ.

Where it's reviewed:
Booklist, March 15, 2011, page 63
Bulletin of the Center for Children's Books, April 2011, page 388
Horn Book Magazine, May/June 2011, page 101
New York Times Book Review, April 10, 2011, page 16
School Library Journal, March 2011, page 168

Other books by the same author:
With the Might of Angels: The Diary of Dawnie Rae Johnson, 2011
Silent Thunder: A Civil War Story, 1999
Hold Fast to Dreams, 1995

Other books you might like:
Christopher Paul Curtis, *Bud, Not Buddy*, 1999
Gail Carson Levine, *Dave at Night*, 1999
Patricia C. McKissack, *A Song for Harlem*, 2007
George Sullivan, *Knockout!: A Photobiography of Boxer Joe Louis*, 2008
Eleanora E. Tate, *Celeste's Harlem Renaissance*, 2007

393

JERRY PINKNEY, Author/Illustrator

Twinkle, Twinkle, Little Star

(New York: Little, Brown Books for Young Readers, 2011)

Story type: Young Readers
Subject(s): Rhyme; Adventure; Animals

Age range(s): 2 - 5+
Summary: Caldecott Medal-winner Jerry Pinkney lends his whimsical and creative illustrations to the beloved nursery rhyme in this picture book for young readers. The story centers on the adventures of an inquisitive young chipmunk that is fascinated by the twilight and glow of the stars. The chipmunk leaves his nest and embarks on a magical, exciting adventure as he chases after the twinkling lights around him during both day and night. His fascination leads him to encounter an array of twinkling beauty, including the glow of fireflies, the sparkle of dew on a spider's web, and the shimmering reflection of the moonlight on the water's surface.

Where it's reviewed:
Booklist, October 2011, page 51
New York Times Book Review, October 16, 2011, page 20
Publishers Weekly, August 29, 2011, page 63
School Library Journal, November 2011, page 107

Other books by the same author:
Three Little Kittens, 2010
The Lion & the Mouse, 2009
The Little Red Hen, 2006

Other books you might like:
Leo Dillon, *Mother Goose: Numbers on the Loose*, 2007
Eugene Field, *Wynken, Blynken and Nod*, 1995
Salley Mavor, *Pocketful of Posies: A Treasury of Nursery Rhymes*, 2010
Jane Yolen, *Switching On the Moon: A Very First Book of Bedtime Poems*, 2010

394

JERRY PINKNEY, Author/Illustrator

The Lion and the Mouse

(New York: Little, Brown Books for Young Readers, 2009)

Subject(s): Fables; Lions; Friendship

Age range(s): 3 - 7+
Locale(s): Kenya; Tanzania

Summary: *The Lion and the Mouse* is author and illustrator Jerry Pinkney's retelling of the classic fable from Aesop. The tale focuses on the unlikely friendship between a lion and a mouse. It is set in the African savannah, which is filled with wild animals and exotic plant life. After the lion shows mercy to a small mouse, he becomes trapped in a net. The mouse then comes to the beast's rescue by chewing through the ropes that have ensnared the creature. *The Lion and the Mouse* contains very little text, but instead relies heavily on Pinkney's stunning and captivating illustrations of the African landscape and wildlife.

Where it's reviewed:
Booklist, July 1, 2009, page 63
Bulletin of the Center for Children's Books, November 2009, page 100
Horn Book Magazine, November/December 2009, Page 658

New York Times Book Review, November 8 2009, page 15

School Library Journal, September 2009, page 146

Other books by the same author:
Three Little Kittens, 2010
Little Red Riding Hood, 2007
The Little Red Hen, 2006
Aesop's Fables, 2000
The Ugly Duckling, 1999

Awards the book has won:
Blue Ribbon Awards: Picture Books, 2008
Off the Cuff Awards, 2009
Book Sense Book of the Year Award: Children's Book, 2010
Caldecott Medal, 2010

Other books you might like:
James Daugherty, *Andy and the Lion*, 1938
Meredith Gary, *Sometimes You Get What You Want*, 2008
Carter Goodrich, *The Hermit Crab*, 2009
Leonard S. Marcus, *Pass It Down: Five Picture-Book Families Make Their Mark*, 2006
Lisa Wheeler, *Old Cricket*, 2003

395

PATRICIA POLACCO, Author/Illustrator

January's Sparrow
(New York: Philomel, 2009)

Subject(s): Slavery; Segregation; Racism
Age range(s): 8 - 11+
Major character(s): Sadie Crosswhite, Child, Slave
Time period(s): 19th century; 1840s
Locale(s): Kentucky, United States; Michigan, United States

Summary: In Patricia Polacco's *January's Sparrow*, Sadie Crosswhite is woken up in the middle of the night by her parents. January has been killed, and Sadie's parents are certain that those who are responsible for their friend's death will be coming for them next. They make immediate preparations to leave Kentucky, and they tell Sadie that she can't bring anything with her. Sadie is heartbroken as she says goodbye to her most treasured possession: a sparrow January whittled for her from a block of wood. That night, the Crosswhites use the Underground Railroad to escape. They settle in Michigan and begin their life anew. Sadie soon receives a package at their new home. Inside is January's sparrow with a note attached: "I found you." Terrified, the town must find the courage to come together and defeat the evil that is heading their way.

Where it's reviewed:
Bulletin of the Center for Children's Books, January 2010, page 212
Horn Book Magazine, November/December 2009, page 659
School Library Journal, September 2009, page 71

Other books by the same author:
Just In Time, Abraham Lincoln, 2011

Pink and Say, 1994

Awards the book has won:
Michigan Notable Books Award, 2010

Other books you might like:
Christopher Paul Curtis, *Elijah of Buxton*, 2007
Laurie Halse Anderson, *Chains*, 2008
Jeffrey Kluger, *Freedom Stone*, 2011
Jerdine Nolan, *Eliza's Freedom Road: An Underground Railroad Diary*, 2011

396

PATRICIA POLACCO, Author/Illustrator

Junkyard Wonders
(New York: Philomel Books, 2010)

Subject(s): Learning disorders; Teachers; Schools
Age range(s): 8 - 11+
Major character(s): Trisha, Learning Disabled Child; Mrs. Peterson, Teacher
Time period(s): 21st century; 2010s
Locale(s): Michigan, United States

Summary: Patricia Polacco's *Junkyard Wonders* follows the challenges and triumphs of young Trisha, a special education student who moves to a new town and starts classes a new school. There she is relegated to the special ed classroom—known as "the junkyard"—but she is soon captivated by a kindly teacher, Mrs. Peterson, and the attitudes of her classmates. After a visit to the *real* junkyard, the group rescues and refurbishes a model plane they plan to fly at the upcoming science fair—unless the school bully can be averted, that is. Polacco's illustrations accompany this tale.

Where it's reviewed:
Booklist, May 1, 2010, page 86
Horn Book Guide, Spring 2011, page 42
Publishers Weekly, June 21, 2010, page 45
School Library Journal, July 2010, page 68

Other books by the same author:
Mr. Lincoln's Way, 2001
Thank You, Mr. Falker, 1998

Other books you might like:
Sandra Belton, *Pictures for Miss Josie*, 2003
Juan Felipe Herrera, *The Upside Down Boy, El Nino De Cabeza*, 2000
Gloria Houston, *My Great-Aunt Arizona*, 1992

397

ANTOINETTE PORTIS, Author/Illustrator

A Penguin Story
(New York: HarperCollins, 2009)

Subject(s): Penguins; Adventure
Age range(s): 4 - 8+
Major character(s): Edna, Penguin
Time period(s): 21st century; 2000s

Summary: Edna lives in a world filled with white, black, and blue. Though she loves the softly falling snow, the inky black sky, and the calm blue ocean, Edna wonders if more colors might exist somewhere out there. On a quest to add a little color to her life, Edna takes a journey across the frozen tundra to find some new hues. When Edna finally finds what she's been looking for, she decides to keep up the search for more color in future adventures. *A Penguin Story* is one of several children's books from acclaimed author and illustrator Antoinette Portis.

Where it's reviewed:
Booklist, November 15, 2008, page 52
Horn Book Magazine, March/April 2009, page 184
New York Times Book Review, November 8, 2009, page 20
Publishers Weekly, December 1, 2009, page 45
School Library Journal, January 2009, page 82

Other books by the same author:
Not a Stick, 2007
Not a Box, 2006

Other books you might like:
Elisha Cooper, *Beaver Is Lost*, 2010
Jean-Luc Fromental, *365 Penguins*, 2006
Edel Rodriguez, *Sergio Makes a Splash*, 2008
Cynthia Rylant, *Snow*, 2008
Mo Willems, *Naked Mole Rat Gets Dressed*, 2009

398

ELLEN POTTER

The Kneebone Boy

(New York: Feiwel and Friends, 2010)

Subject(s): Mystery; Adventure; Missing persons

Age range(s): 10 - 13+

Major character(s): Otto Hardscrabble, 13-Year-Old, Brother (older, of Lucia and Max); Lucia Hardscrabble, Sister (of Otto and Max); Max Hardscrabble, Brother (younger, of Otto and Lucia); Casper Hardscrabble, Father (of Otto, Lucia, and Max)

Time period(s): 21st century; 2010s

Locale(s): London, England

Summary: The Hardscrabble children—Otto, Lucia, and Max—live with their father, Casper. Their mother mysteriously disappeared years ago, leaving Casper depressed and Otto mute. Having to go away on business, Casper sends the children to stay with their aunt in London. Upon their arrival in the city, the children find their aunt is away on vacation. The children then decide to go to the home of their eccentric great-aunt, who lives next door to the Kneebone castle. The Hardscrabble children learn that a boy with a physical deformity is locked away in the castle. They decide to rescue him, but their quest to guide the Kneebone boy to freedom leads them to answers that could unlock the mystery surrounding their mother's disappearance.

Where it's reviewed:
Booklist, September 15, 2010, page 67

Bulletin of the Center for Children's Books, October 2010, page 90
Horn Book Magazine, Sept/Oct 2010, page 67
Publishers Weekly, August 23, 2010, page 49
School Library Journal, September 2010, page 161

Other books by the same author:
Slob, 2009
Olivia Kidney and the Secret beneath the City, 2007
Olivia Kidney and the Exit Academy, 2005
Olivia Kidney, 2003

Other books you might like:
Adam Gidwitz, *A Tale Dark and Grimm*, 2010
Chris Grabenstein, *The Hanging Hill*, 2009
Lemony Snicket, *The Bad Beginning*, 1999
Lian Tanner, *Museum of Thieves*, 2010

399

SARAH PRINEAS
ANTONIO JAVIER CAPARO, Illustrator

Lost

(New York: HarperCollins, 2009)

Series: Magic Thief Series. Book 2
Subject(s): Magic; Wizards; Apprenticeship programs

Age range(s): 9 - 11+
Major character(s): Conn, Apprentice; Nevery, Wizard; Aspeling, Sorcerer
Time period(s): Indeterminate

Summary: Wizard's apprentice Conn returns for another adventure in *Lost*, the second book of The Magic Thief series by Sarah Prineas. Bizarre happenings still plague the town of Wellmet, and Conn and his master, the wizard Nevery, are trying to get to the bottom of things. They soon learn that Wellmet is under threat from the evil king Aspeling, and right on the heels of this discovery, Conn gets banished from the town for using fire in his magic. But his banishment brings him into an unexpected confrontation with the sorcerer-king who has been depleting the magical power of Wellmet. Antonio Javier Caparo provides illustrations to this volume.

Where it's reviewed:
Booklist, May 1, 2009, page 78
Horn Book Guide, Fall 2009, page 381
School Library Journal, September 2009, page 172

Other books by the same author:
Found, 2010
The Magic Thief, 2008

Other books you might like:
F.E. Higgins, *The Black Book of Secrets*, 2007
J.K. Rowling, *Harry Potter and the Sorcerer's Stone*, 1998
Angie Sage, *Magyk: Septimus Heap, Book One*, 2005
Mary Frances Zambreno, *A Plague of Sorcerers*, 1991

400

JAMES PROSEK, Author/Illustrator

Bird, Butterfly, Eel

(New York: Simon & Schuster Books for Young Readers, 2009)

Subject(s): Animals; Nature; Wildlife

Age range(s): 5 - 8+
Locale(s): New England, United States

Summary: *Bird, Butterfly, Eel* by James Prosek is an introduction to animal migration intended for young readers. A barn swallow, a monarch butterfly, and an American eel all live on a New England farm. They each spend the summer months preparing for their fall journeys: the swallow flies to Argentina, the butterfly heads for Mexico, and the eel swims across the Atlantic to the Sargasso Sea. When the spring comes around, their offspring return to the New England farm to begin the cycle again. The straightforward, no-frills text is complemented by brilliant watercolors depicting the animals in their natural habitats. Prosek includes a two-page map depicting the characters' journeys, as well as notes containing further information for older readers.

Where it's reviewed:
Booklist, January 1, 2009, page 90
Horn Book Guide, Fall 2009, page 438
New York Times Book Review, February 16, 2009, page 17
School Library Journal, February 2009, page 84

Other books by the same author:
A Good Day's Fishing, 2004

Other books you might like:
Dianna Hutts Aston, *An Egg Is Quiet*, 2006
Pamela F. Kirby, *What Bluebirds Do*, 2009
Antoine O Flatharta, *Hurry and the Monarch*, 2005
Sam Swope, *Gotta Go! Gotta Go!*, 2000

401

BOB RACZKA
PETER REYNOLDS, Illustrator

Guyku: A Year of Haiku for Boys

(Boston, Massachusetts: Houghton Mifflin Books for Children, 2010)

Subject(s): Poetry; Children

Age range(s): 5 - 8+

Summary: In *Guyku: A Year of Haiku for Boys*, Bob Raczka introduces young readers (boys especially) to the joys of the seasons through the simplicity of haiku poetry. Following the traditional 17-syllable form, each haiku in this clever collection captures the essence of a particular outdoor activity, from kite-flying to bike-riding, tree-climbing to stargazing, snowball-throwing to grasshopper-catching. Pen and ink illustrations by Peter Reynolds complement the book's spare text. Each energetic scene is enhanced with just one color, accord-

ing to the season it represents (blue in winter, green in spring, yellow in summer, and brown in autumn).

Where it's reviewed:
Booklist, June 1, 2010, page 84
Horn Book Magazine, Nov/Dec 2010, page 111
Publishers Weekly, September 20, 2010, page 62
School Library Journal, September 2010, page 139

Other books by the same author:
Fall Mixed Up, 2011

Other books you might like:
Andrew Clements, *Dogku*, 2007
John Grandits, *Technically, It's Not My Fault: Concrete Poems*, 2004
Kobayashi Issa, *Today and Today*, 2007

402

BOB RACZKA
NANCY DONIGER, Illustrator

Lemonade and Other Poems Squeezed from a Single Word

(New York: Roaring Brook Press, 2011)

Subject(s): Poetry; Reading; Games

Age range(s): 7 - 10+

Summary: Bob Raczka serves up poetic word games in this collection of children's verse. The words from each poem are derived from the letters in a single word. For example, the poem "Constellation" reads, "a / silent / lion / tells / an / ancient / tale," while the title poem features the lines "made / one / ad / added / one / lemon / load / and / one / mom." Each poem is included twice. In the first instance, the letters appear scattered across the page beneath the corresponding letter in the original word, creating a word puzzle for readers to solve. On the facing page, the letters are arranged in the order in which the poet intended. Illustrations by Nancy Doniger accompany the text.

Where it's reviewed:
Booklist, December 15, 2010, page 45
Bulletin of the Center for Children's Books, February 2011, page 291
Horn Book Magazine, March/April 2011, page 133
School Library Journal, May 2011, page 137

Other books by the same author:
Guyku: A Year of Haiku for Boys, 2010

Other books you might like:
Georgia Heard, *Falling Down the Page: A Book of List Poems*, 2008
Marilyn Singer, *Mirror, Mirror: A Book of Reversible Verse*, 2010
Lee Wardlaw, *Won-Ton: A Cat Tale Told in Haiku*, 2010

403

CALVIN ALEXANDER RAMSEY
FLOYD COOPER, Illustrator

Ruth and the Green Book

(Minneapolis, Minnesota: Carolrhoda Books, 2010)

Story type: Historical
Subject(s): Race relations; Racism; Segregation
Age range(s): 7 - 10+
Major character(s): Ruth, Child
Time period(s): 20th century; 1950s
Locale(s): Alabama, United States; Georgia, United States; Chicago, Illinois

Summary: In this volume by Calvin Alexander Ramsey, Ruth is a young African American girl who embarks with her family on a road trip to visit her grandmother in Alabama in the early 1950s. Along the way, Ruth finds out that black Americans are not treated so well in some places. In fact, many African Americans are often refused service at gas stations or forbidden from lodging at many hotels. As Ruth and her family struggle to make their way through the segregated South, they meet a friendly gas station attendant who sells them something called the Green Book, which turns out to be a guide to all the businesses that are willing to serve black travelers. With Ruth in charge of navigating the family trip with the help of the Green Book, their journey soon becomes much easier and friendlier. Ramsey's story is based on the real history of segregation, the Jim Crow laws, and the actual publication known as The Green Book.

Where it's reviewed:
Booklist, November 1, 2010, page 68
Bulletin of the Center for Children's Books, December 2010, page 203
Horn Book Guide, Spring 2011, page 43
Publishers Weekly, October 11, 2010, page 44
School Library Journal, November 2010, page 79

Other books by the same author:
Belle: The Last Mule at Gee's Bend: A Civil Rights Story, 2011

Other books you might like:
Christopher Paul Curtis, *The Watsons Go to Birmingham—1963*, 1995
Aaron Reynolds, *Back of the Bus*, 2010
Paula Young Shelton, *Child of the Civil Rights Movement*, 2010
Deborah Wiles, *Freedom Summer*, 2001
Jacqueline Woodson, *The Other Side*, 2001

404

DOREEN RAPPAPORT
GARY KELLY, Illustrator

Eleanor, Quiet No More

(New York: Disney Hyperion, 2009)

Subject(s): Presidents (Government); Women
Age range(s): 8 - 10+

Major character(s): Eleanor Roosevelt, Historical Figure (wife of president Franklin Roosevelt)

Summary: Eleanor Roosevelt, who begin life as a neglected and then shy child, learned to find her voice as an adult — a voice that resounded all over the globe as she spoke out for human rights. This spare biography traces that life; luminous illustrations by Gary Kelly depict Eleanor as an unwanted child in the background and as a gradually emerging adult in her own right. Sprinkled with quotations from Eleanor's writings and speeches, the biography shines with praise for Eleanor Roosevelt. Readers can see not only that she changed the role of First Lady but how she did so. Appended with notes from both author and illustrator.

Where it's reviewed:
Booklist, November 1 2008, page 43
Bulletin of the Center for Children's Books, February 2009, page 254
Horn Book Magazine, March/April 2009, page 213
Publishers Weekly, February 16 2009, page 127
School Library Journal, February 2009, page 125

Other books by the same author:
Jack's Path of Courage: The Life of John F. Kennedy, 2010
Abe's Honest Words: The Life of Abraham Lincoln, 2008
Martin's Big Words: The Life of Dr. Martin Luther King, Jr, 2007
John's Secret Dreams: The Life of John Lennon, 2004

Other books you might like:
Barbara Cooney, *Eleanor*, 1996
Pam Munoz Ryan, *Amelia and Eleanor Go for a Ride*, 1999
Tanya Lee Stone, *Elizabeth Leads the Way: Elizabeth Cady Stanton and the Right to Vote*, 2008
Linda Arms White, *I Could Do That! : Esther Morris Gets Women the Vote*, 2005

405

CHRIS RASCHKA, Author/Illustrator

Little Black Crow

(New York: Atheneum Books for Young Readers, 2010)

Subject(s): Birds; Rhyme; Nature

Age range(s): 4 - 8+

Summary: In the picture story *Little Black Crow* by Chris Raschka, a little boy bases a series of inquiries about the world around him on the comings and goings of a crow. In soothing rhyme, the boy wonders where the little black crow goes in the snow, in the sky, and in the night's starry sky. As the boy formulates his own thoughts about the crow, he also wonders what thoughts the crow might have about him. Raschka's muted watercolor illustrations complement the book's reflective tone.

Where it's reviewed:
Booklist, June 1, 2010, page 93
Horn Book Magazine, July/August 2010, page 94

Publishers Weekly, August 23, 2010, page 46
School Library Journal, July 2010, page 69

Other books by the same author:
A Ball for Daisy, 2011
Whaley Whale, 2000
Arlene Sardine, 1998
Yo! Yes?, 1993

Other books you might like:
Kevin Henkes, *Kitten's First Full Moon*, 2004
Kobayashi Issa, *Today and Today*, 2007
Liz Garton Scanlon, *All the World*, 2009
Laura Vaccaro Seeger, *First the Egg*, 2007

406

CHRIS RASCHKA, Author/Illustrator

A Ball for Daisy

(New York: Schwartz & Wade Books, 2011)

Story type: Young Readers
Subject(s): Dogs; Toys; Friendship

Age range(s): 3 - 6+
Major character(s): Daisy, Dog

Summary: Award-winning author and illustrator Chris Ra-schka weaves a tale of friendship in this wordless picture story for children. In rich, vibrant illustrations, Raschka depicts Daisy the dog playing contentedly at home with her red ball. But when her owner takes her to the park with the ball, the fun day takes a sad turn. A brown dog that is visiting the park takes Daisy's ball and breaks it. Daisy is distraught and looks to her owner for comfort. The next time they go to the park, the brown dog is there again playing with a blue ball of its own. The two dogs play together gleefully, and when it's time to leave, Daisy is given the blue ball to take home.

Where it's reviewed:
Booklist, June 1, 2011, page 90
Horn Book Magazine, September/October 2011, page 77
School Library Journal, August 2011, page 82

Other books by the same author:
Hip Hop Dog, 2010
Little Black Crow, 2010
The Blushful Hippopotamus, 1996
Yo! Yes?, 1993

Awards the book has won:
Caldecott Medal, 2012

Other books you might like:
Kevin Henkes, *Owen's Marshmallow Chick*, 2002
Mercer Mayer, *A Boy, a Dog, and a Frog*, 1974
Mark Newgarden, *Bow-Wow Bugs a Bug*, 2007
Komako Sakai, *Emily's Balloon*, 2006
Laura Vaccaro Seeger, *What If?*, 2010

407

MARJORIE KINNAN RAWLINGS
LEO DILLON, Illustrator
DIANE DILLON, Illustrator

The Secret River

(New York: Atheneum Books for Young Readers, 2011)

Story type: Historical; Young Readers
Subject(s): Fishing (Recreation); Business; Rivers

Age range(s): 7 - 9+
Major character(s): Calpurnia, Girl, Writer; Madame Albi-rtha, Neighbor, Advisor
Locale(s): Florida, United States

Summary: The 2011 version of *The Secret River*, produced by illustrators Leo and Diane Dillon, is a newly il-lustrated republication of Pulitzer Prize-winning author Marjorie Kinnan Rawlings's original 1955 novel of the same name. The story follows a young girl named Calpurnia, whose father is a down-on-his-luck fisherman struggling to keep his business afloat. Hoping to help her downtrodden father, Calpurnia seeks out advice on where to find the biggest catfish from her neighbor, Madame Albirtha. Madame Albirtha points Calpurnia to a secret river teeming with fish and, sure enough, Calpurnia comes home with a huge catch. Success does not come easily, however, and Calpurnia must face a bevy of trials if she is to feed the town and save the family business. The original release of *The Secret River* won a 1956 Newberry Honor.

Where it's reviewed:
New York Times Book Review, May 27, 2011, page 24
Publishers Weekly, November 8, 2011, page 57
School Library Journal, January 2011, page 82

Other books you might like:
Becky Birtha, *Lucky Beans*, 2010
Deborah Hopkinson, *Saving Strawberry Farm*, 2005
Fredrick McKissack, *The All-I'll-Ever-Want Christmas Doll*, 2007
Robert D. San Souci, *The Hired Hand*, 1997

408

DEBORAH KOGAN RAY, Author/Illustrator

Dinosaur Mountain: Digging into the Jurassic Age

(New York: Frances Foster Books/Farrar, Straus, Giroux, 2010)

Subject(s): Dinosaurs; Fossils; Paleontology
Age range(s): 7 - 10+

Summary: In *Dinosaur Mountain: Digging into the Juras-sic Age*, author and illustrator Deborah Kogan Ray examines the life and work of Earl Douglass, one of the most successful dinosaur bone hunters in history. When Douglass was a teen, he was intrigued by stories of competition between paleontologists to find dinosaur fossils. Douglass grew up to become a geologist and botanist at the Carnegie Museum in Pittsburgh, Pennsylvania. His research led him to believe that rocky regions in northwestern Utah might hold dinosaur fossils. Sent on a mission by Andrew Carnegie in 1908, Douglass spent 16 years unearthing 350 tons of fossils. *Dinosaur Mountain* educates young adult readers about the fascinating story of Douglass's success.

Where it's reviewed:
Booklist, February 1, 2010, page 40
Horn Book Magazine, May/June 2010, page 111
Publishers Weekly, March 29, 2010, page 57
School Library Journal, May 2010, page 135

Other books by the same author:
Down the Colorado: John Wesley Powell, the One-Armed Explorer, 2007

Other books you might like:
Douglas Florian, *Dinothesaurus*, 2009
Matthew Reinhart, *Encyclopedia Prehistorica: Dinosaurs*, 2005
David Sheldon, *Barnum Brown: Dinosaur Hunter*, 2006
Kathleen Weidner Zoehfeld, *Dinosaur Tracks*, 2007

409

MARY LYN RAY
MARLA FRAZEE, Illustrator

Stars

(New York: Beach Lane Books, 2011)

Story type: Young Readers
Subject(s): Imagination; Nature; Humor

Age range(s): 3 - 6+

Summary: The star, found in many shapes and sizes, is the literal star of this picture book. Author Mary Lyn Ray explains to young readers the many stars are found in nature, both those in the sky and others within reach. Through illustrations by two-time Caldecott Honor recipient Marla Frazee, young readers meander through a garden and find tiny stars that will yield sweet strawberries in a few weeks; discover yellow stars on a vine that will swell from bloom to pumpkin through the summer months; and examine stars that fall from the sky in the winter that will build a base for exhilarating sledding adventures.

Where it's reviewed:
Booklist, October 15, 2011, page 44
Publishers Weekly, August 15, 2011, page 69
School Library Journal, October 2011, page 118

Other books by the same author:
Christmas Farm, 2009
All Aboard!, 2002
Red Rubber Boot Day, 2000
Mud, 1996
Pumpkins: A Story for a Field, 1992

Other books you might like:
Yuyi Morales, *Little Night*, 2007
Jerry Pinkney, *Twinkle, Twinkle, Little Star*, 2011
John Rocco, *Blackout*, 2011
Nancy Elizabeth Wallace, *Stars! Stars! Stars!*, 2009

410

PHILIP REEVE

No Such Things as Dragons

(New York: Scholastic Press, 2010)

Subject(s): Fantasy; Dragons; Suspense

Age range(s): 9 - 12+
Major character(s): Ansel, Boy, Servant (to Brock); Brock, Dragon (slayer)
Time period(s): Indeterminate

Summary: *No Such Things As Dragons* is a fantasy chapter book for young readers. Young Ansel is a mute boy who's been sold as a servant to the mighty dragon slayer, Brock. Although Brock has countless tales of his brave and heroic deeds killing dragons, Ansel has his doubts about whether or not dragons really exist. Is Brock simply capitalizing on the fear of his fellow villagers? Just when Ansel thinks he's discovered the truth, he's shocked to find a ferocious man-eating monster dwelling in the haunted caves of Dragon Mountain. Do he and Brock have what it takes to slay a real-life dragon?

Where it's reviewed:
Booklist, August 1, 2010, page 51
Bulletin of the Center for Children's Books, December 2010, page 204
Horn Book Magazine, Sept/Oct 2010, page 92
Publishers Weekly, July 19, 2010, page 40
School Library Journal, September 2010, page 163

Other books by the same author:
Fever Crumb, 2010
Here Lies Arthur, 2008
Infernal Devices, 2005
Predator's Gold, 2004
Mortal Engines, 2002

Other books you might like:
Avi, *Crispin: The Cross of Lead*, 2002
Shutta Crum, *Thomas and the Dragon Queen*, 2010
Ann Downer, *Hatching Magic*, 2003
Matthew Reinhart, *Encyclopedia Mythologica: Dragons and Monsters Pop-Up*, 2011
Jane Yolen, *The Dragon's Boy*, 1990

411

AARON RENIER, Author/Illustrator

The Unsinkable Walker Bean

(New York: First Second, 2010)

Subject(s): Adventure; Fantasy; Sea stories

Age range(s): 9 - 14+
Major character(s): Walker Bean, Boy, Adventurer
Time period(s): 21st century; 2010s

Summary: In *The Unsinkable Walker Bean*, author and illustrator Aaron Renier presents a graphic novel full of seafaring adventure and magical escapades. Walker Bean is a rather nerdy youngster who has always lived in the shadow of his grandfather's far-flung tales of the seafaring life. But Walker's entire existence is transformed when his grandfather enlists his help in returning a skull to the floor of the ocean, opening the door to a maritime adventure blending fantasy, science fiction, and folklore.

Where it's reviewed:
Booklist, June 1, 2010, page 70
Publishers Weekly, May 3, 2010, page 55
School Library Journal, September 2010, page 180

Other books by the same author:
Spiral Bound, 2005

Other books you might like:
Shannon Hale, *Calamity Jack*, 2010
Herge, *Red Rackham's Treasure: The Adventures of Tintin*, 1944
Brian Selznick, *The Invention of Hugo Cabret: A Novel in Words and Pictures*, 2007
Joann Sfar, *Little Vampire*, 2008
Lewis Trondheim, *Bourbon Island 1730*, 2008

412

LAURA RESAU

Star in the Forest

(New York: Random House, 2010)

Story type: Contemporary
Subject(s): Illegal immigrants; Family; Dogs

Age range(s): 9 - 11+
Major character(s): Zitlally, 11-Year-Old, 5th Grader, Daughter (of Mama and Papa), Friend (of Crystal); Papa, Father (of Zitlally), Immigrant (illegal, deported); Mama, Mother (of Zitlally); Crystal, Friend (of Zitlally)
Time period(s): 21st century; 2000s
Locale(s): Colorado, United States

Summary: Author Laura Resau explores the difficult topic of illegal immigration in this novel for children and young adult readers. Zitlally and her parents have left Mexico for the United States and now live as undocumented aliens in a Colorado trailer park. When the police arrest Papa for a traffic violation, they discover his immigration status and send him back to Mexico. Determined to return to his family, Papa crosses the border and heads north once again with the help of a "coyote." But Papa and his party are captured, and Mama receives a demand for ransom. As Mama works to earn the $10,000 needed for her husband's safe return, Zitlally finds comfort and hope in her new friendship with a neighbor named Crystal and a stray dog she calls Star.

Where it's reviewed:
Booklist, February 1, 2010, page 45
Bulletin of the Center for Children's Books, May 2010, page 396
Horn Book Magazine, March/April 2010, page 69
School Library Journal, February 2010, page 122

Other books by the same author:
The Queen of Water, 2011
The Ruby Notebook, 2010
Red Glass, 2007

What the Moon Saw, 2006

Other books you might like:
Julia Alvarez, *Return to Sender*, 2009
Kate DiCamillo, *Because of Winn-Dixie*, 2000
Elizabeth Starr Hill, *Wildfire!*, 2004
Pam Munoz Ryan, *Esperanza Rising*, 2000

413

AARON REYNOLDS
FLOYD COOPER, Illustrator

Back of the Bus

(New York: Philomel Books, 2010)

Subject(s): African Americans; Civil rights movements; Race relations

Age range(s): 5 - 8+
Time period(s): 20th century; 1950s (1955)
Locale(s): Montgomery, Alabama

Summary: In *Back of the Bus*, author Aaron Reynolds recounts Rosa Parks's heroic actions on a Montgomery, Alabama bus as witnessed by a young African-American passenger. As the boy, a fictional character seated in the back of the bus, engages in a marble-rolling game with Mrs. Parks (who is seated in front), he realizes that she is breaking the rules. When she refuses to surrender her spot to a white male rider, the boy recognizes her defiance and begins to question the fairness of the rules that keep him at the back of the bus. Floyd Cooper's rich oil paintings complement Reynolds's rhythmic text.

Where it's reviewed:
Booklist, February 1, 2010, page 62
Horn Book Guide, Fall 2010, page 312
School Library Journal, February 2010, page 92

Other books you might like:
Andrea Davis Pinkney, *Boycott Blues: How Rosa Parks Inspired a Nation*, 2008
Doreen Rappaport, *Martin's Big Words: The Life of Dr. Martin Luther King, Jr.*, 2001
Paula Young Shelton, *Child of the Civil Rights Movement*, 2010

414

LORI RIES
FRANK W. DORMER, Illustrator

Aggie the Brave

(Watertown, Massachusetts: Charlesbridge, 2010)

Series: Aggie and Ben Series. Book 2
Subject(s): Dogs; Veterinarians; Friendship

Age range(s): 4 - 8+
Major character(s): Ben, Boy; Aggie, Dog
Time period(s): 21st century; 2010s

Summary: The second book in Lori Ries's Aggie and Ben series, this volume continues the adventures of a small boy and his beloved pooch. Ben is worried when he hears Aggie needs surgery, even though everyone assures him that spaying is a simple process that will ensure Aggie remains healthy. Ben and Aggie head to the vet, where Aggie undergoes the procedure. Ben waits and worries over his special pal. *Aggie the Brave* includes illustrations by Frank W. Dormer.

Where it's reviewed:
Horn Book Magazine, September/October 2010, page 92
School Library Journal, August 2010, page 84

Other books by the same author:
Aggie Gets Lost, 2011
Good Dog Aggie, 2009
Aggie and Ben: Three Stories, 2006

Other books you might like:
Lynn Johnston, *Farley Follows His Nose*, 2009
Lynne Rae Perkins, *The Broken Cat*, 2002
Vladimir Radunsky, *You?*, 2009
Jane Yolen, *How Do Dinosaurs Love Their Dogs?*, 2010

415

SHERRI DUSKEY RINKER
TOM LICHTENHELD, Illustrator

Goodnight, Goodnight, Construction Site

(San Francisco: Chronicle Books, 2011)

Story type: Young Readers
Subject(s): Friendship; Work environment; Construction

Age range(s): 3 - 6+

Summary: A cheerful crew of construction vehicles populates this picture book by author Sherri Duskey Rinker and illustrator Tom Lichtenheld. All the big trucks and machines working at the construction site have put in a hard day of work. They lifted beams, mixed cement, and moved dirt. Now, the long workday is over, and the sun is setting. The vehicles get ready to sleep as the night draws near, and they all settle in for a well-earned rest, snuggling with their teddy bears and blankets.

Where it's reviewed:
Booklist, September 1, 2011, page 101
Horn Book Guide, Fall 2011, page 301
School Library Journal, July 2011, page 76

Other books you might like:
Byron Barton, *Dinosaurs, Dinosaurs*, 1989
Hallie Durand, *Mitchell's License*, 2011
Daniel Kirk, *Honk Honk! Beep Beep!*, 2010
William Low, *Machines Go to Work*, 2009
Sally Sutton, *Roadwork*, 2008

416

RICK RIORDAN
ROBERT VENDITTI, Co-Author
ATTILA FUTAKI, Illustrator
JOSE VILLARRUBIA, Illustrator

The Lightning Thief: The Graphic Novel

(New York: Disney/Hyperion Books, 2010)

Series: Percy Jackson and the Olympians Series. Book 1
Subject(s): Fantasy; Mythology; Father-son relations

Age range(s): 9 - 15+
Major character(s): Percy Jackson, 12-Year-Old, Deity (demigod), Son (of Poseidon); Poseidon, Deity, Father (of Percy)
Time period(s): 21st century; 2000s
Locale(s): United States

Summary: Robert Venditti adapts the first book in Rick Riordan's Percy Jackson and the Olympians Series to graphic novel format. As the story begins, 12-year-old Percy has been thrown out of his latest school and now must go to Camp Half-Blood. As the son of the god Poseidon, Percy is a demigod whose everyday adventures include confrontations with some of mythology's greatest figures. When Zeus's lightning bolt is stolen, Percy is blamed and susbsequently leads the quest to recover it and restore order to Mount Olympus. Illustrations by Attila Futaki and coloring by Jose Villarrubia bring the action of Riordan's best-selling novel to life.

Where it's reviewed:
Booklist, December 15, 2010, page 36
Horn Book Guide, Spring 2011, page 81
Publishers Weekly, October 4, 2010, page 51
School Library Journal, March 2011, page 190

Other books you might like:
Charlie Higson, *SilverFin: The Graphic Novel*, 2010
Anthony Horowitz, *Stormbreaker: The Graphic Novel*, 2006
George O'Connor, *Zeus: King of the Gods*, 2010
J.K. Rowling, *Harry Potter and the Half-Blood Prince*, 2005
Doug TenNapel, *Ghostopolis*, 2010

417

RICK RIORDAN

The Lost Hero

(New York: Disney/Hyperion Books, 2010)

Series: Heroes of Olympus Series. Book 1
Subject(s): Mythology; Camps (Recreation); Monsters

Age range(s): 9 - 14+
Major character(s): Jason, Mythical Creature (demigod); Leo, Mythical Creature (demigod); Piper, Mythical Creature (demigod)
Time period(s): Indeterminate
Locale(s): Camp Half-Blood, Fictional Location

Summary: Rick Riordan's *The Lost Hero* finds beloved character Percy Jackson and his pals resurrecting Camp Half-Blood so that a new crop of demigods can start training. Jason, Leo, and Piper are transferred to Camp Half-Blood after encountering problems at their school for unruly children. There, they discover their noble birthright and set out to prepare for their first mission: liberating the goddess Hera from the captivity of Mother Earth. This volume is the first installment in The Heroes of Olympus series.

Where it's reviewed:
Bulletin of the Center for Children's Books, February 2011, page 292
Horn Book Magazine, Jan/Feb 2011, page 99
School Library Journal, February 2011, page 118

Other books by the same author:
The Son of Neptune, 2011
The 39 Clues: The Maze of Bones, 2008
The Kane Chronicles Series
Percy Jackson and the Olympians Series

Other books you might like:
P. D. Baccalario, *Ring of Fire*, 2009
Bruce Coville, *Half-Human*, 2001
Curtis Jobling, *Wereworld: The Rise of the Wolf*, 2011
George O'Connor, *Zeus: King of the Gods*, 2010
Dugal Steer, *Mythology: The Gods, Heroes, and Monsters of Ancient Greece*, 2010

418

RICK RIORDAN

The Red Pyramid

(New York: William Morrow, 2010)

Series: Kane Chronicles Series. Book 1
Subject(s): Egyptian history, to 642 (Ancient period); Fantasy; Adolescence

Age range(s): 9 - 14+
Major character(s): Carter Kane, Teenager, Brother (of Sadie); Sadie Kane, Teenager, Sister (of Carter); Julius Kane, Father (of Carter and Sadie), Historian (Egyptologist)
Time period(s): 21st century; 2010s
Locale(s): London, England

Summary: *The Red Pyramid* is the first book in a new series by Rick Riordan, author of the popular Percy Jackson and the Olympians series. Teenage brother and sister Carter and Sadie have been living apart since their mother passed away; Sadie has stayed with their grandparents in London, and Carter has been traveling with their father Julius, an Egyptologist. One day when they are in town, Julius takes them all to the British History Museum in order to do an "experiment." It goes horribly wrong when Julius accidentally unleashes Set, a vengeful Egyptian god who banishes him, forcing the children to run for their lives. Carter and Sadie realize that Set is not the only Egyptian god who has been awakened, and they begin an adventure that takes them all over the world and begins to reveal their true destiny.

Where it's reviewed:
Booklist, May 15, 2010, page 53
Bulletin of the Center for Children's Books, September 2010, page 41
Horn Book Magazine, July/August 2010, page 121
New York Times Book Review, June 6, 2010, page 23
School Library Journal, June 2010, page 118

Other books by the same author:
The Throne of Fire, 2011
The 39 Clues: The Maze of Bones, 2008
Heroes of Olympus Series
Percy Jackson and the Olympians Series

Other books you might like:
Suzanne Collins, *The Hunger Games*, 2008
James Giblin, *The Riddle of the Rosetta Stone: Key to Ancient Egypt*, 1990
Margaret Peterson Haddix, *Found*, 2008
Matthew Reinhart, *Encyclopedia Mythologica: Gods and Heroes*, 2010
Michael Scott, *The Alchemyst: The Secrets of the Immortal Nicholas Flamel*, 2007

419

JACQUI ROBBINS
MATT PHELAN, Illustrator

Two of a Kind

(New York: Atheneum Books for Young Readers, 2009)

Subject(s): Friendship; Popularity; Schools

Age range(s): 5 - 8+
Major character(s): Anna, Child; Julisa, Child, Friend (of Anna)
Time period(s): 21st century; 2000s

Summary: In *Two of a Kind*, author Jacqui Robbins crafts a timely tale of friendship, identity, and staying true to oneself. Anna and Julisa are the best of friends—until Anna decides she'd much rather be associated with the girls of the school's popular clique. But as she gets to know her new friends, Anna learns just how valuable her friendship with Julisa was. The popular girls are mean-spirited and snobbish—a far cry from the gentleness and humor of Julisa. Now Anna must find a way to win back the affection of her old friend. *Two of a Kind* contains illustrations by Matt Phelan.

Where it's reviewed:
Booklist, September 1, 2009, page 103
Horn Book Magazine, September/October 2009, page 545
School Library Journal, August 2009, page 83

Other books by the same author:
The New Girl . . . And Me, 2006

Other books you might like:
Diana Cain Bluthenthal, *I'm Not Invited?*, 2003
Peter Catalanotto, *The Secret Lunch Special*, 2006
Jennifer Richard Jacobson, *Andy Shane is NOT in Love*, 2008
Lynne Rae Perkins, *The Cardboard Piano*, 2008
Jacqueline Woodson, *The Other Side*, 2001

420

LAURA PEYTON ROBERTS

Green

(New York: Random House, 2010)

Subject(s): Fantasy; Gold; Irish (European people)

Age range(s): 9 - 12+
Major character(s): Lily, 13-Year-Old
Time period(s): 21st century; 2010s
Locale(s): Green, Fictional Location

Summary: *Green* is a clever and humorous fantasy novel for children and young adult readers from author Laura Peyton Roberts. Lily's 13th birthday party is rudely interrupted by an explosion on her front porch and the arrival of three pushy leprechauns. The trio represent the Clan 'O Green, a group of wealthy leprechauns, and Lily is next in line to be the keeper of their gold. That is, if she can pass three different tests. Lily is taken to the land of Green and learns that, before her, her grandmother, Gigi, served as the Keeper of the Clan 'O Green. In this glittering new world, Lily encounters pixies, clovers, and a totally cute boy, but if she can't pass the tests, she may never fulfill her destiny or find her way home.

Where it's reviewed:
Booklist, December 1, 2009, page 44
Bulletin of the Center for Children's Books, December 2010, page 204
Horn Book Guide, Fall 2010, page 352
Publishers Weekly, January 4, 2010, page 47
School Library Journal, February 2010, page 123

Other books you might like:
Frances O'Roark Dowell, *Falling In*, 2010
Lyn Gardner, *Into the Woods*, 2006
Michelle Harrison, *13 Treasures*, 2010
Matthew Reinhart, *Encyclopedia Mythologica: Fairies and Magical Creatures Pop-Up*, 2008

421

JOHN ROCCO, Author/Illustrator

Blackout

(New York: Hyperion Books, 2011)

Subject(s): Family; Family life; Urban life

Age range(s): 5 - 8+

Summary: It's a sweltering night in the city, and one family is spending the evening doing different things; son is watching television, daughter is on the phone, Dad is cooking dinner, and Mom is working on the computer. Suddenly the electricity goes out, and their apartment is plunged into darkness. Looking to escape the heat of their apartment, the family goes to the rooftop, where they see stars overhead. While the family enjoys some stargazing from the roof, the rest of the neighborhood comes to life with an impromptu party on the street below. The family soon learns that getting away from the regular hustle and bustle of life can bring them closer together.

Where it's reviewed:
Booklist, June 1, 2011, page 90
Bulletin of the Center for Children's Books, June 2011, page 487
New York Times Book Review, June 5, 2011, page 26
School Library Journal, July 2011, page 77

Other books by the same author:
Moonpowder, 2008
Wolf! Wolf!, 2007

Other books you might like:
Jonathan Bean, *At Night*, 2007
David McPhail, *Fix-It*, 1984
Komako Sakai, *The Snow Day*, 2009

422

JOANNE ROCKLIN

One Day and One Amazing Morning on Orange Street

(New York: Abrams Books for Young Readers, 2011)

Subject(s): Childhood; Fear; Trees (Plants)

Age range(s): 8 - 10+
Major character(s): Ms. Snoops, Aged Person, Historian
Time period(s): 21st century; 2010s
Locale(s): California, United States

Summary: *One Day and One Amazing Morning on Orange Street* is a novel for young readers about family, friendship, and fear from author Joanne Rocklin. In a small California town that was formerly an orange grove, one lone orange tree remains in an empty lot. The kids of the town gather around the tree with Ms. Snoops, the town's historian, to learn about the past, present, and future of the street. While Ms. Snoops tells them stories of the past, each child confronts a personal concern or worry that's been hounding them. One child deals with an ill sibling while another struggles to become an impressive magician. Through Ms. Snoops' tales about the town's tree, the kids learn to overcome their fear and anxiety.

Where it's reviewed:
Booklist, March 15, 2011, page 61
Bulletin of the Center for Children's Books, April 2011, page 389
Horn Book Magazine, July/August 2011, page 159
Publishers Weekly, February 7, 2011, page 55
School Library Journal, May 2011, page 122

Other books you might like:
Kathi Appelt, *Keeper*, 2010
Jeanne Birdsall, *The Penderwicks: A Summer Tale of Four Sisters, Two Rabbits, and a Very Interesting Boy*, 2005
Katherine Hannigan, *True (...Sort Of)*, 2011
Mary Ann Hoberman, *Strawberry Hill*, 2009

423

ANNE ROCKWELL
MATT PHELAN, Illustrator

Big George: How a Shy Boy Became President Washington

(New York: Harcourt Children's Books, 2008)

Subject(s): Biographies; Presidents (Government); Shyness

Age range(s): 6 - 9+
Time period(s): 18th century
Locale(s): United States

Summary: As a boy, George Washington was virtually fearless. He had no trouble facing dangerous natives, uncertain times, or wild animals. But young George did possess one fear that profoundly shaped his life: he was scared to talk to people. In *Big George: How a Shy Boy Became President Washington*, young readers learn of the first president's early life and the measures he took to overcome his nearly debilitating shyness. Author Anne Rockwell eschews the normal historical trivia (the cherry tree, wooden teeth, crossing the Delaware, etc.) to present a fresh take on America's inaugural Commander-in-Chief. Matt Phelan provides the stylish artwork.

Where it's reviewed:
Booklist, January 1, 2009, page 86
Bulletin of the Center for Children's Books, February 2009, page 256
Horn Book Magazine, March/April 2009, page 214
Publishers Weekly, January 5, 2009, page 50
School Library Journal, February 2009, page 94

Other books by the same author:
What's So Bad About Gasoline?: Fossil Fuels and What They Do, 2009
Clouds, 2008
My Preschool, 2008
Presidents' Day, 2008
Only Passing Through: The Story of Sojourner Truth, 2002

Other books you might like:
Deborah Chandra, *George Washington's Teeth*, 2003
Cheryl Harness, *George Washington*, 2000
Lane Smith, *John, Paul, George and Ben*, 2006
Judith St. George, *So You Want to Be President?: Revised and Updated Edition*, 2004
Peggy Thomas, *Farmer George Plants a Nation*, 2008

424

BEATRICE RODRIGUEZ, Author/Illustrator

The Chicken Thief

(New York: Enchanted Lion, 2010)

Subject(s): Chickens; Foxes; Adventure

Age range(s): 3 - 6+
Time period(s): 21st century; 2010s

Summary: A family of animals is enjoying a bright, sunny morning when an unexpected stranger is discovered lurking in the shadows. It is a fox, and he has his sights set on nabbing the chicken. Fearful for their young charge, the animals grab the chicken and go on the run, pursued by the fox all the way to the ocean. There, a pleasant surprise awaits that the animal family did not see coming. The wordless children's book *The Chicken Thief* contains illustrations by Beatrice Rodriguez.

Where it's reviewed:
Booklist, June 1, 2010, page 30
Horn Book Guide, Fall 2010, page 313
Publishers Weekly, November 8, 2010, page 31
School Library Journal, September 2010, page 127

Other books by the same author:
Fox and Hen Together, 2011
Rooster's Revenge, 2011

Other books you might like:
Mini Grey, *Three by the Sea*, 2010
Mercer Mayer, *A Boy, a Dog, and a Frog*, 1974
Jeff Newman, *The Boys*, 2010
Stephen Savage, *Where's Walrus?*, 2011
Marc Simont, *The Stray Dog*, 2001

425

ERIC ROHMANN, Author/Illustrator

Bone Dog

(New York: Roaring Brook Press, 2011)

Story type: Contemporary
Subject(s): Dogs; Death; Supernatural

Age range(s): 5 - 8+
Major character(s): Gus, Boy; Ella, Dog, Supernatural Being (bone dog)

Summary: Dealing with the death of a beloved pet can be one of the most difficult events in childhood. This illustrated children's book by Eric Rohmann looks at the problem from an unusual perspective, framing the death of a boy's dog within a spooky Halloween adventure. Gus is a young boy saddened by the passing of his dog, Ella. On Halloween, Gus feels so sad he almost stays home, but at last dries his tears and decides to try trick-or-treating. Shortly after going out into the night, Gus is threatened by a group of ghostly skeletons. Just when he thinks he's in serious trouble, a skeletal Ella appears as a "bone dog" and saves the day.

Where it's reviewed:
Horn Book Magazine, July/August 2011, page 136
New York Times Book Review, October 16, 2011, page 19
Publishers Weekly, May 2, 2011, page 55
School Library Journal, July 2011, page 77

Other books by the same author:
My Friend Rabbit, 2002

Other books you might like:
Margery Cuyler, *Skeleton Hiccups*, 2002
Lori Ries, *Aggie and Ben: Three Stories*, 2006
Barbara Walsh, *Sammy in the Sky*, 2011

426

AMY KROUSE ROSENTHAL
TOM LICHTENHELD, Illustrator

Duck! Rabbit!

(San Francisco: Chronicle Books, 2009)

Subject(s): Animals; Identity

Age range(s): 4 - 7+

Summary: In *Duck! Rabbit!*, author Amy Krouse Rosenthal offers a gentle introduction to debate for young readers. The two unnamed characters in the book spot an animal in the distance, but they can't figure out what kind of animal it is. One person claims it's a duck; the other person is sure it's a rabbit. They argue back and forth for a bit, and just as they finally begin to see things from the other's point of view, the animal runs away and is replaced with an anteater (or brachiosaurus). The brightly colored illustrations and playful text belie an excellent learning experience for youngsters about understanding other people's perspectives.

Where it's reviewed:
Booklist, April 1 2009, page 38
Horn Book Magazine, May/June 2009, Page 286
Publishers Weekly, March 23 2009, page 58
School Library Journal, May 2009, page 88

Other books by the same author:
Spoon, 2009

Awards the book has won:
Beehive Awards: Picture Book, 2011

Other books you might like:
Istvan Banyai, *Zoom*, 1995
Beatrice Boutignon, *Not All Animals Are Blue*, 2009
Emily Gravett, *The Odd Egg*, 2009
Laura Ljungkvist, *Follow the Line through the House*, 2007
Herve Tullet, *Press Here*, 2011

427

EILEEN ROSENTHAL
MARC ROSENTHAL, Illustrator

I Must Have Bobo!

(New York: Atheneum Books for Young Readers, 2010)

Story type: Young Readers
Subject(s): Children; Toys; Pets

Age range(s): 3 - 7+

Major character(s): Willy, Boy (looking for Bobo); Earl, Cat (trying to steal Bobo); Bobo, Toy (sock monkey)

Summary: Many children have one special toy that becomes an imaginary confidante, protector, and friend. In this book, Willy has Bobo. Bobo is a sock monkey—but he's much more than that. Bobo protects Willy from scary insects, comforts him when he's sad, and gives him the courage he needs to go down the sliding board. When Bobo goes missing, Willy's life seems to turn upside down. Willy's imagination kicks into overdrive

and he imagines Bobo in a number of perilous situations, such as being captured by pirates. The real captor is actually Willy's cat, Earl. As Willy and Earl compete to get control over the toy monkey, they eventually learn to share. This book features text by Eileen Rosenthal and retro-style illustrations by Marc Rosenthal.

Where it's reviewed:
Booklist, March 15, 2011, page 63
Bulletin of the Center for Children's Books, February 2011, page 293
Horn Book Guide, Fall 2011, page 30
New York Times Book Review, March 13, 2011, page 15
School Library Journal, March 2011, page 133

Other books by the same author:
I'll Save You Bobo, 2012

Other books you might like:
Karen Beaumont, *Where's My T-R-U-C-K?*, 2011
Jon Klassen, *I Want My Hat Back*, 2011
Anita Lobel, *Nini Lost and Found*, 2010
Michael Rosen, *Red Ted and the Lost Things*, 2009
Mo Willems, *Knuffle Bunny: A Cautionary Tale*, 2004

428

STEWART ROSS
STEPHEN BIESTY, Illustrator

Into the Unknown: How Great Explorers Found Their Way by Land, Sea, and Air

(Somerville, Massachusetts: Candlewick Press, 2011)

Subject(s): Discovery and exploration; Travel; Ships

Age range(s): 9 - 14+

Summary: Explorers have traveled by foot, by boat, and by air to discover new places and chart new territory. This book by author Stewart Ross and illustrator Stephen Biesty describes some of the most famous and most influential explorers whose discoveries helped shape the future. The stories of ancient explorers, such as Lief Eriksson and Zheng He, and modern explorers, such as the astronauts who traveled into outer space, fill the pages of this volume. The book describes the time period in which the discoveries took place, and it lists the materials, supplies, and technologies that made the discoveries possible. Ross also describes how each of the explorer's findings affected the world and helped influence future exploration.

Where it's reviewed:
Booklist, July 1, 2011, page 50
Bulletin of the Center for Children's Books, May 2011, page 437
Horn Book Magazine, May/June 2011, page 118
School Library Journal, May 2011, page 138
Voice of Youth Advocates, August 2011, page 303

Other books by the same author:
Ancient China, 2006
Ancient Rome, 2005
Ancient Egypt, 2003

Read About Vikings, 2000
Columbus and the Age of Exploration, 1985

Other books you might like:
Russell Freedman, *The Adventures of Marco Polo*, 2006
Jean Fritz, *Around the World in a Hundred Years: From Henry the Navigator to Magellan*, 1994
J. Patrick Lewis, *A World of Wonders: Geographic Travels in Verse and Rhyme*, 2002
Carla Mooney, *Explorers of the New World: Discover the Golden Age of Exploration With 22 Projects*, 2011
Andrea White, *Surviving Antarctica: Reality TV 2083*, 2005

429

SUSAN GOLDMAN RUBIN
BILL FARNSWORTH, Illustrator

Irena Sendler and the Children of the Warsaw Ghetto
(New York: Holiday House, 2011)

Subject(s): Biographies; World War II, 1939-1945; Polish history

Age range(s): 6 - 9+

Summary: Author Susan Goldman Rubin and illustrator Bill Farnsworth share the true story of a Polish social worker who saved the lives of more than 400 Jewish children from Nazi-occupied Warsaw during World War II. Disguised as a nurse, Irena Sendler developed a number of innovative ways to safely transport children out of the Nazis' grip. She hid them in ambulances, coffins, potato sacks, and suitcases, all in an effort to ensure their delivery to safe havens. In addition, Sendler kept careful, hidden records in hopes of reuniting the children with their families when the war ended. Though Sendler was jailed and tortured, she never gave up on her mission. This volume includes a list of resources, source notes, and an index.

Where it's reviewed:
Booklist, April 15, 2011, page 53
Bulletin of the Center for Children's Books, June 2011, page 488
Publishers Weekly, March 28, 2011, page 55
School Library Journal, May 2011, page 139

Other books by the same author:
The Anne Frank Case: Simon Wiesenthal's Search for the Truth, 2009
Haym Salomon: American Patriot, 2007
The Cat with the Yellow Star: Coming of Age in Terezin, 2006
The Flag with Fifty-Six Stars: A Gift from the Survivors of Mauthausen, 2005
Fireflies in the Dark: The Story of Friedl Dicker-Brandeis and the Children of Terezin, 2000

Other books you might like:
David A. Adler, *Child of the Warsaw Ghetto*, 1995

Tomek Bogacki, *The Champion of Children: The Story of Janusz Korczak*, 2009
Michelle R. McCann, *Luba: The Angel of Bergen-Belsen*, 2003

430

DEBORAH RUDDELL
JOAN RANKIN, Illustrator

A Whiff of Pine, A Hint of Skunk: A Forest of Poems
(New York: Margaret K. McElderry Books, 2009)

Subject(s): Poetry; Forestry; Animals

Age range(s): 6 - 9+

Summary: Author Deborah Ruddell's *A Whiff of Pine, A Hint of Skunk: A Forest of Poems* is a poetry collection for young readers. The collection features 23 poems, each of which discusses various animals and creatures that reside in the forest. The poems in the collection focus a number of different topics such as the seasons as well as individual animals including deer, groundhogs, skunks, raccoons, squirrels, and snails. The comical and simple poems are accompanied by colorful illustrations by Joan Rankin. Ruddell and Rankin also collaborated on the nature-themed poetry collection *Today at the Bluebird Cafe: A Branchful of Birds*.

Where it's reviewed:
Booklist, March 15 2009, page 64
Bulletin of the Center for Children's Books, March 2009, page 233
School Library Journal, April 2009, page 126

Other books by the same author:
Today at the Bluebird Cafe: A Branchful of Birds, 2007

Awards the book has won:
Blue Ribbon Awards: Non-fiction, 2008

Other books you might like:
Jim Arnosky, *Wild Tracks*, 2008
Eve Bunting, *Night Tree*, 1991
Kevin Henkes, *Birds*, 2009
Tan Koide, *May We Sleep Here Tonight?*, 2000
James Prosek, *Bird, Butterfly, Eel*, 2009

431

JAMES RUMFORD, Author/Illustrator

Rain School
(Boston, Massachusetts: Houghton Mifflin Books for Children, 2010)

Subject(s): Africa; Schools; Children

Age range(s): 4 - 7+
Time period(s): 21st century; 2010s
Locale(s): Chad

Summary: *Rain School* is an uplifting and educational picture book for young readers from author and illustrator James Rumford. In a small village in Chad, Africa, a group of children excitedly await their first day of school.

The kids ponder how their first day might go, wondering about their school supplies and the things they might learn, but they're in for a big surprise when they arrive to find a teacher and no building. Before they begin their education, the class must work together to construct the schoolhouse themselves, patching together walls from mud and a roof from grass. Filled with vibrant illustrations, *Rain School* offers children a firsthand glimpse of the culture and education system of Africa.

Where it's reviewed:
Booklist, September 1, 2010, page 97
Bulletin of the Center for Children's Books, November 2010, page 146
Horn Book Guide, Spring 2011, page 44
Romantic Times, October 2010, page 93

Other books by the same author:
Silent Music, 2008
Calabash Cat, 2004
Nine Animals and the Well, 2003

Other books you might like:
Cynthia Cotten, *Rain Play*, 2008
Rita Gray, *One Big Rain: Poems for Rainy Days*, 2010
Margriet Ruurs, *My School in the Rainforest: How Children Attend School around the World*, 2009

432

CHING YEUNG RUSSELL

Tofu Quilt

(New York: Lee & Low Books, 2009)

Subject(s): Poetry; Biographies; History

Age range(s): 9 - 11+
Time period(s): 20th century; 1960s
Locale(s): China

Summary: In *Tofu Quilt*, Ching Yeung Russell describes her life and career in a series of free-verse poems. Raised in Hong Kong in the 1960s, during an era when women's education was a low priority, Russell began her journey as a writer while visiting a relative in mainland China. Her uncle was so impressed by her poetry recitations that he rewarded her with a special sweet. So enamored was Ching with the dessert, she vowed to be a good student. With the support of her uncle and mother, who disagreed with their culture's opinion of women, Ching received a strong education and achieved success as a writer.

Where it's reviewed:
Booklist, November 1, 2009, page 41
Bulletin of the Center for Children's Books, January 2010, page 215
Horn Book Guide, Spring 2010, page 81
School Library Journal, October 2009, page 134

Other books by the same author:
Lichee Tree, 1997
Water Ghost, 1995
First Apple, 1994

Other books you might like:
David Almond, *My Name Is Mina*, 2010

Grace Lin, *The Year of the Dog*, 2006
Patricia MacLachlan, *Word After Word After Word*, 2010

433

MARISABINA RUSSO, Author/Illustrator

I Will Come Back for You: A Family in Hiding during World War II

(New York: Schwartz & Wade, 2011)

Story type: Historical - World War II
Subject(s): World War II, 1939-1945; Jewish history; Jewelry

Age range(s): 7 - 9+
Major character(s): Nonna, Grandmother (of Narrator); Unnamed Character, Granddaughter, Narrator
Time period(s): 21st century; (2010s); 20th century; 1930s-1940s (1939-1945)
Locale(s): Italy

Summary: Based on her own family's history, author and illustrator Marisabina Russo shares the story of a little girl, whose curiosity about her grandmother's unique charm bracelet launches a description of Jewish life in Italy during the Second World War. Throughout this picture story, Nonna explains to her granddaughter what each charm on her bracelet means. For example, the donkey represents the trip Nonna took with her brother and mother to see her father after he had been detained by Nazis. The author takes care to treat the difficult subject matter delicately. Photographs of the author's real family are included at the end of the book.

Where it's reviewed:
Analog, October 1, 2011, page 94
Horn Book Magazine, September/October 2011, page 114
Publishers Weekly, June 20, 2011, page 52
School Library Journal, October 2011, page 119

Other books by the same author:
Always Remember Me: How One Family Survived World War II, 2005
A Visit to Oma, 1991

Other books you might like:
Jo Hoestlandt, *Star of Fear, Star of Hope*, 1995
Doreen Rappaport, *The Secret Seder*, 2005
Ruth Vander Zee, *Erika's Story*, 2003

434

PAM MUNOZ RYAN
PETER SIS, Illustrator

The Dreamer

(New York: Scholastic, 2010)

Subject(s): Poetry; Writers; Father-son relations

Age range(s): 9 - 12+
Major character(s): Pablo Neruda, Writer

Time period(s): 20th century
Locale(s): Chile

Summary: Pablo Neruda was arguably one of the greatest poets of the 20th century. In *The Dreamer*, author Pam Munoz Ryan presents a fictionalized biography of Neruda especially for young readers. This volume follows the legendary wordsmith through his formative years, where he endures a constant stream of negativity from his father. Despite the challenges, Neruda is able to see beauty everywhere he turns, eventually transforming this unique talent into words. The result is some of the most beautiful poetry ever written, and this chronicle is a testament to both Neruda's talent and his indomitable strength. Peter Sis provides the illustrations to this volume.

Where it's reviewed:
Booklist, February 1, 2010, page 44
Bulletin of the Center for Children's Books, July-August 2010, page 498
Horn Book Magazine, March/April 2010, page 85
Publishers Weekly, March 15, 2010, page 55
School Library Journal, April 2010, page 168

Awards the book has won:
Pen Center USA West Literary Awards: Children's Literature, 2011
Pura Belpre Award: Author Award, 2011
Pura Belpre Award: Text Award, 2011

Other books you might like:
Anne-Laure Bondoux, *The Killer's Tears*, 2003
Jen Bryant, *A River of Words: The Story of William Carlos Williams*, 2008
Michael Burgan, *Chile*, 2009
Deborah Kogan Ray, *To Go Singing through the World: The Childhood of Pablo Neruda*, 2006

435

JOANNE RYDER
KATHERINE FENG, Photographer

Panda Kindergarten

(New York: Harper Collins, 2009)

Subject(s): Science; Nature; Wildlife conservation

Age range(s): 4 - 7+

Summary: At the Wolong Nature Preserve, 16 panda cubs are cared for and raised to be strong and independent. The staff at the China Conservation and Research Center for the Giant Panda has raised the group of panda cubs since birth. The staff teaches the cubs the skills necessary for surviving in the wild. In *Panda Kindergarten*, author Joanne Ryder describes a typical day in the life of the panda cubs that inhabit the center. Ryder also explains that the staff releases some of the center's adult pandas back into the wild after they have been taught to care for themselves. *Panda Kindergarten* includes color photographs of the center's pandas.

Where it's reviewed:
Booklist, June 1, 2009, page 58

Horn Book Magazine, Sept/Oct 2009, page 583
School Library Journal, August 2009, page 92
Science Books & Film, November 2009, page 253

Other books by the same author:
Toad by the Road: A Year in the Life of These Amazing Amphibians, 2007
A Pair of Polar Bears: Twin Cubs Find a Home in the San Diego Zoo, 2006
Little Panda: The World Welcomes Hua Mei at the San Diego Zoo, 2001
Without Words, 1995

Other books you might like:
Frances Barry, *Let's Save the Animals: A Flip the Flap Book*, 2010
Nick Dowson, *Tracks of a Panda*, 2007
Renata Liwska, *Little Panda*, 2008
Sandra Markle, *How Many Baby Pandas?*, 2009

436

CYNTHIA RYLANT
NIKKI MCCLURE, Illustrator

All in a Day

(New York: Abrams Books for Young Readers, 2009)

Subject(s): Rhyme; Promises; Beauty

Age range(s): 3 - 6+
Time period(s): 21st century; 2000s

Summary: In *All in a Day*, award-winning author Cynthia Rylant introduces young readers to the promises and possibilities held in the dawning of each new day. Told in whimsical rhyme, this volume celebrates such simple tasks as planting seeds and making wishes and the positive energy these tasks hold. A thrilling testament to the power of the moment, *All in a Day* contains illustrations by Nikki McClure.

Where it's reviewed:
Booklist, April 1, 2009, page 38
Horn Book Guide, Fall 2009, page 344
Publishers Weekly, January 19, 2009, page 59
School Library Journal, May 2009, page 88

Other books by the same author:
Snow, 2008
Bois, 2006
The Stars Will Still Shine, 2005
Long Night Moon, 2004
Silver Packages, 1997

Other books you might like:
Rachel Isadora, *Peekaboo Morning*, 2002
Emily Jenkins, *What Happens on Wednesdays*, 2007
Albert Lamb, *Tell Me the Day Backwards*, 2011
Amy Krouse Rosenthal, *Yes Day!*, 2009

437

KOMAKO SAKAI, Author/Illustrator

The Snow Day

(New York: Arthur A. Levine Books, 2009)

Subject(s): Mothers; Rabbits; Weather

Age range(s): 3 - 6+
Time period(s): 21st century; 2000s

Summary: A heavy snowfall has blanketed the entire town, and a 5-year-old rabbit wakes to find his world shut down for the day. Kindergarten classes have been canceled, and Mom can't get into work, so he has the whole day to spend at home. But Dad has been traveling, and his plane is stuck in a distant city. As the young rabbit waits for his father, he enjoys spending the day with his mother and taking part in all the pleasures and fun of playing in the freshly fallen snow. *Snow Day*, containing warm illustrations by author Komako Sakai, earned the coveted Japanese Book Prize.

Where it's reviewed:
Booklist, January 1 2009, page 77
Bulletin of the Center for Children's Books, February 2009, page 257
Horn Book Guide, Fall 2009, page 345
Publishers Weekly, January 12 2009, page 77
School Library Journal, December 2008, page 101

Other books by the same author:
Mad At Mommy, 2010

Awards the book has won:
Blue Ribbon Awards: Picture Books, 2008

Other books you might like:
Ezra Jack Keats, *The Snowy Day*, 1962
Cynthia Rylant, *Snow*, 2008
Alice Schertle, *All You Need for a Snowman*, 2002
George Shannon, *Rabbit's Gift*, 2007
Uri Shulevitz, *Snow*, 1998

438

GRAHAM SALISBURY
JACQUELINE ROGERS, Illustrator

Calvin Coconut: Trouble Magnet

(New York: Wendy Lamb Books, 2009)

Series: Calvin Coconut Series. Book 1
Series: Calvin Coconut Series. Book 1
Subject(s): Individualism; Family; Schools

Age range(s): 8 - 10+
Major character(s): Calvin Coconut, 4th Grader; Stella, Friend; Tito, Bully; Frank, Bully; Mr. Purdy, Teacher
Time period(s): 21st century; 2000s
Locale(s): Kailua, Hawaii

Summary: Trouble seems to find Calvin Coconut wherever he goes. On the first day of fourth grade, he inadvertently angers the school bullies, lets a centipede loose in his classroom, and forgets all about picking up his younger sister. At home, things aren't much better. Ever since his dad left, Calvin's been the man of the house. Unfortunately, he doesn't think that he's ready for all that responsibility. He's also had to give up his bedroom to the daughter of his mother's friend—and he's far from happy about his new living arrangement. Throughout the book, Calvin struggles to end his streak of bad luck. *Calvin Coconut: Trouble Magnet* is the first book in the Calvin Coconut series.

Where it's reviewed:
Booklist, January 1, 2009, page 82
Bulletin of the Center for Children's Books, April 2009, page 334
Publishers Weekly, March 16, 2009, page 61
School Library Journal, May 2009, page 88

Other books by the same author:
Calvin Coconut Hero of Hawaii, 2011
Calvin Coconut King Fooey, 2011
Calvin Coconuts Zoo Breath, 2010
Calvin Coconut The Zippy Fix, 2009

Other books you might like:
Katy Kelly, *Melonhead*, 2009
Elvira Lindo, *Manolito Four-Eyes*, 2008
Lenore Look, *Alvin Ho: Allergic to Camping, Hiking, and Other Natural Disasters*, 2009
Lisa Yee, *Bobby versus Girls (Accidentally)*, 2009

439

CAROL FISHER SALLER

Eddie's War

(South Hampton, New Hampshire: Namelos, 2011)

Subject(s): World War II, 1939-1945; Rural life; Children and war

Age range(s): 10 - 13+
Major character(s): Eddie Carl, Boy, Brother (of Thomas); Thomas Carl, Pilot, Military Personnel, Brother (of Eddie); Sarah, Girl
Time period(s): 20th century; 1930s-1940s
Locale(s): Ellisville, Illinois

Summary: Eddie Carl is a young boy growing up in Illinois in the 1930s and '40s. When the United States enters World War II, Eddie longs to help his country by fighting the Germans and stopping Hitler. He is too young to join the war, however, and must watch as his brother Thomas leaves to become a fighter pilot. Meanwhile, at home in the small town of Ellisville, Eddie has some battles of his own. He must contend with family secrets, his grandfather's growing animosity, his friendship with a local gypsy, and his crush on a redheaded girl named Sarah. Author Carol Fisher Saller tells Eddie's story through interconnected vignettes that lay the landscape of Eddie's life in small-town America during wartime.

Where it's reviewed:
Horn Book Magazine, September/October 2011, page 100
School Library Journal, September 2011, page 170

Other books you might like:
Avi, *Don't You Know There's a War On?*, 2001

Iain Lawrence, *B for Buster*, 2004
Richard Peck, *On the Wings of Heroes*, 2007
Mary Ann Rodman, *Jimmy's Stars*, 2008

440

COLEEN SALLEY
JANET STEVENS, Illustrator

Epossumondas Plays Possum

(New York: Harcourt Children's Books, 2009)

Subject(s): Adventure; Mothers; Animals

Age range(s): 5 - 8+

Major character(s): Epossumondas, Opossum

Summary: The possum Epossumondas's mama warns him not to go into the swamp because the scary loup-garou lives there. When Epossumondas gets distracted while chasing a butterfly, however, he unintentionally enters the swamp. In the swamp, Epossumondas meets many frightening creatures, but he keeps himself safe by playing possum, or playing dead. Although Epossumondas manages to stay safe for a while, he worries that he might run into the dreaded loup-garou. Epossumondas will have to use all the things his mama taught him if he wants to get home safely. *Epossumondas Plays Possum* is written by Coleen Salley and illustrated by Janet Stevens. Other stories featuring Epossumondas include *Epossumondas* and *Epossumondas Saves the Day*.

Where it's reviewed:
Booklist, January 15, 2009, page 64
Horn Book Magazine, September/October 2009, page 545
Publishers Weekly, September 14, 2009, page 48
School Library Journal, October 2009, page 104

Other books by the same author:
Epossumondas Saves the Day, 2006
Why Epossumondas Has No Hair On His Tail, 2004
Epossumondas, 2002

Other books you might like:
Carmen Agra Deedy, *Martina the Beautiful Cockroach: A Cuban Folktale*, 2007
Anna Dewdney, *Llama Llama Home with Mama*, 2011
Rebecca Emberley, *Chicken Little*, 2009
Coleen Salley, *Epossumondas*, 2002
Anu Stohner, *Brave Charlotte*, 2005

441

DAN SANTAT, Author/Illustrator

Sidekicks

(New York: Arthur A. Levine Books, 2011)

Story type: Adventure

Subject(s): Human-animal relationships; Pets; Adventure

Age range(s): 8 - 12+

Major character(s): Captain Amazing, Hero; Roscoe, Dog; Fluffy, Hamster; Shifty, Reptile (chameleon); Dr. Havoc, Villain; Static Cat, Cat, Sidekick (former, of Captain Amazing)

Locale(s): Metro City, Fictional Location

Summary: Captain Amazing is always busy fighting crime and keeping his arch enemy, Dr. Havoc, in check. All the action leaves Captain Amazing with little time to spend with his pets—dog Roscoe, hamster Fluffy, and chameleon Shifty—so he decides that it's time to hire a new sidekick. In an effort to spend more quality time with their owner, Captain Amazing's pets decide that they will audition for the role. Before long, the pets are fighting with each other, forming pacts, and training in secret. All that changes, however, when Dr. Havoc hatches a plan to defeat Captain Amazing. Can the super-pets put aside their differences to help their master? This graphic novel for children was written and illustrated by Dan Santat.

Where it's reviewed:
Booklist, April 15, 2011, page 43
Horn Book Magazine, July/August 2011, page 160
Publishers Weekly, May 2, 2011, page 59
School Library Journal, July 2011, page 122

Other books by the same author:
Guild of Geniuses, 2004

Other books you might like:
William Boniface, *The Extraordinary Adventures of Ordinary Boy: The Hero Revealed*, 2006
Adam Jay Epstein, *The Familiars*, 2010
Stephen McCranie, *Mal and Chad: The Biggest, Bestest Time Ever!*, 2011
D.J. Steinberg, *Sound Off!*, 2008
Mark Waid, *The Incredibles: Family Matters*, 2009

442

JULIA SARCONE-ROACH, Author/Illustrator

Subway Story

(New York: Alfred A. Knopf, 2011)

Story type: Young Readers

Subject(s): Transportation; Travel; Recycling

Age range(s): 5 - 8+

Major character(s): Jessie, Object (subway car)

Time period(s): 20th century-21st century

Locale(s): Atlantic Ocean, At Sea; New York, New York

Summary: Jessie the subway car enjoys taking people to and from their destinations all day long. She takes her riders to work in the morning and brings them home at night. One of her earliest memories is of transporting people to the World's Fair in New York in 1964. Over the years, Jessie begins noticing new cars on the tracks beside her. After more than 50 years of service, Jessie retires to an empty lot, where she feels sad and bored. One day, she is hauled to the ocean and dropped into the water. Jessie is scared at first, but she soon finds new life as an artificial reef for the sea's many creatures. In this book, author and illustrator Julia Sarcone-Roach teaches children about the history of subway cars and explains how old cars are repurposed into homes for underwater animals.

Where it's reviewed:
Horn Book Magazine, November 2011, page 88

Publishers Weekly, August 22, 2011, page 63
School Library Journal, September 2011, page 129

Other books you might like:
Virginia Lee Burton, *The Little House*, 1942
Heather Lynn Miller, *Subway Ride*, 2009
Christoph Niemann, *Subway*, 2010
Anastasia Suen, author

443

JENNIFER SATTLER, Author/Illustrator

Pig Kahuna

(New York: Bloomsbury USA Children's Books, 2011)

Story type: Young Readers
Subject(s): Surfing; Animals; Brothers

Age range(s): 4 - 7+
Major character(s): Fergus, Pig, Brother (of Dink); Dink, Pig, Brother (of Fergus); Dave, Object (surfboard)

Summary: Brothers Fergus and Dink love the beach. They especially enjoy collecting objects that wash up on the sand. During their visits, the brothers find many interesting items, including seashells, rocks, bottles, and seaweed. However, Fergus does not like the water and carefully stays away from the ocean. One day, the brothers find an old surfboard and name it Dave. The surfboard becomes their most prized possession. The story takes a dramatic turn when Dink decides that Dave belongs in the ocean and casts the surfboard back into the water. Fergus must now decide if saving Dave is worth braving the ocean waves.

Where it's reviewed:
Booklist, April 15, 2011, page 60
Horn Book Guide, Fall 2011, page 329
Publishers Weekly, March 7, 2011, page 60
School Library Journal, May 2011, page 88

Other books by the same author:
Chick 'n Pug, 2010

Other books you might like:
Diane de Groat, *Gilbert, the Surfer Dude*, 2009
Jonathan London, *Froggy Goes to Hawaii*, 2011
Melanie Watt, *Scaredy Squirrel at the Beach*, 2008

444

STEPHEN SAVAGE, Author/Illustrator

Where's Walrus?

(New York: Scholastic Inc., 2011)

Story type: Young Readers
Subject(s): Zoos; Animals; Humor

Age range(s): 2 - 6+
Major character(s): Unnamed Character, Walrus; Unnamed Character, Zoo Keeper

Summary: In this children's book by author and illustrator Stephen Savage, a walrus uses interesting hiding places to avoid being brought back to the zoo. When a walrus escapes from the zoo, the zookeeper must look high and low to find the missing animal. The zookeeper searches all over the city, but the imaginative walrus always finds new places to hide. When the zookeeper tracks the walrus to a diner, the walrus puts on a hat to blend in with the other customers. Then, the walrus joins a group of dancers to hide from the persistent zookeeper. Finally, the walrus hides from the zookeeper by entering a local diving championship.

Where it's reviewed:
Booklist, May 1, 2001, page 97
Bulletin of the Center for Children's Books, February 2011, page 296
Horn Book Magazine, March/April 2011, page 107
School Library Journal, February 2011, page 90

Other books you might like:
Emily Gravett, *Blue Chameleon*, 2011
Kevin Henkes, *Little White Rabbit*, 2011
Satoru Onishi, *Who's Hiding?*, 2007
Bob Staake, *Look! A Book!: A Zany Seek-and-Find Adventure*, 2010

445

ALLEN SAY, Author/Illustrator

Drawing from Memory

(New York: Scholastic Inc., 2011)

Subject(s): Autobiographies; Drawing; Artists

Age range(s): 10 - 14+

Summary: Allen Say is a Caldecott Medal-winning illustrator known for his work in the books *Grandfather's Journey* and *The Bicycle Man*. In this autobiography, Say discusses his life journey from his childhood in World War II Japan, through his relationship with his father who disapproved of his son's desire to become an artist, to his apprenticeship under renowned Japanese cartoonist Noro Shinpei. Say uses watercolors, cartoon illustrations, and photographs and maps from his past to detail the story of how he learned to draw and developed a career as an illustrator. Say is also the author and illustrator of *The Boy of the Three-Year Nap*, which earned a Horn Book Award and a Caldecott Honor, and *Erika-San*, which earned a starred review in *Publisher's Weekly*.

Where it's reviewed:
Booklist, August 2011, page 43
Horn Book Magazine, September/October 2011, page 115
New York Times Book Review, November 13, 2011, page 115
Publishers Weekly, June 20, 2011, page 53
School Library Journal, September 2011, page 185

Other books by the same author:
Kamishibai Man, 2005
The Sign Painter, 2000
The Ink-Keeper's Apprentice, 1979

Other books you might like:
Gary D. Schmidt, *Okay for Now*, 2011
James Sturm, *Adventures in Cartooning: How to Turn*

Your Doodles into Comics, 2009
Ed Young, *The House Baba Built: An Artist's Childhood in China*, 2011

446

ALLEN SAY, Author/Illustrator

The Boy in the Garden

(Boston: Houghton Mifflin Books for Children, 2010)

Subject(s): Dreams; Folklore; Japanese (Asian people)

Age range(s): 7 - 9+
Major character(s): Jiro, Boy; Mr. Ozu, Wealthy
Time period(s): 21st century; 2010s
Locale(s): Japan

Summary: Allen Say's *The Boy in the Garden* offers a modern twist on the classic Japanese folktale *The Grateful Crane*. A little boy named Jiro hears the fable from his mother and is enchanted. He soon encounters a statue of a crane, which he thinks is real—much to his embarrassment. But the presence of a beautiful woman nearby adds further credence to Jiro's belief in the folktale, and his own journey mirroring *The Grateful Crane* begins.

Where it's reviewed:
Booklist, September 1, 2010, page 111
Bulletin of the Center for Children's Books, November 2010, page 146
Horn Book Magazine, Sept/Oct 2010, page 63
Publishers Weekly, October 11, 2010, page 44
School Library Journal, October 2010, page 93

Other books by the same author:
Kamishibai Man, 2005
Stranger in the Mirror, 1995
Grandfather's Journey, 1993
Tree of Cranes, 1991
The Lost Lake, 1989

Other books you might like:
Neil Gaiman, *Instructions*, 2010
Phillis Gershator, *Sky Sweeper*, 2007
Elizabeth Partridge, *Kogi's Mysterious Journey*, 2003
Mark Reibstein, *Wabi Sabi*, 2008

447

APRIL PULLEY SAYRE
HUY VOUN LEE, Illustrator

Honk, Honk, Goose!: Canada Geese Start a Family

(New York: Henry Holt, 2009)

Subject(s): Geese; Birds; Family

Age range(s): 4 - 8+

Summary: In *Honk, Honk, Goose!: Canada Geese Start a Family*, acclaimed children's author April Pulley Sayre tells a story of the lives, habits, and rituals of Canadian geese. The book focuses on a goose couple as they meet, mate, and start their own family unit. Young readers learn about the mating habits of geese, nest-building techniques, and the protective measures undertaken by the male as he strives to keep his offspring safe. When the six unsteady chicks hatch into the world, the new parents are elated. This volume includes an introduction that further illuminates the lives of Canadian geese, as well as collage illustrations by Huy Voun Lee.

Where it's reviewed:
Booklist, March 1, 2009, page 45
Horn Book Magazine, May/June 2009, page 327
School Library Journal, April 2009, page 126

Other books by the same author:
Vulture View, 2007
The Bumblebee Queen, 2005
Army Ant Parade, 2002
Dig, Wait, Listen: A Desert Toad's Tale, 2001
Turtle, Turtle, Watch Out!, 2000

Other books you might like:
Cari Best, *Goose's Story*, 2002
Trudi Braun, *My Goose Betsy*, 1998
Olivier Dunrea, *Gossie and Gertie*, 2002
Elaine Greenstein, *The Goose Man: The Story of Konrad Lorenz*, 2010
Marc Simont, *The Goose That Almost Got Cooked*, 1997

448

LIZ GARTON SCANLON
MARLA FRAZEE, Illustrator

All the World

(New York: Beach Lane Books, 2009)

Subject(s): Poetry; Rhyme; Summer

Age range(s): 3 - 8+

Summary: Written by Liz Garton Scanlon and illustrated by Marla Frazee, *All the World* is a poetic story for young readers. The story focuses on a day in the life of a family, from sunrise to sunset. A mother, father, brother, and sister spend the day at the beach, visit a farmers' market, get caught in a rainstorm, and enjoy dinner together at a restaurant. The rhyming text describes everything that makes up a child's world—nature, family, friends, and a tight-knit community. Frazee's illustrations, a combination of watercolor and pencil, provide the visuals for Scanlon's engaging text.

Where it's reviewed:
Booklist, July 1 2009, page 64
Bulletin of the Center for Children's Books, October 2009, page 57
Horn Book Magazine, September/October 2009, Page 546
Publishers Weekly, August 24 2009, page 59
School Library Journal, August 2009, page 92

Awards the book has won:
Blue Ribbon Awards: Picture Books, 2008

Other books you might like:
Peter Brown, *The Curious Garden*, 2009
Barbara Kerley, *One World One Day*, 2009

Kadir Nelson, *He's Got the Whole World in His Hands*, 2005

Cynthia Rylant, *All in a Day*, 2009

449

ALICE SCHERTLE
PETRA MATHERS, Illustrator

Button Up!: Wrinkled Rhymes

(New York: Harcourt Children's Books, 2009)

Subject(s): Clothing; Animals; Poetry

Age range(s): 4 - 8+

Summary: In this volume of children's verse, acclaimed poet Alice Schertle writes about the different personalities contained in a closetful of clothes. Each article of clothing gets its chance to speak through Schertle's verse: Emily's lacy underwear, Tanya's ragged T-shirt, Bob's bicycle helmet, Joshua's warm pajamas, and many more. Artist Petra Mathers provides the illustrations to *Button Up!: Wrinkled Rhymes*, showing each piece of clothing displayed on various animals, including an ostrich, a mouse, and a bear.

Where it's reviewed:
Booklist, May 15, 2009, page 41
Bulletin of the Center for Children's Books, June 2009, page 419
Horn Book Magazine, May/June 2009, page 316
Publishers Weekly, February 9, 2009, page 48
School Library Journal, May 2009, page 98

Other books you might like:
Margaret Chodos-Irvine, *Ella Sarah Gets Dressed*, 2003
Paul B. Janeczko, *Dirty Laundry Pile: Poems in Different Voices*, 2001
Bob Shea, *New Socks*, 2007
Marilyn Singer, *Shoe Bop!*, 2008

450

LAURA AMY SCHLITZ
ANGELA BARRETT, Illustrator

The Night Fairy

(Somerville, Massachusetts: Candlewick Press, 2010)

Subject(s): Fairies; Magic; Friendship

Age range(s): 8 - 11+
Major character(s): Flory, Fairy
Time period(s): 21st century; 2010s

Summary: In *The Night Fairy*, author Laura Amy Schlitz and illustrator Angela Barrett team up to bring young readers a new take on the classic fairy story. Flory is a sprightly young fairy who loses her wings after a confrontation with a bat. Now she must learn to navigate life as a wingless creature in the garden, and there's no short supply of challenges to be faced. As she comes head to head with a variety of garden creatures, Flory soon learns the benefits of courage and kindness. Schlitz was awarded the 2008 Newbery Medal for *Good*

Masters! Sweet Ladies! Voices from a Medieval Village.

Where it's reviewed:
Booklist, January 1, 2010, page 81
Bulletin of the Center for Children's Books, February 2010, page 260
Horn Book Magazine, March/April 2010, page 72
Publishers Weekly, January 4, 2010, page 47
School Library Journal, April 2010, page 139

Other books by the same author:
The Bearskinner: A Tale of the Brothers Grimm, 2007

Other books you might like:
Roald Dahl, *The Minpins*, 1991
Kathleen Duey, *The Fairies' Promise*, 2010
Ann Earle, *Zipping, Zapping, Zooming Bats*, 1995
Lynne Jonell, *Hamster Magic*, 2010
Susannah Marriott, *A Field Guide to Fairies: Explore the Secret World of the Fairy Realm*, 2009

451

GARY D. SCHMIDT

Okay for Now

(New York: Clarion Books, 2011)

Story type: Coming-of-Age
Subject(s): Abuse; Family relations; Friendship

Age range(s): 10 - 14+
Major character(s): Doug Swieteck, Student, 14-Year-Old, Friend (of Lil), Abuse Victim; Lil Spicer, Friend (of Doug), Student
Time period(s): 20th century; 1960s (1968)
Locale(s): Marysville, New York

Summary: In this companion to *The Wednesday Wars*, troublemaker Doug Swieteck and his family move from Long Island to Marysville, New York. However, the location change doesn't fix Doug's problems. His father is abusive, and his mother is loving but powerless. One of Doug's brothers teases him mercilessly, and his other brother is fighting in Vietnam. All Doug wants is to fit in with his classmates at his new school. After an incident in gym class, Doug finds a friend in Lil Spicer, a spunky girl whose father owns the local deli. Lil takes Doug to the library, where he befriends the librarian. The librarian sees Doug's budding artistic talents and teaches him how to draw. While at the library one day, Doug discovers a book of John James Audubon's beautiful drawings of birds. After Doug learns that the town has sold many of the book's pages to collectors, he devises a plan to get them back.

Where it's reviewed:
Booklist, April 15, 2011, page 62
Bulletin of the Center for Children's Books, May 2011, page 438
Horn Book Magazine, May/June 2011, page 102
New York Times Book Review, May 15, 2011, page 18
School Library Journal, April 2011, page 184

Other books by the same author:
The Wednesday Wars, 2007
First Boy, 2005

Lizzie Bright and the Buckminster Boy, 2004

Other books you might like:
James Prosek, *The Day My Mother Left*, 2007
Dana Reinhardt, *The Things a Brother Knows*, 2010
Pat Schmatz, *Bluefish*, 2011

452

JOSH SCHNEIDER, Author/Illustrator

Tales for Very Picky Eaters
(New York: Clarion Books, 2011)

Story type: Young Readers
Subject(s): Food; Learning; Children

Age range(s): 5 - 8+
Major character(s): James, Child

Summary: Author and illustrator Josh Schneider develops a creative story for children who are picky eaters. James is a picky eater who won't even try any new foods. He will not eat broccoli, saying it's "disgusting." He thinks that mushrooms smell funny, so he won't touch lasagna made with them. He won't drink milk. Eggs are slimy, and oatmeal is lumpy. He refuses his father's encouraging words of, "You might like them if you tried them." His father comes up with a plan to get James to eat the foods. He offers him sweaty socks and chewed gum as an alternative to broccoli. He makes up a story about a troll who makes lasagna, telling him that if he won't eat it, the troll will return to work at the rat circus, where the rats bite the troll. To get him to drink milk, James's father warns that his bones will become soft and mushy. Will his father's plan be enough for James for to try the food?

Where it's reviewed:
Booklist, May 15, 2011, page 51
Bulletin of the Center for Children's Books, July/August 2011, page 538
Horn Book Guide, Fall 2011, page 347
School Library Journal, June 2011, page 95

Other books by the same author:
You'll Be Sorry, 2007

Other books you might like:
Judi Barrett, *Cloudy with a Chance of Meatballs*, 1978
Russell Hoban, *Bread and Jam for Frances*, 1964
Dr. Seuss, *Green Eggs and Ham*, 1960
Robert Weinstock, *Food Hates You Too: And Other Poems*, 2009
Mo Willems, *Should I Share My Ice Cream?*, 2011

453

IAN SCHOENHERR, Author/Illustrator

Read It, Don't Eat It!
(New York: Greenwillow Books, 2009)

Subject(s): Libraries; Animals; Humor

Age range(s): 3 - 7+

Summary: *Read It, Don't Eat It!* is a picture book by Ian Schoenherr that uses simple, rhyming language and illustrations of animals to teach children the proper way to treat library books. On each page, a different animal learns the rules, such as not to dog-ear or tear the pages, not to yell in the library, and to remember to return the books you've borrowed. The book also encourages kids to have fun reading, however, and to share their books with friends and family.

Where it's reviewed:
Booklist, April 1, 2009, page 44
Horn Book Guide, Fall 2009, page 315
Publishers Weekly, April 13, 2009, page 47
School Library Journal, April 2009, page 116

Other books by the same author:
Don't Spill the Beans, 2010
Cat & Mouse, 2008
Pip and Squeak, 2007

Other books you might like:
Denys Cazet, *Will You Read to Me?*, 2007
Leonid Gore, *The Wonderful Book*, 2010
Judy Sierra, *Wild about Books*, 2004
Louise Yates, *Dog Loves Books*, 2010

454

KAREN SCHWABACH

The Storm before Atlanta
(New York: Random House, 2010)

Subject(s): Civil war; United States Civil War, 1861-1865; Children

Age range(s): 9 - 12+
Major character(s): Jeremy DeGroot, 11-Year-Old, Military Personnel (drummer boy), Friend (of Dulcie); Dulcie, Slave, 11-Year-Old; Charlie, Military Personnel (soldier), Teenager
Time period(s): 19th century; 1860s (1864)
Locale(s): Atlanta, Georgia

Summary: In Karen Schwabach's *The Storm Before Atlanta*, two eleven-year-olds leave their homes to take part in the Civil War. Jeremy wants to be a drummer boy, so he joins the 107th New York Infantry and fights for the respect of his peers and the older soldiers who march alongside him. Dulcie is an escaped slave who wishes to be found by the Union army and kept safe from her past. When Jeremy and Dulcie meet, they become friends and agree that something's not right with Charlie, a young boy who seems like he wants to be their friend, but is loyal to the Confederates. Both Jeremy and Dulcie come close to attaining their individual goals, but a life of war is not what either had imagined—it's much worse.

Where it's reviewed:
Booklist, January 1, 2011, page 108
Horn Book Magazine, Jan/Feb 2011, page 101
School Library Journal, February 2011, page 118

Other books by the same author:
A Pickpocket's Tale, 2008
The Hope Chest, 1998

Other books you might like:
Mary Downing Hahn, *Here the Wind Blow*, 2003
Jim Murphy, *The Boys' War: Confederate and Union Soldiers Talk about the Civil War*, 1990
Gary Paulsen, *Nightjohn*, 1993
Rodman Philbrick, *The Mostly True Adventures of Homer P. Figg*, 2009
Carolyn Reeder, *Across the Lines*, 1997

455

ELAINE SCOTT

Space, Stars, and the Beginning of Time: What the Hubble Telescope Saw

(New York: Clarion Books, 2011)

Subject(s): Space exploration; Technology; Science

Age range(s): 8 - 12+

Summary: Many wonders of the universe have been revealed by the Hubble Space Telescope, which was launched in the 1990s. Although the telescope was extremely advanced for its time, it was built based on centuries of technology and insight, including that of great scientific minds like Galileo. In this book, author Elaine Scott tells the history of the telescope and describes how advances in telescope technology eventually led to the Hubble Space Telescope. The book, which includes full-color photographs from Hubble, also describes the developments and discoveries that were made possible because of the telescope. This volume includes a glossary and an index.

Where it's reviewed:
Bulletin of the Center for Children's Books, February 2011, page 64
Horn Book Magazine, March/April 2011, page 142
School Library Journal, March 2011, page 186

Other books by the same author:
Mars and the Search for Life, 2009
When Is a Planet Not a Planet?, 2007
Close Encounters: Exploring Space With the Hubble Telescope, 1998
Adventures in Space: The Flight to Fix the Hubble, 1995

Other books you might like:
Frank Cottrell Boyce, *Cosmic*, 2010
Dan Green, *Astonomy: Out of this World*, 2009
Jack Prelutsky, *The Swamps of Sleethe: Poems from Beyond the Solar System*, 2009

456

LAURA VACCARO SEEGER, Author/Illustrator

Dog and Bear: Three to Get Ready

(New York: Roaring Brook Press, 2009)

Series: Dog and Bear Series. Book 3
Subject(s): Problem solving; Friendship; Humor

Age range(s): 4 - 8+
Major character(s): Dog, Friend (of Bear); Bear, Friend (of Dog)

Summary: Laura Vaccaro Seeger's *Dog and Bear: Three to Get Ready* continues the adventures of best friends Dog and Bear. In the first of three stories in this installment, Bear accidentally gets his head stuck in a bucket. Dog agrees to help Bear and he counts to three and then pulls as hard as he can, but the bucket will not budge. This is going to take some creative thinking on Dog's part. The next two stories involve stunts on a bouncy bed and an organization system that turns out to be anything but organized. *Dog and Bear: Three to Get Ready* is part of Seeger's Dog and Bear series.

Where it's reviewed:
Horn Book Magazine, September/October 2009, page 547
Publishers Weekly, September 14, 2009, page 48
School Library Journal, October 2009, page 105

Other books by the same author:
Dog and Bear: Two's Company, 2008
Dog And Bear: Two Friends, Three Stories, 2007

Other books you might like:
Kate DiCamillo, *Bink and Gollie*, 2010
Sam Lloyd, *Mr. Pusskins and Little Whiskers: Another Love Story*, 2007
Lori Ries, *Aggie and Ben: Three Stories*, 2006
Mo Willems, *Today I Will Fly!*, 2007

457

LAURA VACCARO SEEGER, Author/Illustrator

What If?

(New York: Roaring Brook Press, 2010)

Subject(s): Seals (Animals); Friendship; Beaches

Age range(s): 4 - 7+
Time period(s): 21st century; 2010s

Summary: In Laura Vaccaro Seeger's *What If?*, a little boy goes to the beach and faces a series of fun questions that lead to an unexpected friendship. As the boy plays with a beach ball, he starts asking himself questions about what might happen if he were to kick that ball into the ocean. This leads him on a stream-of-conscious journey to some new acquaintances that further brighten his day at the beach.

Where it's reviewed:
Booklist, February 1, 2010, page 51
Horn Book Magazine, May/June 2010, page 53
Publishers Weekly, March 8, 2010, page 53

Other books by the same author:
Lemons Are Not Red, 2008
One Boy, 2008
Dog and Bear Series, 2007
First the Egg, 2007
Black? White! Day? Night!: A Book of Opposites, 2006

Other books you might like:
Suzanne Bloom, *What about Bear?*, 2010
Emily Gravett, *Orange Pear Apple Bear*, 2006
Tad Hills, *Duck, Duck, Goose*, 2007

Elivia Savadier, *Will Sheila Share?*, 2008
Mo Willems, *Can I Play Too?*, 2010

458

BRIAN SELZNICK, Author/Illustrator

Wonderstruck

(New York: Scholastic, 2011)

Story type: Young Readers
Subject(s): Adventure; Identity; Voyages and travels

Age range(s): 9 - 12+
Major character(s): Ben Wilson, Deaf Person; Rose, Girl
Time period(s): 20th century; (1970s); 20th century; 1920s (1927)
Locale(s): Gunflint Lake, Minnesota; New Jersey, United States; New York, New York

Summary: Brian Selznick's *Wonderstruck* opens in a small Minnesota town in the late 1970s, where a deaf boy named Ben Wilson is grieving the death of his mother. Now living with relatives, Ben is desperate to find his real father. When a clue pops up in the most unlikely of places, Ben decides to follow that clue to New York City, where he hopes he will find his dad. Woven throughout Ben's tale is the picture story of Rose, a girl in 1920s New Jersey, who also ends up in Manhattan. Rose is also looking for someone special to her: the movie star she idolizes. Selznick's illustrations bring to life this alternating tale of identity, belonging, and acceptance.

Where it's reviewed:
Booklist, August 1, 2011, page 45
Horn Book Magazine, September/October 2011, page 101
New York Times Book Review, September 18, 2001, page 18
Publishers Weekly, July 18, 2011, page 1
School Library Journal, August 2011, page 120

Other books by the same author:
The Houdini Box, 2008
The Invention of Hugo Cabret: A Novel in Words and Pictures, 2007

Other books you might like:
Pam Conrad, *Call Me Ahnighito*, 1995
E.L. Konigsburg, *From the Mixed-Up Files of Mrs. Basil E. Frankweiler*, 1967
Jan Mark, *The Museum Book: A Guide to Strange and Wonderful Collections*, 2007
Laura Rankin, *The Handmade Alphabet*, 1991
Delia Ray, *Singing Hands*, 2006

459

MAURICE SENDAK, Author/Illustrator

Bumble-Ardy

(New York: HarperCollins, 2011)

Subject(s): Swine; Birthdays; Adolescent interpersonal relations

Age range(s): 3 - 7+
Major character(s): Bumble-Ardy, Pig
Time period(s): 21st century; 2010s

Summary: Beloved author and illustrator Maurice Sendak tells the entertaining tale of a young pig who has never experienced the joy of a birthday party in *Bumble-Ardy*. The piglet decides to host a party in celebration of his ninth birthday. He invites all his friends to the festivities, which include a masquerade party. But Bumble-Ardy is soon questioning his decision to throw such a big gala: the masquerade escalates into a wildness that the hapless pig is helpless to control. This volume is based upon a cartoon that originally aired on *Sesame Street* during the 1970s and is Sendak's first children's book in 30 years.

Where it's reviewed:
Booklist, July 1, 2011, page 63
Horn Book Magazine, September/October 2011, page 28
Publishers Weekly, May 6, 2011, page 1
School Library Journal, August 2011, page 84

Other books by the same author:
In the Night Kitchen, 1970
Higglety Pigglety Pop, 1967
Where the Wild Things Are, 1963

Other books you might like:
Bonny Becker, *A Birthday for Bear*, 2009
Lynne Jonell, *It's My Birthday, Too!*, 1999
Dan Yaccarino, *The Birthday Fish*, 2005

460

STEVE SHEINKIN
TIM ROBINSON, Illustrator

Which Way to the Wild West?: Everything Your Schoolbooks Didn't Tell You about Westward Expansion

(New York: Flash Point, 2009)

Subject(s): United States history; Louisiana Purchase, 1803; Battle of Wounded Knee, 1890

Age range(s): 10 - 14+
Time period(s): 19th century; 1800s-1890s (1803-1890)
Locale(s): United States

Summary: Textbook writer Steve Sheinkin gives readers an in-depth look at the history of westward expansion and the vital facts omitted by most schoolbooks. *Which Way to the Wild West?: Everything Your Schoolbooks Didn't Tell You about Westward Expansion* opens with the Louisiana Purchase and charts the ensuing American journey to California, all the way to the time of the Wounded Knee Massacre. With wit and historical sensitivity, this volume presents a fresh take and little-known information on a pivotal period in American history. Tim Robinson provides cartoonish illustrations to accompany the text. *Which Way to the Wild West?* includes appendices and notes.

Where it's reviewed:
Horn Book Magazine, September/October 2009, page 585
School Library Journal, September 2009, page 185

Other books by the same author:
King George: What Was His Problem? The Whole Hilarious Story of the Revolution, 2008
Two Miserable Presidents: The Amazing, Terrible and Totally True Story of the Civil War, 2008

Other books you might like:
Karen Cushman, *The Ballad of Lucy Whipple*, 1996
John Fleischman, *Phineas Gage: A Gruesome but True Story about Brain Science*, 2002
Sid Fleischman, *The Trouble Begins at 8: A Life of Mark Twain in the Wild, Wild West*, 2008
Russell Freedman, *Children of the Wild West*, 1983
Albert Marrin, *Sitting Bull and His World*, 2000

461

JOYCE SIDMAN
PAMELA ZAGARENSKI, Illustrator

Red Sings from Treetops: A Year in Colors

(Boston, Massachusetts: Houghton Mifflin Books for Children, 2009)

Subject(s): Seasons; Poetry; Time
Age range(s): 4 - 8+
Time period(s): 21st century; 2000s
Summary: In *Red Sings from Treetops: A Year in Colors*, author Joyce Sidman and illustrator Pamela Zagarenski craft a loving homage to the four seasons. Focusing on the colors associated with spring, summer, winter, and fall, this volume brings vibrant energy and poetic sensibilities to the changing of the seasons and the passage of time.

Where it's reviewed:
Booklist, May 1 2009, page 81
Bulletin of the Center for Children's Books, March 2009, page 296
Horn Book Magazine, January/February 2009, page 14
Publishers Weekly, February 16 2009, page 127
School Library Journal, April 9 2009, page 126

Awards the book has won:
Blue Ribbon Awards: Non-fiction, 2008
Minnesota Book Awards, 2010

Other books you might like:
Ashley Bryan, *Beautiful Blackbird*, 2003
Kevin Henkes, *Old Bear*, 2008
Kathryn Lasky, *Georgia Rises: A Day in the Life of Georgia O'Keeffe*, 2009
Melissa Sweet, *Carmine: A Little More Red*, 2005

462

JOYCE SIDMAN
BECKIE PRANGE, Illustrator

Ubiquitous: Celebrating Nature's Survivors

(Boston: Houghton Mifflin Books for Children, 2010)

Subject(s): Biology; Nature; Insects
Age range(s): 8 - 11+

Summary: Utilizing poetry and artwork, Joyce Sidman's *Ubiquitous: Celebrating Nature's Survivors* offers young readers an up-close-and-personal glimpse at nature's most enduring species. Accompanied by Beckie Prange's art, this volume examines the survival skills of everything from the tiniest bacteria to the majestic coyote. Sidman's verses whimsically capture the scientific data and unique abilities of each profiled species. *Ubiquitous* includes a glossary and a note from the author.

Where it's reviewed:
Booklist, January 1, 2010, page 82
Bulletin of the Center for Children's Books, May 2010, Page 399
Horn Book Magazine, May/June 2010, Page 100
School Library Journal, March 2010, page 144
Science Books & Film, Nobember 2010, page 300

Other books by the same author:
Swirl By Swirl: Spirals in Nature, 2011
Dark Emperor and Other Poems of the Night, 2010
Song of the Water Boatman and Other Pond Poems, 2005
Butterfly Eyes and Other Secrets of the Meadow, 1999

Other books you might like:
Hannah Bonner, *When Fish Got Feet, Sharks Got Teeth, and Bugs Began to Swarm: A Cartoon Prehistory of Life Long Before Dinosaurs*, 2007
Leslie Bulion, *At the Sea Floor Cafe: Odd Ocean Critter Poems*, 2011
Sandra Dutton, *Mary Mae and the Gospel Truth*, 2010
Steve Jenkins, *Life on Earth: The Story of Evolution*, 2002
Lisa Westberg-Peters, *Our Family Tree: An Evolution Story*, 2003

463

JOYCE SIDMAN
BETH KROMMES, Illustrator

Swirl by Swirl: Spirals in Nature

(Boston: Houghton Mifflin Books for Children, 2011)

Subject(s): Nature; Beauty; Imagination
Age range(s): 5 - 8+

Summary: This is a creative and educational picture book for young readers from Newbery honoree Joyce Sidman and Caldecott medalist Beth Krommes. Through the use of captivating language and vivid illustrations, Sidman and Krommes explore the practical use and amazing beauty of spirals in nature. Readers are taken on a journey through lands near and far to see the unique and interesting ways that the shape shows itself in nature. The spiral is used for protection, as is the case with the porcupine's curved back, and grasp, as with a monkey's tail or elephant's trunk, and it fits neatly into small spaces, allowing animals to burrow deep inside of trees. From tornados to flower buds to the ear canal, spirals can be seen all around the natural world.

Where it's reviewed:
Booklist, September 1, 2011, page 103

Horn Book Magazine, September/October 2011, page 116

School Library Journal, September 2011, page 137

Other books by the same author:
Dark Emperor and Other Poems of the Night, 2010
Red Sings from Treetops: A Year in Colors, 2009
Meow Ruff: A Story in Concrete Poetry, 2006

Other books you might like:
Francisco X Alarcon, *Animal Poems of the Iguazu/Animalario del Iguazu*, 2008
Betsy Franco, *Bees, Snails and Peacock Tails*, 2008
Michael Hall, *Perfect Square*, 2011

464

JOYCE SIDMAN
RICK ALLEN, Illustrator

Dark Emperor and Other Poems of the Night

(Boston, Massachusetts: Houghton Mifflin Books for Children, 2010)

Subject(s): Animals; Poetry; Forestry

Age range(s): 8 - 11+

Summary: A 2011 Newberry Honor Book, *Dark Emperor and Other Poems of the Night* is a collection of chilling and educational poems for young readers from author Joyce Sidman. The anthology of poetry celebrates the creatures and happenings of the night. Children learn about nocturnal life and the activities of nighttime in the forest through the 12 unique and compelling poems. Nine different nocturnal animals are highlighted in *Dark Emperor and Other Poems of the Night*, including the great horned owl, shelled snails, the young porcupette, and the night spider. The book is filled with bold and colorful illustrations from artist Rick Allen.

Where it's reviewed:
Booklist, June 1, 2010, page 68
Bulletin of the Center for Children's Books, Sepember 2010, page 44
Horn Book Magazine, Septrmbrt/October 2009, page 104
School Library Journal, August 2010, page 122

Other books by the same author:
Swirl By Swirl: Spirals in Nature, 2011
Ubiquitous: Celebrating Nature's Survivors, 2010
Song of the Water Boatman and Other Pond Poems, 2005
Butterfly Eyes and Other Secrets of the Meadow, 1999

Awards the book has won:
Blue Ribbon Awards: Non-fiction, 2010

Other books you might like:
Nicola Davies, *Bat Loves the Night*, 2001
Nicola Davies, *Extreme Animals: The Toughest Creatures on Earth*, 2006
Nicola Davies, *White Owl, Barn Owl*, 2007

465

JUDY SIERRA
MARC BROWN, Illustrator

ZooZical

(New York: Alfred A. Knopf, 2011)

Story type: Young Readers
Subject(s): Animals; Friendship; Plays

Age range(s): 3 - 6+

Summary: It's wintertime, and children are not visiting the zoo as often as the animals would like. Most of the animals are unhappy because of the bad weather and the lack of visitors. However, some of the animals have an idea for lifting spirits at the zoo. A young kangaroo and a hippo decide to put on a show to get their animal friends up and moving. The animals' idea is a success, and soon the seals are singing and rolling around the stage, the bears are walking tightropes, and the flamingos are on the trapeze. The audience loves the show, and the animals are happy that they worked together to beat the winter blues. This children's book is written by Judy Sierra and illustrated by Marc Brown.

Where it's reviewed:
Booklist, July 1, 2011, page 67
Publishers Weekly, June 6, 2011, page 41
School Library Journal, July 2011, page 78

Other books by the same author:
Ballyhoo Bay, 2009
The Sleepy Little Alphabet: A Bedtime Story from Alphabet Town, 2009
Born to Read, 2008
Mind Your Manners, B. B. Wolf, 2007
Thelonius Monster's Sky-High Fly-Pie, 2006

Other books you might like:
Michael Ian Black, *A Pig Parade Is a Terrible Idea*, 2010
Jeff Newman, *Hippo! No, Rhino!*, 2006
Peggy Rathmann, *Good Night, Gorilla*, 1994
Stephen Savage, *Where's Walrus?*, 2011
Johanna Wright, *The Secret Circus*, 2009

466

JUDY SIERRA
MELISSA SWEET, Illustrator

The Sleepy Little Alphabet: A Bedtime Story from Alphabet Town

(New York: Alfred A. Knopf, 2009)

Subject(s): Rhyme; Sleep; Education

Age range(s): 2 - 6+
Time period(s): 21st century; 2000s

Summary: The letters of the alphabet take center stage in this whimsical volume by Judy Sierra. *The Sleepy Little Alphabet: A Bedtime Story from Alphabet Town* chronicles the adventures of the ABCs as they get ready for bed. But each letter faces unique challenges before the adults (portrayed by capital letters) tuck them in for the night. Presented in lighthearted rhyming verse, this book is ideal for reading out loud at bedtime. *The Sleepy Little Alphabet* contains illustrations by Melissa Sweet.

Where it's reviewed:
Booklist, July 1 2009, page 56
Horn Book Magazine, July/August 2009, Page 414
Publishers Weekly, May 11 2009, page 50
School Library Journal, June 2009, page 100

Other books by the same author:
Counting Crocodiles, 1997

Other books you might like:
John Archambault, *Chicka Chicka Boom Boom*, 1989
Ina Cumpiano, *Quinito, Day and Night/Quinito, dia y noche*, 2008
Mem Fox, *Where Is the Green Sheep?*, 2004
Susan Marie Swanson, *The House in the Night*, 2008
Jane Yolen, *Switching On the Moon: A Very First Book of Bedtime Poems*, 2010

467

SHEL SILVERSTEIN

Every Thing On It

(New York: HarperCollins, 2011)

Subject(s): Poetry; Rhyme; Humor

Age range(s): 8 - 12+

Summary: The late children's writer Shel Silverstein is world renowned for such books as *Where the Sidewalk Ends* and *A Light in the Attic*. Now, Silverstein fans will rejoice with the publication of *Every Thing On It*, a new collection of poetry found in the author's unpublished archives after his death. These poems capture all the whimsy, fun, and adventure of childhood, as told from the sometimes skewed, always witty perspective of Shel Silverstein's pen. Accompanied by the author's trademark pencil illustrations, this volume includes the verses "Years From Now," "My Zoootch," "The One Who Invented Trick or Treat," and the title poem.

Where it's reviewed:
Booklist, September 1, 2011, page 97
Horn Book Magazine, November/December 2011, page 122
Publishers Weekly, July 25, 2011, page 50
School Library Journal, September 2011, page 186

Other books by the same author:
Runny Babbit: A Billy Sook, 2005
Falling Up, 1996
A Light in the Attic, 1989
Where the Sidewalk Ends, 1975

Other books you might like:
Jon Agee, *Orangutan Tongs: Poems to Tangle Your Tongue*, 2009
Calef Brown, *Hallowilloween: Nefarious Silliness from Calef Brown*, 2010
Jack Prelutsky, *The New Kid on the Block: Poems*, 1984
Judith Viorst, *If I Were in Charge of the World and*

Other Worries: Poems for Children and Their Parents, 1981

468

MARILYN SINGER
JOSEE MASSEE, Illustrator

Mirror, Mirror: A Book of Reversible Verse

(New York: Dutton Children's Books, 2010)

Subject(s): Poetry; Fairy tales

Age range(s): 8 - 12+

Summary: In *Mirror, Mirror: A Book of Reversible Verse*, author Marilyn Singer presents 14 sets of poems centering on various fairy tale characters. Each poem is presented in a unique duplicate form, allowing them to be read either up or down the page. Reading in one direction tells a different perspective on the same poem read in the reverse direction. Verses include the adventures of Snow White, Little Red Riding Hood, and Cinderella. *Mirror, Mirror* contains illustrations by Josee Massee.

Where it's reviewed:
Booklist, January 1, 2010, page 81
Bulletin of the Center for Children's Books, April 2010, page 353
Horn Book Magazine, March/April 2010, page 79
School Library Journal, January 2010, page 90

Other books by the same author:
A Stick Is an Excellent Thing: Poems Celebrating Outdoor Play, 2012
Twosomes: Love Poems from the Animal Kingdom, 2010
Fireflies at Midnight, 2003
How to Cross a Pond: Poems about Water, 2003

Other books you might like:
Georgia Heard, *Falling Down the Page: A Book of List Poems*, 2008
Paul B. Janeczko, *A Kick in the Head: An Everyday Guide to Poetic Forms*, 2005
Ann Jonas, *Round Trip*, 1983

469

MATTHEW SKELTON

The Story of Cirrus Flux

(New York: Delacorte Press, 2010)

Subject(s): Orphans; Supernatural; Adventure

Age range(s): 9 - 12+

Major character(s): Cirrus Flux, 12-Year-Old, Orphan; Pandora, Orphan; Madame Orrery, Hypnotist (mesmerist)

Time period(s): 18th century; 1780s (1783)

Locale(s): London, England

Summary: Set in late 18th-century London, Matthew Skelton's *The Story of Cirrus Flux* chronicles the adventures of the title hero and a fellow orphan named Pandora as they make their way through a string of magical adventures. Cirrus finds himself the target of a mysterious group of magic-seekers, who believe he is in possession of a precious mystical artifact. Meanwhile, Pandora becomes ensnared with the case when she is dispatched from the orphanage to work with a powerful mesmerist called Madame Orrery.

Where it's reviewed:
Booklist, February 1, 2010, page 46
Bulletin of the Center for Children's Books, April 2010, page 353
Horn Book Magazine, May/June 2010, page 91
School Library Journal, March 2010, page 166

Other books by the same author:
Endymion Spring, 2006

Other books you might like:
F.E. Higgins, *The Black Book of Secrets*, 2007
Katherine Langrish, *The Shadow Hunt*
Marie Rutkoski, *The Cabinet of Wonders: The Kronos Chronicles: Book I*, 2008
Roderick Townley, *The Blue Shoe: A Tale of Thievery, Villainy, Sorcery, and Shoes*, 2009

470

JOSEPH SLATE
E.B. LEWIS, Illustrator

I Want to Be Free

(New York: G.P. Putnam's Sons, 2009)

Subject(s): Slavery; Friendship; Adventure

Age range(s): 6 - 9+
Time period(s): 19th century
Locale(s): American South, United States

Summary: Author Joseph Slate relocates a classic Buddhist tale from ancient India to the pre-Civil War South. *I Want to Be Free* tells the story of a runaway slave as he flees the clutches of a very mean master. Along the way, he encounters a sickly orphan, whom he takes under his wing. As he nurses the child to health, the slave grows empowered by the youngster's presence, sharing the story of his escape and his desperate desire to be free. The child, in turn, fills him with hope and gratitude, and finally liberates him from the physical and emotional bondage to which he has been held for so long.

Where it's reviewed:
Booklist, December 2009, page 50
Bulletin of the Center for Children's Books, July/August 2009, page 216
Horn Book Guide, Fall 2009, page 347
Publishers Weekly, January 19, 2009, page 59
School Library Journal, January 2009, page 86

Other books by the same author:
What Star Is This?, 2005
The Great Big Wagon That Rang: How the Liberty Bell Was Saved, 2002

Other books you might like:
Shane W. Evans, *Underground: Finding the Light to Freedom*, 2011

Ellen Levine, *Henry's Freedom Box: A True Story from the Underground Railroad*, 2007
Alice McGill, *Way Up and over Everything*, 2008
Andrea Davis Pinkney, *Sojourner Truth's Step-Stomp Stride*, 2009
Anne Rockwell, *Only Passing Through: The Story of Sojourner Truth*, 2000

471

JANE SMILEY

The Georges and the Jewels

(New York: Knopf, 2009)

Subject(s): Horses; Schools; Family

Age range(s): 10 - 13+
Major character(s): Abby Lovitt, Horse Trainer, 7th Grader
Time period(s): 20th century; 1960s
Locale(s): California, United States

Summary: Abby Lovitt is finding out that growing up can be hard. Now that Abby is in seventh grade, her problems with the popular girls at school are on rise. To make matters worse, Abby's older brother Danny had a fight with their parents and left the house, and Abby worries she might not see him again. Abby finds some comfort working on her parents' horse ranch, where she trains, rides, feeds, grooms, and otherwise cares for the horses. Although Abby interacts with the horses every day, her father warns her not to get attached to them. Her father names all of the female horses "Jewel" and all of the male horses "George," because eventually they will all be sold from the ranch. Even caring for one of the horses — whom Abby names "Ornery George" — becomes difficult for Abby when the horse refuses to be trained. *The Georges and the Jewels* is written by author Jane Smiley.

Where it's reviewed:
Booklist, September 15, 2009, page 60
Bulletin of the Center for Children's Books, October 2009, page 83
Horn Book Magazine, November/December 2009, page 686
Publishers Weekly, July 20, 2009, page 140
School Library Journal, October 2009, page 136

Other books by the same author:
A Good Horse, 2011

Other books you might like:
Juliet Clutton-Brock, *Horse*, 2008
Patricia Reilly Giff, *Wild Girl*, 2009
Annie Wedekind, *A Horse of Her Own*, 2008

472

CHARLES R. SMITH JR.
SHANE W. EVANS, Illustrator

Black Jack: The Ballad of Jack Johnson

(New York: Roaring Brook Press, 2010)

Subject(s): Biographies; Boxing; African Americans
Age range(s): 7 - 9+

Summary: *Black Jack: The Ballad of Jack Johnson* is a biographical picture book for young readers by author Charles R. Smith, Jr. The book tells the story of Arthur "Jack" Johnson, an African-American man from Texas who made history in the beginning of the 20th century. Johnson was a very successful boxer who dedicated himself to an unlikely goal: becoming the first black heavyweight champion. In July of 1910, his dream became a reality. Filled with collage illustrations from Shane W. Evans, *Black Jack* tells the true story of Johnson's career and success.

Where it's reviewed:
Booklist, April 2010, page 40
Horn Book Magazine, Jan.-Feb. 2010, page 137
Publishers Weekly, June 21, 2010, page 45
School Library Journal, July 2010, page 76

Other books by the same author:
Winning Words, 2008
Twelve Rounds to Glory, 2007

Other books you might like:
David A. Adler, *Joe Louis: America's Fighter*, 2005
Lesa Cline-Ransome, *Major Taylor, Champion Cyclist*, 2004
Patsi B. Trollinger, *Perfect Timing: How Isaac Murphy Became One of the World's Greatest Jockeys*, 2006
Jonah Winter, *Muhammad Ali*, 2008

473

HOPE ANITA SMITH, Author/Illustrator

Mother Poems
(New York: Henry Holt and Co., 2009)

Subject(s): Mothers; Death; Grief

Age range(s): 9 - 13+

Summary: In *Mother Poems*, author Hope Anita Smith explores the devastating grief of a young African American girl whose mother tragically dies. Presented entirely through verse, this collection of poems follows the girl through the stages of grief as she struggles to come to terms with the loss of her beloved mother. Following the central character over a period of years, young readers witness her pain and recovery, and her eventual transition to womanhood. Poems include "What My Mom Says," "Let's Make a Deal," "My Mother's Rule Book," "My Mother's Kitchen," and "Memory." Illustrations accompany the poems.

Where it's reviewed:
Bulletin of the Center for Children's Books, April 2009, page 366
Horn Book Guide. Fall 2009, page 466
School Library Journal, April 2009, page 150

Other books by the same author:
The Way a Door Closes, 2011
Keeping the Night Watch, 2008

Other books you might like:
Zetta Elliott, *Bird*, 2008
K.L. Going, *The Garden of Eve*, 2007
Nikki Grimes, *What Is Goodbye?*, 2004

Kimberly Willis Holt, *Keeper of the Night*, 2003
Jacqueline Woodson, *Locomotion*, 2003

474

JEFF SMITH, Author/Illustrator

Little Mouse Gets Ready
(New York: RAW Junior, 2009)

Subject(s): Animals; Clothing; Humor

Age range(s): 4 - 7+
Major character(s): Little Mouse, Mouse
Time period(s): 21st century; 2000s

Summary: In *Little Mouse Gets Ready*, author and illustrator Jeff Smith uses an amusing rodent to introduce young readers to the basic skills of dressing. When Mama announces that the family is making a trip to the barn to munch on some oats and take a dip in the cow's drinking water, Little Mouse can barely contain his excitement. He hurries to put on his clothes—underwear, pants, shirt, socks, and shoes—taking care with each button, snap, and tail hole. When Little Mouse is finally fully dressed he stands upright, proud of his accomplishment until he realizes his one big mistake: Mice don't wear clothes.

Where it's reviewed:
Booklist, August 1, 2009, page 79
Horn Book Guide, Spring 2010, page 65
Publishers Weekly, September 21, 2009, page 57
School Library Journal, November 2009, page 140

Other books by the same author:
Bone, Vol. 1: Out from Boneville, 2005

Other books you might like:
Judi Barrett, *Animals Should Definitely Not Wear Clothing*, 1970
David Kirk, *Little Mouse, Biddle Mouse*, 2002
Beatrix Potter, *The Tale of Peter Rabbit*, 1902
Ellen Stoll Walsh, *Mouse Paint*, 1989

475

LANE SMITH, Author/Illustrator

It's a Book
(New York: Roaring Brook Press, 2010)

Subject(s): Books; Reading; Publishing industry

Age range(s): 5 - 9+

Summary: *It's a Book* is an entertaining picture book for young readers from best-selling author and Caldecott honoree Lane Smith. This humorous and charming picture book offers a lighthearted take on the changes of reading in the digital age. Lane Smith addresses the concern of electronic publishing and the importance of tangible, printed materials in *It's a Book*. The picture book also includes whimsical and stylish illustrations by Smith, and is a thoughtful story that is entertaining and educational to readers of all ages.

Where it's reviewed:
Booklist, September 15, 2010, page 70

Bulletin of the Center for Children's Books, September 2010, page 44

Horn Book Magazine, September/October 2010, page 64

New York Times Book Review, October 17, 2010, page 16

School Library Journal, August 2010, page 86

Other books by the same author:
It's a Little Book, 2011
The Big Elephant in the Room, 2009
Madame President, 2008

Other books you might like:
Barbara Bottner, *Miss Brooks Loves Books (And I Don't)*, 2010
Mordicai Gerstein, *A Book*, 2009
David McPhail, *Fix-It*, 1984
James Proimos, *Todd's TV*, 2010
Mo Willems, *We Are in a Book!*, 2010

476

LANE SMITH, Author/Illustrator

Grandpa Green

(New York: Roaring Book Press, 2011)

Story type: Young Readers
Subject(s): Family; Grandfathers; Family history

Age range(s): 5 - 8+
Major character(s): Green, Grandfather, Gardener
Time period(s): 21st century; 2010s

Summary: Bestselling author and illustrator Lane Smith takes readers on an exciting and heartwarming journey through familial history in this whimsical and engaging picture book for young readers. Long before he was Grandpa Green, he was a young boy who got chicken pox, dreamed of the future, and longed to be an artist. A young boy ruminates on the upbringing of his great-grandfather, Grandpa Green, in this tale of family, heritage, and respect. Grandpa Green grew up to become a magnificent gardener and as his great-grandson wanders through the artfully sculpted topiaries and flowers, he tells the story of how Grandpa Green's life took shape.

Where it's reviewed:
Booklist, July 1, 2011, page 64
Horn Book Magazine, September/October 2011, page 78
New York Times Book Review, August 21, 2011, page 14
Publishers Weekly, July 18, 2011, page 153
School Library Journal, August 2011, page 86

Other books you might like:
Karen Ackerman, *Song and Dance Man*, 1988
Peter Brown, *The Curious Garden*, 2009
Judith Caseley, *Dear Annie*, 1991
Benjamin Alire Saenz, *A Perfect Season for Dreaming: Una Temporado Perfecta Para Sonar*, 2008
Dan Yaccarino, *All the Way to America: The Story of a Big Italian Family and a Little Shovel*, 2011

477

LAUREL SNYDER
ABIGAIL HALPIN, Illustrator

Penny Dreadful

(New York: Random House, 2010)

Subject(s): Wealth; Wishes; Rural life

Age range(s): 8 - 12+
Major character(s): Penelope Gray, Child, Wealthy, Impoverished
Time period(s): 21st century; 2010s
Locale(s): Tennessee, United States

Summary: *Penny Dreadful* is a thought-provoking, humorous, and uplifting novel for children and young adults from author Laurel Snyder and illustrator Abigail Halpin. Penelope Gray has all the worldly possessions money can buy, but she soon discovers that being wealthy and living in a fancy house don't equal happiness. Feeling as though something's missing, Penelope makes a wish that things will change—and change they do. Her father loses his job and the family is forced to move to a rural part of Tennessee where they live in a dilapidated old house with a slew of unusual tenants. Even though Penelope and her family are poorer than they've ever been, they discover a deep happiness they never knew existed.

Where it's reviewed:
Booklist, October 1, 2010, page 81
Bulletin of the Center for Children's Books, November 2010, page 151
Horn Book Guide, Spring 2011, page 83
Publishers Weekly, September 13, 2010, page 45
School Library Journal, January 2011, page 116

Other books by the same author:
Bigger Than a Bread Box, 2011

Other books you might like:
Jeanne Birdsall, *The Penderwicks: A Summer Tale of Four Sisters, Two Rabbits, and a Very Interesting Boy*, 2005
Barbara O'Connor, *Greetings from Nowhere*, 2008
Ruth White, *Way Down Deep*, 2007

478

JAMES SOLHEIM
SIMON JAMES, Illustrator

Born Yesterday: The Diary of a Young Journalist

(New York: Philomel Books, 2010)

Subject(s): Journalism; Humor; Infants

Age range(s): 6 - 9+
Time period(s): 21st century; 2010s

Summary: In *Born Yesterday: The Diary of a Young Journalist*, author James Solheim and illustrator Simon James team up to tell the laugh-out-loud story of an infant-age journalist just beginning to discover the world around him. As the baby makes more and more finds in a larger world, he records his experiences in a whimsical diary, putting down in print his wry observations about life and people.

Where it's reviewed:
Booklist, March 1, 2010, page 76
Bulletin of the Center for Children's Books, May 2010, page 367
Horn Book Guide. Fall 2010, page 315
Publishers Weekly, February 22, 2010, page 63
School Library Journal, March 2010, page 132

Other books by the same author:
Santa's Secrets Revealed, 2004

Awards the book has won:
Blue Ribbon Awards: Picture Books, 2010

Other books you might like:
Allan Ahlberg, *Everybody Was a Baby Once and Other Poems*, 2010
Simon James, *Baby Brains: The Smartest Baby in the Whole World*, 2004
Susan Orlean, *Lazy Little Loafers*, 2008

479

KEAN SOO, Author/Illustrator

Jellaby: Monster in the City

(New York: Hyperion, 2009)

Series: Jellaby Series. Book 2
Subject(s): Comic books; Adventure; Friendship

Age range(s): 8 - 12+
Major character(s): Portia, Friend (of Jason); Jason, Friend (of Portia); Jellaby, Monster
Time period(s): 21st century; 2000s
Locale(s): Toronto, Ontario

Summary: *Jellaby: Monster in the City* is the second book in Kean Soo's Jellaby series. In this installment, Portia and Jason accompany their new friend—a cute purple monster named Jellaby—as he searches for his home. On their journey around Toronto, the young humans begin to realize that the likeable creature belongs to a species that may not be as innocent as they look. When Portia and Jason encounter another monster that looks like Jellaby, they are horrified to learn that this purple creature enjoys eating children. Meanwhile, Portia also attempts to discover the whereabouts of her missing father.

Where it's reviewed:
Canadian Children's Book News, Summer 2009, page 30

Other books by the same author:
Jellaby, Volume 1, 2008

Other books you might like:
Neil Gaiman, *Coraline*, 2002
Kazu Kibuishi, *The Stonekeeper's Curse*, 2009
Andy Runton, *Owly: A Time to Be Brave*, 2007
Jeff Smith, *Bone: Rock Jaw: Master of the Eastern Border*, 1998

480

NADJA SPIEGELMAN
TRADE LOEFFLER, Illustrator

Zig and Wikki in Something Ate My Homework

(New York: Toon Books, 2010)

Story type: Young Readers
Subject(s): Comic books; Pets; Science fiction

Age range(s): 4 - 8+
Major character(s): Zig, Alien; Wikki, Alien

Summary: This comic book for young readers, written by Nadja Spiegelman and illustrated by Trade Loeffler, shares the entertaining and educational story of two aliens who take a field trip to Earth. Zig and Wikki, a pair of school-aged extraterrestrials, come to the world of humans as part of a class project. As the curious friends search for an Earth creature to bring to their teacher, they discover the strange wildlife that populates the planet, such as raccoons and dragonflies. Through simple text and engaging cartoon panels, Spiegelman and Loeffler—and their amusing alien characters—share real-world science facts with readers.

Where it's reviewed:
Booklist, March 15, 2010, page 62
Horn Book Guide. Fall 2010, page 322
Publishers Weekly, January 4, 2010, page 49
School Library Journal, July 2010, page 108

Other books you might like:
Frank Cammuso, *Otto's Orange Day*, 2008
Eric Carle, *The Very Hungry Caterpillar*, 1969
Joanna Cole, *The Magic School Bus: Inside a Beehive*, 1996
P. D. Eastman, *Sam and the Firefly*, 1958
Mike Mc Clintock, *A Fly Went By*, 1958

481

EILEEN SPINELLI
JOANNE LEW-VRIETHOFF, Illustrator

The Dancing Pancake

(New York: Alfred A. Knopf, 2010)

Subject(s): Family; Restaurants; Cooking

Age range(s): 9 - 11+
Major character(s): Belinda "Bindi" Winkler, 11-Year-Old Girl; Mom, Mother (of Bindi); Dad, Father (of Bindi)
Time period(s): 21st century; 2010s
Locale(s): United States

Summary: In the novel in verse *The Dancing Pancake* by Eileen Spinelli, an 11-year-old girl's life is changed when her parents separate and she moves into an apartment with her mother. Belinda "Bindi" Winkler now lives above The Dancing Pancake restaurant—a restaurant newly opened by her mother and aunt. The friendly shop attracts a variety of interesting patrons and workers who become Bindi's friends and mentors. At The Dancing Pancake, Bindi witnesses a range of human experiences from the humorous to the heartbreaking. As she gains a better understanding of herself and the world around her, Bindi watches the gradual healing of her parents' relationship.

Where it's reviewed:
Bulletin of the Center for Children's Books, June 2010, page 456
Horn Book Guide. Fall 2010, page 354
Publishers Weekly, May 17, 2010, page 49
School Library Journal, May 2010, page 124

Other books by the same author:
Where I Live, 2007

Other books you might like:
A.C.E. Bauer, *No Castles Here*, 2007
Kate DiCamillo, *Because of Winn-Dixie*, 2000
Susan Patron, *The Higher Power of Lucky*, 2006
Laurel Snyder, *Penny Dreadful*, 2010
Julie Sternberg, *Like Pickle Juice on a Cookie*, 2011

482

ASHLEY SPIRES, Author/Illustrator

Binky the Space Cat

(Tonawanda, New York: Kids Can Press, 2009)

Subject(s): Humor; Pets; Imagination

Age range(s): 5 - 9+
Major character(s): Binky, Cat

Summary: *Binky the Space Cat* is a graphic novel for children by Ashley Spires. Binky, the family pet, finds an application at the bottom of a bag of his cat food for the program "Felines of the Universe Ready for Space Travel." Binky decides that he wants to join to program and have an adventure. So, Binky gets to ready to blast off into space to fight aliens, which humans think are simply bugs. He is accepted to the program and begins to covertly build his spaceship in the backyard, determined to protect his human owners from the alien invasion. Just when it seems he is ready to go, though, Binky realizes he has forgotten something very important.

Where it's reviewed:
Booklist, August 1, 2009, page 65
Horn Book Guide, Spring 2010, page 60
School Library Journal, November 2009, page 142

Other books by the same author:
Binky Under Pressure, 2011
Small Saul, 2011
Binky to the Rescue, 2010
Penguin and the Cupcake, 2009

Other books you might like:
Barbara Jean Hicks, *The Secret Life of Walter Kitty*, 2007
Laura Joffe Numeroff, *If You Give a Cat a Cupcake*, 2008
Judy Schachner, *Skippyjon Jones*, 2003
Rob Scotton, *Splat the Cat*, 2008

483

R.A. SPRATT
DAN SANTAT, Illustrator

The Adventures of Nanny Piggins

(New York: Little, Brown and Company, 2010)

Subject(s): Child care; Brothers and sisters; Swine

Age range(s): 8 - 11+
Major character(s): Nanny Piggins, Child-Care Giver; Derrick Green, Brother (of Samantha and Michael); Samantha Green, Sister (of Derrick and Michael); Michael Green, Brother (of Derrick and Samantha); Mr. Green, Father (of Derrick, Samantha, and Michael), Employer (of Nanny Piggins)
Time period(s): 21st century; 2010s

Summary: Nanny Piggins isn't a typical nanny. She eats chocolate nonstop, she posses an unquenchable yen for adventure, and she captivates everyone she meets. And she's a pig! R.A. Spratt's *The Adventures of Nanny Piggins* charts the exploits of the title heroine as she charms the children of the Green family and takes them on a series of escapades that range from impromptu dances to rehabilitating robbers. This volume includes illustrations by Dan Santat. First novel.

Where it's reviewed:
Booklist, August 2010, page 54
Horn Book Guide, Spring 2011, page 84
Publishers Weekly, August 9, 2010, page 53
School Library Journal, August 2010, page 113

Other books you might like:
Michael Ian Black, *A Pig Parade Is a Terrible Idea*, 2010
Paul Fleischman, *The Dunderheads*, 2009
Polly Horvath, *The Pepins and Their Problems*, 2004
Lois Lowry, *The Willoughbys*, 2008
Kristin Clark Venuti, *Leaving the Bellweathers*, 2009

484

TRICIA SPRINGSTUBB

What Happened on Fox Street

(New York: Balzer + Bray, 2010)

Subject(s): Neighborhoods; Father-daughter relations; Friendship

Age range(s): 9 - 12+
Major character(s): Mo Wren, Girl, 10-Year-Old, Sister (of Dottie), Daughter (of Mr. Wren); Mr. Wren, Father (of Mo and Dottie); Dottie Wren, Sister (of Mo), Daughter (of Mr. Wren); Mercedes, Friend (of Mo); Da, Grandmother (of Mercedes)
Time period(s): 21st century; 2010s
Locale(s): Cleveland, Ohio

Summary: In *What Happened on Fox Street* by Tricia Springstubb, ten-year-old Mo Wren appears to be enjoying a perfect childhood. She lives on a friendly street where all of the neighbors take care of one another. Mo has a great dad and a busy little sister, but she no longer has a mother. To Mo, Fox Street holds not only the memories of her childhood, but also those of her deceased mother. When Mr. Wren considers selling their home to a realtor, Mo is crushed. Mo experiences another shock when her friend Mercedes comes for her annual visit to her grandmother's house and seems to be losing her affection for Fox Street.

Where it's reviewed:
Booklist, September 1, 2010, page 97
Horn Book Guide, Sept/Oct 2010, page 95
Publishers Weekly, August 9, 2010, page 52
School Library Journal, September 2010, page 165

Other books by the same author:
Mo Wren Lost And Found, 2011

Other books you might like:
A.C.E. Bauer, *No Castles Here*, 2007
Katherine Hannigan, *Ida B.: . . . and Her Plans to Maximize Fun, Avoid Disaster, and (Possibly) Save the World*, 2004
Jennifer L. Holm, *Turtle in Paradise*, 2010
Marlane Kennedy, *Me and the Pumpkin Queen*, 2007
Jacqueline Woodson, *After Tupac and D Foster*, 2008

485

MARK ALAN STAMATY, Author/Illustrator

Shake, Rattle & Turn That Noise Down: How Elvis Shook Up Music, Me and Mom

(New York: Knopf, 2010)

Subject(s): Rock music; Popular culture; Biographies

Age range(s): 8 - 12+

Summary: Mark Alan Stamaty shares his lifelong love of all things Elvis Presley in this lively picture book for children and young adults. When Stamaty turned eight, his parents gave him a radio that allowed him access to the emerging sounds of rock music. The author describes how his life was further transformed after he heard Presley's "Hound Dog" for the first time. To the horror of his mother, young Mark Stamaty began copying the pop star's signature moves and hairstyle. The author parallels his personal journey through Elvis Presley fandom with rock history facts and trivia. Illustrations depict the author's antics and some rock legends.

Where it's reviewed:
Booklist, November 1, 2009, page 59
Horn Book Guide. Fall 2010, page 429
Publishers Weekly, December 14, 2009, page 57
School Library Journal, May 2010, page 142

Other books by the same author:
Alia's Mission: Saving the Books of Iraq, 2010
Who Needs Donuts?, 2003
Too Many Time Machines, 1999

Other books you might like:
Holly George-Warren, *Shake, Rattle and Roll: The Founders of Rock and Roll*, 2001
Jennifer L. Holm, *Babymouse: Rock Star*, 2006

Peter H. Reynolds, *Zebrafish*, 2010
Bob Spitz, *Yeah! Yeah! Yeah!: The Beatles, Beatlemania, and the Music That Changed the World*, 2007

486

DIANE STANLEY

Saving Sky

(New York: Harper, 2010)

Subject(s): Wars; Terrorism; Children and war

Age range(s): 10 - 13+
Major character(s): Sky Brightman, 13-Year-Old, Outcast
Time period(s): Indeterminate Future
Locale(s): Santa Fe, New Mexico

Summary: *Saving Sky* is a thought-provoking futuristic novel for children and young adults about war, racism, and prejudice from author Diane Stanley. Despite the fact that the United States is at war, there's been a significant increase in terrorist attacks, the nation is reduced to rationing supplies, and the power grid is down, life is carrying on as normal for 13-year old Sky Brightman. Her isolated Santa Fe farm, free of all technological advances, is peaceful and calming for Sky and her family, even though her alternative lifestyle has made her an outcast at school. But when prejudice runs rampant, leading to the arrests of her Middle Eastern neighbors and classmates, Sky is forced to confront the harsh reality of the world she lives in.

Where it's reviewed:
Booklist, June 1, 2010, page 69
Horn Book Guide, Spring 2011, page 84
School Library Journal, September 2010, page 165

Other books by the same author:
A Time Apart, 1999

Other books you might like:
Leslie Connor, *Crunch*, 2010
Dean Hughes, *Missing in Action*, 2010
Cynthia Kadohata, *Weedflower*, 2006
Kristin Levine, *The Best Bad Luck I Ever Had*, 2009
Rosanne Parry, *Heart of a Shepherd*, 2009

487

SUE STAUFFACHER
PRISCILLA LAMONT, Illustrator

Gator on the Loose!

(New York: Knopf Books for Young Readers, 2010)

Series: Animal Rescue Team Series. Book 1
Subject(s): Animals; Wildlife rescue; Family

Age range(s): 8 - 11+

Major character(s): Keisha Carter, 10-Year-Old, Animal Lover; Mrs. Carter, Mother (of Keisha); Mr. Carter, Father (of Keisha); Grandma Alice, Grandmother (of Keisha); Razi Carter, 5-Year-Old, Brother (of Keisha); Paolo Carter, Baby, Brother (of Keisha)

Time period(s): 21st century; 2010s
Locale(s): Michigan, United States

Summary: In Sue Stauffacher's *Gator on the Loose!*, ten-year-old Keisha and her family must devise a plan to get an alligator out of the community pool. Keisha's family—which includes her mother, father, grandmother, and two younger brothers—run Carters' Urban Rescue, a business that specializes in rescuing animals from areas where they really shouldn't be. Since Keisha lives in Michigan, it's safe to say that the alligator is definitely lost. If Keisha and her family don't move fast, the community pool is going to have to push back its grand opening for the summer. This will surely disappoint everyone looking forward to cooling off in the pool. Can Keisha come up with a way to rescue the alligator and save the start of summer? This book is the first in Stauffacher's Animal Rescue Team series.

Where it's reviewed:
Horn Book Magazine, May/June 2010, page 92
Publishers Weekly, April 26, 2010, page 109
School Library Journal, August 2010, page 113

Other books by the same author:
Animal Rescue Team: Show Time, 2011
Animal Rescue Team: Hide and Seek, 2010
Animal Rescue Team: Special Delivery, 2010

Other books you might like:
Jean Craighead George, *There's an Owl in the Shower*, 1995
Susan E. Goodman, *Animal Rescue: The Best Job There Is*, 2000
Kelly Milner Halls, *Saving the Baghdad Zoo*, 2010
Laurence Pringle, *Alligators and Crocodiles!: Strange and Wonderful*, 2009
Sue Stauffacher, *Animal Rescue Team: Special Delivery*, 2010

████ **488**

SUE STAUFFACHER
SARAH MCMENEMY, Illustrator

Tillie the Terrible Swede: How One Woman, a Sewing Needle, and a Bicycle Changed History

(New York: Alfred A. Knopf, 2011)

Subject(s): Bicycles; Women; Biographies

Age range(s): 5 - 8+

Summary: This biography by author Sue Stauffacher and illustrator Sarah McMenemy shares the story of a woman who made her own path in life, despite the disapproval of others. Tillie Anderson came to the United States from Europe as a young woman. Upon her arrival, she took a job in a tailor shop. Although she was happy to have found a job, she wanted something exciting to happen in her life. When she saw a man riding on a bicycle, Tillie knew she had found what she wanted to do with her life. Many people did not approve of Tillie's riding a bike because she did not wear "ladylike" clothes and she rode at fast speeds. In fact, Tillie started racing her bike,
and she broke a number of speed records. As Tillie got older, she became interested in motorcycles, and she stayed adventurous for the rest of her years.

Where it's reviewed:
Booklist, February 1, 2011, page 65
Bulletin of the Center for Children's Books, February 2011, page 298
Horn Book Magazine, March/April 2011, page 142
School Library Journal, February 2011, page 99

Other books by the same author:
Nothing but Trouble: The Story of Althea Gibson, 2007
Bessie Smith and the Night Raiders, 2006

Other books you might like:
David A. Adler, *America's Champion Swimmer: Gertrude Ederle*, 2000
Kathleen Krull, *Wilma Unlimited: How Wilma Rudolph Became the World's Fastest Woman*, 1996
Jane Kurtz, *Bicycle Madness*, 2003
Barb Rosenstock, *Fearless: The Story of Racing Legend Louise Smith*, 2010
Tanya Lee Stone, *Elizabeth Leads the Way: Elizabeth Cady Stanton and the Right to Vote*, 2008

████ **489**

PHILIP C. STEAD
ERIN E. STEAD, Illustrator

A Sick Day for Amos McGee

(New York: Roaring Brook, 2010)

Subject(s): Zoos; Animals; Aging (Biology)

Age range(s): 4-8+
Major character(s): Amos McGee, Zoo Keeper
Time period(s): 21st century; 2010s

Summary: Philip C. Stead's *A Sick Day for Amos McGee* follows an aged zookeeper through his rounds as he pays personal visits to all the animals in his zoo. From the elephants to the penguins, Amos makes time for everyone... until, one day, he calls in sick. Suddenly the animals are missing their friend, who is home with an illness and unable to pay them their daily visits. Thus the animals decide that it is time for them to finally visit Amos at home and return the favor for his many years of kind care and attention. Following a bus ride, the animals wait on Amos hand and foot, mirroring the many ways that Amos cares for them at the zoo. This volume includes illustrations by Erin Stead.

Where it's reviewed:
Booklist, May 1, 2010, page 72
Horn Book Magazine, May/June 2010, page 72
Publishers Weekly, May 10, 2010, page 41
School Library Journal, May 2010, page 92

Awards the book has won:
Caldecott Medal, 2011

Other books you might like:
Olivier Dunrea, *Old Bear and His Cub*, 2010
Gilbert Ford, *Flying Lessons*, 2010
Mem Fox, *Night Noises*, 1989

William Steig, *Amos and Boris*, 1971
Jackie Urbanovic, *Duck at the Door*, 2007

490

REBECCA STEAD

When You Reach Me

(New York: Wendy Lamb Books, 2009)

Subject(s): Children; Schools; Friendship

Age range(s): 10 - 13+

Major character(s): Miranda, 6th Grader; Sal, 6th Grader, Friend (of Miranda)

Time period(s): 20th century; 1970s (1978)

Locale(s): New York, New York

Summary: *When You Reach Me*, a novel for younger readers, takes place in New York City in 1978. Sixth-grader Miranda is dealing with the issues of middle school, including changing friendships and first crushes, and living with her single mother who dreams of becoming a contestant on a game show. Miranda is obsessed with Madeleine L'Engle's *A Wrinkle in Time*. She begins receiving mysterious notes that claim to be from someone who wants to save her life, and Miranda believes that the notes are coming from someone who can see the future. She attempts to solve the mystery as she deals with all the other issues in her life. *When You Reach Me* is author Rebecca Stead's second novel.

Where it's reviewed:
Booklist, June 1, 2009, page 66
Bulletin of the Center for Children's Books, September 2009, page 41
Horn Book Magazine, July/August 2009, page 432
Publishers Weekly, June 22, 2009, page 45
School Library Journal, July 2009, page 93

Other books by the same author:
First Light, 2007

Awards the book has won:
Off the Cuff Awards, 2009
Boston Globe - Horn Book Awards: Fiction or Poetry, 2010
Newbery Medal, 2010

Other books you might like:
Susan Cooper, *King of Shadows*, 1999
Susan Cooper, *Victory*, 2006
Madeleine L'Engle, *A Wrinkle in Time*, 1962
Kate Thompson, *The New Policeman*, 2005

491

DAVID EZRA STEIN, Author/Illustrator

Interrupting Chicken

(Somerville, Massachusetts: Candlewick Press, 2010)

Subject(s): Chickens; Books and reading; Fairy tales

Age range(s): 5 - 8+

Major character(s): Little Red Chicken, Chicken; Papa,

Chicken, Father (of Little Red Chicken)

Time period(s): 21st century; 2010s

Summary: Little Red Chicken is having a tough time listening patiently to Papa's fairy tales. Every time he reads her a bedtime story, be it *Little Red Riding Hood*, *Hansel and Gretel*, or *Chicken Little*, she can't help but interrupt the storytelling and cry out to the characters, warning of the dangers that lie in wait for them. Papa grows increasingly frustrated until he inspires Little Red Chicken to write a fairy tale of her own. *Interrupting Chicken* contains illustrations by author David Ezra Stein.

Where it's reviewed:
Booklist, September 15, 2010, page 69
Horn Book Guide, Spring 2011, page 47
Publishers Weekly, July 19, 2010, page 126
School Library Journal, july 2010, page 69

Other books by the same author:
Monster Hug, 2007

Other books you might like:
Jennifer Brutschy, *Just One More Story*, 2002
Peter Catalanotto, *Ivan the Terrier*, 2007
Denys Cazet, *The Octopus*, 2005
Kate DiCamillo, *Louise, The Adventures of a Chicken*, 2008
Mo Willems, *Don't Let the Pigeon Stay Up Late!*, 2006

492

PETER STEIN
BOB STAAKE, Illustrator

Cars Galore

(Somerville, Massachusetts: Candlewick Press, 2011)

Story type: Young Readers
Subject(s): Automobiles; Rhyme; Imagination

Age range(s): 3 - 6+

Summary: Author Peter Stein and illustrator Bob Staake present cars, cars, and more cars in this picture story for young readers. Engaging rhymes and brightly colored cartoon illustrations give this story gas, sending readers on a fun, car-filled journey. Children will encounter a menagerie of wild and wacky cars—and equally strange drivers— as they search for each car mentioned in Stein's rhyme, from the "new car" to the "old car" to the "has-a-cold car!" Staake's illustrations feature bold colors and clean lines, which pop off the solid white background and stand out against the jet-black streets that crisscross the pages.

Where it's reviewed:
Booklist, March 1, 2011, page 91
Horn Book Magazine, March/April 2011, page 206
Publishers Weekly, January 31, 2011, page 48
School Library Journal, February 2011, page 91

Other books by the same author:
Bugs Galore, 2011

Other books you might like:
Brian Biggs, *Everything Goes: On Land*, 2011
Jamie Harper, *Miles to Go*, 2010

G. Brian Karas, *The Village Garage*, 2010
Roxie Munro, *Go! Go! Go!: More Than 70 Flaps to Uncover & Discover!*, 2009
Bob Staake, *Trucks Go Pop!*, 2008

493

JOHN STEPHENS

The Emerald Atlas

(New York: Knopf, 2011)

Series: Books of Beginning Series. Book 1
Subject(s): Adventure; Good and evil; Orphans

Age range(s): 9 - 12+
Major character(s): Emma, Orphan; Kate, Orphan; Michael, Orphan
Time period(s): 21st century; 2010s

Summary: The first installment in the Books of Beginning series, John Stephens's *The Emerald Atlas* chronicles the voyage of three orphans who set out to claim their noble birthright. Emma, Kate, and Michael are unknowingly protected from an evil force that soon reveals itself to them. Intrigued, the trio sets out to learn more about this evil—and why they have been so carefully protected from its clutches. Their journey takes them around the globe, where they unearth the truth of their heritage and the special powers they possess.

Where it's reviewed:
Booklist, March 15, 2011, page 60
Bulletin of the Center for Children's Books, May 2011, page 137
Horn Book Magazine, March/April 2011, page 126
New York Times Book Review, April 10, 2011, page 17
School Library Journal, June 2011, page 137

Other books you might like:
P. D. Baccalario, *Ring of Fire*, 2009
Ted Bell, *Nick of Time*, 2008
Linda Buckley-Archer, *Gideon the Cutpurse*, 2006
P.B. Kerr, *The Akhenaten Adventure*, 2004
Marie Rutkoski, *The Cabinet of Wonders: The Kronos Chronicles: Book I*, 2008

494

JULIE STERNBERG
MATTHEW CORDELL, Illustrator

Like Pickle Juice on a Cookie

(New York: Amulet Books, 2011)

Story type: Young Readers
Subject(s): Babysitters; Children; Childhood

Age range(s): 7 - 9+
Major character(s): Eleanor, Girl; Bibi, Babysitter
Time period(s): 21st century; 2010s
Locale(s): New York, New York

Summary: Eleanor is very upset. Her whole world has been turned upside down because her beloved babysitter, Bibi, is moving away to Florida. The thought of life without Bibi is simply unbearable to young Eleanor and, to make matters even worse, it's the end of the school year, which means she will somehow have to endure the entire summer without favorite sitter. Though her mother takes time off from work to try and appease her, Eleanor remains indignant and refuses to do any of the things she once did with Bibi. As the summer wanes and the new school year approaches, however, Eleanor finally begins to realize that life must go on and that Bibi will always be with her.

Where it's reviewed:
Bulletin of the Center for Children's Books, March 2011, page 346
Horn Book Magazine, May/June 2011, page 105
Publishers Weekly, January 24, 2011, page 153
School Library Journal, April 2011, page 154

Other books you might like:
Annie Barrows, *Ivy and Bean Take Care of the Babysitter*, 2008
Charise Mericle Harper, *Just Grace*, 2007
Lois Lowry, *Gooney Bird Greene*, 2002
Megan McDonald, *Judy Moody*, 2000
Sara Pennypacker, *Clementine*, 2006

495

APRIL STEVENS
SOPHIE BLACKALL, Illustrator

Edwin Speaks Up

(New York: Schwartz & Wade Books, 2011)

Story type: Young Readers
Subject(s): Animals; Family; Shopping

Age range(s): 5 - 8+
Major character(s): Edwin Finnemore, Ferret, Baby; Mrs. Finnemore, Ferret, Mother; Finney Finnemore, Ferret; Franny Finnemore, Ferret; Fergus Finnemore, Ferret

Summary: Edwin is a baby ferret with much to say—if only anyone would listen. In this picture story for young readers by April Stevens, Edwin knows exactly what's happening all around him as he accompanies his mother and siblings on a hectic trip to the grocery store. Unfortunately, no one seems to understand his gurgling and babbling. He tries to tell his mom that her keys are in brother Fergus's shoe ("Gloo poop SHOE noogie froo KEY") and that she left her pocketbook on the roof of the car ("Figbutton noo noo POCKY BOOKY froppin ROOF"), but she just doesn't get it. Fun nonsense words will keep children entertained throughout the book, which features illustrations from award-winning illustrator Sophie Blackall.

Where it's reviewed:
Booklist, May 15, 2011, page 45
Bulletin of the Center for Children's Books, July/August 2011, page 541
Horn Book Magazine, July/August 2011, page 136
New York Times Book Review, June 5, 2011, page 27
School Library Journal, July 2011, page 80

Other books by the same author:
Waking Up Wendell, 2007

Other books you might like:
Marla Frazee, *The Boss Baby*, 2010
Kevin Henkes, *Julius, the Baby of the World*, 1990
Sally Lloyd-Jones, *How to Be a Baby—by Me the Big Sister*, 2007
Amy Schwartz, *A Teeny Tiny Baby*, 1994
Sarah Weeks, *Sophie Peterman Tells the Truth*, 2009

496

PHOEBE STONE

The Romeo and Juliet Code

(New York: Arthur A. Levine Books, 2011)

Subject(s): World War II, 1939-1945; Mystery; Family

Age range(s): 9 - 11+

Major character(s): Felicity Bathburn Budwig, 11-Year-Old, Granddaughter (of Gram); Miami, Aunt (of Felicity); Gideon, Uncle (of Felicity), Teacher; The Gram, Grandmother (of Felicity); Captain Derek, Patient (recovering from polio)

Time period(s): 20th century; 1940s

Locale(s): London, England; Maine, United States

Summary: Eleven-year-old Felicity Bathburn Budwig is not happy when her parents tell her that she has to leave her home in London because of the bombing from the Germans. Felicity goes to Maine in the United States to stay with her relatives. Aunt Miami, Uncle Gideon, Felicity's grandmother, and Captain Derek (a 12-year-old who is recovering from polio) all live in Felicity's new home. As she begins to explore her new surroundings, Felicity finds that everything is not always as it appears. Then, she and Derek find a letter that looks like it was written by Felicity's father. Felicity and Derek are determined to shed light on the mysteries that fill their household. This novel is written by author Phoebe Stone.

Where it's reviewed:
Booklist, January 1, 2011, page 108
Bulletin of the Center for Children's Books, February 2011, page 299
Horn Book Magazine, March/April 2011, page 166
Publishers Weekly, December 6, 2010, page 48
School Library Journal, February 2011, page 120

Other books by the same author:
Deep Down Popular, 2008
All the Blue Moons at the Wallace Hotel, 2000

Other books you might like:
Gary L. Blackwood, *Mysterious Messages: A History of Codes and Ciphers*, 2009
Paul B. Janeczko, *The Dark Game: True Spy Stories*, 2010
Ellen Klages, *The Green Glass Sea*, 2006
Janet Taylor Lisle, *The Art of Keeping Cool*, 2000
Clare Vanderpool, *Moon over Manifest*, 2010

497

TANYA LEE STONE

Almost Astronauts: 13 Women Who Dared to Dream

(Somerville, Massachusetts: Candlewick Press, 2009)

Subject(s): Women; Women's rights; Space flight

Age range(s): 10 - 14+
Time period(s): 20th century; 1950s-1960s
Locale(s): United States

Summary: In the late 1950s, a group of talented, determined young women took on the male-dominated National Aeronautics and Space Administration (NASA). *Almost Astronauts: 13 Women Who Dared to Dream* by Tanya Lee Stone tells the story of these women (known as the Mercury 13) and how their trailblazing work influenced both the American space program and the blossoming women's movement. Though they were ridiculed by the press, spurned by their male counterparts, and rejected by the vice president of the United States, these women worked tirelessly to become astronauts. Despite never making it into space, their legacy is an inspiration to men and women unlike. The book contains photographs, notes on the text, and bibliographical references.

Where it's reviewed:
Booklist, February 15 2009, page 77
Bulletin of the Center for Children's Books, April 2009, page 337
Horn Book Magazine, March/April 2009, page 214
School Library Journal, March 2009, page 169
Science Books & Film, September 2009, page 175

Awards the book has won:
Jane Addams Children's Book Award, 2010

Other books you might like:
Michael Ferrari, *Born to Fly*, 2009
Candace Fleming, *Amelia Lost: The Life and Disappearance of Amelia Earhart*, 2011
Ellen Klages, *The Green Glass Sea*, 2006
Sherri L. Smith, *Flygirl*, 2009
Catherine Thimmesh, *The Sky's the Limit: Stories of Discovery by Women and Girls*, 2002

498

STUART STOTTS
TERRANCE CUMMINGS, Illustrator

We Shall Overcome: A Song That Changed the World

(Boston: Clarion Books, 2010)

Subject(s): Music; Civil rights; African Americans

Age range(s): 10 - 14+

Summary: In this book, author Stuart Stotts provides an in-depth look at the well-known, traditional African American protest song "We Shall Overcome." Stotts traces the legendary song's history from its roots as a simple spiritual in 1863, through the crucial role it played in a 1909 labor movement, to its eventual adoption as the anthem of the civil rights movement and beyond. The text is accompanied by a collection of photographs that reflect the song's long and storied history, a full transcript of the song's lyrics, primary sources, paintings, and more. The volume also comes packaged with a compact disc recording of the titular song by folk singer Pete Seeger.

Where it's reviewed:
Booklist, November 1, 2009, page 59
Horn Book Guide, Fall 2010, page 429
Publishers Weekly, November 30, 2010, page 46
School Library Journal, February 2010, page 135

Other books you might like:
Ashley Bryan, *Let It Shine : Three Favorite Spirituals*, 2007
Russell Freedman, *Voice That Challenged a Nation: Marian Anderson and the Struggle for Equal Rights*, 2004
Elizabeth Partridge, *Marching for Freedom: Walk Together, Children, and Don't You Grow Weary*, 2009
Elizabeth Partridge, *This Land Was Made for You and Me: The Life and Songs of Woody Guthrie*, 2002

499

JONATHAN STROUD

The Amulet of Samarkand: A Bartimaeus Graphic Novel
(2010)

Subject(s): Apprentices; Children; Fantasy

Age range(s): 9 - 14+

Major character(s): Bartimaeus, Supernatural Being (djinni); Nathaniel Underwood, Apprentice; Simon Lovelace, Magician

Time period(s): 21st century; 2000s

Locale(s): London, England

Summary: Taken from his parents when he was only five and apprenticed to a rather middling magician, Nathaniel has been left with enough free time that he reads all the books in his master's library. His ability soars beyond that of his master so when the visiting magician Simon Lovelace makes fun of him, Nathaniel plots revenge. He summons a 5000-year-old djinni named Bartimaeus to do his bidding and steal the Amulet of Samarkand from Simon Lovelace, who murdered the previous owner to obtain this valuable magical artifact. Stealing it is easy, but keeping it is something else as Simon stalks the Amulet to repossess it. This sets in motion danger and tragedy as Nathaniel's house and master are blown to bits; now he's left on his own with only Bartimaeus to help prove Lovelace's plans to assume control of the government in this first of a trilogy.

Where it's reviewed:
Booklist, January 1, 2011, page 67

Horn Book Guide, Spring 2011, page 113
Publishers Weekly, November 1, 2010, page 47
School Library Journal, March 2011, page 190
Voice of Youth Advocates, February 2011, page 580

Other books you might like:
Andrew Donkin, *Artemis Fowl: The Graphic Novel*, 2007
Kazu Kibuishi, *The Stonekeeper*, 2008
Mark Andrew Smith, *The New Brighton Archeological Society*, 2009
Jeanette Winterson, *Tanglewreck*, 2006

500

JAMES STURM, Author/Illustrator
ANDREW ARNOLD, Author/Illustrator
ALEXIS FREDERICK-FROST, Author/Illustrator

Adventures in Cartooning: How to Turn Your Doodles into Comics
(New York: First Second, 2009)

Subject(s): Comic books; Art; Drawing

Age range(s): 7 - 12+

Summary: *Adventures in Cartooning: How to Turn Your Doodles into Comics*, crafted by James Sturm, the director for the Center for Cartoon Studies, and two of his protegees—Andrew Arnold and Alexis Frederick-Frost—is a magical tale that instructs young readers on the best methods of creating memorable comic drawings. A princess is struggling to illustrate a comic, but she just can't make it work. Luckily, an artistic little elf comes to her rescue and shows her how to draw. With the elf's advice and guidance, the princess makes her way through a series of magical encounters and fantastic perils. This unique volume blends how-to and fairy tale to show youngsters the joys of comic art.

Where it's reviewed:
Booklist, March 1, 2009, page 6
Bulletin of the Center for Children's Books, July/August 2009, page 461
Publishers Weekly, May 18, 2009, page 35
School Library Journal, April 2009, page 127

Other books by the same author:
James Sturm's America: God, Gold and Golems, 2007

Other books you might like:
Willow Dawson, *Lila and Ecco's Do-It-Yourself Comics Club*, 2010
Ed Emberley, *Ed Emberley's Drawing Book: Make a World*, 1972
Crockett Johnson, *Harold's Fairy Tale: Further Adventures with the Purple Crayon*, 1956
Scott McCloud, *Understanding Comics: The Invisible Art*, 1993

501

MELISSA SWEET, Author/Illustrator

Balloons over Broadway: The True Story of the Puppeteer of Macy's Parade

(Boston: Houghton Mifflin Books for Children, 2011)

Subject(s): Biographies; History; Americana

Age range(s): 4 - 8+

Summary: The Macy's Thanksgiving Day Parade has been an American tradition since the 1920s. And no element of the parade is more popular than the enormous balloons that float amid the city's skyscraper-lined streets. In this picture book, author and illustrator Melissa Sweet shares the story of Tony Sarg—the man who created the first balloons that sailed over Broadway. Born in Germany, Sarg engineered mechanical contraptions as a young boy and later moved to London where he became a puppeteer. When Tony arrived in New York City, his work attracted the attention of the owners of Macy's department store who were planning a parade for their immigrant staffers. Working for Macy's, Sarg created giant helium balloons that performed like upside-down marionettes in the parade. Sarg's vision remains a foundation of the annual celebration.

Where it's reviewed:
Booklist, September 15, 2011, page 61
Horn Book Magazine, November/December 2011, page 129
Publishers Weekly, August 8, 2011, page 46
School Library Journal, December 2011, page 138

Other books by the same author:
Tupelo Rides the Rails, 2008
Carmine: A Little More Red, 2005

Awards the book has won:
Orbis Pictus Award for Outstanding Nonfiction for Children, 2011

Other books you might like:
Eileen Spinelli, *The Perfect Thanksgiving*, 2003
Tanya Lee Stone, *Sandy's Circus: A Story About Alexander Calder*, 2008

502

CARMEN TAFOLLA
AMY CORDOVA, Illustrator

Fiesta Babies

(Berkeley, California: Tricycle Press, 2010)

Story type: Young Readers
Subject(s): Children; Holidays; Family

Age range(s): 2 - 5+

Summary: The fiesta babies take part in an exciting celebration in this children's book by author Carmen Tafolla and illustrator Amy Cordova. The book includes rhyming verse that tells the story of the fiesta babies and their experiences at a local Hispanic celebration. The fiesta babies march in a parade at the celebration, and they wear special clothes just for the occasion. At the celebration they watch people dance, sing, and play instruments. Although the fiesta babies enjoy being part of the exciting celebration, they also enjoy going home to rest. This volume includes a glossary of Spanish words that are used throughout the text.

Where it's reviewed:
Booklist, February 15, 2010, page 80
Horn Book Guide, Fall 2010, page 288
School Library Journal, March 2010, page 134

Other books by the same author:
What Can You Do With A Paleta?, 2009
What Can You Do With A Rebozo?, 2008

Other books you might like:
Global Fund for Children, *Global Babies*, 2007
Ginger Foglesong Guy, *Bravo!*, 2010
Rachel Isadora, *Say Hello*, 2010
Mario Lopez, *Mario and Baby Gia*, 2011

503

NANCY TAFURI, Author/Illustrator

All Kinds of Kisses

(New York: Little, Brown Books for Young Readers, 2011)

Story type: Young Readers
Subject(s): Animals; Children; Family

Age range(s): 2 - 5+

Summary: Caldecott winner Nancy Tafuri writes and illustrates a children's book about animals' affections. Human families aren't the only ones who express their love to one another in the form of kisses, hugs, and snuggles—animals do, too. Tafuri shows animals giving their young ones special kisses. A mother duck snuggles with her ducklings to keep them warm and loved. A bunny shows love by sniffing its young ones. She also depicts the way other animals such as cows, dogs, lambs, and birds, articulate their love. She ends the book with a mother kissing her child.

Where it's reviewed:
Horn Book Magazine, January/February 2012, page 81
Publishers Weekly, November 7, 2011, page 65
School Library Journal, December 2011, page 94

Other books by the same author:
Whose Chick are You?, 2007
Goodnight My Duckling, 2005
You Are Special Little One, 2003
Mama's Little Bears, 2002
I Love You Little One, 1998

504

HUDSON TALBOTT, Author/Illustrator

River of Dreams: The Story of the Hudson River

(New York: G.P. Putnam's Sons, 2009)

Subject(s): Rivers; History; Science

Age range(s): 8 - 11+
Locale(s): United States

Summary: In *River of Dreams: The Story of the Hudson River*, author Hudson Talbott presents a visually and verbally engaging history of one of America's great rivers. Using rich drawings and paintings to augment the text and convey additional information, Talbott follows the story of the Hudson River from the era before European colonization to the 21st century. The author explains the river's impact on the lives of the Native Americans and subsequent Dutch and English colonists, the rise and decline of its use as a transportation artery, the environmental ills it has suffered in its lifespan, and its current era of revitalization.

Where it's reviewed:
Booklist, December 15, 2008, page 43
Horn Book Magazine, March/April 2009, page 214
Publishers Weekly, January 5, 2009, page 49
School Library Journal, March 2009, page 170

Other books you might like:
Robert C. Baron, *Hudson: The Story of a River*, 2004
Joan Elizabeth Goodman, *Beyond the Sea of Ice: The Voyages of Henry Hudson*, 1999
Thomas Locker, *Where the River Begins*, 1984

505

SHAUN TAN, Author/Illustrator
JOHN MARSDEN, Co-Author

Lost and Found

(New York: Arthur A. Levine Books, 2011)

Story type: Collection
Subject(s): Short stories; Allegories; Psychology

Age range(s): 9 - 12+

Summary: This volume collects three previously published short stories: "The Red Tree" and "The Lost Thing," written and illustrated by Shaun Tan, and "The Rabbits," written by John Marsden and illustrated by Tan. "The Red Tree" focuses on a young girl who is suffering through a very gloomy day. "The Lost Thing" revolves around a boy who assists an odd creature in finding its way home. In "The Rabbits," which centers on the theme of imperialism, oddly dressed rabbits threaten to take over the land they have invaded. Tan's surreal illustrations include paintings and mixed-media images, and the various stories allow room for imagination and interpretation. Both Tan and Marsden includes notes to help explain the stories.

Other books you might like:
Doug TenNapel, *Bad Island*, 2011

506

SHAUN TAN, Author/Illustrator

Tales from Outer Suburbia

(New York: Arthur A. Levine Books, 2009)

Subject(s): Neighborhoods; Magic; Childhood

Age range(s): 10 - 16+
Time period(s): 21st century; 2000s
Locale(s): Australia

Summary: This book is a collection of stories about strange goings-on in suburbia. Told in a straightforward manner, the dreamy illustrations show such oddities as a deep-sea diver wandering the neighborhood in his diving gear, a dugong (large sea mammal) who appears on a neighbor's lawn one morning, and the "inner courtyard" garden that can be accessed inside each nondescript suburban home. The narrator's voice carries through all the stories, even though they feature different people.

Where it's reviewed:
Booklist, December 1, 2008, page 50
Horn Book Magazine, March-April 2009, page 204
New York Times Book Review, November 8, 2009, page 25
Publishers Weekly, November 3, 2008, page 59
School Library Journal, March 2009, page 156

Other books by the same author:
Lost and Found, 2011
The Arrival, 2007

Awards the book has won:
Australian Children's Book of the Year Awards: Older Readers, 2009
Blue Ribbon Awards: Fiction, 2009
Off the Cuff Awards, 2009

Other books you might like:
Judi Barrett, *Cloudy with a Chance of Meatballs*, 1978
Neil Gaiman, *Instructions*, 2010
Adam Rex, *The True Meaning of Smekday*, 2007
Chris Van Allsburg, *The Garden of Abdul Gasazi*, 1979

507

JANET TASHJIAN
JAKE TASHJIAN, Author/Illustrator
JAKE TASHJIAN, Illustrator

My Life as a Book

(New York: Henry Holt, 2010)

Subject(s): Books and reading; Family; Animals

Age range(s): 9 - 12+
Major character(s): Derek Fallon, 12-Year-Old
Time period(s): 21st century; 2010s
Locale(s): Martha's Vineyard, Massachusetts

Summary: In *My Life as a Book*, author Janet Tashjian tells the story of 12-year-old Derek Fallon, who is far less interested in reading than in his own adventures. With the summer starting and a list of required summer reading assigned by his teacher, Derek is focused on continuing his own escapades and avoiding the requisite books at all cost. He soon unearths a years-old mystery surrounding the death of his former babysitter, which he becomes intent on solving. Derek's investigation eventually teaches him about the relationship between life and literature. *My Life as a Book* contains illustrations by Jake Tashjian.

Where it's reviewed:
Booklist, August 2010, page 54
Bulletin of the Center for Children's Books, September 2010, page 46
Horn Book Magazine, July/August 2010, page 124
Publishers Weekly, June 28. 2010, page 129
School Library Journal, August 2010, page 114

Other books by the same author:
My Life as a Stuntboy, 2011

Other books you might like:
Maribeth Boelts, *The PS Brothers*, 2010
Steve Cotler, *Cheesie Mack Is Not a Genius or Anything*, 2011
Lisa Graff, *The Thing about Georgie*, 2006
Jeff Kinney, *Diary of a Wimpy Kid: Greg Heffley's Journal*, 2007

508

MATT TAVARES

Henry Aaron's Dream

(Somerville, Massachusetts: Candlewick Press, 2010)

Subject(s): Baseball; African Americans; Civil rights

Age range(s): 7 - 10+

Summary: The life of baseball great Hank Aaron is brought to vivid life for young readers in Matt Tavares's *Henry Aaron's Dream*. This biography chronicles the legendary athlete's childhood in the segregated South, where he dreams of becoming a baseball star. Undeterred by the fact that no African Americans were in the major leagues, young Henry holds fast to his dream. He is eventually drafted by the Negro Leagues and then by the mainstream, demolishing racial divides and becoming a trailblazer—not only for his prowess as a baseball player, but as a civil rights pioneer. Tavares's illustrations accompany this biography.

Where it's reviewed:
Booklist, February 15, 2010, page 73
Horn Book Magazine, March/April 2010, page 82
School Library Journal, January 2010, page 91

Other books by the same author:
Mudball, 2005
Oliver's Game, 2004
Zachary's Ball, 2000

Other books you might like:
Lesa Cline-Ransome, *Young Pele: Soccer's First Star*, 2007
Gene Fehler, *Change-Up: Baseball Poems*, 2009
Margot Theis Raven, *Let Them Play*, 2005
Sharon Robinson, *Promises to Keep: How Jackie Robinson Changed America*, 2004
Jonah Winter, *Roberto Clemente: Pride of the Pittsburgh Pirates*, 2005

509

DAVID TEAGUE
BORIS KULIKOV, Illustrator

Franklin's Big Dreams

(New York: Hyperion, 2010)

Subject(s): Dreams; Children; Sleep

Age range(s): 4 - 6+

Summary: In *Franklin's Big Dreams*, author David Teague tells the story of Franklin, a little boy with a big imagination. One night while Franklin is trying to sleep, a bunch of construction workers smash through his bedroom wall, followed by a chugging train. But when Franklin wakes up the following morning, his wall appears to be untouched, his room completely train- and construction worker-free. Yet a few days later, the same thing happens again, this time with a buzzing airplane. Soon Franklin realizes that things can happen in his imagination while he sleeps, but that these things only happen in his mind. *Franklin's Big Dreams* is illustrated by Boris Kulikov.

Where it's reviewed:
Booklist, June 1, 2010, page 68
Horn Book Guide, Spring 2011, page 40
Publishers Weekly, July 5, 2010, page 40
School Library Journal, July 2010, page 70

Other books you might like:
Peter McCarty, *Moon Plane*, 2006
Jean Reidy, *Light Up the Night*, 2011
Faith Ringgold, *Tar Beach*, 1991
Chris Van Allsburg, *The Polar Express*, 1985

510

MARK TEAGUE, Author/Illustrator

The Doom Machine

(New York: Blue Sky Press, 2009)

Subject(s): Extraterrestrial life; Science fiction; Adventure

Age range(s): 9 - 12+

Major character(s): Jack Creedle, Nephew (of Bud); Uncle Bud, Uncle (of Jack); Dr. Shumway, Scientist, Mother (of Isadora); Isadora, Daughter (of Dr. Shumway)

Time period(s): 20th century; 1950s (1956)

Summary: Jack Creedle's Uncle Bud is always inventing new things, but Jack never imagined his uncle's inventions would garner much attention. But, when a group of evil alien skreeps land on planet Earth, it is one of Uncle Bud's machines that they are after. The evil skreeps abduct Jack, Uncle Bud, scientist Dr. Shumway, and her daughter Isadora. The humans are taken on a wild adventure through outer space where they meet up with more skreeps, space pirates, royalty, and more. When the group learns that they skreeps want to use Uncle Bud's machine to take over Earth, they realize they must do something to stop their evil plans. *The Doom Machine* is written and illustrated by Mark Teague.

Where it's reviewed:
Bulletin of the Center for Children's Books, January 2010, page 221
Horn Book Magazine, January/February 2009, page 95
School Library Journal, October 2009, page 138

Other books you might like:
Margaret Peterson Haddix, *Found*, 2008
Mark Haddon, *Boom!*, 2010
Adam Rex, *The True Meaning of Smekday*, 2007
Willo Davis Roberts, *The Girl with the Silver Eyes*, 1980

511

RAINA TELGEMEIER, Author/Illustrator

Smile
(New York: Graphix, 2010)

Subject(s): Dentistry; Adolescence; Schools

Age range(s): 9 - 14+
Major character(s): Raina, 6th Grader
Time period(s): 20th century; 1990s
Locale(s): United States

Summary: *Smile*, by Raina Telgemeier, is a graphic novel based on the author's own experiences while she was growing up. In sixth grade, Raina tripped and fell, knocking out both of her front teeth. In the years that followed, she would endure multiple dental surgeries and be forced to wear braces, headgear, and false teeth. In the midst of all this dental drama, Raina also suffered through puberty, which entailed developing crushes on boys and enduring constant teasing from friends. Raina shares her story of adolescent struggles and demonstrates how overcoming her problems made her a better person in the end.

Where it's reviewed:
Booklist, December 15, 2009, page 37
Horn Book Guide. Fall 2010, page 442
New York Times Book Review, May 16, 2010, page 2
School Library Journal, March 2010, page 186

Other books you might like:
Judy Blume, *Are You There God? It's Me, Margaret*, 1970
Louise Carey, *Confessions of a Blabbermouth*, 2007
Siena Cherson Siegel, *To Dance: A Ballerina's Graphic Novel*, 2006
Lauren Weinstein, *Girl Stories*, 2006
Jane Yolen, *Foiled*, 2010

512

CATHERINE THIMMESH

Lucy Long Ago: Uncovering the Mystery of Where We Came From
(Boston: Houghton Mifflin Harcourt, 2009)

Subject(s): Evolution (Biology); Anthropology; Nature
Age range(s): 10 - 14+

Summary: In *Lucy Long Ago: Uncovering the Mystery of Where We Came From*, Catherine Thimmish discusses the discovery in Ethiopia of an early hominid fossil who came to be known as Lucy and what this discovery meant for the fields of anthropology and evolution. Scientists learned that Lucy walked on two legs before her brain had evolved to the size of a brain in other prehistoric humans, meaning that she was part of a missing evolutionary step. Thimmesh discusses first how the bones were recovered, transported, and then put back together to give scientists a more complete picture of what Lucy looked like. She then discusses the questions scientists had and how the skeletal remains helped to solve some evolutionary mysteries. Many scientists from different fields contribute to the discussions in the text. The different ideas and perspectives show how important a single discovery can be.

Where it's reviewed:
Booklist, January 1, 2009, page 65
Bulletin of the Center for Children's Books, July-August 2009, page 463
Horn Book Magazine, July/August 2009, page 442
School Library Journal, July 2009, page 102
Science Books & Film, February-March 2009, page 62

Other books by the same author:
Team Moon: How 40,000 People Landed Apollo 11 on the Moon, 2006
The Sky's the Limit: Stories of Discovery by Women and Girls, 2002
Girls Think of Everything: Stories of Ingenious Inventions By Women, 2000

Other books you might like:
James M. Deem, *Bodies from the Ice: Melting Glaciers and the Recovery of the Past*, 2008
Siobhan Dowd, *Bog Child*, 2008
Deborah Heiligman, *Charles and Emma: The Darwins' Leap of Faith*, 2009
Steve Jenkins, *Life on Earth: The Story of Evolution*, 2002
William Lindsay, *Prehistoric Life*, 2000

513

JAN THOMAS, Author/Illustrator

Rhyming Dust Bunnies
(New York: Beach Lane Books, 2009)

Subject(s): Rhyme
Age range(s): 2 - 6+

Major character(s): Ed, Object (dust bunny); Ned, Object (dust bunny); Ted, Object (dust bunny); Bob, Object (dust bunny)

Summary: In Jan Thomas's *Rhyming Dust Bunnies*, three dust bunnies named Ed, Ned, and Ted enjoy nothing more than a good rhyme. They love playing with rhyming sounds and even try to teach rhyming to a fourth dust bunny named Bob. But Bob doesn't seem to understand their game. He simply cries, "Look!" and "Look out!" even though his words don't rhyme with theirs. The others think he's silly—until a broom and a vacuum cleaner catch them by surprise. Ed, Ned, and Ted must eat humble pie and turn to Bob for an escape plan. Bright illustrations accompany the preschooler-friendly text, which playfully mixes word games with some real-life common sense.

Where it's reviewed:
Bulletin of the Center for Children's Books, January 2009, page 218
Horn Book Guide, Fall 2009, page 316
Publishers Weekly, December 1, 2008, page 45
School Library Journal, February 2009, page 87

Other books by the same author:
Here Comes the Big, Mean Dust Bunny, 2010

Awards the book has won:
Buckeye Children's Book Award: Grades K-2, 2010

Other books you might like:
Terry Golson, *Tillie Lays an Egg*, 2008
Nina Laden, *Peek-a Who?*, 2000
Antoinette Portis, *Not a Box*, 2006
Amy Krouse Rosenthal, *Duck! Rabbit!*, 2009

514

KATE THOMPSON
ROBERT DRESS, Illustrator

Highway Robbery

(New York, New York: Greenwillow Books, 2009)

Subject(s): Morality; Horses; Criminals

Age range(s): 9 - 12+
Major character(s): Dick Turpin, Highwayman

Summary: A dark and mysterious stranger leaves his stunning horse in the care of a young boy, promising him a golden guinea if he looks after it. The boy agrees to the arrangement, but then he is immediately confronted with moral conflicts. He considers charging people for the opportunity to pet the horse, earning himself even more money than the promised reward. At the same time, he is pursued by villains who try to talk him into selling them the horse. Worst of all, the boy learns that the mysterious man may have been a notorious criminal, and he must consider whether or not he should help the King's soldiers lay a trap. With short chapters and pen-and-ink drawings to accompany the fast-paced story, Kate Thompson's *Highway Robbery* is intended for young readers just beginning to enter the world of chapter books.

Where it's reviewed:
Booklist, June 1, 2009, page 55

Bulletin of the Center for Children's Books, July/August 2009, page 463
Horn Book Magazine, July/August 2009, page 432-433
Publishers Weekly, June 8, 2009, page 44
School Library Journal, June 2009, page 100

Other books by the same author:
Most Wanted, 2010

Other books you might like:
Natalie Babbitt, *Jack Plank Tells Tales*, 2007
Melvin Burgess, *The Copper Treasure*, 2000
Brock Cole, *Good Enough to Eat*, 2007
Jacqueline Davies, *Tricking the Tallyman*, 2009
Kaye Umansky, *The Silver Spoon of Solomon Snow*, 2005

515

BILL THOMSON, Author/Illustrator

Chalk

(Tarrytown, New York: Marshall Cavendish Corporation, 2010)

Subject(s): Drawing; Imagination; Games

Age range(s): 6 - 8+

Summary: In *Chalk*, author Bill Thompson tells the story of a trio of children who use chalk to draw a magical world one stormy afternoon. Thompson uses illustrations, with no text, to depict the children as they find chalk and use it to create their imaginary world. A girl draws a sun, and suddenly the rain stops falling; other items are sketched, and they come to life. The real fun begins, however, when a boy draws a picture of a Tyrannosaurus Rex. This book shows the power of make-believe and how children can entertain themselves within their own imaginations. Thompson is also the author of *Baseball Hour* and *Building with Dad*.

Where it's reviewed:
Horn Book Guide, Fall 2010, page 31
Publishers Weekly, January 25, 2010, page 117
School Library Journal, March 2010, page 134

Other books you might like:
Raymond Briggs, *The Snowman*, 1978
Ross Collins, *Doodleday*, 2011
Paul Fleischman, *Sidewalk Circus*, 2004
Vivian French, *T Rex*, 2004
David Wiesner, *Art and Max*, 2010

516

ANNIKA THOR
LINDA SCHENCK, Translator

A Faraway Island

(New York: Random House, 2009)

Subject(s): Jews; Holocaust, 1933-1945; Family relations

Age range(s): 10 - 13+
Major character(s): Stephie Steiner, 12-Year-Old, Refugee, Sister (of Nellie); Nellie Steiner, 8-Year-Old, Sister

(of Stephie); Auntie Alma, Foster Parent (of Nellie); Auntie Marta, Foster Parent (of Stephie)

Time period(s): 20th century; 1930s-1940s

Locale(s): Sweden

Summary: In *A Faraway Island* by Annika Thor, two Jewish girls leave their Austrian homeland for Sweden to escape the approaching Nazi invasion. Though 12-year-old Stephie and 8-year-old Nellie know that their parents' drastic action is an act of love, the adjustment to their new rustic island home is a challenge. Nellie gradually adapts to life with her "Auntie Alma," even forgoing her native German to speak Swedish. For Stephie, whose foster mother, "Auntie Marta," is sterner, the isolated island feels impossibly far from Vienna. Throughout their exile, both girls eagerly await the end of the war and the promise of a reunion with their parents.

Where it's reviewed:
Booklist, October 1, 2009, page 44
Horn Book Magazine, January/February 2009, page 96
New York Times Book Review, March 4, 2009, page 14
School Library Journal, December 2009, page 135

Other books by the same author:
The Lily Pond, 2011

Awards the book has won:
Mildred L. Batchelder Award, 2010

Other books you might like:
Patricia Reilly Giff, *Lily's Crossing*, 1997
Lois Lowry, *Number the Stars*, 1989
Ian Serraillier, *The Silver Sword*, 1956
Joan M. Wolf, *Someone Named Eva*, 2007

517

TIM TINGLE
KAREN CLARKSON, Illustrator

Saltypie: A Choctaw Journey from Darkness into Light

(El Paso, Texas: Cinco Puntos Press, 2010)

Subject(s): Native Americans; Family; Race relations

Age range(s): 8 - 10+

Summary: Author Tim Tingle takes readers into his own past as he remembers his beloved Mawmaw in this book for young readers. Tim recalls his surprise when he found out as a six-year-old that Mawmaw, his grandmother, was blind. Years later, as Tim and his relatives sit in a hospital room with Mawmaw as she prepares to undergo an eye transplant, they reflect on their family history. Among the topics they discuss is the race-related incident that led to Mawmaw's blindness. Many years ago, when Mawmaw first moved to Texas from Oklahoma, a young boy threw a rock at her as she opened her front door. The family stories continue until Mawmaw finally emerges from surgery with her vision restored.

Where it's reviewed:
Booklist, May 1, 2010, page 83
Horn Book Guide, Fall 2010, page 452
Publishers Weekly, April 26, 2010, page 108
School Library Journal, May 2010, page 101

Other books by the same author:
Crossing Bok Chitto: A Choctaw Tale of Friendship and Freedom, 2006
Walking the Choctaw Road: Stories From Red People Memory, 2003

Other books you might like:
Menena Cottin, *The Black Book of Colors*, 2008
Sarah DeCapua, *The Choctaw*
Robert Andrew Parker, *Piano Starts Here: The Young Art Tatum*, 2008

518

DUNCAN TONATIUH

Diego Rivera: His World and Ours

(New York: Abrams Books for Young Readers, 2011)

Subject(s): Painting (Art); Artists; Mexicans

Age range(s): 6 - 8+

Summary: Diego Rivera was a Mexican artist known for his fresco paintings and his political views. Rivera rose to iconic status in Mexican history because of his murals—and because of his heroism on behalf of the Mexican worker. In this picture story, author Duncan Tonatiuh presents the artist's life to young readers via brightly colored illustrations and descriptive text. The author describes Rivera's early life and his career as a painter, and also invites young readers to imagine how Rivera's artwork would translate in today's art world. A glossary of key words and phrases helps readers understand important concepts introduced in the text.

Where it's reviewed:
Booklist, May 1, 2011, page 80
Horn Book Guide, Fall 2011, page 454
Publishers Weekly, March 28, 2011, page 55
School Library Journal, April 2011, page 165

Other books by the same author:
Dear Primo: A Letter to My Cousin, 2010

Awards the book has won:
Pura Belpre Award: Illustrator Award, 2012

Other books you might like:
Campbell Geeslin, *Clara & Senor Frog*, 2007
Guadalupe Rivera Marin, *My Papa Diego and Me/Mi Papa Diego y yo*, 2009
Amy Novesky, *Me, Frida*, 2010
Jonah Winter, *Diego*, 1991

519

DUNCAN TONATIUH, Author/Illustrator

Dear Primo: A Letter to My Cousin

(New York: Abrams Books for Young Readers, 2010)

Story type: Multicultural

Subject(s): Cousins; Letters (Correspondence); Culture

Age range(s): 7 - 9+

Major character(s): Charlie, Cousin (of Carlitos), Boy;

Carlitos, Cousin (of Charlie), Boy
Time period(s): 21st century; 2010s
Locale(s): Mexico; United States

Summary: In this children's book by Duncan Tonatiuh, Charlie and Carlitos are cousins who live in two very different places, but they find out that they have many similarities. Charlie lives in America, and his cousin Carlitos lives in Mexico. They write each other letters to describe where they live, what they do, and what they like. Charlie tells his cousin that he lives in the city and rides the subway to school. Carlitos lives in the country, and he rides his bicycle to school. They both enjoy playing sports, but they play different sports. The boys also find out that while they each have unique traditions, both enjoy spending time with their families. In the end, the boys decide that they should visit each other so they can experience different things.

Where it's reviewed:
Booklist, February 1, 2010, page 48
Horn Book Guide, Fall 2010, page 316
Publishers Weekly, March 15, 2010, page 52
School Library Journal, March 2010, page 134

Other books by the same author:
Diego Rivera: His World and Ours, 2011

Other books you might like:
Jeannie Baker, *Mirror*, 2010
Eve Bunting, *Going Home*, 1996
Nikki Grimes, *Danitra Brown Leaves Town*, 2002
Elissa Haden Guest, *Iris and Walter*, 2000
Charlotte Herman, *First Rain*, 2010

520

RODERICK TOWNLEY
MARY GRANDPRE, Illustrator

The Blue Shoe: A Tale of Thievery, Villainy, Sorcery, and Shoes
(New York: Alfred A. Knopf, 2009)

Subject(s): Fables; Clothing; Adventure
Age range(s): 9 - 12+
Major character(s): Hap Barlo, 13-Year-Old, Apprentice (of Grel); Grel, Worker (cobbler)
Time period(s): Indeterminate

Summary: In *The Blue Shoe: A Tale of Thievery, Villainy, Sorcery, and Shoes*, author Roderick Townley teams up with illustrator Mary GrandPre to offer a story of fantasy and environmental responsibility. Shortly after 13-year-old Hap Barlo is arrested for begging, he is bailed out by Grel, the town cobbler. Hap works as Grel's apprentice in order to pay off his debt, but life grows dangerously complicated when the duo is hired to make a single, magical, blue shoe. This one seemingly simply job leads Hap and Grel on the greatest adventure of their lives.

Where it's reviewed:
Booklist, September 1, 2009, page 88
Bulletin of the Center for Children's Books, November 2009, page 131
Horn Book Guide, Spring 2010, page 85

Publishers Weekly, October 26, 2009, page 58
School Library Journal, December 2009, page 135

Other books by the same author:
The Door in the Forest, 2011

Other books you might like:
Lyn Gardner, *Into the Woods*, 2006
Shannon Hale, *Rapunzel's Revenge*, 2008
Emily Rodda, *The Key to Rondo*, 2008
Matthew Skelton, *The Story of Cirrus Flux*, 2010
J. M. Trewellard, *Butterfingers*, 2007

521

MICHAEL TOWNSEND, Author/Illustrator

Kit Feeny: On the Move
(New York: Knopf Books for Young Readers, 2009)

Subject(s): Schools; Friendship; Children
Age range(s): 5 - 9+
Major character(s): Kit Feeny, Child; Arnold, Friend (of Kit); Devon, Bully

Summary: *Kit Feeny: On the Move*, written and illustrated by Michael Townsend, features Kit Feeny, who is forced to move out of his house and into the big city with his family. The worst part of the move is that he has to leave his best friend Arnold behind. Kit quickly devises a plan to find a "Replacement Arnold" who can be his new best friend, but he mistakenly catches the eye of the school bully, Devon, who likes nothing more than to play mean practical jokes on Kit.

Where it's reviewed:
Bulletin of the Center for Children's Books, November 2009, page 131
Horn Book Guide, Spring 2010, page 85
School Library Journal, March 2010, page 187

Other books by the same author:
Monkey and Elephant's Worst Fight Ever!, 2011
Kit Feeny: The Ugly Necklace, 2009
Billy Tartle in Say Cheese!, 2007

Awards the book has won:
Blue Ribbon Awards: Fiction, 2009

Other books you might like:
Frank Cammuso, *Knights of the Lunch Table: The Dodgeball Chronicles*, 2008
Erik Craddock, *BC Mambo: Stone Rabbit #1*, 2009
Jennifer L. Holm, *Babymouse: Our Hero*, 2005
Jeff Kinney, *Diary of a Wimpy Kid: Greg Heffley's Journal*, 2007
Sara Varon, *Chicken and Cat*, 2006

522

WENDY TOWNSEND

The Sundown Rule
(South Hampton, New Hampshire: Namelos, 2011)

Story type: Family Saga; Young Adult
Subject(s): Father-daughter relations; Travel; Family life

Age range(s): 10 - 13+
Major character(s): Louise, Child, Naturalist
Time period(s): 21st century; 2010s
Locale(s): Michigan, United States

Summary: Louise loves animals and nature. She owes this love to her father, who works for the Park Service in Michigan and writes about nature and wildlife. He allows her to capture the wild animals that surround their home as long as she releases them by sundown. She enjoys tending to injured creatures and nurturing them back to health. She also enjoys communicating with crows. When Louise's father travels to Brazil on an assignment, he sends his daughter to stay with her aunt and uncle in the suburbs. She is sad when she learns that she must leave her cat, Cash, behind because her aunt is allergic to animals. He father assures her that everything will be fine. After spending some time with her aunt and uncle, she eventually makes a friend, but she longs for her father's return, so they can return to their home.

Where it's reviewed:
Bulletin of the Center for Children's Books, March 2011, page 315
Horn Book Guide, Fall 2011, page 369
Publishers Weekly, January 10, 2011, page 50
School Library Journal, April 2011, page 186

Other books you might like:
Lucy Christopher, *Flyaway*, 2011
Adrian Fogelin, *The Sorta Sisters*, 2007
Gill Lewis, *Wild Wings*, 2011
Jerry Spinelli, *Wringer*, 1997
Margaret Willey, *A Summer of Silk Moths*, 2009

523

KRISTEN TRACY

Camille McPhee Fell Under the Bus

(New York: Delacorte Press, 2009)

Subject(s): Friendship; Schools; Family

Age range(s): 8 - 10+
Major character(s): Camille McPhee, Child
Time period(s): 21st century; 2000s
Locale(s): Idaho, United States

Summary: When Camille McPhee slides on the ice and slips underneath her bus, it is only another problem to add to her lit of many. Although Camille is fine after the incident, she worries about her other problems. Camille's best friend just moved to Japan, and Camille isn't sure if she'll ever find another friend like her old one. Camille's parents are constantly fighting, and they've decided to try living separately for a time. Camille, however, is determined to stay optimistic. She decides to appreciate some of the things that she enjoys in life, such as being allowed to carry around a cooler of food in school because she has low blood sugar. Finally, Camille's problems begin to turn around, and she may even find a new friend. *Camille McPhee Fell Under the Bus* is a novel by author Kristen Tracy.

Where it's reviewed:
Booklist, August 2009, page 65
Bulletin of the Center for Children's Books, September 2009, page 42
Horn Book Guide, Spring 2010, page 86
School Library Journal, November 2009, page 90

Other books by the same author:
The Reinvention of Bessica Lefter, 2011

Other books you might like:
Katie Davis, *The Curse of Addy McMahon*, 2008
Lisa Graff, *The Life and Crimes of Bernetta Wallflower*, 2008
Barbara O'Connor, *Greetings from Nowhere*, 2008
Rebecca Rupp, *Sarah Simpson's Rules for Living*, 2008
Lauren Tarshis, *Emma-Jean Lazarus Fell out of a Tree*, 2007

524

MAXINE TROTTIER
ISABELLE ARSENAULT, Illustrator

Migrant

(Toronto: Groundwood Books, 2011)

Story type: Young Readers
Subject(s): Migrant labor; Working conditions; Animals

Age range(s): 5 - 8+
Major character(s): Anna, Child (of migrant workers)
Time period(s): 21st century; 2010s
Locale(s): Canada; Mexico

Summary: Maxine Trottier tells the story of a child who comes from a family of migrant workers with illustrations by Isabelle Arsenault. Anna and her family are Mennonite migrant workers who travel to Canada each year from Mexico for work. While her family harvests fruits and vegetables like buzzing bees, Anna dreams about what it would be like to live in one place. She hates the traveling, which makes her feel like an animal. She feels like a bird, flying from one place to another. She feels like a kitten because she has to share a sleeping space with her sisters. She feels like a jackrabbit because they live in an empty farmhouse. Anna wishes to be a tree, deeply rooted in one place. This title was named a *New York Times* Best Illustrated Children's Book of 2011.

Other books by the same author:
The Long White Scarf, 2005
The Paint Box, 2003
The Tiny Kite of Eddie Wing, 1995

Other books you might like:
Alma Flor Ada, *Gathering the Sun: An Alphabet in Spanish and English*, 1997
Kathleen Krull, *Harvesting Hope: The Story of Cesar Chavez*, 2003
Laurie Lawlor, *Muddy As a Duck Puddle and Other American Similes*, 2010
Pat Mora, *Tomas and the Library Lady*, 1997

525

CINDY TRUMBORE
SUSAN L. ROTH, Author/Illustrator

The Mangrove Tree: Planting Trees to Feed Families

(New York: Lee & Low Books, 2011)

Subject(s): Agriculture; Africa; Biology

Age range(s): 6 - 9+
Locale(s): Hargigo, Eritrea

Summary: The people and animals of Hargigo were hungry. There was not enough rain to grow crops to feed the residents of the African village in Eritrea or to feed their animals. Dr. Gordon Soto, a scientist, had an idea. He helped the village women plant mangrove trees, which live in saltwater, along the coast. The women were paid to plant and nurture the seedlings. As the trees grew, their leaves were harvested to feed the villagers' goats and sheep. The roots of the mangrove trees provided shelter for sea creatures, which attracted fish, and local fishermen were able to harvest more food from the sea to feed the people of Hargigo. Dead mangrove trees could also be used for firewood, and the trees provided oxygen as they grew. The authors describe the events in verse and prose. An extensive afterward includes many photographs of Soto and the people of Hargigo.

Where it's reviewed:
Booklist, May 15, 2011, page 44
Horn Book Guide, Fall 2011, page 433
Publishers Weekly, February 28, 2011, page 54
School Library Journal, May 2011, page 100

Other books by the same author:
Listen for the Wind, 2009

Other books you might like:
Lynne Cherry, *The Great Kapok Tree: A Tale of the Amazon Rain Forest*, 1990
Kristine O'Connell George, *Old Elm Speaks: Tree Poems*, 1998
Donna Jo Napoli, *Mama Miti*, 2010
Nicholas Oldland, *Big Bear Hug*, 2009
Margi Preus, *Celebritrees: Historic and Famous Trees of the World*, 2011

526

HERVE TULLET, Author/Illustrator

Press Here

(New York: San Francisco, 2011)

Story type: Young Readers
Subject(s): Imagination; Games; Children

Summary: Herve Tullet celebrates the power of the imagination with this whimsical and uniquely interactive volume created especially for young readers. As children turn the pages of the book, they are encouraged to press the yellow buttons printed throughout. Readers are then invited to stretch the boundaries of their imaginations and open themselves to the worlds of creativity presented to them by the simple act of pressing a button. The buttons, of course, are simple inked dots on the page, but they aim to inspire young readers to expand the horizons of their imaginative capabilities.

Where it's reviewed:
Booklist, April 1, 2011, page 76
Horn Book Magazine, July/August 2011, page 138
Publishers Weekly, January 31, 2011, page 46
School Library Journal, April 2011, page 155

Other books by the same author:
The Book With a Hole, 2011
The Game of Finger Worms, 2011
The Game of Light, 2011
The Game of Mix-Up Art, 2011
The Game of Patterns, 2011

Other books you might like:
Margaret Wise Brown, *Goodnight Moon*, 1991
Dean Hacohen, *Tuck Me In*, 2010
Michael Hall, *My Heart Is Like a Zoo*, 2009
Bob Staake, *Look! A Book!: A Zany Seek-and-Find Adventure*, 2010
Melanie Watt, *You're Finally Here!*, 2011

527

NAHOKO UEHASHI
YUKO SHIMIZU, Illustrator

Moribito II: Guardian of the Darkness

(New York: Arthur A. Levine Books, 2009)

Series: Moribito Series. Book 2
Subject(s): Adventure; Foster parents; Politics

Age range(s): 10 - 14+
Major character(s): Balsa, Warrior; Jiguro, Guardian (of Balsa)
Time period(s): Indeterminate Past
Locale(s): Kanbal, Fictional Location

Summary: *Morbito II: Guardian of the Darkness* is the second installment in Nahoko Uehashi's Morbito series. This outing finds Balsa heading back to her home country of Kanbal in an attempt to restore honor to her former guardian's name. Jiguro had taken her in as a child and taught her everything he knew, but now Balsa has learned of his dangerous affiliation with King Rogsam's henchmen. She has no idea, however, of the conspiracy surrounding Jiguro—and that she may be the only one who can unearth the truth.

Where it's reviewed:
Booklist, April 1, 2009, page 60
Publishers Weekly, April 27, 2009, page 82
School Library Journal, August 2009, page 115

Other books by the same author:
Morbito: Guardian of the Spirit, 2008

Other books you might like:
Kristin Cashore, *Graceling*, 2008

Suzanne Collins, *The Hunger Games*, 2008
Cindy Pon, *Silver Phoenix: Beyond the Kingdom of Xia*, 2009
Terry Pratchett, *Nation*, 2008
Maya Snow, *Sisters of the Sword*, 2008

528

DEBORAH UNDERWOOD
RENATA LIWSKA, Illustrator

The Quiet Book

(New York: Houghton Mifflin Books for Children, 2010)

Subject(s): Animals; Children; Friendship

Age range(s): 2 - 7+

Summary: In *The Quiet Book*, author Deborah Underwood and illustrator Renata Liwska come together to show young readers the many opportunities for quietude and reflection throughout the course of a day. Various animals are shown in moments of quiet, from the rabbit who relishes being the first one to wake in the morning, to the awe-inspiring joy felt by the woodland creatures during a winter snowfall.

Where it's reviewed:
Booklist, February 15, 2010, page 127
Bulletin of the Center for Children's Books, May 2010, page 403
Publishers Weekly, February 15, 2010, page 127
School Library Journal, March 2010, page 134

Other books by the same author:
The Loud Book, 2011

Other books you might like:
Carin Berger, *The Little Yellow Leaf*, 2008
Lynne Rae Perkins, *Snow Music*, 2003
Susan Marie Swanson, *The House in the Night*, 2008

529

LINDA URBAN

Hound Dog True

(Boston, Massachusetts: Harcourt Children's Books, 2011)

Story type: Young Readers
Subject(s): Friendship; Schools; Students

Age range(s): 8 - 11+

Major character(s): Mattie Breen, 5th Grader, Student—Elementary School
Time period(s): 21st century; 2010s
Locale(s): United States

Summary: A fifth grader struggles to find her place at a new school in this endearing novel for young readers from author Linda Urban. The countdown is on. There's only one week until classes resume at Mitchell P. Anderson Elementary School, and Mattie Breen must once again play the role of new girl. Eager for anything that will keep her from the uncomfortable encounters that await her, Mattie begins studying the art of custodial work in hopes that her Uncle Potluck will take her on as

his assistant. The job isn't ideal, but it will give Mattie something to keep her busy during otherwise awkward lunches and recess outings. When Mattie's custodial attempts fall short, her only hope of surviving at the new school is to be bold and brave among her new classmates.

Where it's reviewed:
Booklist, September 1, 2011, page 120
Horn Book Magazine, September/October 2011, page 104
Publishers Weekly, July 25, 2011, page 54
School Library Journal, October 2011, page 150

Other books by the same author:
A Crooked Kind of Perfect, 2007

Other books you might like:
Jennifer L. Holm, *Turtle in Paradise*, 2010
Kate Klise, *Deliver Us from Normal*, 2005
Claudia Mills, *How Oliver Olson Changed the World*, 2009
Richard Peck, *A Season of Gifts*, 2009

530

ANNE URSU
ERIN MCGUIRE, Illustrator

Breadcrumbs

(New York: Walden Pond Press, 2011)

Story type: Fantasy; Young Readers
Subject(s): Friendship; Fantasy; Fairy tales

Age range(s): 10 - 12+
Major character(s): Hazel, 11-Year-Old, 5th Grader, Adoptee, Friend (of Jack); Jack, 5th Grader, Friend (of Hazel), 11-Year-Old
Locale(s): Minnesota, United States

Summary: Anne Ursu borrows from Hans Christian Andersen's fairy tale, The Snow Queen, for this fantasy adventure. Hazel, an awkward 11-year-old adopted from India, struggles to fit in at her new school. At home, her parents are in the midst of a divorce and argue about money all the time. When Hazel's best friend, Jack, starts acting coldly toward her, her mom pushes her to make some new female friends. Hazel is heartbroken by Jack's actions and tries to heed her mother's advice. When a mysterious woman kidnaps Jack and takes him into the woods, however, Hazel knows she must go find her friend. As she travels deep into the forest, she finds a magical world filled with many beautiful, yet frightening, people and things. Erin Mcguire provides illustrations for the book.

Where it's reviewed:
Booklist, November 15, 2011, page 56
Horn Book Magazine, January/February 2011, page 104
Publishers Weekly, August 29, 2011, page 66
School Library Journal, November 2011, page 141

Other books by the same author:
The Immortal Fire, 2009
The Siren Song, 2008
The Shadow Thieves, 2006
Spilling Clarence, 2002

Other books you might like:
Frank Cottrell Boyce, *The Un-Forgotten Coat*, 2011
Katherine Hannigan, *True (...Sort Of)*, 2011
Madeleine L'Engle, *A Wrinkle in Time*, 1962
L.S. Matthews, *A Dog for Life*, 2006
Rebecca Stead, *When You Reach Me*, 2009

531

RACHEL VAIL
MATTHEW CORDELL, Illustrator

Justin Case: School, Drool, and Other Daily Disasters

(New York: Feiwel and Friends, 2010)

Subject(s): Outcasts; Childhood; Adolescent interpersonal relations
Age range(s): 8 - 11+
Major character(s): Justin "Justin Case" Krzeszewski, 3rd Grader
Time period(s): 21st century; 2010s
Locale(s): United States

Summary: Third grader Justin Krzeszewski—also known as Justin Case—is a quiet, perceptive boy with a long list of hopes and fears. In *Justin Case: School, Drool, and Other Daily Disasters*, author Rachel Vail chronicles a year in the hero's life, presented in diary form and offering readers an intimate peek into Justin's innermost thoughts. As he navigates the terrain of childhood, Justin encounters a series of adventures and discovers his own unique place in the world. *Justin Case* includes illustrations by Matthew Cordell.

Where it's reviewed:
Booklist, March 1, 2010, page 71
Bulletin of the Center for Children's Books, May 2010, page 404
Horn Book Magazine, May/June 2010, page 94
School Library Journal, May 2010, page 93

Other books by the same author:
Do-Over, 1992

Other books you might like:
Judy Blume, *Tales of a Fourth Grade Nothing*, 1972
Jacqueline Davies, *The Lemonade War*, 2007
Katy Kelly, *Melonhead*, 2009
Lenore Look, *Alvin Ho: Allergic to Girls, School, and Other Scary Things*, 2008

532

CATHERYNNE M. VALENTE
ANA JUA, Illustrator

The Girl Who Circumnavigated Fairyland in a Ship of Her Own Making

(New York: Feiwel and Friends, 2011)

Subject(s): Fantasy; Fairies; Adolescent interpersonal relations

Age range(s): 9 - 12+
Major character(s): September, 12-Year-Old, Girl
Locale(s): Omaha, Nebraska

Summary: In this young adult novel, September is normal preteen girl living a mundane life in Middle America. That is, until her life is turned upside by her father shipping off to war and her mother starting a new job to help support the family. September's life gets even more complicated, when a mysterious man in a green suit coat shows up at her house. The man, who is called the Green Wind, tells September that she must help save the inhabitants of Fairyland. The stranger explains that the Marquess is a fickle ruler, and she will make Fairyland a horrible place to live if she does not get what she wants. The Green Wind goes on to explain that the Marquess wants a talisman that only September can retrieve. Now September must go on an extraordinary journey to locate the talisman, and she will have to rely on her courage, her know-how, and her newfound friends.

Where it's reviewed:
Booklist, April 15, 2011, page 52
Bulletin of the Center for Children's Books, June 2011, page 494
Horn Book Magazine, May/June 2011, page 106
New York Times Book Review, June 19, 2011, page 16
School Library Journal, May 2011, page 125

Other books you might like:
L. Frank Baum, *The Wizard of Oz*, 1996
Elise Broach, *Missing on Superstition Mountain*, 2011
Paul Crilley, *The Invisible Order, Book One: Rise of the Darklings*, 2010
Katherine Paterson, *The Flint Heart*, 2011
Laura Peyton Roberts, *Green*, 2010

533

SAMANTHA R. VAMOS
RAFAEL LOPEZ, Illustrator

The Cazuela That the Farm Maiden Stirred

(Watertown, Massachusetts: Charlesbridge, 2011)

Story type: Young Readers
Subject(s): Animals; Food; Cooking

Age range(s): 5 - 8+
Major character(s): Farm Maiden, Cook

Summary: A farm maiden cooks a batch of rice pudding in a pot, or cazuela. Yet she is not the only one responsible for the dish everyone enjoys at the celebration. From the contributions of the hen, goat, donkey, cow, and other farm animals, readers see the cooperation that is needed to make the pudding. Author Samantha R. Vamos constructed her story in a momentum-building style, adding each animal's contribution to the process until the dish is complete. The donkey picks the lime, for example, and the hen grates its peel, in the cheerful illustrations by Rafael Lopez. Vamos builds the reader's vocabulary by introducing a character or object in English, then in subsequent references replacing these words with their Spanish translations. A glossary of Spanish words at the back of the book reinforces the language lesson, and a recipe for arroz con leche is included.

Where it's reviewed:
Booklist, April 15, 2011, page 58
Horn Book Guide, Fall 2011, page 334
Publishers Weekly, February 21, 2011, page 131
School Library Journal, March 2011, page 137

Other books by the same author:
Before You Were Here, Mi Amor, 2009

Other books you might like:
Nancy Andrews-Goebel, *The Pot That Juan Built*, 2002
Eric A. Kimmel, *Cactus Soup*, 2004
Pat Mora, *Yum! Mmmm! Que Rico!*, 2007

534

CHRIS VAN ALLSBURG, Author/Illustrator
Queen of the Falls
(Boston, Massachusetts: Houghton Mifflin Books for Children, 2011)

Subject(s): Women; Biographies; Adventure

Age range(s): 6 - 9+

Summary: *Queen of the Falls* is a biography for young readers from author and illustrator Chris Van Allsburg. In 1901, at the age of 61, former charm-school teacher and widower Annie Edson Taylor was on a quest for fame and fortune. Her brilliant idea? Go over Niagara Falls in a pillow-lined wooden barrel, a feat that had never been accomplished in history! Calling on the media, a public-relations team, and a support squad, Annie embarked on a death-defying mission to become a surprising and unglamorous daredevil and history-maker. In *Queen of the Falls*, Van Allsburg recounts her daring adventures.

Where it's reviewed:
Booklist, January 1, 2011, page 82
Horn Book Guide, March/April 2011, page 153
Publishers Weekly, January 24, 2011, page 153
School Library Journal, March 2011, page 145

Other books by the same author:
The Widow's Broom, 1992

Other books you might like:
Julie Cummins, *Women Daredevils: Thrills, Chills, and Frills*, 2008
Marissa Moss, *The Bravest Woman in America*, 2011
Sara Sheridan, *I'm Me!*, 2011
Jane Yolen, *Not All Princesses Dress in Pink*, 2010

535

CHRIS VAN ALLSBURG, Author/Illustrator
The Chronicles of Harris Burdick: Fourteen Amazing Authors Tell the Tales
(Boston: Houghton Mifflin Harcourt, 2011)

Story type: Collection
Subject(s): Storytelling; Writers; Mystery

Age range(s): 10 - 14+

Summary: In this collection of short stories, various popular and award-winning authors create new tales from the drawings in Chris Van Allsburg's classic picture story *The Mysteries of Harris Burdick* . As the original story goes, Harris Burdick left a series of illustrations with a book publisher that were later transformed into a book by Van Allsburg. The author accompanied these illustrations not with an actual story, but with mere captions, thus encouraging readers to create their own story. In this book, 14 authors write stories inspired by different drawings. Their tales include "Archie Smith, Boy Wonder" by Tabitha King, "Missing in Venice" by Gregory Maguire, "The Seven Chairs" by Lois Lowry, "Captain Tory" by Louis Sachar, and more. The book also includes an introduction by Lemony Snicket.

Where it's reviewed:
Horn Book Magazine, September/October 2011, page 14
New York Times Book Review, November 13, 2011, page 38
Publishers Weekly, July 25, 2011, page 54
School Library Journal, August 2011, page 123
Voice of Youth Advocates, October 2011, page 412

Other books by the same author:
The Mysteries of Harris Burdick, 1984

Other books you might like:
Jon Scieszka, *Guys Read: Thriller*, 2011

536

KATIE VAN CAMP
LINCOLN AGNEW, Illustrator
CookieBot! A Harry and Horsie Adventure
(New York: Balzer & Bray, 2011)

Series: Harry and Horsie Adventure Series. Book 2
Story type: Series; Young Readers
Subject(s): Horses; Robots; Friendship

Age range(s): 3 - 6+
Major character(s): Harry, Friend (of Horsie); Horsie, Friend (of Harry); CookieBot, Robot

Summary: In this second book from the Harry and Horsie Adventure Series by author Katie Van Camp and illustrator Lincoln Agnew, Harry and Horsie must find a way to stop Horsie's belly from growling. As they play with their building blocks, they hear a strange noise—which they quickly realize is coming from Horsie's tummy. Horsie is hungry—and so is Harry, so the two friends go into the kitchen in search of a snack. They could have fruit or carrot sticks, but the two buddies really want the cookies on the counter. Since neither of them is tall enough to reach the cookie jar, they come up with a plan to build the best robot ever—CookieBot. CookieBot will help Harry and Horsie obtain the snack they want. Unfortunately, they lose control of the robot, and CookieBot zooms all over town looking for cookies and other baked goods. Can Harry and Horsie stop CookieBot before it eats everything in sight?

Where it's reviewed:

Booklist, June 1, 2011, page 96

Horn Book Guide, Fall 2011, page 334

Publishers Weekly, March 21, 2011, page 74

School Library Journal, June 2011, page 97

Other books by the same author:

Harry and Horsie, 2009

Other books you might like:

Susan E. Goodman, *All in Just One Cookie*, 2006

Mini Grey, *Traction Man Is Here!*, 2005

Oliver Jeffers, *Stuck*, 2011

Mo Willems, *The Duckling Gets a Cookie!?*, 2012

Karma Wilson, *The Cow Loves Cookies*, 2010

537

KATHLEEN VAN CLEVE

Drizzle

(New York: Dial Books for Young Readers, 2010)

Subject(s): Magic; Self perception; Animals

Age range(s): 9 - 12+

Major character(s): Polly Peabody, 11-Year-Old; Edith, Aunt (of Polly); Harry, Friend (of Polly); Freddy, Brother (of Polly)

Time period(s): 21st century; 2010s

Locale(s): United States

Summary: In *Drizzle* by Kathleen Van Cleve, a young girl learns that her family's farm holds many surprises and challenges. A bit of an outcast at school, 11-year-old Polly Peabody finds comfort and love on the farm with family members and her friend Harry (a rhubarb plant). Visitors flock to the farm to take a spin on the colossal umbrella ride and witness the rain shower that arrives promptly each Monday at 1 p.m. After Aunt Edith shows Polly the farmhouse's enchanted room, the rain stops coming and the farm faces drought. Polly must learn to fix the broken charm that will save the farm and her family. First novel.

Where it's reviewed:

Bulletin of the Center for Children's Books, June 2010, page 415

Horn Book Guide. Fall 2010, page 356

School Library Journal, April 2010, page 170

Other books you might like:

Cheryl Bardoe, *Gregor Mendel: The Friar Who Grew Peas*, 2006

Joy Cowley, *Chicken Feathers*, 2008

Betsy Hearne, *Wishes, Kisses, and Pigs*, 2001

Ingrid Law, *Savvy*, 2008

Kaye Umansky, *Clover Twig and the Magical Cottage*, 2009

538

CLARE VANDERPOOL

Moon over Manifest

(New York: Random House, 2010)

Subject(s): Father-daughter relations; Mystery; Great Depression, 1929-1934

Age range(s): 10 - 12+

Major character(s): Abilene Tucker, 12-Year-Old, Girl; Gideon Tucker, Father (of Abilene), Railroad Worker; Pastor Shady Howard, Religious (pastor); Miss Sadie, Psychic (diviner); Jinx, Young Man, Con Artist; Ned Gillen, Friend (of Jinx), Young Man; Ruthanne, Friend (of Abilene); Lettie, Friend (of Abilene)

Time period(s): 20th century; (1930s); 20th century; 1910s (1917)

Locale(s): Manifest, Kansas

Summary: In this tale of historical fiction, set during the American Great Depression, twelve-year-old Abilene Tucker, the book's narrator, rides the rails to the small, immigrant town of Manifest, Kansas. The year is 1936, Abilene's father, Gideon, an itinerant worker, has sent his daughter to live with his old friend Pastor Shady Howard while he takes a job working on the railroad in Iowa. Abilene's mother left years earlier, and the father-daughter pair have spent the years wandering across the United States, looking for work. After Pastor Howard takes Abilene in, she finds a box of keepsakes from 20 years earlier that sheds light on her father's mysterious past with the town of Manifest. Abilene begins working for Miss Sadie, Manifest's resident fortune-teller, and the narrative breaks off into two distinct paths. One path follows Abilene and her new friends, Ruthanne and Lettie, as they piece together the mystery of the keepsake box, which involves the World War I-era story of a boy named Jinx and a possible spy called the "Rattler" who might be hiding in Manifest. The other path follows Miss Sadie's recounting of Jinx's arrival in Manifest in 1917. Her story is supplemented by several newspaper articles from the era. As the two narrative paths converge, Abilene learns many lessons about her father's past and his relationship to the quirky town of immigrant Americans.

Where it's reviewed:

Booklist, October 15, 2010, page 63

Bulletin of the Center for Children's Books, November 2010, page 152

Horn Book Guide, Spring 2011, page 86

Publishers Weekly, September 27 2010, page 60

School Library Journal, November 2010, page 131

Awards the book has won:

Newbery Medal, 2011

Spur Awards: Best Western Juvenile Book, 2011

Other books you might like:

Susan Campbell Bartoletti, *They Called Themselves the K.K.K.: The Birth of an American Terrorist Group*, 2010

Christopher Paul Curtis, *Bud, Not Buddy*, 1999

Russell Freedman, *Children of the Great Depression*, 2005

Jennifer L. Holm, *Turtle in Paradise*, 2010

Sarah Weeks, *So B. It*, 2004

539

SARA VARON, Author/Illustrator

Bake Sale

(New York: First Second, 2011)

Story type: Young Readers
Subject(s): Cooking; Friendship; Business

Age range(s): 8 - 12+
Major character(s): Cupcake, Musician (drummer), Friend (of Eggplant), Baker; Eggplant, Friend (of Cupcake)

Summary: Cupcake has grown bored of life at the bakery; he's tired of making the same treats every day. His spirits lift when his friend, Eggplant, suggests that they visit Eggplant's aunt in Turkey. His aunt is friends with Turkish Delight, Cupcake's favorite celebrity chef. If Cupcake can spend some time with Turkish Delight, he's certain he'll find his love for pastries again. Though Cupcake is excited about the upcoming trip, he doesn't know how he will afford it. The bakery hasn't been making many profits, and all his spare time is spent practicing the drums with his band. Eggplant suggests that Cupcake extend his bakery's hours and cater local events, but that would mean giving up his spot in the band. Defeated, Cupcake sacrifices his music for the future of his bakery and gets to work. He makes treats for dog shows and boxing fights and soon he has enough money for the trip. Then he hits another snag—Eggplant cannot afford to go see his aunt. What is a cupcake to do? Does Cupcake give his hard-earned money to his best friend so Eggplant can go see his family? Or should Cupcake keep it for himself and take a solo journey to visit his inspiration?

Where it's reviewed:
Booklist, September 15, 2011, page 55
Publishers Weekly, July 4, 2011, page 67
School Library Journal, November 2011, page 154

Other books by the same author:
Chicken and Cat Clean Up, 2009
Robot Dreams, 2007
Chicken and Cat, 2006
Sweaterweather, 2003

Other books you might like:
Jennifer L. Holm, *Babymouse: Cupcake Tycoon*, 2010
Maurice Sendak, *In the Night Kitchen*, 1970
Ashley Spires, *Binky the Space Cat*, 2009
Rosemary Wells, *Bunny Cakes*, 1997
Mo Willems, *Should I Share My Ice Cream?*, 2011

540

ERIC VELASQUEZ, Author/Illustrator

Grandma's Gift

(Walker Publishing Company, 2010)

Subject(s): Artists; Grandmothers; Gifts

Age range(s): 6 - 9+
Major character(s): Eric Velasquez, Child; Grandma, Grandmother (of Eric)
Time period(s): 20th century
Locale(s): New York, New York

Summary: Author and illustrator Eric Velasquez looks back on his childhood and recounts a visit with his grandmother, who lives in the New York neighborhood of Spanish Harlem. Eric and his grandmother get ready to celebrate the holidays, shopping for all the food they will need to prepare the Christmas feast, as well as a surprise stop-off at a famous art museum. This visit inspires young Eric to become a painter, and he begins to think of all the supplies he will need to make his dream come true. *Grandma's Gift* was awarded the Pura Belpre Award for illustration.

Where it's reviewed:
Booklist, November 15, 2010, page 51
Horn Book Guide, Spring 2010, page 48
School Library Journal, October 2010, page 77

Other books by the same author:
Grandma's Records, 2001

Awards the book has won:
Pura Belpre Award: Illustrator Award, 2011

Other books you might like:
Janet Costa Bates, *Seaside Dream*, 2010
Jane Johnson, *The Princess and the Painter*, 1994
Jacqueline Preiss Weitzman, *You Can't Take a Balloon into the Metropolitan Museum*, 1998

541

COLLEEN A.F. VENABLE
STEPHANIE YUE, Illustrator

Hamster and Cheese

(Minneapolis: Lerner Publishing, 2010)

Series: Guinea Pig, Pet Shop Private Eye Series. Book 1
Story type: Series; Young Readers
Subject(s): Comic books; Hamsters; Pets

Age range(s): 5 - 8+
Major character(s): Sasspants, Guinea Pig, Detective; Hamisher, Hamster, Sidekick (to Sasspants); Mr. Venezi, Store Owner (pet shop)

Summary: In this first graphic novel in Colleen A.F. Venable's Guinea Pig, Private Eye Series for young readers, Mr. Venezi's pet shop becomes the scene of a puzzling crime. An unknown thief has been stealing Mr. Venezi's sandwiches, and Hamisher the hamster wants Sasspants the guinea pig to help solve the crime. (Hamisher has mistaken Sasspants for a PI because the letter "g" has fallen off the end of her "guinea pig" sign.) The two furry rodents interview the shop's other animal residents as they search for clues. Sasspants comes up with a clever plan to catch the crook that requires the shop's turtle to pose as a sandwich. Illustrations by Stephanie Yue capture the action of the silly caper.

Where it's reviewed:
Horn Book Guide, Fall 2010, page 327
School Library Journal, May 2010, page 143

Other books by the same author:
The Ferret's a Foot, 2011
Fish You Were Here, 2011
And Then There Were Gnomes, 2010

Other books you might like:
David A. Adler, *Young Cam Jansen and the Missing Cookie*, 1996
Alix Berenzy, *Sammy: The Classroom Guinea Pig*, 2005
Elizabeth Levy, *Something Queer at the Lemonade Stand*, 1982
Megan McDonald, *Judy Moody, Girl Detective*, 2010
Ashley Spires, *Binky the Space Cat*, 2009

542

JUDITH VIORST
LANE SMITH, Illustrator

Lulu and the Brontosaurus

(New York: Atheneum, 2010)

Subject(s): Dinosaurs; Children; Birthdays

Age range(s): 4 - 8+
Major character(s): Lulu, Child; Mr. Brontosaurus, Dinosaur

Summary: In *Lulu and the Brontosaurus*, written by Judith Viorst and illustrated by Lane Smith, it is Lulu's birthday, and she has decided that she wants a brontosaurus for a pet. Her parents tell her that is impossible, but Lulu doesn't believe them and walks off into the forest to find a dinosaur. At first, she sees a bear, a tiger, and a snake, but she just walks right past them. Then, just as she wanted, she finds a big, beautiful brontosaurus named Mr. Brontosaurus; he also thinks that having a pet would be a great idea. Lulu soon realizes, however, that Mr. Brontosaurus wants to keep her as his pet! Now Lulu must find a way out of this peculiar situation.

Where it's reviewed:
Booklist, September 1, 2010, page 105
Bulletin of the Center for Children's Books, October 2010, page 99
Horn Book Magazine, Nov/Dec 2010, page 107
Publishers Weekly, August 30, 2010, page 53
School Library Journal, September 2010, page 135

Other books by the same author:
Earrings, 2010
If I Were In Charge of the World and Other Worries: Poems for Children and Their Parents, 1981
Alexander, Who Used to Be Rich Last Sunday, 1978

Alexander and the Terrible, Horrible, No Good, Very Bad Day, 1972
I'll Fix Anthony, 1969

Other books you might like:
Annie Barrows, *Ivy and Bean: Bound to Be Bad*, 2009
Oliver Butterworth, *The Enormous Egg*, 1956
Stephanie Greene, *Happy Birthday, Sophie Hartley*, 2010
Megan McDonald, *Judy Moody, Girl Detective*, 2010
Sara Pennypacker, *Clementine, Friend of the Week*, 2010

543

FRANK VIVA, Author/Illustrator

Along a Long Road

(New York: Little, Brown Books for Young Readers, 2011)

Story type: Young Readers
Subject(s): Bicycles; Travel; Recreation

Age range(s): 3 - 6+

Summary: This book, by author and illustrator Frank Viva, shares the story of a leisurely journey down a long road. The book contains images that Viva created using one continuous piece of art. The art shows a biker traveling down a long road, enjoying the beautiful scenery. Minimal text accompanies the art and shares the story of the biker's travels.

Where it's reviewed:
Booklist, May 1, 2011, page 89
New York Times Book Review, May 15, 2011, page 19
Publishers Weekly, April 4, 2011, page 49
School Library Journal, June 2011, page 97

Other books you might like:
Allan Ahlberg, *The Pencil*, 2008
Laura Ljungkvist, *Follow the Line*, 2006
Roxie Munro, *Go! Go! Go!: More Than 70 Flaps to Uncover & Discover!*, 2009
David Shannon, *Duck on a Bike*, 2002

544

STEVE VOAKE
CHARLOTTE VOAKE, Illustrator

Insect Detective

(London: Walker Books, 2009)

Subject(s): Insurance; Nature; Ants

Age range(s): 5 - 8+

Summary: In *Insect Detective*, author Steve Voake and illustrator Charlotte Voake persuade young readers to get out of the house and into nature to better examine the bounty it offers—specifically, the insects it houses. Several varieties of insect are profiled in this volume, including dragonflies, caterpillars, beetles, and ants. Steve's detailed information and Charlotte's accurate drawings further help youngsters identify these creatures in the wild.

Where it's reviewed:
Booklist, May 1, 2010, page 88
Horn Book Guide, Fall 2010, page 413
School Library Journal, June 2010, page 92
Science Books & Film, December 2010, page 322

Other books you might like:
David Biedrzycki, *Ace Lacewing, Bug Detective: The Big Swat*, 2010
Vivian French, *Yucky Worms*, 2009
Ruth Horowitz, *Breakout at the Bug Lab*, 2001

545

CYNTHIA VOIGT
LOUISE YATES, Illustrator

Young Fredle

(New York: Alfred A. Knopf, 2011)

Story type: Adventure; Young Readers
Subject(s): Adventure; Self awareness; Freedom

Age range(s): 8 - 12+
Major character(s): Fredle, Mouse

Summary: Fredle is a young mouse who goes on an adventure of self-discovery in this picture book by author Cynthia Voigt and illustrator Louise Yates. When Fredle, who is known to be a troublemaker, eats so much that he gets sick, his family kicks him out of the nest. Then, the owner of the house releases him outside. Fredle is young and inexperienced, so the outside world seems overwhelming and scary. At first, it's difficult for Fredle to decide who his friends are and who his enemies are. Over time, however, Fredle learns to take care of himself outside, and he even learns to enjoy the beauty and freedom he finds there.

Where it's reviewed:
Booklist, January 1, 2011, page 111
Bulletin of the Center for Children's Books, June 2011, page 495
Horn Book Magazine, March/April 2011, page 129
Publishers Weekly, November 29, 2010, page 49
School Library Journal, February 2011, page 121

Other books by the same author:
Angus and Sadie, 2005
The Rosie Stories, 2003

Other books you might like:
Betty G. Birney, *The World According to Humphrey*, 2004
Elise Broach, *Masterpiece*, 2008
E.B. White, *Stuart Little*, 1945
William Wise, *Christopher Mouse: The Tale of a Small Traveler*, 2004

546

BERNARD WABER
PAULIS WABER, Illustrator

Lyle Walks the Dogs: A Counting Book

(Boston: Houghton Mifflin Books for Children, 2010)

Subject(s): Crocodiles; Dogs; Mathematics
Age range(s): 3 - 6+
Major character(s): Lyle, Crocodile
Time period(s): 21st century; 2010s

Summary: Lyle the Crocodile lands a new job that combines his two biggest interests. He adores dogs and he adores walking, and his gig as a dog walker is a perfect fit for Lyle. Soon everyone in the community hears word of Lyle's gift with pooches, and his dog-walking business grows by leaps and bounds. With ten dogs in his charge, however, Lyle has to find a way to keep them all in line. Bernard Waber's *Lyle Walks the Dogs: A Counting Book* contains illustrations by Paulis Waber.

Where it's reviewed:
Publishers Weekly, April 19, 2010, page 50

Other books by the same author:
Lyle at Christmas, 1998
Lyle at the Office, 1994
Lyle Finds His Mother, 1978
Lovable Lyle, 1969
Lyle, Lyle, Crocodile, 1965

Other books you might like:
Julia Durango, *Go-Go Gorillas*, 2010
Tana Hoban, *26 Letters and 99 Cents*, 1987
Mij Kelly, *One More Sheep*, 2006
Laura Vaccaro Seeger, *One Boy*, 2008
Caroline Stutson, *Cats' Night Out*, 2010

547

TIM WADHAM
KADY MACDONALD DENTON, Illustrator

The Queen of France

(Somerville, Massachusetts: Candlewick Press, 2011)

Story type: Young Readers
Subject(s): Children; Imagination; Royalty

Age range(s): 5 - 8+
Major character(s): Rose, Girl (who pretends to be Queen of France)

Summary: Imagination is a big part of growing up. In this picture book by Tim Wadham, a little girl named Rose engages in a flight of fancy. On an otherwise regular morning, Rose imagines that she has transformed into the Queen of France. For the rest of the day, she alternates between the queen and Rose as she interacts with her parents, who lovingly play along. In the end, Rose wins out and the queen retires as Rose heads to dinner to talk about her busy day. This book features illustrations by Kady MacDonald Denton.

Where it's reviewed:
Booklist, April 15, 2011, page 61
Horn Book Magazine, May/June 2011, page 78
Publishers Weekly, January 10, 2011, page 49
School Library Journal, February 2011, page 91

Other books you might like:
Victoria Kann, *Silverlicious*, 2011
Sara Sheridan, *I'm Me!*, 2011
Jane Yolen, *Not All Princesses Dress in Pink*, 2010

548

HILARY WAGNER
OMAR RAYYAN, Illustrator

Nightshade City

(New York: Holiday House, 2010)

Series: Nightshade Chronicles Series. Book 1
Subject(s): Fantasy; Rats; Dictators

Age range(s): 9 - 12+
Major character(s): Victor Nightshade, Rat, Brother (to
  Vincent); Vincent Nightshade, Rat, Brother (to Vic-
  tor); Juniper Belancort, Rat, Friend (of Victor and
  Vincent), Leader
Locale(s): Catacombs, Fictional Location

Summary: *Nightshade City*, a suspenseful and action-
packed fantasy novel for children and young adults, is
the first installment in the Nightshade Chronicles series
from author Hilary Wagner and illustrator Omar Rayyan.
In the Catacombs, an underground community of rats, a
malevolent dictator named High Minister Killdeer and
his band of baddies has taken control over the city and is
abusing his power. Vincent and Victor Nightshade, two
brothers whose father used to govern the Catacombs, are
desperate for an escape from Killdeer's oppressive
regime. They team up with their father's old pal, Juniper
Belancort, to overthrow the leaders and establish a new,
democratic way of life in Nightshade City.

Where it's reviewed:
Booklist, September 15, 2010, page 67
Bulletin of the Center for Children's Books, December
  2010, page 210
Horn Book Guide, Spring 2011, page 86
School Library Journal, January 2011, page 118
Voice of Youth Advocates, December 2010, page 477

Other books by the same author:
The White Assassin, 2011

Other books you might like:
Suzanne Collins, *Gregor the Overlander*, 2003
Erin Hunter, *Warriors: Into the Wild*, 2003
Brian Jacques, *Redwall*, 1986
Albert Marrin, *Oh, Rats!: The Story of Rats and People*,
  2006
Robert C. O'Brien, *Mrs. Frisby and the Rats of NIMH*,
  1971

549

SALLY M. WALKER

Blizzard of Glass: The Halifax Explosion of 1917

(New York: Henry Holt and Co., 2011)

Subject(s): Shipwrecks; Wars; Death

Age range(s): 10 - 14+

Summary: Disasters, both maritime and natural, caused
massive death and destruction in Halifax Harbour in
Nova Scotia, Canada, on December 6, 1917. An empty
Belgian relief ship, the *Imo*, was leaving the busy harbor;
at the same time, the *Mont-Blanc*, which had been waiting all night, was entering Halifax Harbour. The latter
vessel was laden with explosives destined for the war effort, and was preparing to join a convoy to cross the
Atlantic. There was a communication breakdown, and
the ships collided. Many residents of the towns around
the harbor were watching 20 minutes later when the
burning *Mont-Blanc* exploded. The explosion triggered a
tsunami. An area of more than 16 square miles was
leveled. Flooding and fires killed many people, and
rescue efforts were hampered by a storm that dropped
more than a foot of snow on the scene. Nearly 2,000
were dead when it was all over. Author Sally M. Walker
breathes life into the events of the day and the months
that followed, exploring the impact on the community
with a focus on five families.

Where it's reviewed:
Horn Book Magazine, November/December 2011, page
  130
New York Times Book Review, December 18, 2011, page
  23
School Library Journal, October 2011, page 163

Other books by the same author:
Frozen Secrets: Antarctica Revealed, 2010
*Written in Bone: Buried Lives of Jamestown and
  Colonial Maryland*, 2009
*Secrets of a Civil War Submarine: Solving the Mysteries
  of the H.L. Hunley*, 2005
Fossil Fish Found Alive: Discovering the Coelacanth,
  2002

Other books you might like:
Brenda Z. Guiberson, *Disasters: Natural and
  Man-Made Catastrophes through the Centuries*, 2010
Jim Murphy, *The Great Fire*, 1995
Diana Preston, *Remember the Lusitania!*, 2003

550

LEE WARDLAW
EUGENE YELCHIN, Illustrator

Won-Ton: A Cat Tale Told in Haiku

(New York: Henry Holt, 2010)

Story type: Contemporary
Subject(s): Animals; Pets; Poetry

Age range(s): 7 - 10+
Major character(s): Won-Ton, Cat (Siamese)

Summary: In this illustrated children's book by Lee Wardlaw, a series of haiku tell the story of Won-Ton, a black Siamese cat that embarks on an adventure. Won-Ton begins the journey at a shelter for homeless pets. He then travels to a home with a family when a boy adopts him from the shelter. At first, Won-Ton is not sure if he can trust his new owners and his place to live. However, Won-Ton quickly learns that his owners are kind and caring. Over time, Won-Ton comes to love his new home and his new family. Wardlaw's three-line poems show Won-Ton's travels and transformation. The text is supported by illustrations by Eugene Yelchin.

Where it's reviewed:
Booklist, February 1, 2011, page 69
Horn Book Magazine, March/April 2011, page 134
Publishers Weekly, December 6, 2011, page 47
School Library Journal, February 2011, page 92

Other books you might like:
Antonia Barber, *Catkin*, 1994
Nick Bruel, *Bad Kitty Gets a Bath*, 2008
Betsy Byars, *Cat Diaries: Secret Writings of the MEOW Society*, 2010
Clare Turlay Newberry, *April's Kittens*, 1940

551

RENEE WATSON

What Momma Left Me

(New York: Bloomsbury USA Children's Books, 2010)

Subject(s): African Americans; Death; Grandparents
Age range(s): 10 - 13+
Major character(s): Serenity, 13-Year-Old, Sister (of Danny); Danny, Brother (of Serenity)

Summary: *What Momma Left Me*, by author Renee Watson, is the story of a tight-knit African-American family and the strength they must show to cope with the loss of a loved one. Thirteen-year-old Serenity is left practically an orphan after her mother dies and her father runs away, leaving Serenity and her brother Danny behind. The siblings go to live with their grandparents, who teach them the importance of faith in God. As Serenity comes to terms with her mother's death, her brother begins hanging out with some unsavory characters. Can Serenity help lead Danny back onto the right path? Watson is also the author of *A Place Where Hurricanes Happen*.

Where it's reviewed:
Booklist, May 1, 2010, page 87
Horn Book Guide, Spring 2011, page 258
Publishers Weekly, June 28, 2010, page 129
School Library Journal, August 2010, page 115

Other books by the same author:
A Place Where Hurricanes Happen, 2010

Other books you might like:
Carolyn Coman, *What Jamie Saw*, 1995
K.L. Going, *The Garden of Eve*, 2007
Julius Lester, *When Dad Killed Mom*, 2001

Jacqueline Woodson, *I Hadn't Meant to Tell You This*, 1994

552

SARAH WEEKS

Pie

(New York: Scholastic Press, 2011)

Story type: Mystery; Young Readers
Subject(s): Mystery fiction; Mystery; Detective fiction
Age range(s): 9 - 12+
Major character(s): Polly Portman, Baker (deceased), Aunt (of Alice); Alice, 10-Year-Old, Detective—Amateur, Friend (of Charlie); Charlie, Detective—Amateur, Friend (of Alice)
Time period(s): 20th century; 1950s
Locale(s): Ipswitch, Pennsylvania

Summary: The death of baker and pie queen Polly Portman turns the small town of Ipswitch, Pennsylvania, upside down. Polly's pies won numerous awards over the years. She gained a following for her famed confections—which she made free of charge. She made any flavor a customer requested, but she refused to give out her secret pie crust recipe. After her death, everyone in the small town wants the prized recipe, and some go to great lengths to procure it. In her will, Polly left the secret recipe to her cat Lardo, and she left Lardo in the care of her 10-year-old niece, Alice. Alice was devastated by her aunt's death, but she vowed to take care of Lardo, and she does just that—until the cat goes missing. Lardo has likely been kidnapped by someone who wants the secret pie crust recipe. Alice and her friend Charlie put on detective hats and search for the missing cat. Author Sarah Weeks includes pie recipes in each chapter of the book.

Where it's reviewed:
Booklist, September, 1 2011, page 122
Publishers Weekly, August 29, 2011, page 67
School Library Journal, September 2011, page 176

Other books by the same author:
As Simple As It Seems, 2010
Jumping the Scratch, 2006
So B. It, 2004

Other books you might like:
Joan Bauer, *Close to Famous*, 2011
Marlane Kennedy, *Me and the Pumpkin Queen*, 2007
Suzanne Selfors, *Smells Like Dog*, 2010

553

DAVID L. WEITZMAN, Author/Illustrator

Pharaoh's Boat

(Boston: Houghton Mifflin Harcourt, 2009)

Subject(s): Shipbuilding; Ships; Ancient history
Age range(s): 9 - 11+
Major character(s): Cheops, Ruler (pharaoh)

Time period(s): 16th century; 20th century
Locale(s): Egypt

Summary: In *Pharaoh's Boat*, author and illustrator David Weitzman tells the tale of ancient history's most famous boat. 4,000 years in the past, the most talented artisans in Egypt work tirelessly on building the perfect ship for Cheops, the revered pharaoh. Cheops plans on taking the ship on an unparalleled expedition to a bright new land. As this story unfolds, Weitzman tells another tale involving the same ship. It is the 20th century, and archaeologists are working to recover and rebuild the famed boat belonging to the pharaoh. Filled with historical information about boats and shipbuilding, this volume contains illustrated endpapers detailing Egyptian life along the Nile.

Where it's reviewed:
Booklist, May 15, 2009, page 41
Bulletin of the Center for Children's Books, September 2009, page 45
Horn Book Magazine, May/June 2009, page 329
School Library Journal, April 2009, page 151

Other books by the same author:
Model T: Henry Ford Built a Legend, 2002
Locomotion: Building an Eight Wheeler, 1999
Old Ironsides: Americans Build A Fighting Ship, 1997
Superpower: The Making of a Steam Locomotive, 1995

Awards the book has won:
Blue Ribbon Awards: Non-fiction, 2009

Other books you might like:
David Kennett, *Pharaoh: Life and Afterlife of a God*, 2008
David Macaulay, *Pyramid*, 1975
Robert Sabuda, *Tutankhamen's Gift*, 1994
Edwin Tunis, *Oars, Sails and Steam: A Picture Book of Ships*, 1952

554

ROSEMARY WELLS
GAGRAM IBATOULLINE, Illustrator

On the Blue Comet

(Somerville, Massachusetts: Candlewick Press, 2010)

Subject(s): Time travel; Adventure; Railroads

Age range(s): 9 - 12+
Major character(s): Oscar Ogilvie, Time Traveler, 11-Year-Old, Nephew (of Carmen), Cousin (of Willa Sue); Harold Applegate, Vagrant; Carmen, Aunt (of Oscar); Willa Sue, Cousin (of Oscar)
Time period(s): Multiple Time Periods
Locale(s): California, United States; Cairo, Illinois; New York, United States

Summary: As the Great Depression bears down on America, 11-year-old Oscar Ogilvie is left in the care of his aunt while his father sets out for California in search of work. A chance encounter with a vagrant named Harold Applegate leads to a run-in with some dangerous bank robbers, and the event opens a mysterious portal in time that transports Oscar to California. When he gets there, however, he is 21 years old, and Oscar must travel

back and forth in time to find his father and the happy life they once shared. Rosemary Wells's *On the Blue Comet* includes illustrations by Bagram Ibatoulline.

Where it's reviewed:
Booklist, July 1, 2010, page 61
Bulletin of the Center for Children's Books, November 2010, page 154
Horn Book Magazine, Sept/Oct 2010, page 116
New York Times Book Review, December 9, 2010, page 14
School Library Journal, September 2010, page 167

Other books by the same author:
Lincoln and His Boys, 2008
Red Moon at Sharpsburg, 2007
Mary on Horseback: Three Mountain Stories, 2000
Leave Well Enough Alone, 1977

Other books you might like:
John Claude Bemis, *The Nine Pound Hammer*, 2009
Susan Cooper, *Victory*, 2006
Russell Freedman, *Children of the Great Depression*, 2005
Margaret Peterson Haddix, *Found*, 2008
Rebecca Stead, *When You Reach Me*, 2009

555

JACQUELINE WEST
POLY BERNATENE, Illustrator

The Shadows

(New York: Dial Books for Young Readers, 2010)

Series: Book of Elsewhere Series. Book 1
Subject(s): Fantasy; Magic; Ghosts

Age range(s): 9 - 12+
Major character(s): Olive Dunwoody, 11-Year-Old
Time period(s): 21st century; 2010s
Locale(s): United States

Summary: *The Books of Elsewhere: The Shadows* is the first novel in a series for young readers by Jacqueline West. In the novel, eleven-year-old Olive Dunwoody has just moved into an old Victorian mansion with her parents, who are mathematicians. Immediately, something doesn't seem quite right in the house—and that's not just because all of the furnishings from the last owner are still there. There is a group of talking cats that has taken up residence in the home, and Olive also notices that there is something strange about the paintings in the walls. She decides to investigate, and realizes that she can go through the paintings into a whole other world. Once through, however, she begins to worry that she won't be able to return home from Elsewhere.

Where it's reviewed:
Booklist, June 1, 2010, page 78
Bulletin of the Center for Children's Books, September 2010, page 50
Horn Book Guide. Fall 2010, page 78
Publishers Weekly, May 31, 2010, page 48
School Library Journal, May 2010, page 124

Other books by the same author:
Spellbound, 2011

Other books you might like:
Cornelia Funke, *Reckless*, 2010
Neil Gaiman, *Coraline*, 2002
Nykko, *The Shadow Spies*, 2009
Emily Rodda, *The Wizard of Rondo*, 2009
Maureen Sherry, *Walls within Walls*, 2010

556

LISA WHEELER
SOPHIE BLACKALL, Illustrator

Spinster Goose: Twisted Rhymes for Naughty Children
(New York: Atheneum Books, 2011)

Story type: Collection; Young Readers
Subject(s): Discipline; Poetry; Children

Age range(s): 6 - 8+

Summary: Lisa Wheeler reimagines the Mother Goose rhymes with illustrations by Sophie Blackall. Spinster Goose—Mother Goose's sister—shares alternative nursery rhymes for naughty children while teaching at a reform school for troublemakers. She deals with dirty children, whose hair harbors lice and feet are caked with toe jam, cigarette-smoking juveniles, and children who use swear words and tell white lies. Little Miss Muffet likes to eat chalk, while Mary tells tall tales about her little lamb. She twists classics such as Old Mother Hubbard, who becomes a custodian, and Little Jack Horner, who is a thumb-sucker. She also adds new rhymes such as "The Gum-Chewer," which is about a little girl who loves to chew gum and blow bubbles, and "The Swearer," which is about someone who likes to use curse words.

Where it's reviewed:
Booklist, February 15, 2011, page 114
Bulletin of the Center for Children's Books, July/August 2011, page 546
Horn Book Magazine, May/June 2011, page 114
Publishers Weekly, January 10, 2011, page 49
School Library Journal, March 2011, page 146

Other books by the same author:
Boogie Knights, 2008
Where Oh Where Is Santa Claus?, 2007
Castaway Cats, 2006
Sea Dogs: An Epic Ocean Operetta, 2004

Other books you might like:
Harry Allard, *Miss Nelson Is Missing!*, 1977
Chris Duffy, *Nursery Rhyme Comics: 50 Timeless Rhymes from 50 Celebrated Cartoonists*, 2011
Jenny Offill, *17 Things I'm Not Allowed to Do Anymore*, 2007
Michael Rex, *Goodnight Goon*, 2008
J. Otto Seibold, *Other Goose: Re-Nurseired!! and Re-Rhymed!!*, 2010

557

GLORIA WHELAN

After the Train
(New York: HarperCollins, 2009)

Subject(s): Antisemitism; Jews; Germans

Age range(s): 11 - 14+
Major character(s): Peter Liebig, 8th Grader, Adoptee; Dieter Kroner, 8th Grader; Herr Schmidt, Teacher; Mr. Liebig, Father (adopted Peter); Mrs. Liebig, Mother (adopted Peter)
Time period(s): 20th century; 1950s
Locale(s): Rolfen, Germany

Summary: In *After the Train*, a young man struggles to understand his identity after a shocking family secret comes to light. As Herr Schmidt drones on about the evils of the Nazis, eighth-grader Peter Liebig daydreams about how he'll spend his summer vacation. It's 1955 and the war doesn't seem relevant to Peter anymore. The young man soon discovers a secret his parents have kept from him for years—one that will consume his life. After having a horrible nightmare, Peter finds out that his was adopted and that his mother was a Jew who died in a concentration camp. Now, Peter must grapple with accepting his origins in a town where anti-Semitism is rampant and dangerous.

Where it's reviewed:
Booklist, December 1, 2008, page 41
Bulletin of the Center for Children's Books, January 2009, page 222
Horn Book Guide. Fall 2009, page 387
Publishers Weekly, December 22, 2008, page 52
School Library Journal, March 2009, page 158

Other books by the same author:
See What I See, 2011
Small Acts of Amazing Courage, 2011
The Locked Garden, 2009
The Disappeared, 2008
Summer of the War, 2006

Other books you might like:
Susan Campbell Bartoletti, *The Boy Who Dared*, 2008
Ann Clare LeZotte, *T4: A Novel*, 2008
Michael Morpurgo, *The Mozart Question*, 2008
Uri Orlev, *The Man from the Other Side*, 1991
Joan M. Wolf, *Someone Named Eva*, 2007

558

RUTH WHITE

A Month of Sundays
(New York: Farrar, Straus and Giroux, 2011)

Subject(s): Family; Cancer; Mother-daughter relations
Age range(s): 12 - 14+
Major character(s): April Garnet Rose, 14-Year-Old (girl), Daughter (of Betty and August), Niece (of June and Otis); Betty Rose, Mother (of April), Spouse (of August); June, Aunt (of April), Sister (of August),

Spouse (of Otis), Mother (of two boys)
Time period(s): 20th century; 1950s (1956)
Locale(s): Black River, Virginia

Summary: April Garnet Rose is apprehensive when she comes home from school and finds her mom and mom's best friend deep in conversation. Betty Rose has decided to leave Kentucky, where she's been working in a grocery store, to find a better job in Daytona Beach, Florida. While Betty and her friend look for work, 14-year-old April is sent to Black River, Virginia. She spends the summer of 1956 with Aunt June, the sister of the father April has never met, and June's husband and sons. At first resentful, April eventually warms to her aunt and the rural community. June, who has been diagnosed with terminal cancer, takes April along as she visits area churches of different faiths in search of God and maybe a miracle.

Where it's reviewed:
Booklist, August 1, 2011, page 44
Publishers Weekly, September 26, 2011, page 74
School Library Journal, October 2011, page 152
Voice of Youth Advocates, October 2011, page 396

Other books by the same author:
Way Down Deep, 2007
The Search for Belle Prater, 2005
Tadpole, 2003
Belle Prater's Boy, 1996

Other books you might like:
Peter Dickinson, *Healer*, 1983
Tess Hilmo, *With a Name Like Love*, 2011
Kimberly Griffiths Little, *The Healing Spell*, 2010
Sheila O'Connor, *Sparrow Road*, 2011
Clare Vanderpool, *Moon over Manifest*, 2010

559

RUTH WHITE

You'll Like It Here (Everybody Does)

(New York: Delacorte Press, 2011)

Subject(s): Science fiction; Utopian communities; Family

Age range(s): 9 - 12+

Major character(s): Meggie Blue, Sister (of David), Alien; David Blue, Brother (of Meggie), Alien
Time period(s): 21st century; 2010s
Locale(s): Fashion City, Planet—Imaginary; North Carolina, United States

Summary: Meggie and her family moved from California to North Carolina a long time ago because they didn't fit in with everyone else. Now, people in her hometown are starting to talk about how Meggie, her brother, her mother, and her grandfather are different from the other people in the town. In fact, Meggie and her family are aliens, and they have to leave their home quickly so they can escape in their spaceship. After leaving Earth, the family lands in Fashion City, a planet that seems a lot like Earth—except that all the people there are very similar. It doesn't take Meggie long to find out that the citizens of Fashion City are being brainwashed to keep

them all the same. Meggie must save her family from Fashion City before they become just like everyone else. This is a novel by Newbery Honor winner Ruth White.

Where it's reviewed:
Booklist, June 1, 2011, page 90
Bulletin of the Center for Children's Books, June 2011, page 498
Publishers Weekly, May 2, 2011, page 55
School Library Journal, July 2011, page 316

Other books by the same author:
A Month of Sundays, 2011
The Seach For Belle Prater, 2007
Way Down Deep, 2007
Belle Prater's Boy, 1998

Other books you might like:
Ellen Booraem, *The Unnameables*, 2008
Nina Kiriki Hoffman, *Thresholds*, 2010
Rebecca Stead, *First Light*, 2007
Sylvia Waugh, *Space Race*, 2000

560

DAVID WEISNER, Author/Illustrator

Art and Max

(Boston: Clarion Books, 2010)

Story type: Arts
Subject(s): Art; Drawing; Painting (Art)

Age range(s): 5 - 9+
Major character(s): Art, Reptile, Artist; Max, Reptile

Summary: Reptilian portrait painter Art and his artistically challenged lizard friend Max star in this picture story by David Wiesner. Art is a persnickety painter who quickly finds himself transformed when Max decides he wants to try his hand at painting, too. Though Max is excited to get started, he has one problem: He has no idea what to paint. When Art says, "You could paint me," Max takes the suggestion a little too literally and actually paints directly on Art, a move that results in a series of artistic complications that end with Art reduced to little more than a jumbled outline. Will Max be able to restore his friend, or will Art forever remain an abstract rendering of his former self?

Where it's reviewed:
Booklist, October 15, 2010, page 50
Bulletin of the Center for Children's Books, November 2010, page 156
Horn Book Magazine, Nov/Dec 2010, page 81
Publishers Weekly, November 8, 2010, page 32
School Library Journal, September 2010, page 135

Other books by the same author:
Free Fall, 2008
Flotsam, 2006
The Three Pigs, 2001
Sector 7, 1999
Tuesday, 1991

Other books you might like:
Allan Ahlberg, *The Pencil*, 2008

Crockett Johnson, *Harold and the Purple Crayon*, 1955
Tom Lichtenheld, *Bridget's Beret*, 2010
Agnes Rosenstiehl, *Silly Lilly and the Four Seasons*, 2008
Barney Saltzberg, *Beautiful Oops!*, 2010

561

DEBORAH WILES

Countdown

(New York: Scholastic, 2010)

Series: Sixties Trilogy. Book 1
Subject(s): United States history; Coming of age; Family

Age range(s): 10 - 13+
Major character(s): Franny Chapman, 12-Year-Old, Sister (of Jo Ellen and Drew); Jo Ellen, Sister (of Franny and Drew); Drew, Brother (of Franny and Jo Ellen)
Time period(s): 20th century; 1960s (1962)
Locale(s): Maryland, United States

Summary: Deborah Wiles's *Countdown*, the first novel in the Sixties Trilogy, centers on 12-year-old Franny Chapman, who comes of age in Maryland during the 1960s. As fears surrounding the Cuban Missile Crisis weigh heavily on the nation, Franny must also confront a series of personal dramas. Her relationship with her best friend is on the rocks, and Franny's older sister has mysteriously vanished. With air-raid drills growing commonplace at her school, Franny's inner and outer fears collide, sending her on a journey of discovery and redemption.

Where it's reviewed:
Booklist, May 1, 2010, page 84
Bulletin of the Center for Children's Books, July-August 2010, page 503
Horn Book Magazine, May\June 2010, page 95
Journal of Adolescent and Adul, May 2011, page 634
School Library Journal, July 2010, page 98

Other books by the same author:
Freedom Summer, 2001

Other books you might like:
David Almond, *The Fire-Eaters*, 2003
Elizabeth Partridge, *Marching for Freedom: Walk Together, Children, and Don't You Grow Weary*, 2009
Gary D. Schmidt, *The Wednesday Wars*, 2007
Ellen Wittlinger, *This Means War!*, 2010

562

MO WILLEMS
JON J. MUTH, Illustrator

City Dog, Country Frog

(New York: Hyperion Books for Children, 2010)

Subject(s): Frogs; Dogs; Friendship

Age range(s): 4 - 8+

Major character(s): Country Frog, Frog; City Dog, Dog
Time period(s): 21st century; 2010s
Locale(s): United States

Summary: *City Dog, Country Frog* is a story for young readers from bestselling author and Caldecott honoree, Mo Willems. The story follows the sweet and unlikely friendship of City Dog and Country Frog. It's springtime when City Dog meets Country Frog for the first time. Country Frog is eagerly awaiting a friend when he sees City Dog set free in the country. The pair enjoys playing games with one another. Their friendship and fun continues in the summer and fall, but something changes for the two animals when winter rolls around.

Where it's reviewed:
Booklist, March 15, 2010, page 48
Bulletin of the Center for Children's Books, July-August 2010, page 504
Horn Book Magazine, July\August 2010, page 97
Publishers Weekly, May 24, 2010, page 50
School Library Journal, May 2010, page 94

Awards the book has won:
Mitten Award (Michigan Library Association's Children's Services Division), 2011

Other books you might like:
Carin Berger, *Forever Friends*, 2010
Jan Brett, *Town Mouse, Country Mouse*, 1994
G. Brian Karas, *The Village Garage*, 2010
Barney Saltzberg, *All Around the Seasons*, 2010

563

MO WILLEMS, Author/Illustrator

Knuffle Bunny Free: An Unexpected Diversion

(New York: Balzer + Bray, 2010)

Subject(s): Toys; Coming of age; Grandparents
Age range(s): 4 - 7+
Major character(s): Trixie, Girl; Knuffle Bunny, Toy
Time period(s): 21st century; 2010s
Locale(s): Netherlands

Summary: Trixie and her adored stuffed rabbit, Knuffle Bunny, head off to Holland to visit Trixie's grandparents. Once they arrive, Trixie is shocked to discover Knuffle Bunny is missing: He has been left on the airplane. Suddenly, young Trixie is forced to grow up and contemplate a life without her much-loved companion. *Knuffle Bunny Free: An Unexpected Diversion* includes illustrations by the author, multiple Caldecott Honor-winning writer and illustrator Mo Willems.

Where it's reviewed:
Booklist, July 1, 2010, page 62
Bulletin of the Center for Children's Books, December 2010, page 213
Horn Book Guide, Sept/Oct 2010, page 68
Publishers Weekly, September 13, 2010, page 41
School Library Journal, October 2010, page 96

Other books by the same author:
Knuffle Bunny Too, 2007

Knuffle Bunny: A Cautionary Tale, 2004

Other books you might like:
Samantha Berger, *Martha Doesn't Share*, 2010
Susan Middleton Elya, *Adios, Tricycle*, 2009
Geoffrey Hayes, *Benny and Penny in the Toy Breaker*, 2010
Anita Lobel, *Nini Lost and Found*, 2010
Michael Rosen, *Red Ted and the Lost Things*, 2009

564

MO WILLEMS, Author/Illustrator

Naked Mole Rat Gets Dressed

(New York: Hyperion Book CH, 2009)

Subject(s): Individualism; Freedom; Imagination

Age range(s): 3 - 7+
Major character(s): Wilbur, Animal (naked mole rat)

Summary: In *Naked Mole Rat Gets Dressed*, a naked mole rat by the name of Wilbur has a fetish for clothing, which is unusual for a naked mole rat. He loves to dress up in different costumes that help him pretend that he is a variety of characters from his imagination. The other naked mole rats do not understand. They consult the eldest member of their community for advice on how to change Wilbur. They are all surprised when the elder proclaims that everyone is free to wear or not wear clothing. This opens the door to a new profession for Wilbur, who opens a clothing boutique and provides the naked mole rats who want to dress up with stylish new attire.

Where it's reviewed:
Booklist, November 15 2009, page 52
Horn Book Guide, Fall 2009, Page 351
Publishers Weekly, November 3 2009, page 57
School Library Journal, February 2009, page 88

Other books by the same author:
Edwina, The Dinosaur Who Didn't Know She Was Extinct, 2006
Knuffle Bunny: A Cautionary Tale, 2004

Other books you might like:
Lynne Rae Perkins, *The Cardboard Piano*, 2008
Amy Krouse Rosenthal, *Little Oink*, 2009
Marisabina Russo, *A Very Big Bunny*, 2010
Ellen Stoll Walsh, *For Pete's Sake*, 1998

565

MO WILLEMS, Author/Illustrator

Pigs Make Me Sneeze!

(New York: Hyperion, 2009)

Series: Elephant and Piggie Series. Book 10
Subject(s): Friendship; Animals; Elephants

Age range(s): 3 - 6+
Major character(s): Gerald, Elephant; Piggie, Pig; Dr. Cat, Doctor, Cat

Time period(s): 21st century; 2000s

Summary: In *Pigs Make Me Sneeze!* by Mo Willems, Gerald the elephant and Piggie are fast friends until the pachyderm comes down with a fit of sneezing. Gerald uses his gloomy logic to diagnose his condition as an allergy to pigs. The obvious cure means an end to Gerald's friendship with Piggie. But when Gerald seeks professional advice from Dr. Cat, he learns that he's not allergic to pigs—he simply has a cold. When Gerald races to Piggie to share to good news, he finds that he has shared his cold with his best friend. *Pigs Make Me Sneeze* is the 10th book in the Elephant and Piggie series.

Where it's reviewed:
Horn Book Magazine, January/December 2009, page 96
School Library Journal, December 2009, page 94

Other books by the same author:
I Share My Ice Cream, 2011
Elephants Cannot Dance, 2009
I Am Invited to a Party!, 2007
There Is a Bird on Your Head, 2007
Today I Will Fly, 2007

Other books you might like:
Irene Breznak, *Sneezy Louise*, 2009
Olga Cabral, *The Seven Sneezes*, 2009
Alexandra Siy, *Sneeze!*, 2007

566

MO WILLEMS, Author/Illustrator

Hooray for Amanda and Her Alligator!

(New York: Balzer + Bray, 2011)

Subject(s): Friendship; Toys; Alligators

Age range(s): 4 - 7+
Major character(s): Amanda, Girl; Alligator, Toy, Alligator; Panda, Toy (plu), Panda

Summary: In *Hooray for Amanda and Her Alligator!*, a little girl and her stuffed toy alligator share everyday adventures as they learn lessons together. Amanda and her cuddly green alligator like books, tickling, and talking. When Alligator learns that he was purchased on sale because no other child had chosen him, he realizes how important his friendship with Amanda is. Although Amanda and Alligator like surprises, an unexpected addition to their household threatens their friendship. Panda, Amanda's new toy, seems to be competing for his owner's attention and Alligator must try to understand that they can all be friends. Willems is also the author of the Knuffle Bunny books and the Elephant and Piggie series.

Where it's reviewed:
Booklist, March 1, 2011, page 74
Bulletin of the Center for Children's Books, May 2011, page 445
Horn Book Magazine, July/August 2011, page 139
Publishers Weekly, March 28, 2011, page 54
School Library Journal, May 2011, page 92

Other books by the same author:
Knuffle Bunny Free: An Unexpected Diversion, 2010
Knuffle Bunny Too, 2007
Edwina, the Dinosaur Who Didn't Know She Was Extinct, 2005
Leonardo, the Terrible Monster, 2005
Knuffle Bunny, 2004

Other books you might like:
Richard Egielski, *Captain Sky Blue*, 2010
Paul Hoppe, *The Woods*, 2011
Shirley Hughes, *Jonadab and Rita*, 2010
Satomi Ichikawa, *Come Fly with Me*, 2008
Michael Rosen, *Red Ted and the Lost Things*, 2009

567

MO WILLEMS, Author/Illustrator

I Broke My Trunk!

(New York: Hyperion, 2011)

Series: Elephant and Piggie Series. Book 14
Story type: Young Readers
Subject(s): Friendship; Imagination; Accidents

Age range(s): 3 - 6+

Major character(s): Gerald, Elephant, Friend (of Piggie); Piggie, Pig, Friend (of Gerald); Hippo, Hippopotamus, Friend (of Gerald); Rhino, Rhinoceros, Friend (of Gerald)

Summary: Gerald the elephant is fretful and cautious. His best friend, Piggie, is joyful and enthusiastic. When Piggie wants to know how Gerald broke his trunk, the elephant spins a wild tale that involves Hippo, Rhino, a piano, and Hippo's big sister. As Gerald describes the events that led to his injury, his story gets longer and more complicated. Big speech bubbles and simple text make it easy for young readers to become familiar with the words through repeat readings of this addition to the Elephant and Piggie series.

Where it's reviewed:
Booklist, April 15, 2011, page 60
Horn Book Guide, Fall 2011, page 342
School Library Journal, May 2011, page 92

Other books by the same author:
Happy Pig Day!, 2011
I am Going!: An Elephant and Piggie Book, 2010
We are in a Book!, 2010
Pigs Make Me Sneeze!, 2009
Today I Will Fly!, 2007

Other books you might like:
Denys Cazet, *The Octopus*, 2005
Simon James, *Dear Mr. Blueberry*, 1991
David Ezra Stein, *Interrupting Chicken*, 2010

568

KAREN LYNN WILLIAMS
FLOYD COOPER, Illustrator

A Beach Tail

(Honesdale, Pennsylvania: Boyds Mills Press, 2010)

Subject(s): Beaches; Father-son relations; Drawing

Age range(s): 4 - 7+
Major character(s): Greg, Child

Summary: *A Beach Tail* is a clever picture book for young readers from author Karen Lynn Williams and illustrator Floyd Cooper. Greg loves visiting the beach with his father, but there are two very important rules he must obey. The first is not to go into the water. The second is never to leave Sandy, the lion that Greg has drawn in the sand. Sandy was created with a stick and has a long tail that follows Greg wherever he goes. Fortunately, when Greg gets lost, he's able to follow Sandy's tail back to the beach umbrella where his dad remains. Cooper complements the story with realistic pastel illustrations of Greg's seaside adventures.

Where it's reviewed:
Horn Book Guide. Fall 2010, page 318
Publishers Weekly, January 11, 2010, page 46
School Library Journal, March 2010, page 136

Other books by the same author:
My Name Is Sangoel, 2009
Painted Dreams, 1998
Galimoto, 1990

Other books you might like:
Elisha Cooper, *Beach*, 2006
Laura Ljungkvist, *Follow the Line through the House*, 2007
Peter McCarty, *Jeremy Draws a Monster*, 2009
Laura Vaccaro Seeger, *What If?*, 2010
Deborah Underwood, *The Quiet Book*, 2010

569

RITA WILLIAMS-GARCIA

One Crazy Summer

(New York: Amistad, 2010)

Subject(s): Sisters; Mothers; African Americans

Age range(s): 9 - 12+
Major character(s): Delphine, 11-Year-Old; Vonetta, Sister (of Delphine); Fern, Sister (of Delphine); Cecile "Sister Izilla", Mother (of Delphine, Vonetta, and Fern)
Time period(s): 20th century; 1960s (1968)
Locale(s): Oakland, California

Summary: In *One Crazy Summer* by Rita Williams-Garcia, three young girls journey to Oakland, California, in 1968 to see their estranged mother. At just 11 years old, Delphine is used to playing caregiver to her little sisters, Vonetta and Fern, but she can't deny her disappointment when their mother, Cecile, makes it clear that their visit is unwelcome. Living on take-out and forced to follow Cecile's strict rules, Delphine and her sisters are puzzled by their mother's many mysterious guests. Cecile's involvement in a radical group is revealed when she enrolls her daughters in a Black Panther camp.

Where it's reviewed:
Booklist, February 1, 2010, page 61
Bulletin of the Center for Children's Books, February 2010, page 266
Horn Book Magazine, March/April 2010, page 77
New York Times Book Review, January 17, 2009, page 12
School Library Journal, March 2010, page 170

Awards the book has won:
Coretta Scott King Book Award: Author Award, 2011
Coretta Scott King Book Award: Text Award, 2011
Scott O'Dell Historical Fiction Award, 2011

Other books you might like:
Ruby Bridges, *Through My Eyes*, 1999
Christopher Paul Curtis, *The Watsons Go to Birmingham—1963*, 1995
Phillip M. Hoose, *Claudette Colvin: Twice Toward Justice*, 2009
Langston Hughes, *My People*, 2009
Kekla Magoon, *The Rock and the River*, 2009

570

KARMA WILSON
MARCELLUS HALL, Illustrator

The Cow Loves Cookies

(New York: Margaret K. McElderry Books, 2010)

Subject(s): Animals; Cows (Cattle); Humor

Age range(s): 3 - 7+
Time period(s): 21st century; 2010s
Locale(s): United States

Summary: *The Cow Loves Cookies* is a fun, entertaining, and humorous picture book for young readers from author Karma Wilson. This unique barnyard tale explores a bizarre situation happening on the farm. When the farmer checks on the animals, most of them are eating their expected food. The horses have their hay, the chickens eat their feed, the geese are content with corn, the pigs are fed slop, but something unusual is happening with the cows. They'll only eat cookies! Beautiful watercolor illustrations from Marcellus Hall accompanies the text in *The Cow Loves Cookies*.

Where it's reviewed:
Bulletin of the Center for Children's Books, July/August 2010, page 505
Horn Book Guide, Spring 2011, page 141
Publishers Weekly, June 28. 2010, page 126
School Library Journal, August 2010, page 88

Other books by the same author:
Hogwash!, 2011
Moose Tracks, 2006
Hilda Must Be Dancing, 2004
Bear Wants More, 2003

Awards the book has won:
Blue Ribbon Awards: Picture Books, 2010

Other books you might like:
Susan E. Goodman, *All in Just One Cookie*, 2006
John Himmelman, *Pigs to the Rescue*, 2010
Eric Litwin, *Pete the Cat: I Love My White Shoes*, 2010
Laura Joffe Numeroff, *If You Give a Mouse a Cookie*, 1985
Jean Reidy, *Too Pickley*, 2010

571

N.D. WILSON

The Dragon's Tooth

(New York: Random House, 2011)

Series: Ashtown Burials Series. Book 1
Subject(s): Family; Questing; Alternative worlds

Age range(s): 10 - 13+
Major character(s): Cyrus Smith, 12-Year-Old, Brother (of Daniel and Antigone); Antigone Smith, Sister (of Daniel and Cyrus), 13-Year-Old; Daniel, Brother (of Antigone and Cyrus); Dr. Phoenix, Villain

Summary: *The Dragon's Tooth* is the first book in author N.D. Wilson's Ashtown Burials series. Since the disappearance of their parents several years before, Cyrus and Antigone have lived in a crumbling motel operated by their older brother, Daniel. Then one evening, a mysterious man checks in and then dies in his room. The motel burns down, and Cyrus and Antigone are swept away to a bizarre town called Ashtown. There, a secret society invites the siblings to join and help conquer the world's greatest villains, particularly the sinister Dr. Phoenix. As Cyrus and Antigone embark on the adventure of their lives, they begin to wonder if this society is the key to finding out the truth about their parents. Wilson is also the author of the 100 Cupboards series.

Where it's reviewed:
Booklist, October 15, 2011, page 230
School Library Journal, November 2011, page 143

Other books by the same author:
The Chestnut King, 2010
Dandelion Fire, 2008
100 Cupboards, 2007
Leepike Ridge, 2007

Other books you might like:
Dan Gutman, *Mission Unstoppable*, 2011
Brandon Mull, *A World without Heroes*, 2011
Rick Riordan, *The Red Pyramid*, 2010

572

NATASHA WING
JULIA BRECKENREID, Illustrator

An Eye for Color: The Story of Josef Albers

(New York: Henry Holt and Co., 2008)

Subject(s): Artists; Art; Germans
Age range(s): 8 - 10+

Time period(s): 19th century-20th century
Locale(s): Germany; United States

Summary: Josef Albers was an artist, teacher, and pioneer in the field of color theory. In *An Eye for Color: The Story of Josef Albers*, author Natasha Wing and illustrator Julie Breckenreid join forces to bring young readers the remarkable story of Albers's passion for art and fascination with color. As a child in Germany, Josef was mesmerized by the way his housepainter father used color to change the mood and feel of clients' homes. When he came to America, Josef continued exploring his captivation with color, inspiring him to become a renowned scholar on the subject and an esteemed artist in his own right. Notes on the text and a list of activities accompany this volume.

Where it's reviewed:
Booklist, July 1, 2009, page 59
Horn Book Magazine, January/February 2010, page 106
School Library Journal, September 2009, page 149

Other books you might like:
M.T. Anderson, *Strange Mr. Satie*, 2003
David A. Carter, *Yellow Square: A Pop-up Book for Children of All Ages*, 2008
Menena Cottin, *The Black Book of Colors*, 2008
Jan Greenberg, *Action Jackson*, 2002
Rachel Victoria Rodriguez, *Through Georgia's Eyes*, 2006

573

JEANETTE WINTER, Author/Illustrator

Biblioburro: A True Story from Colombia

(New York: Beach Lane Books, 2010)

Subject(s): Libraries; Biographies; Books

Age range(s): 5 - 8+
Locale(s): Colombia

Summary: In *Biblioburro: A True Story from Colombia*, author and illustrator, Jeanette Winter relates the tale of Luis Soriano, a Colombian teacher who devises a unique method for bringing books to rural children. When Luis realizes that his own home is overrun with books, he puts two burros, Alpha and Beta, to work—one to carry him and the other to carry a supply of books to children in the nearby mountain communities. On his journey, Soriano faces challenges from would-be robbers as well as the burros' stubbornness. Winter's bold illustrations capture the beauty and diversity of the Colombian landscape.

Where it's reviewed:
Booklist, May 1, 2010, page 84
Horn Book Guide. Fall 2010, page 452
Publishers Weekly, May 24, 2010, page 52
School Library Journal, June 2010, page 92

Other books by the same author:
Nasreen's Secret School: A True Story from Afghanistan, 2009

The Librarian of Basra: A True Story from Iraq, 2005

Other books you might like:
Mary Virginia Fox, *A Visit to Colombia*, 2000
Heather Henson, *That Book Woman*, 2008
Margriet Ruurs, *My Librarian Is a Camel: How Books Are Brought to Children around the World*, 2005
Melanie Watt, *Have I Got a Book for You!*, 2009

574

JONAH WINTER
ANDRE CARRILHO, Illustrator

You Never Heard of Sandy Koufax?!

(New York: Schwartz & Wade Books, 2009)

Subject(s): Biographies; Baseball; Sports

Age range(s): 6 - 9+
Time period(s): 20th century-21st century; 1930s-2000s

Summary: In *You Never Heard of Sandy Koufax?!*, author Jonah Winter relates the story of the great Major League pitcher as told by an unnamed narrator. Beginning his career with the Brooklyn Dodgers in the 1950s, Sandy Koufax had a pitch and personality that were often unpredictable. After a brief hiatus, Koufax rejoined the Dodgers—who had relocated to L.A.—with with a steadier arm. Despite his career successes, Koufax, one of the league's few Jewish players, experienced prejudice but adhered to the rules of his faith, even when doing so resulted in his sitting out a 1965 World Series game. Andre Carrilho's illustrations capture the book's nostalgia and energy.

Where it's reviewed:
Booklist, December 15, 2009, page 197
Bulletin of the Center for Children's Books, March 2009, page 265
Horn Book Magazine, March/April 2009, page 216
Publishers Weekly, March 16, 2009, page 61
School Library Journal, March 2009, page 139

Other books by the same author:
Roberto Clemente: Pride of the Pittsburgh Pirates, 2008
Beisbol: Latino Baseball Poneers and Leagues, 2001
Fair Ball: 14 Great Stars from American Negro League, 1999

Other books you might like:
Lesa Cline-Ransome, *Satchel Paige*, 2000
Alan Gratz, *The Brooklyn Nine: A Novel in Nine Innings*, 2009
Paul B. Janeczko, *That Sweet Diamond: Baseball Poems*, 1998
Yona Zeldis McDonough, *Hammrin' Hank: The Story of Hank Greenberg*, 2006
Jack Norworth, *Take Me Out to the Ballgame*, 1993

575

JONAH WINTER
RED NOSE STUDIO, Illustrator

Here Comes the Garbage Barge

(New York: Schwartz & Wade Books, 2010)

Subject(s): Recycling; Environmental history; Humor

Age range(s): 5 - 8+

Summary: *Here Comes the Garbage Barge* is an award-winning picture book for young readers. The tale, based on a true story, teaches kids how to be more environmentally conscious in their actions. *Here Comes the Garbage Barge* tells the story of a small town that had so much garbage, all of its landfills were overflowing. With over 3,000 tons of garbage, the town had no choice but to load its refuse on a giant garbage barge and send it out to sea. The comical story, filled with lively illustrations from Red Nose Studio, highlights the importance of recycling and repurposing old items.

Where it's reviewed:
Bulletin of the Center for Children's Books, April 2010, page 358
Horn Book Guide, Fall 2010, page 318
New York Times Book Review, November 7, 2010, page 31
Publishers Weekly, January 11, 2010, page 47
School Library Journal, January 2010, page 84

Other books by the same author:
Steel Town, 2008

Awards the book has won:
Blue Ribbon Awards: Picture Books, 2010

Other books you might like:
Steven Kroll, *Stuff!: Reduce, Reuse, Recycle*, 2009
Paul Showers, *Where Does the Garbage Go?*, 1994
Janet S. Wong, *The Dumpster Diver*, 2007
Andrea Zimmerman, *Trashy Town*, 1999

576

MEG WIVIOTT
JOSEE BISAILLON, Illustrator

Benno and the Night of Broken Glass

(Minneapolis: Kar-Ben Publishing, 2010)

Subject(s): Holocaust, 1933-1945; Jews; Domestic cats

Age range(s): 7 - 9+
Major character(s): Benno, Cat; Sophie, Girl (Jewish)
Time period(s): 20th century; 1930s (1938)
Locale(s): Berlin, Germany

Summary: In this picture story, author Meg Wiviott tells the terrible story of *Kristallnacht* from the perspective of a feline witness named Benno. Benno likes his Berlin neighborhood where Jewish and Christian families live together serenely, and he is free to roam the bustling streets. But one horrifying night, a sea of black boots and brown shirts invades Benno's world, destroying property, burning the synagogue, and smashing the glass of storefronts. After the night of broken glass, Benno no longer sees the little girl Sophie or other Jewish families from the neighborhood. Rich illustrations by Josee Bisaillon convey the fear and violence of the infamous event; an afterword further explains the Holocaust to young readers.

Where it's reviewed:
Booklist, May 1, 2010, page 95
Horn Book Guide, Fall 2010, page 318
School Library Journal, May 2010, page 95

Other books you might like:
Karen Hesse, *The Cats in Krasinski Square*, 2004
Jo Hoestlandt, *Star of Fear, Star of Hope*, 1995
Tomi Ungerer, *Otto: The Autobiography of a Teddy Bear*, 2010

577

SALLIE WOLF, Author/Illustrator

The Robin Makes a Laughing Sound: A Birder's Journal

(Watertown, Massachusetts: Charlesbridge, 2010)

Subject(s): Nature; Birds; Science

Age range(s): 10 - 13+

Summary: *The Robin Makes a Laughing Sound: A Birder's Journal* is a collection of thoughtful musings and illustrations on the joys of nature for children and young adults from author Sallie Wolf. The journal entries included in this anthology offer reflections on the relaxation and tranquility that can be found in nature, specifically through the art of bird-watching. Wolf includes a list of North American birds that can be observed throughout the changing seasons, as well as artistic watercolor and ink sketches and illustrations. The journal entries offer pensive reflection, in the form of personal experiences or poetry, about encountering the beauty of nature.

Where it's reviewed:
Horn Book Guide. Fall 2010, page 438
School Library Journal, June 2010, page 139

Other books you might like:
Jim Arnosky, *Field Trips: Bug Hunting, Animal Tracking, Bird-Watching, Shore Walking*, 2002
Susan Blackaby, *Nest, Nook and Cranny*, 2010
Kristine O'Connell George, *Hummingbird Nest: A Journal of Poems*, 2004
Michael J. Rosen, *The Cuckoo's Haiku and Other Birding Poems*, 2009
Sophie Webb, *Looking for Seabirds: Journal from an Alaskan Voyage*, 2004

578

MEG WOLITZER

The Fingertips of Duncan Dorfman

(New York: Dutton Children's Books, 2011)

Story type: Young Adult; Young Readers
Subject(s): Games; Friendship; Contests

Age range(s): 9 - 12+
Major character(s): Duncan Dorfman, 12-Year-Old (magical); April Blunt, 12-Year-Old (nerd); Nate Saviano, 12-Year-Old (homeschooled)
Time period(s): 21st century; 2010s
Locale(s): United States

Summary: A competition brings together three kids with nothing in common but their love for the game of Scrabble in this book for young readers by Meg Wolitzer. Nate Saviano is a homeschooled boy, lonely and desperate for his father's approval. April Blunt is the only nerd in her family of sports enthusiasts, vying for the affections of a boy she has seen only once. Duncan Dorfman is new to town and worries about his single mother while they adjust to a new life. Duncan possesses the magical ability to feel and see words that he places his fingers on, knowing what they are without having to look at them. This power comes in handy during the national Youth Scrabble Tournament, where he crosses paths with fellow competitors Nate and April.

Where it's reviewed:
Booklist, September, 15 2011, page 178
Publishers Weekly, August, 1 2011, page 48
School Library Journal, September 2011, page 178

Other books you might like:
Jody Feldman, *The Seventh Level*, 2010
Dan Gutman, *The Million Dollar Kick*, 2001
E.L. Konigsburg, *The View from Saturday*, 1996
Louis Sachar, *The Cardturner: A Novel about a King, a Queen, and a Joker*, 2010
Adam Selzer, *I Put a Spell On You*, 2008

579

MARYROSE WOOD

JON KLASSEN, Illustrator

The Mysterious Howling

(New York: Balzer + Bray, 2010)

Series: Incorrigible Children of Ashton Place Series. Book 1
Subject(s): Orphans; Feral children; Christmas

Age range(s): 9 - 12+
Major character(s): Miss Penelope Lumley, 15-Year-Old, Governess; Alexander, Child (feral); Cassiopeia, Child (feral); Beowulf, Child (feral)
Time period(s): 19th century
Locale(s): United Kingdom

Summary: Governess Miss Penelope Lumley has her work cut out for her in Maryrose Wood's *The Mysterious Howling*, the first installment in a series. This outing finds the 15-year-old nanny placed in charge of three wild siblings—and wild they certainly are. Alexander, Cassiopeia, and Beowulf were raised by wolves, and now Penelope must tame these feral creatures in time for a lavish Christmas ball. *The Mysterious Howling* includes illustrations by Jon Klassen.

Where it's reviewed:
Booklist, December 15, 2009, page 39
Bulletin of the Center for Children's Books, April 2010, page 359
Horn Book Magazine, May/June 2010, page 97
School Library Journal, May 2010, page 125

Other books by the same author:
The Hidden Gallery, 2011

Other books you might like:
Vivian French, *The Robe of Skulls*, 2008
Lynne Jonell, *Emmy and the Home for Troubled Girls*, 2008
Lemony Snicket, *The Bad Beginning*, 1999
Paul Stewart, *Curse of the Night Wolf*, 2007

580

JACQUELINE WOODSON
SOPHIE BLACKALL, Illustrator

Pecan Pie Baby

(New York: G.P. Putnam's Sons, 2010)

Subject(s): Pregnancy; Mother-daughter relations; Single parent family

Age range(s): 3 - 7+
Major character(s): Gia, Child
Time period(s): 21st century; 2010s

Summary: In Jacqueline Woodson's *Pecan Pie Baby*, young Gia is frustrated with all the hoopla surrounding her pregnant mother and the impending birth of her sibling. When she expresses her feelings, she is banished to her room, where she eventually has a long talk with her mother about the changes on the horizon, the hopes and fears surrounding the new baby, and the unique joys the event holds for the whole family. This volume includes illustrations by Sophie Blackall.

Where it's reviewed:
Booklist, August 2010, page 61
Bulletin of the Center for Children's Books, January 2011, page 256
Horn Book Magazine, Nov/Dec 2010, page 82
Publishers Weekly, September 27, 2010, page 59
School Library Journal, October 2010, page 97

Other books by the same author:
Show Way, 2005
Our Gracie Aunt, 2002

Other books you might like:
Martha Alexander, *Nobody Asked Me If I Wanted a Baby Sister*, 1977
Kathi Appelt, *Brand-New Baby Blues*, 2010
John Burningham, *There's Going to Be a Baby*, 2010
Lynn Reiser, *My Baby and Me*, 2008

581

JACQUELINE WOODSON

Peace, Locomotion

(New York: G.P. Putnam's Sons, 2009)

Subject(s): Family; Death; Grief

Age range(s): 9 - 11+

Major character(s): Lonnie, Orphan, Brother (of Lili), Foster Child; Lili, Foster Child, Orphan, Sister (of Lonnie)

Time period(s): 21st century; 2000s

Locale(s): New York, New York

Summary: Jacqueline Woodson's *Peace, Locomotion* is the sequel to *Locomotion*, which was a National Book Award finalist in 2003. In this book, the two siblings from the first book, Lonnie and Lili, are now living with different foster families, a result of the death of their parents in a fire. Lonnie is in sixth grade and writes letters to his little sister at her new home. The letters focus on the simple everyday things that remind him of her, their parents, and their former life together. These simple observations remind readers of the things they take for granted in their communities and families and explore issues related to separation and war.

Where it's reviewed:
Bulletin of the Center for Children's Books, January 2009, page 223
Horn Book Magazine, January/February 2009, Page 105
School Library Journal, January 2009, Page 124

Other books by the same author:
After Tupac and D Foster, 2008
Locomotion, 2003

Other books you might like:
Andrew Clements, *Extra Credit*, 2009
Monalisa DeGross, *Donavan's Double Trouble*, 2008
Cynthia Lord, *Touch Blue*, 2010
Rosanne Parry, *Heart of a Shepherd*, 2009

582

ERIC WRIGHT, Author/Illustrator

Frankie Pickle and the Closet of Doom

(New York: Simon and Schuster, 2009)

Subject(s): Adventure; Humor; Imagination

Age range(s): 7 - 10+

Major character(s): Franklin "Frankie Picke" Lorenzo Piccolini, Child; Argyle, Sidekick (of Frankie Pickle)

Time period(s): 21st century; 2000s

Summary: In Eric Wight's *Frankie Pickle and the Closet of Doom*, Franklin Lorenzo Piccolini—otherwise known as Frankie Pickle—is a kid with a big imagination and an absolute abhorrence for cleaning his room. Fed up, his mother tells Frankie to leave the room as dirty as can be, and the little scamp obliges. The messy room soon captures his imagination, and he and his pal Argyle are navigating the wild terrain of the bedroom, which is transformed into jungle. Wight provides the illustrations to this volume.

Where it's reviewed:
Publishers Weekly, May 19, 2009, page 55
School Library Journal, July 2009, page 69

Other books by the same author:
Frankie Pickle and the Mathematical Menace, 2011
Frankie Pickle and the Pine Run 3000, 2010

Other books you might like:
Frank Cammuso, *Knights of the Lunch Table: The Dodgeball Chronicles*, 2008
Betty MacDonald, *Hello, Mrs. Piggle Wiggle*, 1957
Peggy Parish, *Amelia Bedelia*, 1963
Dav Pilkey, *The Adventures of Captain Underpants: An Epic Novel*, 1997
J. Torres, *Alison Dare: Little Miss Adventures*, 2002

583

DAN YACCARINO, Author/Illustrator

All the Way to America: The Story of a Big Italian Family and a Little Shovel

(New York: Alfred A. Knopf, 2011)

Subject(s): Family; Immigrants; United States

Age range(s): 4 - 8+

Summary: In this book, Dan Yaccarino shares the story of how his family came to America. When Yaccarino's great-grandfather was a young man, he left Italy and traveled to Ellis Island in New York. He could only take a few things with him on his journey, but he managed to bring a small shovel. When he arrived in America, immigrant Michele Iaccarino changed his name to Michael Yaccarino. He worked hard and made a life for himself and his family. Over the years, Yaccarino passed the shovel and his work ethic down through the many generations of his family.

Where it's reviewed:
Booklist, March 1, 2011, page 146
Publishers Weekly, January 24, 2011, page 19
School Library Journal, March 2011, page 146

Other books by the same author:
The Fantastic Undersea World of Jacques Cousteau, 2009
Every Friday, 2007

Other books you might like:
Crescent Dragonwagon, *Home Place*, 1990
Susan E. Goodman, *On This Spot: An Expedition Back through Time*, 2006
Kathleen Krull, *The Boy on Fairfield Street*, 2004
Susan Kuklin, *How My Family Lives in America*, 1992
Bonnie Pryor, *The Dream Jar*, 1996

584

DAN YACCARINO, Author/Illustrator

The Fantastic Undersea Life of Jacques Cousteau

(New York: Knopf Books for Young Readers, 2009)

Subject(s): Oceanography; Marine biology; Biographies

Age range(s): 5 - 8+

Summary: Celebrated children's author and illustrator Dan Yaccarino presents a picture-filled biography of renowned oceanographer Jacques Cousteau. *The Fantastic Undersea Life of Jacques Cousteau* gives young readers a glimpse of the man behind the myth, exploring Cousteau's wide-ranging work and thrilling adventures. With his team of assistants and colleagues, he developed new equipment for capturing undersea life on film and for diving. In creating television shows, movies, and books, Cousteau and his team gave the world an unparalleled view of life under the sea and the efforts that need to be undertaken to preserve it.

Where it's reviewed:
Booklist, January 1, 2009, page 86
Bulletin of the Center for Children's Books, March 2009, page 302
Horn Book Magazine, July/August 2009, page 442
Publishers Weekly, March 16, 2009, page 61
School Library Journal, March 2009, page 139

Other books you might like:
Jennifer Berne, *Manfish*, 2008
Douglas Florian, *In the Swim*, 1997
Steve Jenkins, *Down, Down, Down: A Journey to the Bottom of the Sea*, 2009

585

AL YANKOVIC
WES HARGIS, Illustrator

When I Grow Up

(New York: HarperCollins, 2011)

Story type: Young Readers
Subject(s): Rhyme; Children; Schools

Age range(s): 5 - 8+
Major character(s): Billy, 8-Year-Old, Student (of Mrs. Krupp); Mrs. Krupp, Teacher (of Billy)

Summary: Comedian Al "Weird Al" Yankovic's first children's book focuses on a child's imagination. During show-and-tell at school, eight-year-old Billy discusses in rhyme what he wants to be when he grows up. He has many interests and some of his varied career choices include snail trainer, pickle inspector, sumo wrestler, giraffe milker, gorilla masseuse, chef, deodorant tester, artist, and rodeo clown. Billy keeps listing occupations even after his teacher, Mrs. Krupp, tries to tell him that he is out of time. He finally concludes that he'd like to be a teacher just like Mrs. Krupp.

Where it's reviewed:
Booklist, January 1, 2011, page 114
Horn Book Guide, Fall 2011, page 336
Publishers Weekly, December 6, 2010, page 47
School Library Journal, January 2011, page 86

Other books you might like:
Jon Agee, *The Retired Kid*, 2009
Elizabeth Cody Kimmel, *The Top Job*, 2007
Sally Lloyd-Jones, *How to Get a Job...by Me, the Boss*, 2011
Kate McMullan, *Bulldog's Big Day*, 2011

586

LOUISE YATES, Author/Illustrator

Dog Loves Books

(New York: Alfred A. Knopf, 2010)

Subject(s): Dogs; Books and reading; Shopping

Age range(s): 4 - 8+
Major character(s): Dog, Dog, Store Owner
Time period(s): 21st century; 2010s

Summary: In *Dog Loves Books*, author and illustrator Louise Yates tells the story of a little white pooch with a passion for the written word. Dog adores books to such an extent that he opens his own bookshop. As he waits for the customers to pour in, he becomes engrossed in the books surrounding him. When his patrons arrive, Dog is filled with information and advice on which books they would enjoy.

Where it's reviewed:
Horn Book Guide, Spring 2011, page 51
School Library Journal, August 2010, page 88

Other books you might like:
Leonid Gore, *The Wonderful Book*, 2010
Will Hillenbrand, *My Book Box*, 2006
Tad Hills, *How Rocket Learned to Read*, 2010
Anna McQuinn, *Lola Loves Stories*, 2010

587

LISA YEE
DAN SANTAT, Illustrator

Bobby versus Girls (Accidentally)

(New York: Arthur A. Levine Books, 2009)

Subject(s): Friendship; Schools; Social conditions

Age range(s): 9 - 11+
Major character(s): Robert "Bobby" Carver Ellis-Chan, Brother (of Annie and Casey), Friend (of Holly and Chess), Student (of Mrs. Carlson), Son (of Mrs. and Mrs. Ellis-Chan), 4th Grader; Holly Harper, Friend (of Bobby); Mr. Ellis-Chan, Father (of Bobby, Annie, and Casey), Football Player (former); Mrs. Ellis-Chan, Mother (of Bobby, Annie, and Casey), Businesswoman; Annie, Sister (of Bobby and Casey), Football Player, Daughter (of Mr. and Mrs. Ellis-

Chan); Casey, Daughter (of Mr. and Mrs. Ellis-Chan), Sister (of Bobby and Annie), 4-Year-Old; Chess Kapur, Friend (of Bobby); Mrs. Carlson, Teacher (of Bobby's class)
Time period(s): 21st century; 2000s
Locale(s): Rancho Rosetta, California

Summary: In *Bobby Versus Girls (Accidentally)* by Lisa Yee, Robert Carver Ellis-Chan—Bobby to his friends—is a fourth grader with aspirations of popularity and secrets to keep. His classmates might find his family a bit unusual, with a former pro-football player for a father, a mother who runs the Go Girly Girl company, an older sister who plays high school football, and a younger sister who adores him. Then there's his best friend, Holly Harper, a girl who has witnessed Bobby in his most embarrassing moments—wearing curlers, for instance. When Bobby and Holly both run for student council, the election escalates into an all-out battle of the sexes with more than the position of student council representative at stake.

Where it's reviewed:
Booklist, October 15, 2009, page 52
Bulletin of the Center for Children's Books, December 2009, page 174
Horn Book Magazine, September/October 2009, page 577
Publishers Weekly, August 31, 2009, page 58
School Library Journal, November 2009, page 91

Other books by the same author:
Bobby the Brave (Sometimes), 2010

Other books you might like:
Andrew Clements, *Extra Credit*, 2009
Andrew Clements, *No Talking*, 2007
Jennifer L. Holm, *The Trouble with May Amelia*, 2011
Eric Luper, *Jeremy Bender vs the Cupcake Cadets*, 2011

588

EUGENE YELCHIN

Breaking Stalin's Nose

(New York: Henry Holt, 2011)

Story type: Historical
Subject(s): Father-son relations; History; Communism

Age range(s): 9 - 11+
Major character(s): Sasha Zaichik, 10-Year-Old
Time period(s): 20th century; 1920s-1950s (1928-1953)
Locale(s): Russia

Summary: Ten-year-old Sasha Zaichik is just like any other typical boy living in Stalin-era Russia. He has known the laws of the Soviet Young Pioneers since he was a little boy. Like his father, a state security secret police officer, he is a devoted Communist. When the day finally arrives for Sasha to join the Soviet Young Pioneers, however, nothing seems to go right. Sasha accidentally breaks his classmate's glasses in a friendly snowball fight. Then he inadvertently mars the Stalin statue at his school. To make matters worse, his father

was arrested. Illustrator and author Eugene Yelchin received several awards through the years, including a 2012 Newbery Honor award for this title.

Where it's reviewed:
Booklist, October 15, 2011, page 56
Horn Book Magazine, September/October 2011, page 106
Publishers Weekly, August 1, 2011, page 48
School Library Journal, August 2011, page 125

Other books you might like:
Peter Sis, *The Wall: Growing up behind the Iron Curtain*, 2007
Guo Yue, *Little Leap Forward*, 2008

589

THOMAS F. YEZERSKI, Author/Illustrator

Meadowlands: A Wetlands Survival Story

(New York: Farrar, Straus, Giroux, 2011)

Subject(s): Wildlife conservation; Animals; Swamps

Summary: Author and illustrator Thomas F. Yezerski shares the history of New Jersey's Meadowlands—an area near and dear to his heart—in this volume for young readers. Prior to the arrival of European settlers, the 20,000-acre marshland was home to hundreds of different types of plants and animals. Over time, however, an increase in human activity and pollution in the area resulted in near-total destruction of the wetland by the 1960s. Since then, conservationists have worked tirelessly to restore the Meadowlands to its former glory, and their efforts are starting to make a difference. The wetland area and its many plants and animals are starting to bounce back. Yezerski's watercolor illustrations provide visual support for the text, detailing both the destruction and the revival of the Meadowlands.

Where it's reviewed:
Booklist, March 1, 2011, page 54
Bulletin of the Center for Children's Books, May 2011, page 447
Horn Book Magazine, March/April 2011, page 145
Publishers Weekly, February 28, 2011, page 54
School Library Journal, March 2011, page 46

Other books by the same author:
A Full Hand, 2002

Other books you might like:
Jim Arnosky, *The Brook Book: Exploring the Smallest Streams*, 2008
Mary Brown, *Wings along the Waterway*, 1999
Andrew Campbell, *Protecting Wetlands*, 2005
Betsy Franco, *Pond Circle*, 2009
Megan McDonald, *Judy Moody Saves the World!*, 2002

590

JANE YOLEN
HEIDI E. Y. STEMPLE, Co-Author
ANNE-SOPHIE LANQUETIN, Illustrator

Not All Princesses Dress in Pink

(New York: Simon & Schuster, 2010)

Subject(s): Feminism; Children: Childhood

Age range(s): 4 - 8+

Summary: In *Not All Princesses Dress in Pink*, Caldecott-winning author Jane Yolen—along with co-author Heidi E.Y. Stemple and illustrator Anne-Sophie Lanquetin—show young girls everywhere that they don't have to subscribe to the traditional image of frilly dresses and pink bows to be considered princesses. Through lyrical rhymes such as "some princesses wear their jewels while fixing things with power tools," the authors show that girls can do anything they set their minds to.

Where it's reviewed:
Catholic Library World, June 2011, page 231
School Library Journal, June 2010, page 86

Other books by the same author:
The Barefoot Book of Dance Stories, 2010
Not One Damsel In Distress, 2000
Sleeping Ugly, 1991

Other books you might like:
Babette Cole, *Prince Cinders*, 1987
Kelly DiPucchio, *Grace for President*, 2008
Florence Parry Heide, *Princess Hyacinth: The Surprising Tale of a Girl Who Floated*, 2009
Anna Quindlen, *Happily Ever After*, 1997
Charlotte Zolotow, *William's Doll*, 1972

591

CYBELE YOUNG

Ten Birds

(Toronto: Kids Can Press, 2011)

Story type: Young Readers
Subject(s): Birds; Learning; Children

Age range(s): 6 - 8+
Major character(s): Highly Satisfactory, Bird; Brilliant, Bird; Needs Improvement, Bird

Summary: In this counting book for young readers, author and illustrator Cybele Young teaches problem-solving skills. Ten birds try to determine the best way to cross a river. A bridge lies right in front of them, but they do not seem to be able to see it, so they brainstorm other ways to cross the body of water. The birds use items tossed along the sides of the riverbank to help them cross the river. A bird named Highly Satisfactory builds a raft, while Brilliant assembles a pair of stilts. All of the birds develop unique contraptions to get across the river, except for a bird named Needs Improvement, who uses the most obvious route. Young won the 2011 Governor General's Literary Award for Children's Literature—

Illustration for the pen-and-ink artwork used throughout the book.

Where it's reviewed:
Booklist, May 1, 2011, page 97
Horn Book Magazine, May/June 2011, page 79
School Library Journal, April 2011, page 165

Other books by the same author:
A Few Blocks, 2011

Awards the book has won:
Governor General's Literary Awards: Children's Literature (Text and Illustration), 2011

Other books you might like:
Mitsumasa Anno, *Anno's Magic Seeds*, 1995
David A. Carter, *One Red Dot*, 2005
Arthur Geisert, *Pigs from 1 to 10*, 1992
Masayuki Sebe, *Let's Count to 100!*, 2011

592

ED YOUNG, Author/Illustrator

The House Baba Built: An Artist's Childhood in China

(New York: Little, Brown Books for Young Readers, 2011)

Subject(s): Autobiographies; Artists; China

Age range(s): 7 - 10+

Summary: Award-winning illustrator Ed Young recounts his unusual and enchanting childhood in this picture story for young readers. Born in China in 1931, Young spent most of his early years in an enclave built by his father to keep their extended family safe from the dangers of war. A sprawling construction of brick and imagination, the house that Young's "baba" created grew and adapted to accommodate its inhabitants' needs. Within its walls, Young and his siblings raised silkworms, roller skated, played, danced, and shared their good fortune with neighbors in need. Foldout spreads reveal the intricacies of the house and the delights of Ed Young's boyhood.

Where it's reviewed:
Booklist, September 1, 2011, page 102
Horn Book Magazine, September/October 2011, page 118
Publishers Weekly, August 15, 2011, page 118
School Library Journal, September 2011, page 187

Other books by the same author:
Beyond the Great Mountains: A Visual Poem about China, 2005
Voices of the Heart, 1997

Other books you might like:
Andrea Cheng, *Shanghai Messenger*, 2005
Jean Fritz, *Homesick: My Own Story*, 1982

Jessica Gunderson, *The Emperor's Painting: A Story of Ancient China*, 2009

Philip Sendak, *In Grandpa's House*, 1985

593

HYEWON YUM, Author/Illustrator

The Twins' Blanket

(New York: Farrar Straus Giroux, 2011)

Story type: Contemporary
Subject(s): Children; Twins; Childhood

Age range(s): 3 - 6+

Summary: In this illustrated children's book, author Hyewon Yum tells a story about two twin toddlers who grow up together, sharing everything including their bed and their blanket. When the twins are five, however, their parents decide it's time for them to become more independent. So, the two twins are given separate blankets. This is a difficult transition at first, as the twins only know how to share their old, single blanket. With some trial and error, however, they learn that they do not have to share everything. In fact, they learn it can be rewarding to have some of your things, too.

Where it's reviewed:
Booklist, August 2011, page 56
Horn Book Magazine, September/October 2011, page 81
Publishers Weekly, May 23, 2011, page 42
Publishers Weekly, August 2011, page 56

Other books by the same author:
There Are No Scary Wolves, 2010
Last Night, 2008

Other books you might like:
Kevin Henkes, *Owen*, 1993
Grace Lin, *Ling and Ting: Not Exactly the Same!*, 2010
Alison McGhee, *Bye-Bye, Crib*, 2008
Charlotte Voake, *Hello Twins*, 2008

594

NAOMI FLINK ZUCKER

Callie's Rules

(New York: Egmont USA, 2011)

Subject(s): Individualism; Family life; Middle schools
Age range(s): 9 - 11+
Major character(s): Callie Jones, 11-Year-Old, 6th Grader, Classmate (of Valeri); Valeri Van Dine, Classmate (of Callie), Daughter (of Sandy); Sandy Van Dine, Mother (of Valeri)
Time period(s): 21st century; 2000s
Locale(s): New Jersey, United States

Summary: In this novel for children and young adults by Naomi Zucker, 11-year-old Callie Jones must learn the rules of middle school when she starts sixth grade. In the Joneses' home, Callie's artist mother and attorney father impose few rules on their seven children. So when free-spirited Callie is ridiculed for biking to school, she learns the first of several painful lessons about acceptable middle school behavior. Wanting to fit in, Callie keeps a running list of these silly rules and tries to follow them. When a classmate's mother sets out to replace Halloween with a patriotic harvest festival, however, Callie decides it's time to stand up for the principles of individuality that she and her family have always embraced.

Where it's reviewed:
Booklist, September 1, 2009, page 88
Horn Book Guide, Spring 2010, page 87
Publishers Weekly, August 10, 2009, page 55
School Library Journal, August 2009, page 117

Other books by the same author:
Write On, Callie Jones, 2010
Benno's Bear, 2001

Other books you might like:
Meg Cabot, *Allie Finkle's Rules for Girls*, 2008
Martha Freeman, *The Year My Parents Ruined My Life*, 1997
Ann Haywood Leal, *Also Known as Harper*, 2009
Phyllis Reynolds Naylor, *Faith, Hope, and Ivy June*, 2009

Books, Reading and Publishing: 2009 to 2011
by
Pam Spencer Holley

The past three years have seen a lot of changes in the world of books, but the most disruptive to many was the bankruptcy and closing of all the Borders bookstores in 2011. Fortunately there are independents, other chains, and online stores that provide many different avenues for purchase of a book. Libraries are still prominent and anyone can check out a book from them at no cost. Ebooks, which were dismissed several years ago, are suddenly the hot new way to read and many devices are being produced to meet the demand. As with any new industry, there are problems as publishers are imposing limits on what and how libraries can loan ebooks—and, in some instances, are not allowing libraries access to any of their publications. It's probably safe to say that the decade of the 2010s will be a roller coaster ride for books, publishers, and readers as everyone adjusts to change.

The YA field is burgeoning with sales and many new authors writing for teens, including some seasoned authors from the adult field and others making their debut. The members of such prominent committees as the Printz, Morris and Edwards from the Young Adult Library Services Association (YALSA) of the American Library Association (ALA) have had a wealth of books and authors from which to select the award winners. The Margaret A. Edwards is given to an author based on his or her output of work for young adults; over the past three years it has been awarded to a writer of contemporary problem novels (Laurie Halse Anderson), a writer known for his nonfiction works (Jim Murphy), and a fantasy author (Sir Terry Pratchett). The recipients of the Printz Award, for the best literary work for young adults, have been a work of dystopian fiction (*Ship Breaker* by Paolo Bacigalupi), a dark comedy (*Going Bovine* by Libba Bray) and a first novel (*Where Things Come Back* by John Corey Whaley). The Morris, awarded to a debut work by a first-time author writing for teens, has been received by two contemporary works, one of grief solved by the laws of physics (*The Freak Observer* by Blythe Woolston) and another of love, friendship, and photography (L.K. Madigan's *Flash Burnout*) as well as a supernatural retelling of Rumpelstiltskin (*A Curse Dark as Gold* by Elizabeth C. Bunce). At long last YA nonfiction received its own award with the first YALSA Award for Excellence in Nonfiction for Young Adults granted in 2010. Although the first three have been received by biographies, each subject has been uniquely different and from different centuries. These three include *Charles and Emma* by Deborah Heiligman, *Janis Joplin* by Ann Angel, and Steve Sheinken's *Notorious Benedict Arnold*. Suffice it to say that YA books are "alive and well."

Censorship, or Being Politically Correct?

Long a staple in required reading for high school students, as political correctness has become the norm, Mark Twain's works *Tom Sawyer* and *Huckleberry Finn* have met increasing resistance from parents and students because of the "n" word, or nigger. One Twain scholar, Alan Gribben, began to feel uncomfortable with the word after moving to the South and meeting his daughter's best friend, an African-American girl. When he realized that there were 219 instances of the "n" word in *Huck Finn*, he switched them all to the word "slave." His expurgated versions of *Tom* and *Huck* have been printed by New South, although he did express some concerns about what other scholars may think (Schultz, 2011).

Graphic Novels

In the first decade of the 2000s, manga was popular in the United States, but recently there has been an ebbing in sales and closure of some publishing houses. Part of the problem can be traced to the illegally scanned manga (called scanlations) that has become available free online. In addition, there are fewer female fans and new readers (PW, 2010). Tor Publishers, however, has joined with the manga house Seven Seas to release a series of graphic novels. The initial volume will be *The Eye of the World* by Robert Jordan. Noted sci-fi author Orson Scott Card and his daughter Emily will write a manga science fiction series entitled *Laddertop*. In addition, two original graphic novels were scheduled for released in 2011: a steampunk entry by Jared Axelrod and Steve Walker called *Battle of Blood and Ink* while Jonathan Case is working on a mashup of beach and monster movies from the 1960s to be titled *Dear Creature* (Reid, 2011).

YALSA offers a yearly selection list entitled Great Graphic Novels, which is helpful in collection development. Some of YALSA's recent choices on the selected Top Ten Great Graphic Novels for Teens include the ghost story entitled *Anya's Ghost* and a more realistic account concerning a missing brother in Iran in *Zahra's Paradise*. The 2011 list included *Yummy*, the true story of a young gangster's life; an undead person living on "the other side" in *Ghostopolis*; and, from the 2010 list, a fantasy world under a bayou in a book of the same name and the devastation after Katrina in *A.D.: New Orleans after the Deluge*.

Middle and high school boys, often classified as reluctant readers, appear to be more likely to pick up a graphic novel about war or true crime (Maury, 2011). When reviewing the Great Graphic Novel lists for 2010-2012 it is encouraging that the number of nonfiction titles on the lists is increasing steadily, from only four in 2010 to ten on the most recent list. The nonfiction titles on these three lists include selections about Sacco and Vanzetti, violence, gangs, war in Afghanistan as well as Iran, and, perhaps a stretch, two books about mythology, which often involve war. http://www.ala.org/yalsa/ggnt)

How Do Teens Choose What to Read Next?

A study of various reading habits indicated the biggest factor in helping a teen decide what to pick up or buy is whether or not the book is next in a series, or sequel to a title already read. The least influential were celebrity endorsements. In between influences ranged from being familiar with the author or verbiage on the jacket copy and continuing downwards to an award sticker, praiseworthy quotes on the book, or its display on a special table in a store.

People are also important in the book selection process as teens do turn to their parents, teachers, and close friends for reading ideas. Librarians were able to affect 24% of the teen decisions about what to read next, although bookstores did not fare as well. In many cases, booksellers don't have the opportunity to develop a relationship with a teen that is strong enough that the teen trusts their opinion or thinks the bookstore employee knows what they might like (Rosen, 2011).

Online Activity

There is a great deal of activity in the online arena, especially in what publishers are offering teens online as well as in ebooks. In 2010 several children's publishing houses were offering apps for YA, although most being produced by publishers were for children. Bloomsbury's first app aligned with the paranormal romance series by Carrie Jones called Need, which includes pixies, but not the sweet kind. The free app enables tweens and teens to send an online kiss to a friend from one of the three main characters: Zara, Nick, or Astley. Little, Brown also has apps slated for the YA market that were developed to match *Beautiful Creatures and Beautiful Darkness* by Kami Garcia and Margaret Stohl and will include tests about the books, audio versions, photographs, art, some deleted scenes, and recipes. (Deahl, 2010)

Marketing for teens is moving to the online venue rather than remaining with print teen magazines, many of which, such as such as *Elle Girl* and *Teen People*, have ceased publication. Several publishers have launched online products designed for teens. RandomBuzzers.com, which originated in 2007, is designed for teens to chat with authors, view book trailers, and win Buzz Bucks that can be swapped for review galleys or signed copies of finished books. For Simon and Schuster, Pulse It is a combination teen advisory board and book program. Begun in June of 2009, the program moved online in July of that year and has grown from 3,000 to 26,000 members. This site offers many free ebooks that teens are quick to download.

Other publishers are following suit. Houghton Mifflin Harcourt developed a teen Facebook page and is considering more ways to interact online, and Abrams conducted an online poll, responded to by 10,000 teens, to determine the next title in The Strange Case of Origami Yoda series. Of course publishers continue to make use of their own web sites and sometimes add a website specifically for an important author, as Abrams has done for Lauren Myracle (Rosen, 2011).

Ebooks have seen an increase in activity for teens, although not as great as in the adult market. This is understandable for many reasons, ranging from the cost of ebook readers and ebooks for teens who do not have steady jobs and perhaps wish to spend their money in other areas to the fact that several teen favorites are not yet available in ebook format, such as the Harry Potter series or Sherman Alexie's popular *The Absolutely True Diary of a Part-Time Indian*.

For some teens, their preference is to hold the book in their hands. As one teen from Illinois said about using his Kindle, "It feels sacrilegious." Other teens worry that they can't loan an ebook to a good friend. Some grew up with hardback books being special and prefer having a hard copy on their bookshelf where they can see and reread it. A few teens mentioned their preference for turning a page, disliking having to charge their ebook, being distracted by the percent progress at the bottom of the page, or complaining that their eyes hurt and water when using an e-reader.

There is a belief that when ebooks become cheaper more teens will turn to them. At the moment, the smart phones and tablets are used by teens more for social communication rather than the individual task of reading. That might change when there is more interaction within the reading process. As Linda Braun, past president of YALSA said, "Imagine a book discussion inside the book. Why not have it while you're actually reading? It's like posting on Facebook, but it's inside your book" (Springen, 2011).

Publishers are doing their best to offer enticements to teens to read more digitally. Some offer the first title in a series for free, gambling that teens or adults will then buy the next in a series. Llewellyn offered a free download of Linda Joy's book *Don't Die, Dragonfly*, the first in her Seer series, and achieved a spot on the top 100 free for Amazon's Kindle. Scholastic provided a free download of Alexandra Bullet's first book, *Wish*, and publicized the offer through its Facebook page and Twitter feed, which sent the news flying through the blogs and Web sites for teens. And Little, Brown offered a free download of Stephenie Meyer's *The Short Second Life of Bree Tanner* for one month (Springen, 2011).

Authors and librarians and teachers now have a much more economical way to allow their students to interact with an author: Skype! Many authors are willing to speak with teens, either for free or for a fee, which allows them to stay home and continue writing rather than traveling and enables teens to interact with favorite authors. In fact, most authors have their own web sites, many of which are interactive, which provides yet another way for them to meet with their readers. As one illustrator commented, now she is able to share more of her work with young people rather than standing in front of three hundred readers seated in an auditorium. It's a win-win situation for everyone (Messner, 2010).

Self-Publishing

Self-publishing, which used to be looked down upon, has achieved enough success that it is no longer regarded as a stigma in the book publishing world. Success by authors such as Christopher Paolini with *Eragon* or Michael Hoeye's *Time Stops for No Mouse* has convinced publisher and the public that there are worthwhile books to be enjoyed by authors whose works were not originally brought out by a large publishing house. Several titles that were self-published and are now being marketed by large houses include Colleen Houck's *Tiger's Curse*, which initiated Sterling's Splinter YA line. This paranormal romance was originally available only for the Kindle but developed such a large online fan group that Sterling picked it up, along with the sequels *Tiger's Quest* and *Tiger's Voyage* (Lodge, 2011).

On October 19, 2009, *Publishers Weekly* announced that Cory Doctorow would begin a column entitled "With a Little Help" in the first issue of each month. Doctorow is a big fan of self-publishing and has filled his column with lessons he's learned from the venture of self-publishing a collection of short stories also entitled *With a Little Help*. A fan of online publishing , Doctorow does not hesitate to share the pluses and minuses of the online world for authors (Doctorow, 2009).

Series

No one would contest the popularity of series fiction, even though readers often have a hard time waiting for the next title to be published. In middle-grade fiction, series are released more quickly than they have been in the YA realm, but in recent years several popular ones were speeded up in order to retain their eager readers. The Escape from Furnace series by Alexander Gordon Smith is becoming available every six to eight months rather than on a yearly basis, as is the norm. *Lockdown*, first in the series, was published in October 2010, and the fifth and last in the series, *Execution*, will be released in fall of 2012, just two years later. All three of Colleen Houck's books in her tiger series, *Tiger's Curse*, *Tiger's Quest*, and *Tiger's Voyage*, were released during 2011, partly because they had been self-published and were ready to become the lead in Sterling's new Splinter imprint. In a similar fashion, Penguin released the Relic Master series, written by Catherine Fisher of *Incarceron and Sapphique* fame, within a four month period. With *Incarceron* scheduled for release in 2013 as a film, the company wanted to build on the current interest in Fisher's writing. This month-by-month release was possible because the series had been published in the UK in the late 1990s and early 2000s as the Dark Crow, allowing Penguin great flexibility in how they chose to publish in the United States. Although it is nice that some series are released in such quick succession, there is nothing wrong with waiting and anticipating a sequel, just as we all await special holidays and birthdays.

In 2010, series fiction were the big sellers with ones by authors such as Stephenie Meyer for her Twilight Saga, Suzanne Collins with The Hunger Games series and PC and Kristin Cast's House of Night series, all selling more than a million copies. What makes these numbers amazing for Stephenie Meyer is that Twilight Saga concluded in 2008; perhaps the release of the Twilight movies is keeping the popularity going, especially as young girls become older and are ready to read the series (Roback, 2011). Unfortunately, the series sales information for 2011 was not available when this introduction was written (February 20, 2012).

YA Trends in Genre

In the late 1990s, when Harry Potter appeared and set off a reading explosion, book after book that followed featured yet another wizard or boarding school as writers and publishers tried to hop on the enchanted flying car with the same success that J.K. Rowling was enjoying. Then in 2005 came Twilight, the first of four volumes in the Twilight Saga by Stephenie Meyer, and suddenly teen books were filled with paranormal romances, vampires, and werewolves, which in turn has expanded to include mermaids, zombies, angels, revenants, and other paranormal creatures. Some favorite titles in this genre include *Dust and Decay* (zombies), *Daughter of Smoke and Bone* (angels and human/animal combinations), the Wolves of Mercy Falls series [werewolves], the Vampire Kisses series [vampires], and the Forgive My Fins series [mermaids].

Angels

Lauren Kate has four novels coming out about fallen angels who became romantically involved with mortals and so were kicked out of heaven. The first in the series, *Fallen*, had 200,000 titles in print at the end of December, and was followed by *Torment* (2010) and *Passion* (2011) with *Rapture* to follow in 2012. As mentioned above, *Daughter of Smoke and Bone* by Laini Taylor is a powerful story of an angel who falls for a mortal with unusual power. Lee Weatherly writes the Angel Burn series which has its second book out in 2012, titled *Angel Fire*. In an unusual twist, Weatherly has created killer angels, one of whom becomes enamored of a teen named Willow who doesn't realize she's a half-angel.

Vampires

For all the Stephenie Meyer fans, an illustrated guide entitled *The Twilight Saga: The Official Illustrated Guide* was released in 2011 and is filled with information about the characters, family charts, maps, and nearly 100 color photographs. Other authors enjoying success with vampires include Richelle Mead whose Vampire Academy series features two kinds of vampires: the good, living ones and the evil, undead. Other authors have long standing series, such as Rachel Caine who just signed to produce the 15th title in the Morganville Vampires series in 2013, which is set in the vampire-controlled town of Morganville, Texas. Darren Shan has several series, but his Saga of Larten Crepsley, which is up to the fourth volume, details Larten's 200 years as a vampire before meeting Shan at Cirque du Freak. Adult author Kelly Keaton, who writes the mystery series featuring Charlie Madigan, has a new YA series called Darkness Becomes Her, which is set in a post-Katrina New Orleans, now said to be populated by paranormals and renamed New 2. Although the publishing world may be a little tired of vampires, it seems the reading public is not, although many readers are interested only in vampire tales with an approach different than the typical paranormal romance.

Zombies

In addition to paranormal romance, and perhaps to partly offset all the mushy stuff, or to react to the constant threats teens hear about global warming, worry over oil reserves and cost, bacteria that eat our bodies, dystopian fiction is surging. Many titles with zombies fit right in to the dystopian scene, where plague and pestilence rule, such as *Ashes, Ashes* or *The Dead-Tossed Waves*. However, not every zombie emerges into an area that's overrun with plague or some sort of post-apocalyptic horror. Titles such as *I Kissed a Zombie, and I Liked It* and *Undead Much* all take place in typical high schools with normal teen angst, the difference being that the undead have become part of the society. *Publishers Weekly* (1/18/2010, p. 9) reported on a professor at Harvard's Medical School who has even lectured on zombies for the National Academy of Science (Diehl, 2010).

Dystopian

The majority of the dystopian tales do not feature zombies and the worlds in which they are set vary widely. *Incarceron* by Catherine Fisher takes place inside a sentient prison where an inmate finds a key that allows him to communicate with the daughter of the warden and allows him to hope for escape. First in Susan Beth Pfeffer's trilogy is *Life as We Knew It* that begins with diary entries revealing worries about prom and school work, but after an asteroid collides with the moon and tsunamis and earthquakes devastate the Earth, Melinda's attention turns to basics such as food, water, and shelter. Global warming, or climate change, is the impetus for Saci Lloyd's book *The Carbon Diaries 2015* in which the British government resorts to rationing carbon, thereby limiting travel, heat, food, and the way of life.

The release of the film version of *Hunger Games*, first in a trilogy by Suzanne Collins, in the spring of 2012 should ensure dystopian popularity for several years. As an example of how popular this series is, when *Mockingjay*, the third volume was released, it sold 450,000 copies during the first week. This compares to 250,000 the first week that *Eclipse*, the third in Stephenie Meyer's Twilight Saga, was released (Mockingjay, 2010). There are many series in the dystopian pipeline: Ally Condie's *Matched*, where boys and girls have assigned partners, which is followed by *Crossed*; the Gone series by Michael Grant, where anyone over the age of 14 is "gone"; or Marissa Meyer's *Cinder*, a cyborg, which is the first of four, each building on a different fairy tale. Paolo Bacigalupi's Printz-winning novel *Ship Breaker* has been followed by the companion novel *The Drowned Cities* and features the return of the half-man Tool.

Steampunk

Steampunk fiction has also gained in popularity in recent years and is characterized by being set either in Victorian England, or perhaps the Wild West of America, where mechanical devices are powered by steam, hence the term Steampunk. Of course, the settings are changing as the field becomes more popular and the Steampunk world naturally expands. Favorite titles include *Leviathan* by Scott Westerfeld, a trilogy with airships, some mechanical and some living animals; and Philip Reeve's *A Web of Air* where engineer Fever Crumb tries to help a young boy build a flying machine. *Clockwork Angel* by Cassandra Clare combines steampunk with vampires and warlocks, such to attract a wide assortment of readers. An easy introduction to the steampunk world is the collection of short stories in *Steampunk!: An Anthology of Fantastically Rich and Strange Stories* edited by Kelly Link and Gavin J. Grant.

Mashups

Then there are the mashups where a classic title or a historical event suddenly has a zombie or other strange creature in its midst, such as Jane Austen and Seth

Grahame-Smith's *Pride and Prejudice and Zombies* (which in 2010 had more than one million copies in print) featuring the rise of the reanimated dead following a plague with an Elizabeth determined to eradicate them. *Abraham Lincoln Vampire Hunter* tells how Abe handles the knowledge that it was vampires who caused his mother's death. Let's not forget Louisa May Alcott as credit is given to Louisa and Porter Grand for *Little Women and Werewolves* where the four sisters are kept busy exterminating werewolves.

Collaboration

David Levithan and John Green set a very high standard when they collaborated on the work *Will Grayson, Will Grayson*, a novel about two boys with the same name and the peculiarities that arise from that. Although Levithan had collaborated before with Rachel Cohn on *Nick and Norah's Infinite Playlist*, he reached out to Green before John's first book, *Looking for Alaska*, had even been published (Corbett, 2010). More collaborations are evident when looking at recent titles, from a paranormal romance in *Beautiful Creatures* by Kami Garcia and Margaret Stohl to *A Sword in Her Hand*, the story of an unwanted child born in the 1300s by Jean-Claude Van Rijckeghem and Pat Van Beirs, or the Wolf Springs Chronicles by Nancy Holder and Debbie Viguie who write about a small town where, as one might expect, werewolves abide.

Author Memorials

2009

Best known to teens as the co-author of *Farewell to Manzanar: A True Story of Japanese American Experience during and after the World War II Internment*, written with his wife Jeanne, James D. Houston died on April 16.

Adult author David Eddings, whose work was enjoyed by teen fantasy fans, died at the age of 78 on June 2. A favorite series of his was The Belgariad.

Esther Hautzig, whose memoir, *The Endless Steppe: Growing Up in Siberia*, was enjoyed by all ages, died on November 1. The memoir received both a National Book Award and a Boston Globe-Horn Book Honor citation.

The author of *Angela's Ashes*, a memoir that related his miserable Irish childhood and attracted many teen readers, Frank McCourt died on July 19 at the age of 78.

Young adult novelist Norma Fox Mazer, noted for her YA problem novels, including Best Books for Young Adults titles *After the Rain* (1987 list), *Silver* (1988 list), and *Up in Seth's Room* (1979 list), and the recent *The Missing Girl* (2009 list), died on October 17 at the age of 78.

2010

In 1970 *Love Story* was the top-selling work of fiction in the United States and went on to be a favorite tear-jerker movie; it was also a 1970 Best Book for Young Adults. Author Erich Segal, a university professor, died at the age of 72 on January 17.

The reclusive J.D. Salinger, known for his classic work *The Catcher in the Rye*, died at the age of 91 on January 27, 2010.

Recognized as a children's author, Sid Fleischman's books also appealed to teens, as evidenced by the inclusion of *The Abracadabra Kid: A Writer's Life* (1997 list) and *Escape!: The Story of the Great Houdini* (2007 list) on two Best Books for Young Adults lists. He died on March 17 at the age of 90.

Author of mathematical puzzle books and other titles of scientific oddities, which became standards in school and public libraries, Martin Gardner died at the age of 95 on May 22.

Australian author Ruth Park, included on the Best Books for Young Adults list (1982) for her time travel novel *Playing Beatie Bow*, which also won the Boston Globe-Horn Book Award, died on December 14 at the age of 93.

2011

On February 5 Brian Jacques died at the age of 71. He was noted for his fantasy Redwall series; the first in the series, *Redwall*, was a Best Book for Young Adults (1987 list).

William Perry Moore, IV, known as Perry Moore in his writing and movie producer role of *The Chronicles of Narnia*, died at the age of 39 in New York on February 17.

Lisa Wolfson, who wrote under the pseudonym L.K. Madigan, died on February 23 in Portland, Oregon, at the age of 47. Her first book, entitled *Flash Burnout*, was published in 2009 and won the William C. Morris Debut Award for best first novel.

Fantasy writer Diane Wynne Jones, who wrote for both children's and young adults, died on March 26 in Bristol, England. Several of her books were selected as a Best Book for Young Adults including *Archer's Goon* (1984 list), *Howl's Moving Castle* (1986 list), *The Homeward Bounders* (1981 list) and *Castle in the Air* (1992 list).

Popular adult mystery author Lillian Jackson Braun died at the age of 97 on June 4. Cat fanciers of all ages loved her The Cat WholPOseries.

Fantasy and science fiction author William Sleator died at the age of 66 on August 2 in Bua Chet, Thailand. Several of his novels were selected as a Best Book for Young Adults including *Interstellar Pig* (1984 list), *House of Stairs* (1974 list), *Strange Attractors* (1991 list) and *The Duplicate* (1989 list).

Known for her series on dragons, Anne McCaffrey died on November 22 in her home Dragonhold in County Wicklow, Ireland. *Dragonsinger* (1977) and *Pegasus in Flight* (1992) were named to the Best Books for Young Adults lists.

Books to Movies

2009

Call of the Wild by Jack London is based on the book by the same name, a classic adventure tale in American literature that was first published in 1903 and takes place during the Klondike Gold Rush. Christopher Lloyd and Timothy Bottoms star.

Cirque du Freak: The Vampire's Assistant by Darren Shan is a fantasy that continues his Saga of Darren Shan series, specifically the *Vampire Blood* trilogy. The cast includes John C. Reilly, Chris Massoglia, and Salma Hayek.

Harry Potter and the Half-Blood Prince by J.K. Rowling is a fantasy that features Harry in his sixth year at Hogwarts when he is given a textbook that has been annotated by the Half-Blood Prince. In addition to stalwarts Daniel Radcliffe, Rupert Grint and Emma Watson, the cast also includes Helena Bonham Carter. *Harry Potter and the Half-Blood Prince* is a 2006 Best Book for Young Adults.

The Lovely Bones by Alice Sebold is a supernatural drama film adaptation of the book with the same name featuring Susie, a young teen who is killed by a neighbor and falls between life and death, enabling her to watch her friends and family. Saoirse Ronan, Mark Wahlberg, Rachel Weisz, Susan Sarandon, and Stanley Tucci comprise the cast. *The Lovely Bones* is a 2003 Best Book for Young Adults.

My Sister's Keeper by adult author Jodi Picoult is a drama that tells of two sisters, the younger of whom was born to be a perfect match for her older sister who suffers from leukemia. Cameron Diaz, Abigail Breslin, Alec Baldwin, and Sofia Vassilieva star in this film. *My Sister's Keeper* is a 2005 Alex Award winner.

New Moon by Stephenie Meyer is based on her 2006 novel of the same name and continues the romantic vampire fantasy, Twilight Saga, which began with *Twilight*. The three principal actors are Kristen Stewart, Robert Pattinson and Taylor Lautner. *New Moon* is a 2007 Quick Pick for Young Adults.

Precious is based on the novel *Push*, written in 1996 by Sapphire, and features Precious who is raised in horrible circumstances but, with help from others, tries to rise above the squalor and illiteracy. The cast included Gabourey Sidibe in her debut as Precious, Mariah Carey as the social worker and Mo'Nique as Precious's mother, a role that earned her an Academy Award for Best Supporting Actress.

The Road by Cormac McCarthy is a dystopian survival story based on his 2006 Pulitzer Prize winning book of the same name. The film features Viggo Mortensen and Kodi Smit-McPhee as a father and son team who fight to live after all plant and animal life on Earth have been destroyed. 2010

Alice in Wonderland is a computer animated, live action fantasy that drew its inspiration from the 1865 title Alice's Adventures in Wonderland and the 1871 sequel *Through the Looking Glass*, both by Lewis Carroll, and explains Alice's adventures when she falls down a rabbit hole. Cast members include Mia Wasikowska, Johnny Depp, Helena Bonham Carter and Anne Hathaway.

Eclipse by Stephenie Meyer continues the romantic vampire fantasy films made for the Twilight Saga with this third installment. The stars are Kristen Stewart, Robert Pattinson, and Taylor Lautner.

Flipped by Wendelin Van Draanen is a romantic comedy directed by Rob Reiner. Callan McAuliffe and Madeline Carroll star in this film about a young girl's crush on her neighbor that fizzles when he finally becomes interested in her.

Gulliver's Travels by Jonathan Swift, originally written in the eighteenth century, is a fantasy comedy loosely based on the original work but in a modern setting. Jack Black, Emily Blunt, Jason Segel, and Amanda Peet have roles in this film.

Harry Potter and the Deathly Hallows, part 1, by J.K. Rowling, continues the fantasy about Harry Potter, the remarkable wizard, as he tries to destroy the horcruxes which are the secret to Lord Voldemort's immortality. Daniel Radcliffe, Rupert Grint and Emma Watson continue their roles.

It's Kind of a Funny Story by Ned Vizzini is a comedy drama that begins when a teen thinks of committing suicide, but instead seeks help from a hospital. Keir Gilchrist, Zach Galifianakis, Emma Roberts, and Viola Davis are featured in this film. *It's Kind of a Funny Story* was named to the 2007 Best Books for Young Adults list.

Robin Hood by Howard Pyle, an 1883 book that is based on Medieval legends of Robin Hood, is used as the basis for this British/American adventure film starring Russell Crowe and Cate Blanchett. 2011

Beastly is a romantic fantasy, adapted from the book of the same name written by Alex Flinn, which in turn is based on *Beauty and the Beast*. Cast members Vanessa Hudgens and Alex Pettyfer star.

Breaking Dawn, part 1, by Stephenie Meyer, continues in this fourth film devoted to the series. Kristen Stewart, Robert Pattinson, and Taylor Lautner reprise their roles.

The Eagle, based on the 1954 historical fiction titled *The Eagle of the Ninth* by Rosemary Sutcliff, is an historical epic of the search for a lost Roman eagle standard. Channing Tatum, Jamie Bell and Donald Sutherland star in this British-American production.

Harry Potter and the Deathly Hallows, part 2, by J.K. Rowling is the eighth and final film in this epic fantasy and is the first of the series to be filmed entirely in 3D. Daniel Radcliffe, Rupert Grint, and Emma Watson continue their starring roles.

I Am Number Four by Pittacus Lore, pseudonym for Jobie Hughes and James Frey, is a teen action science fiction tale derived from the book by the same name. Actors include Alex Pettyfer, Timothy Olyphant, Teresa Palmer, Dianna Agron and Callan McAuliffe.

Sherlock Holmes: A Game of Shadows by Sir Arthur Conan Doyle is a British-American action mystery from Doyle's "The Final Problem." Actors include Robert Downey, Jr., Jude Law, and Jared Harris.

Soul Surfer is based on Bethany Hamilton's autobiography of the same name which describes losing her arm to a shark attack while surfing. Actors in this film include AnnaSophia Robb, Dennis Quaid, Helen Hunt, and Carrie Underwood.

Thor originates from the comic book character of the same name developed by Marvel Comics and describes when he is exiled to Earth but must prevent his brother Loki from taking over Asagard. Chris Hemsworth, Natalie Portman, Tom Hiddleston, Anthony Hopkins, and Stellan Skarsgard star in the film.

The Three Musketeers is a 3D adventure film from the book by the same name, originally written by Alexandre Dumas in 1844. Actors in the film include Matthew Macfadyen, Ray Stevenson, Luke Evans, Milla Jovovich, and Orlando Bloom.

War Horse is now available in both play [2007]and film format, in addition to the 1982 book by Michael Morpurgo of the same name. Set during World War I, the cast includes David Thewlis, Benedict Cumberbatch, Jeremy Irvine, Emily Watson, and Tom Hiddleston.

Water for Elephants by Sara Gruen features Reese Witherspoon, Robert Pattinson, and Christopher Waltz in addition to Hal Holbrook. Adapted from the 2007 Alex winner book of the same name. Professional Reading Listed below are some titles that will aid in discussing, collecting, and learning more about young adult literature. Professional ResourcesListed below are some titles that will aid in discussing, collecting, and learning more about young adult literature.

Professional Resources

Bartel, Julie, and Pam Spencer Holley (2010). *Annotated Book Lists for Every Teen Reader: The Best from the Experts at YALSA-BK*. New York: Neal-Schuman.

Bodart, Joni Richards (2010). *Radical Reads 2: Working with the Newest Edge Titles for Teens*. Lanham, Md: Scarecrow Press.

———(2011). *They Suck, They Bite, They Eat, They Kill: The Psychological Meaning of Supernatural Monsters in Young Adult Fiction*. Lanham, Md: Scarecrow Press.

Bott, C.J. (2009). *More Bullies in More Books*. Lanham, Md: Scarecrow Press.

Campbell, Patty (2010). *Campbell's Scoop: Reflections on Young Adult Literature*. Lanham, Md: Scarecrow Press.

Cart, Michael (2011). *Young Adult Literature: From Romance to Realism*. Chicago: ALA Editions.

Goldsmith, Francisca (2009). *The Readers' Advisory Guide to Graphic Novels*. Chicago: ALA Editions.

Hogan, Walter (2009). *Animals in Young Adult Fiction*. Lanham, Md: Scarecrow Press.

Holley, Pam Spencer, Ed. (2009). *Quick and Popular Reads for Teens*. Chicago: ALA Editions.

Silver, Linda R. (2010). *Best Jewish Books for Children and Teens*. Philadelphia: The Jewish Publication Society.

Sullivan, Michael (2009). *Connecting Boys with Books 2: Closing the Reading Gap*. Chicago: ALA Editions.

———(2010). *Serving Boys through Readers' Advisory*. Chicago: ALA Editions

Sutton, Roger, and Martha Parravanno, eds. (2010). *A Family of Readers: The Book Lover's Guide to Children's and Young Adult Literature*. Boston: Candlewick.

Webber, Carlisle K. (2010). *Gay, Lesbian, Bisexual and Questioning Teen Literature: A Guide to Reading Interests*. Englewood, Colo.: Libraries Unlimited.

Wilson, Leah, Ed. (2011). *The Girl Who Was on Fire: Your Favorite Authors on Suzanne Collins' "Hunger Games" Trilogy*. Dallas, Tex.: Smart Pop/Ben Bella Books.

Wolf, Shelby A.; Karen Coats; Patricia Enciso; and Christine Jenkins, eds. (2011). *Handbook of Research on Children's and Young Adult Literature*. New York: Routledge.

Works Cited

American Library Association. Young Adult Library Services Association. "Great Graphic Novels for Teens." (http://www.ala.org/yalsa/ggnt).

American Library Association. Young Adult Library Services Association. Michael L. Printz Award for Excellence in YA Literature. (http://www.ala.org/yalsa/printz)

American Library Association. Young Adult Library Services Association. William C. Morris YA Debut Award. (http://www.ala.org/yalsa/morris).(http://www.ala.org/yalsa/printz)

American Library Association. Young Adult Library Services Association. YALSA Award for Excellence in Nonfiction for Young Adults. (http://www.ala.org/yalsa/nonfiction)

Cart, Michael. "A New Literature for a New Millennium?: The First Decade of the Printz Awards." *Young Adult Library Services* (YALS), Spring 2010.

Cha, Kai-Ming. "Down, but Not Out: Manga Holds On in a Tough Market." *Publishers Weekly*, June 14, 2010.

Corbett, Sue. "Double Identity." *Publishers Weekly*, February 15, 2010.

Deahl, Rachel. "Why the Mashups and Zombies Won't Stop." *Publishers Weekly*, January 19, 2010.

———. "What Children's Publishers Are Doing in the Apps Space." *Publishers Weekly*, November 22, 2010.

Doctorow, Cory. "Doctorow's Project: With a Little Help." *Publishers Weekly*, October 19, 2009.

Maury, Laurel. "Hot Fall Graphic Novels for Libraries at BEA." *Publishers Weekly*, May 31, 2011. (http://www.publishersweekly.com)

Messner, Kate. "An Author in Every Classroom." *School Library Journal*, September 2010.

"Mockingjay Sells More than 450,000 Copies in First Week." *Publishers Weekly*, September 2, 2010. (http://www.publishersweekly.com)

Reid, Calvin. "Tor Flies High with Comics and Manga." *Publishers Weekly*, January 24, 2011.

Roback, Diane. "Franchises Flying High." Publishers Weekly, March 21, 2010.

Rosen, Judith. "What Do children's Book Consumers Want Next?" *Publishers Weekly*, January 31, 2011.

———. "Where the Kids Are: Marketing Online." *Publishers Weekly*, February 21, 2011.

Schultz, Marc. "Upcoming NewSouth 'Huck Finn' Eliminates the 'N' Word" *Publishers Weekly*, January 3, 2011.

Springen, Karen. "Reaching the e-Teen." *Publishers Weekly*, February 21, 2011.

"U.S. Graphic Novel Sales Down 6%." Publishers Weekly, April 26, 2010.

Young Adult Titles

595

RANDA ABDEL-FATTAH

Ten Things I Hate about Me

(London: Marion Lloyd, 2009)

Subject(s): Islam; High schools; Father-daughter relations

Age range(s): 13 - 16+

Major character(s): Jamilah "Jamie" Towfeek, 16-Year-Old, Religious (Muslim), Sister (to Shereen and Bilal), Daughter (of a strict widower), Musician (drummer); Shereen, Sister (of Jamie and Bilal); Bilal, Brother (of Jamie and Shereen)

Time period(s): 21st century; 2000s

Locale(s): Sydney, Australia

Summary: A young girl struggles to find her identity in *Ten Things I Hate about Me.* Sixteen-year-old Jamilah Towfeek is a Lebanese Muslim living in Sydney, Australia. Since the death of her mother, Jamilah and her siblings have been under the control of their stern, traditional father. Though she loves her heritage, Jamilah despises the strict rules that her father embraces as part of their culture. Jamilah's sister Shereen wears her hijab as a badge of pride and faith, but shuns college in exchange for activism. Her brother Bilal is more interested in drinking and partying. At home, Jamilah is the dutiful daughter who tries to respect her father's wishes. At school, however, it's a different story. Answering to the name of Jamie, Jamilah wears blue contacts and shows off her dyed blonde hair. Desperate to fit in and avoid the racial taunting that runs rampant in her school, Jamie does nothing while her classmates taunt and torture Muslims and other students who are "different." Soon, the two worlds that Jamie has carefully built for herself begin to collide, and she needs to decide who she really wants to be.

Where it's reviewed:
Booklist, December 1, 2008, page 45
Publishers Weekly, January 12, 2009, page 48
School Library Journal, February 2009, page 96
Voice of Youth Advocates, June 2009, page 131

Other books by the same author:
Where the Streets Had a Name, 2010
Does My Head Look Big in This?, 2005

Other books you might like:
Yvonne Collins, *Love, Inc.,* 2011

Sheba Karim, *Skunk Girl,* 2009
Neesha Meminger, *Shine, Coconut Moon,* 2009

596

PETER ABRAHAMS

Reality Check

(New York: Harper Teen, 2009)

Subject(s): Missing persons; Mystery; Detective fiction

Age range(s): 14 - 18+

Major character(s): Cody, 16-Year-Old, Boyfriend (of Clea), Football Player; Clea, Student—Boarding School, Girlfriend (of Cody)

Time period(s): 21st century; 2000s

Locale(s): Little Bend, Colorado; North Dover, Vermont

Summary: *Reality Check* is a mystery novel for young adults from author Peter Abrahams. Sixteen-year-old Cody only cares about two things in life—sports and Clea, his girlfriend. Cody lives in Little Bend, Colorado, and Clea, who comes from a wealthy family, is attending a boarding school in North Dover, Vermont. A serious injury forces Cody to give up his dreams of earning an athletic scholarship because without one, he has no chance of getting into college. As a result, he decides to quit school. Then, Clea is reported missing from her school, and Cody decides to drive to Vermont to find her. Forced by circumstances to look at life differently, he is able to solve the case when even the most educated crime solvers cannot.

Where it's reviewed:
Booklist, July 1, 2009, page 56
Publishers Weekly, May 25, 2009, page 58
School Library Journal, May 2009, page 100

Other books by the same author:
Bullet Point, 2010
Down the Rabbit Hole: An Echo Falls Mystery, 2005

Awards the book has won:
Edgar Allan Poe Awards: Best Young Adult Novel, 2010

Other books you might like:
Eireann Corrigan, *Accomplice,* 2010
John Feinstein, *Vanishing Act,* 2006
Gregory Galloway, *As Simple as Snow,* 2005

John Green, *Paper Towns*, 2008
Carol Plum-Ucci, *The Body of Christopher Creed*, 2000

597

PETER ABRAHAMS

Bullet Point

(New York: HarperTeen, 2010)

Story type: Mystery
Subject(s): Fathers; Father-son relations; Criminals

Age range(s): 15 - 18+
Major character(s): Wyatt Lathem, Boyfriend (of Greer), Son (of Sonny), 16-Year-Old; Greer, 19-Year-Old, Girlfriend (of Wyatt); Sonny, Father (of Wyatt), Prisoner
Time period(s): 21st century; 2010s
Locale(s): Silver City, United States

Summary: After cuts to the school budget leave East Canton High School without a baseball team, Wyatt Lathem decides to move to another town to try to improve his chances at receiving a baseball scholarship in college. In Silver City, Wyatt realizes that he is now living in the town that houses a prison where his biological father, Sonny, is serving a life sentence for murder. In his new home, Wyatt meets an older girl, Greer, whose father is in the same prison as Sonny. Greer arranges a meeting between Wyatt and his father, who is nothing like the hardened criminal Wyatt always thought him to be. As Wyatt gets to know Sonny better, he is certain that Sonny is innocent. When Wyatt decides that he'll do anything to prove his father's innocence, he sets off on a dangerous journey.

Where it's reviewed:
Booklist, May 1, 2010, page 49
Horn Book Guide, Fall 2010, page 359
School Library Journal, June 2010, page 93
Voice of Youth Advocates, August 2010, page 240

Other books by the same author:
Reality Check, 2009
Into the Dark, 2008

Other books you might like:
John C. Ford, *The Morgue and Me*, 2009
John Green, *Looking for Alaska*, 2005
C.K. Kelly Martin, *The Lighter Side of Life and Death*, 2010
Walter Dean Myers, *Somewhere in the Darkness*, 1992

598

ALEXANDRA ADORNETTO

Halo

(New York: Feiwel & Friends, 2010)

Subject(s): Angels; Interpersonal relations; High schools

Age range(s): 13 - 18+
Major character(s): Bethany, Angel; Gabriel, Angel; Ivy, Angel; Xavier, Boyfriend (of Bethany)

Time period(s): 21st century; 2010s
Locale(s): Venus Cove, United States

Summary: Alexandra Adornetto's *Halo* chronicles the adventures of Bethany, an angel who has been sent to Earth to protect a small town from evil. Bethany, who is inexperienced, is accompanied on her journey by the more-seasoned seraphs Gabriel and Ivy. On Earth, Bethany is tasked with safeguarding the small town of Venus Cove from the dark forces that threaten to overtake it. But when Bethany lays eyes on a cute boy named Xavier, her immortal heart skips a beat. Soon, Bethany and Xavier are in love, and Bethany is distracted from her mission on Earth—which is something that could mean trouble for Venus Cove.

Where it's reviewed:
New York Times Book Review, November 7, 2010, page 22
Publishers Weekly, August 2, 2010, page 47
Reading Time, November 2010, page 32
School Library Journal, November 2010, page 100

Other books by the same author:
Hades, 2011

Other books you might like:
Becca Fitzpatrick, *Crescendo*, 2010
Lauren Kate, *Fallen*, 2009
Suzanne Selfors, *Coffeehouse Angel*, 2009

599

ANN AGUIRRE

Enclave

(New York: Feiwel and Friends, 2011)

Series: Razorland Series. Book 1
Subject(s): Science fiction; Dystopias; Adventure

Age range(s): 14 - 17+
Major character(s): Deuce, 15-Year-Old, Hunter (Huntress); Fade, Teenager, Hunter
Time period(s): Indeterminate Future
Locale(s): Enclave, Fictional Location; Topside, Fictional Location

Summary: In the young-adult novel *Enclave* by Ann Aguirre, a deadly epidemic and devastating wars have transformed the earth into a harsh wasteland. Most of the plague survivors live underground, where they endure the strict rule of the elders and the threat of attack by the Freaks. In Enclave, children aren't given names until they turn 15—the age at which they choose the role of Breeder, Builder, or Hunter. Deuce, a new huntress, fulfills her duties of finding meat and fighting Freaks well, despite being partnered with the disliked hunter Fade. When Deuce comes to the defense of a friend, the unforgiving elders exile her and Fade to a place where death is almost certain. *Enclave* is the first book in Aguirre's Razorland series.

Where it's reviewed:
Booklist, March 15, 2011, page 54
Publishers Weekly, February 7, 2011, page 58
School Library Journal, April 2011, page 166

Other books you might like:
Steve Augarde, *X Isle*, 2010

Suzanne Collins, *The Hunger Games*, 2008
Catherine Fisher, *Incarceron*, 2007
Alison Goodman, *Eona: The Last Dragoneye*, 2011
Malinda Lo, *Huntress*, 2011

600

JILL S. ALEXANDER

The Sweetheart of Prosper County

(New York: Feiwel and Friends, 2009)

Subject(s): Adolescence; Rural life; Beauty contests

Age range(s): 13 - 16+

Major character(s): Austin Gray, 14-Year-Old, 9th Grader, Beauty Pageant Contestant, Outcast

Time period(s): 21st century; 2000s

Locale(s): Texas, United States

Summary: *The Sweetheart of Prosper County* is a young adult novel from author Jill S. Alexander. High school freshman Austin Gray's life is anything but charmed. Still recovering from the death of her father years earlier, she has an overbearing mother and a best friend who will no longer speak to her. Unpopular and friendless, Austin's an easy target for the school bullies. Finally, she decides to do something to end her torment. Determined to become the Sweetheart of Prosper County, Austin joins the Future Farmers of America. The teen begins raising a rooster, and rallies her peers to support her. Now, all she needs to do is make her mother realize why becoming the town sweetheart is so important.

Where it's reviewed:
Booklist, August 1, 2009, page 61
Horn Book Guide, Spring 2010, page 88
Journal of Adolescent & Adult, October 2010, page 154
Publishers Weekly, October 5, 2009, page 50
School Library Journal, September 2009, page 150

Other books by the same author:
Paradise, 2011

Other books you might like:
Shauna Cross, *Derby Girl*, 2007
Randi Hacker, *Life as I Knew It*, 2006
Lauren Kate, *The Betrayal of Natalie Hargrove*, 2009
Julie Ann Linker, *Crowned*, 2008
Tobey Sloane, *Appetite for Detention*, 2008

601

THOMAS B. ALLEN
ROGER MACBRIDE ALLEN, Co-Author

Mr. Lincoln's High-Tech War: How the North Used the Telegraph, Railroads, Surveillance Balloons, Ironclads, High-Powered Weapons, and More to Win the Civil War

(Washington, D.C.: National Geographic, 2009)

Subject(s): History; United States Civil War, 1861-1865; Technology

Age range(s): 11 - 16+

Time period(s): 19th century; 1850s-1860s

Locale(s): United States

Summary: In *Mr. Lincoln's High-Tech War: How the North Used the Telegraph, Railroads, Surveillance Balloons, Ironclads, High-Powered Weapons, and More to Win the Civil War*, Thomas Allen and Roger MacBride Allen describe the military innovations of the mid-19th century. As the authors explain, Lincoln was deeply involved with war strategy and technology, communicating via telegraph with officers in battle, inspecting newly built warships, and personally testing new weapons. The era's latest technologies were utilized in the war effort, from railroad trains to hot air balloons. Illustrated with period photographs and art, this fascinating volume provides a unique perspective on Civil War history.

Where it's reviewed:
Booklist, December 15, 2008, page 50
School Library Journal, February 2009, page 114
Voice of Youth Advocates, February 2009, page 548

Other books by the same author:
Harriet Tubman, Secret Agent: How Daring Slaves and Free Blacks Spied for the Union during the Civil War, 2007
Remember Valley Forge: Patriots, Tories, and Redcoats Tell Their Stories, 2007
George Washington, Spymaster: How the Americans Outspied the British and Won the Revolutionary War, 2005

Other books you might like:
Gail Jarrow, *Lincoln's Flying Spies: Thaddeus Lowe and the Civil War Balloon Corps*, 2010
Shane Mountjoy, *Technology and the Civil War*, 2009
Sally M. Walker, *Secrets of a Civil War Submarine: Solving the Mysteries of the H.L. Hunley*, 2005

602

DAVID ALMOND

Raven Summer

(New York: Delacorte Press, 2009)

Subject(s): Foster children; Interpersonal relations; Conduct of life

Age range(s): 13 - 18+

Major character(s): Liam, Child; Oliver, Foster Child, Refugee; Crystal, Foster Child; Allison, Foster Child, Baby

Time period(s): 21st century; 2000s

Locale(s): Northumbrian Coast, United Kingdom

Summary: David Almond's *Raven Summer* charts the emotional odyssey of young Liam, who is led by a raven to an abandoned baby in a nearby forest. He brings the baby to safety, where she is put in the care of a foster family. Liam visits her and makes the acquaintance of the family's two other foster children, a girl named Crystal and a Liberian refugee named Oliver. Through his friendship with Crystal and Oliver, Liam learns of the cruelty and danger running rampant through the world and sets out to help his new friends overcome their troubled histories.

Where it's reviewed:
Booklist, September 15, 2009, page 59
Horn Book Magazine, November/December 2009, page 662
Publishers Weekly, November 9, 2009, page 47
School Library Journal, December 2009, page 105
Voice of Youth Advocates, December 2009, page 402

Other books by the same author:
Clay, 2006
The Fire-Eaters, 2003
Heaven Eyes, 2001
Kit's Wilderness, 2000
Skellig, 1999

Other books you might like:
Kevin Brooks, *Kissing the Rain*, 2004
Siobhan Dowd, *Bog Child*, 2008
Ron Koertge, *Margaux with an X*, 2004
Barry Lyga, *Hero-Type*, 2008
Jerry Spinelli, *Wringer*, 1997

603

DAVID ALMOND

My Name Is Mina
(London: Hodder Children's Books, 2010)

Subject(s): Mother-daughter relations; Single parent family; Family life
Age range(s): 11 - 14+
Major character(s): Mina, 9-Year-Old, Writer, Student (home-schooled)
Time period(s): 21st century; 2010s
Locale(s): England

Summary: In this prequel to the children's novel *Skellig* (1999), author David Almond follows the self-discovery of a precocious nine-year-old named Mina. Taught at home by her widowed mother, Mina exhibits boundless creativity and curiosity and eventually begins to record her thoughts in a journal. In this simple notebook, she puzzles out the mysteries of the universe and the world—and of her own mind and body. Mina uses her newfound adeptness with words to explore her unusual relationship with her mother and the trappings of her solitary life as she prepares to take her place in the greater world.

Where it's reviewed:
Booklist, February 15, 2010, page 47
Horn Book Guide, Fall 2010, page 371
New York Times Book Review, October 16, 2011, page 20
School Library Journal, August 2010, page 104
Voice of Youth Advocates, August 2010, page 248

Other books by the same author:
Raven Summer, 2009
Clay, 2006
The Fire-Eaters, 2003
Heaven Eyes, 2001
Skellig, 1999

Other books you might like:
E.L. Konigsburg, *The Outcasts of 19 Schuyler Place*, 2004
Gordon Korman, *Schooled*, 2007
Hilary McKay, *Forever Rose*, 2008
Stephanie S. Tolan, *Surviving the Applewhites*, 2002

604

SANDRA ALONZO
NATHAN HUANG, Illustrator

Riding Invisible
(New York: Hyperion, 2010)

Subject(s): Mental health; Brothers; Runaways
Age range(s): 13 - 18+
Major character(s): Yancy Aparacio, 15-Year-Old, Abuse Victim, Runaway; Will Aparacio, Brother (of Yancy), Mentally Ill Person; Tavo, Worker
Time period(s): 21st century; 2010s
Locale(s): California, United States

Summary: In the young adult novel *Riding Invisible* by Sandra Alonzo, 15-year-old Yancy Aparacio leaves his family's home where his emotionally disturbed brother inflicts constant abuse. Will is mentally ill, but as his main victim, Yancy feels he must get away to protect himself. He rides his horse, Shy, into the California desert, searching for a solution to his problem. Yancy is befriended by a Mexican man named Tavo, who shares wise advice on Yancy's family situation as well as his love life. The author tells Yancy's story in journal format. The book's handwritten pages are illustrated with drawings by Nathan Huang that complement the text and reveal Yancy's complex emotions. First novel.

Where it's reviewed:
Booklist, February 1, 2010, page 38
Horn Book Guide, Fall 2010, page 359
Publishers Weekly, February 8, 2010, page 52
Voice of Youth Advocates, August 2010, page 240

Other books you might like:
Tim Bowler, *Midget*, 1995
K.A. Nuzum, *A Small White Scar*, 2006
S.L. Rottman, *Shadow of a Doubt*, 2003

605

TARA ALTEBRANDO

Dreamland Social Club
(New York: Dutton Books, 2011)

Story type: Coming-of-Age
Subject(s): Interpersonal relations; Family life; Amusement parks
Major character(s): Jane Dryden, 16-Year-Old, Twin (of Marcus); Marcus Dryden, Twin (of Jane)
Time period(s): 21st century; 2010s
Locale(s): New York, New York

Summary: Coney Island provides an unlikely sanctuary for a grieving family in this young adult novel by Tara

Altebrando. Sixteen-year-old twins Jane and Marcus Dryden have journeyed around the world with their father in the years since they lost their mother. But the unexpected inheritance of their mother's childhood home has brought the Drydens to Coney Island. The plan is for the family to live in the house for a year while they fix it up for resale. But in the quirky community of amusement park workers, Jane, her brother, and father begin to experience a sense of belonging. As Jane searches her new home for information about her mother's past, she finds romance and friendship on the boardwalk.

Where it's reviewed:
Girls' Life, June/July 2011, page 57
Horn Book Guide, Fall 2011, page 372
Publishers Weekly, March 28, 2011, page 59
School Library Journal, July 2011, page 91
Voice of Youth Advocates, June 2011, page 177

Other books by the same author:
The Best Night of Your (Pathetic) Life, 2012
What Happens Here, 2008
The Pursuit of Happiness, 2006

Other books you might like:
Cecilia Galante, *The Sweetness of Salt*, 2010
David Lubar, *Dunk*, 2002
Sarah Ockler, *Fixing Delilah*, 2010

606

AMIR AMIR
KHALIL KHALIL, Illustrator

Zahra's Paradise

(New York: First Second, 2011)

Subject(s): Middle East; Revolutions; Politics

Age range(s): 15 - 18+

Major character(s): Mehdi, Activist, Missing Person, Brother (of Hassan), Son (of Zahra); Zahra, Mother (of Mehdi and Hassan); Hassan, Writer (blogger), Son (of Zahra), Brother (of Mehdi)

Time period(s): 21st century; 2000s (2009)

Locale(s): Tehran, Iran

Summary: Just outside Iran's capital city, Tehran, is a massive cemetery called Zahra's Paradise. Borrowing its name from the final resting place of countless Iranians, this graphic novel focuses on a family's search for a missing loved one. Mehdi, a young protestor, disappears amid the political chaos following the 2009 presidential elections in Iran. His mother—also called Zahra—searches Iran's streets for her missing son, never once believing that he may have met a deadly fate at the hands of the Iranian secret police. Meanwhile, Zahra's eldest son, Hassan, a blogger, turns to the Internet for help in finding his younger brother. The graphic novel blends fact and fiction, personifying the all-too-real political turmoil that many faced in the aftermath of the fraudulent elections. For political reasons, both author Amir and illustrator Khalil have opted to protect their anonymity.

Where it's reviewed:
Booklist, October 15, 2011, page 36

Library Journal, November 15, 2011, page 58
Publishers Weekly, October 20, 2011, page 39
Voice of Youth Advocates, December 2011, page 486

Other books you might like:
Sarah Glidden, *How to Understand Israel in 60 Days or Less*, 2010
Azadeh Moaveni, *Lipstick Jihad: A Memoir of Growing Up Iranian in America and American in Iran*, 2005
Joe Sacco, *Palestine*, 2001
Marjane Satrapi, *Persepolis: The Story of a Childhood*, 2003
Art Spiegelman, *Maus I: A Survivor's Tale: My Father Bleeds History*, 1986

607

LAURIE HALSE ANDERSON

Forge

(New York: Atheneum Books for Young Readers, 2010)

Subject(s): Slavery; Runaways; Coming of age

Age range(s): 12 - 16+

Major character(s): Curzon, 15-Year-Old, Runaway, Slave, Military Personnel; Isabel, Friend (of Curzon), Runaway, Slave

Time period(s): 19th century

Locale(s): Valley Forge, Pennsylvania

Summary: *Forge*, the sequel to Laurie Halse Anderson's acclaimed 2008 novel *Chains*, continues the adventures of runaway slaves Curzon and Isabel. Curzon, now 15, has joined the Continental Army stationed at Valley Forge and makes his first tentative steps into manhood. Meanwhile, his friend Isabel is also at Valley Forge but under much different—and far more dangerous—circumstances. Now the two must navigate their own respective challenges to attain the freedom they so desperately seek.

Where it's reviewed:
Booklist, September 15, 2010, page 67
Horn Book Magazine, November-December 2010, page 84
New York Times Book Review, February 13, 2011, page 18
Publishers Weekly, September 13, 2010, page 46
School Library Journal, October 2010, page 106

Other books by the same author:
Chains, 2008
Fever 1793, 2002

Other books you might like:
Christopher Paul Curtis, *Elijah of Buxton*, 2007
Marty Rhodes Figley, *Prisoner for Liberty*, 2009
Russell Freedman, *Washington at Valley Forge*, 2008
Gary Paulsen, *Woods Runner*, 2010

608

LAURIE HALSE ANDERSON

Wintergirls

(New York: Viking Juvenile, 2009)

Subject(s): Eating disorders; Family relations; Self esteem

Age range(s): 14 - 18+

Major character(s): Lia, 18-Year-Old, Student—High School, Friend (of Cassie); Cassie, Friend (of Lia, deceased), Spirit; Ellijah, Young Man (last to see Cassie alive)

Time period(s): 21st century; 2000s

Summary: Laurie Halse Anderson's *Wintergirls* gives voice to the inner turmoil that comes along with anorexia. The lies flow like dark poetry from Lia, an 18-year old who struggles with anorexia and self-mutilation. Lia's self-destructive behavior isolates her from her family and her classmates. Even the death of former best friend and weight-loss competitor Cassie can't prevent Lia from sinking further into starvation. Feeling guilty about refusing to answer her ex-friend's calls for help on the night of her death, Lia begins hallucinating. Everywhere she turns, Cassie is there, reminding her that she's not skinny enough or good enough for anyone to love her. In her desperation, Lia turns to Elijah, the last person to see Cassie alive, for help.

Where it's reviewed:
Booklist, December 15, 2008, page 51
Horn Book Magazine, March/April 2009, page 189
Publishers Weekly, January 26, 2009, page 120
School Library Journal, February 2009, page 96

Other books by the same author:
Twisted, 2007
Prom, 2005
Catalyst, 2003
Speak, 1999

Awards the book has won:
Blue Ribbon Awards: Fiction, 2009

Other books you might like:
Gayle Forman, *If I Stay*, 2009
Madeleine George, *Looks*, 2008
Sarah Darer Littman, *Purge*, 2009
Cynthea Liu, *Paris Pan Takes the Dare*, 2009
Mal Peet, *Exposure*, 2009

609

ANN ANGEL

Janis Joplin: Rise Up Singing

(New York: Amulet Books, 2010)

Subject(s): Rock music; Biographies; Musicians

Age range(s): 14 - 18+

Summary: Written by Ann Angel, this engaging biography of Janis Joplin introduces the rock legend to a young adult audience. Although Joplin died at the age of 27—ending a career that had lasted just three years—she made an impact on music and culture that endures four decades after her death. The author studies the many facets of Joplin's persona—the brilliant performer, the rebellious '60s woman, the loving daughter—to create a complete and honest portrait of the soulful singer who helped define her generation. This generously illustrated volume includes personal photos, album covers, period graphics, a time line, and a bibliography.

Where it's reviewed:
Booklist, November 1, 2010, page 54
Horn Book Guide, Spring 2011, page 184
Publishers Weekly, October 11, 2010, page 47
School Library Journal, October 2010, page 130

Other books by the same author:
Amy Tan: Weaver of Asian-American Tales, 2009
Robert Cormier: Author of The Chocolate War, 2007

Other books you might like:
Dynise Balcavage, *Janis Joplin*, 2001
Cecil Castellucci, *Beige*, 2007
Barbara Hall, *Tempo Change*, 2009
Edward Willett, *Janis Joplin: Take Another Little Piece of My Heart*, 2008

610

JENNIFER ARCHER

Through Her Eyes

(New York: HarperTeen, 2011)

Subject(s): Supernatural; Grandfathers; Photography

Age range(s): 14 - 17+

Major character(s): Tansy Piper, 16-Year-Old, Granddaughter (of Grandpa Dan), Daughter (of Millicent); Millicent Moon, Mother (of Tansy), Daughter (of Dan), Writer (horror novelist); Grandpa Dan, Grandfather (of Tansy), Father (of Millicent); Bethany, Friend (of Tansy); Henry Peterson, 17-Year-Old, Spirit

Time period(s): 21st century; 2010s

Locale(s): Cedar Canyon, Texas

Summary: Jennifer Archer's young-adult novel *Through Her Eyes* is a tale of mystery, the supernatural, and family secrets set in the remote Texas town of Cedar Canyon. Tansy Piper and her mother, the famous horror novelist Millicent Moon, have come to Cedar Canyon to stay at an old family home while Millicent works on her latest book. Tansy, who has moved many times with her mother, is immediately put off by the boring town and her eerie new home. As she explores the towering house where her Grandpa Dan was raised, Tansy finds a camera that transports her back in time, where she meets a ghost who has not rested since his death decades ago. As Tansy tries to learn her grandfather's role in a mystery from the past, she begins to slip permanently from the present.

Where it's reviewed:
Booklist, March 15, 2011, page 57
Publishers Weekly, February 14, 2011, page 58
School Library Journal, August 2011, page 94
Voice of Youth Advocates, April 2011, page 74

Other books you might like:
Katie Alender, *Bad Girls Don't Die*, 2009
Sarah Dessen, *What Happened to Goodbye*, 2011
Lois Ruby, *The Secrets of Laurel Oaks*, 2008
Jon Skovron, *Struts and Frets*, 2009
Carol Snow, *Snap*, 2009

611

ARISTOPHANE, Author/Illustrator
MATT MADDEN, Translator

The Zabime Sisters

(New York: First Second, 2010)

Subject(s): Sisters; Adolescent interpersonal relations; Islands

Age range(s): 12 - 16+
Major character(s): Celina, Sister (of Elle and M'Rose); Elle, Sister (of Celina and M'Rose); M'Rose, Sister (of Celina and Elle)
Time period(s): 20th century; 1990s
Locale(s): Guadeloupe

Summary: In the graphic novel *The Zabime Sisters*, author and artist Aristophane tells the story of three sisters over the course of one auspicious summer day on the island of Guadeloupe. Celina, Elle, and M'Rose are teenagers on the brink of womanhood, and they find more than their fair share of interesting situations on the island. They fish for crab, watch a fight between some local boys, and experiment with alcohol. Accompanied by the author's vivid images, this story chronicles those small moments in life that inevitably alter one's perception of the world and help usher in new eras of growth and self-understanding. *The Zabime Sisters* is translated from French by Matt Madden, who also includes an afterword.

Where it's reviewed:
Booklist, October 15, 2010, page 38
School Library Journal, November 2010, page 44

Other books you might like:
Marguerite Abouet, *Aya*, 2007
Michael Anthony, *Green Days by the River*, 1985
Zee Edgell, *Beka Lamb*, 1982
Lewis Trondheim, *Bourbon Island 1730*, 2008

612

MARC ARONSON
MARINA BUDHOS, Co-Author

Sugar Changed the World: A Story of Magic, Spice, Slavery, Freedom, and Science

(Boston: Clarion Books, 2010)

Subject(s): Food; Slavery; Abolition of slavery

Age range(s): 14 - 18+

Summary: Sugar is perhaps the most recognizable taste and most popular treat in the world. In *Sugar Changed the World: A Story of Magic, Spice, Slavery, Freedom, and Science*, authors Marc Aronson and Marina Budhos reveal the history of this celebrated flavoring, tracing its path from the spiritual rites of India to the castles of the Medieval period, from the horrors of the slave trade to the freedom of the emancipation. The authors include a trove of additional helpful information on the history of sugar, including an essay on how they wrote the book, a timeline, notes on the text, a bibliography, a listing of useful Web sites, and a full index.

Where it's reviewed:
Booklist, October 15, 2010, page 43
Horn Book Magazine, January-February 2011, page 107
School Library Journal, October 2010, page 130
Voice of Youth Advocates, October 2010, page 375

Other books by the same author:
Trapped: How the World Rescued 33 Miners from 2,000 Feet below the Chilean Desert, 2011
War Is...: Soldiers, Survivors and Storytellers Talk About War, 2009
Unsettled: The Problem of Loving Israel, 2008
Race: A History Beyond Black and White, 2007

Other books you might like:
R.G. Grant, *Slavery: Real People and Their Stories of Enslavement*, 2009
Barbara Hambly, *Sold Down the River*, 2000
Milton Meltzer, *They Came in Chains: The Story of the Slave Ships*, 2000
Kim L. Siegelson, *Honey Bea*, 2010

613

JAY ASHER
CAROLYN MACKLER, Co-Author

The Future of Us

(New York: Razorbill, 2011)

Story type: Contemporary
Subject(s): Computers; Internet; Adolescence

Age range(s): 14 - 18+
Major character(s): Emma, Teenager, Friend (of Josh); Josh, Teenager, Friend (of Emma)
Time period(s): 21st century; (2010s); 20th century; 1990s (1996)
Locale(s): United States

Summary: Authors Jay Asher and Carolyn Mackler create a thought-provoking story about the future and life in the digital age in this young adult novel. Teenagers in 1996, Emma and Josh are best friends. They're also among the few teens that have access to a computer or the Internet. When Emma gets her first computer and a CD-ROM for America Online, she and Josh decide to surf the World Wide Web—but they're not prepared for what they're about to find. With the click of a button, they soon discover their Facebook profiles from 15 years in the future, revealing to them the paths they're on and causing them to think long and hard about what's in store.

Where it's reviewed:
Booklist, October 15, 2011, page 43

New York Times Book Review, November 13, 2011, page 31

Publishers Weekly, September 12, 2011, page 78

School Library Journal, November 2011, page 112

Other books you might like:

Lauren Baratz-Logsted, *Secrets of My Suburban Life*, 2008

Catherine Hapka, *At First Sight*, 2010

Maili Anne McBride, *Wait! He's Real?*, 2011

Sarah Mlynowski, *Gimme a Call*, 2010

614

JEANNINE ATKINS

Borrowed Names: Poems About Laura Ingalls Wilder, Madam C. J. Walker, Marie Curie, and Their Daughters

(New York: Henry Holt, 2010)

Subject(s): Poetry; Women; Mother-daughter relations

Age range(s): 12 - 16+

Summary: *Borrowed Names: Poems About Laura Ingalls Wilder, Madam C. J. Walker, Marie Curie, and Their Daughters* is a collection of historical and inspirational poems for young adult readers from author Jeannine Atkins. Celebrated *Little House on the Prairie* author Laura Ingalls Wilder, beauty entrepreneur Madam C. J. Walker, and Nobel prize-winning scientist Marie Curie were all born in 1867. Despite the male-dominated societies they grew up in, each woman found great success in her field due to the assistance, encouragement, and support of her daughter. In *Borrowed Names*, Atkins celebrates the accomplishments and mother-daughter bonds of these remarkable women through a series of heartfelt and historical poems.

Where it's reviewed:

Booklist, February 1, 2010, page 44

Horn Book Magazine, May-June 2010, page 99

School Library Journal, February 2010, page 127

Voice of Youth Advocates, August 2010, page 276

Other books by the same author:

How High Can We Climb?: The Story of Women Explorers, 2005

Becoming Little Women: Louisa May at Fruitlands, 2001

Awards the book has won:

Blue Ribbon Awards: Non-fiction, 2010

Other books you might like:

Tananarive Due, *The Black Rose*, 2000

Rose Wilder Lane, *Let the Hurricane Roar*, 1985

Carla Killough McClafferty, *Something out of Nothing: Marie Curie and Radium*, 2006

615

SWATI AVASTHI

Split

(New York: Alfred A. Knopf, 2010)

Subject(s): Child abuse; Family; Brothers

Age range(s): 15 - 18+

Major character(s): Jace Witherspoon, 16-Year-Old, Abuse Victim, Brother (of Christian); Christian, Brother (of Jace)

Time period(s): 21st century; 2010s

Locale(s): Chicago, Illinois; Albuquerque, New Mexico

Summary: Swati Avasthi's *Split* tells the emotional story of 16-year-old Jace Witherspoon, who moves in with his older brother after their violent father kicks him out of the house. Jace and Christian's mother vows to leave her abusive spouse and sets a date for her departure. As Jace waits with baited breath for his mother's safe arrival, he attempts to forge a relationship with his brother and move on with life. But Jace is hiding a dark secret—a secret that is slowly eating away at him and jeopardizing the life he is struggling to reconstruct. First novel.

Where it's reviewed:

Booklist, January 1, 2010, page 70

Horn Book Magazine, May-June 2010, page 74

School Library Journal, March 2010, page 151

Other books you might like:

Kathi Baron, *Shattered*, 2009

David Hernandez, *Suckerpunch*, 2008

Jaye Murray, *Bottled Up*, 2003

Joyce Carol Oates, *Freaky Green Eyes*, 2003

Nancy Werlin, *The Rules of Survival*, 2006

616

HEIDI AYARBE

Compromised

(New York: HarperTeen, 2010)

Subject(s): Urban life; Runaways; Foster children

Age range(s): 15 - 18+

Major character(s): Maya, 15-Year-Old, Daughter (of con man), Foster Child, Runaway; Dad, Father (of Maya)

Time period(s): 21st century; 2010s

Locale(s): United States

Summary: *Compromised* is a gritty urban novel for young adult readers from author Heidi Ayarbe. Life has never been normal or easy for 15-year-old Maya, especially since she's been raised by her con-artist father. Whenever his schemes go wrong, the pair hit the road, while scientifically minded Maya always tries to figure out a way to fix the problem. When her dad gets busted for one of his cons and is sent to federal prison, Maya can't bear the thought of living in foster care so she decides to set out on a cross-country adventure in search of a distant relative. With an unlikely partner and 20 dollars to her name, Maya is forced to face the hard realities of life on the streets as she searches for a woman who might not even exist.

Where it's reviewed:
Booklist, April 1, 2010, page 32
Horn Book Guide, Fall 2010, page 360
Publishers Weekly, May 3, 2010, page 53
School Library Journal, July 2010, page 81

Other books by the same author:
Compulsion, 2011
Freeze Frame, 2008

Other books you might like:
Jessica Blank, *Almost Home*, 2007
Siobhan Dowd, *Solace of the Road*, 2009
Eric Walters, *Sketches*, 2008

617

HEIDI AYARBE

Compulsion

(New York: HarperCollins, 2011)

Story type: Contemporary
Subject(s): Soccer; Interpersonal relations; High schools

Age range(s): 15 - 18+
Major character(s): Jake Martin, Student—High School, Soccer Player, Mentally Ill Person (obsessive-compulsive disorder), Friend (of Luc); Luc, Friend (of Jake)
Time period(s): 21st century; 2010s
Locale(s): Carson City, Nevada

Summary: In this young adult novel by Heidi Ayarbe, high school soccer player Jake Martin knows that his future rides on the upcoming state championship game. His skills on the soccer field have attracted the attention of college recruiters, but his battle with obsessive-compulsive disorder has created frustration in his family. His father and sister are aware of the daily rituals Jake performs—all relating to prime numbers—that are necessary to his success at soccer. But Jake has come to believe that the numbers have made him magical and that the need for rituals will end when his team wins the championship. As the game approaches, Jake grows increasingly anxious as he wonders what will happen if he is wrong.

Where it's reviewed:
Booklist, March 15, 2011, page 52
School Library Journal, June 2011, page 108
Voice of Youth Advocates, August 2011, page 262

Other books by the same author:
Wanted, 2012
Compromised, 2010
Freeze Frame, 2008

Other books you might like:
Crissa-Jean Chappell, *Total Constant Order*, 2007
George Harrar, *Not as Crazy as I Seem*, 2003
Alfred C. Martino, *Over the End Line*, 2009
Walter Dean Myers, *Kick*, 2011

618

PAOLO BACIGALUPI

Ship Breaker: A Novel

(New York: Little, Brown and Company, 2010)

Subject(s): Science fiction; Conduct of life; Recycling

Age range(s): 14 - 18+
Major character(s): Nailer, Teenager, Scavenger; Lucky Girl, Heiress
Time period(s): Indeterminate Future
Locale(s): New Orleans, Louisiana

Summary: In *Ship Breaker* by Paolo Bacigalupi, the future world is a bleak and watery wasteland dominated by powerful shipping companies. In the Gulf Coast region of the U.S., a teenage boy known as Nailer spends his days salvaging copper from ships that have run aground. It is difficult, dangerous work, but it is Nailer's only means of survival. When a violent hurricane grounds a majestic clipper ship in the gulf, Nailer is shocked to find a pretty girl among its cargo. Nailer dubs her "Lucky Girl," and the two forge a friendship destined for disaster. Lucky Girl is the daughter of a rich shipping family— the enemy of Nailer's people. To escape the fury of the scavengers and the upper classes, Nailer and Lucky Girl set off for the devastated city of New Orleans.

Where it's reviewed:
Booklist, May 15, 2010, page 50
Horn Book Magazine, July-August 2010, page 98
School Library Journal, June 2010, page 94
Voice of Youth Advocates, August 2010, page 260

Other books by the same author:
Pump Six and Other Stories, 2010

Awards the book has won:
Michael L. Printz Award, 2011

Other books you might like:
Nancy Farmer, *The Ear, the Eye, and the Arm*, 1994
Catherine Fisher, *Incarceron*, 2007
Richard Harland, *Worldshaker*, 2010

619

LAUREN BARATZ-LOGSTED

Crazy Beautiful

(Boston: Houghton Mifflin, 2009)

Subject(s): Physically disabled persons; Bullying; High schools

Age range(s): 13 - 17+
Major character(s): Lucius Wolfe, 10th Grader, Amputee; Aurora, Classmate (of Lucius); Jessup, Classmate (of Lucius); Cecelia, Girlfriend (of Jessup)
Time period(s): 21st century; 2000s
Locale(s): United States

Summary: In *Crazy Beautiful* by Lauren Baratz-Logsted, Lucius Wolfe faces the first day at a new school with more anxiety than most teenagers. Lucius has no hands.

He wears hooks in place of the limbs he lost in an explosion he caused at his family's home. Angry and bitter, Lucius hopes his hooks will frighten anyone who tries to get too close to him. But Lucius's artificial limbs don't intimidate Aurora, another new student who seems to have no trouble making friends. In a twist on "Beauty and the Beast," Aurora (who recently lost her mother) and Lucius discover an unexpected attraction for one another.

Where it's reviewed:
Horn Book Guide, Spring 2010, page 88
Publishers Weekly, September 21, 2009, page 60
School Library Journal, December 2009, page 106
Voice of Youth Advocates, December 2009, page 402

Other books by the same author:
The Education of Bet, 2010
The Twin's Daughter, 2010
Secrets of My Suburban Life, 2008
Angel's Choice, 2006

Other books you might like:
Alex Flinn, *Beastly*, 2007
Donald R. Gallo, *Owning It: Stories about Teens with Disabilities*, 2008
Brent Runyon, *The Burn Journals*, 2004

620

JOHN BARNES

Tales of the Madman Underground: An Historical Romance 1973

(New York: Viking Juvenile, 2009)

Subject(s): Coming of age; Students; Adolescence

Age range(s): 15 - 18+
Major character(s): Karl Shoemaker, Student—High School
Time period(s): 20th century; 1970s (1973)
Locale(s): Lightsburg, Ohio

Summary: Encompassing six days in the life of a high school senior in small-town America, *Tales of the Madman Underground: An Historical Romance 1973* by John Barnes is the story of recent arrival Karl Shoemaker. For reasons unknown to him, Karl has always been part of a group of kids who must take part in group therapy sessions during the school day (he dubs his group "the Madman Underground"). But once arrived at his new school in Lightsburg, Ohio, he is determined to break out of the Underground at all costs. This volume charts Karl's adventures as he tries to fit in with his classmates, make sense of his chaotic home life, and find a sense of normalcy in his crazy world.

Where it's reviewed:
Booklist, May 1, 2009, page 81
Horn Book Guide, Sept.-October 2009, page 550
Publishers Weekly, June 1, 2009, page 49
School Library Journal, July 2009, page 78

Other books by the same author:
Daybreak Zero, 2011
Directive 51, 2010
The Arms of Memory, 2006

Other books you might like:
Aidan Chambers, *The Toll Bridge*, 1995
Brendan Halpin, *How Ya Like Me Now*, 2007
Ken Kesey, *One Flew over the Cuckoo's Nest*, 1962

621

TRACY BARRETT

King of Ithaka

(New York: Henry Holt, 2010)

Subject(s): Mythology; Legends; Adventure

Age range(s): 13 - 16+
Major character(s): Telemachos, 16-Year-Old, Son (of Odysseus and Penelopeia), Friend (of Brax and Polydora); Brax, Mythical Creature (centaur), Friend (of Telemachos and Polydora); Polydora, Young Woman, Artisan (weaver), Friend (of Telemachos and Brax); Penelopeia, Ruler (of Ithaka), Spouse (of Odysseus), Mother (of Telemachos)
Time period(s): Indeterminate Past
Locale(s): Ithaka, Greece

Summary: Based on Homer's *The Odyssey*, this adventure tale by Tracy Barrett follows 16-year-old Telemachos's quest to find his father. Odysseus left Ithaka at the start of the Trojan War, leaving behind his infant son, Telemachos, and his wife, Penelopeia. For 16 years, Penelopeia has done her best to rule Ithaka and provide a pleasant life for her son. But the citizens have come to believe that Odysseus is dead and want Penelopeia to marry and give Ithaka a new king. Telemachos is roused from his complacent lifestyle and embarks on a journey to find his missing father. Telemachos's friends Brax, a centaur, and Polydora, a weaver, join him on the quest that will take them far from the familiar land of Ithaka.

Where it's reviewed:
Booklist, October 1, 2010, page 86
Publishers Weekly, September 6, 2010, page 41
School Library Journal, November 2010, page 102
Voice of Youth Advocates, December 2010, page 464

Other books by the same author:
Dark of the Moon, 2011
Cold in Summer, 2005
On Etruscan Time, 2005
Anna of Byzantium, 1999

Other books you might like:
Adele Geras, *Ithaka*, 2005
Gareth Hinds, *The Odyssey*, 2010
Clemence McLaren, *Waiting for Odysseus*, 2000
Theresa Tomlinson, *The Moon Riders*, 2006

622

SUSAN CAMPBELL BARTOLETTI

They Called Themselves the K.K.K.: The Birth of an American Terrorist Group

(Boston: Houghton Mifflin Harcourt, 2010)

Subject(s): Ku Klux Klan; Racism; Terrorism

Age range(s): 13 - 18+

Time period(s): 19th century-21st century

Locale(s): United States

Summary: In *They Called Themselves the K.K.K.: The Birth of an American Terrorist Group*, author Susan Campbell Bartoletti records the history of the notorious organization responsible for some of the most appalling attacks on American citizens. From the turbulent post-Civil War years to the present day, Bartoletti profiles individuals on both sides of the Klan's divisive actions, presenting a comprehensive look at the influence, power, and eventual decline of this homegrown terrorist faction. *They Called Themselves the K.K.K.* includes a timeline, a bibliography, and an index.

Where it's reviewed:
Booklist, August 1, 2010, page 48
Horn Book Magazine, September-October 2010, page 106
Publishers Weekly, July 26, 2010, page 77
School Library Journal, August 2010, page 117
Voice of Youth Advocates, October 2010, page 375

Other books by the same author:
Hitler Youth: Growing Up in Hitler's Shadow, 2004
Black Potatoes: The Story of the Great Irish Famine 1845-1850, 2001
Kids on Strike, 1999
Growing Up in Coal Country, 1996

Other books you might like:
Ann Heinrichs, *The Ku Klux Klan: A Hooded Brotherhood*, 2003
Karen Hesse, *Witness*, 2001
George Edward Stanley, *Night Fires*, 2009

623

JOAN BAUER

Close to Famous

(New York: Viking, 2011)

Story type: Contemporary - Mainstream

Subject(s): Learning disorders; Mother-daughter relations; Single parent family

Age range(s): 10 - 14+

Major character(s): Foster McFee, 12-Year-Old, Daughter (of Rayka McFee), Baker; Rayka "Mama" McFee, Mother (of Foster McFee), Single Mother, Singer, Abuse Victim; Miss Charleena, Actress (retired), Friend (of Foster McFee); Macon Dillard, Child, Filmmaker, Friend (of Foster McFee); Huck,

Boyfriend (of Rayka McFee)

Time period(s): 21st century; 2010s

Locale(s): Culpepper, West Virginia

Summary: Culpepper, West Virginia, becomes the new home of 12-year-old Foster McFee and her mother in this novel for older children and young adults by Joan Bauer. Foster and Mama flee Memphis, Tennessee, to get away from Mama's abusive boyfriend, and they end up in a tiny, rural town populated by folks with big dreams and bigger hearts. There, Foster—an aspiring baker who dreams of having her own show on the Food Network—surrounds herself with an eccentric group of friends and starts to feel at home. She begins to conquer her learning disability and even lands a job baking cupcakes for a local business. Meanwhile, she encourages Mama to step out of the shadows as a backup singer and take her rightful place in the spotlight. Can Foster and Mama's happiness last? Or will their past come back to haunt them?

Where it's reviewed:
Bulletin of the Center for Children's Books, January 2011, page 226
Horn Book Magazine, January/February 2011, page 87
Publishers Weekly, December 13, 2010, page 58
School Library Journal, March 2010, page 154

Other books by the same author:
Hope Was Here, 2001
Squashed, 1992

Other books you might like:
Marlane Kennedy, *Me and the Pumpkin Queen*, 2007
Michelle D. Kwasney, *Itch*, 2008
Karon Luddy, *Spelldown*, 2007
Barbara O'Connor, *Greetings from Nowhere*, 2008
Lisa Schroeder, *It's Raining Cupcakes*, 2010

624

BETH ANN BAUMAN

Rosie and Skate

(New York: Wendy Lamb Books, 2009)

Subject(s): Alcoholism; Sisters; Father-daughter relations

Age range(s): 14 - 18+

Major character(s): Rosie, 15-Year-Old, Sister (of Skate); Skate, Sister (of Rosie), 16-Year-Old

Time period(s): 21st century; 2000s

Locale(s): New Jersey, United States

Summary: Against the backdrop of the Jersey shore, two sisters find strength, hope, and support during a dark period in their lives. Beth Ann Bauman's *Rosie and Skate* charts the experiences of two teenage siblings as they try to come to terms with their father's alcoholism and subsequent jailing. Cared for by their cousin, Rosie and Skate navigate the rough waters of young adulthood—and, along the way, discover the joy and pain of first love. First novel.

Where it's reviewed:
Booklist, October 1, 2009, page 43
Horn Book Guide, Spring 2010, page 89

New York Times Book Review, January 17, 2010, page 13

School Library Journal, November 2009, page 100

Other books you might like:

Susane Colasanti, *Waiting for You*, 2009

Maureen Johnson, *The Key to the Golden Firebird*, 2004

David Lubar, *Dunk*, 2002

Amy Kathleen Ryan, *Zen and Xander Undone*, 2010

Zu Vincent, *The Lucky Place*, 2008

625

CRIS BEAM

I Am J

(New York: Little, Brown and Company, 2011)

Subject(s): Sexuality; Identity; Adolescence

Age range(s): 15 - 18+
Major character(s): J, 17-Year-Old
Time period(s): 21st century; 2010s
Locale(s): United States

Summary: Since childhood, J has felt certain that he was a boy who was mistakenly born into a female's body. Now, at the age of 17, his body has developed into a woman's, but his heart and mind are unmistakably male. Despite his best efforts to hide his female anatomy, by binding his breasts and wearing baggy clothing, J feels tormented that his body doesn't match his heart. With his parents feeling upset, angry, and confused, J decides to run away from home to find the answers he needs. He's soon enrolled at a school for transgender and homosexual kids and attending counseling as he searches for the strength he needs to confront himself and the people he loves the most. First novel.

Where it's reviewed:

Booklist, December 1, 2010, page 44

Horn Book Magazine, March-April 2011, page 111

Publishers Weekly, January 31, 2011, page 51

School Library Journal, February 2011, page 101

Voice of Youth Advocates, April 2011, page 74

Other books you might like:

Betsy Franco, *Falling Hard: 100 Love Poems by Teenagers*, 2008

Catherine Ryan Hyde, *Jumpstart the World*, 2010

Ellen Wittlinger, *Parrotfish*, 2007

626

SEAN BEAUDOIN

Fade to Blue

(New York: Little, Brown and Company, 2009)

Subject(s): Identity; Computer programming; High schools

Age range(s): 14 - 17+
Major character(s): Sophie Blue, Teenager; Kenny Fade, Classmate (of Sophie), Teenager

Time period(s): 21st century; 2000s
Locale(s): United States

Summary: In *Fade to Blue*, author Sean Beaudoin tells the story of Goth girl Sophie Blue, whose 17th birthday turns out to be the worst day of her life. Her father vanishes, a stranger injects her with an unknown serum, and a strange truck is staking out her house. A year passes, and Sophie has started to be plagued with extrasensory abilities—abilities she shares with a very unlikely schoolmate: popular jock Kenny Fade. Together, Sophie and Kenny set out to find what exactly has happened to them—before they lose what's left of their minds.

Where it's reviewed:

Booklist, June 1, 2009, page 50

Horn Book Magazine, Sept-Oct 2009, page 551

School Library Journal, October 2009, page 119

Other books by the same author:

Going Nowhere Faster, 2007

You Killed Wesley Payne, 2001

Other books you might like:

Beth Fantaskey, *Jekel Loves Hyde*, 2010

James Kennedy, *The Order of Odd-Fish*, 2008

James Moloney, *The Book of Lies*, 2004

Scott Westerfeld, *Extras*, 2007

627

MARY JANE BEAUFRAND

The River

(New York: Little, Brown and Company, 2010)

Subject(s): Mystery; Rural life; Murder

Age range(s): 14 - 16+
Major character(s): Veronica "Ronnie" Severance, 16-Year-Old, Detective—Amateur; Karen, 8-Year-Old, Crime Victim
Time period(s): 21st century; 2010s
Locale(s): Oregon, United States

Summary: After her father suffers a breakdown, 16-year-old Veronica "Ronnie" Severance is forced to move away from the bright lights of Portland, Oregon, to a new home in the country. Surrounded by nothing but wilderness and the Santiam River, Ronnie is desperately lonely and longs to leave behind this strange place. Her only solace comes in the form of Karen, a lively 8-year-old girl whom Ronnie babysits. The pair begin to build an unlikely friendship as they explore their surroundings. On an afternoon run, Ronnie discovers Karen's body on the banks of the Santiam and, although her death is ruled an accident, Ronnie is determined to find out what really happened. Her investigation leads her deep into the rural town as she uncovers the truth about its residents and the hidden secrets lurking in the woods.

Where it's reviewed:

Booklist, December 15, 2009, page 36

Horn Book Magazine, May-June 2010, page 76

School Library Journal, February 2010, page 104

Voice of Youth Advocates, April 2010, page 54

Other books by the same author:
Primavera, 2008

Other books you might like:
Josh Berk, *The Dark Days of Hamburger Halpin*, 2010
Anna Jarzab, *All Unquiet Things*, 2010
Melissa Lion, *Swollen*, 2004
Linda Newbery, *Flightsend*, 1999

628

MARTYN BEDFORD

Flip

(New York: Walker & Company, 2011)

Subject(s): Adolescent interpersonal relations; Identity; Supernatural

Age range(s): 14 - 16+
Major character(s): Alex Gray, 14-Year-Old
Time period(s): 21st century; 2010s
Locale(s): England

Summary: In the young adult novel *Flip* by Martyn Bedford, Alex Gray is a 14-year-old boy with an identity crisis. Unlike most kids his age, though, Alex's identity is a complete mystery because one day he woke up in another boy's body. Now he is called Philip, aka "Flip," and his life couldn't be more different. Alex was in the school band and chess club, whereas Flip is a jock and a popular student. Flip also juggles two girls at a time, and Alex has never had a girlfriend in his life. Now Alex must figure out what happened to his own body, and why he inhabits someone else's—before the flip is permanent.

Where it's reviewed:
Booklist, May 15, 2011, page 55
Horn Book Magazine, May-June 2011, page 82
Publishers Weekly, February 21, 2011, page 135
School Library Journal, June 2011, page 108
Voice of Youth Advocates, April 2011, page 74

Other books you might like:
Peter Dickinson, *Eva*, 1988
Carol Snow, *Switch*, 2008
Nancy Springer, *Possessing Jessie*, 2010
Laura Whitcomb, *A Certain Slant of Light*, 2005

629

MICHAEL D. BEIL

The Red Blazer Girls: The Ring of Rocamadour

(New York: Alfred A. Knopf, 2009)

Subject(s): Mystery; Schools; Friendship

Age range(s): 11 - 14+
Major character(s): Sophie St. Pierre, 12-Year-Old, Detective—Amateur, Writer, Student; Margaret Wrobel, 12-Year-Old, Student, Detective—Amateur; Rebecca Chen, 12-Year-Old, Student, Artist, Detective—

Amateur; Lee Ann Jaimes, 12-Year-Old, Student, Detective—Amateur, Actress
Time period(s): 21st century; 2000s
Locale(s): New York, New York

Summary: *The Red Blazer Girls: The Ring of Rocamadour* is a humorous and adventurous young adult mystery and the debut novel from author Michael D. Beil. Sophie, Margaret, Rebecca, and Leigh Ann are the Red Blazer Girls, four 12-year-old friends who attend St. Veronica's on the Upper East Side. The four girls are drawn into a puzzling mystery when they offer to help the unusual woman who neighbors their school and church. The preteen detectives must use math and language skills to solve a series of clues, which lead them on a wild, exciting, and sometimes terrifying scavenger hunt. As if that's not enough, they still have to keep up their grades, outsmart their enemies, and deal with boys. First novel.

Where it's reviewed:
Booklist, January 1, 2009, page 77
Horn Book Guide, Spring 2010, page 90
Publishers Weekly, December 15, 2008, page 40
School Library Journal, August 2009, page 98
Voice of Youth Advocates, December 2009, page 403

Other books by the same author:
The Red Blazer Girls: The Mistaken Masterpiece, 2011
The Red Blazer Girls: The Vanishing Violin, 2010

Other books you might like:
Eric Berlin, *The Potato Chip Puzzles: The Puzzling World of Winston Breen*, 2009
Leslie Margolis, *Girl's Best Friend*, 2010
Susan Runholt, *The Mystery of the Third Lucretia*, 2008
Diane Stanley, *The Mysterious Case of the Allbright Academy*, 2007
Trenton Lee Stewart, *The Mysterious Benedict Society and the Perilous Journey*, 2008

630

CHARLES BENOIT

You

(New York: HarperTeen, 2010)

Subject(s): Conduct of life; High schools; Social conditions

Age range(s): 14 - 18+
Major character(s): Kyle Chase, 15-Year-Old, Student—High School; Zack McDade, Student—High School, Friend (of Kyle)
Time period(s): 21st century; 2010s
Locale(s): United States

Summary: In the young adult novel *You* by Charles Benoit, high-school sophomore Kyle Chase realizes that his life is spinning out of control. He's hanging out with a bad crowd, doing poorly in class, and getting in trouble at school and at home. When Zack McDade comes to Midlands High School, Kyle presumes that the new student's smooth personality and sophisticated intelligence make him a good choice for a friend. But once again, Kyle is wrong. When Kyle's accumulation of bad decisions results in a devastating event, he tries to sort through his experiences to discover where his life's downward spiral began. Told in the second person, *You* brings readers into the story, making them feel as if they are participants in Kyle's world.

Where it's reviewed:
Booklist, June 1, 2010, page 62
Horn Book Magazine, July-August 2010, page 100
Publishers Weekly, September 6, 2010, page 41
School Library Journal, August 2010, page 94
Voice of Youth Advocates, December 2010, page 444

Other books by the same author:
Relative Danger, 2004

Other books you might like:
Tim Bowler, *Blade: Playing Dead*, 2008
Alex Flinn, *Breaking Point*, 2002
Gail Giles, *Shattering Glass*, 2002

631

ROBIN BENWAY

The Extraordinary Secrets of April, May and June

(New York: Razorbill, 2010)

Subject(s): Sisters; Psychics; High schools

Age range(s): 15 - 18+

Major character(s): April, 16-Year-Old, Sister (of May and June); May, 15-Year-Old, Sister (of April and June); June, 14-Year-Old, Sister (of April and May)

Time period(s): 21st century; 2010s

Locale(s): California, United States

Summary: In the young adult novel *Extraordinary Secrets of April, May and June* by Robin Benway, three teenage sisters share a close relationship and paranormal powers. After the girls' parents divorced, their father moved to Houston and the girls stayed in California with their mother. The strain of their situation has resurrected mysterious powers that they hadn't used in years. April can look into the future, May can make herself vanish, and June can perceive what those around her are thinking. At first the sisters waste their strange talents on such adolescent concerns as popularity and social status. But when one of April's visions predicts a potential tragedy, the girls unite to protect their family.

Where it's reviewed:
Booklist, July 1, 2010, page 50
Publishers Weekly, July 5, 2010, page 44
Voice of Youth Advocates, October 2010, page 361

Other books by the same author:
Audrey, Wait!, 2008

Other books you might like:
Aimee Friedman, *The Year My Sister Got Lucky*, 2008
Phoebe Kitanidis, *Whisper*, 2010
Myra McEntire, *Hourglass*, 2011
Inara Scott, *The Candidates*, 2010

632

JOSH BERK

The Dark Days of Hamburger Halpin

(New York: Alfred A. Knopf, 2010)

Subject(s): Murder; Mystery; High schools

Age range(s): 14 - 17+

Major character(s): Will Halpin, Deaf Person, Teenager, Student—High School, Detective—Amateur; Devon, Teenager, Student—High School, Detective—Amateur

Time period(s): 21st century; 2010s

Locale(s): United States

Summary: Being deaf and overweight aren't helpful to Will Halpin's social status as the new kid at Coaler High School. When he befriends the dorkiest guy in school, Devon, he seals his fate. Will spends his days "eavesdropping" on conversations with his impressive lip-reading abilities and thinking about girls, until the school's star quarterback is murdered on a field trip. Will and Devon set out to solve the crime, putting their geeky heads together to investigate the murder, weed through the suspects, and find the person responsible. First novel.

Where it's reviewed:
Booklist, December 15, 2009, page 34
Horn Book Guide, Fall 2010, page 360
Publishers Weekly, January 18, 2010, page 49
School Library Journal, January 2010, page 96
Voice of Youth Advocates, June 2010, page 146

Other books by the same author:
Guy Langman, Crime Scene Procrastinator, 2012

Other books you might like:
Donald R. Gallo, *Owning It: Stories about Teens with Disabilities*, 2008
K.L. Going, *Fat Kid Rules the World*, 2003
Paul Griffin, *The Orange Houses*, 2009
Antony John, *Five Flavors of Dumb*, 2010

633

JULIE BERTAGNA

Zenith

(New York: Walker Books, 2009)

Subject(s): Environmental engineering; Disasters; Survival

Age range(s): 15 - 18+

Major character(s): Mara, 16-Year-Old, Refugee, Friend (of Tuck), Lover (of Fox); Fox, Lover (of Mara), Refugee, Activist (against political corruption), Teenager; Tuck, Pirate, Teenager, Refugee

Time period(s): Indeterminate Future

Locale(s): Greenland

Summary: *Zenith* imagines a world in which nothing has been done to stop global warming and most of the world's landmass lies beneath violent waves. In this portion of the story, Mara, her family, and her fellow refugees continue tracking the North Star in an attempt to find dry land somewhere near Greenland. Their ship accidentally collides with a small pirate community, forcing the refugees to bring a young boy, Tuck, onboard. Although Tuck shows a propensity for construction, he finds it hard to shake his pirate heritage. At the same time, Mara's lover, Fox, is off fighting for an uncorrupted new regime, as the world's survivors attempt to coalesce into a new government body.

Where it's reviewed:
Booklist, February 15, 2009, page 90
School Library Journal, July 2009, page 78

Other books by the same author:
Exodus, 2008

Other books you might like:
James Patterson, *The Final Warning*, 2008
Susan Beth Pfeffer, *Life as We Knew It*, 2006
Terry Pratchett, *Nation*, 2008
Suzanne Weyn, *Empty*, 2010

634

FRANNY BILLINGSLEY

Chime

(New York: Dial Books, 2011)

Story type: Fantasy
Subject(s): Twins; Sisters; Supernatural

Age range(s): 14 - 18+
Major character(s): Briony Larkin, 17-Year-Old, Twin (of Rose); Rose, Twin (of Briony), Mentally Challenged Person; Mr. Clayborne, Engineer, Father (of Eldric); Eldric Clayborne, Student—College (dropout)
Time period(s): 20th century
Locale(s): Swampsea, England

Summary: Seventeen-year-old Briony Larkin struggles to hide her shame and fear from the residents of her village in this young adult novel by Franny Billingsley. At the turn of the 20th century, the English community of Swampsea is feeling the effects of scientific advancements. But superstition still rules, and Briony knows that she must keep her terrible secrets at any cost. Briony is a witch, and her wickedness caused her stepmother's death and her twin sister Rose's debilitating injury—at least, that's what Briony has been led to believe. But when a young man comes to Swampsea with his engineer father, Mr. Clayborne, to drain the nearby bogs, Briony finds herself drawn to the fair-haired Eldric. As she deals with the swamp ghosts who have been unsettled by Clayborne's work, Briony must also confront the truths that Eldric reveals.

Where it's reviewed:
Booklist, February 1, 2011, page 68
Horn Book Magazine, March-April 2011, page 111
Publishers Weekly, January 17, 2011, page 49
School Library Journal, March 2011, page 154
Voice of Youth Advocates, April 2011, page 74

Other books by the same author:
The Folk Keeper, 1999
Well Wished, 1997

Other books you might like:
Beth Kephart, *Dangerous Neighbors*, 2010
Jacquelyn Mitchard, *The Midnight Twins*, 2008
Michael Scott, *The Alchemyst: The Secrets of the Immortal Nicholas Flamel*, 2007
Michelle Zink, *Guardian of the Gate*, 2010

635

HOLLY BLACK, Editor
ELLEN KUSHNER, Co-Editor

Welcome to Bordertown: New Stories and Poems of the Borderlands

(New York: Random House, 2011)

Story type: Collection; Fantasy
Subject(s): Short stories; Poetry; Supernatural

Age range(s): 15 - 18+
Locale(s): Borderlands, Fictional Location

Summary: Editors Holly Black and Ellen Kushner collect new tales, poems, and a graphic story that revisit the fantastic realm of the Borderlands, which was created in the 1980s by Terri Windling. The magical region that lies between the elfin and human worlds, the Borderlands is a haven for roaming adolescents of both dominions. Though the place holds promise, it is also filled with danger posed by the unpredictable fairy magic at work there. The collection includes "Shannon's Law" by Cory Doctorow, "Night Song for a Halfie" by Jane Yolen, "The Rowan Gentleman" by Holly Black and Cassandra Clare, and "The Song of the Song" by Neil Gaiman. Terri Windling provides the book's introduction.

Where it's reviewed:
Booklist, March 15, 2011, page 60
School Library Journal, June 2011, page 109

Other books you might like:
Ellen Datlow, *The Beastly Bride: Tales of the Animal People*, 2010
Gavin J. Grant, *Steampunk!: An Anthology of Fantastically Rich and Strange Stories*, 2011
Sharyn November, *Firebirds Rising: An Anthology of Original Fantasy and Science Fiction*, 2003

636

HOLLY BLACK

Red Glove

(New York: Margaret K. McElderry, 2011)

Series: Curse Workers Series. Book 2
Story type: Fantasy; Series
Subject(s): Science fiction; Criminals; Magic

Age range(s): 14 - 18+
Major character(s): Cassel Sharpe, Teenager, Magician (transformation worker), Boyfriend (of Lila); Lila, Girlfriend (of Cassel)

Time period(s): 21st century; 2010s
Locale(s): United States

Summary: In this second young adult novel in Holly Black's Curse Workers Series, 17-year-old Cassel Sharpe continues to adjust to life as a potent magician. Cassel can transform whatever he touches into another object or being. It was this extraordinary power that changed his girlfriend Lila into a white cat. Now that Cassel's brother, an informant for the government, is dead, the authorities want Cassel to carry on in his place. But members of the organized crime world recognize Cassel's value as an assassin and also seek his services. Meanwhile, Lila has become human again but now carries a new curse that makes her as dangerous as the government agents and mob bosses.

Where it's reviewed:
Booklist, April 1, 2011, page 70
Publishers Weekly, February 14, 2011, page 59
School Library Journal, May 2011, page 106
Voice of Youth Advocates, June 2011, page 156

Other books by the same author:
Black Heart, 2012
White Cat, 2010
Ironside: A Modern Faery's Tale, 2007
Valiant: A Modern Tale of Faerie, 2006

Other books you might like:
Shannon Delany, *Bargains and Betrayals*, 2011
Kimberly Derting, *Desires of the Dead*, 2011
Gordon Korman, *Son of the Mob*, 2002

637

HOLLY BLACK, Editor
CECIL CASTELLUCCI, Co-Editor

Geektastic: Stories from the Nerd Herd

(New York: Little, Brown and Company, 2009)

Subject(s): Short stories; Comic books; Fantasy

Age range(s): 15 - 18+

Summary: In *Geektastic: Stories from the Nerd Herd*, editors Holly Black and Cecil Castellucci present a collection of short stories centering on all things great and geeky. Interspersed with comics, the tales of this volume cover such themes as *Star Wars*, *Star Trek*, and *Dungeons and Dragons*, just to name a few. Titles in *Geektastic* include "Once You're a Jedi, You're a Jedi All the Way," "The King of Pelinesse," and "It's Just a Jump to the Left."

Where it's reviewed:
Booklist, September 1, 2009, page 81
Horn Book Guide, Sept.-Oct. 2009, page 553
Publishers Weekly, August 3, 2009, page 45
School Library Journal, August 2009, page 98
Voice of Youth Advocates, August 2009, page 224

Other books you might like:
Barry Lyga, *The Astonishing Adventures of Fanboy and Goth Girl*, 2006
Robin Palmer, *Geek Charming*, 2009

Laura Preble, *Queen Geeks in Love*, 2007
Kieran Scott, *Geek Magnet*, 2008
Charity Tahmaseb, *The Geek Girl's Guide to Cheerleading*, 2009

638

HOLLY BLACK, Editor
JUSTINE LARBALESTIER, Co-Editor

Zombies vs. Unicorns

(New York: Margaret K. McElderry Books, 2010)

Subject(s): Unicorns; Zombies; Short stories

Age range(s): 14 - 18+

Summary: In *Zombies vs. Unicorns*, editors Holly Black and Justine Larbalestier present a collection of short stories for young adults that explore the disputed superiority of two mythical creatures. Half of the dozen stories in the anthology extol the virtues of the zombie, while the remaining tales reveal a pro-unicorn point of view. The stories in this clever collection include "The Highest Justice" by Garth Nix, "Inoculata" by Scott Westerfeld, "Princess Prettypants" by Meg Cabot, "The Purity Test" by Naomi Novik, "Love Will Tear Us Apart" by Alaya Dawn Johnson, "A Thousand Flowers" by Margo Lanagan, and "Care and Feeding of Your Baby Killer Unicorn" by Diana Peterfreund.

Where it's reviewed:
Booklist, September 1, 2010, page 103
Publishers Weekly, August 23, 2010, page 51
Reading Time, February 2011, page 35
School Library Journal, October 2010, page 108

Other books you might like:
Bruce Coville, *Oddest of All: Stories*, 2008
Jonathan Maberry, *Rot and Ruin*, 2010
Trisha Telep, *Kiss Me Deadly: 13 Tales of Paranormal Love*, 2010
Jane Yolen, *Here There Be Unicorns*, 1994

639

HOLLY BLACK

White Cat

(New York: Margaret K. McElderry Books, 2010)

Series: Curse Workers Series. Book 1
Subject(s): Memory; Criminals; Brothers

Age range(s): 13 - 18+
Major character(s): Cassel Sharpe, Teenager
Time period(s): 21st century; 2010s
Locale(s): United States

Summary: *White Cat* is the first installment in Holly Black's Curse Workers series. This volume introduces teenager Cassel Sharpe, who belongs to a family that possesses the dark power to alter the memories and emotions of others. But Cassel doesn't have this same ability, and he's something of a black sheep among the Sharpes. Cassel is also struggling with his guilt over murdering his best friend, Lila, several years ago. Soon a series of strange events prompts Cassel to investigate the magical powers of his family, leading him to question his role in Lila's death—and if there's a chance she could still be alive.

Where it's reviewed:
Booklist, April 1, 2010, page 36
Horn Book Guide, Fall 2010, page 361
Locus, July 2010, page 27
New York Times Book Review, September 12, 2010, page 19
School Library Journal, June 2010, page 94

Other books by the same author:
Red Glove, 2011
The Poison Eaters: And Other Stories, 2010
The Good Neighbors: Kin, 2008
Ironside, 2008
Valiant: A Modern Tale of Faerie, 2006
Tithe, 2002

Other books you might like:
Robert Asprin, *Dragons Wild*, 2008
Ally Carter, *Heist Society*, 2010
Eoin Colfer, *Artemis Fowl Series*, 2001
Shannon Hale, *Calamity Jack*, 2010
Gordon Korman, *Son of the Mob*, 2002

640

KENDARE BLAKE

Anna Dressed in Blood

(New York: Tor Books, 2011)

Story type: Paranormal; Young Adult
Subject(s): Ghosts; Supernatural; Family

Age range(s): 15 - 18+
Major character(s): Cas Lowood, Hunter (of ghosts); Anna "Anna Dressed in Blood" Korlov, Spirit
Locale(s): Thunder Bay, Ontario

Summary: In this novel by Kendare Blake, Cas Lowood isn't like other teens. Following in his deceased father's footsteps, Cas hunts and kills ghosts and specters who are intent on harming the living. The work is dangerous—after all, Cas's father died in an altercation with one of his targets—but Cas has two helpful sidekicks: his mother (an amateur witch) and their cat (who has the ability to detect paranormal activity). Under normal circumstances, Cas has no qualms about killing ghosts with his father's mysterious dagger. When the Lowood clan tracks a legendary ghost named Anna Dressed in Blood, however, Cas cannot bring himself to end the specter's reign of terror. Cas knows that behind Anna's haunting lies pain and anger, and now it is up to him to try to help her find solace in the afterlife. The only question is, will Anna let Cas help, or will he become yet another victim of the girl dressed in blood?

Where it's reviewed:
Booklist, June 1, 2011, page 79

Publishers Weekly, August 15, 2011, page 73
School Library Journal, November 15, 2011, page 113

Other books by the same author:
Girl of Nightmares, 2012

Other books you might like:
Rosemary Clement-Moore, *Texas Gothic*, 2011
Marley Gibson, *The Awakening: Ghost Huntress*, 2009
Tara Hudson, *Hereafter*, 2011
Maureen Johnson, *The Name of the Star*, 2011

641

FRANCESCA LIA BLOCK

Pretty Dead

(New York: HarperTeen, 2009)

Subject(s): Vampires; Supernatural; Death

Age range(s): 15 - 18+
Major character(s): Charlotte Emerson, 17-Year-Old, Vampire; Emily, Friend (of Charlotte); Jared, Boyfriend (of Emily); William Stone Eliot, Vampire
Time period(s): 21st century; 2000s
Locale(s): Los Angeles, California

Summary: In *Pretty Dead* by Francesca Lia Block, Charlotte Emerson has lived for a century with the horrible choice she made in a state of grief. Having lost her twin brother when they were 17, Charlotte became a vampire to escape her human suffering. Now, 100 years later, Charlotte is still a pretty teenager living alone in Los Angeles. When another of her loved ones—best friend Emily—dies, Charlotte and Emily's boyfriend, Jared, offer mutual support. Gradually, Charlotte realizes that blood has begun to course through her body again, and that her vampiric condition may not be as permanent as she believed.

Where it's reviewed:
Horn Book Magazine, January/February 2010, page 82
Publishers Weekly, October 5, 2009, page 52
School Library Journal, October 2009, page 120
Voice of Youth Advocates, October 2009, page 325

Other books by the same author:
The Frenzy, 2010
The Waters and the Wild, 2009
Blood Roses, 2008
I Was a Teenage Fairy, 1998

Other books you might like:
Beth Fantaskey, *Jessica's Guide to Dating on the Dark Side*, 2009
Catherine Jinks, *The Reformed Vampire Support Group*, 2009
Martine Leavitt, *Keturah and Lord Death*, 2006
Trisha Telep, *The Eternal Kiss: 13 Vampire Tales of Blood and Desire*, 2009

642

KAREN BLUMENTHAL

Bootleg: Murder, Moonshine, and the Lawless Years of Prohibition

(New York: Flash Point, 2011)

Subject(s): History; United States; Prohibition

Age range(s): 13 - 16+

Summary: In this nonfiction work, Karen Blumenthal discusses Prohibition and its effects on the nation. The book explains that, in the early 1900s, reformers were interested in ridding the country of evils that they believed were caused by alcohol. At first, these social reformers supported bans on drinking in public. Then the cause spread, and people began campaigning for a ban on all alcohol. Finally the Eighteenth Amendment, which banned the sale and production of alcohol, was passed. Although the law had good intentions, Prohibition caused increases in crime throughout the country. Gangsters and criminals made money from illegally making and selling alcohol, and everyday citizens broke the law so they could have a drink. Throughout the book, Blumenthal describes how the era of Prohibition changed America forever.

Where it's reviewed:
Booklist, April 15, 2007, page 52
Horn Book Magazine, May/June 2011, page 116
School Library Journal, July 2011, page 111
Voice of Youth Advocates, June 2011, page 116

Other books by the same author:
Mr. Sam: How Sam Walton Built Wal-Mart and Became America's Richest Man, 2011
Let Me Play: The Story of Title IX: The Law That Changed the Future of Girls in America, 2005
Six Days in October: The Stock Market Crash of 1929, 2002

Other books you might like:
Stephen Feinstein, *The 1920s from Prohibition to Charles Lindbergh*, 2001
David C. King, *Al Capone and the Roaring Twenties*, 1999
Tamra B. Orr, *Prohibition*, 2004

643

JUDY BLUNDELL

Strings Attached

(New York: Scholastic Inc., 2011)

Story type: Coming-of-Age
Subject(s): Acting; Dance; Family

Age range(s): 15 - 18+
Major character(s): Kit Corrigan, Dancer, Girlfriend (ex, of Billy); Billy, Boyfriend (ex, of Kit), Son (of Nate); Nate, Father (of Billy), Organized Crime Figure
Time period(s): 20th century; 1950s

Locale(s): New York, New York

Summary: Seventeen-year-old Kit Corrigan wants more than anything to leave behind the small-town feel of Providence, Rhode Island and her oppressive family and relationships there, and to set off for a life of fame and fortune in New York City. Once she arrives in the Big Apple, however, Kit finds that her dreams are much harder to accomplish than she ever realized. She is able to score nothing more than a small role as a chorus girl in a minor Broadway show. Then she meets an old friend of the family named Nate who just might be able to help her. Nate is also the father of her horrible ex-boyfriend Billy, but he offers her so much help that she can't refuse his request to get back in touch with Billy. Unfortunately, Nate is also mixed up in organized crime, and the favors that he does for Kit begin to come at a very steep price. Should she continue to follow her dream at all costs, or fight for what little control she has left of her life?

Where it's reviewed:
Booklist, March 1, 2011, page 59
Publishers Weekly, January 17, 2011, page 50
School Library Journal, March 2011, page 156
Voice of Youth Advocates, February 2011, page 578

Other books by the same author:
What I Saw and How I Lied, 2008

Other books you might like:
James Docherty, *The Ice Cream Con*, 2008
Anna Fienberg, *Number 8*, 2007
Gordon Korman, *Son of the Mob*, 2002
April Lurie, *Brothers, Boyfriends and Other Criminal Minds*, 2007
Robert Newton, *Runner*, 2007

644

CAROLINE BOCK

LIE

(New York: St. Martin's Press, 2011)

Story type: Young Adult
Subject(s): Immigrants; Adolescent interpersonal relations; Violence

Age range(s): 13 - 16+
Major character(s): Skylar Thompson, Teenager, Girlfriend (of Jimmy); Jimmy Seeger, Boyfriend (of Skylar), Teenager, Crime Suspect, Friend (of Sean); Lisa Marie Murano, Friend (of Skylar), Girlfriend (of Sean); Sean, Friend (of Jimmy), Boyfriend (of Lisa Marie), Crime Suspect
Time period(s): 21st century; 2010s
Locale(s): New York, New York

Summary: This novel by author Caroline Bock tells the story of a teenage girl caught in the aftermath of a violent act of racism. During an evening out, Long Island teen Skylar Thompson, her boyfriend Jimmy Seeger, her friend Lisa Marie Murano, and Lisa's boyfriend Sean speed down the Long Island Expressway (LIE) in search of fun. What happens next is unthinkable: The group happens upon two El Salvadorian brothers, whom Jimmy and Sean brutally assault. The novel picks up as Skylar explains to the police her role in the events that unfolded that night. At first loyal to her pledge not to tell anybody about what happened, Skylar soon understands the severity of the situation and the cruelty of Jimmy and Sean's act. Now Skylar must question everything she believed in, including Jimmy's ethics and anger issues and her own unwavering love for someone who could be so violent.

Where it's reviewed:
Booklist, November 15, 2011, page 49
Publishers Weekly, July 4, 2011, page 66
School Library Journal, September 2011, page 146
Voice of Youth Advocates, October 2011, page 74

Other books you might like:
Cynthia DeFelice, *Under the Same Sky*, 2003
Alex Flinn, *Fade to Black*, 2005
James Lecesne, *Absolute Brightness*, 2008
Lauren Myracle, *Shine*, 2011
Gretchen Olson, *Joyride*, 1998

645

S.A. BODEEN

The Gardener
(New York: Feiwel and Friends, 2010)

Subject(s): Science fiction; Science experiments (Education); Fathers

Age range(s): 13 - 16+

Major character(s): Mason, Student—High School, 10th Grader; Unnamed Character, Girl, Teenager, Patient (nursing home); "Gardener", Scientist

Time period(s): 21st century; 2010s

Locale(s): Oregon, United States

Summary: In the young adult novel *The Gardener* by S.A. Bodeen, tenth-grader Mason is drawn into a mystery surrounding his missing father and the nursing home that employs his mother. Mason doesn't know who his father is or even what he looks like. Though Mason has a video of his father reading a book aloud, the man's face is never revealed. When Mason visits his mother at work one day, he plays the DVD for the catatonic teenagers who reside there. One girl is roused to consciousness by the sound of Mason's father's voice but doesn't know who she is. As Mason helps the amnesiac girl escape, he begins to discover unsettling links between his father, the strange facility where his mother works, and the scientist known as the Gardener.

Where it's reviewed:
Horn Book Guide, Fall 2010, page 361
Journal of Adolescent & Adult, February 2011, page 384
School Library Journal, June 2010, page 94
Voice of Youth Advocates, August 2010, page 262

Other books by the same author:
The Compound, 2008

Other books you might like:
Beth Fantaskey, *Jekel Loves Hyde*, 2010
Mary E. Pearson, *The Adoration of Jenna Fox*, 2008
Neal Shusterman, *Unwind*, 2007
Nancy Werlin, *Double Helix*, 2004

646

PETER BOGNANNI

The House of Tomorrow
(New York: G.P. Putnam's Sons, 2010)

Subject(s): Coming of age; Social conditions; Grandmothers

Age range(s): 15 - 18+

Major character(s): Sebastian Prendergast, Grandson (of Nana), 16-Year-Old, Outcast; Nana, Grandmother (of Sebastian); Jared Whitcomb, 16-Year-Old, Patient (heart transplant), Musician, Son (of Janice), Brother (of Meredith); Janice Whitcomb, Single Mother (of Jared and Meredith); Meredith Whitcomb, Sister (of Jared), Daughter (of Janice)

Time period(s): 21st century; 2010s

Locale(s): Iowa, United States

Summary: Sebastian Prendergast, a 16-year-old misfit, lives in a geodesic dome with his R. Buckminster Fuller-worshipping grandmother and gives tours of their unusual home to the Iowa locals. Nana believes that Sebastian will save the world one day, but her dream is derailed when she suffers a stroke as her grandson guides Jared Whitcomb on a tour of the dome. While Nana recovers, Sebastian accompanies Jared to the Whitcomb home even though he knows nothing of the family—or anyone else outside the dome, for that matter. Now Jared is Sebastian's guide in a world that contains such unknown wonders as soda, cigarettes, and punk music. The two boys form a band, The Rash, and line up a gig at a church talent show. As Sebastian experiences the intricacies of friendship and family life, he struggles to remain faithful to Nana's wishes. First novel.

Where it's reviewed:
Booklist, March 1, 2010, page 48
New York Times Book Review, April 4, 2010, page 17
Publishers Weekly, November 16, 2009, page 33

Awards the book has won:
Los Angeles Times Book Award: Art Seidenbaum Award for First Fiction, 2010
Alex Awards, 2011

Other books you might like:
Jonathan Coe, *The Rotters' Club*, 2002
K.L. Going, *Fat Kid Rules the World*, 2003
Gordon Korman, *Born to Rock*, 2006

647

ANNE-LAURE BONDOUX
Y. MAUDET, Translator

A Time of Miracles
(New York: Delacorte Press, 2010)

Story type: Historical
Subject(s): Refugees; Wars; Survival

Age range(s): 14 - 18+

Major character(s): Blaise "Koumail" Fortune, Boy, Refugee; Gloria, Refugee, Caregiver (to Koumail)

Time period(s): 20th century; 1990s
Locale(s): France; Georgia

Summary: In this young adult novel by Anne-Laure Bondoux, the fall of the Soviet Union provides the backdrop for the story of one boy's search for his identity. Koumail has lived under the care of Gloria in the Republic of Georgia since the train wreck that claimed the life of his mother. As Gloria tells it, Koumail's gravely injured mother gave her baby—born in France as Blaise Fortune—to Gloria at the scene of the accident. But the happiness of the years that followed are now threatened as the Soviet government falls and violence spreads. Blaise and Gloria embark on a dangerous five-year trek to the boy's homeland. Along the way, the growing boy and resilient woman follow a painful and hopeful path to the truth. Translated from French by Y. Maudet.

Where it's reviewed:
Booklist, December 15, 2010, page 50
Horn Book Magazine, January/February 2011, page 89
Publishers Weekly, November 8, 2010, page 63
School Library Journal, January 2011, page 100

Other books by the same author:
Life as It Comes, 2007
The Killer's Tears, 2006
The Princetta, 2006

Awards the book has won:
Mildred L. Batchelder Award, 2011

Other books you might like:
Linda Sue Park, *A Long Walk to Water: Based on a True Story*, 2010
Gudrun Pausewang, *Dark Hours*, 2006
Marjorie White Pellegrino, *Journey of Dreams*, 2009
N. H. Senzai, *Shooting Kabul*, 2010

648

COE BOOTH

Bronxwood

(New York: Scholastic, 2011)

Story type: Coming-of-Age
Subject(s): Family; Abuse; Prisons

Age range(s): 15 - 18+

Major character(s): Tyrell, Teenager, Friend (of Jasmine), Son (of Pops), Brother (of Troy); Troy, Son (of Pops), Brother (younger, of Tyrell), Foster Child; Jasmine, Friend (of Tyrell); Pops, Criminal, Father (of Tyrell)

Time period(s): 21st century; 2010s
Locale(s): New York, New York

Summary: In this follow-up to author Coe Booth's novel *Tyrell*, Tyrell's life is about to change as his father is released from jail. Tyrell is looking forward to having Pops back in his life, but he is confused when his father doesn't contact him. The whole time Tyrell's father was in prison, Tyrell acted like a father to his younger brother, Troy, who has been placed in foster care. Tyrell is also trying to deal with girls and romance in his life. Meanwhile, his mother shows little interest in what he's going through, and his other two brothers are busy dealing drugs. When Pops beats up Tyrell's mother and places the family in jeopardy with social services, Tyrell rejects his father's authority. He then decides to focus on helping his friend Jasmine escape a predator.

Where it's reviewed:
Booklist, September 1, 2011, page 115
Horn Book Magazine, November-December 2011, page 93
School Library Journal, October 2011, page 131

Other books by the same author:
Kendra, 2010
Tyrell, 2006

Other books you might like:
Peggy Kern, *No Way Out*, 2008
Sofia Quintero, *Efrain's Secret*, 2010
Earl Sewell, *If I Were Your Boyfriend*, 2008

649

ALBERT BORRIS

Crash into Me

(New York: Simon Pulse, 2009)

Subject(s): Suicide; Friendship; Adolescence

Age range(s): 14 - 18+

Major character(s): Owen, Narrator, Teenager; Jin-Ae, Lesbian, Teenager, Student; Frank, Teenager, Student; Audrey, Teenager, Student

Time period(s): 21st century; 2000s
Locale(s): United States

Summary: *Crash into Me* is a young adult novel from author Albert Borris. After each experiences a failed suicide attempt, teens Owen, Frank, Audrey, and Jin-Ae meet in an online chat room. Bonding over their mutual desire to die, the four young people make a pact; they'll take a summer road trip to the sites of famous suicides and take their own lives at their final stop in Death Valley, California. While driving across the country, the four develop an intense friendship. They share their darkest secrets, and slowly begin to question whether ending it all is really the right decision.

Where it's reviewed:
Booklist, May 15, 2009, page 34
Horn Book Guide, Spring 2010, page 90
Publishers Weekly, December 15, 2008, page 40
School Library Journal, August 2009, page 98
Voice of Youth Advocates, December 2009, page 403

Other books you might like:
Ellen Hopkins, *Impulse*, 2007
Nick Hornby, *A Long Way Down*, 2005
Julie Anne Peters, *By the Time You Read This, I'll Be Dead*, 2010
Brent Runyon, *The Burn Journals*, 2004
Courtney Summers, *Cracked Up to Be*, 2009

650

ERIN BOW

Plain Kate

(New York: Arthur A. Levine Books, 2010)

Subject(s): Witchcraft; Orphans; Outcasts

Age range(s): 12 - 17+

Major character(s): Kate, Orphan, Witch (suspected), Outcast

Time period(s): Indeterminate

Summary: Plain Kate, the orphaned daughter of a wood carver, is definitely an outcast in her strange, superstitious village. Her impressive knife-wielding and wood-carving skills have even caused some to speculate that she might be a witch, a dangerous accusation in the small community. When a supernatural sickness befalls the town, Kate becomes the chief suspect. In an attempt to save her own life, Kate agrees to sell her shadow to a stranger in exchange for freedom and her "heart's desire." Making her new home with a gypsy group known as the Roamers, Kate discovers that she can't live without her shadow and must fight to get it back. First novel.

Where it's reviewed:
Booklist, October 15, 2010, page 61
Horn Book Magazine, September-October 2010, page 72
Locus, December 2010, page 29
Publishers Weekly, August 16, 2010, page 54
School Library Journal, October 2010, page 108

Other books you might like:
Shannon Hale, *The Goose Girl*, 2003
Steven Knight, *The Last Words of Will Wolfkin*, 2011
Gail Carson Levine, *Ella Enchanted*, 1997
Garth Nix, *Lirael: Daughter of the Clayr*, 2001

651

RICK BOWERS

Spies of Mississippi: The True Story of the Spy Network That Tried to Destroy the Civil Rights Movement

(Washington, DC: National Geographic, 2010)

Subject(s): Civil rights movements; African Americans; Race relations

Age range(s): 12 - 16+

Summary: In this volume, author Rick Bowers explains the Mississippi State Sovereignty Commission, which was created in 1956 as a propaganda machine that turned into the most extensive state spy network in US history. Bowers uses firsthand accounts, primary source information, and interviews from surviving members to explain to young adults how the commission was created by the Mississippi state government with the mission of stopping racial integration at any cost. He discusses the origins of the commission, the reasons it was formed, the members of the commission and their positions, the African Americans who were targeted by the group, and more. The text includes black-and-white photographs in addition to a bibliography and source notes.

Where it's reviewed:
Booklist, February 1, 2010, page 58
Horn Book Magazine, May-June, page 102
School Library Journal, February 2010, page 128
Voice of Youth Advocates, February 2010, page 516

Other books by the same author:
Superman versus the Ku Klux Klan: The True Story of How the Iconic Superhero Battled the Men of Hate, 2011

Other books you might like:
David Aretha, *Freedom Summer*, 2008
Stephen Currie, *Murder in Mississippi: The 1964 Freedom Summer Killings*, 2006
Phillip M. Hoose, *Claudette Colvin: Twice Toward Justice*, 2009
Elizabeth Partridge, *Marching for Freedom: Walk Together, Children, and Don't You Grow Weary*, 2009

652

MARIA BOYD

Will

(New York: Alfred A. Knopf, 2010)

Subject(s): Humor; Plays; Adolescence

Age range(s): 12 - 16+

Major character(s): Will Armstrong, 17-Year-Old, Student—High School, Musician

Time period(s): 21st century; 2010s

Locale(s): Sydney, Australia

Summary: *Will* is a novel for young adult readers from author Maria Boyd. In the year since his father's death, 17-year-old Will Armstrong has masked his grief through hilarious antics and mischievous pranks. His latest misconduct—mooning a bus from a nearby all-girls school—has really landed him in hot water. The faculty at St. Andrew's is fed up with his class clowning, but one English teacher steps to Will's defense and comes up with a punishment worthy of the crime: Will has to put his guitar skills to use as a band member for the school musical. His fun Saturday nights are a thing of the past as Will devotes all of his free time to rehearsal at the all-girls school. Will soon finds himself surrounded by an unusual cast of characters, including a 7th-grade trombone player who admires Will and is in need of his protection, the beautiful female star of the play, and the studly football hero with the beautiful voice and a shocking secret.

Where it's reviewed:
Horn Book Guide, Spring 2011, page 91
School Library Journal, August 2010, page 96

Other books you might like:
Melina Marchetta, *Jellicoe Road*, 2008
Kieran Scott, *Geek Magnet*, 2008

Rebecca Sparrow, *The Year Nick McGowan Came to Stay*, 2008

John Van de Ruit, *Spud*, 2007

653

ALAN BRADLEY

The Sweetness at the Bottom of the Pie

(New York: Delacorte Press, 2009)

Series: Flavia de Luce Mystery Series. Book 1
Subject(s): Children; Science; Mystery

Age range(s): 15 - 18+
Major character(s): Flavia de Luce, 11-Year-Old, Detective—Amateur
Time period(s): 20th century; 1950s
Locale(s): United Kingdom

Summary: *The Sweetness at the Bottom of the Pie* is Alan Bradley's debut novel, which he published at the age of 70. The book is the first in a series by the author featuring Flavia de Luce, an 11-year-old science wiz with many notable talents, including sleuthing. Flavia overhears a disturbing discussion between her father and a stranger that implicates her father in the suicide of one of his former school teachers. When the stranger turns up dead, Flavia decides to solve the mystery herself, causing trouble for the local police in the process. First novel.

Where it's reviewed:
Booklist, May 1, 2009, page 35
Entertainment Weekly, May 15, 2009, page 60
Publishers Weekly, February 23, 2009, page 38
School Library Journal, May 2009, page 140

Other books by the same author:
A Red Herring Without Mustard, 2011
The Weed that Strings the Hangman's Bag, 2010

Awards the book has won:
Agatha Award: Best First Mystery Novel, 2009
Arthur Ellis Award: Best First Novel, 2010
Dilys Award, 2010
Macavity Awards: Best First Mystery Novel, 2010

Other books you might like:
John Grisham, *Theodore Boone: Kid Lawyer*, 2010
Tamar Myers, *The Headhunter's Daughter*, 2011
Helen Simonson, *Major Pettigrew's Last Stand*, 2011
Alexander McCall Smith, *The Double Comfort Safari Club: The New No. 1 Ladies' Detective Agency Novel*, 2010
Richard Yancey, *The Highly Effective Detective Crosses the Line*, 2011

654

ROBIN BRANDE

Fat Cat

(New York: Alfred A. Knopf, 2009)

Subject(s): Science experiments (Education); Food; Humor
Age range(s): 14 - 18+
Major character(s): Cat Locke, 11th Grader, Student—High School; Matt McKinney, Student—High School, 11th Grader
Time period(s): 21st century; 2000s
Locale(s): United States

Summary: Cat, a high-school junior with a fierce sweet tooth and more than a few excess pounds around her waistline, has multiple motives—some academic, most personal—for her top-secret science experiment. Cat is hoping to beat her nemesis, Matt McKinney, at the science fair by spending 200+ days eating and living as primitive humans did. If swearing off processed foods and motorized transportation helps Cat drop a few pounds and gain the attention of dozens of boys in the process, so be it. As Cat navigates the challenges of her experiment and the newfound admiration of a slew of hunky peers, she learns some valuable lessons about herself, her diet, and her happiness. First novel.

Where it's reviewed:
Horn Book Guide, Spring 2010, page 553
Publishers Weekly, October 12, 2009, page 50
School Library Journal, January 2010, page 96

Other books by the same author:
Evolution, Me and Other Freaks of Nature, 2007

Other books you might like:
Joyce Maynard, *The Cloud Chamber*, 2005
Erica S. Perl, *Vintage Veronica*, 2010
Suzanne Supplee, *Artichoke's Heart*, 2008
Marissa Walsh, *Does This Book Make Me Look Fat?*, 2008

655

LIBBA BRAY

Going Bovine

(New York: Delacorte Press, 2009)

Subject(s): Dwarfs; Gnomes; Diseases

Age range(s): 14 - 18+
Major character(s): Cameron, 16-Year-Old, Friend (of Dulcie, Gonzo, and Balder); Dulcie, Angel, Friend (of Cameron, Gonzo, and Balder); Gonzo, Dwarf, Friend (Cameron, Dulcie, and Balder); Balder, Friend (of Cameron, Dulcie, and Gonzo)
Time period(s): 21st century; 2000s (2009)
Locale(s): Texas, United States

Summary: In *Going Bovine*, by Libba Bray, 16-year-old Cameron is dying from Creutzfeldt-Jacob, or "mad cow" disease, which will eventually eat holes through his brain. He's determined to do some living before his time

---

is up, so he takes a little trip. Cam leaves his Texas hospital room (in his dreams) in search of Dr. X—the man who can cure him—with his new friends at his side. There's Dulcie, a pink-haired angel, a hypochondriac dwarf named Gonzo, and Balder, a Norse god turned garden gnome. While on their way, the four battle a jazz musician, bowl a few good games, and eat lots of ice cream. Will Cam find what he's looking for before it's too late?

Where it's reviewed:
Booklist, August 1, 2009, page 67
Horn Book Magazine, September/October 2009, page 553
Publishers Weekly, August 3, 2009, page 46
School Library Journal, September 2009, page 151
Voice of Youth Advocates, October 2009, page 326

Other books by the same author:
Beauty Queens, 2011
The Sweet Far Thing, 2007
Rebel Angels, 2005
A Great and Terrible Beauty, 2003

Awards the book has won:
Michael L. Printz Award, 2010

Other books you might like:
Ellen Jensen Abbott, *Watersmeet*, 2009
Daniel Ehrenhaft, *Ten Things to Do Before I Die*, 2004
Keith Gray, *Ostrich Boys*, 2010
Lynne Rae Perkins, *As Easy as Falling off the Face of the Earth*, 2010
Neal Shusterman, *Antsy Does Time*, 2008

656

LIBBA BRAY

Beauty Queens

(New York: Scholastic, 2011)

Subject(s): Beauty contests; Adolescent interpersonal relations; Humor
Age range(s): 14 - 18+
Major character(s): Taylor, Beauty Pageant Contestant
Time period(s): 21st century; 2010s

Summary: In *Beauty Queens*, prize-winning author Libba Bray tells the witty, insightful tale of a group of teenage beauty pageant contestants caught up in the most dangerous—and hilarious—of circumstances. When their plane goes down on a remote tropical island, it's every beauty queen for herself. Suddenly, the competition is no longer about winning a pretty, bejeweled crown—but about staying alive. As the girls struggle to survive the trying circumstances, allegiances are made and broken, unexpected challenges arise, and their respective abilities to express poise under pressure are put to the ultimate test.

Where it's reviewed:
Booklist, May 15, 2011, page 46
Horn Book Magazine, July-August 2011, page 140
New York Times Book Review, May 15, 2011, page 19
Publishers Weekly, March 21, 2011, page 78
School Library Journal, July 2011, page 92

Other books by the same author:
Going Bovine, 2009
Vacations from Hell, 2009
The Sweet Far Thing, 2007
Rebel Angels, 2005
A Great and Terrible Beauty, 2003

Other books you might like:
M.T. Anderson, *Feed*, 2002
Susan Juby, *Miss Smithers*, 2004
Terry Pratchett, *Nation*, 2008
Andrea White, *Surviving Antarctica: Reality TV 2083*, 2005

657

SARAH REES BRENNAN

The Demon's Lexicon

(New York: Margaret K. McElderry Books, 2009)

Subject(s): Demons; Brothers; Magic

Age range(s): 15 - 18+
Major character(s): Nick Ryves, 16-Year-Old, Hunter (demons); Alan Ryves, Brother (of Nick); Jamie, Friend (of Nick), Brother (of Mae); Mae, Friend (of Nick), Sister (of Jamie); Mum, Mother (of Nick and Alan)
Time period(s): 21st century; 2000s
Locale(s): Exeter, England

Summary: In Sarah Rees Brennan's *The Demon's Lexicon*, Nick Ryves has a secret. The 16-year-old is a demon slayer, moving from place to place with his older brother Alan and mentally ill mother and trying to elude the wicked magicians responsible for his father's death. The demons want the amulet that Mrs. Ryves wears, and whenever they get too close, Nick uses his powerful sword against them. Now Alan is in peril, bearing a demon's mark he gained after helping their new friends, Jamie and Mae. As Nick tries to protect his mother and brother from the band of magicians, his family's shocking story is revealed. First novel.

Where it's reviewed:
Booklist, April 15, 2009, page 35
Horn Book Magazine, September/October 2009, page 554
School Library Journal, July 2009, page 79

Other books by the same author:
The Demon's Surrender, 2011
The Demon's Covenant, 2010

Other books you might like:
Cassandra Clare, *City of Ashes: The Mortal Instruments*, 2009
Rosemary Clement-Moore, *Highway to Hell*, 2009
D.M. Cornish, *Lamplighter*, 2008
Kami Garcia, *Beautiful Creatures*, 2009
Stacey Jay, *Undead Much*, 2010

658

STEVE BREZENOFF

Brooklyn, Burning

(Minneapolis, Minnesota: Carolrhoda Books, 2011)

Story type: Gay - Lesbian Fiction; Young Adult
Subject(s): Summer; Runaways; Music

Age range(s): 13 - 18+
Major character(s): Kid, Streetperson, Lover (of Scout), Runaway; Scout, Streetperson, Lover (of Kid)
Locale(s): New York, New York

Summary: This young adult novel by author Steve Brezenoff focuses on the life of a homeless teen. After being kicked out, Kid lives on the streets of Greenpoint, Brooklyn. Times are tough, but being able to play the drums brings Kid happiness. When Kid meets Scout, a fellow street kid with an amazing voice, love is in the air. During the next two summers, Kid comes of age, learning about friendship, love, sexual orientation, and heartbreak. Through relationships with friends, Kid even finds the strength and courage to return home and talk to the parents who, in the past, never quite understood Kid. Throughout the novel, Brezenoff never explicitly reveals the genders or the sexual identities of Kid or Scout.

Where it's reviewed:
Booklist, September 1, 2011, page 115
Horn Book Magazine, November/December 2011, page 94
Publishers Weekly, July 4, 2011, page 66
School Library Journal, September 2011, page 146
Voice of Youth Advocates, October 2011, page 374

Other books by the same author:
The Absolute Value of -1, 2010

Other books you might like:
Tara Kelly, *Harmonic Feedback*, 2010
Todd Strasser, *Can't Get There from Here*, 2004
Tim Wynne-Jones, *Blink & Caution*, 2011

659

LARRY DANE BRIMNER

Black and White: The Confrontation between Reverend Fred L. Shuttlesworth and Eugene "Bull" Connor

(Honesdale, Pennsylvania: Boyds Mills Press, 2011)

Subject(s): Civil rights movements; Violence; Social class

Age range(s): 12 - 16+

Summary: The struggles and advances of civil rights during the turbulent 1950s and 1960s are viewed through the lives of two figures in this book by Larry Dane Brimner. Brimner describes how Reverend Fred L. Shuttlesworth, a Baptist minister in Alabama, fought for civil rights in the South. He gathered groups of supporters and used nonviolent methods to protest the unfair treatment of blacks in the South. The book also describes Eugene "Bull" Connor, the Birmingham, Alabama, Commissioner of Public Safety. Connor was a Southern white who opposed integration in the South and used fire hoses, fists, and dogs to quash nonviolent protests. The book describes how Connor's actions horrified the nation and helped Shuttlesworth's cause. Brimner develops his account of the times through interviews, newspapers, police and FBI reports, court documents, and photographs.

Where it's reviewed:
Booklist, October 15, 2011, page 43
School Library Journal, November 2011, page 145

Other books by the same author:
Birmingham Sunday, 2010
We Are One: The Story of Bayard Rustin, 2007

Other books you might like:
David A. Adler, *Heroes For Civil Rights*, 2010
Charlayne Hunter-Gault, *To the Mountaintop!: My Journey through the Civil Rights Movement*, 2012
Robert H. Mayer, *When the Children Marched: The Birmingham Civil Rights Movement*, 2008
Elizabeth Partridge, *Marching for Freedom: Walk Together, Children, and Don't You Grow Weary*, 2009

660

KEVIN BROOKS

iBoy

(New York: Scholastic Inc., 2011)

Story type: Science Fiction
Subject(s): Technology; Gangs; Violence

Age range(s): 15 - 18+
Major character(s): Tom Harvey, 16-Year-Old, Friend (of Lucy); Lucy, Friend (of Tom), Crime Victim
Time period(s): 21st century; 2010s
Locale(s): London, England

Summary: This novel by author Kevin Brooks tells the story of a teenager who suffers a brain injury in a freak accident. Sixteen-year-old Tom Harvey is living the life of an ordinary London teenager until the day an Apple iPhone falls from a skyscraper and lands on his head, embedding itself in Tom's brain. When Tom awakes in the hospital, he finds that he now has the power to tap into Internet technology from his own mind. Tom also learns that his friend Lucy has been sexually assaulted by street gang members, and the assault may have had something to do with his accident. Now Tom is determined to use his newfound powers to defeat the gang that harmed his friend. Will his iPowers be enough to take down these dastardly thugs?

Where it's reviewed:
Booklist, September 1, 2011, page 102
Publishers Weekly, October 10, 2011, page 59
School Library Journal, October 2011, page 131
Voice of Youth Advocates, December 2011, page 507

Other books by the same author:
Dawn, 2009
Black Rabbit Summer, 2008

Being, 2007
The Road of the Dead, 2006

Other books you might like:
M.T. Anderson, *Feed*, 2002
Libba Bray, *Beauty Queens*, 2011
Robert A. Heinlein, *Tunnel in the Sky*, 1955
David Lubar, *Hidden Talents*, 1999
Melinda Metz, *Gifted Touch*, 2001
Anne Schraff, *Shadows of Quiet*, 2010
Charles Sheffield, *The Billion Dollar Boy*, 1997

661

MARTHA BROOKS

Queen of Hearts

(Toronto: Groundwood Books, 2010)

Story type: Historical - World War II
Subject(s): Frontier life; World War II, 1939-1945; Family

Age range(s): 13 - 16+
Major character(s): Marie Claire, Patient, Teenager
Time period(s): 20th century; 1940s
Locale(s): Canada

Summary: This novel by Canadian author Martha Brooks tells the story of a World War II-era frontier family stricken with the dreaded disease tuberculosis, or TB. When Marie Claire and her brother and sister are diagnosed with TB, they must live at a sanatorium with other patients suffering from the illness. While there, Marie Claire must fight the loneliness that sets in, and the sadness of watching others who share her affliction succumb to the disease. Then Marie Claire's young brother passes away, and she is overcome with grief. Yet her seemingly insurmountable sense of despair is the exact thing that brings her together with someone who just may help her become healthy once again. Can this young woman fight hard enough to get well again and live the life she has always dreamed of?

Where it's reviewed:
Booklist, June 1, 2011, page 82
Horn Book Magazine, July-August 2011, page 142
Publishers Weekly, June 6, 2011, page 43
School Library Journal, July 2011, page 93
Voice of Youth Advocates, February 2011, page 549

Other books by the same author:
Mistik Lake, 2007
True Confessions of a Heartless Girl, 2003
Bone Dance, 1999
Traveling on into the Light, 1994

Other books you might like:
T. Degens, *On the Third Ward*, 1990
Ella Thorp Ellis, *The Year of My Indian Prince*, 2001
Marsha Hayles, *Breathing Room*, 2012

662

VERA BROSGOL

Anya's Ghost

(New York: First Second, 2011)

Subject(s): Ghosts; Friendship; Family
Age range(s): 13 - 18+
Major character(s): Anya, Teenager; Emily, Spirit

Summary: *Anya's Ghost* is a young adult graphic novel written and illustrated by Vera Brosgol. Anya faces many typical adolescent experiences, including the pressure of being normal among the rest of her peers. Anya finds it hard to make friends, until a new friend comes along. Her friend is named Emily, and Anya meets her after falling in a well. The only problem is, Emily is a ghost who died nearly a century before. Anya confides in Emily, and Emily helps her try to get along better with the people at school and even helps her become somewhat popular. But soon Anya learns that no matter how normal people act on the outside, most teens feel awkward deep down. First book.

Where it's reviewed:
Booklist, March 15, 2011, page 34
Horn Book Magazine, July/August 2011, page 142
Library Journal, July 2011, page 63
Publishers Weekly, April 11, 2011, page 36
School Library Journal, July 2011, page 120

Other books you might like:
Susan Kim, *Brain Camp*, 2010
Hope Larson, *Mercury*, 2010
Marjane Satrapi, *Persepolis 2: The Story of a Return*, 2004
Gene Luen Yang, *American Born Chinese*, 2006
Jane Yolen, *Foiled*, 2010

663

JENNIFER BROWN

Bitter End

(New York: Little, Brown and Company, 2011)

Subject(s): Adolescent interpersonal relations; High schools; Abuse

Age range(s): 15 - 18+
Major character(s): Alex, Teenager, Student—High School, Girlfriend (of Cole); Cole, Teenager, Student—High School, Boyfriend (of Alex)

Summary: When a cute new guy asks Alex out, she cannot believe her luck: Cole is athletic, instantly popular, and has a great sense of humor. Best of all, he seems to think Alex is the most beautiful girl in the world. Unfortunately, as their relationship continues, Cole reveals an uglier side of himself: he is quick to anger, jealous of Alex's friends, and has a tendency to be a bit rough with her. Soon Alex finds herself in the midst of an abusive relationship with Cole, but can she turn her back on the only boy who has ever made her feel truly loved—no matter how dangerous he is?

Where it's reviewed:
Booklist, April 15, 2011, page 54
New York Times Book Review, May 15, 2011, page 21
Publishers Weekly, March 28, 2011, page 59
School Library Journal, April 2011, page 168
Voice of Youth Advocates, June 2011, page 158

Other books by the same author:
Hate List, 2009

Other books you might like:
Sarah Dessen, *Dreamland*, 2000
Alex Flinn, *Breathing Underwater*, 2001
Patrick Jones, *Things Change*, 2004
Suzanne Weyn, *Beaten*, 2011

664

JENNIFER BROWN

Hate List

(New York: Little, Brown and Company, 2009)

Subject(s): High schools; Family relations; Forgiveness

Age range(s): 15 - 18+

Major character(s): Valerie Leftman, 16-Year-Old; Nick, Boyfriend (of Valerie); Jessica, Classmate (of Valerie)

Time period(s): 21st century; 2000s

Locale(s): Garvin County, American Midwest

Summary: In *Hate List* by Jennifer Brown, Valerie Leftman tries to readjust to life as a high school senior. Five months ago, her boyfriend Nick went on a shooting rampage in the school cafeteria, killing six students, a teacher, and himself. Although Valerie was also shot while protecting another student, she was interrogated for her role in the incident. Valerie had helped Nick create a "hate list" of people he didn't like, but she never imagined that he was compiling a list of targets. Eventually cleared, Valerie now must deal with the repercussions of Nick's unthinkable act on her friends, her family, and the entire community.

Where it's reviewed:
Booklist, September 1, 2009, page 82
Publishers Weekly, September 14, 2009, page 50
School Library Journal, October 2009, page 121
Voice of Youth Advocates, December 2009, page 403

Other books by the same author:
Bitter End, 2011

Other books you might like:
Jay Asher, *Thirteen Reasons Why*, 2007
Anne Cassidy, *Looking for JJ*, 2007
Cynthea Liu, *Paris Pan Takes the Dare*, 2009
Susan Shaw, *One of the Survivors*, 2009
Brooke Taylor, *Undone*, 2008

665

ELIZABETH C. BUNCE

Star Crossed

(New York: Arthur A. Levine Books, 2010)

Subject(s): Fantasy; Politics; Theft

Age range(s): 14 - 17+

Major character(s): Digger, 16-Year-Old, Orphan, Thief, Magician

Time period(s): Indeterminate

Summary: Digger is a teenage orphan with a gift of magic and a penchant for stealing. When Digger and her lover/partner, Tegen, are caught in the middle of a major heist, Digger manages to escape and fears that Tegen is dead. Desperate to get away, Digger finds herself aboard a boat with a group of young aristocrats heading for their mountain home. During her stay with the young nobles, Digger crosses paths with an ambitious lord who knows her secret. He blackmails Digger to find out political secrets about the royal family, forcing her to choose between her own protection and the far-reaching danger the secrets could invoke.

Where it's reviewed:
Booklist, November 15, 2010, page 44
Bulletin of the Center for Children's Books, October 2010, page 66
Horn Book Magazine, September-October, page 73
School Library Journal, January 2011, page 102
Voice of Youth Advocates, February 2011, page 567

Other books by the same author:
Liar's Moon, 2011
A Curse Dark as Gold, 2008

Other books you might like:
Ally Carter, *Heist Society*, 2010
Tamora Pierce, *Lady Knight*, 2002
Celia Rees, *Sovay*, 2008
Eleanor Updale, *Montmorency: Thief, Liar, Gentleman?*, 2004

666

ELIZABETH C. BUNCE

Liar's Moon

(New York: Arthur A. Levine Books, 2011)

Subject(s): Fantasy; Murder; Magic

Age range(s): 14 - 18+

Major character(s): Digger, Thief; Durrel Decath, Prisoner

Locale(s): Gerse, Fictional Location

Summary: Almost immediately after making her return home to the civil war-torn city of Gerse, young pickpocket Digger finds herself imprisoned with no clear explanation of the charges against her. While she's behind bars, Digger has an unexpected encounter with Lord Durrel Decath, a man to whom she already owes her life. Durrel has also been jailed, allegedly for murdering his wife. Convinced of his innocence, Digger vows to repay her debt to Durrel and launches her own investigation into his wife's death when she is freed. As she sifts through the case, Digger learns that Durrel's wife was involved with a smuggling ring that has been using the promise of an escape to freedom to lure people with magical powers into their hands, only to exploit them for their abilities, or worse. As a result of the smuggling ring's activities, many of Gerse's magic users have gone missing and it's now up to Digger to find them. *Liar's Moon* is a sequel to author Elizabeth C. Bunce's *Star Crossed*.

Where it's reviewed:
Horn Book Magazine, November-December 2011, page 94
School Library Journal, January 2012, page 106

Other books by the same author:
Starcrossed, 2010
A Curse Dark as Gold, 2008

Other books you might like:
Hilari Bell, *Shield of Stars*, 2007
Rae Carson, *The Girl of Fire and Thorns*, 2011
Ally Carter, *Heist Society*, 2010
Tamora Pierce, *Lady Knight*, 2002
Megan Whalen Turner, *The Thief*, 1996

667

NICK BURD

The Vast Fields of Ordinary

(New York: Dial Books, 2009)

Subject(s): Homosexuality; Adolescence; Self esteem

Age range(s): 15 - 18+
Major character(s): Dade, Boyfriend (of Alex), Lover (former, of Pablo), Graduate, Teenager, Homosexual; Alex Kincaid, Boyfriend (of Dade), Homosexual; Pablo, Football Player, Homosexual, Lover (of Dade)
Time period(s): 21st century; 2000s
Locale(s): Cedarville, Iowa

Summary: *The Vast Fields of Ordinary* is a young adult novel from author Nick Burd. The story follows Dade, a recent high school graduate living in Cedarville, Iowa. Struggling with his hidden sexuality, his parents' marital issues, and a secret romance with football star Pablo, Dade can't wait for college. He's desperate to get out of his small Midwestern town and make a fresh start. Despite their steady hook-ups, Pablo insists on keeping their homosexual relationship under wraps. When Dade meets and falls for the handsome and charming Alex Kincaid, their relationship is motivation enough to encourage Dade to come out of the closet, stirring up intense jealousy in Pablo. Just as Dade tries to find his footing as an openly gay man, he faces a shocking tragedy that threatens to destroy his new life.

Where it's reviewed:
Booklist, May 15, 2009, page 41
New York Times Book Review, July 12, 2009, page 13
Publishers Weekly, May 11, 2009, page 53
School Library Journal, June 2009, page 116
Voice of Youth Advocates, October 2009, page 311

Other books you might like:
Lee F. Bantle, *David Inside Out*, 2009
Susan Juby, *Another Kind of Cowboy*, 2007
Kathe Koja, *Talk*, 2005
Bill Konigsberg, *Out of the Pocket*, 2008
P.E. Ryan, *In Mike We Trust*, 2009

668

ANN BURG

All the Broken Pieces

(New York: Scholastic Press, 2009)

Subject(s): Vietnam War, 1959-1975; Adoption; Poetry

Age range(s): 12 - 14+
Major character(s): Matt Pin, Adoptee (from Vietnam), 12-Year-Old
Time period(s): 20th century; 1970s (1977)
Locale(s): United States

Summary: *All the Broken Pieces* is a young adult novel by Ann Burg written in free verse. Twelve-year-old Matt Pin was recently adopted by an American family after being airlifted out of Vietnam—his mother was Vietnamese, and his father was an American soldier. It is 1977, and though Matt loves his adoptive family and playing on his school's baseball team, he frequently must deal with the school bully and even other adults who make fun of him or blame him for the deaths of their loved ones. Matt often feels guilty for what happened to his younger brother, and he is still haunted by the images and sounds of the war.

Where it's reviewed:
Booklist, February 15, 2009, page 80
Horn Book Magazine, May/June 2009, page 292
Publishers Weekly, April 13, 2009, page 49
School Library Journal, May 2009, page 101

Other books you might like:
Katherine Applegate, *Home of the Brave*, 2007
Mike Lupica, *Safe at Home: A Comeback Kids Novel*, 2008
Donna Jo Napoli, *Alligator Bayou*, 2009
Katherine Paterson, *Park's Quest*, 1988
Andrew Smith, *In the Path of Falling Objects*, 2009

669

DON CALAME

Swim the Fly

(Somerville, Massachusetts: Candlewick Press, 2009)

Subject(s): Adolescence; Humor; Sexuality

Age range(s): 14 - 16+
Major character(s): Matt Gratton, 15-Year-Old, Swimmer
Time period(s): 21st century; 2000s
Locale(s): United States

Summary: In Don Calame's *Swim the Fly*, 15-year-old Matt Gratton and his two best friends, Sean and Coop, have a tradition of setting a summertime goal for themselves every year. This year, they create their most difficult challenge yet: to see a naked girl in the flesh. This is no small feat considering the boys are all way too intimidated to even ask a girl on a date. Finding a girl who is willing to shed her clothes for them starts to seem easy in light of Matt's other summer ambition, however: swimming the 100-meter butterfly stroke to win the heart of Kelly West, the swim team's newest hottie. *Swim the Fly* is filled with hilarious and crude action as the adolescent boys race to accomplish their goals.

Where it's reviewed:
Booklist, March 15, 2009, page 55
Publishers Weekly, April 20, 2009, page 49
School Library Journal, April 2009, page 129
Voice of Youth Advocates, August 2009, page 221

Other books by the same author:
Beat the Band, 2010

Other books you might like:
Catherine Forde, *Fat Boy Swim*, 2004
Steven Goldman, *Two Parties, One Tux, and a Very Short Film about The Grapes of Wrath*, 2008
Pete Hautman, *Rash*, 2006
Paul Many, *These Are the Rules*, 1997
Randy Powell, *Three Clams and an Oyster*, 2002

670

DON CALAME

Beat the Band

(Somerville, Massachusetts: Candlewick Press, 2010)

Subject(s): Humor; Adolescent interpersonal relations; Music

Age range(s): 15 - 18+

Major character(s): Coop, 10th Grader, Musician, Narrator; Helen, 10th Grader, Outcast, Classmate (of Coop); Matt, 10th Grader, Musician; Sean, 10th Grader, Musician

Time period(s): 21st century; 2010s

Locale(s): United States

Summary: *Beat the Band*, a humorous novel for young adult readers, is the sequel to *Swim the Fly* from author Don Calame. It's sophomore year and Matt, Coop, and Sean, the musically challenged members of Arnold Murphy's Bologna Dare, have two goals: keep the school year from becoming a disaster and meet as many chicks as possible. Things start off pretty rocky for Coop when a semester-long health project has him working side-by-side with social leper, "Hot Dog" Helen, on a project about safe sex. He's desperately hoping that winning the school's Battle of the Bands contest will save him from social suicide, but first the guys have to actually learn how to play their instruments.

Where it's reviewed:
Booklist, September 1, 2010, page 101
Horn Book Guide, Spring 2011, page 92
School Library Journal, December 2010, page 104
Voice of Youth Advocates, December 2010, page 446

Other books by the same author:
Swim the Fly, 2009

Other books you might like:
Andy Behrens, *Beauty and the Bully*, 2008
Mark Peter Hughes, *Lemonade Mouth*, 2007
Gordon Korman, *Born to Rock*, 2006
Chris Lynch, *Scratch and the Sniffs*, 1997

671

DEB CALETTI

Stay

(New York: Simon Pulse, 2011)

Subject(s): Father-daughter relations; Islands; Dating (Social customs)

Age range(s): 15 - 18+

Major character(s): Clara Oates, Graduate (high school), Girlfriend (of Christian, former), Daughter (of Bobby); Bobby Oates, Writer, Father (of Clara); Christian, Boyfriend (of Clara, former); Sylvie, Employer (of Clara)

Time period(s): 21st century; 2010s

Locale(s): Bishop Rock, Washington

Summary: Clara Oates moves with her father to Bishop Rock, an island off the Washington coast, to escape a dangerous relationship in *Stay*, a young adult novel by Deb Caletti. Clara, a recent high-school graduate, realizes how unstable Christian is after their breakup, and agrees to accompany her crime writer father, Bobby Oates, to the isolated beach community. Though Christian continues to stalk her by phone, Clara embarks on another romantic relationship and her father reacquaints himself with Bishop Rock. The island provides an emotional refuge for Clara but also reveals secrets about Bobby's past and Clara's mother's death. Father and daughter must reconcile with one another and the past if they are to move forward together.

Where it's reviewed:
Booklist, March 15, 2011, page 57
Horn Book Magazine, March-April 2011, page 112
School Library Journal, May 2011, page 106
Voice of Youth Advocates, June 2011, page 158

Other books by the same author:
The Six Rules of Maybe, 2010
The Secret Life of Prince Charming, 2009
The Fortunes of Indigo Skye, 2008
The Queen of Everything, 2008
The Nature of Jade, 2007

Other books you might like:
Jennifer Brown, *Bitter End*, 2011
Alane Ferguson, *The Dying Breath*, 2009
Nancy Springer, *My Sister's Stalker*, 2011

672

DEB CALETTI

The Six Rules of Maybe

(New York: Simon Pulse, 2010)

Subject(s): Interpersonal relations; Sisters; Pregnancy

Age range(s): 14 - 18+

Major character(s): Scarlet Hughes, 17-Year-Old; Juliet, Sister (of Scarlet), Spouse (of Hayden); Hayden, Spouse (of Juliet)
Time period(s): 21st century; 2010s
Locale(s): Oregon, United States

Summary: In Deb Caletti's *The Six Rules of Maybe*, Scarlet Hughes is a shy 17-year-old whose life is transformed when her older sister, Juliet, moves back home. Juliet is pregnant and has suddenly married the baby's father, Hayden, who also moves into the Hughes household. Scarlet soon finds herself drawn to her sister's new husband, and though he is passionately in love with Juliet, she can't help but be captivated by Hayden's charisma and romantic nature. With Juliet's due date growing ever closer, Scarlet is impelled to explore her relationships with her mother, sister, and the brother-in-law who has captured her heart.

Where it's reviewed:
Booklist, February 15, 2010, page 72
Horn Book Magazine, May-June, page 78
Publishers Weekly, February 22, 2010, page 69
School Library Journal, August 2010, page 60

Other books by the same author:
Stay, 2011
The Secret Life of Prince Charming, 2009
The Fortunes of Indigo Skye, 2008
The Nature of Jade, 2007
Wild Roses, 2005

Other books you might like:
Sarah Dessen, *That Summer*, 1996
Susan Donovan, *Not That Kind of Girl*, 2010
Colby Rodowsky, *Spindrift*, 2000
Denise Vega, *Fact of Life #31*, 2008

673

ELISA CARBONE

Jump

(New York: Viking, 2010)

Subject(s): Mountaineering; Runaways; Adolescence
Age range(s): 14 - 17+
Major character(s): P.K., 16-Year-Old, Runaway, Mountaineer; Critter, Runaway, Teenager
Time period(s): 21st century; 2010s
Locale(s): United States

Summary: Sixteen-year-old P.K. runs away from home to escape her overbearing parents and a miserable future at boarding school. She has a chance encounter with Critter, a fellow teen runaway. Together, the two leave behind their old lives and embark on a wild adventure, mountain climbing their way across the western United States. As they confront the dangers and excitement of their new-found passion, they're also consumed by passion for one another. But their picturesque escapade is brought to a startling halt when the police arrive with shocking allegations about Critter's dark past.

Where it's reviewed:
Booklist, May 1, 2010, page 76
Horn Book Guide, Fall 2010, page 362

Publishers Weekly, May 3, 2010, page 54
School Library Journal, June 2010, page 96
Voice of Youth Advocates, June 2010, page 148

Other books by the same author:
Last Dance on Holladay Street, 2005

Other books you might like:
Sarah Dessen, *Along for the Ride*, 2009
V. M. Jones, *Out of Reach*, 2008
Margaret I. Rostkowski, *Moon Dancer*, 1995
Eric Walters, *Sketches*, 2008

674

ORSON SCOTT CARD

Pathfinder

(New York: Simon Pulse, 2010)

Series: Pathfinders Series. Book 1
Subject(s): Adventure; Voyages and travels; Magic
Age range(s): 14 - 18+
Major character(s): Rigg, 13-Year-Old; Umbo, Friend (of Rigg)
Time period(s): Indeterminate

Summary: In Orson Scott Card's *Pathfinder*, 13-year-old Rigg's father is dying. On the elder man's deathbed, he urges Rigg to venture to the capital and seek out his long-lost sister. Rigg agrees, and sets off with his friend Umbo. Aiding Rigg on his odyssey is a unique mystical talent: Rigg can telepathically see people's pasts. Umbo, too, possesses the useful magical gift of time manipulation. Together the two friends embark on an epic journey that is peppered with new friends, lethal enemies, and more adventures than either boy could have ever imagined. This volume is the first book in a series.

Where it's reviewed:
Booklist, November 1, 2010, page 53
Horn Book Magazine, January-February 2011, page 90
Publishers Weekly, October 18, 2010, page 50
School Library Journal, December 2010, page 104

Other books by the same author:
The Lost Gate, 2011
Ender's Shadow, 1999
Seventh Son, 1987
Ender's Game, 1985

Other books you might like:
Beth Revis, *Across the Universe*, 2011
Robert Silverberg, *Lord Valentine's Castle*, 1980
Dom Testa, *The Comet's Curse*, 2009

675

JANET LEE CAREY

Stealing Death

(New York: Egmont USA, 2009)

Subject(s): Death; Brothers and sisters; Adventure
Age range(s): 13 - 16+

Major character(s): Kipp, 17-Year-Old
Time period(s): Indeterminate

Summary: Janet Lee Carey's *Stealing Death* is set in an enchanted fantasy world, where 17-year-old Kipp is devastated by the loss of his parents and brother in a fire that destroys their home. Fortunately, Kipp is able to rescue his sister, but his adventures are only just beginning. His innate powers put him in touch with the Gwali, the Collector of Souls, who carries the souls of the dead in a special sack. Kipp knows he can't get his family back, but he sets out to steal the sack and keep his parents and brother close to him. This brazen act leads Kipp on a journey of discovery where he learns much about the meaning of love and loss.

Where it's reviewed:
Booklist, September 15, 2009, page 52
Horn Book Guide, Spring 2010, page 91
Publishers Weekly, October 5, 2009, page 52
School Library Journal, September 2009, page 152
Voice of Youth Advocates, October 2009, page 326

Other books by the same author:
Wenny Has Wings, 2002
Molly's Fire, 2000

Other books you might like:
Piers Anthony, *On a Pale Horse*, 1983
Terry Pratchett, *Wintersmith*, 2006
Markus Zusak, *The Book Thief*, 2006

676

PATRICK CARMAN

Thirteen Days to Midnight
(New York: Little, Brown and Company, 2010)

Subject(s): Supernatural; Death; Orphans

Age range(s): 13 - 16+
Major character(s): Jacob Fielding, Foster Child; Ophelia "Oh", Friend (of Jacob); Milo, Friend (of Jacob); Mr. Fielding, Foster Parent (of Jacob), Accident Victim
Time period(s): 21st century; 2010s
Locale(s): United States

Summary: Patrick Carman's *Thirteen Days to Midnight* finds high schooler Jacob Fielding dealing with the aftermath of his foster father's sudden death. Just before Mr. Fielding died, he muttered to Jacob: "You are indestructible." This phrase transforms Jacob's life, and he sets out to discover if Mr. Fielding's last words were indeed true. Jacob and his friends are soon playing dangerous games to test their indestructibility. His new-found powers take on unexpected proportions with each test, and soon Jacob is questioning the "gift" he seems to possess.

Where it's reviewed:
Booklist, May 1, 2010, page 50
Horn Book Guide, Fall 2010, page 362
School Library Journal, May 2010, page 106
Voice of Youth Advocates, June 2010, page 162

Other books by the same author:
Dark Eden, 2011

Other books you might like:
Sarah Cross, *Dull Boy*, 2009
Francine Pascal, *Fearless*, 1999
Carol Snow, *Snap*, 2009

677

RAE CARSON

The Girl of Fire and Thorns
(New York: Greenwillow Books, 2011)

Story type: Fantasy
Subject(s): Royalty; Suspense; Fantasy

Age range(s): 14 - 18+
Major character(s): Elisa, 16-Year-Old, Royalty (princess)

Summary: A princess fights to become a brave hero in this romantic fantasy novel for young adults from debut author Rae Carson. Shocking as it may be, 16-year-old Elisa, the younger of two princesses and a disappointment to her family and nation, bears the enigmatic God-stone—a rare mark that shows that she is chosen for greatness. Despite her status, Elisa fears she lacks the ambition or bravery to do anything truly remarkable. When she becomes the wife of a handsome king, strictly for political reasons, she's wounded to learn he wants to keep their union a secret. Elisa is hunted by dark magicians, and her very life is in danger. When a mysterious revolutionary comes for Elisa, certain she can save his people, she soon discovers that her heart is in danger, too. First novel.

Where it's reviewed:
Booklist, October 1, 2011, page 86
Publishers Weekly, August 1, 2011, page 49
School Library Journal, August 2011, page 96
Voice of Youth Advocates, December 2011, page 507

Other books you might like:
Catherine Fisher, *Incarceron*, 2007
Catherine Gilbert Murdock, *Princess Ben: Being a Wholly Truthful Account of Her Various Discoveries and Misadventures, Recounted to the Best of Her Recollection, in Four Parts*, 2008
Tamora Pierce, *Lady Knight*, 2002

678

ALLY CARTER

Heist Society
(New York: Hyperion, 2010)

Subject(s): Art; Adolescence; Theft

Age range(s): 12 - 16+
Major character(s): Katarina Bishop, Teenager, Thief (art)
Time period(s): 21st century; 2010s
Locale(s): England

Summary: *Heist Society* is a young adult novel by Ally Carter. Since she was three years old, Katarina Bishop has been part of the family business of stealing valuable pieces of art and jewels from around the world. When she turns fifteen, however, Katarina decides she has had enough and scams her way into a boarding school in England. Before long, however, Katarina learns that her father has been falsely accused of stealing paintings from a dangerous Italian billionaire. Katarina decides to find the paintings and clear her father's name; along with a number of her friends from boarding school, she sets off on an adventure across Europe to recover the stolen property through yet another art heist.

Where it's reviewed:
Booklist, January 1, 2010, page 67
Publishers Weekly, December 21, 2009, page 61
Reading Time, May 2010, page 34
School Library Journal, June 2010, page 98
Voice of Youth Advocates, April 2010, page 54

Other books by the same author:
Uncommon Criminals, 2011
Only the Good Spy Young, 2010
Don't Judge a Girl by Her Cover, 2009

Other books you might like:
Julie Hearn, *Ivy*, 2008
Gordon Korman, *Son of the Mob*, 2002
Susan Runholt, *The Mystery of the Third Lucretia*, 2008
Elizabeth Scott, *Stealing Heaven*, 2008

679

KRISTIN CASHORE

Fire

(New York: Dial Books, 2009)

Subject(s): Feuds; Magic; Adventure

Age range(s): 15 - 18+
Major character(s): Fire, Young Woman; King Nash, Royalty (king)
Time period(s): Indeterminate

Summary: In *Fire*, author Kristin Cashore tells a mystical tale revolving around the adventures of a magical, unforgettable girl. Her name is Fire, the last of her kind. She has flame-red hair and lives in total isolation in a place rife with danger. She can also control the mind of anyone she chooses. But in the land of the Dells, war is imminent, and the fledgling King Nash is struggling to hold onto his title. Could Fire be his last hope—both for his reign and for the fate of the entire land? *Fire* is the companion novel to 2008's *Graceling*.

Where it's reviewed:
Publishers Weekly, July 20, 2009, page 141
School Library Journal, August 2009, page 99
Voice of Youth Advocates, October 2009, page 327

Other books by the same author:
Graceling, 2008

Other books you might like:
Suzanne Collins, *Mockingjay*, 2010
Shannon Hale, *Enna Burning*, 2004
Frances Hardinge, *The Lost Conspiracy*, 2009
Mike Lupica, *Safe at Home: A Comeback Kids Novel*, 2008
Patrick Ness, *Monsters of Men*, 2010

680

CECIL CASTELLUCCI

First Day on Earth

(New York: Scholastic Inc., 2011)

Story type: Coming-of-Age
Subject(s): Adolescent interpersonal relations; High schools; Extraterrestrial life

Age range(s): 13 - 16+
Major character(s): Mal, Teenager; Hooper, Streetperson
Time period(s): 21st century; 2010s
Locale(s): United States

Summary: This novel by author Cecil Castellucci tells the story of a hurt teenager who finds relief and happiness in an unexpected place. Still smarting from the breakup of his parents' marriage and his mother's subsequent turn to alcohol, teenager Mal wants nothing more than to leave the world behind. Things at school aren't great, either; Mal is a social outcast who just doesn't fit in anywhere. Then Mal bumps into Hooper, a street person who confides that he is actually an alien waiting to return to his home planet. Although Mal is initially doubtful, he finds solace in Hooper's claims. Going to another planet would be the best way to flee his troubles. As Mal forms a friendship with this supposed alien, he begins to learn how to deal with his feelings about his father's abandonment and his social status at school.

Where it's reviewed:
Booklist, October 1, 2011, page 85
Horn Book Magazine, Nov.-Dec. 2011, page 95
Publishers Weekly, October 3, 2011, page 69

Other books by the same author:
The Year of the Beast, 2012
Rose Sees Red, 2010
Beige, 2007
The Queen of Cool, 2006
Boy Proof, 2005

Other books you might like:
Donald R. Gallo, *On the Fringe*, 2001
Ron Koertge, *Strays*, 2007
Ursula K. Le Guin, *Very Far Away from Anywhere Else*, 1976
Sarah Nathan, *Out of This World*, 2009

681

JENNIFER CASTLE

The Beginning of After

(New York: HarperCollins, 2011)

Story type: Coming-of-Age
Subject(s): Family; Grief; Death

Age range(s): 15 - 18+
Major character(s): Laurel, 16-Year-Old, Orphan, Neighbor (of David); David Kaufman, Neighbor (of Laurel), Son (of Mr. and Mrs. Kaufman); Mr. Kaufman, Accident Victim, Father (of David); Mrs. Kaufman, Mother (of David), Accident Victim

Time period(s): 21st century; 2010s
Locale(s): New York, United States

Summary: This debut novel by author Jennifer Castle tells the story of a teenage girl coping with grief after the sudden death of her family. When 16-year-old Laurel's parents and brother die in a car crash, she becomes an orphan overnight. Adding to the pain is the fact that the driver of the other car was their neighbor Mr. Kaufman, the father of the boy she secretly likes but has never pursued. David Kaufman is the resident juvenile delinquent at Laurel's school, and his bad-boy status has kept her from acting on her crush. Yet after the accident, which also claimed the life of David's mother and put Mr. Kaufman in a coma, the teenagers find that they have some common ground. As Laurel attempts to come to terms with the loss of her family, she also must deal with the changes the accident's aftermath brings to her life. But can she forgive the Kaufmans for a tragedy that harmed both families? First novel.

Where it's reviewed:
Booklist, September 15, 2011, page 73
Publishers Weekly, August 8, 2011, page 49
School Library Journal, November 2011, page 114
Voice of Youth Advocates, October 2011, page 376

Other books you might like:
Susan Colebank, *Black Tuesday*, 2007
Gayle Forman, *If I Stay*, 2009
Marthe Jocelyn, *Would You*, 2008

682

THALIA CHALTAS

Because I Am Furniture
(New York: Viking, 2009)

Subject(s): Poetry; Child abuse; Abuse

Age range(s): 15 - 18+
Major character(s): Anke, Teenager
Time period(s): 21st century; 2000s
Locale(s): United States

Summary: *Because I Am Furniture* is a young adult novel written in free verse by Thalia Chaltas. Anke is a teenager living in her home with her family, which includes her brother, sister, mother, and father. Her father physically abuses everyone in her family except for her, because she doesn't even warrant that much attention. Anke is completely lacking in self-esteem, but when she joins the volleyball team, where she needs to yell "Mine!" to ever play in the game, she begins gaining more strength and self-confidence. She starts looking forward to the day when she can stand up to her father and protect her family.

Where it's reviewed:
Publishers Weekly, March 9, 2009, page 49
School Library Journal, June 2009, page 118

Other books by the same author:
Displacement, 2011

Other books you might like:
Katherine Applegate, *Home of the Brave*, 2007
Patricia Cumbie, *Where People Like Us Live*, 2008

Ellen Hopkins, *Identical*, 2008
Mike Lupica, *Safe at Home: A Comeback Kids Novel*, 2008
Laura Wiess, *Such a Pretty Girl*, 2007

683

FERN SCHUMER CHAPMAN

Is It Night or Day?
(New York: Farrar Straus Giroux, 2010)

Subject(s): Refugees; Jews; Children

Age range(s): 12 - 16+
Major character(s): Edith Westerfeld, 12-Year-Old, Refugee (German-Jew); Jacob, Uncle (of Edith); Mildred, Aunt (of Edith)
Time period(s): 20th century; 1930s-1940s
Locale(s): Germany; Chicago, Illinois

Summary: In the young adult novel *Is It Night or Day?* by Fern Schumer Chapman, a young Jewish girl is sent to live with relatives in Chicago as the Nazi campaign of anti-Semitism spreads across Germany. When 12-year-old Edith Westerfeld arrives in the U.S. in 1938, she finds many of her fears realized. She misses her parents. She misses her country. In the home of her Uncle Jacob and Aunt Mildred, Edith is treated like a servant. In school, she is demeaned for her inability to speak English and harassed because of her ethnicity. As she gradually adjusts to her new surroundings, she awaits news from her family. But when the war concludes, Edith learns that she has lost more than she could have imagined. *Is It Night or Day?* is based on the experiences of the author's mother, who came to America as a war refugee.

Where it's reviewed:
Booklist, February 1, 2010, page 45
Horn Book Guide, Fall 2010, page 332
Publishers Weekly, February 22, 2010, page 68
School Library Journal, May 2010, page 107
Voice of Youth Advocates, June 2010, page 148

Other books you might like:
Sarah Darer Littman, *Life, After*, 2010
Norma Fox Mazer, *Good Night, Maman*, 1999
Annika Thor, *A Faraway Island*, 2009
Kim Ablon Whitney, *The Other Half of Life: A Novel Based on the True Story of the MS St. Louis*, 2009

684

GEOFFREY CHAUCER
SEYMOUR CHWAST, Author/Illustrator

The Canterbury Tales
(New York: Bloomsbury USA Children's Books, 2011)

Subject(s): Literature; Storytelling; Short stories

Age range(s): 14 - 18+

Summary: Author Seymour Chwast updates Geoffrey Chaucer's classic tales about a group of pilgrims traveling to Canterbury in graphic novel format. In Chwast's version, which includes 24 tales, the voyagers rendezvous at the Tabard Inn and travel on motorcycles to their destination—the gravesite of Thomas Becket, the Archbishop of Canterbury. As in Chaucer's literary classic, the characters pass the time during their long journey by telling stories. Among the many pilgrims are the naughty Wife of Bath, a starving academic, and a knight who questions his duty to the king. Chwast has also adapted Dante's *The Divine Comedy*.

Other books by the same author:
Dante's Divine Comedy: A Graphic Adaptation, 2010
Seymour: The Obsessive Images of Seymour Chwast, 2009

Other books you might like:
Robert Crumb, *The Book of Genesis*, 2009
Timothy Decker, *Run Far, Run Fast*, 2007
Gareth Hinds, *King Lear*, 2007
Gene Luen Yang, *The Eternal Smile*, 2009

685

EISHES CHAYIL

Hush

(New York: Walker Books, 2010)

Subject(s): Adolescent interpersonal relations; Abuse; Suicide

Age range(s): 16 - 18+

Major character(s): Gittel, 13-Year-Old; Devory, Friend (of Gittel), Abuse Victim

Time period(s): 21st century; 2000s-2010s

Locale(s): New York, New York

Summary: In *Hush*, Eishes Chayil tells the powerful tale of 13-year-old Gittel, a girl who lives in a heavily cloistered, very orthodox Jewish community in modern-day New York City. Gittel learns that her best friend Devory has been the victim of abuse, but the strict laws of the community forbid either girl from safely coming forward. Suddenly Gittel is helpless in witnessing her friend's pain, standing feebly by as Devory slips further into depression and suicidal thoughts. As Devory suffers at the hands of her abuser, the harsh, dangerous, and potentially fatal realities of cloistered religious life reveal themselves to Gittel. First novel.

Where it's reviewed:
Booklist, October 15, 2010, page 59
Horn Book Guide, Spring 2011, page 93
School Library Journal, September 2010, page 148
Voice of Youth Advocates, December 2010, page 448

Other books you might like:
Patrick Jones, *Chasing Tail Lights*, 2007
Sonia Levitin, *Strange Relations*, 2007
Dana Reinhardt, *A Brief Chapter in My Impossible Life*, 2006
Naomi Rich, *Alis*, 2009

686

TRACY CHEVALIER

Remarkable Creatures

(London: Hammersmith, 2010)

Subject(s): Science; Women; Friendship

Age range(s): 15 - 18+

Major character(s): Mary Anning, Young Woman, Scientist, Friend (of Elizabeth); Elizabeth Philpot, Young Woman, Scientist, Friend (of Mary)

Time period(s): 19th century

Locale(s): United Kingdom

Summary: In *Remarkable Creatures*, bestselling author Tracy Chevalier tells the story of Mary Anning, a young 19th century woman with a scandalous fascination for science. When she is combing the beaches of her native England, Mary comes across a rare fossil that sets the scientific world on fire, causing the members of her small community to cast a suspicious eye upon her. But soon Mary meets Elizabeth Philpot, a Londoner who shares Mary's interest in walking the beaches. The two form an unlikely alliance that is marked by devotion, respect, and, oftentimes, jealousy. But as these two young women struggle to find their places in a profession ruled by men, they rely on and draw strength from the power of their unique friendship.

Where it's reviewed:
Booklist, October 15, 2009, page 5
Kirkus Reviews, October 15, 2009, page 1087
Library Journal, November 1, 2009, page 54
Publishers Weekly, September 28, 2009, page 42
Publishers Weekly, February 22, 2010, page 60

Other books by the same author:
Burning Bright, 2007
The Lady and the Unicorn, 2003
Falling Angels, 2001
Girl with a Pearl Earring, 1999
The Virgin Blue, 1996

Other books you might like:
Tessa Barclay, *A Tissue of Lies*, 2008
Shelley Emling, *The Fossil Hunter: Dinosaurs, Evolution, and the Woman Whose Discoveries Changed the World*, 2009
Steve Fiffer, *Tyrannosaurus Sue: The Extraordinary Saga of Largest, Most Fought Over T. Rex Ever Found*, 2000
Janice Graham, *The Tailor's Daughter*, 2006
Patrick McGrath, *Martha Peake: A Novel of the Revolution*, 2000
Diane Smith, *Pictures from an Expedition*, 2002

687

CINDA WILLIAMS CHIMA

The Demon King

(New York: Disney/Hyperion Books, 2009)

Series: Seven Realms Series. Book 1
Subject(s): Wizards; Royalty; Conspiracy

Age range(s): 13 - 17+
Major character(s): Han Allister, Thief (reformed); Raisa ana'Marianna, Royalty (princess)
Time period(s): Indeterminate

Summary: *The Demon King* is the first book in Cinda Williams Chima's Seven Realms series. This volume charts the adventures of Han Allister, a onetime thief struggling to straighten out his life. When out on a hunt with a friend, Han witnesses three wizards setting a holy mountain on fire. He manages to meet the boy-wizards head-on and, fearing the youngsters will use their magical pendant on him, steals the amulet. Now the wizards and their people will stop at nothing to get their precious stone back. In the meantime, Princess Raisa has unearthed a sinister plot within the Grey Wolf Court—a plot that only she can prevent before disaster strikes.

Where it's reviewed:
Horn Book Guide, Spring 2010, page 91
School Library Journal, December 2009, page 108
Voice of Youth Advocates, October 2009, page 328

Other books by the same author:
The Gray Wolf Throne, 2011
The Exiled Queen, 2010
The Dragon Heir, 2008
The Wizard Heir, 2007
The Warrior Heir, 2006

Other books you might like:
Jaclyn Dolamore, *Magic Under Glass*, 2010
Dave Duncan, *Children of Chaos*, 2006
Frewin Jones, *The Sorcerer King*, 2008
K.S. Nikakis, *The Song of the Silvercades*, 2008
Jonathan Stroud, *The Amulet of Samarkand: A Bartimaeus Graphic Novel*, 2010

688

CARA CHOW

Bitter Melon

(New York: Penguin, 2010)

Subject(s): Mother-daughter relations; Self knowledge; Child abuse

Age range(s): 14 - 17+
Major character(s): Fei Ting "Frances", Student—High School; Mom, Mother (of Frances)
Time period(s): 20th century; 1980s
Locale(s): San Francisco, California

Summary: In this young adult novel by Cara Chow, Fei Ting, who goes by the American name "Frances," lives with her demanding Chinese mother in 1980s San Francisco. Mom has made extraordinary efforts to get Frances into her prestigious high school and has planned out her daughter's life through Berkeley and medical school to a lucrative career. Although Frances is frustrated by her mother's constant disapproval and harsh discipline, she is resigned to her future. But when she is inadvertently placed in a speech class and discovers a talent for public speaking, Frances realizes that she wants to take control of her life. Frances hides the truth about her new plan from her mother until her deception pushes

their relationship to the breaking point.

Where it's reviewed:
Booklist, December 1, 2010, page 52
Publishers Weekly, November 22, 2010, page 59
School Library Journal, January 2011, page 102
Voice of Youth Advocates, February 2011, page 550

Other books you might like:
Justina Chen Headley, *Nothing but the Truth (and a Few White Lies)*, 2010
Joyce Lee Wong, *Seeing Emily*, 2005
Many Ly, *Roots and Wings*, 2008
Lisa Yee, *Absolutely Maybe*, 2009
Paula Yoo, *Good Enough*, 2008

689

LUCY CHRISTOPHER

Stolen

(New York: Chicken House, 2010)

Subject(s): Kidnapping; Interpersonal relations; Adventure

Age range(s): 15 - 18+
Major character(s): Gemma, 16-Year-Old, Kidnap Victim; Ty, Kidnapper
Time period(s): 21st century; 2010s
Locale(s): Australia; Bangkok, Thailand

Summary: In Lucy Christopher's *Stolen*, Gemma is an average 16-year-old who finds her life forever altered after being abducted from a Bangkok airport. She is taken to a remote stretch of the Australian Outback, where she meets her captor, Ty, a grown man who is dangerously obsessed with her. As she tries to decipher his motives, Gemma finds solace in the beauty of the Outback—and struggles to maintain her sanity when she slowly starts warming up to the mentally unhinged Ty.

Where it's reviewed:
Booklist, March 15, 2010, page 40
Horn Book Guide, Fall 2010, page 364
Journal of Adolescent & Adult, September 2010, page 67
School Library Journal, July 2010, page 84
Voice of Youth Advocates, June 2010, page 149

Other books you might like:
Norma Fox Mazer, *The Missing Girl*, 2008
Gail Giles, *What Happened to Cass McBride?*, 2006
Adele Griffin, *Overnight*, 2003
April Henry, *Girl, Stolen*, 2010
Kristina McBride, *The Tension of Opposites*, 2010

690

CASSANDRA CLARE

Clockwork Angel

(New York: Margaret K. McElderry Books, 2010)

Series: Infernal Devices Series. Book 1
Subject(s): Supernatural; Demons; Orphans

Age range(s): 14 - 18+
Major character(s): Tessa Gray, 16-Year-Old, Shape-Shifter; James, Friend (of Tessa); Will, Friend (of Tessa)
Time period(s): 19th century; 1800s
Locale(s): London, England

Summary: Victorian-era teenager Tessa Gray is on a mission to find her missing brother. She sets sail for England, where she becomes acquainted with London's supernatural Downworld, a place where witches, vampires, and other magical beings run rampant. As she attempts to track down her brother, Tessa gets kidnapped by a secret organization. During her time with the group, called the Dark Sisters, Tessa learns that she too is a Downworlder—and she possesses unique powers of her own. As Tessa continues her search for her brother, she meets two new friends that will change her life forever. *Clockwork Angel* is the first installment in Cassandra Clare's Infernal Devices series.

Where it's reviewed:
Publishers Weekly, July 19, 2010, page 131
School Library Journal, October 2010, page 110
Voice of Youth Advocates, October 2010, page 364

Other books by the same author:
City of Fallen Angels, 2011
Clockwork Prince, 2011
City of Glass, 2009
City of Ashes, 2008
City of Bones, 2007

Other books you might like:
Dia Reeves, *Bleeding Violet*, 2010
Michelle Zink, *Guardian of the Gate*, 2010

691

CASSANDRA CLARE
City of Glass
(New York: Margaret K. McElderry, 2009)

Series: Mortal Instruments Series. Book 3
Subject(s): Adolescence; Family relations; Supernatural

Age range(s): 16 - 18+
Major character(s): Clary, Heroine, Girlfriend (of Jace); Jace, Boyfriend (of Clary); Sebastian, Supernatural Being (Shadowhunter; Clary's ally); Valentine, Supernatural Being (wants to destroy Shadowhunters)
Locale(s): City of Glass, Fictional Location

Summary: *City of Glass*, the third and final book in the Mortal Instruments series by Cassandra Clare, tells the story of Clary, a young woman who must risk her own life in the supernatural world to save her dying mother. To obtain an elixir that will return her mother to normal health, Clary must delve recklessly into an underworld known as the City of Glass. The city is inhabited by dangerous creatures known as Shadowhunters, who do not take kindly to unauthorized entry into their land. Clary treads carefully, despite disapproval from her love Jace, and begins to uncover family secrets that can aid her in her quest. When enemy Valentine begins to follow through on an evil plot to end the Shadowhunters forever,

they find an ally in Clary, who must now work to save their world to preserve both her mother's life and her own.

Where it's reviewed:
Booklist, March 1, 2009, page 46
Library Journal, February 1, 2009, page 45
School Library Journal, July 2009, page 80

Other books by the same author:
City of Fallen Angels, 2011
City of Ashes, 2008
City of Bones, 2007

Other books you might like:
Meg Cabot, *Abandon*, 2011
Richelle Mead, *Frostbite*, 2008
Cindy Pon, *Fury of the Phoenix*, 2011
Lili St. Crow, *Betrayals: A Strange Angels Novel*, 2009

692

JUDITH CLARKE
The Winds of Heaven
(New York: Henry Holt, 2010)

Subject(s): Friendship; Adolescence; Cousins

Age range(s): 14 - 18+
Major character(s): Fan, Cousin (of Clementine); Clementine, Cousin (of Fan)
Time period(s): 20th century; 1950s-2000s
Locale(s): Australia

Summary: Written by award-winning author Judith Clarke, *The Winds of Heaven* is a moving tale of friendship, loyalty, and identity for young adult readers. When uptight and nervous Clementine spends the summer of 1952 with her ten-year-old cousin, Fan, she's smitten by the lively young girl's carefree nature and zeal for life. She's also dismayed to see how Fan's cold and abusive mother belittles and mistreats her. The girls form a unique bond, promising to continue their relationship even after they're apart, but life's circumstances take them in two very different directions. While both girls deal with the ups and downs of adolescence and adulthood, they're continually shaped and changed by their three impacting encounters with one another.

Where it's reviewed:
Booklist, October 15, 2010, page 52
Horn Book Magazine, September-October 2010, page 74
Publishers Weekly, October 4, 2010, page 50
Voice of Youth Advocates, August 2010, page 244

Other books by the same author:
One Whole and Perfect Day, 2007
Night Train, 2000

Other books you might like:
Rachel Cohn, *You Know Where to Find Me*, 2008
Melina Marchetta, *Saving Francesca*, 2003
Meg Rosoff, *How I Live Now*, 2004
Gloria Whelan, *Summer of the War*, 2006

693

ROSEMARY CLEMENT-MOORE

Texas Gothic

(New York: Random House, 2011)

Story type: Paranormal
Subject(s): Supernatural; Ghosts; Witchcraft

Age range(s): 14 - 18+
Major character(s): Amy Goodnight, Sister (of Phin), Niece (of Aunt Hy), 17-Year-Old; Phin Goodnight, Sister (of Amy), Niece (of Aunt Hy); Hy, Aunt (of Amy and Phin), Rancher
Time period(s): 21st century; 2010s
Locale(s): Texas, United States

Summary: In this young adult novel by Rosemary Clement-Moore, Amy Goodnight hails from a family of witches. Thus far, she has been the only one to lend some sense of normalcy to an otherwise extraordinary clan. Amy serves as the Goodnight family Gatekeeper, and her job is to keep the rest of her family somewhat grounded. When she agrees to watch her Aunt Hy's ranch for the summer with her sister Phin, Amy finds herself the subject of gossip around the tiny Texan town. To make matters worse, paranormal activity is on the rise since the arrival of the Goodnight girls, and a ghost may be following Amy around. When things become even more bizarre, Amy begins to wonder if she will ever truly know what normal is.

Where it's reviewed:
Horn Book Magazine, September -October 2011, Page 84
Publishers Weekly, June 6, 2011, page 43
School Library Journal, August 2011, page 98

Other books by the same author:
Hell Week, 2009
Highway to Hell, 2009
The Splendor Falls, 2009
Prom Dates from Hell, 2008

Other books you might like:
Kendare Blake, *Anna Dressed in Blood*, 2011
Meg Cabot, *Jinx*, 2007
Carolyn MacCullough, *Once a Witch*, 2009
Terry Pratchett, *I Shall Wear Midnight*, 2010

694

ROSEMARY CLEMENT-MOORE

Highway to Hell

(New York: Delacorte Press, 2009)

Series: Maggie Quinn: Girl vs. Evil Series. Book 3
Subject(s): Horror; Journalism; Monsters

Age range(s): 14 - 16+
Major character(s): Maggie Quinn, Student—College (freshman); Lisa, Friend (of Maggie)
Time period(s): 21st century; 2000s
Locale(s): Dulcina, Texas

Summary: *Highway to Hell* is the third installment in Rosemary Clement-Moore's Maggie Quinn: Girl vs Evil series. In this novel, Maggie, a psychic, and her friend Lisa are en route to spring break in Texas when their vehicle breaks down in the tiny town of Dulcina. The girls have arrived just in time to help with an investigation into the suspicious deaths of local animals. The residents of Dulcina believe the killings are the work of a chupacabra—a legendary canine monster. To solve the stubborn and increasingly dangerous mystery, Maggie calls on her demonologist boyfriend, a clergyman, and the grandson of a local psychic for assistance.

Where it's reviewed:
Booklist, July 1, 2009, page 55
School Library Journal, April 2009, page 130
Voice of Youth Advocates, February 2009, page 538

Other books by the same author:
Texas Gothic, 2011
The Splendor Falls, 2009
Hell Week, 2008
Prom Dates from Hell, 2007

Other books you might like:
Sarah Rees Brennan, *The Demon's Covenant*, 2010
David Macinnis Gill, *Soul Enchilada*, 2009
Stacey Jay, *Undead Much*, 2010
Christopher Pike, *Thirst No. 2: Phantom, Evil Thirst, Creatures of Forever*, 2010
Greg Taylor, *Killer Pizza*, 2009

695

LENA COAKLEY

Witchlanders

(New York: Atheneum Books for Young Readers, 2011)

Subject(s): Fantasy; Witches; Wars

Age range(s): 13 - 16+
Major character(s): Ryder, Hero, Brother (of Skyla); Falpian, Royalty; Skyla, Sister (of Ryder); Mabis, Witch, Mother (of Ryder and Skyla)
Locale(s): Witchlands, Fictional Location

Summary: For many years, the Witchlands have been protected by the red witches, oracles who worship the Goddess and roll the bones to make their prophecies about the future of the kingdom. Ryder, a young man whose own mother was once a witch, has never been one to believe in their supposed magical abilities and doesn't think they truly deserve the tithes they require his fellow villagers to pay. His feelings about the witches are amplified by the fact that there no longer appears to be anything for the witches to protect the Witchlands from now that their sole enemy, the Baen, have been defeated. That all changes when a deadly new threat descends upon the kingdom, forcing Ryder to put all his faith in the witches, and in particular, the alluring, yet mysteriously quiet witch who holds the greatest secrets. While cooperating with the witches to help his people overcome the enemy threat, Ryder is shocked to learn that the prophecies he once scoffed at may have a much greater impact on his life than he ever thought possible.

Where it's reviewed:
Booklist, October 15, 2011, page 59
Bulletin of the Center for Children's Books, September 2011, page 12
Publishers Weekly, July 11, 2011, page 59
School Library Journal, December 2011, page 108
Voice of Youth Advocates, August 2011, page 286

Other books you might like:
Rae Carson, *The Girl of Fire and Thorns*, 2011
Stuart Hill, *The Cry of the Icemark*, 2005
Frewin Jones, *Warrior Princess*, 2009

696

JUDITH ORTIZ COFER

If I Could Fly

(New York: Farrar Straus Giroux, 2011)

Subject(s): Singing; Family relations; Self reliance
Age range(s): 13 - 16+
Major character(s): Doris, 15-Year-Old
Time period(s): 21st century; 2010s
Locale(s): New Jersey, United States

Summary: In the young-adult novel *If I Could Fly* by Judith Ortiz Cofer, 15-year-old Doris deals with separation from her mother and her distant relationship with her father. Both of Doris's parents are singers, and their frequent absences from home have prompted her to learn to take care of herself. But now that her mother has returned to her native Cuba to recuperate from an illness and her father is spending his time with a new girlfriend, Doris's solitude has become loneliness. When she starts to take care of the pigeons that a neighbor keeps on the roof of their New Jersey apartment building, Doris begins to understand her place in the world.

Where it's reviewed:
Booklist, May 15, 2011, page 46
Horn Book Magazine, May/June 2011, page 84
School Library Journal, June 2011, page 112
Voice of Youth Advocates, June 2011, page 160

Other books by the same author:
An Island Like You: Stories of the Barrio, 2006
Call Me Maria, 2004

Other books you might like:
Barbara Garland Polikoff, *Why Does the Coqui Sing?*, 2011
Danette Vigilante, *The Trouble with Half a Moon*, 2011
Julie Williams, *Escaping Tornado Season: A Story in Poems*, 2004

697

JOSHUA COHEN

Leverage

(New York: Dutton Children's Books, 2011)

Subject(s): Violence; Football; Gymnastics
Age range(s): 14 - 17+
Major character(s): Danny, 10th Grader, Gymnast, Friend (of Kurt); Kurt, Student—High School, Football Player, Friend (of Danny)
Time period(s): 21st century; 2010s
Locale(s): United States

Summary: In the young adult novel *Leverage* by Joshua Cohen, Oregrove High School is run by the football team. A band of bullies fueled by steroids, the players intimidate their fellow students and ridicule the school's other athletes, especially the gymnasts. Danny, the gymnastics squad's high-bar specialist, realizes that the rivalry between the two groups has become volatile. But when one of his teammates is the target of a disastrous act of vengeance, Danny hesitates to reveal the culprits. Kurt, a new student and a member of the football team, also knows the truth about the incident. His disfigured face, awkward speech, and troubled past keep him at a distance from his teammates, but a new friendship with Danny could begin the healing process at Oregrove High. First novel.

Where it's reviewed:
Booklist, December 15, 2010, page 45
Publishers Weekly, December 6, 2010, page 50
School Library Journal, April 2011, page 170
Voice of Youth Advocates, February 2011, page 550

Other books you might like:
Robert Cormier, *The Chocolate War*, 1974
Michael Harmon, *Brutal*, 2009
Pete Hautman, *Blank Confession*, 2010
Catherine Ryan Hyde, *Diary of a Witness*, 2009
Robert Lipsyte, *Raiders Night*, 2007
Paul Volponi, *Crossing Lines*, 2011

698

PAT LOWERY COLLINS

Hidden Voices: The Orphan Musicians of Venice

(Somerville, Massachusetts: Candlewick Press, 2009)

Subject(s): Orphans; Adolescence; History

Age range(s): 14 - 18+
Major character(s): Luisa, Singer, Teenager; Anetta, Teenager; Rosalba, Teenager
Time period(s): 18th century; 1700s
Locale(s): Venice, Italy

Summary: *Hidden Voices: The Orphan Musicians of Venice,* by Pat Lowery Collins, is a young adult novel that takes place in Venice at an orphange/home for abandoned girls during the early 18th century. Three teenagers, Anetta, Luisa, and Rosalba, are talented singers but all want something different. Anetta enjoys taking care of the younger girls and develops an attraction to Luisa. Luisa survives an illness and briefly falls in love with a man, but it does not last. And Rosalba, after meeting a man she thinks loves her, is brutally raped. The chapters are told by the three girls in shifting perspectives as they try to survive their difficult lives and take care of each other.

Where it's reviewed:
Booklist, April 15, 2009, page 49
Horn Book Magazine, July/August 2009, page 419
School Library Journal, May 2009, page 102
Voice of Youth Advocates, June 2009, page 134

Other books by the same author:
Daughter of Winter, 2010
The Fattening Hut, 2003

Other books you might like:
Peter W. Hassinger, *Shakespeare's Daughter*, 2004
Kimberley Heuston, *Dante's Daughter*, 2003
Carolyn Meyer, *In Mozart's Shadow: His Sister's Story*, 2008
Carolyn Meyer, *Marie, Dancing*, 2005

699

SUZANNE COLLINS

Catching Fire
(New York: Scholastic Press, 2009)

Series: Hunger Games Trilogy. Book 2
Subject(s): Dystopias; Survival; Television programs

Age range(s): 13 - 18+
Major character(s): Katniss Everdeen, 16-Year-Old, Contestant (in the Hunger Games); Peeta Mellark, Contestant (in the Hunger Games), Teenager; President Coriolanus Snow, Political Figure, Villain; Gale Hawthorne, Teenager, Hunter, Rebel; Haymitch Abernathy, Contestant (in the Hunger Games); Cinna, Worker (stylist); Finnick Odair, Contestant (in the Hunger Games); Mags, Contestant (in the Hunger Games); Johanna Mason, Contestant (in the Hunger Games); Beetee, Contestant (in the Hunger Games); Wiress, Contestant (in the Hunger Games)
Time period(s): Indeterminate Future
Locale(s): District 11, Fictional Location; District 12, Fictional Location; Panem, Fictional Location; The Capitol, Fictional Location

Summary: In *Catching Fire*, the sequel to Suzanne Collins's best-selling novel, *The Hunger Games*, the United States has been replaced by a dystopian dictatorship called Panem. Every year, the controlling Capitol forces Panem's 12 districts to send two teenaged contestants into a televised competition called the Hunger Games, where only one contestant makes it out alive each year. After winning the last Hunger Games in a rule-bending victory that allowed two victors, District 12's Katniss Everdeen and Peeta Mellark have secured a safe future for their families, but they have also come to symbolize a revolution that is brewing in their district and beyond. Panem's ruler, President Snow, is not pleased with the teenagers and plans retribution even as the pair embarks on their Victory Tour throughout the twelve districts. But Katniss and Peeta's tour is cut short by the spreading rebellion and by a surprise announcement about the next Hunger Games - a 75th anniversary competition called the "Quarter Quell", which brings together past victors of past games for another winner-takes-all fight to the death.

Where it's reviewed:
Booklist, July 1, 2009, page 62
Horn Book Magazine, September-October 2009, page 555
Locus, September 2009, page 25
School Library Journal, September 2009, page 154
Voice of Youth Advocates, December 2009, page 418

Other books by the same author:
Mockingjay, 2010
The Hunger Games, 2008
Gregor the Overlander, 2003

Awards the book has won:
Off the Cuff Awards, 2009

Other books you might like:
Suzanne Collins, *Mockingjay*, 2010
James Dashner, *The Scorch Trials*, 2010
Alison Goodman, *Eon: Dragoneye Reborn*, 2008
Lise Haines, *Girl in the Arena*, 2009
Elana Johnson, *Possession*, 2011

700

SUZANNE COLLINS

Mockingjay
(New York: Scholastic, 2010)

Series: Hunger Games Trilogy. Book 3
Subject(s): Futuristic society; Contests; Adolescence

Age range(s): 13 - 18+
Major character(s): Katniss Everdeen, 16-Year-Old, Contestant (in the Hunger Games; former), Rebel; President Coriolanus Snow, Political Figure, Villain; Peeta Mellark, Teenager, Contestant (in the Hunger Games; former), Rebel; Gale Hawthorne, Teenager, Hunter, Rebel; Haymitch Abernathy, Contestant (in the Hunger Games; former), Rebel; Primrose Everdeen, 12-Year-Old, Sister (of Katniss), Nurse; Alma Coin, Political Figure; Finnick Odair, Contestant (in the Hunger Games; former), Rebel; Annie Cresta, Contestant (in the Hunger Games; former); Boggs, Rebel; Cressida, Rebel, Filmmaker
Time period(s): Indeterminate Future
Locale(s): District 12, Fictional Location; District 13, Fictional Location; Panem, Fictional Location; The Capitol, Fictional Location

Summary: *Mockingjay* is the third and final book in The Hunger Games trilogy by Suzanne Collins. The novels take place in a future in which the United States has been replaced by a dystopian dictatorship called Panem. Every year, the controlling Capitol forces Panem's 12 districts to send two teenaged contestants into a televised competition called the Hunger Games, where only one contestant makes it out alive each year. Katniss Everdeen, a teen from the poorest region of Panem, District 12, has participated in the games twice and survived, which has transformed her into a symbol of rebellion for the oppressed masses in the twelve districts. However, after Katniss participated in an escape from the Hunger Games arena at the end of *Catching Fire*, her love interest Peeta was captured by the Capitol and the heartless President Snow ordered the destruction of Katniss' home, District 12. Katniss and a few remaining survivors from

District 12 have now rallied around the rebellion forces of District 13, a district long rumored to have been destroyed by the Capitol years earlier. Due to her celebrity status as the girl who survived the Hunger Games, Katniss is now the public face of the rebellion, a role that makes the young teenager uncomfortable. As District 13 prepares for a final all-out assault on the Capitol, Katniss must deal with her desire for vengeance, the questionable war-time tactics of the rebellion, and her feelings for Peeta and her old friend Gale, particularly after Peeta escapes from his imprisonment and returns to District 13 as a drastically changed man.

Where it's reviewed:
Horn Book Magazine, November-December 2010, page 86
Locus, October 2010, page 25
New York Times Book Review, September 12, 2010, page 12
People, September 13, 2010, page 69
Publishers Weekly, November 8, 2010, page 32

Other books by the same author:
Catching Fire, 2009
The Hunger Games, 2008

Other books you might like:
M.T. Anderson, *Feed*, 2002
Suzanne Collins, *Catching Fire*, 2009
James Dashner, *The Maze Runner*, 2009
Nancy Farmer, *The House of the Scorpion*, 2002
Catherine Fisher, *Incarceron*, 2007

701

ELISABETH COMBRES

Broken Memory: A Novel of Rwanda
(Toronto: Groundwood Books, 2009)

Subject(s): Genocide; Grief; Friendship

Age range(s): 12 - 15+
Major character(s): Emma, Survivor
Time period(s): 20th century-21st century; 1990s-2000s
Locale(s): Rwanda

Summary: In Elisabeth Combres's *Broken Memory: A Novel of Rwanda*, Emma is just five years old when her mother is killed before her eyes. Fleeing the genocide overtaking her community, Emma finds safety in the arms of a stranger—a kindly, aged Hutu woman. Emma is burdened with horrific memories of what she witnessed, but when she has the chance to face her mother's killer in court, she's not sure she possesses the strength. With the help of two new friends, Emma rallies the courage to face her tormentor and put the past to rest. First novel.

Where it's reviewed:
Booklist, September 1, 2009, page 80
Horn Book Guide, Spring 2010, page 92
School Library Journal, December 2009, page 110
Voice of Youth Advocates, February 2010, page 491

Other books you might like:
Elizabeth D. Crawford, *Over a Thousand Hills I Walk with You*, 2006
Christina Fisanick, *The Rwanda Genocide*, 2004
Laura Manivong, *Escaping the Tiger*, 2010
Jean-Philippe Stassen, *Deogratias*, 2000

702

YING CHANG COMPESTINE

A Banquet for Hungry Ghosts
(New York: Henry Holt and Co., 2009)

Subject(s): Ghosts; Short stories; Chinese (Asian people)

Age range(s): 12 - 16+

Summary: In *A Banquet for Hungry Ghosts*, Ying Chang Compestine serves up a chilling menu of horror stories based on Chinese cuisine. The collection is inspired by the ancient Chinese belief that a person who dies before he eats a suitable last meal will return as a ghost to seek vengeance. Keeping with the culinary theme, the collection follows the format of an eight-course Chinese banquet complete with appetizers, main courses, and dessert. Each gruesome tale is set in a different era of Chinese history, from the construction of the Great Wall to the present. Recipes and pertinent cultural information accompany the stories.

Where it's reviewed:
Booklist, November 15, 2009, page 31
Horn Book Magazine, Nov.-Dec. 2009, page 664
Publishers Weekly, November 9, 2009, page 47
School Library Journal, December 2009, page 110

Other books by the same author:
Revolution Is Not a Dinner Party, 2007

Other books you might like:
Fredrick McKissack, *The Dark-Thirty: Southern Tales of the Supernatural*, 1992
Diane Muldrow, *On the Back Burner*, 2003
Shinji Saijyo, *Iron Wok Jan Volume 1*, 2002
Jane Yolen, *Here There Be Ghosts*, 1998

703

ALLY CONDIE

Matched
(New York: Dutton, 2010)

Subject(s): Romances (Fiction); Love; Poetry

Age range(s): 15 - 18+
Major character(s): Cassia, Young Woman, Friend (of Xander); Xander, Young Man, Friend (of Cassia); Ky, Orphan
Time period(s): Indeterminate Future
Summary: In Ally Condie's *Matched*, readers meet Cassia, a young woman whose whole life has been planned for her. She knows what she will eat, where she will work, and which man she will one day marry. The Society Officials have removed choice from people's lives as a way to simplify things. Cassia is fine with everything that has

been determined for her—until a poem written by her dying grandfather and an image of a boy change everything. Cassia knows that she is supposed to marry her best friend, Xander, but she can't stop thinking about an orphan named Ky. This leads her to question whether her predetermined life is really the life she wants.

Where it's reviewed:
Booklist, September 15, 2010, page 72
Horn Book Guide, Spring 2011, page 94
Publishers Weekly, October 4, 2010, page 49
School Library Journal, December 2010, page 110
Voice of Youth Advocates, December 2010, page 467

Other books by the same author:
Crossed, 2011

Other books you might like:
James DeVita, *The Silenced*, 2007
Catherine Fisher, *Incarceron*, 2007
Melinda Lo, *Ash*, 2009
Lois Lowry, *The Giver*, 1993
Caragh M. O'Brien, *Birthmarked*, 2010

704

NEIL CONNELLY

The Miracle Stealer

(New York: Arthur A. Levine Books, 2010)

Subject(s): Miracles; Religion; Brothers and sisters

Age range(s): 15 - 18+
Major character(s): Andi Grant, 19-Year-Old, Sister (of Daniel); Daniel Grant, 6-Year-Old, Brother (of Andi)
Time period(s): 21st century; 2010s
Locale(s): Paradise, Pennsylvania

Summary: A teenager struggles with issues of faith and family loyalty in this young adult novel by Neil Connelly. When 19-year-old Andi Grant's brother Daniel was a toddler, he was trapped in a deep shaft for three days while their town of Paradise, Pennsylvania, prayed for his rescue. When Daniel was pulled alive from the ground, he was dubbed "Miracle Boy." Soon after, the residents of the town began crediting Daniel with their own miracles—physical healings they believed resulted from prayers and proximity to Daniel. By the time Daniel is six, Andi believes that his miracles are nothing more than coincidences and that her mother and their neighbors are using the boy to bring travelers back to Paradise. To save her brother from exploitation, Andi hatches a plan that will expose the Miracle Boy and put her own life at risk.

Where it's reviewed:
Booklist, November 1, 2010, page 52
Horn Book Magazine, November-December 2010, page 87
Publishers Weekly, October 18, 2010, page 51
School Library Journal, December 2010, page 110
Voice of Youth Advocates, December 2010, page 448

Other books by the same author:
St. Michael's Scales, 2002

Other books you might like:
Peter Dickinson, *Healer*, 1983
Laura Langston, *Hannah's Touch*, 2009
Henning Mankell, *Shadows in the Twilight*, 2008

705

MICHELLE COOPER

The FitzOsbornes in Exile

(New York: Random House, 2011)

Series: Montmaray Journals Series. Book 2
Subject(s): World War II, 1939-1945; Social class; Culture

Age range(s): 15 - 18+
Major character(s): Sophia FitzOsborne, Royalty, Debutante
Time period(s): 20th century; 1930s (1937)
Locale(s): London, England

Summary: *The FitzOsbornes in Exile* is the second book the Montmaray Journals series by Michelle Cooper. After their small island was invaded by Nazis, the FitzOsbornes, Montmaray's royal family, sent their children to live with an aunt in London. Now it is the height of the 1937 social season, and the FitzOsborne children are able to temporarily tuck away their cares as they enjoy the height of English culture. Yet again, Sophia finds herself struggling to be accepted by her peers—her bookishness sets her apart from other middle-class English girls who only wish to marry well. When the Germans begin to pose a threat to the rest of Europe, the FitzOsbornes wonder if they will ever be able to return home or if they will have a home to return to.

Where it's reviewed:
Booklist, May 1, 2011, page 83
Horn Book Magazine, May-June 2011, page 84
School Library Journal, May 2011, page 110
Voice of Youth Advocates, August 2011, page 266

Other books by the same author:
A Brief History of Montmaray, 2009

Other books you might like:
Meg Cabot, *Nicola and the Viscount*, 2004
Ruth Elwin Harris, *Gwen's Story: Sisters of the Quantock Hills*, 2002
Melissa Jensen, *Falling in Love with English Boys*, 2010
Sarah MacLean, *The Season*, 2009

706

MICHELLE COOPER

A Brief History of Montmaray

(New York: Random House, 2009)

Series: Montmaray Journals Series. Book 1
Subject(s): World War II, 1939-1945; Family; Royalty

Age range(s): 13 - 16+
Major character(s): Sophie FitzOsborne, Royalty, Debutante

Time period(s): 20th century; 1930s (1936)
Locale(s): Montmaray, Fictional Location

Summary: Author Michelle Cooper is a young adult novelist from Australia. *A Brief History of Montmaray* is her second novel. Set during the beginning of World War II, the book features Sophie Fitzosborne, a member of the royal family of the island of Montmaray, who lives with her eccentric relatives. Sophie receives a journal as a 16th birthday present and decides to chronicle her day-to-day life on the island. Her daily existence changes dramatically, however, when two German officers land a boat on Montmaray.

Where it's reviewed:
Booklist, September 15, 2009, page 66
Horn Book Magazine, November-December 2009, page 665
Publishers Weekly, October 19, 2009, page 53
School Library Journal, December 2009, page 110
Voice of Youth Advocates, April 2010, page 54

Other books by the same author:
The FitzOsbornes in Exile, 2011

Other books you might like:
Meg Cabot, *Princess Mia: The Princess Diaries, Volume IX*, 2007
Siobhan Dowd, *Solace of the Road*, 2009
Jean Ferris, *Twice upon a Marigold*, 2008
Shannon Hale, *Princess Academy*, 2005
Carlos Ruiz Zafon, *The Prince of Mist*, 2010

707

D.M. CORNISH, Author/Illustrator

Factotum

(New York: G. P. Putnam's Sons, 2010)

Series: Foundling's Tale Trilogy. Book 3
Subject(s): Monsters; Fantasy; Orphans

Age range(s): 13 - 18+
Major character(s): Rossamund Bookchild, Orphan, Monster, Human; Europe, Hunter (monster), Friend (of Rossamund)
Time period(s): Indeterminate
Locale(s): Brandenbrass, Fictional Location

Summary: *Factotum* is the third and final installment in the Foundling's Tale Trilogy (formerly known as the Monster Blood Tattoo Series). Rossamund Bookchild cannot escape dangerous accusations, regardless of how far he travels or with whom he associates. The young orphan has been dogged by allegations that he's a monster disguised as a human. Befriending Europe, one of the most revered monster hunters in the area, doesn't do much to help Rossamund's case. Together, Rossamund and Europe travel to Brandenbrass where Rossamund is forced to confront his heritage and identity, finding out for himself whether or not all monsters are truly evil. The book includes more than 100 pages of maps, charts, and vocabulary to supplement the story.

Where it's reviewed:
Horn Book Guide, Spring 2011, page 95
Locus, December 2010, page 21

School Library Journal, February 2011, page 104

Other books by the same author:
Lamplighter, 2008
Foundling, 2007

Other books you might like:
Gill Arbuthnott, *The Keepers' Tattoo*, 2010
Bruce Coville, *The Last Hunt*, 2010
Neil Gaiman, *Coraline*, 2002
Ursula K. Le Guin, *A Wizard of Earthsea*, 1968
China Mieville, *Un Lun Dun*, 2007
Philip Pullman, *The Golden Compass*, 1995

708

EIREANN CORRIGAN

Accomplice

(New York: Scholastic, 2010)

Subject(s): Friendship; High schools; Conduct of life

Age range(s): 13 - 16+
Major character(s): Finn, Student—High School, 11th Grader, Friend (of Chloe); Chloe, Student—High School, 11th Grader, Friend (of Finn); Dean, Friend (of Chloe)
Time period(s): 21st century; 2010s
Locale(s): New Jersey, United States

Summary: In the young adult novel *Accomplice* by Eireann Corrigan, two high-school juniors take their guidance counselor's advice too far as they try to enhance their college applications. Chloe and Finn are good students and best friends, but they need to make themselves more interesting to impress college-admissions officers. Borrowing an idea from recent headlines, the girls plot Chloe's phony abduction. According to the plan, Chloe will hide out in an empty house for 11 days while Finn brings her food and carries on the charade. Before Finn can rescue Chloe triumphantly, the police presume that Chloe is dead and charge her friend Dean with the crime. Eventually Chloe returns from hiding and Dean is released, but the cruel hoax has already inflicted serious damage on everyone involved.

Where it's reviewed:
Booklist, May 1, 2010, page 49
Horn Book Guide, Spring 2011, page 95
Publishers Weekly, August 23, 2010, page 51
School Library Journal, October 2010, page 110
Voice of Youth Advocates, October 2010, page 344

Other books by the same author:
Ordinary Ghosts, 2007
Splintering, 2004
You Remind Me of You: A Poetry Memoir, 2002

Other books you might like:
Judy Blundell, *What I Saw and How I Lied*, 2008
S.A. Bodeen, *The Compound*, 2008
Dana Reinhardt, *Harmless*, 2007

709

SARAH CORTEZ, Editor

You Don't Have a Clue: Latino Mystery Stories for Teens

(Houston, Texas: Pinata Books, 2011)

Subject(s): Short stories; Mystery; Hispanic Americans

Age range(s): 15 - 18+

Summary: This short fiction collection of 18 short stories, all featuring Latino characters, explores many of the common and not-so-common problems faced by typical teenagers from across the United States. Among the characters readers will meet in the various tales found in this compilation include a young woman who is forced to live with a "family" she cannot remember, a nerdy high school student who must investigate the mysterious appearance of a severed arm in his locker, a baseball player who has started hearing voices in his head after getting hit with the ball, a girl who has been kidnapped and forced into a life of prostitution, and others. Included among this collection's many contributing authors are such accomplished writers as Mario Acevedo, Alicia Gaspar de Alba, Diana Lopez, and Sergio Troncoso.

Where it's reviewed:
Booklist, May 1, 2011, page 43
Bulletin of the Center for Children's Books, May 2011, page 411
School Library Journal, June 2011, page 112
Voice of Youth Advocates, August 2011, page 266

Other books by the same author:
Windows into My World: Latino Youths Write Their Lives, 2007

Other books you might like:
Kelly Link, *Pretty Monsters: Stories*, 2008
Lyn Miller-Lachmann, *Once Upon a Cuento*, 2003
Judith Ortiz Cofer, *An Island Like You: Stories of the Barrio*, 1995
Theresa Saldana, *The Almost Murder and Other Stories*, 2008

710

JENNIFER COWAN

Earthgirl

(Toronto: Groundwood Books, 2009)

Subject(s): Ecology; Friendship; Interpersonal relations

Age range(s): 15 - 18+

Major character(s): Sabine Solomon, 16-Year-Old; Vray Forest, Environmentalist (co-worker of Sabine), Musician

Time period(s): 21st century; 2000s

Locale(s): United States

Summary: Jennifer Cowan's *Earthgirl* tells the story of 16-year-old Sabine Solomon, whose awakening environmental awareness radically transforms her life and the lives of those around her. After a run-in involving litter and an angry motorist, Sabine commits herself to becoming more conscious of environmental matters. She lands a job at a local co-op, where she connects with co-worker Vray Forest. But Vray's activism is far more radical than Sabine's, and she soon must make some complicated choices about her newfound role—and her relationship with Vray. First novel.

Where it's reviewed:
Booklist, June 1, 2009, page 50
Canadian Children's Book News, Spring 2009, page 118
New York Times Book Review, page 16, page September 13, 2009
School Library Journal, June 2009, page 118

Other books you might like:
Lisa Greenwald, *My Life in Pink and Green*, 2009
April Henry, *Torched*, 2009
Saci Lloyd, *The Carbon Diaries 2015*, 2009

711

BRENT CRAWFORD

Carter Finally Gets It

(New York: Hyperion, 2009)

Subject(s): Adolescence; Schools; Love

Age range(s): 14 - 16+

Major character(s): Will Carter, 14-Year-Old

Time period(s): 21st century; 2000s

Locale(s): United States

Summary: 14-year-old Will Carter is about to start high school—and has more than a few worries about it. First of all, Carter isn't exactly a smooth-talking Lothario; he stutters—usually around girls. Second, he has Attention Deficit Disorder—especially around girls. And third, the fact that he is still a virgin plagues him constantly—principally when he's around girls. Narrated by the hapless hero himself, *Carter Finally Gets It* by Brent Crawford chronicles Will's first year of high school as he navigates the waters of adolescence: first, awkward love, academics, the school bully, plenty of discoveries, and, of course, girls. First novel.

Where it's reviewed:
Publishers Weekly, April 20, 2009, page 49
School Library Journal, October 2009, page 60

Other books by the same author:
Carter's Big Break, 2010

Other books you might like:
Bill Brittain, *The Fantastic Freshman*, 1988
Stephen Chbosky, *The Perks of Being a Wallflower*, 1999
David Lubar, *Sleeping Freshmen Never Lie*, 2005

712

GILLIAN CROSS

Where I Belong

(New York: Holiday House, 2011)

Story type: Child-in-Peril

Subject(s): Kidnapping; Fashion models; Fashion design

Age range(s): 14 - 17+
Major character(s): Khadija, 13-Year-Old, Model, Sister (of Mahmoud); Mahmoud, Brother (of Khadija); Sandy Dexter, Designer, Mother (of Freya); Freya, Daughter (of Sandy); Abdi, 14-Year-Old
Time period(s): 21st century; 2010s
Locale(s): London, England; Somalia

Summary: Hoping to give his child an opportunity for a better life, the father of 13-year-old Khadija sends his daughter from their home in Somalia to the streets of London, where she is to become a student. Once there, Khadija has a chance encounter with fashion designer Sandy Dexter, who offers her a modeling job as the face of her upcoming Somalia-themed clothing line. Khadija reluctantly agrees and quickly becomes a well-known figure in the fashion world, only to learn that her fame has a price. Looking to cash in on her celebrity, a group of criminals kidnaps Khadija's brother Mahmoud back in Somalia, demanding that she pay them a $10,000 ransom if she ever wants to see him again. Desperate to rescue her brother, Khadija enlists the help of friends Abdi and Freya to uncover the truth surrounding Mahmoud's abduction, all while preparing to take part in a potentially dangerous London Fashion Week appearance in Somalia.

Where it's reviewed:
Booklist, May 15, 2011, page 43
Horn Book Guide, Fall 2011, page 378
School Library Journal, June 2011, page 114
Voice of Youth Advocates, June 2011, page 160

Other books by the same author:
The Nightmare Game, 2007
The Black Room, 2002
Phoning a Dead Man, 2002
Tightrope, 1999
On the Edge, 1985

Other books you might like:
Kim Antieau, *Broken Moon*, 2007
Julia DeVillers, *Lynn Visible*, 2010
Catherine Johnson, *Face Value*, 2006
Naima B. Robert, *From Somalia, with Love*, 2009

713

CATH CROWLEY

A Little Wanting Song

(New York: Knopf, 2010)

Subject(s): Adolescent interpersonal relations; Music; Neighborhoods

Age range(s): 15 - 18+
Major character(s): Charlie, 16-Year-Old; Rose, Neighbor (of Charlie); Luke, Boyfriend (of Rose); Dave, Friend (of Rose and Luke)
Time period(s): 21st century; 2010s
Locale(s): Melbourne, Victoria

Summary: In Cath Crowley's *A Little Wanting Song*, Charlie is a music-crazy 16-year-old who is spending the summer with her grandfather in Melbourne, Australia. She observes the goings-on of the neighbor girl, Rose,

and her friends. One friend in particular catches Charlie's eye, a handsome young man named Dave, and he becomes an inspiration in her songwriting. Soon Rose reaches out to Charlie and the two form a tentative friendship, but it isn't long before Charlie begins to wonder about Rose's real motivations for befriending her.

Where it's reviewed:
Booklist, May 1, 2010, page 77
Horn Book Guide, Fall 2010, page 364
School Library Journal, June 2010, page 98
Voice of Youth Advocates, June 2010, page 150

Other books by the same author:
Graffiti Moon, 2012

Other books you might like:
Rebecca Burton, *Leaving Jetty Road*, 2006
Patrick Jones, *Chasing Tail Lights*, 2007
Maureen McCarthy, *Rose by Any Other Name*, 2008
Jandy Nelson, *The Sky Is Everywhere*, 2010
Ryan Potter, *Exit Strategy*, 2010

714

SUZANNE CROWLEY

The Stolen One

(New York: Greenwillow Books, 2009)

Subject(s): Family; Family history; Death

Age range(s): 14 - 18+
Major character(s): Kat, 16-Year-Old, Foster Child; Elizabeth I, Royalty (Queen of England)
Time period(s): 16th century; 1500s
Locale(s): London, England

Summary: In Suzanne Crowley's *The Stolen One*, the death of 16-year old Kat's foster mother prompts her to leave her home in the country and set out for London in search of her real parents. Along the way she meets Queen Elizabeth I, a redhead such as herself, and her embroidery skills gain her a job in the Queen's court. Kat learns new customs and meets new people, but is torn between the life she was looking for and this new world made possible by the queen. Soon Kat finds herself in the middle of a dangerous world of jealousy, with those around her questioning if the queen is actually Kat's mother. The mystery unfolds through Kat's first-person narration and entries from an old journal.

Where it's reviewed:
Booklist, May 1, 2009, page 75
Horn Book Magazine, July/August 2009, page 419
School Library Journal, August 2009, page 100

Other books by the same author:
The Very Ordered Existence of Merilee Marvelous, 2007

Other books you might like:
Jacqueline Kolosov, *The Red Queen's Daughter*, 2007
Jacqueline Kolosov, *A Sweet Disorder*, 2009
Carolyn Meyer, *Beware, Princess Elizabeth*, 2001
Sarah L. Thomson, *The Secret of the Rose*, 2006

715

CHRIS CRUTCHER

Angry Management
(New York: Greenwillow Books, 2009)

Subject(s): Short stories; Counseling; Adolescence

Age range(s): 13 - 17+
Time period(s): 21st century; 2000s
Locale(s): United States

Summary: In *Angry Management*, acclaimed young adult author Chris Crutcher presents three novellas starring memorable characters from earlier books and short stories. Bound together by their common membership in Mr. Nakatani's Angry Management group, the troubled teenage characters share their stories of heartbreak, courage, and humor. For overweight Angus Bethune, a boy with four gay parents, Mr. Nak's group gives him the opportunity to meet Sarah Byrnes, a girl who bears the visible scars of her father's abuse. Conservative Christian Matt Miller connects with Marcus James, who is black and gay. For Montana West, Matt Miller, and others, Mr. Nak's Angry Management will impact their young lives forever.

Where it's reviewed:
Booklist, September 1, 2009, page 38
Horn Book Magazine, November/December 2009, page 666
Voice of Youth Advocates, August 2009, page 222

Other books by the same author:
Deadline, 2007
The Sledding Hill, 2005
Athletic Shorts, 2001
Whale Talk, 2001
Ironman, 1995

Other books you might like:
Alex Flinn, *Breathing Underwater*, 2001
James W. Loewen, *Sundown Towns: A Hidden Dimension of Segregation in America*, 2005
Robert B. Parker, *Chasing the Bear*, 2009

716

ALAN CUMYN

Tilt
(Toronto: Groundwood Books, 2011)

Story type: Contemporary; Young Adult
Subject(s): Adolescent interpersonal relations; Adolescence; Dating (Social customs)

Age range(s): 15 - 18+
Major character(s): Stan, 16-Year-Old, Basketball Player; Janine Igwash, Teenager
Time period(s): 21st century; 2010s

Summary: Written by author Alan Cumyn, this young adult novel shares the story of a 16-year-old boy named Stan. Stan doesn't have many friends and isn't very popular, but he knows all that will change once he makes the JV basketball team. As Stan works to perfect his playing techniques, he begins to think that he may just have a chance at making the team after all. Then spiky-haired punk girl Janine Igwash begins to show interest in him. How is Stan supposed to concentrate on his goal when he is awash in a sea of teenage hormones that don't always help him make the best decisions? Stan's home life doesn't make things any easier; his mother's boyfriend is a bum, and his sister is as annoying as ever. When Stan's dad arrives with Stan's half-brother in tow, things get even more confusing. Now Stan isn't worried as much about making the team; he just wants to survive high school!

Where it's reviewed:
Horn Book Magazine, November/December 2011, page 98
Voice of Youth Advocates, October 2011, page 376

Other books you might like:
Carolyn MacCullough, *Stealing Henry*, 2005
Rich Wallace, *Playing without the Ball*, 2000
Ellen Wittlinger, *Hard Love*, 1999

717

LEAH CYPESS

Nightspell
(New York: HarperCollins, 2011)

Series: Mistwood Series. Book 2
Story type: Paranormal; Series
Subject(s): Ghosts; Supernatural; Sisters

Age range(s): 12 - 15+
Major character(s): Darri, Warrior, Sister (of Callie); Callie, Sister (of Darri)
Time period(s): Indeterminate
Locale(s): Ghostland, Fictional Location; Raellia, Fictional Location

Summary: This book is the second title in the Mistwood Series by author Leah Cypess. For as long as Darri can remember, her sister Callie has lived in the Ghostland. Now the girls' father, the king of Raellia, has come up with a plan to retrieve Callie: Darri will marry the prince of the dead. Upon arriving in the Ghostland, however, Darri quickly discovers that Callie has been transformed by this secret world practically beyond recognition. Furthermore, she doesn't seem entirely ready to leave a land in which she has lived most of her life. Can Darri stick to her father's plan to unite the world of the dead and the living, or will the secrets of Ghostland throw her off her quest?

Where it's reviewed:
Booklist, April 1, 2011, page 70
School Library Journal, August 2011, page 98
Voice of Youth Advocates, August 2011, page 287

Other books by the same author:
Mistwood, 2010

Other books you might like:
Jenna Burtenshaw, *Shadowcry*, 2011
Rosemary Clement-Moore, *Texas Gothic*, 2011
Juliet Marillier, *Cybele's Secret*, 2008

718

CAROLE ESTBY DAGG

The Year We Were Famous

(Boston: Clarion Books, 2011)

Subject(s): United States history, 1865-1901; Mother-daughter relations; Travel

Age range(s): 13 - 16+

Major character(s): Clara Estby, 17-Year-Old, Daughter (of Helga); Helga Estby, Mother (of Clara)

Time period(s): 19th century; 1890s (1896)

Locale(s): United States

Summary: *The Year We Were Famous* by Carole Estby Dagg is a novelized account of the historic 1896 walk across America undertaken by Clara and Helga Estby. This book is based on the real journey made by the author's great-grandmother and great-aunt. In the story, the mother-and-daughter duo travels from Washington State to New York City on foot in less than seven months. Because of their amazing accomplishment, the ladies win $10,000 in prize money, which they use to save the family's property from foreclosure. On their arduous journey, the two women encounter dangerous weather, wild animals, and criminals, and they learn about human generosity and their own evolving relationship. First novel.

Where it's reviewed:
Booklist, April 15, 2011, page 63
Horn Book Magazine, May-June 2011, page 86
Publishers Weekly, February 7, 2011, page 57
School Library Journal, May 2011, page 110
Voice of Youth Advocates, April 2011, page 56

Other books you might like:
Kathleen Karr, *The Great Turkey Walk*, 1998
Dana Reinhardt, *The Things a Brother Knows*, 2010
Ellen Wittlinger, *Zigzag*, 2003

719

KEREN DAVID

When I Was Joe

(London, England: Frances Lincoln Children's Books, 2010)

Subject(s): Murder; Identity; Adolescence

Age range(s): 12 - 15+

Major character(s): Ty, 13-Year-Old, Witness (of murder)

Time period(s): 21st century; 2010s

Locale(s): England

Summary: *When I Was Joe* is a suspenseful novel for young adult readers from author Keren David. Ty is a quiet and unassuming teenage boy, but when he witnesses a brutal murder, his whole life is turned upside down. After helping the police find the killer, Ty's life is put in danger, forcing the authorities to send him and his mother into the witness protection program. Ty gets a makeover and a new identity, turning him into Joe, an attractive new kid who garners attention at his new school. Soon, Ty/Joe is turning too many heads in his

new life, as he becomes a popular student and a star athlete. When his grandmother is attacked back in London, Ty/Joe knows that the killers are trying to pull him out of hiding, and he has to decide if he's willing to risk everything, including his exciting new life, to protect his family.

Where it's reviewed:
Booklist, November 1, 2010, page 65
Reading Time, August 2010, page 33
School Librarian, Summer 2010, page 109
School Library Journal, November 2010, page 108

Other books by the same author:
Almost True, 2011

Other books you might like:
James Heneghan, *Safe House*, 2006
Roland Smith, *Zach's Lie*, 2001
James Stevenson, *The Unprotected Witness*, 1997
Tony Varrato, *Fakie*, 2008

720

JACQUELINE DAVIES

Lost

(Tarrytown, New York: Marshall Cavendish, 2009)

Subject(s): Immigrants; History; Sisters

Age range(s): 14 - 16+

Major character(s): Essie Rosenfeld, 16-Year-Old, Seamstress; Freyda, Seamstress, Friend (of Essie); Mama, Mother (of Essie); Zelda Rosenfeld, 6-Year-Old, Sister (of Essie); Harriet Abbott, Seamstress, Friend (of Essie)

Time period(s): 20th century; 1900s-1910s

Locale(s): New York, New York; Manhattan

Summary: In *Lost* by Jacqueline Davies, Essie Rosenfeld, her widowed immigrant mother, and siblings struggle to survive in Manhattan's Lower East Side. In 1911, the 16-year-old takes a job as a seamstress at the Triangle Waist Company, toiling under harsh conditions for six dollars a day. With best friend Freyda at her side, Essie endures the hardships of life at work and home, while the truth about her emotional instability is gradually revealed. Essie makes friends with the new girl at work, Harriet Abbott (an heiress on the run), neither girl aware that they will soon play a part in a tragic chapter in American history.

Where it's reviewed:
Booklist, March 15, 2009, page 54
School Library Journal, April 2009, page 132
Voice of Youth Advocates, August 2009, page 223

Other books by the same author:
Where the Ground Meets the Sky, 2002

Other books you might like:
Mary Jane Auch, *Ashes of Roses*, 2002
Margaret Peterson Haddix, *Uprising*, 2007
Deborah Hopkinson, *Hear My Sorrow: The Diary of Angela Denoto, a Shirtwaist Worker: New York City 1909*, 2004

Suzanne Lieurance, *The Locket: Surviving the Triangle Shirtwaist Fire*, 2008

721

ARIC DAVIS

Nickel Plated

(Seattle, Washington: AmazonEncore, 2010)

Subject(s): Detective fiction; Mystery; Missing persons

Age range(s): 14 - 17+

Major character(s): Nickel, 12-Year-Old, Detective—Private; Arrow, Client, Sister (of Shelby); Shelby, Missing Person, Sister (of Arrow)

Time period(s): 21st century; 2010s

Locale(s): Michigan, United States

Summary: Nickel has been through a lot for a 12-year-old, but this kid doesn't let anything stand in his way. A victim of abuse and a prisoner of the foster-care system, he manages to escape from the foster home, determined never to go back to that miserable life again. Left to his own devices on the streets of suburban Michigan, Nickel makes a living selling drugs and blackmailing online pedophiles so that he has enough money to do what he really enjoys: work as a private eye. Though he is busy with a number of different cases, one in particular holds his attention. The case in question centers around a young girl named Shelby who has gone missing. While Nickel believes that it's probably already too late to find her alive, he is driven to track down her abductors both by his desire to bring them to justice for hurting a child and by his interest in pleasing his client, Shelby's attractive older sister Arrow.

Where it's reviewed:
Booklist, March 1, 2011, page 48
School Library Journal, August 2011, page 100
Voice of Youth Advocates, June 2011, page 162

Other books you might like:
Sara Beitia, *The Last Good Place of Lily Odilon*, 2010
Julia Platt Leonard, *Cold Case*, 2011
Rachel Wright, *You've Got Blackmail*, 2007
Tim Wynne-Jones, *Blink & Caution*, 2011

722

TANITA S. DAVIS

Mare's War

(New York: Knopf, 2009)

Subject(s): Grandmothers; Travel; World War II, 1939-1945

Age range(s): 13 - 16+

Major character(s): Mare, Grandmother; Octavia, Granddaughter (of Mare), Sister (of Tali); Tali, Sister (of Octavia), Granddaughter (of Mare)

Time period(s): 21st century; (2000s); 20th century; 1940s

Locale(s): United States

Summary: Teenage sisters Octavia and Tali are forced to take a road trip with their unusual grandmother in Tanita S. Davis's young adult novel *Mare's War*. The girls reluctantly set out with their grandmother—whom they call Mare—across the open roads of America, but along the way, the sisters are about to learn a thing or two about their freewheeling Mare. Mare tells her granddaughters of her youthful determination to leave the oppression of the American South—and the series of events that led her to enlist in the African-American division of the Women's Army Corp in the Second World War. Octavia and Tali slowly develop a new appreciation for their grandmother, and the road trip becomes a family event that none of them will ever forget.

Where it's reviewed:
Christian Science Monitor, July 6, 2009, page 25
School Library Journal, July 2009, page 81
Voice of Youth Advocates, June 2009, page 134

Other books by the same author:
A la Carte, 2008

Other books you might like:
Laura Malone Elliott, *A Troubled Peace*, 2009
Angela Johnson, *Toning the Sweep: A Novel*, 1993
Sherri L. Smith, *Flygirl*, 2009
Ellen Wittlinger, *Zigzag*, 2003

723

KATE DE GOLDI

The 10 PM Question

(Dunedin, New Zealand: Longacre Press, 2010)

Subject(s): Adolescence; Family relations; Family life

Age range(s): 12 - 15+

Major character(s): Frankie Parsons, 12-Year-Old; Ma, Mother (of Frankie)

Time period(s): 21st century; 2000s

Locale(s): New Zealand

Summary: In *The 10 PM Question* by Kate De Goldi, 12-year-old Frankie Parsons is bright, reasonable, and plagued by troubling questions. Rooted in fears about fatal illness and catastrophe, Frankie's queries typically present themselves at 10 o'clock in the evening, when he seeks his mother's counsel. While other family members seem free from worry, Ma is the only one who listens to his concerns about smoke alarm batteries, tumors, and pandemics. Though unusual, their relationship is predictable and familiar. But a new girl at school threatens to change everything when Frankie realizes that her brain is also overrun with difficult questions.

Where it's reviewed:
Booklist, August 1, 2010, page 54
Horn Book Magazine, November-December 2010, page 88
School Librarian, Autumn 2010, page 175
School Library Journal, September 2010, page 150
Voice of Youth Advocates, December 2010, page 450

Awards the book has won:
Montana New Zealand Book Awards, 2009

Other books you might like:
Thomas Bloor, *The Memory Prisoner*, 2001

Doug MacLeod, *I'm Being Stalked by a Moonshadow*, 2007

Jaclyn Moriarty, *The Spell Book of Listen Taylor: And the Secrets of the Family Zing*, 2007

724

NINA DE GRAMONT

Every Little Thing in the World

(New York: Atheneum Books for Young Readers, 2010)

Subject(s): Pregnancy; Friendship; Camps (Recreation)

Age range(s): 15 - 18+

Major character(s): Sydney Biggs, 16-Year-Old, Pregnant Teenager, Friend (of Natalia), Camper; Natalia Miksa, Camper, 16-Year-Old, Friend (of Sydney); Margit Miksa, Sister (of Natalia); Brendan, Camper, Actor; Mick, Camper

Time period(s): 21st century; 2010s

Locale(s): Canada; Linden Hill, New Jersey

Summary: In the young adult novel *Every Little Thing in the World* by Nina de Gramont, 16-year-old friends Sydney Biggs and Natalia Miksa leave their lives of privilege in Linden Hill, New Jersey, to spend six weeks at a wilderness camp in Canada. After the girls had a run-in with the police, their parents decided that time away in nature might do them some good. Sydney hasn't told her parents that she is pregnant. And Natalia hasn't told her parents that she has discovered her sister's true identity. When the girls arrive at Camp Bell, they find other teenagers struggling with their own problems. As they spend their days boating, hiking, and swimming, Sydney and Natalia consider the decisions that await them back in the real world.

Where it's reviewed:
Booklist, March 15, 2010, page 38
Horn Book Guide, Fall 2010, page 365
School Library Journal, August 2010, page 58
Voice of Youth Advocates, June 2010, page 152

Other books by the same author:
Gossip of the Starlings, 2008

Other books you might like:
Pat Brisson, *The Best and Hardest Thing*, 2010
Sarah Dessen, *Someone Like You*, 1998
Abby McDonald, *Boys, Bears, and a Serious Pair of Hiking Boots*, 2010

725

MATT DE LA PENA

We Were Here

(New York: Delacorte Press, 2009)

Subject(s): Juvenile detention homes; Runaways; Friendship

Age range(s): 13 - 18+

Major character(s): Miguel, Teenager; Rondell, Friend (of Miguel); Mong, Friend (of Miguel)

Time period(s): 21st century; 2000s

Locale(s): California, United States

Summary: In *We Were Here*, author Matt de la Pena crafts a story of identity and redemption. After being involved in a violent crime, Miguel is sentenced to a year in a juvenile detention facility. Since he was eager to get away from his home life anyway, he doesn't regard the sentence as much of a punishment. He meets Mong and Rondell, two fellow offenders. The three break out together and head to Mexico. But the trip doesn't quite go as planned—and Miguel soon learns the journey is sometimes more important than the destination.

Where it's reviewed:
Booklist, September 1, 2009, page 87
Horn Book Magazine, November-December 2009, page 667
Publishers Weekly, November 2, 2009, page 54
School Library Journal, December 2009, page 112
Voice of Youth Advocates, December 2009, page 404

Other books by the same author:
I Will Save You, 2010
Mexican WhiteBoy, 2008
Ball Don't Lie, 2005

Other books you might like:
LouAnne Johnson, *Muchacho*, 2009
Gordon Korman, *The Juvie Three*, 2008
Francisco X. Stork, *Behind the Eyes*, 2006
Paul Volponi, *Homestretch*, 2009

726

DELPHINE DE VIGAN

No and Me

(New York: Bloomsbury USA Children's Books, 2010)

Subject(s): Homeless persons; Adolescence; Gifted children

Age range(s): 15 - 18+

Major character(s): Lou, Teenager, Genius; No, Teenager, Streetperson (homeless)

Time period(s): 21st century; 2010s

Locale(s): Paris, France

Summary: Lou is a brilliant, albeit socially awkward, teenage genius living in Paris. While working on a project for school, she begins researching homelessness in her city. During her studies, she crosses paths with No, a homeless teen whom she befriends and grows fond of. Determined to make a difference, Lou asks her parents if No can live with them and is shocked when they agree. As No settles in with Lou's family, everyone is forced to confront the dark secrets they've been hiding. As Lou and her parents finally begin to deal with a painful tragedy, No comes face to face with her shocking past.

Where it's reviewed:
Horn Book Guide, Spring 2011, page 96
Reading Time, August 2010, page 34
School Librarian, Summer 2010, page 109
School Library Journal, July 2010, page 86

Other books you might like:
Jessica Blank, *Almost Home*, 2007
Catherine Ryan Hyde, *Becoming Chloe*, 2006
Eric Walters, *Sketches*, 2008
Brian Yansky, *Wonders of the World*, 2007

727

MATT DEMBICKI, Editor

Trickster: Native American Tales: A Graphic Collection

(Golden, Colorado: Fulcrum Publishing, 2010)

Subject(s): Folklore; Native Americans; Comic books

Age range(s): 11 - 18+

Summary: The trickster is a familiar figure in Native American folklore. Sometimes cast as an animal, other times as a supernatural being, the trickster is a mischievous or malicious figure who somehow upsets the world's natural order. In this graphic novel for young readers, editor Matt Dembicki presents a collection of 21 trickster tales retold by Native American storytellers and illustrated in comic book format. The pairing of ancient lore with contemporary illustration introduces the tradition of the trickster to a new generation of readers. The collection includes, among others, "Coyote and the Pebbles" by Dayton Edmonds and Micah Farritor, "Raven the Trickster" by John Active and Jason Copland, "How the Alligator Got His Brown, Scaly Skin" by Joyce Bear and Megan Baehr, and "Rabbit's Choctaw Tail Tale" by Tim Tingle and Pat Lewis.

Where it's reviewed:
Booklist, May 1, 2010, page 85
Publishers Weekly, April 26, 2010, page 95
School Library Journal, May 2010, page 139

Awards the book has won:
Aesop Prize, 2011

Other books you might like:
Sherman Alexie, *The Absolutely True Diary of a Part-Time Indian*, 2007
Joseph Bruchac, *Dawn Land*, 1993
Louise Erdrich, *The Birchbark House*, 1999
Virginia Hamilton, *A Ring of Tricksters: Animal Tales from America, the West Indies, and Africa*, 1997

728

KIMBERLY DERTING

The Body Finder

(New York: HarperCollins, 2010)

Series: Body Finder Series. Book 1
Subject(s): Murder; Serial murders; Friendship

Age range(s): 15 - 18+

Major character(s): Violet Ambrose, Student—High School, Friend (of Jay); Jay Heaton, 11th Grader, Friend (of Violet)

Time period(s): 21st century; 2010s
Locale(s): Washington, United States

Summary: In Kimberly Derting's *The Body Finder*, high school student Violet Ambrose experiences some strange feelings. Ever since she was young, she could sense when the body of a dead animal was around. Now that she's older, her ability has developed to allow her to locate the bodies of dead people. Normally this would disturb Violet, but with the recent events happening in town, she finds it to be somewhat of a blessing. A serial killer is on the loose, killing innocent young teens, and Violet is able to connect to his victims and find their bodies. When she shares her secret with her childhood best friend, Jay, he grows concerned but agrees to help her track down the killer. As the two teens get closer to the killer, the nature of their relationship changes and they struggle to keep things platonic.

Where it's reviewed:
Booklist, October 15, 2010, page 58
Horn Book Guide, Fall 2010, page 365
School Library Journal, May 2010, page 110
Voice of Youth Advocates, August 2010, page 264

Other books by the same author:
Desires of the Dead, 2011
The Pledge, 2011

Other books you might like:
Jenny Carroll, *When Lightning Strikes*, 2001
Lois Duncan, *The Third Eye*, 1984
Jen Nadol, *The Mark*, 2010
Marlene Perez, *Dead Is a State of Mind*, 2009
Rachel Vincent, *My Soul to Take*, 2009

729

SARAH DESSEN

Along for the Ride

(New York: Viking, 2009)

Subject(s): Summer; Friendship; Adolescence
Age range(s): 14 - 18+
Major character(s): Auden, 18-Year-Old, Graduate, Student; Eli, Teenager, Friend
Time period(s): 21st century; 2000s
Locale(s): United States

Summary: Sarah Dessen's *Along for the Ride* is a young adult novel about growing up and connecting with others. A recent high school grad and all-star student, Auden decides to spend her last summer before college with her father, a writer, his young new wife, Heidi, and their brand-new baby, Thisbe. Still recovering from her parents' divorce three years earlier, Auden is looking forward to getting through the summer and throwing herself into her college studies in the fall. But when her new stepmother, Heidi, offers her a job working at the boutique she owns, Auden agrees, mostly out of feelings of pity and obligation. Working as the store's bookkeeper thrusts Auden into a huge group of new friends, which include the boutique's teenage salesgirls and the cute boys from the bike rental shop next door. Auden instantly bonds with adorable and brooding Eli, who teaches her to ride a bike, bowl, and experience the life of a typical teenager—one that Auden's parents forced her to miss out on. As Auden and Eli's friendship blossoms, they're both able to embark on a journey of self-discovery and healing.

Where it's reviewed:
Booklist, April 15, 2009, page 35
Horn Book Magazine, May/June 2009, page 295
New York Times Book Review, August 16, 2009, page 13
School Library Journal, June 2009, page 120
Voice of Youth Advocates, June 2009, page 134

Other books by the same author:
What Happened to Goodbye, 2011
Lock and Key, 2008
Just Listen, 2006
The Truth about Forever, 2004
This Lullaby, 2002

Other books you might like:
Deb Caletti, *The Secret Life of Prince Charming*, 2009
Elisa Carbone, *Jump*, 2010
Garret Freymann-Weyr, *After the Moment*, 2009
Cheryl Renee Herbsman, *Breathing*, 2009
James Patterson, *Fang*, 2010

730

SARAH DESSEN

What Happened to Goodbye

(New York: Random House, 2011)

Subject(s): Divorce; Identity; High schools

Age range(s): 14 - 18+

Major character(s): McLean Sweet, 17-Year-Old, Girl; Mr. Sweet, Father (of McLean); Dave, Friend (of McLean)

Time period(s): 21st century; 2010s

Locale(s): United States

Summary: In *What Happened to Goodbye* by Sarah Dessen, 17-year-old McLean Sweet struggles to find herself in the aftermath of her mother's betrayal and her parents' divorce. McLean's mother's extramarital affair with a basketball coach has shocked their community and left their family in a shambles. After the divorce, McLean moves in with her father—but her father is always moving. A restaurant consultant, Mr. Sweet must relocate often. At first, the arrangement suits McLean well. In each town she creates a new identity for herself. After playing the roles of cheerleader and actress, McLean and her father move again. This time, McLean wants to stop pretending to be someone else, but she will need the help of her new neighbor, Dave, to discover the person she has become.

Where it's reviewed:
Booklist, May 1, 2011, page 85
Horn Book Magazine, July-August 2011, page 147
Kirkus Reviews, April 15, 2011, page 28
Publishers Weekly, February 21, 2011, page 134
School Library Journal, June 2011, page 114

Other books by the same author:
Along for the Ride, 2011

Lock and Key, 2008
Just Listen, 2006
That Summer, 2006
The Truth about Forever, 2006
Dreamland, 2004
Someone Like You, 2004
This Lullaby, 2002

Other books you might like:
Joan Bauer, *Hope Was Here*, 2000
Robin Benway, *The Extraordinary Secrets of April, May and June*, 2010
Cheryl Dellasega, *Nugrl90 (Sadie)*, 2007

731

LAUREN DESTEFANO

Wither

(New York: Simon and Schuster, 2011)

Series: Chemical Garden Trilogy. Book 1
Story type: Science Fantasy; Series
Subject(s): Science fiction; Fantasy; Genetic engineering

Age range(s): 15 - 18+
Major character(s): Rhine, 16-Year-Old, Spouse (of Linden); Linden, Spouse (of Rhine)
Time period(s): Indeterminate Future

Summary: This book is the first title in author Lauren DeStefano's Chemical Garden Trilogy. In a world where the quest for the perfect human species has gone awry, genetic mutations dictate that female humans can only live for 20 years, while male humans live to be 25 years old. As scientists scramble to reverse the effects of this mutation, the world is plagued by corruption and destitution, and populated by children whose parents have succumbed to the defect. Worse yet, young women are being kidnapped and forced into bigamous marriages. Rhine is one of those young women, and although her husband Linden loves her deeply, she cannot ignore the tension between her and Linden's other wives. Nor can she overlook the bizarre secrets that characterize Linden's world. Rhine is certain that there must be a better life for her than this. But with less than four years of survival left, can Rhine find freedom before her time runs out?

Where it's reviewed:
Booklist, February 1, 2011, page 79
Publishers Weekly, January 10, 2011, page 51
School Library Journal, April 2011, page 170
Voice of Youth Advocates, April 2011, page 79

Other books by the same author:
Fever, 2012

Other books you might like:
Ian Beck, *Pastworld*, 2009
Garth Nix, *Shade's Children*, 1997
David Patneaude, *Epitaph Road*, 2010
Kathy Reichs, *Virals*, 2010
Neal Shusterman, *Unwind*, 2007

732

CARL DEUKER

Payback Time

(Boston, Massachusetts: Houghton Mifflin, 2010)

Subject(s): Sports; Journalism; Mystery

Age range(s): 13 - 16+

Major character(s): Mitch, Journalist, 12th Grader, Student—High School; Angel, Football Player, Student—High School

Time period(s): 21st century; 2010s

Locale(s): United States

Summary: *Payback Time* is a sports novel for young adults. Mitch isn't exactly Mr. Popularity at Lincoln High School, but the overweight journalist does have a gift for finding a great story. At the beginning of senior year, he begrudgingly accepts his assignment as sports reporter for the school's newspaper. It doesn't take long for him to realize the assignment might be exactly what he needs to capture the attention of the town's local newspaper. On the football field, a new transfer student named Angel really shines, but his life off the field remains a mystery to everyone. When Mitch decides to investigate Angel's background, he's not prepared for the shocking surprise he uncovers.

Where it's reviewed:
Booklist, May 1, 2010, page 45
Booklist, September 1, 2010, page 119
Christian Century, December 14, 2010, page 27
Horn Book Magazine, November/December 2010, page 88
School Library Journal, September 2010, page 150

Other books by the same author:
Gym Candy, 2007
Heart of a Champion, 2007
Runner, 2005
High Heat, 2003
Night Hoops, 2000

Other books you might like:
Joan Bauer, *Peeled*, 2008
Ben Esch, *Sophomore Undercover*, 2009
Tim Green, *Football Champ*, 2009
Robert Lipsyte, *One Fat Summer*, 1977

733

IVY DEVLIN

Low Red Moon

(New York: Bloomsbury USA Children's Books, 2010)

Story type: Fantasy

Subject(s): Fantasy; Werewolves; Wilderness areas

Age range(s): 13 - 16+

Major character(s): Avery Hood, 17-Year-Old, Orphan, Girlfriend (of Ben); Ben Dusic, Werewolf, Boyfriend (of Avery)

Time period(s): 21st century; 2010s

Locale(s): Woodlake, United States

Summary: In this young adult novel by Ivy Devlin, 17-year-old Avery Hood has been left an orphan in the wake of her parents' vicious murders. Avery, her mother, and father had lived in the forest outside of Woodlake and enjoyed their quiet seclusion. Avery didn't even attend school, and she was taught by her parents. Then, Avery's life changed forever when her parents were killed in their home. Although Avery was there and saw the blood and carnage, she can recall nothing but the color silver. Now living with her grandmother in Woodlake, Avery has fallen fast and hard for a boy named Ben Dusic, who lives in the woods. When Ben reveals to Avery that he is a werewolf, she becomes increasingly troubled by his silvery eyes and the true nature of their bond.

Where it's reviewed:
Horn Book Guide, Spring 2011, page 96
Publishers Weekly, August 23, 2010, page 50
School Librarian, Summer 2011, page 116
School Library Journal, November 2010, page 110
Voice of Youth Advocates, December 2010, page 468

Other books you might like:
Andrea Cremer, *Nightshade*, 2010
Rachel Hawthorne, *Dark Guardian: Moonlight*, 2009
Jackson Pearce, *Sweetly*, 2011
Aprilynne Pike, *Spells*, 2010
Vivian Vande Velde, *Witch Dreams*, 2005

734

EMILY DIAMAND

Raiders' Ransom

(New York: Scholastic Inc., 2009)

Age range(s): 11 - 14+

Major character(s): Lilly Melkun, 13-Year-Old, Fisherman; Andy, Friend (of Lilly); Zeph, Pirate

Time period(s): 22nd century

Locale(s): England

Summary: In *Raiders' Ransom* by Emily Diamand, a devastating "Collapse" in the 21st century has left Great Britain a watery wasteland. Technology is banned (except in certain areas of Scotland) and massive floods have submerged most of England. A young fisher girl, Lilly, is at sea when her village is attacked by pirates, who also take the prime minister's daughter hostage. In her quest to rescue the kidnapped girl, Lilly contacts Zeph, the son of pirate raider, for help. With only a jewel salvaged from an old computer as ransom, Lilly holds the life of the prime minister's daughter and the future of her village in her hands.

Where it's reviewed:
Booklist, December 1, 2009, page 46
Horn Book Guide, Spring 2010, page 68
Publishers Weekly, November 30, 2009, page 48
School Library Journal, December 2009, page 112

Other books by the same author:
Flood and Fire, 2011

Other books you might like:
Julie Bertagna, *Exodus*, 2008
Erin Bow, *Plain Kate*, 2010
Tim Downs, *Nick of Time*, 2011

Sam Llewellyn, *Dark Solstice*, 2010
Kenneth Oppel, *Skybreaker*, 2005

735

CHRISTINA DIAZ GONZALEZ

The Red Umbrella

(New York: Alfred A. Knopf, 2010)

Subject(s): Cuban history; Family life; Voyages and travels

Age range(s): 12 - 15+
Major character(s): Lucia Alvarez, 14-Year-Old, Refugee
Time period(s): 20th century; 1960s
Locale(s): Cuba; Nebraska, United States

Summary: In *The Red Umbrella*, author Christina Diaz Gonzalez shares the story of 14-year-old Lucia Alvarez, a spirited girl who becomes part of Cuba's mass evacuation plan in the early 1960s. Fidel Castro has taken power, and Lucia sees her idyllic life undergo some startling transformations. Fearing for their children's future, Lucia's parents send them to America as part of Operation Pedro Pan, in which 14,000 children flee the country without guardians. Suddenly forced into a new life in Nebraska, Lucia is left wondering what happened to her family and if she will be able to remain true to her native culture. First novel.

Where it's reviewed:
Horn Book Guide, Fall 2010, page 339
Publishers Weekly, May 3, 2010, page 53
School Library Journal, May 2010, page 114
Voice of Youth Advocates, June 2010, page 154

Other books you might like:
Maria Acierno, *Children of Flight Pedro Pan*, 2004
Enrique Flores-Galbis, *90 Miles to Havana*, 2010
Kathlyn Gay, *Leaving Cuba: From Operation Pedro Pan to Elian*, 2010

736

HEATHER DIXON

Entwined

(New York: Greenwillow Books, 2011)

Subject(s): Royalty; Dance; Father-daughter relations

Age range(s): 13 - 16+
Major character(s): Azalea, Royalty (princess)
Locale(s): Eathesbury, Fictional Location

Summary: In the young adult novel *Entwined* by Heather Dixon, Azalea is the eldest daughter of the king of the enchanted world of Eathesbury. After her mother succumbs to an illness, Azalea and her 11 other sisters are required to mourn for a given period of time. Then they uncover a magical location just beyond the castle walls, a place where they can dance in their mother's memory. The dancing place is controlled by an enigmatic man named Keeper, who seems not to have the sisters' best interests in mind. Will Azalea fall prey to this mysteri-

ous man's plans? This book is based on the Grimm fairytale "The Twelve Dancing Princesses," also known as "The Worn-Out Dancing Shoes." First novel.

Where it's reviewed:
Booklist, February 1, 2011, page 68
Horn Book Magazine, May/June 2011, page 87
Publishers Weekly, February 28, 2011, page 58
School Library Journal, May 2011, page 112
Voice of Youth Advocates, April 2011, page 79

Other books you might like:
Dia Calhoun, *The Phoenix Dance*, 2005
Jessica Day George, *Princess of the Midnight Ball*, 2009
Suzanne Weyn, *The Night Dance*, 2005

737

CORY DOCTOROW

For the Win

(New York: Tor, 2010)

Subject(s): Virtual reality; Adventure; Feuds

Age range(s): 15 - 18+
Major character(s): Mala, Teenager (virtual combatant); Matthew, Teenager (virtual combatant); Leonard "Wei Dong", Teenager (virtual combatant); Big Sister Nor, Leader
Time period(s): Indeterminate Future

Summary: Cory Doctorow's *For the Win* is set in a futuristic virtual realm, where a group of young people come together to take on a menacing force that threatens the safety and security of the entire world. Mala, Matthew, Leonard, and several other teens possess extraordinary skills in virtual combat, which brings them to the attention of the mystifying Big Sister Nor. To take on the evil system, she assembles the group of elite fighters for an elaborate, dangerous plan to save the world—if it doesn't destroy it first.

Where it's reviewed:
Booklist, May 1, 2010, page 84
Horn Book Magazine, May/June 2010, page 80
School Library Journal, July 2010, page 86

Other books by the same author:
With a Little Help, 2011
Makers, 2009
Little Brother, 2008
Overclocked, 2007
Eastern Standard Tribe, 2004
Down and Out in the Magic Kingdom, 2003

Other books you might like:
Conor Kostick, *Epic*, 2007
Rune Michaels, *Genesis Alpha*, 2007
Walter Jon Williams, *This is Not a Game*, 2009

738

SHARON DOGAR

Annexed

(Boston, MA: Houghton Mifflin, 2010)

Subject(s): World War II, 1939-1945; Holocaust, 1933-1945; Adolescence

Age range(s): 13 - 18+

Major character(s): Anne Frank, Girl; Peter, Boy

Time period(s): 20th century; 1940s

Locale(s): Amsterdam, Netherlands

Summary: While movies, books, and seminars have investigated the stories of diarist Anne Frank, few pieces of literature have explored the lives of the other people hiding with Frank during the writing of her diary. *Annexed*, a novel by Sharon Dogar, tells the imagined story of Peter—the adolescent boy who hid with Frank. In *The Diary of Anne Frank*, Peter and Anne come of age at the same time and share a first love. Dogar imagines Peter's frustration at Anne's writing and at the constant confines of their shared environment. In this novel, readers get a chance to hear Peter's contemplation on what it means to be Jewish during World War II. Dogar continues the story of Anne Frank and the other annex occupants through their capture and their final days in Auschwitz.

Where it's reviewed:
Booklist, September 1, 2010, page 98
Horn Book Magazine, Sept.-Oct. 2010, page 76
Publishers Weekly, September 20, 2010, page 67
School Library Journal, September 2010, page 150
Voice of Youth Advocates, October 2010, page 345

Other books by the same author:
Waves, 2007

Other books you might like:
Anne Frank, *The Diary of Anne Frank*, 1952
Alison Leslie Gold, *Memories of Anne Frank: Reflections of a Childhood Friend*, 1997
Eric Heuvel, *A Family Secret*, 2009
Ruth Jacobsen, *Rescued Images: Memories of a Childhood in Hiding*, 2001

739

JENNIFER DONNELLY

Revolution

(New York: Delacorte Press, 2010)

Subject(s): French Revolution, 1789; Grief; Family

Age range(s): 14 - 18+

Major character(s): Andi Alpers, 17-Year-Old, Musician; Alexandrine Paradis, Actress

Time period(s): 18th century; (1780s); 21st century; 2010s

Locale(s): Paris, France

Summary: In *Revolution*, author Jennifer Donnelly crafts the interwoven tales of two young women who lead parallel lives in vastly different eras. In contemporary Paris, American teen Andi Alpers has just arrived with her famous scientist father, who has been commissioned to trace the history of a heart reportedly belonging to the final heir to the French throne. Andi stumbles upon a journal belonging to Alexandrine Paradis, who lived during the French Revolution and became determined to rescue the prince—and herself—from certain death. The lives of Andi and Alexandrine intersect as the two young women struggle to find their respective voices, purposes, and happily-ever-afters.

Where it's reviewed:
Booklist, October 1, 2010, page 89
New York Times Book Review, November 7, 2010, page 22
Publishers Weekly, September 13, 2010, page 47
School Library Journal, September 2010, page 150
Voice of Youth Advocates, December 2010, page 450

Other books by the same author:
A Northern Light, 2003

Awards the book has won:
Blue Ribbon Awards: Fiction, 2010

Other books you might like:
Patricia Elliott, *The Pale Assassin*, 2009
Sally Gardner, *The Silver Blade*, 2009
Jandy Nelson, *The Sky Is Everywhere*, 2010
Staton Rabin, *The Curse of the Romanovs*, 2007

740

SUSAN DONOVAN

Not That Kind of Girl

(New York: St. Martin's Press, 2010)

Subject(s): Love; Dogs; Interpersonal relations

Age range(s): 15 - 18+

Major character(s): Roxanne "Roxie" Bloom, Writer (blogger); Eli Gallagher, Trainer (dog trainer)

Time period(s): 21st century; 2010s

Locale(s): United States

Summary: Susan Donovan's *Not That Kind of Girl* charts the romance between a man-hating blogger and a handsome dog trainer. Roxanne Bloom has had her heart shattered one too many times, prompting her to start a Web site devoted to man-bashing. When her dog Lilith starts misbehaving (mostly toward men), Roxie reluctantly hires dog trainer Eli Gallagher to help tame the pooch. But the closer Roxie and Eli get, the more Roxie realizes that maybe *she* is the one who is being tamed by this sensitive, sexy man.

Where it's reviewed:
Booklist, September 15, 2010, page 73
Horn Book Guide, Spring 2011, page 114
Publishers Weekly, August 30, 2010, page 55
School Library Journal, November 2010, page 132
Voice of Youth Advocates, December 2010, page 463

Other books by the same author:
The Girl Most Likely To ..., 2008
He Loves Lucy, 2005

Other books you might like:
Kristin Billerbeck, *Perfectly Dateless: A Universally Misunderstood Novel*, 2010

Meg Cabot, *Princess on the Brink: The Princess Diaries, Volume VIII*, 2007
Deb Caletti, *The Six Rules of Maybe*, 2010
Carolyn Mackler, *Vegan Virgin Valentine*, 2004
Daria Snadowsky, *Anatomy of a Boyfriend*, 2007

741

SIOBHAN DOWD

Solace of the Road

(New York: David Fickling Books, 2009)

Subject(s): Runaways; Foster children; Voyages and travels

Age range(s): 14 - 18+

Major character(s): Holly "Solace" Hogan, 14-Year-Old, Foster Child

Time period(s): 21st century; 2000s

Locale(s): United Kingdom

Summary: Siobhan Dowd's *Solace of the Road* tells the story of 14-year-old Holly Hogan, a distressed girl living in an unbearable foster home. As she deals with her disingenuous foster family and the trials of school, Holly longs to escape. And she finds that escape in a very unlikely place: a blond wig. Once the wig is atop her head, Holly becomes Solace, a straight-talking wild child who lives life to the fullest. With this new persona, Holly sets off across England to find her birth mother, and, along the way, she meets a series of unforgettable characters that force her to confront the truth of her troubled past.

Where it's reviewed:
Booklist, October 1, 2009, page 43
Publishers Weekly, September 28, 2009, page 66
School Library Journal, October 2009, page 124

Other books by the same author:
Bog Child, 2008
The London Eye Mystery, 2007
A Swift Pure Cry, 2007

Other books you might like:
Heidi Ayarbe, *Compromised*, 2010
Alden R. Carter, *Walkaway*, 2008
Michelle Cooper, *A Brief History of Montmaray*, 2009
Joseph Monninger, *Baby*, 2007
Martine Murray, *How to Make a Bird*, 2003

742

FRANCES O'ROARK DOWELL

Ten Miles Past Normal

(New York: Atheneum Books for Young Readers, 2011)

Subject(s): Rural life; Adolescent interpersonal relations; High schools

Age range(s): 12 - 16+

Major character(s): Janie Gorman, 14-Year-Old, Student—High School; Sarah, Student—High School, Friend (of Janie)

Time period(s): 21st century; 2010s

Locale(s): North Carolina, United States

Summary: *Ten Miles Past Normal* is a young adult novel by author Frances O'Roark Dowell. As a young girl, Janie Gorman wanted nothing more than to live on a farm with tons of animals. Now that she is in high school, she wants nothing more than to a live a normal life like the rest of her peers. In an effort to fit in, Janie joins the school Jam Band and with the help of her best friend Sarah starts making new friends. Will Janie actually be able to weather the pressures of her first year of high school? O'Roark is also the author of *The Secret Language of Girls*, *Dovey Coe*, and *Chicken Boy*.

Where it's reviewed:
Booklist, March 1, 2011, page 59
Bulletin of the Center for Children's Books, March 2011, page 326
Horn Book Magazine, March-April 2011, page 115
School Library Journal, March 2011, page 160
Voice of Youth Advocates, April 2011, page 56

Other books by the same author:
The Kind of Friends We Used to Be, 2009
Shooting the Moon, 2008
The Secret Language of Girls, 2004

Other books you might like:
Antony John, *Five Flavors of Dumb*, 2010
Gordon Korman, *Schooled*, 2007
Catherine Gilbert Murdock, *Dairy Queen*, 2006
Joyce Raskin, *My Misadventures as a Teenage Rock Star*, 2011

743

JENNY DOWNHAM

You Against Me

(New York: David Fickling Books, 2010)

Subject(s): Rape; Revenge; Brothers and sisters

Age range(s): 14 - 18+

Major character(s): Mikey, 18-Year-Old, Brother (of Karyn), Boyfriend (of Ellie Parker); Karyn, 15-Year-Old, Sister (of Mikey), Crime Victim; Tom Parker, Student—College, Brother (of Ellie), Crime Suspect; Ellie Parker, Brother (of Tom), Girlfriend (of Mikey)

Time period(s): 21st century; 2010s

Locale(s): England

Summary: Set in England, Jenny Downham's *You Against Me* follows the impact of an alleged rape on the victim, the accused, and their siblings. When 15-year-old Karyn tells her 18-year-old brother, Mikey, that she was raped by Tom Parker, a college student, Mikey intends to get revenge. But when he arrives at Parker's opulent home he meets Tom's younger sister, Ellie, and finds his emotions muddled. Mikey and Ellie form an immediate bond, despite the fact that Tom has been accused of assaulting Karyn, and Ellie may have to testify at the hearing. Torn by their love for each other and their sense of family duty, Mikey and Ellie wrestle with the social issues raised by the case.

Where it's reviewed:
Booklist, August 1, 2011, page 45
Horn Book Magazine, November-December 2011, page 98
New York Times Book Review, August 21, 2011, page 13
Publishers Weekly, July 18, 2011, page 155
School Library Journal, November 2011, page 116

Other books by the same author:
Before I Die, 2009

Other books you might like:
Carolyn Mackler, *The Earth, My Butt, and Other Big Round Things*, 2003
Kimberly Marcus, *Exposed*, 2011
Anne Schraff, *Shadows of Quiet*, 2010

744

WENDELIN VAN DRAANEN

The Running Dream

(New York: Alfred A. Knopf, 2011)

Story type: Coming-of-Age
Subject(s): Coming of age; Track and field; Sports

Age range(s): 13 - 16+
Major character(s): Jessica, 16-Year-Old, Accident Victim (loses leg in car crash), Runner (track star); Rosa, Young Woman (with cerebral palsy)
Time period(s): 21st century; 2010s
Locale(s): United States

Summary: In this young-adult novel by Wendelin Van Draanen, Jessica is a 16-year-old high-school track star who seems to have her whole life in order. She's successful and fit and is too busy with her own goals and accomplishments to acknowledge others who aren't as fortunate such as her classmate, Rosa, who suffers from cerebral palsy. One day, everything changes for Jessica: She loses a leg in a horrible automobile accident. Now the star runner is devastated with the notion that she may never run again—she may never even walk again! After learning some lessons, Jessica gathers her resolve and decides to rebuild her life. With support from her parents, teammates, and even Rosa, Jessica is fitted with a prosthetic leg. But, even though Jessica has the leg, will she be able to run like she used to?

Where it's reviewed:
Booklist, January 1, 2011, page 98
Horn Book Magazine, March-April 2011, page 128
Running Times, March 2011, page 12
School Library Journal, February 2011, page 121
Voice of Youth Advocates, February 2011, page 563

Other books by the same author:
Confessional of a Serial Kisser, 2008
Runaway, 2006
Flipped, 2001

Other books you might like:
Kelly Bingham, *Shark Girl*, 2007
Mary Hershey, *The One Where the Kid Nearly Jumps to*

His Death and Lands in California, 2007
Cynthia Voigt, *Izzy, Willy-Nilly*, 1986

745

SHARON M. DRAPER

Just Another Hero

(New York: Atheneum Books for Young Readers, 2009)

Series: Jericho Prescott Trilogy. Book 3
Subject(s): High schools; Crime; Courage

Age range(s): 13 - 16+
Major character(s): Arielle, Student—High School; Kofi, Student—High School; November, Student—High School; Jericho, Student—High School
Time period(s): 21st century; 2000s
Locale(s): United States

Summary: *Just Another Hero* is the final novel in Sharon Draper's award-winning trilogy that includes *The Battle of Jericho* and *November Blues*. Arielle, Kofi, November, and their entire circle of friends have had to face some horrific challenges during their high school years, but none as terrifying as the armed gunman who walks into the girls' senior year English class. There are precious seconds in which to act, and the question is: who among them will stand up to the sniper and defend the school? This volume tells the story of unshakable friendships, fearless determination, and what it means to be a hero.

Where it's reviewed:
Booklist, June 1, 2009, page 51
Publishers Weekly, September 28, 2009, page 51
School Library Journal, July 2009, page 82
Voice of Youth Advocates, June 2009, page 134

Other books by the same author:
November Blues, 2007
The Battle of Jericho, 2003

Other books you might like:
Paul Langan, *Brothers in Arms*, 2004
Denene Miller, *Hotlanta*, 2008
Walter Dean Myers, *Shooter*, 2004
Rita Williams-Garcia, *Jumped*, 2009

746

DAVID L. DUDLEY

Caleb's Wars

(New York: Houghton Mifflin Harcourt, 2011)

Story type: Historical - World War II
Subject(s): Blacks; Civil rights; World War II, 1939-1945

Age range(s): 14 - 18+
Major character(s): Caleb, 15-Year-Old, Brother (of Randall); Randall, Military Personnel, Brother (of Caleb)
Time period(s): 20th century; 1940s
Locale(s): Georgia, United States

Summary: In this novel, author David L. Dudley tells the story of a young black teenager growing up during World War II. Caleb lives in Georgia in the time of Jim Crow laws and segregation, yet right now everyone in his town is thinking more about the war going on in Europe. When Caleb's family receives news that Caleb's older brother Randall may be drafted, Caleb begins to think about the similarities between the war being waged overseas and the one he fights at home every day against prejudice. When a German prisoner of war takes a job at the diner where Caleb works, Caleb must come to terms with working with someone from the enemy side. All the while, he continues to struggle with racism and his father's expectations.

Where it's reviewed:
Booklist, October 1, 2011, page 83
School Library Journal, November 2011, page 116
Voice of Youth Advocates, October 2011, page 378

Other books you might like:
Cynthia Kadohata, *Kira-Kira*, 2004
Sophie Littlefield, *Banished*, 2010
Mildred D. Taylor, *The Road to Memphis*, 1990

747

CLARE B. DUNKLE
PATRICK ARRASMITH, Illustrator

The House of Dead Maids

(New York: Henry Holt and Co., 2010)

Story type: Ghost Story
Subject(s): Ghosts; England; Supernatural

Age range(s): 13 - 16+
Major character(s): Tabby Aykroyd, Governess, 11-Year-Old; Jack, Boy
Time period(s): 19th century; 1800s
Locale(s): Yorkshire, England

Summary: In this young adult novel, author Clare B. Dunkle presents a prequel to Emily Bronte's classic novel *Wuthering Heights*. Dunkle tells the story of Tabby Aykroyd, an 11-year-old girl in Victorian Britain who is put into service at a rambling manor called Seldom House. In her own voice, Tabby tells how she arrives at Seldom House to take care of a troublesome boy who is the house's new master. The boy, who will later become Bronte's Heathcliff, has a fiery temperament and penchant for making life difficult for Tabby—but he is the least of her problems. Seldom House is haunted by the ghost of the former maid and several other lost spirits. As Tabby reaches out to the young master, he becomes more alienated and swears that Seldom House will not be taken over by those from the hereafter.

Where it's reviewed:
Booklist, August 1, 2010, page 47
Horn Book Magazine, Nov.-Dec. 2010, page 90
School Library Journal, November 2010, page 112
Voice of Youth Advocates, December 2010, page 468

Other books by the same author:
The Walls Have Eyes, 2009
By These Ten Bones, 2005
In the Coils of the Snake, 2005
Close Kin, 2004
The Hollow Kingdom, 2003

Other books you might like:
Emily Bronte, *Wuthering Heights*, 1847
Phyllis Reynolds Naylor, *Jade Green: A Ghost Story*, 2000
Paul Stewart, *Barnaby Grimes: Legion of the Dead*, 2010

748

JANE EAGLAND

Wildthorn

(London: Young Picador, 2010)

Story type: Gothic
Subject(s): Mental health; Memory disorders; Medical care

Age range(s): 15 - 18+
Major character(s): Louisa Cosgrove, Patient, 17-Year-Old
Time period(s): 19th century; 1800s
Locale(s): England

Summary: In this young adult novel set in 19th century England, author Jane Eagland tells the story of Louisa Cosgrove, a young woman who is sent to a mental hospital. Louisa grew up in a tumultuous household and faced much criticism from her mother and brother, who protested against her father's efforts to help Louisa rise above her lot in life. Soon, Louisa finds herself at the Wildthorn Hall asylum. Louisa protests when her doctors and nurses insist that she is actually a woman named Lucy Child. Louisa's protesting further convinces the doctors of her illness. But have they really mistaken Louisa for another young lady, or does she belong at Wildthorn as they claim she does?

Where it's reviewed:
Booklist, September 15, 2010, page 73
Horn Book Guide, Spring 2011, page 97
Publishers Weekly, September 6, 2010, page 42
School Library Journal, November 2010, page 112
Voice of Youth Advocates, December 2010, page 451

Other books by the same author:
Whisper My Name, 2010

Other books you might like:
Y.S. Lee, *A Spy in the House*, 2010
Malinda Lo, *Ash*, 2009
Barbara Quick, *A Golden Web*, 2010

749

DEBBY DAHL EDWARDSON

My Name Is Not Easy

(Tarrytown, New York: Marshall Cavendish Publishing, 2011)

Story type: Ethnic; Young Adult
Subject(s): Native North Americans; Interpersonal relations; Adolescent interpersonal relations

Age range(s): 13 - 16+
Major character(s): Luke, Narrator (Inupiaq), Student—Boarding School, Brother (of Bunna and Isaac);

Donna, Narrator (white), Student—Boarding School; Sonny, Narrator (Native American), Student—Boarding School; Chickie, Narrator (white), Student—Boarding School; Amiq, Narrator (Native American), Student—Boarding School; Bunna, Brother (of Luke and Isaac), Student—Boarding School; Isaac, Brother (of Luke and Bunna)

Time period(s): 20th century; 1960s (1960-1965)
Locale(s): Alaska, United States

Summary: In this young adult novel, author Debby Dahl Edwardson weaves the story of a group of Alaskan teens from different backgrounds, who come of age just after Alaska reaches statehood. The narrative shifts amid five narrators: Luke and Amiq, who are Inupiaq; Donna and Chickie, who are white; and Sonny, who is Native American. Although they hail from various cultures, all are subject to the prejudice, homesickness, and other hardships that result from traveling hundreds of miles from their homes to attend a Catholic boarding school. The students at Sacred Heart School are not allowed to speak in their native tongues nor use their native names. These five students, however, are able to reach common ground and form a family from the friendships they discover within the walls of the school. Edwardson was the 2011 National Book Award Finalist for this title.

Where it's reviewed:
Booklist, September 15, 2011, page 63
School Library Journal, November 2011, page 118
Voice of Youth Advocates, October 2011, page 378

Other books by the same author:
Blessing's Bead, 2009

Other books you might like:
Marlene Carvell, *Sweetgrass Basket*, 2005
Kirkpatrick Hill, *Minuk: Ashes in the Pathway*, 2002
Denise Gosliner Orenstein, *Unseen Companion*, 2003

750

DEBBY DAHL EDWARDSON

Blessing's Bead

(New York: Farrar, Straus, and Giroux, 2009)

Subject(s): Eskimos; Arctic; Family

Age range(s): 14 - 17+
Major character(s): Aaluk, Sister (of Nutaaq); Nutaaq, Sister (of Aaluk), Grandmother (great, of Blessing); Blessing, Granddaughter (great, of Nutaaq)
Locale(s): Alaska, United States

Summary: *Blessing's Bead* by Debby Dahl Edwardson is the intergenerational saga of a family indigenous to the Arctic Circle region. Aaluk is a native Inupiaq who has recently married a Siberian man, and is leaving her small village to live with him. As her sister Nutaaq watches, she begins to realize that her life will never be the same again. Seven decades later, Nutaaq's own great-granddaughter flees from some dramatic circumstances in Anchorage to live with her grandmother in an Inupiaq village. There, she endures the stares and gossip of girls she cannot relate to, until she discovers a blue bead in her grandmother's sewing kit. This is the story of the connection that exists between generations and the bond that family always holds.

Where it's reviewed:
Horn Book Magazine, November-December 2009, page 667
Publishers Weekly, November 23, 2009, page 57
School Library Journal, November 2009, page 104
Voice of Youth Advocates, April 2010, page 56

Other books by the same author:
My Name Is Not Easy, 2011

Other books you might like:
Helen Frost, *The Braid*, 2006
Helen Frost, *Diamond Willow*, 2008
Laura Resau, *What the Moon Saw*, 2006
John Smelcer, *The Great Death*, 2009
Rebecca Stead, *First Light*, 2007

751

AMY EFAW

After

(New York: Viking, 2009)

Subject(s): Pregnancy; Teenage parents; Murder

Age range(s): 14 - 18+
Major character(s): Devon Davenport, 15-Year-Old

Summary: *After* is a young adult novel written by Amy Efaw. In it, Efaw tells the story of Devon Davenport, a teenager who has just woken up covered in blood and is being arrested for trying to kill her newborn baby. Devon can barely remember what happened, but that doesn't mean she isn't in for the fight of her life. Now, her public attorney must defend her against charges that even she believes may stick, and Devon must remember exactly what happened that night, as well as what led up to that fateful evening, if she is ever going to move on and heal.

Where it's reviewed:
Booklist, August 1, 2009, page 52
Horn Book Guide, Spring 2010, page 94
Publishers Weekly, August 3, 2009, page 45
School Library Journal, September 2009, page 156
Voice of Youth Advocates, October 2009, page 313

Other books by the same author:
Battle Dress, 2000

Other books you might like:
George Eliot, *Adam Bede*, 1859
Jo Knowles, *Jumping Off Swings*, 2009
Nina LaCour, *Hold Still*, 2009
Walter Dean Myers, *Monster*, 1999
Jodi Picoult, *Plain Truth*, 2000

752

PAMELA EHRENBERG

Tillmon County Fire

(Grand Rapids, Michigan: Eerdmans Books for Young Readers, 2009)

Subject(s): Appalachian people (Southern States); Arson; Rural life

Age range(s): 14 - 18+

Time period(s): 21st century; 2000s

Locale(s): Tillmon County, United States

Summary: *Tillmon County Fire* is a young adult novel from author Pamela Ehrenberg. Nothing very exciting ever happens in the rural area of Tillmon County, so when a multimillion-dollar home is destroyed in a fire, everyone pays attention. When the fire chief labels the incident an act of arson, everyone is intrigued. The story of the mystery surrounding the crime is told from the perspectives of several local teens. The wide range of voices includes a homosexual teen who recently moved from Manhattan and a mentally challenged student who is concerned about his brother's new friendship. *Tillmon County Fire* is an examination of rural life, revenge, and abuse.

Where it's reviewed:
Booklist, April 15, 2009, page 39
School Library Journal, April 2009, page 132

Other books by the same author:
Ethan Suspended, 2009

Other books you might like:
Kevin Brooks, *Black Rabbit Summer*, 2008
James Lecesne, *Absolute Brightness*, 2008
Carol Plum-Ucci, *What Happened to Lani Garver*, 2002
Paul Volponi, *Response*, 2009

753

DANIEL EHRENHAFT

Friend Is Not a Verb

(New York: HarperTeen, 2010)

Subject(s): Family; Friendship; Romances (Fiction)

Age range(s): 13 - 17+

Major character(s): Henry "Hen" Birnbaum, Brother (of Sarah), Neighbor (of Emma), Teenager; Sarah Birnbaum, Sister (of Hen); Emma Wood, Neighbor (of Hen), Teenager

Time period(s): 21st century; 2010s

Locale(s): New York, New York

Summary: In Daniel Ehrenhaft's *Friend is Not a Verb*, Henry "Hen" Birnbaum's sister has returned home after having been missing for nearly a year. She returned in the same style she left: silent and without an excuse. Hen wants to know what Sarah has been up to this whole time, but she refuses to tell anyone where she was or who she was with while she was gone. When Hen's not questioning Sarah, he's spending time with Emma, his neighbor. They pass the time watching VH1 reruns and

talking. At first, Hen's preoccupied with Sarah's mysterious disappearance and his recent breakup, but he soon finds that spending time with Emma is more important than sulking and even annoying his sister.

Where it's reviewed:
Horn Book Guide, Fall 2010, page 366
Publishers Weekly, April 26, 2010, page 109
School Library Journal, May 2010, page 110

Other books by the same author:
Dirty Laundry, 2009
The After Life, 2006
Drawing a Blank, or, How I Tried to Solve a Mystery, End a Feud, and Land the Girl of My Dreams, 2006
Tell It to Naomi, 2004
Ten Things to Do Before I Die, 2004

Other books you might like:
K.L. Going, *Fat Kid Rules the World*, 2003
John Green, *An Abundance of Katherines*, 2006
Nina Malkin, *6X: The Uncensored Confessions*, 2005
Jon Skovron, *Struts and Frets*, 2009

754

DANIEL EHRENHAFT

Dirty Laundry

(New York: HarperTeen, 2009)

Subject(s): Schools; Friendship; Outcasts

Age range(s): 14 - 17+

Major character(s): Carli Gemz, Student, Actress; Fellini "Fun" Udall Newport, Student, Artist (Graffiti); Darcy Novak, Student, Missing Person

Time period(s): 21st century; 2000s

Locale(s): New England, United States

Summary: A young student has disappeared from Winchester, a private school known as the last resort for students expelled from other wealthy private schools. Out to solve the mystery of what happened to the popular senior are Carli Gemz and Fellini Udall Newport ("Fun" for short). Carli is a young actress researching an upcoming role by going incognito. Fun is an artist whose main medium is graffiti. He has been assigned to assist Carli or be expelled for his latest prank. The mystery takes the two down a path filled with a series of false clues. Though their frustration mounts at every turn, they also grow closer together. Author Daniel Ehrenhaft winds dark humor into the numerous plot twists, making this an enjoyable read for teens.

Where it's reviewed:
Booklist, December 15, 2008, page 38
School Library Journal, March 2009, page 143
Voice of Youth Advocates, February 2009, page 526

Other books by the same author:
Friend Is Not a Verb, 2010
The After Life, 2006
Drawing a Blank, or, How I Tried to Solve a Mystery, End a Feud, and Land the Girl of my Dreams, 2006
Tell It to Naomi, 2004
Ten Things to Do Before I Die, 2004

Other books you might like:
Peter Abrahams, *Reality Check*, 2009
Jen Calonita, *Secrets of My Hollywood Life*, 2006
Carol Plum-Ucci, *The Body of Christopher Creed*, 2000
Lee Weatherly, *Missing Abby*, 2004

755

SIMONE ELKELES

Perfect Chemistry
(New York: Walker, 2009)

Subject(s): Social class; Dating (Social customs); Gangs
Age range(s): 16 - 18+
Major character(s): Brittany Ellis, 12th Grader; Alex Fuentes, 12th Grader, Gang Member; Shelley Ellis, Sister (of Brittany), Handicapped
Time period(s): 21st century; 2000s
Locale(s): Colorado, United States; Chicago, Illinois

Summary: When high school seniors Brittany Ellis and Alex Fuentes are thrown together as lab partners in *Perfect Chemistry* by Simone Elkeles, the pair—at first—seem completely mismatched. But when gang member Alex tries to seduce the rich and pretty Brittany on a bet, the two teenagers soon find themselves falling in love. Alex learns that Brittany's life is not as perfect as it seems; her parents' marriage is strained and her handicapped sister requires much of Brittany's time. Brittany is surprised to discover that hoodlum Alex secretly hopes to quit his gang and go to college. As Alex and Brittany follow their dreams through high school and beyond, their improbable relationship defies the doubts of their family and friends.

Where it's reviewed:
Booklist, November 15, 2008, page 38
School Library Journal, January 2009, page 100

Other books by the same author:
Chain Reaction, 2011
Return to Paradise, 2010
Rules of Attraction, 2010
How to Ruin Your Boyfriend's Reputation, 2009
Leaving Paradise, 2007

Awards the book has won:
Rita Awards: Best Young Adult Romance, 2010

Other books you might like:
Jennifer R. Hubbard, *The Secret Year*, 2010
Kathe Koja, *Headlong*, 2008
Stephenie Meyer, *Twilight Saga*, 2005
D. James Smith, *Fast Company*, 1999

756

PATRICIA ELLIOTT

The Pale Assassin
(New York: Holiday House, 2009)

Subject(s): French Revolution, 1789; Brothers and sisters; Orphans

Age range(s): 13 - 16+
Major character(s): Eugenie de Boncouer, Orphan, Teenager; Armand de Boncoeur, Brother (older, of Eugenie); Le Fantome, Revolutionary
Time period(s): 18th century; 1790s
Locale(s): France

Summary: *The Pale Assassin* is a historical young adult novel by Patricia Elliott that takes place in France during the French Revolution. Eugenie and Armand de Boncoeur are two orphaned siblings; Eugenie is sent to a convent school to live when their home becomes too dangerous while Armand stays behind. Eugenie is a very spoiled and beautiful teenager who refuses to let the revolution affect her life in any way. She soon learns, however, that Armand has promised her hand in marriage to a revolutionary known only as La Fantome, a violent and angry man who is holding a grudge against their family. Eugenie is forced to rise to the occasion and survive on her own, finding a way to escape France and La Fantome.

Where it's reviewed:
Booklist, October 1, 2009, page 42
Horn Book Guide, Spring 2010, page 95
School Library Journal, December 2009, page 114

Other books by the same author:
The Traitor's Smile, 2010
Ambergate, 2007
Murkmere, 2005

Other books you might like:
Kimberly Brubaker Bradley, *The Lacemaker and the Princess*, 2007
Sally Gardner, *The Red Necklace: A Story of the French Revolution*, 2008
Celia Rees, *Sovay*, 2008

757

DEBORAH ELLIS

No Safe Place
(Toronto: Groundwood Books, 2010)

Subject(s): Emigration and immigration; England; Social conditions

Age range(s): 14 - 17+
Major character(s): Abdul, 15-Year-Old, Immigrant; Rosalia, Teenager, Slave (escaped); Cheslav, Teenager, Student (military school), Runaway; Jonah, 10-Year-Old, Nephew (of boat pilot)
Time period(s): 21st century; 2010s
Locale(s): English Channel, At Sea; Calais, France

Summary: In the young adult novel *No Safe Place* by Deborah Ellis, a teenager from Baghdad leaves his Iraqi home after wartime violence claims the lives of his family. Abdul makes his way to Calais, France, where he meets other young people also seeking refuge. Rosalia has escaped from the bonds of slavery. Cheslav has run away from his Russian military school. Together the three board a boat headed for England, where they hope to make new starts. When their vessel encounters trouble in the English Channel, the pilot is killed and his ten-year-old nephew is the only person on board qualified to take his place. As the four young people struggle for survival, the grim details of their previous lives are divulged.

Where it's reviewed:
Booklist, September 15, 2010, page 64
Horn Book Guide, Spring 2010, page 97
Reading Time, May 2012, page 34
School Library Journal, September 2010, page 152

Other books by the same author:
Lunch with Lenin and Other Stories, 2008

Other books you might like:
LeeAnne Gelletly, *The Kurds*, 2009
Paul Griffin, *The Orange Houses*, 2009
Ann Jaramillo, *La Linea: A Novel*, 2006
Carol Matas, *The Whirlwind*, 2007
Patricia McCormick, *Sold*, 2006

758

STEPHEN EMOND

Winter Town

(New York: Little, Brown and Company, 2011)

Story type: Young Adult
Subject(s): Adolescent interpersonal relations; Self awareness; Friendship

Age range(s): 15 - 18+
Major character(s): Lucy, 17-Year-Old; Evan, 17-Year-Old
Time period(s): 21st century; 2010s

Summary: In this young adult novel, author Stephen Emond shares the story of Evan and Lucy, two childhood friends who were forced to part ways after Lucy's parents' divorce. The two continue to reunite once each year, and Evan always looks forward to Lucy's visits. This year, however, things have changed. At 17, Evan is a budding cartoonist; unfortunately, his fear of the future forces him to slide his dreams to the back burner. Instead, he is obeying his father's wishes and will pursue a degree at an Ivy League university. Meanwhile, when Lucy arrives for her annual visit, Evan barely recognizes her. The girl next door that he remembers is buried beneath jet-black hair, facial piercings, and Goth makeup. Will Evan be able to reach the Lucy he once knew? More importantly, can Lucy help Evan realize that he doesn't have to be perfect all the time? Includes illustrations.

Where it's reviewed:
Booklist, September 15, 2011, page 76
Publishers Weekly, October 24, 2011, page 55
School Library Journal, December 2011, page 116

Other books by the same author:
Happyface, 2010
Steverino: The Complete Collection, 2010
Emo Boy Series, 2006-

Other books you might like:
Susane Colasanti, *When It Happens*, 2008
John Green, *Looking for Alaska*, 2005
Sara Zarr, *Sweethearts*, 2008

759

STEPHEN EMOND

Happyface

(New York: Little, Brown Books for Young Readers, 2010)

Subject(s): Adolescence; Friendship; Popularity

Age range(s): 13 - 16+
Major character(s): Happyface, Teenager, Student—High School; Gretchen, Friend (of Happyface)
Time period(s): 21st century; 2010s
Locale(s): United States

Summary: In Stephen Emond's *Happyface*, a teenage boy known to readers simply as Happyface struggles with a life-changing move to a new school and new neighborhood. No one knows him in his location, so he decides to hide his life as an avid video gamer and comic book reader. With a fake smile on his face, he soon falls in with the popular kids at his new school. They know nothing of his past, nor are they aware of the rundown apartment he shares with his mother, a recovering alcoholic. All they know is what he tells them—and most if it isn't even true. When Happyface falls for Gretchen, a mysterious girl who hangs out with his group, he must decide if concealing all of his secrets is really the way he wants to live his life.

Where it's reviewed:
Horn Book Guide, Fall 2010, page 366
Publishers Weekly, January 25, 2010, page 120
School Library Journal, March 2010, page 156
Voice of Youth Advocates, June 2010, page 152

Other books by the same author:
Winter Town, 2011

Other books you might like:
Marlene Carvell, *Caught Between the Pages*, 2008
Betsy Franco, *Metamorphosis: Junior Year*, 2009
Peter Moore, *Caught in the Act*, 2005
Jennifer Lynn Ziegler, *How Not to Be Popular*, 2008

760

MARGARITA ENGLE

Tropical Secrets: Holocaust Refugees in Cuba

(New York: Henry Holt and Co., 2009)

Subject(s): Jews; Holocaust, 1933-1945; Refugees

Age range(s): 12 - 17+
Major character(s): Daniel, 13-Year-Old, Refugee; Paloma, 12-Year-Old, Refugee
Time period(s): 20th century; 1940s
Locale(s): Cuba

Summary: In *Tropical Secrets: Holocaust Refugees in Cuba*, Margarita Engle spins a historical tale revolving around 13-year-old Daniel, a Jewish refugee who flees Nazi Germany. Daniel's ship is destined for New York, but a cruel twist of fate intervenes: the United States refuses to allow the ship to enter. This forces Daniel and his fellow passengers to seek asylum in Cuba. After settling in this strange new place, Daniel begins to connect with those around him. Daniel eventually makes friends, and he even gets involved in protecting an accused spy. But through it all, Daniel is determined to find out what happened to the family he was forced to leave behind.

Where it's reviewed:
Booklist, September 1, 2009, page 122
Bulletin of the Center for Children's Books, April 2009, page 318
Publishers Weekly, April 6, 2009, page 48
School Library Journal, June 2009, page 122
Voice of Youth Advocates, April 2009, page 50

Other books by the same author:
The Firefly Letters: A Suffragette's Journey to Cuba, 2010
The Surrender Tree: Poems of Cuba's Struggle for Freedom, 2008

Awards the book has won:
Sydney Taylor Children's Book Awards, 2009

Other books you might like:
Anne L. Fox, *Ten Thousand Children: True Stories Told by Children Who Escaped the Holocaust on the Kindertransport*, 1999
Jamila Gavin, *See No Evil*, 2008
Scott Miller, *Refuge Denied: The St. Louis Passengers and the Holocaust*, 2006
Kim Ablon Whitney, *The Other Half of Life: A Novel Based on the True Story of the MS St. Louis*, 2009

761

MARGARITA ENGLE

Hurricane Dancers

(New York: Henry Holt, 2011)

Story type: Adventure
Subject(s): Pirates; Shipwrecks; Slavery

Age range(s): 11 - 14+
Major character(s): Quebrado, Indian (Taino), Slave, Orphan; Bernardino de Talavera, Pirate (captain), Kidnapper; Alonso de Ojeda, Hostage (of Bernardino)
Time period(s): 16th century
Locale(s): At Sea; Cuba

Summary: Margarita Engle's novel, which is told in verse, follows young Quebrado, the son of a Spanish father and a Taino mother. In 1510, Quebrado lives on an island in the Caribbean with his mother, and he is kidnapped from his village and traded among pirate ships for many years. Finally, he becomes a slave to Bernardino de Talavera. This brutal pirate captain uses Quebrado as a translator as they sail the Caribbean. In the belly of the pirate ship is a conquistador, Alonso de Ojeda, who is being held for ransom. When a hurricane pummels the ship, only three survivors wash up on shore. After the storm, the roles of slave and master are reversed. In the aftermath, Quebrado determines the fate of the pirate captain, and he rediscovers himself and the home he lost.

Where it's reviewed:
Booklist, January 1, 2011, page 88
Bulletin of the Center for Children's Books, April 2011, page 369
Horn Book Magazine, March/April 2011, page 116
School Library Journal, March 2011, page 369
Voice of Youth Advocates, June 2011, page 162

Other books by the same author:
The Firefly Letters: A Suffragette's Journey to Cuba, 2010
The Surrender Tree: Poems of Cuba's Struggle for Freedom, 2008
The Poet Slave of Cuba: A Biography of Juan Francisco Manzano, 2006

Other books you might like:
Daniel Conner, *The Tempest (Graphic Shakespeare)*, 2008
Michael Dorris, *Morning Girl*, 1992
Sherry Garland, *Indio*, 1995
Kathleen Krull, *Lives of the Pirates: Swashbucklers, Scoundrels (Neighbors Beware)*, 2010
Scott O'Dell, *The King's Fifth*, 1966

762

MARGARITA ENGLE

The Firefly Letters: A Suffragette's Journey to Cuba

(New York: Henry Holt and Co., 2010)

Story type: Historical
Subject(s): Women's rights; Women; Wealth

Age range(s): 12 - 15+
Major character(s): Fredrika Bremer, Suffragette; Cecilia, Slave; Elena, 12-Year-Old, Daughter (of sugar baron), Wealthy
Time period(s): 19th century; 1850s (1851)
Locale(s): Cuba

Summary: This young adult novel by author Margarita Engle meshes real historical events with original fiction in a retelling of the life story of Swedish suffragette Fredrika Bremer. Engle's story begins as Fredrika leaves her comfortable existence in Sweden for the largely impoverished island of Cuba. Accompanying Fredrika is Cecilia, a pregnant African slave who is assigned to be her translator. Once in Cuba, the pair is joined by 12-year-old Elena, a fictional character created just for the novel, who is the daughter of the wealthy sugar baron who serves as host to Fredrika and Cecilia. As the three women learn about the rampant systemic injustice in the island nation, Cecilia and Elena both draw inspiration from Fredrika's independent nature and begin to find the strength to strive for similar independence in their own lives.

Where it's reviewed:
Booklist, December 15, 2009, page 32
Bulletin of the Center for Children's Books, April 2010, page 334
Horn Book Magazine, March/April 2010, page 54
Publishers Weekly, March 15, 2010, page 55

School Library Journal, February 2010, page 129

Other books by the same author:
Summer Birds: The Butterflies of Maria Merian, 2010
The Surrender Tree: Poems of Cuba's Struggle for Freedom, 2008
The Poet Slave of Cuba: A Biography of Juan Francisco Manzano, 2006

Other books you might like:
Jennifer L. Holm, *Boston Jane: An Adventure*, 2001
Kirby Larson, *Hattie Big Sky*, 2006
Nancy Springer, *The Case of the Missing Marquess: An Enola Holmes Mystery*, 2006

763

BETH FANTASKEY

Jessica's Guide to Dating on the Dark Side

(New York: Harcourt, 2009)

Subject(s): Vampires; Dating (Social customs); High schools

Age range(s): 13 - 18+

Major character(s): Jessica Packwood, 17-Year-Old, 12th Grader; Lucius Vladescu, Student—Exchange

Time period(s): 21st century; 2000s

Locale(s): Pennsylvania, United States

Summary: High school senior Jessica Packwood finds the new exchange student at Woodrow Wilson High School intriguing. With Old World manners and a predominantly black wardrobe, Lucius Vladescu charms the school's female population but seeks only Jessica's attention. Adopted from Eastern Europe and raised in Pennsylvania, Jessica is stunned when Lucius tells her that they both are vampire royalty, betrothed since birth. Gaining self-assurance with her new role (and her copy of *Growing Up Undead: A Teen Vampire's Guide to Dating, Health, and Emotions*), Jessica battles warring vampire families and a jealous cheerleader to protect her prince.

Where it's reviewed:
Booklist, March 1, 2009, page 38
Journal of Adolescent & Adult, October 2009, page 180
Publishers Weekly, January 5, 2009, page 51
School Library Journal, March 2009, page 144
Voice of Youth Advocates, June 2009, page 149

Other books by the same author:
Jessica Rules the Dark Side, 2012
Jekel Loves Hyde, 2010

Awards the book has won:
Carolyn W. Field Award, 2010

Other books you might like:
Heather Brewer, *Eighth Grade Bites: The Chronicles of Vladimir Tod*, 2007
Kate Cary, *Bloodline*, 2005
Brendan Halpin, *Forever Changes*, 2008
Will Hill, *Department 19*, 2011

764

BRIAN FARREY

With or Without You

(New York: Simon Pulse, 2011)

Subject(s): Bullying; Homosexuality; Gay and lesbian rights

Age range(s): 15 - 18+

Major character(s): Evan Weiss, 18-Year-Old, Student—High School, Homosexual, Boyfriend (of Erik), Friend (of Davis); Davis Grayson, Friend (of Evan), Student—High School, Homosexual; Erik, Boyfriend (of Evan), Homosexual, Teenager

Time period(s): 21st century; 2010s

Locale(s): Madison, Wisconsin

Summary: For many years, Evan Weiss has been the victim of bullying. He's been thrown into lockers, beaten until he's knocked unconscious, and verbally abused for being gay. He's never shed a tear during a beating, however, and as graduation approaches, he doesn't plan to. When high school is over, he plans to move away with his boyfriend, Erik, who he has kept a secret from everyone for a full year. Before he can leave town, he and his best friend, Davis, hear of a group called the Chasers. The members are proud of being gay and offer protection to those who are treated poorly because of their sexuality. Davis convinces Evan to join with him and enthusiastically follows the Chasers' rules. Evan sees through the group and realizes it's just another place where he doesn't belong. Evan doesn't want to leave Davis behind, but he also isn't willing to give up his future with Erik. As everything seems to fall apart, secrets come out and Evan struggles to hold on to those who are most important to him.

Where it's reviewed:
Booklist, July 1, 2011, page 57
Bulletin of the Center for Children's Books, June 2011, page 467
School Library Journal, September 2011, page 152

Other books you might like:
Pamela Ehrenberg, *Tillmon County Fire*, 2009
Davida Wills Hurwin, *Freaks and Revelations*, 2009
Lauren Myracle, *Shine*, 2011
Andrew Smith, *Stick*, 2011

765

JACK D. FERRAIOLO

Sidekicks

(New York: Amulet Books, 2011)

Subject(s): Good and evil; Supernatural; Rescue work

Age range(s): 13 - 16+

Major character(s): Scott "Bright Boy" Hutchinson, Sidekick (of Phantom Justice), Student—High School, Boyfriend (of Allison); Allison "Monkey-wrench" Mendez, Sidekick (of Dr. Chaotic), Student—High School, Girlfriend (of Scott);

Phantom Justice, Hero (superhero); Dr. Chaotic, Villain
Time period(s): 21st century; 2010s
Locale(s): United States

Summary: At night, high school student Scott Hutchinson becomes Bright Boy, Phantom Justice's sidekick. He's held this position for many years and for the longest time, he was content with his responsibilities. After an embarrassing incident with his superhero costume, Bright Boy wonders if he still has the passion required for being a superhero's sidekick. He wants to protect people, but is there another way to do it? With this on his mind, Bright Boy is easily distracted and is unmasked during a battle with Dr. Chaotic and his sidekick, Monkeywrench. Acting quickly, Bright Boy is able to reveal Monkeywrench's identity, as well, and both sidekicks realize they know each other from school. In fact, Scott has always had a crush on Allison Mendez. Their newfound commonality reinforces their friendship and soon they're spending all their free time together. Monkeywrench is supposed to be Bright Boy's enemy, but Scott can't stop himself from falling for Allison. As his relationship with Allison progresses, Scott wonders if being Phantom Justice's sidekick is worth giving up the chance of having a normal, civilian life.

Where it's reviewed:
Booklist, April 15, 2011, page 55
Bulletin of the Center for Children's Books, April 2011, page 370
Horn Book Guide, Fall 2011, page 38
Publishers Weekly, March 21, 2011, page 77
School Library Journal, July 2011, page 97

Other books by the same author:
The Big Splash, 2008

Other books you might like:
Mike Lupica, *Hero*, 2010
Barry Lyga, *Archvillain*, 2010
Perry Moore, *Hero*, 2007

766

CATHERINE FISHER

The Dark City

(New York: Dial Books, 2011)

Series: Relic Master Series. Book 1
Subject(s): Fantasy; Imagination; Adventure

Age range(s): 12 - 15+
Major character(s): Galen, Collector (of relics), Adventurer (in search of relics); Raffi, 16-Year-Old, Apprentice (to Galen)
Locale(s): Anara, Planet—Imaginary

Summary: *The Dark City* by Catherine Fisher is all about a mysterious faraway world known as Anara. Anara is full of wondrous and bizarre places, people, and events. There are artifacts from long-ago civilizations that still resonate with magical powers. These so-called "relics" are sacred to the people of Anara, who have invested their care in a wise keeper named Galen as well as his impetuous teenage sidekick Raffi. The two need to care for the relics and find new ones—a process that takes

them on incredible adventures and exposes them to terrible dangers. One of these dangers is the evil Watch, a group of people who hunt the leaders of the society.

Where it's reviewed:
Booklist, May 15, 2011, page 53
Horn Book Guide, Fall 2011, page 380
Publishers Weekly, March 7, 2011, page 65
School Library Journal, July 2011, page 97

Other books by the same author:
The Hidden Coronet, 2011
The Lost Heiress, 2011
The Margrave, 2011

Other books you might like:
Jenna Burtenshaw, *Shadowcry*, 2011
John Flanagan, *Ranger's Apprentice: Ruins of Gorlan*, 2005
Marie Lu, *Legend*, 2011

767

BECCA FITZPATRICK

Hush, Hush

(New York: Simon & Schuster Books for Young Readers, 2009)

Subject(s): Angels; Friendship; Dating (Social customs)

Age range(s): 14 - 18+
Major character(s): Nora Grey, Student—High School; Patch, Classmate (of Nora); Mom, Mother (of Nora)
Time period(s): 21st century; 2000s
Locale(s): Portland, Maine

Summary: In *Hush, Hush* by Becca Fitzpatrick, Nora Grey has lived with her mother in their rural home near Portland, Maine since her father died. A high school sophomore who studies hard with her sights set on a college scholarship, Nora has always lived her life carefully. But when the new boy at school, Patch, is assigned as her biology lab partner, she finds herself uncharacteristically attracted to him even though she suspects the brooding teenager hides a secret. Nora ignores the advice of faculty and friends and surrenders to the connection she feels with Patch, gradually discovering his true supernatural identity.

Where it's reviewed:
Horn Book Guide, Spring 2010, page 95
Publishers Weekly, October 12, 2009, page 51
School Librarian, Spring 2010, page 47
School Library Journal, December 2009, page 116
Voice of Youth Advocates, December 2009, page 419

Other books by the same author:
Silence, 2011
Crescendo, 2010

Other books you might like:
Elizabeth Chandler, *Kissed by an Angel*, 2008
Amber Kizer, *Meridian*, 2009
Cliff McNish, *Angel*, 2008
Cynthia Leitich Smith, *Eternal*, 2009
Laini Taylor, *Daughter of Smoke and Bone*, 2011

768

NANCY BO FLOOD

Warriors in the Crossfire

(Honesdale, Pennsylvania: Front Street, 2010)

Subject(s): Friendship; World War II, 1939-1945; Loyalty

Age range(s): 12 - 15+

Major character(s): Joseph, 13-Year-Old, Son (of a chief), Friend (of Kento); Kento, 13-Year-Old, Son (of a Japanese soldier), Friend (of Joseph)

Time period(s): 20th century; 1940s

Locale(s): Saipan, Japan

Summary: *Warriors in the Crossfire* is a suspenseful and historical novel for young adult readers about friendship, loyalty, and war from author Nancy Bo Flood. Set on the island of Saipan at the end of World War II, the novel follows the friendships and trials of two young boys from very different backgrounds. Thirteen-year old Joseph is the son of a native chief, while Kento is the son of an occupying Japanese soldier. Despite their differences, the boys are friends and learn to trust one another in the midst of war. They share secrets and survival tactics, but their friendship is put to the ultimate test when the American army invades and both families' lives are put at risk.

Where it's reviewed:
Booklist, April 15, 2010, page 57
Horn Book Guide, Fall 2010, page 367
School Library Journal, May 2010, page 112

Other books you might like:
Barry Denenberg, *Early Sunday Morning: The Pearl Harbor Diary of Amber Billows*, 2001
D. Dina Friedman, *Escaping into the Night*, 2006
Graham Salisbury, *Under the Blood-Red Sun*, 1994

769

JOHN C. FORD

The Morgue and Me

(New York: Viking Juvenile, 2009)

Subject(s): Murder; Suicide; Mystery fiction

Age range(s): 15 - 18+

Major character(s): Christopher, Detective—Amateur; Tina, Journalist; Mitch Blaylock, Crime Victim

Time period(s): 21st century; 2000s

Locale(s): United States

Summary: *The Morgue and Me* is the debut novel from author John C. Ford. After graduating from high school, Christopher has a summer to kill. What better way to pass the time than to work in the local morgue? But Christopher has no idea what lies in store for him when he takes the janitor's position. The first body he comes in contact with is a man named Mitch Blaylock. The documentation labels him a suicide, but Christopher isn't so sure. With the help of a sexy upstart reporter from an area newspaper, he dives into the case with gusto. And the deeper in they get, the more dangerous the investiga-

tion becomes. Not bad for a guy who was certain he'd spend the summer sweeping floors. First novel.

Where it's reviewed:
Booklist, May 1, 2009, page 39
Journal of Adolescent & Adult, March 2010, page 522
Publishers Weekly, June 15, 2009, page 51
School Library Journal, August 2009, page 102
Voice of Youth Advocates, August 2009, page 224

Other books you might like:
Peter Abrahams, *Bullet Point*, 2010
Christopher Golden, *Body Bags*, 1999
Nancy Werlin, *Black Mirror*, 2001
Rachel Wright, *You've Got Blackmail*, 2007

770

MICHAEL FORD

The Poisoned House

(Park Ridge, Illinois: Albert Whitman & Company, 2011)

Subject(s): Ghosts; Orphans; Child abuse

Age range(s): 12 - 15+

Major character(s): Abigail "Abi" Tamper, Servant (of Lord Greave), 14-Year-Old, Friend (of Samuel), Orphan; Samuel Greave, Son (of Lord Greave), Military Personnel (injured soldier), Friend (of Abi); Lord Greave, Mentally Ill Person, Father (of Samuel), Householder; Mrs. Cotton, Housekeeper

Time period(s): 19th century; 1850s (1855)

Locale(s): London, England

Summary: After attempting to escape from Greave Hall, Abigail Tamper is under the abusive watch of Mrs. Cotton, the mansion's housekeeper. Depressed after her failure, Abi attempts to throw herself into her work as a servant girl, but many occurrences in the house keep her thoughts churning. Her master, Lord Greave, is slowly losing his mind and Abi's convinced a ghost is haunting the mansion. As the anniversary of her mother's death approaches, she wonders if the spirit could belong to her mother, who used to be the household's nurse. A sense of calm washes over her when she is told that Lord Greave's son, Samuel, is finally coming home after serving during the Crimean War. She and Samuel were raised together and she hopes that his presence in the house will bring her some peace. The young man who returns to the house is not the boy she remembers, however, and Abi worries that danger lies ahead for the residents of Greave Hall.

Where it's reviewed:
Booklist, August 1, 2011, page 58
School Library Journal, August 2011, page 102
Voice of Youth Advocates, October 2011, page 401

Other books by the same author:
Legacy of Blood, 2009
Birth of a Warrior, 2008
The Fire of Aves, 2008

Other books you might like:
Marthe Jocelyn, *Folly*, 2010

Phyllis Reynolds Naylor, *Jade Green: A Ghost Story*, 2000

Deborah Noyes, *The Ghosts of Kerfol*, 2008

771

GAYLE FORMAN

Where She Went

(New York: Dutton, 2011)

Subject(s): Love; Grief; Music

Age range(s): 15 - 18+

Major character(s): Mia, Orphan, Musician (cellist), Student (Juilliard); Adam, Musician (rock star), Narrator

Time period(s): 21st century; 2010s

Locale(s): Los Angeles, California; New York, New York

Summary: *Where She Went*, a moving young adult novel, is the sequel to *If I Stay* from bestselling author Gayle Forman. It's been three years since Mia lost her family in a tragic accident and ended things with Adam. Mia, now a budding cellist star at Juilliard in New York City, has moved on, but Adam is still coping with losing the love of his life. After throwing his emotion into songwriting, Adam managed to land a lucrative record deal and become a Los Angeles rock star, but his thoughts still linger with Mia. When Adam gets stuck in Manhattan for a night, fate brings he and Mia together once more to tour the city and revisit the ghosts of their past.

Where it's reviewed:
Booklist, April 15, 2011, page 57
Horn Book Magazine, May-June 2011, page 89
Publishers Weekly, February 28, 2011, page 59
School Library Journal, March 2011, page 161
Voice of Youth Advocates, June 2011, page 162

Other books by the same author:
If I Stay, 2009
Sisters in Sanity, 2007

Other books you might like:
Robin Benway, *Audrey, Wait!*, 2008
Rachel Cohn, *Nick and Norah's Infinite Playlist*, 2006
Danielle Joseph, *Indigo Blues*, 2010
Sara Zarr, *Sweethearts*, 2008

772

GAYLE FORMAN

If I Stay

(New York: Dutton Children's Books, 2009)

Subject(s): Death; Medical care; Musicians

Age range(s): 14 - 18+

Major character(s): Mia, 17-Year-Old, Musician (cellist), Accident Victim (in a coma); Adam, Boyfriend (of Mia)

Time period(s): 21st century; 2000s

Locale(s): Oregon, United States

Summary: Mia is a 17-year old cellist with a bright future ahead of her. She needs to make the same choices presented to most adolescents, but, on average, her life is good. It is a typical winter day, and Mia and her family get into the car to drive to a bookstore. Unbeknownst to Mia, this would be her last "normal" day. A collision with another vehicle kills both of Mia's parents and her younger brother. Mia is in a coma. As she tells the story of the day her life changed—all information presented is within a 24-hour period—she narrates what her existence was like and what the future might entail. Friends and family, and her boyfriend, Adam, visit her in the hospital and offer encouraging words and support. Taking everything into account, Mia must make the most important decision of her life—to survive or to succumb to death and be with the family she loves and misses.

Where it's reviewed:
Booklist, December 15, 2008, page 50
Horn Book Magazine, July-August 2009, page 422
Publishers Weekly, March 2, 2009, page 64
School Library Journal, May 2009, page 106
Voice of Youth Advocates, February 2009, page 526

Other books by the same author:
Where She Went, 2011
Sisters in Sanity, 2007

Other books you might like:
Laurie Halse Anderson, *Wintergirls*, 2009
James Hannaham, *God Says No*, 2009
Nina LaCour, *Hold Still*, 2009
Walter Dean Myers, *Dope Sick*, 2009
Mary E. Pearson, *The Miles Between*, 2009

773

HILLARY FRANK

The View from the Top

(New York: Dutton Books, 2010)

Subject(s): Friendship; Interpersonal relations; Dating (Social customs)

Age range(s): 13 - 18+

Major character(s): Anabelle, Graduate (high school), 18-Year-Old; Matt, Boyfriend (of Anabelle), Artist; Jonah, Friend (of Matt); Lexi, Sister (of Matt); Mary-Tyler, Friend (of Anabelle); Tobin, Friend (of Anabelle)

Time period(s): 21st century; 2010s

Locale(s): Normal, Maine

Summary: In the young adult novel *The View from the Top* by Hillary Frank, a group of friends in Normal, Maine, face new social challenges in the wake of high-school graduation. Aloof Annabelle seems to attract the emotional and physical interests of everyone in her circle, and each of the novel's chapters examines Annabelle from a different character's perspective. Their intentions range from boyfriend Matt's need for artistic energy to Jonah's pure lust to Tobin's patient devotion. The girls are not immune to Annabelle's mysterious draw. Mary-Tyler seeks her friendship; Lexi hopes for romance. As Annabelle deals with the drama that swirls around her, she learns more about her friends and herself.

Where it's reviewed:
Booklist, June 1, 2010, page 70
Horn Book Guide, Fall 2010, page 367
Publishers Weekly, May 17, 2010, page 52
School Library Journal, August 2010, page 100
Voice of Youth Advocates, August 2010, page 246

Other books by the same author:
I Can't Tell You, 2004
Better Than Running at Night, 2002

Other books you might like:
Carolyn Mackler, *Tangled*, 2010
Lynne Rae Perkins, *Criss Cross*, 2005
Natalie Standiford, *How to Say Goodbye in Robot*, 2009

774

RUSSELL FREEDMAN

The War to End All Wars: World War I

(New York: Clarion Books, 2010)

Subject(s): World War I, 1914-1918; Weapons; Military life

Age range(s): 12 - 16+
Time period(s): 20th century; 1910s

Summary: Nationalism was at its height, and Europe was ready for an all-out war. It was 1914, and all signs suggested that the First World War would be a brief skirmish that would separate the weak from the strong. It turned out much differently, however, and in *The War to End All Wars: World War I*, author Russell Freedman discusses just how this occurred. Freedman chronicles the events leading up to the war, the nations and various personalities involved, and the implications of a war that would encompass the entire world. This volume also charts the advent of new types of weapons that would inevitably make fighting a much more violent affair. *The War to End All Wars* includes notes on the text, a bibliography, and an index.

Where it's reviewed:
Booklist, March 1, 2010, page 73
Horn Book Guide, Spring 2011, page 193
Publishers Weekly, November 8, 2010, page 35
School Library Journal, June 2010, page 127

Other books by the same author:
Lafayette and the American Revolution, 2010
Washington at Valley Forge, 2008
Freedom Walkers: The Story of the Montgomery Bus Boycott, 2006
Children of the Great Depression, 2005
In Defense of Liberty: The Story of America's Bill of Rights, 2003

Awards the book has won:
Blue Ribbon Awards: Non-fiction, 2010

Other books you might like:
Jack Batten, *The War to End All Wars: The Story of World War I*, 2009

Jonathan Gawne, *Over There!: The American Soldier in World War I*, 1997
Iain Lawrence, *Lord of the Nutcracker Men*, 2001
Michael Morpurgo, *Private Peaceful*, 2004
Michael Morpurgo, *War Horse*, 1982

775

DONNA FREITAS

The Survival Kit

(New York: Farrar, Straus and Giroux, 2011)

Story type: Coming-of-Age
Subject(s): Death; Grief; Mother-daughter relations

Age range(s): 13 - 16+
Major character(s): Rose, Teenager
Time period(s): 21st century; 2010s
Locale(s): United States

Summary: After the death of her mother, Rose feels that she has lost everything that mattered in her life. She is not sure how she will cope with her own grief, until she opens a survival kit her mother made before her death to help Rose deal with the loss. The kit contains five simple items: a photograph of flowers, a heart made of crystal, a star crafted out of paper, a kite, and an iPod. As Rose makes her way through the five items, she learns what each one stands for and how it will help her heal. Meanwhile, she builds her iPod's playlist with songs that soothe her grief and help her remember her mother.

Where it's reviewed:
Booklist, October 1, 2011, page 89
Publishers Weekly, August 29, 2011, page 67
School Library Journal, November 2011, page 120
Voice of Youth Advocates, October 2011, page 380

Other books by the same author:
This Gorgeous Game, 2010
The Possibilities of Sainthood, 2008

Other books you might like:
Gillian Cummings, *Somewhere in Blue*, 2010
Maureen Johnson, *13 Little Blue Envelopes*, 2005
Norma Fox Mazer, *Girlhearts*, 2001
Ellen Wittlinger, *Blind Faith*, 2006

776

GARRET FREYMANN-WEYR

After the Moment

(Boston, Massachusetts: Houghton Mifflin Harcourt, 2009)

Subject(s): Love; Dating (Social customs); Adolescent interpersonal relations

Age range(s): 15 - 18+
Major character(s): Leigh Hunter, Boyfriend (of Maia Morland), Stepbrother, 17-Year-Old, 12th Grader, Student—High School; Maia Morland, Teenager, Student—High School, Girlfriend (of Leigh Hunter), Crime Victim
Time period(s): 21st century; 2000s

Locale(s): District of Columbia, United States

Summary: *After the Moment* is a moving and honest novel for young adults from author Garrett Freymann-Weyr. Leigh Hunter is intelligent, well-liked, and kind. When his stepsister's father dies, he moves from New York City to Washington D.C. to be with her. While finishing his senior year there, he falls for Maia Morland, a smart and beautiful girl with her fair share of problems. Recovering from an eating disorder, Maia is a self-mutilator who is terrified of germs. As the two fall in love, Leigh is overwhelmed with his desire to protect her. At first, their love is sweet, pure, and wonderful, but when Maia endures a horrific act and needs Leigh more than ever, he betrays her confidence and puts their relationship at risk. *After the Moment* explores the power of love and what happens when it just isn't enough.

Where it's reviewed:
Booklist, June 1, 2009, page 64
Horn Book Magazine, May/June 2009, page 296
Publishers Weekly, May 4, 2009, page 51
School Library Journal, May 2009, page 106
Voice of Youth Advocates, August 2009, page 224

Other books by the same author:
Stay with Me, 2006
The Kings Are Already Here, 2003
My Heartbeat, 2002
When I was Older, 2000

Other books you might like:
Sarah Dessen, *Along for the Ride*, 2009
Natasha Friend, *Bounce*, 2007
Lisa Jahn-Clough, *Me, Penelope*, 2007
Celia Rees, *The Wish House*, 2006
Courtney Summers, *Cracked Up to Be*, 2009

HELEN FROST

Crossing Stones

(New York: Farrar, Straus, and Giroux, 2009)

Subject(s): United States history; World War I, 1914-1918; Civil rights

Age range(s): 12 - 16+

Major character(s): Muriel Jorgensen, Young Woman; Ollie Jorgensen, Military Personnel (soldier); Frank Norman, Military Personnel (soldier)

Time period(s): 20th century; 1910s

Locale(s): American Midwest, United States

Summary: *Crossing Stones* is a young adult novel by author Helen Frost, in which she tells the story of two families, the Normans and the Jorgensens, who grow up together during the early 20th century. As the Great War begins to rage in Europe, Frank Norman and Ollie Jorgensen are called up to join the military. Yet Muriel, the main character and the family's rock, stands up against the war as her mother goes to work for the family. As protests rage in the nation's capital for women's rights and a halt to the U.S. involvement overseas, a great flu epidemic threatens the lives of those in Muriel's Midwestern community. Frost tells the story of two

interconnected families and the trials and tribulations they face.

Where it's reviewed:
Booklist, October 1, 2009, page 42
Horn Book Magazine, November-December 2009, page 671
School Library Journal, October 2009, page 126
Voice of Youth Advocates, October 2009, page 314

Other books by the same author:
Hidden, 2011
Diamond Willow, 2008
The Braid, 2006
Keesha's House, 2003

Other books you might like:
Marian Hale, *The Goodbye Season*, 2009
Stephanie Hemphill, *Your Own Sylvia: A Verse Portrait of Sylvia Plath*, 2007
Angela Johnson, *Sweet, Hereafter*, 2010
Kathryn Lasky, *A Time for Courage: The Suffragette Diary of Kathleen Bowen*, 2002
Cynthia Rylant, *I Had Seen Castles*, 1993

HELEN FROST

Hidden

(New York: Farrar Straus Giroux, 2011)

Subject(s): Interpersonal relations; Camps (Recreation); Memory

Age range(s): 13 - 16+

Major character(s): Wren Abbott, 14-Year-Old, Camper; Darra Monson, 14-Year-Old, Camper

Time period(s): 21st century; 2010s

Locale(s): Michigan, United States

Summary: The young-adult novel in verse *Hidden* by Helen Frost explores the complex relationship of two girls who experience opposite sides of a tragic crime. At the age of eight, Wren Abbott waits outside a convenience store for her mother. The store is robbed and the thief drives away in the Abbotts' van, not realizing that Wren is hidden inside. Wren ends up trapped in the robber's garage, where his eight-year-old daughter, Darra, tries to plot her release. Wren escapes on her own, Darra's father is sent to jail, and Darra blames her father's conviction on Wren. Six years later, Wren and Darra meet again, this time at a summer camp in Michigan. As they work through the painful mysteries of the past, the girls sort out the feelings they have for one another.

Where it's reviewed:
Booklist, April 1, 2011, page 64
Bulletin of the Center for Children's Books, May 2011, page 415
Horn Book Guide, Fall 2011, page 381
School Library Journal, June 2011, page 116
Voice of Youth Advocates, June 2011, page 164

Other books by the same author:
Crossing Stones, 2009

Diamond Willow, 2008
The Braid, 2006
Keesha's House, 2003

Other books you might like:
Ian Bone, *The Song of an Innocent Bystander*, 2004
April Henry, *Girl, Stolen*, 2010
Kathryn Williams, *The Lost Summer*, 2009

779

CRISTINA GARCIA

Dreams of Significant Girls

(New York: Simon and Schuster, 2011)

Story type: Coming-of-Age
Subject(s): Friendship; Summer; Boarding schools

Age range(s): 16 - 18+

Major character(s): Ingrid, Student—Boarding School, Friend (of Vivien and Shirin); Shirin, Student—Boarding School, Royalty, Friend (of Ingrid and Vivien); Vivien, Student—Boarding School, Friend (of Ingrid and Shirin)

Time period(s): 20th century; 1970s
Locale(s): Switzerland

Summary: In this novel by Cristina Garcia, three adolescent girls from very different backgrounds share their summers together at a Swiss boarding school. Shirin is a princess from Iran who is relatively shielded from her country's culture by her wealthy parents. Ingrid is an offbeat Canadian whose family celebrates their German heritage. Vivien is a Cuban-American who balks at her family's traditional background and longs to become a chef. When the girls are forced to share a room they wonder if they will ever find any common ground, yet soon a series of circumstances bonds them in a way they never expected. Together, these three girls learn about friendship and cultural identity as they attempt to navigate the trickiest aspects of adolescence. Garcia is also the author of *Dreaming in Cuban* and *The Lady Matador's Hotel*.

Where it's reviewed:
Booklist, July 1, 2011, page 55
New York Times Book Review, July 17, 2011, page 13
Publishers Weekly, May 30, 2011, page 70
School Library Journal, July 2011, page 98
Voice of Youth Advocates, August 2011, page 268

Other books by the same author:
I Wanna Be Your Shoebox, 2008

Other books you might like:
Lily Archer, *The Poison Apples*, 2007
Ann Brashares, *The Sisterhood of the Traveling Pants*, 2001
Maureen Johnson, *The Name of the Star*, 2011
Mary E. Pearson, *The Miles Between*, 2009

780

KAMI GARCIA
MARGARET STOHL, Co-Author

Beautiful Creatures

(New York: Little, Brown and Company, 2009)

Subject(s): Supernatural; Psychics; Love

Age range(s): 15 - 18+
Major character(s): Ethan Wate, Teenager; Lena Duchannes, Teenager, Psychic
Time period(s): 21st century; 2010s
Locale(s): Gatlin, South Carolina

Summary: In *Beautiful Creatures*, authors Kami Garcia and Margaret Stohl craft an eerie tale of young love and the supernatural. Teenager Ethan Wate despises life in his tiny South Carolina town, and he finds escape in his nighttime dreams of a mysterious girl. He is shocked when that girl—Lena Duchannes—shows up as a new student at his school. The unabashed Lena stands out in the repressed town of Gatlin, and Ethan can't help but be drawn to her. He soon learns that Lena possesses strange powers and a shocking secret, but his heart won't let him abandon her. At all costs, Ethan is determined to help Lena and set her free from the grip of the past. First novel.

Where it's reviewed:
Booklist, November 1, 2009, page 31
Journal of Adolescent & Adult, October 2010, page 154
Publishers Weekly, November 16, 2009, page 55
School Library Journal, December 2009, page 118
Voice of Youth Advocates, December 2009, page 419

Other books by the same author:
Beautiful Chaos, 2011
Beautiful Darkness, 2010

Other books you might like:
Aimee Friedman, *Sea Change*, 2009
Paula Morris, *Ruined: A Ghost Story*, 2009
Jerry Spinelli, *Stargirl*, 2000

781

JEANNINE GARSEE

Say the Word

(New York: Bloomsbury USA Children's Books, 2009)

Subject(s): Homosexuality; Death; Family relations

Age range(s): 14 - 18+
Major character(s): Shawna Gallagher, Student—High School, Abandoned Child, 17-Year-Old
Time period(s): 21st century; 2000s
Locale(s): United States

Summary: *Say the Word* is a coming-of-age novel for young adults from author Jeannine Garsee. At 17, high school senior Shawna Gallagher is pretty much perfect. She does great in school, dates the right guys, and obeys every one of her domineering father's rules. When a tragedy strikes, Shawna is forced to face secrets from her past that include painful betrayal. A middle-of-the-night phone call informs Shawna that her estranged mother, who left her father ten years earlier for another woman, has died. The sadness over her death and the anger over being abandoned overwhelm Shawna as she deals with the loss and confronts her mom's other family. As old pain, memories, and secrets are uncovered, Shawna soon learns a valuable lesson about who she really is and the kind of person she wants to be.

Where it's reviewed:
Booklist, April 1, 2009, page 39
Publishers Weekly, February 23, 2009, page 51
School Library Journal, June 2009, page 124
Voice of Youth Advocates, June 2009, page 135

Other books by the same author:
The Unquiet, 2012
Before, After, and Somebody in Between, 2007

Other books you might like:
Barbara Hall, *The Noah Confessions*, 2007
Margot McDonnell, *Torn to Pieces*, 2008
Joyce Carol Oates, *Freaky Green Eyes*, 2003
Julie Anne Peters, *Between Mom and Jo*, 2006
Jacqueline Woodson, *From the Notebooks of Melanin Sun*, 1995

782

XAVIER GARZA

Maximilian and the Mystery of the Guardian Angel: A Bilingual Lucha Libre Thriller

(El Paso, Texas: Cinco Puntos Press, 2011)

Subject(s): Mystery fiction; Family; Wrestling
Age range(s): 12 - 15+
Major character(s): Maximilian "Max", 6th Grader, Fanatic (of Mexican wrestling); Guardian Angel, Wrestler
Time period(s): 21st century; 2010s
Locale(s): San Antonio, Texas

Summary: Maximilian's loves lucha libre, or Mexican wrestling. He plans to spend the entire summer before sixth grade watching lucha libre movies, wearing lucha libre masks, and even attending a few lucha libre matches. His favorite wrestler is the Guardian Angel and he will do anything it takes to meet him someday. While watching the Guardian Angel wrestle in San Antonio, Texas, Max gets too excited and falls over the railing that separates the fans from the wrestlers. While in the ring, he spots multiple clues that lead him to a conclusion about the true identity of the Guardian Angel. This thrills Max, as he is slowly realizing that he may be related to his favorite wrestler in the world! This book is written in both English and Spanish.

Where it's reviewed:
School Library Journal, January 2012, page 103

Other books by the same author:
The Man in the Silver Mask, 2005

Other books you might like:
Todd Strasser, *Help! I'm Trapped in a Professional Wrestler's Body*, 2000
Rich Wallace, *Takedown*, 2006
John Whitman, *The Mask of Zorro*, 1998

783

MAURICE GEE

Salt

(Victoria, British Columbia: Orca Book Publishers, 2009)

Series: Salt Trilogy. Book 1
Subject(s): Dystopias; Futuristic society; Adolescence
Age range(s): 13 - 18+
Major character(s): Hari, Teenager; Pearl, Teenager; Tealeaf, Assistant (maid of Pearl)
Time period(s): Indeterminate

Summary: *Salt* by Maurice Gee is the first book in a trilogy of the same name. In this fantasy young adult novel, the reader is introduced to Hari, a young man whose father has just been taken to work in the mines of Deep Salt. It is virtually impossible to return from Deep Salt once one is captured. Hari is determined to find his father, and along the way, he meets another young woman. Pearl is traveling with her maid, Tealeaf, escaping her home to avoid being forced into an arranged marriage. Hari, Pearl, and Tealeaf choose to travel together, soon realizing that Pearl and Hari each have the gift of mind-speaking, or ESP. Along the way, the two develop a close bond, and often find themselves in danger when trying to learn more about Deep Salt and find Hari's father.

Where it's reviewed:
Horn Book Guide, Spring 2010, page 96
Publishers Weekly, September 7, 2009, page 48
School Library Journal, November 2009, page 106
Voice of Youth Advocates, October 2009, page 330

Other books by the same author:
Gool, 2010
The Limping Man, 2007

Awards the book has won:
New Zealand Post Children's Book Awards: Fiction Categories, 2008

Other books you might like:
Pam Bachorz, *Drought*, 2011
Catherine Fisher, *Incarceron*, 2007
Tamora Pierce, *Terrier*, 2006

784

JESSICA DAY GEORGE

Princess of the Midnight Ball

(New York: Bloomsbury USA Children's Books, 2009)

Subject(s): Fairy tales; Dance; Good and evil
Age range(s): 12 - 16+
Major character(s): Galen, Gardener; Rose, Royalty (princess)

Time period(s): 19th century

Summary: *Princess of the Midnight Ball* is a retelling of the classic Brothers Grimm fairy tale "The 12 Dancing Princesses." Set in 19th-century Europe, the story follows a young man named Galen, who has just returned from war. On his way home, he meets an old woman and shares his food with her. In return for his kindness, the woman presents him with an invisibility cloak and magical yarn. Later, Galen takes a job as a gardener at the palace, where he discovers that a princess named Rose and her 11 sisters are under a curse that forces them to dance each night until they wear out their shoes. Galen falls in love with Rose and uses his magical yarn to rescue Rose and her sisters from their nightly fate.

Where it's reviewed:
Booklist, January 1, 2009, page 71
School Library Journal, April 2009, page 133
Voice of Youth Advocates, June 2009, page 150

Other books by the same author:
Princess of Glass, 2010
Sun and Moon, Ice and Snow, 2008

Awards the book has won:
Beehive Awards: Young Adult Book, 2011

Other books you might like:
Kirsten Boie, *The Princess Plot*, 2009
Heather Dixon, *Entwined*, 2011
Alex Flinn, *A Kiss in Time*, 2009
Mandy Hubbard, *Prada and Prejudice*, 2009
Janette Rallison, *My Fair Godmother*, 2009

785

JESSICA DAY GEORGE

Princess of Glass

(New York: Bloomsbury USA Children's Books, 2010)

Subject(s): Royalty; Fairy tales; Romances (Fiction)

Age range(s): 11 - 14+

Major character(s): Eleanora, Noblewoman, Servant; Poppy, Royalty (princess); Christian, Royalty (prince)

Time period(s): Indeterminate Past

Locale(s): Breton, Fictional Location

Summary: The follow-up to *Princess of the Midnight Ball*, *Princess of Glass* offers a unique spin on the classic Cinderella story. Eleanora is a wealthy woman of noble birth who is forced to spend her days as a maid after her father squanders the family's inheritance and subsequently passes away. When Princess Poppy of Westfalin is shipped off to visit her cousins in Breton, she immediately recognizes something different about their maid. When a magical ball creates an opportunity for Eleanora to trade her rags for a beautiful gown, she immediately accepts, unaware that her fairy godmother is really organizing a sinister plan against her. Princess Poppy and Prince Christian recognize that something is awry and it's up to them to save Eleanora from a dastardly future.

Where it's reviewed:
Booklist, May 15, 2010, page 51

Horn Book Guide, Fall 2010, page 367
School Library Journal, August 2010, page 100
Voice of Youth Advocates, August 2010, page 265

Other books by the same author:
Princess of the Midnight Ball, 2009
Sun and Moon, Ice and Snow, 2008

Other books you might like:
Cameron Dokey, *Before Midnight: A Retelling of "Cinderella"*, 2007
Margaret Peterson Haddix, *Just Ella*, 1999
Diane Stanley, *Bella at Midnight*, 2006

786

GARY GHISLAIN

How I Stole Johnny Depp's Alien Girlfriend

(San Francisco: Chronicle Books, 2011)

Subject(s): Extraterrestrial life; Mental health; Actors

Age range(s): 14 - 16+

Major character(s): David Gershwin, Teenager; Zelda, Mentally Ill Person

Summary: In *How I Stole Johnny Depp's Alien Girlfriend*, author Gary Ghislain tells the story of a teen boy named David Gershwin, whose father is a psychologist. When David meets Zelda, one of his father's patients, she confides in him that she is, in fact, an alien who came to Earth to get Johnny Depp, the actor from such movies as *Alice in Wonderland* and *Pirates of the Caribbean*. Her mission, she claims, is to take Johnny back to her planet, and although David is sure she is nuts, he is also intrigued. Soon he finds himself jetting off to Paris with Zelda as they seek out Johnny Depp. Is Zelda really crazy, or is there some truth to her outlandish story?

Where it's reviewed:
Booklist, June 1, 2011, page 80
Publishers Weekly, May 9, 2011, page 55
School Library Journal, July 2011, page 98
Voice of Youth Advocates, June 2011, page 182

Other books you might like:
Pittacus Lore, *I Am Number Four*, 2010
Sasha Watson, *Vidalia in Paris*, 2008
Brian Yansky, *Alien Invasion and Other Inconveniences*, 2010

787

KERSTIN GIER
ANTHEA BELL, Translator

Ruby Red

(New York: Henry Holt, 2011)

Series: Ruby Red Trilogy. Book 1
Subject(s): Time travel; Family life; Organizations

Age range(s): 13 - 16+

Major character(s): Gwyneth Shepherd, 16-Year-Old, Time

Traveler, Cousin (of Charlotte); Charlotte, Cousin (of Gwyneth); Gideon, Time Traveler
Time period(s): 21st century; (2000s); Multiple Time Periods
Locale(s): England

Summary: Originally published in Germany in 2009, *Ruby Red* is the first book in Kerstin Gier's Ruby Red Trilogy for young adults. Gwyneth Shepherd's family has been grooming her cousin Charlotte since childhood to assume the role of time traveler. But when Gwyneth suddenly jumps back in time during a school day, she and her family realize that Charlotte has not inherited the gift of time travel—Gwyneth has. Gwyneth is ill-prepared for her new role, and relies on fellow time traveler Gideon as they journey through England's past trying to reveal an ancient secret. Gwyneth also endeavors to solve the mystery of her own falsified birth date.

Where it's reviewed:
Booklist, April 15, 2011, page 53
New York Times Book Review, May 15, 2011, page 23
Publishers Weekly, March 7, 2011, page 65
School Library Journal, June 2011, page 116
Voice of Youth Advocates, April 2011, page 79

Other books you might like:
Linda Buckley-Archer, *Gideon the Cutpurse*, 2006
Katie Crouch, *The Magnolia League*, 2011
Mary Hoffman, *City of Masks*, 2002
James A. Owen, *Here, There Be Dragons*, 2006

788

GAIL GILES

Dark Song

(New York: Little, Brown and Company, 2010)

Subject(s): Family; Betrayal; Abuse

Age range(s): 14 - 17+
Major character(s): Ames Ford, 15-Year-Old
Time period(s): 21st century; 2010s
Locale(s): Texas, United States

Summary: Fifteen-year-old Ames Ford leads the perfect life with the perfect family in a wealthy Boulder suburb, until Ames's dad loses his job, the family is disowned by most of their friends, and they're all forced to relocate to a rundown rental in Texas. Furthering their miserable situation is a plethora of lies that come to the surface upon their relocation. The stress and betrayal begins to wear on their family bond. Making matters worse is Ames's new friend, Marc, a sexy and dangerous guy who wants nothing more than to protect Ames while also leading her astray. As Ames becomes more and more infatuated with Marc, she has trouble telling right from wrong and remembering where her true loyalty lies.

Where it's reviewed:
Booklist, September 1, 2010, page 98
Horn Book Guide, Spring 2011, page 9i8
Publishers Weekly, September 6, 2010, page 42
School Library Journal, October 2010, page 116
Voice of Youth Advocates, October 2010, page 347

Other books by the same author:
Right Behind You, 2007
What Happened to Cass McBride?, 2006
Playing in Traffic, 2004
Dead Girls Don't Write Letters, 2003
Shattering Glass, 2002

Other books you might like:
Holly Black, *White Cat*, 2010
Carolee Dean, *Take Me There*, 2010
Eliot Schrefer, *The Deadly Sister*, 2010
Michael Simmons, *Pool Boy*, 2003
Brian Yansky, *Wonders of the World*, 2007

789

DAVID MACINNIS GILL

Black Hole Sun

(New York: Greenwillow Books, 2010)

Subject(s): Mars (Planet); Science fiction; Adventure

Age range(s): 14 - 17+
Major character(s): Durango, 16-Year-Old, Military Personnel (regulator); Vienne, Sidekick (to Durango); Mimi, Artificial Intelligence
Time period(s): Indeterminate
Locale(s): Mars, Outer Space

Summary: *Black Hole Sun* is an action-packed science fiction novel for young adult readers from author David Macinnis Gill. Durango is a 16-year old Regulator on Mars, disgraced after his father's very public arrest and subsequent imprisonment. The only jobs Durango can get are the ones no one else wants, like protecting a group of miners from the cannibalistic Draeu, whose queen is desperate to get her hands on the alleged treasure possessed by the miners. Along with his gorgeous sidekick, Vienne, and Mimi, his former chief who is now an artificial intelligence brain chip, Durango must take on this dangerous and deadly mission, knowing that it could be his last.

Where it's reviewed:
Booklist, June 1, 2010, page 68
Horn Book Magazine, Sept.-Oct. 2010, page 77
Publishers Weekly, August 30, 2010, page 55
School Library Journal, November 2010, page 114
Voice of Youth Advocates, December 2010, page 469

Other books by the same author:
Soul Enchilada, 2009

Other books you might like:
John Barnes, *The Sky So Big and Black*, 2002
Joe Haldeman, *Marsbound*, 2008
Chris Roberson, *Iron Jaw and Hummingbird*, 2008

790

DAVID MACINNIS GILL

Soul Enchilada

(New York: HarperCollins, 2009)

Subject(s): Good and evil; Devil; Love
Age range(s): 14 - 18+

Major character(s): Eunice "Bug" Smoot, Young Woman, Worker (pizza delivery); Pesto, Agent (for International Supernatural Immigration Service), Manager (of car wash); Papa C, Grandfather (of Bug; deceased); Lucifer "Scratch", Demon (devil); Beelzebub "Mr. Beals", Demon (devil)
Time period(s): 21st century; 2000s
Locale(s): El Paso, Texas

Summary: *Soul Enchilada* is author David Macinnis Gill's daring and humorous debut novel. The book's protagonist is Eunice "Bug" Smoot, a pizza delivery girl in danger of losing her job. That is the least of her problems, however, when two devils show up to repossess her car, a 1958 Cadillac Biarritz, which she inherited from her grandfather. One devil is Scratch, also known as Lucifer, who sent Beelzebub, "Beals" for short, to collect on a debt owed to them by Bug's grandfather. Now, Bug has until the witching hour on Halloween to get her grandfather's soul to pay up and go to hell like it was supposed to, or she will be taking his place. Enter Pesto, who works at a car wash—and just so happens to moonlight for an agency that deports illegal supernatural beings such as devils. Until now, Pesto and Bug have shared monosyllabic conversations and hurled insults at each other as a way of flirting. With Scratch and Beals in the picture, however, Pesto will try to help Bug survive her face off with the devils.

Where it's reviewed:
Booklist, November 15, 2008, page 55
Publishers Weekly, January 26, 2009, page 121
School Library Journal, April 2009, page 133

Other books by the same author:
Black Hole Sun, 2010

Other books you might like:
Rosemary Clement-Moore, *Highway to Hell*, 2009
Chris Humphreys, *Possession*, 2008
Donna Jo Napoli, *The Wager*, 2010
Rachel Vail, *Gorgeous*, 2009

791

MORRIS GLEITZMAN

Once

(New York: Henry Holt, 2010)

Series: Felix and Zelda Series. Book 1
Subject(s): World War II, 1939-1945; Jews; Children and war

Age range(s): 12 - 16+
Major character(s): Felix, Child, Orphan
Time period(s): 20th century; 1940s (1942)
Locale(s): Poland

Summary: *Once* is a historical novel for young adult readers about World War II and the Nazi regime. It's 1942 and Poland is occupied by the Nazis. Felix, a young Jewish boy, is sent into hiding at a Catholic orphanage, unaware of the horrific atrocities happening outside of the orphanage's walls. To him, he's simply biding his time until his parents return from a work-related trip. When he catches wind of what's really going on, he fears for his parents' safety and sets out on a dangerous journey to warn them. Felix uses stories to cope with his surroundings, making up plots and characters to explain away everything happening around him, but soon he's confronted with a very real terror that's impossible to fictionalize.

Where it's reviewed:
Booklist, February 15, 2010, page 71
Horn Book Magazine, March-April 2010, page 55
Publishers Weekly, March 8, 2010, page 58
Voice of Youth Advocates, April 2010, page 57

Other books by the same author:
Then, 2011

Other books you might like:
John Boyne, *The Boy in the Striped Pajamas*, 2006
Uri Orlev, *Run, Boy, Run*, 2003
Jennifer Roy, *Yellow Star*, 2006
Jerry Spinelli, *Milkweed*, 2003

792

MORRIS GLEITZMAN

Then

(London: Puffin, 2009)

Series: Felix and Zelda Series. Book 2
Subject(s): World War II, 1939-1945; Refugees; Jews

Age range(s): 13 - 16+
Major character(s): Felix, 10-Year-Old, Refugee; Zelda, 6-Year-Old, Orphan; Genia, Farmer
Time period(s): 20th century; 1940s (1942)
Locale(s): Poland

Summary: On the run from the Nazis who killed his Jewish family, 10-year-old Felix befriends Zelda, a six-year-old orphan whose parents were Nazis. In 1942 Poland, the children form a familial bond that helps them survive until they make their way to a farm run by Genia, a kind woman who takes them in. As they witness shocking acts of war and prejudice around them, Felix and Zelda find themselves in increasing danger, compounded by Zelda's outspoken nature and an enemy bent on exposing Felix as a Jew. The second book in a trilogy, *Then*, which follows *Once*, Gleitzman's terrifying and touching story introduces young readers to the horrors of the Holocaust and World War II.

Where it's reviewed:
Booklist, April 15, 2011, page 63
Horn Book Magazine, May-June 2011, page 90
Publishers Weekly, March 28, 2011, page 58
School Library Journal, June 2011, page 118

Other books by the same author:
Once, 2005

Other books you might like:
John Boyne, *The Boy in the Striped Pajamas*, 2006
Uri Orlev, *Run, Boy, Run*, 2003
Mirjam Pressler, *Malka*, 2003
Jennifer Roy, *Yellow Star*, 2006

793

SARAH GLIDDEN, Author/Illustrator

How to Understand Israel in 60 Days or Less

(New York: Vertigo/DC Comics, 2010)

Subject(s): Autobiographies; Jews; Comic books

Age range(s): 15 - 18+

Summary: This memoir, told in graphic novel format, chronicles Sarah Glidden's soul-searching, eye-opening travels through Israel. An American Jewish author and artist, Glidden had long struggled to understand her culture and religion. Determined to find answers at the heart of the issues, she embarked on a "Birthright Israel" tour—a government-sponsored program that provides young Jews with the opportunity to visit Israel. Glidden's insightful account of her journey, told in comic book panels, reveals the disconnect between her expectations of the trip and the realities she encountered. Instead of finding unambiguous confirmation of her heritage and faith, Glidden discovers contradictions and uncertainty that force her to reexamine her identity as a Jew.

Where it's reviewed:
Booklist, December 15, 2010, page 35
Library Journal, March 15, 2011, page 104
Publishers Weekly, August 30, 2010, page 36
School Library Journal, November 2010, page 147

Other books you might like:
Guy Delisle, *Pyongyang: A Journey in North Korea*, 2005
J.A. Jance, *Exit Wounds*, 2003
Lars Martinson, *Tonoharu: Part One*, 2008
Joe Sacco, *Palestine*, 2001
Casey Scieszka, *To Timbuktu: Nine Countries, Two People, One True Story*, 2011

794

K.L. GOING

King of the Screwups

(New York: Harcourt Children's Books, 2009)

Subject(s): Father-son relations; Identity; Homosexuality

Age range(s): 14 - 18+
Major character(s): Liam Gellar, Student—High School; "Aunt" Pete, Uncle
Time period(s): 21st century; 2000s
Locale(s): New York, United States

Summary: In this unique coming-of-age tale by K.L. Going, high school senior Liam Gellar challenges the notions of identity and popularity with his wild adventures. *King of the Screwups* centers on Liam's journey as he goes from being the most popular kid in school to being booted out of the house by his domineering father. With nowhere else to go, he tracks down and moves in with "Aunt" Pete, who is actually his gay transvestite uncle. In a bid to gain his father's approval, Liam tries to become a nerdy student, but the stunt doesn't pay off. With Pete's help, Liam learns about the special things he has to offer his family, his friends, and the world.

Where it's reviewed:
Booklist, April 15, 2009, page 37
Journal of Adolescent & Adult, April 2010, page 611
Publishers Weekly, February 9, 2009, page 49
School Library Journal, April 2009, page 134
Voice of Youth Advocates, June 2009, page 136

Other books by the same author:
Saint Iggy, 2006
Fat Kid Rules the World, 2003

Other books you might like:
Sean Beaudoin, *Going Nowhere Faster*, 2007
Ben Bo, *The Edge*, 1999
Alden R. Carter, *Up Country*, 1989
Ron Koertge, *The Arizona Kid*, 1988
Jennifer Lynn Ziegler, *How Not to Be Popular*, 2008

795

CHRISTOPHER GOLDEN
TIM LEBBON, Co-Author
GREG RUTH, Illustrator

The Wild

(New York: HarperCollins, 2011)

Series: Secret Journeys of Jack London Series. Book 1
Story type: Literary; Young Adult
Subject(s): Adventure; Supernatural; Survival

Age range(s): 13 - 16+
Major character(s): Jack London, Adventurer, 17-Year-Old
Time period(s): 19th century
Locale(s): Yukon Territory, Canada

Summary: Authors Christopher Golden and Tim Lebbon weave a fictionalized account of author Jack London's adventures in the Alaskan wilderness in this young adult novel, the first in the Secret Journeys of Jack London series. In this outing, Jack finds himself in the midst of the Yukon Territory's Gold Rush. Jack is sure he'll be able to get rich quick, and he ventures far into the territory to stake his claim. When winter falls early, however, Jack must fight to survive along with the rest of the prospectors. Along the way, Jack encounters things he never imagined: slavery, kidnapping, and a supernatural beast known as the Wendigo, a creature so fearsome that even the wolves run from it. As Jack's mind turns from gold fever to survival, he wonders if he'll make it out of the Yukon alive. Includes illustrations by Greg Ruth.

Where it's reviewed:
Booklist, February 15, 2011, page 73
Horn Book Guide, Fall 2011, page 382
School Library Journal, April 2011, page 173
Voice of Youth Advocates, April 2011, page 80

Other books by the same author:
The Secret Journeys of Jack London: The Sea Wolves, 2012

Other books you might like:
Will Hobbs, *Jason's Gold*, 1999

Jack London, *The Call of the Wild*, 1903
Rick Yancey, *The Curse of the Wendigo*, 2010

JULIA GOLDING

Dragonfly

(New York: Marshall Cavendish, 2009)

Subject(s): Interpersonal relations; Royalty; Kidnapping

Age range(s): 13 - 16+

Major character(s): Taoshira "Tashi", Royalty (Princess of the Blue Crescent Islands); Ramil, Royalty (Prince of Gerfal)

Time period(s): Indeterminate

Summary: Julia Golding's *Dragonfly* recounts the tale of two spirited royals whose arranged marriage leads to the adventure of a lifetime. Princess Taoshira of the Blue Crescent Islands is 16 years old when she is married off to 18-year-old Prince Ramil of Gerfal. Though their union is politically advantageous, the two detest one another immediately. But when they are kidnapped, Tashi and Ramil must put their differences aside and learn to work together to save their lives—and their native countries.

Where it's reviewed:
Booklist, September 1, 2009, page 80
School Library Journal, November 2009, page 108
Voice of Youth Advocates, December 2009, page 420

Other books by the same author:
The Silver Sea, 2010
Cat Among the Pigeons, 2008

Other books you might like:
Hilari Bell, *The Farsala Trilogy*, 2004
Shannon Hale, *Book of a Thousand Days*, 2007
Robin McKinley, *The Blue Sword*, 1982

797

LAURA GOODE

Sister Mischief

(Somerville, Massachusetts: Candlewick Press, 2011)

Story type: Gay - Lesbian Fiction; Young Adult
Subject(s): Gay and lesbian rights; Homosexuality; Music

Age range(s): 15 - 18+

Major character(s): Esme Rockett, Teenager, Student—High School, Friend (of Marcy, Tess, and Rowie), Lesbian; Marcy, Friend (of Tess, Esme, and Rowie), Student—High School, Teenager; Tess, Friend (of Rowie, Esme, and Marcy), Teenager, Student—High School; Rowie, Teenager, Friend (of Marcy, Esme, and Tess), Student—High School; Mary Ashley Baumgarten, Teenager, Student—High School, Enemy (of Esme, Marcy, Tess, and Rowie)

Time period(s): 21st century; 2010s
Locale(s): Holyhill, Minnesota

Summary: In this young adult novel by Laura Good, best girlfriends Esme, Marcy, Tess, and Rowie appear to be run-of-the-mill teenagers growing up on the outskirts of Minneapolis, Minnesota. Behind closed doors, however, these girls are major hip-hop fans with alter egos: MC Ferocious, DJ SheStorm, the ConTessa, and MC Rohini. As the friends come of age and rebel against societal norms in the white, middle-class suburb of Holyhill, they explore their sexuality and flirt with the music scene they love so much. When their school adopts a resolution banning hip-hop, the four girls settle in for the fight of their lives as they start a gay-straight alliance for hip-hop lovers. Meanwhile, the girls' worst nemesis, Mary Ashley Baumgarten, threatens to expose the girls as lesbians and stop their club in its tracks.

Where it's reviewed:
Booklist, June 1, 2011, page 69
Publishers Weekly, May 23, 2011, page 47
School Library Journal, November 2011, page 122
Voice of Youth Advocates, August 2011, page 268

Other books you might like:
Antony John, *Five Flavors of Dumb*, 2010
Jennifer McMahon, *My Tiki Girl*, 2008
Alex Sanchez, *Rainbow Boys*, 2001
Alan Lawrence Sitomer, *Hip-Hop High School*, 2006

798

BEATRICE GORMLEY

Poisoned Honey: A Story of Mary Magdalene

(New York: Knopf Books for Young Readers, 2010)

Subject(s): Bible stories; Jewish history; Jesus Christ
Age range(s): 15 - 18+
Major character(s): Mariamne, Daughter (of a Sardine merchant), Magician, Biblical Figure
Time period(s): 1st century
Locale(s): Jerusalem, Israel

Summary: In *Poisoned Honey: A Story of Mary Magdalene*, Beatrice Gormley takes readers back to first century Jerusalem to share the story of a young woman named Mariamne. Although Mariamne believes she has powers of her own (after all, she frequency hears voices in her head), she succumbs to the wishes of her father and brother. After their deaths, however, her remaining family members promise her to a man she does not love and does not wish to marry. Having turned to an Egyptian fortune teller for advice, Mariamne takes control of her future and embraces a life of charms, curses, and spirits.

Where it's reviewed:
Booklist, May 15, 2010, page 36
Horn Book Guide, Fall 2010, page 367
School Library Journal, February 2010, page 110

Other books by the same author:
Salome, 2007

Other books you might like:
Anita Diamant, *The Red Tent*, 1997
Donna Freitas, *The Possibilities of Sainthood*, 2008

Cecilia Galante, *The Patron Saint of Butterflies*, 2008
Donna Jo Napoli, *Song of the Magdalene*, 1996

799

HIROMI GOTO

Half World

(New York: Viking, 2010)

Subject(s): Afterlife; Death; Fantasy

Age range(s): 13 - 16+

Major character(s): Melanie, 14-Year-Old, Outcast; Mr. Glueskin, Villain, Kidnapper

Time period(s): Indeterminate

Summary: Fourteen-year-old Melanie is an overweight outcast being raised by an impoverished single mother. Her father is trapped in the Half World, a terrifying limbo between life and death where inhabitants are forced to relive traumatic experiences over and over again. When Melanie's mother is kidnapped by the sinister Mr. Glueskin, Melanie must travel to the Half World and try to rescue her parents. Confronted by terrible creatures and Glueskin's horrific schemes, Melanie must find a well of inner strength and bridge the gap between life and death, freeing the Half World's residents once and for all.

Where it's reviewed:
Booklist, March 1, 2010, page 60
Horn Book Magazine, July-August 2010, page 104
The Magazine of Fantasy and Sc, March 2009, page 30
Publishers Weekly, March 8, 2010, page 58
Voice of Youth Advocates, June 2010, page 164

Other books you might like:
Holly Black, *Ironside: A Modern Faery's Tale*, 2007
Frewin Jones, *The Seventh Daughter*, 2009
Sharon Shinn, *Gateway*, 2009

800

CANDY GOURLAY

Tall Story

(New York: Random House, 2010)

Subject(s): Brothers; Sisters; Family

Age range(s): 12 - 15+

Major character(s): Amandolina "Andi", Sister (half, of Bernardo), Basketball Player; Bernardo, Brother (half, of Andi)

Time period(s): 21st century; 2010s

Locale(s): London, England

Summary: Amandolina "Andi" has always wanted her half-brother to live with her family in London, but for many years he's been in the Philippines, protecting his city from earthquakes. Now Bernardo is finally going to move in with them in London and Andi couldn't be more excited. As a short girl with a passion for basketball, she hopes Bernardo is tall and will be able to help her practice. When she sees her older brother in London for the first time, she realizes she got her wish: Bernardo is

eight feet tall. However, he suffers from gigantism and is unhappy with his height. He thinks witches in his village put a curse on him when he was younger, which resulted in his exaggerated height. Andi hopes to convince Bernardo that his height is a blessing, not a curse, as she helps him fit in with his new family. Andi also realizes that having an older brother will take some getting used to on her part.

Where it's reviewed:
Booklist, January 1, 2011, page 90
Bulletin of the Center for Children's Books, February 2011, page 277
Horn Book Magazine, May-June 2011, page 90
School Library Journal, March 2011, page 161

Other books you might like:
Edward Averett, *The Rhyming Season*, 2005
Pat Flynn, *Out of His League*, 2008
Nikki Grimes, *Planet Middle School*, 2011
Laura Manivong, *Escaping the Tiger*, 2010

801

GAVIN J. GRANT, Editor
KELLY LINK, Co-Editor

Steampunk!: An Anthology of Fantastically Rich and Strange Stories

(Somerville, Massachusetts: Candlewick Press, 2011)

Story type: Collection; Steampunk
Subject(s): Steampunk; Short stories; Fantasy

Age range(s): 14 - 18+

Summary: Editors Gavin J. Grant and Kelly Link collect stories by 14 renowned authors, including two graphic novelists, in the first ever steampunk anthology for young adult readers. These short stories offer inventive new twists on the traditional elements of the steampunk genre, creating an exciting blend of science fiction, fantasy, romance, and history. In Holly Black's story "Everything Amiable and Obliging," an automaton finds love with an unexpected mate. Kelly Link's "The Summer People" takes readers to Appalachia where a young girl must care for the bizarre residents of a strange house. Other authors include Libba Bray, Garth Nix, and Cory Doctorow.

Where it's reviewed:
Horn Book Magazine, September/October 2011, page 90
Publishers Weekly, August 8, 2011, page 50
School Library Journal, September 2011, page 160

Other books by the same author:
Pretty Monsters: Stories, 2008
The Year's Best Fantasy and Horror, 2006

Other books you might like:
Philip Reeve, *Hungry City Chronicles*, 2001
Trisha Telep, *Corsets and Clockwork: 13 Steampunk Romances*, 2011

802

HELEN GRANT

The Vanishing of Katharina Linden

(New York: Delacorte Press, 2010)

Subject(s): Missing persons; Children; Mystery

Age range(s): 15 - 18+

Major character(s): Pia Kolvenbach, 10-Year-Old; Stink-Stefan, Friend (of Pia)

Time period(s): 20th century; 1990s (1998)

Locale(s): Bad Munstereifel, Germany

Summary: In *The Vanishing of Katharina Linden* by Helen Grant, the death of 10-year-old Pia Kolvenbach's grandmother in Bad Munstereifel, Germany, makes her a social outcast. Pia's grandmother was burned to death, but reports that the woman also exploded draw suspicion on the Kolvenbach family. Suddenly ostracized, Pia forges a friendship with fellow outcast "StinkStefan." The two children start calling on an old man in town who tells them tales of local folklore. When Katharina Linden disappears after a parade, Pia and StinkStefan believe that ghosts are involved. The investigation takes a dangerous turn when another person goes missing. First novel.

Where it's reviewed:
Booklist, June 1, 2010, page 42
Library Journal, June 15, 2010, page 42
New York Times Book Review, August 15, 2010, page 22

Other books by the same author:
The Glass Demon, 2011

Awards the book has won:
Alex Awards, 2011

Other books you might like:
Alan Bradley, *The Sweetness at the Bottom of the Pie*, 2009
Gail Giles, *Dead Girls Don't Write Letters*, 2003
Chevy Stevens, *Still Missing*, 2010

803

MICHAEL GRANT

Hunger

(New York: HarperTeen, 2009)

Series: Gone Series. Book 2
Subject(s): Good and evil; Supernatural; Survival
Age range(s): 13 - 17+
Major character(s): Sam Temple, Teenager; Quinn, Teenager; Edilio Escobar, Teenager; Lana, Teenager
Time period(s): 21st century; 2000s
Locale(s): Perdido Beach, California

Summary: In *Hunger*, the second book in Michael Grant's Gone series, a nuclear episode known as the FAYZ has eradicated all residents of Perdido Beach, California, who are older than 14. Though the young people left behind have managed to survive for three months without any adult presence, their resources are dwindling and their social structure has begun to erode. As the children divide themselves into two groups—those with psychic abilities and those with normal mental function—Sam Temple and his friends Quinn, Edilio, Albert, and Lana struggle to stay alive in their increasingly violent world. Meanwhile a ravenous specter has emerged from hiding to prey on the weak.

Where it's reviewed:
Booklist, August 1, 2009, page 60
Publishers Weekly, June 15, 2009, page 51
School Library Journal, July 2009, page 84
Voice of Youth Advocates, June 2009, page 150

Other books by the same author:
Plague, 2011
Lies, 2010
Gone, 2008

Other books you might like:
John Brindley, *The Rule of Claw*, 2007
William Golding, *Lord of the Flies*, 1954
Stephen King, *The Stand: The Complete and Uncut Edition*, 1990
Cameron Stracher, *The Water Wars*, 2011

804

KEITH GRAY

Ostrich Boys

(New York: Random House, 2010)

Subject(s): Friendship; Death; Grief

Age range(s): 14 - 18+

Major character(s): Blake, Teenager, Friend (of Ross); Sam, Teenager, Friend (of Ross); Kenny, Teenager, Friend (of Ross)

Time period(s): 21st century; 2010s

Locale(s): England; Ross, Scotland

Summary: In Keith Gray's *Ostrich Boys*, three teenagers are devastated by the death of one of their best friends, Ross. Blake, Sam, and Kenny are distraught over the loss of their friend, and they become even more upset when members of the community, who ignored Ross during his life, come forward to mourn Ross's death. The friends are certain they are the only people in the town who cared for Ross, so they steal their friend's ashes. Knowing that Ross had always wanted to visit the town of Ross in Scotland, they begin a road trip. They steal rides on trains, hitchhike, and meet a variety of people along the way. As they approach the village of Ross, information about the reason behind Ross's death emerges. The boys begin to question how well any of them ever really knew Ross—and each other.

Where it's reviewed:
Booklist, February 1, 2010, page 38
Horn Book Guide, Fall 2010, page 368
Publishers Weekly, February 8, 2010, page 52
School Library Journal, February 2010, page 110

Other books by the same author:
The Fearful, 2006
Creepers, 1997

Other books you might like:
Heidi Ayarbe, *Freeze Frame*, 2008
Libba Bray, *Going Bovine*, 2009
Morgan Matson, *Amy and Roger's Epic Detour*, 2010
Francisco X. Stork, *The Last Summer of The Death Warriors*, 2010
Jenny Valentine, *Me, the Missing, and the Dead*, 2007

805

MICHELE DOMINGUEZ GREENE

Keep Sweet

(New York: Simon Pulse, 2010)

Subject(s): Mormons; Child abuse; Romances (Fiction)

Age range(s): 14 - 17+

Major character(s): Alva Jane, 14-Year-Old, Daughter, Girlfriend (of John Joseph), Cult Member; John Joseph, Teenager, Boyfriend (of Alva Jane), Cult Member

Time period(s): 21st century; 2010s

Locale(s): Pineridge, Utah

Summary: In Michele Greene's *Keep Sweet*, Alva Jane is a smart, respectable girl whose one father has seven wives and 29 children. Although her family may appear unconventional to anyone not living in Pineridge, Alva Jane has never challenged the way they live. She enjoys her life. She's one of the smartest girls at school, and she is given many freedoms because of her intelligence. She works outside the home, she earns money, and she spends time with the boy she has had a crush on for many years. Luckily, John Joseph also has feelings for Alva, and they agree to marry once they get permission. Before they are married, they sneak a quick kiss and are caught. Alva is imprisoned, beaten, and promised to a man nearly 40 years older than she. For the first time, she questions the everyday events that occur in Pineridge, and she wonders if she would be better off on the other side of its walls.

Where it's reviewed:
Horn Book Guide, Fall 2010, page 368
Publishers Weekly, February 15, 2010, page 133
School Library Journal, April 2010, page 156

Other books you might like:
Eishes Chayil, *Hush*, 2010
Ellen Hopkins, *Burned*, 2006
Shelley Hrdlitschka, *Sister Wife*, 2008
Naomi Rich, *Alis*, 2009
Carol Lynch Williams, *The Chosen One*, 2009

806

LISA GREENWALD

Sweet Treats and Secret Crushes

(New York: Amulet Books, 2010)

Story type: Contemporary
Subject(s): Friendship; Adolescence; Apartments

Age range(s): 12 - 14+

Major character(s): Kate, 7th Grader, Friend (of Olivia and Georgia); Olivia, 7th Grader, Friend (of Kate and Georgia); Georgia, 7th Grader, Friend (of Kate and Olivia)

Time period(s): 21st century; 2010s

Locale(s): New York, New York

Summary: A Valentine's Day blizzard strands three seventh-grade girls in their Brooklyn apartment building in this young adult novel by Lisa Greenwald. Although Kate, Olivia, and Georgia are very different, the three girls are the best of friends. All agree that the unexpected snow day is a disappointment; now they'll have no chance of seeing their crushes on Valentine's Day. But with a recipe supplied by Georgia's mother, the girls bake some special fortune cookies that they deliver to their snowbound neighbors. As the friends share their uncannily accurate Valentine fortunes, they enjoy some in-depth conversations about feelings they've been holding inside.

Where it's reviewed:
Booklist, September 15, 2010, page 73
Horn Book Guide, Spring 2011, page 99
Publishers Weekly, October 18, 2010, page 49
School Library Journal, December 2010, page 114

Other books by the same author:
Reel Life Starring Us, 2011
My Life in Pink and Green, 2009

Other books you might like:
Avi, *Never Mind!: A Twin Novel*, 2004
Amy Goldman Koss, *Gossip Times Three*, 2003
Wendy Mass, *The Candymakers*, 2010
Rachel Vail, *What Are Friends For?*, 1999

807

ADELE GRIFFIN

Tighter

(New York: Alfred A. Knopf, 2011)

Subject(s): Death; Ghosts; Social class

Age range(s): 15 - 18+

Major character(s): Jamie Atkinson, 17-Year-Old, Child-Care Giver (au pair); Isa, 11-Year-Old, Sister (of Milo); Milo, Brother (of Isa, older); Jessie, Child-Care Giver (au pair, deceased), Spirit

Time period(s): 21st century; 2010s

Locale(s): Little Bly, Rhode Island

Summary: Adele Griffin's young adult novel *Tighter*, a contemporary version of Henry James's *The Turn of the Screw*, recounts 17-year-old Jamie Atkinson's summer spent as an au pair in a home with a tragic past. Jamie arrives at Little Bly, an islet off the Rhode Island coast, armed with a cache of pills swiped from her family's medicine cabinets to help ease her broken heart. She hopes a summer spent on beautiful Little Bly caring for 11-year-old Isa will also be therapeutic. But Little Bly's secrets soon emerge, and Jamie deals with a crotchety housekeeper, Isa's bold brother, and the spirits of a teenage couple who killed themselves on the island the previous year. Jessie, the female ghost, was Isa's nanny last year and she looks remarkably like Jamie. As Jamie's drug habit worsens, anxiety and danger tighten their grip.

Where it's reviewed:
Booklist, March 15, 2011, page 58
Horn Book Guide, Fall 2011, page 382
Publishers Weekly, March 21, 2011, page 78
School Library Journal, June 2011, page 118
Voice of Youth Advocates, June 2011, page 184

Other books by the same author:
The Julian Game, 2010
My Almost Epic Summer, 2006
Where I Want to Be, 2005

Other books you might like:
Victoria Ashton, *Confessions of a Teen Nanny*, 2006
April Lindner, *Jane*, 2010
Lizabeth Zindel, *A Girl, a Ghost, and the Hollywood Hills*, 2010

808

ADELE GRIFFIN
LISA BROWN, Illustrator

Picture the Dead
(Naperville, Illinois: Sourcebooks, 2010)

Story type: Ghost Story
Subject(s): United States Civil War, 1861-1865; Ghosts; Orphans

Age range(s): 12 - 16+
Major character(s): Jennie, Orphan, Fiance(e) (of Will); Will, Fiance(e) (of Jennie), Military Personnel (Civil War soldier), Brother (of Quinn); Quinn, Military Personnel (Civil War soldier), Brother (of Will); Clara, Aunt (of Jennie); Mr. Geist, Photographer
Time period(s): 19th century; 1860s
Locale(s): Massachusetts, United States

Summary: In this young adult novel by Adele Griffin, the Civil War has brought misery to the life of an orphaned young woman. Having lost her parents, Jennie lives in the home of her cruel Aunt Clara. Jennie is still grieving the death of her twin brother in battle when her cousin Quinn returns from the front with more bad news. Quinn has been injured, but his brother Will—who was Jennie's fiance—is dead. With the prospect of marriage gone, Jennie becomes the target of her aunt's malice. Meanwhile, Jennie begins to sense the presence of Will's spirit in the house. Is he unhappy about the relationship that has developed between Jennie and Quinn? Jennie turns to paranormal photographer Mr. Geist to help her uncover the real reason for Will's unrest.

Where it's reviewed:
Booklist, May 1, 2010, page 49
Horn Book Guide, Fall 2010, page 368
Publishers Weekly, May 17, 2010, page 52
Voice of Youth Advocates, August 2010, page 266

Other books by the same author:
Tighter, 2011
The Julian Game, 2010

My Almost Epic Summer, 2006
Where I Want to Be, 2005

Other books you might like:
Elaine Marie Alphin, *Ghost Soldier*, 2001
Iain Lawrence, *The Seance*, 2008
Gary Paulsen, *Soldier's Heart*, 1998

809

PAUL GRIFFIN

Stay with Me
(New York: Dial Books, 2011)

Story type: Coming-of-Age
Subject(s): Romances (Fiction); Adolescent interpersonal relations; Dating (Social customs)

Age range(s): 15 - 18+
Major character(s): Cece, 15-Year-Old, Girlfriend (of Mack); Mack, 15-Year-Old, Boyfriend (of Cece)
Time period(s): 21st century; 2010s
Locale(s): New York, New York

Summary: In this novel, author Paul Griffin tells the story of a pair of teenage lovers who come from opposite sides of the tracks. Cece is the typical girl next door; a perfect student and daughter, she rarely does anything wrong and has her future all planned out. Meanwhile, her brother's friend Mack has dropped out of school, and his quick temper often gets him in trouble. These teenagers seem as though they have nothing in common until a stray dog Mack has rescued brings them together. As Cece and Mack's relationship develops, they begin to realize that they are more alike than they ever realized. But can their relationship withstand a bad decision by Mack, or will their differences drive them apart?

Where it's reviewed:
Booklist, November 1, 2011, page 72
School Library Journal, August 2011, page 104
Voice of Youth Advocates, October 2011, page 381

Other books by the same author:
The Orange Houses, 2009
Ten Mile River, 2008

Other books you might like:
Ingrid Lee, *Dog Lost*, 2008
Chris Lynch, *Anger Management*, 2009
Sylvia McNicoll, *Last Chance for Paris*, 2008
Robin Wasserman, *Wrath*, 2006

810

PAUL GRIFFIN

The Orange Houses
(New York: Dial Books, 2009)

Subject(s): Urban life; Outcasts; Adolescence

Age range(s): 15 - 18+
Major character(s): Tamika Sykes, 15-Year-Old, Deaf Person, Outcast, Artist; Fatima Esperer, 16-Year-Old, Refugee (Africa), Newspaper Carrier; Jimmi Sixes,

18-Year-Old, Addict, Veteran
Time period(s): 21st century; 2000s
Locale(s): New York, New York

Summary: *The Orange Houses* is Paul Griffin's tale of three teenage social misfits and the unlikely friendship they build. Tamika Sykes is 15 years old, partially deaf, and utterly hopeless. She doesn't have a single friend in school and, although her mother is working two jobs to pay for it, she's not sure she wants the auditory surgery that will restore her hearing. Fatima Esperer is 16 years old and a refugee from the violent and dangerous African country she used to call home. Retreating from the war-torn place, she has made a new home in the Bronx, selling newspapers on Tamika's street. Jimmi Sixes is 18 years old, a homeless war veteran, and a drug-addicted, self-proclaimed artist. Set against the harsh backdrop of inner-city Bronx, *The Orange Houses* follows the unusual bond that these three outcasts form as they connect artistically to one another and fight against unwanted gang violence that hounds their streets.

Where it's reviewed:
Booklist, May 1, 2009, page 80
Publishers Weekly, June 22, 2009, page 46
School Library Journal, June 2009, page 126
Voice of Youth Advocates, October 2009, page 314

Other books by the same author:
Stay with Me, 2011
Ten Mile River, 2008

Other books you might like:
Josh Berk, *The Dark Days of Hamburger Halpin*, 2010
Deborah Ellis, *No Safe Place*, 2010
K.L. Going, *Saint Iggy*, 2006
Paul Volponi, *Black and White*, 2005
Rita Williams-Garcia, *Jumped*, 2009

811

JESSICA GRUNER
ROB REGER, Co-Author
BUZZ PARKER, Illustrator

Emily the Strange: The Lost Days

(New York: Harper, 2009)

Subject(s): Adventure; Identity; Runaways

Age range(s): 13 - 16+
Major character(s): Emily, 13-Year-Old, Amnesiac
Time period(s): 21st century; 2000s

Summary: Told in the form of a diary, Rob Reger and Jessica Runer's *Emily the Strange: The Lost Days* chronicles the further adventures of the 13-year-old goth heroine. At the story's onset, Emily finds herself in the throes of amnesia, and she has no idea who or where she is. All she knows is that the mysterious town of Blackrock is a dangerous place for a girl alone. But Emily is nothing if not resourceful, and she has soon hatched a plan that will hopefully lead her out of Blackrock for good. Author Rob Reger and Buzz Parker provide the illustrations to this volume.

Where it's reviewed:
Booklist, May 1, 2009, page 47

Publishers Weekly, June 1, 2009, page 136
School Library Journal, June 2009, page 136
Voice of Youth Advocates, August 2009, page 231

Other books by the same author:
Emily the Strange: Piece of Mind, 2011
Emily the Strange: Dark Times, 2010
Emily the Strange: Stranger and Stranger, 2010

Other books you might like:
Nancy Kilpatrick, *The Goth Bible: A Compendium for the Darkly Inclined*, 2004
Kelly McClymer, *Must Love Black*, 2008
Ted Naifeh, *Courtney Crumrin's Monstrous Holiday*, 2009
Douglas Rees, *Vampire High: Sophomore Year*, 2011
Gabrielle Zevin, *Memoirs of a Teenage Amnesiac*, 2007

812

MAURISSA GUIBORD

Warped

(New York: Delacorte Press, 2011)

Story type: Fantasy
Subject(s): Witchcraft; Magic; Adolescent interpersonal relations

Age range(s): 13 - 16+
Major character(s): Tessa Brody, 17-Year-Old; William de Chaucy, Nobleman; Gray Lily, Witch
Time period(s): 21st century; 16th century
Locale(s): Maine, United States

Summary: In her debut novel, author Maurissa Guibord tells the story of a young woman who discovers a secret world hidden beyond the weavings of an old tapestry. One of Tessa's favorite things is to attend auctions and estate sales with her art dealer father. When an antique tapestry comes into their possession, Tessa immediately feels that the piece was meant to be hers, and she hangs it in her room. During the nights that follow she is plagued by odd dreams about medieval times. She finally pulls at a thread in the tapestry and reveals an ancient world. Instantly before her a man appears who says he is William de Chaucy, a nobleman imprisoned in the textile by an evil witch. Now Tessa finds herself on a quest more than five centuries in the making as she attempts to get William back to where he belongs. But can she help him before the witch known as Gray Lily exacts her revenge on the tapestry's newest owner? First novel.

Where it's reviewed:
Booklist, January 1, 2011, page 100
Horn Book Magazine, March-April 2011, page 117
Publishers Weekly, November 15, 2011, page 58
School Library Journal, March 2011, page 162
Voice of Youth Advocates, April 2011, page 81

Other books you might like:
Bonnie Dobkin, *Dream Spiiner*, 2006
Jennifer Donnelly, *Revolution*, 2010
Kerstin Gier, *Ruby Red*, 2011

813

MATT HAIG

The Radleys: A Novel

(New York: Free Press, 2010)

Subject(s): Vampires; Family; Family relations

Age range(s): 15 - 18+

Major character(s): Peter Radley, Doctor, Vampire, Father (to Rowan and Clara), Spouse (to Helen); Helen Radley, Spouse (to Peter), Mother (to Rowan and Clara), Housewife, Vampire; Rowan Radley, 17-Year-Old, Vampire, Son (of Peter and Helen); Clara Radley, Vampire, Teenager, Crime Suspect, Daughter (of Peter and Helen); Will, Brother (of Peter)

Time period(s): 21st century; 2010s

Locale(s): England

Summary: Written by Matt Haig, *The Radleys* provides dark humor about family dysfunction, age-old secrets, and vampires. The Radleys seem like an average family, complete with a workaholic patriarch, Peter; a discontent housewife, Helen; and two moody and withdrawn teenagers, Rowan and Clara. The thing that sets the Radley family apart from their neighbors is that they're secretly vampires. Peter and Helen have been abstaining from their traditional blood-filled diet for 17 years in hopes of giving their kids a normal life, but when Clara is attacked by classmates and commits a horrific act of violence, the truth is revealed. As the town investigates the crime and legends about vampires begin surfacing, the Radleys face serious trouble. Making matters worse is the return of Peter's brother, Will, a devious character who knows enough secrets to destroy the Radley family forever.

Where it's reviewed:
Booklist, November 1, 2010, page 35
Entertainment Weekly, December 17, 2010, page 80
Library Journal, October 1, 2010, page 67
New York Times Book Review, January 1, 2011, page 17
Publishers Weekly, October 4, 2010, page 27

Other books by the same author:
The Labrador Pact, 2008
The Dead Father's Club, 2006

Awards the book has won:
Alex Awards, 2011

Other books you might like:
Gail Carriger, *Heartless*, 2011
Alyxandra Harvey, *Hearts at Midnight*, 2010
C.C. Hunter, *Born at Midnight*, 2011

814

KATHRYN MILLER HAINES

The Girl Is Murder

(New York: Roaring Brook Press, 2011)

Story type: Private Detective

Subject(s): Detective fiction; Mystery; World War II, 1939-1945

Age range(s): 13 - 16+

Major character(s): Iris Anderson, 15-Year-Old, Detective

Time period(s): 20th century; 1940s

Locale(s): New York, New York

Summary: In this young adult novel by Kathryn Miller Haines, Iris Anderson's life of privilege on Manhattan's Upper East Side disappears after her mother's suicide. When Iris's father returns from the frontlines of World War II, his wounds prevent him from fully performing his former duties as a detective. That's where Iris comes in. Although she is only 15, she has inherited her father's private-eye instincts. Iris is especially anxious to pitch in and do the legwork for her dad when she learns that a mystery he is working on deals with her missing schoolmate. Mr. Anderson doesn't want his daughter to follow in his footsteps, though, so Iris must keep her investigative activities from him. Iris relies on her wits and street smarts to figure her way out of one mess after another, but could this case be too dangerous even for a plucky girl like her?

Where it's reviewed:
Booklist, May 1, 2011, page 42
Publishers Weekly, October 31, 2011, page 53
School Library Journal, August 2011, page 104

Other books you might like:
Judy Blundell, *What I Saw and How I Lied*, 2008
Harlan Coben, *Shelter*, 2011
Daniel Ehrenhaft, *Dirty Laundry*, 2009
Christine Fletcher, *Ten Cents a Dance*, 2008

815

JULIE HALPERN

Into the Wild Nerd Yonder

(New York: Feiwel and Friends, 2009)

Subject(s): Friendship; High schools; Adolescent interpersonal relations

Age range(s): 15 - 18+

Major character(s): Jess, Teenager, Student—High School, 10th Grader, Outcast, Friend (former, of Char and Bizza); Bizza, Teenager, Student—High School, 10th Grader, Friend (former, of Jess), Friend (of Char); Char, Teenager, Student—High School, 10th Grader, Friend (former, of Jess), Friend (of Bizza)

Time period(s): 21st century; 2000s

Locale(s): United States

Summary: In Julie Halpern's *Into the Wild Nerd Yonder*, longtime friends Jess, Bizza, and Char realize that as they get older they have less in common. While Jess has a growing interest in sewing and studying, Bizza and Char are drawn toward partying and boys. When sophomore year begins, Bizza and Char adopt a punk lifestyle of shaved heads, oral sex, and rock bands over the friendship they once shared with Jess. Hurt and confused, Jess decides to go looking for friends elsewhere and finds herself in the middle of "nerdville" with a group of Dungeons and Dragons-obsessed peers. As Jess wrestles with the thought of what this new clique could do to her reputation, she learns a valuable lesson about true friendship, trust, and loyalty.

Where it's reviewed:
Booklist, November 15, 2009, page 35
Horn Book Magazine, November-December 2009, page 673
Publishers Weekly, October 19, 2009, page 55
School Library Journal, September 2009, page 161

Other books by the same author:
Don't Stop Now, 2011
Get Well Soon, 2007

Other books you might like:
A.J. Byrd, *Chasing Romeo*, 2009
Sarah Dessen, *What Happened to Goodbye*, 2011
Mandy Hubbard, *You Wish*, 2010
Leila Sales, *Mostly Good Girls*, 2010
Libby Schmais, *The Pillow Book of Lotus Lowenstein*, 2009

816

KERSTEN HAMILTON

Tyger Tyger
(New York: Clarion Books, 2010)

Series: Goblin Wars Series. Book 1
Story type: Fantasy; Series
Subject(s): Folklore; Fairy tales; Celts

Age range(s): 14 - 16+
Major character(s): Teagan Wylltson, 16-Year-Old, Friend (of Abby); Abby, Friend (of Teagan); Finn Mac Cumhaill, Traveler
Time period(s): 21st century; 2010s
Locale(s): Michigan, United States

Summary: This first novel in author Kersten Hamilton's Goblin Wars Series for young adults introduces 16-year-old Teagan Wylltson—a serious student whose world is about to take a fantastic turn. Teagan works hard at school and her part-time job and is looking forward to college unencumbered by teenage romance. When Teagan learns that her friend Abby is having nightmares about goblins that want to harm Teagan, Teagan attributes the dreams to Abby's strange imagination. Then Finn Mac Cumhaill, a handsome Irish boy, comes to stay with the Wyllstons. He reveals to Teagan that he is a goblin hunter and warns her that Abby's dreams are true. Teagan joins Finn on a quest that will uncover the truth about her family's magical past.

Where it's reviewed:
Booklist, November 1, 2010, page 65
Horn Book Guide, Spring 2010, page 368
Publishers Weekly, October 18, 2010, page 50
School Library Journal, December 2010, page 144
Voice of Youth Advocates, December 2010, page 471

Other books by the same author:
In the Forests of the Night, 2011

Other books you might like:
Hilari Bell, *The Goblin Gate*, 2010
Ann Coburn, *Glint*, 2007
Clare B. Dunkle, *The Hollow Kingdom*, 2003
O.R. Melling, *Chronicles of Faerie*, 2006

817

JENNY HAN

The Summer I Turned Pretty
(New York: Simon & Schuster Books for Young Readers, 2009)

Series: Summer Trilogy. Book 1
Subject(s): Coming of age; Interpersonal relations; Beaches

Age range(s): 13 - 16+
Major character(s): Mom, Mother (of Belly); Steven, Brother (of Belly); Susannah Fisher, Friend (of Belly's mother); Jeremiah, Son (of Susannah); Conrad, Son (of Susannah); Cam, Boyfriend (of Belly)
Time period(s): 21st century; 2000s
Locale(s): Cousins Beach, United States

Summary: In *The Summer I Turned Pretty* by Jenny Han, 15-year-old Isabel (Belly) looks forward to her family's annual trip to Cousins Beach, never imagining the surprises the summer will hold. When Belly, her mom, and her older brother Steven arrive at Susannah Fisher's familiar seaside house, they are reunited with Susannah's sons Jeremiah and Conrad. Both boys immediately recognize the physical changes in Belly, who will turn 16 over the summer. Jeremiah reveals his attraction to her while Belly pines for long-time crush Conrad. Meanwhile Belly falls for Cam, a new boy summering at Cousins Beach. This book is the first in a planned trilogy.

Where it's reviewed:
Publishers Weekly, April 27, 2009, page 133
School Librarian, Autumn 2010, page 176
School Library Journal, April 2009, page 134
Voice of Youth Advocates, August 2009, page 225

Other books by the same author:
We'll Always Have Summer, 2011
It's Not Summer Without You, 2010
Shug, 2006

Other books you might like:
Sarah Dessen, *Along for the Ride*, 2009
Sarah Dessen, *What Happened to Goodbye*, 2011
Garret Freymann-Weyr, *After the Moment*, 2009
Jenny Han, *It's Not Summer Without You*, 2010
Carolyn Mackler, *Tangled*, 2010

818

JENNY HAN

It's Not Summer Without You
(New York: Simon & Schuster Books for Young Readers, 2010)

Series: Summer Trilogy. Book 2
Subject(s): Romances (Fiction); Death; Grief

Age range(s): 13 - 16+
Major character(s): Isobel "Belly" Conklin, 16-Year-Old, Friend (of Jeremiah and Conrad); Jeremiah, Brother (of Conrad); Conrad, Brother (of Jeremiah), Runaway
Time period(s): 21st century; 2010s
Locale(s): Cousins Beach, United States

Summary: In *It's Not Summer Without You*, the sequel to *The Summer I Turned Pretty*, 16-year-old Isobel (Belly) is looking forward to another summer at Cousins Beach with two of her closest friends, Jeremiah and his brother, Conrad. Last summer, Conrad and Belly began dating, but this summer, the relationship is heading down a devastating road. This summer is not like last summer for many reasons, but mostly because last summer Conrad and Jeremiah's mother was alive. As the school year comes to an end, Conrad suddenly disappears. Jeremiah turns to Belly, who immediately agrees to help him find his brother. As they search, Belly and Jeremiah's relationship alters and when they find Conrad, they must come to terms with what has happened in the past and what will happen in the future.

Where it's reviewed:
Horn Book Guide, Fall 2010, page 368
Publishers Weekly, March 15, 2010, page 56
School Library Journal, October 2010, page 57

Other books by the same author:
We'll Always Have Summer, 2011
The Summer I Turned Pretty, 2009

Other books you might like:
Hailey Abbott, *Next Summer*, 2005
Pam Conrad, *Taking the Ferry Home*, 1988
Stewart O'Nan, *Wish You Were Here*, 2002

819

CYNTHIA HAND

Unearthly

(New York: HarperTeen, 2011)

Series: Unearthly Series. Book 1
Story type: Fantasy; Series
Subject(s): Angels; Supernatural; High schools

Age range(s): 13 - 16+
Major character(s): Clara Gardner, Angel (quarter-angel), 16-Year-Old; Christian, Classmate (of Clara), Football Player; Tucker, Classmate (of Clara), Twin (of Wendy); Wendy, Twin (of Tucker), Friend (of Clara); Angela, Friend (of Clara), Angel
Time period(s): 21st century; 2010s
Locale(s): California, United States; Jackson, Wyoming

Summary: In this young adult fantasy novel, the first book in Cynthia Hand's Unearthly Series, 16-year-old Clara Gardner discovers that she is an angel. The daughter of a half-angel mother, Clara is a quarter-angel—a Quartarius—who has been put on Earth to fulfill a specific mission. Her angelic duty begins to emerge in dreams of a forest fire that threatens a boy's life. With her mother's help, Clara determines that the fire will take place in Wyoming. The family immediately moves from California to Jackson so Clara can begin her work. There, she discovers that the boy who has haunted her dreams is a football player named Christian. Clara also learns that despite the strength and wings that her angel status brings, her job will not be an easy one. She must find out how she can protect Christian, but teenage distractions threaten to throw her off course. First novel.

Where it's reviewed:
Booklist, December 1, 2010, page 55
Publishers Weekly, November 15, 2010, page 58
School Library Journal, January 2011, page 106
Voice of Youth Advocates, February 2011, page 569

Other books by the same author:
Hallowed, 2012

Other books you might like:
Alexandra Adornetto, *Halo*, 2010
Becca Fitzpatrick, *Hush, Hush*, 2009
Lauren Kate, *Fallen*, 2009
Heather Terrell, *Fallen Angel*, 2011

820

ELIZABETH HAND

Illyria

(Hornsea, England, United Kingdom: PS Publishing, 2010)

Subject(s): Cousins; Love; Theater
Age range(s): 16 - 18+
Major character(s): Maddy, Teenager, Cousin (of Rogan); Rogan, Teenager, Cousin (of Maddy)
Time period(s): 20th century; 1970s
Locale(s): New York, New York

Summary: *Illyria* is a novella by Elizabeth Hand. Maddy and Rogan are cousins who were born on the same day. They like to think of themselves as twins. The two refer to themselves as the light and the dark, respectively, and pretend to be characters from ill-fated romances that fit that description. They have an unnatural love for one another that their parents forbid. When their high school drama teacher holds auditions for a romantic Shakespearean play, Maddy and Rogan try out for the two main characters, seeing it as a way to fulfill their secret desires. However, like the characters in the play, their relationship comes to a dramatic and tragic conclusion.

Where it's reviewed:
Booklist, May 15, 2010, page 46
Horn Book Magazine, July/August 2010, page 108
Publishers Weekly, April 26, 2010, page 111
Voice of Youth Advocates, August 2010, page 266

Awards the book has won:
World Fantasy Awards: Best Novella, 2008

Other books you might like:
Francesca Lia Block, *Wasteland*, 2003
Kathe Koja, *Talk*, 2005
Madeleine L'Engle, *The Joys of Love*, 2008
Linda Newbery, *Set in Stone*, 2006

821

DANIEL HANDLER
MAIRA KALMAN, Illustrator

Why We Broke Up

(New York: Little, Brown and Company, 2011)

Story type: Contemporary
Subject(s): Romances (Fiction); High schools; Dating (Social customs)

Age range(s): 15 - 18+
Major character(s): Min Green, Student—High School, Narrator, Girlfriend (former, of Ed); Ed Slaterton, Student—High School, Boyfriend (former, of Min)
Time period(s): 21st century; 2010s
Locale(s): United States

Summary: High school sweethearts Min Green and Ed Slaterton are calling it quits, and Min wants to make sure the reasons for their breakup are very clear in this young adult novel from author Daniel Handler. The book is written as a letter from Min to Ed outlining the various reasons for their failed relationship. Min drops a shoebox full of old mementos on Ed's porch, accompanied by the note. Min recounts their entire relationship, from their first chance meeting, to falling in love, losing her virginity, and recognizing the signs that they weren't destined for a happily-ever-after. The box's contents, including movie tickets, bottle caps, a toy truck, earrings, and a protractor, are vividly illustrated by Maira Kalman as Min explains their significance to the romance.

Where it's reviewed:
Publishers Weekly, November 14, 2011, page 55
School Library Journal, November 2011, page 124
Voice of Youth Advocates, December 2011, page 492

Other books by the same author:
The Basic Eight, 2006

Other books you might like:
Liz Gallagher, *The Opposite of Invisible*, 2008
Pete Hautman, *The Big Crunch*, 2011
Jandy Nelson, *The Sky Is Everywhere*, 2010
Adriana Trigiani, *Viola in Reel Life*, 2009

822

FRANCES HARDINGE

The Lost Conspiracy

(New York: Harper, 2009)

Subject(s): Sisters; Adventure; Colonialism
Age range(s): 10 - 14+
Major character(s): Arilou, Prophetess (oracle), Sister (of Hathin); Hathin, Sister (of Arilou), Assistant (to Arilou), 12-Year-Old
Time period(s): Indeterminate

Summary: Francis Hardinge's *The Lost Conspiracy* is a fantasy-adventure tale revolving around two sisters, Arilou and Hathin, who live on a mystical island plagued by ruthless colonials, traitorous natives, and violent mercenaries. Arilou has been recognized as a Lost, an esteemed oracle. But both sisters are harboring some dangerous secrets, and when they mistakenly become ensnared in a political plot, their lives are turned upside-down. Now they must venture forth into the wild of the island to save their own lives and fulfill their destinies.

Where it's reviewed:
Booklist, May 15, 2009, page 48
Bulletin of the Center for Children's Books, November 2009, page 112
Horn Book Magazine, September/October 2009, page 562

Publishers Weekly, September 7, 2009, page 47
School Library Journal, September 2009, page 161

Other books by the same author:
Fly Trap, 2011
Well Witched, 2008
Fly by Night, 2006
Fly by Night, 2006

Awards the book has won:
Blue Ribbon Awards: Fiction, 2009

Other books you might like:
Catherine Fisher, *Incarceron*, 2007
Terry Pratchett, *Nation*, 2008
Michelle Zink, *Prophecy of the Sisters*, 2009

823

RICHARD HARLAND

Worldshaker

(New York: Simon and Schuster, 2010)

Subject(s): Futuristic society; Social class; Friendship
Age range(s): 12 - 16+
Major character(s): Col Porpentine, 16-Year-Old; Riff, 14-Year-Old, Friend (of Col)
Time period(s): Indeterminate Future
Locale(s): United Kingdom

Summary: Set in a futuristic England, Richard Harland's *Worldshaker* finds 16-year-old Col Porpentine poised to take over his grandfather's coveted position within a large, mobile community. But Col's plans for a shining future are thrown off course when he meets 14-year-old Riff, a girl belonging to the lower class. Through his friendship with Riff, Col is introduced to the inner workings of the Worldshaker society, revealing the intricate hierarchies and social classes that he never knew existed.

Where it's reviewed:
Booklist, May 15, 2010, page 51
Publishers Weekly, May 10, 2010, page 47
Reading Time, August 2009, page 37
Voice of Youth Advocates, August 2010, page 266

Other books by the same author:
Liberator, 2012

Other books you might like:
Kenneth Oppel, *Airborn*, 2004
Philip Reeve, *Mortal Engines*, 2001
Scott Westerfeld, *Leviathan*, 2009

824

MICHAEL HARMON

Brutal

(New York, New York: Knopf, 2009)

Subject(s): Bullying; Coming of age; Popularity
Age range(s): 14 - 18+
Major character(s): Poe Holly, 16-Year-Old; Theo, Friend (of Poe); Velveeta, Friend (of Poe); Colby, Bully

Time period(s): 21st century; 2000s
Locale(s): California, United States

Summary: Michael Harmon's young-adult novel *Brutal* is a no-holds barred look at bullying in high schools. Sixteen-year-old Poe is starting over in a new town and a new school. Her well-meaning but slightly self-involved mother has gone to South Africa to practice medicine, leaving Poe in the care of the father she's never met. Her dad is a guidance counselor at Poe's new high school—an institution that favors the athletes and rich kids and ostracizes those who are different. Poe and her new friends are subjected to constant bullying from the other kids at the school. But when the pranks take a dangerous turn, Poe knows she has to do something to stop it.

Where it's reviewed:
Booklist, January 1, 2009, page 64
School Library Journal, June 2009, page 126

Other books by the same author:
The Chamber of Five, 2011
The Last Exit to Normal, 2008
Skate, 2006

Other books you might like:
Cecil Castellucci, *Beige*, 2007
Joshua Cohen, *Leverage*, 2011
J.E. MacLeod, *Waiting to Score*, 2009
Peter Marino, *Magic and Misery*, 2009
Marcella Pixley, *Freak*, 2007

825

KIM HARRINGTON

Clarity

(New York: Point, 2011)

Subject(s): Mystery; Murder; Supernatural

Age range(s): 14 - 17+

Major character(s): Clarity "Clare" Fern, 16-Year-Old, Psychic; Gabriel, Teenager, Son (of detective)

Time period(s): 21st century; 2010s

Locale(s): Massachusetts, United States

Summary: *Clarity* is a paranormal mystery for young adult readers from author Kim Harrington. Sixteen-year-old Clarity "Clare" Fern has a supernatural gift to see visions from the past and uncover emotions whenever she touches an object, something that makes her a bit of a tourist attraction in her small Cape Cod town but carries with it great responsibility. When a young girl is murdered, Clare's cheating ex-boyfriend begs her to help with the investigation. At first, Clare is reluctant until her supernaturally gifted brother is pegged as a suspect. Soon, Clare finds herself teaming up with Gabriel, the hot son of a new detective, to uncover the mysteries surrounding the killing in an attempt to track the murderer and clear her brother's name.

Where it's reviewed:
Booklist, March 15, 2011, page 54
Girls' Life, June-July 2011, page 57
Publishers Weekly, January 24, 2011, page 155
School Library Journal, March 2011, page 162

Other books by the same author:
Perception, 2012

Other books you might like:
Kristi Cook, *Haven*, 2011
Marlene Perez, *Dead Is a State of Mind*, 2009
Linda Joy Singleton, *Magician's Muse*, 2010

826

SONYA HARTNETT

Butterfly

(Somerville, Massachusetts: Candlewick Press, 2010)

Subject(s): Adolescent interpersonal relations; Family; Brothers and sisters

Age range(s): 14 - 18+

Major character(s): Plum, 14-Year-Old; Justin, Brother (of Plum and Cydar); Cydar, Brother (of Plum and Justin); Maureen, Neighbor (of Plum, Justin, and Cydar)

Time period(s): 21st century; 2010s

Locale(s): Australia

Summary: In *Butterfly*, author Sonya Hartnett charts the emotional story of an Australian family, centering on 14-year-old protagonist Plum. Plum is wandering through those years between childhood and adulthood, not entirely ready to give up the pleasures of her youth and also not prepared for the onset of maturity. She is close to her two brothers, Justin and Cydar, and strikes up a friendship with Maureen, the woman living next door. As her birthday approaches, Plum makes startling revelations about Maureen, her brother Justin, and her own relationships with her girlfriends.

Where it's reviewed:
Booklist, May 1, 2010, page 76
Horn Book Magazine, July/August 2010, page 108
Publishers Weekly, August 16, 2010, page 55
School Library Journal, August 2010, page 56
Voice of Youth Advocates, October 2010, page 348

Other books by the same author:
The Ghost's Child, 2008
The Silver Donkey, 2006
Surrender, 2006
Thursday's Child, 2002

Other books you might like:
Stephanie Greene, *Happy Birthday, Sophie Hartley*, 2010
Hilary McKay, *Forever Rose*, 2008
Jaclyn Moriarty, *The Spell Book of Listen Taylor: And the Secrets of the Family Zing*, 2007

827

PETE HAUTMAN

Blank Confession

(New York: Simon and Schuster Books for Young Readers, 2010)

Subject(s): Murder; Drugs; Adolescent interpersonal relations

Age range(s): 14 - 17+
Major character(s): Shayne Blank, 16-Year-Old; Mikey Martin, Friend (of Shayne)
Time period(s): 21st century; 2010s
Locale(s): United States

Summary: Pete Hautman's *Blank Confession* tells the story of 16-year-old Shayne Blank, who one day walks into a police station and confesses to murder. The story of that murder unfolds through flashbacks told by Mikey, Shayne's classmate and a victim of bullying. Readers gradually learn how the two boys get caught up in a drug deal gone wrong, resulting in a split-second decision that alters their lives forever.

Where it's reviewed:
Booklist, October 1, 2010, page 82
Horn Book Magazine, Nov.-Dec. 2010, page 93
Publishers Weekly, November 15, 2010, page 59
School Library Journal, December 2010, page 114
Voice of Youth Advocates, February 2011, page 554

Other books by the same author:
The Obsidian Blade, 2012
The Big Crunch, 2011
How to Steal a Car, 2009
Invisible, 2005
Godless, 2004

Awards the book has won:
Minnesota Book Awards, 2011

Other books you might like:
K.L. Going, *Saint Iggy*, 2006
Catherine Ryan Hyde, *Diary of a Witness*, 2009
Patrick Jones, *Chasing Tail Lights*, 2007
Anthony McGowan, *The Knife That Killed Me*, 2008
Nicky Singer, *Feather Boy*, 2002

828

PETE HAUTMAN

The Big Crunch

(New York: Scholastic Inc., 2011)

Story type: Coming-of-Age
Subject(s): Dating (Social customs); Adolescent interpersonal relations; High schools

Age range(s): 15 - 17+
Major character(s): June, 15-Year-Old, Girlfriend (of Wes); Wes, Boyfriend (of June)
Time period(s): 21st century; 2010s
Locale(s): Minneapolis, Minnesota

Summary: In this young adult novel by Pete Hautman, 15-year-old June is used to moving. She has already lived in six different towns, and now she has arrived in Minneapolis to start the year at another school. She is used to being the new girl and not having many friends. Then she meets Wes, a newly-single guy who broke up with his longtime girlfriend just before the beginning of the fall semester. Although June originally dates Wes's friend, she and Wes eventually cannot deny their attraction to one another. The only problem is, June knows that her family will have to move once again. Can these

teenagers keep their relationship intact even though they live far apart?

Where it's reviewed:
Booklist, January 1, 2011, page 88
Horn Book Magazine, January-February 2011, page 95
Publishers Weekly, November 29, 2011, page 51
School Library Journal, February 2011, page 109
Voice of Youth Advocates, February 2011, page 554

Other books by the same author:
Blank Confession, 2010
How to Steal a Car, 2009
All-In, 2007
Invisible, 2005
Sweetblood, 2003

Other books you might like:
Sarah Dessen, *The Truth about Forever*, 2004
John Green, *An Abundance of Katherines*, 2006
C. Leigh Purtill, *Love, Meg*, 2007

829

PETE HAUTMAN

How to Steal a Car

(New York: Scholastic Inc., 2009)

Subject(s): Adolescent interpersonal relations; Crime; Theft

Age range(s): 15 - 18+
Major character(s): Kelleigh Monahan, 15-Year-Old, Thief

Summary: *How to Steal a Car* is a young adult novel by author Pete Hautman. In it, Hautman tells the story of Kelleigh Monahan, a 15-year-old girl who faces some tough issues in the midst of her adolescence. Among those issues include the recent discovery of her father's affair: a revelation that could shake her seemingly perfect family apart. Unlike most teenagers, who may deal with similar issues through self-mutilation or illegal substances, Kelleigh has found a new way to cope: stealing cars. The first time she does it, it seems so easy. Now she is well on her way to an addiction that she can't cure, and doesn't really want to. Hautman is a winner of the 2004 National Book Award for his story *Godless*.

Where it's reviewed:
Booklist, August 1, 2009, page 57
Horn Book Magazine, November/December 2009, page 675
Publishers Weekly, September 14, 2009, page 50
School Library Journal, November 2009, page 108

Other books by the same author:
Blank Confession, 2010
The Big Crunch, 2008
All-In, 2007
Invisible, 2005
Godless, 2004

Other books you might like:
Cara Haycak, *Living on Impulse*, 2009
Patrick Jones, *Stolen Car*, 2008
Graham Joyce, *TWOC: Taken Without Owner Consent*, 2005

830

JUSTINA CHEN HEADLEY

North of Beautiful

(New York: Little, Brown Young Readers, 2009)

Subject(s): Beauty; Friendship; Courage

Age range(s): 11 - 17+

Major character(s): Terra, 16-Year-Old, Friend (of Jacob); Jacob, Teenager, Friend (of Terra)

Time period(s): 21st century; 2000s

Locale(s): China; United States

Summary: In *North of Beautiful*, two teenagers form a bond around their mutual physical insecurities and learn that true beauty is not something physical. While at the hospital for another failed operation to remove a large, wine-colored birthmark from her cheek, Terra meets Jacob, a handsome teen with a scar where his cleft lip was fixed. Terra and Jacob become friends quickly, and their mothers also form a bond. When Jacob's mother invites the two to join them on a journey to China, the mother and daughter see it as an opportunity to break away from Terra's abusive father. Terra and her mother find strength and companionship in the far east.

Where it's reviewed:
Booklist, February 15, 2009, page 81
Publishers Weekly, December 1, 2008, page 46
School Library Journal, February 2009, page 99
Voice of Youth Advocates, June 2009, page 136

Other books by the same author:
Girl Overboard, 2008
Nothing but the Truth (and a Few White Lies), 2006

Other books you might like:
Cheryl Klam, *The Pretty One*, 2008
Angela Morrison, *Sing Me to Sleep*, 2010
Renee Rosen, *Every Crooked Pot*, 2007
Rachel Vail, *Gorgeous*, 2009

831

KAREN HEALEY

Guardian of the Dead

(New York: Little, Brown and Company, 2010)

Subject(s): Adolescent interpersonal relations; Folklore; Theater

Age range(s): 15 - 18+

Major character(s): Ellie Spencer, 17-Year-Old, Martial Arts Expert; Reka Gordon, Actress; Mark Nolan, Student—College

Time period(s): 21st century; 2010s

Locale(s): New Zealand

Summary: Karen Healey's *Guardian of the Dead* follows 17-year-old Ellie Spencer, a boarding-school student who uses her martial-arts training to help choreograph a production at a nearby college. There she comes face to face with an actress named Reka, who has an eerie effect on Ellie, and the sexy Mark, who seems to be able to hypnotize people at will. As she becomes more and more involved in the production, Ellie begins to realize that Reka, Mark, and the rest of the gang have been swept up in an ancient battle of good and evil that has its roots in Maori folklore.

Where it's reviewed:
Booklist, March 15, 2010, page 38
Horn Book Magazine, July-August 2010, page 110
Publishers Weekly, March 29, 2010, page 60
School Library Journal, May 2010, page 116
Voice of Youth Advocates, June 2010, page 155

Other books by the same author:
The Shattering, 2011

Other books you might like:
Sam Enthoven, *The Black Tattoo*, 2006
Regina McBride, *The Fire Opal*, 2010
Kai Meyer, *The Stone Light*, 2007

832

KAREN HEALEY

The Shattering

(New York: Little, Brown and Company, 2011)

Story type: Paranormal

Subject(s): Suicide; Murder; Supernatural

Age range(s): 12 - 15+

Major character(s): Keri, 17-Year-Old, Sister (of suicide victim); Janna, Friend (of Keri), Sister (of suicide victim); Sione, Tourist, Brother (of suicide victim)

Time period(s): 21st century; 2010s

Locale(s): Summerton, New Zealand

Summary: In this young adult novel by Karen Healey, the seaside New Zealand town of Summerton holds a dark secret. Each year, not long after the annual New Year's celebration, a boy commits suicide. He may be a local or a visitor, but each leaves behind a younger sibling. Seventeen-year-old Keri and her friend Janna have both lost older brothers to apparent suicide. So has Sione, a tourist. But Sione doesn't believe that the deaths are suicides; he thinks they are murders. Together, Keri, Janna, and Sione search for the truth about their brothers' deaths and find unexpected answers. There is an ancient supernatural force at work in Summerton, and with December 31 not far off, the new year may bring a new death.

Where it's reviewed:
Booklist, September 15, 2011, page 64
Publishers Weekly, August 8, 2011, page 49
School Library Journal, September 2011, page 156
Voice of Youth Advocates, October 2011, page 384

Other books by the same author:
Guardian of the Dead, 2010

Other books you might like:
Franny Billingsley, *Chime*, 2011
Holly Black, *Curse Workers Series*, 2010
Joan Lowery Nixon, *Secret, Silent Screams*, 1988
Gregg Olsen, *Envy*, 2011
Dia Reeves, *Slice of Cherry*, 2011

833

DEBORAH HEILIGMAN

Charles and Emma: The Darwins' Leap of Faith

(New York: Henry Holt and Co., 2009)

Subject(s): Biographies; Evolution (Biology); Marriage

Age range(s): 14 - 18+

Major character(s): Charles Darwin, Scientist, Spouse (of Emma); Emma Darwin, Spouse (of Charles)

Time period(s): 19th century

Summary: Charles and Emma: The Darwins' Leap of Faith is a biographical novel for young adults by Deborah Heiligman. The book begins as Charles Darwin attempts to make a decision regarding whether to get married. He uses a pro/con list to help him make the decision. Eventually, he sees the advantages of marriage and weds a young woman named Emma. The two had a mostly happy marriage, despite some religious differences that caused quite the debate between husband and wife. In addition, the book contains many documents and letters from the Darwin family's history. The book also includes information on how Darwin's theory of evolution changed over time.

Where it's reviewed:
Booklist, January 1, 2009, page 68
Horn Book Magazine, January-February 2009, page 115
New York Times, May 10, 2009, page 13
Publishers Weekly, December 15, 2008, page 53
School Library Journal, January 2009, page 127

Other books by the same author:
Holidays around the World, 2007
High Hopes: A Photobiography of John F. Kennedy, 2003

Awards the book has won:
Blue Ribbon Awards: Non-fiction, 2008

Other books you might like:
Jonathan Clements, Darwin's Notebook: The Life, Times and Discoveries of Charles Robert Darwin, 2009
Christopher Hitchens, Hitch-22, 2010
Kathleen Krull, Charles Darwin, 2010
Rebecca Newberger Goldstein, 36 Arguments for the Existence of God: A Work of Fiction, 2010
Rebecca Skloot, The Immortal Life of Henrietta Lacks, 2009

834

STEPHANIE HEMPHILL

Wicked Girls: A Novel of the Salem Witch Trials

(New York: Balzer + Bray, 2010)

Subject(s): Trials; Adolescent interpersonal relations; United States history, 1600-1775 (Colonial period)

Age range(s): 13 - 18+

Major character(s): Mercy Lewis, Teenager; Ann Putnam, 12-Year-Old; Margaret Walcott, Teenager

Time period(s): 17th century; 1690s

Locale(s): Salem, Massachusetts

Summary: In Wicked Girls: A Novel of the Salem Witch Trials, author Stephanie Hemphill chronicles the events of the historic 17th-century witch trials from the perspective of the girls who made the damning accusations. Told in verse, this volume follows the girls as they make claims against their fellow townspeople and watch them hang—all as the group slowly starts to unravel from within, and the accusations the girls make become more and more treacherous.

Where it's reviewed:
Booklist, June 1, 2010, page 70
Horn Book Magazine, July-August 2010, page 111
Publishers Weekly, July 5, 2010, page 44
School Library Journal, August 2010, page 102
Voice of Youth Advocates, October 2010, page 348

Other books by the same author:
Your Own Sylvia: A Verse Portrait of Sylvia Plath, 2007
Things Left Unsaid: A Novel in Poems, 2005

Other books you might like:
Marc Aronson, Witch-Hunt: Mysteries of the Salem Witch Trials, 2003
Julie Hearn, The Minister's Daughter, 2005
Katherine Howe, The Physick Book of Deliverance Dane, 2009
Anna Myers, Time of the Witches, 2009
Elizabeth George Speare, The Witch of Blackbird Pond, 1958

835

APRIL HENRY

Girl, Stolen

(New York: Henry Holt and Company, 2010)

Subject(s): Theft; Kidnapping; Suspense

Age range(s): 13 - 16+

Major character(s): Cheyenne Wilder, 16-Year-Old, Kidnap Victim, Blind Person; Griffin, Thief, Kidnapper, Teenager

Time period(s): 21st century; 2010s

Locale(s): United States

Summary: Girl, Stolen is a suspenseful novel for young adult readers from author April Henry. Cheyenne Wilder's mom makes a quick stop at the pharmacy to fill a prescription, leaving the 16-year-old asleep in the backseat. Before Cheyenne knows what's going on, the Escalade is stolen while she's inside! Rebellious teenager Griffin was sent by his father and a gang of thugs to boost the car, but he never expected to add kidnapping to his rap sheet. Once Griffin and the crew learn that Cheyenne's dad is a powerful and successful businessman, they decide to hold the teen for ransom. But their plans are made increasingly more difficult when they discover that she's blind and suffering from pneumonia.

Where it's reviewed:
Booklist, September 15, 2010, page 64

Publishers Weekly, September 20, 2010, page 67
School Library Journal, October 2010, page 118
Voice of Youth Advocates, August 2010, page 247

Other books by the same author:
Torched, 2009
Shock Point, 2006

Other books you might like:
Andrew Clements, *Things That Are*, 2008
Michael Coleman, *On the Run*, 2004
Norah McClintock, *Taken*, 2009

836

GEOFF HERBACH

Stupid Fast: The Summer I Went from a Joke to a Jock

(Naperville, Illinois: Sourcebooks, 2011)

Subject(s): Sports; Adolescence; Brothers

Age range(s): 13 - 17+

Major character(s): Felton Reinstein, 11th Grader, Brother (of Andrew), Son (of Jerri), Football Player, Runner, Boyfriend (of Aleah); Aleah, Girlfriend (of Felton), Student—High School; Jerri Reinstein, Widow(er), Single Mother, Mother (of Felton and Andrew); Andrew Reinstein, Brother (of Felton)

Time period(s): 21st century; 2010s

Locale(s): United States

Summary: Last year, Felton Reinstein was the last guy picked for teams in gym class. He was also ignored by all the girls in his high school. This year, Felton is hard to miss. He's taller, he's stronger, and he's hairier. The thing that's winning everyone over, however, is his newfound speed. Felton now runs faster than most of the guys in school—and the girls are impressed. The school's coaches ask Felton to try out for their teams, and for the first time in Felton's life, he's receiving respect and praise instead of snide comments from the jocks he passes in the hallways. Even Aleah, the girl he has a crush on, is giving him the attention he's always wanted. These accomplishments don't do much for his home life, though. Felton's brother, Andrew, won't stop being weird and his hippie mom, Jerri, can't let go of the past. In this book, Felton tries to find a way to bring his happiness and success at school into his house to heal his family's wounds.

Where it's reviewed:
Booklist, May 15, 2011, page 48
Bulletin of the Center for Children's Books, June 2011, page 472
Publishers Weekly, April 25, 2011, page 139
School Library Journal, August 2011, page 106
Voice of Youth Advocates, June 2011, page 166

Other books by the same author:
Nothing Special, 2012

Other books you might like:
Jessi Kirby, *Moonglass*, 2011
Han Nolan, *Crazy*, 2010
Tim Tharp, *Knights of the Hill Country*, 2006

837

DAVID HERNANDEZ

No More Us for You

(New York: HarperCollins, 2009)

Subject(s): Friendship; Conduct of life; Death

Age range(s): 15 - 18+

Major character(s): Carlos, Student—High School, 17-Year-Old; Isabel, Student—High School, 17-Year-Old; Vanessa, Student—High School (transfer student), 17-Year-Old

Time period(s): 21st century; 2000s

Locale(s): Long Beach, California

Summary: David Hernandez tells a story of love, friendship, and mortality in *No More Us for You*. Seventeen-year-old Carlos is a part-time museum guard who attends school at Millikan High in Long Beach, California. Carlos's life is seemingly carefree, except for the apparent infidelity of his girlfriend. Isabel attends the same school, but her life is full of worry. The young woman is still trying to move past the terrible car accident that claimed the life of her boyfriend over a year ago. Carlos and Isabel have never met, but their lives intersect when they meet Vanessa—a transfer student who befriends both teens. The lives of all three are turned upside down when they decide to go out together one evening after work.

Where it's reviewed:
Booklist, January 1, 2009, page 70
School Library Journal, July 2009, page 84
Voice of Youth Advocates, February 2009, page 529

Other books by the same author:
Suckerpunch, 2007

Other books you might like:
Justina Chen Headley, *North of Beautiful*, 2009
Emily Horner, *A Love Story Starring My Dead Best Friend*, 2010
Francisco X. Stork, *The Last Summer of The Death Warriors*, 2010
Jenny Valentine, *Broken Soup*, 2009

838

WILL HILL

Department 19

(New York: Razorbill, 2011)

Subject(s): Supernatural; Vampires; Murder

Age range(s): 15 - 18+

Major character(s): Jamie Carpenter, 16-Year-Old, Agent (Department 19); Frankenstein, Monster; Mrs. Carpenter, Mother (of Jamie)

Time period(s): 21st century; 2010s

Locale(s): England

Summary: Sixteen-year-old Jamie Carpenter is conscripted into England's most secret government agency in Will Hill's young-adult novel *Department 19*. Jamie witnesses both his father's murder and his mother's abduction, but is protected from Mrs. Carpenter's terrifying captor by a monster named Frankenstein. When Jamie is brought to Department 19 he learns shocking truths about England's history. Vampires exist and have posed a threat to humans for centuries. Vampire slayers also exist—in fact, Jamie's father was one. The books *Dracula* and *Frankenstein* are not fiction but histories that chronicle England's long battle against supernatural forces. Armed with this new knowledge, Jamie sets out to save his mother from the vampire who holds her.

Where it's reviewed:
Booklist, May 15, 2011, page 55
Publishers Weekly, February 7, 2011, page 59
School Library Journal, June 2011, page 119
Voice of Youth Advocates, June 2011, page 185

Other books you might like:
D.M. Cornish, *Monster Blood Tattoo series*, 2006-
Alyxandra Harvey, *Out for Blood*, 2010
Kenneth Oppel, *This Dark Endeavor: The Apprenticeship of Victor Frankenstein*, 2011
Mary Shelley, *Frankenstein: The Modern Prometheus*, 1818
Lynn Viehl, *After Midnight*, 2011

839

GARETH HINDS, Author/Illustrator

The Odyssey
(Somerville, Massachusetts: Candlewick Press, 2010)

Subject(s): Poetry; Fantasy; Mythology

Age range(s): 14 - 18+

Major character(s): Odysseus, Warrior; Calypso, Deity; Poseidon, Deity

Summary: Gareth Hinds translates Homer's masterpiece *The Odyssey* into graphic novel format. The story revolves around a Greek warrior named Odysseus who has completed battle in the Trojan War. While those he left at home, including his wife Penelope, believe he has died in battle, Odysseus is in fact alive and well. The story begins 10 years after the war ends, and Odysseus is attempting to make his journey home. Along the way, he experiences a variety of terrifying ordeals, including captivity at the hands of Calypso and a very angry sea god named Poseidon. Hinds is also the author of the graphic novel adaptation of *Beowulf*.

Where it's reviewed:
Booklist, September 15, 2010, page 56
Horn Book Magazine, November/December 2010, page 114
Publishers Weekly, September 6, 2010, page 43
School Library Journal, November 2010, page 145

Other books by the same author:
King Lear, 2009
The Merchant of Venice, 2008
Beowulf, 2007

Other books you might like:
Edith Hamilton, *Mythology: Timeless Tales of Gods and Heroes*, 1942

George O'Connor, *Zeus: King of the Gods*, 2010
Rick Riordan, *The Lightning Thief*, 2005
Anne Ursu, *The Shadow Thieves*, 2006
Jane Yolen, *Odysseus in the Serpent Maze*, 2001

840

CHRISTINE HINWOOD

The Returning
(New York: Dial Books, 2011)

Subject(s): Wars; Interpersonal relations; Family

Age range(s): 15 - 18+

Major character(s): Cam Attling, 18-Year-Old, Amputee; Graceful Fenister, Fiance(e) (of Cam); Diido, Young Woman; Lord Gyaar, Nobleman

Time period(s): 11th century

Locale(s): Kayforl, Fictional Location

Summary: Set in a fictional medieval era, Christine Hinwood's young adult novel *The Returning* examines the effects of war on a young survivor and the people in his life. Cam Attling was just 12 years old when he left Kayforl to fight in the ongoing battle between the Uplanders and Downlanders. His young body was whole then, and he was engaged to Graceful Fenister. Six years later he has returned to his village after losing an arm in a conflict that killed all the other soldiers from Kayforl. Cam's mysterious survival and his disfiguring injury draw the distrust of his family and neighbors, and Graceful's father reneges on the marriage pact. Confused and disheartened, Cam journeys back to Lord Gyaar, the son of the man who cut off his arm and saved his life. First novel.

Where it's reviewed:
Booklist, May 1, 2011, page 84
Bulletin of the Center for Children's Books, April 2011, page 375
Horn Book Magazine, May-June 2011, page 93
Publishers Weekly, February 14, 2011, page 58
Voice of Youth Advocates, June 2011, page 186

Other books you might like:
Katy Moran, *Bloodline*, 2009
Marcus Sedgwick, *My Swordhand Is Singing*, 2007
Jonathan Stroud, *Heroes of the Valley*, 2009

841

WILL HOBBS

Take Me to the River
(New York: Harper, 2011)

Subject(s): Canoeing; Cousins; Adventure

Age range(s): 10 - 14+

Major character(s): Dylan Sands, 14-Year-Old, Cousin (of Rio); Rio, 15-Year-Old, Cousin (of Dylan); Carlos, Kidnapper

Time period(s): 21st century; 2010s

Locale(s): Rio Grande, American Southwest

Summary: *Take Me to the River*, an adventure novel for children and young adults by Will Hobbs, follows the ill-fated Rio Grande canoe trip of teenage cousins Dylan and Rio. Dylan Sands comes to Texas from North Carolina to run the river with his older cousin Rio. The trip will be a dangerous one, but Rio knows the river well and shrugs off warnings about an approaching hurricane. On their 10-day journey, the boys learn that weather and wildlife are not the only dangers on the river. A man named Carlos arrives at their campsite on the riverbank accompanied by a frightened young boy, and Dylan and Rio must think fast if they are to survive their adventure.

Where it's reviewed:
Booklist, Feburary 1, 2011, page 80
Horn Book Magazine, March/April 2011, page 118
School Library Journal, April 2011, page 174
Voice of Youth Advocates, June 2011, page 166

Other books by the same author:
Go Big or Go Home, 2008
Jackie's Wild Seattle, 2003
Down the Yukon, 2001
Jason's Gold, 1999
Downriver, 1991

Other books you might like:
Tom Birdseye, *Storm Mountain*, 2010
Dee Garretson, *Wildfire Run*, 2010
Charlie Higson, *Hurricane Gold: A James Bond Adventure*, 2009
P.J. Petersen, *White Water*, 1997
S.L. Rottman, *Rough Waters*, 1998

842

ALICE HOFFMAN

Green Witch

(New York: Scholastic Press, 2010)

Age range(s): 14 - 18+
Major character(s): Green, 16-Year-Old; Heather, Friend (of Green); Diamond, Lover (of Green)
Time period(s): Indeterminate
Locale(s): Fictional Location

Summary: In *Green Witch* by Alice Hoffman, an attack by an invading force called the Horde left the city in ruins and the surrounding villages struggling for survival. In the year since the catastrophe, Green, a teenage girl with supernatural powers, nurtures her garden back to life as she gathers the tales of fellow survivors. Knowing that there are other survivors being held captive by the Horde in an island prison, Green sets out on a dangerous journey to set them free. But Green is also on another quest—to find the silent young man named Diamond who took her heart with him when he disappeared.

Where it's reviewed:
Booklist, January 1, 2010, page 67
Horn Book Guide, Fall 2010, page 370
Publishers Weekly, February 22, 2010, page 69
School Library Journal, May 2010, page 116
Voice of Youth Advocates, October 2010, page 366

Other books by the same author:
Incantation, 2006
Green Angel, 2003
Indigo, 2002
Aquamarine, 2001

Other books you might like:
Francesca Lia Block, *Blood Roses*, 2008
Penny Blubaugh, *Serendipity Market*, 2009
Beth Kephart, *Nothing but Ghosts*, 2009
Melissa Marr, *Ink Exchange*, 2008
Chris Wooding, *Poison*, 2005

843

ELLEN HOPKINS

Tricks

(New York: Margaret K. McElderry, 2009)

Subject(s): Adolescence; Adolescent interpersonal relations; Parent-child relations

Age range(s): 16 - 18+
Major character(s): Eden, Teenager, Religious; Seth, Teenager, Homosexual; Whitney, Teenager; Ginger, Teenager, Daughter (of a prostitute); Cody, Teenager, Addict
Time period(s): 21st century; 2000s
Locale(s): United States

Summary: *Tricks* is a young adult novel in verse by Ellen Hopkins. The book focuses on the lives of five unconnected teenagers facing difficult situations. When Eden's religious parents discover that she has a boyfriend, they decide to send her to a home for troubled teens. After the death of his mother, gay teen Seth struggles to relate to his distant, traditional father. Whitney feels stifled by her older sister's success and seeks companionship in inappropriate places. Ginger and her siblings move in with their grandmother when their prostitute mother can no longer provide for them. Cody seems to have his life together, but he's hiding a secret that could endanger himself and his loved ones.

Where it's reviewed:
Booklist, August 1, 2009, page 62
Publishers Weekly, July 20, 2009, page 141
School Library Journal, October 2009, page 128
Voice of Youth Advocates, August 2009, page 226

Other books by the same author:
Fallout, 2010
Identical, 2008
Glass, 2007
Impulse, 2007
Burned, 2006

Other books you might like:
Julia Bell, *Dirty Work*, 2007
E.R. Frank, *Life Is Funny*, 2000
Barry Lyga, *Boy Toy*, 2007
Adam Rapp, *33 Snowfish*, 2003
Willo Davis Roberts, *Blood on His Hands*, 2004

844

SILAS HOUSE

Eli the Good

(Somerville, Massachusetts: Candlewick Press, 2009)

Subject(s): Vietnam War, 1959-1975; Adolescence; Family relations

Age range(s): 14 - 18+

Major character(s): Eli Book, Teenager, Friend (of Edie); Edie, Friend (of Eli), Teenager

Time period(s): 20th century; 1970s (1976)

Summary: *Eli the Good* is a young adult novel by author Silas House. In this novel, House tells the story of a teenage boy named Eli Book. In the summer of 1976, Eli is eager to celebrate America's Bicentennial with the rest of the country, but issues within his family dampen the excitement. His father, a veteran of the Vietnam conflict, regularly argues with his aunt, who opposed the war and has recently come to live with their family. His sister is becoming more antiestablishmentarian by the moment. Worst of all, his best friend Edie is facing her parent's divorce, and Eli has lost his longtime confidante. Now it's up to Eli to grow up and come of age as everyone around him seems to be falling apart.

Where it's reviewed:
Booklist, October 1, 2009, page 34
Horn Book Guide, Spring 2010, page 98
Publishers Weekly, September 21, 2009, page 59
School Library Journal, January 2010, page 104

Other books you might like:
Kathryn Jensen, *Pocket Change*, 1989
Lyn Miller-Lachmann, *Gringolandia*, 2009
Gary Paulsen, *Soldier's Heart*, 1998

845

JAMES HOWE

Addie on the Inside

(New York: Atheneum Books for Young Readers, 2011)

Story type: Coming-of-Age

Subject(s): Coming of age; Adolescence; Adolescent interpersonal relations

Age range(s): 10 - 13+

Major character(s): Addie Carle, 13-Year-Old

Time period(s): 21st century; 2010s

Locale(s): Paintbrush Falls, United States

Summary: In this young adult novel by James Howe, a young girl changes as she becomes a teenager and begins to leave her childish ways behind. The girl is 13-year-old Addie Carle, who grew up hanging out with male friends and always enjoyed being outgoing, loud, and bossy. As she becomes a teenager, however, she starts feeling uncomfortable with that role. She starts having a hard time being as forthright as she used to be now that she is experiencing some of the hard parts of life, such as bullying, a broken heart, and the death of a pet. Addie eases off her old tough image and starts writing poetry to

sort out her feelings. Soon, Addie concludes that she's growing up and it's up to her to define her own personality before other people try to do so for her.

Where it's reviewed:
Booklist, June 1, 2011, page 85
New York Times Book Review, August 21, 2011, page 12
Publishers Weekly, May 16, 2011, page 73
School Library Journal, August 2011, page 107

Other books by the same author:
Totally Joe, 2005
The Misfits, 2001

Other books you might like:
Marion Dane Bauer, *Am I Blue?: Coming out from the Silence*, 1994
Catherine Gilbert Murdock, *Princess Ben: Being a Wholly Truthful Account of Her Various Discoveries and Misadventures, Recounted to the Best of Her Recollection, in Four Parts*, 2008
Kimberly Willis Holt, *When Zachary Beaver Came to Town*, 1999
Hilary McKay, *Permanent Rose*, 2005
Naomi Shihab Nye, *A Maze Me: Poems for Girls*, 2005

846

HOLLY NICOLE HOXTER

The Snowball Effect

(New York: HarperTeen, 2010)

Story type: Contemporary

Subject(s): Death; Brothers and sisters; Family life

Age range(s): 14 - 17+

Major character(s): Lainey Pike, 17-Year-Old, Sister (of Collin), Stepsister (of Vallery), Girlfriend (of Riley); Collin, 5-Year-Old, Brother (of Lainey and Vallery), Emotionally Impaired Child; Vallery, Stepsister (of Lainey), Sister (of Collin); Riley, Boyfriend (of Lainey)

Time period(s): 21st century; 2010s

Locale(s): Maryland, United States

Summary: Author Holly Nicole Hoxter explores the topic of teenage grief in this young adult novel. At 17, Lainey Pike has experienced more tragedy in a year than many people do in a lifetime. Her stepfather was killed in a motorcycle wreck, her grandmother died from a stroke, and her mother committed suicide shortly after Lainey's high school graduation. The surviving figures in Lainey's world are her emotionally troubled brother Collin, her stepsister Vallery, and her too-good-to-be-true boyfriend Riley. As Lainey tries to make sense of her family's misfortune, she breaks up with Riley and embarks on a relationship with an older guy she meets at a convenience store. Over hamburgers and snowballs, Lainey and her new friend try to sort out her complicated life. First novel.

Where it's reviewed:
Booklist, February 15, 2010, page 72
Horn Book Guide, Fall 2010, page 371
Publishers Weekly, March 22, 2010, page 70

School Library Journal, April 2010, page 160

Other books you might like:
Jillian Cantor, *The Life of Glass*, 2010
Kimberly Willis Holt, *Keeper of the Night*, 2003
Jandy Nelson, *The Sky Is Everywhere*, 2010

847

JENNIFER R. HUBBARD

The Secret Year

(New York: Viking Juvenile, 2010)

Subject(s): Love; Death; Social class

Age range(s): 15 - 18+

Major character(s): Colton "Colt" Morrissey, 16-Year-Old, Boyfriend (of Julia); Julia Vernon, Girlfriend (of Colt)

Time period(s): 21st century; 2010s

Locale(s): United States

Summary: A young man mourns the loss of his girlfriend in *The Secret Year*. Colt and Julia seem like the most unlikely couple. While Julia is popular and rich, Colt is poor and unknown. But despite these differences, the two share a romance that only they know about. However, their relationship ends tragically when Julia dies in a car accident. Now, Colt must learn how to cope, but how can he properly mourn the love of his life when no one else was aware of their love? During Colt's struggle, he is given Julia's diary, which recounts the year they spent together. Colt relives that year through Julia's eyes and slowly comes to terms with his grief. First novel.

Where it's reviewed:
Booklist, December 1, 2009, page 37
Horn Book Guide, Fall 2010, page 371
Publishers Weekly, December 14, 2009, page 60
School Library Journal, February 2010, page 112

Other books you might like:
Simone Elkeles, *Perfect Chemistry*, 2009
Sarah Ockler, *Twenty Boy Summer*, 2009
Todd Strasser, *Stolen Kisses, Secrets, and Lies*, 2007

848

JENNY HUBBARD

Paper Covers Rock

(New York: Random House, 2011)

Story type: Coming-of-Age

Subject(s): Conduct of life; Death; Boarding schools

Age range(s): 15 - 18+

Major character(s): Alex, 16-Year-Old, Student—Boarding School, Friend (of Glenn); Glenn, Student—Boarding School, Friend (of Alex); Miss Dovecott, Teacher

Time period(s): 20th century; 1980s

Locale(s): North Carolina, United States

Summary: In her debut novel, author Jenny Hubbard tells the story of a young man who must deal with both grief and shame after his friend is killed in a freak accident. Alex is a 16-year-old high school junior who attends a boarding school. While swimming at a nearby river, a fellow classmate drowns as Alex and his friend Glenn look on. Ashamed that they couldn't do more to save their friend, both Glenn and Alex evade questions from the police, and attempt to hide the truth of their failed rescue. Meanwhile, Alex shelters himself in a world filled with his own poetry. When Alex's English teacher, Miss Dovecott, discovers his writings, she attempts to draw Alex out of his shell. But will Alex's talent threaten his reputation at school and his tenuous friendship with Glenn? First novel.

Where it's reviewed:
Booklist, July 1, 2011, page 53
Horn Book Magazine, July-August 2011, page 150
Publishers Weekly, April 25, 2011, page 139
School Library Journal, June 2011, page 120
Voice of Youth Advocates, June 2011, page 166

Other books you might like:
Ariela Anhalt, *Freefall*, 2010
John Knowles, *A Separate Peace*, 1959
Nancy Werlin, *Black Mirror*, 2001

849

MANDY HUBBARD

You Wish

(New York: Razorbill, 2010)

Subject(s): Wishes; Birthdays; Adolescence

Age range(s): 12 - 15+

Major character(s): Kayla McHenry, 16-Year-Old

Time period(s): 21st century; 2010s

Locale(s): United States

Summary: *You Wish* is a humorous novel for young adult readers from author Mandy Hubbard. Kayla McHenry's 16th birthday is less sweet, more sour. Her dad left, her grades are at an all-time low, and her best friend, Nicole, is dating Ben, the guy who Kayla has been in love with for three years. While blowing out her candles, Kayla makes a wish that her birthday wishes would actually come true for once. To Kayla's surprise, the next several days bring the realization of her past birthday wishes. Kayla is overwhelmed by her life-sized My Little Pony, fantastically large breasts, and a year's supply of gumballs. But as her wishes continue to become a reality, she's nervously anticipating the wish from her 15th birthday when she prayed that Ben, the guy who is now her best friend's boyfriend, would finally kiss her.

Where it's reviewed:
Booklist, September 15, 2010, page 73
School Library Journal, February 2011, page 110
Voice of Youth Advocates, October 2010, page 350

Other books by the same author:
Ripple, 2011
Prada and Prejudice, 2009

Other books you might like:
Alexandra Bullen, *Wish*, 2010
Julie Halpern, *Into the Wild Nerd Yonder*, 2009

Jackson Pearce, *As You Wish*, 2009

850

PAT HUGHES

Five 4ths of July

(New York: Viking, 2011)

Story type: Historical - American Revolution
Subject(s): American Revolution, 1775-1783; Adolescent interpersonal relations; United States history

Age range(s): 12+, 14 - 17+
Major character(s): Jake Mallory, Military Personnel, 14-Year-Old
Time period(s): 18th century; 1770s-1780s (1777-1782)
Locale(s): United States; Connecticut, United States

Summary: In this historical young adult novel set in the midst of the American Revolution, author Pat Hughes tells the story of Jake Mallory, a teenager growing up in a small Connecticut town. Although he is thrilled that America has declared its independence from Britain, Jake has more pressing matters to deal with in his personal life. Most importantly, Jack wants to lead a life full of excitement far away from his father's stern, watchful eye. In hopes of finding his longed-for adventure, Jake leaves home to fight the British. Soon after enlisting, Jake finds himself in the middle of his nation's battle for freedom. He is then taken prisoner on a British ship, and he must fight for his own independence. In the years following, he continues to fight and evade danger. Then, he returns to his hometown in Connecticut.

Where it's reviewed:
Booklist, May 15, 2011, page 45
Horn Book Guide, Fall 2011, page 385
School Library Journal, June 2011, page 120
Voice of Youth Advocates, August 2011, page 271

Other books by the same author:
Guerrilla Season, 2009
Seeing the Elephant: A Story of the Civil War, 2007
The Breaker Boys, 2004

Other books you might like:
Laurie Halse Anderson, *Forge*, 2010
Laurie Calkhoven, *Daniel at the Siege of Boston, 1776*, 2010
Bonnie Pryor, *Pirate Hannah Pritchard: Captured!*, 2010
G. Clifton Wisler, *Kings Mountain*, 2002

851

AMY HUNTLEY

The Everafter

(New York: Balzer + Bray, 2009)

Subject(s): Death; Friendship; Interpersonal relations

Age range(s): 14 - 17+
Major character(s): Madison Stanton, 17-Year-Old

Time period(s): 21st century; 2000s
Locale(s): Is, Alternate Universe

Summary: In *The Everafter* by Amy Huntley, 17-year-old Madison Stanton has died unexpectedly and is now adrift in an alternate state she calls "Is." Although not fully conscious of her situation, Maddy gradually becomes aware of her surroundings—a black abyss populated by glowing objects. As Maddy learns, each of these items is a souvenir from her brief life—a baby toy, a barrette, a special sweatshirt. By touching them, Maddy discovers that she can revisit specific moments from her childhood and adolescence—happy, sad, and painful—and even manipulate the outcomes. Maddy also learns that she is not alone on her journey through "Is." First novel.

Where it's reviewed:
Booklist, August 1, 2009, page 55
Horn Book Guide, Spring 2010, page 98
Publishers Weekly, October 26, 2009, page 59
School Library Journal, December 2009, page 122

Other books you might like:
Kim Harrison, *Once Dead, Twice Shy*, 2009
Lauren Oliver, *Before I Fall*, 2010
Neal Shusterman, *Everlost*, 2006
Neal Shusterman, *Everwild*, 2009
Gabrielle Zevin, *Elsewhere*, 2005

852

KIM DONG HWA

The Color of Earth

(New York: First Second, 2009)

Subject(s): Mother-daughter relations; Love; Koreans

Age range(s): 15 - 18+
Major character(s): Ehwa, Daughter; Mother, Mother (of Ehwa); Picture Man, Salesman, Boyfriend (of Ehwa's mother)
Time period(s): 21st century; 2000s
Locale(s): Korea, South

Summary: Graphic novelist Kim Dong Hwa crafts a tender tale of mothers, daughters, and the unbreakable bonds they share. *The Color of Earth* traces the experiences of Ehwa and her widowed mother as they work in a local pub to make ends meet. Ehwa is heartbroken that those around her condemn her mother for being single, and the two slowly find themselves alienated from the rest of the community. But as the two women age, Ehwa watches her mother fall in love with a traveling salesman. Witnessing such passion in her normally staid parent, Ehwa is inspired and begins to hope for that kind of love in her own life.

Where it's reviewed:
Booklist, June 1, 2009, page 64
Publishers Weekly, April 20, 2009, page 38
School Library Journal, September 2009, page 192
Teacher Librarian, April 2010, page 27

Other books by the same author:
The Color of Heaven, 2009
The Color of Water, 2009

Other books you might like:
Derek Kirk Kim, *Good as Lily*, 2007
Anne Sibley O'Brien, *The Legend of Hong Kil Dong: The Robin Hood of Korea*, 2008
Mariko Tamaki, *Skim*, 2008
Mi-Kyung Yun, *Bride of the Water God*, 2007

853

DAISUKE IGARASHI, Author/Illustrator

Children of the Sea, Volume 1

(San Francisco: VIZ Media, 2009)

Series: Children of the Sea Series. Book 1
Story type: Adventure; Fantasy
Subject(s): Fishes; Mystery; Oceanography

Age range(s): 12 - 16+
Major character(s): Ruka, Teenager; Umi, Boy, Friend (of Sora and Ruka); Sora, Boy, Friend (of Umi and Ruka)
Time period(s): 21st century; 2010s

Summary: Strange disappearances and unexplained occurrences combine in this manga mystery. Fish are disappearing from aquariums worldwide, and children living in the oceans are being discovered. Lonely Ruka saw one such disappearance when she was a young child, but nobody believed her story that the fish disappeared in a flash of light. Now the teen has met two young boys raised in the ocean by dugongs, aquatic mammals. Like Ruka, Umi and Sora can hear the call of the sea. The three work together to find answers to these mysteries, despite the disregard of adults too preoccupied by their work to see the clues in front of them. This book serves as an introduction to the Children of the Sea series.

Where it's reviewed:
Booklist, November 1, 2009, page 34
Publishers Weekly, April 20, 2009, page 38

Other books by the same author:
Children of the Sea, Volume 3, 2010
Children of the Sea, Volume 4, 2010
Children of the Sea, Volume 2, 2009

Other books you might like:
Diane Duane, *Deep Wizardry*, 1985
Hisae Iwaoka, *Saturn Apartments*, 2010
Kazuhiro Okamoto, *Translucent, Volume 1*, 2007
Shaun Tan, *Tales from Outer Suburbia*, 2009
Craig Thompson, *Good-bye, Chunky Rice*, 2004

854

CARLA JABLONSKI
LELAND PURVIS, Illustrator

Resistance

(New York: First Second, 2010)

Series: Resistance Trilogy. Book 1
Subject(s): World War II, 1939-1945; Friendship; French (European people)

Age range(s): 12 - 16+
Major character(s): Paul, Brother (of Marie), Friend (of Henri); Marie, Sister (of Paul), Friend (of Henri); Henri, Friend (of Marie and Paul)
Time period(s): 20th century; 1940s (1942)
Locale(s): France

Summary: During World War II, teenage siblings Paul and Marie do their best to stay out of the way, but this becomes increasingly difficult when their father is taken prisoner. It becomes even more of a challenge when their Jewish friend Henri comes to them for help after his parents disappear. It soon becomes obvious that these teenagers cannot continue to keep silent, and must fight for their own safety and beliefs during this trying time. *Resistance: Book 1* is the first book in the Resistance trilogy from author Carla Jablonski.

Where it's reviewed:
Booklist, May 15, 2010, page 57
School Library Journal, May 2010, page 140

Other books by the same author:
Defiance: Resistance, 2011

Other books you might like:
Claire Huchet Bishop, *Twenty and Ten*, 1952
Lois Lowry, *Number the Stars*, 1989
Art Spiegelman, *The Complete Maus*, 1996
Jane Yolen, *The Devil's Arithmetic*, 1988
Markus Zusak, *The Book Thief*, 2006

855

JENNIFER RICHARD JACOBSON

The Complete History of Why I Hate Her

(New York: Atheneum/Richard Jackson Books, 2010)

Subject(s): Friendship; Family; Cancer

Age range(s): 13 - 16+
Major character(s): Nola, Sister (of Song), Friend (of Carly), 17-Year-Old; Carly, Friend (of Nola); Song, 13-Year-Old, Cancer Patient, Sister (of Nola)
Time period(s): 21st century; 2010s
Locale(s): Maine, United States

Summary: In *The Complete History of Why I Hate Her*, readers meet 17-year-old Nola, a young girl who is struggling to find herself. It's been difficult for Nola to deal with the fact that her younger sister, Song, has been diagnosed with cancer. Nola decides to go to Maine to take a summer job and take some time away from her responsibilities at home. While there, she meets Carly, an energetic and friendly co-worker around Nola's age. At first, Nola's ecstatic to make a new friend so quickly, until she starts to notice how clingy Carly has become. Carly also starts to copy Nola and seems to be stealing Nola's life. When Song suddenly appears in Maine, Nola knows Carly has something to do with it, but what can she do to stop her obsessive friend from completely taking over?

Where it's reviewed:
Booklist, February 15, 2010, page 47
Horn Book Guide, Fall 2010, page 371
School Library Journal, August 2010, page 104

Voice of Youth Advocates, August 2010, page 248

Other books by the same author:
Stained, 2005

Other books you might like:
Gail Giles, *Shattering Glass*, 2002
D. Anne Love, *Defying the Diva*, 2008
Janette Rallison, *Just One Wish*, 2009

856

PAUL B. JANECZKO

The Dark Game: True Spy Stories
(Somerville, Massachusetts: Candlewick Press, 2010)

Subject(s): Espionage; Suspense; United States history

Age range(s): 12 - 16+

Summary: Author Paul B. Janeczko compiles 20 true and exciting stories of espionage from the annals of U.S. history. Written for young adult readers, the tales are arranged in chapters by subject matter. The first chapter, "Outspying the British," includes stories about Founding Fathers George Washington and Benjamin Franklin, renowned traitor Benedict Arnold, and other stories during the Revolutionary War. In "Spies in Blue and Gray," Janeczko shares information about spying during the Civil War. "Espionage Comes of Age in World War I," shares information about forms of spying during the First World War, including Native American code talking and Dutch spy Mata Hari. Subsequent chapters discuss spying during World War II and the Cold War Era, including the Berlin Tunnel and the U-2 Spy Plane. The final chapter focuses on cases of double agents who spied against the United States, including CIA agent Aldrich Ames and FBI agent Robert Hanssen.

Where it's reviewed:
Booklist, September 15, 2010, page 58
School Library Journal, August 2011, page 120
Voice of Youth Advocates, October 2010, page 376

Other books by the same author:
Requiem: Poems of the Terezin Ghetto, 2011
Top Secret: A Handbook of Codes, Ciphers, and Secret Writing, 2004
Worlds Afire, 2004
Loads of Codes and Secret Ciphers, 1984

Other books you might like:
Bill Doyle, *Behind Enemy Lines*, 2009
Adrian Gilbert, *Spy School*, 2009
Marissa Moss, *Nurse, Soldier, Spy: The Story of Sarah Edmonds, a Civil War Hero*, 2011

857

ROBERT T. JESCHONEK

My Favorite Band Does Not Exist
(New York: Clarion Books, 2011)

Story type: Fantasy; Young Adult
Subject(s): Fantasy; Imagination; Books

Age range(s): 14 - 17+
Major character(s): Idea Deity, 16-Year-Old

Summary: Idea Deity is a 16-year-old boy living in a fantasy world. Idea thinks he exists within the pages of a book penned by a Godlike author who writes Idea's existence page by page. As part of his character's plot, Idea has created a fake Internet sensation through a band he calls Youforia. What Idea does not realize, however, is that Youforia is actually a real band. When the members of the real band read Idea's online posts about the band, they wonder who could know such personal information about them. They are determined to find out who the culprit is. Idea's life is complicated even further because he believes that he will die in chapter 64 of the novel. Will Idea's fears come true, or is it all just in his mind?

Where it's reviewed:
Booklist, May 15, 2011, page 45
Horn Book Guide, Fall 2011, page 385
School Library Journal, June 2011, page 120
Voice of Youth Advocates, August 2011, page 271

Other books you might like:
Libba Bray, *Going Bovine*, 2009
Michael Ende, *The Neverending Story*, 1983
Jasper Fforde, *The Eyre Affair: A Novel*, 2001

858

CATHERINE JINKS

Living Hell
(New York, New York: Harcourt, 2010)

Subject(s): Space flight; Family; Survival

Age range(s): 13 - 16+
Major character(s): Cheney, Child
Time period(s): Indeterminate
Locale(s): Plexus, Spaceship

Summary: Onboard the spaceship Plexus, the crew and their families form a unique, carefully controlled society as they travel further and further away from the doomed planet Earth. The ship's inhabitants have adjusted to their unorthodox lives, but everything changes when Plexus passes through a radiation field. Now this once-inanimate ship has taken on human characteristics, including emotions and an immune system. And most frightening of all is the fact that the ship believes its human crew is an infection—an infection to be destroyed at all costs. *Living Hell* is a work of young adult sci-fi from celebrated author Catherine Jinks.

Where it's reviewed:
Booklist, February 15, 2010, page 71
Horn Book Magazine, March-April 2010, page 58
Publishers Weekly, March 29, 2010, page 60
School Library Journal, April 2010, page 160
Voice of Youth Advocates, June 2010, page 166

Other books by the same author:
The Abused Werewolf Rescue Group, 2011
The Reformed Vampire Support Group, 2009
Babylonne, 2008
Evil Genius, 2007

Pagan's Curse, 2002

Other books you might like:
Elizabeth Bear, *Chill*, 2010
Anne McCaffrey, *The Ship Who Sang*, 1969
Dom Testa, *The Comet's Curse*, 2009

859

CATHERINE JINKS

The Reformed Vampire Support Group

(New York: Houghton Mifflin Harcourt, 2009)

Subject(s): Vampires; Supernatural; Satire

Age range(s): 13 - 18+

Major character(s): Nina, 15-Year-Old, Vampire; Dave, Vampire, Musician; Father Ramon, Religious (priest), Leader (group sponsor)

Time period(s): 21st century; 2000s

Locale(s): Australia

Summary: Even the terminally fanged must learn how to behave themselves if they plan to coexist in polite society. In *The Reformed Vampire Support Group* by Catherine Jinks, Nina is a member of the title group. Thirty-five years ago, she took a vow never to drink human blood again. Stuck a perpetual teenager, Nina subsists on guinea pigs, because they breed like crazy and are easy to dispose of. Nina is nothing like the sexy, powerful vampires in the romance novels she writes. She and the other seven members of her support group are all weak, homely, and full of complaints. All languish in their boring lives—until one of the vampires is killed by a silver bullet. Now, Nina, Dave—the cute, former member of a punk band—and the rest of the group set out to find the killer. Along the way, they rescue a werewolf and contend with a geeky vampire hunter. The group may even realize that vampires have more potential than they ever thought possible. Catherine Jinks presents the antithesis to the smooth, perfect vampires of other novels in her quirky tale of whiny, outcast supernatural beings.

Where it's reviewed:
Booklist, January 1, 2009, page 71
Publishers Weekly, January 26, 2009, page 120
USA Today, April 16, 2009, page 7D
Voice of Youth Advocates, October 2009, page 332

Other books by the same author:
The Abused Werewolf Rescue Group, 2011
The Genius Wars, 2010
Living Hell, 2010

Other books you might like:
Lucienne Diver, *Vamped*, 2009
Rachel Hawkins, *Hex Hall*, 2010
Stacey Jay, *My So-Called Death*, 2010
R.A. Nelson, *Throat*, 2011
Adam Rex, *Fat Vampire: A Never Coming of Age Story*, 2010

860

LOUANNE JOHNSON

Muchacho

(New York: Alfred A. Knopf, 2009)

Subject(s): High schools; Urban life; Hispanic Americans

Age range(s): 15 - 18+

Major character(s): Eddie Corazon, Student—High School; Enrique, Cousin (of Eddie); Lupe Garcia, Girlfriend (of Eddie); Papi, Father (of Eddie); Mami, Mother (of Eddie)

Time period(s): 21st century; 2000s

Locale(s): New Mexico, United States

Summary: In *Muchacho* by LouAnne Johnson, Eddie Corazon has been transferred to Bright Horizons, an alternative school that his family hopes will steer him away from their drug-plagued New Mexico neighborhood. Intelligent but easily influenced by his criminal cousins, Eddie brings his tough-guy act to his new school. But when he meets Lupe Garcia, Eddie finds hope in her ambitious plans. An accident throws his relationship with Lupe off track and threatens to derail Eddie's future. But now that the resilient teenager has glimpsed potential beyond a life of drugs and crime, he searches for a way to reinvent himself and start over.

Where it's reviewed:
Booklist, August 1, 2009, page 58
Horn Book Guide, Spring 2010, page 99
School Library Journal, September 2009, page 162
Voice of Youth Advocates, December 2009, page 407

Other books by the same author:
My Posse Don't Do Homework, 1992

Other books you might like:
Matt de la Pena, *We Were Here*, 2009
Lorraine M. Lopez, *Call Me Henri*, 2006
Alex Sanchez, *Bait*, 2009
Gary Soto, *Facts of Life: Stories*, 2008

861

MAUREEN JOHNSON

The Last Little Blue Envelope

(New York: HarperCollins, 2011)

Story type: Contemporary

Subject(s): Travel; Voyages and travels; Theft

Age range(s): 14 - 17+

Major character(s): Ginny Blackstone, Traveler, Teenager, Niece (of Aunt Peg); Oliver, Thief; Aunt Peg, Aunt (of Ginny)

Time period(s): 21st century; 2010s

Locale(s): England

Summary: When Ginny Blackstone's beloved Aunt Peg passed away, she left Ginny with one task: to travel Europe by following the instructions left for her in a series of 13 letters. Yet during Ginny's journey her backpack is stolen, along with the final letter that tells her how to complete her adventure. An English boy named Oliver reaches out to Ginny and lets her know that he has the final letter. Ginny is thrilled to be able to complete her aunt's wish, but her quest for the letter has unexpected consequences. Without the help of Aunt Peg's guidance, Ginny is on her own. She must now deal with Oliver's trickery—and the twists and turns of the real world—if she is to complete her task.

Where it's reviewed:
Booklist, May 1, 2011, page 88
Horn Book Magazine, May-June 2011, page 94
Publishers Weekly, April 18, 2011, page 54
School Library Journal, August 2011, page 108
Voice of Youth Advocates, April 2011, page 61

Other books by the same author:
The Name of the Star, 2011
Scarlett Fever, 2010
Suite Scarlett, 2008
Devilish, 2006
13 Little Blue Envelopes, 2005

Other books you might like:
Ally Carter, *Uncommon Criminals*, 2011
Suzanne Harper, *The Juliet Club*, 2008
Beth Kephart, *Undercover*, 2007
Wendy MacIntyre, *Apart*, 2007
Valerie Zenatti, *A Bottle in the Gaza Sea*, 2008

862

MAUREEN JOHNSON

The Name of the Star

(New York: Penguin, 2011)

Series: Shades of London Series. Book 1
Story type: Mystery; Series
Subject(s): Murder; Serial murders; Boarding schools

Age range(s): 14 - 17+
Major character(s): Rory Deveaux, Student—Boarding School
Time period(s): 21st century; 2010s
Locale(s): London, England

Summary: In this first novel from author Maureen Johnson's Shades of London Series, Southern teenager Rory Deveaux goes to England to attend a prestigious boarding school. Yet Rory's excitement about her new life turns to fear when a copycat killer begins imitating the murders committed by Jack the Ripper more than a century ago. Soon Rory must watch her own back after she encounters the person London detectives believe committed the crimes. But no one besides Rory seems to be able to see the man. Is Rory truly seeing the ghost of Jack the Ripper? And if so, how can she keep herself from becoming the notorious killer's next victim?

Where it's reviewed:
Booklist, September 1, 2011, page 117
Horn Book Magazine, November-December 2011, page 103
Publishers Weekly, June 27, 2011, page 158
School Library Journal, September 2011, page 157
Voice of Youth Advocates, October 2011, page 404

Other books by the same author:
The Last Little Blue Envelope, 2011
Scarlett Fever, 2010
Suite Scarlett, 2008
Devilish, 2006
13 Little Blue Envelopes, 2005

Other books you might like:
Rosemary Clement-Moore, *Texas Gothic*, 2011
Claudia Gray, *Afterlife*, 2011
Jeri Smith-Ready, *Shade*, 2010

863

TRACI L. JONES

Silhouetted by the Blue

(New York: Farrar, Straus and Giroux, 2011)

Story type: Coming-of-Age; Family Saga
Subject(s): Depression (Mood disorder); Parent-child relations; Death

Age range(s): 12 - 15+
Major character(s): Serena Shaw, 7th Grader, Sister (of Henry), Singer; Henry Shaw, Brother (of Serena)
Time period(s): 21st century; 2010s
Locale(s): United States

Summary: Serena Shaw's mother died a year ago, and her father has recently plunged further into his depression. Since her mother's death, Serena has taken on more responsibilities than most girls her age. At 13 years old, she does the grocery shopping, makes her family meals, and looks after her younger brother, Henry, while her father fights "the blue" just to get out of bed. In addition to being the head of a very broken household, she is also a middle-school student attempting to keep her grades up and stay active in extracurricular activities. When Serena earns the lead role in the spring play, she becomes overwhelmed with all that is demanded of her at school and home. She's tried as hard as she can to handle everything by herself, but now she thinks the only way to move forward is to ask someone for help. But who is she supposed to turn to when her mother is gone and her father is part of the problem?

Where it's reviewed:
Booklist, June 1, 2011, page 68
Bulletin of the Center for Children's Books, July-August 2011, page 524
Horn Book Magazine, July-August 2011, page 153
Publishers Weekly, May 30, 2011, page 69
School Library Journal, August 2011, page 108

Other books by the same author:
Finding My Place, 2010
Standing Against the Wind, 2006

Other books you might like:
Joanne Bell, *Breaking Trail*, 2005
Andrea Davis Pinkney, *Bird in a Box*, 2011
Rita Williams-Garcia, *One Crazy Summer*, 2010

864

SHEBA KARIM

Skunk Girl

(New York: Farrar, Straus, and Giroux, 2009)

Subject(s): Muslims; Cultural identity; Identity

Age range(s): 13 - 16+

Major character(s): Nina Khan, 11th Grader, Student—High School, Religious (Muslim); Asher Ricelli, Student—High School

Time period(s): 20th century; 1990s

Locale(s): Deer Hook, New York

Summary: *Skunk Girl* is a humorous debut novel for young adults from author Sheba Karim. Nina Khan, an eleventh grader at Deer Hook High in upstate New York, is trying to come to terms with her Pakistani-Muslim identity. Her parents are incredibly strict and forbid her to date, her sister is a total nerd whose academic prowess makes Nina look like a dunce, and her face and body are covered in an abundance of dark hair. When Asher Ricelli, the totally crush-worthy new guy, begins to show interest in Nina, she's shocked and torn about what to do. Finding herself in a major dilemma between respecting her parents' cultural and religious beliefs and desperately wanting to be her own person, Nina must make a choice that will impact her future and family forever. First novel.

Where it's reviewed:
Booklist, April 15, 2009, page 39
School Library Journal, April 2009, page 137

Other books you might like:
Randa Abdel-Fattah, *Does My Head Look Big in This?*, 2007
Randa Abdel-Fattah, *Ten Things I Hate about Me*, 2009
Tanuja Desai Hidier, *Born Confused*, 2002
Neesha Meminger, *Shine, Coconut Moon*, 2009
Mitali Perkins, *First Daughter: Extreme American Makeover*, 2007

865

BRIAN KATCHER

Almost Perfect

(New York: Delacorte Press, 2009)

Subject(s): Sexuality; Dating (Social customs); High schools

Age range(s): 14 - 17+

Major character(s): Logan Witherspoon, 18-Year-Old; Brenda, Girlfriend (of Logan, former); Sage Hendricks, Student—High School; Tim, Friend (of Logan)

Time period(s): 21st century; 2000s

Locale(s): Missouri, United States

Summary: In *Almost Perfect* by Brian Katcher, Logan Witherspoon's life is in a definite slump. Single (he recently found out his longtime girlfriend was cheating) and unhappy at home (his mother is depressed over a failed relationship of her own), Logan needs to find some excitement in his Missouri town. The new student at school, Sage Hendricks, may be just what Logan needs. Previously homeschooled, Sage is a bit eccentric and mysterious, but Logan decides to make a move. Immediately after their momentous kiss, Sage reveals a shocking surprise—she is a boy. As Logan tries to sort out his feelings about his sexuality, Sage's own confusion leads to a suicide attempt.

Where it's reviewed:
Horn Book Guide, Spring 2010, page 99
School Library Journal, December 2009, page 122
Voice of Youth Advocates, February 2010, page 495

Other books by the same author:
Playing with Matches, 2008

Other books you might like:
Jean Ferris, *Eight Seconds*, 2000
Julie Anne Peters, *Luna*, 2004
Ellen Wittlinger, *Parrotfish*, 2007

866

MARILYN KAYE

Gifted: Better Late than Never

(New York: Kingfisher, 2009)

Series: Gifted Series. Book 2
Subject(s): Adolescence; Adolescent interpersonal relations; Alcoholism

Age range(s): 12 - 15+

Major character(s): Jenna Kelly, Telepath, Teenager, Child of an Alcoholic

Time period(s): 21st century; 2000s

Locale(s): United States

Summary: *Gifted: Better Late than Never* is the second book in the Gifted series. Jenna Kelly is a telepathic teenager who attends Meadowbrook Middle School, a school that caters to gifted students. Reading other peoples' minds is easier than doing her science homework, but it can't help her escape from her alcoholic mother. After a particularly hard binge, Jenna's mom lands in the hospital. Days later, a stranger turns up at Jenna's door claiming to be the father she has never known. He says that he wants to take care of her and give her a better life. While the idea of having a normal family life is extremely appealing to Jenna, her gifted friends have a bad feeling about Jenna's dad.

Where it's reviewed:
School Library Journal, June 2009, page 128

Other books by the same author:
Speak No Evil, 2011
Finders Keepers, 2010
Now You See Me, 2010
Here Today, Gone Tomorrow, 2009
Out of Sight, Out of Mind, 2009

Other books you might like:
Joan Ackerman, *In the Space Left Behind*, 2007
Jennifer Lynn Barnes, *Golden*, 2006
Carla Jablonski, *Thicker than Water*, 2006
David Lubar, *True Talents*, 2007

867

JOE KELLY
J. M. MILLIKEN NIIMURA, Illustrator

I Kill Giants

(Berkeley: Image Comics, 2009)

Subject(s): Giants; Adolescent interpersonal relations; Fairies

Age range(s): 14 - 18+
Major character(s): Barbara Thorson, 5th Grader, Warrior
Time period(s): 21st century; 2000s
Locale(s): United States

Summary: In *I Kill Giants*, author Joe Kelly tells the story of Barbara Thorson, an unorthodox fifth grader who slays monsters in her spare time. Barbara is an outcast among her classmates and leads a life fueled by fantasy—and the headstrong young warrior would have it no other way. As Barbara deals with problems at home, she channels her energies into her giant-killing training and finds solace in communicating with fairies. Barbara's journey gradually progresses to a thrilling climax, where the lines between fantasy and reality begin to blur, and the indomitable heroine must face her demons—real and imaginary. *I Kill Giants* includes illustrations by J.M. Milliken Niimura.

Other books by the same author:
Spider Man: American Son, 2009
Captain Stoneheart and the Truth Fairy, 2008
Batman: Black and White, Volume 3, 2007
Space Ghost, 2005

Other books you might like:
David Almond, *The Savage*, 2008
Brian Fies, *Mom's Cancer*, 2006
Jeff Lemire, *The Complete Essex County*, 2009
David Small, *Stitches: A Memoir*, 2009

868

TARA KELLY

Harmonic Feedback

(New York: Henry Holt and Co., 2010)

Subject(s): Adolescent interpersonal relations; Music; Diseases

Age range(s): 15 - 18+
Major character(s): Drea, Student—High School; Naomi, Friend (of Drea); Justin, Boyfriend (of Drea)
Time period(s): 21st century; 2010s
Locale(s): Bellingham, Washington

Summary: Tara Kelly's *Harmonic Feedback* follows high-school junior Drea as she relocates to Bellingham, Washington, from San Francisco and taps into her passion for music. Drea has been diagnosed with Asperger's syndrome, which makes her socially awkward but causes her to find solace in music. Once settled in her new town, she strikes up friendships with wild-child Naomi and fellow new kid Justin, and the trio decides to form a band. As the group grows closer, Drea gets a taste of

Naomi's carefree lifestyle and a shot at romance with Justin. First novel.

Where it's reviewed:
Booklist, June 1, 2010, page 53
Horn Book Guide, Fall 2010, page 372
School Library Journal, August 2010, page 104
Voice of Youth Advocates, October 2010, page 351

Other books by the same author:
Amplified, 2011

Other books you might like:
Rachel Cohn, *Nick and Norah's Infinite Playlist*, 2006
Cath Crowley, *A Little Wanting Song*, 2010
Antony John, *Five Flavors of Dumb*, 2010
Francisco X. Stork, *Marcelo in the Real World*, 2009

869

TRILBY KENT

Stones for My Father

(Toronto: Tundra Books, 2011)

Subject(s): Boer War, 1899-1902; Concentration camps; Mother-daughter relations

Age range(s): 11 - 14+
Major character(s): Corlie Roux, Girl, Daughter (of Mrs. Roux), Friend (of Sipho); Mrs. Roux, Widow(er), Mother (of Corlie and two boys); Sipho, Servant, Child, Friend (of Corlie)
Time period(s): 19th century; 1890s
Locale(s): South Africa

Summary: Corlie Roux knew love once, but then her father died of an illness and left her in the care of her mother, a mysterious woman with a mean streak. Corlie has two younger brothers who are spared their mother's wrath for reasons Corlie can't quite comprehend. In times of confusion or anger, Corlie turns to her friend, Sipho, and they pass the time in remote areas of her family's South African farm. Any chance Corlie has at happiness is snatched away when the Boers rebel against British rule, thus starting a war that forces her family and their neighbors to flee their farms. They are captured, however, and sent to live at Kroonstad, an internment camp. At the camp, Corlie's mother makes it clear to Corlie that she is concerned about the well-being of her sons, not her daughter. Corlie can now rely only on her own wit and insights to survive the conditions of the camp. A chance friendship with a British soldier from Canada helps Corlie through the rougher days at Kroonstad, while she spends the rest of her time envisioning what life has in store for her when the war ends.

Where it's reviewed:
Booklist, July 1, 2011, page 56
School Library Journal, July 2011, page 101

Other books by the same author:
Medina Hill, 2009

Other books you might like:
Anton Ferreira, *Zulu Dog*, 2002
Cynthia Kadohata, *Weedflower*, 2006
Lauren St. John, *The White Giraffe*, 2007

870

BETH KEPHART

Dangerous Neighbors

(New York: Egmont USA, 2010)

Subject(s): History; Twins; Sisters

Age range(s): 14 - 18+

Major character(s): Katherine, 17-Year-Old, Twin (of Anna); Anna, Twin (of Katherine); Bennett, Apprentice (baker), Boyfriend (of Anna)

Time period(s): 19th century; 1870s (1876)

Locale(s): Philadelphia, Pennsylvania

Summary: In the young adult novel *Dangerous Neighbors* by Beth Kephart, a young woman grieving her sister's loss considers killing herself to relieve her pain. It is 1876 and Philadelphia's Centennial Exhibition has brought an air of excitement to the city. But Katherine, a 17-year-old girl whose twin sister Anna died months ago in an ice-skating accident, refuses to be distracted in her task. Believing that she is to blame for Anna's death, Katherine plots her own spectacular demise. Before she can make her fatal leap, Anna's former boyfriend, Bennett, intercedes. Katherine had resented her sister's relationship with Bennett but now searches her heart for the power to forgive.

Where it's reviewed:
Booklist, September 1, 2010, page 98
Horn Book Guide, Fall 2010, page 372
Publishers Weekly, August 9, 2010, page 54
School Library Journal, October 2010, page 120
Voice of Youth Advocates, October 2010, page 351

Other books by the same author:
You Are My Only, 2011
One Heart Is Not a Size, 2010
Nothing but Ghosts, 2009
House of Dance, 2008
Undercover, 2007

Other books you might like:
Carolyn MacCullough, *Drawing the Ocean*, 2006
Jacquelyn Mitchard, *Watch for Me by Moonlight*, 2010
Richard Peck, *Fair Weather*, 2001

871

KODY KEPLINGER

The DUFF: Designated Ugly Fat Friend

(New York: Little, Brown Books for Young Readers, 2010)

Subject(s): Adolescence; Adolescent interpersonal relations; Coming of age

Age range(s): 16 - 18+

Major character(s): Bianca Piper, Student, Teenager; Wesley Rush, Student, Teenager; Casey, Student, Teenager, Friend (of Bianca); Jessica, Student, Teenager, Friend (of Bianca)

Time period(s): 21st century; 2010s

Locale(s): United States

Summary: Keplinger addresses issues of self-esteem, male-female friendships, and body image in this cynical, engaging teen romance. High-schooler Bianca Piper is convinced that she's unattractive and, while loyal to her two conventionally beautiful best friends, she perpetually stands in their shadow. Her self-perception isn't improved when her school's slick ladies' man, Wesley Rush, calls her a "DUFF", which stands for "designated ugly fat friend." However, during a tumultuous period when Bianca's parents decide to get divorced, Wesley starts to pursue the outspoken Bianca romantically and the two engage on a secret relationship that neither of them fully understand. And both teens are quickly surprised that neither is completely what the other expected.

Where it's reviewed:
Horn Book Guide, Spring 2011, page 103
Publishers Weekly, August 16, 2010, page 55
School Library Journal, November 2010, page 118
Voice of Youth Advocates, October 2010, page pge 351

Other books by the same author:
Shut Out, 2011

Other books you might like:
Celia Banting, *I Only Said "Yes" So They'd Like Me*, 2006
Simone Elkeles, *Perfect Chemistry*, 2009
Elizabeth Scott, *Perfect You*, 2008
Daria Snadowsky, *Anatomy of a Boyfriend*, 2007

872

CAITLIN R. KIERNAN

Low Red Moon

(New York: ROC, 2007)

Subject(s): Horror; Paleontology; Parapsychology

Age range(s): 16 - 18+

Major character(s): Chance Silvey, Scientist (paleontologist); Deacon Silvey, Psychic; Narcissa Snow, Serial Killer

Time period(s): 21st century; 2000s

Locale(s): Birmingham, Alabama

Summary: Narcissa Snow, a serial killer with supernatural talents, is convinced that her offerings of child sacrifices to sinister gods will gain her respect and acceptance into their realm. Her latest quarry is the unborn child of Chance and Deacon Silvey, but Deacon has psychometric skills that give him an unusual advantage in foreseeing Narcissa's devious scheme and trying to subvert it. Sequel to the author's award-winning novel *Threshold* (1991).

Where it's reviewed:
Horn Book Guide, Spring 2010, page 96
Publishers Weekly, August 23, 2010, page 50
School Librarian, Summer 2010, page 50
School Library Journal, November 2010, page 110
Voice of Youth Advocates, December 2010, page 468

Other books you might like:
Andrea Cremer, *Nightshade*, 2010

Rachel Hawthorne, *Dark Guardian: Moonlight*, 2009
Jackson Pearce, *Sweetly*, 2011
Aprilynne Pike, *Spells*, 2010
Vivian Vande Velde, *Witch Dreams*, 2005

873

SUSAN KIM
LAURENCE KLAVAN, Co-Author
FAITH ERIN HICKS, Illustrator

Brain Camp

(New York: Macmillan, 2010)

Subject(s): Comic books; Camps (Recreation); Horror

Age range(s): 12 - 16+
Major character(s): Lucas, Teenager, Camper; Jenna, Teenager, Camper
Time period(s): 21st century; 2010s
Locale(s): United States

Summary: In the young adult graphic novel *Brain Camp* by authors Susan Kim, Laurence Klavan, and illustrator Faith Erin Hicks, Camp Fielding claims that it can rehabilitate even the worst adolescent offenders. Exiled there by their frustrated families, Lucas and Jenna find romance, adventure, and danger as they uncover the camp's darker side. While it's true that Camp Fielding increases the brain power of many of its campers, it's also true that some campers seem to vanish mysteriously. Syringe-wielding staff members and smart but stupefied campers eventually lead Lucas and Jenna to the horrifying truth. Hicks's illustrations capture the camp's creepy atmosphere.

Where it's reviewed:
Booklist, May 15, 2010, page 33
School Library Journal, August 2010, page 106
Voice of Youth Advocates, August 2010, page 268

Other books by the same author:
City of Spies, 2010

Other books you might like:
Vera Brosgol, *Anya's Ghost*, 2011
Anthony Horowitz, *Point Blank: The Graphic Novel*, 2007
R.L. Stine, *The Curse of Camp Cold Lake*, 1997
Gene Luen Yang, *Prime Baby*, 2010

874

A.S. KING

The Dust of 100 Dogs

(Woodbury, Minnesota: Flux, 2009)

Subject(s): Pirates; Reincarnation; Dogs

Age range(s): 15 - 18+
Major character(s): Emer Morrisey, Pirate; Saffron Adams, Teenager
Time period(s): 17th century-20th century
Locale(s): South Seas, At Sea; Jamaica; United States

Summary: A.S. King's *The Dust of 100 Dogs* tells the humorous and poignant tale of Emer Morrisey, a 17th century pirate who is finally ready to turn in her sword and eye-patch and live off the treasure she has buried in Jamaica. But Emer is suddenly killed and cursed to live as a dog for the next 100 lifetimes. Now it is the present day, and Emer has been reborn as Saffron Adams, a normal teenager in a typical community. But Saffron is haunted by dreams of Emer's long-buried treasure, and she sets out to recover it in hopes of building a better life for herself. First novel.

Where it's reviewed:
Booklist, February 15, 2009, page 71
Journal of Adolescent & Adult, April 2010, page 611
Publishers Weekly, February 16, 2009, page 129
School Library Journal, May 2009, page 110

Other books by the same author:
Please Ignore Vera Dietz, 2010

Other books you might like:
W. Bruce Cameron, *A Dog's Purpose*, 2010
Linda Francis Lee, *Emily and Einstein*, 2011
L.A. Meyer, *Under the Jolly Roger: Being an Account of the Further Nautical Adventures of Jacky Faber*, 2005
Suzanne Weyn, *Reincarnation*, 2008
Danielle Younge-Ullman, *Falling Under*, 2008

875

A.S. KING

Everybody Sees the Ants

(New York: Little, Brown and Company, 2011)

Story type: Coming-of-Age
Subject(s): Self confidence; Family life; Bullying

Age range(s): 15 - 18+
Major character(s): Lucky Linderman, Teenager; Nader McMillan, Bully
Time period(s): 21st century; 2010s
Locale(s): Arizona, United States

Summary: Lucky Linderman is an ordinary teenager living a fairly ordinary life in suburban Arizona. Like many teens, however, Lucky has crosses to bear that make him not so lucky after all. The local tough guy, Nader McMillan, has set Lucky in his sights as a prime target for bullying. Making matters worse are Lucky's family troubles and his father's mental illness, which emerged after the loss of Lucky's grandfather during the Vietnam conflict. As Lucky's misfortunes begin to take their toll on his own psyche and self-confidence, he takes shelter in a dream world where he saves his grandfather from the Vietcong and becomes a national hero. Can Lucky ever translate the self-worth he feels in his dreams into reality, or is he destined to live an unlucky life?

Where it's reviewed:
Booklist, August 1, 2011, page 43
Publishers Weekly, September 19, 2011, page 158
School Library Journal, October 2011, page 140
Voice of Youth Advocates, October 2011, page 385

Other books by the same author:
Please Ignore Vera Dietz, 2010
The Dust of 100 Dogs, 2009

Other books you might like:
Karen Bass, *Run Like Jager*, 2008
Aidan Chambers, *Postcards from No Man's Land*, 1999
Graham Gardner, *Inventing Elliot*, 2003

876

A.S. KING

Please Ignore Vera Dietz

(New York: Knopf, 2010)

Subject(s): Adolescent interpersonal relations; Friendship; Family

Age range(s): 15 - 18+

Major character(s): Vera Dietz, Student—High School; Charlie, Student—High School; Jenny Flick, Student—High School

Time period(s): 21st century; 2010s

Locale(s): United States

Summary: The complex ties that bind two best friends are the focus of A.S. King's *Please Ignore Vera Dietz*. Vera and her neighbor Charlie had been best friends for most of their lives, but after a disastrous attempt at dating during their junior year, they went their separate ways. Now seniors, Vera and Charlie must deal with the nasty Jenny Flick, who, after Charlie refuses her advances, spreads word of his father's abusive behavior all around the school—and promptly blames Vera for the indiscretion. Charlie, wanting vengeance, then tells people about Vera's mother's former gig as a stripper, much to Vera's anger and embarrassment. Will Vera survive this insult to her pride and reputation? Can she and Charlie ever mend the rift between them?

Where it's reviewed:
Booklist, November 15, 2010, page 37
Horn Book Guide, Spring 2011, page 103
Publishers Weekly, October 11, 2010, page 46
School Library Journal, December 2010, page 116
Voice of Youth Advocates, October 2010, page 352

Other books by the same author:
Everybody Sees the Ants, 2011
The Dust of 100 Dogs, 2009

Other books you might like:
Ariela Anhalt, *Freefall*, 2010
Elizabeth Scott, *Love You Hate You Miss You*, 2009
Jeri Smith-Ready, *Shade*, 2010
Siobhan Vivian, *A Little Friendly Advice*, 2008

877

JESSI KIRBY

Moonglass

(New York: Simon and Schuster, 2011)

Story type: Coming-of-Age

Subject(s): Beaches; Household moving; Father-daughter relations

Age range(s): 14 - 16+

Major character(s): Anna, Teenager; Tyler, Teenager

Time period(s): 21st century; 2010s

Locale(s): California, United States

Summary: In her debut novel, author Jessi Kirby tells the story of a teenager who finally comes to terms with the death of her mother after nearly a decade. For more than 10 years, Anna has mourned her mother's tragic passing, and has remembered their special walks on the beach. When her father moves the family back to that same beach, Anna is haunted by the memories of her mother. She attempts to cope with her grief by jogging along the beach, where she encounters a lifeguard her own age named Tyler. Tyler and Anna soon fall in love, and Anna realizes that it is okay to become close to another person. Yet when Anna learns a secret about her mother, she must reconcile her grief once again. First novel.

Where it's reviewed:
Booklist, April 15, 2011, page 54
School Library Journal, September 2011, page 158
Voice of Youth Advocates, June 2011, page 167

Other books by the same author:
In Honor, 2012

Other books you might like:
Gwendolyn Heasley, *Where I Belong*, 2011
Celeste O. Norfleet, *Fast Forward*, 2009
Cathy Ostlere, *Karma*, 2011
Courtney Summers, *Fall for Anything*, 2011

878

MATTHEW J. KIRBY

Icefall

(New York: Scholastic Inc., 2011)

Subject(s): Brothers and sisters; Wars; Royalty

Age range(s): 11 - 15+

Major character(s): Solveig, Daughter (of the king), Sister (of the crown prince)

Summary: *Icefall* is a young adult novel by author Matthew J. Kirby. A group of siblings, all children of the king, hide deep within a stronghold as they await word from their father about the outcome of his latest battle. Meanwhile, dissension grows within the ranks of those who were entrusted by the king to protect his offspring. A conspirator is suspected among the warriors, and tensions mount people turn against each other. Now it is up to Solveig, the king's daughter, and her brother and sister to maintain peace, at least for as long as it takes for the chilling winter to pass and the king to return for them. Kirby is also the author of *The Clockwork Three*.

Where it's reviewed:
Booklist, November 15, 2011, page 58
Publishers Weekly, September 26, 2011, page 73
School Library Journal, November 2011, page 128
Voice of Youth Advocates, October 2011, page 405

Other books by the same author:
The Clockwork Three, 2010

Other books you might like:
Nancy Farmer, *The Sea of Trolls*, 2004

John Flanagan, *Ranger's Apprentice: Ruins of Gorlan*, 2005

Stuart Hill, *The Cry of the Icemark*, 2005

879

CAITLIN KITTREDGE

The Iron Thorn

(New York: Delacorte Press, 2011)

Series: Iron Codex Series. Book 1
Subject(s): Steampunk; Technology; Mental disorders

Age range(s): 13 - 18+
Major character(s): Aoife Grayson, Orphan
Time period(s): 20th century; 1950s
Locale(s): United States

Summary: *Iron Thorn* is the first book in author Caitlin Kittredge's Iron Codex series. Aoife Grayson is almost 16 years old, and for her family that means something very serious. For her relatives in each generation, including her mother and her brother before her, have completely lost their sanity upon turning 16. As the only girl at Lovecraft Academy's School of Engines, Aoife has a lot of reasons for wanting to beat the odds of heredity. As she looks for answers, she finds herself heading toward the home of her father, whom she has never met. Along the way, she encounters a variety of magical forces that make her wonder if her mother's insane visions were in fact a reality.

Where it's reviewed:
Booklist, January 1, 2011, page 96
Publishers Weekly, December 13, 2010, page 59
School Library Journal, March 2011, page 164
Voice of Youth Advocates, April 2011, page 83

Other books you might like:
Cassandra Clare, *Clockwork Angel*, 2010
Gavin J. Grant, *Steampunk!: An Anthology of Fantastically Rich and Strange Stories*, 2011
H.P. Lovecraft, *The Best of H.P. Lovecraft*, 1963
Philip Reeve, *Mortal Engines*, 2001

880

SHEILA SOLOMON KLASS

Soldier's Secret: The Story of Deborah Sampson

(New York: Henry Holt, 2009)

Subject(s): United States history; American Revolution, 1775-1783; Women

Age range(s): 12 - 16+
Major character(s): Deborah Sampson, Historical Figure, Military Personnel (soldier), Young Woman
Time period(s): 18th century; 1780s (1782-1783)
Locale(s): United States

Summary: Written by Shelia Solomon Klass, *Soldier's Secret: The Story of Deborah Sampson* is a historical novel based on the true account of a Revolutionary soldier. In the 1700s, the role of women was easily defined as childcare giver and housekeeper. Deborah Sampson wanted more from life than that. Abandoned as a baby, she spent her child as a servant. At the age of 22, in the midst of the Revolutionary War, she began serving her country, going undercover as a man to enlist in the Continental Army. Taking the alias Robert Shurtliff, she served for one year before receiving an honorable discharge. Told as a first-person account, *Soldier's Secret* is a fictionalized account of this remarkable woman's bravery and accomplishments.

Where it's reviewed:
Booklist, February 15, 2009, page 81
Publishers Weekly, January 12, 2009, page 48
School Library Journal, April 2009, page 138

Other books by the same author:
Next Stop, Nowhere, 1995
Rhino, 1993

Other books you might like:
Aileen Kilgore Henderson, *Hard Times for Jake Smith: A Story of the Depression Era*, 2004
Gloria Houston, *Mountain Valor*, 1994
Sally M. Keehn, *Anna Sunday*, 2002
L.A. Meyer, *Bloody Jack: Being an Account of the Curious Adventures of Mary "Jacky" Faber, Ship's Boy*, 2002
Anita Silvey, *I'll Pass For Your Comrade: Women Soldiers in the Civil War*, 2008

881

JO KNOWLES

Jumping Off Swings

(Somerville, Massachusetts: Candlewick Press, 2009)

Subject(s): Sexual behavior; Adolescent interpersonal relations; Adolescence

Age range(s): 15 - 18+
Major character(s): Ellie, Friend (of Corinne, Caleb, and Liz), Pregnant Teenager; Josh, Father (of Ellie's baby), Teenager; Caleb, Friend (of Josh and Ellie), Son (of Liz), Boyfriend (of Corinne), Teenager; Corinne, Girlfriend (of Caleb), Friend (of Ellie), Teenager; Liz, Mother (of Caleb), Friend (of Ellie)
Time period(s): 21st century; 2000s

Summary: In *Jumping Off Swings* by Jo Knowles, an experienced teenage girl gets far more than she is looking for from a one-night stand with a young virgin. Ellie decides to give Josh the night of his dreams, but what follows is a nightmare for both of them. Ellie becomes pregnant and Josh is filled with regret and embarrassment. Josh abandons Ellie when he hears the news. Ellie turns to her best friend, Corinne, and Liz, the mother of her childhood friend, Caleb, for advice. Josh turns to Caleb for support. The news draws Corinne and Caleb together. The story follows each of the teens as they sort through the complicated issues related to teenage pregnancy, which forces them to make adult decisions they are not prepared to make.

Where it's reviewed:
Booklist, July 1, 2009, page 54
Horn Book Guide, Spring 2010, page 100
Publishers Weekly, August 10, 2009, page 58
School Library Journal, August 2009, page 107
Voice of Youth Advocates, December 2009, page 408

Other books by the same author:
Pearl, 2011
Lessons from a Dead Girl, 2007

Other books you might like:
Amy Efaw, *After*, 2009
Nick Hornby, *Slam*, 2007
Carrie Jones, *Love (and Other Uses for Duct Tape)*, 2008
Sara Zarr, *Story of a Girl*, 2007

882

JO KNOWLES

Pearl

(New York: Henry Holt, 2011)

Story type: Contemporary
Subject(s): Friendship; Single parent family; Death

Age range(s): 13 - 16+
Major character(s): Bean "Pearl", 15-Year-Old, Daughter (of Lexie), Granddaughter (of Gus), Friend (of Henry), Outcast; Henry, 15-Year-Old, Son (of Sally), Friend (of Pearl), Outcast; Gus, Grandfather (of Pearl), Father (of Lexie), Aged Person; Lexie, Single Mother (of Pearl), Waiter/Waitress, Daughter (of Gus); Sally, Single Mother (of Henry), Recluse
Time period(s): 21st century; 2010s
Locale(s): United States

Summary: Author Jo Knowles explores the complexities of single-parent families and teen friendships in this thought-provoking novel for young adult readers. Out of their misfit status and similar upbringings, 15-year-olds Bean, aka Pearl, and Henry have developed a deep friendship. While Pearl deals with the struggles of sharing a home with her 30-year-old waitress mother and her cranky grandfather Gus, Henry wrestles with his own problems—namely, his obese recluse mother who hasn't left their home since his dad walked out on them. When Gus dies unexpectedly, shocking family secrets are revealed that threaten Pearl's relationships with everyone she holds dear, especially Henry.

Where it's reviewed:
Booklist, September 15, 2011, page 75
School Library Journal, September 2011, page 158
Voice of Youth Advocates, August 2011, page 272

Other books by the same author:
See You at Harry's, 2012
Jumping Off Swings, 2009
Lessons from a Dead Girl, 2007

Other books you might like:
Jessica Lee Anderson, *Calli*, 2011
Tonya Bolden, *Finding Family*, 2010
Julie Anne Peters, *Between Mom and Jo*, 2006

Jacqueline Woodson, *From the Notebooks of Melanin Sun*, 1995

883

RON KOERTGE

Now Playing: Stoner & Spaz II

(Somerville, Massachusetts: Candlewick Press, 2011)

Story type: Contemporary
Subject(s): Romances (Fiction); Humor; Cerebral palsy
Age range(s): 14 - 18+
Major character(s): Ben Bancroft, Teenager, Mentally Ill Person (cerebral palsy); Colleen Minou, Teenager, Friend (of Ben); A.J., Teenager, Wealthy, Friend (of Ben)
Time period(s): 21st century; 2010s
Locale(s): United States

Summary: Celebrated children's author Ron Koertge follows up the award-winning *Stoner & Spaz* with a young adult novel centered on Ben Bancroft as he wrestles with a major romantic dilemma. Gorgeous Colleen Minou, troubled as she may be, is the only person who has ever looked past Ben's cerebral palsy and seen him as a person and a friend. As their differences become more and more obvious, Ben is conflicted about his true feelings for Colleen. Does he love her or simply appreciate her? Meanwhile, his grandmother is rooting for A.J., a smart, straightlaced, wealthy girl who shares Ben's affinity for films. A.J. and Colleen are as different as night and day, but Ben is drawn towards both girls for reasons he can't quite understand.

Where it's reviewed:
Booklist, August 1, 2011, page 45
Horn Book Magazine, September-October 2011, page 88
Publishers Weekly, June 27, 2011, page 159
School Library Journal, September 2011, page 158
Voice of Youth Advocates, August 2011, page 272

Other books by the same author:
Lies, Knives and Girls in Red Dresses, 2012
Strays, 2007
Boy Girl Boy, 2005
Margaux with an X, 2004
Stoner and Spaz, 2002

Other books you might like:
Mark Fink, *The Summer I Got a Life*, 2009
Harriet McBryde Johnson, *Accidents of Nature*, 2006
Barry Lyga, *The Astonishing Adventures of Fanboy and Goth Girl*, 2006
Ben Mikaelsen, *Petey*, 1998
Blake Nelson, *Recovery Road*, 2011

884

RON KOERTGE

Shakespeare Makes the Playoffs

(Someville, Massachusetts: Candlewick Press, 2010)

Subject(s): Adolescent interpersonal relations; Poetry; Baseball

Age range(s): 12 - 15+
Major character(s): Kevin Boland, 14-Year-Old; Mira, Girlfriend (of Kevin); Amy, Friend (of Kevin)
Time period(s): 21st century; 2010s
Locale(s): United States

Summary: Rob Koertge's *Shakespeare Makes the Playoffs* tells the story of 14-year-old Kevin Boland, who loves to write poetry and play baseball. His relationship with his girlfriend Mira enters shaky ground when Kevin meets Amy at an open-mic poetry event. As he comes to terms with his feelings for Amy and his loss of interest in Mira, Kevin realizes he has a big decision to make—and that there's no way at least one person won't be hurt in the process.

Where it's reviewed:
Booklist, January 1, 2010, page 68
Horn Book Magazine, March-April 2010, page 61
Publishers Weekly, February 15, 2010, page 133
School Library Journal, February 2010, page 114

Other books by the same author:
Now Playing: Stoner & Spaz II, 2011
Deadville, 2008
Strays, 2007
Boy Girl Boy, 2005
Shakespeare Bats Cleanup, 2002

Other books you might like:
Alan Gratz, *Samurai Shortstop*, 2006
Lisa Schroeder, *Chasing Brooklyn*, 2010
Jacqueline Woodson, *Locomotion*, 2003

885

GORDON KORMAN

Pop

(New York: Balzer + Bray, 2009)

Subject(s): Sports; Football; Friendship

Age range(s): 13 - 15+
Major character(s): Marcus, Teenager, Football Player; Charlie Popovich, Football Player (former), Father (of Marcus); Troy Popovich, Football Player, Teenager, Son (of Charlie)
Time period(s): 21st century; 2000s
Locale(s): United States

Summary: In Gordon Korman's young adult novel *Pop*, a young man starts a friendship with a former football star. As the new kid in town, Marcus hopes that making the football team will help him make friends at his new school. While practicing one day, he strikes up a conversation with a man named Charlie. As they become friends, Marcus discovers that Charlie is actually Charlie Popovich, or "the King of Pop," a famous ex-NFL linebacker. When school starts, Marcus learns that Troy Popovich, Charlie's son, is the quarterback of the football team. Surprisingly, Troy he does not appreciate Marcus's friendship with his father. The Popovich family is guarding a secret, and they fear that Marcus will learn the painful truth about what's happened to Charlie.

Where it's reviewed:
Booklist, September 1, 2009, page 105
Publishers Weekly, September 21, 2009, page 59
School Library Journal, November 2009, page 113
Voice of Youth Advocates, August 2009, page 227

Other books by the same author:
The Juvie Three, 2008
Born to Rock, 2006
Son of the Mob, 2004
Jake, Reinvented, 2003

Other books you might like:
Elena Yates Eulo, *The Great Receiver*, 2008
Tim Green, *Football Champ*, 2009
Bill Konigsberg, *Out of the Pocket*, 2008
Gary Soto, *Taking Sides*, 1991

886

DANIEL KRAUS

Rotters

(New York: Delacorte Press, 2011)

Subject(s): Father-son relations; Bullying; High schools

Age range(s): 15 - 18+
Major character(s): Joey Crouch, 16-Year-Old, Son (of Ken Harnett); Ken Harnett, Father (of Joey), Thief (grave robber)
Time period(s): 21st century; 2010s
Locale(s): Iowa, United States

Summary: In *Rotters*, which is a young adult novel by Daniel Kraus, Joey Crouch learns about his estranged father's bizarre occupation. Joey has been living in Chicago with his mother, but when she is killed in a bus accident, he is forced to move to small-town Iowa with his father. Joey soon learns that his father, Ken Harnett, is an outcast in the community, and Joey is treated cruelly by his classmates and teachers. When Ken goes away on business, Joey is often left alone in their filthy house. Curious about his father's absences, Joey asks to accompany Ken at his work. That's when Joey learns that his father is a grave robber. Joey is not repulsed. Instead, he shares his father's fascination with the decaying human bodies they encounter on the job.

Where it's reviewed:
Booklist, April 15, 2011, page 55
Publishers Weekly, February 28, 2011, page 59
School Library Journal, July 2011, page 102
Voice of Youth Advocates, June 2011, page 186

Other books by the same author:
The Monster Variations, 2009

Other books you might like:
Kathleen Karr, *Skullduggery*, 2000
Jonathan Maberry, *Rot and Ruin*, 2010
Rick Yancey, *The Monstrumologist*, 2009

887

NINA LACOUR

Hold Still

(New York: Dutton, 2009)

Subject(s): Grief; Suicide; Friendship

Age range(s): 15 - 18+

Major character(s): Caitlin, Teenager; Ingrid, Friend (of Caitlin)

Time period(s): 21st century; 2010s

Locale(s): United States

Summary: Nina LaCour's *Hold Still* tells the emotionally driven tale of Caitlin, a teenager who has just lost her best friend, Ingrid, to suicide. Withdrawn from the world, Caitlin rejects the idea of therapy and chooses instead to forge ahead on her own, alone with her grief and pain. When she finds Ingrid's diary, she is forced to confront the darkness that once plagued her friend, and by going through this darkness herself, Caitlin may just find a reason to live again. First novel.

Where it's reviewed:
Horn Book Guide, Spring 2010, page 100
Publishers Weekly, August 13, 2009, page 1
School Library Journal, December 2009, page 124
Voice of Youth Advocates, February 2010, page 496

Other books you might like:
Lauren Bjorkman, *My Invented Life*, 2009
Amy Efaw, *After*, 2009
Gayle Forman, *If I Stay*, 2009
Emily Horner, *A Love Story Starring My Dead Best Friend*, 2010
Lili Wilkinson, *Pink*, 2011

888

THANHHA LAI

Inside Out and Back Again

(New York: HarperCollins, 2011)

Subject(s): Refugees; Cultural conflict; Vietnam War, 1959-1975

Age range(s): 10 - 12+

Major character(s): Ha, 10-Year-Old, Refugee

Time period(s): 20th century; 1970s

Locale(s): Alabama, United States; Saigon, Vietnam

Summary: In this award-winning volume by Thanhha Lai, Ha is a 10-year-old Vietnamese girl who becomes a refugee during the Vietnam War. Saigon has fallen, and Ha, her mother, and her brothers must flee the increasingly violent city. They find passage on a ship bound for America, eventually landing in Alabama. Though they are given shelter and are thousands of miles away from the terror of war, Ha is baffled and frightened by the new country. She is suddenly an outcast and must deal with the challenges of a new language, style of dress, and culture. Told in free verse poems, this powerful story also chronicles Ha's heartbreak for her missing soldier-father, whom she hasn't seen since she was an infant. First novel.

Where it's reviewed:
Booklist, January 1, 2011, page 88
Horn Book Magazine, March/April 2011, page 120
Publishers Weekly, January 31, 2011, page 49
School Library Journal, March 2011, page 164

Awards the book has won:
National Book Awards: Young People's Literature, 2011

Other books you might like:
Katherine Applegate, *Home of the Brave*, 2007
Cynthia Kadohata, *Kira-Kira*, 2004
Annika Thor, *A Faraway Island*, 2009
Andrea Warren, *Escape from Saigon: How a Vietnam War Orphan Became an American Boy*, 2004

889

ELIZABETH LAIRD

The Betrayal of Maggie Blair

(Boston: Houghton Mifflin, 2011)

Subject(s): Betrayal; Witchcraft; Scottish history

Age range(s): 14 - 17+

Major character(s): Maggie Blair, 16-Year-Old, Niece (of Uncle Blair), Orphan; Hugh Blair, Uncle (of Maggie)

Time period(s): 17th century

Locale(s): Scotland

Summary: In Elizabeth Laird's young-adult novel *The Betrayal of Maggie Blair*, the severe religious and political atmosphere of seventeenth-century Scotland brings tragedy to the life of 16-year-old Maggie Blair. Orphaned as a baby, Maggie lives with her grandmother on Scotland's Isle of Bute until the old woman is accused of witchcraft. When her grandmother is hanged, Maggie escapes the same fate by fleeing to the home of another relative, Uncle Blair. When her grandmother's accuser, who claims that Maggie is a witch as well, comes to Uncle Blair's home, Maggie must go on the run again, for now her relatives distrust her. Maggie later puts her own life in danger when Uncle Blair becomes the target of the King's men.

Where it's reviewed:
Booklist, April 15, 2011, page 62
Horn Book Magazine, September-October 2011, page 89
Publishers Weekly, February 28, 2011, page 58
School Library Journal, April 2011, page 177
Voice of Youth Advocates, April 2011, page 62

Other books by the same author:
Secret Friends, 1999
Kiss the Dust, 1992

Other books you might like:
Douglas Bond, *Duncan's War*, 2002
K.M. Grant, *How the Hangman Lost His Heart*, 2007
Kathryn Lasky, *Beyond the Burning Time*, 1994

890

ANDREW LANE

Death Cloud

(New York: Farrar Straus Giroux, 2011)

Series: Sherlock Holmes: The Legend Begins Series. Book 1

Subject(s): Detective fiction; Murder; Adventure

Age range(s): 12 - 15+

Major character(s): Sherlock Holmes, 14-Year-Old, Student—Boarding School, Detective—Amateur; Amyus Crowe, Tutor (of Holmes); Matthew, Runaway

Time period(s): 19th century; 1860s (1868)

Locale(s): Farnham, England

Summary: The young-adult novel *Death Cloud* by Andrew Lane is the first book in the Sherlock Holmes: The Legend Begins series, which was authorized by Arthur Conan Doyle's estate. In 1868, Sherlock Holmes is a 14-year-old boarding-school student spending a holiday at his uncle's home in Farnham. There, young Sherlock is tutored by Amyus Crowe, an American who also becomes the boy's mentor in the field of detection. When two local residents die of plague-like symptoms, Sherlock suspects the victims were murdered. He follows a trail of clues that leads to an evil criminal with an equally wicked plot.

Where it's reviewed:
Booklist, January 1, 2011, page 95
New York Times Book Review, March 13, 2011, page 14
Publishers Weekly, January 3, 2011, page 52
School Library Journal, February 2011, page 112
Voice of Youth Advocates, April 2011, page 62

Other books by the same author:
Rebel Fire, 2012

Other books you might like:
Charlie Higson, *SilverFin: A James Bond Adventure*, 2005
Y.S. Lee, *A Spy in the House*, 2010
Eleanor Updale, *Montmorency: Thief, Liar, Gentleman?*, 2004

891

JUSTINE LARBALESTIER

Liar

(New York: Bloomsbury USA Children's Books, 2009)

Subject(s): Science fiction; Law; Crime

Age range(s): 15 - 18+

Major character(s): Micah Wilkins, 17-Year-Old, Wolf (half); Zach, Boyfriend (of Micah)

Time period(s): 21st century; 2000s

Locale(s): New York, New York

Summary: In *Liar* by Justine Larbalestier, 17-year-old Micah Wilkins is a student at a private school in Manhattan and a habitual liar with a shocking secret. First trying to pass as a boy at her new school, eccentric Micah becomes involved with Zach Rubin (who's already involved with the popular—and more "normal"—Sarah). When Zach is killed in a vicious Central Park attack, Micah soon falls under suspicion. As details of the case emerge, and rumors of a Manhattan werewolf on the prowl begin to surface, Micah finds that her lies may not be able to protect her and her secrets this time.

Where it's reviewed:
Horn Book Guide, Spring 2010, page 101
Publishers Weekly, August 24, 2009, page 63
School Library Journal, October 2009, page 129
Voice of Youth Advocates, December 2009, page 422

Other books by the same author:
How to Ditch Your Fairy, 2008
Magic's Child, 2007
Magic Lessons, 2006
Magic or Madness, 2005

Other books you might like:
Anastasia Hollings, *Beautiful World*, 2009
E. Lockhart, *Dramarama*, 2007
Stefan Petrucha, *Split*, 2010
Sara Shepard, *Wanted*, 2010
Ellen Wittlinger, *Love and Lies: Marisol's Story*, 2008

892

HOPE LARSON

Mercury

(New York: Atheneum Books for Young Readers, 2010)

Subject(s): Cousins; Genealogy; Comic books

Age range(s): 12 - 18+

Major character(s): Tara Fraser, Student—High School, 10th Grader; Josey Fraser, Young Woman, Relative (ancestor of Tara); Asa Curry, Prospector

Time period(s): Multiple Time Periods; 21st century; (2000s); 19th century; 1850s (1859)

Locale(s): French Hill, Nova Scotia

Summary: In the young adult graphic novel *Mercury*, author and illustrator Hope Larson tells the story of two young women separated by 150 years and united by a family secret. In 2009, Tara Fraser comes to live at her family's ancestral farm in French Hill, Nova Scotia, after her own home is destroyed in a fire. While Tara's mother works at a job far away from French Hill, Tara acquaints herself with her family's history, which may include a cache of gold buried somewhere on their land. In 1859, Tara's ancestor Josey Fraser is smitten with Asa Curry, a gold dowser whom Josey's parents don't trust. Past and present intersect as Tara learns Josey's fate and discovers her own talent for finding gold.

Where it's reviewed:
Booklist, November 1, 2009, page 35
Horn Book Guide, Fall 2010, page 373
Publishers Weekly, November 4, 2010, page 49
School Library Journal, March 2010, page 185

Other books by the same author:
Chiggers, 2008
Gray Horses, 2006
Salamander Dream, 2005

Other books you might like:
Gilbert Hernandez, *Sloth*, 2006
Mariko Tamaki, *Skim*, 2008
Craig Thompson, *Good-bye, Chunky Rice*, 2004
Jane Yolen, *Foiled*, 2010

893

KATHRYN LASKY

Ashes

(New York: Viking, 2010)

Subject(s): Germans; Holocaust, 1933-1945; Family
Age range(s): 12 - 16+
Major character(s): Gabriella "Gaby", 13-Year-Old
Time period(s): 20th century; 1930s (1932)
Locale(s): Berlin, Germany

Summary: Kathryn Lasky's *Ashes* is set in 1932 Berlin, where 13-year-old Gabriella bears witness to Hitler's terrifying ascension to power. As the world around her rapidly changes into a frightening place, Gaby dives into her love for both literature and movies, offering her a respite from the unsettling reality she must face every day.

Where it's reviewed:
Booklist, January 1, 2010, page 80
Horn Book Magazine, March-April 2010, page 62
Publishers Weekly, January 4, 2010, page 47
School Library Journal, February 2010, page 114
Voice of Youth Advocates, April 2010, page 58

Other books by the same author:
Broken Song, 2005
Blood Secret, 2004
Dreams in the Golden Country: The Diary of Zipporah Feldman, a Jewish Immigrant Girl, 1998
Beyond the Burning Time, 1994

Other books you might like:
Susan Campbell Bartoletti, *The Boy Who Dared*, 2008
Lois Lowry, *Number the Stars*, 1989
Markus Zusak, *The Book Thief*, 2006

894

LINDSEY LEAVITT

Sean Griswold's Head

(New York: Bloomsbury USA Children's Books, 2011)

Subject(s): Multiple sclerosis; Parent-child relations; Friendship
Age range(s): 12 - 15+
Major character(s): Payton Gritas, 15-Year-Old, Student—High School, Genius, Basketball Player, Friend (of Sean and Jac); Sean Griswold, Student—High School, Friend (of Payton); Trent Gritas, Brother (of Payton); Jac, Girl, Student—High School, Friend (of Payton)
Time period(s): 21st century; 2010s
Locale(s): Pennsylvania, United States

Summary: Payton Gritas is a 15-year-old genius. Though she may be academically gifted, she is emotionally immature. For this reason, her parents decided to keep her father's diagnosis of multiple sclerosis from her. Now that Payton knows, she feels betrayed and decides to cut her parents out of her life. At school, her frustration is evident and the guidance counselor suggests that when Payton feels angry or hurt, she find an object to focus on until she is calm. Then she should write about how her focus object makes her feel. Payton has been staring at the back of Sean Griswold's head for years and it seems only natural to her that it would be a good, reliable focus object. After a few days of consistently watching the back of Sean's head, however, Payton finds herself wanting to know more about him. The two begin speaking regularly and Payton records their conversations in her new journal. If she lets it, Sean's friendship—along with existing relationships Payton has with her brother, Trent, and best friend, Jac—may be able to help her cope with her father's diagnosis.

Where it's reviewed:
Booklist, March 1, 2011, page 61
Bulletin of the Center for Children's Books, February 2011, page 284
Horn Book Guide, Fall 2011, page 387
Publishers Weekly, January 31, 2011, page 51
Voice of Youth Advocates, April 2011, page 62

Other books by the same author:
A Farewell to Charms, 2012
The Royal Treatment, 2011
Princess for Hire, 2010

Other books you might like:
Cheryl Dellasega, *Nugrl90 (Sadie)*, 2007
Daphne Grab, *Alive and Well in Prague, New York*, 2008
Lurlene McDaniel, *Kathleen's Story*, 2005

895

Y.S. LEE

A Spy in the House

(Somerville, Massachusetts: Candlewick Press, 2010)

Series: Agency Series. Book 1
Subject(s): England; Spies; Mystery
Age range(s): 13 - 17+
Major character(s): Mary Quinn, Heroine, Spy (for The Agency), Teacher (at Miss Scrimshaw's Academy for Girls)
Time period(s): 19th century-20th century
Locale(s): London, England

Summary: As a child in Victorian London, orphan Mary Quinn was rescued from a life on the streets by a stranger and taken to Miss Scrimshaw's Academy for Girls, where she not only received shelter but also an education. Now, five years later, the same foundation that saved her life wants something from 17-year-old Mary in return. In *A Spy in the House* by Y.S. Lee, Mary, now a teacher at the academy, believes that her life couldn't be any duller. However, more is going on at the school than meets the eye, and Mary is offered a position in a secret spy society known only as "The Agency." Soon, Mary receives her first training mission. Will she succeed? And what obstacles lie in her way of assuming the exciting life of a spy?

Where it's reviewed:
Booklist, January 1, 2010, page 70
Horn Book Guide, Fall 2010, page 373
Publishers Weekly, February 1, 2010, page 51
School Library Journal, April 2010, page 162
Voice of Youth Advocates, October 2010, page 352

Other books by the same author:
The Body at the Tower, 2010

Other books you might like:
Ally Carter, *I'd Tell You I Love You, but Then I'd Have to Kill You*, 2006
Marthe Jocelyn, *Folly*, 2010
L.A. Meyer, *Curse of the Blue Tattoo: Being an Account of the Misadventures of Jacky Faber, Midshipman and Fine Lady*, 2004
Nancy Springer, *The Case of the Cryptic Crinoline*, 2009

896

JEFF LEMIRE, Author/Illustrator

The Complete Essex County
(Marietta, Georgia: Top Shelf Productions, 2009)

Subject(s): Rural life; Interpersonal relations; Family
Age range(s): 14 - 18+
Major character(s): Lester, Boy; Lou LeBeuf, Brother (of Vince); Vince LeBeuf, Brother (of Lou); Anne Byrne, Nurse
Time period(s): 20th century
Locale(s): Essex County, Canada

Summary: Author and artist Jeff Lemire presents a powerful chronicle of small-town life and the individuals and events that populate it. *The Complete Essex County* contains all three novels of Lemire's Essex County trilogy, a series of graphic novels set in a rural farming town in Ontario, Canada. Readers are introduced to Lester, a small boy dealing with overwhelming grief and a new life in the care of his uncle; Lou and Vince LeBeuf, two brothers harboring a painful secret; and Anne Byrne, a nurse who tends to the residents of Essex County while juggling the heartache of a private life lived in solitude. Titles in this volume are *Tales from the Farm*, *Ghost Stories*, and *The Country Nurse*.

Where it's reviewed:
Artforum International, October 2008, page S49
Booklist, March 15, 2007, page 39
Booklist, January 1, 2008, page 52
Booklist, October 1, 2008, page 33
Teacher Librarian, June 2010, page 65

Other books by the same author:
Out of the Woods, 2011
The Nobody, 2009

Other books you might like:
Hope Larson, *Mercury*, 2010

Matt Phelan, *The Storm in the Barn*, 2009
David Small, *Stitches: A Memoir*, 2009
Craig Thompson, *Blankets*, 2003

897

DAVID LEVITHAN
JONATHAN FARMER, Photographer

Every You, Every Me
(New York: Alfred A. Knopf, 2011)

Story type: Psychological Suspense
Subject(s): Stalking; Missing persons; Psychology
Age range(s): 14 - 18+
Major character(s): Evan, Student—High School, Teenager; Ariel, Friend (of Evan, missing)
Time period(s): 21st century; 2010s
Locale(s): United States

Summary: Author David Levithan and photographer Jonathan Farmer team up to create this psychological thriller for young adult readers. Evan has been wrestling with insomnia, brought on by overwhelming guilt and grief over the disappearance of his best friend Ariel. In Ariel's absence, Evan is tormented with unanswered questions and unrelenting sadness that he can't quite handle. When he discovers a series of creepy photographs, many of which feature him, Evan begins to realize someone is stalking him. But who? As the pictures begin piling up, Evan grows increasingly paranoid that Ariel is somehow connected to the stalker, and she's paying him back for not saving her.

Where it's reviewed:
Booklist, October 15, 2011, page 45
Publishers Weekly, August 15, 2011, page 73
School Library Journal, October 2011, page 140
Voice of Youth Advocates, October 2011, page 386

Other books by the same author:
Love Is the Higher Law, 2009
How They Met, and Other Stories, 2008
Wide Awake, 2006
Boy Meets Boy, 2003

Other books you might like:
Matt Blackstone, *A Scary Scene in a Scary Movie*, 2011
John Green, *Paper Towns*, 2008
Ransom Riggs, *Miss Peregrine's Home for Peculiar Children*, 2011

898

DAVID LEVITHAN
JOHN GREEN, Co-Author

Will Grayson, Will Grayson
(New York: Dutton, 2010)

Subject(s): Friendship; High schools; Adolescence
Age range(s): 15 - 18+
Major character(s): Will Grayson, Teenager, Student—High School; Will Grayson, Teenager, Student—High

School; Tiny Cooper, Homosexual, Teenager, Friend (of Will Grayson), Student—High School
Time period(s): 21st century; 2000s
Locale(s): Chicago, Illinois

Summary: *Will Grayson, Will Grayson* is a young adult novel from authors John Green and David Levithan. The story follows two teenage boys with the same name—Will Grayson—whose paths cross in an unexpected way. Despite having the same moniker, the two boys have little to nothing in common, but they forge an unlikely friendship that helps them gain insight into their own lives, hearts, and identities. Alternating between each Will's perspective, the story reveals the way their lives are changed by their chance meeting. *Will Grayson, Will Grayson* is about life's unexpected surprises and the journey of discovering one's unique identity and place in the world.

Where it's reviewed:
Booklist, January 1, 2010, page 82
Horn Book Magazine, May-June 2010, page 81
New York Times Book Review, June 20, 2010, page 12
School Library Journal, March 2010, page 158
Voice of Youth Advocates, February 2010, page 494

Other books you might like:
Michael Cart, *How Beautiful the Ordinary: Twelve Stories of Identity*, 2009
Maureen Johnson, *Suite Scarlett*, 2008
Jennifer E. Smith, *The Comeback Season*, 2008

899

DAVID LEVITHAN

Love Is the Higher Law
(New York: Alfred A. Knopf, 2009)

Subject(s): Terrorism; Death; Survival

Age range(s): 14 - 18+
Major character(s): Claire, Student—High School, Friend (of Peter and Jasper), 11th Grader; Peter, Friend (of Claire and Jasper), 11th Grader, Classmate (of Claire), Student—High School; Jasper, Student—College, Friend (of Claire and Peter)
Time period(s): 21st century; 2000s (2001)
Locale(s): New York, New York

Summary: In David Levithan's *Love Is the Higher Law*, three young New Yorkers are changed forever by the terroristic attacks on the World Trade Center on September 11, 2001. Claire, a junior in high school, is frantic to find her little brother in the chaos. Claire's fellow classmate, Peter, is caught in the middle of everything and trying to get to school, as he thinks he will be safer there. Jasper, who is a college junior, is trying to help in any way he can. The three find each other and become close as they are confronted by the horrors of reality. The story follows the characters on that tragic day as they find ways to cope in the weeks that follow.

Where it's reviewed:
Booklist, June 1, 2009, page 51
Horn Book Magazine, Sept.-Oct. 2009, page 566
Publishers Weekly, August 3, 2009, page 45
School Library Journal, September 2009, page 164

Other books by the same author:
How They Met, and Other Stories, 2008
Wide Awake, 2006
Are We There Yet?, 2005
The Realm of Possibility, 2004
Boy Meets Boy, 2003

Other books you might like:
Caroline B. Cooney, *The Terrorist*, 1997
Juan Felipe Herrera, *Cinnamon Girl: Letters Found Inside a Cereal Box*, 2005
Joyce Maynard, *The Usual Rules*, 2003
Neesha Meminger, *Shine, Coconut Moon*, 2009
Catherine Stine, *Refugees*, 2005

900

ROBERT LIPSYTE

Center Field
(New York: HarperTeen, 2010)

Subject(s): Adolescent interpersonal relations; Baseball; Friendship

Age range(s): 14 - 18+
Major character(s): Mike Semak, Student—High School, Baseball Player; Katherine "Kat" Herold, Student—High School; Oscar Ramirez, Student—High School
Time period(s): 21st century; 2010s
Locale(s): United States

Summary: In Robert Lipsyte's *Center Field*, Mike Semak is a junior in high school who seems to have it all: a beautiful girlfriend, a circle of good friends, and a prime spot on the school's baseball team. But Mike also has a hair-trigger temper, which lands him in hot water after a run-in with a nerdy classmate. Now Mike must serve detention with a band of misfits, where he meets the enigmatic Katherine Herold and eventually develops a crush on her. Soon Mike is torn between his status as a star jock and his newfound alliances within the school's less popular community.

Where it's reviewed:
Booklist, February 15, 2010, page 47
Horn Book Guide, Fall 2010, page 374
New York Times Book Review, May 16, 2010, page 19
School Library Journal, April 2010, page 162
Voice of Youth Advocates, June 2010, page 162

Other books by the same author:
An Accidental Sportswriter: A Memoir, 2011
Yellow Flag, 2007
Raiders Night, 2006
Heroes of Baseball: The Men Who Made It America's Favorite Game, 2005

Other books you might like:
Matt de la Pena, *Mexican WhiteBoy*, 2008
Gene Fehler, *Beanball*, 2008
Will Weaver, *Hard Ball*, 1998

901

SACI LLOYD

The Carbon Diaries 2015

(New York: Holiday House, 2009)

Subject(s): Futuristic society; Natural resource conservation; Adolescence

Age range(s): 13 - 18+

Major character(s): Laura Brown, 16-Year-Old, Writer; Kim Brown, Sister (of Laura)

Time period(s): 21st century; 2010s (2015)

Locale(s): London, England

Summary: It is now the year 2015, and the United Kingdom is the first to begin carbon rationing. Laura Brown, a 16-year-old musician living in London with her family, must now adjust to the new way of life, and describes it in her diary. Her father loses his job, her mother joins the new Women Moving Forward club, and her sister almost dies from a cholera epidemic. The weather is impossible to predict, and the carbon limitations prevent travel, cell phone use, and even the heating of homes. However, the family has no choice but to continue on as usual—Laura plays in her rock band and develops a crush on her new neighbor. Also included in the diary are mock newspaper clippings from the year 2015, which describe current events and carbon rationing.

Where it's reviewed:
Booklist, February 15, 2009, page 89
Horn Book Magazine, MayJune 2009, page 301
Publishers Weekly, April 6, 2009, page 48
School Library Journal, May 2009, page 112

Other books by the same author:
Momentum, 2011
The Carbon Diaries 2017, 2010

Other books you might like:
John Joseph Adams, *Seeds of Change*, 2008
Julie Bertagna, *Exodus*, 2008
Jennifer Cowan, *Earthgirl*, 2009
Susan Beth Pfeffer, *This World We Live In*, 2010
Rachel Ward, *The Chaos*, 2011

902

MALINDA LO

Ash

(New York: Little, Brown and Company, 2009)

Subject(s): Fairy tales; Love; Fairies

Age range(s): 14 - 18+

Major character(s): Aisling "Ash", Orphan; Sidhean, Fairy; Kaisa, Hunter (King's Huntress)

Time period(s): 4th century-15th century

Summary: In *Ash*, a retelling of the Cinderella tale by Malinda Lo, Aisling ("Ash") is forced to live with her cruel stepmother after her father dies. Consoling herself by the fireplace reading fairy tales from her childhood, Ash dreams of the day a fairy will rescue her from her fate. When Sidhean, a handsome fairy arrives, Ash thinks her fortune has changed. Then she meets Kaisa, Huntress to the King. With Kaisa, Ash learns how to hunt—and how to love. Despite her attraction to Sidhean and his magical realm, Ash realizes that it is her relationship with Kaisa that promises lasting love. First novel.

Where it's reviewed:
Booklist, September 15, 2009, page 66
Horn Book Magazine, Nov.-Dec. 2009, page 677
Publishers Weekly, August 31, 2009, page 60
School Library Journal, September 2009, page 164
Voice of Youth Advocates, October 2009, page 332

Other books by the same author:
Huntress, 2011

Other books you might like:
Tea Benduhn, *Gravel Queen*, 2003
Julie Berry, *The Amaranth Enchantment*, 2009
Paula Boock, *Dare Truth or Promise*, 1999

903

MALINDA LO

Huntress

(New York: Little, Brown and Company, 2011)

Story type: Fantasy

Subject(s): Fairies; Fantasy; Magic

Age range(s): 14 - 17+

Major character(s): Taisin, Teenager, Magician; Kaede, Teenager, Warrior

Time period(s): Indeterminate

Locale(s): Tanlili, Fictional Location

Summary: The prequel to author Malinda Lo's acclaimed novel *Ash*, this fantastical tale for young adult readers finds two teenage girls setting out on a perilous mission to save their kingdom. For two years, Earth has suffered under the heavy hand of an unrelenting winter. The sun hasn't shone, the crops are dead, trade has slowed, and the balance of life itself is off. Two girls are selected from the kingdom's citizens to travel to Tanlili, the city of the Fairy Queen. Taisin, a magical sage, and Kaede, a courageous warrior, lead a team on the treacherous journey, encountering hardships and surprises along the way. In addition to unearthly attacks and fairy traps, Taisin and Kaede must also confront the attraction that has grown between them.

Where it's reviewed:
Booklist, March 15, 2011, page 54
Horn Book Magazine, May-June 2011, page 96
Publishers Weekly, February 28, 2011, page 59
School Library Journal, June 2011, page 122
Voice of Youth Advocates, June 2011, page 188

Other books by the same author:
Ash, 2009

Other books you might like:
Kristin Cashore, *Graceling*, 2008
Ursula K. LeGuin, *Tales of Earthsea*, 2001
Garth Nix, *Abhorsen Series*, 1995

904

E. LOCKHART

Real Live Boyfriends: Yes, Boyfriends, Plural. If My Life Weren't Complicated I Wouldn't Be Ruby Oliver

(New York: Random House, 2010)

Series: Ruby Oliver Quartet. Book 4
Story type: Coming-of-Age; Series
Subject(s): High schools; Dating (Social customs); Self perception

Age range(s): 15 - 18+
Major character(s): Ruby Oliver, Student—High School, 12th Grader, Girlfriend (of Noel); Noel, Boyfriend (of Ruby)
Time period(s): 21st century; 2010s
Locale(s): Seattle, Washington

Summary: In this fourth installment in the Ruby Oliver Quartet by author E. Lockhart, Ruby interviews her peers and pals as she puts together a documentary about high school life. It's finally senior year, and Ruby thinks she has found the perfect boyfriend in Noel. But she's still worried about her popularity with boys, so when a new guy starts flirting with her she begins to question her relationship. Then Ruby's grandmother passes away, and her father falls into a deep depression. Things are hard enough at home, but now her mother seems to have forgotten that Ruby won't eat meat. As Ruby puts together her documentary, she begins to find out more about herself and her friends—some of which she doesn't really want to know. With so much going on in Ruby's life, how will she ever find time to fill out college applications?

Where it's reviewed:
Booklist, November 15, 2010, page 47
Horn Book Guide, Spring 2011, page 104

Other books by the same author:
The Treasure Map of Boys: Noel, Jackson, Finn, Hutch, Gideon—and Me, Ruby Oliver, 2009
The Boy Book: A Study of Habits and Behaviors, Plus Techniques for Taming Them, 2006
Fly on the Wall: How One Girl Saw Everything, 2006

Other books you might like:
Deb Caletti, *The Nature of Jade*, 2007
Susane Colasanti, *Something Like Fate*, 2010
Susie Day, *My Invisible Boyfriend*, 2010
Robin Palmer, *Little Miss Red*, 2010

905

E. LOCKHART

The Treasure Map of Boys: Noel, Jackson, Finn, Hutch, Gideon—and Me, Ruby Oliver

(New York: Delacorte Press, 2009)

Series: Ruby Oliver Quartet. Book 3
Subject(s): Interpersonal relations; Dating (Social customs); High schools

Age range(s): 15 - 18+
Major character(s): Ruby Oliver, 16-Year-Old; Noel, Friend; Gideon, Friend; Finn, Friend
Time period(s): 21st century; 2000s
Locale(s): Seattle, Washington

Summary: In E. Lockhart's *The Treasure Map of Boys: Noel, Jackson, Finn, Hutch, Gideon—and Me, Ruby Oliver*, Ruby returns for the third installment in a series that captures her attempts to find health, happiness, and mental stability. She has just started another year at Tate Prep School, and Ruby is bereft about not having a boyfriend. Not that there's a shortage of boys, however; in fact, there are several young men seeking Ruby's attention. Ruby, however, isn't interested in any of them. She's too busy dealing with panic attacks, going to her therapist, spearheading the school bake sale—and searching desperately for that one true love.

Where it's reviewed:
Horn Book Guide, Spring 2010, page 101
Publishers Weekly, July 6, 2009, page 53
School Library Journal, September 2009, page 165
Voice of Youth Advocates, October 2009, page 318

Other books by the same author:
Real Live Boyfriends: Yes, Boyfriends, Plural. If My Life Weren't Complicated, I Wouldn't Be Ruby Oliver, 2010
The Boy Book: A Study of Habits and Behaviors, Plus Techniques for Taming Them, 2006
The Boyfriend List: 15 Guys, 11 Shrink Appointments, 4 Ceramic Frogs and Me, Ruby Oliver, 2005

Other books you might like:
Julie Halpern, *Get Well Soon*, 2007
Susan Juby, *Alice, I Think*, 2003
Sue Limb, *Girl, 15, Charming but Insane*, 2004

906

PITTACUS LORE

I Am Number Four

(New York: Harper, 2010)

Series: Lorien Legacies Series. Book 1
Subject(s): Extraterrestrial life; High schools; Friendship

Age range(s): 15 - 18+
Major character(s): Number Four "John Smith", Alien, 15-Year-Old
Time period(s): 21st century; 2010s

Locale(s): Paradise, Ohio

Summary: In the small town of Paradise, Ohio, 15-year-old John Smith is on the run from an evil band of aliens intent on destroying him and those like him. John is from the planet Lorien and, a decade earlier, arrived on Earth with a group of other children in hopes of expanding his supernatural powers. John is not only attempting to steer clear of the sinister Mogadorians, but now the unexpected trials of human adolescence present further complications to his quest. *I Am Number Four* is the first installment in Pittacus Lore's Lorien Legacies series.

Where it's reviewed:
Booklist, June 1, 2010, page 53
Horn Book Magazine, Sept.-Oct. 2010, page 82
Publishers Weekly, July 19, 2010, page 131
School Library Journal, January 2011, page 111
Voice of Youth Advocates, December 2010, page 473

Other books by the same author:
The Power of Six, 2011

Other books you might like:
Gail Giles, *Right Behind You*, 2007
David Klass, *Caretaker Trilogy*, 2006-2009
Dennis Pepper, *The Young Oxford Book of Aliens*, 1998
Neal Shusterman, *The Dark Side of Nowhere*, 1997

907

JEREMY LOVE, Author/Illustrator
PATRICK MORGAN, Illustrator

Bayou: Volume 1
(New York: DC Comics, 2009)

Subject(s): Southern United States; Race relations; United States history, 1921-1945

Age range(s): 14 - 18+

Major character(s): Lee Wagstaff, Heroine; Lily Westmoreland, Friend (of Lee); Bayou, Monster; Bog, Monster

Time period(s): 20th century; 1930s (1933)

Locale(s): Dixie, Fictional Location; Charon, Mississippi

Summary: In *Bayou: Volume 1*, readers are taken back to the racially charged Southern United States of the 1930s. Lee Wagstaff is the daughter of an African-American sharecropper living in Charon, Mississippi. When her white friend, Lily Westmoreland, is kidnapped by a monster called Bog, fingers point at Lee's father. Now Lee must prove his innocence by entering a fantasy world known as Dixie, where she meets a kindly creature named Bayou. Can Bayou help Lee find Lily and save her father's life?

Where it's reviewed:
Booklist, July 1, 2009, page 62
Library Journal, September 15, 2009, page 45
Publishers Weekly, May 25, 2009, page 43

Other books by the same author:
Bayou: Volume 2, 2011
Shadow Rock, 2006
Fierce, 2005

Other books you might like:
Lilli Carre, *The Lagoon*, 2008

Akira Hiramoto, *Me and the Devil Blues 1: The Unreal Life of Robert Johnson*, 2008
Mat Johnson, *Incognegro: A Graphic Mystery*, 2008
Lewis Trondheim, *Bourbon Island 1730*, 2008

908

MARIE LU

Legend
(New York: G.P. Putnam's Sons, 2011)

Subject(s): Futuristic society; Crime; Revenge

Age range(s): 12 - 18+

Major character(s): Day, 15-Year-Old, Criminal; June, 15-Year-Old, Military Personnel

Time period(s): Indeterminate Future

Locale(s): The Republic, Fictional Location

Summary: *Legend* is a suspenseful futuristic novel for young adult readers from author Marie Lu. The Republic now reigns in what was formerly the western United States, constantly at war with its neighbors and home to two very different teenagers. June, a 15-year-old prodigy, is being trained to serve in the Republic's elite military force, while 15-year-old Day is the nation's most wanted criminal. Born into an impoverished area, Day has legitimate reasons for his criminal activity. The two should never meet, but when June's brother is killed and Day is the prime suspect, a dangerous game of cat-and-mouse begins. Day is struggling to protect his family, while June wants to avenge hers, but these two young people will soon learn how much they have in common and how sinister their government really is.

Where it's reviewed:
Booklist, October 15, 2011, page 58
Horn Book Magazine, November-December 2011, page 105
Publishers Weekly, October 10, 2011, page 59
School Library Journal, October 2011, page 140
Voice of Youth Advocates, October 2011, page 405

Other books you might like:
Suzanne Collins, *The Hunger Games*, 2008
Teri Hall, *The Line*, 2010
Gemma Malley, *The Declaration*, 2007
Lauren Oliver, *Delirium*, 2011

909

BARRY LYGA
COLLEEN DORAN, Illustrator

Mangaman
(Boston: Houghton Mifflin, 2011)

Story type: Fantasy; Young Adult

Subject(s): Comic books; Cartoons; Adolescent interpersonal relations

Age range(s): 14 - 18+

Major character(s): Ryoko, Teenager (manga character); Marissa Montaigne, Student—High School

Locale(s): United States

Summary: Written by author Barry Lyga and illustrated by Colleen Doran, this graphic novel looks at what might happen if a Japanese manga character were suddenly thrust into the world of American teenagers. Ryoko is a manga character from a popular graphic novel who falls through a rip in the divider between real and fantasy. After falling through the rip, Ryoko ends up in an American high school, where he tries to fit in as much as possible. Fitting in is a difficult task for Ryoko, though, because he looks so different from all the other students at the school. The other students aren't very welcoming to the new, strange student, and Ryoko quickly feels the pressure of being an outcast. Meanwhile, he finds himself falling for Marissa Montaigne, the prettiest girl at school. Can Ryoko ever show her that there is more to him than meets the eye?

Where it's reviewed:
Booklist, October 15, 2011, page 35
Publishers Weekly, August 1, 2011, page 51
School Library Journal, November 2011, page 155
Voice of Youth Advocates, October 2011, page 386

Other books you might like:
Holly Black, *The Good Neighbors: Kin*, 2008
Daisuke Igarashi, *Children of the Sea, Volume 1*, 2009
Antony Johnston, *Wolverine: Prodigal Son*, 2009
Tsugumi Ohba, *Death Note, Volume 1: Boredom*, 2005
Raina Telgemeier, *X-Men: Misfits 1*, 2009

BARRY LYGA

Goth Girl Rising
(Boston: Houghton Mifflin Harcourt, 2009)

Subject(s): High schools; Mothers; Friendship

Age range(s): 14 - 18+
Major character(s): Kyra "Goth Girl" Sellers, Teenager; Fanboy, Friend (of Kyra)
Time period(s): 21st century; 2000s
Locale(s): United States

Summary: Barry Lyga's *Goth Girl Rising* continues the escapades of teenager Kyra Sellers, first begun in 2006's *The Astonishing Adventures of Fanboy and Goth Girl*. Kyra has just been released from a psychiatric hospital, and she's ready to dive back into life at her old high school. But Kyra is wholly unprepared for the discoveries she is about to make. Her friend Fanboy has gone behind her back and started producing the comic book they had originally created together. Her father's chain-smoking weighs heavily on her mind and causes her to think about her mother's death. Additionally, Kyra is plagued by the objectification of women, which seems to be happening all around her. Who said getting better was going to be easy?

Where it's reviewed:
Booklist, November 15, 2009, page 34
Horn Book Magazine, Jan.-Feb. 2010, page 88
Publishers Weekly, October 12, 2009, page 51

Other books by the same author:
Hero-Type, 2008
The Astonishing Adventures of Fanboy and Goth Girl, 2006

Other books you might like:
Cecil Castellucci, *Boy Proof*, 2005
Catherine Ryan Hyde, *The Year of My Miraculous Reappearance*, 2007
Martine Leavitt, *Heck Superhero*, 2004
Anne Spollen, *The Shape of Water*, 2008

CHRIS LYNCH

Hothouse
(New York: HarperCollins, 2010)

Subject(s): Father-son relations; Death; Grief

Age range(s): 14 - 17+
Major character(s): Russell, Friend (of DJ), Teenager; DJ, Friend (of Russell), Teenager
Time period(s): 21st century; 2010s
Locale(s): United States

Summary: *Hothouse* is a young adult novel written by author Chris Lynch. Russell and DJ were best friends once upon a time, but since reaching adolescence have grown apart. A tragedy that befalls their fathers, both firefighters, during a fire call brings the former pals back together. As both teens struggle to handle their individual losses, the people of their town show nothing but support. Both men are considered heroes until the facts surrounding their death are called into question, and it's up to Russell to uncover the truth about the night of the fire that claimed his father's life. Why, then, is DJ unwilling to help out with Russell's investigation? Can these boys work together in true friendship in order to learn the truth about their fathers?

Where it's reviewed:
Booklist, May 15, 2010, page 36
Horn Book Magazine, Sept.-Oct. 2010, page 83
Publishers Weekly, September 13, 2010, page 47
School Library Journal, September 2010, page 157
Voice of Youth Advocates, October 2010, page 352

Other books by the same author:
Angry Young Man, 2011
The Big Game of Everything, 2008
Sins of the Fathers, 2006
Me, Dead Dad and Alcatraz, 2005
Who the Man, 2003

Awards the book has won:
Blue Ribbon Awards: Fiction, 2010

Other books you might like:
Tim Bowler, *Firmament*, 2004
Jonathan Friesen, *Rush*, 2010
Barry Lyga, *Hero-Type*, 2008

912

CHRIS LYNCH

Angry Young Man

(New York: Simon & Schuster Books for Young Readers, 2011)

Story type: Contemporary
Subject(s): Terrorism; Outcasts; Sibling rivalry

Age range(s): 15 - 18+
Major character(s): Robert, Brother (of Alexander), Student—College, 18-Year-Old; Alexander "Xan", 17-Year-Old, Outcast, Student—College, Activist
Time period(s): 21st century; 2010s
Locale(s): United States

Summary: Award-winning author Chris Lynch examines the complexities of sibling rivalry and homegrown terrorism in this chilling novel for young adult readers. Robert and Alexander (Xan) are half-brothers, a year apart in age, and the sons of a financially strapped single mother. But the pair couldn't be more different. While Robert is a responsible hard worker with good grades and a pretty girlfriend, Xan is a social outcast with a great deal of pent-up anger and no visible ambition in life. Robert is hopeful when he discovers that Xan has signed up for classes at the local community college. But Xan's growing involvement in a social activist group that shows signs of extremism and violence has Robert worried for the safety of his brother and his entire family.

Where it's reviewed:
Booklist, January 1, 2011, page 92
Publishers Weekly, December 20, 2010, page 54
School Library Journal, February 2011, page 113
Voice of Youth Advocates, February 2011, page 556

Other books by the same author:
Pledge Allegiance, 2011
Hothouse, 2010
Sins of the Fathers, 2006
Who the Man, 2003
Freewill, 2001

Other books you might like:
Swati Avasthi, *Split*, 2010
April Henry, *Torched*, 2009
Kekla Magoon, *The Rock and the River*, 2009
Dana Reinhardt, *The Things a Brother Knows*, 2010

913

JANET NICHOLS LYNCH

Messed Up

(New York: Holiday House, 2009)

Subject(s): Foster children; Death; Grief

Age range(s): 13 - 16+
Major character(s): R.D., 15-Year-Old, Foster Child; Earl, Guardian (of R.D.), Boyfriend (of R.D.'s grandmother)
Time period(s): 21st century; 2000s
Locale(s): United States

Summary: In Janet Nichols Lynch's *Messed Up*, 15-year-old R.D. has experienced more hardships than most. His entire family is dead. He lives with his grandmother's ex-boyfriend, Earl, and tries to stay out of trouble. When Earl suddenly dies, R.D. finds himself completely alone and in danger of social services finding out about his situation. He knows he can't tell anyone about his situation or he'll end living in a group home. R.D. sets out on a journey of self-discovery, learning how to go to the grocery store, cook for himself, pay the bills, and orchestrate a funeral. It is more than a 15-year-old should know how to handle, but it beats the alternative.

Where it's reviewed:
Booklist, April 1, 2009, page 33
School Library Journal, August 2009, page 108

Other books by the same author:
Addicted to Her, 2010
Peace Is a Four-Letter Word, 2005

Other books you might like:
Kevin Brooks, *Martyn Pig*, 2002
Sarah Dessen, *Lock and Key*, 2008
J. Adams Oaks, *Why I Fight*, 2009
Danny Santiago, *Famous All over Town*, 1983

914

JONATHAN MABERRY

Rot and Ruin

(New York: Simon and Schuster Books for Young Readers, 2010)

Subject(s): Zombies; Survival; Brothers

Age range(s): 14 - 17+
Major character(s): Benny Imura, Hunter (of zombies); Tom, Brother (of Benny)
Time period(s): Indeterminate Future
Locale(s): United States

Summary: Jonathan Maberry's *Rot and Ruin* is set in a futuristic America that has been overtaken by zombies. Teenager Benny Imura is desperate to find a job to stay within the bounds of the law, which dictates that all citizens must have a job by the age of 15 or risk starvation. Through his brother, Tom, Benny gets an apprenticeship as a zombie hunter, a position that doesn't exactly thrill him—but it is, after all, a job. Benny can't fathom the danger he is about to face—and how it will transform and invigorate his entire life.

Where it's reviewed:
Booklist, October 15, 2010, page 51
Horn Book Guide, Spring 2010, page 105
Publishers Weekly, September 27, 2010, page 62
School Library Journal, November 2010, page 121

Other books by the same author:
Dust and Decay, 2011

Other books you might like:
Charlie Higson, *The Enemy*, 2009
Sherrilyn Kenyon, *Infinity: Chronicles of Nick*, 2010
Jackson Pearce, *Sisters Red*, 2010
Carrie Ryan, *The Forest of Hands and Teeth*, 2009

915

CAROLYN MACCULLOUGH

Once a Witch

(New York: Clarion Books, 2009)

Subject(s): Witches; Sibling rivalry; Identity

Age range(s): 14 - 17+

Major character(s): Tamsin Greene, 17-Year-Old, Witch; Rowena Greene, Sister (of Tamsin), Witch, Kidnap Victim; Gabriel, Friend (of Tamsin)

Time period(s): Multiple Time Periods

Locale(s): United States

Summary: In *Once a Witch*, Carolyn MacCullough presents the adventures of Tamsin Greene, a 17-year-old girl who comes from a long line of powerful witches. The only problem is that Tamsin is the one person in her family who appears to be devoid of magical powers. Struggling to find a place within her own family, Tamsin finally discovers her destiny after her sister Rowena is kidnapped. Suddenly, Tamsin is faced with the knowledge that she might be the only one who can save her sister.

Where it's reviewed:
Booklist, October 1, 2009, page 37
Horn Book Guide, Spring 2010, page 102
School Library Journal, October 2009, page 130
Voice of Youth Advocates, October 2009, page 333

Other books by the same author:
Always a Witch, 2011

Other books you might like:
Debbie Federici, *L.O.S.T.*, 2004
Lynne Hansen, *A Time for Witches*, 2007
Terry Pratchett, *I Shall Wear Midnight*, 2010
Gillian Shields, *Waters Dark and Deep*, 2009

916

CAROLYN MACKLER

Tangled

(New York: HarperCollins, 2010)

Subject(s): Adolescent interpersonal relations; Romances (Fiction); Vacations

Age range(s): 15 - 18+

Major character(s): Jena, Teenager; Skye, Teenager, Actress; Dakota, Teenager; Owen, Teenager, Computer Game Player

Time period(s): 21st century; 2010s

Locale(s): Caribbean Islands

Summary: *Tangled* by Carolyn Mackler is a coming-of-age novel about four adolescents who interconnect during a holiday in the Caribbean. Featured in the book are Jena, a shy, introverted teen who feels overwhelmed by the increasing popularity of her best friend, Skye; Skye, a depressed teen searching for the truth about her father; Dakota, a young man who uses his playboy ways to cope with the death of his girlfriend; and Dakota's younger brother Owen, a computer geek who hides behind his onscreen persona. Mackler is also the author

of *The Earth, My Butt, and Other Round Things* and *Vegan Virgin Valentine*.

Where it's reviewed:
Booklist, January 1, 2010, page 71
Horn Book Guide, Fall 2010, page 375
Publishers Weekly, November 23, 2009, page 59
School Library Journal, January 2010, page 108
Voice of Youth Advocates, February 2010, page 498

Other books by the same author:
Guyaholic: A Story of Finding, Flirting, Forgetting — and the Boy Who Changes Everything, 2007
Vegan Virgin Valentine, 2004
The Earth, My Butt, and Other Big Round Things, 2003
Love and Other Four-Letter Words, 2000

Other books you might like:
Garret Freymann-Weyr, *After the Moment*, 2009
Jenny Han, *The Summer I Turned Pretty*, 2009
Steve Kluger, *My Most Excellent Year: A Novel of Love, Mary Poppins, and Fenway Park*, 2008

917

SUE MACY

Wheels of Change: How Women Rode the Bicycle to Freedom (with a Few Flat Tires along the Way)

(Washington, DC: National Geographic, 2011)

Subject(s): Bicycles; Women; Women's rights

Age range(s): 12 - 15+

Summary: This book for young readers by Sue Macy examines the role that the bicycle played in the women's rights movement. Macy examines the invention of the bicycle and describes how the machine's invention gave many more women the freedom of mobility. Although some people protested women's use of bicycles, the trend continued for many years. Women often used their bikes to vote, to participate in women's rights activities, and even to work outside the home. The author uses a variety of media including old photos, reprints of advertisements, and animation stills to convey how women used bicycles in their daily lives and how this use affected their personal lives, their rights and freedoms, and even their fashion sense.

Where it's reviewed:
Booklist, February 15, 2011, page 64
Horn Book Guide, Fall 2011, page 458
New York Times Book Review, May 15, 2011, page 19
School Library Journal, April 2011, page 193
Voice of Youth Advocates, August 2011, page 302

Other books by the same author:
Basketball Belles: How Two Teams and One Scrappy Player Put Women's Hoops on the Map, 2010
Swifter, Higher, Stronger: A Photographic History of the Summer Olympics, 2008
Freeze Frame: A Photographic History of the Winter Olympics, 2006
Girls Got Game: Sports Stories and Poems, 2001

Other books you might like:
Bill Haduch, *Go Fly a Bike!: The Ultimate Book about Bicycle Fun, Freedom and Science*, 2004
Philip Steele, *A History of Fashion and Costume: The Nineteenth Century*, 2005
Frances Willard, *Wheel within a Wheel*, 1997

918

L.K. MADIGAN

The Mermaid's Mirror

(Boston: Houghton Mifflin Books for Children, 2010)

Subject(s): Mermaids; Sea stories; Identity

Age range(s): 14 - 16+
Major character(s): Lena, Teenager
Time period(s): 21st century; 2010s
Locale(s): United States

Summary: L.K. Madigan's *The Mermaid's Mirror* tells the story of Lena, a teenager with an abiding fascination with the sea who wants more than anything to learn how to surf. Her father, however, is leery of allowing his daughter to partake in the dangerous sport and prefers she stick close to shore. Lena's determination eventually gets the best of her, and she takes to the waves where she makes a shocking discovery: a beautiful mermaid who gives Lena a key. When the teen seeks out the lock that the key opens, the secret of her past is, at last, revealed.

Where it's reviewed:
Booklist, September 15, 2010, page 63
Horn Book Magazine, November/December 2010, page 94
Publishers Weekly, October 4, 2010, page 49
School Library Journal, December 2010, page 120
Voice of Youth Advocates, October 2010, page 368

Other books by the same author:
Flash Burnout, 2009

Other books you might like:
Tera Lynn Childs, *Forgive My Fins*, 2011
Peter Dickinson, *Water: Tales of Elemental Spirits*, 2002
Alice Hoffman, *Aquamarine*, 2001
Donna Jo Napoli, *Sirena*, 1998

919

L.K. MADIGAN

Flash Burnout

(Boston: Houghton Mifflin, 2009)

Subject(s): Photography; High schools; Friendship

Age range(s): 15 - 18+
Major character(s): Blake, 15-Year-Old, Photographer, Friend (of Marissa), Boyfriend (of Shannon); Marissa, Friend (of Blake); Shannon, Girlfriend (of Blake)
Time period(s): 21st century; 2000s
Locale(s): United States

Summary: L.K. Madigan's *Flash Burnout* tells the story of 15-year-old photographer Blake, his best friend Marissa, and his girlfriend Shannon. When Blake takes a picture of a homeless woman, he is shocked to find that Marissa recognizes the person in the photo. It is her mother, whom she hasn't seen in years. As Marissa deals with this startling discovery, Blake is drawn closer to her—creating problems in his relationship with Shannon. *Flash Burnout* was the recipient of the 2010 William C. Morris Award. First novel.

Where it's reviewed:
Booklist, September 15, 2009, page 68
Horn Book Guide, Spring 2010, page 102
School Library Journal, November 2009, page 114

Other books by the same author:
The Mermaid's Mirror, 2010

Awards the book has won:
William C. Morris Award, 2010

Other books you might like:
Joan Bauer, *Thwonk*, 1995
Joyce Carol Oates, *Big Mouth & Ugly Girl*, 2002
Lauren Strasnick, *Nothing Like You*, 2009
Ellen Wittlinger, *Razzle*, 2001

920

KEKLA MAGOON

The Rock and the River

(New York: Aladdin, 2009)

Subject(s): Civil rights; African Americans; Family

Age range(s): 12 - 16+
Major character(s): Sam Childs, 13-Year-Old; Stephen "Stick" Childs, 17-Year-Old, Brother (of Sam)
Time period(s): 20th century; 1960s (1968)
Locale(s): Chicago, Illinois

Summary: It is 1968 and Sam Childs is 13, living in Chicago. His father is one of Dr. Martin Luther King's colleagues, and Sam and his family have been involved in peaceful protests. When Sam sees a brutal police beating of an African-American man, followed soon by Dr. King's assassination, however, he begins to listen to his older brother Stephen, who is leaving home to join the violent Black Panthers. Sam's father does not support Stephen's decision. *The Rock and the River* provides a fictionalized first-person perspective of living through the civil rights movement. First novel.

Where it's reviewed:
Booklist, February 1, 2009, page 50
New York Times Book Review, April 12, 2009, page 15
School Library Journal, February 2009, page 104
Voice of Youth Advocates, October 2009, page 318

Other books by the same author:
Camo Girl, 2011
Abraham Lincoln, 2007

Other books you might like:
Julius Lester, *Guardian*, 2008
Chris Lynch, *Angry Young Man*, 2011

Margaret McMullan, *Cashay*, 2009
Paul Volponi, *Response*, 2009
Rita Williams-Garcia, *One Crazy Summer*, 2010

921

MELINA MARCHETTA

Finnikin of the Rock

(Somerville, Massachusetts: Candlewick Press, 2010)

Series: Lumatere Chronicles. Book 1
Subject(s): Fantasy; Adventure; Love

Age range(s): 14 - 17+
Major character(s): Finnikin, 19-Year-Old; Evanjalin, Psychic; Balthazar, Friend (of Finnikin); Froi, Thief
Time period(s): Indeterminate Past
Locale(s): Lumatere, Fictional Location

Summary: In *Finnikin of the Rock* by Melina Marchetta, the killing of Lumatere's royal family a decade ago has left the kingdom under fraudulent rule. Finnikin, once the friend of royal heir Balthazar, is now banished from the kingdom and serves as an apprentice to an exiled knight. When Finnikin, now 19, meets a young psychic woman called Evanjalin, he learns that Balthazar may have escaped assassination. With Evanjalin, Finnikin formulates a plan to shatter the spell that holds Lumatere in darkness and reinstate rightful order. *Finnikin of the Rock* is the first book in the Lumatere series. Originally published in Australia.

Where it's reviewed:
Booklist, March 1, 2010, page 73
Publishers Weekly, January 11, 2010, page 50
School Library Journal, March 2010, page 163
Voice of Youth Advocates, April 2010, page 72

Other books by the same author:
The Piper's Son, 2011
Jellicoe Road, 2008
Saving Francesca, 2004
Looking for Alibrandi, 1999

Other books you might like:
Kristin Cashore, *Graceling*, 2008
Catherine Fisher, *Incarceron*, 2007
Jenny Moss, *Shadow*, 2010
Tamora Pierce, *Lady Knight*, 2002

922

MELINA MARCHETTA

The Piper's Son

(Somerville, Massachusetts: Candlewick Press, 2011)

Story type: Contemporary
Subject(s): Friendship; Family; Forgiveness

Age range(s): 15 - 18+
Major character(s): Thomas Mackee, Teenager, Child of an Alcoholic, Musician
Time period(s): 21st century; 2010s
Locale(s): Sydney, Australia

Summary: Award-winning author Melina Marchetta follows up *Saving Francesca* with this moving young adult novel set five years later. Francesca's friend Thomas Mackee has watched his entire family fall apart in the two years since a suicide bomber killed his uncle in a foreign city. Thomas's mom left town with his sister in tow, his father has succumbed to alcoholism, and his aunt is in denial about her pregnancy. As a result, Thomas has dropped out of school, given up his music, and cut himself off from all of his friends. Now, he's living with his aunt, working at the Union Pub, and trying desperately to forget about the love of his life. Can Thomas's friends step in to rescue him, or is he simply too far gone for saving?

Where it's reviewed:
Booklist, February 15, 2011, page 72
Publishers Weekly, January 31, 2011, page 51
School Library Journal, March 2011, page 166
Voice of Youth Advocates, April 2011, page 63

Other books by the same author:
Finnikin of the Rock, 2010
Jellicoe Road, 2008
Saving Francesca, 2004
Looking for Alibrandi, 1999

Other books you might like:
Michael Cadnum, *Edge*, 1997
Maureen McCarthy, *Rose by Any Other Name*, 2008
Martine Murray, *How to Make a Bird*, 2003
Gabrielle Williams, *Beatle Meets Destiny*, 2010

923

KIMBERLY MARCUS

Exposed

(New York: Random House, 2011)

Story type: Coming-of-Age
Subject(s): Rape; Friendship; Photography

Age range(s): 13 - 16+
Major character(s): Liz, 16-Year-Old, Student—High School, Photographer, Friend (of Kate); Kate, 16-Year-Old, Student—High School, Dancer, Friend (of Liz)
Time period(s): 21st century; 2010s
Locale(s): United States

Summary: Two best friends are ripped apart by a shocking accusation in this chilling novel for young adult readers from debut author Kimberly Marcus. Told entirely in free verse, the story centers on aspiring photographer Liz and her best friend Kate. As the two 16-year-old girls begin preparing for college, Liz knows without question that she's going to study photography, but she can't understand why Kate won't pursue her dream of becoming a dancer. When the girls get into a huge fight over the matter, Kate begins avoiding Liz. Her behavior seems unreasonable until Kate reveals the real reason for her evasion: she was raped by Liz's brother. Shocked and unsure what to believe, Liz tries desperately to uncover the truth and salvage her family, friendships, and future. First novel.

Where it's reviewed:
Booklist, February 1, 2011, page 76
Horn Book Magazine, May-June 2011, page 97
Publishers Weekly, January 3, 2011, page 52
School Library Journal, April 2011, page 179
Voice of Youth Advocates, April 2011, page 63

Other books you might like:
Laurie Halse Anderson, *Speak*, 1999
Heidi Ayarbe, *Freeze Frame*, 2008
Ellen Hopkins, *Identical*, 2008
Carolyn Mackler, *The Earth, My Butt, and Other Big Round Things*, 2003

924

C.K. KELLY MARTIN

The Lighter Side of Life and Death

(New York: Random House, 2010)

Subject(s): Adolescent interpersonal relations; Friendship; Family

Age range(s): 15 - 18+
Major character(s): Mason, Teenager, Friend (of Kat and Jamie), Boyfriend (of Colette); Kat, Teenager, Friend (of Mason); Jamie, Teenager, Friend (of Mason); Colette, Girlfriend (of Mason)
Time period(s): 21st century; 2010s
Locale(s): United States

Summary: In C.K. Kelly Martin's *The Lighter Side of Life and Death*, high-school students Kat and Mason are best friends who have a sexual liaison after getting drunk at a party. Suddenly, their entire relationship changes. Kat is aloof and moody, while Mason—who's always been in love with Kat—can't get her out of his head. As the two deal with the fallout of their affair, Mason must also contend with problems at home, a strained friendship with his pal Jamie, and the turbulence of a new relationship with a much older woman.

Where it's reviewed:
Booklist, March 15, 2010, page 43
Horn Book Magazine, July/August 2010, page 114
School Library Journal, August 2010, page 107
Voice of Youth Advocates, October 2010, page 353

Other books by the same author:
My Beating Teenage Heart, 2011
One Lonely Degree, 2009
I Know It's Over, 2008

Other books you might like:
Melvin Burgess, *Doing It*, 2004
Janette Rallison, *Fame, Glory, and Other Things on My To-Do List*, 2005
Lauren Strasnick, *Nothing Like You*, 2009
Aury Wallington, *Pop!*, 2006

925

JESSICA MARTINEZ

Virtuosity

(New York: Simon Pulse, 2011)

Subject(s): Music; Mother-daughter relations; Drug abuse
Age range(s): 14 - 17+
Major character(s): Carmen Bianchi, Musician (violinist), Student—High School, Addict, Friend (of Jeremy), Daughter (of Diana); Jeremy King, Teenager, Musician (violinist), Friend (of Carmen); Diana Bianchi, Mother (of Carmen), Singer
Time period(s): 21st century; 2010s
Locale(s): Chicago, Illinois

Summary: Carmen is a stellar violin player. She's also a teenager with an overprotective mother, a cowardly stepfather, and an overwhelming class schedule. No matter what else is going on in Carmen's life, though, she knows she can rely on her music to get her through the day. Then she meets Jeremy. Jeremy is good looking and fun to be around, but he is also the first person in years who presents a challenge to her on the stage. Carmen knows that due to the schedule her mother has made for her life, a relationship with Jeremy is impossible. She also fears that growing close to Jeremy will leave her vulnerable and will distract her from reaching her goals. Nervous that she'll crack under the pressure, Carmen takes anti-anxiety medication and soon finds herself addicted to the pills. Jeremy is getting closer, her mother is suffocating her, and Carmen is certain that she has only a short amount of time left at the top. She sees herself falling—failing—and needs to find a way to make it all stop.

Where it's reviewed:
Booklist, December 1, 2011, page 63
School Library Journal, October 2011, page 143

Other books you might like:
Michelle Baldini, *Unraveling*, 2008
Deb Caletti, *Wild Roses*, 2005
Sophie Flack, *Bunheads*, 2011

926

ALFRED C. MARTINO

Over the End Line

(New York: Houghton Mifflin Harcourt, 2009)

Subject(s): Soccer; High schools; Adolescence
Age range(s): 14 - 17+
Major character(s): Jonny Fehey, Student—High School, Soccer Player; Kyle Saint-Claire, Friend (of Jonny), Soccer Player

Summary: *Over the End Line* is a young adult novel by author Alfred C. Martino. In it, the author tells the story of a high-school student named Jonny Fehey, who must deal with several unexpected issues in his adolescent life. His best friend, Kyle, is not only a better athlete than he but also more popular. Jonny is sick of sitting on the bench both at the soccer field and in life. Things get worse, however, as Jonny learns to deal with his father's estrangement as well as the rape of a girlfriend and even more than his share of teenage trauma. Can Fehey juggle issues that life keeps lobbing at him? Martino is also the author of *Pinned* and *Perfected by Girls*.

Where it's reviewed:
Booklist, September 15, 2009, page 51
Horn Book Guide, Spring 2010, page 102
School Library Journal, September 2009, page 166
Voice of Youth Advocates, October 2009, page 318

Other books by the same author:
Perfected by Girls, 2011
Pinned, 2005

Other books you might like:
Laurie Halse Anderson, *Speak*, 1999
Chris Crutcher, *Staying Fat for Sarah Byrnes*, 1993
Gail Giles, *What Happened to Cass McBride?*, 2006
Tom Hazuka, *Last Chance for First*, 2008
Coert Voorhees, *The Brothers Torres*, 2008

927

MORGAN MATSON

Amy and Roger's Epic Detour

(New York: Simon & Schuster, 2010)

Subject(s): Travel; Grief; Death

Age range(s): 15 - 18+
Major character(s): Amy Curry, Teenager; Roger, 19-Year-Old; Mom, Mother (of Amy)
Time period(s): 21st century; 2010s
Locale(s): United States

Summary: In *Amy and Roger's Epic Detour* by Morgan Matson, a cross-country road trip provides a getaway for a teenager dealing with her father's death. After Amy Curry's dad is killed in a car accident, the high school student thinks her life can't get any worse. Then her brother is admitted to a rehab program and her mother announces that the family is moving from California to Connecticut. To get Amy—and the family car—to the East Coast, Amy's mother recruits her friend's 19-year-old son, Roger, to drive. As Amy and Roger's relationship grows, the couple strays from their assigned route to see the sights and drive her mother crazy.

Where it's reviewed:
Horn Book Guide, Fall 2010, page 376
Publishers Weekly, May 10, 2010, page 47
School Library Journal, June 2010, page 112

Other books you might like:
Sarah Dessen, *The Truth about Forever*, 2004
Jonathan Friesen, *Jerk, California*, 2008
Mary E. Pearson, *The Miles Between*, 2009
Ellen Wittlinger, *Zigzag*, 2003

928

LISH MCBRIDE

Hold Me Closer, Necromancer

(New York: Henry Holt and Co., 2010)

Subject(s): Adventure; Death; Supernatural
Age range(s): 15 - 18+
Major character(s): Sam, Sorcerer (necromancer); Douglas, Sorcerer (necromancer)
Time period(s): 21st century; 2010s
Locale(s): Seattle, Washington

Summary: In Lish McBride's *Hold Me Closer, Necromancer*, Sam is a college dropout who passes his days working at a Seattle fast food restaurant. After a run-in with a customer named Douglas, Sam makes a startling discovery about himself: He is a necromancer, one with the ability to raise the dead. Not only is Douglas a necromancer, too, but he wants Sam to come work alongside him in resurrecting the dead. Douglas gives Sam has just once week to learn all he can about his long-dormant powers and come to a decision as to whether or not he wants to work with Douglas. If Sam declines, there could very well be hell to pay. First novel.

Where it's reviewed:
Booklist, November 15, 2010, page 36
Horn Book Guide, Spring 2011, page 106
Publishers Weekly, September 13, 2010, page 47
School Library Journal, January 2011, page 111
Voice of Youth Advocates, February 2011, page 574

Other books you might like:
Kelley Armstrong, *The Summoning*, 2008
Garth Nix, *Sabriel*, 1995
Michael Scott, *The Necromancer: The Secrets of the Immortal Nicholas Flamel*, 2010

929

GUADALUPE GARCIA MCCALL

Under the Mesquite

(New York: Lee & Low, 2011)

Story type: Ethnic; Young Adult
Subject(s): Poetry; Cancer; Mother-daughter relations

Age range(s): 13 - 16+
Major character(s): Lupita, Teenager, Student—High School
Time period(s): 21st century; 2010s
Locale(s): Texas, United States

Summary: Lupita is an aspiring actress who lands a lead role in the school play, but her dreams are dampened by the news that her mother has cancer. Now Lupita must face her fears of losing her mother while she attempts to maintain control of her emotions for the sake of her seven younger siblings. When Lupita's father takes her mother out of town for treatments, Lupita is responsible for caring for her brothers and sisters. Although Lupita is caring for her siblings, she needs to take some time for herself so she can let her emotions run their course.

McCall tells Lupita's story through poetic prose as she described the heartache and worry experienced by a teenage girl faced with a parent's mortality.

Where it's reviewed:
Booklist, October 1, 2011, page 90
School Library Journal, October 2011, page 142
Voice of Youth Advocates, October 2011, page 388

Awards the book has won:
Pura Belpre Award: Author Award, 2012

Other books you might like:
Jennifer Donnelly, *A Northern Light*, 2003
Anne Estevis, *Down Garrapata Road*, 2003
Kimberly Willis Holt, *Keeper of the Night*, 2003
Alan Lawrence Sitomer, *The Secret Story of Sonia Rodriguez*, 2008

930

CARLA KILLOUGH MCCLAFFERTY

The Many Faces of George Washington: Remaking a Presidential Icon

(Minneapolis, Minnesota: Carolrhoda Books, 2011)

Subject(s): Presidents (Government); Biographies; Science

Age range(s): 11 - 14+

Summary: This book describes an effort to preserve the legacy of George Washington—America's first president. Historians have found that different paintings and sculptures of George Washington portray his looks in various ways. Therefore, a group of historians and other professionals worked together to create three life-sized replicas of the first US president that were as accurate as possible. Historians, artists, anthropologists, artisans, and others worked together to create the replicas. The team used advanced technology and old-fashioned research to develop sculptures of Washington as a young man, as a middle-aged man, and as an elderly man. In addition to telling the story of the creation of the statues, the book gives biographical information about Washington's life.

Where it's reviewed:
Booklist, May 15, 2011, page 40
Bulletin of the Center for Children's Books, June 2011, page 478
Horn Book Guide, Fall 2011, page 469
School Library Journal, May 2011, page 134

Other books by the same author:
In Defiance of Hitler: The Secret Mission of Varian Fry, 2008
Something Out of Nothing: Marie Curie and Radium, 2006

Other books you might like:
Frank Keating, *George: George Washington, Our Founding Father*, 2012
Sterling North, *George Washington, Frontier Colonel*, 2006
Andrew Santella, *Mount Vernon*, 2011

931

NORAH MCCLINTOCK

She Said/She Saw

(Victoria, British Columbia: Orca Book Publishers, 2011)

Story type: Psychological Suspense
Subject(s): Murder; Memory; Mystery

Age range(s): 14 - 17+
Major character(s): Tegan, Teenager, Witness (to double murder), Narrator; Kelly, Sister (of Tegan), Narrator
Time period(s): 21st century; 2010s
Locale(s): United States

Summary: After witnessing a double murder, a young woman struggles to remember the details of the crime in this psychological thriller for young adults from award-winning author Norah McClintock. While Tegan watched, horrified, from the backseat, her two best friends were murdered by gunshot. As speculation begins circulating about the motive for the murders—illegal drugs, a lasting fight, random violence—all eyes are on Tegan. But the teenager claims that she never saw the person who pulled the trigger, and she has absolutely no idea why her friends were killed. The police, the victims' families, and Tegan's sister Kelly all question her story, believing she knows more than she's telling. As everyone shuns Tegan, she tries to recover her memory from that terrifying night, feeling more alone and desperate than ever.

Where it's reviewed:
School Library Journal, April 2011, page 179
Voice of Youth Advocates, June 2011, page 168

Other books by the same author:
Homicide Related, 2009
Taken, 2009
Dooley Takes the Fall, 2008
Bang, 2007
Tell, 2006

Other books you might like:
Peter Abrahams, *Bullet Point*, 2010
Robert Cormier, *The Rag and Bone Shop*, 2001
Lois Duncan, *I Know What You Did Last Summer*, 1973
Maureen Johnson, *The Name of the Star*, 2011

932

NORAH MCCLINTOCK

Taken

(Victoria, British Columbia, Canada: Orca Book Publishers, 2009)

Subject(s): Kidnapping; Wilderness survival; Suspense

Age range(s): 13 - 16+
Major character(s): Stephanie, Teenager, Kidnap Victim, Survivor
Time period(s): 21st century; 2000s
Locale(s): United States

Summary: Despite the recent disappearance of two teenage girls from her small town and constant warnings from police, Stephanie is confident she won't reach the same fate—until she takes a shortcut home from a friend's house and is kidnapped. She wakes up in an abandoned house, tied up and terrified. Desperate to see her family again and make amends with her mother, Stephanie manages to escape only to realize the true terror is just beginning. Stephanie is alone in the middle of nowhere, miles from help and without food, shelter, or water. Recalling the survival skills she learned from her grandfather and determined to make things right at home, Stephanie fights for her life in this haunting and suspenseful tale.

Where it's reviewed:
Booklist, September 15, 2009, page 53
Resource Links, December 2009, page 37
School Library Journal, December 2009, page 126

Other books by the same author:
Masked, 2010
Back, 2009
Bang, 2007
Tell, 2006
Snitch, 2005

Other books you might like:
Robert Cormier, *Tenderness: A Novel*, 1997
April Henry, *Girl, Stolen*, 2010
Stephen King, *The Girl Who Loved Tom Gordon*, 1999
Jacquelyn Mitchard, *Now You See Her*, 2007
Elizabeth Scott, *Living Dead Girl*, 2008

933

PATRICIA MCCORMICK

Purple Heart

(New York: Balzer and Bray, 2009)

Subject(s): Military life; Military science; Military bases
Age range(s): 15 - 18+
Major character(s): Matt Duffy, Military Personnel (soldier)
Time period(s): 21st century; 2000s
Locale(s): Iraq

Summary: A young solider confronts the harsh realities of war in *Purple Heart*. Matt Duffy is awarded the Purple Heart after he is injured in combat in Iraq. For some reason that he cannot explain, he does not feel that he deserves the honor. He suffered a major head injury during an attack, which affected his memory. One image, however, continues to haunt him: a vision of the death of a young Iraqi boy. Matt can't help but feel as if he was involved in the boy's murder, but he can't remember what happened. He eventually returns to combat, but Matt isn't the soldier he used to be. Matt's fears begin to overwhelm him, putting him and his fellow soldiers in grave danger.

Where it's reviewed:
Booklist, July 1, 2009, page 56
Horn Book Magazine, November-December 2009, page 679
Publishers Weekly, August 24, 2009, page 63
School Library Journal, November 2009, page 114
Voice of Youth Advocates, August 2009, page 228

Other books by the same author:
Sold, 2006
My Brother's Keeper, 2004
Cut, 2000

Other books you might like:
Walter Dean Myers, *Sunrise over Fallujah*, 2008
Rosanne Parry, *Heart of a Shepherd*, 2009
Dana Reinhardt, *The Things a Brother Knows*, 2010
Ryan Smithson, *Ghosts of War: The True Story of a 19-Year-Old GI*, 2009
Tim Tharp, *Badd*, 2011

934

LURLENE MCDANIEL

Breathless

(New York: Delacorte Press, 2009)

Subject(s): Cancer; Friendship; Brothers and sisters
Age range(s): 13 - 16+
Major character(s): Travis Morrison, Teenager, Diver, Cancer Patient
Time period(s): 21st century; 2000s
Locale(s): United States

Summary: In Lurlene McDaniel's *Breathless*, a teenage diving star must confront the biggest challenge of his life: his own mortality. Travis Morrison dives off a boat while vacationing with some friends, but the dive goes terribly wrong, and Travis suspects he's broken his leg. But when he's taken to the hospital, he learns something far more disturbing: he has cancer, and the doctors want to amputate the leg. Travis, however, isn't going down without a fight. He hatches an extreme plan of action that he hopes can save his leg. But is anyone willing to go along with his crazy plan?

Where it's reviewed:
Booklist, July 1, 2009, page 52
School Library Journal, April 2009, page 139

Other books by the same author:
Reaching through Time: Three Novellas, 2011
Heart to Heart, 2010
Prey, 2008
Hit and Run, 2007
Garden of Angels, 2003

Other books you might like:
Chris Crutcher, *Deadline*, 2007
Barbara Snow Gilbert, *Stone Water*, 1996
Amy Goldman Koss, *Side Effects*, 2006
Terry Trueman, *Inside Out*, 2003

935

ABBY MCDONALD

Boys, Bears, and a Serious Pair of Hiking Boots

(Somerville, Massachusetts: Candlewick Press, 2010)

Subject(s): Adolescent interpersonal relations; Ecology; Intergenerational relations

Age range(s): 15 - 18+
Major character(s): Jenna, Teenager, Activist (environmentalist); Susie, Godmother (of Jenna), Manager (of bed-and-breakfast)
Time period(s): 21st century; 2010s
Locale(s): Canada

Summary: In *Boys, Bears, and a Serious Pair of Hiking Boots*, author Abby McDonald introduces readers to Jenna, a teen environmental crusader and member of the Green Teens, a New Jersey-based activist organization. Jenna cannot wait until summer, when she'll have more time to devote to her activism, until she finds out that she must spend the summer at her godmother's bed-and-breakfast in Canada. Jenna instantly feels like an outcast; locals see her "green" activism as an imposition on their way of life, and her godmother, Susie, quickly tires of Jenna's suggestions for making the bed-and-breakfast more environmentally friendly—suggestions which Susie simply cannot afford. Soon Jenna learns that there is more than one side to the environmental issue, and she learns a valuable lesson in forming relationships while championing a cause.

Where it's reviewed:
Booklist, July 1, 2010, page 51
Horn Book Guide, Fall 2010, page 376
Publishers Weekly, March 22, 2010, page 72
School Library Journal, April 2010, page 164
Voice of Youth Advocates, August 2010, page 251

Other books by the same author:
The Anti-Prom, 2011
Sophomore Switch, 2009

Other books you might like:
Sneed B. Collard III, *Flash Point*, 2006
Janet Fox, *Faithful*, 2010
David Gilman, *The Devil's Breath*, 2007
Blake Nelson, *Destroy All Cars*, 2009

936

ANTHONY MCGOWAN

The Knife That Killed Me

(New York: Random House, 2008)

Subject(s): Gangs; Violence; Weapons

Age range(s): 10 - 15+
Major character(s): Roth, Bully, Gang Member, Young Man; Paul Varderman, Bullied Child, Narrator
Time period(s): 21st century; 2000s
Locale(s): United Kingdom

Summary: Paul doesn't fit into any particular "clique" at school. He likes the "freaks" because they talk about interesting things and don't get into fights. However, he is drawn to the likes of Roth, a terrifying bully. Roth is made even scarier by the fact that he openly carries weapons and is not afraid to use them. When Roth persuades Paul to be his messenger to a rival gang leader, it sets off a chain reaction of terrible events. Paul is afraid—too afraid to back away from the gang. Roth gives him a knife—a gesture of initiation, a means of protection, and a dangerous weapon.

Where it's reviewed:
Booklist, March 15, 2010, page 42
Horn Book Guide, Fall 2010, page 376
Publishers Weekly, March 29, 2010, page 61
School Library Journal, June 2010, page 110

Other books by the same author:
Jack Tumor, 2009
Hellbent, 2006

Other books you might like:
Tim Bowler, *Blade: Playing Dead*, 2008
Yxta Maya Murray, *The Good Girl's Guide to Getting Kidnapped*, 2010
Jeff Rivera, *Forever My Lady*, 2007
Todd Strasser, *If I Grow Up*, 2009

937

SHARON E. MCKAY

Thunder over Kandahar

(Toronto: Annick Press, 2010)

Story type: Historical
Subject(s): Middle East; Afghanistan Conflict, 2001-; Marriage

Age range(s): 13 - 16+
Major character(s): Yasmine, 14-Year-Old, Friend (of Tamanna); Tamanna, Friend (of Yasmine)
Time period(s): 21st century
Locale(s): Afghanistan

Summary: In this young adult novel, Sharon E. McKay tells the story of a 14-year-old Afghani girl who flees the Taliban with her friend. Yasmine and Tamanna are best friends living in a small Afghani village. Yasmine's parents have been educated in Britain and America and have passed their learning down to their daughter; Tamanna is smart but poor and lacks a formal education. A school is built in their village and both girls are excited to attend, but their chance to learn is taken away when the Taliban torches the building. Then Yasmine's parents are attacked, and she and Tamanna must leave their village and search for safe haven in the city of Kandahar. Along the way, they travel through the Taliban-controlled mountain regions where they encounter suicide bombers, mines, and the wrath of Tamanna's husband-to-be. McKay explores the realities faced by young people living in the war-torn Middle East through Yasmine and Tamanna's saga.

Where it's reviewed:
Booklist, December 1, 2010, page 54
Horn Book Guide, Spring 2011, page 106
School Library Journal, December 2010, page 118

Other books by the same author:
War Brothers, 2008
Esther, 2004
Penelope: Terror in the Harbor, 2001

Other books you might like:
Judie Oron, *Cry of the Giraffe*, 2010

Suzanne Fisher Staples, *Under the Persimmon Tree*, 2005

Catherine Stine, *Refugees*, 2005

938

VICTORIA MCKERNAN

The Devil's Paintbox

(New York: Alfred A. Knopf, 2009)

Subject(s): Frontier life; Brothers and sisters; Orphans

Age range(s): 12 - 16+, 13 - 16+

Major character(s): Aiden, 15-Year-Old, Brother (of Maddy); Maddy, 13-Year-Old, Sister (of Aiden)

Time period(s): 19th century; 1860s (1865)

Locale(s): American West, United States; Kansas, United States

Summary: In *The Devil's Paintbox*, author Victoria McKernan crafts a tale of adventure set in 1865 America. Here readers are introduced to 15-year-old Aiden and his kid sister Maddy, two orphans barely getting by on a drought-plagued Kansas farm. Desperate for new opportunities, the siblings hop a wagon train heading to Washington State, where Aiden plans on getting work as a logger. But the journey is an arduous one, putting the siblings' loyalty, strength, and determination to the test.

Where it's reviewed:
Booklist, July 1, 2009, page 52
School Library Journal, April 2009, page 139

Other books by the same author:
Shackleton's Stowaway, 2005

Other books you might like:
Stephen E. Ambrose, *This Vast Land: A Young Man's Journal of the Lewis and Clark Expedition*, 2003
Kimberly Willis Holt, *The Water Seeker*, 2010
Michael Spooner, *Daniel's Walk*, 2002

939

ROBIN MCKINLEY
PETER DICKINSON, Co-Author

Fire: Tales of Elemental Spirits

(New York: G. P. Putnam's Sons, 2009)

Subject(s): Short stories; Fires; Fantasy

Age range(s): 14 - 17+

Summary: *Fire: Tales of Elemental Spirits* by is a collection of five short stories by Robin McKinley and Peter Dickinson. Each story features different characters and takes place during a different time period, but in every story, the main character encounters a magical creature affiliated with fire. For instance, in the story "Phoenix," Ellie meets Dave and Welly, who have become caretakers of an ancient phoenix. In "Fireworm," Tandin is forced to fight the fireworm to save his village, but finds that he feels sympathy towards the creature. In "First Flight," a man helps a one-eyed dragon find its way home.

Where it's reviewed:
Booklist, September 1, 2009, page 81
Horn Book Magazine, November-December 2009, page 681
Journal of Adolescent & Adult, September 2010, page 72
School Library Journal, September 2009, page 166
Voice of Youth Advocates, December 2009, page 422

Other books by the same author:
Water: Tales of Elemental Spirits, 2002

Other books you might like:
Marianne Carus, *Fire and Wings: Dragon Tales from the East and West*, 2002
Bruce Coville, *Half-Human*, 2001
Shannon Hale, *Enna Burning*, 2004
Anne Ursu, *The Immortal Fire*, 2009

940

ROBIN MCKINLEY

Pegasus

(New York: G. P. Putnam's Sons, 2010)

Subject(s): Adventure; Human-animal relationships; Magic

Age range(s): 14 - 17+

Major character(s): Sylviianel "Sylvi", Royalty (princess); Ebon, Mythical Creature (Pegasus)

Time period(s): Indeterminate Past

Locale(s): Balsinland, Fictional Location

Summary: Robin McKinley's *Pegasus* is set in a magical land where Pegasi and royal-born children are united in loyalty on the child's 12th birthday. Princess Sylviianel is no exception to this tradition, and she is bound to her beloved Pegasus, Ebon. Svlvi and Ebon share a bond that is much deeper than the other human-Pegasus unions in Balsinland; they can actually communicate with one another without the use of a highly skilled magician. When word spreads of Sylvi and Ebon's unique ability to speak to one another, it challenges long-held traditions about the Pegasi and threatens the normal order of life in Balsinland.

Where it's reviewed:
Booklist, October 1, 2010, page 88
Horn Book Magazine, November/December 2010, page 96
Publishers Weekly, October 11, 2010, page 45
School Library Journal, December 2010, page 119
Voice of Youth Advocates, February 2011, page 574

Other books by the same author:
Chalice, 2008
Dragonhaven, 2007
Spindle's End, 2000

Other books you might like:
Mette Ivie Harrison, *The Princess and the Snowbird*, 2010
Anne McCaffrey, *Dragonriders of Pern Series*, 1968
Tamora Pierce, *Emperor Mage*, 1995

941

FREDRICK MCKISSACK JR.

Shooting Star

(New York: Atheneum Books for Young Readers, 2009)

Subject(s): Steroids (Organic compounds); African Americans; Football

Age range(s): 14 - 18+

Major character(s): Jomo Rodgers, Teenager, Friend (of Jayson Caldwell), Football Player, Addict; Jayson Caldwell, Teenager, Football Player, Friend (of Jomo Rodgers); Virgil Ganz, Drug Dealer

Time period(s): 21st century; 2000s (2009)

Locale(s): United States

Summary: In Fredrick McKissack Jr.'s *Shooting Star*, Jomo Rodgers is a struggling defense player for his high school's football team. The son of a former college athlete and a teacher, Jomo is embarrassed at his performance on the field. When his best friend and teammate Jayson Caldwell gets more attention than he does, Jomo makes a risky decision. With the help of drug dealer Virgil Ganz, Jomo gets his hands on steroids. Jomo's whole life changes in an instant. He quickly packs on pounds of muscle, and becomes faster and more agile on the field. A few weeks later, he is in over his head and no one seems to notice until it's too late.

Where it's reviewed:
Booklist, September 1, 2009, page 105
School Library Journal, September 2009, page 166
Voice of Youth Advocates, December 2009, page 411

Other books you might like:
Carl Deuker, *Gym Candy*, 2007
Robert Lipsyte, *Raiders Night*, 2007
Robert B. Parker, *The Boxer and the Spy*, 2008
Marlene Perez, *Dead Is So Last Year*, 2009

942

LISA MCMANN

Cryer's Cross

(New York: Simon Pulse, 2011)

Subject(s): Mystery; Missing persons; Supernatural

Age range(s): 14 - 18+

Major character(s): Kendall Fletcher, Teenager, Student—High School, Mentally Ill Person (OCD), Soccer Player; Nico, Friend (of Kendall), Teenager, Kidnap Victim

Time period(s): 21st century; 2010s

Locale(s): Cryer's Cross, Montana

Summary: *Cryer's Cross* is a supernatural mystery for young adult readers from best-selling author Lisa McMann. As a teenager in the tiny town of Cryer's Cross, Montana, Kendall Fletcher enjoys playing soccer, dreams of making it big on Broadway, and struggles daily with obsessive-compulsive disorder. When two students disappear without a trace, including Kendall's best friend, Nico, Kendall's symptoms worsen and her life begins spiraling out of control. Shortly after Nico's disappearance, Kendall is haunted by terrifying visions and supernatural messages that hint at an ominous presence in Cryer's Cross. Kendall is certain that Nico can be saved, and the rest of the community spared, if she can uncover the dark forces at work in the sleepy town.

Where it's reviewed:
Booklist, February 15, 2011, page 70
Journal of Adolescent & Adult, May 2011, page 635
Publishers Weekly, January 3, 2011, page 52
School Library Journal, February 2011, page 114

Other books by the same author:
Dead to You, 2012
The Unwanteds, 2011
Gone, 2010
Fade, 2009
Wake, 2008

Other books you might like:
George Harrar, *Not as Crazy as I Seem*, 2003
D.J. MacHale, *The Light*, 2010
F. Paul Wilson, *Jack: Secret Circles*, 2010
Brenna Yovanoff, *The Replacement*, 2010

943

MARGARET MCMULLAN

Sources of Light

(New York: Houghton Mifflin, 2010)

Subject(s): Race relations; Adolescent interpersonal relations; Civil rights movements

Age range(s): 13 - 16+

Major character(s): Samantha, 14-Year-Old

Time period(s): 20th century; 1960s (1962-1963)

Locale(s): Jackson, Mississippi

Summary: Margaret McMullan's *Sources of Light* is the story of a 14-year-old girl growing up in the racially charged southern United States. Samantha and her mother move to Mississippi in 1962, and Samantha is taken aback at the social differences between her new town and her native Pennsylvania. She is determined to stay removed from the volatile race riots, but when Samantha's mother begins a professorship at a nearby black college, both are harassed by white supremacists. Samantha soon finds solace in photography, as her mother's new colleague shows her how to capture the civil rights experience on film.

Where it's reviewed:
Horn Book Magazine, May-June 2010, page 87
Publishers Weekly, April 5, 2010, page 61
School Library Journal, May 2010, page 120
Voice of Youth Advocates, August 2010, page 252

Other books by the same author:
Cashay, 2009
When I Crossed No-Bob, 2007
How I Found the Strong, 2004

Other books you might like:
Shana Burg, *A Thousand Never Evers*, 2008

Kristi Collier, *Jericho Walls*, 2002
Trudy Krisher, *Spite Fences*, 1994

944

BRIAN MEEHL

You Don't Know About Me

(New York: Delacorte Press, 2011)

Subject(s): Christian life; Self knowledge; Mother-son relations

Age range(s): 15 - 18+

Major character(s): Billy Allbright, 15-Year-Old, Traveler; Ruah Branch, Baseball Player, Homosexual, Companion (of Billy)

Time period(s): 21st century; 2010s

Locale(s): United States

Summary: In the young-adult novel *You Don't Know About Me* by Brian Meehl, 15-year-old Billy Allbright learns about life, faith, and family on a road trip through the American West. Billy has been raised by his mother, who teaches him at home and takes him on her evangelical pilgrimages around the country. Though Billy is a devout Christian, he wants to experience the greater world and gets his chance when he receives a package from his presumably deceased father. Billy teams up with gay pro-baseball player Ruah Branch as he follows the trail of clues left by his father that lead to a literary treasure. As Billy reconsiders his beliefs in light of his friendship with Ruah and encounters a diverse cast of characters on the road, the teenager's journey becomes more important than his destination.

Where it's reviewed:
Booklist, May 15, 2011, page 48
Publishers Weekly, March 14, 2011, page 75
School Library Journal, June 2011, page 124
Voice of Youth Advocates, June 2011, page 170

Other books by the same author:
Suck It Up, 2008

Other books you might like:
Helen Hemphill, *Long Gone Daddy*, 2006
Catherine Ryan Hyde, *Becoming Chloe*, 2006
Maureen Johnson, *13 Little Blue Envelopes*, 2005
Mark Twain, *The Adventures of Huckleberry Finn*, 1884

945

MAILE MELOY

IAN SCHOENHERR, Illustrator

The Apothecary

(New York: Penguin USA, 2011)

Subject(s): Cold War, 1945-1991; Magic; Espionage

Age range(s): 12 - 15+

Major character(s): Janie Scott, 14-Year-Old, Friend (of Benjamin), Expatriate; Benjamin Burrows, Teenager, Son (of Mr. Burrows), Friend (of Janie); Mr. Bur-rows, Apothecary, Father (of Benjamin), Kidnap Victim

Time period(s): 20th century; 1950s (1952)

Locale(s): London, England

Summary: The year is 1952, and Janie Scott is not thrilled to have to move from Los Angeles all the way to London, especially since the reason the Scotts must move there is because her parents have been accused of being communists. Fortunately for Janie, she meets Benjamin Burrows, a teenager with plans to become a spy against the Soviet Union when he grows up. Mr. Burrows, Benjamin's father, is the local apothecary, but when he disappears, Janie begins to wonder if there is more to him than meets the eye. Now Benjamin and Janie must risk their lives to save his father, and the key to Mr. Burrows's whereabouts could lie within a mysterious book called *The Pharmacopoeia*. Can Janie and Benjamin figure out this puzzling book before the Soviet spies steal it away? This book is illustrated by Ian Schoenherr.

Where it's reviewed:
Booklist, September 1, 2011, page 114
Girls' Life, December 2011, page 43
Publishers Weekly, September 5. 2011, page 50
School Library Journal, December 2011, page 125
Voice of Youth Advocates, October 2011, page 406

Other books you might like:
Andrew Clements, *Things Not Seen*, 2002
Ronald Kidd, *The Year of the Bomb*, 2009
Angie Sage, *Physik*, 2007

946

NEESHA MEMINGER

Shine, Coconut Moon

(New York: Margaret K. McElderry Books, 2009)

Subject(s): Racism; Indians (Asian people); Cultural identity

Age range(s): 12 - 16+

Major character(s): Samar "Sam", 17-Year-Old, Student—High School, Indian

Time period(s): 21st century; 2000s

Locale(s): New Jersey, United States

Summary: *Shine, Coconut Moon* is a young adult novel about identity, heritage, and acceptance from author Neesha Meminger. Seventeen-year-old Samar ("Sam") has never known much about her Indian heritage. Growing up in America, her mom has deliberately kept her from her traditional relatives, a fact that has never bothered the teenager, who is typically consumed with school, friendships, and dating. But everything changes after September 11. A turban-wearing man, who turns out to be Sam's uncle, shows up at her door eager to teach her about her Sikh heritage. Sam isn't interested until a racial slur propels her to understand more about her culture. When her uncle is the victim of a racist attack, Sam quickly realizes how powerful and dangerous ignorance can be.

Where it's reviewed:
Booklist, February 15, 2009, page 72
Publishers Weekly, February 9, 2009, page 49

School Library Journal, April 2009, page 139
Voice of Youth Advocates, June 2009, page 140

Other books by the same author:
Jazz in Love, 2011

Other books you might like:
Randa Abdel-Fattah, *Ten Things I Hate about Me*, 2009
Tanuja Desai Hidier, *Born Confused*, 2002
Uma Krishnaswami, *Naming Maya*, 2004
Daphne Muse, *Prejudice: Stories About Hate, Ignorance, Revelation, and Transformation*, 1995
Mitali Perkins, *Secret Keeper*, 2009

947

ANTONIA MICHAELIS
ANTHEA BELL, Translator

Dragons of Darkness

(New York: Amulet Books, 2010)

Subject(s): Sibling rivalry; Dragons; Fantasy

Age range(s): 12 - 18+

Major character(s): Niya, Teenager, Revolutionary; Jumar, Teenager, Royalty (prince of Nepal); Christopher, 14-Year-Old, Brother (Arne); Arne, Brother (of Christopher)

Locale(s): Nepal

Summary: *Dragons of Darkness*, written by Antonia Michaelis and translated by Anthea Bell, is the story of two siblings: Arne and his younger brother, Christopher. When Arne suddenly vanishes, Christopher sets out on a journey to Nepal to find his older brother. Once there, he encounters a boy named Jumar, who claims to be the royal prince of Nepal on the run from Maoist rebels, and a Maoist named Niya. The trio must find their way through a country rocked by treacherous political turmoil as Christopher seeks out his brother, Jumar aims for vengeance against a friend's murder, and Niya looks for justice for his people.

Where it's reviewed:
Booklist, March 1, 2010, page 72
Horn Book Guide, Fall 2010, page 377
Publishers Weekly, December 14. 2009, page 61
School Librarian, Spring 2010, page 52
School Library Journal, March 2010, page 164

Other books by the same author:
Tiger Moon, 2008

Other books you might like:
Ann Coburn, *Glint*, 2007
Megan Whalen Turner, *A Conspiracy of Kings*, 2010
Carrie Vaughn, *Voices of Dragons*, 2010

948

GLENDA MILLARD

A Small Free Kiss in the Dark

(Crows Nest, New South Wales, Australia: Allen & Unwin, 2009)

Subject(s): Refugees; Survival; Runaways

Age range(s): 13 - 16+

Major character(s): Skip, 11-Year-Old, Runaway; Billy, Vagrant; Max, 6-Year-Old; Tia, 15-Year-Old, Dancer (ballet), Mother (of Sixpence); Sixpence, Daughter (of Tia)

Time period(s): Indeterminate

Locale(s): Australia

Summary: Acclaimed young adult novelist Glenda Millard crafts a tale of friendship and survival in *A Small Free Kiss in the Dark*. Skip, an 11-year-old runaway, teams up with a vagrant named Billy when bombs descend on the Australian city they call home. The devastation left by the bombs adds more members to their team: six-year-old Max, teenage ballet dancer Tia, and Tia's newborn daughter, Sixpence. The group makes an unlikely family as they struggle to survive in the aftermath of war-torn Australia. *A Small Free Kiss in the Dark* was awarded the Queensland Premier's Literary Awards Young Adult Book Award in 2009.

Where it's reviewed:
Booklist, March 1, 2010, page 61
Horn Book Guide, Fall 2010, page 337
School Library Journal, March 2010, page 164

Awards the book has won:
Queensland Premier's Literary Awards, 2009

Other books you might like:
Anne-Laure Bondoux, *A Time of Miracles*, 2010
Linda Sue Park, *A Long Walk to Water: Based on a True Story*, 2010
Katherine Paterson, *The Day of the Pelican*, 2009
Wendelin Van Draanen, *Runaway*, 2006

949

KIRSTEN MILLER

The Eternal Ones

(New York: Razorbill, 2010)

Subject(s): Reincarnation; Faith; Love

Age range(s): 14 - 18+

Major character(s): Haven Moore, 17-Year-Old; Iain Morrow, Wealthy; Beau, Friend (of Haven)

Time period(s): 21st century; 2010s

Locale(s): New York, New York; Tennessee, United States

Summary: Kirsten Miller's *The Eternal Ones* charts the romantic escapades of 17-year-old Haven Moore, who sets out to find the man she suspects was her true love in a previous life. Leaving her small Tennessee town behind, Haven makes her way to New York City, where she plans to attend fashion school. There she meets Iain Morrow, a handsome billionaire who calls forth unusual memories for Haven. Soon she is convinced Iain is her soul mate, but the mysterious stranger is surrounded by danger—and he may just be trying to kill her.

Where it's reviewed:
Booklist, June 1, 2010, page 50
Horn Book Guide, Spring 2011, page 106
Publishers Weekly, July 19, 2010, page 131
School Library Journal, August 2010, page 108
Voice of Youth Advocates, August 2010, page 121

Other books by the same author:
Kiki Strike: The Empress's Tomb, 2007
Kiki Strike: Inside the Shadow City, 2006

Other books you might like:
Lauren Kate, *Fallen*, 2009
Nancy Werlin, *Impossible*, 2008
Scott Westerfeld, *Love Is Hell*, 2008
Suzanne Weyn, *Reincarnation*, 2008

950

LYN MILLER-LACHMANN
Gringolandia
(Willimantic, Connecticut: Curbstone Press, 2009)

Subject(s): Mental disorders; Violence; Hispanic
Americans

Age range(s): 15 - 18+

Major character(s): Daniel Aguilar, 12-Year-Old; Marcelus
Aguilar, Father (of Daniel), Journalist; Courtney,
Girlfriend (of Daniel)

Time period(s): 20th century; 1980s (1980-1986)

Locale(s): Santiago, Chile; Madison, Wisconsin

Summary: *Gringolandia* by Lyn Miller-Lachmann begins
in Santiago, Chile, in 1980. Daniel Aguilar is 12 years
old, and his father Marcelus is captured at gunpoint for
starting an underground newspaper. While Marcelus is in
prison, Daniel and his family flee to Madison, Wisconsin,
or "Gringolandia," as they call it. Six years pass and
Daniel is relatively happy with a girlfriend and a part in
a rock band, though he blames himself for his father's
capture. When Marcelus is finally freed and comes to
their home in Wisconsin, he thinks everything will be
fine, but he appears to be suffering from post-traumatic
stress disorder. Daniel also worries that his girlfriend
Courtney is trying to get his father to start another
underground newspaper.

Where it's reviewed:
Booklist, July 1, 2009, page 54
Horn Book Magazine, November/December 2009, page
681
School Library Journal, April 2009, page 139
Voice of Youth Advocates, August 13, 2009, page 229

Other books by the same author:
Dirt Cheap, 2006

Other books you might like:
Julia Alvarez, *Before We Were Free*, 2002
Beverly Birch, *Rift*, 2006
Gary Paulsen, *Soldier's Heart*, 1998
James Watson, *Talking in Whispers*, 1983

951

SARAH MLYNOWSKI
*Ten Things We Did (and Probably
Shouldn't Have)*
(New York: HarperTeen, 2011)

Story type: Contemporary; Young Adult

Subject(s): Adolescent interpersonal relations; Sexuality;
Dating (Social customs)

Age range(s): 15 - 18+

Major character(s): April, Teenager, Friend (of Vi); Vi,
Teenager, Friend (of April)

Time period(s): 21st century; 2010s

Summary: This young adult novel by author Sarah
Mlynowski tells the story of what happens when a group
of teenagers are allowed to housesit for the first time.
When April wakes up with a strange boy in her bed and
a house trashed by partygoers, she and her best friend Vi
must retrace their steps to remember exactly how they
got into this predicament. They don't have much time,
either. April's father has called to let her know he will
be stopping by in a few minutes. As the girls scramble to
clean up the house, April recounts the wild night before
and how she handled—or mishandled—her first experience on her own.

Where it's reviewed:
Booklist, May 15, 2011, page 48
Horn Book Guide, Fall 2011, page 390
Publishers Weekly, May 9, 2011, page 55
School Library Journal, August 2011, page 112
Voice of Youth Advocates, August 2011, page 274

Other books by the same author:
Gimme a Call, 2010
Magic in Manhattan, 2005-2009

Other books you might like:
Jan Blazanin, *A and L Do Summer*, 2011
Ann Brashares, *Sisterhood of the Traveling Pants
Series*, 2001
Ted Staunton, *Acting Up*, 2010

952

FABIO MOON
GABRIEL BA, Co-Author
Daytripper
(New York: DC Comics, 2011)

Subject(s): Death; Friendship; Love

Age range(s): 15 - 18+

Major character(s): Bras de Olivias Dominguez, Young
Man

Time period(s): 21st century; 2010s

Locale(s): Brazil

Summary: *Daytripper* is a thought-provoking graphic
novel from authors Fabio Moon and Gabriel Ba. The
story, about living life to its fullest and the inevitability
of death, focuses on a Brazilian man named Bras de
Olivias Dominguez. Each chapter of the book follows
some adventure, whether big or small, good or bad, in
the life of Bras and ultimately ends with his death. The
next chapter picks up with another event in Bras' life
and again ends with his death. Ba and Moon shed light
on Bras' connections with his family, friends, career,
life, and art by showcasing how differently death would
affect him and those around him at various points in his
life.

Where it's reviewed:
Booklist, March 15, 2011, page 3
Library Journal, September 15. 2011, page 58

Publishers Weekly, January 20, 2011, page 37

Other books by the same author:
De: Tales: Stories from Urban Brazil, 2006

Other books you might like:
Luis Alberto Urrea, *Mr. Mendoza's Paintbrush*, 2010
Aristophane, *The Zabime Sisters*, 2010
Kathryn Immonen, *Moving Pictures*, 2010
David Mazzucchelli, *Asterios Polyp*, 2009
Josh Neufeld, *A.D.: New Orleans after the Deluge*, 2009

953

JESSICA MORGAN
HEATHER COCKS, Co-Author
Spoiled
(New York: Little, Brown and Company, 2011)

Subject(s): Sisters; Father-daughter relations; Schools
Age range(s): 15 - 18+
Major character(s): Molly Dix, 16-Year-Old, Sister (of Brooke), Daughter (of Brick); Brooke Berlin, Sister (of Molly); Brick Berlin, Father (of Molly and Brooke), Actor
Time period(s): 21st century; 2010s
Locale(s): Hollywood, California; Indiana, United States

Summary: *Spoiled* is a novel by authors Jessica Morgan and Heather Cocks. Having grown up the only daughter of a single mom, Molly Dix and couldn't be closer to her mother. When Molly's mom dies, however, the 16-year-old discovers her extraordinary heritage: she is the illegitimate daughter of superstar Brick Berlin. Now she is being whisked away from her small town life in Indiana to Hollywood, where nothing seems real. She has a new sister named Brooke and an amazing new life. Yet the love she felt from her mother is missing, and the smiles on the faces of her new family hide some secrets about how lonely each of them is.

Where it's reviewed:
Booklist, July1, 2011, page 53
Horn Book Guide, Fall 2011, page 377
Publishers Weekly, April 1, 2011, page 55
School Library Journal, December 2011, page 112
Voice of Youth Advocates, August 2011, page 364

Other books you might like:
Lauren Conrad, *Sweet Little Lies: An L.A. Candy Novel*, 2010
Carolyn Mackler, *Vegan Virgin Valentine*, 2004
Cecily Von Ziegesar, *Gossip Girl: The Carlyles*, 2008
Lizabeth Zindel, *The Secret Rites of Social Butterflies*, 2008

954

JACLYN MORIARTY
The Ghosts of Ashbury High
(New York: Arthur A. Levine Books, 2010)

Series: Ashbury High Series. Book 4
Subject(s): Interpersonal relations; High schools; History
Age range(s): 14 - 18+
Major character(s): Emily Thompson, Student—High School; Amelia, Student—High School; Riley, Student—High School, Boyfriend (of Amelia); Lydia, Friend (of Emily); Cassie, Friend (of Emily)
Time period(s): 21st century; 2010s
Locale(s): Australia

Summary: In *The Ghosts of Ashbury High* by Jaclyn Moriarty, the arrival of two new students at Ashbury High arouses the interest of students and faculty alike. Amelia and Riley, transfers from notorious Brookfield High, come to Ashbury for their senior year. Deeply in love, they stay out late, skip class, and still win admiration from the Ashbury community for their unparalleled coolness. Emily Thompson wants to find out more about the strange couple. As she tries to dig up dirt on Amelia and Riley, Emily also investigates a mysterious haunting at the school. *The Ghosts of Ashbury High* is the fourth book in the Ashbury High series.

Where it's reviewed:
Booklist, April 1, 2010, page 32
Horn Book Magazine, July/August 2010, page 115
Publishers Weekly, June 28, 2010, page 129
School Library Journal, September 2010, page 158

Other books by the same author:
The Spell Book of Listen Taylor: And the Secrets of the Family Zing, 2007
The Murder of Bindy Mackenzie, 2006
The Year of Secret Assignments, 2004
Feeling Sorry for Celia, 2001

Other books you might like:
Charles de Lint, *The Blue Girl*, 2004
Deborah Noyes, *The Ghosts of Kerfol*, 2008
Nina Schindler, *An Order of Amelie, Hold the Fries*, 2004

955

PAULA MORRIS
Ruined: A Ghost Story
(New York: Scholastic, 2009)

Subject(s): Ghosts; Friendship; Schools
Age range(s): 12 - 16+
Major character(s): Rebecca, 10th Grader; Lisette, Spirit; Anton Grey, Friend (of Rebecca)
Time period(s): 21st century; 2000s
Locale(s): New Orleans, Louisiana

Summary: In Paula Morris's *Ruined: A Ghost Story*, teenager Rebecca is forced to live with her aunt for a year while her father travels on business. Stuck in New Orleans and ignored at school, Rebecca decides to explore the city. In a graveyard, she meets Lisette, a ghost who is anxious to make friends with Rebecca. As Rebecca's unusual new friend shows her around New Orleans, she learns that Lisette has secrets and agendas of her own. Meanwhile, at school, Rebecca is drawn to handsome Anton Grey, and with his help, she not only unearths Lisette's dark history—but her own.

Where it's reviewed:
Booklist, September 15, 2009, page 51
Horn Book Guide, Spring 2010, page 103
Publishers Weekly, July 20, 2009, page 141
School Library Journal, November 2009, page 115

Other books by the same author:
Dark Souls, 2011

Other books you might like:
Tony Abbott, *City of the Dead*, 2009
Kim Antieau, *Ruby's Imagine*, 2008
Joanne Dahme, *Creepers*, 2008
Terry Pratchett, *Johnny and the Dead*, 1993
Anne Spollen, *Light Beneath Ferns*, 2010

956

JEAN-CLAUDE MOURLEVAT

Winter's End

(Somerville, Massachusetts: Candlewick Press, 2009)

Subject(s): Dystopias; Fantasy; Orphans

Age range(s): 14 - 18+

Major character(s): Milena, Teenager, Orphan; Bartolomeo, Teenager, Orphan; Helen, Teenager, Orphan; Milos, Teenager, Orphan

Time period(s): Indeterminate Future

Locale(s): Fictional Location

Summary: In *Winter's End* by Jean-Claude Mourlevat, a bleak, dystopian future has left many children orphans. Held as captives for 15 years in an oppressive boarding school after the murder of their parents, Milena, Bartolomeo, Helen, and Milos, now teenagers, finally break out to take a stand against the ruling regime. Their flight toward resistance headquarters and away from the dogmen that are tracking them leads them through treacherous, frozen terrain. Their journey is complicated when Milos is seized by Phalange government officials who want to force him to participate in state-sponsored death matches. Milos's friends must fight for his freedom and the survival of their generation. Translated from the French by Anthea Bell.

Where it's reviewed:
Publishers Weekly, November 2, 2009, page 54
School Library Journal, December 2009, page 128

Other books you might like:
Suzanne Collins, *The Hunger Games*, 2008
James DeVita, *The Silenced*, 2007
John Marsden, *Tomorrow Series*, 1993
Neal Shusterman, *Unwind*, 2007

957

ANDY MULLIGAN

Trash

(New York: David Fickling Books, 2010)

Subject(s): Futuristic society; Scandals; Mystery

Age range(s): 12 - 15+

Major character(s): Raphael, Friend (of Rat and Gordo); Rat, Friend (of Raphael and Gordo); Gordo, Friend (of Raphael and Rat)

Time period(s): Indeterminate Future

Locale(s): Behala, Fictional Location

Summary: Andy Mulligan's *Trash* takes place in a futuristic third-world country, where three boys—Raphael, Rat, and Gordo—forage a living by sifting through the mounds of garbage that surround their community. One day, Raphael makes a startling find: a strange bag that immediately catches the boys' attention. They decide to keep the bag for themselves, even when the local authorities put out an all-points bulletin seeking the safe return of the object. This triggers a series of events that lead Raphael and his friends to some shocking truths about the society in which they live—and about those who are supposed to be looking after their best interests. First novel.

Where it's reviewed:
Booklist, September 15, 2010, page 64
Horn Book Magazine, November/December 2010, page 97
Publishers Weekly, October 4, 2010, page 49
Reading Time, November 2010, page 38
School Library Journal, October 2010, page 123

Other books you might like:
Nancy Farmer, *The Ear, the Eye, and the Arm*, 1994
Daniel Finn, *She Thief*, 2010
Jess Mowry, *Babylon Boyz*, 1997

958

MIKE MULLIN

Ashfall

(Terre Haute, Indiana: Tanglewood, 2011)

Story type: Disaster
Subject(s): Volcanoes; Adolescence; Suspense

Age range(s): 14 - 18+

Major character(s): Alex, Teenager, Survivor; Darla, Companion (to Alex)

Time period(s): 21st century; 2010s

Locale(s): Iowa, United States

Summary: A teenage boy must fight for survival amidst an epic natural disaster in this suspenseful novel for young adults from author Mike Mullin. Alex is relishing the freedom of an entire weekend alone while his parents are away. Intent on doing nothing but hang out with his friends and play video games, Alex is in for a major surprise when his hometown turns into a scene from a horror movie. Far beneath the boiling springs of Yellowstone National Park lies a long-dormant supervolcano. When the volcano erupts, Alex's town—and the entire state of Iowa—is covered in darkness, debris, and ash. Desperate to find his family, Alex sets out on a harrowing journey aided by Darla, a surprisingly resourceful travel companion he meets along the way.

Where it's reviewed:
Booklist, October 1, 2011, page 82

Publishers Weekly, September 12, 2011, page 79
School Library Journal, November 2011, page 133
Voice of Youth Advocates, December 2011, page 498

Other books you might like:
Joelle Anthony, *Restoring Harmony*, 2010
Paolo Bacigalupi, *Ship Breaker: A Novel*, 2010
David Brin, *The Postman*, 1985
Anna Carey, *Eve*, 2011
Susan Beth Pfeffer, *Life as We Knew It*, 2006

959

CATHERINE GILBERT MURDOCK

Wisdom's Kiss: A Thrilling and Romantic Adventure Incorporating Magic, Villainy and a Cat

(New York: Houghton Mifflin Harcourt, 2011)

Story type: Fantasy; Young Adult
Subject(s): Adventure; Supernatural; Royalty

Age range(s): 13 - 16+
Major character(s): Princess Dizzy, Royalty; Tips, Military Personnel; Fortitude, Housekeeper; Magic, Cat

Summary: Princess Wisdom, or Dizzy as most of her friends call her, is a young princess whose life is turned upside down when she learns she must help save her kingdom and her family from an evil duchess. The duchess is planning to overthrow Dizzy's family to gain the thrown. Dizzy decides to go on adventure to stop the duchess, but she can't do it alone. Dizzy teams up with a warrior named Tips, a housekeeper named Fortitude, and a cat named Magic. This unlikely foursome must embark on a perilous journey to stop their kingdom's total destruction, but will their differences drive them apart before they can accomplish their goals?

Where it's reviewed:
Booklist, August 1, 2011, page 45
Horn Book Magazine, September/October 2011, page 92
Publishers Weekly, August 8, 2011, page 50
School Library Journal, October 2011, page 143
Voice of Youth Advocates, October 2011, page 407

Other books by the same author:
Princess Ben: Being a Wholly Truthful Account of Her Various Discoveries and Misadventures, Recounted to the Best of Her Recollection, in Four Parts, 2008

Other books you might like:
Michelle Cooper, *A Brief History of Montmaray*, 2009
Jean Ferris, *Once upon a Marigold*, 2002
Jessica Day George, *Princess of Glass*, 2010
Michaela MacColl, *Prisoners in the Palace: How Victoria Became Queen with the Help of Her Maid, a Reporter, and a Scoundrel: A Novel of Intrigue and Romance*, 2010

960

CATHERINE GILBERT MURDOCK

Front and Center

(New York: Houghton Mifflin, 2009)

Series: Dairy Queen Series. Book 3
Subject(s): Basketball; Dating (Social customs); Interpersonal relations

Age range(s): 12 - 16+
Major character(s): D.J. Schwenk, 11th Grader; Brian Nelson, Friend (of D.J.)
Time period(s): 21st century; 2010s
Locale(s): American Midwest, United States

Summary: In *Front and Center* by Catherine Gilbert Murdock, high-school junior D.J. Schwenk likes playing basketball, but she doesn't like the fanfare that accompanies her accomplishments on the court. When the hectic season ends at Red Bend High School, D.J. is eager to return to her anonymous life. But her coach thinks D.J. has a future in basketball, and the college scouts who have been coming to watch her play agree. Even the Red Bend basketball fans take an interest in D.J.'s career. Meanwhile, Brian Nelson, her ex-boyfriend, provides an unwelcome distraction. *Front and Center* is the third book in the Dairy Queen series.

Where it's reviewed:
Booklist, October 1, 2009, page 34
Horn Book Magazine, Sept.-Oct. 2009, page 569
School Library Journal, September 2009, page 167
Voice of Youth Advocates, December 2009, page 412

Other books by the same author:
The Off Season, 2007
Dairy Queen, 2006

Other books you might like:
Kate Jaimet, *Slam Dunk*, 2009
Kathryn Mackel, *Boost*, 2008
Phyllis Reynolds Naylor, *Intensely Alice*, 2009
Janette Rallison, *Life, Love, and the Pursuit of Free Throws*, 2004

961

WALTER DEAN MYERS

Lockdown

(New York: HarperCollins, 2010)

Subject(s): Juvenile detention homes; Conduct of life; Friendship

Age range(s): 14 - 18+
Major character(s): Reese, 15-Year-Old; Toon, Friend (of Reese)
Time period(s): 21st century; 2010s
Locale(s): United States

Summary: In *Lockdown* by Walter Dean Myers, a 14-year-old inmate at a juvenile detention center looks forward to completing his sentence and setting his life back on course. Sent to the Progress center for stealing prescription pads, Reese realizes that he could be imprisoned in a much tougher facility if he breaks the law again. As Reese has learned at Progress, being locked up has not only limited his personal freedom, it has also narrowed his choice of companions considerably. When his friend, Toon, is threatened, Reese must decide if he should intervene, even though his actions could endanger his record of good behavior.

Where it's reviewed:
Booklist, December 1, 2009, page 38
Horn Book Guide, Fall 2010, page 378
Publishers Weekly, January 11, 2010, page 49
School Library Journal, February 2010, page 118
Voice of Youth Advocates, February 2010, page 496

Other books by the same author:
Dope Sick, 2009
Shooter, 2004
Dream Bearer, 2003

Other books you might like:
LouAnne Johnson, *Muchacho*, 2009
Jordan Sonnenblick, *Notes from the Midnight Driver*, 2006
Paul Volponi, *Rikers High*, 2010

962

WALTER DEAN MYERS

Dope Sick

(New York: HarperTeen, 2009)

Subject(s): Conduct of life; Drug abuse; Supernatural
Age range(s): 14 - 18+
Major character(s): Jeremy "Lil J" Dance, 17-Year-Old, Crime Suspect, Addict, Drug Dealer, Impoverished, Fugitive; Rico, Drug Dealer, Prisoner, Friend (of Lil J), 19-Year-Old; Anthony Gaffione, Police Officer (undercover); Kelly, Supernatural Being (sees past and future)
Time period(s): 21st century; 2000s
Locale(s): New York, New York

Summary: With blood dripping from his arm and sweat soaking his clothes, 17-year-old Jeremy "Lil J" Dance seeks temporary refuge in a crack house in Harlem, New York, after a petty drug deal becomes violent and ends with an undercover cop shot and Lil J pegged as the trigger man. So much for making a little quick cash. In the building, Lil J meets a man named Kelly, who is somehow able to watch past scenes from Lil J's life and, stranger yet, scenes of what may come. For example, Kelly shows Lil J that if he continues on his current route, he will commit suicide as a SWAT team bears down on the very building in which he is hiding. With that, Kelly questions Lil J about his wasted existence, what went wrong, and what he would change. Geared toward young adults, this book covers poverty, addiction, parenting, and decision making. Author Walter Dean Myers, a two-time National Book Award finalist for *Monster* (1999) and *Autobiography of My Dead Brother* (2005), uses a blend of fantasy and real-life urban ills to tell a tale of what is and what can be.

Where it's reviewed:
Booklist, November 15, 2009, page 37

Horn Book Magazine, March/April 2009, page 201
Horn Book Magazine, March-April 2009, page 201
Publishers Weekly, January 19, 2009, page 61
School Library Journal, April 2009, page 140

Other books by the same author:
Kick, 2011
Lockdown, 2010
Street Love, 2006
Autobiography of My Dead Brother, 2005
The Dream Bearer, 2003

Other books you might like:
Gayle Forman, *If I Stay*, 2009
Gordon Korman, *The Juvie Three*, 2008
Sofia Quintero, *Efrain's Secret*, 2010
Todd Strasser, *If I Grow Up*, 2009
Allison Van Diepen, *Snitch*, 2007

963

WALTER DEAN MYERS

Riot

(New York: Egmont USA, 2009)

Age range(s): 13 - 17+
Major character(s): Claire, 15-Year-Old
Time period(s): 19th century; 1860s (1863)

Summary: *Riot* is a young adult story by author Walter Dean Myers based around the 1863 race riots in New York City. In this book, Myers tells the story of Claire, a teenage biracial girl who is the daughter of a black man and an Irish woman. After President Lincoln declares a draft that allows those who pay $300 to be exempt, tensions in New York City grow between the poor, the rich, the black, the Irish, and other ethnic and racial groups. Now Claire must watch as New York tears itself apart, and wonder where she has a place in the world. Myers is also the author of *Monster* and *Lockdown*.

Where it's reviewed:
Booklist, August 1, 2009, page 67
Publishers Weekly, September 7, 2009, page 48
School Library Journal, September 2009, page 168
Voice of Youth Advocates, December 2009, page 412

Other books by the same author:
Harlem Summer, 2007
The Journal of Joshua Loper: A Black Cowboy, 1999
The Glory Field, 1994

Other books you might like:
Jennifer Armstrong, *The Dreams of Mairhe Mehan*, 1996
Isabelle Holland, *Behind the Lines*, 1994
Carolyn Meyer, *Jubilee Journey*, 1997
Ann Rinaldi, *The Last Full Measure*, 2010

964

WALTER DEAN MYERS

Carmen

(New York: Egmont USA, 2011)

Story type: Young Adult
Subject(s): Music; Entertainment industry; Abuse

Age range(s): 15 - 18+

Major character(s): Carmen, Girlfriend (of Jose); Jose, Boyfriend (of Carmen); Escamillo, Producer (music)
Locale(s): New York, New York

Summary: In this Young Adult novel, author Walter Dean Myers modernizes the classic French opera by Georges Bizet. This time, Carmen is a sassy and streetwise mama from Spanish Harlem. Carmen is in love with Jose, but she knows he will never let her out of the ghetto to pursue her dreams of becoming a pop star. Then Escamillo comes along. A P. Diddy-type hip-hop mogul, Escamillo is able to make anyone he touches transform into an overnight sensation. Everyone in the neighborhood vies for his attention, but the only one who gets it is Carmen. Now Carmen is finally poised to leave Spanish Harlem for good—but will Jose let her leave it all behind without a fight?

Where it's reviewed:
Booklist, April 15, 2011, page 54
Horn Book Magazine, May/June 2011, page 98
School Library Journal, May 2011, page 135
Voice of Youth Advocates, June 2011, page 170

Other books by the same author:
Amiri and Odette: A Love Story, 2009
Riot, 2009
What They Found: Love on 145th Street, 2007
Street Love, 2006
Monster, 1999

Other books you might like:
Jen Bryant, *The Fortune of Carmen Navarro*, 2010
Simone Elkeles, *Rules of Attraction*, 2010
Julius Lester, *Othello: A Novel*, 1995

965

LAUREN MYRACLE

Shine

(New York: Amulet Books, 2011)

Subject(s): Homosexuality; Crime; Friendship

Age range(s): 16 - 18+

Major character(s): Cat, 16-Year-Old, Abuse Victim, Friend (of Patrick); Patrick, Friend (of Cat), Homosexual, Crime Victim
Time period(s): 21st century; 2010s
Locale(s): North Carolina, United States

Summary: In the young adult novel *Shine* by Lauren Myracle, 16-year-old Cat must overcome painful events from her past to help a friend who has been brutally beaten by an unknown attacker. Cat and Patrick were best friends until three years ago, when friends of Cat's brother sexually assaulted her and the then 13-year-old withdrew from the outside world. Now Patrick, who is gay, is in a coma after an attack prompted by his homosexuality. Cat emerges from her isolated existence to find those responsible for Patrick's injuries. The suspects are many in their North Carolina town, and as Cat looks for answers she also reveals the town's problems of poverty and drugs.

Where it's reviewed:
Publishers Weekly, March 14, 2011, page 75
School Library Journal, June 2011, page 128
Voice of Youth Advocates, April 2011, page 65

Other books by the same author:
Peace, Love, and Baby Ducks, 2009
Bliss, 2008
L8r,g8r, 2008
Rhymes with Witches, 2005

Other books you might like:
Pamela Ehrenberg, *Tillmon County Fire*, 2009
Katherine Holubitsky, *Tweaked*, 2008
Ellen Hopkins, *Glass*, 2007
James Lecesne, *Absolute Brightness*, 2008

966

LAUREN MYRACLE

Peace, Love, and Baby Ducks

(New York: Dutton Books, 2009)

Subject(s): Sisters; Interpersonal relations; Individualism

Age range(s): 13 - 18+

Major character(s): Carly, 15-Year-Old; Anna, 14-Year-Old, Sister (of Carly); Peyton, Friend (of Carly)
Time period(s): 21st century; 2000s
Locale(s): Atlanta, Georgia

Summary: In *Peace, Love, and Baby Ducks* by Lauren Myracle, teenage sisters deal with their changing relationship as their lives begin to take divergent paths. Carly, a 15-year-old idealist fresh from a volunteer assignment at Lookout Mountain, is surprised to find how much her younger sister Anna—and her chest—have grown over the summer. While Carly is determined to move beyond the materialism of her affluent Atlanta neighborhood and elite prep school, she can't help but feel jealous of Anna's emerging beauty. Carly and Anna find humor and heartache as they try to establish individual identities and heal their wounded relationship.

Where it's reviewed:
Booklist, April 15, 2009, page 38
Horn Book Magazine, July-August 2009, page 427
Publishers Weekly, March 30, 2009, page 51
Voice of Youth Advocates, February 2009, page 532

Other books by the same author:
Shine, 2011
Bliss, 2008
L8r,g8r, 2007

Other books you might like:
Sarah Dessen, *Lock and Key*, 2008
Justina Chen Headley, *North of Beautiful*, 2009

Cecily Von Ziegesar, *Gossip Girl, The Carlyles Series*, 2008

967

BEVERLEY NAIDOO

Burn My Heart

(New York: Amistad, 2009)

Subject(s): Apartheid; Friendship; Adolescence

Age range(s): 10 - 15+

Major character(s): Mathew Grayson, Son (of white landowner), 11-Year-Old, Friend (of Mugo), Classmate (of Lance); Mr. Grayson, Landlord, Father (of Mathew); Mugo, Servant (for the Graysons), Friend (of Mathew); Kamau, Servant (for the Graysons), Father (of Mugo); Lance Smithers, Classmate (of Mathew), Son (of Frank); Frank Smithers, Inspector, Father (of Lance)

Time period(s): 20th century; 1950s (1951-1954)

Locale(s): Kenya

Summary: Two young boys struggle to maintain their friendship amidst the growing violence of the Mau Mau rebellion in 1950s Kenya. Mathew Grayson, son of a white landowner, has been friends with Mugo, an African servant, for many years, but rumors of plots against white settlers put the boys' bond in jeopardy. Things only become more complicated after Mathew and a classmate blame a fire they started on Mau Mau rebels. As tensions mount throughout the colony, Mathew and Mugo question their loyalty to one another and wonder whether their friendship can survive the changes to come. *Burn My Heart* is the seventh young adult novel from author Beverley Naidoo.

Where it's reviewed:
School Library Journal, February 2009, page 106
Voice of Youth Advocates, February 2009, page 532

Other books by the same author:
Web of Lies, 2006
The Other Side of Truth, 2001
No Turning Back: A Novel of South Africa, 1997
Journey to Jo'burg: A South African Story, 1985

Other books you might like:
Sheila Gordon, *Waiting for the Rain: A Novel of South Africa*, 1987
Ben Mikaelsen, *Countdown*, 1996
Meja Mwangi, *The Mzungu Boy*, 2005

968

DONNA JO NAPOLI

Alligator Bayou

(New York: Wendy Lamb Books, 2009)

Subject(s): Race relations; Immigrants; Family

Age range(s): 12 - 16+

Major character(s): Calogero, 14-Year-Old, Immigrant; Patricia, Girlfriend

Time period(s): 19th century; 1890s (1899)

Locale(s): Tallulah, Louisiana

Summary: In Donna Jo Napoli's *Alligator Bayou*, newly motherless, 14-year-old Calogero sets off from Sicily to the deep bayous of Louisiana to help his male relatives run their grocery store. It's 1899, and Tallulah, Louisiana, is not a welcoming place for outsiders, especially those who are noticeably different. Almost immediately, Calogero senses the hostility between the black and white members of the community. And for his own part, Calogero doesn't fit in with either group; he's too bizarre for the whites and too suspicious for the blacks. But life in the bayou presents some very unexpected adventures: the excitement of an alligator hunt and the thrill of first love as Calogero meets a charming black girl named Patricia.

Where it's reviewed:
Booklist, February 15, 2009, page 69
Journal of Adolescent & Adult, September 2010, page 68
Publishers Weekly, February 2, 2009, page 50
School Library Journal, May 2009, page 116

Other books by the same author:
The King of Mulberry Street, 2005
North, 2004
Jack, 1999

Other books you might like:
Jay Asher, *Thirteen Reasons Why*, 2007
Ann Burg, *All the Broken Pieces*, 2009
Suzanne Collins, *The Hunger Games*, 2008
Kristin Levine, *The Best Bad Luck I Ever Had*, 2009
Rita Williams-Garcia, *Jumped*, 2009

969

BLAKE NELSON

Recovery Road

(New York: Scholastic Press, 2011)

Story type: Contemporary

Subject(s): Addiction; Rehabilitation; Adolescent interpersonal relations

Age range(s): 15 - 18+

Major character(s): Madeline, Teenager, Student—High School, 11th Grader, Alcoholic, Patient (rehab facility); Stewart, Teenager, Addict, Patient (rehab facility), Boyfriend (of Madeline)

Time period(s): 21st century; 2010s

Locale(s): United States

Summary: In this novel for young adult readers, award-winning author Blake Nelson weaves a dark tale of romance, sobriety, and tragedy. Madeline isn't an average high school junior. For starters, she has a serious problem with alcohol and rage. Secondly, she's spending 11th grade in a secluded rehab center called Spring Meadows. Madeline immediately bonds with a fellow patient and the two girls sneak out every week to see a movie in the nearby town. On one such night, Madeline meets Stewart, a handsome teen with some serious issues of his own. As the two addicts fall for one another, they realize their romance is in for a serious test—especially when they're released from rehab and must fight to stay sober in the real world.

Where it's reviewed:
Booklist, February 15, 2011, page 72
Horn Book Magazine, March-April 2011, page 121
Publishers Weekly, January 10, 2011, page 51
School Library Journal, May 2011, page 119
Voice of Youth Advocates, April 2011, page 52

Other books by the same author:
Destroy All Cars, 2009
Gender Blender, 2006
Prom Anonymous, 2006
Paranoid Park, 2005

Other books you might like:
Amy Reed, *Beautiful*, 2010
Randi Reisfeld, *Rehab*, 2008
Benjamin Alire Saenz, *Last Night I Sang to the Monster*, 2009
Elizabeth Scott, *Love You Hate You Miss You*, 2009

970

JANDY NELSON

The Sky Is Everywhere
(New York: Dial Books, 2010)

Subject(s): Sisters; Grief; Death

Age range(s): 14 - 18+
Major character(s): Lennie, 17-Year-Old; Bailey, Sister (of Lennie); Toby, Boyfriend (of Bailey); Joe, Friend (of Lennie), Musician
Time period(s): 21st century; 2010s
Locale(s): California, United States

Summary: In *The Sky Is Everywhere* by Jandy Nelson, a 17-year-old girl deals with the complicated emotions she experiences in the wake of her sister's death. Lennie, bookish and quiet, was accustomed to living in the shadow of her beautiful sister Bailey. When Bailey dies unexpectedly of a heart problem, Lennie is distraught. But as Lennie struggles with her sister's death, she finds herself drawn to Bailey's boyfriend, even as a new boy in town starts to fall for Lennie. Bailey's death also prompts Lennie to reexamine her feelings for her mother, who walked out on the family years ago. First novel.

Where it's reviewed:
Booklist, January 1, 2010, page 70
Horn Book Magazine, April/May 2010, page 65
Publishers Weekly, February 22, 2010, page 69
School Library Journal, March 2010, page 165
Voice of Youth Advocates, August 2010, page 242

Awards the book has won:
Blue Ribbon Awards: Fiction, 2010

Other books you might like:
Jennifer Armstrong, *What a Song Can Do: 12 Riffs on the Power of Music*, 2004
Sarah Dessen, *This Lullaby*, 2002
Loretta Ellsworth, *In a Heartbeat*, 2010
Marthe Jocelyn, *Would You*, 2008

971

MARILYN NELSON
JERRY PINKNEY, Illustrator

Sweethearts of Rhythm: The Story of the Greatest All-Girl Swing Band in the World
(New York: Dial Books, 2009)

Subject(s): Poetry; Biographies; Women

Age range(s): 12 - 18+

Summary: Marilyn Nelson's *Sweethearts of Rhythm: The Story of the Greatest All-Girl Swing Band in the World* recounts the true story of the female jazz musicians, known as the International Sweethearts of Rhythm, who entertained audiences during World War II. Nelson shares the story of the bands' members through poems told from the perspectives of their instruments. Nelson doesn't shy away from the hardships the women faced—segregation, racism—but she portrays how the music helped people temporarily forget the negativity of the time and have fun. Illustrations by Jerry Pinkney complement the rhyming text.

Where it's reviewed:
Horn Book Guide, Spring 2010, page 167
School Library Journal, October 2009, page 150
Voice of Youth Advocates, December 2009, page 431

Other books by the same author:
Beautiful Ballerina, 2009
Miss Crandall's School for Young Ladies and Little Misses of Color, 2007
Fortune's Bones: The Manumission Requiem, 2004
Carver, Life in Poems, 2001

Other books you might like:
Tonya Bolden, *Take-off!: American All-Girl Bands During WWII*, 2007
Leslie Gourse, *Sophisticated Ladies: The Great Women of Jazz*, 2007
Carole Boston Weatherford, *Becoming Billie Holiday*, 2008

972

R.A. NELSON

Days of Little Texas
(New York: Alfred A. Knopf, 2009)

Subject(s): Ghosts; Christian life; Slavery

Age range(s): 13 - 17+
Major character(s): Ronald "Little Texas" Earl, 16-Year-Old, Religious (evangelist)
Time period(s): 21st century; 2000s
Locale(s): American South, United States

Summary: In *Days of Little Texas*, author R.A. Nelson tells the story of a teenage evangelist faced with doubt and uncertainty and a mysterious specter that haunts his revival meetings. By the tender age of 10, Ronald Earl was an exhilarating preacher, drawing in crowds that hailed him as a miraculous orator and healer. But now at 16, Ronald, who is known by the nickname Little Texas, has come to question his abilities. This questioning comes to a head when he notices a strange girl—a girl he supposedly cured years earlier—showing up at his services. When he realizes she is a ghost, Ronald is thrust into a war between the tenets of his faith and what he feels in his heart.

Where it's reviewed:
Publishers Weekly, July 6, 2009, page 52
School Library Journal, October 2009, page 132

Other books by the same author:
Throat, 2011
Breathe My Name, 2007
Teach Me, 2005

Other books you might like:
Cathryn Clinton, *The Calling*, 2001
Peter Dickinson, *Healer*, 1983
Judd Holt, *A Promise to Catie*, 1992

973

G. NERI
RANDY DUBURKE, Illustrator

Yummy: The Last Days of a Southside Shorty

(New York: Lee & Low Books, 2010)

Subject(s): Gangs; Violence; Murder

Age range(s): 11 - 16+
Major character(s): Roger, 11-Year-Old, Narrator, Classmate (of Robert); Robert "Yummy" Sandifer, 11-Year-Old, Gang Member, Murderer
Time period(s): 20th century; 1990s (1994)
Locale(s): Chicago, Illinois

Summary: *Yummy: The Last Days of a Southside Shorty* is a thought-provoking urban graphic novel for young adult readers from author G. Neri. Based on a true story, *Yummy* centers on the shocking gang-related murder of a 14-year old girl in Chicago. In 1994 in Roseland, a neighborhood on the south side of Chicago, 14-year-old Shavon Dean, was shot by her 11-year-old neighbor, Robert "Yummy" Sandifer, a young boy who carried around a teddy bear and earned his nickname because of his penchant for candy. Relying on public records, personal accounts, and media from the event, Neri tells the story of Yummy's three-day evasion of the police and his descent into violence through the eyes of his fictional classmate, Roger.

Where it's reviewed:
Horn Book Guide, Spring 2010, page 107
Publishers Weekly, July 19, 2010, page 119
Skipping Stones, January/February 2011, page 33

Other books by the same author:
Ghetto Cowboy, 2011
Surf Mules, 2009
Chess Rumble, 2007

Other books you might like:
Mat Johnson, *Incognegro: A Graphic Mystery*, 2008
Marybeth Lorbiecki, *Just One Flick of a Finger*, 1996
Walter Dean Myers, *Scorpions*, 1988
Todd Strasser, *If I Grow Up*, 2009
Rita Williams-Garcia, *Jumped*, 2009

974

PATRICK NESS

Monsters of Men

(New York: Walker, 2010)

Series: Chaos Walking Series. Book 3
Subject(s): Fantasy; Suspense; Wars

Age range(s): 15 - 18+
Major character(s): Mayor, Leader, Murderer; Mistress Coyle, Leader, Terrorist; Todd, Young Man, Leader; Viola, Leader, Young Woman

Summary: A 2011 Carnegie Medal Winner, *Monsters of Men*, a suspenseful fantasy novel for young adult readers, is the third and final installment in the Chaos Walking trilogy from author Patrick Ness. The fate of the world hangs in the balance as three powerful and terrifying armies go head-to-head in a devastating war. A murderous tyrant known as Mayor and a scheming terrorist named Mistress Coyle lead their respective factions against Spackle, a powerful army of telepathic peoples native to the planet. Meanwhile, another colony of humans approach the planet and Todd and Viola must use their newfound power to negotiate with the three armies to protect the planet and save the lives of thousands of innocent victims.

Where it's reviewed:
Booklist, May 15, 2010, page 49
Horn Book Magazine, December 2010, page 99
Publishers Weekly, August 2, 2010, page 46
School Librarian, Fall 2010, page 180
School Library Journal, September 2010, page 149

Other books by the same author:
A Monster Calls, 2011
The Ask and the Answer, 2009
The Knife of Never Letting Go, 2008

Awards the book has won:
Carnegie Medal, 2011

Other books you might like:
Kristin Cashore, *Fire*, 2009
Adrian McKinty, *The Lighthouse Trilogy*, 2006
Lindsey Priestley, *Tales of Heresy*, 2009

975

PATRICK NESS

The Ask and the Answer

(Somerville, Massachusetts: Candlewick Press, 2009)

Series: Chaos Walking Series. Book 2
Subject(s): Social conditions; Telepathy; Space colonies

Age range(s): 15 - 18+
Major character(s): Todd, Prisoner, Military Personnel (soldier), Friend (of Viola); Viola, Activist, Friend (of Todd); Mayor Prentiss, Political Figure (mayor)
Time period(s): Indeterminate Future

Summary: *The Ask and the Answer* is the sophomore installment in author Patrick Ness's science fiction series that explores the adventures of Tom and Viola. The duo has just entered New Prentisstown, a strange community overseen by the malevolent Mayor Prentiss. While Todd is imprisoned, Viola is exiled to a healing house where her injuries are looked after. Soon Viola finds herself caught up in a radical movement planning to depose Prentisstown's oppressive new government system. Meanwhile, Tom is pushed into the Mayor's army, becoming part of the tyranny Viola is seeking to overthrow. Will Tom and Viola be able to find one another and save Prentisstown at the same time?

Where it's reviewed:
Booklist, August 1, 2009, page 66
Horn Book Magazine, Sept.-Oct. 2009, page 570
Publishers Weekly, August 31, 2009, page 59
School Library Journal, January 2010, page 110

Other books by the same author:
Monsters of Men, 2010
The Knife of Never Letting Go, 2008

Other books you might like:
L.J. Adlington, *The Diary of Pelly D.*, 2005
Melvin Burgess, *Bloodtide*, 2001
Orson Scott Card, *Pathfinder*, 2010
Neal Shusterman, *Unwind*, 2007

976

PATRICK NESS
JIM KAY, Illustrator

A Monster Calls

(London: Walker Books, 2011)

Story type: Fantasy
Subject(s): Monsters; Cancer; Fantasy

Age range(s): 13 - 16+
Major character(s): Conor, Boy; Monster, Monster

Summary: In this novel, author Patrick Ness tells the story of a boy coming to grips with his mother's cancer diagnosis and treatments. When Conor learns his mother has cancer, he is devastated by the news. He worries about the situation all the time. Eventually, his worries turn into nightmares. When a monster wanders into Conor's backyard, Conor assumes he must be having a nightmare. To his surprise, however, he is not. The monster does not terrorize Conor. Instead, the monster helps Conor understand that life is not always fair and facing difficult times is something that everyone must go through. As Conor listens to the monster's revelations, he starts to prepare himself for the toughest time in his life.

Where it's reviewed:
Booklist, July 1, 2011, page 52

Horn Book Magazine, September-October 2011, page 93
New York Times Book Review, October 16, 2011, page 18
Publishers Weekly, June 20, 2011, page 54
School Library Journal, September 2011, page 164

Other books by the same author:
Monsters of Men, 2010
The Ask and the Answer, 2009
The Knife of Never Letting Go, 2009

Other books you might like:
Amy Ackley, *Sign Language*, 2011
Rune Michaels, *Nobel Genes*, 2010
Ransom Riggs, *Miss Peregrine's Home for Peculiar Children*, 2011

977

JOSH NEUFELD

A.D.: New Orleans after the Deluge

(New York: Pantheon Books, 2009)

Subject(s): Hurricanes; Survival; Disasters

Age range(s): 15 - 18+
Time period(s): 21st century; 2000s (2005)
Locale(s): New Orleans, Louisiana

Summary: In *A.D.: New Orleans After the Deluge*, graphic artist Josh Neufeld presents a series of true stories that take place during the nightmare of Hurricane Katrina. As the storm destroys the city, everyday citizens are required to make the most heartbreaking decisions of their lives: whether to stay in their beloved town or escape to safety. This volume captures the experiences of seven New Orleans residents whose lives were forever changed by the hurricane, serving as both a powerful testament to the fortitude of the human spirit and a tribute to those who did not survive the tragedy.

Where it's reviewed:
Booklist, July 1, 2009, page 46
Mother Jones, September/October 2009, page 74
New York Times, August 24, 2009, page C1
Publishers Weekly, June 1, 2009, page 38
Teacher Librarian, June 2010, page 65

Other books by the same author:
A Few Perfect Hours and Other Stories from Southeast Asia and Central Europe, 2011

Other books you might like:
Rebeca Antoine, *Voices Rising: Stories from the Katrina Narrative Project*, 2008
Dan Baum, *Nine Lives: Mystery, Magic, Death, and Life in New Orleans*, 2009
Alison Bechdel, *Fun Home: A Family Tragicomic*, 2006
Dave Eggers, *Zeitoun*, 2009

978

RACHEL NEUMEIER

The Floating Islands

(New York: Alfred A. Knopf, 2011)

Story type: Fantasy
Subject(s): Islands; Dragons; Fantasy

Age range(s): 12 - 16+
Major character(s): Trei, 14-Year-Old, Orphan, Cousin (of Araene); Araene, Teenager, Cousin (of Trei)
Time period(s): Indeterminate
Locale(s): Floating Islands, Fictional Location

Summary: A teenage boy discovers a magical land and the family he never knew he had in this fantasy novel for young adult readers from author Rachel Neumeier. When Trei's family is killed in a tragic accident, the 14-year-old boy has no one to care for him. When his uncle turns him away, his last resort is to track down his mother's family on the Floating Islands, a series of airborne isles kept aloft by the wind power of dragons. Trei is fascinated by this magical and beautiful new land and its inhabitants, particularly the kajurai, a group of men who are able to fly. Despite only being a half-islander, Trei is determined to become a kajurai. Eliciting help from his new cousin, Araene, a girl with secret ambitions of her own, Trei embarks on a wild and courageous journey to pursue his passions and realize his dreams.

Where it's reviewed:
Booklist, February 15, 2011, page 70
Horn Book Magazine, May-June 2011, page 98
School Library Journal, February 2011, page 115

Other books by the same author:
The City in the Lake, 2008

Other books you might like:
Alison Goodman, *Eon: Dragoneye Reborn*, 2008
Tamora Pierce, *Circle of Magic Quartet*, 1996
Carole Wilkinson, *Dragon Keeper*, 2003

979

HAN NOLAN

Pregnant Pause

(Boston, Massachusetts: Harcourt, 2011)

Story type: Coming-of-Age
Subject(s): Teenage parents; Pregnancy; Adolescence

Age range(s): 14 - 18+
Major character(s): Eleanor Crowe, 16-Year-Old, Pregnant Teenager
Time period(s): 21st century; 2010s
Locale(s): United States

Summary: Award-winning author Han Nolan tackles the challenges of teenage pregnancy in this poignant and thought-provoking novel for young adult readers. Sixteen-year-old Eleanor Crowe is a stubborn risk taker, which is probably why she a) got knocked up as a teenager and b) refuses to accept her parents' ultimatums.

They give her two options: Eleanor can move to Kenya with them and work as a missionary or move to California to live with her older sister. Either way, she's expected to give her baby up for adoption. Disregarding their plans, Eleanor decides to marry her boyfriend and takes a job at his family's camp for overweight kids where she discovers new skills and passions. When a horrible tragedy strikes, Eleanor is forced to make some difficult choices about her life and future that may not please anyone.

Where it's reviewed:
Booklist, August 1, 2011, page 48
Publishers Weekly, July 4, 2011, page 67
School Library Journal, September 2011, page 164
Voice of Youth Advocates, October 2011, page 390

Other books by the same author:
Crazy, 2010
A Summer of Kings, 2006
Born Blue, 2001
Dancing on the Edge, 1997
Send Me Down a Miracle, 1996

Other books you might like:
Pat Brisson, *The Best and Hardest Thing*, 2010
Jo Knowles, *Jumping Off Swings*, 2009
Charnan Simon, *Plan B*, 2011

980

HAN NOLAN

Crazy

(New York: Harcourt, 2010)

Subject(s): Mental disorders; Father-son relations; Adolescent interpersonal relations

Age range(s): 14 - 17+
Major character(s): Jason, 15-Year-Old; Dad, Father (of Jason)
Time period(s): 21st century; 2010s
Locale(s): United States

Summary: *Crazy* is a young adult novel by author Han Nolan. In it, Nolan tells the story of Jason, a 15-year-old who takes care of his mentally ill father. When he was six years old, Jason's father put him through a harrowing experience. Since then, his father's condition has only gotten worse, and his mother's recent death as a result of a stroke leaves Jason's father entirely in his care. In order to survive, Jason imagines a group of friends that includes several characters from his favorite television programs. When Jason's behavior finally gets out of control, his school sends him to therapy to deal with his issues. Now Jason must learn to deal with the guilt he feels over attempting to get better, even as his father is sent to get some help of his own.

Where it's reviewed:
Booklist, August 1, 2010, page 64
Horn Book Magazine, November/December 2010, page 100
Publishers Weekly, September 13, 2010, page 46
School Library Journal, September 2010, page 160
Voice of Youth Advocates, October 2010, page 380

Other books by the same author:
Pregnant Pause, 2011
A Summer of Kings, 2006
Born Blue, 2001
A Face in Every Window, 1999
Dancing on the Edge, 1997

Other books you might like:
John Barnes, *Tales of the Madman Underground: An Historical Romance 1973*, 2009
Elizabeth Fensham, *Helicopter Man*, 2005
Judy Gregerson, *Bad Girls Club*, 2007
Robin Merrow MacCready, *Buried*, 2006
Laura McNeal, *The Decoding of Lana Morris*, 2007

981

MICHAEL NORTHROP

Gentlemen

(New York: Scholastic Press, 2009)

Subject(s): High schools; Missing persons; Teachers

Age range(s): 16 - 18+
Major character(s): Mike, Student—High School; Tommy, Student—High School; Mixer, Student—High School; Bones, Student—High School; Mr. Haberman, Teacher (of English)
Time period(s): 21st century; 2000s
Locale(s): United States

Summary: In *Gentlemen*, a young adult novel by Michael Northrop, four delinquent teenagers, Mike, Mixer, Bones, and Tommy, find themselves in a remedial English class taught by Mr. Haberman. Though the school's other teachers and students want nothing to do with them, it seems like Mr. Haberman actually respects them and wants them to learn. Then, Tommy mysteriously vanishes, and Mr. Haberman starts acting strangely. Mike, Mixer, and Bones are determined to find out what happened to Tommy and do something about it.

Where it's reviewed:
Booklist, May 1, 2009, page 38
Journal of Adolescent & Adult, May 2010, page 699
New York Times Book Review, June 14, 2009, page 13
Publishers Weekly, April 6, 2009, page 49
School Library Journal, August 2009, page 112

Other books by the same author:
Trapped, 2011

Other books you might like:
Kevin Brooks, *Black Rabbit Summer*, 2008
Eve Bunting, *Blackwater*, 1999
Fyodor Dostoyevsky, *Crime and Punishment*, 1866
Lois Duncan, *Killing Mr. Griffin*, 1978
Walter Dean Myers, *Monster*, 1999

982

CARAGH M. O'BRIEN

Birthmarked

(New York: Roaring Brook Press, 2010)

Series: Birthmarked Trilogy. Book 1
Subject(s): Dystopias; Genetic engineering; Science fiction

Age range(s): 15 - 18+
Major character(s): Gaia Stone, 16-Year-Old, Midwife; Captain Grey, Friend (of Gaia)
Time period(s): Indeterminate Future
Locale(s): Wharfton, Fictional Location

Summary: In *Birthmarked* by Caragh O'Brien, Earth has suffered a devastating climate shift that has propelled human society into a struggle for survival. In Wharfton, 16-year-old Gaia Stone learns midwifing skills from her mother. Every month, her mother brings the allotted three infants into the nearby Enclave to be raised with the privileged. Gaia, who bears a burn scar, could never be worthy of admission to the Enclave. But when her parents are taken prisoner and brought inside, Gaia knows she is their only hope for rescue. Inside the Enclave, Gaia realizes that her parents' captors want information from the Stones about one of the babies they delivered.

Where it's reviewed:
Booklist, February 15, 2010, page 47
Horn Book Guide, Fall 2010, page 379
People, February 15, 2010, page 132
School Library Journal, May 2010, page 120
Voice of Youth Advocates, April 2010, page 74

Other books by the same author:
Prized, 2011

Other books you might like:
Charlotte Agell, *Shift*, 2008
Patrick Carman, *Atherton: The House of Power*, 2007
James DeVita, *The Silenced*, 2007
Carrie Ryan, *The Forest of Hands and Teeth*, 2009

983

CARAGH M. O'BRIEN

Prized

(New York: Roaring Brook Press, 2011)

Series: Birthmarked Trilogy. Book 2
Subject(s): Science fiction; Dystopias; Women

Age range(s): 14 - 18+
Major character(s): Gaia Stone, Sister (of Maya), Heroine, 16-Year-Old, Midwife; Matrarc, Ruler; Maya, Sister (of Gaia), Baby
Locale(s): Sylum, Fictional Location

Summary: In the second book of author Caragh M. O'Brien's Birthmarked Trilogy, Gaia Stone, after her escape from the Enclave, heads for the Dark Forest with little more than her baby sister Maya and the few supplies she can carry with her. Before long, she finds herself in the village of Sylum, a matriarchy led by Matrarc, a blind, dictatorial ruler. While she initially believes Sylum is a veritable paradise, she quickly realizes it is a dystopic society where men are oppressed and denied many of the rights and privileges its women enjoy. She also learns that she has no way to escape, as a mysterious element in the air proves fatal for anyone who attempts to leave the village. With no other options, Gaia turns to the few rebellious women in Sylum who refuse to follow the town's moral code for help. With their support, Gaia investigates the mystery surrounding the town, encouraging their dissident movement in return and ultimately ending up at the center of a political struggle that pits her against the tyrannical Matrarc.

Where it's reviewed:
Booklist, December 1, 2011, page 58
Voice of Youth Advocates, December 2011, page 517

Other books by the same author:
Birthmarked, 2010

Other books you might like:
Margaret Atwood, *The Handmaid's Tale*, 1985
Kristin Cashore, *Graceling*, 2008
Lauren DeStefano, *Wither*, 2011

984

CAITLIN O'CONNELL
DONNA M. JACKSON, Co-Author
TIMOTHY RODWELL, Photographer

The Elephant Scientist
(Boston: Houghton Mifflin Books for Children, 2011)

Subject(s): Africa; Animals; Elephants
Age range(s): 11 - 16+

Summary: American scientist Caitlin O'Connell spends her days in the Namibian desert, stealthily observing the glory and wonder of the nation's elephants. In Etosha National Park, a particularly arid region of Africa, O'Connell discovered something that would change the way elephants are studied forever. As the elephants traveled across the wasteland, led by "the mother of all elephants," as many call her, O'Connell noticed that when the matronly animal stopped to study her surroundings, all stopped and remained motionless. This plainly viewed interaction led O'Connell to a critical conclusion concerning how elephants communicate with one another. O'Connell provides readers with an eyewitness account of the majestic African elephant in its natural habitat.

Where it's reviewed:
Booklist, September 15, 2011, page 56
Horn Book Magazine, November-December 2011, page 127
Natural History, November 2011, page 40
School Library Journal, November 2011, page 149

Other books you might like:
Mary Kay Carson, *Emi and the Rhino Scientist*, 2007
Ann Downer, *Elephant Talk*, 2011
Dereck Joubert, *Face to Face with Elephants*, 2009
Jody Morgan, *Elephant Rescue: Changing the Future*

for Endangered Wildlife, 2004

985

SHEILA O'CONNOR

Sparrow Road
(New York: G.P. Putnam's Sons, 2011)

Story type: Coming-of-Age
Subject(s): Mother-daughter relations; Coming of age; Family life

Age range(s): 10 - 13+
Major character(s): Raine O'Rourke, 12-Year-Old, Daughter (of Molly O'Rourke); Molly O'Rourke, Mother (of Raine), Worker (at Sparrow Road); Viktor Berglund, Overseer (of Sparrow Road); Grandpa Mac, Grandfather (of Raine); Lillian, Artist, Friend (of Raine); Diego, Artist, Friend (of Raine); Josie, Artist, Friend (of Raine)
Locale(s): Comfort, Michigan

Summary: In this coming-of-age novel by Sheila O'Connor, Raine O'Rourke's mother takes a job at Sparrow Road, an out-of-the-way artists' colony near Lake Michigan, forcing 12-year-old Raine to move away from her beloved Grandpa Mac in Milwaukee for the whole summer. At Sparrow Road, Raine struggles under the strict rules of Sparrow Road's owner, Viktor Berglund, but she manages to find a quirky group of friends in artists Josie, Diego, and Lillian. She even stumbles upon a mystery when she learns that Sparrow Road used to be an orphanage. Then Raine's mother shares a secret—her real reason for bringing Raine to Sparrow Road—and Raine's life may never be the same again.

Where it's reviewed:
Booklist, July 1, 2011, page 53
Bulletin of the Center for Children's Books, June 2011, page 483
Horn Book Guide, Fall 2011, page 364
School Library Journal, July 2011, page 104

Other books by the same author:
Where No Gods Came, 2003

Other books you might like:
Catherine Bateson, *Being Bee*, 2007
Audrey Couloumbis, *Lexie*, 2011
Polly Horvath, *My One Hundred Adventures*, 2008

986

ELLIS O'NEAL

The False Princess
(New York City: Egmont USA, 2011)

Story type: Fantasy
Subject(s): Fantasy; Magic; Wizards

Age range(s): 13 - 16+
Major character(s): Sinda/Nalia, Teenager, Magician, Royalty (former, princess); Kiernan, Friend (Sinda/Nalia); Neomar Ostralis, Wizard; Melaina Harandron,

Wizard; Varil Azaway, Aunt (of Sinda/Nalia); Cornalus, Servant (to the royal court)

Time period(s): Indeterminate

Locale(s): Thorvaldor, Fictional Location

Summary: Princess Nalia has never felt comfortable in her role as royalty. She has always been clumsy and unkempt, happier in a library than mingling at court. Her privileged life is soon turned upside down when she is told she is not, in fact, the real princess of Thorvaldor. The real princess has been hidden for the last 16 years to protect her from a deadly prophecy. Nalia, whose real name is Sinda, is swiftly separated from her royal life and her best friend Kiernan and placed with her Aunt Varil, who is less than welcoming. She may not have royal blood, but something else courses through Sinda's veins, a deep, dark magic that has been restrained for too long. Sinda will soon discover she is not just some cast-off peasant girl, but harbors tremendous powers. Her quest for answers takes her back to the palace, where she discovers a long-buried secret that will send ripples through Thorvaldor's history. First novel.

Where it's reviewed:

Booklist, May 15, 2011, page 61

Bulletin of the Center for Children's Books, May 2011, page 433

Horn Book Magazine, May-June 2011, page 99

Publishers Weekly, November 1, 2011, page 44

School Library Journal, June 2011, page 128

Other books you might like:

Kirsten Boie, *The Princess Plot*, 2009

Shannon Hale, *The Goose Girl*, 2003

Angie Sage, *Magyk: Septimus Heap, Book One*, 2005

987

J. ADAMS OAKS

Why I Fight

(New York: Atheneum Books for Young Readers, 2009)

Subject(s): Family; Boxing; Parent-child relations

Age range(s): 14 - 18+

Major character(s): Wyatt Reaves, Teenager; Fever, Father (of Wyatt); Ma, Mother (of Wyatt); Uncle Spade, Uncle (of Wyatt)

Time period(s): 21st century; 2000s

Locale(s): United States

Summary: In *Why I Fight*, a young adult novel by J. Adams Oaks, teenager Wyatt Reaves has been on the road with his Uncle Spade for six years after leaving his neglectful parents, Fever and Ma, behind. Wyatt is incapable of displaying any emotion other than rage, and his uncle predominantly ignores him as they travel the country in favor of meeting up with different women in each town. Spade then encourages Wyatt, because of his unnatural size, to become a bare-knuckle fighter, and Wyatt is surprisingly successful. Soon, though, Wyatt begins to get tired of his life alone on the road, and he decides he wants to return to his parents—but it may be too late.

Where it's reviewed:

Booklist, April 15, 2009, page 43

School Library Journal, July 2009, page 90

Voice of Youth Advocates, June 2009, page 141

Other books you might like:

K.L. Going, *King of the Screwups*, 2009

Joseph Helgerson, *Crows and Cards*, 2009

Janet Nichols Lynch, *Messed Up*, 2009

Coert Voorhees, *The Brothers Torres*, 2008

Kate Wild, *Fight Game*, 2007

988

NNEDI OKORAFOR

Akata Witch

(New York: Viking, 2011)

Subject(s): Supernatural; Magic; Serial murders

Age range(s): 12 - 15+

Major character(s): Sunny Nwazue, 12-Year-Old (albino); Orlu, Classmate (of Sunny); Chichi, Classmate (of Sunny); Sasha, Classmate (of Sunny); Black Hat Otokoto, Serial Killer, Witch

Time period(s): 21st century; 2010s

Locale(s): Nigeria

Summary: Set in Nigeria, Nnedi Okorafor's young-adult novel *Akata Witch* blends fantasy, mystery, and contemporary issues in a story about a young girl who discovers her cultural and spiritual heritage. American-born Sunny Nwazue moved to her parents' native Nigeria when she was nine. Now 12, the young albino girl continues to deal with the suspicion of her classmates because of her appearance. When fellow students Orlu, Chichi, and Sasha befriend Sunny, they tell her they have magical powers—and that she does too. With her newly discovered gifts of time travel and clairvoyance, Sunny joins her new friends on a dangerous quest to stop a serial killer who uses his young victims for black magic.

Where it's reviewed:

Booklist, May 15, 2011, page 54

Publishers Weekly, February 14, 2011, page 59

School Library Journal, June 2011, page 128

Voice of Youth Advocates, June 2011, page pag 54

Other books by the same author:

The Shadow Speaker, 2007

Zahrah the Windseeker, 2005

Other books you might like:

Nancy Farmer, *A Girl Named Disaster*, 1996

F.E. Higgins, *The Bone Magician*, 2011

Nalo Hopkinson, *Mojo*, 2003

Karen Kincy, *Other*, 2010

989

LAUREN OLIVER

Delirium

(New York: HarperCollins, 2011)

Subject(s): Love; Adventure; Dystopias

Age range(s): 15 - 18+

Major character(s): Lena Haloway, Teenager; Alex, Boyfriend (of Lena)
Time period(s): Indeterminate Future
Locale(s): Portland, Maine

Summary: Set in a not-too-distant dystopian America, Lauren Oliver's *Delirium* tells the story of teenager Lena Haloway, who has all but accepted the sanctions placed upon humanity by the controlling government. Love is forbidden, and, according to Lena, that's just fine; she can look forward to a routine life of work and an arranged marriage. When she turns 18, the government will cure her of any feelings of love, and Lena is looking forward to that day...until she meets Alex. Suddenly Lena is questioning the motives of the government—and determined to follow the demands of her heart.

Where it's reviewed:
Booklist, May 15, 2011, page 61
Horn Book Magazine, March-April 2011, page 121
Publishers Weekly, December 20, 2010, page 55
School Library Journal, April 2011, page 182
Voice of Youth Advocates, April 2011, page 85

Other books by the same author:
Pandemonium, 2012
Before I Fall, 2010

Other books you might like:
Ally Condie, *Matched*, 2010
James DeVita, *The Silenced*, 2007
Graham Marks, *Omega Place*, 2008
Caragh M. O'Brien, *Birthmarked*, 2010
Neal Shusterman, *Unwind*, 2007

990

LAUREN OLIVER

Before I Fall

(New York: HarperCollins, 2010)

Subject(s): High schools; Bullying; Death

Age range(s): 15 - 18+

Major character(s): Samantha Kingston, Student—High School, Bully; Lindsey, Friend (of Samantha); Elody, Friend (of Samantha)
Time period(s): 21st century; 2010s
Locale(s): United States

Summary: Samantha Kingston is used to holding the world in her hands. From the cutest boyfriend to the best of friends and the coolest clothes, she never regretted a single decision she made in her life—until the day she died. In *Before I Fall*, Sam is a typical mean girl: she picks on those who have less than her and those who may not agree with her views of the world. She believes that she deserves the hot boyfriend, ideal parking spot, and praise from the student body. Others, however, surely disagree. After her death, Sam gets to rethink the way she lived her life and the horrible ways she treated people. Sam is granted the privilege of reliving the day she died seven times. As each day passes, she grows closer to the truth of her death—why did she have to die? And how will her death affect those closest to her, and those whom she bullied while alive? *Before I Fall* is

Lauren Oliver's debut novel.

Where it's reviewed:
Booklist, October 15, 2010, page 67
Horn Book Magazine, Fall 2010, page 379
Publishers Weekly, January 25, 2010, page 121
School Library Journal, November 2010, page 56
Voice of Youth Advocates, April 2010, page 60

Other books by the same author:
Pandemonium, 2012
Delirium, 2011

Other books you might like:
Amy Huntley, *The Everafter*, 2009
Rosalind Wiseman, *Boys, Girls, and Other Hazardous Materials*, 2010
Gabrielle Zevin, *Elsewhere*, 2005

991

C.J. OMOLOLU

Dirty Little Secrets

(New York: Walker & Co., 2010)

Subject(s): Mother-daughter relations; Death; Self reliance
Age range(s): 14 - 18+
Major character(s): Lucy, 16-Year-Old; Mom, Mother (of Lucy)
Time period(s): 21st century; 2010s
Locale(s): United States

Summary: In *Dirty Little Secrets* by C.J. Omololu, a teenager takes drastic measures to protect her family's shocking secret. Lucy, 16, lives with her mentally ill mother in a house that is overrun with junk and trash. Unable to throw anything out, Lucy's mother has been letting things accumulate in their home. Repairmen can't get in and Lucy, of course, can't let friends in either. When Lucy's mother dies in their home, Lucy is determined to keep the outside world from learning about their situation and decides to clean the house before calling emergency services to report her mother's death. First novel.

Where it's reviewed:
Horn Book Guide, Fall 2010, page 379
Publishers Weekly, January 11, 2010, page 48
School Library Journal, February 2010, page 121
Voice of Youth Advocates, April 2010, page 60

Other books you might like:
Robin Merrow MacCready, *Buried*, 2006
Mary E. Pearson, *The Miles Between*, 2009
Nancy Werlin, *The Rules of Survival*, 2006

992

KENNETH OPPEL

Half Brother

(New York: Scholastic Press, 2010)

Subject(s): Chimpanzees; Human-animal relationships; Family

Age range(s): 13 - 17+
Major character(s): Ben Tomlin, 13-Year-Old; Zan, Chimpanzee
Time period(s): 20th century; 1970s
Locale(s): Canada

Summary: *Half Brother* is a moving novel for young adult readers from award-winning author Kenneth Oppel. Thirteen-year-old Ben Tomlin is less than thrilled when his parents uproot the family to relocate to Canada and introduce him to his new "baby brother." Zan is actually an 8-day-old chimpanzee that will be living with the Tomlin family so Ben's father, a behavioral scientist, can research the animal's ability to learn sign language. Ben is reluctant to share his parents' attention and love, but soon Zan starts to grow on him and Ben begins to view him as a real member of the family. When Zan's life is threatened, Ben will stop at nothing to protect his adopted baby brother from harm.

Where it's reviewed:
Booklist, September 1, 2010, page 99
Horn Book Magazine, September/October 2010, page 88
Publishers Weekly, August 23, 2010, page 51
School Library Journal, September 2010, page 160
Voice of Youth Advocates, December 2010, page 458

Other books by the same author:
This Dark Endeavor: The Apprenticeship of Victor Frankenstein, 2011
Darkwing, 2007
Firewing, 2003
Sunwing, 2000
Silverwing, 1997

Awards the book has won:
CLA (Canadian Library Association) Book of the Year Award for Children, 2011
CLA (Canadian Library Association) Young Adult Book Award, 2011

Other books you might like:
Peter Dickinson, *Eva*, 1988
Elizabeth Hess, *Nim Chimpsky: The Chimp Who Would Be Human*, 2008
Lottie L. Riekehof, *The Joy of Signing: The Illustrated Guide for Mastering Sign Language and the Manual Alphabet*, 1987

993

KENNETH OPPEL

This Dark Endeavor: The Apprenticeship of Victor Frankenstein

(New York: Simon & Schuster Books for Young Readers, 2011)

Story type: Fantasy
Subject(s): Alchemy; Twins; Adventure

Age range(s): 14 - 18+
Major character(s): Victor Frankenstein, Twin (of Konrad), Teenager, Adventurer; Konrad Frankenstein, Twin (of

Victor), Teenager; Henry, Friend (of Victor and Konrad); Elizabeth, Adoptee, Friend (of Victor and Konrad)
Time period(s): 19th century

Summary: A brave teenager faces great danger and adventure to save his brother's life in this historical fantasy novel for young adult readers from author Kenneth Oppel. Victor Frankenstein and his twin brother, Konrad, are inseparable thrill-seekers. When their adventures lead them to the Dark Library, they're intrigued by the secret books on alchemy and ancient remedies, despite the fact that their father warns them never to return. When Konrad falls deathly ill, Victor returns to the Dark Library in search of a cure for his ailing twin. When he discovers an ancient formula for the Elixir of Life, he recruits his friend Henry and his beautiful adopted sister, Elizabeth, to help him track down the necessary ingredients, a dangerous task that leads them to the tallest trees in Strumwald and the deep caves of Switzerland.

Where it's reviewed:
Booklist, June 1, 2011, page 84
Horn Book Magazine, July-August 2011, page 155
Publishers Weekly, June 6, 2011, page 42
School Library Journal, October 2011, page 144
Voice of Youth Advocates, October 2011, page 390

Other books by the same author:
Such Wicked Intent, 2012
Half Brother, 2010
Starclimber, 2009
Airborn, 2004

Other books you might like:
Will Hill, *Department 19*, 2011
Philip Pullman, *Lyra's Oxford*, 2003
Michael Scott, *The Alchemyst: The Secrets of the Immortal Nicholas Flamel*, 2007
Mary Shelley, *Frankenstein: The Modern Prometheus*, 1818

994

CATHY OSTLERE

Karma

(New York: Penguin USA, 2011)

Subject(s): Indians (Asian people); Religion; Indian history

Age range(s): 15 - 18+
Major character(s): Maya, 15-Year-Old
Time period(s): 20th century; 1980s (1984)
Locale(s): India

Summary: *Karma*, written by Cathy Ostlere, is a novel told in journal format by the narrator and main character, 15-year-old Maya. Maya is the daughter of two Indian parents, one who was raised Hindu and the other who is of the Sikh religion. Maya's mother's parents disapprove of the marriage, and eventually the pressures of disapproval lead to Maya's mother's suicide. Determined to give his wife a proper Indian burial, Maya's father takes them to India on the very night that Prime

Minister Indira Gandhi is murdered by Sikhs. Now stranded in an angry city suspicious of its Sikh population, Maya must fend for herself when her father is abducted. Ostlere is also the author of *Lost: A Memoir*.

Where it's reviewed:
Booklist, February 15, 2011, page 68
Horn Book Magazine, July-August 2011, page 156
Publishers Weekly, January 31, 2011, page 51
School Library Journal, March 2011, page 167
Voice of Youth Advocates, April 2011, page 66

Other books you might like:
E.L. Konigsburg, *Silent to the Bone*, 2000
Walter Dean Myers, *Riot*, 2009
Kashmira Sheth, *Keeping Corner*, 2007
Padma Venkatraman, *Climbing the Stairs*, 2008

995

MICOL OSTOW
DAVID OSTOW, Illustrator

So Punk Rock (and Other Ways to Disappoint Your Mother)

(Woodbury, Minnesota: Flux, 2009)

Subject(s): Rock music; Jews; Interpersonal relations

Age range(s): 14 - 18+
Major character(s): Ari Abramson, Musician, Teenager
Time period(s): 21st century; 2000s
Locale(s): United States

Summary: Micol Ostow's *So Punk Rock (and Other Ways to Disappoint Your Mother)* chronicles the surprising rise to fame of a teenage punk band. Headed by Ari Abramson, the Tribe is a group of upper-middle-class Jewish teens who watch their success skyrocket after playing a single song at a bar mitzvah. Now Ari and the gang are forced to confront the harsh realities of the music world, with its shallowness, easy fame, and access to vices of all kinds. *So Punk Rock* contains illustrations by David Ostow.

Where it's reviewed:
Booklist, June 1, 2009, page 66
School Library Journal, November 2009, page 116
Voice of Youth Advocates, August 2009, page 230

Other books by the same author:
Family, 2011
Emily Goldberg Learns to Salsa, 2006
Westminster Abbey, 2005

Other books you might like:
Melody Carlson, *What Matters Most*, 2009
Lesley Choyce, *Thunderbowl*, 2004
Simone Elkeles, *How to Ruin My Teenage Life*, 2007
Antony John, *Five Flavors of Dumb*, 2010

996

JIM OTTAVIANI
LELAND MYRICK, Illustrator

Feynman

(New York: First Second, 2011)

Subject(s): Biographies; Physics; Science
Age range(s): 15 - 18+

Summary: In this graphic novel, author Jim Ottaviani and illustrator Leland Myrick provide a biographical account of the life of physicist Richard Feynman through the unique format of graphic novelization. Feynman played an integral role in many of the most important scientific developments of not only the 20th century, but of all time. A key player in the development of the atomic bomb, Feynman also made great strides in the fields of quantum mechanics and particle physics. His report on the Space Shuttle Challenger disaster of 1996 helped reveal the key reasons that the space shuttle broke apart seconds after launching. Beyond his life as a scientist, however, Feynman was also a musician and an avid storyteller. In this book, Ottaviani and Myrick depict Feynman's life through illustrations from his beginnings growing up on New York's Long Island to his life as one of the most influential scientists in the world.

Where it's reviewed:
Booklist, March 15, 2011, page 29
Horn Book Magazine, September/October 2011, page 113
Publishers Weekly, May 30, 2011, page 54
Voice of Youth Advocates, August 2011, page 302

Other books you might like:
Nick Abadzis, *Laika*, 2007
Larry Gonick, *The Cartoon Guide to Physics*, 1991
Ralph Leighton, *"Surely You're Joking, Mr. Feynman!": Adventures of a Curious Character*, 1985
Gene Luen Yang, *Prime Baby*, 2010

997

MARIA PADIAN

Jersey Tomatoes Are the Best

(New York: Alfred A. Knopf, 2011)

Story type: Coming-of-Age
Subject(s): Adolescence; Ballet; Tennis

Age range(s): 13 - 16+
Major character(s): Eva Smith, Dancer (ballerina), Teenager, Student—High School; Henriette "Henry" Lloyd, Teenager, Student—High School, Tennis Player
Time period(s): 21st century; 2010s
Locale(s): Florida, United States; New York, New York

Summary: Two teenage girls must confront the pressure of pursuing dreams and striving for perfection in this young adult novel from author Maria Padian. Best friends Eva and Henriette ("Henry") have a lot in common: both have overbearing parents, both are involved in highly competitive extracurricular activities, and both have amazing opportunities the summer before junior year. Henriette spends her summer at a tennis camp in Florida, enjoying the time away from her parents. Meanwhile, Eva spends her break at a New York City ballet school, where the monumental pressure to look and act the part of the perfect ballerina begins to wear her down and push her down a dangerous path.

Where it's reviewed:
Booklist, March 1, 2011, page 57
Publishers Weekly, January 24, 2011, page 154
School Library Journal, May 2011, page 120
Voice of Youth Advocates, April 2011, page 66

Other books by the same author:
Brett McCarthy: Work in Progress, 2008

Other books you might like:
Ann Brashares, *The Sisterhood of the Traveling Pants*, 2001
Rebecca Burton, *Leaving Jetty Road*, 2006
Cecil Castellucci, *Rose Sees Red*, 2010
Megan Shull, *Amazing Grace*, 2006

998

SIOBHAN PARKINSON

Long Story Short

(New York: Roaring Brook Press, 2011)

Subject(s): Brothers and sisters; Runaways; Family life
Age range(s): 13 - 16+
Major character(s): Jonathan "Jono" Kinahan, 14-Year-Old, Brother (of Julie), Narrator; Julie Kinahan, 8-Year-Old, Sister (of Jono)
Time period(s): 21st century; 2010s
Locale(s): Ireland

Summary: In the young adult novel *Long Story Short* by Siobhan Parkinson, 14-year-old narrator Jonathan (Jono) Kinahan, who has learned a lot about telling a story in creative writing class, sets out to relate his personal tale of tragedy. The older brother of eight-year-old Julie, Jono has spent his young life protecting his sister from the fallout of their dysfunctional family—which includes an absent father, an alcoholic mother, and a recently deceased grandmother. When their mother hits Julie and breaks her cheekbone, Jono takes his sister on the run. His ill-conceived plan begins with a failed stint of street living, followed by a visit to their father. When the need for money spurs Jono to robbery, he is arrested and his story is revealed—but which version of his tale is the truth?

Where it's reviewed:
Booklist, May 1, 2010, page 84
Horn Book Magazine, July-August 2011, page 156
Publishers Weekly, April 11, 2011, page 54
School Library Journal, June 2011, page 128
Voice of Youth Advocates, August 2011, page 275

Other books you might like:
Ben Bo, *Skullcrack*, 2000
Siobhan Dowd, *A Swift Pure Cry*, 2006
Carolyn MacCullough, *Stealing Henry*, 2005

999

GARY PAULSEN

Liar, Liar: The Theory, Practice and Destructive Properties of Deception

(New York: Wendy Lamb Books, 2011)

Story type: Contemporary - Mainstream
Subject(s): Deception; Friendship; Love

Age range(s): 9 - 12+
Major character(s): Kevin Spencer, 14-Year-Old, Student
Time period(s): 21st century; 2010s
Summary: In this short novel by Gary Paulsen, 14-year-old Kevin Spencer is a liar. The teen's string of falsehoods and half-truths is seemingly endless; in fact, he's the self-proclaimed "best liar you'll ever meet." When Kevin isn't busy making up stories that work to his benefit, such as convincing a classmate that he has a disease that prevents him from helping with a school project or tricking his father into giving him permission to attend a concert after his mother denied his request, he's thinking of ways to win a girl's heart. It seems like only a matter of time before Kevin's fountain of fibs will catch up to him, but an unlikely source may just help him see the value in telling the truth.

Where it's reviewed:
Booklist, March 1, 2011, page 80
Bulletin of the Center for Children's Books, March 2011, page 342
Horn Book Magazine, March/April 2011, page 122
School Library Journal, June 2011, page 129

Other books by the same author:
Flat Broke: The Theory, Practice and Destructive Properties of Greed, 2011
Masters of Disaster, 2011
Mudshark, 2009
Lawn Boy, 2007
The Amazing Life of Birds, 2006

Other books you might like:
Eric Luper, *Jeremy Bender vs the Cupcake Cadets*, 2011
Chris Rylander, *The Fourth Stall*, 2011
Eleanor Updale, *Johnny Swanson*, 2010
Meg Wolitzer, *The Fingertips of Duncan Dorfman*, 2011

1000

JACKSON PEARCE

Sisters Red

(New York: Little, Brown and Company, 2010)

Subject(s): Fantasy; Werewolves; Sisters

Age range(s): 14 - 18+
Major character(s): Scarlett March, Sister (of Rosie), Orphan, Hunter (of werewolves), 18-Year-Old; Rosie March, 16-Year-Old, Sister (of Scarlett), Hunter (of werewolves), Orphan; Silas, Neighbor (of Scarlett & Rosie), Hunter (of werewolves), Teenager

Time period(s): 21st century; 2010s
Locale(s): Atlanta, Georgia

Summary: Written for young adults, *Sisters Red* is a violent adaptation of Little Red Riding Hood from author Jackson Pearce. The fantasy novel follows sisters, Scarlett and Rosie March, hellbent on a mission to rid the world of werewolves known as Fenris. Scarlett's vendetta is the strongest since she was injured in the Fenris attack that took her grandmother's life. Along with their neighbor, Silas, the sisters hunt down the vicious enemies and take their lives. When the Fenris begin gathering together and killing off innocent young girls in nearby Atlanta, the trio has no choice but to travel there together to put an end to the vicious attacks. During their stay in the city, shocking revelations come to light about their pasts, futures, and hidden desires.

Where it's reviewed:
Booklist, April 15, 2010, page 43
Horn Book Magazine, September/October 2010, page 89
Publishers Weekly, June 28, 2010, page 131
School Library Journal, May 2010, page 120
Voice of Youth Advocates, June 2010, page 169

Other books by the same author:
Purity, 2012
Sweetly, 2011
As You Wish, 2009

Other books you might like:
Kelley Armstrong, *The Reckoning*, 2010
Shannon Delany, *Secrets and Shadows*, 2011
Porter Grand, *Little Women and Werewolves*, 2010
Shannon Hale, *Book of a Thousand Days*, 2007
Marianne Mancusi, *Girls That Growl*, 2007

1001

MARY E. PEARSON

The Miles Between

(New York: Henry Holt, 2009)

Subject(s): Friendship; Fate; Adolescence

Age range(s): 15 - 18+
Major character(s): Destiny Faraday, 17-Year-Old, Student—Boarding School
Time period(s): 21st century; 2000s
Locale(s): United States

Summary: *The Miles Between* is a young adult novel from author Mary E. Pearson. Destiny Faraday is a 17-year-old boarding school student who finds comfort in her consistent routine. However, her curiosity is piqued when she finds a pink convertible with the keys in the ignition and cash in the glove box. Along with three of her peers, Destiny escapes on a one-day road trip, hoping to find excitement, adventure, and freedom. Along the way, the four teenagers discover valuable lessons about friendship and fate, and Destiny gains new insight into herself as a shocking secret from her past surfaces.

Where it's reviewed:
Booklist, July 1, 2009, page 43

Horn Book Magazine , September/October 2009, page 572
Journal of Adolescent & Adult, May 2010, page 691
School Library Journal, September 2009, page 170

Other books by the same author:
The Fox Inheritance, 2011
The Adoration of Jenna Fox, 2008
A Room on Lorelei Street, 2005
David v. God, 2000

Other books you might like:
Scott William Carter, *The Last Great Getaway of the Water Balloon Boys*, 2011
Gayle Forman, *If I Stay*, 2009
Morgan Matson, *Amy and Roger's Epic Detour*, 2010
C.J. Omololu, *Dirty Little Secrets*, 2010
Jessica Warman, *Where the Truth Lies*, 2010

1002

MAL PEET

Exposure

(Somerville, Massachusetts: Candlewick Press, 2009)

Series: Paul Faustino Series. Book 3
Subject(s): Sports; Popularity; Journalism

Age range(s): 15 - 18+
Major character(s): Paul Faustino, Journalist (sports writer); Otello, Soccer Player
Time period(s): 21st century; 2000s

Summary: *Exposure* is the third book in the series by Mal Peet to feature the character of Paul Faustino, a South American journalist. If you believe what the newspapers say, South American football star Otello has the perfect life. Someone, however, is out to destroy the world-renowned athlete's reputation. When Otello is implicated in a salacious scandal, both his career and his marriage are threatened. As top-notch sports writer Faustino chronicles the events surrounding the scandal, he begins to understand how much power the media has over people who are in the spotlight. *Exposure* is the winner the 2009 Guardian Children's Fiction Prize.

Where it's reviewed:
Booklist, August 1, 2009, page 56
Horn Book Magazine, Nov.-Dec. 2009, page 129
Publishers Weekly, October 26, 2009, page 59
School Library Journal, December 2009, page 129
Voice of Youth Advocates, February 2010, page 499

Other books by the same author:
The Penalty, 2007
Tamar: A Novel of Espionage, Passion, and Betrayal, 2007
Keeper, 2005

Awards the book has won:
Guardian Award for Children's Fiction, 2009
Blue Ribbon Awards: Fiction, 2010

Other books you might like:
Malorie Blackman, *Naughts and Crosses*, 2005
Caroline B. Cooney, *If the Witness Lied*, 2009
Julius Lester, *Othello: A Novel*, 1995

1003

MAL PEET

Life: An Exploded Diagram

(Somerville, Massachusetts: Candlewick Press, 2011)

Subject(s): Love; Cold War, 1945-1991; Nuclear warfare

Age range(s): 15 - 18+

Major character(s): Clem Ackroyd, Worker; Frankie Mortimer, Wealthy, Heiress

Time period(s): 21st century; (2000s); 20th century; 1940s

Locale(s): England

Summary: In this novel, author Mal Peet looks at three generations of one family living through several key eras in time: World War II, the onset of the Cold War, and the day and aftermath of 9/11. When Clem Ackroyd first meets the love of his life, Frankie Mortimer, he never expects it to last forever. After all, in a world that could end any minute at the hands of the Russians during the Cold War, he has no reason to believe in forever. His mother experienced those same fears nearly 20 years before during the London Blitz. Yet Clem knows that even with so much violence in the world, and in fact especially because of that violence, he must grab every bit of happiness he can. This book follows Clem and his family as they experience the trials and tribulations of the volatile world around them and make the most of their love for one another.

Where it's reviewed:
Booklist, September 15, 2011, page 62
Horn Book Magazine, November/December 2011, page 108
Publishers Weekly, September 19, 2011, page 62
School Library Journal, October 2011, page 145

Other books by the same author:
Exposure, 2009
Tamar: A Novel of Espionage, Passion, and Betrayal, 2007

Other books you might like:
David Almond, *The Fire-Eaters*, 2003
Malorie Blackman, *Naughts and Crosses*, 2005
Simone Elkeles, *Perfect Chemistry*, 2009

1004

ANNA PERERA

Guantanamo Boy

(Park Ridge, Illinois: Albert Whitman & Company, 2011)

Subject(s): Prisoners; Abuse; Psychology

Age range(s): 14 - 18+

Major character(s): Khalid, 15-Year-Old, Student—High School, Cousin (of Tariq), Soccer Player, Prisoner (at Guantanamo Bay); Tariq, Cousin (of Khalid)

Time period(s): 21st century; 2000s (2002)

Locale(s): Guantanamo Bay, Cuba

Summary: Khalid is a 15-year-old boy born into a Muslim family and raised in England. He's passionate about soccer, has an interest in a particular girl at school, and likes to play video games with his cousin, Tariq. He's never met Tariq, who lives in Pakistan, but they talk to each other frequently when they play war games together online. Six months after the terrorist attacks of September 11, 2001, in the United States, Khalid and his family travel to Pakistan to visit Tariq's family. When Khalid's father doesn't return to the house, Khalid goes looking for him and finds a protest. He is then arrested on the grounds of being an "enemy combatant." After hours of questioning at a prison in Pakistan and a camp in Afghanistan, Khalid is taken to Guantanamo Bay, Cuba. There, he is water boarded, beaten, and deprived of sleep. To stop the torture, Khalid confesses to a crime he didn't commit and is thrown into jail. For two years, Khalid endures beatings on a daily basis and waits for his family to find a way to free him.

Where it's reviewed:
Booklist, September 1, 2011, page 101
Library Media Connection, November-December 2011, page 75
Publishers Weekly, November-December 2011, page 89
School Library Journal, July 2011, page 89
Voice of Youth Advocates, December 2011, page 498

Other books you might like:
Paula Jolin, *In the Name of God*, 2007
Alexander Gordon Smith, *Solitary*, 2010
Allan Stratton, *Borderline*, 2010
Matt Whyman, *Icecore*, 2007

1005

ASHLEY HOPE PEREZ

What Can't Wait

(Minneapolis, Minnesota: Carolrhoda Books, 2011)

Subject(s): Universities and colleges; College environment; Family life

Age range(s): 15 - 18+

Major character(s): Marisa, 17-Year-Old, Student—High School, Aunt, Daughter, Sister

Time period(s): 21st century; 2010s

Locale(s): Houston, Texas

Summary: Marisa has one decision to make. This decision will change everything in her life and will affect everyone closest to her. The decision to go to college can hurt her relationship with her parents, who are depending on her to get a job when she's done with high school. The income will help their growing household, which includes Marisa's niece, whom she adores. Marisa is then to marry another Mexican American and bring joy to the family through their future children. The decision not to go to college will disappoint her teachers, who know she has what it takes to be a successful engineer someday. What she learns in college could make her a well-rounded person and open her up to a future full of possibilities. Pressure from her family combined with pressure from people at school becomes too much for Marisa to bear, so she starts to shut down. She doesn't know what to do, but she knows if she can just find someone who understands her, she'll come to the right decision eventually.

Where it's reviewed:
Booklist, March 15, 2011, page 60
Bulletin of the Center for Children's Books, April 2011, page 388
Library Media Connection, August-September 2011, page 77
School Library Journal, May 2011, page 120
Voice of Youth Advocates, April 2011, page 498

Other books by the same author:
The Knife and the Butterfly, 2012

Other books you might like:
Guadalupe Garcia McCall, *Under the Mesquite*, 2011
Rene Saldana Jr., *A Good Long Way*, 2010
Alan Lawrence Sitomer, *The Secret Story of Sonia Rodriguez*, 2008

1006

MITALI PERKINS

Bamboo People

(Watertown, Massachusetts: Charlesbridge, 2010)

Subject(s): Children and war; Refugees; Military life

Age range(s): 13 - 16+

Major character(s): Chiko, Teenager, Teacher, Military Personnel; Tu Reh, Teenager, Refugee, Military Personnel

Time period(s): 21st century; 2010s

Locale(s): Myanmar

Summary: Set in modern-day Myanmar (formerly Burma), *Bamboo People* follows the lives of two similar boys on two very different sides of a conflict. Chiko, the educated son of a doctor, dreams of becoming a teacher, but when he answers an ad for educators, he is unwillingly duped into joining the Burmese army, the same military that imprisoned his father for treason. Meanwhile, Tu Reh, a teenage Karenni refugee, is nursing a deep hatred for the Burmese government for destroying his land and displacing his people. When the two boys are sent on opposing missions, they come face-to-face in the jungle and must confront their fears, their ideals, and their hopes for the future.

Where it's reviewed:
Booklist, May 15, 2010, page 38
Horn Book Magazine, July/August 2010, page 119
School Library Journal, November 2010, page 124

Other books by the same author:
Secret Keeper, 2009
First Daughter: White House Rules, 2008
First Daughter: Extreme American Makeover, 2007
Monsoon Summer, 2004

Other books you might like:
Philip Gross, *The Lastling*, 2003
Nathaniel Harris, *Burma (Myanmar)*, 2010
John Marsden, *The Other Side of Dawn*, 1999
Linda Sue Park, *A Long Walk to Water: Based on a True Story*, 2010
Roland Smith, *Elephant Run*, 2007

1007

STEPHANIE PERKINS

Lola and the Boy Next Door

(New York: Dutton, 2011)

Story type: Coming-of-Age
Subject(s): Adolescence; Romances (Fiction); Dating (Social customs)
Major character(s): Lola Nolan, Designer (fashion), Teenager, 11th Grader, Neighbor (of Cricket); Cricket Bell, Neighbor (of Lola), Twin, Inventor
Time period(s): 21st century; 2010s
Locale(s): United States

Summary: This companion novel to *Anna and the French Kiss* is a witty story of adolescent romance and angst from author Stephanie Perkins. High school junior and aspirant costume designer Lola Nolan is an eccentric and trail-blazing individual who couldn't care less about fitting in among her peers. Her biggest dilemma is figuring out a way to get her father to approve of the 22-year-old rocker she's been dating—that is, until Cricket Bell moves back in next door to Lola. He broke her heart two years ago and, as much as she hates to admit it, her feelings for him aren't gone. When Cricket steps out from his twin sister's shadow and reenters Lola's life with a bang, she has to sort out her feelings for the boy next door.

Where it's reviewed:
Booklist, September 15, 2011, page 75
Publishers Weekly, July 25, 2011, page 55
School Library Journal, October 2011, page 146

Other books by the same author:
Anna and the French Kiss, 2010

Other books you might like:
Catherine Gilbert Murdock, *Front and Center*, 2009
Robin Palmer, *Cindy Ella*, 2008
Coleen Murtagh Paratore, *From Willa with Love*, 2011
Erica S. Perl, *Vintage Veronica*, 2010

1008

STEPHANIE PERKINS

Anna and the French Kiss

(New York: Dutton, 2010)

Subject(s): Boarding schools; Adolescent interpersonal relations; Dating (Social customs)

Age range(s): 15 - 18+

Major character(s): Anna Oliphant, Teenager

Time period(s): 21st century; 2010s

Locale(s): Paris, France; Atlanta, Georgia

Summary: Anna Oliphant is excited to begin her senior year in high school, a year she expects to be filled with fun and flirting in her hometown of Atlanta, Georgia. Then her father gives her an unwelcome surprise by sending her off to a boarding school in Paris, France. As Anna attempts to navigate her way around high school in a foreign country, she finds herself not only making friends but also finding a passion for French cinema. But when she arrives home to the United States for Christmas break, will she be able to readjust to the life she left behind?

Where it's reviewed:
Booklist, November 15, 2010, page 41
Horn Book Guide, Spring 2011, page 108
Reading Time, May 2011, page 36
School Library Journal, December 2010, page 112
Voice of Youth Advocates, December 2010, page 458

Other books by the same author:
Lola and the Boy Next Door, 2011

Other books you might like:
Lisa Barham, *Project Paris*, 2007
Sabine Durrant, *Bon Voyage, Connie Pickles*, 2008
Abby McDonald, *Sophomore Switch*, 2009
Lucy Silag, *Beautiful Americans*, 2009
Sasha Watson, *Vidalia in Paris*, 2008

1009

ERICA S. PERL

Vintage Veronica

(New York: Alfred A. Knopf, 2010)

Subject(s): Friendship; Fashion; Work environment

Age range(s): 15 - 18+
Major character(s): Veronica Walsh, Worker (vintage clothing shop); Zoe, Worker (vintage clothing shop); Ginger, Worker (vintage clothing shop); Lenny, Worker (vintage clothing shop)
Time period(s): 21st century; 2010s
Locale(s): United States

Summary: In *Vintage Veronica* by Erica S. Perl, a 15-year-old girl overcomes the insecurities created by her plus-size body to pursue her passion for fashion. To land the coveted position at Clothing Bonanza, a vintage apparel shop, Veronica Walsh lies about her age. Assigned to sort incoming clothing items as they arrive in the store via an enormous chute, Veronica proves her fashion expertise as she finds vintage pieces among the junk. Demonstrating her unique style in her own wardrobe, Veronica impresses her coworkers despite their misgivings about her weight. As Veronica adjusts to her new social status, she examines her feelings about herself, her appearance, and the new romantic interest in her life.

Where it's reviewed:
Booklist, February 15, 2010, page 72
Horn Book Guide, Fall 2010, page 360
School Library Journal, February 2010, page 122

Other books you might like:
Julia DeVillers, *Lynn Visible*, 2010
Yvonne Prinz, *The Vinyl Princess*, 2010
Susan Vaught, *Big Fat Manifesto*, 2008
Marissa Walsh, *Does This Book Make Me Look Fat?*, 2008

1010

JULIE ANNE PETERS

By the Time You Read This, I'll Be Dead

(New York: Disney/Hyperion Books, 2010)

Subject(s): Suicide; Bullying; Peer pressure

Age range(s): 15 - 18+
Major character(s): Daelyn Rice, 15-Year-Old; Santana, Friend (of Daelyn)
Time period(s): 21st century; 2010s
Locale(s): United States

Summary: In *By the Time You Read This, I'll Be Dead* by Julie Anne Peters, a suicidal teenager finds comfort in a friendship with a gravely ill classmate. Fifteen-year-old Daelyn Rice has been trying to kill herself for five years. A lifelong victim of bullying because of her weight and reclusive personality, Daelyn has attempted suicide several times. Her last experience has left her seriously injured and intent on completing her mission. She finds encouragement on a Web site that offers graphic suicide instruction. But as she counts the days to her final suicide attempt, Daelyn finds her plan thrown off course by Santana, a cancer patient who wants to be her friend.

Where it's reviewed:
Horn Book Magazine, March/April 2010, page 68
Publishers Weekly, November 30, 2009, page 49
School Library Journal, May 2010, page 121
Voice of Youth Advocates, February 2010, page 499

Other books by the same author:
She Loves You, She Loves You Not..., 2011
Rage: A Love Story, 2009
Grl2grl:Short Fictions, 2007
Far from Xanadu, 2005
Keeping You a Secret, 2000

Other books you might like:
Jay Asher, *Thirteen Reasons Why*, 2007
Albert Borris, *Crash into Me*, 2009
Rachel Cohn, *You Know Where to Find Me*, 2008

1011

JULIE ANNE PETERS

She Loves You, She Loves You Not...

(New York: Little, Brown and Company, 2011)

Story type: Lesbian Contemporary
Subject(s): Homosexuality; Adolescence; Mother-daughter relations
Major character(s): Alyssa, 17-Year-Old, Lesbian, Waiter/Waitress
Time period(s): 21st century; 2010s
Locale(s): Colorado, United States

Summary: National Book Award finalist Julie Anne Peters confronts the trials of teenage homosexuality in this poignant novel for young adult readers. Despite keeping a monumental secret from her family and friends, 17-year-old Alyssa is happy with her life. She has a great girlfriend named Sarah, with whom she hopes to spend the rest of her life. When the truth about Alyssa comes out, however, she loses everything and everyone she cares about. Her homophobic father kicks her out, forcing her to move to Colorado to live with the mother she never knew, and Sarah is out of her life forever. Alyssa fights to find her place in a new town as she comes to terms with her sexual identity, the secrets of the past, and her dreams for the future.

Where it's reviewed:
Booklist, May 15, 2011, page 45
Publishers Weekly, April 18, 2011, page 55
School Library Journal, June 2011, page 130
Voice of Youth Advocates, August 2011, page 276

Other books by the same author:
It's Our Prom (So Deal With It), 2012
By the Time You Read This, I'll Be Dead, 2010
Rage: A Love Story, 2009
Far from Xanadu, 2005
Keeping You a Secret, 2003

Other books you might like:
Joan Bauer, *Hope Was Here*, 2000
Sarah Dessen, *Keeping the Moon*, 1999
Mayra Lazara Dole, *Down to the Bone*, 2008
Lauren Myracle, *Kissing Kate*, 2003

1012

SUSAN BETH PFEFFER

This World We Live In

(Boston: Harcourt, 2010)

Series: Last Survivor Series. Book 3
Subject(s): Science fiction; Survival; Family life

Age range(s): 13 - 16+
Major character(s): Miranda Evans, Teenager; Alex Morales, Friend (of Miranda); Dad, Father (of Miranda); Lisa, Stepmother (of Miranda); Mom, Mother (of Miranda); Matt, Brother (of Miranda); Jon, Brother (of Miranda)
Time period(s): Indeterminate Future
Locale(s): Howell, Pennsylvania

Summary: In *This World We Live In* by Susan Beth Pfeffer, an asteroid strike on the moon has had a devastating impact on the Earth's climate. The planet has become a frigid wasteland where only the strongest survive. In the year since the moon's orbit shifted, Miranda Evans has adjusted to the hard life she shares with her mother and two brothers. When her father and stepmother arrive with other refugees seeking a place to stay, Miranda's world is thrown off balance again—especially by her feelings for one of the travelers, Alex Morales. *This World We Live In* is the third book in the Last Survivor series.

Where it's reviewed:
Booklist, March 1, 2010, page 64
Horn Book Guide, Fall 2010, page 380
School Librarian, Winter 2010, page 246

School Library Journal, April 2010, page 166
Voice of Youth Advocates, August 2010, page 270

Other books by the same author:
Blood Wounds, 2011
The Dead and the Gone, 2008
Life as We Knew It, 2006

Other books you might like:
Susan Butler, *The Hermit Thrush Sings*, 1999
Catherine Jinks, *Living Hell*, 2010
Saci Lloyd, *The Carbon Diaries 2015*, 2009
Terry Pratchett, *Nation*, 2008
Jo Treggiari, *Ashes, Ashes*, 2011

1013

TAMORA PIERCE

Bloodhound

(New York: Random House, 2009)

Series: Legend of Beka Cooper Trilogy. Book 2
Subject(s): Crime; Criminals; Law enforcement

Age range(s): 13 - 18+
Major character(s): Beka Cooper, Hero (member of the Provost's Guard), Police Officer (rookie police officer in search of counterfeiters), 16-Year-Old; Dale Rowan, Banker (Beka's love interest); Achoo, Police Officer (member of Provost's Guard); Clary, Police Officer (Beka Cooper's partner)
Locale(s): Corus, Fictional Location; Port Caynn, Fictional Location

Summary: *Bloodhound*, the second book in the Beka Cooper trilogy by Tamora Pierece, finds Beka in a good place; she has reached her goal and has finally become a member of Provost's Guard. She is officially a Dog, and now she must perform her duties and help keep her town and its residents safe. When gamblers begin to wreak havoc by using counterfeit money, she must infiltrate the underground world in nearby Port Caynn to discover who is behind the operation and how it can be stopped. She soon finds herself enamored with Dale Rowan, a local bank employee. Beka must learn to keep her wits about her and deal with the matter at hand, however, to become the true Bloodhound she was meant to be. Told through a series of journal entries from Beka's first-person point of view, *Bloodhound* sets the stage for the third and final book in the trilogy.

Where it's reviewed:
Booklist, March 1, 2009, page 46
Horn Book Magazine, May-June 2009, page 305
Locus, June 2009, page 27
School Library Journal, May 2009, page 116
Voice of Youth Advocates, August 2009, page 242

Other books by the same author:
Mastiff, 2011
Tortall and Other Lands: A Collection of Tales, 2011
Melting Stones, 2008
Terrier, 2006
Shatterglass, 2004
Cold Fire, 2003
Lady Knight, 2002

Other books you might like:
Erin Bow, *Plain Kate*, 2010
Eoin Colfer, *Artemis Fowl*, 2001
Herve Jubert, *Dance of the Assassins*, 2004
Robin McKinley, *The Blue Sword*, 1982

1014

D.C. PIERSON

The Boy Who Couldn't Sleep and Never Had To

(New York: Vintage Books, 2010)

Subject(s): Friendship; High schools; Sleep

Age range(s): 15 - 18+

Major character(s): Darren Bennett, 15-Year-Old; Eric Lederer, Friend (of Darren)

Time period(s): 21st century; 2010s

Locale(s): United States

Summary: In *The Boy Who Couldn't Sleep and Never Had To* by D.C. Pierson, 15-year-old Darren Bennett lives the life of an anonymous, unpopular 10th-grade student. When he meets classmate Eric Lederer, Darren finds a co-creator for his science-fiction book and a friend with an amazing secret. Eric can't sleep—ever. Weirder still, his body doesn't require sleep. Though Darren knows that exposing Eric's anomaly could put his new friend in danger, he does just that—unintentionally, of course. When a mysterious man in sunglasses shows interest in Eric, the teenagers realize that their sci-fi imaginings have come to life. First novel.

Where it's reviewed:
Booklist, December 15, 2009, page 18
Publishers Weekly, December 7, 2009, page 36

Awards the book has won:
Alex Awards, 2011

Other books you might like:
L. Ron Hubbard, *Slaves of Sleep*, 1948
Barry Lyga, *The Astonishing Adventures of Fanboy and Goth Girl*, 2006
William Sleator, *The Boy Who Couldn't Die*, 2004

1015

APRILYNNE PIKE

Spells

(New York: HarperTeen, 2010)

Series: Wings Series. Book 2
Subject(s): Fairies; Schools; Interpersonal relations

Age range(s): 13 - 16+

Major character(s): Laurel, Fairy, 16-Year-Old; Tamani "Tam", Friend (of Laurel)

Time period(s): Indeterminate

Summary: Aprilynne Pike's *Spells*, the second novel in a series, continues the journey of Laurel, a bright-eyed youth who has recently discovered she's a faerie. Her newly uncovered heritage leads her to study at the Academy of Avalon, where she learns more and more about her magical birthright. But when she returns home, Laurel finds the sinister trolls are wreaking havoc on her family. With her newfound knowledge, she sets out to take on the trolls and protect her loved ones.

Where it's reviewed:
Booklist, March 15, 2010, page 43
Horn Book Guide, Fall 2010, page 380
School Library Journal, August 2010, page 109
Voice of Youth Advocates, August 2010, page 270

Other books by the same author:
Illusions, 2011
Wings, 2009

Other books you might like:
Cyn Balog, *Fairy Tale*, 2009
Holly Black, *Valiant: A Modern Tale of Faerie*, 2005
Julie Kagawa, *The Iron King*, 2010
Lisa Mantchev, *Perchance to Dream*, 2010

1016

AMY PLUM

Die for Me

(New York: HarperCollins, 2011)

Series: Revenants Series. Book 1
Subject(s): Supernatural; Adolescence; Orphans

Age range(s): 14 - 18+

Major character(s): Kate Mercier, Teenager, Sister (of Georgia), Orphan, Girlfriend (of Vincent); Vincent, Boyfriend (of Kate), Supernatural Being (revenant); Georgia Mercier, Sister (of Kate)

Time period(s): 21st century; 2010s

Locale(s): Paris, France

Summary: Kate Mercier shuts down after the death of her parents. Plagued by memories of time spent with them before the tragic accident, Kate loses herself in her books. When she moves to Paris with her sister, Georgia, to live with their grandparents, Kate discovers something else that helps take her mind off her loss: Parisian art. Though she knows her life will never be normal again, she hopes that it will someday—somehow—get better. Meeting Vincent makes her realize that finding happiness again is a real possibility. Vincent is handsome and careful with her fragile emotions. Before she can fall for him completely, he tells her a secret that threatens to keep them apart. Vincent is a revenant, an undead being that must put himself in danger time and time again to save others. He is hunted by evil revenants who make it difficult for him to do his job and who may target Kate if they learn about their relationship. Kate doesn't want to lose Vincent, but staying with him will put her and her family in danger.

Where it's reviewed:
Booklist, March 1, 2011, page 56
Horn Book Guide, Fall 2011, page 393
Publishers Weekly, March 28, 2011, page 59
School Library Journal, May 2011, page 121
Voice of Youth Advocates, June 2011, page 190

Other books by the same author:
Until I Die, 2012

Other books you might like:
Amy Garvey, *Cold Kiss*, 2011
Nova Ren Suma, *Imaginary Girls*, 2011
Yvonne Woon, *Life Eternal*, 2012

1017

CINDY PON

Silver Phoenix: Beyond the Kingdom of Xia

(New York: Greenwillow Books, 2009)

Subject(s): Chinese history; Supernatural; Voyages and travels

Age range(s): 13 - 17+

Major character(s): Ai Ling, 17-Year-Old; Mother, Mother (of Ai Ling); Father, Father (of Ai Ling); Chen Yong, Young Man; Zhong Ye, Supernatural Being

Time period(s): Indeterminate Past

Locale(s): China

Summary: In *Silver Phoenix: Beyond the Kingdom of Xia* by Cindy Pon, 17-year-old Ai Ling embarks on a journey to find her father and discovers shocking truths about her heritage. Believing that her father is a captive in the emperor's palace, Ai Ling sets off on a dangerous mission in long-ago China that brings her in contact with a frightening presence—and a fascinating young man, Chen Yong. But another man, the cruel Zhong Ye, wants Ai Ling for his bride. Already instructed by her mother in the secrets of the bed chamber, Ai Ling is aware of the expectations of a marital relationship. As she struggles to resist Zhong Ye's advances, she realizes his true identity—and her own. First novel.

Where it's reviewed:
Booklist, April 1, 2009, page 39
Bulletin of the Center for Children's Books, June 2009, page 414
Magazine of Fantasy & Science Fiction, October 2009, page 46
School Library Journal, December 2009, page 129
Voice of Youth Advocates, August 2009, page 242

Other books by the same author:
Fury of the Phoenix, 2011

Other books you might like:
Da Chen, *Forbidden Tales: Sword*, 2008
Suzanne Collins, *Gregor the Overlander*, 2003
Alison Goodman, *Eon: Dragoneye Reborn*, 2008
Juliet Marillier, *Cybele's Secret*, 2008
Garth Nix, *Sabriel*, 1995

1018

TRACEY PORTER

Lark

(New York: Laura Geringer Books, 2011)

Story type: Paranormal; Young Adult
Subject(s): Supernatural; Death; Grief

Age range(s): 14 - 17+
Major character(s): Lark Austin, 16-Year-Old (murder victim), Supernatural Being (ghost), Friend (of Nyetta and Eve); Nyetta, Friend (of Lark and Eve); Eve, Friend (of Lark and Nyetta)
Time period(s): 21st century; 2010s
Locale(s): Virginia, United States

Summary: The lives of two teenage girls are never the same after the death of their friend. A man kidnaps 16-year-old Lark Austin, stabs and sexually assaults her, and then leaves her to freeze to death in the snowy Virginia woods. Her death devastates her friends, Nyetta and Eve, who try to cope with what has happened. Men in their lives have hurt both Nyetta and Eve. Nyetta's father left when she was a child, and a trusted coach molested Eve. When Lark's ghost visits Nyetta and begs her to help her find her way to the supernatural world, the friends vow to help her and in doing so, come to terms with the cards they've been dealt.

Where it's reviewed:
Booklist, June 1, 2011, page 80
Horn Book Magazine, May-June 2011, page 101
Publishers Weekly, April 18, 2011, page 54
School Library Journal, August 2011, page 117
Voice of Youth Advocates, August 2011, page 295

Other books by the same author:
A Dance of Sisters, 2012

Other books you might like:
Kimberly Derting, *The Body Finder*, 2010
Lauren Oliver, *Before I Fall*, 2010
Alice Sebold, *The Lovely Bones*, 2002
Jessica Warman, *Between*, 2011

1019

FRANK PORTMAN

Andromeda Klein

(New York: Delacorte Press, 2009)

Subject(s): Occultism; Psychics; Adolescence

Age range(s): 15 - 18+

Major character(s): Andromeda Klein, Occultist, Psychic (tarot card reader), Teenager; Daisy, Spirit

Time period(s): 21st century; 2000s

Locale(s): United States

Summary: *Andromeda Klein* is a dark and humorous young adult novel from author Frank Portman. In some ways, Andromeda is a typical teenage girl dealing with typical teenage issues. She's far from being popular, her crush lost interest and disappeared, and her mom is a tad overbearing. In other ways, Andromeda is far from normal. She's obsessed with the occult and reads tarot cards. More importantly, the young woman is still dealing with the tragic death of her best friend Daisy a year earlier. Now, it seems that Daisy is back, trying to communicate to Andromeda from the other side. Andromeda begins recognizing "signs" in everything and her tarot card readings start becoming eerily accurate. Is Daisy really trying to get a message through to Andromeda?

Where it's reviewed:
Booklist, August 1, 2009, page 66
Publishers Weekly, July 27, 2009, page 64
School Library Journal, November 2009, page 118

Other books by the same author:
King Dork, 2006

Other books you might like:
Mariah Fredericks, *In the Cards: Love*, 2006
Leslie D. Guccione, *Tell Me How the Wind Sounds*, 1989
Jaclyn Moriarty, *The Spell Book of Listen Taylor: And the Secrets of the Family Zing*, 2007
Susan Whitcher, *The Fool Reversed*, 2000

1020

J. L. POWERS

This Thing Called the Future

(El Paso, Texas: Cinco Puntos Press, 2011)

Subject(s): AIDS (Disease); Healing; Medical care

Age range(s): 15 - 18+
Major character(s): Khosi, 14-Year-Old, Girl, Sister (of Zi); Zi, Sister (of Khosi); Mama, Mother (of Khosi and Zi); Gogo, Grandmother (of Khosi and Zi); Little Man, Classmate (of Khosi)
Time period(s): 21st century; 2010s
Locale(s): Pietermaritzburg, South Africa

Summary: Contemporary South Africa provides the setting for *This Thing Called the Future*, a young-adult novel by J.L. Powers that follows a young girl's struggle between old customs and new threats. Khosi and her little sister, Zi, live with their grandmother in a shanty outside Pietermaritzburg. The girls' mother teaches in a faraway city, and when she comes to stay each weekend Khosi sees how quickly Mama's disease is progressing. Though she lives in poverty and in constant danger of rapists looking for virgins, Khosi remains determined to pursue her education and her interest in science. But she is also respectful of her Zulu culture, and seeks help from her ancestors as she faces overwhelming obstacles.

Where it's reviewed:
Booklist, June 1, 2011, page 85
Horn Book Magazine, July-August 2011, page 158
Publishers Weekly, March 21, 2011, page 78
School Library Journal, May 2011, page 121
Voice of Youth Advocates, August 2011, page 276

Other books by the same author:
The Confessional, 2007

Other books you might like:
Linzi A. Glass, *The Year the Gypsies Came*, 2006
Beverley Naidoo, *No Turning Back: A Novel of South Africa*, 1997
Allan Stratton, *Chanda's Secrets*, 2004

1021

TERRY PRATCHETT

I Shall Wear Midnight

(New York: HarperCollins, 2010)

Series: Discworld Series. Book 38
Subject(s): Witches; Magic; Good and evil

Age range(s): 14 - 18+
Major character(s): Tiffany Aching, Witch, 15-Year-Old; The Cunning Man, Mythical Creature; Preston, Guard, Student (medical); Roland, Nobleman, Son (of the Baron of the Chalk); Letitia Keepsake, Fiance(e) (of Roland), Noblewoman; Lady Keepsake, Noblewoman (also known as Deirdre Parsley); Amber Petty, 13-Year-Old, Girl; Rob Anybody, Mythical Creature (Nac Mac Feegle; Big Man of the Chalk Clan); Daft Wullie, Mythical Creature (Nac Mac Feegle); William the Gonnagle, Mythical Creature (Nac Mac Feegle); Jeannie, Mythical Creature (Nac Mac Feegle; Kelda of the Chalk Clan); Wee Mad Arthur, Police Officer, Mythical Creature (Nac Mac Feegle); Granny Weatherwax, Witch; Nanny Ogg, Witch; Eskarina Smith, Witch; Mrs. Proust, Witch, Store Owner (of Boffo's Joke Shop); Carrot Ironfoundersson, Police Officer (Captain of the City Watch); Angua von Uberwald, Police Officer, Werewolf
Time period(s): Indeterminate
Locale(s): Ankh-Morpork, Fictional Location; Ramtop Mountains, Fictional Location; The Chalk, Fictional Location; Discworld, Planet—Imaginary

Summary: Fifteen-year-old Tiffany is finally a full-fledged witch, performing her standard mix of magic and social work in her home country of The Chalk. However, following the death of the local Baron, anti-witch hysteria begins spreading across Discworld, propelled by the magical entity known as The Cunning Man. As Tiffany prepares to facedown the eyeless evil Cunning Man - in a battle that Granny Weatherwax and her fellow witches aren't sure that Tiffany can win - she also must contend with the impending marriage of the Baron's son, Roland, her former flame, to Letitia, his soppy fiancee who might just be a witch herself. But Tiffany has does have allies during her darkest days (whether she likes it or not) in the miniature Nac Mac Feegles and Preston, a childhood friend and reluctant castle guard.

Where it's reviewed:
Booklist, October 1, 2010, page 86
Horn Book Magazine, November/December 2010, page 101
Publishers Weekly, September 20, 2010, page 66
School Library Journal, November 2010, page 125
Voice of Youth Advocates, December 2010, page 474

Other books by the same author:
The Illustrated Wee Free Men, 2008
Wintersmith, 2006
A Hat Full of Sky, 2004
The Wee Free Men, 2003

Awards the book has won:
Blue Ribbon Awards: Fiction, 2010

Other books you might like:
Marianne Curley, *Old Magic*, 2002
Robin Jarvis, *The Whitby Witches*, 2006
Carolyn MacCullough, *Always a Witch*, 2011
Donna Jo Napoli, *The Magic Circle*, 1993

1022

JAMES PRELLER

Bystander
(New York: Feiwel and Friends, 2009)

Subject(s): Bullying; Conduct of life; Middle schools
Age range(s): 11 - 14+
Major character(s): Eric Hayes, Student—Middle School;
  Griffin Connelly, Bully, Friend (of Eric); Mary,
  Friend (of Eric)
Time period(s): 21st century; 2000s
Locale(s): New York, New York

Summary: James Preller's *Bystander* tells the story of
middle school student Eric Hayes, who is struggling to
adjust to life at his new Long Island school. Eric is
thrilled to make a friend in the magnetic Griffin Connelly, but it doesn't take long for Eric to realize Griffin
is a bully. As he watches his new friend terrorize the
other students, Eric is thrown into a moral dilemma.
Does he remain a bystander and bear witness to Griffin's
bullying? Or does he speak out and lose his only friend?

Where it's reviewed:
Booklist, October 1, 2009, page 41
Horn Book Guide, Spring 2010, page 80
Publishers Weekly, November 2, 2009, page 54
School Library Journal, January 2010, page 111

Other books by the same author:
Six Innings, 2008

Other books you might like:
James Howe, *The Misfits*, 2001
Gordon Korman, *Schooled*, 2007
Joyce Sweeney, *The Guardian*, 2009

1023

MARGI PREUS

Heart of a Samurai
(New York: Amulet Books, 2010)

Subject(s): Japanese (Asian people); Shipwrecks; United
  States
Age range(s): 12 - 16+
Major character(s): Manjiro Nakahama, Survivor (of
  shipwreck), 14-Year-Old
Time period(s): 19th century; 1840s
Locale(s): Japan; United States

Summary: A 2011 Newberry Honor Book, *Heart of a
Samurai* is an adventurous historical novel for young
adult readers from author Margi Preus. Based on a true
story, *Heart of a Samurai* follows the adventures of the
first known Japanese man to step foot on American soil.

In 1841, 14-year-old Manjiro Nakahama is among the
survivors of a shipwreck off the Japanese coast. After
swimming to an unknown island, the crew is rescued by
a passing American whaling ship and taken to the United
States. Although his fellow men are terrified of the
"barbarians," Manjiro is intrigued by this fascinating
new culture and he works hard to create a new life for
himself in America. However, everything changes years
later when he decides to return to his native land.

Where it's reviewed:
Booklist, July 1, 2010, page 62
Horn Book Magazine, September/October 2010, page
  91
Publishers Weekly, July 26, 2010, page 76
School Library Journal, September 2010, page 162

Other books you might like:
Rhoda Blumberg, *Shipwrecked!: The True Adventures of
  a Japanese Boy*, 2001
Emily Crofford, *Born in the Year of Courage*, 1991
Emily Arnold McCully, *Manjiro*, 2008
Michele Torrey, *Voyage of Ice: Chronicles of Courage*,
  2004

1024

CHARLIE PRICE

The Interrogation of Gabriel James
(New York: Farrar, Straus, Giroux Books, 2010)

Subject(s): Detective fiction; Adolescence; Adolescent
  interpersonal relations
Age range(s): 13 - 18+
Major character(s): Gabriel James, 14-Year-Old, Witness
  (to double murder)
Time period(s): 21st century; 2000s
Locale(s): Montana, United States

Summary: *The Interrogation of Gabriel James* is a young
adult mystery novel by author Charlie Price. In this book,
Price tells the story of Gabriel James, a teenager who,
since witnessing a double homicide that occurred right
in front of him, has taken it upon himself to become a
top informant for the local police department. In the
meantime, Gabriel struggles to deal with what he saw
that fateful day, as he attempts to traverse the typical
pitfalls of teenage-hood—including girls, school, and
popularity. However, as he becomes closer to a fellow
student, he begins to find a correlation between the
crimes occurring within the town and his new friend's
rocky relationship with his family. Price was awarded
the 2011 Young Adult Edgar Award for this book.

Where it's reviewed:
Booklist, July 1, 2010, page 52
Horn Book Guide, Spring 2011, page 109
Publishers Weekly, July 26, 2010, page 77
School Library Journal, September 2010, page 162
Voice of Youth Advocates, October 2010, page 356

Other books by the same author:
Desert Angel, 2011
Lizard People, 2007
Dead Connection, 2006

Awards the book has won:
Edgar Allan Poe Awards: Best Young Adult Novel, 2011

Other books you might like:
Peter Abrahams, *Bullet Point*, 2010
Robert Cormier, *The Rag and Bone Shop*, 2001
Norah McClintock, *She Said/She Saw*, 2011

1025

CHARLIE PRICE

Desert Angel

(New York: Farrar, Straus and Giroux, 2011)

Story type: Mystery
Subject(s): Suspense; Abuse; Mystery

Age range(s): 15 - 18+
Major character(s): Angel, 14-Year-Old, Abuse Victim, Runaway; Scotty, Murderer
Time period(s): 21st century; 2010s
Locale(s): United States

Summary: A young girl must fight for her life against a deranged murderer in this thriller for young adult readers from Edgar Award-winning author Charlie Price. Fourteen-year-old Angel narrowly escapes when her trailer is set ablaze by a deranged lunatic named Scotty. He murdered her mother and, in an effort to eliminate any witnesses, he has attempted to kill Angel as well. Discovering her mother's body and realizing it's only a matter of time until Scotty realizes she has escaped, Angel flees the desert that she has called home in search of help. Braving the harsh elements, Angel makes her way to civilization, where she encounters people who are willing to help her—if only she can find a way to trust them.

Where it's reviewed:
Publishers Weekly, August 22, 2011, page 67
Voice of Youth Advocates, October 2011, page 292

Other books by the same author:
The Interrogation of Gabriel James, 2010
Lizard People, 2007
Dead Connection, 2006

Other books you might like:
Andrew Smith, *In the Path of Falling Objects*, 2009
Alex Van Tol, *Knifepoint*, 2010
Robb White, *Deathwatch*, 1972

1026

MATTHEW QUICK

Sorta Like a Rock Star

(New York: Little, Brown and Company, 2010)

Subject(s): Homeless persons; Depression (Mood disorder); High schools

Age range(s): 14 - 17+
Major character(s): Amber Appleton, 17-Year-Old; Mom, Mother (of Amber)
Time period(s): 21st century; 2010s

Locale(s): Childress, United States

Summary: In *Sorta Like a Rockstar* by Matthew Quick, a 17-year-old girl finds hope despite overwhelming challenges in her life. Amber Appleton has been living with her dog in the school bus that her mother drives but maintains a positive attitude and a deep faith in God. Though homeless, Amber finds time to do volunteer work at a nursing home and at the local Korean Catholic church. Friendly to a fault and proud of her Catholic faith, Amber considers herself a rock star of hope. A devastating event sends Amber into a dark depression that causes her to question her faith.

Where it's reviewed:
Horn Book Guide, Fall 2010, page 381
Publishers Weekly, May 17, 2010, page 52
School Library Journal, May 2010, page 122
Voice of Youth Advocates, October 2010, page 356

Other books by the same author:
Boy21, 2012
The Silver Linings Playbook, 2008

Other books you might like:
Gennifer Choldenko, *Al Capone Does My Shirts*, 2004
C.J. Omololu, *Dirty Little Secrets*, 2010
Coleen Murtagh Paratore, *Forget Me Not: From the Life of Willa Havisham*, 2009

1027

SOFIA QUINTERO

Efrain's Secret

(New York: Alfred A. Knopf, 2010)

Subject(s): Drugs; Violence; High schools

Age range(s): 14 - 17+
Major character(s): Efrain Rodriguez, 17-Year-Old, Student—High School; Mom, Mother (of Efrain); Dad, Father (of Efrain); Candace, Friend (of Efrain); Nestor, Friend (of Efrain)
Time period(s): 21st century; 2010s
Locale(s): New York, New York

Summary: In *Efrain's Secret* by Sofia Quintero, a South Bronx teenager dreaming of an Ivy League education starts selling drugs to make some fast cash. For star student Efrain Rodriguez, son of an absent father and overworked mother, Harvard's astronomical tuition seems out of reach. At school, he works on improving his standardized test scores so he has a chance at admission. Efrain spends his nights dealing drugs with his old friend Nestor to build up a tuition fund. Though Efrain sees his drug selling as a quick and easy solution to his problem, his actions may do permanent damage to his future.

Where it's reviewed:
Booklist, March 1, 2010, page 72
Horn Book Guide, Fall 2010, page 381
Publishers Weekly, March 15, 2010, page 56
School Library Journal, June 2010, page 117

Other books you might like:
Oscar Hijuelos, *Dark Dude*, 2008

Janet Mcdonald, *Harlem Hustle*, 2006
Walter Dean Myers, *Dope Sick*, 2009

1028

CHERYL RAINFIELD

Scars

(Lodi, New Jersey: WestSide Books, 2010)

Subject(s): Self mutilation; Adolescent interpersonal relations; Abuse

Age range(s): 13 - 17+

Major character(s): Kendra, 15-Year-Old; Meghan, Friend (of Kendra)

Time period(s): 21st century; 2010s

Locale(s): United States

Summary: Cheryl Rainfield's *Scars* chronicles the emotional journey of 15-year-old Kendra, a young woman with a history of abuse who finds relief by cutting herself. Memories of a long-ago rape haunt Kendra and plague nearly every facet of her young life. The only respite she finds from the terrifying shards of memory comes in the form of a blade against her skin, drawing blood and releasing her pent-up pain. As she struggles to understand what happened to her, Kendra makes an unexpected friend in Meghan, and the relationship soon evolves into something more than friendship. Attempting to find out who she is and what she has endured, Kendra finds the strength to heal at last.

Where it's reviewed:
Booklist, March 1, 2010, page 61
Canadian Women Studies, Fall 2009, page 147
School Library Journal, May 2010, page 122
Voice of Youth Advocates, April 2010, page 62

Other books by the same author:
Hunted, 2011

Other books you might like:
Cynthia D. Grant, *Uncle Vampire*, 1993
Julia Hoban, *Willow*, 2009
Patricia McCormick, *Cut*, 2000
Holly Schindler, *A Blue So Dark*, 2010

1029

JANETTE RALLISON

My Fair Godmother

(New York: Walker, 2009)

Story type: Adventure

Subject(s): Fairies; Adolescence; Magic

Age range(s): 11 - 14+

Major character(s): Savannah Delano, 10th Grader; Chrysanthemum "Chrissy" Everstar, Godmother (fairy), Student (fairy school); Tristan, Student, Runner (track team)

Time period(s): Multiple Time Periods

Summary: Sophomore Savannah Delano is devastated when her boyfriend dumps her for, of all people, her responsible older sister. She longs for a prince, a fairy tale-worthy guy who will like the true Savannah, flaws and all. Into the teen's life pops Chrysanthemum "Chrissy" Everstar, her fair godmother. Yes, she's magical, but only fair in her skills, as can be understood from the comments and notes provided throughout the book by her professors. Chrissy's responses to her godchild's wishes involve putting her into such stories as Cinderella and Snow White. Then the fairy sends Tristan, a member of the track team at Savannah's school, to the past to become a perfect prince. He faces an ogre, a dragon, and other challenges. Savannah goes to his rescue, learning some valuable lessons through the experience.

Where it's reviewed:
Booklist, January 1, 2009, page 70
Journal of Adolescent & Adult, April 2009, page 639
Publishers Weekly, December 1, 2008, page 46

Other books by the same author:
My Unfair Godmother, 2011
My Double Life, 2010
Just One Wish, 2009
How to Take the Ex Out of Ex-Boyfriend, 2007
It's a Mall World After All, 2006

Other books you might like:
Julie Berry, *The Amaranth Enchantment*, 2009
Jessica Day George, *Princess of the Midnight Ball*, 2009
Justine Larbalestier, *How to Ditch Your Fairy*, 2008
Abby McDonald, *The Anti-Prom*, 2011

1030

ADAM RAPP

Punkzilla

(Somerville, Massachusetts: Candlewick Press, 2009)

Subject(s): Brothers; Drugs; Letters (Correspondence)

Age range(s): 16 - 18+

Major character(s): Jamie "Punkzilla", 14-Year-Old, Addict, Runaway, Criminal

Time period(s): 21st century; 2000s

Locale(s): United States

Summary: *Punkzilla* is a young adult novel from author Adam Rapp. Jamie is a 14-year-old, pot-smoking, meth-using runaway living in Portland, Oregon. Going by the nickname Punkzilla, Jamie leads a life of petty crime and drug addiction. When he learns that his homosexual older brother is dying of cancer, Jamie cleans up his act to head across the country to see him one last time. Along his journey, filled with hitched rides, shady motels, and scary bus stops, Jamie chronicles his adventure and feelings in a series of letters to his brother. The entire novel, comprised of Jamie's letters and supplemented by the correspondence of other family members, follows Jamie on his quest to make it to his brother on time. Gritty and raw, *Punkzilla* is an examination of family relationships, America, and surprising chance encounters.

Where it's reviewed:
Booklist, April 15, 2009, page 43
Horn Book Magazine, May/June 2009, page 305

Publishers Weekly, May 25, 2009, page 59
School Library Journal, July 2009, page 90
Voice of Youth Advocates, August 2009, page 231

Other books by the same author:
Under the Wolf, Under the Dog, 2004
33 Snowfish, 2003
Little Chicago, 2002
The Buffalo Tree, 1993

Other books you might like:
Melvin Burgess, *Smack*, 1998
Katherine Holubitsky, *Tweaked*, 2008
Kathe Koja, *The Blue Mirror*, 2004
Ranulfo, *Nirvana's Children*, 2003

1031

AMY REED

Clean

(New York: Simon Pulse, 2011)

Story type: Contemporary
Subject(s): Drug abuse; Addiction; Rehabilitation

Age range(s): 15 - 18+
Major character(s): Olivia, Wealthy, Addict (diet pills), Socialite; Kelly, Teenager, Addict; Christopher, Addict, Teenager, Religious, Homosexual; Eva, Teenager, Addict (prescription painkillers); Jason, Alcoholic, Addict, Teenager
Time period(s): 21st century; 2010s
Locale(s): United States

Summary: Five addicts must face their fears and overcome their pasts in this darkly humorous and thought-provoking novel for young adult readers from author Amy Reed. Despite drastically different backgrounds and lifestyles, five teens are drawn together by one common identifier: they're all addicts. Olivia is a high-society snob who can't stop taking diet pills, Kelly is a wild party girl who will try anything, Christopher is a church-raised homosexual with a meth problem, Eva is a prescription pill-popping drama queen, and Jason is an alcoholic tough guy wracked with guilt. Told in alternating narratives from each character's perspective, the story follows these five kids as they face their demons and strive to get clean.

Where it's reviewed:
Booklist, October 1, 2011, page 83
School Library Journal, October 2011, page 146
Voice of Youth Advocates, August 2011, page 276

Other books by the same author:
Beautiful, 2009

Other books you might like:
Ellen Hopkins, *Crank*, 2004
Blake Nelson, *Recovery Road*, 2011
Randi Reisfeld, *Rehab*, 2008

1032

M.K. REED
JONATHAN DAVID HILL, Illustrator

Americus

(New York: First Second, 2011)

Story type: Young Adult
Subject(s): Books; Censorship; Courage

Age range(s): 13 - 17+
Major character(s): Neal Barton, Teenager, Student—High School, Outcast, 9th Grader; Charlotte Murphy, Librarian (youth services)
Time period(s): 21st century; 2010s
Locale(s): Americus, Fictional Location

Summary: In this graphic novel for young adult readers from author M.K. Reed and illustrator Jonathan David Hill, a shy teenager must find the courage to stand up for what he believes in. A introverted outsider beginning his freshman year of high school, Neal Barton finds solace and escape from his everyday woes in the pages of his favorite fantasy series, Ravenchilde. Unfortunately, a local Christian activist group is boycotting the series and trying to get the Americus public library to ban the books due to their immoral content. Desperate to protect his beloved books and stand up for what is right, Neal elicits help from youth services librarian Charlotte Murphy to square off with the organization.

Where it's reviewed:
Booklist, September 15, 2011, page 54
Publishers Weekly, August 1, 2011, page 33
School Library Journal, September 2011, page 190

Other books you might like:
Vera Brosgol, *Anya's Ghost*, 2011
Cecil Castellucci, *The Plain Janes*, 2007
Barry Lyga, *Mangaman*, 2011
Jeff Smith, *Bone Prequel: Rose*, 2009

1033

TRENT REEDY

Words in the Dust

(New York: Arthur A. Levine Books, 2011)

Subject(s): Culture; Disadvantaged persons; Family life

Age range(s): 11 - 14+
Major character(s): Zulaikha, Sister (of Zeynab), 13-Year-Old (with a deformity), Student (of Meena); Meena, Professor (former), Teacher (of Zulaikha); Zeynab, 15-Year-Old, Sister (of Zulaikha)
Time period(s): 21st century; 2010s
Locale(s): Afghanistan

Summary: Zulaikha is a 13-year-old Afghanistan teenager with a cleft lip. While her birth defect puts her at a risk of being ridiculed and teased—even by her own brother—it also has its advantages. Unlike her 15-year-old sister, Zeynab, who will soon be married to an older man, Zulaikha can leave the house as she pleases. One day she meets a woman named Meena, a former professor who knew Zulaikha's mother before the Taliban killed her for hiding books. She offers to teach Zulaikha how to read and write, and the two begin working together. After American soldiers arrive in the country, Zulaikha gets a chance at a new life. She undergoes surgery to fix her lip and begins to realize what it feels like to look normal. First novel.

Where it's reviewed:
Booklist, January 1, 2011, page 111
Bulletin of the Center for Children's Books, January 2011, page 250
Horn Book Guide, Fall 2011, page 366
Publishers Weekly, November 29, 2011, page 50
School Library Journal, February 2011, page 118

Other books you might like:
Deborah Ellis, *Parvana's Journey*, 2002
Rukhsana Kahn, *Wanting Mor*, 2009
Sharon E. McKay, *Thunder over Kandahar*, 2010

1034

PHILIP REEVE

A Web of Air
(New York: Scholastic Inc., 2010)

Series: Fever Crumb Series. Book 1
Subject(s): Steampunk; Technology; Alternative worlds

Age range(s): 12 - 16+
Major character(s): Fever Crumb, Engineer, Young Woman
Locale(s): Mayda, Fictional Location

Summary: *A Web of Air* is the first book in the Fever Crumb series by Philip Reeves, which is the preceding series leading up to the author's Mortal Engines series. In this book, the author revisits the character of Fever Crumb, the adopted daughter of Dr. Crumb and his former apprentice. After leaving her apprenticeship for a mission and fleeing a crumbling London, Fever finds herself arriving at Mayda, a metropolis built upon the slopes of a seemingly bottomless crater. There she meets a hermit who is building a flying machine, and Fever's engineering know-how is just what the hermit needs to get his invention running. Yet there are some who would rather that the duo never complete their project. Will Fever be able to finish before her foes catch up to her?

Where it's reviewed:
Booklist, October 15, 2011, page 47
Horn Book Magazine, September-October 2011, page 98
School Library Journal, September 2011, page 168

Other books by the same author:
Fever Crumb, 2010
A Darkling Plain, 2006
Infernal Devices, 2005
Predator's Gold, 2004
Mortal Engines, 2003

Other books you might like:
Eoin Colfer, *Airman*, 2008
Rachel Neumeier, *The Floating Islands*, 2011

Terry Pratchett, *Nation*, 2008
Scott Westerfeld, *Leviathan*, 2009

1035

KATHY REICHS

Virals
(New York: Razorbill, 2010)

Series: Virals Series. Book 1
Subject(s): Diseases; Adolescence; Science fiction

Age range(s): 13 - 17+
Major character(s): Tory Brennan, Friend (of Ben, Hi, and Shelton), Teenager; Ben, Friend (of Tory); Hi, Friend (of Tory); Shelton, Friend (of Tory)
Time period(s): 21st century; 2010s
Locale(s): South Carolina, United States

Summary: *Virals* is the first book in a planned series for young adults by Kathy Reichs. In the novel, teenager Tory Brennan is sent to live with her father on a remote island off the South Carolina coast after the death of her mother. Her father is a respected forensic anthropologist. Fortunately, Tory loves studying science and is interested in her father's work. Once on the island, she befriends a group of teenagers: Ben, Hi, and Shelton. When the friends discover military ID tags that belong to a missing person, they begin piecing together additional clues and soon find themselves in an illegal canine research lab. There, they accidentally contract a type of parvovirus, which mutates and begins to cause changes, giving the teens special powers that allow them to predict danger and increases their senses of sight and smell. When they attempt to get to the bottom of things, they find themselves in grave danger from people who will do anything to keep the research lab a secret.

Where it's reviewed:
Booklist, October 1, 2010, page 89
Horn Book Guide, Spring 2011, page 109
Publishers Weekly, October 18, 2010, page 50
School Library Journal, December 2010, page 125
Voice of Youth Advocates, December 2010, page 475

Other books by the same author:
Seizure, 2011

Other books you might like:
Daniel Ehrenhaft, *The Last Dog on Earth*, 2003
Alex Flinn, *Fade to Black*, 2005
Dean R. Koontz, *Watchers*, 1987
Gemma Malley, *The Legacy*, 2011
Celia Thomson, *The Chosen*, 2005

1036

DANA REINHARDT

The Things a Brother Knows
(New York: Wendy Lamb Books, 2010)

Subject(s): Wars; Brothers; Armed forces

Age range(s): 15 - 18+

Major character(s): Levi Katznelson, Brother (to Boaz), Narrator; Boaz Katznelson, Military Personnel (Marine), Brother (to Levi)

Time period(s): 21st century; 2010s

Locale(s): United States

Summary: *The Things a Brother Knows* is a heartfelt book about the impact of war for young adult readers from author Dana Reinhardt. Levi Katznelson is thrilled to have his brother, Boaz, back home after three years of serving in the Marines in the Middle East, but it doesn't take long for Levi to realize that Boaz isn't the same person he was when he joined the armed forces. A hero in their Boston suburb, Boaz is withdrawn, isolated, and uncommunicative since his return. When Boaz shares his plans to hike the Appalachian Trail alone, Levi knows that he's not telling the truth. Desperate to understand the person his brother has become, Levi secretly follows Boaz on a surprising and heartbreaking journey to Washington D.C.

Where it's reviewed:
Booklist, October 1, 2010, page 81
Horn Book Magazine, November/December 2010, page 102
Publishers Weekly, August 30, 2010, page 55
School Library Journal, December 2010, page 125
Voice of Youth Advocates, October 2010, page 356

Other books by the same author:
The Summer I Learned to Fly, 2011
How to Build a House, 2008
Harmless, 2007
A Brief Chapter in My Impossible Life, 2006

Awards the book has won:
Sydney Taylor Children's Book Awards, 2011

Other books you might like:
Kelly Easton, *The Life History of a Star*, 2001
Patricia McCormick, *Purple Heart*, 2009
Michael Morpurgo, *Private Peaceful*, 2004
Walter Dean Myers, *Sunrise over Fallujah*, 2008
Tim Tharp, *Badd*, 2011

1037

DANA REINHARDT

The Summer I Learned to Fly

(New York: Wendy Lamb Books, 2011)

Story type: Coming-of-Age

Subject(s): Coming of age; Friendship; Rats

Age range(s): 12 - 15+

Major character(s): Drew Robin Solo, 13-Year-Old, Friend (of Emmett); Emmett Crane, Teenager, Friend (of Drew)

Time period(s): 20th century; 1980s (1986)

Locale(s): United States

Summary: In this young adult novel, author Dana Reinhardt tells the story of an eccentric adolescent girl whose life is turned upside down by the arrival of an interesting stranger. Drew Robin Solo is not an average 13-year-old girl. For starters, she has a pet rat. She also works at her mother's cheese shop, which is one of the most unglam-

orous jobs she can imagine. Drew spends her time mourning her deceased father and trying to make sense of his life's work—a huge book full of lists. As Drew prepares to start eighth grade, her life seems set on a course for quiet boredom. That is, until she meets a strange soul mate, a rat-loving boy named Emmett Crane. This unexpected, unusual friendship jump-starts Drew's life and sets her on a new course toward adulthood.

Where it's reviewed:
Booklist, June 1, 2011, page 89
Horn Book Magazine, July-August 2011, page 148
Publishers Weekly, May 23, 2011, page 46
School Library Journal, June 2011, page 131
Voice of Youth Advocates, June 2011, page 172

Other books by the same author:
The Things a Brother Knows, 2010
How to Build a House, 2008
Harmless, 2007
A Brief Chapter in My Impossible Life, 2006

Other books you might like:
Michael Harmon, *Skate*, 2006
Angela Johnson, *Bird*, 2004
Marilyn Taylor McDowell, *Carolina Harmony*, 2009
Nnedi Okorafor-Mbachu, *Zahrah the Windseeker*, 2005
Brian Selznick, *Wonderstruck*, 2011

1038

LAURA RESAU
MARIA VIRGINIA FARINANGO, Co-Author

The Queen of Water

(New York: Delacorte Press, 2011)

Story type: Coming-of-Age

Subject(s): Coming of age; Racism; Poverty

Age range(s): 14 - 18+

Major character(s): Virginia, Young Woman, Servant

Time period(s): 20th century

Locale(s): Andes Mountains, Ecuador

Summary: This young adult novel by Laura Resau and Maria Virginia Farinango is based on the true story of Farinango's childhood. It tells the story of Virginia, a young girl growing up in an Indian family in the Andes Mountains of Ecuador. Her family is so poor that they live in a mud hut and even the children have to put in long hours of labor in the fields. All the while, they face the disparaging attitudes of the Spanish mestizo families in the area. When Virginia is seven years old, her parents send her to work for a mestizo family—but her troubles are far from over. Now Virginia is alone, subject to insulting and abusive employers. She is still working hard for little money or respect. Four years later, Virginia has the opportunity to return to her family. By then, however, she has learned and changed so much she no longer fits in her parents' world. How will Virginia resolve her conflict and find her place in the big, confusing world?

Where it's reviewed:
Booklist, February 15, 2011, page 68
Horn Book Magazine, July-August 2011, page 149

School Library Journal, June 2011, page 132
Voice of Youth Advocates, February 2011, page 559

Other books you might like:
Sharon M. Draper, *Copper Sun*, 2006
Patricia McCormick, *Sold*, 2006
Suzanne Fisher Staples, *Shabanu: Daughter of the Wind*, 1989

1039

NAOMI RICH

Alis

(New York: Viking Children's Books, 2009)

Subject(s): Religious life; Marriage; Cults

Age range(s): 14 - 18+
Major character(s): Alis, 14-Year-Old, Religious, Runaway
Time period(s): Indeterminate Past

Summary: *Alis* is the debut novel from British author Naomi Rich. Growing up in the strict religious community known as Freeborne, 14-year-old Alis has never experienced life outside its walls. But when her parents arrange a marriage to the 40-year-old minister, Alis decides to join her runaway brother in the city. She soon learns that the only way to survive on the streets is to steal—or worse. Faced with the dilemma of an arranged marriage to a much older man or life on the dangerous city streets, Alis tries desperately to take control. Her choices lead to disastrous results, though, and she soon finds herself accused of murder. Will she betray someone she loves or sacrifice herself?

Where it's reviewed:
Booklist, December 15, 2008, page 40
Publishers Weekly, December 22, 2008, page 52
School Library Journal, March 2009, page 152

Other books you might like:
Michele Dominguez Greene, *Keep Sweet*, 2010
Shelley Hrdlitschka, *Sister Wife*, 2008
Carol Lynch Williams, *The Chosen One*, 2009

1040

JAME RICHARDS

Three Rivers Rising: A Novel of the Johnstown Flood

(New York: Alfred A. Knopf, 2010)

Subject(s): Floods; Hittites; Social class

Age range(s): 14 - 17+
Major character(s): Celestia, 16-Year-Old; Whitcombe, Father (of Celestia); Maura, Mother (of four children); Kate, Nurse; Peter, Worker (hired hand)
Time period(s): 19th century; 1880s (1888-1889)
Locale(s): Allegheny Mountains, Pennsylvania

Summary: In *Three Rivers Rising: A Novel of the Johnstown Flood* by Jame Richards, the Johnstown Flood of 1889 provides the setting for a story of romance and a clash between classes. Celestia, age 16, summers each year at the Allegheny Mountains' South Fork Fishing and Hunting Club with her family. To the great disappointment of her parents, Celestia meets and falls in love with Peter, a member of the club's staff. When her parents refuse to accept Celestia and Peter's relationship, the defiant young woman decides to live with Peter in Johnstown. A devastating flood further tests Celestia's strength and determination. First novel.

Where it's reviewed:
Booklist, August 1, 2010, page 67
Horn Book Guide, Fall 2010, page 381
Publishers Weekly, March 29, 2010, page 60
School Library Journal, April 2010, page 168
Voice of Youth Advocates, August 2010, page 255

Other books you might like:
Steve Augarde, *X Isle*, 2010
Jennifer Donnelly, *A Northern Light*, 2003
Janet Fox, *Faithful*, 2010
Marian Hale, *Dark Water Rising*, 2006

1041

RANSOM RIGGS

Miss Peregrine's Home for Peculiar Children

(Philadelphia: Quirk Books, 2011)

Subject(s): Fear; Children; Adventure

Age range(s): 14 - 18+
Major character(s): Jacob Portman, 16-Year-Old
Time period(s): 21st century; 2010s
Locale(s): Wales, United Kingdom

Summary: In *Miss Peregrine's Home for Peculiar Children*, author Ransom Riggs tells the story of a ramshackle old house and the eerie inhabitants who just may still be alive. Circumstances force 16-year-old Jacob Portman to take to the seas, where he happens upon an isolated island near the coast of Wales. There he finds the ruins of Miss Peregrine's Home for Peculiar Children, but the more information he unearths about the home's strange residents, the more he is haunted by the idea that they may be alive—and they may be after him. First novel.

Where it's reviewed:
Booklist, May 15, 2011, page 17
Publishers Weekly, April 25, 2011, page 139
School Library Journal, June 2011, page 133
Voice of Youth Advocates, August 2011, page 297

Other books by the same author:
Talking Pictures: Images and Messages Rescued from the Past, 2012

Other books you might like:
Kelly Keaton, *Darkness Becomes Her*, 2011
David Levithan, *Every You, Every Me*, 2011
Graham McNamee, *Bonechiller*, 2008

1042

VERONICA ROTH

Divergent

(New York: Katherine Tegen Books, 2011)

Series: Divergent Trilogy. Book 1
Subject(s): Science fiction; Identity; Family

Age range(s): 15 - 18+
Major character(s): Beatrice "Tris" Prior, 16-Year-Old; Four, Teacher (of Tris)
Time period(s): Indeterminate Future
Locale(s): Chicago, Illinois

Summary: In *Divergent* by Veronica Roth, Beatrice Prior has been born into an Abnegation family, meaning that she and her people follow a philosophy of selflessness. At the age of 16, according the rules of the dystopian society that now governs a Chicago of the future, Beatrice must choose her own path. Besides Abnegation, her choices include Amity, Candor, Erudite, and Dauntless. Although Beatrice knows that her decision will be binding, she decides to leave her family and join the Dauntless using her new name, "Tris." As Tris undergoes the grueling initiation rites of the Dauntless, she realizes that she is a Divergent who possesses attributes of several factions. *Divergent* is the first book in Roth's Divergent series. First novel.

Where it's reviewed:
Booklist, March 1, 2011, page 56
New York Times Book Review, May 15, 2011, page 17
Publishers Weekly, February 21, 2011, page 4
School Library Journal, June 2011, page 133
Voice of Youth Advocates, August 2011, page 297

Other books you might like:
Suzanne Collins, *The Hunger Games*, 2008
Ally Condie, *Crossed*, 2011
Richard Harland, *Worldshaker*, 2010

1043

S.L. ROTTMAN

Out of the Blue

(Atlanta, Georgia: Peachtree, 2009)

Subject(s): Military bases; Adolescence; Neighborhoods

Age range(s): 14 - 17+
Major character(s): Stuart Ballentyne, 15-Year-Old; Billy, 8-Year-Old, Neighbor (of Stuart)
Time period(s): 21st century; 2000s
Locale(s): North Dakota, United States

Summary: *Out of the Blue* is a young adult novel by S. L. Rottman. In the novel, 15-year-old Stuart Ballentyne has spent most of his life moving around, and this year is no different. He is now living at the Minot Air Force Base, where his mother is a commander. Since his father left and his older brother went to college, Stu has started feeling more alone than ever. His feelings are magnified when his mother is deployed. The lonely teen decides to get to know his neighbors better, and he soon befriends a troubled eight-year-old named Billy. When he realizes that Billy may be suffering at the hands of his family members, Stu makes a decision that could lead to tragedy.

Where it's reviewed:
Horn Book Guide, Spring 2010, page 106
School Library Journal, October 2009, page 134

Other books by the same author:
Hero, 2007
Shadow of a Doubt, 2005
Slalom, 2004
Stetson, 2002
Head Above Water, 1999

Other books you might like:
Michael B. Harmon, *The Last Exit to Normal*, 2008
Alice Mead, *Soldier Mom*, 1999
Marilyn Reynolds, *Shut Up!*, 2009

1044

JENNIFER ROY

Mindblind

(New York: Marshall Cavendish, 2010)

Subject(s): Mental disorders; Gifted children; Adolescence

Age range(s): 12 - 16+
Major character(s): Nathaniel Clark, 14-Year-Old, Genius
Time period(s): 21st century; 2010s
Locale(s): United States

Summary: With an IQ of 182, 14-year-old Nathaniel Clark is a genius by definition. He can play the keyboard, is a self-taught Mandarin Chinese speaker, and can solve mathematical equations that would stump some graduate students. His Asperger's makes all of these things a breeze for him, but to Nathaniel, being a real genius isn't about his IQ or proficiency in foreign languages or math. He once read that real geniuses are the people who make a difference in the world. Determined to become that kind of genius, Nathaniel sets out to contribute to the people and world around him in a tangible way, and if he happens to win the heart of a cute girl along the way, so be it.

Where it's reviewed:
Booklist, October 1, 2010, page 80
Horn Book Magazine, November/December 2010, page 103
School Library Journal, March 2011, page 170
Voice of Youth Advocates, October 2010, page 357

Other books by the same author:
Yellow Star, 2006

Other books you might like:
Emily Franklin, *The Half-Life of Planets*, 2010
Tara Kelly, *Harmonic Feedback*, 2010
Francisco X. Stork, *Marcelo in the Real World*, 2009

1045

JILL RUBALCABA

I.M. Pei: Architect of Time, Place, and Purpose

(New York: Marshall Cavendish, 2011)

Subject(s): Biographies; Architecture; Buildings

Age range(s): 13 - 17+

Summary: Author Jill Rubalcaba provides young adult readers with a biography of I.M. Pei, one of the most influential and successful architects of the 20th and 21st centuries. This biography showcases Pei's talent, range, and professional success by examining six of his most famous and recognizable buildings. Using photographs and illustrations, Rubalcaba recounts the trials, conflict, and determination that contributed to the construction of the National Center for Atmospheric Research in Boulder, Colorado; the John F. Kennedy Presidential Library in Boston, Massachusetts; the East Building of the National Gallery of Art in Washington, D.C.; the Fragrant Hill Hotel in China; the Miho Museum in Japan; and the Louvre in Paris, France.

Where it's reviewed:
Publishers Weekly, September 12, 2009, page 79
School Library Journal, October 2011, page 161

Other books by the same author:
Digging for Troy: From Homer to Hisarlik, 2011
Every Bone Tells a Story: Hominin Discoveries, Deductions, and Debates, 2010
Empires of the Maya, 2009
Ancient Egypt: Archaeology Unlocks the Secrets of Egypt's Past, 2006

Other books you might like:
Jan Adkins, *Frank Lloyd Wright (Up Close)*, 2007
Julie Dunlap, *Parks for the People: The Life of Frederick Law Olmsted*, 2011
Susan Goldman Rubin, *There Goes the Neighborhood: Ten Buildings People Loved to Hate*, 2001
Louise Chipley Slavicek, *I.M. Pei*, 2010

1046

JILL RUBALCABA
PETER ROBERTSHAW, Co-Author

Every Bone Tells a Story: Hominin Discoveries, Deductions, and Debates

(Watertown, Massachusetts: Charlesbridge, 2010)

Subject(s): Fossils; Archaeology; Paleontology

Age range(s): 14 - 18+

Summary: In *Every Bone Tells a Story: Hominin Discoveries, Deductions, and Debates*, authors Jill Rubalcaba and Peter Robertshaw guide young adult readers through the fascinating history of humanity's origins. The authors tell the stories of four remarkable hominin discoveries—those of Turkana Boy, Otzi the Iceman, Lapedo Child, and Kennewick Man—and detail the enormous scientific contributions of each finding. Rubalcaba and Robertshaw also chart the emerging debate surrounding the hominins and the countless hours of research and conversation they have inspired.

Where it's reviewed:
Booklist, February 15, 2010, page 47
Horn Book Guide, Fall 2010, page 409
School Library Journal, March 2010, page 180

Other books by the same author:
The Early Human World, 2005

Other books you might like:
Linda Goldenberg, *Little People and a Lost World: An Anthropological Mystery*, 2007
Kelly Milner Halls, *Mysteries of the Mummy Kids*, 2007
Robin Place, *Bodies from the Past*, 1995
Sally M. Walker, *Written in Bone: Buried Lives of Jamestown and Colonial Maryland*, 2009
Charlotte Wilcox, *Mummies, Bones and Body Parts*, 2000

1047

SUSAN GOLDMAN RUBIN

Music Was It: Young Leonard Bernstein

(Watertown, Massachusetts: Charlesbridge, 2011)

Subject(s): Music; Musicians; Biographies

Age range(s): 12 - 15+

Summary: Author Susan Goldman Rubin teaches young readers about the life, determination, trials, and success of Jewish American composer, pianist, and conductor Leonard Bernstein in this comprehensive biography. From the earliest stages of childhood, Bernstein was passionate about music and determined to pursue it, despite adamant protests from his father. Unwilling to give up on his dream, Bernstein worked to pay for his own piano lessons, sought out opportunities, and stayed strong in the face of prejudice and racism. At the age of 25, his hard work paid off and he made his professional conducting debut at Carnegie Hall with the New York Philharmonic. Rubin tells the complete story of Bernstein's rise to fame in this detailed tome, complemented with photographs, illustrations, and primary documents, including telegrams, sheet music, and concert programs.

Where it's reviewed:
Booklist, February 15, 2011, page 68
Horn Book Magazine, May/June 2011, page 120
School Library Journal, March 2011, page 186

Other books by the same author:
Wideness and Wonder: The Life and Art of Georgia O'Keeffe, 2010
Delicious: The Art and Life of Wayne Thiebaud, 2007
Edward Hopper: Painter of Light and Shadow, 2007
Andy Warhol: Pop Painter, 2006

Other books you might like:
Elizabeth Partridge, *John Lennon: All I Want Is the Truth*, 2005
Eleanora E. Tate, *African American Musicians*, 2000
Robert Ziegler, *Great Musicians*, 2008

1048

LAURA RUBY

Bad Apple

(New York: HarperTeen, 2009)

Subject(s): Teacher-student relations; Bullying; High schools
Age range(s): 15 - 18+
Major character(s): Tola Riley, 11th Grader; Mr. Mymer, Teacher (art)
Time period(s): 21st century; 2000s
Locale(s): United States

Summary: In *Bad Apple* by Laura Ruby, a high-school scandal involving an 11th-grade student and her teacher plays out on the Internet. With her green hair, pierced nose, and curious tastes in art and literature, Tola Riley stands out at her high school. When rumors that she and her art teacher, Mr. Mymer, are involved in an inappropriate relationship emerge, a scurrilous Web site goes up—thetruthabouttolariley.com—allowing anyone with Internet access to weigh in. Through Tola's narration and comments left by students and family members, the real story of what happened between Tola and Mr. Mymer is gradually revealed.

Where it's reviewed:
Booklist, November 15, 2009, page 31
Horn Book Magazine, January-February 2010, page 91
Publishers Weekly, October 12, 2009, page 50
School Library Journal, December 2009, page 131

Other books by the same author:
Hero, 2007
Shadow of a Doubt, 2005
Slalom, 2004
Stetson, 2002
Head Above Water, 1999

Other books you might like:
Liz Gallagher, *The Opposite of Invisible*, 2008
Jody Gehrman, *Triple Shot Bettys in Love*, 2009
Isabel Kaplan, *Hancock Park*, 2009
Andrew Matthews, *A Winter Night's Dream*, 2004
Lisa Ann Sandell, *A Map of the Known World*, 2009

1049

BRENT RUNYON

Surface Tension: A Novel in Four Summers

(New York: Alfred A. Knopf, 2009)

Subject(s): Vacations; Adolescence; Coming of age
Age range(s): 15 - 18+

Major character(s): Lucas, Teenager, Narrator
Time period(s): 20th century; 1990s
Locale(s): United States

Summary: Written by Brent Runyon, *Surface Tension: A Novel in Four Summers* follows Lucas from ages 13 to 16 as he spends two weeks every summer at a lake house with his parents. This coming-of-age novel for young adults traces the outward and inward changes that take place in one boy's life over the course of four years. At the age of 13, Lucas is passionate about everything and loves his time at the lake. He's thrilled to have the opportunity to swim, skip rocks, fish, and search for stones. At the age of 14, he's grown a bit more cynical and is more interested in girls than skipping rocks. At 15, Lucas has grown angrier, and the friend he brings to the lake challenges his view on the once idyllic place. At 16, Lucas has found love until he receives a break-up letter from his girlfriend that sends him into a depression. *Surface Tension* is a moving novel about a person's journey in life and how it's molded by the people and places encountered along the way.

Where it's reviewed:
Booklist, February 15, 2009, page 76
Horn Book Magazine, May/June 2009, page 307
Publishers Weekly, February 23, 2009, page 51
School Library Journal, April 2009, page 141

Other books by the same author:
Maybe, 2006
The Burn Journals, 2004

Other books you might like:
Garret Freymann-Weyr, *After the Moment*, 2009
Han Nolan, *A Summer of Kings*, 2006
Maria Padian, *Brett McCarthy: Work in Progress*, 2008
Celia Rees, *The Wish House*, 2006

1050

AMY KATHLEEN RYAN

Glow

(New York: St. Martin's Griffin, 2011)

Series: Sky Chasers Series. Book 1
Story type: Fantasy
Subject(s): Science fiction; End of the world; Space flight
Age range(s): 14 - 17+
Major character(s): Waverly, 15-Year-Old, Girlfriend (of Kieran); Kieran, Boyfriend (of Waverly); Seth, Boy (Waverly likes)
Time period(s): Indeterminate Future
Locale(s): New Earth, Planet—Imaginary

Summary: In this young adult novel, which is an entry in the Sky Chasers series, Earth has been ruined and the surviving humans have rocketed away in several giant spaceships, heading toward a New Earth. Their chances of making a harmonious new start look slim, however, when various factions begin to argue. One group begins trying to kidnap young women to use as reproductive slaves. One of the women targeted is 15-year-old Waverly, who embarks on a quest with her teenage boyfriend Kieran to stop this rash of abductions and violence. Waverly and Kieran have many dangerous, action-packed missions, while Waverly starts to notice another boy, Seth, who she might like better.

Where it's reviewed:
Booklist, September 1, 2011, page 117
Publishers Weekly, July 11, 2011, page 58
School Library Journal, September 2011, page 169

Other books by the same author:
Zen and Xander Undone, 2010
Vibes, 2008
Shadow Falls, 2005

Other books you might like:
Megan McCafferty, *Bumped*, 2011
Beth Revis, *Across the Universe*, 2011
Dom Testa, *The Comet's Curse*, 2009

1051

CARRIE RYAN

The Forest of Hands and Teeth

(New York: Delacorte Press, 2009)

Series: Forest of Hands and Teeth Series. Book 1
Subject(s): Horror; Fantasy; Alternative worlds

Age range(s): 15 - 18+
Major character(s): Mary, Orphan; Harry, Friend (of Mary); Travis, Friend (of Mary)
Time period(s): Indeterminate

Summary: Carrie Ryan's debut novel, *The Forest of Hands and Teeth*, takes place seven generations after The Return, a zombie outbreak that has nearly wiped out humanity. Now, a sole village exists, separated from the hoards of undead in the woods by only a chain-link fence. Mary, a young villager, has lost her mother to the zombies. Now an orphan, Mary goes to the Sisters, a religious order that controls the village, to be prepared for marriage. Then the zombies break into the village, and chaos ensues. Mary, who had been wondering what life might have been like before The Return, decides to venture into the surrounding forest to see if there are any other humans beyond the borders of her town. Accompanying her are her brother and his wife, her friends Travis and Harry, and an orphan boy. First novel.

Where it's reviewed:
Booklist, January 1, 2009, page 66
Publishers Weekly, February 2, 2009, page 51
School Library Journal, May 2009, page 117

Other books by the same author:
The Dark and Hollow Places, 2011
The Dead-Tossed Waves, 2010

Other books you might like:
Gail Dayton, *Heart's Blood*, 2010
Faith Hunter, *Blood Cross*, 2010
Jonathan Maberry, *Rot and Ruin*, 2010
Eileen Rendahl, *Don't Kill the Messenger*, 2010
Skyler White, *And Falling, Fly*, 2010

1052

DARLENE RYAN

Five Minutes More

(Victoria, British Columbia: Orca Book Publishers, 2009)

Subject(s): Diseases; Suicide; Family relations
Age range(s): 14 - 18+
Major character(s): D'Arcy, Teenager; Seth, Friend (of D'Arcy)
Time period(s): 21st century; 2000s
Locale(s): United States

Summary: In *Five Minutes More* by Darlene Ryan, a teenage girl struggles to deal with her father's tragic death. Though it seems apparent that D'Arcy's father drove off a bridge to his death on purpose, she can't believe that he committed suicide. Compounding her grief is D'Arcy's anger at her mother and half-sister and the ease with which they seem to accept his loss. Leaning on her friends for support, D'Arcy learns that her father had received a devastating diagnosis of Lou Gehrig's disease. As D'Arcy questions how well she knew her father, she acts out by drinking and running away.

Where it's reviewed:
Best Books for Kids & Teens, Annual 2010, page 24

Other books by the same author:
Responsible, 2007
Saving Grace, 2006
Rules for Life, 2004

Other books you might like:
Delia Ephron, *Frannie in Pieces*, 2007
Maureen Johnson, *The Key to the Golden Firebird*, 2004
Julie Williams, *Escaping Tornado Season: A Story in Poems*, 2004

1053

LOUIS SACHAR

The Cardturner: A Novel about a King, a Queen, and a Joker

(New York: Delacorte Press, 2010)

Subject(s): Recreation; Gambling; Summer

Age range(s): 13 - 15+
Major character(s): Alton Richards, 12th Grader, 17-Year-Old, Nephew (of Lester Trapp), Unemployed; Lester Trapp, Wealthy (old man), Uncle (great), Gambler (bridge player); Toni Castenada, Teenager, Friend (of Alton; love interest)
Time period(s): 21st century; 2010s
Locale(s): California, United States

Summary: Alton Richards' great-uncle Lester Trapp is rich—really rich. And people know it. Forced to spend the summer with Uncle Lester, Alton sees firsthand what people will do for money, or for a spot in the old man's will. In Louis Sachar's *The Cardholder: A Novel about a King, a Queen, and a Joker*, Alton begins his summer in a slump. His girlfriend has broken up with him, having developed feelings for his best friend. He has no job, no money of his own to spend, and his parents have managed to talk him into taking his great-uncle to play bridge four times a week. Alton is to be Uncle Lester's card-turner, though he's not quite sure what the duty entails. Alton has no interest in playing cards, or in his uncle, and he is certain that this will be the worst summer of his life. Until he meets Toni Castaneda, that is. Even though Toni's family appears to be mostly interested in the old man's wallet, Alton can see that Toni is different. At her side, his perspective is altered, and he begins to see the benefits of being his uncle's cardholder.

Where it's reviewed:
Booklist, May 15, 2010, page 40
Bulletin of the Center for Children's Books, June 2010, page 453
Horn Book Magazine, May/June, 2010, page 90
New York Times Book Review, May 16, 2010, page 51

Other books by the same author:
Holes, 1998

Other books you might like:
Patrick Carman, *Thirteen Days to Midnight*, 2010
Cory Doctorow, *For the Win*, 2010
A.M. Jenkins, *Repossessed*, 2007
Robert F. MacKinnon, *Bridge, Probability, and Information*, 2010
Paul Volponi, *The Hand You're Dealt*, 2008

1054

BENJAMIN ALIRE SAENZ

Last Night I Sang to the Monster

(El Paso, Texas: Cinco Puntos Press, 2009)

Subject(s): Addiction; Rehabilitation; Psychology

Age range(s): 15 - 18+
Major character(s): Zachariah Johnson Gonzalez, 18-Year-Old, Alcoholic, Narrator
Time period(s): 21st century; 2000s
Locale(s): United States

Summary: At the age of 18, Zachariah Johnson Gonzalez wakes up to find himself in a mental institution and rehab center with absolutely no recollection of his reason for being there. Told from Zachariah's perspective, *Last Night I Sang to the Monster* follows Zach's challenging and emotional journey to discover the secrets of his past and find healing and wholeness. Guided by his long-suffering therapist and his fatherly roommate, Zach digs deep within his heart to confront his personal demons of grief, abuse, and addiction and find restoration for his soul.

Where it's reviewed:
Booklist, September 15, 2009, page 49
Horn Book Guide, Spring 2010, page 107
Publishers Weekly, September 28, 2009, page 66
School Library Journal, October 2009, page 136
Voice of Youth Advocates, December 2009, page 414

Other books by the same author:
He Forgot to Say Goodbye, 2008
Sammy and Juliana in Hollywood, 2004

Other books you might like:
Catherine Ryan Hyde, *The Day I Killed James*, 2008
Blake Nelson, *Recovery Road*, 2011
Monica M. Roe, *Thaw*, 2008
Brent Runyon, *The Burn Journals*, 2004
Elizabeth Scott, *Love You Hate You Miss You*, 2009

1055

LEILA SALES

Past Perfect

(New York: Simon Pulse, 2011)

Story type: Contemporary
Subject(s): Interpersonal relations; Dating (Social customs); Summer

Age range(s): 14 - 18+
Major character(s): Chelsea Glaser, Friend (of Fiona), Girlfriend (of Ezra, former), Worker (historic reenactor), 16-Year-Old; Fiona, Friend (of Chelsea), Worker (historic reenactor), Teenager; Ezra, Teenager, Worker (historic reenactor), Boyfriend (of Chelsea, former); Dan, Teenager, Worker (historic reenactor)
Time period(s): 21st century; 2010s
Locale(s): New England, United States

Summary: In this young-adult novel by Leila Sales, 16-year-old Chelsea Glaser looks forward to her summer job at Colonial Essex Village. There, dressed in period costume, she can spend time with her friend Fiona, guide visiting tourists, and try to forget about her painful breakup with her former boyfriend, Ezra. Chelsea's plans take a turn when she discovers that Ezra is working at the same historic village. Not far away, another tourist attraction—a Civil War site—competes with Essex for patrons. The teenage staffs of both villages engage in combat, trying to outdo one another's pranks. While Chelsea joins the historic summertime battle and deals with her feelings for Ezra, she finds romance with Dan, a Confederate re-enactor from Essex Village's enemy camp.

Where it's reviewed:
Horn Book Magazine, November-December 2011, page 111
School Library Journal, October 2011, page 147

Other books by the same author:
Mostly Good Girls, 2010

Other books you might like:
Brad Barkley, *Dream Factory*, 2007
Margaret Peterson Haddix, *Running out of Time*, 1995
Sydney Salter, *Swoon at Your Own Risk*, 2010
Stephanie Kate Strohm, *Pilgrims Don't Wear Pink*, 2012

1056

ALEX SANCHEZ

Boyfriends with Girlfriends

(New York: Simon & Schuster, 2011)

Story type: Coming-of-Age
Subject(s): Coming of age; Sexuality; Sex roles

Age range(s): 15 - 18+
Major character(s): Lance, Teenager, Lover (of Sergio); Sergio, Teenager, Lover (of Lance); Kimiko, Teenager, Lover (of Allie); Allie, Teenager, Lover (of Kimiko)
Time period(s): 21st century; 2010s
Locale(s): United States

Summary: A group of teens ponder their sexual preferences as they test the waters of same-sex relationships in high school in this young adult novel by author Alex Sanchez. The book follows four teens—Sergio, Lance, Kimiko, and Allie—as they try to determine what they want in their romantic relationships. Although Sergio and Lance feel an attraction toward each other, their differences threaten to keep them apart. To make matter worse, Sergio is bisexual and has no experience dating another man. Meanwhile, Kimiko finds a mutual attraction with Allie, who believed she was heterosexual but now has to second-guess her longstanding beliefs. While Allie tries to understand her new feelings for Kimiko, Kimiko tries to understand how someone as beautiful as Allie could be attracted to her.

Where it's reviewed:
Booklist, March 1, 2011, page 48
Publishers Weekly, March 7, 2011, page 65
School Library Journal, April 2011, page 183
Voice of Youth Advocates, April 2011, page 68

Other books by the same author:
Bait, 2009
Getting It, 2006
Rainbow Road, 2005
So Hard to Say, 2004
Rainbow Boys, 2001

Other books you might like:
M.E. Kerr, *"Hello," I Lied*, 1997
Julie Anne Peters, *Rage: A Love Story*, 2009
Sara Ryan, *Empress of the World*, 2001

1057

ALEX SANCHEZ

Bait

(New York: Simon & Schuster Books for Young Readers, 2009)

Subject(s): Abuse; Child abuse; Rape

Age range(s): 13 - 16+
Major character(s): Diego Rivera, 16-Year-Old; Mr. Vidas, Counselor
Time period(s): 21st century; 2000s
Locale(s): United States

Summary: Alex Sanchez's novel *Bait* tells the story of a young man coming to terms with his troubled past. After beating up a classmate, 16-year-old Diego Rivera is put on probation and referred to a counselor named Mr. Vidas. In speaking with Mr. Vidas, Diego encounters the first person in his entire life who has ever genuinely wanted to help him. Diego opens up to Vidas about the reasons for his anger and begins to manage his emotions properly. As the bond between Diego and Vidas grows, Diego admits that he cuts himself with a sharp shark's tooth given to him by his stepfather. Later, Diego acknowledges that his stepfather beat and raped him for many years. Diego has long dealt with fears that he will also become an abuser or a homosexual. When Diego finds out that Mr. Vidas is himself homosexual, he again loses faith in those closest to him. Diego must learn to let go of anger and accept suffering as a part of life.

Where it's reviewed:
Booklist, May 15, 2009, page 34
Publishers Weekly, June 1, 2009, page 49
School Library Journal, July 2009, page 92

Other books by the same author:
Boyfriends with Girlfriends, 2011
Rainbow Road, 2007
Getting It, 2006
So Hard to Say, 2004
Rainbow High, 2003

Other books you might like:
M. Sindy Felin, *Touching Snow*, 2007
Ellen Hopkins, *Identical*, 2008
LouAnne Johnson, *Muchacho*, 2009
Patrick Jones, *Chasing Tail Lights*, 2007
Suzanne Phillips, *Burn*, 2008

1058

ROSALYN SCHANZER, Author/Illustrator

Witches!: The Absolutely True Tale of Disaster in Salem

(Washington, DC: National Geographic Society, 2011)

Subject(s): Witchcraft; History; Religion

Age range(s): 12 - 16+

Summary: The Salem Witch Trials were an unforgettable event in American history. In this book, author Rosalyn Schanzer describes the trials for young readers. During 1692 and 1693 in Salem, Massachusetts, more than 150 people were arrested on suspicion of practicing witchcraft. The trouble started when two young girls began twitching and saying strange things. Officials in the town declared that the two girls had been bewitched, which caused all of the townspeople to suspect each other of cavorting with the devil. During the trials, girls as young as four years old were accused of being witches, and some of the accused were executed for their suspected crimes. This book gives details about the trials and the hysteria they caused throughout the small town of Salem.

Where it's reviewed:
School Library Journal, December 2011, page 142

Voice of Youth Advocates, December 2011, page 523

Other books by the same author:
What Darwin Saw: The Journey That Changed the World, 2009
George vs. George: The American Revolution As Seen from Both Sides, 2004
How We Crossed the West: The Adventures of Lewis & Clark, 1997

Other books you might like:
Marc Aronson, *Witch-Hunt: Mysteries of the Salem Witch Trials*, 2003
Judith Bloom Fradin, *The Salem Witch Trials*, 2009
Anna Myers, *Time of the Witches*, 2009
Louise Chipley Slavicek, *The Salem Witch Trials: Hysteria in Colonial America*, 2011

1059

HOLLY SCHINDLER

A Blue So Dark

(Woodbury, Minnesota: Flux, 2010)

Subject(s): Mental disorders; Mother-daughter relations; Artists

Age range(s): 14 - 17+
Major character(s): Aura Ambrose, 15-Year-Old, Artist
Time period(s): 21st century; 2010s
Locale(s): United States

Summary: Holly Schindler's *A Blue So Dark* charts the emotional journey of 15-year-old Aura Ambrose, a devoted artist and high school student who is forced to confront her mother's devastating mental illness. Aura's mother, who is also an accomplished artist, suffers from schizophrenia, and the teenager watches helplessly as her parent slips deeper into the abyss of insanity. Convinced that the combination of art and family history will deter her own sanity, Aura stops painting. But before long, she yearns for a way to express herself and reconnect with her struggling mother. First novel.

Where it's reviewed:
Booklist, May 1, 2010, page 84
School Library Journal, June 2010, page 119

Other books by the same author:
Playing Hurt, 2011

Other books you might like:
Brad Barkley, *Jars of Glass*, 2008
Jennifer Donnelly, *Revolution*, 2010
Robin Merrow MacCready, *Buried*, 2006
Liz Rosenberg, *17: A Novel in Prose Poems*, 2002

1060

PAT SCHMATZ

Bluefish

(Somerville, Massachusetts: Candlewick Press, 2011)

Story type: Contemporary
Subject(s): Learning disorders; Teachers; Middle schools

Age range(s): 13 - 15+
Major character(s): Travis, 13-Year-Old, Orphan, Friend (of Velveeta), Learning Disabled Child, 8th Grader; Velveeta, Friend (of Travis), 8th Grader; Mr. McQueen, Teacher (of Travis); Grandpa, Grandfather (of Travis), Alcoholic
Time period(s): 21st century; 2010s
Locale(s): United States

Summary: A 13-year-old boy deals with the loss of a pet, his grandfather's alcoholism, and the challenges of being the new kid at school in this young adult novel by Pat Schmatz. For Travis, joining the eighth grade class at a new school is especially intimidating because he doesn't know how to read. At his previous school, Travis was able to hide his disability, but his new teacher, Mr. McQueen, can't be fooled. As Mr. McQueen helps Travis learn how to read, another school fixture—a spunky student named Velveeta—befriends the troubled boy. Travis discovers that he's not the only one who's been keeping secrets, and he and Velveeta together learn important lessons about friendship and healing.

Where it's reviewed:
Horn Book Magazine, November-December 2011, page 111
Library Media Connection, November-December 2011, page 74
School Library Journal, December 2011, page 129

Other books by the same author:
Mousetraps, 2008
Circle the Truth, 2007

Other books you might like:
Elizabeth Stow Ellison, *Flight*, 2008
Rodman Philbrick, *Freak the Mighty*, 1993
Markus Zusak, *The Book Thief*, 2006

1061

ANNE SCHRAFF

A Boy Called Twister

(Costa Mesa, California: Saddleback Educational, 2010)

Series: Urban Underground Series. Book 3
Subject(s): Adolescent interpersonal relations; Family; High schools

Age range(s): 13 - 16+
Major character(s): Kevin Walker, 16-Year-Old; Marko Lane, Bully
Time period(s): 21st century; 2010s
Locale(s): California, United States

Summary: Sixteen-year-old Kevin Walker has just moved from Texas to California, and he's looking forward to leading an anonymous life at his new school. Kevin possesses a dark secret that he is determined to keep to himself. As he settles in at Tubman High, Kevin finds himself becoming popular with his classmates, falling for a beautiful girl, and rising to a star spot on the school's track team. When school bully Marko learns of Kevin's secret, Kevin is faced with a momentous decision: be terrorized by Marko—or confess. Anne Schraff's *A Boy Called Twister* is the third volume in the Urban Underground series.

Where it's reviewed:
Booklist, April 15, 2010, page 40
School Library Journal, September 2010, page 164

Other books by the same author:
If You Really Loved Me, 2010
One of Us, 2010
Outrunning the Darkness, 2010

Other books you might like:
Paul Langan, *The Bully*, 2002
Chris Lynch, *Who the Man*, 2002
Walter Dean Myers, *Somewhere in the Darkness*, 1992
Cynthia Voigt, *The Runner*, 1985
Rich Wallace, *One Good Punch*, 2007

1062

ELIOT SCHREFER

The Deadly Sister

(New York: Scholastic, 2010)

Subject(s): Sisters; Murder; Family

Age range(s): 14 - 18+

Major character(s): Abby Goodwin, Teenager, Sister (of Maya); Maya Goodwin, Teenager, Sister (of Abby); Jefferson Andrews, Tutor (of Maya)

Time period(s): 21st century; 2010s

Locale(s): Florida, United States

Summary: In the young adult novel *The Deadly Sister* by Eliot Schrefer, the death of golden boy Jefferson Andrews shocks a Florida town. Abby Goodwin discovers his lifeless body and the incriminating evidence that lies close by—a cell phone that belongs to Abby's sister Maya. With her history of substance abuse and other personal problems, Maya seems like a probable suspect, especially since Jefferson had been her tutor and the object of her infatuation. Abby has long been Maya's protector and remains loyal to her sister even though their parents and the authorities believe that Maya killed Jefferson. Abby's careful investigation reveals surprising information about the victim as well as the accused.

Where it's reviewed:
Booklist, June 1, 2010, page 50
Horn Book Guide, Fall 2010, page 382
School Library Journal, August 2010, page 112

Other books by the same author:
The School for Dangerous Girls, 2009

Other books you might like:
Kim Harrington, *Clarity*, 2011
Antonio Pagliarulo, *The Celebutantes: On the Avenue*, 2007
Sara Shepard, *Wanted*, 2010
Walter Sorrells, *White-Out*, 2009
Katie Williams, *The Space between Trees*, 2010

1063

JOE SCHREIBER

Au Revoir, Crazy European Chick

(Boston, Massachusetts: Houghton Mifflin, 2011)

Story type: Adventure
Subject(s): Assassination; Proms (Parties); Suspense

Age range(s): 14 - 17+
Major character(s): Perry Stormaire, 18-Year-Old, 12th Grader; Gobija Zaksauskas, Teenager, Student—Exchange, Assassin
Time period(s): 21st century; 2010s
Locale(s): New York, New York

Summary: A teenager's prom night goes from promising to disaster to action-packed adventure in this fast-paced novel for young adult readers from author Joe Schreiber. In one month, everything is going to change for Perry Stormaire. The eighteen-year-old will graduate from high school and head off to college (hopefully Columbia), so all he wants is a fun, carefree prom night with his friends. When his mom forces him to take a Lithuanian foreign exchange student as his date, he thinks the night can't possibly get any worse. He soon discovers, however, that his mysterious date is actually a trained assassin with a long list of targets she needs to eliminate.

Where it's reviewed:
Booklist, October 15, 2011, page 56
Horn Book Magazine, November/December 2011, page 112
Publishers Weekly, August 15, 2011, page 72
School Library Journal, August 2011, page 120
Voice of Youth Advocates, October 2011, page 393

Other books you might like:
Ally Carter, *I'd Tell You I Love You, but Then I'd Have to Kill You*, 2006
Kristin Cashore, *Graceling*, 2008
Gary Ghislain, *How I Stole Johnny Depp's Alien Girlfriend*, 2011
Anthony Horowitz, *Scorpia Rising*, 2011
Robin LaFevers, *Grave Mercy*, 2012

1064

SAMANTHA SCHUTZ

You Are Not Here

(New York: PUSH, 2010)

Subject(s): Death; Love; Grief

Age range(s): 15 - 18+
Major character(s): Annaleah, Teenager, Student—High School
Time period(s): 21st century; 2010s
Locale(s): United States

Summary: Annaleah and Brian have been physically and emotionally involved with one another for months, sharing what Annaleah assumed was a very special connection, but when Brian dies unexpectedly, the secrecy shrouding their relationship prevents Annaleah from grieving publicly or receiving the comfort she so desperately needs. As she struggles to make sense of the tragedy and visits Brian's grave daily, she rehashes the minutiae of their relationship and comes to the harsh reality that what they shared might not have been so special after all.

Where it's reviewed:
Booklist, October 15, 2010, page 62
Horn Book Guide, Spring 2011, page 118
School Library Journal, February 2011, page 118
Voice of Youth Advocates, December 2010, page 460

Other books by the same author:
I Don't Want to Be Crazy, 2006

Other books you might like:
Kevin Brooks, *Lucas*, 2003
Sarah Ockler, *Twenty Boy Summer*, 2009
Lisa Schroeder, *Chasing Brooklyn*, 2010

1065

ELIZABETH SCOTT

Between Here and Forever
(New York: Simon Pulse, 2011)

Subject(s): Coming of age; Sisters; Self perception

Age range(s): 15 - 18+

Major character(s): Abby, 17-Year-Old, Sister (of Tess); Tess, Sister (of Abby, older), Accident Victim, Patient (hospital); Eli, Worker (hospital)

Time period(s): 21st century; 2010s

Summary: In Elizabeth Scott's young-adult novel *Between Here and Forever*, 17-year-old Abby believes that she can never be as popular or pretty as her older sister, Tess. When Tess is involved in a car accident that leaves her comatose, Abby realizes how important her relationship with her sister is. For six weeks Abby visits Tess, dealing with her grief and low self-esteem, and desperately hoping for a return to normalcy. When Abby meets Eli, a good-looking guy who works at the hospital gift shop, she persuades him to visit Tess, thinking that a male voice might coax her back to consciousness. Abby's attempts to heal Tess reveal surprising truths about her sister and herself.

Where it's reviewed:
Booklist, June 1, 2011, page 79
Publishers Weekly, May 2, 2011, page 59
School Library Journal, June 2011, page 134
Voice of Youth Advocates, June 2011, page 172

Other books by the same author:
As I Wake, 2011
Grace, 2010
The Unwritten Rule, 2010
Love You Hate You Miss You, 2009
Something, Maybe, 2009

Other books you might like:
Marthe Jocelyn, *Would You*, 2008
Jandy Nelson, *The Sky Is Everywhere*, 2010
Julie Anne Peters, *Rage: A Love Story*, 2009

1066

ELIZABETH SCOTT

The Unwritten Rule
(New York: Simon Pulse, 2010)

Subject(s): Friendship; Dating (Social customs); Interpersonal relations

Age range(s): 15 - 18+

Major character(s): Sarah, 17-Year-Old; Brianna, Friend (of Sarah); Ryan, Boyfriend (of Brianna)

Time period(s): 21st century; 2010s

Locale(s): United States

Summary: In *The Unwritten Rule* by Elizabeth Scott, two teenagers find their friendship threatened by their mutual attraction to a boy. Beautiful Brianna has claimed Ryan as her official boyfriend, but that doesn't stop average-looking Sarah from falling for him. Sarah is used to living in Brianna's shadow, but her feelings for Ryan drive her to break the rules of friendship. Secretly liking Ryan is one thing, but kissing your best friend's boyfriend is another—and that's exactly what happens one night after a party. Sarah knows that the truth will crush Brianna, but her feelings for Ryan may run deeper than her loyalty to Brianna.

Where it's reviewed:
Booklist, March 1, 2010, page 64
Horn Book Guide, Fall 2010, page 382
School Library Journal, April 2010, page 166
Voice of Youth Advocates, October 2010, page 158

Other books by the same author:
As I Wake, 2011
Love You Hate You Miss You, 2009
Perfect You, 2008
Bloom, 2007

Other books you might like:
Ed Briant, *Choppy Socky Blues*, 2010
Susane Colasanti, *Something Like Fate*, 2010
Jody Gehrman, *Triple Shot Bettys in Love*, 2009
Carolyn Mackler, *Tangled*, 2010
Rachel Vail, *If We Kiss*, 2005

1067

ELIZABETH SCOTT

Love You Hate You Miss You
(New York: HarperTeen, 2009)

Subject(s): Death; Self perception; Alcoholism

Age range(s): 14 - 18+

Major character(s): Amy, Teenager, Sister (of Julia); Julia, Accident Victim, Sister (of Amy)

Time period(s): 21st century; 2000s

Locale(s): United States

Summary: In Elizabeth Scott's *Love You Hate You Miss You*, teenager Amy is forced to deal with a grief so profound that she can barely discuss it. With her parents incessantly nagging her, Amy decides to follow her therapist's advice by starting a journal of her thoughts as a way of healing. But Amy uses her diary to construct letters to her older sister Julia, who was killed in a car accident—a car Amy was driving. After the accident, Amy was sent to rehab, but she has managed to keep her unbearable feelings of guilt firmly buried. That is, until she starts writing to her beloved sister.

Where it's reviewed:
Booklist, April 1, 2009, page 33
Horn Book Magazine, July/August 2009, page 431
Publishers Weekly, June 29, 2009, page 130
School Library Journal, June 2009, page 137
Voice of Youth Advocates, October 2009, page 322

Other books by the same author:
Between Here and Forever, 2011
Grace, 2010
The Unwritten Rule, 2010
Something, Maybe, 2009
Living Dead Girl, 2008

Other books you might like:
A.S. King, *Please Ignore Vera Dietz*, 2010
Tricia Mills, *Heartbreak River*, 2009
Blake Nelson, *Recovery Road*, 2011
Benjamin Alire Saenz, *Last Night I Sang to the Monster*, 2009
Courtney Summers, *Cracked Up to Be*, 2009

1068

MARCUS SEDGWICK

Revolver
(New York: Macmillan, 2010)

Subject(s): Arctic; Family relations; Father-son relations
Age range(s): 13 - 16+
Major character(s): Sig Andersson, Teenager; Einar Andersson, Father (of Sig); Gunther Wolff, Businessman (former partner of Einar)
Time period(s): 20th century; 1910s (1910)
Locale(s): Giron, Sweden

Summary: In *Revolver* by Marcus Sedgwick, the discovery by Sig Andersson of his father's frozen body sets off a chain of events that endangers the teenager's life. It is 1910 and Sig's father, Einar, had been crossing a frozen lake near their Swedish village when his sled crashed through the ice. Sig brings his father's corpse back to their cabin and sends his stepmother and sister to find help. While keeping vigil, an angry stranger enters the cabin accusing Einar of being a thief. As Sig tries to sort out the facts of the stranger's allegations, he considers using the gun that is hidden in the cabin.

Where it's reviewed:
Booklist, May 1, 2010, page 49
Horn Book Magazine, March/April 2010, page 73
Publishers Weekly, March 15, 2010, page 56
School Library Journal, September 2010, page 181

Other books by the same author:
White Crow, 2011
My Swordhand Is Singing, 2006
The Book of Dead Days, 2004

Other books you might like:
Michael Cadnum, *Blood Gold*, 2004
Jack London, *The Call of the Wild*, 1903
Gary Paulsen, *The Rifle*, 1995
Monique Polak, *The Middle of Everywhere*, 2009
John Smelcer, *The Trap*, 2006

1069

MARCUS SEDGWICK

White Crow
(New York: Roaring Brook Press, 2011)

Subject(s): Fantasy; Horror; Afterlife
Age range(s): 14 - 18+
Major character(s): Rebecca, Teenager, Friend (of Ferelith); Ferelith, Friend (of Rebecca)
Time period(s): 21st century; (2010s); 18th century; 1790s (1798)
Locale(s): Winterfold, England

Summary: In this young adult novel by Marcus Sedgwick, Rebecca is a young girl living in modern-day England. When she moves to a small seaside town, she wants to get to know her new surroundings. Another girl from the town, Ferelith, promises to teach Rebecca about all of Winterfold's darkest secrets. Rebecca thinks Ferelith, who joined a commune after leaving school at age 14, is a bit strange. Nevertheless, Rebecca agrees to go with her new friend to learn more about the town. Rebecca doesn't realize, however, that an old priest who lived more than two hundred years ago will impact her life in ways she never thought possible.

Where it's reviewed:
Booklist, May 1, 2011, page 85
Horn Book Magazine, July-August 2011, page 161
Publishers Weekly, May 9, 2011, page 54
School Library Journal, August 2011, page 120

Other books by the same author:
Revolver, 2010
The Foreshadowing, 2006
My Swordhand Is Singing, 2006
The Book of Dead Days, 2004

Other books you might like:
David Almond, *Kit's Wilderness*, 2000
Amy Garvey, *Cold Kiss*, 2011
Tara Hudson, *Hereafter*, 2011
Deborah Noyes, *The Ghosts of Kerfol*, 2008

1070

SUZANNE SELFORS

Coffeehouse Angel
(New York: Walker and Company, 2009)

Subject(s): Angels; Adolescence; Love
Age range(s): 14 - 18+
Major character(s): Katrina, 16-Year-Old, Waiter/Waitress; Malcolm, Angel

Time period(s): 21st century; 2000s
Locale(s): United States

Summary: *Coffeehouse Angel* is a young adult novel from author Suzanne Selfors. While working at her grandma's coffee shop, 16-year-old Katrina feels compassion for a homeless man sleeping behind the building. Each day, she brings him coffee and pastries, unaware of the massive impact her kindness is going to have. The homeless man isn't what he seems. The man is really a guardian angel named Malcolm who is taking a quick break between assignments. To pay Katrina back for her thoughtfulness and generosity, Malcolm agrees to give her anything she wants. The young woman, however, has no idea what her heart desires most.

Where it's reviewed:
Booklist, September 15, 2009, page 49
Horn Book Guide, Spring 2010, page 107
Publishers Weekly, August 17, 2009, page 64
School Library Journal, August 2009, page 114
Voice of Youth Advocates, December 2009, page 423

Other books by the same author:
Mad Love, 2011
Saving Juliet, 2008

Other books you might like:
Jody Gehrman, *Triple Shot Bettys in Love*, 2009
Sid Hite, *Answer My Prayer*, 1995
Graham Marks, *How It Works: Everyone Gets the Angel They Deserve*, 2004
Cynthia Leitich Smith, *Eternal*, 2009

1071

RUTA SEPETYS

Between Shades of Gray

(New York: Philomel Books, 2011)

Subject(s): Prisoners of war; Family; Concentration camps

Age range(s): 13 - 18+
Major character(s): Lina, 16-Year-Old, Prisoner
Time period(s): 20th century; 1930s (1939)
Locale(s): Lithuania; Siberia, Russia

Summary: In *Between Shades of Gray*, Ruta Sepetys tells the story of Lina, a 16-year-old Lithuanian girl whose family is imprisoned in a Siberian labor camp during the 1939 Russian genocide. Lina sustains the hope of her family through her artwork—a series of pictures that she believes will somehow reach her father, who was arrested by the secret police. The novel sheds light on a dark point in history when a double genocide committed first by Nazi Germany and then by Soviet Russia devastated the Baltic region. First novel.

Where it's reviewed:
Booklist, February 1, 2011, page 68
Horn Book Magazine, May-June 2011, page 103
Publishers Weekly, January 3, 2011, page 51
School Library Journal, March 2011, page 170

Other books you might like:
Anne Fine, *The Road of Bones*, 2008

Morris Gleitzman, *Once*, 2010
Anne Isaacs, *Torn Thread*, 2000
Lyll Becerra de Jenkins, *The Honorable Prison*, 1988

1072

DARREN SHAN

Birth of a Killer

(London: HarperCollins, 2010)

Series: Saga of Larten Crepsley Series. Book 1
Story type: Horror; Series
Subject(s): Vampires; Horror; Adolescence

Age range(s): 12 - 16+
Major character(s): Larten Crepsley, Teenager, Vampire, Assistant (to Seba Nile); Seba Nile, Vampire
Locale(s): England

Summary: The first volume in the Saga of Larten Crepsley Series by Darren Shan, this young adult novel chronicles the evolution of the vampire star of Shan's Cirque du Freak Series. As a child, Larten Crepsley spends his days toiling in a factory and his nights huddled with his poor family in their cramped home. Larten endures his plight with little protest until the cruelty of his boss pushes him to retaliate with violence. Though he escapes the factory, Larten must hide in a cemetery. There, he encounters the centuries-old vampire Seba Nile and joins him on his travels. Larten's journey takes him into the dark world of the undead and, ultimately, to the freak show known as Cirque du Freak.

Where it's reviewed:
Horn Book Guide, Spring 2011, page 111
School Librarian, Winter 2010, page 247
Voice of Youth Advocates, February 2011, page 577

Other books by the same author:
City of the Snakes, 2011
Ocean of Blood, 2011
Palace of the Damned, 2011
Sons of Destiny, 2006
Cirque du Freak, 2001

Other books you might like:
Rachel Caine, *Kiss of Death*, 2010
P.C. Cast, *The Fledgling Handbook 101*, 2010
C.C. Hunter, *Born at Midnight*, 2011
Cynthia Leitich Smith, *Blessed*, 2011
Lynn Viehl, *After Midnight*, 2011

1073

ROBERT SHARENOW

The Berlin Boxing Club

(New York: HarperTeen, 2011)

Story type: Historical; Historical - World War II
Subject(s): Coming of age; Boxing; Sports

Age range(s): 13 - 16+
Major character(s): Karl Stern, 14-Year-Old, Boxer,

Student (of Max); Max Schmeling, Boxer, Trainer (of Karl)
Time period(s): 20th century; 1930s
Locale(s): Berlin, Germany

Summary: Karl Stern is a 14-year-old from a nonpracticing Jewish family. He barely considers himself Jewish, but his neighbors and classmates do. As more and more Jews are being repressed because of Nazism, people in his town begin to bully and scorn Karl. Karl tries to escape his pain by taking boxing lessons with the great German champion Max Schmeling. Although he is opposed to Nazism, Schmeling is required to represent the party and its criminal leaders. When the Nazis increase their violence against Germany's Jews, Karl's family comes into direct danger. Karl must choose between the boxing greatness he might achieve under Schmeling and his duties as a son. This is young adult novel by author Robert Sharenow.

Where it's reviewed:
Booklist, April 15, 2011, page 62
Publishers Weekly, April 25, 2011, page 139
School Library Journal, June 2011, page 135
Voice of Youth Advocates, August 2011, page 278

Other books by the same author:
My Mother the Cheerleader, 2007

Other books you might like:
Susan Campbell Bartoletti, *The Boy Who Dared*, 2008
Bryce Courtenay, *The Power of One*, 1989
Paul Dowswell, *The Auslander*, 2011
Kathleen Karr, *The Boxer*, 2000
Markus Zusak, *Fighting Ruben Wolfe*, 2001

1074

STEVE SHEINKIN

The Notorious Benedict Arnold

(New York: Flash Point, 2010)

Subject(s): United States history; American Revolution, 1775-1783; Adventure
Age range(s): 11 - 16+
Time period(s): 18th century-19th century
Locale(s): United States

Summary: In *The Notorious Benedict Arnold*, author Steve Sheinkin presents an all-encompassing biography of the man long known as the United States' first turncoat. But Sheinkin peels away the veneer of this mythology to reveal the complex—and heroic—man underneath. From his challenging childhood to his rise to the highest ranks of the military, Arnold's life was marked by success and admiration. But it was a single act that forever marred his legacy, and Sheinkin exposes the truth—at last—behind Arnold's adventures. *The Notorious Benedict Arnold* contains excerpts from correspondence, diaries, and first-person accounts.

Where it's reviewed:
Booklist, October 15, 2010, page 43
Horn Book Magazine, January/February 2011, page 115
School Library Journal, November 2010, page 142
Voice of Youth Advocates, December 2010, page 461

Awards the book has won:
Boston Globe - Horn Book Awards: Nonfiction, 2011

Other books you might like:
Thomas B. Allen, *George Washington, Spymaster: How the Americans Outspied the British and Won the Revolutionary War*, 2004
Laurie Halse Anderson, *Chains*, 2008
Jim Murphy, *The Real Benedict Arnold*, 2007
Ann Rinaldi, *Finishing Becca: A Story of Peggy Shippen and Benedict Arnold*, 1994

1075

BONNIE SHIMKO

The Private Thoughts of Amelia E. Rye

(New York: Farrar, Straus and Giroux, 2010)

Subject(s): Friendship; Racism; African Americans
Age range(s): 10 - 14+
Major character(s): Amelia E. Rye, Child, 13-Year-Old, Outcast; Fancy Nelson, 13-Year-Old, Friend (of Amelia)
Time period(s): 20th century; 1960s
Locale(s): New York, United States

Summary: Set in the 1960s in a small town in northeastern New York, *The Private Thoughts of Amelia E. Rye* follows the miserable life of Amelia E. Rye, a young girl with a lousy family and a lonely existence. Grandpa Thomas reassures Amelia that her luck will change and all she really needs to get through life is one true friend. When Fancy Nelson arrives in school, not only is she the first African-American girl that Amelia has ever seen, she's also quite suitable as a friend. As the two girls learn more about their starkly different lives, they soon learn to love and accept themselves and understand their places in the world.

Where it's reviewed:
Horn Book Guide, Fall 2010, page 353
Publishers Weekly, March 29, 2010, page 59
Voice of Youth Advocates, August 2010, page 256

Other books by the same author:
Letters in the Attic, 2007
Kat's Promise, 2006

Other books you might like:
Trudy Krisher, *Spite Fences*, 1994
Patricia C. McKissack, *A Friendship for Today*, 2007
Han Nolan, *Born Blue*, 2001
Jane St. Anthony, *The Summer Sherman Loved Me*, 2006

1076

SHARON SHINN

Gateway

(New York: Viking, 2009)

Subject(s): Alternative worlds; Spacetime; Fantasy
Age range(s): 14 - 17+

Major character(s): Daiyu, Teenager, Adoptee; Ombri, Time Traveler; Aurora, Time Traveler; Kalen, Friend (of Daiyu)
Time period(s): 21st century; 2000s
Locale(s): Shenglang, Alternate Universe; St. Louis, Missouri

Summary: In *Gateway* by Sharon Shinn, Daiyu, a Chinese-American girl living in St. Louis with her adoptive parents, purchases a piece of black jade jewelry that soon reveals its magical powers. After passing under the St. Louis Arch, Daiyu emerges on the other side to find that the arch is now a pagoda-shaped gate and her familiar city has seemingly been transported to 19th-century China. Gradually, Daiyu learns the rules of Shenglang, her new city, and the two supernatural servants, Ombri and Aurora, who travel creation's varied worlds. When Daiyu meets Ombri and Aurora's attractive assistant, Kalen, she must choose between her old life and the new love that she has found.

Where it's reviewed:
Booklist, September 15, 2009, page 66
Horn Book Guide, Spring 2010, page 108
Publishers Weekly, October 19, 2009, Page 53
School Library Journal, December 2009, page 131
Voice of Youth Advocates, December 2009, page 423

Other books by the same author:
The Dream-Maker's Magic, 2006
The Truth-Teller's Tale, 2005
The Safe-Keeper's Secret, 2004

Other books you might like:
Malorie Blackman, *Naughts and Crosses*, 2005
Chitra Lekha Banerjee Divakaruni, *Shadowland*, 2009
Alison Goodman, *Eon: Dragoneye Reborn*, 2008
Hiromi Goto, *Half World*, 2010
Paul McCusker, *Ripple Effect*, 2008

1077

MARK SHULMAN

Scrawl

(New York: Roaring Brook Press, 2010)

Subject(s): Bullying; Adolescent interpersonal relations; Diaries
Age range(s): 13 - 16+
Major character(s): Tod Munn, Bully; Mrs. Woodrow, Counselor
Time period(s): 21st century; 2010s
Locale(s): United States

Summary: Mark Shulman's *Scrawl* is the fictionalized personal notebook of a bully named Tod Munn. As the school initiates new attempts to stop bullying in its halls, Tod and his friends soon find themselves without a purpose. And after a run-in with school authorities, Tod lands himself in detention, overseen by guidance counselor Mrs. Woodrow. Mrs. Woodrow is insistent that Tod begin keeping a notebook of his thoughts and ideas, a notion that he at first abhors. But the more Tod writes, the more deeply entrenched he becomes in this challenging project, which eventually reveals some startling

insights into the young man's behavior.
Where it's reviewed:
Horn Book Guide, Spring 2011, page 112
Publishers Weekly, September 13, 2010, page 47
School Library Journal, November 2010, page 147
Voice of Youth Advocates, October 2010, page 358

Other books you might like:
Carl Deuker, *Runner*, 2005
Margaret Peterson Haddix, *Don't You Dare Read This, Mrs. Dunphrey*, 1996
Glen Huser, *Stitches*, 2003
Anthony McGowan, *The Knife That Killed Me*, 2008
Richard Scrimger, *Me and Death: An Afterlife Adventure*, 2010

1078

POLLY SHULMAN

The Grimm Legacy

(New York: G. P. Putnam's Sons, 2010)

Subject(s): Adolescent interpersonal relations; Magic; Libraries
Age range(s): 12 - 15+
Major character(s): Elizabeth Rew, Teenager
Time period(s): 21st century; 2010s
Locale(s): New York, New York

Summary: In Polly Shulman's *The Grimm Legacy*, young Elizabeth Rew is relieved to land a job as a page at the New York Circulating Material Repository. Her new gig gives her a chance to escape her painful home life, where she feels alienated from her family. Elizabeth is intrigued by the section of the library that holds magical artifacts from Grimm's famous fairy tales. When the objects start to disappear, she and her coworkers set out to find them. But their adventure lands them in hot water: soon Elizabeth and the gang are the chief suspects in the disappearance of the precious artifacts.

Where it's reviewed:
Booklist, May 15, 2010, page 48
Horn Book Magazine, July/August 2010, page 121
Publishers Weekly, June 28, 2010, page 129
School Library Journal, June 2010, page 120
Voice of Youth Advocates, June 2010, page 170

Other books by the same author:
Enthusiasm, 2007

Other books you might like:
John Connolly, *The Book of Lost Things*, 2006
Jasper Fforde, *The Eyre Affair: A Novel*, 2001
Frank Portman, *Andromeda Klein*, 2009

1079

CRAIG SILVEY

Jasper Jones

(New York: Alfred A. Knopf, 2011)

Story type: Coming-of-Age
Subject(s): Coming of age; Friendship; Outcasts

Age range(s): 13 - 18+
Major character(s): Charlie Bucktin, 13-Year-Old, Friend (of Jasper); Jasper Jones, Outcast, Friend (of Charlie)
Time period(s): 20th century; 1960s
Locale(s): Western Australia, Australia

Summary: In this novel by Craig Silvey, a boy stumbles across a terrible secret that could lead to doom for a misunderstood man in his town. Charlie Bucktin is a normal 13-year-old who stays out of trouble and tries to do well in school. Charlie's life is normal and mundane until Jasper Jones, an eccentric neighbor, asks him for help. Charlie can tell that Jasper is desperate so he agrees to help. The task Jasper need help with puts Charlie and Jasper in danger of getting into deep trouble. Charlie and Jasper have to figure out what to do with a horrible secret that threatens to rip apart their hometown. Can they manage to save the town and clear their names of any wrongdoing?

Where it's reviewed:
Booklist, March 15, 2011, page 53
Publishers Weekly, February 7, 2011, page 58
School Library Journal, June 2011, page pge 136
Voice of Youth Advocates, April 2011, page 70

Other books you might like:
Karen Foxlee, *The Anatomy of Wings*, 2007
Steven Herrick, *The Wolf*, 2007
Jennifer R. Hubbard, *The Secret Year*, 2010

| 1080 |

JON SKOVRON

Misfit

(New York: Amulet Books, 2011)

Story type: Coming-of-Age; Paranormal
Subject(s): Demons; Adolescence; Outcasts

Age range(s): 14 - 17+
Major character(s): Jael Thompson, 16-Year-Old, Demon, Student—High School
Time period(s): 21st century; 2010s
Locale(s): Seattle, Washington

Summary: A teenage girl must embrace a dark family secret in this novel for young adult readers from author Jon Skovron. After a lifetime of moving around, missing her mom, and having zero romantic interests, sixteen-year-old Jael Thompson is eager for a normal life. She just wants to go to high school, make friends, and find a cute boyfriend. Unfortunately, a simple life is hard to come by when you're a half demon who is expected to ward off the Duke of Hell. Jael must face her dark lineage when a mysterious birthday present reveals her strong powers and demonic destiny. To be successful against the Duke, Jael must dig into her parents' mysterious past and unlock the secrets about her newfound potential.

Where it's reviewed:
Publishers Weekly, June 27, 2011, page 159
School Library Journal, October 2011, page 149

Other books by the same author:
Struts and Frets, 2009

Other books you might like:
Alexandra Adornetto, *Hades*, 2011
Rachel Hawkins, *Demonglass*, 2011
Michelle Rowen, *Demon Princess: Reign or Shine*, 2009
Brenna Yovanoff, *The Space Between*, 2011

| 1081 |

ARTHUR G. SLADE

The Hunchback Assignments

(New York: Wendy Lamb Books, 2009)

Subject(s): History; Espionage; Adolescence
Age range(s): 13 - 16+
Major character(s): Modo, 14-Year-Old, Shape-changer (hunchback); Mr. Socrates, Agent (for Permanent Association, spy agency); Octavia Milkweed, 14-Year-Old, Agent (for Permanent Association)
Time period(s): 19th century
Locale(s): London, England

Summary: *The Hunchback Assignments* by Arthur Slade is a young adult novel that is a combination of steampunk, historical fiction, and fantasy. Modo is a hunchback who was rescued from a traveling freak show by the strange Mr. Socrates, who then raised Modo and trained him to be an agent for the Permanent Association, a spy agency in London determined to protect Great Britain. Modo has the unique ability to shape-shift and alter his appearance. When he is 14 years old, Modo is sent to fend for himself on the streets of London, along with Octavia Milkweed, another teenage agent. The two teens find themselves thrown into an adventure when they learn that the group known as the Clockword Guild is working against them and attempting to turn children into automatons.

Where it's reviewed:
Booklist, August 1, 2009, page 57
Horn Book Guide, Spring 2010, page 108
Publishers Weekly, September 14, 2009, page 50
School Library Journal, December 2009, page 132

Other books by the same author:
Empire of Ruins, 2011
The Dark Deeps, 2010

Other books you might like:
Philip Reeve, *Mothstorm: The Horror from Beyond Georgium Sidus!*, 2008
Justin Richards, *The Death Collector*, 2006
Eleanor Updale, *Montmorency: Thief, Liar, Gentleman?*, 2004
Scott Westerfeld, *Leviathan*, 2009
Rick Yancey, *The Monstrumologist*, 2009

| 1082 |

FRAN CANNON SLAYTON

When the Whistle Blows

(New York: Philomel Books, 2009)

Subject(s): Railroads; Family relations; Adolescence
Age range(s): 12 - 16+

Major character(s): Jimmy Cannon, Teenager, Football Player
Time period(s): 20th century; 1940s (1943-1949)
Locale(s): Rowlesburg, West Virginia

Summary: *When the Whistle Blows* is a collection of seven short stories that make up this novel for children and young adults. The narrative follows seven consecutive Halloween nights in the life of Jimmy Cannon. Growing up in a small West Virginia town that's built around the railroad, Jimmy experiences the highs and lows of his teenage years from 1943 to 1949. He recounts his involvement in the high school championship football game, the danger and excitement of his part-time job, the hilarious teenage pranks, and his relationship with his hardworking father, who desires for Jimmy to have a different life than he did. As he grows older, he also grows suspicious about the secret society in which his father and brothers take part. As Jimmy transforms from a boy to a man, he begins to question the future that lies ahead of him and accept that it might be much different than the one he's always imagined.

Where it's reviewed:
Booklist, July 1, 2009, page 57
Reading Today, June/July 2009, page 24
School Library Journal, June 2009, page 138
Voice of Youth Advocates, October 2009, page 322

Other books you might like:
Stephen Krensky, *The Iron Dragon Never Sleeps*, 1994
Robert Newton Peck, *A Day No Pigs Would Die*, 1972
Cynthia Rylant, *A Blue-Eyed Daisy*, 1985
Laurence Yep, *Dragon's Gate*, 1993

1083

HOLLY GOLDBERG SLOAN

I'll Be There

(New York: Little, Brown and Company, 2011)

Story type: Contemporary
Subject(s): Brothers; Family; Father-son relations

Age range(s): 14 - 18+

Major character(s): Sam Border, 17-Year-Old, Brother (of Riddle), Son (of Clarence), Friend (of Emily); Riddle Border, Brother (of Sam), Autistic; Clarence Border, Father (of Sam and Riddle), Mentally Ill Person; Emily Bell, 17-Year-Old, Friend (of Sam)
Time period(s): 21st century; 2010s
Locale(s): United States

Summary: In this debut young adult novel by Holly Goldberg Sloan, 17-year-old Sam Border and his autistic brother, Riddle, spend their young lives wandering from place to place with their mentally ill father, Clarence. The boys don't attend school, but Sam takes good care of Riddle, who communicates by drawing pictures, and satisfies his own interest in music by attending church services. At one church, when Sam hears Emily Bell perform a solo in the choir, his life is forever changed. Not because Emily has a beautiful voice—her performance is a failure—but because the two form an instant friendship based on kindness. As Sam becomes more involved with Emily, he and Riddle spend more time

with the Bell family and begin to realize what "normal" feels like. First novel.

Where it's reviewed:
Booklist, April 1, 2011, page 65
Horn Book Magazine, July/August 2011, page 162
Publishers Weekly, April 11, 2011, page 54
School Library Journal, May 2011, page 125
Voice of Youth Advocates, June 2011, page 174

Other books you might like:
Alden R. Carter, *Walkaway*, 2008
Rune Michaels, *Fix Me*, 2011
Robert Newton Peck, *Bro*, 2004
Sara Zarr, *Sweethearts*, 2008

1084

DAVID SMALL, Author/Illustrator

Stitches: A Memoir

(New York: Norton, 2009)

Subject(s): Autobiographies; Cancer; Father-son relations

Age range(s): 15 - 18+

Summary: In *Stitches: A Memoir*, author David Small uses illustrations in the style of a graphic novel in order to create an account of his young life. Small's life story is both sad and remarkable because of the obstacles he had to overcome. Small, who was the son of a radiologist, was exposed to unnecessary x-ray treatments for a variety of illnesses that did not call for such excessive action. Later, Small developed cancer because of the overexposure to radiology, and he remained untreated for a long period of time. In pictures and sparse prose, Small recounts the ordeal for readers.

Where it's reviewed:
Booklist, July 1, 2009, page 6
The Christian Century, December 15, 2009, page 25
Newsweek, October 19, 2009, page 54
Publishers Weekly, August 10, 2009, page 42
School Library Journal, September 2009, page 193

Other books by the same author:
Imogene's Antlers, 2010
So You Want to be President?, 2004
Fenwick's Suit, 1996
George Washington's Cows, 1994

Awards the book has won:
Alex Awards, 2010
Michigan Notable Books Award, 2010
Reference and User Service Association Awards: Nonfiction, 2010

Other books you might like:
David B., *Epileptic*, 2005
Alison Bechdel, *Fun Home: A Family Tragicomic*, 2006
Leland Myrick, *Missouri Boy*, 2006
Laurie Sandell, *The Impostor's Daughter: A True Memoir*, 2009
Craig Thompson, *Blankets*, 2003

1085

ALEXANDER GORDON SMITH

Lockdown

(New York: Farrar, Straus and Giroux, 2009)

Series: Escape from Furnace Series. Book 1
Subject(s): Prisons; Adventure; Crime

Age range(s): 15 - 18+
Major character(s): Alex Sawyer, 14-Year-Old, Prisoner (Furnace Penitentiary)
Time period(s): 21st century; 2010s
Locale(s): Earth

Summary: In *Lockdown* by Alexander Gordon Smith, a bungled robbery prompts 14-year-old Alex Sawyer's entry to the juvenile detention system. When he is also convicted of murder, Alex is sentenced to life in Furnace Penitentiary, a horrifying subterranean facility designed to hold the worst criminals. In the Furnace, Alex learns that he is not the only falsely convicted inmate. He also discovers that life in the Furnace is dangerous. Violent mutants patrol the passages and inmates vanish. Alex must join with other prisoners—some good, some truly evil—if he hopes to survive and escape. *Lockdown* is the first book in the Escape from Furnace series.

Where it's reviewed:
Booklist, February 1, 2010, page 38
Horn Book Guide, Spring 2010, page 108
School Library Journal, February 2010, page 124
Voice of Youth Advocates, February 2010, page 513

Other books by the same author:
Death Sentence, 2011
Execution, 2011
Solitary, 2010

Other books you might like:
Lesley Choyce, *The Book of Michael*, 2008
James Dashner, *The Scorch Trials*, 2010
Catherine Fisher, *Incarceron*, 2007
Andrew Klavan, *The Last Thing I Remember*, 2009
Kristen Landon, *The Limit*, 2010

1086

ANDREW SMITH

In the Path of Falling Objects

(New York: Feiwel and Friends, 2009)

Subject(s): Brothers; Survival; Vietnam War, 1959-1975

Age range(s): 15 - 18+
Major character(s): Jonah, 16-Year-Old, Brother (of Simon); Simon, Brother (of Jonah); Mitch, Driver (sociopath), Boyfriend (of Lilly); Lilly, Girlfriend (of Mitch)
Time period(s): 20th century; 1970s (1970)
Locale(s): American Southwest, United States

Summary: In Andrew Smith's *In the Path of Falling Objects*, teenager Jonah and his little brother Simon embark upon a perilous journey to find their father. It is 1970, and Jonah and Simon's eldest brother has been sent to fight in Vietnam. With their mother no longer on the scene, the boys set out to pick up their ex-con father from an Arizona prison. In order to get there, however, the siblings must hitchhike. When Mitch offers them a ride, it doesn't take long for Jonah and Simon to realize their driver is more than a little psychotic. Will they make it to Arizona safely?

Where it's reviewed:
Booklist, November 1, 2009, page 32
Horn Book Magazine, January-February 2010, page 93
Journal of Adolescent & Adult, December 2010, page 301
Publishers Weekly, October 12, 2009, page 50
School Library Journal, November 2009, page 120

Other books by the same author:
Stick, 2011
The Marbury Lens, 2010
Ghost Medicine, 2008

Other books you might like:
Ann Burg, *All the Broken Pieces*, 2009
Scott William Carter, *The Last Great Getaway of the Water Balloon Boys*, 2011
Thomas Pendleton, *Mason*, 2008
Darren Shan, *The Thin Executioner*, 2010
Francisco X. Stork, *The Last Summer of The Death Warriors*, 2010

1087

ANDREW SMITH

The Marbury Lens

(New York: Feiwel and Friends, 2010)

Subject(s): Fantasy; Kidnapping; Murder

Age range(s): 15 - 18+
Major character(s): Jack, 16-Year-Old, Kidnap Victim; Conner, Friend (of Jack), 16-Year-Old
Time period(s): 21st century; 2010s
Locale(s): London, England; Marbury, Fictional Location

Summary: *The Marbury Lens* is a chilling fantasy novel for young adult readers from author Andrew Smith. While at a party, 16-year-old Jack gets drunk and is kidnapped by a sadistic serial killer who tortures and nearly rapes him. Jack makes a harrowing escape and recounts the whole ordeal to his best friend, Conner, only to come face-to-face with his kidnapper the next day. Desperate to make him pay, Jack and Conner kidnap the criminal and accidentally kill him. Vowing to keep it a secret, Jack and Conner continue on with their summer plans to visit a prep school in London, but shortly after arriving, Jack is greeted by a mysterious stranger who gives him a pair of odd glasses. The glasses transform Jack to a dark land called Marbury where Conner is manifesting as a venomous murderer and it's up to Jack to save the lives of two young boys.

Where it's reviewed:
Booklist, November 1, 2010, page 52
Publishers Weekly, October 25, 2010, page 51
School Library Journal, January 2011, page 115
Voice of Youth Advocates, February 2011, page 578

Other books by the same author:
Stick, 2011
In the Path of Falling Objects, 2009
Ghost Medicine, 2008

Other books you might like:
Nancy Coffelt, *Listen*, 2009
Kristina McBride, *The Tension of Opposites*, 2010
Tom Pow, *The Pack*, 2004
Elizabeth Scott, *Living Dead Girl*, 2008

1088

ANDREW SMITH

Stick

(New York: Feiwel and Friends, 2011)

Story type: Coming-of-Age
Subject(s): Coming of age; Brothers; Bullying
Age range(s): 14 - 17+
Major character(s): Stark "Stick" McClellan, Brother (of Bosten), 14-Year-Old (with one ear); Bosten McClellan, Young Man, Brother (of Stark)
Time period(s): 21st century
Locale(s): United States
Summary: Stark McClellan, a 14-year-old boy, grew up as the target of merciless bullying. For starters, he was born with only one ear, causing people to label him a freak. On top of that, he grew so tall and skinny that his classmates changed his name from Stark to "Stick." Stark can't even find peace at home, since his parents are cruel to him and his brother. Stark's only salvation is his friendship with his older brother and protector, Bosten. However, when Bosten admits that he's homosexual, neighbors and classmates turn on him as well. Now Stark and Bosten are both left outcasts, venturing out into the world to find meaning, acceptance, and a place where they can belong.

Where it's reviewed:
Booklist, September 1, 2011, page 117
Publishers Weekly, August 15, 2011, page 74
Voice of Youth Advocates, October 2011, page 394

Other books by the same author:
The Marbury Lens, 2010
In the Path of Falling Objects, 2009
Ghost Medicine, 2008

Other books you might like:
Siobhan Parkinson, *Long Story Short*, 2011
Adam Rapp, *Punkzilla*, 2009
Nigel Richardson, *The Wrong Hands*, 2006
Will Weaver, *Defect*, 2007

1089

JENNIFER E. SMITH

You Are Here

(New York: Simon & Schuster Books for Young Readers, 2009)

Subject(s): Identity; Death; Twins
Age range(s): 14 - 17+

Major character(s): Emma Healy, 16-Year-Old; Mom, Mother (of Emma); Dad, Father (of Emma); Patrick, Brother (of Emma)
Time period(s): 21st century; 2000s
Locale(s): New Jersey, United States; New York, New York; North Carolina, United States

Summary: In *You Are Here* by Jennifer E. Smith, 16-year-old Emma Healy feels that her relationship with her family is somehow incomplete. The discovery of a birth certificate for her twin—a baby boy who lived just two days—confirms Emma's sense of displacement and prompts her to find the part of her that has been lost. Setting off from her home in New York for North Carolina, Emma gets to New Jersey when her car breaks down. Desperate, she calls on her neighbor Peter for assistance. Driving in an illegally acquired car, the pair makes their way south, finding friendship, a dog, and surprising answers along the way.

Where it's reviewed:
Booklist, June 1, 2009, page 53
School Library Journal, August 2009, page 114

Other books by the same author:
The Statistical Probability of Love at First Sight, 2010
The Comeback Season, 2008

Other books you might like:
John Green, *An Abundance of Katherines*, 2006
E. Lockhart, *How to Be Bad*, 2008
Maureen McCarthy, *Rose by Any Other Name*, 2008
Lynn Weingarten, *Wherever Nina Lies*, 2009

1090

SHERRI L. SMITH

Flygirl

(New York: G.P. Putnam's Sons, 2009)

Subject(s): World War II, 1939-1945; African Americans; Women

Age range(s): 13 - 17+
Major character(s): Ida Mae Jones, Young Woman
Time period(s): 20th century; 1940s
Locale(s): Louisiana, United States

Summary: Sherri L. Smith's young adult novel *Flygirl* tells the story of a young girl named Ida Mae Jones, growing up during World War II in the United States. Ida is African American but still dreams of flying planes like her father did. When the government creates a program for women to join the Air Force, Ida sees her chance to make her dreams come true. In order to join, however, she must pretend to be white. Ida must decide what is more important to her: her family and heritage or her dreams. The themes of identity and goals will engage the readers as they learn about a historical moment as well.

Where it's reviewed:
Horn Book Magazine, May-June 2009, page 308
Publishers Weekly, December 8, 2008, page 59
School Library Journal, February 2009, page 110
Voice of Youth Advocates, February 2009, page 534

Other books by the same author:

Hot, Sour, Salty, Sweet, 2008

Sparrow, 2006

Lucy the Giant, 2002

Other books you might like:

Tanita S. Davis, *Mare's War*, 2009

Phillip M. Hoose, *Claudette Colvin: Twice Toward Justice*, 2009

M.E. Kerr, *Your Eyes in Stars: A Novel*, 2006

Julia Moberg, *Skies over Sweetwater*, 2008

Tanya Lee Stone, *Almost Astronauts: 13 Women Who Dared to Dream*, 2009

1091

JERI SMITH-READY

Shade

(New York: Simon Pulse, 2010)

Series: Shade Series. Book 1
Subject(s): Ghosts; Trials; Musicians

Age range(s): 15 - 18+
Major character(s): Aura, 16-Year-Old; Logan, Boyfriend (of Aura); Zachary, Friend (of Aura)
Time period(s): Indeterminate Future
Locale(s): United States

Summary: In *Shade* by Jeri Smith-Ready, a cosmic event known as the Shift gives humans the ability to communicate with the spirit world. Aura, 16, has a job at a law office that seeks legal aid for ghosts who may have died prematurely. As she plans a birthday surprise for her soon-to-be-17-year-old boyfriend, Logan, Aura has no idea that he will soon need her services. When Logan dies suddenly, Aura must face the purple phantom that now holds her boyfriend's spirit. As she tries to help Logan into the afterlife, Aura deals with feelings she has for her new classmate, Zachary. *Shade* is the first book in the Shade series.

Where it's reviewed:

Booklist, April 1, 2010, page 45

Horn Book Guide, Fall 2010, page 383

Publishers Weekly, May 3, 2010, page 54

School Library Journal, August 2010, page 112

Other books by the same author:

Shine, 2012

Shift, 2011

Other books you might like:

Megan Crewe, *Give Up the Ghost*, 2009

Richie Tankersley Cusick, *Shadow Mirror*, 2010

Heather Davis, *The Clearing*, 2010

Judd Holt, *A Promise to Catie*, 1992

Maureen Johnson, *The Name of the Star*, 2011

1092

RYAN SMITHSON

Ghosts of War: The True Story of a 19-Year-Old GI

(New York: HarperCollins, 2009)

Subject(s): Middle East; Wars; Terrorism

Age range(s): 14 - 18+

Summary: *Ghosts of War: The True Story of a 19-Year-Old GI* is an autobiographical account of Ryan Smithson's time as a soldier in the Iraq War. Smithson was in high school during the September 11th terrorist attacks, and immediately joined the military after graduation. He was assigned many different missions in Iraq, primarily working on rebuilding areas destroyed by homemade bombs and salvaging equipment for other missions. He writes of his personal experiences, the night terrors he suffered through, and his experiences with the Iraqi children. Smithson discovered that writing this novel and sharing his experiences of the war were helpful in recovering from post-traumatic stress disorder.

Where it's reviewed:

Booklist, June 1, 2009, page 49

Publishers Weekly, May 25, 2009, page 59

School Library Journal, March 2009, page 169

Voice of Youth Advocates, August 2009, page 250

Other books you might like:

Lauri S. Friedman, *Iraq War: An Opposing Viewpoints Guide*, 2008

Walter Dean Myers, *Sunrise over Fallujah*, 2008

Tim O'Brien, *The Things They Carried*, 1990

James Rumford, *Silent Music*, 2008

1093

THOMAS SNIEGOSKI

Legacy

(New York: Random House, 2009)

Subject(s): Supernatural; Father-son relations; Family

Age range(s): 14 - 17+
Major character(s): Lucas, 18-Year-Old, Son (of Clayton); Clayton "The Raptor" Hartwell, Wealthy, Hero, Father (of Lucas)

Summary: *Legacy* is a young adult novel by author Thomas Sniegoski. In it, the author tells the story of Lucas, a teenager whose father has not been a part of his life for some time. When his father breezes back into his life, however, Lucas is in for a shock. His father, billionaire Clayton Hartwell, claims to be the Raptor, a superhero who protects the city of Seraph. Clayton asks Lucas to carry on his good work because he is dying, a task that Lucas isn't sure he is ready for. Yet when evil forces launch an assault on his trailer park, killing his mother in the process, Lucas must decide to fight—if for no other reason than to avenge his mother's death.

Where it's reviewed:
Booklist, September 1, 2009, page 82
Horn Book Guide, Spring 2010, page 108
School Library Journal, December 2009, page 133
Voice of Youth Advocates, August 2009, page 232

Other books by the same author:
Sleeper Agenda, 2006
Sleeper Code, 2006
Leviathan, 2003

Other books you might like:
Chelsea M. Campbell, *The Rise of Renegade X*, 2010
Sarah Cross, *Dull Boy*, 2009
Perry Moore, *Hero*, 2007
Markus Zusak, *I Am the Messenger*, 2005

1094

JORDAN SONNENBLICK

After Ever After

(New York: Scholastic Press, 2010)

Subject(s): Cancer; Adolescence; Friendship

Age range(s): 12 - 15+
Major character(s): Jeffrey Alper, 8th Grader, Cancer Patient; Tad, Friend (of Jeffrey), Cancer Patient
Time period(s): 21st century; 2010s
Locale(s): United States

Summary: *After Ever After*, a heartfelt novel for young adult readers, is the sequel to *Drums, Girls, and Dangerous Pie* from author Jordan Sonnenblick. Eighth grader Jeffrey Alper has won the battle against leukemia, for now anyway, but his intense treatment left him with a few disturbing aftereffects, namely the fact that his brain is a bit scrambled and he walks with a limp. When Jeffrey learns that his only chance of moving onto ninth grade is to pass a standardized test, he agrees to receive tutoring from fellow cancer survivor, Tad. Unfortunately, Tad begins behaving strangely and missing a lot of school, Jeffrey's girlfriend is keeping her distance until after the test, and Jeffrey's brother, Steven, has disappeared on a mission to Africa to "find himself," leaving Jeffrey to struggle through the woes of eighth grade alone.

Where it's reviewed:
Booklist, December 15, 2009, page 39
Horn Book Magazine, March/April 2010, page 73
Publishers Weekly, January 4, 2010, page 48
Reading Time, August 2010, page 39
School Library Journal, January 2010, page 114

Other books by the same author:
Zen and the Art of Faking It, 2007
Notes from the Midnight Driver, 2006
Drums, Girls and Dangerous Pie, 2004

Other books you might like:
Maureen Johnson, *Suite Scarlett*, 2008
James Preller, *Six Innings*, 2008
Francisco X. Stork, *The Last Summer of The Death Warriors*, 2010

1095

ELIZABETH SPIRES

I Heard God Talking to Me: William Edmondson and His Stone Carvings

(New York: Farrar, Straus and Giroux, 2009)

Subject(s): Artists; Art; Poetry

Age range(s): 12 - 18+

Summary: William Edmondson's name may be virtually forgotten today, but in the 1930s and beyond, his stone carvings made him a sensation in the art world. In *I Heard God Talking to Me: William Edmondson and His Stone Carvings*, author Elizabeth Spires reflects on Edmondson's life and career through a series of poems profiling the great artist's struggles and triumphs. Through Spires's verse, readers learn of the middle-aged Edmondson receiving what he considered a message from God, urging him to carve a tombstone. The artist followed that urging and went on to create breathtaking sculptures that eventually landed him a solo show at the Museum of Modern Art in New York—a first for an African-American artist. This volume includes photos of Edmondson's work.

Where it's reviewed:
Booklist, February 1, 2009, page 49
Christianity Today, February 2009, page 58
Publishers Weekly, December 1, 2008, page 45
School Library Journal, March 2009, page 169

Other books you might like:
Jan Greenberg, *Heart to Heart: New Poems Inspired by Twentieth-Century American Art*, 2001
Steven Naifeh, *Van Gogh: The Life*, 2011
Alan Schroeder, *In Her Hands: The Story of Sculptor Augusta Savage*, 2009
Ntozake Shange, *We Troubled the Waters*, 2009
Carole Boston Weatherford, *Becoming Billie Holiday*, 2008

1096

NATALIE STANDIFORD

Confessions of the Sullivan Sisters

(New York: Scholastic, 2010)

Subject(s): Conduct of life; Inheritance and succession; Grandmothers

Age range(s): 15 - 18+
Major character(s): Norrie Sullivan, 18-Year-Old, Sister (of Sassy and Jane); Sassy Sullivan, 16-Year-Old, Sister (of Norrie and Jane); Jane Sullivan, 15-Year-Old, Sister (of Norrie and Sassy); Mrs. "Almighty" Beckendorf, Grandmother (of Norrie, Sassy, and Jane)
Time period(s): 21st century; 2010s
Locale(s): Baltimore, Maryland

Summary: In the young adult novel *Confessions of the Sullivan Sisters* by Natalie Standiford, the Sullivan siblings' wealthy grandmother delivers a Christmas surprise that could determine that family's financial future. Mrs. Arden Louisa Norris Sullivan Weems Maguire Hightower Beckendorf, the six-times-married family matriarch known as "Almighty," is nearing the end of her days. As she settles her estate, she reveals that one of her granddaughters has committed an offense so grave that the whole clan may be removed from her will. So instead of opening presents, 18-year-old Norrie, 16-year-old Sassy, and 15-year-old Jane spend the holidays preparing written confessions of their many transgressions. Their shocking revelations include betrayal, murder, and more, but they may not be enough to appease their almighty grandmother.

Where it's reviewed:
Booklist, September 1, 2010, page 98
Horn Book Magazine, September/October 2010, page 95
Publishers Weekly, September 6, 2010, page 41
School Library Journal, September 2010, page 165
Voice of Youth Advocates, October 2010, page 359

Other books by the same author:
How to Say Goodbye in Robot, 2009
Breaking Up Is Really, Really Hard to Do, 2005
Can True Love Survive High School?, 2005

Other books you might like:
Autumn Cornwell, *Carpe Diem*, 2007
Jennifer Echols, *Love Story*, 2011
Anna Godbersen, *The Luxe*, 2007
Libby Sternberg, *Finding the Forger*, 2004

1097

NATALIE STANDIFORD

How to Say Goodbye in Robot
(New York: Scholastic, 2009)

Subject(s): Friendship; Family; Death

Age range(s): 15 - 18+
Major character(s): Beatrice Szabo, Student—High School; Jonas Tate, Friend (of Beatrice), Student—High School
Time period(s): 21st century; 2000s
Locale(s): Baltimore, Maryland

Summary: In Natalie Standiford's *How to Say Goodbye in Robot*, high school student Beatrice Szabo finds herself relocating yet again with her constantly moving family. Now in Baltimore, Beatrice begins her senior year of high school, maintaining the aloofness and steely demeanor that keeps her safe from forming any lasting relationships. But her resolve melts when she meets Jonas Tate, a withdrawn classmate who captivates Beatrice. As the two become friends, she slowly grows enmeshed in Jonas's troubled world, leading them both on an emotional odyssey of love and self-discovery.

Where it's reviewed:
Booklist, November 1, 2009, page 32
Horn Book Guide, Spring 2010, page 109

Horn Book Magazine, January-February 2009, page 94
Publishers Weekly, October 26, 2009, page 59
School Library Journal, October 2009, page 136

Other books by the same author:
Confessions of the Sullivan Sisters, 2010
Can True Love Survive High School?, 2005
Dating Game Series, 2005-2006

Other books you might like:
Cecil Castellucci, *Boy Proof*, 2005
Hillary Frank, *The View from the Top*, 2010
K.A. Nuzum, *A Small White Scar*, 2006
Sara Zarr, *Sweethearts*, 2008

1098

TAMMAR STEIN

Kindred
(New York: Alfred A. Knopf, 2011)

Story type: Contemporary - Fantasy
Subject(s): Twins; Coming of age; Religion

Age range(s): 14 - 17+
Major character(s): Mo, Twin (of Miriam), Supernatural Being (visited by demons); Miriam, Twin (of Mo), Supernatural Being (visited by angels); Raphael, Angel (archangel)
Time period(s): 21st century
Locale(s): Tennessee, United States

Summary: Miriam is a troubled student who drops out of college and has to scramble to find a job. Then, Miriam is dealt another blow when she finds out she has Crohn's disease. On top of all that, something extraordinarily strange has happened: Miriam believes that she was visited by an angel named Raphael. Can it be real? And if it is what business could a supernatural being have with her? Worse yet, Miriam learns that she wasn't the only one to receive a bizarre visitation. Her twin brother, Mo, also was visited by an otherworldly spirit—but an evil one. Mo was visited by a satanic being that threatens to take over his mind. Can Miriam save him while fulfilling her own destiny?

Where it's reviewed:
Booklist, January 1, 2011, page 96
Horn Book Magazine, March-April 2011, page 125
Publishers Weekly, December 20, 2010, page 54
School Library Journal, March 2011, page 171
Voice of Youth Advocates, April 2011, page 70

Other books by the same author:
High Dive, 2008
Light Years, 2005

Other books you might like:
Sarwat Chadda, *Dark Goddess*, 2011
Michael Grant, *Gone*, 2008
R.A. Nelson, *Days of Little Texas*, 2009
Laini Taylor, *Daughter of Smoke and Bone*, 2011
Michelle Zink, *Prophecy of the Sisters*, 2009

1099

MAGGIE STIEFVATER

The Scorpio Races

(New York: Scholastic Press, 2011)

Story type: Fantasy
Subject(s): Fantasy; Adventure; Horse racing

Age range(s): 14 - 18+

Major character(s): Sean Kendrick, 19-Year-Old,
   Equestrian (champion); Puck Connolly, Teenager,
   Equestrian
Locale(s): Thisby, Fictional Location

Summary: In this young adult fantasy novel by Maggie
Stiefvater, it is time once again for the island of Thisby's
yearly water horse competition known as the Scorpio
Races. Young contestants race their steeds—dangerous,
enchanted, carnivorous beasts—along the sea cliffs. Sean
Kendrick, now 19, has held his place as champion for
several seasons while others have died in their attempts
to win. This November, Puck Connolly has entered the
race. She desperately needs to win the prize money for
her family despite the race's risks. Sean, who on the
surface seems fearless, has faced the challenges of the
Scorpio Races before, but he has never raced against a
competitor like Puck.

Where it's reviewed:
Booklist, September 1, 2011, page 102
Horn Book Magazine, November-December 2011, page
   114
New York Times Book Review, November 13, 2011,
   page 40
Publishers Weekly, August 22, 2011, page 67
School Library Journal, November 2011, page 140

Other books by the same author:
Forever, 2011
Linger, 2010
Ballad: A Gathering of Faerie, 2009
Shiver, 2009
Lament: The Faerie Queen's Deception, 2008

Other books you might like:
K.M. Grant, *Blood Red Horse*, 2005
Victoria Holmes, *The Horse from the Sea*, 2005
Prue Mason, *Camel Rider*, 2004
Diane Lee Wilson, *I Rode a Horse of Milk White Jade*,
   1998

1100

MAGGIE STIEFVATER

Shiver

(New York: Scholastic, 2009)

Subject(s): Werewolves; Love; Courage

Age range(s): 15 - 18+

Major character(s): Grace, Young Woman, Girlfriend (of
   Sam); Sam, Boyfriend (of Grace), Werewolf
Time period(s): 21st century; 2000s

Locale(s): United States

Summary: *Shiver* tells the story of a forbidden love
between a young woman and a wolf. When Grace was a
small child, a wolf saved her life in the woods behind
her house. Now a young woman, Grace obsessively
watches the wolves in the winter, always searching for
the one with yellow eyes. Sam leads two lives. In the
winter, he is a wolf, but for a few brief months during
the summer, he is a boy. When Grace meets Sam as a
young man, she recognizes his yellow eyes and knows
that he is her wolf. The two soon fall in love, but Sam
knows his time with Grace is short. At the end of this
summer, he will turn back into a wolf forever. Now,
Grace must find a way to prevent Sam from changing
back.

Where it's reviewed:
Booklist, August 1, 2009, page 61
Horn Book Magazine, March/April 2009, page 84
Journal of Adolescent & Adult, May 2010, page 692
Publishers Weekly, August 3, 2009, page 46
Reading Time, May 2010, page 39

Other books by the same author:
Forever, 2011
The Scorpio Races, 2011
Linger, 2010
Ballad: A Gathering of Faerie, 2009
Lament: The Faerie Queen's Deception, 2008

Other books you might like:
Holly Black, *Kith*, 2009
John Farris, *High Bloods*, 2009
Elizabeth Hand, *Illyria*, 2010
Cynthea Liu, *Paris Pan Takes the Dare*, 2009
Rebecca York, *Dragon Moon*, 2009

1101

R.L. STINE, Editor

Fear: 13 Stories of Suspense and Horror

(New York: Dutton Children's Books, 2010)

Story type: Collection
Subject(s): Horror; Short stories; Fantasy

Age range(s): 13 - 16+

Summary: Horror master R.L. Stine edits and contributes
a story to this collection of spooky tales for young adults.
From vampires and werewolves to creepy kids and
bloodthirsty neighbors, the stories explore a variety of
horror and science fiction themes. In "The Night Hunter"
by Meg Cabot, a masked bank robber takes a girl
hostage, but the girl has strange ideas of her own. In
"Piney Power" by F. Paul Wilson, a rural clan imposes
law and order on local offenders. In "Tuition" by Walter
Sorrells, a young criminal's birthday celebration is truly
surprising. The collection also includes Stine's "Welcome
to the Club," Heather Graham's "She's Different
Tonight," and Suzanne Weyn's "Suckers."

Where it's reviewed:
Booklist, September 1, 2010, page 98

Horn Book Guide, Spring 2011, page 179
Publishers Weekly, August 30, 2010, page 54
School Library Journal, November 2010, page 129
Voice of Youth Advocates, August 2010, page 275

Other books by the same author:
Secret Admirer, 2006
Beware! R.L. Stine Picks His Favorite Scary Stories, 2002
Nightmare Hour: Time for Terror, 2000

Other books you might like:
Peter Carver, *The Horrors: Terrifying Tales*, 2006
Deborah Noyes, *The Restless Dead: Ten Original Stories of the Supernatural*, 2007
Neal Shusterman, *Darkness Creeping: Twenty Twisted Tales*, 2007
Trisha Telep, *The Eternal Kiss: 13 Vampire Tales of Blood and Desire*, 2009

1102

TANYA LEE STONE

The Good, the Bad, and the Barbie: A Doll's History and Her Impact on Us

(New York: Viking Juvenile, 2010)

Subject(s): Dolls; Popular culture; Women

Age range(s): 13 - 18+

Summary: For generations, the Barbie doll has captured the imaginations of young people around the world. In *The Good, the Bad, and the Barbie: A Doll's History and Her Impact on Us*, author Tanya Lee Stone offers an incisive look at Barbie's evolution and her place in the popular consciousness. With a foreword by bestselling author Meg Cabot, this volume traces Barbie's journey from the mind of inventor Ruth Handler to her position as one of the most sought-after toys in the world. Stone also includes Barbie-themed observances from women of all ages who were profoundly impacted by the famously blond-haired, blue-eyed doll.

Where it's reviewed:
Booklist, November 15, 2010, page 36
Horn Book Magazine, November/December 2010, page 119
Publishers Weekly, November 1, 2010, page 45
School Library Journal, October 2010, page 133

Other books by the same author:
Almost Astronauts: 13 Women Who Dared to Dream, 2009
Laura Ingalls Wilder, 2009
Abraham Lincoln, 2005

Awards the book has won:
Golden Kite Awards: Nonfiction, 2011

Other books you might like:
Robin Gerber, *Barbie and Ruth: The Story of the World's Most Famous Doll and the Woman Who Created Her*, 2009

Kristine Hooks, *Dolls*, 2000
Jerry Oppenheimer, *Toy Monster: The Big, Bad World of Mattel*, 2009

1103

FRANCISCO X. STORK

Marcelo in the Real World

(New York: Arthur A. Levine Books, 2009)

Subject(s): Learning disorders; Adolescence; Work environment

Age range(s): 15 - 18+

Major character(s): Marcelo Sandoval, 17-Year-Old, Worker (at father's law firm)

Time period(s): 21st century; 2000s

Summary: In Francisco X. Stork's *Marcelo in the Real World*, a 17-year-old boy with an autistic spectrum disorder gets a dose of the "real world" at his summer job. As a high-functioning teen with a disorder similar to Asperger's syndrome, Marcelo Sandoval enjoys life at his special school. He would like to spend the summer working with the ponies there, but his lawyer father has other plans, and sticks Marcelo in the mailroom at his law firm to give him an idea of what life is like outside his comfort zone. There, Marcelo must juggle work, new relationships, and other challenges, and as the summer progresses, he learns not only about himself, but also about society, trust, and injustice.

Where it's reviewed:
Booklist, April 1, 2009, page 38
Horn Book Magazine, March/April 2009, page 204
New York Times Book Review, May 10, 2009, page 17
Publishers Weekly, January 15, 2009, page 51
School Library Journal, March 2009, page 156

Other books by the same author:
The Last Summer of the Death Warriors, 2010
Behind the Eyes, 2006

Awards the book has won:
Off the Cuff Awards, 2009

Other books you might like:
Andrew Auseon, *Freak Magnet*, 2010
Emily Franklin, *The Half-Life of Planets*, 2010
Mark Haddon, *The Curious Incident of the Dog in the Night-Time*, 2003
Tara Kelly, *Harmonic Feedback*, 2010
Olugbemisola Rhuday-Perkovich, *Eighth-Grade Superzero*, 2010

1104

FRANCISCO X. STORK

The Last Summer of The Death Warriors

(New York: Arthur A. Levine Books, 2010)

Subject(s): Revenge; Cancer; Orphans

Age range(s): 14 - 18+

Major character(s): Pancho, 17-Year-Old, Orphan, Friend (of D.Q.); D.Q., Cancer Patient, Friend (of Pancho); Marisol, Caregiver (of D.Q.)
Time period(s): 21st century; 2010s
Locale(s): Las Cruces, New Mexico

Summary: In *The Last Summer of the Death Warriors* by Francisco Stork, 17-year-old Pancho has one goal—to take revenge on the man who killed his older sister, Rosa. When Pancho is sent to an orphanage for boys in Las Cruces, he meets another teenager, D.Q., with a goal of his own—staying alive. Afflicted with a lethal form of brain cancer, D.Q. lives life according to his own "Death Warrior's Manifesto," which includes appreciating life's gifts (especially the presence of his caregiver, Marisol). When Pancho and D.Q. travel to Albuquerque, each boy has his own motivations but both find the answers they need.

Where it's reviewed:
Booklist, February 1, 2010, page 45
Horn Book Magazine, March/April 2010, page 74
New York Times Book Review, April 11, 2010, page 15
Publishers Weekly, January 11, 2010, page 49
School Library Journal, March 2010, page 166

Other books by the same author:
Irises, 2012
Marcelo in the Real World, 2009
Behind the Eyes, 2006

Other books you might like:
Miguel de Cervantes, *Don Quixote*, 1605
Matt Haig, *The Dead Fathers Club*, 2007
Andrew Smith, *In the Path of Falling Objects*, 2009
Paul Volponi, *The Hand You're Dealt*, 2008

1105

JONATHAN STRAHAN, Editor

Life on Mars: Tales from the New Frontier

(New York: Viking, 2011)

Subject(s): Science fiction; Mars (Planet); Short stories

Age range(s): 15 - 18+
Locale(s): Mars, Outer Space

Summary: Editor Jonathan Strahan collects 13 science-fiction stories for young adults in the anthology *Life on Mars: Tales from the New Frontier*. Written by celebrated science-fiction authors, the tales are set in different times but all focus on the theme of Martian travel and colonization. "Goodnight Moons" by Ellen Klage tells the story of the first baby born on Mars. "The Old Man and the Martian Sea" by Alastair Reynolds describes a teenage runaway's encounter with a Martian explorer. Other titles in the anthology include "Attlee and the Long Walk" by Kage Baker, "First Principle" by Nancy Kress, "Discovering Life" by Kim Stanley Robinson, and "Untitled Story" by Garth Nix.

Where it's reviewed:
Booklist, May 15, 2011, page 55
Publishers Weekly, February 28, 2011, page 58

School Library Journal, July 2011, page 108
Voice of Youth Advocates, June 2011, page 193

Other books by the same author:
The Starry Rift: Tales of New Tomorrows, 2008

Other books you might like:
David Macinnis Gill, *Black Hole Sun*, 2010
Patrick Nielsen Hayden, *New Skies*, 2004
Chris Roberson, *Iron Jaw and Hummingbird*, 2008
Brad Strickland, *Marsquake!*, 2005

1106

TODD STRASSER

Blood on My Hands

(New York: Egmont USA, 2010)

Series: Wish You Were Dead Trilogy. Book 2
Subject(s): Murder; Crime; High schools

Age range(s): 14 - 18+
Major character(s): Callie, Crime Suspect; Katherine Remington-Day, Crime Victim
Time period(s): 21st century; 2010s

Summary: *Blood on My Hands* is the second novel from Todd Strasser's Wish You Were Dead series. When teen queen Katherine Remington-Day is found dead during a high-school party, her frenemy Callie is the one caught holding the murder weapon. The only problem is, Callie knows she didn't do it, even if everyone has pictures of her standing over Katherine's dead body. As the incriminating photos make their way around town, Callie must evade the police as she sets out to find who really killed Katherine. Can Callie figure out who the real murderer is before she goes to jail for a crime she didn't commit?

Where it's reviewed:
Booklist, October 15, 2010, page 51
Horn Book Guide, Spring 2011, page 113
School Library Journal, December 2010, page 128
Voice of Youth Advocates, February 2011, page 562

Other books by the same author:
Famous, 2011
Kill You Last, 2011
If I Grow Up, 2009
Wish You Were Dead, 2009
Book Camp, 2007

Other books you might like:
Shannon Cowan, *Tin Angel*, 2007
Lauren Henderson, *Kiss Me Kill Me*, 2008
Anthony McGowan, *The Knife That Killed Me*, 2008
Eliot Schrefer, *The Deadly Sister*, 2010

1107

TODD STRASSER

Wish You Were Dead

(New York: Egmont USA, 2009)

Series: Wish You Were Dead Trilogy. Book 1
Subject(s): Missing persons; Kidnapping; High schools

Age range(s): 15 - 18+
Major character(s): Madison Archer, Student—High School, Detective—Amateur; Lucy Cunningham, Friend (of Madison), Kidnap Victim; Tyler, Student—High School
Time period(s): 21st century; 2000s
Locale(s): New York, United States

Summary: The first book in a trilogy, Todd Strasser's *Wish You Were Dead* tells the story of high school senior Madison Archer, who finds herself at the center of a dangerous mystery. Her friend Lucy has disappeared after a mysterious blogger posted threatening messages about her online. When two more students vanish, Madison fears the worst and sets out to find the truth. But the determined teen must proceed cautiously, as it becomes more and more clear that she just might be the next victim.

Where it's reviewed:
Booklist, October 1, 2009, page 39
Horn Book Guide, Spring 2010, page 109
School Library Journal, October 2009, page 138

Other books by the same author:
Famous, 2011
Blood on My Hands, 2010
If I Grow Up, 2009
Boot Camp, 2007
Stolen Kisses, Secrets, and Lies, 2007

Other books you might like:
Melissa Kantor, *Invisible I*, 2009
Shana Norris, *Something to Blog About: A Novel*, 2008
Laurie Faria Stolarz, *Deadly Little Secret: A Touch Novel*, 2009
Lynn Weingarten, *Wherever Nina Lies*, 2009

`1108`

ALLAN STRATTON

Borderline

(New York: HarperTeen, 2010)

Subject(s): Mystery; Prejudice; Social conditions

Age range(s): 13 - 17+
Major character(s): Sami Sabiri, 15-Year-Old, Religious (Muslim)
Time period(s): 21st century; 2000s
Locale(s): Rochester, New York

Summary: *Borderline* is a novel set in present-day New York. Sami Sabiri is a 15-year-old boy who is used to being bullied and harassed at school because of his Muslim faith. His strict father, an active member of the Muslim community, has always supported Sami. One day, something unthinkable happens—Sami's father is accused of being part of a terrorist ring known as the Brotherhood of Martyrs, and the FBI raids the family's home, ruining their things, and taking Sami's father into custody. Sami decides to do some investigating of his own, and discovers his father recently lied about a business trip, making Sami question what he believes about his father.

Where it's reviewed:
Booklist, January 1, 2010, page 58
Horn Book Guide, Fall 2010, page 384
Publishers Weekly, February 1, 2010, page 35
Resource Links, February 2010, page 35
School Library Journal, March 2010, page 167

Other books by the same author:
Chanda's Wars, 2008
Chanda's Secrets, 2004

Other books you might like:
Randa Abdel-Fattah, *Does My Head Look Big in This?*, 2007
Marina Tamar Budhos, *Ask Me No Questions*, 2006
Paula Jolin, *In the Name of God*, 2007
Neesha Meminger, *Shine, Coconut Moon*, 2009
Carol Plum-Ucci, *Streams of Babel*, 2008

`1109`

JONATHAN STROUD

The Ring of Solomon

(New York: Disney/Hyperion Books, 2010)

Subject(s): History; Magic; Wizards

Age range(s): 11 - 16+
Major character(s): King Solomon, Royalty; Bartimaeus, Supernatural Being (djinni)
Time period(s): 10th century B.C.; 950s B.C.
Locale(s): Jerusalem, Israel

Summary: *The Ring of Solomon: A Bartimaeus Novel* by Jonathan Stroud is the fourth novel to feature the character of Bartimaeus, a djinni. This novel is set in Jerusalem in 950 B.C. Bartimaeus is now serving King Solomon. Stories from the Old Testament are interwoven in this novel, with Bartimaeus serving as the comic relief. In this novel, Bartimaeus is dealing with an extremely challenging master and a servant who seems out to get him. The King requests that he build a temple for him, but then Bartimaeus has an issue with the King's magic ring and finds himself in an even worse situation. This novel serves as a prequel to the other three novels in the first Bartimaeus trilogy.

Where it's reviewed:
Booklist, March 15, 2011, page 66
Booklist, November 15, 2010, page 34
The Horn Book Guide, Spring 2011, page 85
School Library Journal, March 2011, page 190
Voice of Youth Advocates, February 2011, page 580

Other books by the same author:
Heroes of the Valley, 2009
Ptolemy's Gate, 2006
The Golem's Eye, 2004
The Leap, 2004
The Amulet of Samarkand, 2003

Awards the book has won:
Blue Ribbon Awards: Fiction, 2010

Other books you might like:
Maurissa Guibord, *Warped*, 2011
John Lenahan, *Shadowmagic*, 2009

Kai Meyer, *The Stone Light*, 2007
Andre Norton, *Dragon Mage*, 2008
Michael Scott, *The Alchemyst: The Secrets of the Immortal Nicholas Flamel*, 2007

1110

JONATHAN STROUD

Heroes of the Valley

(New York: Hyperion Book CH, 2009)

Subject(s): Folklore; Family history; Questing

Age range(s): 12 - 17+

Major character(s): Halli Sveinsson, 15-Year-Old, Hero

Summary: In *Heroes of the Valley*, the descendants of 12 heroes of Nordic folklore build a community together in a valley to protect each other from the dreaded Trows. Now, the community faces no more threats, and the descendents of the heroes thrive on telling old stories of heroic deeds. Halli Sveinsson is the youngest son of the house of Svein. He has grown up listening to folklore and longing to have adventures of his own. He decides to set out on a quest to find the man who killed his uncle and avenge his death. Halli soon discovers that reality has little in common with the heroic tales that come after the fact.

Where it's reviewed:
Booklist, December 1, 2008, page 50
Horn Book Magazine, January/February 2009, page 103
Publishers Weekly, November 24, 2008, page 58
School Library Journal, January 2009, page 118
Voice of Youth Advocates, February 2009, page 548

Other books by the same author:
Ptolemy's Gate, 2006
The Golem's Eye, 2004
The Leap, 2004
The Amulet of Samarkand, 2003
The Last Siege, 2003

Other books you might like:
Ellen Jensen Abbott, *Watersmeet*, 2009
Cinda Williams Chima, *The Wizard Heir*, 2007
Christine Hinwood, *The Returning*, 2011
Brian Meehl, *Suck It Up*, 2008
Jonathan Stroud, *The Ring of Solomon*, 2010

1111

BARBARA STUBER

Crossing the Tracks

(New York: Margaret K. McElderry Books, 2010)

Subject(s): Rural life; Family; Friendship

Age range(s): 12 - 15+

Major character(s): Iris, 15-Year-Old, Housekeeper, Friend (of Leroy); Leroy, Friend (of Iris)

Time period(s): 20th century; 1920s (1926)

Locale(s): Missouri, United States

Summary: *Crossing the Tracks* is a young adult novel from author Barbara Stuber. This debut novel focuses on 15-year-old Iris, a young girl suffering a great deal of hardship. After her mother's death, Iris's father no longer has room for her in his life. Focused on his career and his new girlfriend, he sends Iris to live in Missouri as the housekeeper to the elderly mother of a country doctor. Miles from her family, her home, and her only friend, Leroy, Iris is devastated. Before long, her heart is softened and moved by the compassion and kindness of the doctor and his mother. Just as she's growing content in her new life, a horrible tragedy strikes, teaching Iris a valuable lesson about love, faith, and confidence. First novel.

Where it's reviewed:
Booklist, July 1, 2010, page 50
Horn Book Guide, Spring 2011, page 113
School Library Journal, August 2010, page 114
Voice of Youth Advocates, October 2010, page 359

Other books you might like:
Gillian Cummings, *Somewhere in Blue*, 2010
Marian Hale, *The Goodbye Season*, 2009
Kathryn Lasky, *Hannah: Daughters of the Sea*, 2009

1112

KATHERINE STURTEVANT

The Brothers Story

(New York: Farrar, Straus and Giroux, 2009)

Subject(s): Brothers; Twins; Mentally disabled persons

Age range(s): 14 - 18+

Major character(s): Kit, 15-Year-Old, Apprentice (to artist); Christy, Twin (of Kit), Mentally Challenged Person

Time period(s): 17th century; 1680s

Locale(s): England

Summary: In *The Brothers Story* by Katherine Sturtevant, the Great Frost of 1683 and 1684 has brought misery and a scarcity of food to an Essex community. Having already lost one brother, 15-year-old Kit acts as sole protector of his mentally handicapped twin, Christy. But when Kit has an opportunity to escape his harsh existence and move to London as an artist's apprentice, he decides to leave Christy to fend for himself. As Kit learns the rules of city life, he is haunted by memories of his brother. His remorse over his desertion of Christy and his sexual feelings for a girl he meets are accentuated by his frequent study of the Bible.

Where it's reviewed:
Booklist, November 1, 2009, page 34
Horn Book Magazine, November-December 2009, page 687
Publishers Weekly, November 2, 2009, page 54
School Library Journal, January 2010, page 115
Voice of Youth Advocates, December 2009, page 415

Other books by the same author:
A True and Faithful Narrative, 2006
At the Sign of the Star, 2000

Other books you might like:
Mary Hooper, *At the Sign of the Sugared Plum*, 2003
Ann M. Martin, *A Corner of the Universe*, 2002
Michael Morpurgo, *Private Peaceful*, 2004
Pamela Porter, *The Crazy Man*, 2005

1113

NOVA REN SUMA

Imaginary Girls

(New York: Dutton, 2011)

Subject(s): Sisters; Supernatural; Death

Age range(s): 15 - 18+

Major character(s): Chloe, 16-Year-Old, Sister (of Ruby); Ruby, Sister (of Chloe, older), Friend (of London); London, Friend (of Ruby)

Time period(s): 21st century; 2010s

Locale(s): New York, United States

Summary: In the young-adult novel *Imaginary Girls* by Nova Ren Suma, 16-year-old Chloe, like many younger sisters, looks up to her older sister, Ruby. The girls have recently been reunited in their Hudson River Valley town after two years—a separation prompted by the death of Ruby's friend, London, at a party that Chloe attended with Ruby. Back in her hometown, Chloe learns that Ruby is still as popular as ever. She also discovers that London is alive. Gradually, Chloe realizes that Ruby's powerful influence, which seems to have altered the events surrounding London's tragic death, may be a talent from the supernatural realm.

Where it's reviewed:
Booklist, May 1, 2011, page 84
Publishers Weekly, April 4, 2011, page 54
School Library Journal, July 2011, page 109
Voice of Youth Advocates, June 2011, page 174

Other books by the same author:
Dani Noir, 2009

Other books you might like:
Margo Lanagan, *Black Juice*, 2004
Marlene Perez, *Dead Is So Last Year*, 2009
Amy Plum, *Die for Me*, 2011

1114

COURTNEY SUMMERS

Some Girls Are

(New York: St. Martin's Griffin, 2010)

Subject(s): Bullying; High schools; Popularity

Age range(s): 15 - 18+

Major character(s): Regina Afton, Friend (of Anna, Marta, Jeanette, and Kara), Student—High School; Anna Morrison, Friend (of Regina, Marta, Kara, and Jeanette), Girlfriend (of Donnie); Donnie Henderson, Boyfriend (of Anna); Kara, Friend (of Regina, Anna, Jeanette, and Marta); Jeanette, Friend (of Regina, Anna, Kara, and Marta); Marta, Friend (of Regina,

Anna, Kara, and Jeanette); Michael Hayden, Friend (of Regina)

Time period(s): 21st century; 2010s

Locale(s): Hallowell, Connecticut

Summary: In the young adult novel *Some Girls Are* by Courtney Summers, Regina Afton's reign of terror as one of Hallowell High School's "Fearsome Fivesome" comes to a spectacular end. Since middle school, Regina and her friends Anna, Marta, Kara, and Jeanette have enjoyed life at the top of the social food chain, intimidating the unfortunate girls beneath them with cruelty and bullying. Everything changes when Anna's boyfriend assaults Regina at a party. When the circumstances of Donnie's brutal treatment are revealed, Regina receives no sympathy from her friends but is ostracized instead. Now one of the unpopular kids, Regina forges a friendship with Michael Hayden, a boy well acquainted with her darker side.

Where it's reviewed:
Booklist, February 1, 2010, page 39
Publishers Weekly, December 14, 2009, page 60
School Library Journal, February 2010, page 124

Other books by the same author:
Fall for Anything, 2010
Cracked Up to Be, 2009

Other books you might like:
Kay Cassidy, *The Cinderella Society*, 2010
D. Anne Love, *Defying the Diva*, 2008
Courtney Summers, *Some Girls Are*, 2010
Rita Williams-Garcia, *Jumped*, 2009

1115

SUZANNE SUPPLEE

Somebody Everybody Listens To

(New York: Dutton Books, 2010)

Subject(s): Singing; Self confidence; Country music

Age range(s): 12 - 16+

Major character(s): Retta Lee Jones, Graduate (high school), Singer (country music); Daddy, Father (of Retta Lee); Mama, Mother (of Retta Lee)

Time period(s): 21st century; 2010s

Locale(s): Nashville, Tennessee; Starling, Tennessee

Summary: In the young adult novel *Somebody Everybody Listens To* by Suzanne Supplee, high-school graduate Retta Lee Jones leaves Sparling, Tennessee, to pursue her dream of country music stardom in Nashville. Though Retta Lee knows her departure will probably further strain her parents' marriage, she decides that she must do what's in her own best interest. In Nashville, Retta Lee finds friends, hard work, and heartache, but she relies on her country music idols to maintain her strength and optimism. Written especially for the young country music fan, *Somebody Everybody Listens To* features a succinct bio of an iconic performer in each chapter. Supplee is also the author of *Artichoke's Heart*.

Where it's reviewed:
Booklist, June 1, 2010, page 60
Horn Book Guide, Fall 2010, page 384

Publishers Weekly, May 24, 2010, page 54
School Library Journal, October 2010, page 126

Other books by the same author:
Artichoke's Heart, 2008
When Irish Guys Are Smiling, 2008

Other books you might like:
Kristin Harmel, *When You Wish*, 2008
Sophia Lowell, *Glee: The Beginning: An Original Novel*, 2010
Nerissa Nields, *Plastic Angel*, 2005

1116

TABITHA SUZUMA

Forbidden

(New York: Simon Pulse, 2011)

Story type: Contemporary
Subject(s): Brothers and sisters; Family relations; Alcoholism

Age range(s): 16 - 18+
Major character(s): Lochan, 17-Year-Old, Brother (of Maya), Lover (of Maya); Maya, 16-Year-Old, Sister (of Lochan), Lover (of Lochan)
Time period(s): 21st century; 2000s
Locale(s): England

Summary: Author Tabitha Suzuma explores a complex and controversial family relationship in the novel for young adults. Because of their dysfunctional family's circumstances, 17-year-old Lochan and his 16-year-old sister, Maya, have been thrown into the roles of surrogate parents to their three younger brothers and sisters. Their father has left, and their mother has a serious drinking problem that distances her from the rest of the family. As Lochan and Maya try to hold their lives and their family together, they develop a deep friendship that evolves into romantic love. Despite the conflicting emotions and their guilt about the relationship, Lochan and Maya act on their feelings and journey down a dangerous path.

Where it's reviewed:
Booklist, June 1, 2011, page 80
Publishers Weekly, April 18, 2011, page 55
School Library Journal, October 2011, page 150
Voice of Youth Advocates, August 2011, page 280

Other books by the same author:
Without Looking Back, 2009
From Where I Stand, 2008
Voice in the Distance, 2008
A Note of Madness, 2007

Other books you might like:
Francesca Lia Block, *Wasteland*, 2003
Elizabeth Hand, *Illyria*, 2010
Ellen Hopkins, *Identical*, 2008
Linda Newbery, *Set in Stone*, 2006

1117

GREG TAYLOR

The Girl Who Became a Beatle

(New York: Feiwel and Friends, 2011)

Subject(s): Music; Wishes; Fantasy

Age range(s): 12 - 15+
Major character(s): Regina, Teenager, Musician
Time period(s): 21st century; 2010s

Summary: High-school musician Regina wants nothing more than for her band to succeed, but when the Caverns part ways for good, she makes a simple wish—for her music to become as popular as the Beatles' music. When she wakes the following day, her entire world has changed: the Beatles' catalog is now credited to the Caverns, and Regina is as famous as John Lennon and Paul McCartney. The only problem is, she may have left her real-world anonymity behind but she still has the memories of the good and the bad, including her parents' breakup and her high-school crush. As Regina's fame gets trickier to navigate, she begins to wonder if some wishes are better off not granted.

Where it's reviewed:
Booklist, January 1, 2011, page 95
Publishers Weekly, December 20, 2010, page 54
School Library Journal, April 2011, page 186
Voice of Youth Advocates, February 2011, page 562

Other books by the same author:
Killer Pizza, 2011

Other books you might like:
Cecil Castellucci, *Beige*, 2007
Grace Dent, *LBD: Live and Fabulous!*, 2006
Janette Rallison, *My Unfair Godmother*, 2011
Jane Yolen, *Pay the Piper: A Rock 'n' Roll Fairy Tale*, 2005

1118

GREG TAYLOR

Killer Pizza

(New York: Feiwel and Friends, 2009)

Subject(s): Fantasy; Work environment; Monsters

Age range(s): 12 - 15+
Major character(s): Toby, 14-Year-Old; Annabel, Worker (at Killer Pizza); Strobe, Worker (at Killer Pizza)
Time period(s): 21st century; 2000s
Locale(s): United States

Summary: Toby gets a summer job at the local pizza joint, Killer Pizza. He likes learning to make pizza and gets along well with his co-workers, Annabel and Strobe. Soon, however, Toby begins having strange and vivid dreams about monsters invading his small town. Eventually, it is revealed that Killer Pizza is just a front for a monster-hunting enterprise, and that he, Annabel, and Strobe are all being recruited. The town is full of monsters taking the shape of humans and killing people, and it is up to the three teenagers to stop them.

Where it's reviewed:
Booklist, May 15, 2009, page 55
Publishers Weekly, June 15, 2009, page 50
School Library Journal, September 2009, page 174

Other books by the same author:
The Girl Who Became a Beatle, 2011
Killer Pizza: The Slice, 2011

Other books you might like:
Royce Buckingham, *Demonkeeper*, 2007
Rosemary Clement-Moore, *Highway to Hell*, 2009
D.M. Cornish, *Foundling*, 2006
Dean Lorey, *Monster Madness*, 2008
Charles Ogden, *Split Ends*, 2009

1119

LAINI TAYLOR

Lips Touch: Three Times

(New York: Arthur A. Levine Books, 2009)

Subject(s): Short stories; Supernatural; Fantasy

Age range(s): 14 - 18+

Summary: In *Lips Touch: Three Times*, author Laini Taylor presents three short stories featuring the theme of kissing and the very different outcomes the act holds for three heroines. "Goblin Fruit" recalls the Victorian belief that goblins can trick girls into surrendering their souls with a gift of fruit. Modern Kizzy disregards the old traditions she was taught and is fooled by a clever goblin. In "Spicy Little Curses," Anamique, a British girl who lives in colonial India, is stricken mute by an evil spell. The stirrings of young love empower Anamique to challenge the curse. In "Hatchling," 13-year-old Esme experiences strange physical changes that reveal the presence of the sinister being she carries within.

Where it's reviewed:
Booklist, October 1, 2009, page 42
Horn Book Guide, Spring 2010, page 110
Horn Book Magazine, January-February 2010, page 94
Publishers Weekly, September 21, 2009, page 59
Voice of Youth Advocates, December 1, 2009, page 425

Other books by the same author:
Daughter of Smoke and Bone, 2011
Silksinger, 2009
Blackbringer, 2007

Other books you might like:
Rachel Caine, *Carpe Corpus*, 2009
P.C. Cast, *Chosen*, 2008
Melissa de la Cruz, *Blue Bloods*, 2006
Alex Flinn, *A Kiss in Time*, 2009
Lauren Henderson, *Kiss Me Kill Me*, 2008

1120

LAINI TAYLOR

Daughter of Smoke and Bone

(New York: Little, Brown and Company, 2011)

Subject(s): Demons; Monsters; Fantasy

Age range(s): 14 - 18+

Major character(s): Karou, 17-Year-Old, Student—Boarding School, Artist; Brimstone, Supernatural Being; Akiva, Angel

Time period(s): 21st century; 2010s

Locale(s): Prague, Czech Republic

Summary: In the young adult fantasy novel *Daughter of Smoke and Bone* by Laini Taylor, 17-year-old Karou pursues her interest in art at a Prague boarding school as she tries to unravel the mystery of her heritage. Tattooed and blue-haired, Karou chooses a collection of frightening creatures as inspiration for her drawings—but the monsters are very real. Raised by a being called Brimstone, Karou fulfills her family duties—including the retrieval of human teeth—without fully understanding her place in her grotesque family tree. While on an assignment for Brimstone, Karou meets an angel, Akiva, one of the many heavenly beings who have come to earth. Akiva may have the answers Karou seeks, but the information will forever change the teenager's world.

Where it's reviewed:
Booklist, September 1, 2011, page 115
Horn Book Magazine, November-December 2011, page 115
New York Times Book Review, October 16, 2011, page 20
Publishers Weekly, July 25, 2011, page 55
School Library Journal, November 2011, page 140

Other books by the same author:
Lips Touch: Three Times, 2009
Silksinger, 2009
Blackbringer, 2007

Other books you might like:
Josephine Angelini, *Starcrossed*, 2011
Lisa Papademetriou, *Siren's Storm*, 2011
Heather Terrell, *Fallen Angel*, 2011
L.A. Weatherly, *Angel Burn*, 2011

1121

JANNE TELLER
MARTIN AITKEN, Translator

Nothing

(New York: Atheneum Books for Young Readers, 2010)

Subject(s): Adolescence; Values (Philosophy); Children

Age range(s): 13 - 18+

Major character(s): Pierre Anthon, 7th Grader

Time period(s): 21st century; 2010s

Locale(s): Denmark

Summary: A 2011 Michael L. Printz Honor Book and Batchelder Honor Book, *Nothing* is a chilling novel for young adult readers about the meaning of life from author Janne Teller. When seventh-grader Pierre Anthon decides that nothing in the world really matters in the grand scheme of things, he runs out of school and climbs into a plum tree, vowing never to come down. His peers are desperate to prove him wrong and get him to come down from the tree so they form a plan to compile a hidden stash of "meaningful" objects that represent the importance of life. When the children struggle with parting with their beloved items, they resort to choosing which items their peers must give up. The activity starts innocently enough, with sneakers and books, but takes a dark and sinister turn as the stakes are raised and the kids grow more desperate to see Pierre return to normal civilization.

Where it's reviewed:
Booklist, December 1, 2009, page 44
Horn Book Guide, Spring 2011, page 113
Publishers Weekly, January 4, 2010, page 48
School Library Journal, April 2010, page 169
Voice of Youth Advocates, June 2010, page 159

Other books by the same author:
Odin's Island, 2006

Other books you might like:
David Almond, *Kit's Wilderness*, 2000
Lesley Choyce, *Random: If You Think Life Makes Sense, Do Not Read This Book*, 2010
William Golding, *Lord of the Flies*, 1954
Carol Plum-Ucci, *The Body of Christopher Creed*, 2000

1122

DOUG TENNAPEL, Author/Illustrator

Ghostopolis

(New York: Scholastic, 2010)

Subject(s): Comic books; Horror; Adventure

Age range(s): 11 - 15+

Major character(s): Frank Gallows, Worker (Supernatural Immigration Task Force); Garth Hale, Boy

Locale(s): Ghostopolis, Fictional Location

Summary: In the young adult graphic novel *Ghostopolis*, author and illustrator Doug TenNapel creates an eerie hereafter known as Ghostopolis. The Supernatural Immigration Task Force is supposed to keep the spirits who reside there from wandering back to the world of the living. But one of its staff, Frank Gallows, has made a serious error and brought a mortal to Ghostopolis prematurely. Garth Hale had always feared death. Having recently been diagnosed with a terminal illness, he fully expected to be passing into the afterlife soon—but not via a deceased horse. On the other side, Garth meets the despicable ruler of the realm as well as the spirit of Cecil, his grandfather.

Where it's reviewed:
Booklist, March 15, 2010, page 60
Horn Book Guide, Spring 2010, page 113
School Library Journal, July 2010, page 108

Other books by the same author:
Bad Island, 2011
Creature Tech, 2010
Power Up, 2009
Monster Zoo, 2008
Iron West, 2006

Other books you might like:
Otis Frampton, *Oddly Normal: Volume One*, 2006
Kazu Kibuishi, *The Stonekeeper*, 2008
D.J. MacHale, *The Merchant of Death*, 2002

Nykko, *The Shadow Door*, 2009
Neal Shusterman, *Everlost*, 2006

1123

DOUG TENNAPEL

Bad Island

(New York: Graphix, 2011)

Story type: Adventure
Subject(s): Islands; Boating; Vacations

Age range(s): 11 - 16+
Major character(s): Reese, Teenager, Accident Victim (boating)
Time period(s): 21st century; 2010s

Summary: A teenage boy must rely on his family when he's shipwrecked on a bizarre and dangerous island in this graphic novel for young adult readers from award-winning illustrator and author Doug TenNapel. The last thing Reese wants to do on his school break is go on a boating trip with his family. Expecting a boring week of forced family bonding, Reese is shocked and more than a little miffed when the gang is shipwrecked on a strange island. As Reese and his family try to hatch a plan of escape, they discover that they're not alone on the island. A slew of unusual and hostile inhabitants troll the land, and they're not fond of these unexpected guests. To stay alive, Reese and his family must rely on one another and each person's individual strengths to outwit the creatures, unlock the island's hidden secrets, and find a way home.

Where it's reviewed:
Booklist, March 15, 2011, page 38
Publishers Weekly, May 2, 2011, page 59
School Library Journal, November 2011, page 154

Other books by the same author:
Ghostopolis, 2010
Gear, 2007
Iron West, 2006
Earthboy Jacobus, 2005
Creature Tech, 2002

Other books you might like:
Jodi Lynn Anderson, *May Bird and the Ever After*, 2005
Kazu Kibuishi, *Amulet: The Cloud Searchers*, 2010
Christopher Lincoln, *Billy Bones: Tales from the Secrets Closet*, 2008
Shaun Tan, *Lost and Found*, 2011
Don Wood, *Into the Volcano*, 2008

1124

DOM TESTA

The Comet's Curse

(New York: Tor Teen, 2009)

Series: Galahad Series. Book 1
Subject(s): Futuristic society; Adolescence; Adventure

Age range(s): 13 - 16+
Major character(s): Roc, Computer; Triana, 16-Year-Old,

Leader (commander of ship)
Time period(s): 23rd century
Locale(s): Galahad, Spaceship

Summary: *The Comet's Curse* is the first novel in the Galahad series for young adults by Dom Testa. The series begins approximately 200 years in the future, when Earth's near miss with a comet leads to toxic particles being left behind in the atmosphere. This causes a virus deadly to everyone over the age of 16. The government's solution is to choose 251 promising teenagers and send them off on a spaceship known as Galahad in search of a safer planet. The ship is commanded by Triana, a 16-year-old girl who has just lost her family, and a computer known as Roc. In the first novel, the commanders of the ship discover that an adult has somehow gotten aboard Galahad—an adult with the potential to bring the deadly virus to the new location.

Where it's reviewed:
Booklist, December 15, 2008, page 38
School Library Journal, September 2009, page 174

Other books by the same author:
Cosmic Storm, 2011
The Dark Zone, 2011
The Cassini Code, 2010
The Web of Titan, 2010

Other books you might like:
Orson Scott Card, *Pathfinder*, 2010
Catherine Jinks, *Living Hell*, 2010
Beth Revis, *Across the Universe*, 2011

1125

TIM THARP

Badd

(New York: Alfred A. Knopf, 2011)

Story type: Coming-of-Age
Subject(s): Coming of age; Family; Brothers and sisters

Age range(s): 15 - 18+
Major character(s): Ceejay McDermott, Young Woman, Sister (of Bobby); Bobby McDermott, Veteran (of Iraq conflict), Brother (of Ceejay)
Time period(s): 21st century; 2010s
Locale(s): United States

Summary: In this young adult novel by Tim Tharp, a teenage girl discovers how war can change a person forever. Ceejay McDermott grew up idolizing her big brother Bobby, who was a "bad boy" in the best way: He was a fun, zany, charming boy who was generally a pleasure to be around. Ceejay called him "badd," a special, good kind of "bad." However, things change when Bobby joins the armed forces and is shipped to Iraq. He returns early and won't say why. He wasn't physically injured, but his personality has changed significantly. Bobby now finds little pleasure in life and seems to force himself to act in his old ways. Instead of being fun and silly, though, his "badd" attitude is now dark and dangerous. Ceejay has to come to terms with the changes in her brother and understand what happened to him if she wants any chance to help him readjust to civilian life.

Where it's reviewed:
Booklist, January 1, 2011, page 92
School Library Journal, April 2011, page 186
Voice of Youth Advocates, February 2011, page 562

Other books by the same author:
The Spectacular Now, 2008
Knights of the Hill Country, 2006

Other books you might like:
Patricia McCormick, *Purple Heart*, 2009
Walter Dean Myers, *Sunrise over Fallujah*, 2008
Dana Reinhardt, *The Things a Brother Knows*, 2010

1126

CRAIG THOMPSON, Author/Illustrator

Habibi

(New York: Pantheon Books, 2011)

Subject(s): Adventure; Allegories; Love
Age range(s): 16 - 18+
Major character(s): Dodola, Refugee, Orphan, Lover (of Zam); Zam, Refugee, Orphan, Lover (of Dodola)
Time period(s): 21st century; 2010s

Summary: At the heart of author and illustrator Craig Thompson's powerful allegory is the love story of orphans Dodola and Zam. Their epic tale unfolds against a variety of backgrounds, including the open desert, a shadowy brothel, and an industrial dumping ground. Through poetic storytelling and imaginative imagery, Thompson brings to life this unique celebration of love's enduring power as it reveals the dangers of the material world and the tentative ties between humans and the environment. While Dodola and Zam make their way toward their mutual destiny, the world around them offers up no shortage of challenges, tests, and moral lessons.

Where it's reviewed:
Booklist, September 15, 2011, page 53
New York Times Book Review, October 16, 2011, page 26
Publishers Weekly, July 11, 2011, page 42

Other books by the same author:
Good-bye, Chunky Rice, 2006
Blankets, 2003

Other books you might like:
Jeff Lemire, *Ghost Stories: Essex County*, 2007
David Mazzucchelli, *Asterios Polyp*, 2009
Jordan Mechner, *Prince of Persia: The Graphic Novel*, 2008
G. Willow Wilson, *Cairo*, 2007

1127

HOLLY THOMPSON
GRADY MCFERRIN, Illustrator

Orchards

(New York: Delacorte Press, 2011)

Story type: Coming-of-Age
Subject(s): Coming of age; Suicide; Bullying

Major character(s): Kana Goldberg, Young Woman
Time period(s): 21st century; 2010s
Locale(s): Japan; New York, New York

Summary: Kana Goldberg, a girl of mixed Jewish and Japanese heritage, is part of the "in crowd" at her high school. As such, she participates in the bullying of a mentally ill girl who ultimately commits suicide. Kana and her friends, never having considered their actions, are left with shock and guilt. Kana's parents, understanding Kana's guilt over the incident, arrange for her to visit family in Japan. During her trip, Kana learns all about Japanese culture. She also learns to work in her family's orchard, and she learns a lot while living with her brash, xenophobic grandmother. Through her trip, Kana gains a broader perspective on life, but will she be able to apply the lesson she's learned to her life back in America? This book by Holly Thompson features illustrations by Grady McFerrin.

Where it's reviewed:
Booklist, January 1, 2011, page 97
Publishers Weekly, January 3, 2011, page 51
School Library Journal, March 2011, page 172
Voice of Youth Advocates, February 2011, page 562

Other books by the same author:
Tomo: Friendship through Fiction: An Anthology of Japan Teen Stories, 2012

Other books you might like:
Jodi Lynn Anderson, *The Secrets of Peaches*, 2007
Jay Asher, *Thirteen Reasons Why*, 2007
Kelly Easton, *Hiroshima Dreams*, 2007
Mary Beth Miller, *Aimee*, 2002
Cathy Ostlere, *Karma*, 2011

1128

KATE THOMPSON

Creature of the Night

(New York: Roaring Brook Press, 2009)

Subject(s): Ireland; Adolescence; Fantasy

Age range(s): 14 - 18+
Major character(s): Bobby, 14-Year-Old
Time period(s): 21st century; 2000s
Locale(s): Ireland

Summary: In *Creature of the Night*, a young adult novel by Kate Thompson, teenager Bobby is moved out of Dublin and into rural Ireland in an attempt by his mother to make him stop drinking, doing drugs, and getting into trouble. His mother has never been a good parent to him, and they fight constantly. Bobby begins to adjust to the quieter, rural setting, but then he learns that a murder took place in their new home. A couple killed their child there, believing that she was an evil changeling. Though at first he is unconcerned with the history of the house, he starts to notice someone in the shadows at night, and starts to think that strange things may be happening in the dwelling after all.

Where it's reviewed:
Booklist, April 1, 2009, page 38
Horn Book Magazine, May/June 2009, page 309

School Library Journal, August 2009, page 115

Other books by the same author:
Most Wanted, 2010
The White Horse Trick, 2010
Highway Robbery, 2009
Beguilers, 2008
The New Policeman, 2007

Other books you might like:
Cathy Cassidy, *Scarlett*, 2006
Patrick Jones, *Stolen Car*, 2008
Gordon Korman, *The Juvie Three*, 2008
O.R. Melling, *The Summer King*, 2006

1129

RUTH THOMSON

Terezin: Voices from the Holocaust

(Somerville, Massachusetts: Candlewick Press, 2011)

Subject(s): Holocaust, 1933-1945; World War II, 1939-1945; Concentration camps

Age range(s): 11 - 14+

Summary: Author Ruth Thomson uses first-hand accounts to tell the story of Terezin, a town in Czechoslovakia commandeered by the Nazis as a transit camp during World War II. Though there were no gas chambers at Terezin, its story is no less shocking. The camp was used to confine Jewish artists, writers, and performers who were ordered to produce works that would assure outside observers of the Nazis' fair treatment. The "show camp" fulfilled its purpose, but the Nazis did not know that their prisoners were secretly documenting the camp's true horrors in journals and drawings. The words and pictures of those Jewish prisoners are collected here to reveal a deplorable chapter from Holocaust history to a middle school audience.

Where it's reviewed:
Booklist, February 15, 2011, page 64
Bulletin of the Center for Children's Books, February 2011, page 303
Horn Book Magazine, Fall 2011, page 476
School Library Journal, March 2011, page 187

Other books you might like:
Paul B. Janeczko, *Requiem: Poems of the Terezin Ghetto*, 2011
Karen Levine, *Hana's Suitcase*, 2002
Monique Polak, *What World is Left*, 2008
Hana Volavkova, *I Never Saw Another Butterfly: Children's Drawings and Poems from Terezin Concentration Camp, 1942-1944*, 1962

1130

CATE TIERNAN

Immortal Beloved

(New York: Little, Brown and Company, 2010)

Subject(s): Immortality; Rehabilitation; Fantasy
Major character(s): Nastasya, Immortal; Reyn, Immortal

Time period(s): 21st century; 2010s
Locale(s): London, England; Massachusetts, United States

Summary: *Immortal Beloved* is a suspenseful fantasy novel for young adult readers from author Cate Tiernan. Born in 1551, Nastasya has spent centuries living the wild, carefree, and often devious life of an immortal, but a moment of cruelty has her questioning her lifestyle. In an attempt to regain a sense of humanity and moral compass, Nastasya checks herself into River's Edge, a rural Massachusetts rehab center for misguided immortals. Nastasya immerses herself in the program, befriending her peers and confronting the demons of her past. But just as she begins to feel comfortable—and fall for a sexy immortal named Reyn—her family and the secrets of her past force her to return home to take care of unfinished business.

Where it's reviewed:
Booklist, August 1, 2010, page 47
Horn Book Guide, Spring 2011, page 114
Publishers Weekly, August 30, 2010, page 54
School Library Journal, November 2010, page 130
Voice of Youth Advocates, October 2010, page 372

Other books by the same author:
Darkness Falls, 2012
Balefire, 2011
A Chalice of Wind, 2005
Night's Child, 2003
Origins, 2002

Other books you might like:
R.J. Anderson, *Spell Hunter*, 2009
Penni Russon, *Undine*, 2006
Cynthia Leitich Smith, *Eternal*, 2009

1131

ALEX VAN TOL

Knifepoint
(Victoria, British Columbia, Canada: Orca Book Publishers, 2010)

Subject(s): Suspense; Horses; Murder

Age range(s): 13 - 17+
Major character(s): Jill, Teenager, Horse Trainer
Time period(s): 21st century; 2010s
Locale(s): United States

Summary: Jill is thrilled about her summer job at a mountain ranch, leading customers on trail rides by horseback. That is, until she actually starts the job and discovers that the work is harder than she imagined, the pay is way less, and the people are downright impossible to deal with. When she gets into a huge fight with her boss, Jill makes a bad judgment call and takes out a good-looking and mysterious guy for an isolated ride, despite the fact that he hasn't filled out the proper paperwork. Her impulsive decision leads to disastrous results when the lone rider turns out to be a malicious killer with violent plans for Jill.

Where it's reviewed:
Booklist, October 15, 2010, page 60
Horn Book Guide, Spring 2011, page 114
School Library Journal, January 2011, page 118

Other books by the same author:
Viral, 2011

Other books you might like:
Mary Jane Beaufrand, *The River*, 2010
Kevin Brooks, *Black Rabbit Summer*, 2008
Vicki Grant, *Pigboy*, 2006

1132

HEATHER TOMLINSON

Toads and Diamonds
(New York: Henry Holt, 2010)

Subject(s): Fantasy; Gifted persons; Stepfamilies

Age range(s): 14 - 18+
Major character(s): Diribani, 15-Year-Old, Stepsister (to Tana); Tana, 16-Year-Old, Stepsister (to Diribani)
Time period(s): Indeterminate
Locale(s): India

Summary: *Toads and Diamonds* is a fantasy novel for young adult readers from author Heather Tomlinson. Set in India, the story centers on teenage stepsisters, Diribani and Tana, and their very different encounters with magic and fortune. When the sweet and tenderhearted Diribani encounters a goddess, she is blessed with a rare gift. Flowers and precious stones fall from her mouth every time she speaks. Tana, on the other hand, finds it fitting that her brush with the goddess results in a curse. Whenever Tana speaks, snakes and toads appear. Both girls' new abilities are filled with both blessings and curses. Diribani finds a prince, but her life is put at risk. Meanwhile, Tana is banished from their village; but when a rat plague breaks out, her newfound gift could save the entire community.

Where it's reviewed:
Booklist, February 15, 2010, page 77
Horn Book Guide, Fall 2010, page 384
School Library Journal, July 2010, page 98
Voice of Youth Advocates, April 2010, page 46
Voice of Youth Advocates, April 2010, page 76

Other books by the same author:
Aurelie: A Fairy Tale, 2008
The Swan Maiden, 2007

Other books you might like:
Elizabeth C. Bunce, *A Curse Dark as Gold*, 2008
Shannon Hale, *Book of a Thousand Days*, 2007
Marilyn Kaye, *Penelope*, 2007
William Nicholson, *Seeker*, 2006
Suzanne Weyn, *Water Song*, 2006

1133

ADRIANA TRIGIANI

Viola in Reel Life
(New York: HarperTeen, 2009)

Subject(s): Boarding schools; Dating (Social customs); Interpersonal relations

Age range(s): 13 - 16+
Major character(s): Viola, 14-Year-Old, Student—Boarding School
Time period(s): 21st century; 2000s
Locale(s): South Bend, Indiana

Summary: In Adriana Trigiani's *Viola in Reel Life*, 14-year-old Viola is apprehensive about making the move from her native Brooklyn to a remote Indiana boarding school. But her parents are insistent that she must spend her ninth grade year there, so she reluctantly attends. Hiding behind her video camera, Viola chronicles her experiences. Leaving behind her best friend Andrew, she now must contend with three annoyingly cheerful roommates...as well as the ghost that only she can see. But as her freshman year progresses, Viola's feelings about life at boarding school begin to change. She makes new friends and even goes on a date. Now if only she could put down that video camera.

Where it's reviewed:
Booklist, August 1, 2009, page 62
Publishers Weekly, August 10, 2009, page 58
School Library Journal, September 2009, page 156
Voice of Youth Advocates, December 2009, page 415

Other books by the same author:
Viola in the Spotlight, 2011

Other books you might like:
Ann Brashares, *The Sisterhood of the Traveling Pants*, 2001
Jen Calonita, *Sleepaway Girls*, 2009
John Green, *Looking for Alaska*, 2005
E. Lockhart, *The Disreputable History of Frankie Landau-Banks: A Novel*, 2008
Tracy Mack, *Birdland*, 2003

1134

MEGAN WHALEN TURNER

A Conspiracy of Kings
(New York: Greenwillow Books, 2010)

Series: Queen's Thief Series. Book 4
Subject(s): Monarchs; Adolescence; Adventure
Age range(s): 13 - 18+
Major character(s): Sophos, Teenager, Heir (to throne of Sounis); Eugenides, Friend (of Sophos), Royalty (King of Attolia)
Time period(s): Indeterminate Past
Locale(s): Sounis, Fictional Location

Summary: *A Conspiracy of Kings* is the fourth novel in The Queen's Thief series by Megan Whalen Turner. Perspective shifts in this book to Sophos, a teenager who is heir to the throne in the kingdom of Sounis. Sophos does not want this responsibility. He is sent to live in the country, where he is eventually captured and placed in slavery after an attack on the kingdom leads to the rest of his family being killed. As time passes, Sophos realizes the error of his ways and decides to escape and try to reclaim his rightful place on the throne. Sophos goes to see his friend Eugenides, ruler of the kingdom of Attolia, to request his help in taking the kingdom of Sounis back. This is no easy undertaking, but Sophos is now

determined to do everything he can to fulfill his responsibility.

Where it's reviewed:
Booklist, February 1, 2010, page 76
Horn Book Magazine, March/April 2010, page 75
Publishers Weekly, February 15, 2010, page 132
Voice of Youth Advocates, August 2010, page 275

Other books by the same author:
The King of Attolia, 2006
The Queen of Attolia, 2000
The Thief, 1996

Awards the book has won:
Los Angeles Times Book Award: Young Adult Fiction, 2010

Other books you might like:
Leah Cypess, *Mistwood*, 2010
John Dickinson, *The Fatal Child*, 2008
Catherine Fisher, *Incarceron*, 2007
Zoe Marriott, *Daughter of the Flames*, 2009

1135

PAMELA S. TURNER
ANDY COMINS, Illustrator

The Frog Scientist
(Boston: Houghton Mifflin Books for Children, 2009)

Subject(s): Science; Frogs; Nature

Age range(s): 11 - 15+

Summary: In *The Frog Scientist*, author Pamela Turner chronicles the career of amphibian scientist Tyrone Hayes as he investigates the cause of increased frog deaths around the world. Now a respected authority in his field, Hayes began collecting frogs in Columbia, South Carolina, and eventually pursued his interest in science at Harvard University, where a professor noticed the young African-American man's unique challenges and potential. Through his lab work at Berkeley, Hayes discovered a connection between the pesticide atrazine and the decline in frog populations. Photographs by Andy Comins supplement the text.

Where it's reviewed:
Booklist, August 1, 2009, page 66
Horn Book Magazine, Sept.-Oct. 2009, page 585
School Library Journal, September 2009, page 185

Other books by the same author:
Project Seahorse, 2010
Prowling the Seas: Exploring the Hidden World of Ocean Predators, 2009
A Life in the Wild: George Schaller's Struggle to Save the Last Great Beasts, 2008

Other books you might like:
Nic Bishop, *Nic Bishop Frogs*, 2008
Garry Hamilton, *Frog Rescue: Changing the Future for Endangered Wildlife*, 2004
Mark W. Moffett, *Face to Face with Frogs*, 2008

1136

JENNY VALENTINE

Broken Soup

(New York: HarperCollins, 2009)

Subject(s): Grief; Friendship; Mystery

Age range(s): 14 - 18+

Major character(s): Rowan, 15-Year-Old; Stroma, Sister; Bee, Friend

Time period(s): 21st century; 2000s

Locale(s): United Kingdom

Summary: In Jenny Valentine's *Broken Soup*, Rowan is a 15-year-old girl struggling to get by. Her beloved older brother has recently died, and her mother is so paralyzed with grief that she can't get out of bed. Her father has abandoned the family, leaving Rowan to care for her kid sister, Stroma. Rowan is just trying to make it through each day without falling apart, but her life is further complicated by a young man on the street who hands her a photo negative. After getting the negative developed, Rowan finds that it is a picture of her late brother. This propels the young woman into the biggest adventure of her life, filled with mystery, healing, and unexpected friendship.

Where it's reviewed:
Booklist, February 15, 2009, page 71
Horn Book Magazine, May/June 2009, page 309
Publishers Weekly, April 6, 2009, page 49
School Library Journal, April 2009, page 143

Other books by the same author:
Me, the Missing, and the Dead, 2008
Finding Violet Park, 2007

Other books you might like:
Karen Foxlee, *The Anatomy of Wings*, 2007
E.R. Frank, *Wrecked: A Novel*, 2005
David Hernandez, *No More Us for You*, 2009
Sarah Ockler, *Twenty Boy Summer*, 2009
Ellen Yeomans, *Rubber Houses*, 2007

1137

SUSAN VANHECKE

Raggin' Jazzin' Rockin': A History of American Musical Instrument Makers

(Honesdale, Pennsylvania: Boyds Mills Pres, 2011)

Subject(s): Music; Musicians; History

Age range(s): 11 - 14+

Summary: Music writer Susan VanHecke introduces young-adult readers to some of history's most important musical instrument innovations, and the men who created them. The Zildjian name is prominently displayed on cymbals played by popular bands around the world, but the company's roots lie in 17th century Turkey where Avedis Zildjian created the instrument's unique alloy. The world-renowned Steinway piano is the realization of a German carpenter's goal when he immigrated to America. Illustrated with more than 200 color photos, this volume describes the amazing stories of our best-loved instruments, including Fender electric guitars, Martin acoustic guitars, Moog synthesizers, and Ludwig drums.

Where it's reviewed:
Booklist, May 1, 2011, page 73
Bulletin of the Center for Children's Books, May 2011, page 443
Horn Book Guide, Fall 2011, page 455
School Library Journal, May 2011, page 140
Voice of Youth Advocates, April 2011, page 93

Other books you might like:
Neil Ardley, *Music*, 1989
     Stephen M. Tomecek, author
Robert Ziegler, *Great Musicians*, 2008

1138

PADMA VENKATRAMAN

Island's End

(New York: G.P. Putnam's Sons, 2011)

Story type: Coming-of-Age

Subject(s): Islands; Tribalism; Modern Life

Age range(s): 13 - 16+

Major character(s): Uido, 15-Year-Old, Leader (spiritual)

Time period(s): 21st century; 2010s

Summary: A young woman from an isolated island tribe must confront the challenges and dangers of modernity in this coming-of-age novel for young adult readers from author Padma Venkatraman. Uido is a fifteen-year-old girl living on an isolated island where her tribe, composed of forty families, enjoys a simple, primitive way of life, unaffected by the advances of the modern world. When Uido is appointed to the post of spiritual leader of the tribe—thanks to her Otherworldly dreams—her older brother and her best friend turn their backs on her. As tourists from the mainland begin visiting the island, the natives are swayed by their gifts and modern way of life. When Uido's brother becomes deathly ill, Uido must travel to the mainland in search of medical help, but once she observes their way of life, how will she return to the simple existence she's known for so long?

Where it's reviewed:
Booklist, September 15, 2011, page 61
Publishers Weekly, June 13, 2011, page 50
School Library Journal, August 2011, page 124
Voice of Youth Advocates, October 2011, page 396

Other books by the same author:
Climbing the Stairs, 2008

Other books you might like:
Jamie Bastedo, *On Thin Ice*, 2006
Kathleen O'Neal Gear, *Children of the Dawnland*, 2009
Patrick Ness, *Monsters of Men*, 2010
Celia Rees, *Sorceress*, 2002

1139

SHIRLEY REVA VERNICK

The Blood Lie

(El Paso, Texas: Cinco Puntos Press, 2011)

Story type: Historical
Subject(s): Antisemitism; Prejudice; Jews

Age range(s): 13 - 16+
Major character(s): Jack Pool, 16-Year-Old, Crime Suspect; Emaline, Teenager, Sister (of Daisy); Daisy, Child, Missing Person, Sister (of Emaline)
Time period(s): 20th century; 1920s (1928)
Locale(s): Massena, New York

Summary: In this historical novel for young adults by Shirley Reva Vernick, 16-year-old Jack Pool looks forward to leaving the stifling atmosphere of his upstate New York town. It is the autumn of 1928, and the season's Jewish holidays have commanded extra attendance at temple where Jack distracts himself with fantasies about his future as a cellist. He also spends a lot of time thinking about his feelings for Emaline, a Christian girl, although he knows his love for her is futile. When Emaline's younger sister Daisy disappears, Jack becomes a suspect. Fueled by gossip and a spirit of anti-Semitism, a false story of Jack's involvement in a blood libel spreads, and the Pools find themselves in danger in their own community. A 2012 Sydney Taylor Award Honor Book, this novel is based on events from the author's family history. First novel.

Where it's reviewed:
Booklist, November 15, 2011, page 52
School Library Journal, November 2011, page 142

Other books you might like:
Karen Hesse, *Witness*, 2001
Alice Hoffman, *Incantation*, 2006
Kathryn Lasky, *Blood Secret*, 2004
Mirjam Pressler, *Let Sleeping Dogs Lie*, 2007

1140

SIOBHAN VIVIAN

Same Difference

(New York: PUSH, 2009)

Subject(s): Artists; Self confidence; Self esteem

Age range(s): 14 - 17+
Major character(s): Emily, 16-Year-Old, Student—High School, Friend (of Meg), Artist; Meg, Friend (of Emily), Student—High School, Girlfriend (of Rick); Fiona, Student, Artist; Robyn, Student, Artist; Adrian, Student, Artist; Rick, Boyfriend (of Meg); Yates, Teacher (assistant at Emily's art school)
Time period(s): 21st century; 2000s
Locale(s): Cherry Grove, New Jersey; Philadelphia, Pennsylvania

Summary: For the last five summers, Emily and Meg have been inseparable. This summer, however, is different. Meg has a boyfriend, Rick, and Emily is going to take art classes at the Philadelphia College for Fine Arts.

Even though it is only three days a week, Emily soon learns that the city is entirely different from the gated suburban community where she has spent all of her life. The people Emily meets at the college are unlike any she has ever encountered, especially Fiona, Robyn, and Adrian. At first, Fiona and Emily don't get along, but they soon come to a mutual understanding. Yates, Emily's teaching assistant and first year college student, is interested in Emily's artistic ability. He is also interested in Emily. Before she realizes it, Emily's life changes, and she is not sure she likes the differences. As the summer ends, Emily reflects on the person she was and the artist she has the potential to become.

Where it's reviewed:
Booklist, May 1, 2009, page 74
Publishers Weekly, March 2, 2009, page 62
School Library Journal, May 2009, page 118

Other books by the same author:
Not That Kind of Girl, 2010
A Little Friendly Advice, 2008

Other books you might like:
Autumn Cornwell, *Carpe Diem*, 2007
Julie Halpern, *Into the Wild Nerd Yonder*, 2009
Marisabina Russo, *A Portrait of Pia*, 2007
Sasha Watson, *Vidalia in Paris*, 2008

1141

PAUL VOLPONI

Response

(New York: Viking, 2009)

Subject(s): Racism; Urban life; African Americans

Age range(s): 12 - 16+
Major character(s): Noah, 17-Year-Old, Teenager, Father, Crime Victim
Time period(s): 21st century; 2000s
Locale(s): United States

Summary: *Response* is a young adult novel about racial issues and urban life from author Paul Volponi. Seventeen-year-old Noah, and his two friends—all African Americans—devise a plan to go to a predominately white area to steal a car and sell it for parts. Noah is hesitant to take part in the crime but is in desperate need of money for his young daughter. The three guys head to the Italian-American neighborhood, but before they can steal a car, they are attacked by three white boys. Noah's friends narrowly escape leaving him behind to withstand a vicious and brutal beating that results in a fractured skull. Was the attack a provoked act of self-defense or a malicious hate crime because of Noah's race? These are the questions that are examined in *Response*. With alternating viewpoints, the novel gives readers a glimpse into the minds of individuals on both sides of hate crimes.

Where it's reviewed:
Booklist, November 15, 2008, page 39
School Library Journal, March 2009, page 157

Other books by the same author:
Crossing Lines, 2011

Rikers High, 2010
Homestretch, 2009
Rucker Park Setup, 2007
Black and White, 2005

Other books you might like:
Pamela Ehrenberg, *Tillmon County Fire*, 2009
Bob Krech, *Rebound*, 2006
James Lecesne, *Absolute Brightness*, 2008
Kekla Magoon, *The Rock and the River*, 2009
Robert Sharenow, *My Mother the Cheerleader*, 2007

1142

PAUL VOLPONI

Homestretch

(New York: Atheneum Books for Young Readers, 2009)

Subject(s): Horse racing; Adolescence; Grief

Age range(s): 13 - 16+
Major character(s): Gaston Giambanco, Teenager,
   Runaway
Time period(s): 21st century; 2000s
Locale(s): Arkansas, United States

Summary: In *Homestretch* by Paul Volponi, teenager Gaston Giambanco grew up in Texas; a few months ago, his mother was killed in a car accident when an illegal immigrant, or "beaner" as Gas calls them, ran a stop sign and hit her head on. After that, his father began drinking and became more and more abusive, until Gas finally decides to take off. He finds himself in the back of a pickup truck heading north, realizing to his horror that he's stuck with a bunch of beaners. He ends up at a horseracing farm, where one of the trainers agrees to give Gas a job as well. He works his way up until he becomes a jockey, going through more hardships along the way than he could have imagined. He also addresses his prejudices along the way, however, and begins to find a family in the most unexpected of places.

Where it's reviewed:
Booklist, September 15, 2009, page 49
Horn Book Guide, Spring 2010, page 111
Publishers Weekly, September 21, 2009, page 60
School Library Journal, December 2009, page 135

Other books by the same author:
Crossing Lines, 2011
Rikers High, 2010
Response, 2009
The Hand You're Dealt, 2008
Rucker Park Setup, 2007

Other books you might like:
Matt de la Pena, *We Were Here*, 2009
Will Hobbs, *The Maze*, 1998
Eric Luper, *Bug Boy*, 2009
Alan Watt, *Diamond Dogs*, 2000

1143

PAUL VOLPONI

Rikers High

(New York: Viking, 2010)

Subject(s): Prisons; Prisoners; Crime

Age range(s): 14 - 17+
Major character(s): Martin Stokes, 17-Year-Old, Criminal,
   Prisoner
Time period(s): 21st century; 2010s
Locale(s): New York, New York

Summary: *Rikers High* is a teen version of Paul Volponi's prison-based adult novel, *Rikers*. Seventeen-year-old Martin Stokes is serving time in jail on Rikers Island after unintentionally committing a petty crime. After five months in jail, Martin gets inadvertently caught in the middle of a violent attack between two fellow prisoners that leaves a vicious scar along his face. Martin is transferred to another part of the jail after the altercation, which allows him to attend high school. Although Martin's heart has been hardened from his five months in jail, the slow and steady relationship he builds with an encouraging teacher challenges Martin to reevaluate his life, his future, and his choices.

Where it's reviewed:
Booklist, December 1, 2009, page 38
Horn Book Guide, Fall 2010, page 384
Publishers Weekly, January 18, 2010, page 50
School Library Journal, January 2010, page 115
Voice of Youth Advocates, April 2010, page 64

Other books by the same author:
Crossing Lines, 2011
Response, 2009
The Hand You're Dealt, 2008
Rucker Park Setup, 2007
Rooftop, 2006

Other books you might like:
Paul Griffin, *Ten Mile River*, 2008
Susan Kuklin, *No Choirboy: Murder, Violence, and
   Teenagers on Death Row*, 2008
Walter Dean Myers, *Lockdown*, 2010
Adam Rapp, *The Buffalo Tree*, 1997

1144

ADRIENNE MARIA VRETTOS

Burnout

(New York: Margaret K. McElderry Books, 2011)

Story type: Contemporary
Subject(s): Drug abuse; Alcoholism; Mental disorders

Age range(s): 15 - 18+
Major character(s): Nan Masterson, Student—High
   School, Alcoholic (recovering), Friend (of Seemy);
   Seemy, Friend (of Nan)
Time period(s): 21st century; 2010s
Locale(s): New York, New York

Summary: In this young adult novel by Adrienne Maria Vrettos, a teenage girl battling alcoholism experiences a shocking setback. Nan Masterson's drinking had been completely out of control, but a stay in rehab was supposed to have given her a new start. Now, after months of being sober, she wakes up on a New York subway train with no recollection of the past 24 hours. It is November 1 and Nan's feet are bare, her hair has been chopped off, her arms are scratched, and she's wearing a Halloween costume that isn't hers. Sick and confused, Nan recalls events from the recent and distant past in flashbacks, eventually realizing that her one-time friend, Seemy, is in serious trouble.

Where it's reviewed:
Bulletin of the Center for Children's Books, October 2011, page 116
Library Media Connection, November-December 2011, page 79
School Library Journal, October 2011, page 151
Voice of Youth Advocates, August 2011, page 282

Other books by the same author:
The Exile of Gigi Lane, 2010
Sight, 2007
Skin, 2006

Other books you might like:
Blake Nelson, *Recovery Road*, 2011
Amy Lynn Reed, *Clean*, 2011
Benjamin Alire Saenz, *Last Night I Sang to the Monster*, 2009
Elizabeth Scott, *Love You Hate You Miss You*, 2009

1145

SALLY M. WALKER

Written in Bone: Buried Lives of Jamestown and Colonial Maryland

(Minneapolis, Minnesota: Carolrhoda Books, 2009)

Subject(s): Anthropology; United States history, 1600-1775 (Colonial period); Archaeology

Age range(s): 12 - 16+

Summary: *Written in Bone: Buried Lives of Jamestown and Colonial Maryland*, by Sally M. Walker, is an examination through archaeology and forensic anthropology of the lives of the colonists living in Jamestown and the surrounding area during the 16th and 17th centuries. Walker examines different methods of burial for different classes and discusses the way in which skeletal remains give specific clues to the way of life during this time. Walker also discusses how forensic scientists use skeletal remains to determine age, gender, and ethnicity of a human being. Photographs, maps, drawings, and historic documents illustrate the text and provide additional information.

Where it's reviewed:
Booklist, February 1, 2009, page 41
Horn Book Magazine, May/June 2009, page 328
School Library Journal, February 2009, page 127

Other books by the same author:

Frozen Secrets: Antarctica Revealed, 2010
Secrets of a Civil War Submarine: Solving the Mysteries of the H.L. Hunleyy, 2005
Fossil Fish Found Alive: Discovering the Coelacanth, 2002

Other books you might like:
Marc Aronson, *If Stones Could Speak: Unlocking the Secrets of Stonehenge*, 2010
Janet Buell, *Greenland Mummies*, 1998
Danielle Denega, *Skulls and Skeletons: True-Life Stories of Bone Detectives*, 2007
Robert Gardner, *Forensic Science Projects with a Crime Lab You Can Build*, 2007
Lorraine Jean Hopping, *Bone Detective: The Story of Forensic Anthropologist Diane France*, 2005

1146

JASON WALLACE

Out of Shadows

(New York: Holiday House, 2011)

Subject(s): Race relations; Conduct of life; Bullying

Age range(s): 15 - 18+

Major character(s): Jacklin, Student—Boarding School; Ivan, Classmate (of Jacklin), Bully; Robert Mugabe, Leader (president)

Time period(s): 20th century; 1980s

Locale(s): Zimbabwe

Summary: Jason Wallace's *Out of Shadows* takes place in Zimbabwe during the 1980s and focuses on a young white student who feels the affects of apartheid. Jacklin slowly awakens to both the white population's concerns and the oppression his black schoolmates face every day. Jacklin's moral dilemma reaches epic proportions when President Robert Mugabe pays a visit to his school. Complications arise when Jacklin learns that one of his racist classmates has hatched a plan to assassinate the black leader. First novel.

Where it's reviewed:
Booklist, March 1, 2011, page 57
Horn Book Guide, Fall 2011, page 401
School Library Journal, April 2011, page 187
Voice of Youth Advocates, August 2011, page 282

Other books you might like:
Anton Ferreira, *Zulu Dog*, 2002
John Van de Ruit, *Spud*, 2007
Michael Williams, *Now Is the Time for Running*, 2011

1147

RICH WALLACE

Perpetual Check

(New York: Knopf Books for Young Readers, 2009)

Subject(s): Sibling rivalry; Father-son relations; Brothers

Age range(s): 14 - 17+

Major character(s): Zeke, Brother (of Randy), Student—High School, Chess Player; Randy, Brother (of Zeke), Student—High School, Chess Player
Time period(s): 21st century; 2000s
Locale(s): Scranton, Pennsylvania

Summary: In Rich Wallace's *Perpetual Check*, two brothers, who seem to be polar opposites in every respect, learn about life, love, brotherhood, and how to cope with family struggles through the game of chess. Zeke and Randy have a sibling rivalry that is spurred by their aggressive father and his competitive spirit. Zeke, a senior, is adept at a great many things in life and follows in his father's footsteps. Randy, a freshman, takes a more relaxed approach to everything, and finds his perspective to be an asset, particularly in playing chess against his brother. When the two find themselves competing against each other at the regional high school chess championship, instead of encouraging their sibling rivalry, the match helps the brothers realize the ways in which they can help each other.

Where it's reviewed:
Booklist, January 1, 2009, page 71
School Library Journal, February 2009, page 112
Voice of Youth Advocates, June 2009, page 144

Other books by the same author:
War and Watermelon, 2011
One Good Punch, 2007
Losing Is Not an Option, 2003
Restless, 2003
Wrestling Sturbridge, 1996

Awards the book has won:
Blue Ribbon Awards: Fiction, 2009

Other books you might like:
Garret Freymann-Weyr, *The Kings Are Already Here*, 2003
V. M. Jones, *Out of Reach*, 2008
Alfred C. Martino, *Pinned*, 2005
Daniel Nayeri, *Another Faust*, 2009
Will Weaver, *Hard Ball*, 1998

1148

RACHEL WARD

Numbers

(Somerset, United Kingdom: The Chicken House, 2010)

Series: Numbers Series. Book 1
Subject(s): Adolescent interpersonal relations; Psychics; Death

Age range(s): 14 - 18+
Major character(s): Jem, Psychic; Spider, Friend (of Jem)
Time period(s): 21st century; 2010s
Locale(s): London, England

Summary: Rachel Ward's *Numbers* follows the adventures of Jem, an adolescent girl with an unsettling gift: she can predict when people will die. She soon meets Spider, a black youth who is just as must a loner as she is. The two go to London for the day, where Jem is shocked to find that all those riding the London Eye Ferris Wheel are going to die. Now it's up to Jem and Spider to avert catastrophe while convincing the world Jem's gifts are very real. First novel.

Where it's reviewed:
Booklist, December 15, 2009, page 36
Horn Book Guide, Fall 2010, page 385
Publishers Weekly, January 4, 2010, page 48
School Library Journal, January 2010, page 115

Other books by the same author:
The Chaos, 2011
Infinity, 2011

Other books you might like:
Holly Black, *White Cat*, 2010
Meg Cabot, *Sanctuary*, 2007
Siobhan Dowd, *The London Eye Mystery*, 2008
Alyson Noel, *Evermore: A Novel*, 2009
Alisa Valdes-Rodriguez, *Haters*, 2006

1149

JESSICA WARMAN

Breathless

(New York: Walker Books, 2009)

Subject(s): Boarding schools; Brothers and sisters; Mental disorders

Age range(s): 15 - 18+
Major character(s): Katie Kitrell, Student—Boarding School; Will Kitrell, Brother (of Katie), Mentally Ill Person; Mazzie, Roommate (of Katie)
Time period(s): 21st century; 2000s
Locale(s): Pennsylvania, United States

Summary: In *Breathless* by Jessica Warman, Katie Kitrell leaves her small town in Pennsylvania for boarding school to advance her swimming career. But swimming isn't the only reason Katie leaves home; she's also escaping her family—a psychiatrist father, an alcoholic mother, and a schizophrenic brother, Will. At her new school, Katie makes friends, finds a boyfriend, and shines on the swim team. But lies Katie has told about her family (she has claimed that her brother is dead) quickly catch up with her when Will's violence reaches new heights. Although her roommate Mazzie knows the Kitrells' story, Katie's devout boyfriend may not be able to handle the truth.

Where it's reviewed:
Booklist, September 1, 2009, page 105
Horn Book Guide, Spring 2010, page 111
School Library Journal, November 2009, page 124

Other books by the same author:
Where the Truth Lies, 2010

Other books you might like:
Chris Crutcher, *Stotan!*, 1986
Tessa Duder, *In Lane Three, Alex Archer*, 1987
Ann Gonzalez, *Running for My Life*, 2009
Megan McCafferty, *Sloppy Firsts*, 2001
Mary E. Pearson, *The Miles Between*, 2009

1150

JESSICA WARMAN

Between

(New York: Walker, 2011)

Story type: Contemporary
Subject(s): Death; Family; Afterlife

Age range(s): 16 - 18+
Major character(s): Liz Valchar, 18-Year-Old, Spirit; Alex Berg, Accident Victim, Spirit
Time period(s): 21st century; 2010s
Locale(s): New York, New York

Summary: A teenage girl newly arrived in the afterlife searches for answers about her death and life in this young-adult novel by Jessica Warman. Liz Valchar's last night was spent on her family's yacht on Long Island Sound, where she was celebrating her 18th birthday with a group of friends. The next morning, when she investigates a banging sound on the side of the boat, Nan discovers her own corpse floating in the water. From the spirit realm Nan tries to find out how she died, and in the process learns unpleasant truths about her seemingly ideal life. A deceased classmate, Alex Berg, helps Nan with her investigation.

Where it's reviewed:
Booklist, September 15, 2011, page 75
Bulletin of the Center for Children's Books, July-August 2011, page 545
School Library Journal, September 2011, page 176
Voice of Youth Advocates, October 2011, page 412

Other books by the same author:
Where the Truth Lies, 2010
Breathless, 2009

Other books you might like:
Gayle Forman, *If I Stay*, 2009
Lauren Oliver, *Before I Fall*, 2010
Tracey Porter, *Lark*, 2011
Neal Shusterman, *Everfound*, 2011

1151

ROBISON WELLS

Variant

(New York: HarperCollins, 2011)

Story type: Science Fiction
Subject(s): Boarding schools; Schools; Adolescent interpersonal relations

Age range(s): 14 - 17+
Major character(s): Benson Fisher, Foster Child, Student— Boarding School
Time period(s): 21st century; 2010s
Locale(s): New Mexico, United States

Summary: In this novel, author Robison Wells tells the story of a boarding school that harbors some deadly secrets. Benson Fisher has spent most of his life being shuffled among foster families, and he has never really settled in one place for long. When he earns a scholarship to a boarding school called Maxfield Academy, Benson is sure his life will turn around. Finally he can put down roots and begin to work toward a better future. However, Maxfield Academy is nothing like he expected; the grounds are surrounded by barbed wire and the absence of adults has forced students to fend for themselves by forming three gangs. As Benson seeks escape from this prisonlike school, he begins to learn more and more secrets about Maxfield Academy. Then Benson realizes that the school holds one final—and perhaps deadly—secret that he must learn.

Where it's reviewed:
Booklist, October 15, 2011, page 47
Publishers Weekly, August 15, 2011, page 73
Voice of Youth Advocates, October 2011, page 413

Other books you might like:
James Dashner, *The Maze Runner*, 2009
April Henry, *Shock Point*, 2006
Veronica Roth, *Divergent*, 2011
Alexander Gordon Smith, *Lockdown*, 2009
Todd Strasser, *Boot Camp*, 2007

1152

CONRAD WESSELHOEFT

Adios, Nirvana

(Boston, Massachusetts: Houghton Mifflin Harcourt, 2010)

Subject(s): Twins; Death; Writing

Age range(s): 15 - 18+
Major character(s): Jonathan, 16-Year-Old, Writer, Twin
Time period(s): 21st century; 2010s
Locale(s): United States

Summary: It's been an entire year since the death of Jonathan's twin brother and he's doing everything he can to keep his head above water. Last year, during sophomore year, Jonathan won an esteemed prize for poetry. This year, he's barely passing 11th grade. Jonathan is ready to throw in the towel on school and life, but his friends and family won't allow him to give in so easily. In a last-ditch effort to pass junior year, Jonathan is tasked with writing the biography of a WWII vet, an assignment that his English teacher and principal believe will teach him a lot more than writing technique. First novel.

Where it's reviewed:
Booklist, September 15, 2010, page 64
Horn Book Guide, Spring 2011, page 115
Publishers Weekly, September 27, 2010, page 63
School Library Journal, November 2010, page 133
Voice of Youth Advocates, December 2010, page 464

Other books you might like:
Carolyn MacCullough, *Drawing the Ocean*, 2006
Jandy Nelson, *The Sky Is Everywhere*, 2010
Jeri Smith-Ready, *Shade*, 2010
Rob Thomas, *Rats Saw God*, 1996

1153

SCOTT WESTERFELD
KEITH THOMPSON, Illustrator

Leviathan

(New York: Simon Pulse, 2009)

Series: Leviathan Trilogy. Book 1
Subject(s): World War I, 1914-1918; Love; Loyalty

Age range(s): 11 - 16+
Major character(s): Prince Aleksander "Alek", Orphan,
    Son (of Archduke Ferdinand), Boyfriend (of Deryn);
    Deryn, Girlfriend (of Alek), Orphan (from Scotland)
Time period(s): 20th century; 1900s (1914)
Locale(s): England; *Leviathan*, Fictional Location;
    Switzerland

Summary: Scott Westerfeld's historical novel *Leviathan*
imagines what the battles of the great war, World War I,
would have been like if biotechnology were an option in
the design of military weapons and vehicles. Submarines
are shaped like whales with the capacity to swim to
unknown depths and insect-like planes pluck people right
out of the sky. In this alternate 1914 Edwardian society,
two orphans from very different backgrounds, Alek and
Deryn, form an unlikely bond in order to help one
another survive, while living, breathing ships and planes
wage war all around them. This is the first book in a
trilogy.

Where it's reviewed:
Booklist, August 1, 2009, page 58
Horn Book Magazine, November/December 2009, page
    689
Publishers Weekly, August 24, 2009, page 62
School Library Journal, September 2009, page 176
Voice of Youth Advocates, October 2009, page 336

Other books by the same author:
Goliath, 2011
Behemoth, 2010

Other books you might like:
Anina Bennett, *Boilerplate: History's Mechanical
    Marvel*, 2009
Richard Harland, *Worldshaker*, 2010
Cherie Priest, *Boneshaker*, 2009
Philip Reeve, *A Web of Air*, 2010
Arthur G. Slade, *The Hunchback Assignments*, 2009

1154

SCOTT WESTERFELD
KEITH THOMPSON, Illustrator

Behemoth

(New York: Simon Pulse, 2010)

Series: Leviathan Trilogy. Book 2
Subject(s): Genetic engineering; Wars; Royalty

Age range(s): 13 - 17+
Major character(s): Alek, Royalty (prince); Deryn,
    Military Personnel (British Air Service)

Time period(s): 20th century; 1910s (1914)
Locale(s): *Leviathan*, Fictional Location; Istanbul, Turkey

Summary: The second novel in Scott Westerfeld's
Leviathan series, *Behemoth* continues the adventures of
Alek, a prince being hunted by Germans in an alternative version of World War I Europe. Hoping to avoid
capture, he books passage on the ship called *Leviathan*,
where he meets Deryn, a young man harboring a shocking secret. Together, Alek and Deryn must join forces to
take on the enemy, which gets stronger and more
technologically advanced with each passing day. *Behemoth* includes illustrations by Keith Thompson.

Where it's reviewed:
Booklist, October 15, 2010, page 51
Horn Book Magazine, November/December 2010, page
    107
Publishers Weekly, September 13, 2010, page 46
School Library Journal, October 2010, page 128
Voice of Youth Advocates, October 2010, page 377

Other books by the same author:
Goliath, 2011
Leviathan, 2009

Other books you might like:
Richard Harland, *Worldshaker*, 2010
Caitlin Kittredge, *The Iron Thorn*, 2011
Kenneth Oppel, *Skybreaker*, 2005
Philip Reeve, *A Web of Air*, 2010

1155

JOHN COREY WHALEY

Where Things Come Back

(New York: Atheneum Books, 2011)

Story type: Coming-of-Age
Subject(s): Adolescent interpersonal relations; Birds;
    Extinct animals

Age range(s): 14 - 18+
Major character(s): Cullen Witter, Boy, 17-Year-Old; John
    Barling, Neighbor (bird watcher)
Time period(s): 21st century; 2010s
Locale(s): Lily, Arkansas

Summary: In this book, debut author John Corey Whaley
adapts the true story of the rediscovery of a bird species
into a fictional account of a teenager coming of age in
small-town America. Cullen Witter is a 17-year-old boy
growing up in the tiny community of Lily, Arkansas.
Life seems fairly mundane for Cullen until a local bird
aficionado named John Barling announces that he has
seen a particular species of woodpecker that was previously thought to be extinct. Suddenly, Lily is in an
uproar, and the town becomes packed with visitors,
scientists, and experts trying to determine if Barling's
findings are correct. Meanwhile, thousands of miles
away, an African missionary attempts to regain his faith
in God. As these stories interconnect, Cullen must also
face the devastating discovery that his younger brother
has gone missing. First novel.

Where it's reviewed:
Booklist, July 1, 2011, page 56
Horn Book Guide, Fall 2011, page 402
Publishers Weekly, April 11, 2011, page 55

School Library Journal, July 2011, page 110
Voice of Youth Advocates, June 2011, page 196

Awards the book has won:
Michael L. Printz Award, 2012
William C. Morris Award, 2012

Other books you might like:
Sean Beaudoin, *Fade to Blue*, 2009
Tim Gallagher, *The Grail Bird: Hot on the Trail of the Ivory-Billed Woodpecker*, 2005
Meg Rosoff, *There Is No Dog*, 2011

1156

KIERSTEN WHITE

Paranormalcy
(New York: HarperTeen, 2010)

Series: Paranormalcy Series. Book 1
Story type: Paranormal; Series
Subject(s): Fantasy; Romances (Fiction); Identity

Age range(s): 14 - 18+
Major character(s): Evie, 16-Year-Old, Agent (International Paranormal Containment Agency); Lend, Shape-Shifter, Teenager
Time period(s): 21st century; 2010s
Locale(s): United States

Summary: In this first novel in author Kiersten White's Paranormalcy Series, 16-year-old Evie has become bored with her work for the International Paranormal Containment Agency (IPCA). The human agent is valued for her ability to identify and capture paranormal offenders, but she has begun to find her daily duties monotonous. Then she encounters the shapeshifter Lend, a new captive who has experienced life beyond the realm of the IPCA. As Evie recognizes the emergence of romantic feelings for Lend, a dangerous paranormal foretelling is about to come to pass. Evie and Lend must halt the prophecy's fulfillment and learn its role in their relationship. First novel.

Where it's reviewed:
Booklist, October 15, 2010, page 61
Horn Book Guide, Spring 2011, page 115
Publishers Weekly, September 13, 2010, page 47
School Library Journal, December 2010, page 130
Voice of Youth Advocates, October 2010, page 374

Other books by the same author:
Supernaturally, 2011

Other books you might like:
Steve Augarde, *Winter Wood*, 2010
Kelly Keaton, *Darkness Becomes Her*, 2011
Jeri Smith-Ready, *Shade*, 2010
Robert Paul Weston, *Dust City*, 2010

1157

DAVID WHITLEY

The Midnight Charter
(New York: Roaring Brook Press, 2009)

Subject(s): Prophecy; Conduct of life; Astrology
Age range(s): 13 - 16+
Major character(s): Mark, Astrologer; Lily, Care Giver
Time period(s): Indeterminate
Summary: In *The Midnight Charter*, award-winning author David Whitley presents a powerful fantasy saga set in the plague-infested city-state known as Agora. In the slums of the city, two young people are thrown together. Mark is seeking refuge from the plague, and Lily becomes his caretaker. As they fight for survival in money-driven Agora, they must trade, haggle, and barter for everything in their lives. Both Mark and Lily see a way out, however, when they are given a chance to switch fates and take totally different paths in life. As their journeys seemingly separate, the two soon come to realize that their destinies are forever linked.

Where it's reviewed:
Booklist, August 1, 2009, page 58
Horn Book Guide, Spring 2010, page 111
Publishers Weekly, August 3, 2009, page 45
School Library Journal, October 2009, page 140

Other books by the same author:
The Children of the Lost, 2011

Other books you might like:
Clare B. Dunkle, *The Sky Inside*, 2008
Jeanne DuPrau, *The City of Ember*, 2003
Pearl North, *Libyrinth*, 2009

1158

DAISY WHITNEY

The Mockingbirds
(New York: Little, Brown and Company, 2010)

Subject(s): Rape; Boarding schools; Adolescence
Age range(s): 15 - 18+
Major character(s): Alex, Student—Boarding School, Crime Victim, 11th Grader
Time period(s): 21st century; 2010s
Locale(s): Rhode Island, United States

Summary: At Themis Academy, the elite Rhode Island school where Alex is a junior, the school's strict honor code is upheld by the Mockingbirds, a top-secret society dedicated to keeping students on the straight and narrow. When Alex is date raped after a concert, she wrestles with how to proceed. At first, the events of that night are unclear, but as the details return to her memory, she is horrified at what happened. Unwilling to let the horrendous act go by unpunished, yet terrified to go to the police, Alex enlists the help of the Mockingbirds to see that justice is served. First novel.

Where it's reviewed:
Booklist, October 15, 2011, page 60

Horn Book Guide, Spring 2011, page 116
Publishers Weekly, October 18, 2010, page 51
School Library Journal, March 2011, page 175
Voice of Youth Advocates, December 2010, page 464

Other books by the same author:
The Rivals, 2012

Other books you might like:
Chris Lynch, *Inexcusable*, 2005
C.K. Kelly Martin, *One Lonely Degree*, 2009
Alice Sebold, *Lucky*, 1999
Jack Weyland, *Brittany*, 1997

1159

KIM ABLON WHITNEY

The Other Half of Life: A Novel Based on the True Story of the MS St. Louis

(New York: Alfred A. Knopf, 2009)

Subject(s): Jews; Holocaust, 1933-1945; Refugees

Age range(s): 13 - 16+
Major character(s): Thomas Werkmann, 15-Year-Old, Refugee; Priska Affeldt, 14-Year-Old, Refugee
Time period(s): 20th century; 1930s (1939)
Locale(s): *MS St. Louis*, At Sea; Germany; United States

Summary: Author Kim Ablon Whitney envisions the lives of two passengers aboard a ship fleeing Nazi persecution in *The Other Half of Life: A Novel Based on the True Story of the MS St. Louis*. It is the spring of 1939, and the St. Louis has disembarked from Europe, en route to America and, hopefully, freedom from the Nazis' atrocities. 15-year-old Thomas is distraught at having to leave his parents behind; his Jewish father has been arrested and his Christian mother has chosen to stay. Meanwhile, 14-year-old Priska is the picture of optimism: anticipating the excitement of the journey and the new world that lay beyond. As the ship makes its way to America, no one onboard has an inkling of the cruel twist of fate that awaits them at the other end.

Where it's reviewed:
Booklist, April 15, 2009, page 50
School Library Journal, July 2009, page 96

Awards the book has won:
National Jewish Book Award: Children's Literature, 2009

Other books you might like:
Fern Schumer Chapman, *Is It Night or Day?*, 2010
Margarita Engle, *Tropical Secrets: Holocaust Refugees in Cuba*, 2009
Carol Matas, *Daniel's Story*, 1993
Scott Miller, *Refuge Denied: The St. Louis Passengers and the Holocaust*, 2006

1160

K.J. WIGNALL

Blood

(New York: Egmont USA, 2011)

Series: Mercian Trilogy. Book 1
Story type: Horror; Series
Subject(s): Horror; Vampires; Good and evil

Age range(s): 14 - 17+
Major character(s): Will, 16-Year-Old, Heir (to the Earl of Mercia), Vampire; Eloise, 16-Year-Old, Runaway; Jex, Vagrant; Chris, Restaurateur (cafe owner); Rachel, Restaurateur (cafe owner)
Time period(s): 21st century; 2010s

Summary: In this first book in K.J. Wignall's Mercian Trilogy, 750-year-old vampire Will—who remains forever a 16-year-old—wakes up in the 21st century. He has been sleeping since 1980, when he last roamed the earth to satisfy his thirst for blood, and now needs to feed again. When he meets a teenage runaway named Eloise, Will fights the temptation to bite her and nurture his immortality with her blood. Instead, he befriends the mortal girl and seeks her help in solving the mystery of his past. Centuries after he was cursed as one of the undead, Will is still threatened by evil forces from the 13th century and dangerous characters he encounters in the modern realm.

Where it's reviewed:
Booklist, September 1, 2011, page 114
Horn Book Magazine, November-December 2011, page 117
School Library Journal, August 2011, page 124

Other books by the same author:
Alchemy, 2012

Other books you might like:
Kate Cary, *Bloodline Book Two: Reckoning*, 2007
Gena Showalter, *Intertwined*, 2009
Max Turner, *End of Days*, 2010

1161

LILI WILKINSON

Pink

(New York: HarperTeen, 2011)

Story type: Contemporary
Subject(s): Identity; Adolescent interpersonal relations; High schools

Age range(s): 15 - 18+
Major character(s): Ava, 16-Year-Old, Girlfriend (of Chloe), Student—High School (private); Chloe, Girlfriend (of Ava)
Time period(s): 21st century; 2000s
Locale(s): Australia

Summary: A 16-year-old high school student hatches an unusual plan of rebellion and self-discovery in this young-adult novel by Lili Wilkinson. Raised by liberal parents, Ava is extremely cool, dresses in black, and is comfortable in her lesbian relationship with her girl-friend, Chloe. But when she transfers to a prestigious private high school, Ava seizes the opportunity to create a new identity for herself. At Billy Hughes School for Academic Excellence, Ava dresses in pink, hangs out with the theater geeks, and explores her romantic feelings for a male classmate. But keeping her new persona hidden from her parents and Chloe becomes more challenging than Ava imagined, and her seemingly innocent experiment threatens to hurt the people in both halves of her life.

Where it's reviewed:
Booklist, January 1, 2011, page 97
Bulletin of the Center for Children's Books, January 2011, page 256
Horn Book Guide, Fall 2011, page 402
School Library Journal, March 2011, page 176
Voice of Youth Advocates, April 2011, page 71

Other books by the same author:
A Pocketful of Eyes, 2011
Angel Fish, 2010
Scatterheart, 2007
The (Not Quite) Perfect Boyfriend, 2005

Other books you might like:
Lauren Bjorkman, *My Invented Life*, 2009
Michael Cart, *How Beautiful the Ordinary: Twelve Stories of Identity*, 2009
Emily Horner, *A Love Story Starring My Dead Best Friend*, 2010
Melina Marchetta, *Saving Francesca*, 2003

1162

MIKE WILKS

Mirrorscape

(New York: Egmont USA, 2009)

Subject(s): Adventure; Art; Artists

Age range(s): 10 - 15+
Major character(s): Melkin "Mel" Womper, Apprentice; Ludo, Friend; Wren, Friend; Ambrosius Blenk, Artist
Time period(s): Indeterminate Future

Summary: In *Mirrorscape* by Mike Wilks, weaver Melkin Womper jumps at the chance to work as an apprentice to renowned craftsman Ambrosius Blenk. In a world where pleasurable items are regulated with rigid authority by the Fifth Mystery, Mel is eager to have the chance to work with exciting new colors and ideas. But apprentice life is not what he had hoped, and he butts heads with his fellow novices. Things take an unexpected turn to the dark side when Mel finds himself caught in a power struggle between the Fifth Mystery and the Rainbow Rebellion, a group working to make Pleasure accessible to all citizens. To help the Rebellion's cause, Mel and his friends must enter the world of Blenk's paintings, where logic is defied and nothing is as it seems.

Where it's reviewed:
Booklist, October 1, 2009, page 55
Horn Book Guide, Spring 2010, page 111
Publishers Weekly, October 19, 2009, page 55

School Library Journal, December 2009, page 136
Other books you might like:
Tim Bowler, *River Boy*, 2000
Lewis Carroll, *Alice's Adventures in Wonderland*, 1865
Patricia A. McKillip, *Ombria in Shadow*, 2002
Jenny Nimmo, *Charlie Bone and The Shadow*, 2008

1163

CAROL LYNCH WILLIAMS

Glimpse

(New York: Simon and Schuster Books for Young Readers, 2010)

Subject(s): Sisters; Suicide; Adolescence

Age range(s): 15 - 18+
Major character(s): Hope, Child of an Alcoholic, 12-Year-Old, Narrator, Sister (of Lizzie); Lizzie, 14-Year-Old, Sister (of Hope), Mentally Ill Person, Child of an Alcoholic
Time period(s): 21st century; 2010s
Locale(s): United States

Summary: *Glimpse* is a dark novel for young adult readers from author Carol Lynch Williams. Narrated by 12-year-old Hope, the story begins when Hope's older sister, 14-year-old Lizzie, threatens to kill herself. Lizzie is soon admitted to a mental hospital, while Hope grapples with shock and curiosity about her sister's desired suicide. Through flashbacks, readers gain insight into the difficult and trying upbringing that the two young sisters shared. Their father's death and their mother's alcoholism are just two of the hardships they've had to endure. Throughout the book, Hope struggles to find the true reason for Lizzie's suicide attempt and uncovers it in the final pages.

Where it's reviewed:
Booklist, April 15, 2010, page 47
Bulletin of the Center for Children's Books, July/August 2010, page 504
Horn Book Guide, Fall 2010, page 385
Publishers Weekly, May 24, 2010, page 54
School Library Journal, August 2010, page 116

Other books by the same author:
Miles from Ordinary, 2011
The Chosen One, 2009
Pretty Like Us, 2008

Other books you might like:
Gigi Amateau, *Claiming Georgia Tate*, 2005
Ellen Hopkins, *Identical*, 2008
Ellen Hopkins, *Impulse*, 2007
Suzanne Phillips, *Chloe Doe*, 2007

1164

CAROL LYNCH WILLIAMS

Miles from Ordinary

(New York: St. Martin's Griffin, 2011)

Story type: Psychological
Subject(s): Mother-daughter relations; Mental disorders; Family

Age range(s): 12 - 15+

Major character(s): Lacey, 13-Year-Old, Worker (library), Daughter (of Momma), Niece (of Linda); Momma, Mother (of Lacey), Mentally Ill Person; Aunt Linda, Aunt (of Lacey); Aaron, Neighbor (of Lacey)

Time period(s): 21st century; 2010s

Locale(s): Florida, United States

Summary: In this young-adult novel by Carol Lynch Williams, 13-year-old Lacey must care for her mentally ill mother and try to hold their fragile world together. Momma's condition has disrupted most of Lacey's childhood, and her inability to hold a job has pushed them into financial trouble. When Momma seems to experience an improvement, Lacey lines her up with a job at the local market and Lacey assumes her Aunt Linda's position at the library. With the Florida sun shining brightly on their first day at work, Lacey looks forward to a pivotal day in her difficult young life. When Momma wanders away from the store, Lacey leans on Aaron—a neighborhood boy who helps Lacey look for her mother and recognize the seriousness of her situation.

Where it's reviewed:
Booklist, February 15, 2011, page 72
Horn Book Guide, Fall 2011, page 402
Publishers Weekly, January 17, 2011, page 50
School Library Journal, May 2011, page 126
Voice of Youth Advocates, April 2011, page 72

Other books by the same author:
Waiting, 2012
Glimpse, 2010
The Chosen One, 2009
Pretty Like Us, 2008

Other books you might like:
Robin Merrow MacCready, *Buried*, 2006
Han Nolan, *Crazy*, 2010
Holly Schindler, *A Blue So Dark*, 2010

`1165`

CAROL LYNCH WILLIAMS

The Chosen One

(New York: St. Martin's Griffin, 2009)

Subject(s): Cults; Adolescence; Adolescent interpersonal relations

Age range(s): 15 - 18+

Major character(s): Kyra, 13-Year-Old, Cult Member

Time period(s): 21st century; 2000s

Summary: Thirteen-year-old Kyra is trying to find a way out of her stifling life in a compound. A member of a cult since birth, Kyra longs to leave, knowing that there is another world out there where people are not confined by barbed wire and forced to do things they do not want to do. When she gets involved with a boy in the cult, the leader becomes angry and beats her for her disobedience. Then, he tells her that she must marry a relative who is more than 50 years her senior. Her father tries to help

her, but this only makes the leader angrier. Kyra must flee or die.

Where it's reviewed:
Booklist, February 15, 2009, page 71
Horn Book Magazine, May/June 2009, page 311
Publishers Weekly, May 25, 2009, page 58
School Library Journal, July 2009, page 96
Voice of Youth Advocates, June 2009, page 146

Other books by the same author:
Miles from Ordinary, 2011
Glimpse, 2010
Pretty Like Us, 2008
The True Colors of Caitlyn Jackson, 1997

Other books you might like:
Cecilia Galante, *The Patron Saint of Butterflies*, 2008
Michele Dominguez Greene, *Keep Sweet*, 2010
Shelley Hrdlitschka, *Sister Wife*, 2008
Naomi Rich, *Alis*, 2009
Suzanne Fisher Staples, *Shabanu: Daughter of the Wind*, 1989

`1166`

GABRIELLE WILLIAMS

Beatle Meets Destiny

(Tarrytown, New York: Marshall Cavendish, 2010)

Subject(s): Fate; Adolescent interpersonal relations; Humor

Age range(s): 14 - 18+

Major character(s): John "Beatle" Lennon, 12th Grader, Twin; Destiny McCartney, Teenager, Thief

Time period(s): 21st century; 2010s

Locale(s): Australia

Summary: High-school senior John "Beatle" Lennon is heading home early on Friday the 13th to avoid any bizarre events, when he encounters Destiny McCartney on the tram platform. The pair discovers they have far more in common than their names and are instantly intrigued by one another. Unfortunately, Beatle has a girlfriend, who also happens to be BFFs with his twin sister, and Destiny has more than a few secrets of her own and an older brother with a strange connection to Beatle. Their romance seems fated, but the timing is all wrong. What are Lennon and McCartney to do?

Where it's reviewed:
Booklist, September 15, 2010, page 72
Publishers Weekly, October 11, 2010, page 46
School Library Journal, December 2010, page 131
Voice of Youth Advocates, December 2010, page 464

Other books you might like:
Kate Brian, *Lucky T*, 2005
David Levithan, *Dash and Lily's Book of Dares*, 2010
David Levithan, *Will Grayson, Will Grayson*, 2010
Janette Rallison, *How to Take the Ex out of Ex-Boyfriend*, 2007

1167

KATIE WILLIAMS

The Space between Trees

(San Francisco: Chronicle Books, 2010)

Subject(s): Coming of age; Murder; High schools

Age range(s): 14 - 18+

Major character(s): Evie, 16-Year-Old; Elizabeth "Zabet" McCabe, Friend (of Evie); Jonah Luks, Friend (of Evie), Student—College (dropout)

Time period(s): 21st century; 2010s

Locale(s): American Midwest, United States

Summary: In the young adult novel *Space between Trees* by Katie Williams, 16-year-old Evie is one of the oldest kids in her town with a paper route. The job gives her an easy excuse to get out of the house and easy access to neighborhood news. Bored with her surroundings, Evie seeks excitement and has a history of embellishing her stories just to bring some drama into her life. But when her friend Elizabeth "Zabet" McCabe is found dead, Evie's overactive imagination creates more trouble. Evie is pulled into the investigation into Zabet's murder and in the process finds herself at odds with Zabet's father, her best friend, and Evie's own would-be boyfriend, Jonah Luks. First novel.

Where it's reviewed:
Horn Book Guide, Fall 2010, page 386
Publishers Weekly, May 31, 2010, page 50
School Library Journal, May 2010, page 125
Voice of Youth Advocates, August 2010, page 258

Other books you might like:
Kate Brian, *Perfect Mistake*, 2009
Eliot Schrefer, *The Deadly Sister*, 2010
Walter Sorrells, *First Shot*, 2007
Nancy Werlin, *The Killer's Cousin*, 1998

1168

MICHAEL WILLIAMS

Now Is the Time for Running

(New York: Little, Brown and Company, 2011)

Subject(s): Africa; Brothers; Refugees

Age range(s): 13 - 18+

Major character(s): Deo, 14-Year-Old, Soccer Player, Refugee, Brother (of Innocent); Innocent, Teenager, Mentally Challenged Person, Brother (of Deo)

Time period(s): 21st century; 2010s

Locale(s): Zimbabwe

Summary: Two Zimbabwean brothers must run for their lives in this young adult novel from South African author Michael Williams. Fourteen-year-old Deo and his pals are enjoying a soccer match down the road from his small village in Zimbabwe, while Deo's mentally handicapped brother, Innocent, cheers from the sidelines. When their village is ransacked and destroyed by rebel soldiers, the boys must flee the scene immediately. On the run with no shoes and very little money, the brothers face an onslaught of horrific and dangerous setbacks as they struggle to find safety and refuge. When a horrible tragedy strikes, Deo's love for soccer is his only hope for making it through.

Where it's reviewed:
Booklist, September 15, 2011, page 64
Horn Book Magazine, July/August 2011, page 165
Reading Today, August/September 2011, page 37
School Library Journal, September 2011, page 178
Voice of Youth Advocates, August 2011, page 283

Other books by the same author:
The Genuine Half-Moon Kid, 1996
Crocodile Burning, 1994

Other books you might like:
Colleen Craig, *Afrika*, 2008
Judie Oron, *Cry of the Giraffe*, 2010
Mal Peet, *Keeper*, 2005
Jason Wallace, *Out of Shadows*, 2011

1169

SUZANNE MORGAN WILLIAMS

Bull Rider

(New York: Margaret K. McElderry, 2009)

Subject(s): Bulls (Cattle); Sports; Family

Age range(s): 12 - 15+

Major character(s): Cam O'Mara, 14-Year-Old; Ben O'Mara, Brother, Military Personnel

Time period(s): 21st century; 2000s

Locale(s): Nevada, United States

Summary: In *Bull Rider* by Suzanne Morgan Williams, 14-year-old Cam O'Mara doesn't have much desire to take part in the family pastime: bull riding. He'd much rather be skateboarding, working on his technique and hanging out with his friends. But everything changes when Cam's older brother, Ben, returns home from the war in Iraq. Ben has suffered a debilitating brain injury and only wants one thing from his younger sibling: to see Cam take up bull riding. Now it's up to Cam to quite literally take the bull by the horns, learn this challenging and dangerous sport, and fulfill a promise to his brother—a promise that just may give Ben the will to live again.

Where it's reviewed:
Booklist, January 1, 2009, page 64
School Library Journal, April 2009, page 144

Other books you might like:
Lynn Hall, *Flying Changes*, 1991
Marilyn Halvorson, *Bull Rider*, 2003
Walter Dean Myers, *Sunrise over Fallujah*, 2008
Gary D. Schmidt, *Trouble*, 2008
Tim Tharp, *Badd*, 2011

1170

RITA WILLIAMS-GARCIA

Jumped

(New York: HarperCollins, 2009)

Subject(s): High schools; Urban life; Violence

Age range(s): 15 - 17+

Major character(s): Trina, Student; Dominique, Student, Basketball Player; Leticia, Student

Time period(s): 21st century; 2000s

Locale(s): United States

Summary: Rita Williams-Garcia's *Jumped* is a young adult novel told from three shifting perspectives. Trina, Dominique, and Leticia are all students at an urban high school. The three girls lead very different lives. After a perceived slight from the beautiful, popular, and confident Trina, basketball player Dominique promises to beat her up after school. Trina doesn't hear the threat, gossip hound Leticia does. Leticia then must decide if she should warn Trina or if she should just let things play out. The reader gets an in-depth understanding of each character, as the perspective shifts between the three girls throughout the school day. As the day wears on, it becomes clear that all of the girls feel restricted by the roles they play at school.

Where it's reviewed:
Booklist, February 1, 2009, page 41
Horn Book Magazine, March/April 2009, page 205
Publishers Weekly, February 2, 2009, page 50
School Library Journal, March 2009, page 158
Voice of Youth Advocates, August 2009, page 233

Other books by the same author:
One Crazy Summer, 2010
No Laughter Here, 2004
Every Time a Rainbow Dies, 2001
Like Sisters on the Homefront, 1995

Other books you might like:
Paul Griffin, *The Orange Houses*, 2009
Donna Jo Napoli, *Alligator Bayou*, 2009
G. Neri, *Yummy: The Last Days of a Southside Shorty*, 2010
Courtney Summers, *Some Girls Are*, 2010
Ebony Wilkins, *Sellout*, 2010

1171

ALLAN WOLF

The Watch That Ends the Night: Voices from the Titanic

(Somerville, Massachusetts: Candlewick Press, 2011)

Story type: Historical

Subject(s): History; Shipwrecks; Poetry

Age range(s): 15 - 18+

Major character(s): John Jacob Astor, Historical Figure, Wealthy; Molly Brown, Historical Figure; E.J. Smith, Historical Figure, Sea Captain (captain of *Titanic*)

Time period(s): 20th century; 1910s (1912)

Locale(s): *Titanic*, At Sea

Summary: Written in verse, this young-adult novel by Allan Wolf explores the personal stories of the passengers and crew of the *Titanic* as the ship's doomed voyage unfolds. Using archival material and other historic documents, Wolf has re-created 24 tales of those involved in the historic shipwreck. On board are John Jacob Astor and his pregnant young wife; a Lebanese emigrant traveling with her brother; Margaret "Unsinkable Molly" Brown; Captain E.J. Smith; a tailor; a gambler; and others who are each given a voice in this very personal account of the maritime disaster. A rat and the powerful iceberg also share their perspectives on the human tragedy. The novel includes a Morse code guide, *Titanic* memorabilia, and a bibliography.

Where it's reviewed:
Booklist, September 15, 2011, page 62
Bulletin of the Center for Children's Books, October 2011, page 118
Horn Book Magazine, September-October 2011, page 105
School Library Journal, October 2011, page 152
Voice of Youth Advocates, October 2011, page 396

Other books by the same author:
Zane's Trace, 2007
New Found Land: Lewis and Clark's Voyage of Discovery, 2004

Other books you might like:
Claudia Gray, *Fateful*, 2011
Martin Jenkins, *Titanic*, 2007
Suzanne Weyn, *Distant Waves: A Novel of Titanic*, 2009

1172

VIRGINIA EUWER WOLFF

This Full House

(New York: HarperCollins, 2009)

Series: Make Lemonade Trilogy. Book 3

Subject(s): Urban life; Women; Unmarried mothers

Age range(s): 14 - 18+

Major character(s): LaVaughn, Student—High School; Dr. Moore, Teacher; Jolly, Single Mother

Time period(s): 21st century; 2000s

Locale(s): United States

Summary: *This Full House* is the third and final installment in the "Make Lemonade" trilogy. The novel picks up the story of main character LaVaughn as she is about to finish high school, after surviving a rough childhood growing up in the projects. She has recently been admitted to a program called WIMS, which stands for Women in Medical Science, a program designed to give female students a better appreciation of science and medicine. LaVaughn feels this will be her ticket to college, but sudden events in her personal life threaten to derail those plans permanently. Author Virginia Euwer Wolff is an award-winning writer of books for young readers.

Where it's reviewed:
Booklist, December 1, 2008, page 45

Horn Book Magazine, March-April 2009, page 206
Publishers Weekly, December 22, 2008, page 53
School Library Journal, February 2009, page 114

Other books by the same author:
True Believer, 2001
Make Lemonade, 1993

Other books you might like:
Elisa Carbone, *Last Dance on Holladay Street*, 2005
Cecil Castellucci, *The Queen of Cool*, 2006
Janet Mcdonald, *Spellbound*, 2001

1173

JILL WOLFSON

Cold Hands, Warm Heart

(New York: Henry Holt and Co., 2009)

Subject(s): Medical care; Transplantation; Friendship

Age range(s): 14 - 16+

Major character(s): Dani, 15-Year-Old; Wendy, 8-Year-Old; Milo, 17-Year-Old; Amanda, 14-Year-Old, Accident Victim

Time period(s): 21st century; 2000s

Locale(s): United States

Summary: Fifteen-year-old Dani, 8-year-old Wendy, and 17-year-old Milo are all in a hospital at the same time awaiting organ transplants. When Amanda, a 14-year-old gymnast, is killed at a gymnastics meet, Dani and Wendy receive her organs while Milo continues to wait for a second liver transplant after abusing and destroying his first. In many different plot lines, Dani and Milo develop feelings for each other, letters arrive for Amanda's family from the recipients of her other organs, and Amanda's older brother Tyler learns more about her after going through her computer files. The teens must all deal with their extremely challenging emotional situations.

Where it's reviewed:
Booklist, March 15, 2009, page 54
School Library Journal, May 2009, page 119
Voice of Youth Advocates, June 2009, page 146

Other books by the same author:
Home and Other Big, Fat Lies, 2006

Other books you might like:
Lesley Choyce, *Sudden Impact*, 2005
Loretta Ellsworth, *In a Heartbeat*, 2010
Brendan Halpin, *Forever Changes*, 2008
Marthe Jocelyn, *Would You*, 2008
Lurlene McDaniel, *Saving Jessica*, 1996

1174

BRENDA WOODS

Saint Louis Armstrong Beach

(New York: Nancy Paulsen Books, 2011)

Story type: Historical
Subject(s): Hurricanes; Natural disasters; Musicians

Age range(s): 9 - 12+

Major character(s): Saint Louis Armstrong Beach, 11-Year-Old, Musician; Miz Moran, Aged Person, Diabetic; Shadow, Dog

Time period(s): 21st century; 2000s (2005)

Locale(s): New Orleans, Louisiana

Summary: This novel by Brenda Woods focuses on an 11-year-old boy named Saint Louis Armstrong Beach, who ends up stranded in a neighbor's attic when Hurricane Katrina makes landfall in New Orleans. Saint, a promising musician who earns money playing the clarinet on the street, is supposed to leave town during the mandatory evacuation of the city, but he returns to his Treme neighborhood to look for Shadow, the stray dog who follows him everywhere. The hurricane hits before he can leave, and then the levee breaks and the streets flood with water. Saint finds himself trapped in an attic with Shadow and his diabetic neighbor, Miz Moran. There, the unlikely trio waits for the storm to end and for the waters to recede. When Miz Moran runs out of medicine she needs, however, it's up to Saint to save the day.

Where it's reviewed:
Horn Book Magazine, November/December 2011, page 118
Publishers Weekly, August 22, 2011, page 65
School Library Journal, October 2011, page 152

Other books by the same author:
The Red Rose Box, 2002

Other books you might like:
Jane Paley, *Hooper Finds a Family: A Hurricane Katrina Dog's Survival Tale*, 2011
Jewell Parker Rhodes, *Ninth Ward*, 2010
Myron Uhlberg, *A Storm Called Katrina*, 2011
Renee Watson, *A Place Where Hurricanes Happen*, 2011

1175

BLYTHE WOOLSTON

The Freak Observer

(Minneapolis, Minnesota: Carolrhoda, 2010)

Subject(s): Death; Mental disorders; Students

Age range(s): 14 - 17+

Major character(s): Loa Lindgren, 16-Year-Old

Time period(s): 21st century; 2010s

Locale(s): United States

Summary: In *The Freak Observer*, author Blythe Woolston tells the story of 16-year-old Loa Lindgren, a young woman dealing with the death of her friend and the torturous memories of her sister's death. This set of tragedies has led Loa to a diagnosis of post-traumatic stress disorder, a condition she seeks to understand by delving into her schoolwork and exploring the illness from the standpoints of astrophysics and technology. *The Freak Observer* was awarded the William C. Morris Award. First novel.

Where it's reviewed:
Booklist, June 1, 2010, page 53

Horn Book Magazine, September/October 2010, page 99

Publishers Weekly, August 9, 2010, page 54

School Library Journal, December 2010, page 132

Voice of Youth Advocates, February 2011, page 565

Other books by the same author:
Catch and Release, 2012

Awards the book has won:
William C. Morris Award, 2011

Other books you might like:
Crissa-Jean Chappell, *Total Constant Order*, 2007
Melina Marchetta, *Jellicoe Road*, 2008
Dana Reinhardt, *The Things a Brother Knows*, 2010

1176

PATRICIA C. WREDE

Thirteenth Child

(New York: Scholastic Press, 2009)

Series: Frontier Magic Series. Book 1
Subject(s): Twins; Prophecy; Magic

Age range(s): 13 - 16+
Major character(s): Eff, Magician, Twin (of Lan); Lan, Twin (of Eff), Magician
Time period(s): 19th century; 1800s
Locale(s): United States

Summary: Patricia C. Wrede's *Thirteenth Child* is the first book in the Frontier Magic series. When fraternal twins Eff and Lan are born, they each have a different prophecy related to their birth. Eff is the 13th child in the family, which means that she will bring the family bad luck and difficult times. Lan is the seventh son of the family and their father was also a seventh son, which means that Lan is lucky and possesses great magic. Heeding neither prophecy, their father takes a job as an instructor of magic on the western frontier, dangerously close to where the wild things live. In the end, Eff disproves her prophecy.

Where it's reviewed:
Booklist, June 1, 2009, page 57
Horn Book Magazine, July-August 2009, page 434
Publishers Weekly, April 27, 2009, page 133
School Library Journal, August 2009, page 117

Other books by the same author:
Across the Great Barrier, 2011

Other books you might like:
Orson Scott Card, *Seventh Son*, 1987
Philip Caveney, *Sebastian Darke: Prince of Pirates*, 2009
D.M. Cornish, *Lamplighter*, 2008
Joseph Delaney, *The Last Apprentice Series*, 2005

1177

BIL WRIGHT

Putting Makeup on the Fat Boy

(New York: Simon and Schuster Books For Young Readers, 2011)

Story type: Coming-of-Age
Subject(s): Homosexuality; Cosmetics industry; Hispanic Americans

Age range(s): 14 - 18+
Major character(s): Carlos Duarte, Brother (of Rosalia), 16-Year-Old, Worker (makeup artist at Macy's), Friend (to Angie); Rosalia Duarte, Sister (of Carlos), 15-Year-Old; Angie, Teenager, Friend (of Carlos), Worker (at Macy's); Valentino, Employer (of Carlos)
Time period(s): 21st century; 2010s
Locale(s): New York, New York

Summary: Sixteen-year-old Carlos Duarte is skilled with makeup, a talent his younger sister Rosalia recognizes and encourages. Their mother is less enthusiastic, however, as having a boy interested in makeup raises concern for her. Carlos's friend Angie has a job in the linens department of Macy's. She's intimidated by the women who work in the makeup department of the famed store but suggests that Carlos may be able to get his start in the industry there. Although he lands his dream job, Carlos faces some hurdles. His mother loses her job, his older sister's boyfriend hassles him for being gay, and he starts to develop feelings for a classmate. To make things even worse, Carlos is at odds with his boss, Valentino, who is jealous of the teen's talent. Carlos also encounters violence when he is beaten and continually harassed, but he endures these trials with optimism, inner strength, and the determination to succeed.

Where it's reviewed:
Booklist, September 1, 2011, page 117
Bulletin of the Center for Children's Books, September 2011, page 56
Publishers Weekly, May 16, 2011, page 73
School Library Journal, July 2011, page 110

Other books by the same author:
When the Black Girl Sings, 2007

Awards the book has won:
Stonewall Book Award: Literature, 2012

Other books you might like:
Michael Cart, *How Beautiful the Ordinary: Twelve Stories of Identity*, 2009
Stephen Ertle-Rickard, *Stage Makeup*, 2011
Lisi Harrison, *Massie*, 2008
Erica S. Perl, *Vintage Veronica*, 2010

1178

MELISSA WYATT

Funny How Things Change

(New York: Farrar, Straus and Giroux, 2009)

Subject(s): Coming of age; College environment; Artists
Age range(s): 15 - 18+

Major character(s): Remy Walker, Teenager; Lisa, Teenager, Girlfriend (of Remy); Dana, Artist
Time period(s): 21st century; 2000s
Locale(s): Pennsylvania, United States; Dwyer, West Virginia

Summary: Author Melissa Wyatt offers an in-depth character study in her coming-of-age novel *Funny How Things Change*. Remy Walker has always been happy in his quiet mountain town of Dwyer, West Virginia. But after he graduates from high school, he finds himself at a crossroads. His girlfriend, Lisa, wants to leave Remy behind to attend college in Pennsylvania, and Remy reluctantly agrees to go with her. But when a hip artist visits Dwyer to paint a mural and gives Remy a look at his hometown from another perspective, Remy begins to question everything.

Where it's reviewed:
Booklist, March 15, 2009, page 54
School Library Journal, April 2009, page 145

Other books by the same author:
Raising the Griffin, 2005

Other books you might like:
Cat Bauer, *Harley's Ninth*, 2007
Carla Joinson, *A Diamond in the Dust*, 2001
Richard Uhlig, *Last Dance at the Frosty Queen*, 2007
Will Weaver, *Full Service*, 2005

1179

TIM WYNNE-JONES

The Uninvited

(Somerville, Massachusetts: Candlewick Press, 2009)

Subject(s): Mystery; Family; Suspense
Age range(s): 15 - 18+
Major character(s): Mimi Shapiro, Student—College; Jay Page, Brother (half, of Mimi); Cramer Lee, Brother (half, of Mimi and Jay); Marc Soto, Artist, Father (absent; of Mimi, Jay, and Cramer)
Time period(s): 21st century; 2000s
Locale(s): Ontario, Canada

Summary: Mimi Shapiro leaves New York City after her first year of college, during which she had a tumultuous affair with a professor. She decides to go to her absent father Marc's cottage in Ontario, Canada, but upon her arrival is surprised to discover 22-year-old Jay already living there. Jay is a half-brother she never knew about, but Mimi and Jay get along well and decide to continue to live together. Then, strange events begin happening in the cottage, and it seems that someone is breaking in, stealing their things, and leaving strange items in their place. Mimi and Jay discover a hidden tunnel underneath the house; they also learn that Cramer Lee, a loner in town who spends much of his time taking care of his mother, is another half-brother of theirs who delights in stalking their home. Jay and Mimi wonder if he is the one who has been breaking in—but they learn the truth in an unexpected and violent way.

Where it's reviewed:
Booklist, May 1, 2009, page 41
Horn Book Magazine, May/June 2009, page 311

Publishers Weekly, May 4, 2009, page 51
School Library Journal, July 2009, page 96
Voice of Youth Advocates, June 2009, page 158

Other books by the same author:
Blink & Caution, 2011
A Thief in the House of Memory, 2005
The Boy in the Burning House, 2001
Stephen Fair, 1998

Other books you might like:
Jay Asher, *Thirteen Reasons Why*, 2007
Jo Knowles, *Lessons from a Dead Girl*, 2007
Blake Nelson, *Paranoid Park*, 2006
R.A. Nelson, *Breathe My Name*, 2007
Sara Shepard, *Unbelievable*, 2008

1180

TIM WYNNE-JONES

Blink & Caution

(Somerville, Massachusetts: Candlewick Press, 2011)

Subject(s): Runaways; Kidnapping; Adventure
Age range(s): 15 - 18+
Major character(s): Blink, 16-Year-Old, Runaway; Caution, 16-Year-Old, Runaway
Time period(s): 21st century; 2010s
Locale(s): Toronto, Ontario

Summary: Tim Wynne-Jones's *Blink & Caution* follows the adventures of a pair of teen runaways who find themselves involved in a high-profile kidnapping case. Blink is living on the streets of Toronto, desperate for food and shelter, while Caution has just fled her violent, drug-dealing boyfriend. When the two 16-year-olds meet, Blink shares knowledge of a terrifying event he recently witnessed: the kidnapping of a powerful businessman. Together, Blink and Caution set out to solve the mystery surrounding the abduction, but their good intentions land them in the dark epicenter of the crime—where they don't know where to turn or whom to trust.

Where it's reviewed:
Booklist, February 1, 2011, page 76
Horn Book Magazine, March/April 2011, page 129
Publishers Weekly, January 17, 2011, page 50
School Library Journal, February 2011, page 122
Voice of Youth Advocates, April 2011, page 72

Other books by the same author:
The Uninvited, 2009
A Thief in the House of Memory, 2005
The Boy in the Burning House, 2001
Stephen Fair, 1998

Awards the book has won:
Boston Globe - Horn Book Awards: Fiction or Poetry, 2011

Other books you might like:
Jacquelyn Mitchard, *Now You See Her*, 2007
Eric Walters, *Sketches*, 2008
Rachel Ward, *Numbers*, 2010

1181

RICK YANCEY

The Isle of Blood

(New York: Simon & Schuster Books for Young Readers, 2011)

Series: Monstrumologist Series. Book 3
Story type: Fantasy
Subject(s): Monsters; Islands; Suspense

Age range(s): 15 - 18+
Major character(s): Dr. Pellinore Warthrop, Scientist (monstrumologist); Will Henry, Orphan, Assistant (to Dr. Warthrop)
Time period(s): Indeterminate Past
Locale(s): Socotra, Fictional Location; United States

Summary: In this suspenseful young adult fantasy from author Rick Yancey, the third installment in the Monstrumologist series, Will Henry and his master, Dr. Warthrop, embark on a terrifying adventure to track down the rarest and most elusive creature of all. When Dr. Warthrop learns that a dangerous old pal might hold the secret to the whereabouts of an elusive monster, he can't resist the urge to track the man down. His sleuthing leads him to Socotra, the Isle of Blood, a dangerous island inhabited by a series of bizarre creatures. Could the extraordinary and enigmatic creature that monstrumologists have been seeking for generations live in this strange land? When Will Henry receives word that Dr. Warthorp was killed during his quest, he has no choice but to travel to Socotra for himself in search of the truth.

Where it's reviewed:
Booklist, August 1, 2011, page 57
Horn Book Magazine, November/December 2011, page 119
Voice of Youth Advocates, December 2011, page 522

Other books by the same author:
The Curse of the Wendigo, 2010
The Monstrumologist, 2009
The Extraordinary Adventures of Alfred Kropp, 2005

Other books you might like:
D.M. Cornish, *Monster Blood Tattoo series*, 2006-
Joseph Delaney, *The Last Apprentice Series*, 2005
Patrick Ness, *A Monster Calls*, 2011
Ransom Riggs, *Miss Peregrine's Home for Peculiar Children*, 2011

1182

RICK YANCEY

The Monstrumologist

(New York: Simon & Schuster Books for Young Readers, 2009)

Series: Monstrumologist Series. Book 1
Subject(s): Supernatural; Monsters; Orphans

Age range(s): 14 - 18+
Major character(s): Will Henry, 12-Year-Old, Orphan; Dr. Pellinore Warthrop, Scientist (monstrumologist)
Time period(s): 19th century; 1880s
Locale(s): New England, United States

Summary: In *The Monstrumologist* by Rick Yancey, long-time New England resident Will Henry has died at the age of 131, leaving behind a diary that details his horrifying apprenticeship to Doctor Pellinore Warthrop. In 1888, the journal explains, 12-year-old Will—an orphan—was taken in by the doctor, who specialized in monstrumology. As Will assisted Warhtrop in his monster-hunting activities, the boy encountered a host of terrifying creatures. When a band of Anthropophagi—monsters that walk like men and eat through razor-toothed mouths on their chests—invaded New England, Dr. Warthrop and his young apprentice had to find a way to defeat the beasts before they annihilated the entire country.

Where it's reviewed:
Booklist, September 1, 2009, page 92
Horn Book Guide, Spring 2010, page 112
Publishers Weekly, September 7, 2009, page 48
School Library Journal, November 2009, page 125
Voice of Youth Advocates, February 2010, page 515

Other books by the same author:
The Isle of Blood, 2011
The Curse of the Wendigo, 2010

Other books you might like:
Daniel Kraus, *Rotters*, 2011
Ransom Riggs, *Miss Peregrine's Home for Peculiar Children*, 2011
Michael Scott, *The Necromancer: The Secrets of the Immortal Nicholas Flamel*, 2010
Arthur G. Slade, *The Hunchback Assignments*, 2009
Carlos Ruiz Zafon, *The Prince of Mist*, 2010

1183

RICK YANCEY

The Curse of the Wendigo

(New York: Simon & Schuster Books for Young Readers, 2010)

Series: Monstrumologist Series. Book 2
Subject(s): Monsters; Supernatural; Orphans

Age range(s): 14 - 18+
Major character(s): Will Henry, Apprentice (to Dr. Warthrop), 12-Year-Old; Dr. Pellinore Warthrop, Scientist (monstrumologist)
Time period(s): 19th century; 1880s (1888)
Locale(s): New England, United States

Summary: The year is 1888, and 12-year-old Will Henry is chosen to be an apprentice to the renowned monster-hunter Dr. Warthrop. Will takes readers along for the ride as he and the odd doctor hunt New England's most feared monsters—the most notorious of which is the Wendigo, a beast that feeds on human flesh but is never sated. *The Curse of the Wendigo* is the second installment in Rick Yancey's Monstrumologist series.

Where it's reviewed:
Booklist, September 1, 2010, page 96
Horn Book Magazine, January/February 2011, page 103
Publishers Weekly, October 4, 2010, page 50
School Library Journal, December 2010, page 132
Voice of Youth Advocates, December 2010, page 478

Other books by the same author:
The Isle of Blood, 2011
The Monstrumologist, 2009
The Extraordinary Adventures of Alfred Kropp, 2005

Other books you might like:
N.M. Browne, *Basilisk*, 2004
D.M. Cornish, *Foundling*, 2006
Graham McNamee, *Bonechiller*, 2008
Patrick Ness, *A Monster Calls*, 2011
Bram Stoker, *Dracula*, 1897

1184

GENE LUEN YANG
THIEN PHAM, Illustrator
Level Up
(New York: First Second, 2011)

Story type: Coming-of-Age
Subject(s): Games; Medical professions; Adolescence
Age range(s): 14 - 18+
Major character(s): Dennis Ouyang, Teenager
Time period(s): 21st century; 2010s

Summary: A teenager must choose between his passions and his parents' dreams for him in this graphic novel for young adult readers from award-winning author Gene Luen Yang and illustrator Thien Pham. Dennis Ouyang's parents have incredibly high expectations for him—expectations that include medical school and a successful, lucrative career as a gastroenterologist. Dennis, on the other hand, has no desire to go into medicine, instead wishing he could spend his days devoted to the one thing he's exceptionally good at: playing video games. When four cute, controlling, and sometimes scary angels pay him a surprise visit, he's forced to evaluate his life choices and choose the right path.

Where it's reviewed:
Booklist, March 15, 2011, page 34
Horn Book Guide, Fall 2011, page 403
Publishers Weekly, February 28, 2011, page 41
Voice of Youth Advocates, August 2011, page 300

Other books by the same author:
The Eternal Smile: Three Stories, 2009
American Born Chinese, 2006

Other books you might like:
Jessica Abel, *Life Sucks*, 2008
Derek Kirk Kim, *Good as Lily*, 2007
Bryan Lee O'Malley, *Scott Pilgrim's Precious Little Life*, 2004
Jane Yolen, *Foiled*, 2010

1185

GENE LUEN YANG, Author/Illustrator
DEREK KIRK KIM, Illustrator
The Eternal Smile
(New York: First Second, 2009)

Subject(s): Magic; Imagination; Short stories
Age range(s): 14 - 18+

Summary: In *The Eternal Smile*, graphic novelists Gene Luen Yang and Derek Kirk Kim team up to bring young adult readers a trio of magical tales. In "Duncan's Kingdom," a prince must battle his mortal foe—but he is unprepared for the surprising results. "Gran'pa Greenbax and the Eternal Smile" centers on a frog who spots a smile situated high in the clouds and proceeds to place his hopes and dreams in this unusual phenomena. In "Urgent Request," Janet's life is forever changed after getting an e-mail from Prince Henry of Nigeria. Told through bold artwork and inspired prose, this volume celebrates the power of the imagination and the rich fantasy worlds that live within everyday events.

Where it's reviewed:
Booklist, March 1, 2009, page 56
Library Journal, May 15, 2009, page 55
Teacher Librarian, April 20, 2010, page 75

Other books by the same author:
Level Up, 2011
Prime Baby, 2010
American Born Chinese, 2008

Other books you might like:
Derek Kirk Kim, *Good as Lily*, 2007
Jordan Mechner, *Prince of Persia: The Graphic Novel*, 2008
Linda Medley, *Castle Waiting*, 2006
Joann Sfar, *The Professor's Daughter*, 2007

1186

LISA YEE
Warp Speed
(New York: Arthur A. Levine Books, 2011)

Story type: Contemporary
Subject(s): Bullying; Popularity; Middle schools
Age range(s): 11 - 15+
Major character(s): Marley Sandelski, 7th Grader; Digger Ronster, Bully; Coach Martin, Coach (track)
Time period(s): 21st century; 2010s
Locale(s): California, United States

Summary: A science nerd's sudden encounter with popularity turns his seventh grade world upside down in this young-adult novel by Lisa Yee. *Star Trek* devotee Marley Sandelski is used to the bullying he receives at Rancho Rosetta Middle School. He's been physically and emotionally attacked before. But when he becomes the target of Digger Ronster's cruel treatment, Marley knows that he's in for some serious humiliation. When his frequent sprints from danger catch the eye of the track coach, Marley must decide if he wants to join the dreaded jocks or retain his familiar status as a school geek. Marley faces another dilemma when he learns the reason behind Digger's behavior.

Where it's reviewed:
Booklist, February 15, 2011, page 75
Bulletin of the Center for Children's Books, February 2011, page 306
Horn Book Magazine, March-April 2011, page 130
Publishers Weekly, January 17, 2011, page 49

Other books by the same author:

Absolutely Maybe, 2009

Stanford Wong Flunks Big-Time, 2005

Millicent Min, Girl Genius, 2003

Other books you might like:

M.E. Castle, *Popular Clone*, 2012

Donna Gephart, *How to Survive Middle School*, 2010

Jerry Spinelli, *Maniac Magee*, 1990

Michael Winerip, *Adam Canfield, Watch Your Back!*, 2007

1187

LISA YEE

Absolutely Maybe

(New York: Arthur A. Levine Books, 2009)

Subject(s): Runaways; Rape; Marriage

Age range(s): 12 - 17+

Major character(s): Maybelline "Maybe" Mary Katherine Mary Ann Chestnut, 17-Year-Old; Thammasat "Ted" Tantipinichwong Schneider, Friend; Hollywood, Friend, Filmmaker

Time period(s): 21st century; 2000s

Locale(s): Los Angeles, California; Kissimee, Florida

Summary: In *Absolutely Maybe* by Lisa Yee, Maybelline Mary Katherine Mary Ann Chestnut, known as "Maybe" for short, has never had a boring life. Named for two Miss Americas and a brand of mascara, Maybe is in full-out rebellion mode against her flaky mother. She dyes her hair using Kool-Aid and hides any sign of a girlish figure under oversized clothes and sneakers. Her mom runs an old-fashioned charm school in Florida and prepares to walk down the aisle for a seventh time. When Maybe's latest dad-to-be tries to have sex with her and her mom believes the lowlife over her, Maybe leaves for good. She and her two best friends, Thammasat Tantipinichwong Schneider (Ted) and Hollywood, leave Florida for Los Angeles. Hollywood plans to attend film school, Maybe searches for her father with only a first name to guide her, and Ted goes along for something to do. They all find success in unexpected ways. Hollywood wins a prize for his documentary about Maybe, while Ted is taken under the wing of an aging starlet and begins a successful career. Though Maybe encounters difficulties in finding her dad and runs out of money, she ends up finding something better—herself.

Where it's reviewed:

Booklist, December 1, 2008, page 41

Horn Book Magazine, March-April 2009, page 206

Publishers Weekly, January 26, 2009, page 121

Other books you might like:

Cecil Castellucci, *Beige*, 2007

Deborah Davis, *Not Like You*, 2007

Zoey Dean, *California Dreaming: An A-List Novel, #10*, 2008

Sarah Dessen, *Lock and Key*, 2008

1188

PAUL YEE

Money Boy

(Toronto: Groundwood Books, 2011)

Story type: Contemporary

Subject(s): Social conditions; Father-son relations; Homosexuality

Age range(s): 15 - 18+

Major character(s): Ray Liu, Teenager, Immigrant, Homosexual

Time period(s): 21st century; 2010s

Locale(s): Toronto, Ontario

Summary: In this young-adult novel by Paul Yee, a teenage Chinese immigrant struggles to adapt to his new life in Canada. Ray Liu lives with his strict father and stepmother in Toronto, escaping the stress of learning English and doing well in school by playing video games and surfing the Internet. When Ray's father discovers that his son has been visiting gay websites, the secret that Ray has been hiding is exposed. Furious about his son's sexual orientation, Ray's father throws him out of the house, and the troubled teenager is forced to fend for himself on the streets of Toronto. Naive to the realities of his new lifestyle, Ray is attacked, robbed, and taken in by a man who turns out to be a pimp. Is working as a prostitute the only way Ray can survive?

Where it's reviewed:

Booklist, September 1, 2011, page 117

Bulletin of the Center for Children's Books, October 2011, page 120

School Library Journal, September 2011, page 179

Voice of Youth Advocates, October 2011, page 396

Other books by the same author:

Learnng to Fly, 2008

What Happened This Summer, 2006

The Bone Collector's Son, 2004

Other books you might like:

Jessica Blank, *Almost Home*, 2007

Tim Bowler, *Blade: Playing Dead*, 2008

Tim Wynne-Jones, *Blink & Caution*, 2011

1189

FUMI YOSHINAGA, Author/Illustrator

Ooku: The Inner Chambers, Volume 1

(San Francisco: VIZ Media, 2009)

Series: Ooku: The Inner Chambers Series. Book 1

Story type: Fantasy

Subject(s): Japanese history; Marriage; Poverty

Age range(s): 16 - 18+

Major character(s): Mizuno, Young Man (Japanese), Man (concubine)

Time period(s): 18th century

Locale(s): Japan

Summary: In an alternate history of Japan, a plague kills 75 percent of the male population over several generations. By the 18th century, women have taken on all traditionally male roles, including that of shogun. These female leaders hoard the best-looking men in the Inner Chamber. Other women of means may marry from the remaining men, while poor women who want children are forced to pay for sex. Mizuno, a young and healthy man, does not charge women of his village for his services. Then he is claimed by the shogun for her harem and must leave behind the woman he loves. Mizuno must prove his mettle and find his place in the hierarchy of the concubines living in the men's quarters, or Ooku.

Where it's reviewed:
Publishers Weekly, August 31, 2009, page 42

Other books by the same author:
Ooku: The Inner Chambers, Volume 6, 2011
Not Love but Delicious Foods, 2010
Flower of Life, Volume 4, 2009
Antique Bakery, 2008
Garden Dreams, 2007

Awards the book has won:
James Tiptree, Jr. Memorial Award, 2009

Other books you might like:
James Clavell, *Shogun*, 1977
Kim Dong Hwa, *The Color of Heaven*, 2009
Lisa See, *Snow Flower and the Secret Fan*, 2005
Sa Shan, *Empress*, 2006
Brian K. Vaughan, *Y: The Last Man: Unmanned*, 2003

1190

JANET RUTH YOUNG

The Babysitter Murders
(New York: Atheneum Books for Young Readers, 2011)

Story type: Psychological
Subject(s): Mental disorders; Babysitters; Psychology
Major character(s): Dani Solomon, 17-Year-Old, Babysitter, Mentally Ill Person
Time period(s): 21st century; 2010s
Locale(s): United States

Summary: Janet Ruth Young's psychological novel for young adult readers addresses the dangers and realities of mental illness among teenagers. Suffering from a rare form of obsessive-compulsive disorder (OCD), 17-year-old Dani Solomon struggles with an onslaught of disturbing thoughts, ranging from groping her music teacher to taunting her mother. When her thoughts grow more violent and center on hurting Alex, the little boy she babysits, Dani grows concerned that she might actually try to kill the little boy. Determined to keep him safe, Dani comes clean about her horrifying thoughts to the boy's mother and seeks treatment for her mental condition. While Dani attempts to get the help she needs, rumors about her violent imagination begin swirling and cause a vigilante group to grow obsessed with seeking justice.

Where it's reviewed:
Booklist, March 15, 2011, page 34

Horn Book Guide, Fall 2011, page 403
Publishers Weekly, February 28, 2011, page 41
Voice of Youth Advocates, August 2011, page 300

Other books by the same author:
The Opposite of Music, 2007

Other books you might like:
Crissa-Jean Chappell, *Total Constant Order*, 2007
Julia DeVillers, *Princess of Gossip*, 2008
Terry Spencer Hesser, *Kissing Doorknobs*, 1998
E.L. Konigsburg, *Silent to the Bone*, 2000

1191

MOIRA YOUNG

Blood Red Road
(New York: Margaret K. McElderry Books, 2011)

Series: Dustlands Series. Book 1
Subject(s): Kidnapping; Brothers and sisters; Twins

Age range(s): 15 - 18+
Major character(s): Lugh, 18-Year-Old, Twin (of Saba), Brother (of Emmi); Saba, 18-Year-Old, Twin (of Lugh), Sister (of Emmi); Emmi, 9-Year-Old, Sister (of Lugh and Saba); Jack, Warrior
Time period(s): Indeterminate Future
Locale(s): Hopetown, Fictional Location; Sandsea, Fictional Location; Silverlake, Fictional Location

Summary: In the young adult science-fiction novel *Blood Red Road* by Moira Young, Earth in the far future is a barren desert that is continually ravaged by sandstorms. Humans struggle for survival in the harsh environment, where violence and cruelty have taken hold. In the region known as Silverlake, 18-year-old twins Lugh and Saba care for their little sister, Emmi, and scrounge the nearby garbage dumps for the materials they need. When a fierce dust storm brings four strange men to Silverlake and Lugh is abducted, Saba and Emmi follow the kidnappers' path to Hopetown. There, Saba must work as a cage fighter while she plots a way out for her and her siblings. *Blood Red Road* is the first book in the Dustlands series.

Where it's reviewed:
Booklist, May 1, 2011, page 82
Horn Book Guide, Fall 2011, page 403
New York Times Book Review, June 5, 2011, page 27
Publishers Weekly, April 11, 2011, page 54
School Library Journal, September 2011, page 179

Other books you might like:
Kristin Cashore, *Graceling*, 2008
Suzanne Collins, *Hunger Games Trilogy*, 2008
Donna Jo Napoli, *Hush: An Irish Princess' Tale*, 2007
Tamora Pierce, *Lady Knight*, 2002
Amy Kathleen Ryan, *Glow*, 2011

1192

SUZANNE YOUNG

A Need So Beautiful

(New York: Balzer + Bray, 2011)

Story type: Fantasy
Subject(s): Fantasy; Adolescence; Friendship

Age range(s): 15 - 18+
Major character(s): Charlotte, Teenager, Supernatural Being (one of the Forgotten)
Time period(s): 21st century; 2010s
Locale(s): Portland, Oregon

Summary: A teenage girl must choose between her mortal and supernatural identities in this young-adult fantasy novel by Suzanne Young. Charlotte has been keeping an incredible secret from her best friend and boyfriend. She is one of the Forgotten, a spirit who must fulfill a driving need to come to the aid of a person she doesn't even know. But Charlotte doesn't want to help a stranger—she wants to help her troubled best friend. She wants to stay with her boyfriend in the mortal realm and not be forgotten. The pull of Charlotte's supernatural identity is strong, and she must decide if she should accept her lot or risk the dire repercussions her resistance could bring.

Where it's reviewed:
Booklist, May 15, 2011, page 56
School Library Journal, August 2011, page 126
Voice of Youth Advocates, August 2011, page 300

Other books by the same author:
The Naughty List, 2010
So Many Boys, 2010

Other books you might like:
Jocelyn Davies, *A Beautiful Dark*, 2011
Becca Fitzpatrick, *Crescendo*, 2010
Cat Patrick, *Forgotten*, 2011

1193

BRENNA YOVANOFF

The Space Between

(New York: Razorbill, 2011)

Story type: Fantasy
Subject(s): Demons; Hell; Brothers and sisters

Age range(s): 15 - 18+
Major character(s): Daphne, Supernatural Being (half demon, half fallen angel), Daughter (of Lucifer and Lilith), Sister (of Obie); Lucifer, Demon, Spouse (of Lilith), Father (of Daphne); Lilith, Demon, Spouse (of Lucifer), Mother (of Daphne and Obie); Obie, Supernatural Being, Son (of Lilith), Brother (of Daphne); Truman Flynn, Teenager, Human
Time period(s): 21st century; 2010s
Locale(s): Pandemonium, Fictional Location; Las Vegas, Nevada

Summary: Lucifer's young daughter comes to Earth in search of her lost brother in this young-adult fantasy novel by Brenna Yovanoff. Daphne's existence in the city of Pandemonium with her demon parents Lucifer and Lilith is tedious, alleviated somewhat by her friendship with her brother Obie. When Obie disappears from Hell, Daphne journeys to the strange world of the humans to find him and discovers a place that is both frightening and fantastic. Daphne also meets a human boy named Truman Flynn who has already been saved once from the clutches of the demons. As Daphne pursues Obie and her growing love for Truman, she must face dangerous enemies from Hell and Earth.

Where it's reviewed:
Booklist, October 1, 2011, page 89
Horn Book Magazine, January-February 2012, page 106
Publishers Weekly, September 26, 2011, page 75
School Library Journal, December 2011, page 136
Voice of Youth Advocates, December 2011, page 522

Other books by the same author:
The Replacement, 2010

Other books you might like:
Elizabeth Chandler, *Evercrossed*, 2011
Cassandra Clare, *Clockwork Angel*, 2010
Gwen Hayes, *Falling Under*, 2011

1194

BRENNA YOVANOFF

The Replacement

(New York: Razorbill, 2010)

Subject(s): Fairies; Fantasy; Horror

Age range(s): 15 - 18+
Major character(s): Mackie Doyle, Mythical Creature (fairy); Tate Stewart, Human
Locale(s): Gentry, Fictional Location

Summary: *The Replacement* is a fantastical horror novel for young adult readers from author Brenna Yovanoff. The small town of Gentry has struck a horrifying and secretive deal with the Fairy Court: every seven years, a human baby is exchanged for a fairy child and in return, the town of Gentry experiences prosperity and stability. Mackie Doyle was a Replacement—a fairy that replaced a stolen human baby, and although everyone in the town knows it, not many will acknowledge it. Now, Mackie is struggling to survive among the humans, thanks to a severe allergy to iron and blood. When the baby sister of his crush, Tate Stewart, is replaced, Mackie decides to team up with Tate to confront the authorities of Fairy Court and restore normalcy to the small town of Gentry.

Where it's reviewed:
Booklist, September 1, 2010, page 97
Horn Book Guide, Spring 2011, page 117
Publishers Weekly, August 16, 2010, page 51
School Library Journal, December 2010, page 132
Voice of Youth Advocates, December 2010, page 478

Other books by the same author:
The Space Between, 2011

Other books you might like:
Cyn Balog, *Fairy Tale*, 2009
Ellen Booraem, *The Unnameables*, 2008

Delia Sherman, *Changeling*, 2006
Kate Thompson, *The Last of the High Kings*, 2008

1195

CARLOS RUIZ ZAFON

The Prince of Mist

(New York: Little, Brown and Company, 2010)

Subject(s): Supernatural; Haunted houses; World War II, 1939-1945

Age range(s): 12 - 17+

Major character(s): Max Carver, 13-Year-Old, Brother (to Alicia); Alicia Carver, 15-Year-Old, Sister (to Max)

Time period(s): 20th century; 1940s

Locale(s): Spain

Summary: Recently translated into English, Carlos Ruiz Zafon's *The Prince of Mist* is a chilling tale for young adult readers. Set in Spain during World War II, the story follows teenagers Max and Alicia Carver as they move to a small town with their parents. They soon learn that their new home on the coast is haunted by the spirit of a young boy named Jacob, whose father drowned years before. Max and Alicia, along with their new friend, Roland, begin investigating the local supernatural forces at work. They learn about the Prince of Mist, an evil being who has tormented the area for decades and is seeking revenge for a mistake in the past. The three teens embark on a terrifying adventure to stop the Prince of Mist before he harms another living soul.

Where it's reviewed:
Booklist, September 1, 2010, page 100
Horn Book Guide, Fall 2010, page 386
Publishers Weekly, April 12, 2010, page 209
School Library Journal, July 2010, page 98
Voice of Youth Advocates, April 2010, page 64

Other books by the same author:
The Midnight Palace, 2011

Other books you might like:
Kate Cann, *Possessed*, 2010
Michelle Cooper, *A Brief History of Montmaray*, 2009
Elizabeth Hand, *Illyria*, 2010
William Sleator, *The Last Universe*, 2005
Susan Vaught, *Stormwitch*, 2005

1196

SARA ZARR

Once Was Lost

(New York: Little, Brown Books for Young Readers, 2009)

Subject(s): Adolescence; Kidnapping; Family life

Age range(s): 14 - 17+

Major character(s): Samara "Sam" Taylor, Teenager; Jody, 13-Year-Old, Kidnap Victim, Sister (of Nick); Nick, Teenager, Brother (of Jody)

Time period(s): 21st century; 2000s

Locale(s): United States

Summary: In Sara Zarr's young adult novel *Once Was Lost*, a young girl struggles with family issues as she investigates the strange disappearance of another teenager. A long summer is drawing to a close but Samara Taylor feels completely lost. Her mother is in rehab and her father, the pastor of a church, is too wrapped up in his work and his appearance to give Sam any attention. She is finding it hard to have faith in much of anything. When a 13-year-old girl named Jody is kidnapped, Sam becomes wrapped up in the disappearance and begins spending a great deal of time with Jody's older brother, Nick. When it appears as if Nick may have had something to do with Jody's disappearance, Sam begins questioning her life, her faith, and her relationship with God even more.

Where it's reviewed:
Booklist, November 15, 2009, page 44
Horn Book Magazine, January/February 2010, page 97
Publishers Weekly, August 31, 2009, page 64
School Library Journal, November 2009, page 126
Voice of Youth Advocates, February 2010, page 502

Other books by the same author:
How to Save a Life, 2011
Sweethearts, 2008
Story of a Girl, 2007

Other books you might like:
Kimberly Brubaker Bradley, *Leap of Faith*, 2007
Norma Fox Mazer, *The Missing Girl*, 2008
Olugbemisola Rhuday-Perkovich, *Eighth-Grade Superzero*, 2010
Barbara Shoup, *Wish You Were Here*, 1994
Lara Zielin, *Donut Days*, 2009

1197

SARA ZARR

How to Save a Life

(New York: Little, Brown and Company, 2011)

Story type: Contemporary

Subject(s): Adoption; Pregnancy; Death

Age range(s): 14 - 18+

Major character(s): Jill MacSweeny, 17-Year-Old; Mandy Kalinowski, Teenager, Pregnant Teenager, Abuse Victim

Time period(s): 21st century; 2010s

Locale(s): United States

Summary: Critically acclaimed author Sara Zarr tackles the challenges of death, teenage pregnancy, adoption, and depression in this emotional and thought-provoking novel for young adult readers. Since the unexpected death of her father, 17-year-old Jill MacSweeny has been floating through life, growing more estranged from her boyfriend, closest friends, and mother. Suffocating under the weight of her grief, Jill can't seem to let go of the pain and allow herself to be loved and comforted by those who truly care about her. When Jill's mom decides to adopt a baby, the chasm between them grows even wider. For Mandy Kalinowski, an abused pregnant teenager, Jill's mom seems like the perfect choice to raise and love her unborn baby. As Jill and Mandy's lives collide, these two young women learn more about themselves and the reality of their circumstances than they ever imagined.

Where it's reviewed:
Booklist, November 1, 2011, page 60
Publishers Weekly, October 24, 2011, page 55
School Library Journal, December 2011, page 36
Voice of Youth Advocates, December 2011, page 504

Other books by the same author:
Once Was Lost, 2009
Sweethearts, 2008
Story of a Girl, 2007

Other books you might like:
Deb Caletti, *The Six Rules of Maybe*, 2010
Sarah Dessen, *The Truth about Forever*, 2004
Varian Johnson, *My Life as a Rhombus*, 2008
Carolyn Mackler, *Vegan Virgin Valentine*, 2004

1198

GABRIELLE ZEVIN

All These Things I've Done

(New York: Farrar, Straus and Giroux, 2011)

Story type: Coming-of-Age
Subject(s): Organized crime; Murder; Adolescence
Age range(s): 14 - 18+
Major character(s): Anya Balanchine, 16-Year-Old, Daughter (of a Mafia crime boss), Crime Suspect
Time period(s): 21st century; 2080s (2083)
Locale(s): New York, New York

Summary: The teenage daughter of a notorious Mafia don struggles to fit in with her peers despite her family's illegal activities and a false murder accusation in this futuristic young adult novel from author Gabrielle Zevin. It's 2083 and New York City is a center of poverty and crime. Chocolate, alcohol, and coffee are illegal, making Anya Balanchine's family's contraband chocolate business very lucrative. The daughter of a dead Mafia crime boss, Anya longs for a normal life. It's farther from her reach than ever when her ex-boyfriend is poisoned with a piece of Balanchine chocolate and Anya is accused of murder. Desperate to prove her innocence, Anya must fight against the media attention and the disappointment of her Mafia family.

Where it's reviewed:
Booklist, September 15, 2011, page 73
Horn Book Magazine, September/October 2011, page 107
Publishers Weekly, June 27, 2011, page 158
School Library Journal, November 2011, page 145

Other books by the same author:
Memoirs of a Teenage Amnesiac, 2007
Elsewhere, 2005

Other books you might like:
Gordon Korman, *Son of the Mob*, 2002
April Lurie, *Brothers, Boyfriends and Other Criminal Minds*, 2007
Veronica Roth, *Divergent*, 2011

1199

MICHELLE ZINK

Prophecy of the Sisters

(New York: Little, Brown Young Readers, 2009)

Series: Prophecy of the Sisters Trilogy. Book 1
Subject(s): Twins; Orphans; Death
Age range(s): 13 - 16+
Major character(s): Lia Milthorpe, 16-Year-Old, Twin (of Alice); Alice Milthorpe, 16-Year-Old, Twin (of Lia)

Summary: *The Prophecy of the Sisters* is the first book in the Prophecy of the Sisters Trilogy by Michelle Zink. In this installment, readers are introduced to Lia and Alice Milthorpe, twin 16-year-olds, who have recently lost both of their parents. One day, Lia discovers a mark on her wrist. She uncovers an ancient prophecy and finds that the mark on her wrist is actually a branding. The prophecy says Lia and Alice are sisters who are destined to destroy each other, but not if Lia can help it. She must keep the truth of the prophecy a secret from everyone, especially Alice, until she can devise a way to break the curse, and before Alice destroys her.

Where it's reviewed:
Booklist, May 15, 2009, page 53
Horn Book Guide, Spring 2010, page 112
Publishers Weekly, August 3, 2009, page 46
School Library Journal, January 2010, page 117

Other books by the same author:
Circle of Fire, 2011
Guardian of the Gate, 2010

Other books you might like:
Charles de Lint, *Dingo*, 2008
Jennifer Anne Kogler, *The Otherworldlies*, 2008
Jacquelyn Mitchard, *The Midnight Twins*, 2008
Michael Scott, *The Alchemyst: The Secrets of the Immortal Nicholas Flamel*, 2007

1200

CLAIRE ZULKEY

An Off Year

(New York: Dutton, 2009)

Subject(s): College environment; Psychology; Family life
Age range(s): 15 - 18+
Major character(s): Cecily, 18-Year-Old
Time period(s): 21st century; 2000s
Locale(s): Chicago, Illinois

Summary: In the young adult novel *An Off Year* by Claire Zulkey, a teenager chooses to delay the start of her college career to learn more about herself. Cecily had always been an excellent student. The college application process went smoothly: She was accepted to a good school, enrolled, and arrived at her dorm, ready to move in. But Cecily doesn't move in—she heads home to Chicago where she plans to take a year off from school and explore alternate life paths. As Cecily considers the range of opportunities now open to her, she works to renew relationships with the important people in her life.

Where it's reviewed:
Booklist, August 1, 2009, page 58
Horn Book Guide, Spring 2010, page 112
School Library Journal, November 2009, page 126

Other books you might like:
AV Club, *Inventory: 16 Films Featuring Manic Pixie Dream Girls, 10 Great Songs Nearly Ruined by Saxophone, and 100 More Obsessively Specific Pop-Culture Lists*, 2009

Abby McDonald, *Sophomore Switch*, 2009
The Onion, *Our Front Pages: 21 Years of Greatness, Virtue, and Moral Rectitude from America's Finest News Source*, 2009
Nathan Rabin, *The Big Rewind: A Memoir Brought to You by Pop Culture*, 2009
Rob Sheffield, *Talking to Girls about Duran Duran: One Young Man's Quest for True Love and a Cooler Haircut*, 2010

Series Index

This index alphabetically lists series to which books featured in the entries belong. Beneath each series name, book titles are listed alphabetically, with author names, age-level code(s) and entry numbers also included. The age-level codes are as follows: *p*: ages 1-4, *c*: ages 5-10, *y*: ages 11-18.

Award Index

This index lists major awards given to books featured in the entries. Books are listed alphabetically beneath the name of the award, with author name, age-level code(s) and entry numbers also included. The age-level codes are as follows: *p*: ages 1-4, *c*: ages 5-10, *y*: ages 11-18.

Time Index

This index chronologically lists the time settings in which the featured books take place. Main headings refer to a century; where no specific time is given, the headings MULTIPLE TIME PERIODS, INDETERMINATE PAST, INDETERMINATE FUTURE, AND INDETERMINATE are used. Entries are broken down into decades when possible. (Note: 1800s, for example, refers to the first decade of the 19th century.) Featured titles are listed alphabetically beneath time headings, with author names, age-level code(s) and entry numbers also included. The age-level codes are as follows: *p*: ages 1-4, *c*: ages 5-10, *y*: ages 11-18.

Time Index

21ST CENTURY

2010s

Geographic Index

This index provides access to all featured books by geographic settings—such as countries, continents, oceans, and planets. States and provinces are indicated for the United States and Canada. Also interfiled are headings for fictional place names (Spaceships, Imaginary Planets, etc.). Sections are further broken down by city or the specific name of the imaginary locale. Book titles are listed alphabetically under headings, with author names, age-level code(s) and entry numbers also included. The age-level codes are as follows: *p*: ages 1-4, *c*: ages 5-10, *y*: ages 11-18

AFGHANISTAN
Thunder over Kandahar - Sharon E. McKay *y* 937
Words in the Dust - Trent Reedy *y* 1033

ALABAMA

Birmingham
Low Red Moon - Caitlin R. Kiernan *y* 872

ALTERNATE UNIVERSE

Is
The Everafter - Amy Huntley *y* 851

Lyrian
A World without Heroes - Brandon Mull *c, y* 335

Shenglang
Gateway - Sharon Shinn *y* 1076

AT SEA
Hurricane Dancers - Margarita Engle *y* 761
Secrets at Sea - Richard Peck *c, y* 383

MS St. Louis
The Other Half of Life: A Novel Based on the True Story of the MS St. Louis - Kim Ablon Whitney *y* 1159

Titanic
Titanic Sinks! - Barry Denenberg *c, y* 107
The Watch That Ends the Night: Voices from the Titanic - Allan Wolf *y* 1171

Atlantic Ocean
Subway Story - Julia Sarcone-Roach *c* 442

English Channel
No Safe Place - Deborah Ellis *y* 757

Gulf of Mexico
Keeper - Kathi Appelt *c, y* 10

South Seas
The Dust of 100 Dogs - A.S. King *y* 874

AUSTRALIA
Beatle Meets Destiny - Gabrielle Williams *y* 1166
Butterfly - Sonya Hartnett *y* 826
The Ghosts of Ashbury High - Jaclyn Moriarty *y* 954
Pink - Lili Wilkinson *y* 1161
The Reformed Vampire Support Group - Catherine Jinks *y* 859
A Small Free Kiss in the Dark - Glenda Millard *y* 948
Stolen - Lucy Christopher *y* 689
Tales from Outer Suburbia - Shaun Tan *c, y* 506
The Winds of Heaven - Judith Clarke *y* 692

Sydney
The Piper's Son - Melina Marchetta *y* 922
Ten Things I Hate about Me - Randa Abdel-Fattah *y* 595
Will - Maria Boyd *y* 652

VICTORIA

Melbourne
A Little Wanting Song - Cath Crowley *y* 713

WESTERN AUSTRALIA
Jasper Jones - Craig Silvey *y* 1079

BELGIUM
Truce: The Day the Soldiers Stopped Fighting - Jim Murphy *c, y* 337

BRAZIL
Daytripper - Fabio Moon *y* 952

CANADA
Boys, Bears, and a Serious Pair of Hiking Boots - Abby McDonald *y* 935
Every Little Thing in the World - Nina de Gramont *y* 724
Half Brother - Kenneth Oppel *y* 992
Migrant - Maxine Trottier *c* 524

Queen of Hearts - Martha Brooks *y* 661

Essex County
The Complete Essex County - Jeff Lemire *y* 896

NOVA SCOTIA

French Hill
Mercury - Hope Larson *y* 892

ONTARIO
The Uninvited - Tim Wynne-Jones *y* 1179

Thunder Bay
Anna Dressed in Blood - Kendare Blake *y* 640

Toronto
Blink & Caution - Tim Wynne-Jones *y* 1180
I Know Here - Laurel Croza *p, c* 93
Jellaby: Monster in the City - Kean Soo *c, y* 479
Money Boy - Paul Yee *y* 1188

SASKATCHEWAN
I Know Here - Laurel Croza *p, c* 93

YUKON TERRITORY
The Wild - Christopher Golden *y* 795

CARIBBEAN ISLANDS
Tangled - Carolyn Mackler *y* 916

CHAD
Rain School - James Rumford *p, c* 431

CHILE
The Dreamer - Pam Munoz Ryan *c, y* 434

Santiago
Gringolandia - Lyn Miller-Lachmann *y* 950

CHINA
Kubla Khan: The Emperor of Everything - Kathleen Krull *c, y* 263
A New Year's Reunion - Yu Li-Qiong *c* 276
North of Beautiful - Justina Chen Headley *y* 830

The Runaway Wok - Ying Chang
　　Compestine　c　76
Silver Phoenix: Beyond the Kingdom of Xia -
　　Cindy Pon　y　1017
Tofu Quilt - Ching Yeung Russell　c, y　432

COLOMBIA

Biblioburro: A True Story from Colombia - Jeanette
　　Winter　c　573

CUBA

The Firefly Letters: A Suffragette's Journey to Cuba
　　- Margarita Engle　y　762
Hurricane Dancers - Margarita Engle　y　761
The Red Umbrella - Christina Diaz
　　Gonzalez　y　735
Tropical Secrets: Holocaust Refugees in Cuba -
　　Margarita Engle　y　760

Guantanamo Bay
Guantanamo Boy - Anna Perera　y　1004

CZECH REPUBLIC

Prague
Daughter of Smoke and Bone - Laini
　　Taylor　y　1120

DENMARK

Nothing - Janne Teller　y　1121

EARTH

Big Wolf and Little Wolf - Sharon Phillips
　　Denslow　c　108
Lockdown - Alexander Gordon Smith　y　1085

Starkian Mountains
The Secret of Zoom - Lynne Jonell　c, y　228

ECUADOR

Andes Mountains
The Queen of Water - Laura Resau　y　1038

EGYPT

Pharaoh's Boat - David L. Weitzman　c, y　553

ENGLAND

13 Treasures - Michelle Harrison　c, y　194
Birth of a Killer - Darren Shan　y　1072
The Brothers Story - Katherine
　　Sturtevant　y　1112
Department 19 - Will Hill　y　838
Flip - Martyn Bedford　y　628
Forbidden - Tabitha Suzuma　y　1116
The Ghost of Crutchfield Hall - Mary Downing
　　Hahn　c, y　186
Heist Society - Ally Carter　y　678
In the Belly of an Ox: The Unexpected Photo-
　　graphic Adventures of Richard and Cherry
　　Kearton - Rebecca Bond　c　43
The Last Little Blue Envelope - Maureen
　　Johnson　y　861
Leviathan - Scott Westerfeld　y　1153
Life: An Exploded Diagram - Mal Peet　y　1003
Me . . . Jane - Patrick McDonnell　p, c　314

My Name Is Mina - David Almond　y　603
Ostrich Boys - Keith Gray　y　804
The Radleys: A Novel - Matt Haig　y　813
Raiders' Ransom - Emily Diamand　y　734
Ruby Red - Kerstin Gier　y　787
Season of Secrets - Sally Nicholls　c, y　357
Secrets at Sea - Richard Peck　c, y　383
Sent - Margaret Peterson Haddix　c, y　185
When I Was Joe - Keren David　y　719
Wildthorn - Jane Eagland　y　748
You Against Me - Jenny Downham　y　743

Bootle
The Un-Forgotten Coat - Frank Cottrell
　　Boyce　c, y　85

Exeter
The Demon's Lexicon - Sarah Rees
　　Brennan　y　657

Farnham
Death Cloud - Andrew Lane　y　890

Liverpool
The Christmas Eve Ghost - Shirley
　　Hughes　c　217

London
Alchemy and Meggy Swann - Karen
　　Cushman　c, y　97
The Amulet of Samarkand: A Bartimaeus Graphic
　　Novel - Jonathan Stroud　c, y　499
The Apothecary - Maile Meloy　y　945
The Carbon Diaries 2015 - Saci Lloyd　y　901
The Cheshire Cheese Cat: A Dickens of a Tale -
　　Carmen Agra Deedy　c, y　105
Clockwork Angel - Cassandra Clare　y　690
The FitzOsbornes in Exile - Michelle
　　Cooper　y　705
The Hunchback Assignments - Arthur G.
　　Slade　y　1081
iBoy - Kevin Brooks　y　660
The Kneebone Boy - Ellen Potter　c, y　398
The Marbury Lens - Andrew Smith　y　1087
The Name of the Star - Maureen Johnson　y　862
Numbers - Rachel Ward　y　1148
The Poisoned House - Michael Ford　y　770
The Red Pyramid - Rick Riordan　c, y　418
The Romeo and Juliet Code - Phoebe
　　Stone　c, y　496
A Spy in the House - Y.S. Lee　y　895
The Stolen One - Suzanne Crowley　y　714
The Story of Cirrus Flux - Matthew
　　Skelton　c, y　469
Tall Story - Candy Gourlay　y　800
Where I Belong - Gillian Cross　y　712

Swampsea
Chime - Franny Billingsley　y　634

Winterfold
White Crow - Marcus Sedgwick　y　1069

Yorkshire
The House of Dead Maids - Clare B.
　　Dunkle　y　747

ERITREA

Hargigo
The Mangrove Tree: Planting Trees to Feed Fami-
　　lies - Cindy Trumbore　c　525

ETHIOPIA

A Long Walk to Water: Based on a True Story -
　　Linda Sue Park　c, y　375

FICTIONAL LOCATION

Green Witch - Alice Hoffman　y　842
Winter's End - Jean-Claude Mourlevat　y　956

Leviathan
Behemoth - Scott Westerfeld　y　1154
Leviathan - Scott Westerfeld　y　1153

Americus
Americus - M.K. Reed　y　1032

Ankh-Morpork
I Shall Wear Midnight - Terry Pratchett　y　1021

Balsinland
Pegasus - Robin McKinley　y　940

Behala
Trash - Andy Mulligan　y　957

Borderlands
Welcome to Bordertown: New Stories and Poems of
　　the Borderlands - Holly Black　y　635

Brandenbrass
Factotum - D.M. Cornish　y　707

Breton
Princess of Glass - Jessica Day George　y　785

Camp Half-Blood
The Lost Hero - Rick Riordan　c, y　417

Catacombs
Nightshade City - Hilary Wagner　c, y　548

Christmastown
The Christmas Giant - Steve Light　p, c　279

City of Glass
City of Glass - Cassandra Clare　y　691

Corus
Bloodhound - Tamora Pierce　y　1013

District 11
Catching Fire - Suzanne Collins　y　699

District 12
Mockingjay - Suzanne Collins　y　700

District 13
Mockingjay - Suzanne Collins　y　700

Dixie
Bayou: Volume 1 - Jeremy Love　y　907

Eathesbury
Entwined - Heather Dixon　y　736

Enclave
Enclave - Ann Aguirre　y　599

Floating Islands
The Floating Islands - Rachel Neumeier　y　978

Fruitless Mountain
Where the Mountain Meets the Moon - Grace
　　Lin　c, y　281

Gentry
The Replacement - Brenna Yovanoff　y　1194

Messina
Miss Lina's Ballerinas - Grace Maccarone   *c*   292

Naples
Take Me with You - Carolyn Marsden   *c, y*   302

Venice
Hidden Voices: The Orphan Musicians of Venice -
   Pat Lowery Collins   *y*   698

JAMAICA
The Dust of 100 Dogs - A.S. King   *y*   874

JAPAN
The Boy in the Garden - Allen Say   *c*   446
Heart of a Samurai - Margi Preus   *y*   1023
Ooku: The Inner Chambers, Volume 1 - Fumi
   Yoshinaga   *y*   1189
Tsunami! - Kimiko Kajikawa   *p, c*   236

Saipan
Warriors in the Crossfire - Nancy Bo
   Flood   *y*   768

KENYA
Burn My Heart - Beverley Naidoo   *c, y*   967
The Lion and the Mouse - Jerry
   Pinkney   *p, c*   394
A Long Walk to Water: Based on a True Story -
   Linda Sue Park   *c, y*   375

KOREA, SOUTH
The Color of Earth - Kim Dong Hwa   *y*   852

LITHUANIA
Between Shades of Gray - Ruta Sepetys   *y*   1071

MALI
Never Forgotten - Patricia C.
   McKissack   *c, y*   319

MEXICO
Dear Primo: A Letter to My Cousin - Duncan
   Tonatiuh   *c*   519
Migrant - Maxine Trottier   *c*   524

MIDDLE EAST
Habibi - Craig Thompson   *y*   1126
The Third Gift - Linda Sue Park   *c*   376

MYANMAR
Bamboo People - Mitali Perkins   *y*   1006

NEPAL
Dragons of Darkness - Antonia Michaelis   *y*   947

NETHERLANDS
Knuffle Bunny Free: An Unexpected Diversion - Mo
   Willems   *p, c*   563

Amsterdam
Annexed - Sharon Dogar   *y*   738

NEW ZEALAND
The 10 PM Question - Kate De Goldi   *y*   723
Guardian of the Dead - Karen Healey   *y*   831
*Kakapo Rescue: Saving the World's Strangest Par-
   rot* - Sy Montgomery   *c, y*   332

Summerton
The Shattering - Karen Healey   *y*   832

NIGERIA
Akata Witch - Nnedi Okorafor   *y*   988
Anna Hibiscus - Atinuke   *c*   14

NORTH AMERICA
Before Columbus: The Americas of 1491 - Charles
   C. Mann   *c, y*   296

NORWAY
Asgard
Odd and the Frost Giants - Neil
   Gaiman   *c, y*   154

OUTER SPACE
Mars
Black Hole Sun - David Macinnis Gill   *y*   789
Life on Mars: Tales from the New Frontier -
   Jonathan Strahan   *y*   1105
You Are the First Kid on Mars - Patrick
   O'Brien   *c, y*   363

PLANET—IMAGINARY
Zita the Spacegirl - Ben Hatke   *c, y*   195

Anara
The Dark City - Catherine Fisher   *y*   766

Discworld
I Shall Wear Midnight - Terry Pratchett   *y*   1021

Fashion City
You'll Like It Here (Everybody Does) - Ruth
   White   *c, y*   559

New Earth
Glow - Amy Kathleen Ryan   *y*   1050

POLAND
*The Champion of Children: The Story of Janusz
   Korczak* - Tomek Bogacki   *c*   41
Once - Morris Gleitzman   *y*   791
Then - Morris Gleitzman   *y*   792

RUSSIA
Breaking Stalin's Nose - Eugene
   Yelchin   *c, y*   588

Siberia
Between Shades of Gray - Ruta Sepetys   *y*   1071

RWANDA
Broken Memory: A Novel of Rwanda - Elisabeth
   Combres   *y*   701

SCOTLAND
The Betrayal of Maggie Blair - Elizabeth
   Laird   *y*   889
Wild Wings - Gill Lewis   *c, y*   275

Ross
Ostrich Boys - Keith Gray   *y*   804

SOMALIA
Where I Belong - Gillian Cross   *y*   712

SOUTH AFRICA
Goal! - Mina Javaherbin   *c*   222
Stones for My Father - Trilby Kent   *y*   869

Pietermaritzburg
This Thing Called the Future - J. L.
   Powers   *y*   1020

SOUTH AMERICA
Before Columbus: The Americas of 1491 - Charles
   C. Mann   *c, y*   296
Exposure - Mal Peet   *y*   1002

SPACESHIP
Galahad
The Comet's Curse - Dom Testa   *y*   1124

Plexus
Living Hell - Catherine Jinks   *y*   858

SPAIN
The Prince of Mist - Carlos Ruiz Zafon   *y*   1195

SUDAN
A Long Walk to Water: Based on a True Story -
   Linda Sue Park   *c, y*   375

SWEDEN
A Faraway Island - Annika Thor   *c, y*   516

Giron
Revolver - Marcus Sedgwick   *y*   1068

SWITZERLAND
Dreams of Significant Girls - Cristina
   Garcia   *y*   779
Leviathan - Scott Westerfeld   *y*   1153

TANZANIA
The Lion and the Mouse - Jerry
   Pinkney   *p, c*   394

THAILAND
Bangkok
Stolen - Lucy Christopher   *y*   689

TURKEY

Istanbul

Behemoth - Scott Westerfeld   *y*   1154

UNITED KINGDOM

Broken Soup - Jenny Valentine   *y*   1136
Cosmic - Frank Cottrell Boyce   *c, y*   84
The Knife That Killed Me - Anthony McGowan   *c, y*   936
The Mysterious Howling - Maryrose Wood   *c, y*   579
Remarkable Creatures - Tracy Chevalier   *y*   686
Solace of the Road - Siobhan Dowd   *y*   741
The Sweetness at the Bottom of the Pie - Alan Bradley   *y*   653
Worldshaker - Richard Harland   *y*   823

Northumbrian Coast

Raven Summer - David Almond   *y*   602

WALES

Miss Peregrine's Home for Peculiar Children - Ransom Riggs   *y*   1041

UNITED STATES

Adios, Nirvana - Conrad Wesselhoeft   *y*   1152
After Ever After - Jordan Sonnenblick   *y*   1094
All the Broken Pieces - Ann Burg   *y*   668
Almost Astronauts: 13 Women Who Dared to Dream - Tanya Lee Stone   *c, y*   497
Along for the Ride - Sarah Dessen   *y*   729
Amy and Roger's Epic Detour - Morgan Matson   *y*   927
Andromeda Klein - Frank Portman   *y*   1019
Andy Shane and the Barn Sale Mystery - Jennifer Richard Jacobson   *c*   220
Angry Management - Chris Crutcher   *y*   715
Angry Young Man - Chris Lynch   *y*   912
Anything but Typical - Nora Raleigh Baskin   *y*   27
Bad Apple - Laura Ruby   *y*   1048
Badd - Tim Tharp   *y*   1125
Bait - Alex Sanchez   *y*   1057
Ballet for Martha: Making Appalachian Spring - Jan Greenberg   *c, y*   174
Beat the Band - Don Calame   *y*   670
Because I Am Furniture - Thalia Chaltas   *y*   682
Before I Fall - Lauren Oliver   *y*   990
Benny and Penny in the Big No-No! - Geoffrey Hayes   *c*   196
Big George: How a Shy Boy Became President Washington - Anne Rockwell   *c*   423
Bink and Gollie - Kate DiCamillo   *c*   111
Blank Confession - Pete Hautman   *y*   827
A Blue So Dark - Holly Schindler   *y*   1059
Bluefish - Pat Schmatz   *y*   1060
Book Fiesta!: Celebrate Children's Day/Book Day; Celebremos El dia de los ninos/El dia de los libros - Pat Mora   *p, c*   334
The Boy Who Couldn't Sleep and Never Had To - D.C. Pierson   *y*   1014
Boyfriends with Girlfriends - Alex Sanchez   *y*   1056
Brain Camp - Susan Kim   *y*   873
Breathless - Lurlene McDaniel   *y*   934
Brontorina - James Howe   *p, c*   213
By the Time You Read This, I'll Be Dead - Julie Anne Peters   *y*   1010
Carter Finally Gets It - Brent Crawford   *y*   711
Center Field - Robert Lipsyte   *y*   900

City Dog, Country Frog - Mo Willems   *p, c*   562
Clean - Amy Reed   *y*   1031
The Clockwork Three - Matthew Kirby   *c, y*   249
Coffeehouse Angel - Suzanne Selfors   *y*   1070
Cold Hands, Warm Heart - Jill Wolfson   *y*   1173
Compromised - Heidi Ayarbe   *y*   616
The Cow Loves Cookies - Karma Wilson   *p, c*   570
Crash into Me - Albert Borris   *y*   649
Crazy - Han Nolan   *y*   980
Crazy Beautiful - Lauren Baratz-Logsted   *y*   619
Crunch - Leslie Connor   *c, y*   78
The Dancing Pancake - Eileen Spinelli   *c, y*   481
The Dark Days of Hamburger Halpin - Josh Berk   *y*   632
The Day-Glo Brothers: The True Story of Bob and Joe Switzer's Bright Ideas and Brand-New Colors - Chris Barton   *c, y*   26
Dear Primo: A Letter to My Cousin - Duncan Tonatiuh   *c*   519
Desert Angel - Charlie Price   *y*   1025
Dessert First - Hallie Durand   *c*   123
Dirty Little Secrets - C.J. Omololu   *y*   991
Drizzle - Kathleen Van Cleve   *c, y*   537
The DUFF: Designated Ugly Fat Friend - Kody Keplinger   *y*   871
The Dunderheads - Paul Fleischman   *c, y*   138
The Dust of 100 Dogs - A.S. King   *y*   874
Earthgirl - Jennifer Cowan   *y*   710
Every You, Every Me - David Levithan   *y*   897
Exposed - Kimberly Marcus   *y*   923
An Eye for Color: The Story of Josef Albers - Natasha Wing   *c*   572
Fade to Blue - Sean Beaudoin   *y*   626
Falling In - Frances O'Roark Dowell   *c, y*   115
Fancy Nancy and the Mermaid Ballet - Jane O'Connor   *p, c*   367
Fat Cat - Robin Brande   *y*   654
Finally - Wendy Mass   *c, y*   305
The Fingertips of Duncan Dorfman - Meg Wolitzer   *c, y*   578
First Day on Earth - Cecil Castellucci   *y*   680
Five 4ths of July - Pat Hughes   *y*   850
Five Minutes More - Darlene Ryan   *y*   1052
Flash Burnout - L.K. Madigan   *y*   919
The Freak Observer - Blythe Woolston   *y*   1175
The Future of Us - Jay Asher   *y*   613
Gentlemen - Michael Northrop   *y*   981
Gifted: Better Late than Never - Marilyn Kaye   *y*   866
Girl, Stolen - April Henry   *y*   835
Glimpse - Carol Lynch Williams   *y*   1163
Goth Girl Rising - Barry Lyga   *y*   910
Gracias Thanks - Pat Mora   *p, c*   333
Griff Carver, Hallway Patrol - Jim Krieg   *c, y*   258
Happy Birthday, Sophie Hartley - Stephanie Greene   *c*   175
Happyface - Stephen Emond   *y*   759
Heart of a Samurai - Margi Preus   *y*   1023
Hero - Mike Lupica   *c, y*   290
Hold Still - Nina LaCour   *y*   887
Hothouse - Chris Lynch   *y*   911
Hound Dog True - Linda Urban   *c, y*   529
How to Get Rich on a Texas Cattle Drive - Tod Olson   *c, y*   370
How to Save a Life - Sara Zarr   *y*   1197
I Am J - Cris Beam   *y*   625
I Kill Giants - Joe Kelly   *y*   867
I'll Be There - Holly Goldberg Sloan   *y*   1083
In Memory of Gorfman T. Frog - Gail Donovan   *c*   113
Into the Wild Nerd Yonder - Julie Halpern   *y*   815
The Iron Thorn - Caitlin Kittredge   *y*   879

The Isle of Blood - Rick Yancey   *y*   1181
It's a Secret! - John Burningham   *p, c*   55
Jump - Elisa Carbone   *y*   673
Jumped - Rita Williams-Garcia   *y*   1170
Just Another Hero - Sharon M. Draper   *y*   745
Just Grace Goes Green - Charise Mericle Harper   *c*   191
Justin Case: School, Drool, and Other Daily Disasters - Rachel Vail   *c, y*   531
Killer Pizza - Greg Taylor   *y*   1118
The Kind of Friends We Used to Be - Frances O'Roark Dowell   *c, y*   116
Knifepoint - Alex Van Tol   *y*   1131
Last Night I Sang to the Monster - Benjamin Alire Saenz   *y*   1054
Leverage - Joshua Cohen   *y*   697
The Lighter Side of Life and Death - C.K. Kelly Martin   *y*   924
The Lightning Thief: The Graphic Novel - Rick Riordan   *c, y*   416
Ling and Ting: Not Exactly the Same! - Grace Lin   *p, c*   280
Lockdown - Walter Dean Myers   *y*   961
A Long Walk to Water: Based on a True Story - Linda Sue Park   *c, y*   375
Love You Hate You Miss You - Elizabeth Scott   *y*   1067
Lunch Lady and the League of Librarians - Jarrett J. Krosoczka   *c*   260
Mangaman - Barry Lyga   *y*   909
Mare's War - Tanita S. Davis   *y*   722
The Mermaid's Mirror - L.K. Madigan   *y*   918
Messed Up - Janet Nichols Lynch   *y*   913
The Miles Between - Mary E. Pearson   *y*   1001
Mindblind - Jennifer Roy   *y*   1044
Mission Unstoppable - Dan Gutman   *c, y*   183
Mockingbird - Kathryn Erskine   *c, y*   133
The Morgue and Me - John C. Ford   *y*   769
The Mostly True Adventures of Homer P. Figg - Rodman Philbrick   *c, y*   389
Mr. Lincoln's High-Tech War: How the North Used the Telegraph, Railroads, Surveillance Balloons, Ironclads, High-Powered Weapons, and More to Win the Civil War - Thomas B. Allen   *y*   601
Nikki and Deja: Birthday Blues - Karen English   *c*   131
North of Beautiful - Justina Chen Headley   *y*   830
Not That Kind of Girl - Susan Donovan   *y*   740
The Notorious Benedict Arnold - Steve Sheinkin   *y*   1074
Now Playing: Stoner & Spaz II - Ron Koertge   *y*   883
Once a Witch - Carolyn MacCullough   *y*   915
Once Was Lost - Sara Zarr   *y*   1196
Operation Yes - Sara Lewis Holmes   *c, y*   209
The Other Half of Life: A Novel Based on the True Story of the MS St. Louis - Kim Ablon Whitney   *y*   1159
Our Abe Lincoln - Jim Aylesworth   *c*   17
Out of My Mind - Sharon M. Draper   *c, y*   118
Paranormalcy - Kiersten White   *y*   1156
Payback Time - Carl Deuker   *y*   732
Pearl - Jo Knowles   *y*   882
Please Ignore Vera Dietz - A.S. King   *y*   876
Pond Circle - Betsy Franco   *c*   149
Pop - Gordon Korman   *y*   885
Pregnant Pause - Han Nolan   *y*   979
Princess Posey and the First Grade Parade - Stephanie Greene   *c*   176

CONNECTICUT
Five 4ths of July - Pat Hughes   *y*   850
My Life in Pink and Green - Lisa
Greenwald   *c, y*   178

Hallowell
Some Girls Are - Courtney Summers   *y*   1114

Stamford
Strawberry Hill - Mary Ann Hoberman   *c*   205

DISTRICT OF COLUMBIA
After the Moment - Garret
Freymann-Weyr   *y*   776

Washington
Melonhead - Katy Kelly   *c*   240

FLORIDA
The Deadly Sister - Eliot Schrefer   *y*   1062
Jersey Tomatoes Are the Best - Maria
Padian   *y*   997
Miles from Ordinary - Carol Lynch
Williams   *y*   1164
The Secret River - Marjorie Kinnan
Rawlings   *c*   407

Florida Everglades
Scat - Carl Hiaasen   *c, y*   203

Key West
Turtle in Paradise - Jennifer L. Holm   *c, y*   206

Kissimee
Absolutely Maybe - Lisa Yee   *y*   1187

Pensacola
Piper Reed, Campfire Girl - Kimberly Willis
Holt   *c*   210

Sanibel Island
Junonia - Kevin Henkes   *c, y*   200

GEORGIA
Caleb's Wars - David L. Dudley   *y*   746
Ruth and the Green Book - Calvin Alexander
Ramsey   *c*   403

Atlanta
Anna and the French Kiss - Stephanie
Perkins   *y*   1008
Peace, Love, and Baby Ducks - Lauren
Myracle   *y*   966
Sisters Red - Jackson Pearce   *y*   1000
The Storm before Atlanta - Karen
Schwabach   *c, y*   454

Carter
The Fantastic Secret of Owen Jester - Barbara
O'Connor   *c, y*   366

HAWAII

Kailua
Calvin Coconut: Trouble Magnet - Graham
Salisbury   *c*   438

IDAHO
*The Boy Who Invented TV: The Story of Philo
Farnsworth* - Kathleen Krull   *c*   261

Camille McPhee Fell Under the Bus - Kristen
Tracy   *c*   523

ILLINOIS
A Season of Gifts - Richard Peck   *y*   384

Cairo
On the Blue Comet - Rosemary Wells   *c, y*   554

Chicago
Angel in My Pocket - Ilene Cooper   *c, y*   82
Divergent - Veronica Roth   *y*   1042
Is It Night or Day? - Fern Schumer
Chapman   *y*   683
My Life with the Lincolns - Gayle
Brandeis   *c, y*   46
An Off Year - Claire Zulkey   *y*   1200
Perfect Chemistry - Simone Elkeles   *y*   755
The Rock and the River - Kekla Magoon   *y*   920
Ruth and the Green Book - Calvin Alexander
Ramsey   *c*   403
Split - Swati Avasthi   *y*   615
Virtuosity - Jessica Martinez   *y*   925
Will Grayson, Will Grayson - David
Levithan   *y*   898
Yummy: The Last Days of a Southside Shorty - G.
Neri   *y*   973

Ellisville
Eddie's War - Carol Fisher Saller   *c, y*   439

INDIANA
Spoiled - Jessica Morgan   *y*   953

South Bend
Viola in Reel Life - Adriana Trigiani   *y*   1133

IOWA
Ashfall - Mike Mullin   *y*   958
The House of Tomorrow - Peter Bognanni   *y*   646
Rotters - Daniel Kraus   *y*   886

Cedarville
The Vast Fields of Ordinary - Nick Burd   *y*   667

Hazelwood
The Mostly True Story of Jack - Kelly
Barnhill   *c, y*   23

KANSAS
The Devil's Paintbox - Victoria McKernan   *y*   938
The Storm in the Barn - Matt Phelan   *c, y*   387

Manifest
Moon over Manifest - Clare Vanderpool   *c, y*   538

KENTUCKY
Faith, Hope, and Ivy June - Phyllis Reynolds
Naylor   *c, y*   347
January's Sparrow - Patricia Polacco   *c, y*   395

LOUISIANA
Flygirl - Sherri L. Smith   *y*   1090

New Orleans
A.D.: New Orleans after the Deluge - Josh
Neufeld   *y*   977
*A Nest for Celeste: A Story about Art, Inspiration,
and the Meaning of Home* - Henry
Cole   *c, y*   74

Ruined: A Ghost Story - Paula Morris   *y*   955
Saint Louis Armstrong Beach - Brenda
Woods   *c, y*   1174
Ship Breaker: A Novel - Paolo Bacigalupi   *y*   618

Tallulah
Alligator Bayou - Donna Jo Napoli   *y*   968

MAINE
The Complete History of Why I Hate Her - Jennifer
Richard Jacobson   *y*   855
The Romeo and Juliet Code - Phoebe
Stone   *c, y*   496
Warped - Maurissa Guibord   *y*   812

Bethsaida Island
Touch Blue - Cynthia Lord   *c, y*   286

Normal
The View from the Top - Hillary Frank   *y*   773

Portland
Delirium - Lauren Oliver   *y*   989
Hush, Hush - Becca Fitzpatrick   *y*   767

MARYLAND
Countdown - Deborah Wiles   *c, y*   561
The Grand Plan to Fix Everything - Uma
Krishnaswami   *c, y*   259
The Snowball Effect - Holly Nicole
Hoxter   *y*   846

Baltimore
Confessions of the Sullivan Sisters - Natalie
Standiford   *y*   1096
How to Say Goodbye in Robot - Natalie
Standiford   *y*   1097
Jake - Audrey Couloumbis   *c, y*   88
Murder Afloat - Jane Leslie Conly   *c, y*   77

MASSACHUSETTS
Clarity - Kim Harrington   *y*   825
Picture the Dead - Adele Griffin   *y*   808

Boston
Busing Brewster - Richard Michelson   *c*   329
The Prince of Fenway Park - Julianna
Baggott   *c, y*   18

Cape Cod
The Fires Beneath the Sea - Lydia
Millet   *c, y*   330

Martha's Vineyard
My Life as a Book - Janet Tashjian   *c, y*   507

Salem
Wicked Girls: A Novel of the Salem Witch Trials -
Stephanie Hemphill   *y*   834

MICHIGAN
Gator on the Loose! - Sue Stauffacher   *c, y*   487
Hidden - Helen Frost   *y*   778
January's Sparrow - Patricia Polacco   *c, y*   395
Junkyard Wonders - Patricia Polacco   *c, y*   396
Nickel Plated - Aric Davis   *y*   721
The Sundown Rule - Wendy Townsend   *c, y*   522
Tyger Tyger - Kersten Hamilton   *y*   816

Comfort
Sparrow Road - Sheila O'Connor   *c, y*   985

Grand Rapids
The Brooklyn Nine: A Novel in Nine Innings - Alan
Gratz   *c, y*   171

OHIO

Cleveland
What Happened on Fox Street - Tricia Springstubb   *c, y*   484

Lightsburg
Tales of the Madman Underground: An Historical Romance 1973 - John Barnes   *y*   620

Paradise
I Am Number Four - Pittacus Lore   *y*   906

OKLAHOMA

The Glorious Adventures of the Sunshine Queen - Geraldine McCaughrean   *c, y*   312

OREGON

The Gardener - S.A. Bodeen   *y*   645
Heart of a Shepherd - Rosanne Parry   *c, y*   377
If I Stay - Gayle Forman   *y*   772
The River - Mary Jane Beaufrand   *y*   627
The Six Rules of Maybe - Deb Caletti   *y*   672

Portland
A Need So Beautiful - Suzanne Young   *y*   1192
Wildwood - Colin Meloy   *c, y*   325

PENNSYLVANIA

Breathless - Jessica Warman   *y*   1149
Crow Call - Lois Lowry   *c*   288
Funny How Things Change - Melissa Wyatt   *y*   1178
Jessica's Guide to Dating on the Dark Side - Beth Fantaskey   *y*   763
Sean Griswold's Head - Lindsey Leavitt   *y*   894
Woods Runner - Gary Paulsen   *c, y*   382

Allegheny Mountains
Three Rivers Rising: A Novel of the Johnstown Flood - Jame Richards   *y*   1040

Howell
This World We Live In - Susan Beth Pfeffer   *y*   1012

Ipswitch
Pie - Sarah Weeks   *c, y*   552

Norvelt
Dead End in Norvelt - Jack Gantos   *c, y*   157

Paradise
The Miracle Stealer - Neil Connelly   *y*   704

Philadelphia
Dangerous Neighbors - Beth Kephart   *y*   870
Same Difference - Siobhan Vivian   *y*   1140

Scranton
Perpetual Check - Rich Wallace   *y*   1147

Steele
The Last Newspaper Boy in America - Sue Corbett   *c, y*   83

Valley Forge
Forge - Laurie Halse Anderson   *y*   607

RHODE ISLAND

The Mockingbirds - Daisy Whitney   *y*   1158

Little Bly
Tighter - Adele Griffin   *y*   807

SOUTH CAROLINA

Dave the Potter, Artist, Poet, Slave - Laban Carrick Hill   *c*   204
Freedom Stone - Jeffrey Kluger   *c, y*   255
Virals - Kathy Reichs   *y*   1035

Charleston
Never Forgotten - Patricia C. McKissack   *c, y*   319

Fayette
The Small Adventure of Popeye and Elvis - Barbara O'Connor   *c, y*   365

Gatlin
Beautiful Creatures - Kami Garcia   *y*   780

TENNESSEE

The Eternal Ones - Kirsten Miller   *y*   949
Kindred - Tammar Stein   *y*   1098
Penny Dreadful - Laurel Snyder   *c, y*   477

Nashville
Somebody Everybody Listens To - Suzanne Supplee   *y*   1115

Starling
Somebody Everybody Listens To - Suzanne Supplee   *y*   1115

TEXAS

Dark Song - Gail Giles   *y*   788
The Evolution of Calpurnia Tate - Jacqueline Kelly   *c, y*   239
Going Bovine - Libba Bray   *y*   655
Keeper - Kathi Appelt   *c, y*   10
The Sweetheart of Prosper County - Jill S. Alexander   *y*   600
Texas Gothic - Rosemary Clement-Moore   *y*   693
Under the Mesquite - Guadalupe Garcia McCall   *y*   929

Cedar Canyon
Through Her Eyes - Jennifer Archer   *y*   610

Dulcina
Highway to Hell - Rosemary Clement-Moore   *y*   694

El Paso
Soul Enchilada - David Macinnis Gill   *y*   790

Houston
What Can't Wait - Ashley Hope Perez   *y*   1005

San Antonio
Maximilian and the Mystery of the Guardian Angel: A Bilingual Lucha Libre Thriller - Xavier Garza   *y*   782

UTAH

Pineridge
Keep Sweet - Michele Dominguez Greene   *y*   805

VERMONT

Return to Sender - Julia Alvarez   *c, y*   7

North Dover
Reality Check - Peter Abrahams   *y*   596

Tunbridge
Tricking the Tallyman - Jacqueline Davies   *c*   101

VIRGINIA

Lark - Tracey Porter   *y*   1018

Black River
A Month of Sundays - Ruth White   *y*   558

Charlottesville
Jefferson's Sons: A Founding Father's Secret Children - Kimberly Brubaker Bradley   *c, y*   45

WASHINGTON

The Body Finder - Kimberly Derting   *y*   728
The Trouble with May Amelia - Jennifer L. Holm   *c, y*   207

Bellingham
Harmonic Feedback - Tara Kelly   *y*   868

Bishop Rock
Stay - Deb Caletti   *y*   671

Cascade Mountains
Storm Mountain - Tom Birdseye   *c, y*   36

Seattle
Hold Me Closer, Necromancer - Lish McBride   *y*   928
Misfit - Jon Skovron   *y*   1080
Real Live Boyfriends: Yes, Boyfriends, Plural. If My Life Weren't Complicated I Wouldn't Be Ruby Oliver - E. Lockhart   *y*   904
The Treasure Map of Boys: Noel, Jackson, Finn, Hutch, Gideon—and Me, Ruby Oliver - E. Lockhart   *y*   905

WEST COAST

Stagecoach Sal - Deborah Hopkinson   *c*   212

WEST VIRGINIA

Charleston
Finding Family - Tonya Bolden   *c, y*   42

Culpepper
Close to Famous - Joan Bauer   *c, y*   623

Dwyer
Funny How Things Change - Melissa Wyatt   *y*   1178

Rowlesburg
When the Whistle Blows - Fran Cannon Slayton   *y*   1082

WISCONSIN

Madison
Gringolandia - Lyn Miller-Lachmann   *y*   950
With or Without You - Brian Farrey   *y*   764

WYOMING

Jackson
Unearthly - Cynthia Hand   *y*   819

VIETNAM

Saigon
Inside Out and Back Again - Thanhha Lai   *c, y*   888

ZIMBABWE

Now Is the Time for Running - Michael Williams   *y*   1168
Out of Shadows - Jason Wallace   *y*   1146

Subject Index

This index lists subjects which are covered in the featured titles. These can include such things as family life, animals, personal and social problems, historical events, ethnic groups, and story types, e.g. Mystery and Detective Stories. Book titles are listed alphabetically under headings, with author names, age-level code(s) and entry numbers also included. The age-level codes are as follows: *p*: ages 1-4, *c*: ages 5-10, *y*: ages 11-18.

Abolition of slavery

Sugar Changed the World: A Story of Magic, Spice, Slavery, Freedom, and Science - Marc Aronson *y* 612

Abolitionists

John Brown: His Fight for Freedom - John Hendrix *c, y* 197

Abuse

Bait - Alex Sanchez *y* 1057
Because I Am Furniture - Thalia Chaltas *y* 682
Bitter End - Jennifer Brown *y* 663
Bronxwood - Coe Booth *y* 648
Carmen - Walter Dean Myers *y* 964
Dark Song - Gail Giles *y* 788
Desert Angel - Charlie Price *y* 1025
Guantanamo Boy - Anna Perera *y* 1004
Hush - Eishes Chayil *y* 685
Okay for Now - Gary D. Schmidt *c, y* 451
Scars - Cheryl Rainfield *y* 1028

Accidents

Amelia Lost: The Life and Disappearance of Amelia Earhart - Candace Fleming *c, y* 144
As Easy as Falling off the Face of the Earth - Lynne Rae Perkins *c, y* 386
I Broke My Trunk! - Mo Willems *p, c* 567
Jake - Audrey Couloumbis *c, y* 88

Acting

Operation Yes - Sara Lewis Holmes *c, y* 209
Strings Attached - Judy Blundell *y* 643

Actors

How I Stole Johnny Depp's Alien Girlfriend - Gary Ghislain *y* 786
Sir Charlie Chaplin: The Funniest Man in the World - Sid Fleischman *c, y* 139

Addiction

Clean - Amy Reed *y* 1031
Last Night I Sang to the Monster - Benjamin Alire Saenz *y* 1054
Recovery Road - Blake Nelson *y* 969

Adolescence

The 10 PM Question - Kate De Goldi *y* 723
Addie on the Inside - James Howe *c, y* 845
After Ever After - Jordan Sonnenblick *y* 1094
All These Things I've Done - Gabrielle Zevin *y* 1198
Along for the Ride - Sarah Dessen *y* 729
Andromeda Klein - Frank Portman *y* 1019
Angry Management - Chris Crutcher *y* 715
Annexed - Sharon Dogar *y* 738
Ashfall - Mike Mullin *y* 958
Birth of a Killer - Darren Shan *y* 1072
Burn My Heart - Beverley Naidoo *c, y* 967
The Carbon Diaries 2015 - Saci Lloyd *y* 901
Carter Finally Gets It - Brent Crawford *y* 711
The Chosen One - Carol Lynch Williams *y* 1165
City of Glass - Cassandra Clare *y* 691
Coffeehouse Angel - Suzanne Selfors *y* 1070
The Comet's Curse - Dom Testa *y* 1124
A Conspiracy of Kings - Megan Whalen Turner *y* 1134
Crash into Me - Albert Borris *y* 649
Creature of the Night - Kate Thompson *y* 1128
Die for Me - Amy Plum *y* 1016
The DUFF: Designated Ugly Fat Friend - Kody Keplinger *y* 871
Eli the Good - Silas House *y* 844
The Future of Us - Jay Asher *y* 613
Gifted: Better Late than Never - Marilyn Kaye *y* 866
Glimpse - Carol Lynch Williams *y* 1163
Happyface - Stephen Emond *y* 759
Heist Society - Ally Carter *y* 678
Hidden Voices: The Orphan Musicians of Venice - Pat Lowery Collins *y* 698
Homestretch - Paul Volponi *y* 1142
The Hunchback Assignments - Arthur G. Slade *y* 1081
I Am J - Cris Beam *y* 625
The Interrogation of Gabriel James - Charlie Price *y* 1024
Jersey Tomatoes Are the Best - Maria Padian *y* 997
Jump - Elisa Carbone *y* 673
Jumping Off Swings - Jo Knowles *y* 881
The Kind of Friends We Used to Be - Frances O'Roark Dowell *c, y* 116
Level Up - Gene Luen Yang *y* 1184
Lola and the Boy Next Door - Stephanie Perkins 1007

Marcelo in the Real World - Francisco X. Stork *y* 1103
The Miles Between - Mary E. Pearson *y* 1001
Mindblind - Jennifer Roy *y* 1044
Misfit - Jon Skovron *y* 1080
The Mockingbirds - Daisy Whitney *y* 1158
Mockingjay - Suzanne Collins *y* 700
My Fair Godmother - Janette Rallison *y* 1029
A Need So Beautiful - Suzanne Young *y* 1192
Nikki and Deja: Birthday Blues - Karen English *c* 131
No and Me - Delphine De Vigan *y* 726
Nothing - Janne Teller *y* 1121
Odd and the Frost Giants - Neil Gaiman *c, y* 154
Once Was Lost - Sara Zarr *y* 1196
The Orange Houses - Paul Griffin *y* 810
Out of the Blue - S.L. Rottman *y* 1043
Over the End Line - Alfred C. Martino *y* 926
Pregnant Pause - Han Nolan *y* 979
The Red Pyramid - Rick Riordan *c, y* 418
Salt - Maurice Gee *y* 783
She Loves You, She Loves You Not... - Julie Anne Peters 1011
Smile - Raina Telgemeier *c, y* 511
Stupid Fast: The Summer I Went from a Joke to a Jock - Geoff Herbach *y* 836
Surface Tension: A Novel in Four Summers - Brent Runyon *y* 1049
Sweet Treats and Secret Crushes - Lisa Greenwald *y* 806
The Sweetheart of Prosper County - Jill S. Alexander *y* 600
Swim the Fly - Don Calame *y* 669
Tales of the Madman Underground: An Historical Romance 1973 - John Barnes *y* 620
Tilt - Alan Cumyn *y* 716
Time You Let Me In: 25 Poets under 25 - Naomi Shihab Nye *y* 361
Tricks - Ellen Hopkins *y* 843
The Vast Fields of Ordinary - Nick Burd *y* 667
Virals - Kathy Reichs *y* 1035
When I Was Joe - Keren David *y* 719
When the Whistle Blows - Fran Cannon Slayton *y* 1082
Will - Maria Boyd *y* 652
Will Grayson, Will Grayson - David Levithan *y* 898
The Winds of Heaven - Judith Clarke *y* 692
You Wish - Mandy Hubbard *y* 849

Animals/Wolves

Anthropology

Antisemitism

Ants

Apartheid

Apartments

Appalachian people (Southern States)

Apprentices

Apprenticeship programs

Archaeology

Architecture

Arctic

Armed forces

Arson

Art

Artists

Assassination

Astrology

Authorship

Autobiographies

Automobiles

Aviation

Babysitters

Ballet

Subject Index

Subject Index

Country music

Somebody Everybody Listens To - Suzanne
    Supplee   *y*   1115

Courage

Americus - M.K. Reed   *y*   1032
If I Never Forever Endeavor - Holly
    Meade   *p, c*   323
Just Another Hero - Sharon M. Draper   *y*   745
North of Beautiful - Justina Chen Headley   *y*   830
Shiver - Maggie Stiefvater   *y*   1100
Zita the Spacegirl - Ben Hatke   *c, y*   195

Cousins

Dear Primo: A Letter to My Cousin - Duncan
    Tonatiuh   *c*   519
Illyria - Elizabeth Hand   *y*   820
Mercury - Hope Larson   *y*   892
Storm Mountain - Tom Birdseye   *c, y*   36
Take Me to the River - Will Hobbs   *c, y*   841
The Winds of Heaven - Judith Clarke   *y*   692

Cows (Cattle)

The Cow Loves Cookies - Karma
    Wilson   *p, c*   570

Crime

Blood on My Hands - Todd Strasser   *y*   1106
Bloodhound - Tamora Pierce   *y*   1013
Griff Carver, Hallway Patrol - Jim
    Krieg   *c, y*   258
How to Steal a Car - Pete Hautman   *y*   829
Just Another Hero - Sharon M. Draper   *y*   745
Legend - Marie Lu   *y*   908
Liar - Justine Larbalestier   *y*   891
Lockdown - Alexander Gordon Smith   *y*   1085
Rikers High - Paul Volponi   *y*   1143
Shine - Lauren Myracle   *y*   965

Criminals

Bloodhound - Tamora Pierce   *y*   1013
Bullet Point - Peter Abrahams   *y*   597
Highway Robbery - Kate Thompson   *c, y*   514
Red Glove - Holly Black   *y*   636
The Secret Science Alliance and the Copycat Crook
    - Eleanor Davis   *c, y*   103
Stagecoach Sal - Deborah Hopkinson   *c*   212
White Cat - Holly Black   *y*   639

Crocodiles

Lyle Walks the Dogs: A Counting Book - Bernard
    Waber   *p, c*   546

Cuban history

The Red Umbrella - Christina Diaz
    Gonzalez   *y*   735

Cults

Alis - Naomi Rich   *y*   1039
The Chosen One - Carol Lynch Williams   *y*   1165

Cultural conflict

Inside Out and Back Again - Thanhha
    Lai   *c, y*   888

Cultural identity

*Marisol McDonald Doesn't Match/Marisol Mc-
    Donald no combina* - Monica Brown   *c*   49
Mirror - Jeannie Baker   *c*   19
Shine, Coconut Moon - Neesha Meminger   *y*   946
Skunk Girl - Sheba Karim   *y*   864

Culture

Balarama: A Royal Elephant - Ted Lewin   *c*   274
Dear Primo: A Letter to My Cousin - Duncan
    Tonatiuh   *c*   519
The FitzOsbornes in Exile - Michelle
    Cooper   *y*   705
Words in the Dust - Trent Reedy   *y*   1033

Dance

Ballet for Martha: Making Appalachian Spring -
    Jan Greenberg   *c, y*   174
Brontorina - James Howe   *p, c*   213
Entwined - Heather Dixon   *y*   736
Miss Lina's Ballerinas - Grace Maccarone   *c*   292
Ole Flamenco - George Ancona   *c, y*   8
Princess of the Midnight Ball - Jessica Day
    George   *y*   784
Strings Attached - Judy Blundell   *y*   643

Dating (Social customs)

After the Moment - Garret
    Freymann-Weyr   *y*   776
Almost Perfect - Brian Katcher   *y*   865
Anna and the French Kiss - Stephanie
    Perkins   *y*   1008
The Big Crunch - Pete Hautman   *y*   828
Front and Center - Catherine Gilbert
    Murdock   *y*   960
Hush, Hush - Becca Fitzpatrick   *y*   767
Jessica's Guide to Dating on the Dark Side - Beth
    Fantaskey   *y*   763
Lola and the Boy Next Door - Stephanie
    Perkins   1007
Past Perfect - Leila Sales   *y*   1055
Perfect Chemistry - Simone Elkeles   *y*   755
*Real Live Boyfriends: Yes, Boyfriends, Plural. If My
    Life Weren't Complicated I Wouldn't Be Ruby
    Oliver* - E. Lockhart   *y*   904
Stay - Deb Caletti   *y*   671
Stay with Me - Paul Griffin   *y*   809
Ten Things We Did (and Probably Shouldn't Have)
    - Sarah Mlynowski   *y*   951
Tilt - Alan Cumyn   *y*   716
*The Treasure Map of Boys: Noel, Jackson, Finn,
    Hutch, Gideon—and Me, Ruby Oliver* - E.
    Lockhart   *y*   905
The Unwritten Rule - Elizabeth Scott   *y*   1066
The View from the Top - Hillary Frank   *y*   773
Viola in Reel Life - Adriana Trigiani   *y*   1133
Why We Broke Up - Daniel Handler   *y*   821

Death

Adios, Nirvana - Conrad Wesselhoeft   *y*   1152
Amy and Roger's Epic Detour - Morgan
    Matson   *y*   927
Before I Fall - Lauren Oliver   *y*   990
The Beginning of After - Jennifer Castle   *y*   681
Between - Jessica Warman   *y*   1150
Blizzard of Glass: The Halifax Explosion of 1917 -
    Sally M. Walker   *c, y*   549
Bone Dog - Eric Rohmann   *c*   425
Daytripper - Fabio Moon   *y*   952
Departure Time - Truus Matti   *c, y*   306

Depression (Mood disorder)

Dirty Little Secrets - C.J. Omololu   *y*   991
The Everafter - Amy Huntley   *y*   851
The Freak Observer - Blythe Woolston   *y*   1175
Half World - Hiromi Goto   *y*   799
Hero - Mike Lupica   *c, y*   290
Hold Me Closer, Necromancer - Lish
    McBride   *y*   928
Hothouse - Chris Lynch   *y*   911
How to Save a Life - Sara Zarr   *y*   1197
How to Say Goodbye in Robot - Natalie
    Standiford   *y*   1097
If I Stay - Gayle Forman   *y*   772
Imaginary Girls - Nova Ren Suma   *y*   1113
It's Not Summer Without You - Jenny Han   *y*   818
Lark - Tracey Porter   *y*   1018
Love Is the Higher Law - David Levithan   *y*   899
Love You Hate You Miss You - Elizabeth
    Scott   *y*   1067
Messed Up - Janet Nichols Lynch   *y*   913
Mockingbird - Kathryn Erskine   *c, y*   133
Mother Poems - Hope Anita Smith   *c, y*   473
No More Us for You - David Hernandez   *y*   837
Numbers - Rachel Ward   *y*   1148
Ostrich Boys - Keith Gray   *y*   804
Paper Covers Rock - Jenny Hubbard   *y*   848
Peace, Locomotion - Jacqueline
    Woodson   *c, y*   581
Pearl - Jo Knowles   *y*   882
Pretty Dead - Francesca Lia Block   *y*   641
Prophecy of the Sisters - Michelle Zink   *y*   1199
Say the Word - Jeannine Garsee   *y*   781
The Secret Year - Jennifer R. Hubbard   *y*   847
Silhouetted by the Blue - Traci L. Jones   *y*   863
The Sky Is Everywhere - Jandy Nelson   *y*   970
The Snowball Effect - Holly Nicole
    Hoxter   *y*   846
Stealing Death - Janet Lee Carey   *y*   675
The Stolen One - Suzanne Crowley   *y*   714
The Survival Kit - Donna Freitas   *y*   775
Thirteen Days to Midnight - Patrick
    Carman   *y*   676
Tighter - Adele Griffin   *y*   807
Umbrella Summer - Lisa Graff   *c, y*   167
What Momma Left Me - Renee Watson   *c, y*   551
You Are Here - Jennifer E. Smith   *y*   1089
You Are Not Here - Samantha Schutz   *y*   1064

Deception

*Liar, Liar: The Theory, Practice and Destructive
    Properties of Deception* - Gary
    Paulsen   *c, y*   999

Demons

Clockwork Angel - Cassandra Clare   *y*   690
Daughter of Smoke and Bone - Laini
    Taylor   *y*   1120
The Demon's Lexicon - Sarah Rees
    Brennan   *y*   657
Misfit - Jon Skovron   *y*   1080
The Space Between - Brenna Yovanoff   *y*   1193

Dentistry

Smile - Raina Telgemeier   *c, y*   511

Depression (Mood disorder)

Silhouetted by the Blue - Traci L. Jones   *y*   863
Sorta Like a Rock Star - Matthew Quick   *y*   1026

Deserts

The Third Gift - Linda Sue Park   *c*   376

Detective fiction

Andy Shane and the Barn Sale Mystery - Jennifer Richard Jacobson   *c*   220
The Case of the Case of Mistaken Identity - Mac Barnett   *c, y*   22
City of Orphans - Avi   *c, y*   15
Death Cloud - Andrew Lane   *y*   890
The Girl Is Murder - Kathryn Miller Haines   *y*   814
The Interrogation of Gabriel James - Charlie Price   *y*   1024
Missing on Superstition Mountain - Elise Broach   *c, y*   47
Nickel Plated - Aric Davis   *y*   721
Pie - Sarah Weeks   *c, y*   552
Reality Check - Peter Abrahams   *y*   596

Devil

Soul Enchilada - David Macinnis Gill   *y*   790

Diaries

Faith, Hope, and Ivy June - Phyllis Reynolds Naylor   *c, y*   347
Scrawl - Mark Shulman   *y*   1077

Dictators

Kubla Khan: The Emperor of Everything - Kathleen Krull   *c, y*   263
Nightshade City - Hilary Wagner   *c, y*   548

Dinosaurs

Brontorina - James Howe   *p, c*   213
Dinosaur Mountain: Digging into the Jurassic Age - Deborah Kogan Ray   *c*   408
Dinosaur Woods: Can Seven Clever Critters Save Their Forest Home? - George McClements   *p, c*   313
Dinothesaurus - Douglas Florian   *c*   146
Dinotrux - Chris Gall   *p, c*   156
Lulu and the Brontosaurus - Judith Viorst   *p, c*   542

Disadvantaged persons

No Ordinary Day - Deborah Ellis   *c, y*   126
Words in the Dust - Trent Reedy   *y*   1033

Disasters

A.D.: New Orleans after the Deluge - Josh Neufeld   *y*   977
Disasters: Natural and Man-Made Catastrophes through the Centuries - Brenda Z. Guiberson   *c, y*   181
Titanic Sinks! - Barry Denenberg   *c, y*   107
Zenith - Julie Bertagna   *y*   633

Discipline

Spinster Goose: Twisted Rhymes for Naughty Children - Lisa Wheeler   *c*   556

Discovery and exploration

Into the Unknown: How Great Explorers Found Their Way by Land, Sea, and Air - Stewart Ross   *c, y*   428

Diseases

Five Minutes More - Darlene Ryan   *y*   1052
The Giant Slayer - Iain Lawrence   *c, y*   267
Going Bovine - Libba Bray   *y*   655
Harmonic Feedback - Tara Kelly   *y*   868
No Ordinary Day - Deborah Ellis   *c, y*   126
Virals - Kathy Reichs   *y*   1035

Divorce

Lexie - Audrey Couloumbis   *c, y*   87
What Happened to Goodbye - Sarah Dessen   *y*   730

Dogs

Aggie the Brave - Lori Ries   *p, c*   414
Apple Pie ABC - Alison Murray   *p, c*   339
A Ball for Daisy - Chris Raschka   *p, c*   406
Bone Dog - Eric Rohmann   *c*   425
City Dog, Country Frog - Mo Willems   *p, c*   562
Dog Loves Books - Louise Yates   *p, c*   586
The Dust of 100 Dogs - A.S. King   *y*   874
I'm the Best - Lucy Cousins   *p, c*   91
The Incredible Life of Balto - Meghan McCarthy   *p, c*   308
Itty Bitty - Cece Bell   *p, c*   30
The King's Taster - Kenneth Oppel   *c*   371
Lyle Walks the Dogs: A Counting Book - Bernard Waber   *p, c*   546
Not That Kind of Girl - Susan Donovan   *y*   740
Nubs: The True Story of a Mutt, a Marine, & a Miracle - Mary Nethery   *c*   352
RRRalph - Lois Ehlert   *p, c*   124
Say Hello to Zorro! - Carter Goodrich   *p, c*   164
See Me Run - Paul Meisel   *p, c*   324
Star in the Forest - Laura Resau   *c, y*   412
The Trouble with Chickens - Doreen Cronin   *c*   92
Waiting for the Magic - Patricia MacLachlan   *c*   293

Dolls

The Good, the Bad, and the Barbie: A Doll's History and Her Impact on Us - Tanya Lee Stone   *y*   1102

Domestic cats

Benno and the Night of Broken Glass - Meg Wiviott   *c*   576
The Familiars - Adam Jay Epstein   *c, y*   132
Nini Lost and Found - Anita Lobel   *p, c*   283
Posy - Linda Newbery   *p, c*   354

Dragons

Dragons of Darkness - Antonia Michaelis   *y*   947
The Floating Islands - Rachel Neumeier   *y*   978
Hereville: How Mirka Got Her Sword - Barry Deutsch   *c, y*   110
King Jack and the Dragon - Peter Bently   *p, c*   31
No Such Things as Dragons - Philip Reeve   *c, y*   410
The Runaway Dragon - Kate Coombs   *c, y*   79
Thomas and the Dragon Queen - Shutta Crum   *c*   96
Where the Mountain Meets the Moon - Grace Lin   *c, y*   281

Drawing

Adventures in Cartooning: How to Turn Your Doodles into Comics - James Sturm   *c, y*   500
Art and Max - David Wiesner   *c*   560
A Beach Tail - Karen Lynn Williams   *p, c*   568
A Book about Color: A Clear and Simple Guide for Young Artists - Mark Gonyea   *c*   163
Chalk - Bill Thomson   *c*   515
Drawing from Memory - Allen Say   *c, y*   445

Dreams

Bird in a Box - Andrea Davis Pinkney   *c, y*   392
The Boy in the Garden - Allen Say   *c*   446
A Call for a New Alphabet - Jef Czekaj   *c*   99
Franklin's Big Dreams - David Teague   *p, c*   509

Droughts

The Storm in the Barn - Matt Phelan   *c, y*   387

Drug abuse

Burnout - Adrienne Maria Vrettos   *y*   1144
Clean - Amy Reed   *y*   1031
Dope Sick - Walter Dean Myers   *y*   962
Virtuosity - Jessica Martinez   *y*   925

Drugs

Blank Confession - Pete Hautman   *y*   827
Efrain's Secret - Sofia Quintero   *y*   1027
Punkzilla - Adam Rapp   *y*   1030

Dwarfs

Going Bovine - Libba Bray   *y*   655

Dystopias

Birthmarked - Caragh M. O'Brien   *y*   982
Catching Fire - Suzanne Collins   *y*   699
Delirium - Lauren Oliver   *y*   989
Enclave - Ann Aguirre   *y*   599
Prized - Caragh M. O'Brien   *y*   983
Salt - Maurice Gee   *y*   783
Winter's End - Jean-Claude Mourlevat   *y*   956

Eating disorders

Wintergirls - Laurie Halse Anderson   *y*   608

Ecology

Boys, Bears, and a Serious Pair of Hiking Boots - Abby McDonald   *y*   935
The Curious Garden - Peter Brown   *p, c*   50
Earth: Feeling the Heat - Brenda Z. Guiberson   *c*   182
Earthgirl - Jennifer Cowan   *y*   710
Energy Island: How One Community Harnessed the Wind and Changed Their World - Allan Drummond   *c*   119
My Life in Pink and Green - Lisa Greenwald   *c, y*   178
Panorama: A Foldout Book - Fani Marceau   *c*   297
Years of Dust: The Story of the Dust Bowl - Albert Marrin   *c, y*   301

Education

If Rocks Could Sing: A Discovered Alphabet - Leslie McGuirk   *p, c*   318

Frogs

999 Tadpoles - Ken Kimura   *p, c*   247
City Dog, Country Frog - Mo Willems   *p, c*   562
The Fantastic Secret of Owen Jester - Barbara
 O'Connor   *c, y*   366
The Frog Scientist - Pamela S. Turner   *y*   1135
Hip-Pocket Papa - Sandra Markle   *c*   300
In Memory of Gorfman T. Frog - Gail
 Donovan   *c*   113

Frontier life

The Devil's Paintbox - Victoria McKernan   *y*   938
How to Get Rich on a Texas Cattle Drive - Tod
 Olson   *c, y*   370
Queen of Hearts - Martha Brooks   *y*   661
Stagecoach Sal - Deborah Hopkinson   *c*   212

Futuristic society

The Carbon Diaries 2015 - Saci Lloyd   *y*   901
The Comet's Curse - Dom Testa   *y*   1124
Legend - Marie Lu   *y*   908
Mockingjay - Suzanne Collins   *y*   700
Salt - Maurice Gee   *y*   783
Trash - Andy Mulligan   *y*   957
Worldshaker - Richard Harland   *y*   823

Gambling

*The Cardturner: A Novel about a King, a Queen,
 and a Joker* - Louis Sachar   *y*   1053

Games

Chalk - Bill Thomson   *c*   515
The Fingertips of Duncan Dorfman - Meg
 Wolitzer   *c, y*   578
*Lemonade and Other Poems Squeezed from a
 Single Word* - Bob Raczka   *c*   402
Let's Do Nothing! - Tony Fucile   *c*   153
Level Up - Gene Luen Yang   *y*   1184
*The Potato Chip Puzzles: The Puzzling World of
 Winston Breen* - Eric Berlin   *c, y*   33
Press Here - Herve Tullet   526

Gangs

iBoy - Kevin Brooks   *y*   660
The Knife That Killed Me - Anthony
 McGowan   *c, y*   936
Perfect Chemistry - Simone Elkeles   *y*   755
Yummy: The Last Days of a Southside Shorty - G.
 Neri   *y*   973

Gardening

*First Garden: The White House Garden and How It
 Grew* - Robbin Gourley   *c*   165
My Garden - Kevin Henkes   *p, c*   198
Yucky Worms - Vivian French   *p, c*   152

Gardens

The Curious Garden - Peter Brown   *p, c*   50
The Honeybee Man - Lela Nargi   *c*   345

Gay and lesbian rights

Sister Mischief - Laura Goode   *y*   797
With or Without You - Brian Farrey   *y*   764

Geese

Honk, Honk, Goose!: Canada Geese Start a Family
 - April Pulley Sayre   *p, c*   447

Genealogy

Mercury - Hope Larson   *y*   892

Genetic engineering

Behemoth - Scott Westerfeld   *y*   1154
Birthmarked - Caragh M. O'Brien   *y*   982
Wither - Lauren DeStefano   *y*   731

Genocide

Broken Memory: A Novel of Rwanda - Elisabeth
 Combres   *y*   701

Geography

Panorama: A Foldout Book - Fani
 Marceau   *c*   297

Germans

After the Train - Gloria Whelan   *y*   557
Ashes - Kathryn Lasky   *y*   893
An Eye for Color: The Story of Josef Albers - Na-
 tasha Wing   *c*   572

Ghosts

Anna Dressed in Blood - Kendare Blake   *y*   640
Anya's Ghost - Vera Brosgol   *y*   662
A Banquet for Hungry Ghosts - Ying Chang
 Compestine   *y*   702
The Christmas Eve Ghost - Shirley
 Hughes   *c*   217
Days of Little Texas - R.A. Nelson   *y*   972
Dying to Meet You - Kate Klise   *c, y*   254
The Fires Beneath the Sea - Lydia
 Millet   *c, y*   330
The Ghost of Crutchfield Hall - Mary Downing
 Hahn   *c, y*   186
The House of Dead Maids - Clare B.
 Dunkle   *y*   747
Liesl and Po - Lauren Oliver   *c, y*   369
Nightspell - Leah Cypess   *y*   717
Picture the Dead - Adele Griffin   *y*   808
The Poisoned House - Michael Ford   *y*   770
Ruined: A Ghost Story - Paula Morris   *y*   955
Shade - Jeri Smith-Ready   *y*   1091
The Shadows - Jacqueline West   *c, y*   555
Texas Gothic - Rosemary Clement-Moore   *y*   693
Tighter - Adele Griffin   *y*   807

Giants

The Christmas Giant - Steve Light   *p, c*   279
I Kill Giants - Joe Kelly   *y*   867
The Runaway Dragon - Kate Coombs   *c, y*   79
Stand Straight, Ella Kate - Kate Klise   *c*   252

Gifted children

Mindblind - Jennifer Roy   *y*   1044
No and Me - Delphine De Vigan   *y*   726

Gifted persons

Toads and Diamonds - Heather
 Tomlinson   *y*   1132

Gifts

Andy Shane and the Barn Sale Mystery - Jennifer
 Richard Jacobson   *c*   220
Grandma's Gift - Eric Velasquez   *c*   540

Gnomes

Going Bovine - Libba Bray   *y*   655

Gold

Green - Laura Peyton Roberts   *c, y*   420

Good and evil

Blood - K.J. Wignall   *y*   1160
The Emerald Atlas - John Stephens   *c, y*   493
Hunger - Michael Grant   *y*   803
I Shall Wear Midnight - Terry Pratchett   *y*   1021
Princess of the Midnight Ball - Jessica Day
 George   *y*   784
Sidekicks - Jack D. Ferraiolo   *y*   765
Soul Enchilada - David Macinnis Gill   *y*   790
Summer Birds: The Butterflies of Maria Merian -
 Margarita Engle   *c*   130

Grandfathers

Clara Lee and the Apple Pie Dream - Jenny
 Han   *c*   189
Finding Family - Tonya Bolden   *c, y*   42
Grandpa Green - Lane Smith   *c*   476
Jake - Audrey Couloumbis   *c, y*   88
Ratfink - Marcia Thornton Jones   *c, y*   230
Through Her Eyes - Jennifer Archer   *y*   610

Grandmothers

Confessions of the Sullivan Sisters - Natalie
 Standiford   *y*   1096
Grandma's Gift - Eric Velasquez   *c*   540
The House of Tomorrow - Peter Bognanni   *y*   646
Mare's War - Tanita S. Davis   *y*   722
My Abuelita - Tony Johnston   *p, c*   226
Sleepover at Gramma's House - Barbara
 Joosse   *p, c*   231

Grandparents

Knuffle Bunny Free: An Unexpected Diversion - Mo
 Willems   *p, c*   563
My Abuelita - Tony Johnston   *p, c*   226
What Momma Left Me - Renee Watson   *c, y*   551

Great Depression, 1929-1934

Bird in a Box - Andrea Davis Pinkney   *c, y*   392
Moon over Manifest - Clare Vanderpool   *c, y*   538
Strawberry Hill - Mary Ann Hoberman   *c*   205
Turtle in Paradise - Jennifer L. Holm   *c, y*   206
Years of Dust: The Story of the Dust Bowl - Albert
 Marrin   *c, y*   301

Grief

Amy and Roger's Epic Detour - Morgan
 Matson   *y*   927
Angel in My Pocket - Ilene Cooper   *c, y*   82
The Beginning of After - Jennifer Castle   *y*   681
Broken Memory: A Novel of Rwanda - Elisabeth
 Combres   *y*   701
Broken Soup - Jenny Valentine   *y*   1136
Grounded - Kate Klise   *c, y*   253
Hold Still - Nina LaCour   *y*   887

Homeless persons

No and Me - Delphine De Vigan   *y*   726
Sorta Like a Rock Star - Matthew Quick   *y*   1026

Homosexuality

King of the Screwups - K.L. Going   *y*   794
Mommy, Mama and Me - Leslea
   Newman   *p, c*   356
Money Boy - Paul Yee   *y*   1188
Putting Makeup on the Fat Boy - Bil
   Wright   *y*   1177
Say the Word - Jeannine Garsee   *y*   781
She Loves You, She Loves You Not... - Julie Anne
   Peters   1011
Shine - Lauren Myracle   *y*   965
Sister Mischief - Laura Goode   *y*   797
The Vast Fields of Ordinary - Nick Burd   *y*   667
With or Without You - Brian Farrey   *y*   764

Honesty

The Boy Who Cried Ninja - Alex
   Latimer   *p, c*   266

Horror

Birth of a Killer - Darren Shan   *y*   1072
Blood - K.J. Wignall   *y*   1160
Brain Camp - Susan Kim   *y*   873
Fear: 13 Stories of Suspense and Horror - R.L.
   Stine   *y*   1101
The Forest of Hands and Teeth - Carrie
   Ryan   *y*   1051
The Ghost of Crutchfield Hall - Mary Downing
   Hahn   *c, y*   186
Ghostopolis - Doug TenNapel   *y*   1122
Highway to Hell - Rosemary
   Clement-Moore   *y*   694
Low Red Moon - Caitlin R. Kiernan   *a*   872
The Replacement - Brenna Yovanoff   *y*   1194
White Crow - Marcus Sedgwick   *y*   1069

Horse racing

Homestretch - Paul Volponi   *y*   1142
The Scorpio Races - Maggie Stiefvater   *y*   1099

Horses

CookieBot! A Harry and Horsie Adventure - Katie
   Van Camp   *p, c*   536
Dust Devil - Anne Isaacs   *c*   219
The Georges and the Jewels - Jane
   Smiley   *c, y*   471
Highway Robbery - Kate Thompson   *c, y*   514
Knifepoint - Alex Van Tol   *y*   1131

House mouse

Bless This Mouse - Lois Lowry   *c, y*   289

Household moving

Moonglass - Jessi Kirby   *y*   877

Housing

Goldilocks and the Three Bears - Emma
   Chichester-Clark   *p, c*   65
Itty Bitty - Cece Bell   *p, c*   30

Human behavior

Mine! - Shutta Crum   *p, c*   95

Human-animal relationships

Dust Devil - Anne Isaacs   *c*   219
Half Brother - Kenneth Oppel   *y*   992
*How to Clean a Hippopotamus: A Look at Unusual
   Animal Partnerships* - Robin Page   *c*   372
The Mitten - Jim Aylesworth   *p, c*   16
*A Nest for Celeste: A Story about Art, Inspiration,
   and the Meaning of Home* - Henry
   Cole   *c, y*   74
Pegasus - Robin McKinley   *y*   940
Posy - Linda Newbery   *p, c*   354
RRRalph - Lois Ehlert   *p, c*   124
Sidekicks - Dan Santat   *c, y*   441
Snook Alone - Marilyn Nelson   *c*   349

Humor

Alpha Oops!: H Is for Halloween - Alethea
   Kontis   *c*   257
Beat the Band - Don Calame   *y*   670
Beatle Meets Destiny - Gabrielle
   Williams   *y*   1166
Beauty Queens - Libba Bray   *y*   656
Bink and Gollie - Kate DiCamillo   *c*   111
Binky the Space Cat - Ashley Spires   *c*   482
A Book - Mordicai Gerstein   *c*   161
Born Yesterday: The Diary of a Young Journalist -
   James Solheim   *c*   478
The Boss Baby - Marla Frazee   *p, c*   150
A Call for a New Alphabet - Jef Czekaj   *c*   99
Cosmic - Frank Cottrell Boyce   *c, y*   84
The Cow Loves Cookies - Karma
   Wilson   *p, c*   570
Dog and Bear: Three to Get Ready - Laura Vaccaro
   Seeger   *p, c*   456
Dot - Patricia Intriago   *p, c*   218
E-mergency! - Tom Lichtenheld   *p, c*   277
Emma Dilemma: Big Sister Poems - Kristine
   O'Connell George   *c*   160
Even Monsters Need Haircuts - Matthew
   McElligott   *p, c*   316
Every Thing On It - Shel Silverstein   *c, y*   467
The Extraordinary Mark Twain (According to Susy)
   - Barbara Kerley   *c*   242
Fat Cat - Robin Brande   *y*   654
Frankie Pickle and the Closet of Doom - Eric
   Wright   *c*   582
Griff Carver, Hallway Patrol - Jim
   Krieg   *c, y*   258
Grin and Bear It - Leo Landry   *c*   265
Here Comes the Garbage Barge - Jonah
   Winter   *c*   575
I Spy Fly Guy - Tedd Arnold   *p, c*   11
Itsy Mitsy Runs Away - Elanna Allen   *c*   5
Little Mouse Gets Ready - Jeff Smith   *p, c*   474
Melonhead - Katy Kelly   *c*   240
Monsters Eat Whiny Children - Bruce Eric
   Kaplan   *p, c*   237
My Mom Is Trying to Ruin My Life - Kate
   Feiffer   *c*   135
My Name Is Elizabeth! - Annika
   Dunklee   *p, c*   121
Now Playing: Stoner & Spaz II - Ron
   Koertge   *y*   883
Orangutan Tongs: Poems to Tangle Your Tongue -
   Jon Agee   *c*   3
Pearl and Wagner: One Funny Day - Kate
   McMullan   *c*   321
A Pig Parade Is a Terrible Idea - Michael Ian
   Black   *p, c*   39

Read It, Don't Eat It! - Ian Schoenherr   *p, c*   453
RRRalph - Lois Ehlert   *p, c*   124
A Season of Gifts - Richard Peck   *c, y*   384
Stars - Mary Lyn Ray   *p, c*   409
Swim the Fly - Don Calame   *y*   669
*There's a Princess in the Palace: Five Classic
   Tales* - Zoe B. Alley   *c*   6
Tricking the Tallyman - Jacqueline Davies   *c*   101
Where's Walrus? - Stephen Savage   *p, c*   444
Will - Maria Boyd   *y*   652

Hunting

Crow Call - Lois Lowry   *c*   288

Hurricanes

A.D.: New Orleans after the Deluge - Josh
   Neufeld   *y*   977
Saint Louis Armstrong Beach - Brenda
   Woods   *c, y*   1174

Identity

Divergent - Veronica Roth   *y*   1042
Duck! Rabbit! - Amy Krouse Rosenthal   *p, c*   426
Emily the Strange: The Lost Days - Jessica
   Gruner   *y*   811
Fade to Blue - Sean Beaudoin   *y*   626
Flip - Martyn Bedford   *y*   628
Happenstance Found - P. W. Catanese   *c, y*   63
I Am J - Cris Beam   *y*   625
Itty Bitty - Cece Bell   *p, c*   30
King of the Screwups - K.L. Going   *y*   794
Ling and Ting: Not Exactly the Same! - Grace
   Lin   *p, c*   280
The Mermaid's Mirror - L.K. Madigan   *y*   918
Once a Witch - Carolyn MacCullough   *y*   915
Paranormalcy - Kiersten White   *y*   1156
Pink - Lili Wilkinson   *y*   1161
The Reinvention of Moxie Roosevelt - Elizabeth
   Cody Kimmel   *c, y*   246
Skunk Girl - Sheba Karim   *y*   864
Take Me with You - Carolyn Marsden   *c, y*   302
What Happened to Goodbye - Sarah
   Dessen   *y*   730
When I Was Joe - Keren David   *y*   719
Wonderstruck - Brian Selznick   *c, y*   458
You Are Here - Jennifer E. Smith   *y*   1089

Illegal immigrants

Return to Sender - Julia Alvarez   *c, y*   7
Star in the Forest - Laura Resau   *c, y*   412

Imagination

Big Nate: In a Class by Himself - Lincoln
   Peirce   *c, y*   385
Binky the Space Cat - Ashley Spires   *c*   482
Cars Galore - Peter Stein   *p, c*   492
Chalk - Bill Thomson   *c*   515
The Dark City - Catherine Fisher   *y*   766
The Eternal Smile - Gene Luen Yang   *y*   1185
Frankie Pickle and the Closet of Doom - Eric
   Wright   *c*   582
The Giant Slayer - Iain Lawrence   *c, y*   267
I Broke My Trunk! - Mo Willems   *p, c*   567
Ice - Arthur Geisert   *c*   159
Let's Do Nothing! - Tony Fucile   *c*   153
My Favorite Band Does Not Exist - Robert T.
   Jeschonek   *y*   857
My Garden - Kevin Henkes   *p, c*   198

Pathfinder - Orson Scott Card   *y*   674
Pegasus - Robin McKinley   *y*   940
Red Glove - Holly Black   *y*   636
The Ring of Solomon - Jonathan Stroud   *y*   1109
The Secret Box - Barbara Lehman   *c*   270
The Shadows - Jacqueline West   *c, y*   555
The Silver Blade - Sally Gardner   *y*   158
Tales from Outer Suburbia - Shaun Tan   *c, y*   506
Thirteenth Child - Patricia C. Wrede   *y*   1176
Warped - Maurissa Guibord   *y*   812
Wildwood - Colin Meloy   *c, y*   325
Willoughby and the Lion - Greg Foley   *p, c*   147

Marine biology

The Fantastic Undersea Life of Jacques Cousteau - Dan Yaccarino   *c*   584

Marriage

Absolutely Maybe - Lisa Yee   *y*   1187
Alis - Naomi Rich   *y*   1039
Charles and Emma: The Darwins' Leap of Faith - Deborah Heiligman   *y*   833
Ooku: The Inner Chambers, Volume 1 - Fumi Yoshinaga   *y*   1189
Thunder over Kandahar - Sharon E. McKay   *y*   937

Mars (Planet)

Black Hole Sun - David Macinnis Gill   *y*   789
Life on Mars: Tales from the New Frontier - Jonathan Strahan   *y*   1105
You Are the First Kid on Mars - Patrick O'Brien   *c, y*   363

Mathematics

Growing Patterns: Fibonacci Numbers in Nature - Sarah C. Campbell   *c*   59
Lyle Walks the Dogs: A Counting Book - Bernard Waber   *p, c*   546

Medical care

Cold Hands, Warm Heart - Jill Wolfson   *y*   1173
If I Stay - Gayle Forman   *y*   772
This Thing Called the Future - J. L. Powers   *y*   1020
Wildthorn - Jane Eagland   *y*   748

Medical professions

Level Up - Gene Luen Yang   *y*   1184

Memory

Hidden - Helen Frost   *y*   778
The Memory Bank - Carolyn Coman   *c, y*   75
She Said/She Saw - Norah McClintock   *y*   931
White Cat - Holly Black   *y*   639

Memory disorders

Wildthorn - Jane Eagland   *y*   748

Mental disorders

Anything but Typical - Nora Raleigh Baskin   *y*   27
The Babysitter Murders - Janet Ruth Young   1190
A Blue So Dark - Holly Schindler   *y*   1059
Breathless - Jessica Warman   *y*   1149

Burnout - Adrienne Maria Vrettos   *y*   1144
Crazy - Han Nolan   *y*   980
The Freak Observer - Blythe Woolston   *y*   1175
Gringolandia - Lyn Miller-Lachmann   *y*   950
The Iron Thorn - Caitlin Kittredge   *y*   879
Miles from Ordinary - Carol Lynch Williams   *y*   1164
Mindblind - Jennifer Roy   *y*   1044

Mental health

How I Stole Johnny Depp's Alien Girlfriend - Gary Ghislain   *y*   786
Riding Invisible - Sandra Alonzo   *y*   604
Wildthorn - Jane Eagland   *y*   748

Mentally disabled persons

The Brothers Story - Katherine Sturtevant   *y*   1112

Mermaids

Keeper - Kathi Appelt   *c, y*   10
The Mermaid's Mirror - L.K. Madigan   *y*   918

Mexicans

Diego Rivera: His World and Ours - Duncan Tonatiuh   *c*   518

Middle East

Ghosts of War: The True Story of a 19-Year-Old GI - Ryan Smithson   *y*   1092
Thunder over Kandahar - Sharon E. McKay   *y*   937
Zahra's Paradise - Amir Amir   *y*   606

Middle schools

Bluefish - Pat Schmatz   *y*   1060
Bystander - James Preller   *y*   1022
Callie's Rules - Naomi Flink Zucker   *c, y*   594
Griff Carver, Hallway Patrol - Jim Krieg   *c, y*   258
The Strange Case of Origami Yoda - Tom Angleberger   *c, y*   9
Warp Speed - Lisa Yee   *y*   1186

Migrant labor

Migrant - Maxine Trottier   *c*   524

Military bases

Operation Yes - Sara Lewis Holmes   *c, y*   209
Out of the Blue - S.L. Rottman   *y*   1043
Purple Heart - Patricia McCormick   *y*   933

Military life

Bamboo People - Mitali Perkins   *y*   1006
Nubs: The True Story of a Mutt, a Marine, & a Miracle - Mary Nethery   *c*   352
Purple Heart - Patricia McCormick   *y*   933
The War to End All Wars: World War I - Russell Freedman   *y*   774

Military science

Purple Heart - Patricia McCormick   *y*   933

Mining

Trapped: How the World Rescued 33 Miners from 2,000 Feet below the Chilean Desert - Marc Aronson   *c, y*   12

Miracles

The Miracle Stealer - Neil Connelly   *y*   704

Missing persons

Amelia Lost: The Life and Disappearance of Amelia Earhart - Candace Fleming   *c, y*   144
Cryer's Cross - Lisa McMann   *y*   942
Every You, Every Me - David Levithan   *y*   897
The Fires Beneath the Sea - Lydia Millet   *c, y*   330
Gentlemen - Michael Northrop   *y*   981
The Kneebone Boy - Ellen Potter   *c, y*   398
Nickel Plated - Aric Davis   *y*   721
Reality Check - Peter Abrahams   *y*   596
Scat - Carl Hiaasen   *c, y*   203
The Vanishing of Katharina Linden - Helen Grant   *y*   802
Wish You Were Dead - Todd Strasser   *y*   1107

Modern Life

Island's End - Padma Venkatraman   *y*   1138

Monarchs

A Conspiracy of Kings - Megan Whalen Turner   *y*   1134

Money

Adios, Tricycle - Susan Middleton Elya   *p, c*   128
Money Madness - David A. Adler   *c*   1

Mongol Empire, 1206-1502

Kubla Khan: The Emperor of Everything - Kathleen Krull   *c, y*   263

Monkeys

Happy Birthday, Sophie Hartley - Stephanie Greene   *c*   175

Monsters

The Curse of the Wendigo - Rick Yancey   *y*   1183
Daughter of Smoke and Bone - Laini Taylor   *y*   1120
Even Monsters Need Haircuts - Matthew McElligott   *p, c*   316
Factotum - D.M. Cornish   *y*   707
Highway to Hell - Rosemary Clement-Moore   *y*   694
The Isle of Blood - Rick Yancey   *y*   1181
Killer Pizza - Greg Taylor   *y*   1118
The Lost Hero - Rick Riordan   *c, y*   417
A Monster Calls - Patrick Ness   *y*   976
Monsters Eat Whiny Children - Bruce Eric Kaplan   *p, c*   237
The Monstrumologist - Rick Yancey   *y*   1182
The Prince of Fenway Park - Julianna Baggott   *c, y*   18

Morality

Highway Robbery - Kate Thompson   *c, y*   514

Subject Index

Subject Index

Writing

Adios, Nirvana - Conrad Wesselhoeft *y* 1152

Anything but Typical - Nora Raleigh Baskin *y* 27

A Call for a New Alphabet - Jef Czekaj *c* 99

Pearl verses the World - Sally Murphy *c* 338

Zombies

Rot and Ruin - Jonathan Maberry *y* 914

Zombies vs. Unicorns - Holly Black *y* 638

Zoos

A Sick Day for Amos McGee - Philip C. Stead *p, c* 489

Where's Walrus? - Stephen Savage *p, c* 444

Character Name Index

This index alphabetically lists the major characters in each featured title. Each character name is followed by a description of the character. Citations also provide titles of the books featuring the character, listed alphabetically if there is more than one title, with author names, age-level code(s) and entry numbers also included. The age-level codes are as follows: *p*: ages 1-4, *c*: ages 5-10, *y*: ages 11-18.

A

A.J. (Teenager; Wealthy; Friend)
Now Playing: Stoner & Spaz II - Ron Koertge   *y*   883

Aaluk (Sister)
Blessing's Bead - Debby Dahl Edwardson   *y*   750

Aaron (Foster Child)
Touch Blue - Cynthia Lord   *c, y*   286

Aaron (Neighbor)
Miles from Ordinary - Carol Lynch Williams   *y*   1164

Aaron (Twin)
The Unwanteds - Lisa McMann   *c, y*   320

Abbott, Harriet (Seamstress; Friend)
Lost - Jacqueline Davies   *y*   720

Abbott, Wren (14-Year-Old; Camper)
Hidden - Helen Frost   *y*   778

Abby (17-Year-Old; Sister)
Between Here and Forever - Elizabeth Scott   *y*   1065

Abby (Friend)
Tyger Tyger - Kersten Hamilton   *y*   816

Abdi (14-Year-Old)
Where I Belong - Gillian Cross   *y*   712

Abdul (15-Year-Old; Immigrant)
No Safe Place - Deborah Ellis   *y*   757

Abernathy, Haymitch (Contestant)
Catching Fire - Suzanne Collins   *y*   699

Abernathy, Haymitch (Contestant; Rebel)
Mockingjay - Suzanne Collins   *y*   700

Abramson, Ari (Musician; Teenager)
So Punk Rock (and Other Ways to Disappoint Your Mother) - Micol Ostow   *y*   995

Aching, Tiffany (Witch; 15-Year-Old)
I Shall Wear Midnight - Terry Pratchett   *y*   1021

Achoo (Police Officer)
Bloodhound - Tamora Pierce   *y*   1013

Ackroyd, Clem (Worker)
Life: An Exploded Diagram - Mal Peet   *y*   1003

Adam (Boyfriend)
If I Stay - Gayle Forman   *y*   772

Adam (Musician; Narrator)
Where She Went - Gayle Forman   *y*   771

Adams, Saffron (Teenager)
The Dust of 100 Dogs - A.S. King   *y*   874

Dr. Adnoid (Father; Scientist)
The Secret of Zoom - Lynne Jonell   *c, y*   228

Adnoid, Beth (Mother; Scientist)
The Secret of Zoom - Lynne Jonell   *c, y*   228

Adrian (Student; Artist)
Same Difference - Siobhan Vivian   *y*   1140

Affeldt, Priska (14-Year-Old; Refugee)
The Other Half of Life: A Novel Based on the True Story of the MS St. Louis - Kim Ablon Whitney   *y*   1159

Afton, Regina (Friend; Student—High School)
Some Girls Are - Courtney Summers   *y*   1114

Aggie (Dog)
Aggie the Brave - Lori Ries   *p, c*   414

Aguilar, Daniel (12-Year-Old)
Gringolandia - Lyn Miller-Lachmann   *y*   950

Aguilar, Marcelus (Father; Journalist)
Gringolandia - Lyn Miller-Lachmann   *y*   950

Ai Ling (17-Year-Old)
Silver Phoenix: Beyond the Kingdom of Xia - Cindy Pon   *y*   1017

Aiden (15-Year-Old; Brother)
The Devil's Paintbox - Victoria McKernan   *y*   938

Aisling "Ash" (Orphan)
Ash - Malinda Lo   *y*   902

Ajani (Boy; Soccer Player)
Goal! - Mina Javaherbin   *c*   222

Akiva (Angel)
Daughter of Smoke and Bone - Laini Taylor   *y*   1120

Alderman, Ignatius "Brother" (12-Year-Old)
Heart of a Shepherd - Rosanne Parry   *c, y*   377

Aldwyn (Cat)
The Familiars - Adam Jay Epstein   *c, y*   132

Aleah (Girlfriend; Student—High School)
Stupid Fast: The Summer I Went from a Joke to a Jock - Geoff Herbach   *y*   836

Alek (Royalty)
Behemoth - Scott Westerfeld   *y*   1154

Alex (16-Year-Old; Student—Boarding School; Friend)
Paper Covers Rock - Jenny Hubbard   *y*   848

Alex (Boyfriend)
Delirium - Lauren Oliver   *y*   989

Alex (Brother)
Sent - Margaret Peterson Haddix   *c, y*   185

Alex (Student—Boarding School; Crime Victim; 11th Grader)
The Mockingbirds - Daisy Whitney   *y*   1158

Alex (Teenager; Student—High School; Girlfriend)
Bitter End - Jennifer Brown   *y*   663

Alex (Teenager; Survivor)
Ashfall - Mike Mullin   *y*   958

Alex (Twin)
The Unwanteds - Lisa McMann   *c, y*   320

Alexander (Child)
The Mysterious Howling - Maryrose Wood   *c, y*   579

Alexander "Xan" (17-Year-Old; Outcast; Student—College; Activist)
Angry Young Man - Chris Lynch   *y*   912

Alfred (Bird)
The Money We'll Save - Brock Cole   *c*   73

Alice (10-Year-Old; Detective—Amateur; Friend)
Pie - Sarah Weeks   *c, y*   552

Alis (14-Year-Old; Religious; Runaway)
Alis - Naomi Rich   *y*   1039

Allbright, Billy (15-Year-Old; Traveler)
You Don't Know About Me - Brian Meehl   *y*   944

Allie (Teenager; Lover)
Boyfriends with Girlfriends - Alex Sanchez   *y*   1056

Alligator (Toy; Alligator)
Hooray for Amanda and Her Alligator! - Mo Willems   *p, c*   566

Allison (Foster Child; Baby)
Raven Summer - David Almond   *y*   602

Allister, Han (Thief)
The Demon King - Cinda Williams Chima   *y*   687

Alper, Jeffrey (8th Grader; Cancer Patient)
After Ever After - Jordan Sonnenblick   *y*   1094

Alpers, Andi (17-Year-Old; Musician)
Revolution - Jennifer Donnelly   *y*   739

Alva Jane (14-Year-Old; Daughter; Girlfriend; Cult Member)
Keep Sweet - Michele Dominguez Greene   *y*   805

Alvarez, Lucia (14-Year-Old; Refugee)
The Red Umbrella - Christina Diaz Gonzalez   *y*   735

Alyssa (17-Year-Old; Lesbian; Waiter/Waitress)
She Loves You, She Loves You Not... - Julie Anne Peters   1011

Amanda (14-Year-Old; Accident Victim)
Cold Hands, Warm Heart - Jill Wolfson   *y*   1173

Amanda (5th Grader; Friend)
Ten - Lauren Myracle   *c*   344

Amanda (Girl)
Hooray for Amanda and Her Alligator! - Mo Willems   *p, c*   566

Amandolina "Andi" (Sister; Basketball Player)
Tall Story - Candy Gourlay   *y*   800

Ambrose, Aura (15-Year-Old; Artist)
A Blue So Dark - Holly Schindler   *y*   1059

Ambrose, Violet (Student—High School; Friend)
The Body Finder - Kimberly Derting   *y*   728

Amelia (Student—High School)
The Ghosts of Ashbury High - Jaclyn Moriarty   *y*   954

Ami (Mother)
Big Red Lollipop - Rukhsana Khan   *p, c*   244

Amiq (Narrator; Student—Boarding School)
My Name Is Not Easy - Debby Dahl Edwardson   *y*   749

Amy (Friend)
Shakespeare Makes the Playoffs - Ron Koertge   *y*   884

Amy (Teenager; Sister)
Love You Hate You Miss You - Elizabeth Scott   *y*   1067

ana'Marianna, Raisa (Royalty)
The Demon King - Cinda Williams Chima   *y*   687

Anabelle (Graduate; 18-Year-Old)
The View from the Top - Hillary Frank   *y*   773

Anders (Psychic; Friend)
The Mostly True Story of Jack - Kelly Barnhill   *c, y*   23

Anderson, Iris (17-Year-Old; Detective)
The Girl Is Murder - Kathryn Miller Haines   *y*   814

Andersson, Einar (Father)
Revolver - Marcus Sedgwick   *y*   1068

Andersson, Sig (Teenager)
Revolver - Marcus Sedgwick   *y*   1068

Andrews, Jefferson (Tutor)
The Deadly Sister - Eliot Schrefer   *y*   1062

Andy (Friend)
Raiders' Ransom - Emily Diamand   *y*   734

Anetta (Teenager)
Hidden Voices: The Orphan Musicians of Venice - Pat Lowery Collins   *y*   698

Angel (14-Year-Old; Abuse Victim; Runaway)
Desert Angel - Charlie Price   *y*   1025

Angel (Football Player; Student—High School)
Payback Time - Carl Deuker   *y*   732

Angel, Swamp (Woodsman)
Dust Devil - Anne Isaacs   *c*   219

Angela (Friend; Angel)
Unearthly - Cynthia Hand   *y*   819

Angie (Teenager; Friend; Worker)
Putting Makeup on the Fat Boy - Bil Wright   *y*   1177

Anke (Teenager)
Because I Am Furniture - Thalia Chaltas   *y*   682

Anna (14-Year-Old; Sister)
Peace, Love, and Baby Ducks - Lauren Myracle   *y*   966

Anna (Child)
Migrant - Maxine Trottier   *c*   524
Two of a Kind - Jacqui Robbins   *c*   419

Anna (Child; Animal Lover)
Pond Circle - Betsy Franco   *c*   149

Anna (Teenager)
Moonglass - Jessi Kirby   *y*   877

Anna (Twin)
Dangerous Neighbors - Beth Kephart   *y*   870

Annabel (Worker)
Killer Pizza - Greg Taylor   *y*   1118

Annaleah (Teenager; Student—High School)
You Are Not Here - Samantha Schutz   *y*   1064

Annie (Sister; Football Player; Daughter)
Bobby versus Girls (Accidentally) - Lisa Yee   *c, y*   587

Anning, Mary (Young Woman; Scientist; Friend)
Remarkable Creatures - Tracy Chevalier   *y*   686

Ansel (Boy; Servant)
No Such Things as Dragons - Philip Reeve   *c, y*   410

Anthon, Pierre (7th Grader)
Nothing - Janne Teller   *y*   1121

Anya (Teenager)
Anya's Ghost - Vera Brosgol   *y*   662

Anybody, Rob (Mythical Creature)
I Shall Wear Midnight - Terry Pratchett   *y*   1021

Aparacio, Will (Brother; Mentally Ill Person)
Riding Invisible - Sandra Alonzo   *y*   604

Aparacio, Yancy (15-Year-Old; Abuse Victim; Runaway)
Riding Invisible - Sandra Alonzo   *y*   604

Applegate, Harold (Vagrant)
On the Blue Comet - Rosemary Wells   *c, y*   554

Appleton, Amber (17-Year-Old)
Sorta Like a Rock Star - Matthew Quick   *y*   1026

April (16-Year-Old; Sister)
The Extraordinary Secrets of April, May and June - Robin Benway   *y*   631

April (Teenager; Friend)
Ten Things We Did (and Probably Shouldn't Have) - Sarah Mlynowski   *y*   951

Araene (Teenager; Cousin)
The Floating Islands - Rachel Neumeier   *y*   978

Archer, Madison (Student—High School; Detective—Amateur)
Wish You Were Dead - Todd Strasser   *y*   1107

Argyle (Sidekick)
Frankie Pickle and the Closet of Doom - Eric Wright   *c*   582

Ariel (Friend)
Every You, Every Me - David Levithan   *y*   897

Arielle (Student—High School)
Just Another Hero - Sharon M. Draper   *y*   745

Arilou (Prophetess; Sister)
The Lost Conspiracy - Frances Hardinge   *c, y*   822

Armstrong, Will (17-Year-Old; Student—High School; Musician)
Will - Maria Boyd   *y*   652

Arne (Brother)
Dragons of Darkness - Antonia Michaelis   *y*   947

Arnold (Friend)
Kit Feeny: On the Move - Michael Townsend   *c*   521

Arrow (Client; Sister)
Nickel Plated - Aric Davis   *y*   721

Art (Reptile; Artist)
Art and Max - David Wiesner   *c*   560

Aspeling (Sorcerer)
Lost - Sarah Prineas   *c, y*   399

Astor, John Jacob (Historical Figure; Wealthy)
The Watch That Ends the Night: Voices from the Titanic - Allan Wolf   *y*   1171

Atkinson, Jamie (17-Year-Old; Child-Care Giver)
Tighter - Adele Griffin   *y*   807

Attling, Cam (18-Year-Old; Amputee)
The Returning - Christine Hinwood   *y*   840

Auden (18-Year-Old; Graduate; Student)
Along for the Ride - Sarah Dessen   *y*   729

Audrey (Teenager; Student)
Crash into Me - Albert Borris   *y*   649

Audubon, John James (Naturalist; Historical Figure)
A Nest for Celeste: A Story about Art, Inspiration, and the Meaning of Home - Henry Cole   *c, y*   74

Aunt Linda (Aunt)
Miles from Ordinary - Carol Lynch Williams   *y*   1164

Aunt Peg (Aunt)
The Last Little Blue Envelope - Maureen Johnson   *y*   861

"Aunt" Pete (Uncle)
King of the Screwups - K.L. Going   *y*   794

Auntie Alma (Foster Parent)
A Faraway Island - Annika Thor   *c, y*   516

Auntie Marta (Foster Parent)
A Faraway Island - Annika Thor   *c, y*   516

Auntie Shen (Grandmother)
Carolina Harmony - Marilyn Taylor McDowell   *c, y*   315

Aura (16-Year-Old)
Shade - Jeri Smith-Ready   *y*   1091

Aurora (Classmate)
Crazy Beautiful - Lauren Baratz-Logsted   *y*   619

Aurora (Time Traveler)
Gateway - Sharon Shinn   *y*   1076

Austin, Lark (16-Year-Old; Supernatural Being; Friend)
Lark - Tracey Porter   *y*   1018

Ava (16-Year-Old; Girlfriend; Student—High School)
Pink - Lili Wilkinson   *y*   1161

Avery, Clayton (Bully)
The Mostly True Story of Jack - Kelly Barnhill   *c, y*   23

Aykroyd, Tabby (Governess; 11-Year-Old)
The House of Dead Maids - Clare B. Dunkle   *y*   747

Azalea (Royalty)
Entwined - Heather Dixon   *y*   736

Azaway, Varil (Aunt)
The False Princess - Ellis O'Neal   *y*   986

B

Baby Bear (Narrator)
Me and You - Anthony Browne   *p, c*   51

Bishop, Katarina (Teenager; Thief)
Heist Society - Ally Carter *y* 678

Bitty (Dog)
Waiting for the Magic - Patricia MacLachlan *c* 293

Bizza (Teenager; Student—High School; 10th Grader; Friend; Friend)
Into the Wild Nerd Yonder - Julie Halpern *y* 815

Blackstone, Ginny (Traveler; Teenager; Niece)
The Last Little Blue Envelope - Maureen Johnson *y* 861

Blair, Hugh (Uncle)
The Betrayal of Maggie Blair - Elizabeth Laird *y* 889

Blair, Maggie (16-Year-Old; Niece; Orphan)
The Betrayal of Maggie Blair - Elizabeth Laird *y* 889

Blake (15-Year-Old; Photographer; Friend; Boyfriend)
Flash Burnout - L.K. Madigan *y* 919

Blake (Teenager; Friend)
Ostrich Boys - Keith Gray *y* 804

Blake, Jason (6th Grader; Autistic)
Anything but Typical - Nora Raleigh Baskin *y* 27

Blank, Shayne (16-Year-Old)
Blank Confession - Pete Hautman *y* 827

Blaylock, Mitch (Crime Victim)
The Morgue and Me - John C. Ford *y* 769

Blenk, Ambrosius (Artist)
Mirrorscape - Mike Wilks *c, y* 1162

Blessing (Granddaughter)
Blessing's Bead - Debby Dahl Edwardson *y* 750

Blink (16-Year-Old; Runaway)
Blink & Caution - Tim Wynne-Jones *y* 1180

Bloom, Roxanne "Roxie" (Writer)
Not That Kind of Girl - Susan Donovan *y* 740

Blue, David (Brother; Alien)
You'll Like It Here (Everybody Does) - Ruth White *c, y* 559

Blue, Meggie (Sister; Alien)
You'll Like It Here (Everybody Does) - Ruth White *c, y* 559

Blue, Sophie (Teenager)
Fade to Blue - Sean Beaudoin *y* 626

Blum, Carson (Friend; 8-Year-Old)
The New Kid - Mavis Jukes *c* 233

Blunderboar (Monster)
Calamity Jack - Shannon Hale *c, y* 187

Blunt, April (12-Year-Old)
The Fingertips of Duncan Dorfman - Meg Wolitzer *c, y* 578

Bly, Nellie (Historical Figure; Journalist; Adventurer; Traveler)
Around the World - Matt Phelan *c, y* 388

Bob (Object)
Rhyming Dust Bunnies - Jan Thomas *p, c* 513

Bobby (14-Year-Old)
Creature of the Night - Kate Thompson *y* 1128

Bobo (Toy)
I Must Have Bobo! - Eileen Rosenthal *p, c* 427

Bobs, The (Mythical Creature)
The Prince of Fenway Park - Julianna Baggott *c, y* 18

Bog (Monster)
Bayou: Volume 1 - Jeremy Love *y* 907

Boggs (Rebel)
Mockingjay - Suzanne Collins *y* 700

Boland, Kevin (14-Year-Old)
Shakespeare Makes the Playoffs - Ron Koertge *y* 884

Bones (Student—High School)
Gentlemen - Michael Northrop *y* 981

Book, Eli (Teenager; Friend)
Eli the Good - Silas House *y* 844

Bookchild, Rossamund (Orphan; Monster; Human)
Factotum - D.M. Cornish *y* 707

Border, Clarence (Father; Mentally Ill Person)
I'll Be There - Holly Goldberg Sloan *y* 1083

Border, Riddle (Brother; Autistic)
I'll Be There - Holly Goldberg Sloan *y* 1083

Border, Sam (17-Year-Old; Brother; Son; Friend)
I'll Be There - Holly Goldberg Sloan *y* 1083

Boss (Construction Worker)
Job Site - Nathan Clement *p, c* 71

Boss Baby (Baby)
The Boss Baby - Marla Frazee *p, c* 150

Boy (Son)
The Third Gift - Linda Sue Park *c* 376

Branch, Ruah (Baseball Player; Homosexual; Companion)
You Don't Know About Me - Brian Meehl *y* 944

Brax (Mythical Creature; Friend)
King of Ithaka - Tracy Barrett *y* 621

Miss Breakbone (Teacher)
The Dunderheads - Paul Fleischman *c, y* 138

Bree (Girl; Friend)
Fancy Nancy and the Mermaid Ballet - Jane O'Connor *p, c* 367

Breen, Mattie (5th Grader; Student—Elementary School)
Hound Dog True - Linda Urban *c, y* 529

Breen, Winston (Student)
The Potato Chip Puzzles: The Puzzling World of Winston Breen - Eric Berlin *c, y* 33

Bremer, Fredrika (Suffragette)
The Firefly Letters: A Suffragette's Journey to Cuba - Margarita Engle *y* 762

Brenda (Girlfriend)
Almost Perfect - Brian Katcher *y* 865

Brendan (Camper; Actor)
Every Little Thing in the World - Nina de Gramont *y* 724

Brennan, Tory (Friend; Teenager)
Virals - Kathy Reichs *y* 1035

Brewster (1st Grader)
Busing Brewster - Richard Michelson *c* 329

Brewster, Jebediah (Businessman; Quaker)
The Mostly True Adventures of Homer P. Figg - Rodman Philbrick *c, y* 389

Brianna (Friend)
The Unwritten Rule - Elizabeth Scott *y* 1066

Bridget (Child; Artist)
Bridget's Beret - Tom Lichtenheld *c* 278

Brightman, Sky (13-Year-Old; Outcast)
Saving Sky - Diane Stanley *c, y* 486

Brilliant (Bird)
Ten Birds - Cybele Young *c* 591

Brimstone (Supernatural Being)
Daughter of Smoke and Bone - Laini Taylor *y* 1120

Brixton, Steve (12-Year-Old; Detective—Amateur)
The Case of the Case of Mistaken Identity - Mac Barnett *c, y* 22

Brock (Dragon)
No Such Things as Dragons - Philip Reeve *c, y* 410

Brody, Tessa (17-Year-Old)
Warped - Maurissa Guibord *y* 812

Brontorina (Dinosaur)
Brontorina - James Howe *p, c* 213

Mr. Brontosaurus (Dinosaur)
Lulu and the Brontosaurus - Judith Viorst *p, c* 542

Bronwen (Child; Sister)
The Christmas Eve Ghost - Shirley Hughes *c* 217

Mrs. Brook (Counselor)
Mockingbird - Kathryn Erskine *c, y* 133

Brooks, Tess (11-Year-Old)
Touch Blue - Cynthia Lord *c, y* 286

Brown, Kim (Sister)
The Carbon Diaries 2015 - Saci Lloyd *y* 901

Brown, Laura (16-Year-Old; Writer)
The Carbon Diaries 2015 - Saci Lloyd *y* 901

Brown, Molly (Historical Figure)
The Watch That Ends the Night: Voices from the Titanic - Allan Wolf *y* 1171

Mr. Bruff (Teacher)
Pearl verses the World - Sally Murphy *c* 338

Bryan (Brother)
Busing Brewster - Richard Michelson *c* 329

Bryn (Dog)
Waiting for the Magic - Patricia MacLachlan *c* 293

Bucktin, Charlie (13-Year-Old; Friend)
Jasper Jones - Craig Silvey *y* 1079

Mr. Bud (Dog)
Say Hello to Zorro! - Carter Goodrich *p, c* 164

Bud (Pig; Classmate)
Pearl and Wagner: One Funny Day - Kate McMullan *c* 321

Budwig, Felicity Bathburn (11-Year-Old; Granddaughter)
The Romeo and Juliet Code - Phoebe Stone *c, y* 496

Bumble-Ardy (Pig)
Bumble-Ardy - Maurice Sendak *p, c* 459

Bump, Phineus (Worker)
Tricking the Tallyman - Jacqueline Davies *c* 101

Bunna (Brother; Student—Boarding School)
My Name Is Not Easy - Debby Dahl Edwardson *y* 749

Mr. Burrows (Apothecary; Father; Kidnap Victim)
The Apothecary - Maile Meloy *y* 945

Burrows, Benjamin (Teenager; Son; Friend)
The Apothecary - Maile Meloy *y* 945

Buzz (Child)
I Spy Fly Guy - Tedd Arnold *p, c* 11

Byrne, Anne (Nurse)
The Complete Essex County - Jeff Lemire *y* 896

C

Mr. C'mere (Cat)
Wild Things - Clay Carmichael *c, y* 60

Caitlin (10-Year-Old)
Mockingbird - Kathryn Erskine   *c, y*   133

Caitlin (Teenager)
Hold Still - Nina LaCour   *y*   887

Caldwell, Jayson (Teenager; Football Player; Friend)
Shooting Star - Fredrick McKissack Jr.   *y*   941

Caleb (15-Year-Old; Brother)
Caleb's Wars - David L. Dudley   *y*   746

Caleb (Friend; Son; Boyfriend; Teenager)
Jumping Off Swings - Jo Knowles   *y*   881

Calendar, Julian (11-Year-Old; Friend; Scientist)
The Secret Science Alliance and the Copycat Crook - Eleanor Davis   *c, y*   103

Callie (Crime Suspect)
Blood on My Hands - Todd Strasser   *y*   1106

Callie (Sister)
Nightspell - Leah Cypess   *y*   717

Callum (11-Year-Old; Friend)
Wild Wings - Gill Lewis   *c, y*   275

Calogero (14-Year-Old; Immigrant)
Alligator Bayou - Donna Jo Napoli   *y*   968

Calpurnia (Girl; Writer)
The Secret River - Marjorie Kinnan Rawlings   *c*   407

Calypso (Deity)
The Odyssey - Gareth Hinds   *y*   839

Cam (Boyfriend)
The Summer I Turned Pretty - Jenny Han   *y*   817

Cam (Friend)
Signal - Cynthia DeFelice   *c, y*   106

Cam (Gardener; Friend)
The Runaway Dragon - Kate Coombs   *c, y*   79

Cameron (16-Year-Old; Friend)
Going Bovine - Libba Bray   *y*   655

Camilla "Milla" (5th Grader)
Luv Ya Bunches - Lauren Myracle   *c, y*   343

Candace (Friend)
Efrain's Secret - Sofia Quintero   *y*   1027

Cannon, Jimmy (Teenager; Football Player)
When the Whistle Blows - Fran Cannon Slayton   *y*   1082

Captain Amazing (Hero)
Sidekicks - Dan Santat   *c, y*   441

Captain Grey (Friend)
Birthmarked - Caragh M. O'Brien   *y*   982

Cara (Sister; Child)
The Fires Beneath the Sea - Lydia Millet   *c, y*   330

Carl, Eddie (Boy; Brother)
Eddie's War - Carol Fisher Saller   *c, y*   439

Carl, Thomas (Pilot; Military Personnel; Brother)
Eddie's War - Carol Fisher Saller   *c, y*   439

Carle, Addie (13-Year-Old)
Addie on the Inside - James Howe   *c, y*   845

Carlitos (Cousin; Boy)
Dear Primo: A Letter to My Cousin - Duncan Tonatiuh   *c*   519

Carlos (Kidnapper)
Take Me to the River - Will Hobbs   *c, y*   841

Carlos (Student—High School; 17-Year-Old)
No More Us for You - David Hernandez   *y*   837

Mrs. Carlson (Teacher)
Bobby versus Girls (Accidentally) - Lisa Yee   *c, y*   587

Carly (15-Year-Old)
Peace, Love, and Baby Ducks - Lauren Myracle   *y*   966

Carly (Friend)
The Complete History of Why I Hate Her - Jennifer Richard Jacobson   *y*   855

Carmen (Aunt)
On the Blue Comet - Rosemary Wells   *c, y*   554

Carmen (Girlfriend)
Carmen - Walter Dean Myers   *y*   964

Carolina (10-Year-Old; Runaway)
Carolina Harmony - Marilyn Taylor McDowell   *c, y*   315

Carolyn (14-Year-Old)
The Giant Slayer - Iain Lawrence   *c, y*   267

Mrs. Carpenter (Mother)
Department 19 - Will Hill   *y*   838

Carpenter, Jamie (16-Year-Old; Agent)
Department 19 - Will Hill   *y*   838

Mr. Carter (Father)
Gator on the Loose! - Sue Stauffacher   *c, y*   487

Mrs. Carter (Mother)
Gator on the Loose! - Sue Stauffacher   *c, y*   487

Carter, Keisha (10-Year-Old; Animal Lover)
Gator on the Loose! - Sue Stauffacher   *c, y*   487

Carter, Paolo (Baby; Brother)
Gator on the Loose! - Sue Stauffacher   *c, y*   487

Carter, Razi (5-Year-Old; Brother)
Gator on the Loose! - Sue Stauffacher   *c, y*   487

Carter, Will (14-Year-Old)
Carter Finally Gets It - Brent Crawford   *y*   711

Carver, Alicia (15-Year-Old; Sister)
The Prince of Mist - Carlos Ruiz Zafon   *y*   1195

Carver, Griff (Student—Middle School; 7th Grader)
Griff Carver, Hallway Patrol - Jim Krieg   *c, y*   258

Carver, Max (13-Year-Old; Brother)
The Prince of Mist - Carlos Ruiz Zafon   *y*   1195

Carver Ellis-Chan, Robert "Bobby" (Brother; Friend; Student; Son; 4th Grader)
Bobby versus Girls (Accidentally) - Lisa Yee   *c, y*   587

Casey (Daughter; Sister; 4-Year-Old)
Bobby versus Girls (Accidentally) - Lisa Yee   *c, y*   587

Casey (Student; Teenager; Friend)
The DUFF: Designated Ugly Fat Friend - Kody Keplinger   *y*   871

Cassia (Young Woman; Friend)
Matched - Ally Condie   *y*   703

Cassie (Friend)
The Ghosts of Ashbury High - Jaclyn Moriarty   *y*   954

Cassie (Friend; Spirit)
Wintergirls - Laurie Halse Anderson   *y*   608

Cassiopeia (Child)
The Mysterious Howling - Maryrose Wood   *c, y*   579

Castenada, Toni (Teenager; Friend)
The Cardturner: A Novel about a King, a Queen, and a Joker - Louis Sachar   *y*   1053

Cat (16-Year-Old; Abuse Victim; Friend)
Shine - Lauren Myracle   *y*   965

Cat (Cat; Housekeeper)
Three by the Sea - Mini Grey   *p, c*   179

Cat (Girl; 13-Year-Old; Cousin)
Storm Mountain - Tom Birdseye   *c, y*   36

Caution (16-Year-Old; Runaway)
Blink & Caution - Tim Wynne-Jones   *y*   1180

Cece (15-Year-Old; Girlfriend)
Stay with Me - Paul Griffin   *y*   809

Cecelia (Girlfriend)
Crazy Beautiful - Lauren Baratz-Logsted   *y*   619

Cecile "Sister Izilla" (Mother)
One Crazy Summer - Rita Williams-Garcia   *c, y*   569

Cecilia (Slave)
The Firefly Letters: A Suffragette's Journey to Cuba - Margarita Engle   *y*   762

Cecily (18-Year-Old)
An Off Year - Claire Zulkey   *y*   1200

Celeste (Mouse)
A Nest for Celeste: A Story about Art, Inspiration, and the Meaning of Home - Henry Cole   *c, y*   74

Celestia (16-Year-Old)
Three Rivers Rising: A Novel of the Johnstown Flood - Jame Richards   *y*   1040

Celina (Sister)
The Zabime Sisters - Aristophane   *y*   611

Chameleon (Reptile)
Blue Chameleon - Emily Gravett   *p, c*   172

Dr. Chaotic (Villain)
Sidekicks - Jack D. Ferraiolo   *y*   765

Chapman, Franny (12-Year-Old; Sister)
Countdown - Deborah Wiles   *c, y*   561

Char (Teenager; Student—High School; 10th Grader; Friend; Friend)
Into the Wild Nerd Yonder - Julie Halpern   *y*   815

Miss Charleena (Actress; Friend)
Close to Famous - Joan Bauer   *c, y*   623

Charles (Brother)
The Flint Heart - Katherine Paterson   *c, y*   380

Charlie (16-Year-Old)
A Little Wanting Song - Cath Crowley   *y*   713

Charlie (Cousin; Boy)
Dear Primo: A Letter to My Cousin - Duncan Tonatiuh   *c*   519

Charlie (Detective—Amateur; Friend)
Pie - Sarah Weeks   *c, y*   552

Charlie (Military Personnel; Teenager)
The Storm before Atlanta - Karen Schwabach   *c, y*   454

Charlie (Student—High School)
Please Ignore Vera Dietz - A.S. King   *y*   876

Charlotte (Cousin)
Ruby Red - Kerstin Gier   *y*   787

Charlotte (Teenager; Supernatural Being)
A Need So Beautiful - Suzanne Young   *y*   1192

Chase, Kyle (15-Year-Old; Student—High School)
You - Charles Benoit   *y*   630

Chen, Rebecca (12-Year-Old; Student; Artist; Detective—Amateur)
The Red Blazer Girls: The Ring of Rocamadour - Michael D. Beil   *y*   629

Chen Yong (Young Man)
Silver Phoenix: Beyond the Kingdom of Xia - Cindy Pon   *y*   1017

Cheney (Child)
Living Hell - Catherine Jinks   *y*   858

Cheops (Ruler)
Pharaoh's Boat - David L. Weitzman   *c, y*   553

Crumb, Fever (Engineer; Young Woman)
A Web of Air - Philip Reeve y 1034

Crutchfield, Florence (12-Year-Old; Orphan)
The Ghost of Crutchfield Hall - Mary Downing Hahn c, y 186

Crutchfield, Sophia (Spirit)
The Ghost of Crutchfield Hall - Mary Downing Hahn c, y 186

Crystal (Classmate)
How Oliver Olson Changed the World - Claudia Mills c 331

Crystal (Foster Child)
Raven Summer - David Almond y 602

Crystal (Friend)
Star in the Forest - Laura Resau c, y 412

Cunning Man, The (Mythical Creature)
I Shall Wear Midnight - Terry Pratchett y 1021

Cunningham, Lucy (Friend; Kidnap Victim)
Wish You Were Dead - Todd Strasser y 1107

Cupcake (Musician; Friend; Baker)
Bake Sale - Sara Varon c, y 539

Curry, Amy (Teenager)
Amy and Roger's Epic Detour - Morgan Matson y 927

Curry, Asa (Prospector)
Mercury - Hope Larson y 892

Curtis (Friend)
Wildwood - Colin Meloy c, y 325

Curzon (15-Year-Old; Runaway; Slave; Military Personnel)
Forge - Laurie Halse Anderson y 607

Cydar (Brother)
Butterfly - Sonya Hartnett y 826

D

D'Arcy (Teenager)
Five Minutes More - Darlene Ryan y 1052

D.Q. (Cancer Patient; Friend)
The Last Summer of The Death Warriors - Francisco X. Stork y 1104

Da (Grandmother)
What Happened on Fox Street - Tricia Springstubb c, y 484

Dad (Father)
Compromised - Heidi Ayarbe y 616
Crazy - Han Nolan y 980
The Dancing Pancake - Eileen Spinelli c, y 481
Don't Want to Go! - Shirley Hughes p, c 216
Efrain's Secret - Sofia Quintero y 1027
Itsy Mitsy Runs Away - Elanna Allen c 5
This World We Live In - Susan Beth Pfeffer y 1012
You Are Here - Jennifer E. Smith y 1089

Dad (Father; Spouse; Professor)
Mission Unstoppable - Dan Gutman c, y 183

Daddy (Father)
Crow Call - Lois Lowry c 288
Dessert First - Hallie Durand c 123
Lexie - Audrey Couloumbis c, y 87
Somebody Everybody Listens To - Suzanne Supplee y 1115

Dade (Boyfriend; Lover; Graduate; Teenager; Homosexual)
The Vast Fields of Ordinary - Nick Burd y 667

Daft Wullie (Mythical Creature)
I Shall Wear Midnight - Terry Pratchett y 1021

Daisy (Child; Missing Person; Sister)
The Blood Lie - Shirley Reva Vernick y 1139

Daisy (Dog)
A Ball for Daisy - Chris Raschka p, c 406

Daisy (Spirit)
Andromeda Klein - Frank Portman y 1019

Daiyu (Teenager; Adoptee)
Gateway - Sharon Shinn y 1076

Dakota (Teenager)
Tangled - Carolyn Mackler y 916

Dan (Teenager; Worker)
Past Perfect - Leila Sales y 1055

Dana (Artist)
Funny How Things Change - Melissa Wyatt y 1178

Dance, Jeremy "Lil J" (17-Year-Old; Crime Suspect; Addict; Drug Dealer; Impoverished; Fugitive)
Dope Sick - Walter Dean Myers y 962

Dangerfield, Daniel (Boy)
April and Esme: Tooth Fairies - Bob Graham p, c 168

Dani (15-Year-Old)
Cold Hands, Warm Heart - Jill Wolfson y 1173

Daniel (13-Year-Old; Refugee)
Tropical Secrets: Holocaust Refugees in Cuba - Margarita Engle y 760

Daniel (Brother)
The Dragon's Tooth - N.D. Wilson c, y 571

Daniel, Dyamonde (9-Year-Old; Child of Divorced Parents)
Make Way for Dyamonde Daniel - Nikki Grimes c 180

Danny (10th Grader; Gymnast; Friend)
Leverage - Joshua Cohen y 697

Danny (Brother)
What Momma Left Me - Renee Watson c, y 551

Daphne (Supernatural Being; Daughter; Sister)
The Space Between - Brenna Yovanoff y 1193

Darla (Companion)
Ashfall - Mike Mullin y 958

Darri (Warrior; Sister)
Nightspell - Leah Cypess y 717

Darwin, Charles (Scientist; Spouse)
Charles and Emma: The Darwins' Leap of Faith - Deborah Heiligman y 833

Darwin, Emma (Spouse)
Charles and Emma: The Darwins' Leap of Faith - Deborah Heiligman y 833

Dave (Friend)
A Little Wanting Song - Cath Crowley y 713
What Happened to Goodbye - Sarah Dessen y 730

Dave (Object)
Pig Kahuna - Jennifer Sattler p, c 443

Dave (Vampire; Musician)
The Reformed Vampire Support Group - Catherine Jinks y 859

Davenport, Devon (15-Year-Old)
After - Amy Efaw y 751

David, Wilson "Wil" (12-Year-Old)
The Last Newspaper Boy in America - Sue Corbett c, y 83

Day (15-Year-Old; Criminal)
Legend - Marie Lu y 908

de Boncoeur, Armand (Brother)
The Pale Assassin - Patricia Elliott y 756

de Boncouer, Eugenie (Orphan; Teenager)
The Pale Assassin - Patricia Elliott y 756

de Chaucy, William (Nobleman)
Warped - Maurissa Guibord y 812

de Luce, Flavia (11-Year-Old; Detective—Amateur)
The Sweetness at the Bottom of the Pie - Alan Bradley y 653

Dean (Friend)
Accomplice - Eireann Corrigan y 708

Decath, Durrel (Prisoner)
Liar's Moon - Elizabeth C. Bunce y 666

Dee (Child)
Lunch Lady and the League of Librarians - Jarrett J. Krosoczka c 260

Deer (Deer)
Waiting for Winter - Sebastian Meschenmoser p, c 326

DeGroot, Jeremy (11-Year-Old; Military Personnel; Friend)
The Storm before Atlanta - Karen Schwabach c, y 454

Deity, Idea (16-Year-Old)
My Favorite Band Does Not Exist - Robert T. Jeschonek y 857

Deja (3rd Grader; Student—Elementary School; Friend)
Nikki and Deja: Birthday Blues - Karen English c 131

Delana (12-Year-Old; Orphan)
Finding Family - Tonya Bolden c, y 42

Delano, Savannah (10th Grader)
My Fair Godmother - Janette Rallison y 1029

Delilah (10-Year-Old; Neighbor)
Missing on Superstition Mountain - Elise Broach c, y 47

Delphine (11-Year-Old)
One Crazy Summer - Rita Williams-Garcia c, y 569

Deo (14-Year-Old; Soccer Player; Refugee; Brother)
Now Is the Time for Running - Michael Williams y 1168

Derek, Captain (Patient)
The Romeo and Juliet Code - Phoebe Stone c, y 496

Deryn (Girlfriend; Orphan)
Leviathan - Scott Westerfeld y 1153

Deryn (Military Personnel)
Behemoth - Scott Westerfeld y 1154

Desberg, Lucy (12-Year-Old)
My Life in Pink and Green - Lisa Greenwald c, y 178

Deuce (15-Year-Old; Hunter)
Enclave - Ann Aguirre y 599

Deveaux, Rory (Student—Boarding School)
The Name of the Star - Maureen Johnson y 862

Devon (Bully)
Kit Feeny: On the Move - Michael Townsend c 521

Devon (Teenager; Student—High School; Detective—Amateur)
The Dark Days of Hamburger Halpin - Josh Berk y 632

Devory (Friend; Abuse Victim)
Hush - Eishes Chayil y 685

Eli (Teenager; Friend)
Along for the Ride - Sarah Dessen   y   729

Eli (Worker)
Between Here and Forever - Elizabeth Scott   y   1065

Elinor (4-Year-Old; Sister)
Waiting for the Magic - Patricia MacLachlan   c   293

Eliot, William Stone (Vampire)
Pretty Dead - Francesca Lia Block   y   641

Elisa (16-Year-Old; Royalty)
The Girl of Fire and Thorns - Rae Carson   y   677

Elizabeth (Adoptee; Friend)
This Dark Endeavor: The Apprenticeship of Victor Frankenstein - Kenneth Oppel   y   993

Elizabeth (Girl; Child)
My Name Is Elizabeth! - Annika Dunklee   p, c   121

Elizabeth (Royalty)
The Stolen One - Suzanne Crowley   y   714

Ella (Dog; Supernatural Being)
Bone Dog - Eric Rohmann   c   425

Elle (Sister)
The Zabime Sisters - Aristophane   y   611

Ellie (6th Grader; Friend)
Camo Girl - Kekla Magoon   c, y   294

Ellie (Friend; Pregnant Teenager)
Jumping Off Swings - Jo Knowles   y   881

Ellijah (Young Man)
Wintergirls - Laurie Halse Anderson   y   608

Ellis, Brittany (12th Grader)
Perfect Chemistry - Simone Elkeles   y   755

Ellis, Shelley (Sister; Handicapped)
Perfect Chemistry - Simone Elkeles   y   755

Mr. Ellis-Chan (Father; Football Player)
Bobby versus Girls (Accidentally) - Lisa Yee   c, y   587

Mrs. Ellis-Chan (Mother; Businesswoman)
Bobby versus Girls (Accidentally) - Lisa Yee   c, y   587

Elody (Friend)
Before I Fall - Lauren Oliver   y   990

Eloise (16-Year-Old; Runaway)
Blood - K.J. Wignall   y   1160

Emaline (Teenager; Sister)
The Blood Lie - Shirley Reva Vernick   y   1139

Emerson, Charlotte (17-Year-Old; Vampire)
Pretty Dead - Francesca Lia Block   y   641

Emily (13-Year-Old; Amnesiac)
Emily the Strange: The Lost Days - Jessica Gruner   y   811

Emily (16-Year-Old; Student—High School; Friend; Artist)
Same Difference - Siobhan Vivian   y   1140

Emily (Friend)
Pretty Dead - Francesca Lia Block   y   641

Emily (Spirit)
Anya's Ghost - Vera Brosgol   y   662

Emma (3-Year-Old; Sister)
Emma Dilemma: Big Sister Poems - Kristine O'Connell George   y   160

Emma (Narrator; Girl)
My Mom Is Trying to Ruin My Life - Kate Feiffer   c   135

Emma (Orphan)
The Emerald Atlas - John Stephens   c, y   493

Emma (Survivor)
Broken Memory: A Novel of Rwanda - Elisabeth Combres   y   701

Emma (Teenager; Friend)
The Future of Us - Jay Asher   y   613

Emmi (9-Year-Old; Sister)
Blood Red Road - Moira Young   y   1191

Emmy (Bird; Friend)
Grin and Bear It - Leo Landry   c   265

Enrique (Cousin)
Muchacho - LouAnne Johnson   y   860

Epossumondas (Opossum)
Epossumondas Plays Possum - Coleen Salley   c   440

Ereskigal (Daughter; Villain)
The Call - Michael Grant   c, y   170

Erik (Boyfriend; Homosexual; Teenager)
With or Without You - Brian Farrey   y   764

Escamillo (Producer)
Carmen - Walter Dean Myers   y   964

Escobar, Edilio (Teenager)
Hunger - Michael Grant   y   803

Esperer, Fatima (16-Year-Old; Refugee; Newspaper Carrier)
The Orange Houses - Paul Griffin   y   810

Estby, Clara (17-Year-Old; Daughter)
The Year We Were Famous - Carole Estby Dagg   y   718

Estby, Helga (Mother)
The Year We Were Famous - Carole Estby Dagg   y   718

Eugene (Fox; Neighbor)
Zelda and Ivy: Keeping Secrets - Laura McGee Kvasnosky   c   264

Eugenides (Friend; Royalty)
A Conspiracy of Kings - Megan Whalen Turner   y   1134

Europe (Hunter; Friend)
Factotum - D.M. Cornish   y   707

Eva (Teenager; Addict)
Clean - Amy Reed   y   1031

Evan (17-Year-Old)
Winter Town - Stephen Emond   y   758

Evan (Student—High School; Teenager)
Every You, Every Me - David Levithan   y   897

Evanjalin (Psychic)
Finnikin of the Rock - Melina Marchetta   y   921

Evans, Miranda (Teenager)
This World We Live In - Susan Beth Pfeffer   y   1012

Eve (Friend)
Lark - Tracey Porter   y   1018

Evelyn (Artist)
City of Spies - Susan Kim   c, y   245

Everdeen, Katniss (16-Year-Old; Contestant)
Catching Fire - Suzanne Collins   y   699

Everdeen, Katniss (16-Year-Old; Contestant; Rebel)
Mockingjay - Suzanne Collins   y   700

Everdeen, Primrose (12-Year-Old; Sister; Nurse)
Mockingjay - Suzanne Collins   y   700

Everstar, Chrysanthemum "Chrissy" (Godmother; Student)
My Fair Godmother - Janette Rallison   y   1029

Evie (16-Year-Old)
The Space between Trees - Katie Williams   y   1167

Evie (16-Year-Old; Agent)
Paranormalcy - Kiersten White   y   1156

Ewing, Ella Kate (Teenager)
Stand Straight, Ella Kate - Kate Klise   c   252

Ezra (Teenager; Worker; Boyfriend)
Past Perfect - Leila Sales   y   1055

F

Fade (Teenager; Hunter)
Enclave - Ann Aguirre   y   599

Fade, Kenny (Classmate; Teenager)
Fade to Blue - Sean Beaudoin   y   626

Fallon, Derek (12-Year-Old)
My Life as a Book - Janet Tashjian   c, y   507

Falpian (Royalty)
Witchlanders - Lena Coakley   y   695

Fan (Cousin)
The Winds of Heaven - Judith Clarke   y   692

Fanboy (Friend)
Goth Girl Rising - Barry Lyga   y   910

Fancy Nancy (Girl)
Fancy Nancy and the Mermaid Ballet - Jane O'Connor   p, c   367

Faraday, Destiny (17-Year-Old; Student—Boarding School)
The Miles Between - Mary E. Pearson   y   1001

Farm Maiden (Cook)
The Cazuela That the Farm Maiden Stirred - Samantha R. Vamos   c   533

Father (Father)
Over and Under the Snow - Kate Messner   c   327
Silver Phoenix: Beyond the Kingdom of Xia - Cindy Pon   y   1017

Father Ramon (Religious; Leader)
The Reformed Vampire Support Group - Catherine Jinks   y   859

Faustino, Paul (Journalist)
Exposure - Mal Peet   y   1002

Feeny, Kit (Child)
Kit Feeny: On the Move - Michael Townsend   c   521

Fehey, Jonny (Student—High School; Soccer Player)
Over the End Line - Alfred C. Martino   y   926

Fei Ting "Frances" (Student—High School)
Bitter Melon - Cara Chow   y   688

Felix (10-Year-Old; Refugee)
Then - Morris Gleitzman   y   792

Felix (Child; Orphan)
Once - Morris Gleitzman   y   791

Fenister, Graceful (Fiance(e))
The Returning - Christine Hinwood   y   840

Ferelith (Friend)
White Crow - Marcus Sedgwick   y   1069

Fergus (Pig; Brother)
Pig Kahuna - Jennifer Sattler   p, c   443

Fern (Sister)
One Crazy Summer - Rita Williams-Garcia   c, y   569

Fern, Clarity "Clare" (16-Year-Old; Psychic)
Clarity - Kim Harrington   y   825

Fever (Father)
Why I Fight - J. Adams Oaks   y   987

G

Henry (Uncle; Artist; Doctor)
Wild Things - Clay Carmichael   *c, y*   60

Henry, Will (12-Year-Old; Orphan)
The Monstrumologist - Rick Yancey   *y*   1182

Henry, Will (Apprentice; 12-Year-Old)
The Curse of the Wendigo - Rick Yancey   *y*   1183

Henry, Will (Orphan; Assistant)
The Isle of Blood - Rick Yancey   *y*   1181

Mr. Herbert (Aged Person)
Hero - Mike Lupica   *c, y*   290

Herold, Katherine "Kat" (Student—High School)
Center Field - Robert Lipsyte   *y*   900

Hewitt, Josh (5th Grader)
In Memory of Gorfman T. Frog - Gail Donovan   *c*   113

Hi (Friend)
Virals - Kathy Reichs   *y*   1035

Hibernia (12-Year-Old; Friend)
Bird in a Box - Andrea Davis Pinkney   *c, y*   392

Hibiscus, Anna (Child)
Anna Hibiscus - Atinuke   *c*   14

Highly Satisfactory (Bird)
Ten Birds - Cybele Young   *c*   591

Hildegarde (Mouse)
Bless This Mouse - Lois Lowry   *c, y*   289

Hippo (Hippopotamus; Friend)
I Broke My Trunk! - Mo Willems   *p, c*   567

Ho, Alvin (Child)
Alvin Ho: Allergic to Camping, Hiking, and Other Natural Disasters - Lenore Look   *c*   285

Hogan, Holly "Solace" (14-Year-Old; Foster Child)
Solace of the Road - Siobhan Dowd   *y*   741

Holly, Poe (16-Year-Old)
Brutal - Michael Harmon   *y*   824

Hollywood (Friend; Filmmaker)
Absolutely Maybe - Lisa Yee   *y*   1187

Holmes, Sherlock (14-Year-Old; Student—Boarding School; Detective—Amateur)
Death Cloud - Andrew Lane   *y*   890

Hood, Avery (17-Year-Old; Orphan; Girlfriend)
Low Red Moon - Ivy Devlin   *y*   733

Hooper (Streetperson)
First Day on Earth - Cecil Castellucci   *y*   680

Hope (Child of an Alcoholic; 12-Year-Old; Narrator; Sister)
Glimpse - Carol Lynch Williams   *y*   1163

Horsie (Friend)
CookieBot! A Harry and Horsie Adventure - Katie Van Camp   *p, c*   536

Howard, Pastor Shady (Religious)
Moon over Manifest - Clare Vanderpool   *c, y*   538

Huck (Boyfriend)
Close to Famous - Joan Bauer   *c, y*   623

Hughes, Scarlet (17-Year-Old)
The Six Rules of Maybe - Deb Caletti   *y*   672

Humphrey (Human; Designer)
The Christmas Giant - Steve Light   *p, c*   279

Hunter, Leigh (Boyfriend; Stepbrother; 17-Year-Old; 12th Grader; Student—High School)
After the Moment - Garret Freymann-Weyr   *y*   776

Hutchinson, Scott "Bright Boy" (Sidekick; Student—High School; Boyfriend)
Sidekicks - Jack D. Ferraiolo   *y*   765

Hy (Aunt; Rancher)
Texas Gothic - Rosemary Clement-Moore   *y*   693

I

Ignatius (Mouse)
Bless This Mouse - Lois Lowry   *c, y*   289

Igwash, Janine (Teenager)
Tilt - Alan Cumyn   *y*   716

Imogene (Child; Historian)
Imogene's Last Stand - Candace Fleming   *c*   141

Imura, Benny (Hunter)
Rot and Ruin - Jonathan Maberry   *y*   914

India (14-Year-Old; Sister)
No Passengers beyond This Point - Gennifer Choldenko   *c, y*   68

Dr. Indra (Doctor)
No Ordinary Day - Deborah Ellis   *c, y*   126

Inepta (Mythical Creature)
Small Persons with Wings - Ellen Booraem   *c, y*   44

Ingrid (Friend)
Hold Still - Nina LaCour   *y*   887

Ingrid (Student—Boarding School; Friend)
Dreams of Significant Girls - Cristina Garcia   *y*   779

Innocent (Teenager; Mentally Challenged Person; Brother)
Now Is the Time for Running - Michael Williams   *y*   1168

Iris (15-Year-Old; Housekeeper; Friend)
Crossing the Tracks - Barbara Stuber   *y*   1111

Ironfoundersson, Carrot (Police Officer)
I Shall Wear Midnight - Terry Pratchett   *y*   1021

Isa (11-Year-Old; Sister)
Tighter - Adele Griffin   *y*   807

Isaac (Brother)
My Name Is Not Easy - Debby Dahl Edwardson   *y*   749

Isabel (Friend; Runaway; Slave)
Forge - Laurie Halse Anderson   *y*   607

Isabel (Student—High School; 17-Year-Old)
No More Us for You - David Hernandez   *y*   837

Isadora (Daughter)
The Doom Machine - Mark Teague   *c, y*   510

Itsy Mitsy (Girl; Daughter)
Itsy Mitsy Runs Away - Elanna Allen   *c*   5

Itty Bitty (Dog)
Itty Bitty - Cece Bell   *p, c*   30

Ivan (Classmate; Bully)
Out of Shadows - Jason Wallace   *y*   1146

Ivy (Angel)
Halo - Alexandra Adornetto   *y*   598

Ivy (Fox; Sister)
Zelda and Ivy: Keeping Secrets - Laura McGee Kvasnosky   *c*   264

Izzy (Girl)
Wow! Ocean! - Robert Neubecker   *p, c*   353

J

J (17-Year-Old)
I Am J - Cris Beam   *y*   625

Jac (Girl; Student—High School; Friend)
Sean Griswold's Head - Lindsey Leavitt   *y*   894

Jace (Boyfriend)
City of Glass - Cassandra Clare   *y*   691

Jack (16-Year-Old; Kidnap Victim)
The Marbury Lens - Andrew Smith   *y*   1087

Jack (5th Grader; Friend; 11-Year-Old)
Breadcrumbs - Anne Ursu   *c, y*   530

Jack (Boy)
The House of Dead Maids - Clare B. Dunkle   *y*   747

Jack (Boy; Nephew)
The Mostly True Story of Jack - Kelly Barnhill   *c, y*   23

Jack (Child)
Clever Jack Takes the Cake - Candace Fleming   *c*   140

Jack (Son; Brother)
Don't Want to Go! - Shirley Hughes   *p, c*   216

Jack (Warrior)
Blood Red Road - Moira Young   *y*   1191

Jack (Wizard)
The Familiars - Adam Jay Epstein   *c, y*   132

Jack (Young Man)
Calamity Jack - Shannon Hale   *c, y*   187

Jacklin (Student—Boarding School)
Out of Shadows - Jason Wallace   *y*   1146

Jackson (Brother; Genius; Child)
The Fires Beneath the Sea - Lydia Millet   *c, y*   330

Jackson (Orphan)
Emily's Fortune - Phyllis Reynolds Naylor   *c, y*   346

Jackson, May Amelia (13-Year-Old)
The Trouble with May Amelia - Jennifer L. Holm   *c, y*   207

Jackson, Percy (12-Year-Old; Deity; Son)
The Lightning Thief: The Graphic Novel - Rick Riordan   *c, y*   416

Jacob (Teenager; Friend)
North of Beautiful - Justina Chen Headley   *y*   830

Jacob (Uncle)
Is It Night or Day? - Fern Schumer Chapman   *y*   683

Jacob, Abba (Religious; Human)
Snook Alone - Marilyn Nelson   *c*   349

Jaimes, Lee Ann (12-Year-Old; Student; Detective—Amateur; Actress)
The Red Blazer Girls: The Ring of Rocamadour - Michael D. Beil   *y*   629

Jake (10-Year-Old)
Jake - Audrey Couloumbis   *c, y*   88

Jake (Student)
The Potato Chip Puzzles: The Puzzling World of Winston Breen - Eric Berlin   *c, y*   33

Jam Boy (Child)
Once Upon a Twice - Denise Doyen   *c*   117

James (Child)
Tales for Very Picky Eaters - Josh Schneider   *c*   452

James (Friend)
Clockwork Angel - Cassandra Clare   *y*   690

James, Gabriel (14-Year-Old; Witness)
The Interrogation of Gabriel James - Charlie Price   *y*   1024

Character Name Index

K

Kahlo, Frida (Spouse; Artist; Immigrant)
Me, Frida - Amy Novesky   *c*   360

Kaisa (Hunter)
Ash - Malinda Lo   *y*   902

Kalen (Friend)
Gateway - Sharon Shinn   *y*   1076

Kalinowski, Mandy (Teenager; Pregnant Teenager; Abuse Victim)
How to Save a Life - Sara Zarr   *y*   1197

Kalliovski, Count (Villain)
The Silver Blade - Sally Gardner   *y*   158

Kamau (Servant; Father)
Burn My Heart - Beverley Naidoo   *c, y*   967

Kane, Carter (Teenager; Brother)
The Red Pyramid - Rick Riordan   *c, y*   418

Kane, Julius (Father; Historian)
The Red Pyramid - Rick Riordan   *c, y*   418

Kane, Sadie (Teenager; Sister)
The Red Pyramid - Rick Riordan   *c, y*   418

Kapur, Chess (Friend)
Bobby versus Girls (Accidentally) - Lisa Yee   *c, y*   587

Kara (Friend)
Some Girls Are - Courtney Summers   *y*   1114

Karen (8-Year-Old; Crime Victim)
The River - Mary Jane Beaufrand   *y*   627

Karou (17-Year-Old; Student—Boarding School; Artist)
Daughter of Smoke and Bone - Laini Taylor   *y*   1120

Karyn (15-Year-Old; Sister; Crime Victim)
You Against Me - Jenny Downham   *y*   743

Kat (16-Year-Old; Foster Child)
The Stolen One - Suzanne Crowley   *y*   714

Kat (Teenager; Friend)
The Lighter Side of Life and Death - C.K. Kelly Martin   *y*   924

Kate (16-Year-Old; Student—High School; Dancer; Friend)
Exposed - Kimberly Marcus   *y*   923

Kate (7th Grader; Friend)
Sweet Treats and Secret Crushes - Lisa Greenwald   *y*   806

Kate (7th Grader; Songwriter; Musician)
The Kind of Friends We Used to Be - Frances O'Roark Dowell   *c, y*   116

Kate (Girlfriend)
Hero - Mike Lupica   *c, y*   290

Kate (Nurse)
Three Rivers Rising: A Novel of the Johnstown Flood - Jame Richards   *y*   1040

Kate (Orphan)
The Emerald Atlas - John Stephens   *c, y*   493

Kate (Orphan; Witch; Outcast)
Plain Kate - Erin Bow   *y*   650

Katherine (17-Year-Old; Twin)
Dangerous Neighbors - Beth Kephart   *y*   870

Katherine (Sister)
Sent - Margaret Peterson Haddix   *c, y*   185

Katie-Rose (5th Grader; Filmmaker)
Luv Ya Bunches - Lauren Myracle   *c, y*   343

Katrina (16-Year-Old; Waiter/Waitress)
Coffeehouse Angel - Suzanne Selfors   *y*   1070

Katrina (Dancer; Student)
Miss Lina's Ballerinas - Grace Maccarone   *c*   292

Katznelson, Boaz (Military Personnel; Brother)
The Things a Brother Knows - Dana Reinhardt   *y*   1036

Katznelson, Levi (Brother; Narrator)
The Things a Brother Knows - Dana Reinhardt   *y*   1036

Mr. Kaufman (Accident Victim; Father)
The Beginning of After - Jennifer Castle   *y*   681

Mrs. Kaufman (Mother; Accident Victim)
The Beginning of After - Jennifer Castle   *y*   681

Kaufman, David (Neighbor; Son)
The Beginning of After - Jennifer Castle   *y*   681

Keeper (Girl; 10-Year-Old; Daughter)
Keeper - Kathi Appelt   *c, y*   10

Lady Keepsake (Noblewoman)
I Shall Wear Midnight - Terry Pratchett   *y*   1021

Keepsake, Letitia (Fiance(e); Noblewoman)
I Shall Wear Midnight - Terry Pratchett   *y*   1021

Keller, Bonwit (Friend)
Julia Gillian (and the Quest for Joy) - Alison McGhee   *c*   317

Kelly (Sister; Narrator)
She Said/She Saw - Norah McClintock   *y*   931

Kelly (Supernatural Being)
Dope Sick - Walter Dean Myers   *y*   962

Kelly (Teenager; Addict)
Clean - Amy Reed   *y*   1031

Kelly, Jenna (Telepath; Teenager; Child of an Alcoholic)
Gifted: Better Late than Never - Marilyn Kaye   *y*   866

Kendra (15-Year-Old)
Scars - Cheryl Rainfield   *y*   1028

Kendrick, Sean (19-Year-Old; Equestrian)
The Scorpio Races - Maggie Stiefvater   *y*   1099

Kenny (Teenager; Friend)
Ostrich Boys - Keith Gray   *y*   804

Kento (13-Year-Old; Son; Friend)
Warriors in the Crossfire - Nancy Bo Flood   *y*   768

Keri (17-Year-Old; Sister)
The Shattering - Karen Healey   *y*   832

Ketchvar (Alien)
Stuck on Earth - David Klass   *c, y*   250

Khadija (13-Year-Old; Model; Sister)
Where I Belong - Gillian Cross   *y*   712

Khalid (15-Year-Old; Student—High School; Cousin; Soccer Player; Prisoner)
Guantanamo Boy - Anna Perera   *y*   1004

Khan, Nina (11th Grader; Student—High School; Religious)
Skunk Girl - Sheba Karim   *y*   864

Khosi (14-Year-Old; Girl; Sister)
This Thing Called the Future - J. L. Powers   *y*   1020

Kid (Streetperson; Lover; Runaway)
Brooklyn, Burning - Steve Brezenoff   *y*   658

Kieran (Boyfriend)
Glow - Amy Kathleen Ryan   *y*   1050

Kiernan (Friend)
The False Princess - Ellis O'Neal   *y*   986

Kimiko (Teenager; Lover)
Boyfriends with Girlfriends - Alex Sanchez   *y*   1056

Kinahan, Jonathan "Jono" (14-Year-Old; Brother; Narrator)
Long Story Short - Siobhan Parkinson   *y*   998

Kinahan, Julie (8-Year-Old; Sister)
Long Story Short - Siobhan Parkinson   *y*   998

Kincaid, Alex (Boyfriend; Homosexual)
The Vast Fields of Ordinary - Nick Burd   *y*   667

King, Jeremy (Teenager; Musician; Friend)
Virtuosity - Jessica Martinez   *y*   925

King, The (Royalty)
The King's Taster - Kenneth Oppel   *c*   371

Kingston, Samantha (Student—High School; Bully)
Before I Fall - Lauren Oliver   *y*   990

Kipp (17-Year-Old)
Stealing Death - Janet Lee Carey   *y*   675

Kipper, Moxie Roosevelt (13-Year-Old; Musician)
The Reinvention of Moxie Roosevelt - Elizabeth Cody Kimmel   *c, y*   246

Kit (15-Year-Old; Apprentice)
The Brothers Story - Katherine Sturtevant   *y*   1112

Kitrell, Katie (Student—Boarding School)
Breathless - Jessica Warman   *y*   1149

Kitrell, Will (Brother; Mentally Ill Person)
Breathless - Jessica Warman   *y*   1149

Klein, Andromeda (Occultist; Psychic; Teenager)
Andromeda Klein - Frank Portman   *y*   1019

Knuffle Bunny (Toy)
Knuffle Bunny Free: An Unexpected Diversion - Mo Willems   *p, c*   563

Kofi (Student—High School)
Just Another Hero - Sharon M. Draper   *y*   745

Kolvenbach, Pia (10-Year-Old)
The Vanishing of Katharina Linden - Helen Grant   *y*   802

Kookie (Student; 12-Year-Old; Friend; Student)
The Glorious Adventures of the Sunshine Queen - Geraldine McCaughrean   *c, y*   312

Korlov, Anna "Anna Dressed in Blood" (Spirit)
Anna Dressed in Blood - Kendare Blake   *y*   640

Kroner, Dieter (8th Grader)
After the Train - Gloria Whelan   *y*   557

Mrs. Krupp (Teacher)
When I Grow Up - Al Yankovic   *c*   585

Krzeszewski, Justin "Justin Case" (3rd Grader)
Justin Case: School, Drool, and Other Daily Disasters - Rachel Vail   *c, y*   531

Kurt (Student—High School; Football Player; Friend)
Leverage - Joshua Cohen   *y*   697

Ky (Orphan)
Matched - Ally Condie   *y*   703

Kyra (13-Year-Old; Cult Member)
The Chosen One - Carol Lynch Williams   *y*   1165

L

Lacey (13-Year-Old; Worker; Daughter; Niece)
Miles from Ordinary - Carol Lynch Williams   *y*   1164

Laddy (Runaway; Dragon)
The Runaway Dragon - Kate Coombs   *c, y*   79

Ladybug (Insect)
I'm the Best - Lucy Cousins   *p, c*   91

Lafayette (Bird)
A Nest for Celeste: A Story about Art, Inspiration, and the Meaning of Home - Henry Cole   *c, y*   74

Lamont (Mouse; Brother)
Secrets at Sea - Richard Peck   *c, y*   383

Lan (Twin; Magician)
Thirteenth Child - Patricia C. Wrede   *y*   1176

Lana (Teenager)
Hunger - Michael Grant   *y*   803

Lance (Teenager; Lover)
Boyfriends with Girlfriends - Alex Sanchez   *y*   1056

Lane, Marko (Bully)
A Boy Called Twister - Anne Schraff   *y*   1061

Larkin, Briony (17-Year-Old; Twin)
Chime - Franny Billingsley   *y*   634

Miss Latah (Spouse)
Carolina Harmony - Marilyn Taylor McDowell   *c, y*   315

Lathem, Wyatt (Boyfriend; Son; 16-Year-Old)
Bullet Point - Peter Abrahams   *y*   597

Laurel (16-Year-Old; Orphan; Neighbor)
The Beginning of After - Jennifer Castle   *y*   681

Laurel (Fairy; 16-Year-Old)
Spells - Aprilynne Pike   *y*   1015

LaVaughn (Student—High School)
This Full House - Virginia Euwer Wolff   *y*   1172

Le Fantome (Revolutionary)
The Pale Assassin - Patricia Elliott   *y*   756

Leach, Squinton (Uncle)
The Mostly True Adventures of Homer P. Figg - Rodman Philbrick   *c, y*   389

LeBeuf, Lou (Brother)
The Complete Essex County - Jeff Lemire   *y*   896

LeBeuf, Vince (Brother)
The Complete Essex County - Jeff Lemire   *y*   896

Lederer, Eric (Friend)
The Boy Who Couldn't Sleep and Never Had To - D.C. Pierson   *y*   1014

Lee, Clara (Granddaughter; Student—Elementary School; 3rd Grader)
Clara Lee and the Apple Pie Dream - Jenny Han   *c*   189

Lee, Cramer (Brother)
The Uninvited - Tim Wynne-Jones   *y*   1179

Leetree (Human; Designer)
The Christmas Giant - Steve Light   *p, c*   279

Leftman, Valerie (16-Year-Old)
Hate List - Jennifer Brown   *y*   664

Lena (Teenager)
The Mermaid's Mirror - L.K. Madigan   *y*   918

Lend (Shape-Shifter; Teenager)
Paranormalcy - Kiersten White   *y*   1156

Lennie (17-Year-Old)
The Sky Is Everywhere - Jandy Nelson   *y*   970

Lennon, John "Beatle" (12th Grader; Twin)
Beatle Meets Destiny - Gabrielle Williams   *y*   1166

Lenny (Worker)
Vintage Veronica - Erica S. Perl   *y*   1009

Leo (Mythical Creature)
The Lost Hero - Rick Riordan   *c, y*   417

Leonard "Wei Dong" (Teenager)
For the Win - Cory Doctorow   *y*   737

Leroy (Friend)
Crossing the Tracks - Barbara Stuber   *y*   1111

Lester (Boy)
The Complete Essex County - Jeff Lemire   *y*   896

Leticia (Student)
Jumped - Rita Williams-Garcia   *y*   1170

Lettie (Friend)
Moon over Manifest - Clare Vanderpool   *c, y*   538

Lewis, Mercy (Teenager)
Wicked Girls: A Novel of the Salem Witch Trials - Stephanie Hemphill   *y*   834

Lex (Young Man; Wizard; Friend)
The Runaway Dragon - Kate Coombs   *c, y*   79

Lexi (Sister)
The View from the Top - Hillary Frank   *y*   773

Lexie (10-Year-Old; Child of Divorced Parents)
Lexie - Audrey Couloumbis   *c, y*   87

Lexie (Single Mother; Waiter/Waitress; Daughter)
Pearl - Jo Knowles   *y*   882

Lia (18-Year-Old; Student—High School; Friend)
Wintergirls - Laurie Halse Anderson   *y*   608

Liam (12-Year-Old)
Cosmic - Frank Cottrell Boyce   *c, y*   84

Liam (Child)
Raven Summer - David Almond   *y*   602

Liam (Child; Gardener)
The Curious Garden - Peter Brown   *p, c*   50

Mr. Liebig (Father)
After the Train - Gloria Whelan   *y*   557

Mrs. Liebig (Mother)
After the Train - Gloria Whelan   *y*   557

Liebig, Peter (8th Grader; Adoptee)
After the Train - Gloria Whelan   *y*   557

Liesl (Orphan; Abuse Victim; Friend; 11-Year-Old; Prisoner)
Liesl and Po - Lauren Oliver   *c, y*   369

Lila (Girlfriend)
Red Glove - Holly Black   *y*   636

Lili (Foster Child; Orphan; Sister)
Peace, Locomotion - Jacqueline Woodson   *c, y*   581

Lilith (Demon; Spouse; Mother)
The Space Between - Brenna Yovanoff   *y*   1193

Lillian (Artist; Friend)
Sparrow Road - Sheila O'Connor   *c, y*   985

Lillie (14-Year-Old; Slave; Sister)
Freedom Stone - Jeffrey Kluger   *c, y*   255

Lilly (Girlfriend)
In the Path of Falling Objects - Andrew Smith   *y*   1086

Lily (13-Year-Old)
Green - Laura Peyton Roberts   *c, y*   420

Lily (Care Giver)
The Midnight Charter - David Whitley   *y*   1157

Lily (Child)
Don't Want to Go! - Shirley Hughes   *p, c*   216

Lina (16-Year-Old; Prisoner)
Between Shades of Gray - Ruta Sepetys   *y*   1071

Miss Lina (Dancer; Teacher)
Miss Lina's Ballerinas - Grace Maccarone   *c*   292

Lincoln, Abraham (Historical Figure; Political Figure)
Our Abe Lincoln - Jim Aylesworth   *c*   17

Linden (Spouse)
Wither - Lauren DeStefano   *y*   731

Linderman, Lucky (Teenager)
Everybody Sees the Ants - A.S. King   *y*   875

Lindgren, Loa (16-Year-Old)
The Freak Observer - Blythe Woolston   *y*   1175

Lindsey (Friend)
Before I Fall - Lauren Oliver   *y*   990

Ling (Twin)
Ling and Ting: Not Exactly the Same! - Grace Lin   *p, c*   280

Lion (Friend)
Mouse and Lion - Rand Burkert   *c*   54

Lion, The (Lion)
Willoughby and the Lion - Greg Foley   *p, c*   147

Lisa (Friend)
Highway to Hell - Rosemary Clement-Moore   *y*   694

Lisa (Stepmother)
This World We Live In - Susan Beth Pfeffer   *y*   1012

Lisa (Teenager; Girlfriend)
Funny How Things Change - Melissa Wyatt   *y*   1178

Lisette (Spirit)
Ruined: A Ghost Story - Paula Morris   *y*   955

Little Man (Classmate)
This Thing Called the Future - J. L. Powers   *y*   1020

Little Mouse (Mouse)
Little Mouse Gets Ready - Jeff Smith   *p, c*   474

Little Red Chicken (Chicken)
Interrupting Chicken - David Ezra Stein   *c*   491

Liu, Ray (Teenager; Immigrant; Homosexual)
Money Boy - Paul Yee   *y*   1188

Liz (16-Year-Old; Student—High School; Photographer; Friend)
Exposed - Kimberly Marcus   *y*   923

Liz (9-Year-Old; Daughter)
Crow Call - Lois Lowry   *c*   288

Liz (Mother; Friend)
Jumping Off Swings - Jo Knowles   *y*   881

Lizzie (14-Year-Old; Sister; Mentally Ill Person; Child of an Alcoholic)
Glimpse - Carol Lynch Williams   *y*   1163

Lloyd, Henriette "Henry" (Teenager; Student—High School; Tennis Player)
Jersey Tomatoes Are the Best - Maria Padian   *y*   997

Lochan (17-Year-Old; Brother; Lover)
Forbidden - Tabitha Suzuma   *y*   1116

Locke, Cat (11th Grader; Student—High School)
Fat Cat - Robin Brande   *y*   654

Logan (Boyfriend)
Shade - Jeri Smith-Ready   *y*   1091

Miss Lois (Teacher)
Just Grace Goes Green - Charise Mericle Harper   *c*   191

London (Friend)
Imaginary Girls - Nova Ren Suma   *y*   1113

London, Jack (Adventurer; 17-Year-Old)
The Wild - Christopher Golden   *y*   795

Lonnie (Orphan; Brother; Foster Child)
Peace, Locomotion - Jacqueline Woodson   *c, y*   581

Loompski, Lenny (Villain)
The Secret of Zoom - Lynne Jonell   *c, y*   228

Loosey Goosey (Goose)
Chicken Little - Rebecca Emberley   *p, c*   129

Lou (Teenager; Genius)
No and Me - Delphine De Vigan   *y*   726

Miss Loucien (Teacher; Actress)
The Glorious Adventures of the Sunshine Queen - Geraldine McCaughrean   *c, y*   312

Louis, Joe (Historical Figure; Boxer)
Bird in a Box - Andrea Davis Pinkney   *c, y*   392

Louise (Child; Naturalist)
The Sundown Rule - Wendy Townsend   *c, y*   522

Louise (Mouse; Sister)
Secrets at Sea - Richard Peck   *c, y*   383

Miss Loupe (Teacher)
Operation Yes - Sara Lewis Holmes   *c, y*   209

Lovelace, Simon (Magician)
The Amulet of Samarkand: A Bartimaeus Graphic Novel - Jonathan Stroud   *y*   499

Lovitt, Abby (Horse Trainer; 7th Grader)
The Georges and the Jewels - Jane Smiley   *c, y*   471

Lowood, Cas (Hunter)
Anna Dressed in Blood - Kendare Blake   *y*   640

Luc (Friend)
Compulsion - Heidi Ayarbe   *y*   617

Lucas (18-Year-Old; Son)
Legacy - Thomas Sniegoski   *y*   1093

Lucas (Teenager; Camper)
Brain Camp - Susan Kim   *y*   873

Lucas (Teenager; Narrator)
Surface Tension: A Novel in Four Summers - Brent Runyon   *y*   1049

Lucifer (Demon; Spouse; Father)
The Space Between - Brenna Yovanoff   *y*   1193

Lucifer "Scratch" (Demon)
Soul Enchilada - David Macinnis Gill   *y*   790

Lucky Ducky (Duck)
Chicken Little - Rebecca Emberley   *p, c*   129

Lucky Girl (Heiress)
Ship Breaker: A Novel - Paolo Bacigalupi   *y*   618

Lucy (16-Year-Old)
Dirty Little Secrets - C.J. Omololu   *y*   991

Lucy (17-Year-Old)
Winter Town - Stephen Emond   *y*   758

Lucy (Fox; Child)
Red Wagon - Renata Liwska   *p, c*   282

Lucy (Friend; Crime Victim)
iBoy - Kevin Brooks   *y*   660

Ludo (Friend)
Mirrorscape - Mike Wilks   *c, y*   1162

Lugh (18-Year-Old; Twin; Brother)
Blood Red Road - Moira Young   *y*   1191

Luisa (Singer; Teenager)
Hidden Voices: The Orphan Musicians of Venice - Pat Lowery Collins   *y*   698

Luke (Boyfriend)
A Little Wanting Song - Cath Crowley   *y*   713

Luke (Narrator; Student—Boarding School; Brother)
My Name Is Not Easy - Debby Dahl Edwardson   *y*   749

Luks, Jonah (Friend; Student—College)
The Space between Trees - Katie Williams   *y*   1167

Lula (Cat)
Waiting for the Magic - Patricia MacLachlan   *c*   293

Lulu (Child)
Lulu and the Brontosaurus - Judith Viorst   *p, c*   542

Lumley, Miss Penelope (15-Year-Old; Governess)
The Mysterious Howling - Maryrose Wood   *c, y*   579

Lunch Lady (Worker; Heroine)
Lunch Lady and the League of Librarians - Jarrett J. Krosoczka   *c*   260

Lupita (Teenager; Student—High School)
Under the Mesquite - Guadalupe Garcia McCall   *y*   929

Lydia (Friend)
The Ghosts of Ashbury High - Jaclyn Moriarty   *y*   954

Lyle (Crocodile)
Lyle Walks the Dogs: A Counting Book - Bernard Waber   *p, c*   546

Lynwood (Student—Elementary School; Bully)
Squish: Super Amoeba - Jennifer L. Holm   *c*   208

M

M'Rose (Sister)
The Zabime Sisters - Aristophane   *y*   611

Ma (Mother)
The 10 PM Question - Kate De Goldi   *y*   723
The Money We'll Save - Brock Cole   *c*   73
Why I Fight - J. Adams Oaks   *y*   987

Mabel (Aunt; Spouse)
The Mostly True Story of Jack - Kelly Barnhill   *c, y*   23

Mabel (Girl)
Bubble Trouble - Margaret Mahy   *p, c*   295

Mabis (Witch; Mother)
Witchlanders - Lena Coakley   *y*   695

Mac Cumhaill, Finn (Traveler)
Tyger Tyger - Kersten Hamilton   *y*   816

MacAvoy, Mack (Teenager)
The Call - Michael Grant   *c, y*   170

Mack (15-Year-Old; Boyfriend)
Stay with Me - Paul Griffin   *y*   809

Mackee, Thomas (Teenager; Child of an Alcoholic; Musician)
The Piper's Son - Melina Marchetta   *y*   922

MacSweeny, Jill (17-Year-Old)
How to Save a Life - Sara Zarr   *y*   1197

Madame Albirtha (Neighbor; Advisor)
The Secret River - Marjorie Kinnan Rawlings   *c*   407

Madame Lucille (Teacher)
Brontorina - James Howe   *p, c*   213

Maddie (Friend)
The Grand Plan to Fix Everything - Uma Krishnaswami   *c, y*   259

Maddy (13-Year-Old; Sister)
The Devil's Paintbox - Victoria McKernan   *y*   938

Maddy (Teenager; Cousin)
Illyria - Elizabeth Hand   *y*   820

Madeline (Teenager; Student—High School; 11th Grader; Alcoholic; Patient)
Recovery Road - Blake Nelson   *y*   969

Madison (Brother; Slave; Son)
Jefferson's Sons: A Founding Father's Secret Children - Kimberly Brubaker Bradley   *c, y*   45

Mae (Friend; Sister)
The Demon's Lexicon - Sarah Rees Brennan   *y*   657

Magic (Cat)
Wisdom's Kiss: A Thrilling and Romantic Adventure Incorporating Magic, Villainy and a Cat - Catherine Gilbert Murdock   *y*   959

Mags (Contestant)
Catching Fire - Suzanne Collins   *y*   699

Mahmoud (Brother)
Where I Belong - Gillian Cross   *y*   712

Mal (Student)
The Potato Chip Puzzles: The Puzzling World of Winston Breen - Eric Berlin   *c, y*   33

Mal (Teenager)
First Day on Earth - Cecil Castellucci   *y*   680

Mala (Teenager)
For the Win - Cory Doctorow   *y*   737

Malcolm (Angel)
Coffeehouse Angel - Suzanne Selfors   *y*   1070

Malcolm (Cat)
It's a Secret! - John Burningham   *p, c*   55

Maldor (Ruler)
A World without Heroes - Brandon Mull   *c, y*   335

Maldwyn (Raven)
The Cheshire Cheese Cat: A Dickens of a Tale - Carmen Agra Deedy   *c, y*   105

Malik (Friend)
Ratfink - Marcia Thornton Jones   *c, y*   230

Mallory, Jake (Military Personnel; 14-Year-Old)
Five 4ths of July - Pat Hughes   *y*   850

Malone, Logan (10-Year-Old)
Ratfink - Marcia Thornton Jones   *c, y*   230

Mam (Seamstress; Mother; Widow(er))
The Christmas Eve Ghost - Shirley Hughes   *c*   217

Mama (Mother)
Busing Brewster - Richard Michelson   *c*   329
Lost - Jacqueline Davies   *y*   720
Mommy, Mama and Me - Leslea Newman   *p, c*   356
Somebody Everybody Listens To - Suzanne Supplee   *y*   1115
Star in the Forest - Laura Resau   *c, y*   412
This Thing Called the Future - J. L. Powers   *y*   1020

Mama (Mother; Spouse)
Waiting for the Magic - Patricia MacLachlan   *c*   293

Mami (Mother)
Muchacho - LouAnne Johnson   *y*   860

Maomao (Girl)
A New Year's Reunion - Yu Li-Qiong   *c*   276

Mara (16-Year-Old; Refugee; Friend; Lover)
Zenith - Julie Bertagna   *y*   633

March, Miss May (Teacher)
The Glorious Adventures of the Sunshine Queen - Geraldine McCaughrean   *c, y*   312

March, Rosie (16-Year-Old; Sister; Hunter; Orphan)
Sisters Red - Jackson Pearce   *y*   1000

March, Scarlett (Sister; Orphan; Hunter; 18-Year-Old)
Sisters Red - Jackson Pearce   *y*   1000

Marcus (Teenager; Football Player)
Pop - Gordon Korman   *y*   885

Mendez, Allison "Monkeywrench" (Sidekick; Student—High School; Girlfriend)
Sidekicks - Jack D. Ferraiolo y 765

Mercedes (Friend)
What Happened on Fox Street - Tricia Springstubb c, y 484

Mercier, Georgia (Sister)
Die for Me - Amy Plum y 1016

Mercier, Kate (Teenager; Sister; Orphan; Girlfriend)
Die for Me - Amy Plum y 1016

Mia (17-Year-Old; Musician; Accident Victim)
If I Stay - Gayle Forman y 772

Mia (Orphan; Musician; Student)
Where She Went - Gayle Forman y 771

Miami (Aunt)
The Romeo and Juliet Code - Phoebe Stone c, y 496

Michael (Orphan)
The Emerald Atlas - John Stephens c, y 493

Mick (Camper)
Every Little Thing in the World - Nina de Gramont y 724

Miguel (Teenager)
We Were Here - Matt de la Pena y 725

Mike (Student—High School)
Gentlemen - Michael Northrop y 981

Mikey (18-Year-Old; Brother; Boyfriend)
You Against Me - Jenny Downham y 743

Miksa, Margit (Sister)
Every Little Thing in the World - Nina de Gramont y 724

Miksa, Natalia (Camper; 16-Year-Old; Friend)
Every Little Thing in the World - Nina de Gramont y 724

Mildew, Arthur (Impoverished; Brother; Child; Friend)
Tumtum and Nutmeg: Adventures beyond Nutmouse Hall - Emily Bearn c, y 29

Mildew, Lucy (Friend; Child; Impoverished; Sister)
Tumtum and Nutmeg: Adventures beyond Nutmouse Hall - Emily Bearn c, y 29

Mildred (Aunt)
Is It Night or Day? - Fern Schumer Chapman y 683

Milena (Teenager; Orphan)
Winter's End - Jean-Claude Mourlevat y 956

Milkweed, Octavia (14-Year-Old; Agent)
The Hunchback Assignments - Arthur G. Slade y 1081

Milo (17-Year-Old)
Cold Hands, Warm Heart - Jill Wolfson y 1173

Milo (Brother)
Tighter - Adele Griffin y 807

Milo (Friend)
Thirteen Days to Midnight - Patrick Carman y 676

Milos (Teenager; Orphan)
Winter's End - Jean-Claude Mourlevat y 956

Milthorpe, Alice (16-Year-Old; Twin)
Prophecy of the Sisters - Michelle Zink y 1199

Milthorpe, Lia (16-Year-Old; Twin)
Prophecy of the Sisters - Michelle Zink y 1199

Mimi (3rd Grader; Friend)
Just Grace Goes Green - Charise Mericle Harper c 191

Mimi (Artificial Intelligence)
Black Hole Sun - David Macinnis Gill y 789

Mimi (Friend)
Strawberry Hill - Mary Ann Hoberman c 205

Mina (9-Year-Old; Writer; Student)
My Name Is Mina - David Almond y 603

Mindy (5th Grader; Bully)
Ten - Lauren Myracle c 344

Ming (Boy; Impoverished)
The Runaway Wok - Ying Chang Compestine c 76

Minkus, Andy (7th Grader; Twin)
Angel in My Pocket - Ilene Cooper c, y 82

Minkus, Vivi (7th Grader; Twin)
Angel in My Pocket - Ilene Cooper c, y 82

Minli (Child; Daughter; Friend; Traveler)
Where the Mountain Meets the Moon - Grace Lin c, y 281

Minou, Colleen (Teenager; Friend)
Now Playing: Stoner & Spaz II - Ron Koertge y 883

Mira (Girlfriend)
Shakespeare Makes the Playoffs - Ron Koertge y 884

Miranda (6th Grader)
When You Reach Me - Rebecca Stead c, y 490

Miriam (Twin; Supernatural Being)
Kindred - Tammar Stein y 1098

Mirka (11-Year-Old)
Hereville: How Mirka Got Her Sword - Barry Deutsch c, y 110

Mitch (Driver; Boyfriend)
In the Path of Falling Objects - Andrew Smith y 1086

Mitch (Journalist; 12th Grader; Student—High School)
Payback Time - Carl Deuker y 732

Mixer (Student—High School)
Gentlemen - Michael Northrop y 981

Mr. Mixler (Teacher)
Julia Gillian (and the Quest for Joy) - Alison McGhee c 317

Mizuno (Young Man; Man)
Ooku: The Inner Chambers, Volume 1 - Fumi Yoshinaga y 1189

Mo (Twin; Supernatural Being)
Kindred - Tammar Stein y 1098

Modessa (5th Grader)
Luv Ya Bunches - Lauren Myracle c, y 343

Modo (14-Year-Old; Shape-changer)
The Hunchback Assignments - Arthur G. Slade y 1081

Mole (Mole)
I'm the Best - Lucy Cousins p, c 91
Mouse and Mole, Fine Feathered Friends - Wong Herbert Lee c 269

Molly (Sister; Student)
Season of Secrets - Sally Nicholls c, y 357

Mom (Mother)
Amy and Roger's Epic Detour - Morgan Matson y 927
Are You Awake? - Sophie Blackall p, c 40
Bitter Melon - Cara Chow y 688
The Dancing Pancake - Eileen Spinelli c, y 481
Dirty Little Secrets - C.J. Omololu y 991
Efrain's Secret - Sofia Quintero y 1027
Hush, Hush - Becca Fitzpatrick y 767
Lexie - Audrey Couloumbis c, y 87

Sorta Like a Rock Star - Matthew Quick y 1026
The Summer I Turned Pretty - Jenny Han y 817
This World We Live In - Susan Beth Pfeffer y 1012
You Are Here - Jennifer E. Smith y 1089

Mom (Mother; Spouse)
Mission Unstoppable - Dan Gutman c, y 183

Momma (Mother; Mentally Ill Person)
Miles from Ordinary - Carol Lynch Williams y 1164

Mommy (Mother)
Mommy, Mama and Me - Leslea Newman p, c 356

Monahan, Kelleigh (15-Year-Old; Thief)
How to Steal a Car - Pete Hautman y 829

Mong (Friend)
We Were Here - Matt de la Pena y 725

Monroe, Clem (Con Artist)
Grounded - Kate Klise c, y 253

Monson, Darra (14-Year-Old; Camper)
Hidden - Helen Frost y 778

Monster (Monster)
A Monster Calls - Patrick Ness y 976

Montaigne, Marissa (Student—High School)
Mangaman - Barry Lyga y 909

Moon, Millicent (Mother; Daughter; Writer)
Through Her Eyes - Jennifer Archer y 610

Dr. Moore (Teacher)
This Full House - Virginia Euwer Wolff y 1172

Moore, Haven (17-Year-Old)
The Eternal Ones - Kirsten Miller y 949

Morales, Alex (Friend)
This World We Live In - Susan Beth Pfeffer y 1012

Moran, Miz (Aged Person; Diabetic)
Saint Louis Armstrong Beach - Brenda Woods c, y 1174

Morland, Maia (Teenager; Student—High School; Girlfriend; Crime Victim)
After the Moment - Garret Freymann-Weyr y 776

Morrisey, Emer (Pirate)
The Dust of 100 Dogs - A.S. King y 874

Morrison, Anna (Friend; Girlfriend)
Some Girls Are - Courtney Summers y 1114

Morrison, Travis (Teenager; Diver; Cancer Patient)
Breathless - Lurlene McDaniel y 934

Morrissey, Colton "Colt" (16-Year-Old; Boyfriend)
The Secret Year - Jennifer R. Hubbard y 847

Morrow, Iain (Wealthy)
The Eternal Ones - Kirsten Miller y 949

Mortimer, Frankie (Wealthy; Heiress)
Life: An Exploded Diagram - Mal Peet y 1003

Moseley, Ivy June (7th Grader)
Faith, Hope, and Ivy June - Phyllis Reynolds Naylor c, y 347

Mother (Mother)
The Color of Earth - Kim Dong Hwa y 852
Silver Phoenix: Beyond the Kingdom of Xia - Cindy Pon y 1017

Mother Earth (Guardian)
Never Forgotten - Patricia C. McKissack c, y 319

Mouse (11-Year-Old; Girl)
Departure Time - Truus Matti c, y 306

Oates, Bobby (Writer; Father)
Stay - Deb Caletti   y   671

Oates, Clara (Graduate; Girlfriend; Daughter)
Stay - Deb Caletti   y   671

Obie (Supernatural Being; Son; Brother)
The Space Between - Brenna Yovanoff   y   1193

Octavia (Granddaughter; Sister)
Mare's War - Tanita S. Davis   y   722

Odair, Finnick (Contestant)
Catching Fire - Suzanne Collins   y   699

Odair, Finnick (Contestant; Rebel)
Mockingjay - Suzanne Collins   y   700

Odd (Child)
Odd and the Frost Giants - Neil
   Gaiman   c, y   154

Odysseus (Warrior)
The Odyssey - Gareth Hinds   y   839

Ogg, Nanny (Witch)
I Shall Wear Midnight - Terry Pratchett   y   1021

Ogilvie, Oscar (Time Traveler; 11-Year-Old;
   Nephew; Cousin)
On the Blue Comet - Rosemary Wells   c, y   554

Ojeda, Alonso de (Hostage)
Hurricane Dancers - Margarita Engle   y   761

Ojisan (Wealthy; Farmer)
Tsunami! - Kimiko Kajikawa   p, c   236

Oldham, Roger (Apprentice)
Alchemy and Meggy Swann - Karen
   Cushman   c, y   97

Oliphant, Anna (Teenager)
Anna and the French Kiss - Stephanie
   Perkins   y   1008

Olive (Spirit)
Dying to Meet You - Kate Klise   c, y   254

Oliver (Foster Child; Refugee)
Raven Summer - David Almond   y   602

Oliver (Thief)
The Last Little Blue Envelope - Maureen
   Johnson   y   861

Oliver, Ruby (16-Year-Old)
*The Treasure Map of Boys: Noel, Jackson, Finn,
   Hutch, Gideon—and Me, Ruby Oliver* - E.
   Lockhart   y   905

Oliver, Ruby (Student—High School; 12th Grader;
   Girlfriend)
*Real Live Boyfriends: Yes, Boyfriends, Plural. If My
   Life Weren't Complicated I Wouldn't Be Ruby
   Oliver* - E. Lockhart   y   904

Olivia (7th Grader; Friend)
Sweet Treats and Secret Crushes - Lisa
   Greenwald   y   806

Olivia (Wealthy; Addict; Socialite)
Clean - Amy Reed   y   1031

Olson, Oliver (3rd Grader)
How Oliver Olson Changed the World - Claudia
   Mills   c   331

Ombri (Time Traveler)
Gateway - Sharon Shinn   y   1076

Ophelia "Oh" (Friend)
Thirteen Days to Midnight - Patrick
   Carman   y   676

Orlu (Classmate)
Akata Witch - Nnedi Okorafor   y   988

Orrery, Madame (Hypnotist)
The Story of Cirrus Flux - Matthew
   Skelton   c, y   469

Orville, Benjamin Franklin (Boy; Kidnap Victim;
   14-Year-Old)
Murder Afloat - Jane Leslie Conly   c, y   77

Ostralis, Neomar (Wizard)
The False Princess - Ellis O'Neal   y   986

Otello (Soccer Player)
Exposure - Mal Peet   y   1002

Otis (12-Year-Old; Orphan; Friend)
Bird in a Box - Andrea Davis Pinkney   c, y   392

Otis (Worker)
Otis - Loren Long   p, c   284

Otokoto, Black Hat (Serial Killer; Witch)
Akata Witch - Nnedi Okorafor   y   988

Ouyang, Dennis (Teenager)
Level Up - Gene Luen Yang   y   1184

Owen (Narrator; Teenager)
Crash into Me - Albert Borris   y   649

Owen (Teenager; Computer Game Player)
Tangled - Carolyn Mackler   y   916

Mr. Ozu (Wealthy)
The Boy in the Garden - Allen Say   c   446

P

P.K. (16-Year-Old; Runaway; Mountaineer)
Jump - Elisa Carbone   y   673

Pa (Father)
The Money We'll Save - Brock Cole   c   73

Pablo (Football Player; Homosexual; Lover)
The Vast Fields of Ordinary - Nick Burd   y   667

Packwood, Jessica (17-Year-Old; 12th Grader)
Jessica's Guide to Dating on the Dark Side - Beth
   Fantaskey   y   763

Page, Jay (Brother)
The Uninvited - Tim Wynne-Jones   y   1179

Pale Queen, The (Villain; Mother)
The Call - Michael Grant   c, y   170

Paloma (12-Year-Old; Refugee)
Tropical Secrets: Holocaust Refugees in Cuba -
   Margarita Engle   y   760

Pancho (17-Year-Old; Orphan; Friend)
The Last Summer of The Death Warriors - Francisco X. Stork   y   1104

Panda (Toy; Panda)
Hooray for Amanda and Her Alligator! - Mo
   Willems   p, c   566

Pandora (Orphan)
The Story of Cirrus Flux - Matthew
   Skelton   c, y   469

Papa (Chicken; Father)
Interrupting Chicken - David Ezra Stein   c   491

Papa (Father; Immigrant)
Star in the Forest - Laura Resau   c, y   412

Papa (Father; Spouse; Teacher; Writer)
Waiting for the Magic - Patricia
   MacLachlan   c   293

Papa (Worker; Father)
A New Year's Reunion - Yu Li-Qiong   c   276

Papa C (Grandfather)
Soul Enchilada - David Macinnis Gill   y   790

Papi (Father)
Muchacho - LouAnne Johnson   y   860

Paradis, Alexandrine (Actress)
Revolution - Jennifer Donnelly   y   739

Parker, Ellie (Brother; Girlfriend)
You Against Me - Jenny Downham   y   743

Parker, Tom (Student—College; Brother; Crime
   Suspect)
You Against Me - Jenny Downham   y   743

Parsons, Frankie (12-Year-Old)
The 10 PM Question - Kate De Goldi   y   723

Patch (Classmate)
Hush, Hush - Becca Fitzpatrick   y   767

Patricia (Girlfriend)
Alligator Bayou - Donna Jo Napoli   y   968

Patrick (Brother)
You Are Here - Jennifer E. Smith   y   1089

Patrick (Friend; Homosexual; Crime Victim)
Shine - Lauren Myracle   y   965

Patrick (Friend; Orphan)
Newsgirl - Liza Ketchum   c, y   243

Paul (Brother; Friend)
Resistance - Carla Jablonski   y   854

Peabody, Polly (11-Year-Old)
Drizzle - Kathleen Van Cleve   c, y   537

Pearl (Rabbit; Friend)
Pearl and Wagner: One Funny Day - Kate
   McMullan   c   321

Pearl (Student; Writer; Daughter; Granddaughter)
Pearl verses the World - Sally Murphy   c   338

Pearl (Teenager)
Salt - Maurice Gee   y   783

Peggy (Student—Elementary School; Friend)
Squish: Super Amoeba - Jennifer L. Holm   c   208

Pencil (Student)
The Dunderheads - Paul Fleischman   c, y   138

Penelopeia (Ruler; Spouse; Mother)
King of Ithaka - Tracy Barrett   y   621

Penny (Mouse; Child; Sister)
Benny and Penny in the Big No-No! - Geoffrey
   Hayes   c   196

Mrs. Pepper (Trickster)
Tricking the Tallyman - Jacqueline Davies   c   101

Perry, Pingpong (Child; Writer)
Pingpong Perry Experiences How a Book Is Made
   - Sandy Donovan   c   114

Perry, Winnie (10-Year-Old; 5th Grader; Sister;
   Friend; Bullied Child)
Ten - Lauren Myracle   c   344

Pesto (Agent; Manager)
Soul Enchilada - David Macinnis Gill   y   790

Peter (Boy)
Annexed - Sharon Dogar   y   738

Peter (Friend; 11th Grader; Classmate;
   Student—High School)
Love Is the Higher Law - David Levithan   y   899

Peter (Worker)
*Three Rivers Rising: A Novel of the Johnstown
   Flood* - Jame Richards   y   1040

Mrs. Peterson (Teacher)
Junkyard Wonders - Patricia Polacco   c, y   396

Peterson, Henry (17-Year-Old; Spirit)
Through Her Eyes - Jennifer Archer   y   610

Petros (12-Year-Old; Brother)
War Games - Audrey Couloumbis   c, y   89

Petty, Amber (13-Year-Old; Girl)
I Shall Wear Midnight - Terry Pratchett   y   1021

Peyton (Friend)
Peace, Love, and Baby Ducks - Lauren
   Myracle   y   966

Regina (Dancer; Student)
Miss Lina's Ballerinas - Grace Maccarone *c* 292

Regina (Teenager; Musician)
The Girl Who Became a Beatle - Greg Taylor *y* 1117

Reinstein, Andrew (Brother)
Stupid Fast: The Summer I Went from a Joke to a Jock - Geoff Herbach *y* 836

Reinstein, Felton (11th Grader; Brother; Son; Football Player; Runner; Boyfriend)
Stupid Fast: The Summer I Went from a Joke to a Jock - Geoff Herbach *y* 836

Reinstein, Jerri (Widow(er); Single Mother; Mother)
Stupid Fast: The Summer I Went from a Joke to a Jock - Geoff Herbach *y* 836

Remington-Day, Katherine (Crime Victim)
Blood on My Hands - Todd Strasser *y* 1106

Rew, Elizabeth (Teenager)
The Grimm Legacy - Polly Shulman *y* 1078

Reyn (Immortal)
Immortal Beloved - Cate Tiernan 1130

Rhine (16-Year-Old; Spouse)
Wither - Lauren DeStefano *y* 731

Rhino (Rhinoceros; Friend)
I Broke My Trunk! - Mo Willems *p, c* 567

Rice, Alice (10-Year-Old)
Junonia - Kevin Henkes *c, y* 200

Rice, Daelyn (15-Year-Old)
By the Time You Read This, I'll Be Dead - Julie Anne Peters *y* 1010

Ricelli, Asher (Student—High School)
Skunk Girl - Sheba Karim *y* 864

Richards, Alton (12th Grader; 17-Year-Old; Nephew; Unemployed)
The Cardturner: A Novel about a King, a Queen, and a Joker - Louis Sachar *y* 1053

Richards, Annie (10-Year-Old)
Umbrella Summer - Lisa Graff *c, y* 167

Rick (Boyfriend)
Same Difference - Siobhan Vivian *y* 1140

Rico (Drug Dealer; Prisoner; Friend; 19-Year-Old)
Dope Sick - Walter Dean Myers *y* 962

Riff (14-Year-Old; Friend)
Worldshaker - Richard Harland *y* 823

Rigg (13-Year-Old)
Pathfinder - Orson Scott Card *y* 674

Riley (Boyfriend)
The Snowball Effect - Holly Nicole Hoxter *y* 846

Riley (Student—High School; Boyfriend)
The Ghosts of Ashbury High - Jaclyn Moriarty *y* 954

Riley, Tola (11th Grader)
Bad Apple - Laura Ruby *y* 1048

Rio (15-Year-Old; Cousin)
Take Me to the River - Will Hobbs *c, y* 841

Rivera, Diego (16-Year-Old)
Bait - Alex Sanchez *y* 1057

Rivera, Diego (Spouse; Immigrant; Artist)
Me, Frida - Amy Novesky *c* 360

Robert (Brother; Student—College; 18-Year-Old)
Angry Young Man - Chris Lynch *y* 912

Robyn (Student; Artist)
Same Difference - Siobhan Vivian *y* 1140

Roc (Computer)
The Comet's Curse - Dom Testa *y* 1124

Rockett, Esme (Teenager; Student—High School; Friend; Lesbian)
Sister Mischief - Laura Goode *y* 797

Rodgers, Jomo (Teenager; Friend; Football Player; Addict)
Shooting Star - Fredrick McKissack Jr. *y* 941

Rodriguez, Efrain (17-Year-Old; Student—High School)
Efrain's Secret - Sofia Quintero *y* 1027

Rogan (Teenager; Cousin)
Illyria - Elizabeth Hand *y* 820

Roger (11-Year-Old; Narrator; Classmate)
Yummy: The Last Days of a Southside Shorty - G. Neri *y* 973

Roger (19-Year-Old)
Amy and Roger's Epic Detour - Morgan Matson *y* 927

Rojo (Fox)
Dinosaur Woods: Can Seven Clever Critters Save Their Forest Home? - George McClements *p, c* 313

Roland (Nobleman; Son)
I Shall Wear Midnight - Terry Pratchett *y* 1021

Rondell (Friend)
We Were Here - Matt de la Pena *y* 725

Ronster, Digger (Bully)
Warp Speed - Lisa Yee *y* 1186

Roosevelt, Eleanor (Historical Figure)
Eleanor, Quiet No More - Doreen Rappaport *c* 404

Rosa (Young Woman)
The Running Dream - Wendelin Van Draanen *y* 744

Rosalba (Teenager)
Hidden Voices: The Orphan Musicians of Venice - Pat Lowery Collins *y* 698

Rosalia (Teenager; Slave)
No Safe Place - Deborah Ellis *y* 757

Roscoe (Dog)
Sidekicks - Dan Santat *c, y* 441

Rose (Girl)
The Queen of France - Tim Wadham *c* 547
Wonderstruck - Brian Selznick *c, y* 458

Rose (Neighbor)
A Little Wanting Song - Cath Crowley *y* 713

Rose (Royalty)
Princess of the Midnight Ball - Jessica Day George *y* 784

Rose (Teenager)
The Survival Kit - Donna Freitas *y* 775

Rose (Twin; Mentally Challenged Person)
Chime - Franny Billingsley *y* 634

Rose, April Garnet (14-Year-Old; Daughter; Niece)
A Month of Sundays - Ruth White *y* 558

Rose, Betty (Mother; Spouse)
A Month of Sundays - Ruth White *y* 558

Rose, Lucy (Friend)
Melonhead - Katy Kelly *c* 240

Rosenfeld, Essie (16-Year-Old; Seamstress)
Lost - Jacqueline Davies *y* 720

Rosenfeld, Zelda (6-Year-Old; Sister)
Lost - Jacqueline Davies *y* 720

Rosie (15-Year-Old; Sister)
Rosie and Skate - Beth Ann Bauman *y* 624

Roth (Bully; Gang Member; Young Man)
The Knife That Killed Me - Anthony McGowan *c, y* 936

Mrs. Roux (Widow(er); Mother)
Stones for My Father - Trilby Kent *y* 869

Roux, Corlie (Girl; Daughter; Friend)
Stones for My Father - Trilby Kent *y* 869

Roux, Pepper (14-Year-Old; Adventurer)
The Death-Defying Pepper Roux - Geraldine McCaughrean *c, y* 311

Rowan (15-Year-Old)
Broken Soup - Jenny Valentine *y* 1136

Rowan, Dale (Banker)
Bloodhound - Tamora Pierce *y* 1013

Rowie (Teenager; Friend; Student—High School)
Sister Mischief - Laura Goode *y* 797

Rubia (Girl)
Rubia and the Three Osos - Susan Middleton Elya *p, c* 127

Rubina (Sister; Daughter)
Big Red Lollipop - Rukhsana Khan *p, c* 244

Ruby (Sister; Friend)
Imaginary Girls - Nova Ren Suma *y* 1113

Ruka (Teenager)
Children of the Sea, Volume 1 - Daisuke Igarashi *y* 853

Rush, Wesley (Student; Teenager)
The DUFF: Designated Ugly Fat Friend - Kody Keplinger *y* 871

Russell (Foster Child)
Carolina Harmony - Marilyn Taylor McDowell *c, y* 315

Russell (Friend; Teenager)
Hothouse - Chris Lynch *y* 911

Ruth (Child)
Ruth and the Green Book - Calvin Alexander Ramsey *c* 403

Ruthanne (Friend)
Moon over Manifest - Clare Vanderpool *c, y* 538

Ry (Teenager)
As Easy as Falling off the Face of the Earth - Lynne Rae Perkins *c, y* 386

Ryan (Boyfriend)
The Unwritten Rule - Elizabeth Scott *y* 1066

Ryder (Hero; Brother)
Witchlanders - Lena Coakley *y* 695

Rye, Amelia E. (Child; 13-Year-Old; Outcast)
The Private Thoughts of Amelia E. Rye - Bonnie Shimko *c, y* 1075

Ryoko (Teenager)
Mangaman - Barry Lyga *y* 909

Ryves, Alan (Brother)
The Demon's Lexicon - Sarah Rees Brennan *y* 657

Ryves, Nick (16-Year-Old; Hunter)
The Demon's Lexicon - Sarah Rees Brennan *y* 657

S

Saba (18-Year-Old; Twin; Sister)
Blood Red Road - Moira Young *y* 1191

Sabiri, Sami (15-Year-Old; Religious)
Borderline - Allan Stratton *y* 1108

Signe (Guardian)
Keeper - Kathi Appelt   *c*, *y*   10

Silas (Neighbor; Hunter; Teenager)
Sisters Red - Jackson Pearce   *y*   1000

Silvey, Chance (Scientist)
Low Red Moon - Caitlin R. Kiernan   *a*   872

Silvey, Deacon (Psychic)
Low Red Moon - Caitlin R. Kiernan   *a*   872

Simon (Baker)
Raspberries! - Jay O'Callahan   *p*, *c*   364

Simon (Brother)
In the Path of Falling Objects - Andrew Smith   *y*   1086

Sims, Harry "Dit" (Friend)
The Best Bad Luck I Ever Had - Kristin Levine   *y*   273

Sinda/Nalia (Teenager; Magician; Royalty)
The False Princess - Ellis O'Neal   *y*   986

Sione (Tourist; Brother)
The Shattering - Karen Healey   *y*   832

Sipho (Servant; Child; Friend)
Stones for My Father - Trilby Kent   *y*   869

Sixes, Jimmi (18-Year-Old; Addict; Veteran)
The Orange Houses - Paul Griffin   *y*   810

Sixpence (Daughter)
A Small Free Kiss in the Dark - Glenda Millard   *y*   948

Skate (Sister; 16-Year-Old)
Rosie and Skate - Beth Ann Bauman   *y*   624

Skilley (Cat; Friend)
The Cheshire Cheese Cat: A Dickens of a Tale - Carmen Agra Deedy   *c*, *y*   105

Skip (11-Year-Old; Runaway)
A Small Free Kiss in the Dark - Glenda Millard   *y*   948

Skye (Teenager; Actress)
Tangled - Carolyn Mackler   *y*   916

Skyla (Sister)
Witchlanders - Lena Coakley   *y*   695

Skylar (Bird)
The Familiars - Adam Jay Epstein   *c*, *y*   132

Slaterton, Ed (Student—High School; Boyfriend)
Why We Broke Up - Daniel Handler   *y*   821

Slocum, Joshua (Sailor; Adventurer; Traveler)
Around the World - Matt Phelan   *c*, *y*   388

Small, Cleo (Sister; 8-Year-Old; Narrator)
Underpants On My Head - Jessica Harper   *c*   192

Small, Jenna (Sister)
Underpants On My Head - Jessica Harper   *c*   192

Smith, Antigone (Sister; 13-Year-Old)
The Dragon's Tooth - N.D. Wilson   *c*, *y*   571

Smith, Cyrus (12-Year-Old; Brother)
The Dragon's Tooth - N.D. Wilson   *c*, *y*   571

Smith, E.J. (Historical Figure; Sea Captain)
The Watch That Ends the Night: Voices from the Titanic - Allan Wolf   *y*   1171

Smith, Eskarina (Witch)
I Shall Wear Midnight - Terry Pratchett   *y*   1021

Smith, Eva (Dancer; Teenager; Student—High School)
Jersey Tomatoes Are the Best - Maria Padian   *y*   997

Smith, Willoughby (Child)
Willoughby and the Lion - Greg Foley   *p*, *c*   147

Smithers, Frank (Inspector; Father)
Burn My Heart - Beverley Naidoo   *c*, *y*   967

Smithers, Lance (Classmate; Son)
Burn My Heart - Beverley Naidoo   *c*, *y*   967

Smoot, Eunice "Bug" (Young Woman; Worker)
Soul Enchilada - David Macinnis Gill   *y*   790

Snider, Kat (Mother)
The Brooklyn Nine: A Novel in Nine Innings - Alan Gratz   *c*, *y*   171

Snider, Walter (Father)
The Brooklyn Nine: A Novel in Nine Innings - Alan Gratz   *c*, *y*   171

Snook (Dog; Animal)
Snook Alone - Marilyn Nelson   *c*   349

Ms. Snoops (Aged Person; Historian)
One Day and One Amazing Morning on Orange Street - Joanne Rocklin   *c*   422

Snow, Narcissa (Serial Killer)
Low Red Moon - Caitlin R. Kiernan   *a*   872

Snow, President Coriolanus (Political Figure; Villain)
Catching Fire - Suzanne Collins   *y*   699
Mockingjay - Suzanne Collins   *y*   700

Mr. Socrates (Agent)
The Hunchback Assignments - Arthur G. Slade   *y*   1081

Solo, Drew Robin (13-Year-Old; Friend)
The Summer I Learned to Fly - Dana Reinhardt   *y*   1037

Solomon, Dani (17-Year-Old; Babysitter; Mentally Ill Person)
The Babysitter Murders - Janet Ruth Young   1190

Solomon, King (Royalty)
The Ring of Solomon - Jonathan Stroud   *y*   1109

Solomon, Sabine (16-Year-Old)
Earthgirl - Jennifer Cowan   *y*   710

Solveig (Daughter; Sister)
Icefall - Matthew J. Kirby   *y*   878

Song (13-Year-Old; Cancer Patient; Sister)
The Complete History of Why I Hate Her - Jennifer Richard Jacobson   *y*   855

Sonny (Father; Prisoner)
Bullet Point - Peter Abrahams   *y*   597

Sonny (Narrator; Student—Boarding School)
My Name Is Not Easy - Debby Dahl Edwardson   *y*   749

Sophie (Girl)
Benno and the Night of Broken Glass - Meg Wiviott   *c*   576

Sophos (Teenager; Heir)
A Conspiracy of Kings - Megan Whalen Turner   *y*   1134

Sora (Boy; Friend)
Children of the Sea, Volume 1 - Daisuke Igarashi   *y*   853

Soto, Marc (Artist; Father)
The Uninvited - Tim Wynne-Jones   *y*   1179

Sparksmith, Freddie (Journalist)
Calamity Jack - Shannon Hale   *c*, *y*   187

Spencer, Ellie (17-Year-Old; Martial Arts Expert)
Guardian of the Dead - Karen Healey   *y*   831

Spencer, Kevin (14-Year-Old; Student)
Liar, Liar: The Theory, Practice and Destructive Properties of Deception - Gary Paulsen   *c*, *y*   999

Spicer, Lil (Friend; Student)
Okay for Now - Gary D. Schmidt   *c*, *y*   451

Spider (Friend)
Numbers - Rachel Ward   *y*   1148

Spider (Student)
The Dunderheads - Paul Fleischman   *c*, *y*   138

Spinach (Girl)
The Runaway Dragon - Kate Coombs   *c*, *y*   79

Spree, Twilly (Wealthy; Environmentalist)
Scat - Carl Hiaasen   *c*, *y*   203

Squirrel (Squirrel)
Waiting for Winter - Sebastian Meschenmoser   *p*, *c*   326

Squish (Student—Elementary School)
Squish: Super Amoeba - Jennifer L. Holm   *c*   208

St. Pierre, Sophie (12-Year-Old; Detective—Amateur; Writer; Student)
The Red Blazer Girls: The Ring of Rocamadour - Michael D. Beil   *y*   629

Stan (16-Year-Old; Basketball Player)
Tilt - Alan Cumyn   *y*   716

Stanley (5th Grader)
Piper Reed, Campfire Girl - Kimberly Willis Holt   *c*   210

Stanton, Madison (17-Year-Old)
The Everafter - Amy Huntley   *y*   851

Starbuckle, Dolores (Friend)
Andy Shane and the Barn Sale Mystery - Jennifer Richard Jacobson   *c*   220

Starch, Mrs. Bunny (Teacher)
Scat - Carl Hiaasen   *c*, *y*   203

Static Cat (Cat; Sidekick)
Sidekicks - Dan Santat   *c*, *y*   441

Steiner, Nellie (8-Year-Old; Sister)
A Faraway Island - Annika Thor   *c*, *y*   516

Steiner, Stephie (12-Year-Old; Refugee; Sister)
A Faraway Island - Annika Thor   *c*, *y*   516

Stella (Friend)
Calvin Coconut: Trouble Magnet - Graham Salisbury   *c*   438

Stephanie (Teenager; Kidnap Victim; Survivor)
Taken - Norah McClintock   *y*   932

Stern, Karl (14-Year-Old; Boxer; Student)
The Berlin Boxing Club - Robert Sharenow   *y*   1073

Steven (Brother)
The Summer I Turned Pretty - Jenny Han   *y*   817

Stevens, Thomas (Historical Figure; Adventurer; Traveler)
Around the World - Matt Phelan   *c*, *y*   388

Stewart (Teenager; Addict; Patient; Boyfriend)
Recovery Road - Blake Nelson   *y*   969

Stewart, Grace "Just Grace" (3rd Grader; Friend)
Just Grace Goes Green - Charise Mericle Harper   *c*   191

Stewart, Tate (Human)
The Replacement - Brenna Yovanoff   *y*   1194

StinkStefan (Friend)
The Vanishing of Katharina Linden - Helen Grant   *y*   802

Stokes, Martin (17-Year-Old; Criminal; Prisoner)
Rikers High - Paul Volponi   *y*   1143

Stone, Gaia (16-Year-Old; Midwife)
Birthmarked - Caragh M. O'Brien   *y*   982

Stone, Gaia (Sister; Heroine; 16-Year-Old; Midwife)
Prized - Caragh M. O'Brien   *y*   983

Triana (16-Year-Old; Leader)
The Comet's Curse - Dom Testa   y   1124

Trina (Student)
Jumped - Rita Williams-Garcia   y   1170

Trisha (Learning Disabled Child)
Junkyard Wonders - Patricia Polacco   c, y   396

Tristan (Student; Runner)
My Fair Godmother - Janette Rallison   y   1029

Trixie (Girl)
Knuffle Bunny Free: An Unexpected Diversion - Mo
   Willems   p, c   563

Troy (Son; Brother; Foster Child)
Bronxwood - Coe Booth   y   648

Tu Reh (Teenager; Refugee; Military Personnel)
Bamboo People - Mitali Perkins   y   1006

Tuck (Pirate; Teenager; Refugee)
Zenith - Julie Bertagna   y   633

Tucker (Classmate; Twin)
Unearthly - Cynthia Hand   y   819

Tucker, Abilene (12-Year-Old; Girl)
Moon over Manifest - Clare Vanderpool   c, y   538

Tucker, Gideon (Father; Railroad Worker)
Moon over Manifest - Clare Vanderpool   c, y   538

Tully, J.J. (Dog; Detective—Private)
The Trouble with Chickens - Doreen
   Cronin   c   92

Tumtum (Mouse; Guardian; Spouse)
*Tumtum and Nutmeg: Adventures beyond Nutmouse
   Hall* - Emily Bearn   c, y   29

Turpin, Dick (Highwayman)
Highway Robbery - Kate Thompson   c, y   514

Turpin, Mellie (13-Year-Old)
Small Persons with Wings - Ellen
   Booraem   c, y   44

Turtle (11-Year-Old; Granddaughter)
Turtle in Paradise - Jennifer L. Holm   c, y   206

Ty (13-Year-Old; Witness)
When I Was Joe - Keren David   y   719

Ty (3-Year-Old; Brother)
Ten - Lauren Myracle   c   344

Ty (Boy; 13-Year-Old; Cousin)
Storm Mountain - Tom Birdseye   c, y   36

Ty (Kidnapper)
Stolen - Lucy Christopher   y   689

Tyler (Farmer; Narrator; 13-Year-Old;
   Student—Middle School)
Return to Sender - Julia Alvarez   c, y   7

Tyler (Neighbor)
Princess Posey and the First Grade Parade -
   Stephanie Greene   c   176

Tyler (Student—High School)
Wish You Were Dead - Todd Strasser   y   1107

Tyler (Teenager)
Moonglass - Jessi Kirby   y   877

Tyrell (Teenager; Friend; Son; Brother)
Bronxwood - Coe Booth   y   648

U

Uberwald, Angua von (Police Officer; Werewolf)
I Shall Wear Midnight - Terry Pratchett   y   1021

Uido (15-Year-Old; Leader)
Island's End - Padma Venkatraman   y   1138

Lord Umber (Adventurer; Inventor)
Happenstance Found - P. W. Catanese   c, y   63

Umbo (Friend)
Pathfinder - Orson Scott Card   y   674

Umi (Boy; Friend)
Children of the Sea, Volume 1 - Daisuke
   Igarashi   y   853

Uncle Bud (Uncle)
The Doom Machine - Mark Teague   c, y   510

Uncle Spade (Uncle)
Why I Fight - J. Adams Oaks   y   987

Underhill, April (7-Year-Old; Mythical Creature)
April and Esme: Tooth Fairies - Bob
   Graham   p, c   168

Underhill, Esme (6-Year-Old; Mythical Creature;
   Sister)
April and Esme: Tooth Fairies - Bob
   Graham   p, c   168

Underwood, Nathaniel (Apprentice)
*The Amulet of Samarkand: A Bartimaeus Graphic
   Novel* - Jonathan Stroud   c, y   499

Unity (Sister)
The Flint Heart - Katherine Paterson   c, y   380

Unnamed Character (Baby; Narrator)
Mommy, Mama and Me - Leslea
   Newman   p, c   356

Unnamed Character (Boy)
King Jack and the Dragon - Peter
   Bently   p, c   31

Unnamed Character (Boy; Hairdresser)
Even Monsters Need Haircuts - Matthew
   McElligott   p, c   316

Unnamed Character (Child)
Gracias Thanks - Pat Mora   p, c   333

Unnamed Character (Dog)
See Me Run - Paul Meisel   p, c   324

Unnamed Character (Father; Merchant)
The Third Gift - Linda Sue Park   c   376

Unnamed Character (Girl)
Sea of Dreams - Dennis Nolan   p, c   359

Unnamed Character (Girl; Daughter)
Over and Under the Snow - Kate Messner   c   327

Unnamed Character (Girl; Teenager; Patient)
The Gardener - S.A. Bodeen   y   645

Unnamed Character (Granddaughter; Narrator)
*I Will Come Back for You: A Family in Hiding dur-
   ing World War II* - Marisabina Russo   c   433

Unnamed Character (Grandfather; Narrator)
These Hands - Margaret H. Mason   c   304

Unnamed Character (Narrator)
RRRalph - Lois Ehlert   p, c   124

Unnamed Character (Pig)
Adios, Tricycle - Susan Middleton Elya   p, c   128

Unnamed Character (Turtle)
The Voyage of Turtle Rex - Kurt Cyrus   c   98

Unnamed Character (Walrus)
Where's Walrus? - Stephen Savage   p, c   444

Unnamed Character (Zoo Keeper)
Where's Walrus? - Stephen Savage   p, c   444

V

Valchar, Liz (18-Year-Old; Spirit)
Between - Jessica Warman   y   1150

Valentine (Supernatural Being)
City of Glass - Cassandra Clare   y   691

Valentine, Laurie (11-Year-Old; Friend)
The Giant Slayer - Iain Lawrence   c, y   267

Valentino (Employer)
Putting Makeup on the Fat Boy - Bil
   Wright   y   1177

Vallery (Stepsister; Sister)
The Snowball Effect - Holly Nicole
   Hoxter   y   846

Valli (Girl)
No Ordinary Day - Deborah Ellis   c, y   126

Van Dine, Sandy (Mother)
Callie's Rules - Naomi Flink Zucker   c, y   594

Van Dine, Valeri (Classmate; Daughter)
Callie's Rules - Naomi Flink Zucker   c, y   594

Vanessa (Student—High School; 17-Year-Old)
No More Us for You - David Hernandez   y   837

Varderman, Paul (Bullied Child; Narrator)
The Knife That Killed Me - Anthony
   McGowan   c, y   936

Velasquez, Eric (Child)
Grandma's Gift - Eric Velasquez   c   540

Velveeta (Friend)
Brutal - Michael Harmon   y   824

Velveeta (Friend; 8th Grader)
Bluefish - Pat Schmatz   y   1060

Mr. Venezi (Store Owner)
Hamster and Cheese - Colleen A.F.
   Venable   c   541

Vernon, Julia (Girlfriend)
The Secret Year - Jennifer R. Hubbard   y   847

Vi (Teenager; Friend)
Ten Things We Did (and Probably Shouldn't Have)
   - Sarah Mlynowski   y   951

Vicky (Girlfriend; Mother)
Lexie - Audrey Couloumbis   c, y   87

Victor (Uncle)
Emily's Fortune - Phyllis Reynolds
   Naylor   c, y   346

Mr. Vidas (Counselor)
Bait - Alex Sanchez   y   1057

Vienne (Sidekick)
Black Hole Sun - David Macinnis Gill   y   789

Vincent (Boyfriend; Supernatural Being)
Die for Me - Amy Plum   y   1016

Viola (14-Year-Old; Student—Boarding School)
Viola in Reel Life - Adriana Trigiani   y   1133

Viola (Activist; Friend)
The Ask and the Answer - Patrick Ness   y   975

Viola (Leader; Young Woman)
Monsters of Men - Patrick Ness   y   974

Viola (Neighbor)
The Fantastic Secret of Owen Jester - Barbara
   O'Connor   c, y   366

Violet (5th Grader; Student)
Luv Ya Bunches - Lauren Myracle   c, y   343

Virginia (Young Woman; Servant)
The Queen of Water - Laura Resau   y   1038

Vivien (Student—Boarding School; Friend)
Dreams of Significant Girls - Cristina
   Garcia   y   779

Vladescu, Lucius (Student—Exchange)
Jessica's Guide to Dating on the Dark Side - Beth
   Fantaskey   y   763

Yasaman (5th Grader)
Luv Ya Bunches - Lauren Myracle   *c, y*   343

Yasmine (14-Year-Old; Friend)
Thunder over Kandahar - Sharon E. McKay   *y*   937

Yates (Teacher)
Same Difference - Siobhan Vivian   *y*   1140

Z

Z (6th Grader; Friend)
Camo Girl - Kekla Magoon   *c, y*   294

Zach (Boyfriend)
Liar - Justine Larbalestier   *y*   891

Zachary (Friend)
Shade - Jeri Smith-Ready   *y*   1091

Zagabog (Mythical Creature)
The Flint Heart - Katherine Paterson   *c, y*   380

Zahra (Mother)
Zahra's Paradise - Amir Amir   *y*   606

Zaichik, Sasha (10-Year-Old)
Breaking Stalin's Nose - Eugene Yelchin   *c, y*   588

Zaksauskas, Gobija (Teenager; Student—Exchange; Assassin)
Au Revoir, Crazy European Chick - Joe Schreiber   *y*   1063

Zam (Refugee; Orphan; Lover)
Habibi - Craig Thompson   *y*   1126

Zan (Chimpanzee)
Half Brother - Kenneth Oppel   *y*   992

Zeke (Brother; Student—High School; Chess Player)
Perpetual Check - Rich Wallace   *y*   1147

Zelda (6-Year-Old; Orphan)
Then - Morris Gleitzman   *y*   792

Zelda (Fox; Sister)
Zelda and Ivy: Keeping Secrets - Laura McGee Kvasnosky   *c*   264

Zelda (Mentally Ill Person)
How I Stole Johnny Depp's Alien Girlfriend - Gary Ghislain   *y*   786

Zeph (Pirate)
Raiders' Ransom - Emily Diamand   *y*   734

Zeynab (15-Year-Old; Sister)
Words in the Dust - Trent Reedy   *y*   1033

Zhong Ye (Supernatural Being)
Silver Phoenix: Beyond the Kingdom of Xia - Cindy Pon   *y*   1017

Zi (Sister)
This Thing Called the Future - J. L. Powers   *y*   1020

Zig (Alien)
Zig and Wikki in Something Ate My Homework - Nadja Spiegelman   *p, c*   480

Zita (Girl; Friend; Heroine)
Zita the Spacegirl - Ben Hatke   *c, y*   195

Zitlally (11-Year-Old; 5th Grader; Daughter; Friend)
Star in the Forest - Laura Resau   *c, y*   412

Zoe (11-Year-Old; Orphan)
Wild Things - Clay Carmichael   *c, y*   60

Zoe (Worker)
Vintage Veronica - Erica S. Perl   *y*   1009

Zola (Brother)
War Games - Audrey Couloumbis   *c, y*   89

Zorro (Dog)
Say Hello to Zorro! - Carter Goodrich   *p, c*   164

Zulaikha (Sister; 13-Year-Old; Student)
Words in the Dust - Trent Reedy   *y*   1033

Character Description Index

This index alphabetically lists descriptions of the major characters in featured titles. The descriptions may be occupations (doctor, lawyer, etc.) or may describe persona (amnesiac, runaway, teenager, etc.). For each description, character names are listed alphabetically. Book titles, author names, age-level code(s) and entry numbers are also included. The age-level codes are as follows: *p*: ages 1-4, *c* : ages 5-10, *y*: ages 11-18.

10-YEAR-OLD

Alice
Pie - Sarah Weeks *c, y* 552

Barker, Henry
Missing on Superstition Mountain - Elise Broach *c, y* 47

Barnhardt, Bob
A Season of Gifts - Richard Peck *c, y* 384

Caitlin
Mockingbird - Kathryn Erskine *c, y* 133

Carolina
Carolina Harmony - Marilyn Taylor McDowell *c, y* 315

Carter, Keisha
Gator on the Loose! - Sue Stauffacher *c, y* 487

Christina
The Secret of Zoom - Lynne Jonell *c, y* 228

Delilah
Missing on Superstition Mountain - Elise Broach *c, y* 47

Duchene, Peter Augustus
The Magician's Elephant - Kate DiCamillo *c, y* 112

Felix
Then - Morris Gleitzman *y* 792

Gillian, Julia
Julia Gillian (and the Quest for Joy) - Alison McGhee *c* 317

Ha
Inside Out and Back Again - Thanhha Lai *c, y* 888

Jake
Jake - Audrey Couloumbis *c, y* 88

Jonah
No Safe Place - Deborah Ellis *y* 757

Keeper
Keeper - Kathi Appelt *c, y* 10

Kolvenbach, Pia
The Vanishing of Katharina Linden - Helen Grant *y* 802

Lexie
Lexie - Audrey Couloumbis *c, y* 87

Malone, Logan
Ratfink - Marcia Thornton Jones *c, y* 230

Perry, Winnie
Ten - Lauren Myracle *c* 344

Rice, Alice
Junonia - Kevin Henkes *c, y* 200

Richards, Annie
Umbrella Summer - Lisa Graff *c, y* 167

Sherman, Allie
Strawberry Hill - Mary Ann Hoberman *c* 205

Tammy
Neil Armstrong Is My Uncle and Other Lies Muscle Man McGinty Told Me - Nan Marino *c, y* 299

Wren, Mo
What Happened on Fox Street - Tricia Springstubb *c, y* 484

Zaichik, Sasha
Breaking Stalin's Nose - Eugene Yelchin *c, y* 588

10TH GRADER

Bizza
Into the Wild Nerd Yonder - Julie Halpern *y* 815

Char
Into the Wild Nerd Yonder - Julie Halpern *y* 815

Coop
Beat the Band - Don Calame *y* 670

Danny
Leverage - Joshua Cohen *y* 697

Delano, Savannah
My Fair Godmother - Janette Rallison *y* 1029

Fraser, Tara
Mercury - Hope Larson *y* 892

Helen
Beat the Band - Don Calame *y* 670

Jess
Into the Wild Nerd Yonder - Julie Halpern *y* 815

Mason
The Gardener - S.A. Bodeen *y* 645

Matt
Beat the Band - Don Calame *y* 670

Rebecca
Ruined: A Ghost Story - Paula Morris *y* 955

Sean
Beat the Band - Don Calame *y* 670

Wolfe, Lucius
Crazy Beautiful - Lauren Baratz-Logsted *y* 619

11-YEAR-OLD

Aykroyd, Tabby
The House of Dead Maids - Clare B. Dunkle *y* 747

Barker, Simon
Missing on Superstition Mountain - Elise Broach *c, y* 47

Beach, Saint Louis Armstrong
Saint Louis Armstrong Beach - Brenda Woods *c, y* 1174

Brooks, Tess
Touch Blue - Cynthia Lord *c, y* 286

Budwig, Felicity Bathburn
The Romeo and Juliet Code - Phoebe Stone *c, y* 496

Calendar, Julian
The Secret Science Alliance and the Copycat Crook - Eleanor Davis *c, y* 103

Callum
Wild Wings - Gill Lewis *c, y* 275

Clark, Jack
The Storm in the Barn - Matt Phelan *c, y* 387

de Luce, Flavia
The Sweetness at the Bottom of the Pie - Alan Bradley *y* 653

DeGroot, Jeremy
The Storm before Atlanta - Karen Schwabach *c, y* 454

Delphine
One Crazy Summer - Rita Williams-Garcia *c, y* 569

Dini
The Grand Plan to Fix Everything - Uma Krishnaswami *c, y* 259

Dulcie
The Storm before Atlanta - Karen Schwabach *c, y* 454

Dunwoody, Olive
The Shadows - Jacqueline West *c, y* 555

Grayson, Mathew
Burn My Heart - Beverley Naidoo *c, y* 967

Hazel
Breadcrumbs - Anne Ursu *c, y* 530

Isa
Tighter - Adele Griffin *y* 807

Jack
Breadcrumbs - Anne Ursu *c, y* 530

Jones, Callie
Callie's Rules - Naomi Flink Zucker *c, y* 594

Liesl
Liesl and Po - Lauren Oliver *c, y* 369

McNair, Iona
Wild Wings - Gill Lewis   *c, y* 275

Melody
Out of My Mind - Sharon M. Draper   *c, y* 118

Mirka
Hereville: How Mirka Got Her Sword - Barry Deutsch   *c, y* 110

Mouse
Departure Time - Truus Matti   *c, y* 306

Ogilvie, Oscar
On the Blue Comet - Rosemary Wells   *c, y* 554

Peabody, Polly
Drizzle - Kathleen Van Cleve   *c, y* 537

Pina
Take Me with You - Carolyn Marsden   *c, y* 302

Roger
Yummy: The Last Days of a Southside Shorty - G. Neri   *y* 973

Salva
A Long Walk to Water: Based on a True Story - Linda Sue Park   *c, y* 375

Sandifer, Robert "Yummy"
Yummy: The Last Days of a Southside Shorty - G. Neri   *y* 973

Seymour
Dying to Meet You - Kate Klise   *c, y* 254

Skip
A Small Free Kiss in the Dark - Glenda Millard   *y* 948

Susanna
Take Me with You - Carolyn Marsden   *c, y* 302

Turtle
Turtle in Paradise - Jennifer L. Holm   *c, y* 206

Valentine, Laurie
The Giant Slayer - Iain Lawrence   *c, y* 267

Winkler, Belinda "Bindi"
The Dancing Pancake - Eileen Spinelli   *c, y* 481

Zitlally
Star in the Forest - Laura Resau   *c, y* 412

Zoe
Wild Things - Clay Carmichael   *c, y* 60

11TH GRADER

Alex
The Mockingbirds - Daisy Whitney   *y* 1158

Chloe
Accomplice - Eireann Corrigan   *y* 708

Claire
Love Is the Higher Law - David Levithan   *y* 899

Finn
Accomplice - Eireann Corrigan   *y* 708

Heaton, Jay
The Body Finder - Kimberly Derting   *y* 728

Khan, Nina
Skunk Girl - Sheba Karim   *y* 864

Locke, Cat
Fat Cat - Robin Brande   *y* 654

Madeline
Recovery Road - Blake Nelson   *y* 969

McKinney, Matt
Fat Cat - Robin Brande   *y* 654

Nolan, Lola
Lola and the Boy Next Door - Stephanie Perkins   1007

Peter
Love Is the Higher Law - David Levithan   *y* 899

Reinstein, Felton
Stupid Fast: The Summer I Went from a Joke to a Jock - Geoff Herbach   *y* 836

Riley, Tola
Bad Apple - Laura Ruby   *y* 1048

Schwenk, D.J.
Front and Center - Catherine Gilbert Murdock   *y* 960

12-YEAR-OLD

Aguilar, Daniel
Gringolandia - Lyn Miller-Lachmann   *y* 950

Alderman, Ignatius "Brother"
Heart of a Shepherd - Rosanne Parry   *c, y* 377

Blunt, April
The Fingertips of Duncan Dorfman - Meg Wolitzer   *c, y* 578

Brixton, Steve
The Case of the Case of Mistaken Identity - Mac Barnett   *c, y* 22

Chapman, Franny
Countdown - Deborah Wiles   *c, y* 561

Chen, Rebecca
The Red Blazer Girls: The Ring of Rocamadour - Michael D. Beil   *y* 629

Cissy
The Glorious Adventures of the Sunshine Queen - Geraldine McCaughrean   *c, y* 312

Crutchfield, Florence
The Ghost of Crutchfield Hall - Mary Downing Hahn   *c, y* 186

David, Wilson "Wil"
The Last Newspaper Boy in America - Sue Corbett   *c, y* 83

Delana
Finding Family - Tonya Bolden   *c, y* 42

Desberg, Lucy
My Life in Pink and Green - Lisa Greenwald   *c, y* 178

Dorfman, Duncan
The Fingertips of Duncan Dorfman - Meg Wolitzer   *c, y* 578

Edelman, Mina
My Life with the Lincolns - Gayle Brandeis   *c, y* 46

Egg, Oscar
The Prince of Fenway Park - Julianna Baggott   *c, y* 18

Elena
The Firefly Letters: A Suffragette's Journey to Cuba - Margarita Engle   *y* 762

Everdeen, Primrose
Mockingjay - Suzanne Collins   *y* 700

Fallon, Derek
My Life as a Book - Janet Tashjian   *c, y* 507

Finn
No Passengers beyond This Point - Gennifer Choldenko   *c, y* 68

Flux, Cirrus
The Story of Cirrus Flux - Matthew Skelton   *c, y* 469

Forrester, Amelia
Newsgirl - Liza Ketchum   *c, y* 243

Gantos, Jack
Dead End in Norvelt - Jack Gantos   *c, y* 157

Hathin
The Lost Conspiracy - Frances Hardinge   *c, y* 822

Henry, Will
The Curse of the Wendigo - Rick Yancey   *y* 1183
The Monstrumologist - Rick Yancey   *y* 1182

Hibernia
Bird in a Box - Andrea Davis Pinkney   *c, y* 392

Hope
Glimpse - Carol Lynch Williams   *y* 1163

Jackson, Percy
The Lightning Thief: The Graphic Novel - Rick Riordan   *y* 416

Jaimes, Lee Ann
The Red Blazer Girls: The Ring of Rocamadour - Michael D. Beil   *y* 629

Jester, Owen
The Fantastic Secret of Owen Jester - Barbara O'Connor   *c, y* 366

Kookie
The Glorious Adventures of the Sunshine Queen - Geraldine McCaughrean   *c, y* 312

Liam
Cosmic - Frank Cottrell Boyce   *c, y* 84

McDonald, Coke
Mission Unstoppable - Dan Gutman   *c, y* 183

McDonald, Pepsi
Mission Unstoppable - Dan Gutman   *c, y* 183

McFee, Foster
Close to Famous - Joan Bauer   *c, y* 623

McGuire, Owen
Signal - Cynthia DeFelice   *c, y* 106

Nickel
Nickel Plated - Aric Davis   *y* 721

Nwazue, Sunny
Akata Witch - Nnedi Okorafor   *y* 988

O'Rourke, Raine
Sparrow Road - Sheila O'Connor   *c, y* 985

Oakland, Daralynn
Grounded - Kate Klise   *c, y* 253

Otis
Bird in a Box - Andrea Davis Pinkney   *c, y* 392

Paloma
Tropical Secrets: Holocaust Refugees in Cuba - Margarita Engle   *y* 760

Parsons, Frankie
The 10 PM Question - Kate De Goldi   *y* 723

Petros
War Games - Audrey Couloumbis   *c, y* 89

Pin, Matt
All the Broken Pieces - Ann Burg   *y* 668

Putnam, Ann
Wicked Girls: A Novel of the Salem Witch Trials - Stephanie Hemphill   *y* 834

Saviano, Nate
The Fingertips of Duncan Dorfman - Meg Wolitzer   *c, y* 578

September
The Girl Who Circumnavigated Fairyland in a Ship of Her Own Making - Catherynne M. Valente   *c, y* 532

Smith, Cyrus
The Dragon's Tooth - N.D. Wilson   *c, y* 571

St. Pierre, Sophie
The Red Blazer Girls: The Ring of Rocamadour - Michael D. Beil   *y* 629

Steiner, Stephie
A Faraway Island - Annika Thor   *c, y* 516

Gray, Austin
The Sweetheart of Prosper County - Jill S. Alexander   y 600

Harriman, Zach
Hero - Mike Lupica   c, y 290

Hogan, Holly "Solace"
Solace of the Road - Siobhan Dowd   y 741

Holmes, Sherlock
Death Cloud - Andrew Lane   y 890

India
No Passengers beyond This Point - Gennifer Choldenko   c, y 68

James, Gabriel
The Interrogation of Gabriel James - Charlie Price   y 1024

Jamie "Punkzilla"
Punkzilla - Adam Rapp   y 1030

Jason
A World without Heroes - Brandon Mull   c, y 335

June
The Extraordinary Secrets of April, May and June - Robin Benway   y 631

Khosi
This Thing Called the Future - J. L. Powers   y 1020

Kinahan, Jonathan "Jono"
Long Story Short - Siobhan Parkinson   y 998

Lillie
Freedom Stone - Jeffrey Kluger   c, y 255

Lizzie
Glimpse - Carol Lynch Williams   y 1163

Mallory, Jake
Five 4ths of July - Pat Hughes   y 850

Marriss, Dewey
Crunch - Leslie Connor   c, y 78

McClellan, Stark "Stick"
Stick - Andrew Smith   y 1088

Melanie
Half World - Hiromi Goto   y 799

Milkweed, Octavia
The Hunchback Assignments - Arthur G. Slade   y 1081

Modo
The Hunchback Assignments - Arthur G. Slade   y 1081

Monson, Darra
Hidden - Helen Frost   y 778

Nakahama, Manjiro
Heart of a Samurai - Margi Preus   y 1023

O'Mara, Cam
Bull Rider - Suzanne Morgan Williams   y 1169

Orville, Benjamin Franklin
Murder Afloat - Jane Leslie Conly   c, y 77

Plum
Butterfly - Sonya Hartnett   y 826

Riff
Worldshaker - Richard Harland   y 823

Rose, April Garnet
A Month of Sundays - Ruth White   y 558

Roux, Pepper
The Death-Defying Pepper Roux - Geraldine McCaughrean   c, y 311

Samantha
Sources of Light - Margaret McMullan   y 943

Sands, Dylan
Take Me to the River - Will Hobbs   c, y 841

Sawyer, Alex
Lockdown - Alexander Gordon Smith   y 1085

Scott, Janie
The Apothecary - Maile Meloy   y 945

Spencer, Kevin
Liar, Liar: The Theory, Practice and Destructive Properties of Deception - Gary Paulsen   c, y 999

Stern, Karl
The Berlin Boxing Club - Robert Sharenow   y 1073

Swieteck, Doug
Okay for Now - Gary D. Schmidt   c, y 451

Tamper, Abigail "Abi"
The Poisoned House - Michael Ford   y 770

Toby
Killer Pizza - Greg Taylor   y 1118

Trei
The Floating Islands - Rachel Neumeier   y 978

Viola
Viola in Reel Life - Adriana Trigiani   y 1133

Wendy
The Mostly True Story of Jack - Kelly Barnhill   c, y 23

Yasmine
Thunder over Kandahar - Sharon E. McKay   y 937

15-YEAR-OLD

Abdul
No Safe Place - Deborah Ellis   y 757

Aching, Tiffany
I Shall Wear Midnight - Terry Pratchett   y 1021

Aiden
The Devil's Paintbox - Victoria McKernan   y 938

Allbright, Billy
You Don't Know About Me - Brian Meehl   y 944

Ambrose, Aura
A Blue So Dark - Holly Schindler   y 1059

Anderson, Iris
The Girl Is Murder - Kathryn Miller Haines   y 814

Aparacio, Yancy
Riding Invisible - Sandra Alonzo   y 604

Ballentyne, Stuart
Out of the Blue - S.L. Rottman   y 1043

Bean "Pearl"
Pearl - Jo Knowles   y 882

Bennett, Darren
The Boy Who Couldn't Sleep and Never Had To - D.C. Pierson   y 1014

Blake
Flash Burnout - L.K. Madigan   y 919

Caleb
Caleb's Wars - David L. Dudley   y 746

Carly
Peace, Love, and Baby Ducks - Lauren Myracle   y 966

Carver, Alicia
The Prince of Mist - Carlos Ruiz Zafon   y 1195

Cece
Stay with Me - Paul Griffin   y 809

Chase, Kyle
You - Charles Benoit   y 630

Claire
Riot - Walter Dean Myers   y 963

Curzon
Forge - Laurie Halse Anderson   y 607

Dani
Cold Hands, Warm Heart - Jill Wolfson   y 1173

Davenport, Devon
After - Amy Efaw   y 751

Day
Legend - Marie Lu   y 908

Deuce
Enclave - Ann Aguirre   y 599

Diribani
Toads and Diamonds - Heather Tomlinson   y 1132

Doris
If I Could Fly - Judith Ortiz Cofer   y 696

Duarte, Rosalia
Putting Makeup on the Fat Boy - Bil Wright   y 1177

Ford, Ames
Dark Song - Gail Giles   y 788

Gratton, Matt
Swim the Fly - Don Calame   y 669

Gritas, Payton
Sean Griswold's Head - Lindsey Leavitt   y 894

Henry
Pearl - Jo Knowles   y 882

Iris
Crossing the Tracks - Barbara Stuber   y 1111

Jason
Crazy - Han Nolan   y 980

June
The Big Crunch - Pete Hautman   y 828
Legend - Marie Lu   y 908

Karyn
You Against Me - Jenny Downham   y 743

Kendra
Scars - Cheryl Rainfield   y 1028

Khalid
Guantanamo Boy - Anna Perera   y 1004

Kit
The Brothers Story - Katherine Sturtevant   y 1112

Lumley, Miss Penelope
The Mysterious Howling - Maryrose Wood   c, y 579

Mack
Stay with Me - Paul Griffin   y 809

May
The Extraordinary Secrets of April, May and June - Robin Benway   y 631

Maya
Compromised - Heidi Ayarbe   y 616
Karma - Cathy Ostlere   y 994

Monahan, Kelleigh
How to Steal a Car - Pete Hautman   y 829

Nina
The Reformed Vampire Support Group - Catherine Jinks   y 859

Number Four "John Smith"
I Am Number Four - Pittacus Lore   y 906

R.D.
Messed Up - Janet Nichols Lynch   y 913

Reese
Lockdown - Walter Dean Myers   y 961

Rice, Daelyn
By the Time You Read This, I'll Be Dead - Julie Anne Peters   y 1010

Rio
Take Me to the River - Will Hobbs   *c, y* 841

Rosie
Rosie and Skate - Beth Ann Bauman   *y* 624

Rowan
Broken Soup - Jenny Valentine   *y* 1136

Sabiri, Sami
Borderline - Allan Stratton   *y* 1108

Sullivan, Jane
Confessions of the Sullivan Sisters - Natalie Standiford   *y* 1096

Sveinsson, Halli
Heroes of the Valley - Jonathan Stroud   *y* 1110

Sykes, Tamika
The Orange Houses - Paul Griffin   *y* 810

Tia
A Small Free Kiss in the Dark - Glenda Millard   *y* 948

Uido
Island's End - Padma Venkatraman   *y* 1138

Waverly
Glow - Amy Kathleen Ryan   *y* 1050

Werkmann, Thomas
The Other Half of Life: A Novel Based on the True Story of the MS St. Louis - Kim Ablon Whitney   *y* 1159

Zeynab
Words in the Dust - Trent Reedy   *y* 1033

16-YEAR-OLD

Alex
Paper Covers Rock - Jenny Hubbard   *y* 848

April
The Extraordinary Secrets of April, May and June - Robin Benway   *y* 631

Aura
Shade - Jeri Smith-Ready   *y* 1091

Austin, Lark
Lark - Tracey Porter   *y* 1018

Ava
Pink - Lili Wilkinson   *y* 1161

Balanchine, Anya
All These Things I've Done - Gabrielle Zevin   *y* 1198

Biggs, Sydney
Every Little Thing in the World - Nina de Gramont   *y* 724

Blair, Maggie
The Betrayal of Maggie Blair - Elizabeth Laird   *y* 889

Blank, Shayne
Blank Confession - Pete Hautman   *y* 827

Blink
Blink & Caution - Tim Wynne-Jones   *y* 1180

Brown, Laura
The Carbon Diaries 2015 - Saci Lloyd   *y* 901

Cameron
Going Bovine - Libba Bray   *y* 655

Carpenter, Jamie
Department 19 - Will Hill   *y* 838

Cat
Shine - Lauren Myracle   *y* 965

Caution
Blink & Caution - Tim Wynne-Jones   *y* 1180

Celestia
Three Rivers Rising: A Novel of the Johnstown Flood - Jame Richards   *y* 1040

Charlie
A Little Wanting Song - Cath Crowley   *y* 713

Chloe
Imaginary Girls - Nova Ren Suma   *y* 1113

Cody
Reality Check - Peter Abrahams   *y* 596

Conklin, Isobel "Belly"
It's Not Summer Without You - Jenny Han   *y* 818

Conner
The Marbury Lens - Andrew Smith   *y* 1087

Cooper, Beka
Bloodhound - Tamora Pierce   *y* 1013

Crouch, Joey
Rotters - Daniel Kraus   *y* 886

Crowe, Eleanor
Pregnant Pause - Han Nolan   *y* 979

Deity, Idea
My Favorite Band Does Not Exist - Robert T. Jeschonek   *y* 857

Digger
Star Crossed - Elizabeth C. Bunce   *y* 665

Dix, Molly
Spoiled - Jessica Morgan   *y* 953

Dryden, Jane
Dreamland Social Club - Tara Altebrando   605

Duarte, Carlos
Putting Makeup on the Fat Boy - Bil Wright   *y* 1177

Durango
Black Hole Sun - David Macinnis Gill   *y* 789

Earl, Ronald "Little Texas"
Days of Little Texas - R.A. Nelson   *y* 972

Elisa
The Girl of Fire and Thorns - Rae Carson   *y* 677

Eloise
Blood - K.J. Wignall   *y* 1160

Emily
Same Difference - Siobhan Vivian   *y* 1140

Esperer, Fatima
The Orange Houses - Paul Griffin   *y* 810

Everdeen, Katniss
Catching Fire - Suzanne Collins   *y* 699
Mockingjay - Suzanne Collins   *y* 700

Evie
Paranormalcy - Kiersten White   *y* 1156
The Space between Trees - Katie Williams   *y* 1167

Fern, Clarity "Clare"
Clarity - Kim Harrington   *y* 825

Gardner, Clara
Unearthly - Cynthia Hand   *y* 819

Gemma
Stolen - Lucy Christopher   *y* 689

Glaser, Chelsea
Past Perfect - Leila Sales   *y* 1055

Gray, Tessa
Clockwork Angel - Cassandra Clare   *y* 690

Green
Green Witch - Alice Hoffman   *y* 842

Harvey, Tom
iBoy - Kevin Brooks   *y* 660

Healy, Emma
You Are Here - Jennifer E. Smith   *y* 1089

Holly, Poe
Brutal - Michael Harmon   *y* 824

Jack
The Marbury Lens - Andrew Smith   *y* 1087

Jessica
The Running Dream - Wendelin Van Draanen   *y* 744

Jonah
In the Path of Falling Objects - Andrew Smith   *y* 1086

Jonathan
Adios, Nirvana - Conrad Wesselhoeft   *y* 1152

Kat
The Stolen One - Suzanne Crowley   *y* 714

Kate
Exposed - Kimberly Marcus   *y* 923

Katrina
Coffeehouse Angel - Suzanne Selfors   *y* 1070

Lathem, Wyatt
Bullet Point - Peter Abrahams   *y* 597

Laurel
The Beginning of After - Jennifer Castle   *y* 681
Spells - Aprilynne Pike   *y* 1015

Leftman, Valerie
Hate List - Jennifer Brown   *y* 664

Lina
Between Shades of Gray - Ruta Sepetys   *y* 1071

Lindgren, Loa
The Freak Observer - Blythe Woolston   *y* 1175

Liz
Exposed - Kimberly Marcus   *y* 923

Lucy
Dirty Little Secrets - C.J. Omololu   *y* 991

Mara
Zenith - Julie Bertagna   *y* 633

March, Rosie
Sisters Red - Jackson Pearce   *y* 1000

Maya
Forbidden - Tabitha Suzuma   *y* 1116

McHenry, Kayla
You Wish - Mandy Hubbard   *y* 849

Meg
The Runaway Dragon - Kate Coombs   *c, y* 79

Miksa, Natalia
Every Little Thing in the World - Nina de Gramont   *y* 724

Milthorpe, Alice
Prophecy of the Sisters - Michelle Zink   *y* 1199

Milthorpe, Lia
Prophecy of the Sisters - Michelle Zink   *y* 1199

Morrissey, Colton "Colt"
The Secret Year - Jennifer R. Hubbard   *y* 847

Oliver, Ruby
The Treasure Map of Boys: Noel, Jackson, Finn, Hutch, Gideon—and Me, Ruby Oliver - E. Lockhart   *y* 905

P.K.
Jump - Elisa Carbone   *y* 673

Piper, Tansy
Through Her Eyes - Jennifer Archer   *y* 610

Pool, Jack
The Blood Lie - Shirley Reva Vernick   *y* 1139

Porpentine, Col
Worldshaker - Richard Harland   *y* 823

Portman, Jacob
Miss Peregrine's Home for Peculiar Children - Ransom Riggs   y 1041

Prendergast, Sebastian
The House of Tomorrow - Peter Bognanni   y 646

Prior, Beatrice "Tris"
Divergent - Veronica Roth   y 1042

Raffi
The Dark City - Catherine Fisher   y 766

Rhine
Wither - Lauren DeStefano   y 731

Rivera, Diego
Bait - Alex Sanchez   y 1057

Rosenfeld, Essie
Lost - Jacqueline Davies   y 720

Ryves, Nick
The Demon's Lexicon - Sarah Rees Brennan   y 657

Severance, Veronica "Ronnie"
The River - Mary Jane Beaufrand   y 627

Shepherd, Gwyneth
Ruby Red - Kerstin Gier   y 787

Skate
Rosie and Skate - Beth Ann Bauman   y 624

Solomon, Sabine
Earthgirl - Jennifer Cowan   y 710

Stan
Tilt - Alan Cumyn   y 716

Stone, Gaia
Birthmarked - Caragh M. O'Brien   y 982
Prized - Caragh M. O'Brien   y 983

Sullivan, Sassy
Confessions of the Sullivan Sisters - Natalie Standiford   y 1096

Tana
Toads and Diamonds - Heather Tomlinson   y 1132

Telemachos
King of Ithaka - Tracy Barrett   y 621

Terra
North of Beautiful - Justina Chen Headley   y 830

Thompson, Jael
Misfit - Jon Skovron   y 1080

Towfeek, Jamilah "Jamie"
Ten Things I Hate about Me - Randa Abdel-Fattah   y 595

Triana
The Comet's Curse - Dom Testa   y 1124

Walker, Kevin
A Boy Called Twister - Anne Schraff   y 1061

Whitcomb, Jared
The House of Tomorrow - Peter Bognanni   y 646

Wilder, Cheyenne
Girl, Stolen - April Henry   y 835

Will
Blood - K.J. Wignall   y 1160

Witherspoon, Jace
Split - Swati Avasthi   y 615

Wylltson, Teagan
Tyger Tyger - Kersten Hamilton   y 816

17-YEAR-OLD

Abby
Between Here and Forever - Elizabeth Scott   y 1065

Ai Ling
Silver Phoenix: Beyond the Kingdom of Xia - Cindy Pon   y 1017

Alexander "Xan"
Angry Young Man - Chris Lynch   y 912

Alpers, Andi
Revolution - Jennifer Donnelly   y 739

Alyssa
She Loves You, She Loves You Not... - Julie Anne Peters   1011

Appleton, Amber
Sorta Like a Rock Star - Matthew Quick   y 1026

Armstrong, Will
Will - Maria Boyd   y 652

Atkinson, Jamie
Tighter - Adele Griffin   y 807

Bell, Emily
I'll Be There - Holly Goldberg Sloan   y 1083

Border, Sam
I'll Be There - Holly Goldberg Sloan   y 1083

Brody, Tessa
Warped - Maurissa Guibord   y 812

Carlos
No More Us for You - David Hernandez   y 837

Chestnut, Maybelline "Maybe" Mary Katherine Mary Ann
Absolutely Maybe - Lisa Yee   y 1187

Childs, Stephen "Stick"
The Rock and the River - Kekla Magoon   y 920

Cosgrove, Louisa
Wildthorn - Jane Eagland   y 748

Dance, Jeremy "Lil J"
Dope Sick - Walter Dean Myers   y 962

Emerson, Charlotte
Pretty Dead - Francesca Lia Block   y 641

Estby, Clara
The Year We Were Famous - Carole Estby Dagg   y 718

Evan
Winter Town - Stephen Emond   y 758

Faraday, Destiny
The Miles Between - Mary E. Pearson   y 1001

Gallagher, Shawna
Say the Word - Jeannine Garsee   y 781

Goodnight, Amy
Texas Gothic - Rosemary Clement-Moore   y 693

Greene, Tamsin
Once a Witch - Carolyn MacCullough   y 915

Hood, Avery
Low Red Moon - Ivy Devlin   y 733

Hughes, Scarlet
The Six Rules of Maybe - Deb Caletti   y 672

Hunter, Leigh
After the Moment - Garret Freymann-Weyr   y 776

Isabel
No More Us for You - David Hernandez   y 837

J
I Am J - Cris Beam   y 625

Karou
Daughter of Smoke and Bone - Laini Taylor   y 1120

Katherine
Dangerous Neighbors - Beth Kephart   y 870

Keri
The Shattering - Karen Healey   y 832

Kipp
Stealing Death - Janet Lee Carey   y 675

Larkin, Briony
Chime - Franny Billingsley   y 634

Lennie
The Sky Is Everywhere - Jandy Nelson   y 970

Lochan
Forbidden - Tabitha Suzuma   y 1116

London, Jack
The Wild - Christopher Golden   y 795

Lucy
Winter Town - Stephen Emond   y 758

MacSweeny, Jill
How to Save a Life - Sara Zarr   y 1197

Marisa
What Can't Wait - Ashley Hope Perez   y 1005

Mia
If I Stay - Gayle Forman   y 772

Milo
Cold Hands, Warm Heart - Jill Wolfson   y 1173

Moore, Haven
The Eternal Ones - Kirsten Miller   y 949

Noah
Response - Paul Volponi   y 1141

Nola
The Complete History of Why I Hate Her - Jennifer Richard Jacobson   y 855

Packwood, Jessica
Jessica's Guide to Dating on the Dark Side - Beth Fantaskey   y 763

Pancho
The Last Summer of The Death Warriors - Francisco X. Stork   y 1104

Peterson, Henry
Through Her Eyes - Jennifer Archer   y 610

Pike, Lainey
The Snowball Effect - Holly Nicole Hoxter   y 846

Radley, Rowan
The Radleys: A Novel - Matt Haig   y 813

Richards, Alton
The Cardturner: A Novel about a King, a Queen, and a Joker - Louis Sachar   y 1053

Rodriguez, Efrain
Efrain's Secret - Sofia Quintero   y 1027

Samar "Sam"
Shine, Coconut Moon - Neesha Meminger   y 946

Sandoval, Marcelo
Marcelo in the Real World - Francisco X. Stork   y 1103

Sarah
The Unwritten Rule - Elizabeth Scott   y 1066

Solomon, Dani
The Babysitter Murders - Janet Ruth Young   1190

Spencer, Ellie
Guardian of the Dead - Karen Healey   y 831

Stanton, Madison
The Everafter - Amy Huntley   y 851

Stokes, Martin
Rikers High - Paul Volponi   y 1143

Sweet, McLean
What Happened to Goodbye - Sarah Dessen   y 730

Vanessa
No More Us for You - David Hernandez   y 837

Wilkins, Micah
Liar - Justine Larbalestier   y 891

Witter, Cullen
Where Things Come Back - John Corey Whaley   y 1155

18-YEAR-OLD

Anabelle
The View from the Top - Hillary Frank   y 773

Attling, Cam
The Returning - Christine Hinwood   y 840

Auden
Along for the Ride - Sarah Dessen   y 729

Cecily
An Off Year - Claire Zulkey   y 1200

Gonzalez, Zachariah Johnson
Last Night I Sang to the Monster - Benjamin Alire Saenz   y 1054

Lia
Wintergirls - Laurie Halse Anderson   y 608

Lucas
Legacy - Thomas Sniegoski   y 1093

Lugh
Blood Red Road - Moira Young   y 1191

March, Scarlett
Sisters Red - Jackson Pearce   y 1000

Marriss, Lil
Crunch - Leslie Connor   c, y 78

Mikey
You Against Me - Jenny Downham   y 743

Robert
Angry Young Man - Chris Lynch   y 912

Saba
Blood Red Road - Moira Young   y 1191

Sixes, Jimmi
The Orange Houses - Paul Griffin   y 810

Stormaire, Perry
Au Revoir, Crazy European Chick - Joe Schreiber   y 1063

Sullivan, Norrie
Confessions of the Sullivan Sisters - Natalie Standiford   y 1096

Valchar, Liz
Between - Jessica Warman   y 1150

Weiss, Evan
With or Without You - Brian Farrey   y 764

Witherspoon, Logan
Almost Perfect - Brian Katcher   y 865

19-YEAR-OLD

Finnikin
Finnikin of the Rock - Melina Marchetta   y 921

Grant, Andi
The Miracle Stealer - Neil Connelly   y 704

Greer
Bullet Point - Peter Abrahams   y 597

Kendrick, Sean
The Scorpio Races - Maggie Stiefvater   y 1099

Rico
Dope Sick - Walter Dean Myers   y 962

Roger
Amy and Roger's Epic Detour - Morgan Matson   y 927

1ST GRADER

Brewster
Busing Brewster - Richard Michelson   c 329

Posey
Princess Posey and the First Grade Parade - Stephanie Greene   c 176

3-YEAR-OLD

Emma
Emma Dilemma: Big Sister Poems - Kristine O'Connell George   c 160

Harris
Lexie - Audrey Couloumbis   c, y 87

Ty
Ten - Lauren Myracle   c 344

3RD GRADER

Deja
Nikki and Deja: Birthday Blues - Karen English   c 131

Krzeszewski, Justin "Justin Case"
Justin Case: School, Drool, and Other Daily Disasters - Rachel Vail   c, y 531

Lee, Clara
Clara Lee and the Apple Pie Dream - Jenny Han   c 189

Mimi
Just Grace Goes Green - Charise Mericle Harper   c 191

Nikki
Nikki and Deja: Birthday Blues - Karen English   c 131

Olson, Oliver
How Oliver Olson Changed the World - Claudia Mills   c 331

Stewart, Grace "Just Grace"
Just Grace Goes Green - Charise Mericle Harper   c 191

4-YEAR-OLD

Casey
Bobby versus Girls (Accidentally) - Lisa Yee   c, y 587

Elinor
Waiting for the Magic - Patricia MacLachlan   c 293

4TH GRADER

Carver Ellis-Chan, Robert "Bobby"
Bobby versus Girls (Accidentally) - Lisa Yee   c, y 587

Coconut, Calvin
Calvin Coconut: Trouble Magnet - Graham Salisbury   c 438

Jessica
Emma Dilemma: Big Sister Poems - Kristine O'Connell George   c 160

Sunny
Sunny Holiday - Coleen Murtagh Paratore   c, y 374

5-YEAR-OLD

Carter, Razi
Gator on the Loose! - Sue Stauffacher   c, y 487

Collin
The Snowball Effect - Holly Nicole Hoxter   y 846

5TH GRADER

Amanda
Ten - Lauren Myracle   c 344

Breen, Mattie
Hound Dog True - Linda Urban   c, y 529

Camilla "Milla"
Luv Ya Bunches - Lauren Myracle   c, y 343

Hazel
Breadcrumbs - Anne Ursu   c, y 530

Hewitt, Josh
In Memory of Gorfman T. Frog - Gail Donovan   c 113

Jack
Breadcrumbs - Anne Ursu   c, y 530

Katie-Rose
Luv Ya Bunches - Lauren Myracle   c, y 343

Mindy
Ten - Lauren Myracle   c 344

Modessa
Luv Ya Bunches - Lauren Myracle   c, y 343

Perry, Winnie
Ten - Lauren Myracle   c 344

Reed, Piper
Piper Reed, Campfire Girl - Kimberly Willis Holt   c 210

Stanley
Piper Reed, Campfire Girl - Kimberly Willis Holt   c 210

Thorson, Barbara
I Kill Giants - Joe Kelly   y 867

Violet
Luv Ya Bunches - Lauren Myracle   c, y 343

William
Waiting for the Magic - Patricia MacLachlan   c 293

Yasaman
Luv Ya Bunches - Lauren Myracle   c, y 343

Zitlally
Star in the Forest - Laura Resau   c, y 412

6-YEAR-OLD

Barker, Jack
Missing on Superstition Mountain - Elise Broach   c, y 47

Grant, Daniel
The Miracle Stealer - Neil Connelly   y 704

Max
A Small Free Kiss in the Dark - Glenda Millard   y 948

Mouse
No Passengers beyond This Point - Gennifer Choldenko   c, y 68

Plato
Freedom Stone - Jeffrey Kluger   c, y 255

Rosenfeld, Zelda
Lost - Jacqueline Davies   y 720

Underhill, Esme
April and Esme: Tooth Fairies - Bob Graham   p, c 168

Zelda
Then - Morris Gleitzman   y 792

6TH GRADER

Bailey
Camo Girl - Kekla Magoon   c, y 294

Bean, Isabelle
Falling In - Frances O'Roark Dowell   c, y 115

Blake, Jason
Anything but Typical - Nora Raleigh Baskin   y 27

Chingis
The Un-Forgotten Coat - Frank Cottrell
  Boyce   *c, y* 85

Ellie
Camo Girl - Kekla Magoon   *c, y* 294

Jones, Callie
Callie's Rules - Naomi Flink Zucker   *c, y* 594

Julie
The Un-Forgotten Coat - Frank Cottrell
  Boyce   *c, y* 85

Maximilian "Max"
*Maximilian and the Mystery of the Guardian Angel:
  A Bilingual Lucha Libre Thriller* - Xavier
  Garza   *y* 782

Miranda
When You Reach Me - Rebecca Stead   *c, y* 490

Nergui
The Un-Forgotten Coat - Frank Cottrell
  Boyce   *c, y* 85

Pratt, Benjamin "Ben"
We the Children - Andrew Clements   *c, y* 72

Raina
Smile - Raina Telgemeier   *c, y* 511

Sal
When You Reach Me - Rebecca Stead   *c, y* 490

Tommy
The Strange Case of Origami Yoda - Tom
  Angleberger   *c, y* 9

Z
Camo Girl - Kekla Magoon   *c, y* 294

7-YEAR-OLD

Underhill, April
April and Esme: Tooth Fairies - Bob
  Graham   *p, c* 168

7TH GRADER

Anthon, Pierre
Nothing - Janne Teller   *y* 1121

Bette
Angel in My Pocket - Ilene Cooper   *c, y* 82

Carver, Griff
Griff Carver, Hallway Patrol - Jim Krieg   *c, y* 258

Combs, Catherine
Faith, Hope, and Ivy June - Phyllis Reynolds
  Naylor   *c, y* 347

Georgia
Sweet Treats and Secret Crushes - Lisa
  Greenwald   *y* 806

Joe
Angel in My Pocket - Ilene Cooper   *c, y* 82

Kate
The Kind of Friends We Used to Be - Frances
  O'Roark Dowell   *c, y* 116
Sweet Treats and Secret Crushes - Lisa
  Greenwald   *y* 806

Lovitt, Abby
The Georges and the Jewels - Jane
  Smiley   *c, y* 471

Marilyn
The Kind of Friends We Used to Be - Frances
  O'Roark Dowell   *c, y* 116

Minkus, Andy
Angel in My Pocket - Ilene Cooper   *c, y* 82

Minkus, Vivi
Angel in My Pocket - Ilene Cooper   *c, y* 82

Moseley, Ivy June
Faith, Hope, and Ivy June - Phyllis Reynolds
  Naylor   *c, y* 347

Olivia
Sweet Treats and Secret Crushes - Lisa
  Greenwald   *y* 806

Raines, Travis
The Seventh Level - Jody Feldman   *c, y* 136

Sandelski, Marley
Warp Speed - Lisa Yee   *y* 1186

Shaw, Serena
Silhouetted by the Blue - Traci L. Jones   *y* 863

8-YEAR-OLD

Billy
Out of the Blue - S.L. Rottman   *y* 1043
When I Grow Up - Al Yankovic   *c* 585

Blum, Carson
The New Kid - Mavis Jukes   *c* 233

Karen
The River - Mary Jane Beaufrand   *y* 627

Kinahan, Julie
Long Story Short - Siobhan Parkinson   *y* 998

Schneider, Dessert
Dessert First - Hallie Durand   *c* 123

Small, Cleo
Underpants On My Head - Jessica Harper   *c* 192

Steiner, Nellie
A Faraway Island - Annika Thor   *c, y* 516

Wendy
Cold Hands, Warm Heart - Jill Wolfson   *y* 1173

Wiggins, Emily
Emily's Fortune - Phyllis Reynolds
  Naylor   *c, y* 346

8TH GRADER

Alper, Jeffrey
After Ever After - Jordan Sonnenblick   *y* 1094

Kroner, Dieter
After the Train - Gloria Whelan   *y* 557

Liebig, Peter
After the Train - Gloria Whelan   *y* 557

Travis
Bluefish - Pat Schmatz   *y* 1060

Velveeta
Bluefish - Pat Schmatz   *y* 1060

9-YEAR-OLD

Daniel, Dyamonde
Make Way for Dyamonde Daniel - Nikki
  Grimes   *c* 180

Emmi
Blood Red Road - Moira Young   *y* 1191

Hartley, Sophie
Happy Birthday, Sophie Hartley - Stephanie
  Greene   *c* 175

Liz
Crow Call - Lois Lowry   *c* 288

Mina
My Name Is Mina - David Almond   *y* 603

9TH GRADER

Barton, Neal
Americus - M.K. Reed   *y* 1032

Gray, Austin
The Sweetheart of Prosper County - Jill S.
  Alexander   *y* 600

ABANDONED CHILD

Gallagher, Shawna
Say the Word - Jeannine Garsee   *y* 781

ABUSE VICTIM

Angel
Desert Angel - Charlie Price   *y* 1025

Aparacio, Yancy
Riding Invisible - Sandra Alonzo   *y* 604

Cat
Shine - Lauren Myracle   *y* 965

Devory
Hush - Eishes Chayil   *y* 685

Kalinowski, Mandy
How to Save a Life - Sara Zarr   *y* 1197

Liesl
Liesl and Po - Lauren Oliver   *c, y* 369

McFee, Rayka "Mama"
Close to Famous - Joan Bauer   *c, y* 623

Swieteck, Doug
Okay for Now - Gary D. Schmidt   *c, y* 451

Witherspoon, Jace
Split - Swati Avasthi   *y* 615

ACCIDENT VICTIM

Amanda
Cold Hands, Warm Heart - Jill Wolfson   *y* 1173

Berg, Alex
Between - Jessica Warman   *y* 1150

Mr. Fielding
Thirteen Days to Midnight - Patrick
  Carman   *y* 676

Jessica
The Running Dream - Wendelin Van
  Draanen   *y* 744

Julia
Love You Hate You Miss You - Elizabeth
  Scott   *y* 1067

Mrs. Kaufman
The Beginning of After - Jennifer Castle   *y* 681

Mr. Kaufman
The Beginning of After - Jennifer Castle   *y* 681

Mia
If I Stay - Gayle Forman   *y* 772

Reese
Bad Island - Doug TenNapel   *y* 1123

Tess
Between Here and Forever - Elizabeth
  Scott   *y* 1065

ACTIVIST

Alexander "Xan"
Angry Young Man - Chris Lynch   *y* 912

Fox
Zenith - Julie Bertagna   *y* 633

Jenna
Boys, Bears, and a Serious Pair of Hiking Boots -
  Abby McDonald   *y* 935

Mehdi
Zahra's Paradise - Amir Amir   *y* 606

Viola
The Ask and the Answer - Patrick Ness   *y* 975

ACTOR

Berlin, Brick
Spoiled - Jessica Morgan   y 953

Brendan
Every Little Thing in the World - Nina de Gramont   y 724

Harrison, Jake
Finally - Wendy Mass   c, y 305

ACTRESS

Miss Charleena
Close to Famous - Joan Bauer   c, y 623

Gemz, Carli
Dirty Laundry - Daniel Ehrenhaft   y 754

Gordon, Reka
Guardian of the Dead - Karen Healey   y 831

Jaimes, Lee Ann
The Red Blazer Girls: The Ring of Rocamadour - Michael D. Beil   y 629

Miss Loucien
The Glorious Adventures of the Sunshine Queen - Geraldine McCaughrean   c, y 312

Paradis, Alexandrine
Revolution - Jennifer Donnelly   y 739

Skye
Tangled - Carolyn Mackler   y 916

ADDICT

Bianchi, Carmen
Virtuosity - Jessica Martinez   y 925

Christopher
Clean - Amy Reed   y 1031

Cody
Tricks - Ellen Hopkins   y 843

Dance, Jeremy "Lil J"
Dope Sick - Walter Dean Myers   y 962

Eva
Clean - Amy Reed   y 1031

Jamie "Punkzilla"
Punkzilla - Adam Rapp   y 1030

Jason
Clean - Amy Reed   y 1031

Kelly
Clean - Amy Reed   y 1031

Olivia
Clean - Amy Reed   y 1031

Rodgers, Jomo
Shooting Star - Fredrick McKissack Jr.   y 941

Sixes, Jimmi
The Orange Houses - Paul Griffin   y 810

Stewart
Recovery Road - Blake Nelson   y 969

ADOPTEE

Daiyu
Gateway - Sharon Shinn   y 1076

Elizabeth
This Dark Endeavor: The Apprenticeship of Victor Frankenstein - Kenneth Oppel   y 993

Hazel
Breadcrumbs - Anne Ursu   c, y 530

Liebig, Peter
After the Train - Gloria Whelan   y 557

Pin, Matt
All the Broken Pieces - Ann Burg   y 668

ADVENTURER

Bean, Walker
The Unsinkable Walker Bean - Aaron Renier   c, y 411

Bly, Nellie
Around the World - Matt Phelan   c, y 388

Frankenstein, Victor
This Dark Endeavor: The Apprenticeship of Victor Frankenstein - Kenneth Oppel   y 993

Galen
The Dark City - Catherine Fisher   y 766

Happenstance "Hap"
Happenstance Found - P. W. Catanese   c, y 63

London, Jack
The Wild - Christopher Golden   y 795

Meg
The Runaway Dragon - Kate Coombs   c, y 79

Roux, Pepper
The Death-Defying Pepper Roux - Geraldine McCaughrean   c, y 311

Slocum, Joshua
Around the World - Matt Phelan   c, y 388

Stevens, Thomas
Around the World - Matt Phelan   c, y 388

Lord Umber
Happenstance Found - P. W. Catanese   c, y 63

ADVISOR

Madame Albirtha
The Secret River - Marjorie Kinnan Rawlings   c 407

AGED PERSON

Bett
Freedom Stone - Jeffrey Kluger   c, y 255

Gus
Pearl - Jo Knowles   y 882

Mr. Herbert
Hero - Mike Lupica   c, y 290

Moran, Miz
Saint Louis Armstrong Beach - Brenda Woods   c, y 1174

Ms. Snoops
One Day and One Amazing Morning on Orange Street - Joanne Rocklin   c 422

AGENT

Carpenter, Jamie
Department 19 - Will Hill   y 838

Evie
Paranormalcy - Kiersten White   y 1156

Milkweed, Octavia
The Hunchback Assignments - Arthur G. Slade   y 1081

Pesto
Soul Enchilada - David Macinnis Gill   y 790

Mr. Socrates
The Hunchback Assignments - Arthur G. Slade   y 1081

ALCOHOLIC

Gonzalez, Zachariah Johnson
Last Night I Sang to the Monster - Benjamin Alire Saenz   y 1054

Grandpa
Bluefish - Pat Schmatz   y 1060

Jason
Clean - Amy Reed   y 1031

Madeline
Recovery Road - Blake Nelson   y 969

Masterson, Nan
Burnout - Adrienne Maria Vrettos   y 1144

ALIEN

Blue, David
You'll Like It Here (Everybody Does) - Ruth White   c, y 559

Blue, Meggie
You'll Like It Here (Everybody Does) - Ruth White   c, y 559

Ketchvar
Stuck on Earth - David Klass   c, y 250

Number Four "John Smith"
I Am Number Four - Pittacus Lore   y 906

Wikki
Zig and Wikki in Something Ate My Homework - Nadja Spiegelman   p, c 480

Zig
Zig and Wikki in Something Ate My Homework - Nadja Spiegelman   p, c 480

ALLIGATOR

Alligator
Hooray for Amanda and Her Alligator! - Mo Willems   p, c 566

AMNESIAC

Emily
Emily the Strange: The Lost Days - Jessica Gruner   y 811

Happenstance "Hap"
Happenstance Found - P. W. Catanese   c, y 63

AMPUTEE

Attling, Cam
The Returning - Christine Hinwood   y 840

Wolfe, Lucius
Crazy Beautiful - Lauren Baratz-Logsted   y 619

ANGEL

Akiva
Daughter of Smoke and Bone - Laini Taylor   y 1120

Angela
Unearthly - Cynthia Hand   y 819

Bethany
Halo - Alexandra Adornetto   y 598

Dulcie
Going Bovine - Libba Bray   y 655

Gabriel
Halo - Alexandra Adornetto   y 598

Gardner, Clara
Unearthly - Cynthia Hand   y 819

Ivy
Halo - Alexandra Adornetto   y 598

Malcolm
Coffeehouse Angel - Suzanne Selfors   y 1070

Raphael
Kindred - Tammar Stein   y 1098

ANIMAL

Melina
Benny and Penny in the Big No-No! - Geoffrey Hayes   c 196

Snook
Snook Alone - Marilyn Nelson   c 349

Wilbur
Naked Mole Rat Gets Dressed - Mo Willems   p, c 564

ANIMAL LOVER

Anna
Pond Circle - Betsy Franco   c 149

Carter, Keisha
Gator on the Loose! - Sue Stauffacher   c, y 487

APOTHECARY

Mr. Burrows
The Apothecary - Maile Meloy   y 945

APPRENTICE

Barlo, Hap
The Blue Shoe: A Tale of Thievery, Villainy, Sorcery, and Shoes - Roderick Townley   c, y 520

Bennett
Dangerous Neighbors - Beth Kephart   y 870

Conn
Lost - Sarah Prineas   c, y 399

Frederick
The Clockwork Three - Matthew Kirby   c, y 249

Henry, Will
The Curse of the Wendigo - Rick Yancey   y 1183

Kit
The Brothers Story - Katherine Sturtevant   y 1112

Mason, Joseph
A Nest for Celeste: A Story about Art, Inspiration, and the Meaning of Home - Henry Cole   c, y 74

Oldham, Roger
Alchemy and Meggy Swann - Karen Cushman   c, y 97

Raffi
The Dark City - Catherine Fisher   y 766

Underwood, Nathaniel
The Amulet of Samarkand: A Bartimaeus Graphic Novel - Jonathan Stroud   c, y 499

Will
Liesl and Po - Lauren Oliver   c, y 369

Womper, Melkin "Mel"
Mirrorscape - Mike Wilks   c, y 1162

ARTIFICIAL INTELLIGENCE

Mimi
Black Hole Sun - David Macinnis Gill   y 789

ARTISAN

Polydora
King of Ithaka - Tracy Barrett   y 621

ARTIST

Adrian
Same Difference - Siobhan Vivian   y 1140

Ambrose, Aura
A Blue So Dark - Holly Schindler   y 1059

Art
Art and Max - David Wiesner   c 560

Blenk, Ambrosius
Mirrorscape - Mike Wilks   c, y 1162

Bridget
Bridget's Beret - Tom Lichtenheld   c 278

Chen, Rebecca
The Red Blazer Girls: The Ring of Rocamadour - Michael D. Beil   y 629

Dana
Funny How Things Change - Melissa Wyatt   y 1178

Diego
Sparrow Road - Sheila O'Connor   c, y 985

Emily
Same Difference - Siobhan Vivian   y 1140

Evelyn
City of Spies - Susan Kim   c, y 245

Fiona
Same Difference - Siobhan Vivian   y 1140

Gramma
Sleepover at Gramma's House - Barbara Joosse   p, c 231

Henry
Wild Things - Clay Carmichael   c, y 60

Josie
Sparrow Road - Sheila O'Connor   c, y 985

Kahlo, Frida
Me, Frida - Amy Novesky   c 360

Karou
Daughter of Smoke and Bone - Laini Taylor   y 1120

Lillian
Sparrow Road - Sheila O'Connor   c, y 985

Mason, Joseph
A Nest for Celeste: A Story about Art, Inspiration, and the Meaning of Home - Henry Cole   c, y 74

Matt
The View from the Top - Hillary Frank   y 773

Newport, Fellini "Fun" Udall
Dirty Laundry - Daniel Ehrenhaft   y 754

Rivera, Diego
Me, Frida - Amy Novesky   c 360

Robyn
Same Difference - Siobhan Vivian   y 1140

Soto, Marc
The Uninvited - Tim Wynne-Jones   y 1179

Sykes, Tamika
The Orange Houses - Paul Griffin   y 810

ASSASSIN

Zaksauskas, Gobija
Au Revoir, Crazy European Chick - Joe Schreiber   y 1063

ASSISTANT

Crepsley, Larten
Birth of a Killer - Darren Shan   y 1072

Hathin
The Lost Conspiracy - Frances Hardinge   c, y 822

Henry, Will
The Isle of Blood - Rick Yancey   y 1181

Tealeaf
Salt - Maurice Gee   y 783

ASTROLOGER

Mark
The Midnight Charter - David Whitley   y 1157

AUNT

Aunt Linda
Miles from Ordinary - Carol Lynch Williams   y 1164

Aunt Peg
The Last Little Blue Envelope - Maureen Johnson   y 861

Azaway, Varil
The False Princess - Ellis O'Neal   y 986

Carmen
On the Blue Comet - Rosemary Wells   c, y 554

Clara
Picture the Dead - Adele Griffin   y 808

Edith
Drizzle - Kathleen Van Cleve   c, y 537

Hy
Texas Gothic - Rosemary Clement-Moore   y 693

Josie
Grounded - Kate Klise   c, y 253

June
A Month of Sundays - Ruth White   y 558

Mabel
The Mostly True Story of Jack - Kelly Barnhill   c, y 23

Marisa
What Can't Wait - Ashley Hope Perez   y 1005

Miami
The Romeo and Juliet Code - Phoebe Stone   c, y 496

Mildred
Is It Night or Day? - Fern Schumer Chapman   y 683

Portman, Polly
Pie - Sarah Weeks   c, y 552

Tilly
Finding Family - Tonya Bolden   c, y 42

AUTISTIC

Blake, Jason
Anything but Typical - Nora Raleigh Baskin   y 27

Border, Riddle
I'll Be There - Holly Goldberg Sloan   y 1083

BABY

Allison
Raven Summer - David Almond   y 602

Boss Baby
The Boss Baby - Marla Frazee   p, c 150

Carter, Paolo
Gator on the Loose! - Sue Stauffacher   c, y 487

Finnemore, Edwin
Edwin Speaks Up - April Stevens   c 495

Maya
Prized - Caragh M. O'Brien   y 983

Nicholas
Waiting for the Magic - Patricia MacLachlan   c 293

Sam
Don't Want to Go! - Shirley Hughes   p, c 216

Unnamed Character
Mommy, Mama and Me - Leslea Newman   p, c 356

BABYSITTER

Bibi
Like Pickle Juice on a Cookie - Julie
    Sternberg   *c* 494

Solomon, Dani
The Babysitter Murders - Janet Ruth Young   1190

BAKER

Cupcake
Bake Sale - Sara Varon   *c, y* 539

McFee, Foster
Close to Famous - Joan Bauer   *c, y* 623

Portman, Polly
Pie - Sarah Weeks   *c, y* 552

Simon
Raspberries! - Jay O'Callahan   *p, c* 364

BANKER

Rowan, Dale
Bloodhound - Tamora Pierce   *y* 1013

BASEBALL PLAYER

Branch, Ruah
You Don't Know About Me - Brian Meehl   *y* 944

Semak, Mike
Center Field - Robert Lipsyte   *y* 900

BASKETBALL PLAYER

Amandolina "Andi"
Tall Story - Candy Gourlay   *y* 800

Dominique
Jumped - Rita Williams-Garcia   *y* 1170

Gritas, Payton
Sean Griswold's Head - Lindsey Leavitt   *y* 894

Stan
Tilt - Alan Cumyn   *y* 716

BEAR

Bear
Grin and Bear It - Leo Landry   *c* 265
Lousy Rotten Stinkin' Grapes - Margie
    Palatini   *c* 373
Waiting for Winter - Sebastian
    Meschenmoser   *p, c* 326

Bear, Baby
Goldilocks and the Three Bears - Emma
    Chichester-Clark   *p, c* 65

Bear, Benjamin
Benjamin Bear in Fuzzy Thinking - Philippe
    Coudray   *p, c* 86

Bear, Mama
Goldilocks and the Three Bears - Emma
    Chichester-Clark   *p, c* 65

Bear, Papa
Goldilocks and the Three Bears - Emma
    Chichester-Clark   *p, c* 65

BEAUTY PAGEANT CONTESTANT

Gray, Austin
The Sweetheart of Prosper County - Jill S.
    Alexander   *y* 600

Taylor
Beauty Queens - Libba Bray   *y* 656

BEAVER

Beaver
Beaver Is Lost - Elisha Cooper   *p, c* 80
Lousy Rotten Stinkin' Grapes - Margie
    Palatini   *c* 373

BEEKEEPER

Fred
The Honeybee Man - Lela Nargi   *c* 345

BIBLICAL FIGURE

Mariamne
Poisoned Honey: A Story of Mary Magdalene -
    Beatrice Gormley   *y* 798

Naamah
Naamah and the Ark at Night - Susan Campbell
    Bartoletti   *p, c* 24

Noah
Naamah and the Ark at Night - Susan Campbell
    Bartoletti   *p, c* 24

BIRD

Alfred
The Money We'll Save - Brock Cole   *c* 73

Brilliant
Ten Birds - Cybele Young   *c* 591

Cornelius
*A Nest for Celeste: A Story about Art, Inspiration,
    and the Meaning of Home* - Henry
    Cole   *c, y* 74

Emmy
Grin and Bear It - Leo Landry   *c* 265

Highly Satisfactory
Ten Birds - Cybele Young   *c* 591

Lafayette
*A Nest for Celeste: A Story about Art, Inspiration,
    and the Meaning of Home* - Henry
    Cole   *c, y* 74

Needs Improvement
Ten Birds - Cybele Young   *c* 591

Skylar
The Familiars - Adam Jay Epstein   *c, y* 132

BLACKSMITH

Dinga
Never Forgotten - Patricia C. McKissack   *c, y* 319

BLIND PERSON

Wilder, Cheyenne
Girl, Stolen - April Henry   *y* 835

BOXER

Louis, Joe
Bird in a Box - Andrea Davis Pinkney   *c, y* 392

Schmeling, Max
The Berlin Boxing Club - Robert
    Sharenow   *y* 1073

Stern, Karl
The Berlin Boxing Club - Robert
    Sharenow   *y* 1073

BOY

Ajani
Goal! - Mina Javaherbin   *c* 222

Ansel
No Such Things as Dragons - Philip
    Reeve   *c, y* 410

Bean, Walker
The Unsinkable Walker Bean - Aaron
    Renier   *c, y* 411

Ben
Aggie the Brave - Lori Ries   *p, c* 414

Carl, Eddie
Eddie's War - Carol Fisher Saller   *c, y* 439

Carlitos
Dear Primo: A Letter to My Cousin - Duncan
    Tonatiuh   *c* 519

Charlie
Dear Primo: A Letter to My Cousin - Duncan
    Tonatiuh   *c* 519

Conor
A Monster Calls - Patrick Ness   *y* 976

Crispin
Flora's Very Windy Day - Jeanne Birdsall   *c* 35

Dangerfield, Daniel
April and Esme: Tooth Fairies - Bob
    Graham   *p, c* 168

Fortune, Blaise "Koumail"
A Time of Miracles - Anne-Laure Bondoux   *y* 647

Gus
Bone Dog - Eric Rohmann   *c* 425
*Who Has What?: All about Girls' Bodies and Boys'
    Bodies* - Robie H. Harris   *p, c* 193

Hale, Garth
Ghostopolis - Doug TenNapel   *y* 1122

Henry
Everything Goes: On Land - Brian Biggs   *p, c* 34

Jack
The House of Dead Maids - Clare B.
    Dunkle   *y* 747
The Mostly True Story of Jack - Kelly
    Barnhill   *c, y* 23

Jiro
The Boy in the Garden - Allen Say   *c* 446

Joseph
Zita the Spacegirl - Ben Hatke   *c, y* 195

Lester
The Complete Essex County - Jeff Lemire   *y* 896

Ming
The Runaway Wok - Ying Chang Compestine   *c* 76

Orville, Benjamin Franklin
Murder Afloat - Jane Leslie Conly   *c, y* 77

Peter
Annexed - Sharon Dogar   *y* 738

Seth
Glow - Amy Kathleen Ryan   *y* 1050

Sora
Children of the Sea, Volume 1 - Daisuke
    Igarashi   *y* 853

Tim
The Boy Who Cried Ninja - Alex
    Latimer   *p, c* 266

Ty
Storm Mountain - Tom Birdseye   *c, y* 36

Umi
Children of the Sea, Volume 1 - Daisuke
    Igarashi   *y* 853

Unnamed Character
Even Monsters Need Haircuts - Matthew
    McElligott   *p, c* 316
King Jack and the Dragon - Peter Bently   *p, c* 31

Willy
I Must Have Bobo! - Eileen Rosenthal   *p, c* 427

Witter, Cullen
Where Things Come Back - John Corey Whaley   y 1155

BOYFRIEND

Adam
If I Stay - Gayle Forman   y 772

Alex
Delirium - Lauren Oliver   y 989

Bennett
Dangerous Neighbors - Beth Kephart   y 870

Billy
Strings Attached - Judy Blundell   y 643

Blake
Flash Burnout - L.K. Madigan   y 919

Caleb
Jumping Off Swings - Jo Knowles   y 881

Cam
The Summer I Turned Pretty - Jenny Han   y 817

Christian
Stay - Deb Caletti   y 671

Cody
Reality Check - Peter Abrahams   y 596

Cole
Bitter End - Jennifer Brown   y 663

Dade
The Vast Fields of Ordinary - Nick Burd   y 667

Dusic, Ben
Low Red Moon - Ivy Devlin   y 733

Earl
Messed Up - Janet Nichols Lynch   y 913

Erik
With or Without You - Brian Farrey   y 764

Ezra
Past Perfect - Leila Sales   y 1055

Henderson, Donnie
Some Girls Are - Courtney Summers   y 1114

Huck
Close to Famous - Joan Bauer   c, y 623

Hunter, Leigh
After the Moment - Garret Freymann-Weyr   y 776

Hutchinson, Scott "Bright Boy"
Sidekicks - Jack D. Ferraiolo   y 765

Jace
City of Glass - Cassandra Clare   y 691

Jared
Pretty Dead - Francesca Lia Block   y 641

John Joseph
Keep Sweet - Michele Dominguez Greene   y 805

Jose
Carmen - Walter Dean Myers   y 964

Justin
Harmonic Feedback - Tara Kelly   y 868

Kieran
Glow - Amy Kathleen Ryan   y 1050

Kincaid, Alex
The Vast Fields of Ordinary - Nick Burd   y 667

Lathem, Wyatt
Bullet Point - Peter Abrahams   y 597

Logan
Shade - Jeri Smith-Ready   y 1091

Luke
A Little Wanting Song - Cath Crowley   y 713

Mack
Stay with Me - Paul Griffin   y 809

Mason
The Lighter Side of Life and Death - C.K. Kelly Martin   y 924

Matt
The View from the Top - Hillary Frank   y 773

Mikey
You Against Me - Jenny Downham   y 743

Mitch
In the Path of Falling Objects - Andrew Smith   y 1086

Morrissey, Colton "Colt"
The Secret Year - Jennifer R. Hubbard   y 847

Nick
Hate List - Jennifer Brown   y 664

Noel
Real Live Boyfriends: Yes, Boyfriends, Plural. If My Life Weren't Complicated I Wouldn't Be Ruby Oliver - E. Lockhart   y 904

Picture Man
The Color of Earth - Kim Dong Hwa   y 852

Prince Aleksander "Alek"
Leviathan - Scott Westerfeld   y 1153

Reinstein, Felton
Stupid Fast: The Summer I Went from a Joke to a Jock - Geoff Herbach   y 836

Rick
Same Difference - Siobhan Vivian   y 1140

Riley
The Ghosts of Ashbury High - Jaclyn Moriarty   y 954
The Snowball Effect - Holly Nicole Hoxter   y 846

Ryan
The Unwritten Rule - Elizabeth Scott   y 1066

Sam
Shiver - Maggie Stiefvater   y 1100

Sean
LIE - Caroline Bock   y 644

Seeger, Jimmy
LIE - Caroline Bock   y 644

Sharpe, Cassel
Red Glove - Holly Black   y 636

Slaterton, Ed
Why We Broke Up - Daniel Handler   y 821

Stewart
Recovery Road - Blake Nelson   y 969

Toby
The Sky Is Everywhere - Jandy Nelson   y 970

Vincent
Die for Me - Amy Plum   y 1016

Weiss, Evan
With or Without You - Brian Farrey   y 764

Wes
The Big Crunch - Pete Hautman   y 828

Xavier
Halo - Alexandra Adornetto   y 598

Zach
Liar - Justine Larbalestier   y 891

BROTHER

Aiden
The Devil's Paintbox - Victoria McKernan   y 938

Alex
Sent - Margaret Peterson Haddix   c, y 185

Aparacio, Will
Riding Invisible - Sandra Alonzo   y 604

Arne
Dragons of Darkness - Antonia Michaelis   y 947

Barker, Henry
Missing on Superstition Mountain - Elise Broach   c, y 47

Barker, Jack
Missing on Superstition Mountain - Elise Broach   c, y 47

Barker, Simon
Missing on Superstition Mountain - Elise Broach   c, y 47

Ben
Lexie - Audrey Couloumbis   c, y 87

Benny
Benny and Penny in the Big No-No! - Geoffrey Hayes   c 196

Bernardo
Tall Story - Candy Gourlay   y 800

Beverly
Jefferson's Sons: A Founding Father's Secret Children - Kimberly Brubaker Bradley   c, y 45

Bilal
Ten Things I Hate about Me - Randa Abdel-Fattah   y 595

Birnbaum, Henry "Hen"
Friend Is Not a Verb - Daniel Ehrenhaft   y 753

Blue, David
You'll Like It Here (Everybody Does) - Ruth White   c, y 559

Border, Riddle
I'll Be There - Holly Goldberg Sloan   y 1083

Border, Sam
I'll Be There - Holly Goldberg Sloan   y 1083

Bryan
Busing Brewster - Richard Michelson   c 329

Bunna
My Name Is Not Easy - Debby Dahl Edwardson   y 749

Caleb
Caleb's Wars - David L. Dudley   y 746

Carl, Eddie
Eddie's War - Carol Fisher Saller   c, y 439

Carl, Thomas
Eddie's War - Carol Fisher Saller   c, y 439

Carter, Paolo
Gator on the Loose! - Sue Stauffacher   c, y 487

Carter, Razi
Gator on the Loose! - Sue Stauffacher   c, y 487

Carver, Max
The Prince of Mist - Carlos Ruiz Zafon   y 1195

Carver Ellis-Chan, Robert "Bobby"
Bobby versus Girls (Accidentally) - Lisa Yee   c, y 587

Charles
The Flint Heart - Katherine Paterson   c, y 380

Childs, Stephen "Stick"
The Rock and the River - Kekla Magoon   y 920

Chingis
The Un-Forgotten Coat - Frank Cottrell Boyce   c, y 85

Christian
Split - Swati Avasthi   y 615

Christopher
Dragons of Darkness - Antonia Michaelis   y 947

Collin
The Snowball Effect - Holly Nicole Hoxter   y 846

Conrad
It's Not Summer Without You - Jenny Han   y 818

Crispin
Flora's Very Windy Day - Jeanne Birdsall   c 35

Cydar
Butterfly - Sonya Hartnett   y 826

Daniel
The Dragon's Tooth - N.D. Wilson   c, y 571

Danny
What Momma Left Me - Renee Watson   c, y 551

de Boncoeur, Armand
The Pale Assassin - Patricia Elliott   y 756

Deo
Now Is the Time for Running - Michael Williams   y 1168

Dink
Pig Kahuna - Jennifer Sattler   p, c 443

Drew
Countdown - Deborah Wiles   c, y 561

Duarte, Carlos
Putting Makeup on the Fat Boy - Bil Wright   y 1177

Dylan
The Christmas Eve Ghost - Shirley Hughes   c 217

Fergus
Pig Kahuna - Jennifer Sattler   p, c 443

Figg, Harold
The Mostly True Adventures of Homer P. Figg - Rodman Philbrick   c, y 389

Finn
No Passengers beyond This Point - Gennifer Choldenko   c, y 68

Frankie
Let's Do Nothing! - Tony Fucile   c 153

Freddy
Drizzle - Kathleen Van Cleve   c, y 537

Geless, Maks
City of Orphans - Avi   c, y 15

Grant, Daniel
The Miracle Stealer - Neil Connelly   y 704

Green, Derrick
The Adventures of Nanny Piggins - R.A. Spratt   c, y 483

Green, Michael
The Adventures of Nanny Piggins - R.A. Spratt   c, y 483

Gritas, Trent
Sean Griswold's Head - Lindsey Leavitt   y 894

Gus
Who Has What?: All about Girls' Bodies and Boys' Bodies - Robie H. Harris   p, c 193

Hardscrabble, Max
The Kneebone Boy - Ellen Potter   c, y 398

Hardscrabble, Otto
The Kneebone Boy - Ellen Potter   c, y 398

Harris
Lexie - Audrey Couloumbis   c, y 87

Hassan
Zahra's Paradise - Amir Amir   y 606

Heffley, Greg
Diary of a Wimpy Kid: Cabin Fever - Jeff Kinney   c, y 248

Heffley, Manny
Diary of a Wimpy Kid: Cabin Fever - Jeff Kinney   c, y 248

Heffley, Roderick
Diary of a Wimpy Kid: Cabin Fever - Jeff Kinney   c, y 248

Innocent
Now Is the Time for Running - Michael Williams   y 1168

Isaac
My Name Is Not Easy - Debby Dahl Edwardson   y 749

Jack
Don't Want to Go! - Shirley Hughes   p, c 216

Jackson
The Fires Beneath the Sea - Lydia Millet   c, y 330

Jamie
The Demon's Lexicon - Sarah Rees Brennan   y 657

Jeremiah
It's Not Summer Without You - Jenny Han   y 818

Jon
This World We Live In - Susan Beth Pfeffer   y 1012

Jonah
In the Path of Falling Objects - Andrew Smith   y 1086

Justin
Butterfly - Sonya Hartnett   y 826

Kane, Carter
The Red Pyramid - Rick Riordan   c, y 418

Katznelson, Boaz
The Things a Brother Knows - Dana Reinhardt   y 1036

Katznelson, Levi
The Things a Brother Knows - Dana Reinhardt   y 1036

Kinahan, Jonathan "Jono"
Long Story Short - Siobhan Parkinson   y 998

Kitrell, Will
Breathless - Jessica Warman   y 1149

Lamont
Secrets at Sea - Richard Peck   c, y 383

LeBeuf, Lou
The Complete Essex County - Jeff Lemire   y 896

LeBeuf, Vince
The Complete Essex County - Jeff Lemire   y 896

Lee, Cramer
The Uninvited - Tim Wynne-Jones   y 1179

Lochan
Forbidden - Tabitha Suzuma   y 1116

Lonnie
Peace, Locomotion - Jacqueline Woodson   c, y 581

Lugh
Blood Red Road - Moira Young   y 1191

Luke
My Name Is Not Easy - Debby Dahl Edwardson   y 749

Madison
Jefferson's Sons: A Founding Father's Secret Children - Kimberly Brubaker Bradley   c, y 45

Mahmoud
Where I Belong - Gillian Cross   y 712

Matt
This World We Live In - Susan Beth Pfeffer   y 1012

Max
The Fires Beneath the Sea - Lydia Millet   c, y 330

McClellan, Bosten
Stick - Andrew Smith   y 1088

McClellan, Stark "Stick"
Stick - Andrew Smith   y 1088

McDermott, Bobby
Badd - Tim Tharp   y 1125

McDonald, Coke
Mission Unstoppable - Dan Gutman   c, y 183

Mehdi
Zahra's Paradise - Amir Amir   y 606

Mikey
You Against Me - Jenny Downham   y 743

Mildew, Arthur
Tumtum and Nutmeg: Adventures beyond Nutmouse Hall - Emily Bearn   c, y 29

Milo
Tighter - Adele Griffin   y 807

Mushy
Dessert First - Hallie Durand   c 123

Nergui
The Un-Forgotten Coat - Frank Cottrell Boyce   c, y 85

Nicholas
Waiting for the Magic - Patricia MacLachlan   c 293

Nick
Once Was Lost - Sara Zarr   y 1196

Nightshade, Victor
Nightshade City - Hilary Wagner   c, y 548

Nightshade, Vincent
Nightshade City - Hilary Wagner   c, y 548

O'Mara, Ben
Bull Rider - Suzanne Morgan Williams   y 1169

Obie
The Space Between - Brenna Yovanoff   y 1193

Page, Jay
The Uninvited - Tim Wynne-Jones   y 1179

Parker, Ellie
You Against Me - Jenny Downham   y 743

Parker, Tom
You Against Me - Jenny Downham   y 743

Patrick
You Are Here - Jennifer E. Smith   y 1089

Paul
Resistance - Carla Jablonski   y 854

Petros
War Games - Audrey Couloumbis   c, y 89

Plato
Freedom Stone - Jeffrey Kluger   c, y 255

Quinn
Picture the Dead - Adele Griffin   y 808

Randall
Caleb's Wars - David L. Dudley   y 746

Randy
Perpetual Check - Rich Wallace   y 1147

Reinstein, Andrew
Stupid Fast: The Summer I Went from a Joke to a Jock - Geoff Herbach   y 836

Reinstein, Felton
Stupid Fast: The Summer I Went from a Joke to a Jock - Geoff Herbach   y 836

Robert
Angry Young Man - Chris Lynch   y 912

Ryder
Witchlanders - Lena Coakley   y 695

Ryves, Alan
The Demon's Lexicon - Sarah Rees Brennan   y 657

Sal
Let's Do Nothing! - Tony Fucile   *c* 153

Sam
Don't Want to Go! - Shirley Hughes   *p, c* 216

Shaw, Henry
Silhouetted by the Blue - Traci L. Jones   *y* 863

Simon
In the Path of Falling Objects - Andrew Smith   *y* 1086

Sione
The Shattering - Karen Healey   *y* 832

Smith, Cyrus
The Dragon's Tooth - N.D. Wilson   *c, y* 571

Steven
The Summer I Turned Pretty - Jenny Han   *y* 817

Tom
Rot and Ruin - Jonathan Maberry   *y* 914

Troy
Bronxwood - Coe Booth   *y* 648

Ty
Ten - Lauren Myracle   *c* 344

Tyrell
Bronxwood - Coe Booth   *y* 648

Whitcomb, Jared
The House of Tomorrow - Peter Bognanni   *y* 646

Will
Picture the Dead - Adele Griffin   *y* 808
The Radleys: A Novel - Matt Haig   *y* 813

William
Waiting for the Magic - Patricia MacLachlan   *c* 293

Witherspoon, Jace
Split - Swati Avasthi   *y* 615

Wolfgang
Dessert First - Hallie Durand   *c* 123

Zeke
Perpetual Check - Rich Wallace   *y* 1147

Zola
War Games - Audrey Couloumbis   *c, y* 89

BULLIED CHILD

Filber, Tom
Stuck on Earth - David Klass   *c, y* 250

Perry, Winnie
Ten - Lauren Myracle   *c* 344

Varderman, Paul
The Knife That Killed Me - Anthony McGowan   *c, y* 936

BULLY

Avery, Clayton
The Mostly True Story of Jack - Kelly Barnhill   *c, y* 23

Colby
Brutal - Michael Harmon   *y* 824

Connelly, Griffin
Bystander - James Preller   *y* 1022

Devon
Kit Feeny: On the Move - Michael Townsend   *c* 521

Frank
Calvin Coconut: Trouble Magnet - Graham Salisbury   *c* 438

Ivan
Out of Shadows - Jason Wallace   *y* 1146

Joe
Angel in My Pocket - Ilene Cooper   *c, y* 82

Kingston, Samantha
Before I Fall - Lauren Oliver   *y* 990

Lane, Marko
A Boy Called Twister - Anne Schraff   *y* 1061

Lynwood
Squish: Super Amoeba - Jennifer L. Holm   *c* 208

McMillan, Nader
Everybody Sees the Ants - A.S. King   *y* 875

Mindy
Ten - Lauren Myracle   *c* 344

Munn, Tod
Scrawl - Mark Shulman   *y* 1077

Ronster, Digger
Warp Speed - Lisa Yee   *y* 1186

Roth
The Knife That Killed Me - Anthony McGowan   *c, y* 936

Tito
Calvin Coconut: Trouble Magnet - Graham Salisbury   *c* 438

BUSINESSMAN

Brewster, Jebediah
The Mostly True Adventures of Homer P. Figg - Rodman Philbrick   *c, y* 389

McBride, Drake
Scat - Carl Hiaasen   *c, y* 203

Wolff, Gunther
Revolver - Marcus Sedgwick   *y* 1068

BUSINESSWOMAN

Mrs. Ellis-Chan
Bobby versus Girls (Accidentally) - Lisa Yee   *c, y* 587

CAMPER

Abbott, Wren
Hidden - Helen Frost   *y* 778

Biggs, Sydney
Every Little Thing in the World - Nina de Gramont   *y* 724

Brendan
Every Little Thing in the World - Nina de Gramont   *y* 724

Jenna
Brain Camp - Susan Kim   *y* 873

Lucas
Brain Camp - Susan Kim   *y* 873

Mick
Every Little Thing in the World - Nina de Gramont   *y* 724

Miksa, Natalia
Every Little Thing in the World - Nina de Gramont   *y* 724

Monson, Darra
Hidden - Helen Frost   *y* 778

CANCER PATIENT

Alper, Jeffrey
After Ever After - Jordan Sonnenblick   *y* 1094

D.Q.
The Last Summer of The Death Warriors - Francisco X. Stork   *y* 1104

Morrison, Travis
Breathless - Lurlene McDaniel   *y* 934

Song
The Complete History of Why I Hate Her - Jennifer Richard Jacobson   *y* 855

Tad
After Ever After - Jordan Sonnenblick   *y* 1094

CAPTIVE

Joseph
Zita the Spacegirl - Ben Hatke   *c, y* 195

CARE GIVER

Lily
The Midnight Charter - David Whitley   *y* 1157

CAREGIVER

Gloria
A Time of Miracles - Anne-Laure Bondoux   *y* 647

Marisol
The Last Summer of The Death Warriors - Francisco X. Stork   *y* 1104

CAT

Aldwyn
The Familiars - Adam Jay Epstein   *c, y* 132

Benno
Benno and the Night of Broken Glass - Meg Wiviott   *c* 576

Binky
Binky the Space Cat - Ashley Spires   *c* 482

Mr. C'mere
Wild Things - Clay Carmichael   *c, y* 60

Cat
Three by the Sea - Mini Grey   *p, c* 179

Dr. Cat
Pigs Make Me Sneeze! - Mo Willems   *p, c* 565

Earl
I Must Have Bobo! - Eileen Rosenthal   *p, c* 427

Henry
Henry in Love - Peter McCarty   *p, c* 310

Lula
Waiting for the Magic - Patricia MacLachlan   *c* 293

Magic
Wisdom's Kiss: A Thrilling and Romantic Adventure Incorporating Magic, Villainy and a Cat - Catherine Gilbert Murdock   *y* 959

Malcolm
It's a Secret! - John Burningham   *p, c* 55

Nini
Nini Lost and Found - Anita Lobel   *p, c* 283

Pinch
The Cheshire Cheese Cat: A Dickens of a Tale - Carmen Agra Deedy   *c, y* 105

Posy
Posy - Linda Newbery   *p, c* 354

Shadow
Dying to Meet You - Kate Klise   *c, y* 254

Skilley
The Cheshire Cheese Cat: A Dickens of a Tale - Carmen Agra Deedy   *c, y* 105

Static Cat
Sidekicks - Dan Santat   *c, y* 441

Velasquez, Eric
Grandma's Gift - Eric Velasquez   c 540

CHILD OF AN ALCOHOLIC

Hope
Glimpse - Carol Lynch Williams   y 1163

Kelly, Jenna
Gifted: Better Late than Never - Marilyn Kaye   y 866

Lizzie
Glimpse - Carol Lynch Williams   y 1163

Mackee, Thomas
The Piper's Son - Melina Marchetta   y 922

CHILD OF DIVORCED PARENTS

Daniel, Dyamonde
Make Way for Dyamonde Daniel - Nikki Grimes   c 180

Lexie
Lexie - Audrey Couloumbis   c, y 87

CHILD-CARE GIVER

Atkinson, Jamie
Tighter - Adele Griffin   y 807

Jessie
Tighter - Adele Griffin   y 807

Piggins, Nanny
The Adventures of Nanny Piggins - R.A. Spratt   c, y 483

CHIMPANZEE

Jubilee
Me . . . Jane - Patrick McDonnell   p, c 314

Zan
Half Brother - Kenneth Oppel   y 992

CLASSMATE

Aurora
Crazy Beautiful - Lauren Baratz-Logsted   y 619

Bud
Pearl and Wagner: One Funny Day - Kate McMullan   c 321

Chichi
Akata Witch - Nnedi Okorafor   y 988

Christian
Unearthly - Cynthia Hand   y 819

Crystal
How Oliver Olson Changed the World - Claudia Mills   c 331

Dwight
The Strange Case of Origami Yoda - Tom Angleberger   c, y 9

Fade, Kenny
Fade to Blue - Sean Beaudoin   y 626

Free
Make Way for Dyamonde Daniel - Nikki Grimes   c 180

Gonzalez, Marta
Scat - Carl Hiaasen   c, y 203

Grayson, Mathew
Burn My Heart - Beverley Naidoo   c, y 967

Helen
Beat the Band - Don Calame   y 670

Henry
Pearl and Wagner: One Funny Day - Kate McMullan   c 321

Ivan
Out of Shadows - Jason Wallace   y 1146

Jessica
Hate List - Jennifer Brown   y 664

Jessup
Crazy Beautiful - Lauren Baratz-Logsted   y 619

Jones, Callie
Callie's Rules - Naomi Flink Zucker   c, y 594

Little Man
This Thing Called the Future - J. L. Powers   y 1020

Orlu
Akata Witch - Nnedi Okorafor   y 988

Patch
Hush, Hush - Becca Fitzpatrick   y 767

Peter
Love Is the Higher Law - David Levithan   y 899

Raines, Travis
The Seventh Level - Jody Feldman   c, y 136

Roger
Yummy: The Last Days of a Southside Shorty - G. Neri   y 973

Sara
The Strange Case of Origami Yoda - Tom Angleberger   c, y 9

Sasha
Akata Witch - Nnedi Okorafor   y 988

Scott, Emily
Ratfink - Marcia Thornton Jones   c, y 230

Scrod, Duane "Smoke" Jr.
Scat - Carl Hiaasen   c, y 203

Smithers, Lance
Burn My Heart - Beverley Naidoo   c, y 967

Tucker
Unearthly - Cynthia Hand   y 819

Van Dine, Valeri
Callie's Rules - Naomi Flink Zucker   c, y 594

Waters, Nick
Scat - Carl Hiaasen   c, y 203

CLIENT

Arrow
Nickel Plated - Aric Davis   y 721

COACH

Martin, Coach
Warp Speed - Lisa Yee   y 1186

COLLECTOR

Galen
The Dark City - Catherine Fisher   y 766

COMPANION

Branch, Ruah
You Don't Know About Me - Brian Meehl   y 944

Darla
Ashfall - Mike Mullin   y 958

COMPUTER

Roc
The Comet's Curse - Dom Testa   y 1124

COMPUTER GAME PLAYER

Owen
Tangled - Carolyn Mackler   y 916

CON ARTIST

Bayliss, Jimmy Lee
Scat - Carl Hiaasen   c, y 203

Fleabottom, Fenton J.
The Mostly True Adventures of Homer P. Figg - Rodman Philbrick   c, y 389

Jinx
Moon over Manifest - Clare Vanderpool   c, y 538

McBride, Drake
Scat - Carl Hiaasen   c, y 203

Monroe, Clem
Grounded - Kate Klise   c, y 253

Nibbly, Kate
The Mostly True Adventures of Homer P. Figg - Rodman Philbrick   c, y 389

CONSTRUCTION WORKER

Boss
Job Site - Nathan Clement   p, c 71

CONTESTANT

Abernathy, Haymitch
Catching Fire - Suzanne Collins   y 699
Mockingjay - Suzanne Collins   y 700

Beetee
Catching Fire - Suzanne Collins   y 699

Cresta, Annie
Mockingjay - Suzanne Collins   y 700

Everdeen, Katniss
Catching Fire - Suzanne Collins   y 699
Mockingjay - Suzanne Collins   y 700

Mags
Catching Fire - Suzanne Collins   y 699

Mason, Johanna
Catching Fire - Suzanne Collins   y 699

Mellark, Peeta
Catching Fire - Suzanne Collins   y 699
Mockingjay - Suzanne Collins   y 700

Odair, Finnick
Catching Fire - Suzanne Collins   y 699
Mockingjay - Suzanne Collins   y 700

Wiress
Catching Fire - Suzanne Collins   y 699

COOK

Cook
The King's Taster - Kenneth Oppel   c 371

Farm Maiden
The Cazuela That the Farm Maiden Stirred - Samantha R. Vamos   c 533

Mouse
Three by the Sea - Mini Grey   p, c 179

COUNSELOR

Mrs. Brook
Mockingbird - Kathryn Erskine   c, y 133

Mr. Vidas
Bait - Alex Sanchez   y 1057

Mrs. Woodrow
Scrawl - Mark Shulman   y 1077

COUSIN

Araene
The Floating Islands - Rachel Neumeier   y 978

Character Description Index

Minli
Where the Mountain Meets the Moon - Grace
    Lin   *c, y* 281

Moon, Millicent
Through Her Eyes - Jennifer Archer   *y* 610

O'Rourke, Raine
Sparrow Road - Sheila O'Connor   *c, y* 985

Oates, Clara
Stay - Deb Caletti   *y* 671

Pearl
Pearl verses the World - Sally Murphy   *c* 338

Piper, Tansy
Through Her Eyes - Jennifer Archer   *y* 610

Radley, Clara
The Radleys: A Novel - Matt Haig   *y* 813

Rose, April Garnet
A Month of Sundays - Ruth White   *y* 558

Roux, Corlie
Stones for My Father - Trilby Kent   *y* 869

Rubina
Big Red Lollipop - Rukhsana Khan   *p, c* 244

Sana
Big Red Lollipop - Rukhsana Khan   *p, c* 244

Sixpence
A Small Free Kiss in the Dark - Glenda
    Millard   *y* 948

Solveig
Icefall - Matthew J. Kirby   *y* 878

Towfeek, Jamilah "Jamie"
Ten Things I Hate about Me - Randa
    Abdel-Fattah   *y* 595

Unnamed Character
Over and Under the Snow - Kate Messner   *c* 327

Van Dine, Valeri
Callie's Rules - Naomi Flink Zucker   *c, y* 594

Whitcomb, Meredith
The House of Tomorrow - Peter Bognanni   *y* 646

Wren, Dottie
What Happened on Fox Street - Tricia
    Springstubb   *c, y* 484

Wren, Mo
What Happened on Fox Street - Tricia
    Springstubb   *c, y* 484

Zitlally
Star in the Forest - Laura Resau   *c, y* 412

DEAF PERSON

Halpin, Will
The Dark Days of Hamburger Halpin - Josh
    Berk   *y* 632

Sykes, Tamika
The Orange Houses - Paul Griffin   *y* 810

Wilson, Ben
Wonderstruck - Brian Selznick   *c, y* 458

DEBUTANTE

FitzOsborne, Sophia
The FitzOsbornes in Exile - Michelle
    Cooper   *y* 705

FitzOsborne, Sophie
A Brief History of Montmaray - Michelle
    Cooper   *y* 706

DEER

Deer
Waiting for Winter - Sebastian
    Meschenmoser   *p, c* 326

DEITY

Calypso
The Odyssey - Gareth Hinds   *y* 839

Jackson, Percy
The Lightning Thief: The Graphic Novel - Rick
    Riordan   *c, y* 416

Poseidon
The Lightning Thief: The Graphic Novel - Rick
    Riordan   *c, y* 416
The Odyssey - Gareth Hinds   *y* 839

DEMON

Beelzebub "Mr. Beals"
Soul Enchilada - David Macinnis Gill   *y* 790

Lilith
The Space Between - Brenna Yovanoff   *y* 1193

Lucifer
The Space Between - Brenna Yovanoff   *y* 1193

Lucifer "Scratch"
Soul Enchilada - David Macinnis Gill   *y* 790

Thompson, Jael
Misfit - Jon Skovron   *y* 1080

DESIGNER

Dexter, Sandy
Where I Belong - Gillian Cross   *y* 712

Humphrey
The Christmas Giant - Steve Light   *p, c* 279

Leetree
The Christmas Giant - Steve Light   *p, c* 279

Nolan, Lola
Lola and the Boy Next Door - Stephanie
    Perkins   1007

DETECTIVE

Anderson, Iris
The Girl Is Murder - Kathryn Miller Haines   *y* 814

Sasspants
Hamster and Cheese - Colleen A.F. Venable   *c* 541

DETECTIVE—AMATEUR

Alice
Pie - Sarah Weeks   *c, y* 552

Archer, Madison
Wish You Were Dead - Todd Strasser   *y* 1107

Brixton, Steve
The Case of the Case of Mistaken Identity - Mac
    Barnett   *c, y* 22

Charlie
Pie - Sarah Weeks   *c, y* 552

Chen, Rebecca
The Red Blazer Girls: The Ring of Rocamadour -
    Michael D. Beil   *y* 629

Christopher
The Morgue and Me - John C. Ford   *y* 769

de Luce, Flavia
The Sweetness at the Bottom of the Pie - Alan
    Bradley   *y* 653

Devon
The Dark Days of Hamburger Halpin - Josh
    Berk   *y* 632

Geless, Maks
City of Orphans - Avi   *c, y* 15

Halpin, Will
The Dark Days of Hamburger Halpin - Josh
    Berk   *y* 632

Holmes, Sherlock
Death Cloud - Andrew Lane   *y* 890

Jaimes, Lee Ann
The Red Blazer Girls: The Ring of Rocamadour -
    Michael D. Beil   *y* 629

Pratt, Benjamin "Ben"
We the Children - Andrew Clements   *c, y* 72

Severance, Veronica "Ronnie"
The River - Mary Jane Beaufrand   *y* 627

Shane, Andy
Andy Shane and the Barn Sale Mystery - Jennifer
    Richard Jacobson   *c* 220

St. Pierre, Sophie
The Red Blazer Girls: The Ring of Rocamadour -
    Michael D. Beil   *y* 629

Wrobel, Margaret
The Red Blazer Girls: The Ring of Rocamadour -
    Michael D. Beil   *y* 629

DETECTIVE—PRIVATE

Nickel
Nickel Plated - Aric Davis   *y* 721

Tully, J.J.
The Trouble with Chickens - Doreen Cronin   *c* 92

DIABETIC

Moran, Miz
Saint Louis Armstrong Beach - Brenda
    Woods   *c, y* 1174

DINOSAUR

Brontorina
Brontorina - James Howe   *p, c* 213

Mr. Brontosaurus
Lulu and the Brontosaurus - Judith
    Viorst   *p, c* 542

DIVER

Morrison, Travis
Breathless - Lurlene McDaniel   *y* 934

DOCTOR

Dr. Cat
Pigs Make Me Sneeze! - Mo Willems   *p, c* 565

Henry
Wild Things - Clay Carmichael   *c, y* 60

Dr. Indra
No Ordinary Day - Deborah Ellis   *c, y* 126

Radley, Peter
The Radleys: A Novel - Matt Haig   *y* 813

DOG

Aggie
Aggie the Brave - Lori Ries   *p, c* 414

Bitty
Waiting for the Magic - Patricia
    MacLachlan   *c* 293

Bryn
Waiting for the Magic - Patricia
    MacLachlan   *c* 293

Mr. Bud
Say Hello to Zorro! - Carter Goodrich   *p, c* 164

City Dog
City Dog, Country Frog - Mo Willems   *p, c* 562

Daisy
A Ball for Daisy - Chris Raschka   *p, c* 406

Dog

Dog Loves Books - Louise Yates *p, c* 586
I'm the Best - Lucy Cousins *p, c* 91
Three by the Sea - Mini Grey *p, c* 179

Ella
Bone Dog - Eric Rohmann *c* 425

Grace
Waiting for the Magic - Patricia
    MacLachlan *c* 293

Itty Bitty
Itty Bitty - Cece Bell *p, c* 30

Max
The King's Taster - Kenneth Oppel *c* 371

Neo
Waiting for the Magic - Patricia
    MacLachlan *c* 293

Ralph
RRRalph - Lois Ehlert *p, c* 124

Roscoe
Sidekicks - Dan Santat *c, y* 441

Shadow
Saint Louis Armstrong Beach - Brenda
    Woods *c, y* 1174

Snook
Snook Alone - Marilyn Nelson *c* 349

Tully, J.J.
The Trouble with Chickens - Doreen Cronin *c* 92

Unnamed Character
See Me Run - Paul Meisel *p, c* 324

Zorro
Say Hello to Zorro! - Carter Goodrich *p, c* 164

DONKEY

Donkey
I'm the Best - Lucy Cousins *p, c* 91

DRAGON

Brock
No Such Things as Dragons - Philip
    Reeve *c, y* 410

Laddy
The Runaway Dragon - Kate Coombs *c, y* 79

DRIVER

Mitch
In the Path of Falling Objects - Andrew
    Smith *y* 1086

Sally "Sal"
Stagecoach Sal - Deborah Hopkinson *c* 212

DRUG DEALER

Dance, Jeremy "Lil J"
Dope Sick - Walter Dean Myers *y* 962

Ganz, Virgil
Shooting Star - Fredrick McKissack Jr. *y* 941

Rico
Dope Sick - Walter Dean Myers *y* 962

DUCK

Duck
The Odd Egg - Emily Gravett *p, c* 173

Lucky Ducky
Chicken Little - Rebecca Emberley *p, c* 129

DWARF

Gonzo
Going Bovine - Libba Bray *y* 655

ELEPHANT

Gerald
I Broke My Trunk! - Mo Willems *p, c* 567
Pigs Make Me Sneeze! - Mo Willems *p, c* 565

EMOTIONALLY IMPAIRED CHILD

Collin
The Snowball Effect - Holly Nicole Hoxter *y* 846

EMPLOYER

Mr. Green
The Adventures of Nanny Piggins - R.A.
    Spratt *c, y* 483

Sylvie
Stay - Deb Caletti *y* 671

Valentino
Putting Makeup on the Fat Boy - Bil
    Wright *y* 1177

ENEMY

Baumgarten, Mary Ashley
Sister Mischief - Laura Goode *y* 797

ENGINEER

Mr. Clayborne
Chime - Franny Billingsley *y* 634

Crumb, Fever
A Web of Air - Philip Reeve *y* 1034

ENVIRONMENTALIST

Forest, Vray
Earthgirl - Jennifer Cowan *y* 710

Spree, Twilly
Scat - Carl Hiaasen *c, y* 203

EQUESTRIAN

Connolly, Puck
The Scorpio Races - Maggie Stiefvater *y* 1099

Kendrick, Sean
The Scorpio Races - Maggie Stiefvater *y* 1099

EXPATRIATE

Scott, Janie
The Apothecary - Maile Meloy *y* 945

FAIRY

Flory
The Night Fairy - Laura Amy Schlitz *c, y* 450

Laurel
Spells - Aprilynne Pike *y* 1015

Sidhean
Ash - Malinda Lo *y* 902

FANATIC

Maximilian "Max"
*Maximilian and the Mystery of the Guardian Angel:
    A Bilingual Lucha Libre Thriller* - Xavier
    Garza *y* 782

FARMER

Genia
Then - Morris Gleitzman *y* 792

Harmony, Ray
Carolina Harmony - Marilyn Taylor
    McDowell *c, y* 315

Mari
Return to Sender - Julia Alvarez *c, y* 7

Ojisan
Tsunami! - Kimiko Kajikawa *p, c* 236

Tyler
Return to Sender - Julia Alvarez *c, y* 7

FATHER

Dr. Adnoid
The Secret of Zoom - Lynne Jonell *c, y* 228

Aguilar, Marcelus
Gringolandia - Lyn Miller-Lachmann *y* 950

Andersson, Einar
Revolver - Marcus Sedgwick *y* 1068

Berlin, Brick
Spoiled - Jessica Morgan *y* 953

Border, Clarence
I'll Be There - Holly Goldberg Sloan *y* 1083

Mr. Burrows
The Apothecary - Maile Meloy *y* 945

Mr. Carter
Gator on the Loose! - Sue Stauffacher *c, y* 487

Mr. Clayborne
Chime - Franny Billingsley *y* 634

Dad
Compromised - Heidi Ayarbe *y* 616
Crazy - Han Nolan *y* 980
The Dancing Pancake - Eileen Spinelli *c, y* 481
Don't Want to Go! - Shirley Hughes *p, c* 216
Efrain's Secret - Sofia Quintero *y* 1027
Itsy Mitsy Runs Away - Elanna Allen *c* 5
Mission Unstoppable - Dan Gutman *c, y* 183
This World We Live In - Susan Beth
    Pfeffer *y* 1012
You Are Here - Jennifer E. Smith *y* 1089

Daddy
Crow Call - Lois Lowry *c* 288
Dessert First - Hallie Durand *c* 123
Lexie - Audrey Couloumbis *c, y* 87
Somebody Everybody Listens To - Suzanne
    Supplee *y* 1115

Dinga
Never Forgotten - Patricia C. McKissack *c, y* 319

Edelman, Albert Baruch
My Life with the Lincolns - Gayle
    Brandeis *c, y* 46

Egg, Malachi
The Prince of Fenway Park - Julianna
    Baggott *c, y* 18

Mr. Ellis-Chan
Bobby versus Girls (Accidentally) - Lisa
    Yee *c, y* 587

Father
Over and Under the Snow - Kate Messner *c* 327
Silver Phoenix: Beyond the Kingdom of Xia -
    Cindy Pon *y* 1017

Fever
Why I Fight - J. Adams Oaks *y* 987

Flint, Jimmy
The Brooklyn Nine: A Novel in Nine Innings - Alan
    Gratz *c, y* 171

Grandpa Dan
Through Her Eyes - Jennifer Archer   *y* 610

Grayson, Mr.
Burn My Heart - Beverley Naidoo   *c, y* 967

Lord Greave
The Poisoned House - Michael Ford   *y* 770

Mr. Green
The Adventures of Nanny Piggins - R.A.
   Spratt   *c, y* 483

Gus
Pearl - Jo Knowles   *y* 882

Hardscrabble, Casper
The Kneebone Boy - Ellen Potter   *c, y* 398

Harnett, Ken
Rotters - Daniel Kraus   *y* 886

Hartwell, Clayton "The Raptor"
Legacy - Thomas Sniegoski   *y* 1093

Heffley, Frank
Diary of a Wimpy Kid: Cabin Fever - Jeff
   Kinney   *c, y* 248

Jefferson, Thomas
*Jefferson's Sons: A Founding Father's Secret Chil-
   dren* - Kimberly Brubaker Bradley   *c, y* 45

Josh
Jumping Off Swings - Jo Knowles   *y* 881

Kamau
Burn My Heart - Beverley Naidoo   *c, y* 967

Kane, Julius
The Red Pyramid - Rick Riordan   *c, y* 418

Mr. Kaufman
The Beginning of After - Jennifer Castle   *y* 681

Mr. Liebig
After the Train - Gloria Whelan   *y* 557

Lucifer
The Space Between - Brenna Yovanoff   *y* 1193

Nate
Strings Attached - Judy Blundell   *y* 643

Noah
Response - Paul Volponi   *y* 1141

Oates, Bobby
Stay - Deb Caletti   *y* 671

Pa
The Money We'll Save - Brock Cole   *c* 73

Papa
Interrupting Chicken - David Ezra Stein   *c* 491
A New Year's Reunion - Yu Li-Qiong   *c* 276
Star in the Forest - Laura Resau   *c, y* 412
Waiting for the Magic - Patricia
   MacLachlan   *c* 293

Papi
Muchacho - LouAnne Johnson   *y* 860

Popovich, Charlie
Pop - Gordon Korman   *y* 885

Pops
Bronxwood - Coe Booth   *y* 648

Poseidon
The Lightning Thief: The Graphic Novel - Rick
   Riordan   *c, y* 416

Radley, Peter
The Radleys: A Novel - Matt Haig   *y* 813

Schneider, Felix
The Brooklyn Nine: A Novel in Nine Innings - Alan
   Gratz   *c, y* 171

Smithers, Frank
Burn My Heart - Beverley Naidoo   *c, y* 967

Snider, Walter
The Brooklyn Nine: A Novel in Nine Innings - Alan
   Gratz   *c, y* 171

Sonny
Bullet Point - Peter Abrahams   *y* 597

Soto, Marc
The Uninvited - Tim Wynne-Jones   *y* 1179

Mr. Sweet
What Happened to Goodbye - Sarah Dessen   *y* 730

Tucker, Gideon
Moon over Manifest - Clare Vanderpool   *c, y* 538

Unnamed Character
The Third Gift - Linda Sue Park   *c* 376

Whitcombe
*Three Rivers Rising: A Novel of the Johnstown
   Flood* - Jame Richards   *y* 1040

Wolf, Big
Big Wolf and Little Wolf - Sharon Phillips
   Denslow   *c* 108

Mr. Wren
What Happened on Fox Street - Tricia
   Springstubb   *c, y* 484

FERRET

Mrs. Finnemore
Edwin Speaks Up - April Stevens   *c* 495

Finnemore, Edwin
Edwin Speaks Up - April Stevens   *c* 495

Finnemore, Fergus
Edwin Speaks Up - April Stevens   *c* 495

Finnemore, Finney
Edwin Speaks Up - April Stevens   *c* 495

Finnemore, Franny
Edwin Speaks Up - April Stevens   *c* 495

FIANCE(E)

Fenister, Graceful
The Returning - Christine Hinwood   *y* 840

Jennie
Picture the Dead - Adele Griffin   *y* 808

Keepsake, Letitia
I Shall Wear Midnight - Terry Pratchett   *y* 1021

Will
Picture the Dead - Adele Griffin   *y* 808

FILMMAKER

Cressida
Mockingjay - Suzanne Collins   *y* 700

Dillard, Macon
Close to Famous - Joan Bauer   *c, y* 623

Hollywood
Absolutely Maybe - Lisa Yee   *y* 1187

Katie-Rose
Luv Ya Bunches - Lauren Myracle   *c, y* 343

FISHERMAN

Melkun, Lilly
Raiders' Ransom - Emily Diamand   *y* 734

FLY

Fly Guy
I Spy Fly Guy - Tedd Arnold   *p, c* 11

FOOTBALL PLAYER

Angel
Payback Time - Carl Deuker   *y* 732

Annie
Bobby versus Girls (Accidentally) - Lisa
   Yee   *c, y* 587

Caldwell, Jayson
Shooting Star - Fredrick McKissack Jr.   *y* 941

Cannon, Jimmy
When the Whistle Blows - Fran Cannon
   Slayton   *y* 1082

Christian
Unearthly - Cynthia Hand   *y* 819

Cody
Reality Check - Peter Abrahams   *y* 596

Mr. Ellis-Chan
Bobby versus Girls (Accidentally) - Lisa
   Yee   *c, y* 587

Kurt
Leverage - Joshua Cohen   *y* 697

Marcus
Pop - Gordon Korman   *y* 885

Pablo
The Vast Fields of Ordinary - Nick Burd   *y* 667

Popovich, Charlie
Pop - Gordon Korman   *y* 885

Popovich, Troy
Pop - Gordon Korman   *y* 885

Reinstein, Felton
*Stupid Fast: The Summer I Went from a Joke to a
   Jock* - Geoff Herbach   *y* 836

Rodgers, Jomo
Shooting Star - Fredrick McKissack Jr.   *y* 941

FOSTER CHILD

Aaron
Touch Blue - Cynthia Lord   *c, y* 286

Allison
Raven Summer - David Almond   *y* 602

Crystal
Raven Summer - David Almond   *y* 602

Fielding, Jacob
Thirteen Days to Midnight - Patrick
   Carman   *y* 676

Fisher, Benson
Variant - Robison Wells   *y* 1151

Hogan, Holly "Solace"
Solace of the Road - Siobhan Dowd   *y* 741

Kat
The Stolen One - Suzanne Crowley   *y* 714

Lili
Peace, Locomotion - Jacqueline Woodson   *c, y* 581

Lonnie
Peace, Locomotion - Jacqueline Woodson   *c, y* 581

Maya
Compromised - Heidi Ayarbe   *y* 616

Oliver
Raven Summer - David Almond   *y* 602

R.D.
Messed Up - Janet Nichols Lynch   *y* 913

Russell
Carolina Harmony - Marilyn Taylor
   McDowell   *c, y* 315

Troy
Bronxwood - Coe Booth   *y* 648

FOSTER PARENT

Auntie Alma
A Faraway Island - Annika Thor   *c, y* 516

Auntie Marta
A Faraway Island - Annika Thor   *c, y* 516

Mr. Fielding
Thirteen Days to Midnight - Patrick
Carman   *y* 676

FOX

Eugene
Zelda and Ivy: Keeping Secrets - Laura McGee
Kvasnosky   *c* 264

Fox
Lousy Rotten Stinkin' Grapes - Margie
Palatini   *c* 373

Ivy
Zelda and Ivy: Keeping Secrets - Laura McGee
Kvasnosky   *c* 264

Lucy
Red Wagon - Renata Liwska   *p, c* 282

Rojo
*Dinosaur Woods: Can Seven Clever Critters Save
Their Forest Home?* - George
McClements   *p, c* 313

Stranger, The
Three by the Sea - Mini Grey   *p, c* 179

Zelda
Zelda and Ivy: Keeping Secrets - Laura McGee
Kvasnosky   *c* 264

FRIEND

A.J.
Now Playing: Stoner & Spaz II - Ron
Koertge   *y* 883

Abbott, Harriet
Lost - Jacqueline Davies   *y* 720

Abby
Tyger Tyger - Kersten Hamilton   *y* 816

Afton, Regina
Some Girls Are - Courtney Summers   *y* 1114

Alex
Paper Covers Rock - Jenny Hubbard   *y* 848

Alice
Pie - Sarah Weeks   *c, y* 552

Amanda
Ten - Lauren Myracle   *c* 344

Ambrose, Violet
The Body Finder - Kimberly Derting   *y* 728

Amy
Shakespeare Makes the Playoffs - Ron
Koertge   *y* 884

Anders
The Mostly True Story of Jack - Kelly
Barnhill   *c, y* 23

Andy
Raiders' Ransom - Emily Diamand   *y* 734

Angela
Unearthly - Cynthia Hand   *y* 819

Angie
Putting Makeup on the Fat Boy - Bil
Wright   *y* 1177

Anning, Mary
Remarkable Creatures - Tracy Chevalier   *y* 686

April
Ten Things We Did (and Probably Shouldn't Have)
- Sarah Mlynowski   *y* 951

Ariel
Every You, Every Me - David Levithan   *y* 897

Arnold
Kit Feeny: On the Move - Michael
Townsend   *c* 521

Austin, Lark
Lark - Tracey Porter   *y* 1018

Balder
Going Bovine - Libba Bray   *y* 655

Balthazar
Finnikin of the Rock - Melina Marchetta   *y* 921

Bean "Pearl"
Pearl - Jo Knowles   *y* 882

Bear
Dog and Bear: Three to Get Ready - Laura Vaccaro
Seeger   *p, c* 456
Grin and Bear It - Leo Landry   *c* 265

Beau
The Eternal Ones - Kirsten Miller   *y* 949

Bee
Broken Soup - Jenny Valentine   *y* 1136

Belancort, Juniper
Nightshade City - Hilary Wagner   *c, y* 548

Bell, Emily
I'll Be There - Holly Goldberg Sloan   *y* 1083

Ben
The Secret Science Alliance and the Copycat Crook
- Eleanor Davis   *c, y* 103
Virals - Kathy Reichs   *y* 1035

Bethany
Through Her Eyes - Jennifer Archer   *y* 610

Bianchi, Carmen
Virtuosity - Jessica Martinez   *y* 925

Biggs, Sydney
Every Little Thing in the World - Nina de
Gramont   *y* 724

Bizza
Into the Wild Nerd Yonder - Julie Halpern   *y* 815
Into the Wild Nerd Yonder - Julie Halpern   *y* 815

Blake
Flash Burnout - L.K. Madigan   *y* 919
Ostrich Boys - Keith Gray   *y* 804

Blum, Carson
The New Kid - Mavis Jukes   *c* 233

Book, Eli
Eli the Good - Silas House   *y* 844

Border, Sam
I'll Be There - Holly Goldberg Sloan   *y* 1083

Brax
King of Ithaka - Tracy Barrett   *y* 621

Bree
Fancy Nancy and the Mermaid Ballet - Jane
O'Connor   *p, c* 367

Brennan, Tory
Virals - Kathy Reichs   *y* 1035

Brianna
The Unwritten Rule - Elizabeth Scott   *y* 1066

Bucktin, Charlie
Jasper Jones - Craig Silvey   *y* 1079

Burrows, Benjamin
The Apothecary - Maile Meloy   *y* 945

Caldwell, Jayson
Shooting Star - Fredrick McKissack Jr.   *y* 941

Caleb
Jumping Off Swings - Jo Knowles   *y* 881

Calendar, Julian
The Secret Science Alliance and the Copycat Crook
- Eleanor Davis   *c, y* 103

Callum
Wild Wings - Gill Lewis   *c, y* 275

Cam
The Runaway Dragon - Kate Coombs   *c, y* 79
Signal - Cynthia DeFelice   *c, y* 106

Cameron
Going Bovine - Libba Bray   *y* 655

Candace
Efrain's Secret - Sofia Quintero   *y* 1027

Captain Grey
Birthmarked - Caragh M. O'Brien   *y* 982

Carly
The Complete History of Why I Hate Her - Jennifer
Richard Jacobson   *y* 855

Carver Ellis-Chan, Robert "Bobby"
Bobby versus Girls (Accidentally) - Lisa
Yee   *c, y* 587

Casey
The DUFF: Designated Ugly Fat Friend - Kody
Keplinger   *y* 871

Cassia
Matched - Ally Condie   *y* 703

Cassie
The Ghosts of Ashbury High - Jaclyn
Moriarty   *y* 954
Wintergirls - Laurie Halse Anderson   *y* 608

Castenada, Toni
*The Cardturner: A Novel about a King, a Queen,
and a Joker* - Louis Sachar   *y* 1053

Cat
Shine - Lauren Myracle   *y* 965

Char
Into the Wild Nerd Yonder - Julie Halpern   *y* 815
Into the Wild Nerd Yonder - Julie Halpern   *y* 815

Miss Charleena
Close to Famous - Joan Bauer   *c, y* 623

Charlie
Pie - Sarah Weeks   *c, y* 552

Chingis
The Un-Forgotten Coat - Frank Cottrell
Boyce   *c, y* 85

Chloe
Accomplice - Eireann Corrigan   *y* 708

Cissy
The Glorious Adventures of the Sunshine Queen -
Geraldine McCaughrean   *c, y* 312

Claire
Love Is the Higher Law - David Levithan   *y* 899

Conklin, Isobel "Belly"
It's Not Summer Without You - Jenny Han   *y* 818

Connelly, Griffin
Bystander - James Preller   *y* 1022

Conner
The Marbury Lens - Andrew Smith   *y* 1087

Cooper, Tiny
Will Grayson, Will Grayson - David
Levithan   *y* 898

Corinne
Jumping Off Swings - Jo Knowles   *y* 881

Crane, Emmett
The Summer I Learned to Fly - Dana
Reinhardt   *y* 1037

Crystal
Star in the Forest - Laura Resau   *c, y* 412

Jasper
Love Is the Higher Law - David Levithan   y 899

Jazzy
Sunny Holiday - Coleen Murtagh
Paratore   c, y 374

Jeanette
Some Girls Are - Courtney Summers   y 1114

Jess
Into the Wild Nerd Yonder - Julie Halpern   y 815

Jessica
The DUFF: Designated Ugly Fat Friend - Kody
Keplinger   y 871

Jester, Owen
The Fantastic Secret of Owen Jester - Barbara
O'Connor   c, y 366

Jill
We the Children - Andrew Clements   c, y 72

Joe
The Sky Is Everywhere - Jandy Nelson   y 970

Jonah
The View from the Top - Hillary Frank   y 773

Jones, Jasper
Jasper Jones - Craig Silvey   y 1079

Joseph
Warriors in the Crossfire - Nancy Bo Flood   y 768
Zita the Spacegirl - Ben Hatke   c, y 195

Josh
The Future of Us - Jay Asher   y 613

Josie
Sparrow Road - Sheila O'Connor   c, y 985

Julie
The Un-Forgotten Coat - Frank Cottrell
Boyce   c, y 85

Julisa
Two of a Kind - Jacqui Robbins   c 419

Kalen
Gateway - Sharon Shinn   y 1076

Kapur, Chess
Bobby versus Girls (Accidentally) - Lisa
Yee   c, y 587

Kara
Some Girls Are - Courtney Summers   y 1114

Kat
The Lighter Side of Life and Death - C.K. Kelly
Martin   y 924

Kate
Exposed - Kimberly Marcus   y 923
Sweet Treats and Secret Crushes - Lisa
Greenwald   y 806

Keller, Bonwit
Julia Gillian (and the Quest for Joy) - Alison
McGhee   c 317

Kenny
Ostrich Boys - Keith Gray   y 804

Kento
Warriors in the Crossfire - Nancy Bo Flood   y 768

Kiernan
The False Princess - Ellis O'Neal   y 986

King, Jeremy
Virtuosity - Jessica Martinez   y 925

Kookie
The Glorious Adventures of the Sunshine Queen -
Geraldine McCaughrean   c, y 312

Kurt
Leverage - Joshua Cohen   y 697

Lederer, Eric
The Boy Who Couldn't Sleep and Never Had To -
D.C. Pierson   y 1014

Leroy
Crossing the Tracks - Barbara Stuber   y 1111

Lettie
Moon over Manifest - Clare Vanderpool   c, y 538

Lex
The Runaway Dragon - Kate Coombs   c, y 79

Lia
Wintergirls - Laurie Halse Anderson   y 608

Liesl
Liesl and Po - Lauren Oliver   c, y 369

Lillian
Sparrow Road - Sheila O'Connor   c, y 985

Lindsey
Before I Fall - Lauren Oliver   y 990

Lion
Mouse and Lion - Rand Burkert   c 54

Lisa
Highway to Hell - Rosemary
Clement-Moore   y 694

Liz
Exposed - Kimberly Marcus   y 923
Jumping Off Swings - Jo Knowles   y 881

London
Imaginary Girls - Nova Ren Suma   y 1113

Luc
Compulsion - Heidi Ayarbe   y 617

Lucy
iBoy - Kevin Brooks   y 660

Ludo
Mirrorscape - Mike Wilks   c, y 1162

Luks, Jonah
The Space between Trees - Katie Williams   y 1167

Lydia
The Ghosts of Ashbury High - Jaclyn
Moriarty   y 954

Maddie
The Grand Plan to Fix Everything - Uma
Krishnaswami   c, y 259

Mae
The Demon's Lexicon - Sarah Rees
Brennan   y 657

Malik
Ratfink - Marcia Thornton Jones   c, y 230

Mara
Zenith - Julie Bertagna   y 633

Marcy
Sister Mischief - Laura Goode   y 797

Mari
Return to Sender - Julia Alvarez   c, y 7

Marie
Resistance - Carla Jablonski   y 854

Marissa
Flash Burnout - L.K. Madigan   y 919

Marta
Some Girls Are - Courtney Summers   y 1114

Martha
Strawberry Hill - Mary Ann Hoberman   c 205

Martin, Jake
Compulsion - Heidi Ayarbe   y 617

Martin, Mikey
Blank Confession - Pete Hautman   y 827

Mary
Bystander - James Preller   y 1022

Mary-Tyler
The View from the Top - Hillary Frank   y 773

Mason
The Lighter Side of Life and Death - C.K. Kelly
Martin   y 924

Masterson, Nan
Burnout - Adrienne Maria Vrettos   y 1144

McCabe, Elizabeth "Zabet"
The Space between Trees - Katie Williams   y 1167

McDade, Zack
You - Charles Benoit   y 630

McGuire, Owen
Signal - Cynthia DeFelice   c, y 106

McKeel, Prue
Wildwood - Colin Meloy   c, y 325

McNair, Iona
Wild Wings - Gill Lewis   c, y 275

Meg
Same Difference - Siobhan Vivian   y 1140

Meghan
Scars - Cheryl Rainfield   y 1028

Melanie
Don't Want to Go! - Shirley Hughes   p, c 216

Mercedes
What Happened on Fox Street - Tricia
Springstubb   c, y 484

Miksa, Natalia
Every Little Thing in the World - Nina de
Gramont   y 724

Mildew, Arthur
*Tumtum and Nutmeg: Adventures beyond Nutmouse
Hall* - Emily Bearn   c, y 29

Mildew, Lucy
*Tumtum and Nutmeg: Adventures beyond Nutmouse
Hall* - Emily Bearn   c, y 29

Milo
Thirteen Days to Midnight - Patrick
Carman   y 676

Mimi
Just Grace Goes Green - Charise Mericle
Harper   c 191
Strawberry Hill - Mary Ann Hoberman   c 205

Minli
Where the Mountain Meets the Moon - Grace
Lin   c, y 281

Minou, Colleen
Now Playing: Stoner & Spaz II - Ron
Koertge   y 883

Mong
We Were Here - Matt de la Pena   y 725

Morales, Alex
This World We Live In - Susan Beth
Pfeffer   y 1012

Morrison, Anna
Some Girls Are - Courtney Summers   y 1114

Mouse
Mouse and Lion - Rand Burkert   c 54

Mugo
Burn My Heart - Beverley Naidoo   c, y 967

Murano, Lisa Marie
LIE - Caroline Bock   y 644

Naomi
Harmonic Feedback - Tara Kelly   y 868

Unnamed Character

I Will Come Back for You: A Family in Hiding during World War II - Marisabina Russo   *c* 433

GRANDFATHER

Granddad

Jake - Audrey Couloumbis   *c, y* 88

Grandfather

Clara Lee and the Apple Pie Dream - Jenny Han   *c* 189

Finding Family - Tonya Bolden   *c, y* 42

Grandpa

Bluefish - Pat Schmatz   *y* 1060

Heart of a Shepherd - Rosanne Parry   *c, y* 377

Ratfink - Marcia Thornton Jones   *c, y* 230

Grandpa Dan

Through Her Eyes - Jennifer Archer   *y* 610

Grandpa Mac

Sparrow Road - Sheila O'Connor   *c, y* 985

Green

Grandpa Green - Lane Smith   *c* 476

Gus

Pearl - Jo Knowles   *y* 882

Papa C

Soul Enchilada - David Macinnis Gill   *y* 790

Unnamed Character

These Hands - Margaret H. Mason   *c* 304

GRANDMOTHER

Auntie Shen

Carolina Harmony - Marilyn Taylor McDowell   *c, y* 315

Beckendorf, Mrs. "Almighty"

Confessions of the Sullivan Sisters - Natalie Standiford   *y* 1096

Da

What Happened on Fox Street - Tricia Springstubb   *c, y* 484

Gogo

This Thing Called the Future - J. L. Powers   *y* 1020

Gram, The

The Romeo and Juliet Code - Phoebe Stone   *c, y* 496

Gramma

Sleepover at Gramma's House - Barbara Joosse   *p, c* 231

Grandma

Grandma's Gift - Eric Velasquez   *c* 540

Grandma Alice

Gator on the Loose! - Sue Stauffacher   *c, y* 487

Mare

Mare's War - Tanita S. Davis   *y* 722

Nana

The House of Tomorrow - Peter Bognanni   *y* 646

Nana Philly

Turtle in Paradise - Jennifer L. Holm   *c, y* 206

Nonna

I Will Come Back for You: A Family in Hiding during World War II - Marisabina Russo   *c* 433

Nutaaq

Blessing's Bead - Debby Dahl Edwardson   *y* 750

Webb, Granny

Andy Shane and the Barn Sale Mystery - Jennifer Richard Jacobson   *c* 220

GRANDSON

Joseph

These Hands - Margaret H. Mason   *c* 304

Prendergast, Sebastian

The House of Tomorrow - Peter Bognanni   *y* 646

GUARD

Nort

The Runaway Dragon - Kate Coombs   *c, y* 79

Preston

I Shall Wear Midnight - Terry Pratchett   *y* 1021

GUARDIAN

Earl

Messed Up - Janet Nichols Lynch   *y* 913

Fire

Never Forgotten - Patricia C. McKissack   *c, y* 319

Grandpa

Heart of a Shepherd - Rosanne Parry   *c, y* 377

Jiguro

Moribito II: Guardian of the Darkness - Nahoko Uehashi   *c, y* 527

Mother Earth

Never Forgotten - Patricia C. McKissack   *c, y* 319

Nutmeg

Tumtum and Nutmeg: Adventures beyond Nutmouse Hall - Emily Bearn   *c, y* 29

Signe

Keeper - Kathi Appelt   *c, y* 10

Tumtum

Tumtum and Nutmeg: Adventures beyond Nutmouse Hall - Emily Bearn   *c, y* 29

Water

Never Forgotten - Patricia C. McKissack   *c, y* 319

Willow, Webster B.

The Mostly True Adventures of Homer P. Figg - Rodman Philbrick   *c, y* 389

Wind

Never Forgotten - Patricia C. McKissack   *c, y* 319

GUINEA PIG

Sasspants

Hamster and Cheese - Colleen A.F. Venable   *c* 541

GYMNAST

Danny

Leverage - Joshua Cohen   *y* 697

GYPSY

Yann

The Silver Blade - Sally Gardner   *y* 158

HAIRDRESSER

Unnamed Character

Even Monsters Need Haircuts - Matthew McElligott   *p, c* 316

HAMSTER

Fluffy

Sidekicks - Dan Santat   *c, y* 441

Hamisher

Hamster and Cheese - Colleen A.F. Venable   *c* 541

HANDICAPPED

Ellis, Shelley

Perfect Chemistry - Simone Elkeles   *y* 755

Swann, Meggy

Alchemy and Meggy Swann - Karen Cushman   *c, y* 97

HEDGEHOG

Hedgehog

Waiting for Winter - Sebastian Meschenmoser   *p, c* 326

HEIR

Sophos

A Conspiracy of Kings - Megan Whalen Turner   *y* 1134

Will

Blood - K.J. Wignall   *y* 1160

HEIRESS

Lucky Girl

Ship Breaker: A Novel - Paolo Bacigalupi   *y* 618

Mortimer, Frankie

Life: An Exploded Diagram - Mal Peet   *y* 1003

HEN

Hen

Animal Crackers Fly the Coop - Kevin O'Malley   *p, c* 368

Henny Penny

Chicken Little - Rebecca Emberley   *p, c* 129

HERO

Captain Amazing

Sidekicks - Dan Santat   *c, y* 441

Cooper, Beka

Bloodhound - Tamora Pierce   *y* 1013

Hartwell, Clayton "The Raptor"

Legacy - Thomas Sniegoski   *y* 1093

Phantom Justice

Sidekicks - Jack D. Ferraiolo   *y* 765

Ryder

Witchlanders - Lena Coakley   *y* 695

Sveinsson, Halli

Heroes of the Valley - Jonathan Stroud   *y* 1110

HEROINE

Clary

City of Glass - Cassandra Clare   *y* 691

Lunch Lady

Lunch Lady and the League of Librarians - Jarrett J. Krosoczka   *c* 260

Quinn, Mary

A Spy in the House - Y.S. Lee   *y* 895

Stone, Gaia

Prized - Caragh M. O'Brien   *y* 983

Wagstaff, Lee

Bayou: Volume 1 - Jeremy Love   *y* 907

Zita

Zita the Spacegirl - Ben Hatke   *c, y* 195

HIGHWAYMAN

Turpin, Dick

Highway Robbery - Kate Thompson   *c, y* 514

HIPPOPOTAMUS

Hippo
I Broke My Trunk! - Mo Willems　*p, c* 567

HISTORIAN

Imogene
Imogene's Last Stand - Candace Fleming　*c* 141

Kane, Julius
The Red Pyramid - Rick Riordan　*c, y* 418

Ms. Snoops
One Day and One Amazing Morning on Orange Street - Joanne Rocklin　*c* 422

HISTORICAL FIGURE

Astor, John Jacob
The Watch That Ends the Night: Voices from the Titanic - Allan Wolf　*y* 1171

Audubon, John James
A Nest for Celeste: A Story about Art, Inspiration, and the Meaning of Home - Henry Cole　*c, y* 74

Bly, Nellie
Around the World - Matt Phelan　*c, y* 388

Brown, Molly
The Watch That Ends the Night: Voices from the Titanic - Allan Wolf　*y* 1171

Dickens, Charles
The Cheshire Cheese Cat: A Dickens of a Tale - Carmen Agra Deedy　*c, y* 105

Jefferson, Thomas
Jefferson's Sons: A Founding Father's Secret Children - Kimberly Brubaker Bradley　*c, y* 45

Lincoln, Abraham
Our Abe Lincoln - Jim Aylesworth　*c* 17

Louis, Joe
Bird in a Box - Andrea Davis Pinkney　*c, y* 392

Roosevelt, Eleanor
Eleanor, Quiet No More - Doreen Rappaport　*c* 404

Sampson, Deborah
Soldier's Secret: The Story of Deborah Sampson - Sheila Solomon Klass　*y* 880

Smith, E.J.
The Watch That Ends the Night: Voices from the Titanic - Allan Wolf　*y* 1171

Stevens, Thomas
Around the World - Matt Phelan　*c, y* 388

HOMOSEXUAL

Branch, Ruah
You Don't Know About Me - Brian Meehl　*y* 944

Christopher
Clean - Amy Reed　*y* 1031

Cooper, Tiny
Will Grayson, Will Grayson - David Levithan　*y* 898

Dade
The Vast Fields of Ordinary - Nick Burd　*y* 667

Erik
With or Without You - Brian Farrey　*y* 764

Grayson, Davis
With or Without You - Brian Farrey　*y* 764

Kincaid, Alex
The Vast Fields of Ordinary - Nick Burd　*y* 667

Liu, Ray
Money Boy - Paul Yee　*y* 1188

Pablo
The Vast Fields of Ordinary - Nick Burd　*y* 667

Patrick
Shine - Lauren Myracle　*y* 965

Seth
Tricks - Ellen Hopkins　*y* 843

Weiss, Evan
With or Without You - Brian Farrey　*y* 764

HORSE

Dust Devil
Dust Devil - Anne Isaacs　*c* 219

HORSE TRAINER

Jill
Knifepoint - Alex Van Tol　*y* 1131

Lovitt, Abby
The Georges and the Jewels - Jane Smiley　*c, y* 471

HOSTAGE

Ojeda, Alonso de
Hurricane Dancers - Margarita Engle　*y* 761

HOTEL WORKER

Hannah
The Clockwork Three - Matthew Kirby　*c, y* 249

HOUSEHOLDER

Lord Greave
The Poisoned House - Michael Ford　*y* 770

HOUSEKEEPER

Cat
Three by the Sea - Mini Grey　*p, c* 179

Mrs. Cotton
The Poisoned House - Michael Ford　*y* 770

Fortitude
Wisdom's Kiss: A Thrilling and Romantic Adventure Incorporating Magic, Villainy and a Cat - Catherine Gilbert Murdock　*y* 959

Iris
Crossing the Tracks - Barbara Stuber　*y* 1111

HOUSEWIFE

Radley, Helen
The Radleys: A Novel - Matt Haig　*y* 813

HUMAN

Bookchild, Rossamund
Factotum - D.M. Cornish　*y* 707

Flynn, Truman
The Space Between - Brenna Yovanoff　*y* 1193

Humphrey
The Christmas Giant - Steve Light　*p, c* 279

Jacob, Abba
Snook Alone - Marilyn Nelson　*c* 349

Leetree
The Christmas Giant - Steve Light　*p, c* 279

Stewart, Tate
The Replacement - Brenna Yovanoff　*y* 1194

HUNTER

Deuce
Enclave - Ann Aguirre　*y* 599

Europe
Factotum - D.M. Cornish　*y* 707

Fade
Enclave - Ann Aguirre　*y* 599

Hawthorne, Gale
Catching Fire - Suzanne Collins　*y* 699
Mockingjay - Suzanne Collins　*y* 700

Imura, Benny
Rot and Ruin - Jonathan Maberry　*y* 914

Kaisa
Ash - Malinda Lo　*y* 902

Lowood, Cas
Anna Dressed in Blood - Kendare Blake　*y* 640

March, Rosie
Sisters Red - Jackson Pearce　*y* 1000

March, Scarlett
Sisters Red - Jackson Pearce　*y* 1000

Ryves, Nick
The Demon's Lexicon - Sarah Rees Brennan　*y* 657

Silas
Sisters Red - Jackson Pearce　*y* 1000

HYPNOTIST

Orrery, Madame
The Story of Cirrus Flux - Matthew Skelton　*c, y* 469

IMMIGRANT

Abdul
No Safe Place - Deborah Ellis　*y* 757

Calogero
Alligator Bayou - Donna Jo Napoli　*y* 968

Kahlo, Frida
Me, Frida - Amy Novesky　*c* 360

Liu, Ray
Money Boy - Paul Yee　*y* 1188

Papa
Star in the Forest - Laura Resau　*c, y* 412

Rivera, Diego
Me, Frida - Amy Novesky　*c* 360

IMMORTAL

Nastasya
Immortal Beloved - Cate Tiernan　1130

Reyn
Immortal Beloved - Cate Tiernan　1130

IMPOVERISHED

Dance, Jeremy "Lil J"
Dope Sick - Walter Dean Myers　*y* 962

Gray, Penelope
Penny Dreadful - Laurel Snyder　*c, y* 477

Mildew, Arthur
Tumtum and Nutmeg: Adventures beyond Nutmouse Hall - Emily Bearn　*c, y* 29

Mildew, Lucy
Tumtum and Nutmeg: Adventures beyond Nutmouse Hall - Emily Bearn　*c, y* 29

Ming
The Runaway Wok - Ying Chang Compestine　*c* 76

INDIAN

Quebrado
Hurricane Dancers - Margarita Engle　*y* 761

Samar "Sam"
Shine, Coconut Moon - Neesha Meminger   *y* 946

INSECT

Ladybug
I'm the Best - Lucy Cousins   *p, c* 91

INSPECTOR

Smithers, Frank
Burn My Heart - Beverley Naidoo   *c, y* 967

INVENTOR

Bell, Cricket
Lola and the Boy Next Door - Stephanie Perkins   1007

Melon, Adam "Melonhead"
Melonhead - Katy Kelly   *c* 240

Lord Umber
Happenstance Found - P. W. Catanese   *c, y* 63

JOURNALIST

Aguilar, Marcelus
Gringolandia - Lyn Miller-Lachmann   *y* 950

Bly, Nellie
Around the World - Matt Phelan   *c, y* 388

Faustino, Paul
Exposure - Mal Peet   *y* 1002

Mitch
Payback Time - Carl Deuker   *y* 732

Sparksmith, Freddie
Calamity Jack - Shannon Hale   *c, y* 187

Tina
The Morgue and Me - John C. Ford   *y* 769

KIDNAP VICTIM

Mr. Burrows
The Apothecary - Maile Meloy   *y* 945

Cunningham, Lucy
Wish You Were Dead - Todd Strasser   *y* 1107

Gemma
Stolen - Lucy Christopher   *y* 689

Greene, Rowena
Once a Witch - Carolyn MacCullough   *y* 915

Jack
The Marbury Lens - Andrew Smith   *y* 1087

Jody
Once Was Lost - Sara Zarr   *y* 1196

Nico
Cryer's Cross - Lisa McMann   *y* 942

Orville, Benjamin Franklin
Murder Afloat - Jane Leslie Conly   *c, y* 77

Stephanie
Taken - Norah McClintock   *y* 932

Wilder, Cheyenne
Girl, Stolen - April Henry   *y* 835

KIDNAPPER

Carlos
Take Me to the River - Will Hobbs   *c, y* 841

Mr. Glueskin
Half World - Hiromi Goto   *y* 799

Griffin
Girl, Stolen - April Henry   *y* 835

Talavera, Bernardino de
Hurricane Dancers - Margarita Engle   *y* 761

Ty
Stolen - Lucy Christopher   *y* 689

KNIGHT

Thomas
Thomas and the Dragon Queen - Shutta Crum   *c* 96

LANDLORD

Grayson, Mr.
Burn My Heart - Beverley Naidoo   *c, y* 967

LAWYER

Donck, Bartleby
City of Orphans - Avi   *c, y* 15

LEADER

Belancort, Juniper
Nightshade City - Hilary Wagner   *c, y* 548

Big Sister Nor
For the Win - Cory Doctorow   *y* 737

Coyle, Mistress
Monsters of Men - Patrick Ness   *y* 974

Father Ramon
The Reformed Vampire Support Group - Catherine Jinks   *y* 859

Mayor
Monsters of Men - Patrick Ness   *y* 974

Mugabe, Robert
Out of Shadows - Jason Wallace   *y* 1146

Todd
Monsters of Men - Patrick Ness   *y* 974

Triana
The Comet's Curse - Dom Testa   *y* 1124

Uido
Island's End - Padma Venkatraman   *y* 1138

Viola
Monsters of Men - Patrick Ness   *y* 974

LEARNING DISABLED CHILD

Travis
Bluefish - Pat Schmatz   *y* 1060

Trisha
Junkyard Wonders - Patricia Polacco   *c, y* 396

LESBIAN

Alyssa
She Loves You, She Loves You Not... - Julie Anne Peters   1011

Jin-Ae
Crash into Me - Albert Borris   *y* 649

Rockett, Esme
Sister Mischief - Laura Goode   *y* 797

LIBRARIAN

Murphy, Charlotte
Americus - M.K. Reed   *y* 1032

Miss O'Grady
Busing Brewster - Richard Michelson   *c* 329

LION

Lion, The
Willoughby and the Lion - Greg Foley   *p, c* 147

LOVER

Allie
Boyfriends with Girlfriends - Alex Sanchez   *y* 1056

Dade
The Vast Fields of Ordinary - Nick Burd   *y* 667

Diamond
Green Witch - Alice Hoffman   *y* 842

Dodola
Habibi - Craig Thompson   *y* 1126

Fox
Zenith - Julie Bertagna   *y* 633

Hemings, Sally
Jefferson's Sons: A Founding Father's Secret Children - Kimberly Brubaker Bradley   *c, y* 45

Jefferson, Thomas
Jefferson's Sons: A Founding Father's Secret Children - Kimberly Brubaker Bradley   *c, y* 45

Kid
Brooklyn, Burning - Steve Brezenoff   *y* 658

Kimiko
Boyfriends with Girlfriends - Alex Sanchez   *y* 1056

Lance
Boyfriends with Girlfriends - Alex Sanchez   *y* 1056

Lochan
Forbidden - Tabitha Suzuma   *y* 1116

Mara
Zenith - Julie Bertagna   *y* 633

Maya
Forbidden - Tabitha Suzuma   *y* 1116

Pablo
The Vast Fields of Ordinary - Nick Burd   *y* 667

Scout
Brooklyn, Burning - Steve Brezenoff   *y* 658

Sergio
Boyfriends with Girlfriends - Alex Sanchez   *y* 1056

Zam
Habibi - Craig Thompson   *y* 1126

MAGICIAN

Digger
Star Crossed - Elizabeth C. Bunce   *y* 665

Eff
Thirteenth Child - Patricia C. Wrede   *y* 1176

Lan
Thirteenth Child - Patricia C. Wrede   *y* 1176

Lovelace, Simon
The Amulet of Samarkand: A Bartimaeus Graphic Novel - Jonathan Stroud   *c, y* 499

Mariamne
Poisoned Honey: A Story of Mary Magdalene - Beatrice Gormley   *y* 798

Sharpe, Cassel
Red Glove - Holly Black   *y* 636

Sinda/Nalia
The False Princess - Ellis O'Neal   *y* 986

Taisin
Huntress - Malinda Lo   *y* 903

MAN

Fred
The Honeybee Man - Lela Nargi   *c* 345

Mizuno
Ooku: The Inner Chambers, Volume 1 - Fumi Yoshinaga   *y* 1189

MANAGER

Bayliss, Jimmy Lee
Scat - Carl Hiaasen   *c, y* 203

Pesto
Soul Enchilada - David Macinnis Gill   *y* 790

Susie
Boys, Bears, and a Serious Pair of Hiking Boots - Abby McDonald   *y* 935

MARTIAL ARTS EXPERT

Spencer, Ellie
Guardian of the Dead - Karen Healey   *y* 831

MENTALLY CHALLENGED PERSON

Christy
The Brothers Story - Katherine Sturtevant   *y* 1112

Innocent
Now Is the Time for Running - Michael Williams   *y* 1168

Rose
Chime - Franny Billingsley   *y* 634

MENTALLY ILL PERSON

Aparacio, Will
Riding Invisible - Sandra Alonzo   *y* 604

Bancroft, Ben
Now Playing: Stoner & Spaz II - Ron Koertge   *y* 883

Border, Clarence
I'll Be There - Holly Goldberg Sloan   *y* 1083

Fletcher, Kendall
Cryer's Cross - Lisa McMann   *y* 942

Lord Greave
The Poisoned House - Michael Ford   *y* 770

Kitrell, Will
Breathless - Jessica Warman   *y* 1149

Lizzie
Glimpse - Carol Lynch Williams   *y* 1163

Martin, Jake
Compulsion - Heidi Ayarbe   *y* 617

Momma
Miles from Ordinary - Carol Lynch Williams   *y* 1164

Solomon, Dani
The Babysitter Murders - Janet Ruth Young   1190

Zelda
How I Stole Johnny Depp's Alien Girlfriend - Gary Ghislain   *y* 786

MERCHANT

Unnamed Character
The Third Gift - Linda Sue Park   *c* 376

MIDWIFE

Stone, Gaia
Birthmarked - Caragh M. O'Brien   *y* 982
Prized - Caragh M. O'Brien   *y* 983

MIGRANT WORKER

Mari
Return to Sender - Julia Alvarez   *c, y* 7

MILITARY PERSONNEL

Carl, Thomas
Eddie's War - Carol Fisher Saller   *c, y* 439

Charlie
The Storm before Atlanta - Karen Schwabach   *c, y* 454

Chiko
Bamboo People - Mitali Perkins   *y* 1006

Curzon
Forge - Laurie Halse Anderson   *y* 607

DeGroot, Jeremy
The Storm before Atlanta - Karen Schwabach   *c, y* 454

Deryn
Behemoth - Scott Westerfeld   *y* 1154

Dogie
Keeper - Kathi Appelt   *c, y* 10

Duffy, Matt
Purple Heart - Patricia McCormick   *y* 933

Durango
Black Hole Sun - David Macinnis Gill   *y* 789

Greave, Samuel
The Poisoned House - Michael Ford   *y* 770

Jorgensen, Ollie
Crossing Stones - Helen Frost   *y* 777

June
Legend - Marie Lu   *y* 908

Katznelson, Boaz
The Things a Brother Knows - Dana Reinhardt   *y* 1036

Mallory, Jake
Five 4ths of July - Pat Hughes   *y* 850

Norman, Frank
Crossing Stones - Helen Frost   *y* 777

O'Mara, Ben
Bull Rider - Suzanne Morgan Williams   *y* 1169

Quinn
Picture the Dead - Adele Griffin   *y* 808

Randall
Caleb's Wars - David L. Dudley   *y* 746

Sampson, Deborah
Soldier's Secret: The Story of Deborah Sampson - Sheila Solomon Klass   *y* 880

Tips
Wisdom's Kiss: A Thrilling and Romantic Adventure Incorporating Magic, Villainy and a Cat - Catherine Gilbert Murdock   *y* 959

Todd
The Ask and the Answer - Patrick Ness   *y* 975

Tu Reh
Bamboo People - Mitali Perkins   *y* 1006

Will
Picture the Dead - Adele Griffin   *y* 808

MISSING PERSON

Daisy
The Blood Lie - Shirley Reva Vernick   *y* 1139

Mehdi
Zahra's Paradise - Amir Amir   *y* 606

Novak, Darcy
Dirty Laundry - Daniel Ehrenhaft   *y* 754

Shelby
Nickel Plated - Aric Davis   *y* 721

MODEL

Khadija
Where I Belong - Gillian Cross   *y* 712

MOLE

Mole
I'm the Best - Lucy Cousins   *p, c* 91
Mouse and Mole, Fine Feathered Friends - Wong Herbert Lee   *c* 269

MONSTER

Bayou
Bayou: Volume 1 - Jeremy Love   *y* 907

Blunderboar
Calamity Jack - Shannon Hale   *c, y* 187

Bog
Bayou: Volume 1 - Jeremy Love   *y* 907

Bookchild, Rossamund
Factotum - D.M. Cornish   *y* 707

Frankenstein
Department 19 - Will Hill   *y* 838

Jellaby
Jellaby: Monster in the City - Kean Soo   *c, y* 479

Monster
A Monster Calls - Patrick Ness   *y* 976

MOTHER

Adnoid, Beth
The Secret of Zoom - Lynne Jonell   *c, y* 228

Ami
Big Red Lollipop - Rukhsana Khan   *p, c* 244

Bianchi, Diana
Virtuosity - Jessica Martinez   *y* 925

Mrs. Carpenter
Department 19 - Will Hill   *y* 838

Mrs. Carter
Gator on the Loose! - Sue Stauffacher   *c, y* 487

Cecile "Sister Izilla"
One Crazy Summer - Rita Williams-Garcia   *c, y* 569

Dexter, Sandy
Where I Belong - Gillian Cross   *y* 712

Mrs. Ellis-Chan
Bobby versus Girls (Accidentally) - Lisa Yee   *c, y* 587

Estby, Helga
The Year We Were Famous - Carole Estby Dagg   *y* 718

Mrs. Finnemore
Edwin Speaks Up - April Stevens   *c* 495

Heffley, Susan
Diary of a Wimpy Kid: Cabin Fever - Jeff Kinney   *c, y* 248

Hemings, Sally
Jefferson's Sons: A Founding Father's Secret Children - Kimberly Brubaker Bradley   *c, y* 45

June
A Month of Sundays - Ruth White   *y* 558

Mrs. Kaufman
The Beginning of After - Jennifer Castle   *y* 681

Mrs. Liebig
After the Train - Gloria Whelan   *y* 557

Lilith
The Space Between - Brenna Yovanoff   *y* 1193

Liz
Jumping Off Swings - Jo Knowles   y 881

Ma
The 10 PM Question - Kate De Goldi   y 723
The Money We'll Save - Brock Cole   c 73
Why I Fight - J. Adams Oaks   y 987

Mabis
Witchlanders - Lena Coakley   y 695

Mam
The Christmas Eve Ghost - Shirley Hughes   c 217

Mama
Busing Brewster - Richard Michelson   c 329
Lost - Jacqueline Davies   y 720
Mommy, Mama and Me - Leslea
    Newman   p, c 356
Somebody Everybody Listens To - Suzanne
    Supplee   y 1115
Star in the Forest - Laura Resau   c, y 412
This Thing Called the Future - J. L.
    Powers   y 1020
Waiting for the Magic - Patricia
    MacLachlan   c 293

Mami
Muchacho - LouAnne Johnson   y 860

Marie, Meggie
Keeper - Kathi Appelt   c, y 10

Maura
*Three Rivers Rising: A Novel of the Johnstown
    Flood* - Jame Richards   y 1040

McFee, Rayka "Mama"
Close to Famous - Joan Bauer   c, y 623

Melanie
Don't Want to Go! - Shirley Hughes   p, c 216

Mom
Amy and Roger's Epic Detour - Morgan
    Matson   y 927
Are You Awake? - Sophie Blackall   p, c 40
Bitter Melon - Cara Chow   y 688
The Dancing Pancake - Eileen Spinelli   c, y 481
Dirty Little Secrets - C.J. Omololu   y 991
Efrain's Secret - Sofia Quintero   y 1027
Hush, Hush - Becca Fitzpatrick   y 767
Lexie - Audrey Couloumbis   c, y 87
Mission Unstoppable - Dan Gutman   c, y 183
Sorta Like a Rock Star - Matthew Quick   y 1026
The Summer I Turned Pretty - Jenny Han   y 817
This World We Live In - Susan Beth
    Pfeffer   y 1012
You Are Here - Jennifer E. Smith   y 1089

Momma
Miles from Ordinary - Carol Lynch
    Williams   y 1164

Mommy
Mommy, Mama and Me - Leslea
    Newman   p, c 356

Moon, Millicent
Through Her Eyes - Jennifer Archer   y 610

Mother
The Color of Earth - Kim Dong Hwa   y 852
Silver Phoenix: Beyond the Kingdom of Xia -
    Cindy Pon   y 1017

Mum
The Demon's Lexicon - Sarah Rees
    Brennan   y 657
Don't Want to Go! - Shirley Hughes   p, c 216

Mummy
Dessert First - Hallie Durand   c 123

O'Rourke, Molly
Sparrow Road - Sheila O'Connor   c, y 985

Pale Queen, The
The Call - Michael Grant   c, y 170

Penelopeia
King of Ithaka - Tracy Barrett   y 621

Radley, Helen
The Radleys: A Novel - Matt Haig   y 813

Reinstein, Jerri
*Stupid Fast: The Summer I Went from a Joke to a
    Jock* - Geoff Herbach   y 836

Rose, Betty
A Month of Sundays - Ruth White   y 558

Mrs. Roux
Stones for My Father - Trilby Kent   y 869

Dr. Shumway
The Doom Machine - Mark Teague   c, y 510

Snider, Kat
The Brooklyn Nine: A Novel in Nine Innings - Alan
    Gratz   c, y 171

Tia
A Small Free Kiss in the Dark - Glenda
    Millard   y 948

Van Dine, Sandy
Callie's Rules - Naomi Flink Zucker   c, y 594

Vicky
Lexie - Audrey Couloumbis   c, y 87

Wolf, Mama
Big Wolf and Little Wolf - Sharon Phillips
    Denslow   c 108

Zahra
Zahra's Paradise - Amir Amir   y 606

MOUNTAINEER

P.K.
Jump - Elisa Carbone   y 673

MOUSE

Beatrice
Secrets at Sea - Richard Peck   c, y 383

Benny
Benny and Penny in the Big No-No! - Geoffrey
    Hayes   c 196

Celeste
*A Nest for Celeste: A Story about Art, Inspiration,
    and the Meaning of Home* - Henry
    Cole   c, y 74

Fredle
Young Fredle - Cynthia Voigt   c, y 545

Helena
Secrets at Sea - Richard Peck   c, y 383

Hildegarde
Bless This Mouse - Lois Lowry   c, y 289

Ignatius
Bless This Mouse - Lois Lowry   c, y 289

Lamont
Secrets at Sea - Richard Peck   c, y 383

Little Mouse
Little Mouse Gets Ready - Jeff Smith   p, c 474

Louise
Secrets at Sea - Richard Peck   c, y 383

Mouse
Mouse and Mole, Fine Feathered Friends - Wong
    Herbert Lee   c 269
Three by the Sea - Mini Grey   p, c 179

Nutmeg
*Tumtum and Nutmeg: Adventures beyond Nutmouse
    Hall* - Emily Bearn   c, y 29

Penny
Benny and Penny in the Big No-No! - Geoffrey
    Hayes   c 196

Pip
The Cheshire Cheese Cat: A Dickens of a Tale -
    Carmen Agra Deedy   c, y 105

Tumtum
*Tumtum and Nutmeg: Adventures beyond Nutmouse
    Hall* - Emily Bearn   c, y 29

Wagner
Pearl and Wagner: One Funny Day - Kate
    McMullan   c 321

MURDERER

Mayor
Monsters of Men - Patrick Ness   y 974

Sandifer, Robert "Yummy"
Yummy: The Last Days of a Southside Shorty - G.
    Neri   y 973

Scotty
Desert Angel - Charlie Price   y 1025

MUSICIAN

Abramson, Ari
*So Punk Rock (and Other Ways to Disappoint Your
    Mother)* - Micol Ostow   y 995

Adam
Where She Went - Gayle Forman   y 771

Alpers, Andi
Revolution - Jennifer Donnelly   y 739

Armstrong, Will
Will - Maria Boyd   y 652

Beach, Saint Louis Armstrong
Saint Louis Armstrong Beach - Brenda
    Woods   c, y 1174

Bianchi, Carmen
Virtuosity - Jessica Martinez   y 925

Coop
Beat the Band - Don Calame   y 670

Cupcake
Bake Sale - Sara Varon   c, y 539

Dave
The Reformed Vampire Support Group - Catherine
    Jinks   y 859

Forest, Vray
Earthgirl - Jennifer Cowan   y 710

Giuseppe
The Clockwork Three - Matthew Kirby   c, y 249

Joe
The Sky Is Everywhere - Jandy Nelson   y 970

Kate
The Kind of Friends We Used to Be - Frances
    O'Roark Dowell   c, y 116

King, Jeremy
Virtuosity - Jessica Martinez   y 925

Kipper, Moxie Roosevelt
The Reinvention of Moxie Roosevelt - Elizabeth
    Cody Kimmel   c, y 246

Mackee, Thomas
The Piper's Son - Melina Marchetta   y 922

Matt
Beat the Band - Don Calame   y 670

Mia
If I Stay - Gayle Forman   y 772
Where She Went - Gayle Forman   y 771

Regina

The Girl Who Became a Beatle - Greg Taylor   y 1117

Sean

Beat the Band - Don Calame   y 670

Towfeek, Jamilah "Jamie"

Ten Things I Hate about Me - Randa Abdel-Fattah   y 595

Whitcomb, Jared

The House of Tomorrow - Peter Bognanni   y 646

MYTHICAL CREATURE

Anybody, Rob

I Shall Wear Midnight - Terry Pratchett   y 1021

Bobs, The

The Prince of Fenway Park - Julianna Baggott   c, y 18

Brax

King of Ithaka - Tracy Barrett   y 621

Cunning Man, The

I Shall Wear Midnight - Terry Pratchett   y 1021

Daft Wullie

I Shall Wear Midnight - Terry Pratchett   y 1021

Doyle, Mackie

The Replacement - Brenna Yovanoff   y 1194

Durindana

Small Persons with Wings - Ellen Booraem   c, y 44

Ebon

Pegasus - Robin McKinley   y 940

Fidius

Small Persons with Wings - Ellen Booraem   c, y 44

Inepta

Small Persons with Wings - Ellen Booraem   c, y 44

Jason

The Lost Hero - Rick Riordan   c, y 417

Jeannie

I Shall Wear Midnight - Terry Pratchett   y 1021

Leo

The Lost Hero - Rick Riordan   c, y 417

Marie, Meggie

Keeper - Kathi Appelt   c, y 10

Piper

The Lost Hero - Rick Riordan   c, y 417

Underhill, April

April and Esme: Tooth Fairies - Bob Graham   p, c 168

Underhill, Esme

April and Esme: Tooth Fairies - Bob Graham   p, c 168

Wee Mad Arthur

I Shall Wear Midnight - Terry Pratchett   y 1021

William the Gonnagle

I Shall Wear Midnight - Terry Pratchett   y 1021

Zagabog

The Flint Heart - Katherine Paterson   c, y 380

NARRATOR

Adam

Where She Went - Gayle Forman   y 771

Amiq

My Name Is Not Easy - Debby Dahl Edwardson   y 749

Baby Bear

Me and You - Anthony Browne   p, c 51

Chickie

My Name Is Not Easy - Debby Dahl Edwardson   y 749

Coop

Beat the Band - Don Calame   y 670

Donna

My Name Is Not Easy - Debby Dahl Edwardson   y 749

Emma

My Mom Is Trying to Ruin My Life - Kate Feiffer   c 135

Gonzalez, Zachariah Johnson

Last Night I Sang to the Monster - Benjamin Alire Saenz   y 1054

Green, Min

Why We Broke Up - Daniel Handler   y 821

Hope

Glimpse - Carol Lynch Williams   y 1163

Katznelson, Levi

The Things a Brother Knows - Dana Reinhardt   y 1036

Kelly

She Said/She Saw - Norah McClintock   y 931

Kinahan, Jonathan "Jono"

Long Story Short - Siobhan Parkinson   y 998

Lucas

Surface Tension: A Novel in Four Summers - Brent Runyon   y 1049

Luke

My Name Is Not Easy - Debby Dahl Edwardson   y 749

Owen

Crash into Me - Albert Borris   y 649

Roger

Yummy: The Last Days of a Southside Shorty - G. Neri   y 973

Small, Cleo

Underpants On My Head - Jessica Harper   c 192

Sonny

My Name Is Not Easy - Debby Dahl Edwardson   y 749

Tegan

She Said/She Saw - Norah McClintock   y 931

Tyler

Return to Sender - Julia Alvarez   c, y 7

Unnamed Character

I Will Come Back for You: A Family in Hiding during World War II - Marisabina Russo   c 433

Mommy, Mama and Me - Leslea Newman   p, c 356

RRRalph - Lois Ehlert   p, c 124

These Hands - Margaret H. Mason   c 304

Varderman, Paul

The Knife That Killed Me - Anthony McGowan   c, y 936

NATURALIST

Audubon, John James

A Nest for Celeste: A Story about Art, Inspiration, and the Meaning of Home - Henry Cole   c, y 74

Louise

The Sundown Rule - Wendy Townsend   c, y 522

Tate, Calpurnia Virginia

The Evolution of Calpurnia Tate - Jacqueline Kelly   c, y 239

NEIGHBOR

Aaron

Miles from Ordinary - Carol Lynch Williams   y 1164

Barling, John

Where Things Come Back - John Corey Whaley   y 1155

Bell, Cricket

Lola and the Boy Next Door - Stephanie Perkins   1007

Billy

Out of the Blue - S.L. Rottman   y 1043

Birnbaum, Henry "Hen"

Friend Is Not a Verb - Daniel Ehrenhaft   y 753

Delilah

Missing on Superstition Mountain - Elise Broach   c, y 47

Douglas

Neil Armstrong Is My Uncle and Other Lies Muscle Man McGinty Told Me - Nan Marino   c, y 299

Dowdel, Grandma

A Season of Gifts - Richard Peck   c, y 384

Eugene

Zelda and Ivy: Keeping Secrets - Laura McGee Kvasnosky   c 264

Gabby

Angel in My Pocket - Ilene Cooper   c, y 82

Jester, Owen

The Fantastic Secret of Owen Jester - Barbara O'Connor   c, y 366

Kaufman, David

The Beginning of After - Jennifer Castle   y 681

Laurel

The Beginning of After - Jennifer Castle   y 681

Madame Albirtha

The Secret River - Marjorie Kinnan Rawlings   c 407

Maureen

Butterfly - Sonya Hartnett   y 826

Melina

Benny and Penny in the Big No-No! - Geoffrey Hayes   c 196

Nick

Princess Posey and the First Grade Parade - Stephanie Greene   c 176

Nolan, Lola

Lola and the Boy Next Door - Stephanie Perkins   1007

Rose

A Little Wanting Song - Cath Crowley   y 713

Silas

Sisters Red - Jackson Pearce   y 1000

Timmo

Small Persons with Wings - Ellen Booraem   c, y 44

Tyler

Princess Posey and the First Grade Parade - Stephanie Greene   c 176

Viola

The Fantastic Secret of Owen Jester - Barbara O'Connor   c, y 366

Wood, Emma

Friend Is Not a Verb - Daniel Ehrenhaft   y 753

NEPHEW

Creedle, Jack

The Doom Machine - Mark Teague   c, y 510

Jack
The Mostly True Story of Jack - Kelly Barnhill   c, y 23

Jonah
No Safe Place - Deborah Ellis   y 757

Ogilvie, Oscar
On the Blue Comet - Rosemary Wells   c, y 554

Richards, Alton
The Cardturner: A Novel about a King, a Queen, and a Joker - Louis Sachar   y 1053

NEWSPAPER CARRIER

Esperer, Fatima
The Orange Houses - Paul Griffin   y 810

Geless, Maks
City of Orphans - Avi   c, y 15

NIECE

Blackstone, Ginny
The Last Little Blue Envelope - Maureen Johnson   y 861

Blair, Maggie
The Betrayal of Maggie Blair - Elizabeth Laird   y 889

Goodnight, Amy
Texas Gothic - Rosemary Clement-Moore   y 693

Goodnight, Phin
Texas Gothic - Rosemary Clement-Moore   y 693

Lacey
Miles from Ordinary - Carol Lynch Williams   y 1164

Rose, April Garnet
A Month of Sundays - Ruth White   y 558

Wiggins, Emily
Emily's Fortune - Phyllis Reynolds Naylor   c, y 346

NOBLEMAN

de Chaucy, William
Warped - Maurissa Guibord   y 812

Lord Gyaar
The Returning - Christine Hinwood   y 840

Roland
I Shall Wear Midnight - Terry Pratchett   y 1021

NOBLEWOMAN

Eleanora
Princess of Glass - Jessica Day George   y 785

Lady Keepsake
I Shall Wear Midnight - Terry Pratchett   y 1021

Keepsake, Letitia
I Shall Wear Midnight - Terry Pratchett   y 1021

Sido
The Silver Blade - Sally Gardner   y 158

NURSE

Byrne, Anne
The Complete Essex County - Jeff Lemire   y 896

Everdeen, Primrose
Mockingjay - Suzanne Collins   y 700

Kate
Three Rivers Rising: A Novel of the Johnstown Flood - Jame Richards   y 1040

OBJECT

Bob
Rhyming Dust Bunnies - Jan Thomas   p, c 513

Dave
Pig Kahuna - Jennifer Sattler   p, c 443

Ed
Rhyming Dust Bunnies - Jan Thomas   p, c 513

Gingerbread Man, The
The Gingerbread Man Loose in the School - Laura Murray   p, c 340

Jessie
Subway Story - Julia Sarcone-Roach   c 442

Ned
Rhyming Dust Bunnies - Jan Thomas   p, c 513

Ted
Rhyming Dust Bunnies - Jan Thomas   p, c 513

OCCULTIST

Klein, Andromeda
Andromeda Klein - Frank Portman   y 1019

OPOSSUM

Epossumondas
Epossumondas Plays Possum - Coleen Salley   c 440

Possum
Lousy Rotten Stinkin' Grapes - Margie Palatini   c 373

ORGANIZED CRIME FIGURE

Nate
Strings Attached - Judy Blundell   y 643

ORPHAN

Aisling "Ash"
Ash - Malinda Lo   y 902

Bartolomeo
Winter's End - Jean-Claude Mourlevat   y 956

Blair, Maggie
The Betrayal of Maggie Blair - Elizabeth Laird   y 889

Bookchild, Rossamund
Factotum - D.M. Cornish   y 707

Chip
The Giant Slayer - Iain Lawrence   c, y 267

Crutchfield, Florence
The Ghost of Crutchfield Hall - Mary Downing Hahn   c, y 186

de Boncouer, Eugenie
The Pale Assassin - Patricia Elliott   y 756

Delana
Finding Family - Tonya Bolden   c, y 42

Deryn
Leviathan - Scott Westerfeld   y 1153

Digger
Star Crossed - Elizabeth C. Bunce   y 665

Dodola
Habibi - Craig Thompson   y 1126

Duchene, Peter Augustus
The Magician's Elephant - Kate DiCamillo   c, y 112

Emma
The Emerald Atlas - John Stephens   c, y 493

Felix
Once - Morris Gleitzman   y 791

Figg, Homer P.
The Mostly True Adventures of Homer P. Figg - Rodman Philbrick   c, y 389

Flux, Cirrus
The Story of Cirrus Flux - Matthew Skelton   c, y 469

Grayson, Aoife
The Iron Thorn - Caitlin Kittredge   y 879

Helen
Winter's End - Jean-Claude Mourlevat   y 956

Henry, Will
The Isle of Blood - Rick Yancey   y 1181
The Monstrumologist - Rick Yancey   y 1182

Hood, Avery
Low Red Moon - Ivy Devlin   y 733

Jackson
Emily's Fortune - Phyllis Reynolds Naylor   c, y 346

Jennie
Picture the Dead - Adele Griffin   y 808

Kate
The Emerald Atlas - John Stephens   c, y 493
Plain Kate - Erin Bow   y 650

Ky
Matched - Ally Condie   y 703

Laurel
The Beginning of After - Jennifer Castle   y 681

Liesl
Liesl and Po - Lauren Oliver   c, y 369

Lili
Peace, Locomotion - Jacqueline Woodson   c, y 581

Lonnie
Peace, Locomotion - Jacqueline Woodson   c, y 581

March, Rosie
Sisters Red - Jackson Pearce   y 1000

March, Scarlett
Sisters Red - Jackson Pearce   y 1000

Mary
The Forest of Hands and Teeth - Carrie Ryan   y 1051

Mercier, Kate
Die for Me - Amy Plum   y 1016

Mia
Where She Went - Gayle Forman   y 771

Michael
The Emerald Atlas - John Stephens   c, y 493

Milena
Winter's End - Jean-Claude Mourlevat   y 956

Milos
Winter's End - Jean-Claude Mourlevat   y 956

Otis
Bird in a Box - Andrea Davis Pinkney   c, y 392

Pancho
The Last Summer of The Death Warriors - Francisco X. Stork   y 1104

Pandora
The Story of Cirrus Flux - Matthew Skelton   c, y 469

Patrick
Newsgirl - Liza Ketchum   c, y 243

Pina
Take Me with You - Carolyn Marsden   c, y 302

Prince Aleksander "Alek"
Leviathan - Scott Westerfeld   y 1153

Quebrado
Hurricane Dancers - Margarita Engle   y 761

Susanna
Take Me with You - Carolyn Marsden   *c, y* 302

Tamper, Abigail "Abi"
The Poisoned House - Michael Ford   *y* 770

Travis
Bluefish - Pat Schmatz   *y* 1060

Trei
The Floating Islands - Rachel Neumeier   *y* 978

Wiggins, Emily
Emily's Fortune - Phyllis Reynolds
   Naylor   *c, y* 346

Zam
Habibi - Craig Thompson   *y* 1126

Zelda
Then - Morris Gleitzman   *y* 792

Zoe
Wild Things - Clay Carmichael   *c, y* 60

OUTCAST

Alexander "Xan"
Angry Young Man - Chris Lynch   *y* 912

Barton, Neal
Americus - M.K. Reed   *y* 1032

Bean, Isabelle
Falling In - Frances O'Roark Dowell   *c, y* 115

Bean "Pearl"
Pearl - Jo Knowles   *y* 882

Brightman, Sky
Saving Sky - Diane Stanley   *c, y* 486

Gray, Austin
The Sweetheart of Prosper County - Jill S.
   Alexander   *y* 600

Helen
Beat the Band - Don Calame   *y* 670

Henry
Pearl - Jo Knowles   *y* 882

Jess
Into the Wild Nerd Yonder - Julie Halpern   *y* 815

Jones, Jasper
Jasper Jones - Craig Silvey   *y* 1079

Kate
Plain Kate - Erin Bow   *y* 650

Melanie
Half World - Hiromi Goto   *y* 799

Prendergast, Sebastian
The House of Tomorrow - Peter Bognanni   *y* 646

Rye, Amelia E.
The Private Thoughts of Amelia E. Rye - Bonnie
   Shimko   *c, y* 1075

Sykes, Tamika
The Orange Houses - Paul Griffin   *y* 810

OUTLAW

Bain
The Runaway Dragon - Kate Coombs   *c, y* 79

Bart, Backward
Dust Devil - Anne Isaacs   *c* 219

Poetic Pete
Stagecoach Sal - Deborah Hopkinson   *c* 212

OVERSEER

Berglund, Viktor
Sparrow Road - Sheila O'Connor   *c, y* 985

PANDA

Panda
Hooray for Amanda and Her Alligator! - Mo
   Willems   *p, c* 566

PATIENT

Claire, Marie
Queen of Hearts - Martha Brooks   *y* 661

Cosgrove, Louisa
Wildthorn - Jane Eagland   *y* 748

Derek, Captain
The Romeo and Juliet Code - Phoebe
   Stone   *c, y* 496

Madeline
Recovery Road - Blake Nelson   *y* 969

Stewart
Recovery Road - Blake Nelson   *y* 969

Tess
Between Here and Forever - Elizabeth
   Scott   *y* 1065

Unnamed Character
The Gardener - S.A. Bodeen   *y* 645

Whitcomb, Jared
The House of Tomorrow - Peter Bognanni   *y* 646

PENGUIN

Edna
A Penguin Story - Antoinette Portis   *p, c* 397

Tacky
Tacky Goes to Camp - Helen Lester   *c* 271

PHOTOGRAPHER

Blake
Flash Burnout - L.K. Madigan   *y* 919

Mr. Geist
Picture the Dead - Adele Griffin   *y* 808

Liz
Exposed - Kimberly Marcus   *y* 923

PIG

Bud
Pearl and Wagner: One Funny Day - Kate
   McMullan   *c* 321

Bumble-Ardy
Bumble-Ardy - Maurice Sendak   *p, c* 459

Dink
Pig Kahuna - Jennifer Sattler   *p, c* 443

Fergus
Pig Kahuna - Jennifer Sattler   *p, c* 443

Piggie
I Broke My Trunk! - Mo Willems   *p, c* 567
Pigs Make Me Sneeze! - Mo Willems   *p, c* 565

Unnamed Character
Adios, Tricycle - Susan Middleton Elya   *p, c* 128

PILOT

Carl, Thomas
Eddie's War - Carol Fisher Saller   *c, y* 439

PIRATE

Morrisey, Emer
The Dust of 100 Dogs - A.S. King   *y* 874

Talavera, Bernardino de
Hurricane Dancers - Margarita Engle   *y* 761

Tuck
Zenith - Julie Bertagna   *y* 633

Zeph
Raiders' Ransom - Emily Diamand   *y* 734

POLICE OFFICER

Achoo
Bloodhound - Tamora Pierce   *y* 1013

Clary
Bloodhound - Tamora Pierce   *y* 1013

Cooper, Beka
Bloodhound - Tamora Pierce   *y* 1013

Gaffione, Anthony
Dope Sick - Walter Dean Myers   *y* 962

Ironfoundersson, Carrot
I Shall Wear Midnight - Terry Pratchett   *y* 1021

Uberwald, Angua von
I Shall Wear Midnight - Terry Pratchett   *y* 1021

Wee Mad Arthur
I Shall Wear Midnight - Terry Pratchett   *y* 1021

POLITICAL FIGURE

Coin, Alma
Mockingjay - Suzanne Collins   *y* 700

Lincoln, Abraham
Our Abe Lincoln - Jim Aylesworth   *c* 17

Prentiss, Mayor
The Ask and the Answer - Patrick Ness   *y* 975

Snow, President Coriolanus
Catching Fire - Suzanne Collins   *y* 699
Mockingjay - Suzanne Collins   *y* 700

PORCUPINE

Porcupine
Lousy Rotten Stinkin' Grapes - Margie
   Palatini   *c* 373

PREGNANT TEENAGER

Biggs, Sydney
Every Little Thing in the World - Nina de
   Gramont   *y* 724

Crowe, Eleanor
Pregnant Pause - Han Nolan   *y* 979

Ellie
Jumping Off Swings - Jo Knowles   *y* 881

Kalinowski, Mandy
How to Save a Life - Sara Zarr   *y* 1197

PRISONER

Decath, Durrel
Liar's Moon - Elizabeth C. Bunce   *y* 666

Khalid
Guantanamo Boy - Anna Perera   *y* 1004

Liesl
Liesl and Po - Lauren Oliver   *c, y* 369

Lina
Between Shades of Gray - Ruta Sepetys   *y* 1071

Rico
Dope Sick - Walter Dean Myers   *y* 962

Sawyer, Alex
Lockdown - Alexander Gordon Smith   *y* 1085

Sonny
Bullet Point - Peter Abrahams   *y* 597

Stokes, Martin
Rikers High - Paul Volponi   *y* 1143

Todd
The Ask and the Answer - Patrick Ness   *y* 975

PRODUCER

Escamillo
Carmen - Walter Dean Myers   *y* 964

PROFESSOR

Dad
Mission Unstoppable - Dan Gutman   *c, y* 183

Fleabottom, Fenton J.
The Mostly True Adventures of Homer P. Figg -
   Rodman Philbrick   *c, y* 389

Meena
Words in the Dust - Trent Reedy   *y* 1033

PROPHETESS

Arilou
The Lost Conspiracy - Frances Hardinge   *c, y* 822

PROSPECTOR

Curry, Asa
Mercury - Hope Larson   *y* 892

PSYCHIC

Anders
The Mostly True Story of Jack - Kelly
   Barnhill   *c, y* 23

Duchannes, Lena
Beautiful Creatures - Kami Garcia   *y* 780

Evanjalin
Finnikin of the Rock - Melina Marchetta   *y* 921

Fern, Clarity "Clare"
Clarity - Kim Harrington   *y* 825

Jem
Numbers - Rachel Ward   *y* 1148

Klein, Andromeda
Andromeda Klein - Frank Portman   *y* 1019

Miss Sadie
Moon over Manifest - Clare Vanderpool   *c, y* 538

Silvey, Deacon
Low Red Moon - Caitlin R. Kiernan   *a* 872

QUAKER

Brewster, Jebediah
The Mostly True Adventures of Homer P. Figg -
   Rodman Philbrick   *c, y* 389

RABBIT

Chloe
Henry in Love - Peter McCarty   *p, c* 310

Pearl
Pearl and Wagner: One Funny Day - Kate
   McMullan   *c* 321

Rabbit
Little White Rabbit - Kevin Henkes   *p, c* 199

RAILROAD WORKER

Tucker, Gideon
Moon over Manifest - Clare Vanderpool   *c, y* 538

RANCHER

Hy
Texas Gothic - Rosemary Clement-Moore   *y* 693

RAT

Belancort, Juniper
Nightshade City - Hilary Wagner   *c, y* 548

Nightshade, Victor
Nightshade City - Hilary Wagner   *c, y* 548

Nightshade, Vincent
Nightshade City - Hilary Wagner   *c, y* 548

RAVEN

Maldwyn
The Cheshire Cheese Cat: A Dickens of a Tale -
   Carmen Agra Deedy   *c, y* 105

REBEL

Abernathy, Haymitch
Mockingjay - Suzanne Collins   *y* 700

Boggs
Mockingjay - Suzanne Collins   *y* 700

Cressida
Mockingjay - Suzanne Collins   *y* 700

Everdeen, Katniss
Mockingjay - Suzanne Collins   *y* 700

Hawthorne, Gale
Catching Fire - Suzanne Collins   *y* 699
Mockingjay - Suzanne Collins   *y* 700

Jewell, Elvis
The Small Adventure of Popeye and Elvis - Barbara
   O'Connor   *c, y* 365

Mellark, Peeta
Mockingjay - Suzanne Collins   *y* 700

Odair, Finnick
Mockingjay - Suzanne Collins   *y* 700

RECLUSE

Sally
Pearl - Jo Knowles   *y* 882

REFUGEE

Affeldt, Priska
*The Other Half of Life: A Novel Based on the True
   Story of the* MS St. Louis - Kim Ablon
   Whitney   *y* 1159

Alvarez, Lucia
The Red Umbrella - Christina Diaz
   Gonzalez   *y* 735

Daniel
Tropical Secrets: Holocaust Refugees in Cuba -
   Margarita Engle   *y* 760

Deo
Now Is the Time for Running - Michael
   Williams   *y* 1168

Dodola
Habibi - Craig Thompson   *y* 1126

Esperer, Fatima
The Orange Houses - Paul Griffin   *y* 810

Felix
Then - Morris Gleitzman   *y* 792

Fortune, Blaise "Koumail"
A Time of Miracles - Anne-Laure Bondoux   *y* 647

Fox
Zenith - Julie Bertagna   *y* 633

Gloria
A Time of Miracles - Anne-Laure Bondoux   *y* 647

Ha
Inside Out and Back Again - Thanhha
   Lai   *c, y* 888

Mara
Zenith - Julie Bertagna   *y* 633

Nya
A Long Walk to Water: Based on a True Story -
   Linda Sue Park   *c, y* 375

Oliver
Raven Summer - David Almond   *y* 602

Paloma
Tropical Secrets: Holocaust Refugees in Cuba -
   Margarita Engle   *y* 760

Salva
A Long Walk to Water: Based on a True Story -
   Linda Sue Park   *c, y* 375

Steiner, Stephie
A Faraway Island - Annika Thor   *c, y* 516

Tu Reh
Bamboo People - Mitali Perkins   *y* 1006

Tuck
Zenith - Julie Bertagna   *y* 633

Werkmann, Thomas
*The Other Half of Life: A Novel Based on the True
   Story of the* MS St. Louis - Kim Ablon
   Whitney   *y* 1159

Westerfeld, Edith
Is It Night or Day? - Fern Schumer
   Chapman   *y* 683

Zam
Habibi - Craig Thompson   *y* 1126

REINCARNATED PERSON

Edelman, Albert Baruch
My Life with the Lincolns - Gayle
   Brandeis   *c, y* 46

Edelman, Mina
My Life with the Lincolns - Gayle
   Brandeis   *c, y* 46

RELATIVE

Fraser, Josey
Mercury - Hope Larson   *y* 892

RELIGIOUS

Alis
Alis - Naomi Rich   *y* 1039

Christopher
Clean - Amy Reed   *y* 1031

Earl, Ronald "Little Texas"
Days of Little Texas - R.A. Nelson   *y* 972

Eden
Tricks - Ellen Hopkins   *y* 843

Father Ramon
The Reformed Vampire Support Group - Catherine
   Jinks   *y* 859

Howard, Pastor Shady
Moon over Manifest - Clare Vanderpool   *c, y* 538

Jacob, Abba
Snook Alone - Marilyn Nelson   *c* 349

Khan, Nina
Skunk Girl - Sheba Karim   *y* 864

Murphy, Father
Bless This Mouse - Lois Lowry   *c, y* 289

Sabiri, Sami
Borderline - Allan Stratton   *y* 1108

Towfeek, Jamilah "Jamie"
Ten Things I Hate about Me - Randa
   Abdel-Fattah   *y* 595

Willow, Webster B.
The Mostly True Adventures of Homer P. Figg - Rodman Philbrick   c, y 389

REPTILE

Art
Art and Max - David Wiesner   c 560

Chameleon
Blue Chameleon - Emily Gravett   p, c 172

Max
Art and Max - David Wiesner   c 560

Shifty
Sidekicks - Dan Santat   c, y 441

RESTAURATEUR

Chris
Blood - K.J. Wignall   y 1160

Rachel
Blood - K.J. Wignall   y 1160

REVOLUTIONARY

Le Fantome
The Pale Assassin - Patricia Elliott   y 756

Niya
Dragons of Darkness - Antonia Michaelis   y 947

RHINOCEROS

Rhino
I Broke My Trunk! - Mo Willems   p, c 567

ROBOT

CookieBot
CookieBot! A Harry and Horsie Adventure - Katie Van Camp   p, c 536

ROOMMATE

Mazzie
Breathless - Jessica Warman   y 1149

ROYALTY

Alek
Behemoth - Scott Westerfeld   y 1154

ana'Marianna, Raisa
The Demon King - Cinda Williams Chima   y 687

Azalea
Entwined - Heather Dixon   y 736

Christian
Princess of Glass - Jessica Day George   y 785

Dizzy, Princess
Wisdom's Kiss: A Thrilling and Romantic Adventure Incorporating Magic, Villainy and a Cat - Catherine Gilbert Murdock   y 959

Eleanor
Thomas and the Dragon Queen - Shutta Crum   c 96

Elisa
The Girl of Fire and Thorns - Rae Carson   y 677

Elizabeth
The Stolen One - Suzanne Crowley   y 714

Eugenides
A Conspiracy of Kings - Megan Whalen Turner   y 1134

Falpian
Witchlanders - Lena Coakley   y 695

FitzOsborne, Sophia
The FitzOsbornes in Exile - Michelle Cooper   y 705

FitzOsborne, Sophie
A Brief History of Montmaray - Michelle Cooper   y 706

Jumar
Dragons of Darkness - Antonia Michaelis   y 947

King, The
The King's Taster - Kenneth Oppel   c 371

Nash, King
Fire - Kristin Cashore   y 679

Poppy
Princess of Glass - Jessica Day George   y 785

Ramil
Dragonfly - Julia Golding   y 796

Rose
Princess of the Midnight Ball - Jessica Day George   y 784

Shirin
Dreams of Significant Girls - Cristina Garcia   y 779

Sinda/Nalia
The False Princess - Ellis O'Neal   y 986

Solomon, King
The Ring of Solomon - Jonathan Stroud   y 1109

Sylviianel "Sylvi"
Pegasus - Robin McKinley   y 940

Taoshira "Tashi"
Dragonfly - Julia Golding   y 796

RULER

Cheops
Pharaoh's Boat - David L. Weitzman   c, y 553

Maldor
A World without Heroes - Brandon Mull   c, y 335

Matrarc
Prized - Caragh M. O'Brien   y 983

Penelopeia
King of Ithaka - Tracy Barrett   y 621

RUNAWAY

Alis
Alis - Naomi Rich   y 1039

Angel
Desert Angel - Charlie Price   y 1025

Aparacio, Yancy
Riding Invisible - Sandra Alonzo   y 604

Blink
Blink & Caution - Tim Wynne-Jones   y 1180

Carolina
Carolina Harmony - Marilyn Taylor McDowell   c, y 315

Caution
Blink & Caution - Tim Wynne-Jones   y 1180

Cheslav
No Safe Place - Deborah Ellis   y 757

Conrad
It's Not Summer Without You - Jenny Han   y 818

Critter
Jump - Elisa Carbone   y 673

Curzon
Forge - Laurie Halse Anderson   y 607

Eloise
Blood - K.J. Wignall   y 1160

Giambanco, Gaston
Homestretch - Paul Volponi   y 1142

Isabel
Forge - Laurie Halse Anderson   y 607

Jamie "Punkzilla"
Punkzilla - Adam Rapp   y 1030

Kid
Brooklyn, Burning - Steve Brezenoff   y 658

Laddy
The Runaway Dragon - Kate Coombs   c, y 79

Matthew
Death Cloud - Andrew Lane   y 890

Maya
Compromised - Heidi Ayarbe   y 616

P.K.
Jump - Elisa Carbone   y 673

Skip
A Small Free Kiss in the Dark - Glenda Millard   y 948

RUNNER

Jessica
The Running Dream - Wendelin Van Draanen   y 744

Reinstein, Felton
Stupid Fast: The Summer I Went from a Joke to a Jock - Geoff Herbach   y 836

Tristan
My Fair Godmother - Janette Rallison   y 1029

SAILOR

Slocum, Joshua
Around the World - Matt Phelan   c, y 388

SALESMAN

Picture Man
The Color of Earth - Kim Dong Hwa   y 852

SCAVENGER

Nailer
Ship Breaker: A Novel - Paolo Bacigalupi   y 618

SCIENTIST

Dr. Adnoid
The Secret of Zoom - Lynne Jonell   c, y 228

Adnoid, Beth
The Secret of Zoom - Lynne Jonell   c, y 228

Anning, Mary
Remarkable Creatures - Tracy Chevalier   y 686

Ben
The Secret Science Alliance and the Copycat Crook - Eleanor Davis   c, y 103

Calendar, Julian
The Secret Science Alliance and the Copycat Crook - Eleanor Davis   c, y 103

Darwin, Charles
Charles and Emma: The Darwins' Leap of Faith - Deborah Heiligman   y 833

"Gardener"
The Gardener - S.A. Bodeen   y 645

Greta
The Secret Science Alliance and the Copycat Crook - Eleanor Davis   c, y 103

Philpot, Elizabeth
Remarkable Creatures - Tracy Chevalier   y 686

Dr. Shumway
The Doom Machine - Mark Teague   *c, y* 510

Silvey, Chance
Low Red Moon - Caitlin R. Kiernan   *a*872

Warthrop, Dr. Pellinore
The Curse of the Wendigo - Rick Yancey   *y* 1183
The Isle of Blood - Rick Yancey   *y* 1181
The Monstrumologist - Rick Yancey   *y* 1182

SEA CAPTAIN

Smith, E.J.
The Watch That Ends the Night: Voices from the Titanic - Allan Wolf   *y* 1171

SEAMSTRESS

Abbott, Harriet
Lost - Jacqueline Davies   *y* 720

Freyda
Lost - Jacqueline Davies   *y* 720

Mam
The Christmas Eve Ghost - Shirley Hughes   *c* 217

Rosenfeld, Essie
Lost - Jacqueline Davies   *y* 720

SERIAL KILLER

Otokoto, Black Hat
Akata Witch - Nnedi Okorafor   *y* 988

Snow, Narcissa
Low Red Moon - Caitlin R. Kiernan   *a*872

SERVANT

Ansel
No Such Things as Dragons - Philip Reeve   *c, y* 410

Cornalus
The False Princess - Ellis O'Neal   *y* 986

Eleanora
Princess of Glass - Jessica Day George   *y* 785

Kamau
Burn My Heart - Beverley Naidoo   *c, y* 967

Mugo
Burn My Heart - Beverley Naidoo   *c, y* 967

Sipho
Stones for My Father - Trilby Kent   *y* 869

Tamper, Abigail "Abi"
The Poisoned House - Michael Ford   *y* 770

Virginia
The Queen of Water - Laura Resau   *y* 1038

SHAPE-CHANGER

Modo
The Hunchback Assignments - Arthur G. Slade   *y* 1081

SHAPE-SHIFTER

Gray, Tessa
Clockwork Angel - Cassandra Clare   *y* 690

Lend
Paranormalcy - Kiersten White   *y* 1156

SIDEKICK

Argyle
Frankie Pickle and the Closet of Doom - Eric Wright   *c* 582

Hamisher
Hamster and Cheese - Colleen A.F. Venable   *c* 541

Hutchinson, Scott "Bright Boy"
Sidekicks - Jack D. Ferraiolo   *y* 765

Mendez, Allison "Monkeywrench"
Sidekicks - Jack D. Ferraiolo   *y* 765

Pru
Calamity Jack - Shannon Hale   *c, y* 187

Static Cat
Sidekicks - Dan Santat   *c, y* 441

Vienne
Black Hole Sun - David Macinnis Gill   *y* 789

SINGER

Bianchi, Diana
Virtuosity - Jessica Martinez   *y* 925

Jones, Retta Lee
Somebody Everybody Listens To - Suzanne Supplee   *y* 1115

Luisa
Hidden Voices: The Orphan Musicians of Venice - Pat Lowery Collins   *y* 698

McFee, Rayka "Mama"
Close to Famous - Joan Bauer   *c, y* 623

Naamah
Naamah and the Ark at Night - Susan Campbell Bartoletti   *p, c* 24

Shaw, Serena
Silhouetted by the Blue - Traci L. Jones   *y* 863

SINGLE MOTHER

Jolly
This Full House - Virginia Euwer Wolff   *y* 1172

Lexie
Pearl - Jo Knowles   *y* 882

McFee, Rayka "Mama"
Close to Famous - Joan Bauer   *c, y* 623

Reinstein, Jerri
Stupid Fast: The Summer I Went from a Joke to a Jock - Geoff Herbach   *y* 836

Sally
Pearl - Jo Knowles   *y* 882

Whitcomb, Janice
The House of Tomorrow - Peter Bognanni   *y* 646

SISTER

Aaluk
Blessing's Bead - Debby Dahl Edwardson   *y* 750

Abby
Between Here and Forever - Elizabeth Scott   *y* 1065

Amandolina "Andi"
Tall Story - Candy Gourlay   *y* 800

Amy
Love You Hate You Miss You - Elizabeth Scott   *y* 1067

Anna
Peace, Love, and Baby Ducks - Lauren Myracle   *y* 966

Annie
Bobby versus Girls (Accidentally) - Lisa Yee   *c, y* 587

April
The Extraordinary Secrets of April, May and June - Robin Benway   *y* 631

Arilou
The Lost Conspiracy - Frances Hardinge   *c, y* 822

Arrow
Nickel Plated - Aric Davis   *y* 721

Bailey
The Sky Is Everywhere - Jandy Nelson   *y* 970

Barbra
Angel in My Pocket - Ilene Cooper   *c, y* 82

Beatrice
Secrets at Sea - Richard Peck   *c, y* 383

Berlin, Brooke
Spoiled - Jessica Morgan   *y* 953

Bette
Angel in My Pocket - Ilene Cooper   *c, y* 82

Birnbaum, Sarah
Friend Is Not a Verb - Daniel Ehrenhaft   *y* 753

Blue, Meggie
You'll Like It Here (Everybody Does) - Ruth White   *c, y* 559

Bronwen
The Christmas Eve Ghost - Shirley Hughes   *c* 217

Brown, Kim
The Carbon Diaries 2015 - Saci Lloyd   *y* 901

Callie
Nightspell - Leah Cypess   *y* 717

Cara
The Fires Beneath the Sea - Lydia Millet   *c, y* 330

Carver, Alicia
The Prince of Mist - Carlos Ruiz Zafon   *y* 1195

Casey
Bobby versus Girls (Accidentally) - Lisa Yee   *c, y* 587

Celina
The Zabime Sisters - Aristophane   *y* 611

Chapman, Franny
Countdown - Deborah Wiles   *c, y* 561

Chloe
Imaginary Girls - Nova Ren Suma   *y* 1113

Daisy
The Blood Lie - Shirley Reva Vernick   *y* 1139

Daphne
The Space Between - Brenna Yovanoff   *y* 1193

Darri
Nightspell - Leah Cypess   *y* 717

Dix, Molly
Spoiled - Jessica Morgan   *y* 953

Duarte, Rosalia
Putting Makeup on the Fat Boy - Bil Wright   *y* 1177

Elinor
Waiting for the Magic - Patricia MacLachlan   *c* 293

Elle
The Zabime Sisters - Aristophane   *y* 611

Ellis, Shelley
Perfect Chemistry - Simone Elkeles   *y* 755

Emaline
The Blood Lie - Shirley Reva Vernick   *y* 1139

Emma
Emma Dilemma: Big Sister Poems - Kristine O'Connell George   *c* 160

Emmi
Blood Red Road - Moira Young   *y* 1191

Everdeen, Primrose
Mockingjay - Suzanne Collins   *y* 700

Fern
One Crazy Summer - Rita
    Williams-Garcia   *c, y* 569

Flora
Flora's Very Windy Day - Jeanne Birdsall   *c* 35

Geless, Emma
City of Orphans - Avi   *c, y* 15

Goodnight, Amy
Texas Gothic - Rosemary Clement-Moore   *y* 693

Goodnight, Phin
Texas Gothic - Rosemary Clement-Moore   *y* 693

Goodwin, Abby
The Deadly Sister - Eliot Schrefer   *y* 1062

Goodwin, Maya
The Deadly Sister - Eliot Schrefer   *y* 1062

Grant, Andi
The Miracle Stealer - Neil Connelly   *y* 704

Green, Samantha
The Adventures of Nanny Piggins - R.A.
    Spratt   *c, y* 483

Greene, Rowena
Once a Witch - Carolyn MacCullough   *y* 915

Gretel
A Tale Dark and Grimm - Adam Gidwitz   *c, y* 162

Gritas, Payton
Sean Griswold's Head - Lindsey Leavitt   *y* 894

Hannah
Season of Secrets - Sally Nicholls   *c, y* 357

Hardscrabble, Lucia
The Kneebone Boy - Ellen Potter   *c, y* 398

Hathin
The Lost Conspiracy - Frances Hardinge   *c, y* 822

Helena
Secrets at Sea - Richard Peck   *c, y* 383

Hope
Glimpse - Carol Lynch Williams   *y* 1163

India
No Passengers beyond This Point - Gennifer
    Choldenko   *c, y* 68

Isa
Tighter - Adele Griffin   *y* 807

Ivy
Zelda and Ivy: Keeping Secrets - Laura McGee
    Kvasnosky   *c* 264

Janna
The Shattering - Karen Healey   *y* 832

Jo Ellen
Countdown - Deborah Wiles   *c, y* 561

Jody
Once Was Lost - Sara Zarr   *y* 1196

Julia
Love You Hate You Miss You - Elizabeth
    Scott   *y* 1067

Juliet
The Six Rules of Maybe - Deb Caletti   *y* 672

June
The Extraordinary Secrets of April, May and June -
    Robin Benway   *y* 631
A Month of Sundays - Ruth White   *y* 558

Kane, Sadie
The Red Pyramid - Rick Riordan   *c, y* 418

Karyn
You Against Me - Jenny Downham   *y* 743

Katherine
Sent - Margaret Peterson Haddix   *c, y* 185

Kelly
She Said/She Saw - Norah McClintock   *y* 931

Keri
The Shattering - Karen Healey   *y* 832

Khadija
Where I Belong - Gillian Cross   *y* 712

Khosi
This Thing Called the Future - J. L.
    Powers   *y* 1020

Kinahan, Julie
Long Story Short - Siobhan Parkinson   *y* 998

Lexi
The View from the Top - Hillary Frank   *y* 773

Lili
Peace, Locomotion - Jacqueline Woodson   *c, y* 581

Lillie
Freedom Stone - Jeffrey Kluger   *c, y* 255

Lizzie
Glimpse - Carol Lynch Williams   *y* 1163

Louise
Secrets at Sea - Richard Peck   *c, y* 383

M'Rose
The Zabime Sisters - Aristophane   *y* 611

Maddy
The Devil's Paintbox - Victoria McKernan   *y* 938

Mae
The Demon's Lexicon - Sarah Rees
    Brennan   *y* 657

March, Rosie
Sisters Red - Jackson Pearce   *y* 1000

March, Scarlett
Sisters Red - Jackson Pearce   *y* 1000

Marie
Resistance - Carla Jablonski   *y* 854

Marisa
What Can't Wait - Ashley Hope Perez   *y* 1005

Marriss, Lil
Crunch - Leslie Connor   *c, y* 78

May
The Extraordinary Secrets of April, May and June -
    Robin Benway   *y* 631

Maya
Forbidden - Tabitha Suzuma   *y* 1116
Prized - Caragh M. O'Brien   *y* 983

McDermott, Ceejay
Badd - Tim Tharp   *y* 1125

McDonald, Pepsi
Mission Unstoppable - Dan Gutman   *c, y* 183

McKeel, Prue
Wildwood - Colin Meloy   *c, y* 325

Mercier, Georgia
Die for Me - Amy Plum   *y* 1016

Mercier, Kate
Die for Me - Amy Plum   *y* 1016

Miksa, Margit
Every Little Thing in the World - Nina de
    Gramont   *y* 724

Mildew, Lucy
*Tumtum and Nutmeg: Adventures beyond Nutmouse
    Hall* - Emily Bearn   *c, y* 29

Molly
Season of Secrets - Sally Nicholls   *c, y* 357

Mouse
No Passengers beyond This Point - Gennifer
    Choldenko   *c, y* 68

Nellie
*Who Has What?: All about Girls' Bodies and Boys'
    Bodies* - Robie H. Harris   *p, c* 193

Nola
The Complete History of Why I Hate Her - Jennifer
    Richard Jacobson   *y* 855

Nutaaq
Blessing's Bead - Debby Dahl Edwardson   *y* 750

Octavia
Mare's War - Tanita S. Davis   *y* 722

Penny
Benny and Penny in the Big No-No! - Geoffrey
    Hayes   *c* 196

Perry, Winnie
Ten - Lauren Myracle   *c* 344

Pike, Lainey
The Snowball Effect - Holly Nicole Hoxter   *y* 846

Rosenfeld, Zelda
Lost - Jacqueline Davies   *y* 720

Rosie
Rosie and Skate - Beth Ann Bauman   *y* 624

Rubina
Big Red Lollipop - Rukhsana Khan   *p, c* 244

Ruby
Imaginary Girls - Nova Ren Suma   *y* 1113

Saba
Blood Red Road - Moira Young   *y* 1191

Sana
Big Red Lollipop - Rukhsana Khan   *p, c* 244

Sandra
Ten - Lauren Myracle   *c* 344

Scroggins, Honey
The Memory Bank - Carolyn Coman   *c, y* 75

Scroggins, Hope
The Memory Bank - Carolyn Coman   *c, y* 75

Serenity
What Momma Left Me - Renee Watson   *c, y* 551

Shaw, Serena
Silhouetted by the Blue - Traci L. Jones   *y* 863

Shelby
Nickel Plated - Aric Davis   *y* 721

Shereen
Ten Things I Hate about Me - Randa
    Abdel-Fattah   *y* 595

Skate
Rosie and Skate - Beth Ann Bauman   *y* 624

Skyla
Witchlanders - Lena Coakley   *y* 695

Small, Cleo
Underpants On My Head - Jessica Harper   *c* 192

Small, Jenna
Underpants On My Head - Jessica Harper   *c* 192

Smith, Antigone
The Dragon's Tooth - N.D. Wilson   *c, y* 571

Solveig
Icefall - Matthew J. Kirby   *y* 878

Song
The Complete History of Why I Hate Her - Jennifer
    Richard Jacobson   *y* 855

Steiner, Nellie
A Faraway Island - Annika Thor   *c, y* 516

Steiner, Stephie
A Faraway Island - Annika Thor   *c, y* 516

Stone, Gaia
Prized - Caragh M. O'Brien   *y* 983

Stroma
Broken Soup - Jenny Valentine   *y* 1136

Sullivan, Jane
Confessions of the Sullivan Sisters - Natalie
    Standiford   *y* 1096

Sullivan, Norrie
Confessions of the Sullivan Sisters - Natalie
    Standiford   *y* 1096

Sullivan, Sassy
Confessions of the Sullivan Sisters - Natalie
    Standiford   *y* 1096

Tali
Mare's War - Tanita S. Davis   *y* 722

Tess
Between Here and Forever - Elizabeth
    Scott   *y* 1065

Towfeek, Jamilah "Jamie"
Ten Things I Hate about Me - Randa
    Abdel-Fattah   *y* 595

Underhill, Esme
April and Esme: Tooth Fairies - Bob
    Graham   *p, c* 168

Unity
The Flint Heart - Katherine Paterson   *c, y* 380

Vallery
The Snowball Effect - Holly Nicole Hoxter   *y* 846

Vonetta
One Crazy Summer - Rita
    Williams-Garcia   *c, y* 569

Whitcomb, Meredith
The House of Tomorrow - Peter Bognanni   *y* 646

Wren, Dottie
What Happened on Fox Street - Tricia
    Springstubb   *c, y* 484

Wren, Mo
What Happened on Fox Street - Tricia
    Springstubb   *c, y* 484

Zelda
Zelda and Ivy: Keeping Secrets - Laura McGee
    Kvasnosky   *c* 264

Zeynab
Words in the Dust - Trent Reedy   *y* 1033

Zi
This Thing Called the Future - J. L.
    Powers   *y* 1020

Zulaikha
Words in the Dust - Trent Reedy   *y* 1033

SKATER

Samantha
Samantha on a Roll - Linda Ashman   *p, c* 13

SLAVE

Bett
Freedom Stone - Jeffrey Kluger   *c, y* 255

Beverly
*Jefferson's Sons: A Founding Father's Secret Child-
ren* - Kimberly Brubaker Bradley   *c, y* 45

Cecilia
The Firefly Letters: A Suffragette's Journey to Cuba
    - Margarita Engle   *y* 762

Crosswhite, Sadie
January's Sparrow - Patricia Polacco   *c, y* 395

Curzon
Forge - Laurie Halse Anderson   *y* 607

Dulcie
The Storm before Atlanta - Karen
    Schwabach   *c, y* 454

Fossett, Peter
*Jefferson's Sons: A Founding Father's Secret Chil-
dren* - Kimberly Brubaker Bradley   *c, y* 45

Hemings, Sally
*Jefferson's Sons: A Founding Father's Secret Chil-
dren* - Kimberly Brubaker Bradley   *c, y* 45

Isabel
Forge - Laurie Halse Anderson   *y* 607

Lillie
Freedom Stone - Jeffrey Kluger   *c, y* 255

Madison
*Jefferson's Sons: A Founding Father's Secret Chil-
dren* - Kimberly Brubaker Bradley   *c, y* 45

Musafa "Moses"
Never Forgotten - Patricia C. McKissack   *c, y* 319

Plato
Freedom Stone - Jeffrey Kluger   *c, y* 255

Quebrado
Hurricane Dancers - Margarita Engle   *y* 761

Rosalia
No Safe Place - Deborah Ellis   *y* 757

SOCCER PLAYER

Ajani
Goal! - Mina Javaherbin   *c* 222

Deo
Now Is the Time for Running - Michael
    Williams   *y* 1168

Fehey, Jonny
Over the End Line - Alfred C. Martino   *y* 926

Fletcher, Kendall
Cryer's Cross - Lisa McMann   *y* 942

Khalid
Guantanamo Boy - Anna Perera   *y* 1004

Martin, Jake
Compulsion - Heidi Ayarbe   *y* 617

Otello
Exposure - Mal Peet   *y* 1002

Saint-Claire, Kyle
Over the End Line - Alfred C. Martino   *y* 926

SOCIALITE

Olivia
Clean - Amy Reed   *y* 1031

SON

Ben
Lexie - Audrey Couloumbis   *c, y* 87

Beverly
*Jefferson's Sons: A Founding Father's Secret Chil-
dren* - Kimberly Brubaker Bradley   *c, y* 45

Billy
Strings Attached - Judy Blundell   *y* 643

Border, Sam
I'll Be There - Holly Goldberg Sloan   *y* 1083

Boy
The Third Gift - Linda Sue Park   *c* 376

Burrows, Benjamin
The Apothecary - Maile Meloy   *y* 945

Caleb
Jumping Off Swings - Jo Knowles   *y* 881

Carver Ellis-Chan, Robert "Bobby"
Bobby versus Girls (Accidentally) - Lisa
    Yee   *c, y* 587

Conrad
The Summer I Turned Pretty - Jenny Han   *y* 817

Crouch, Joey
Rotters - Daniel Kraus   *y* 886

Edward
Are You Awake? - Sophie Blackall   *p, c* 40

Flint, Michael
The Brooklyn Nine: A Novel in Nine Innings - Alan
    Gratz   *c, y* 171

Gabriel
Clarity - Kim Harrington   *y* 825

Grayson, Mathew
Burn My Heart - Beverley Naidoo   *c, y* 967

Greave, Samuel
The Poisoned House - Michael Ford   *y* 770

Harris
Lexie - Audrey Couloumbis   *c, y* 87

Hassan
Zahra's Paradise - Amir Amir   *y* 606

Heffley, Greg
Diary of a Wimpy Kid: Cabin Fever - Jeff
    Kinney   *c, y* 248

Heffley, Manny
Diary of a Wimpy Kid: Cabin Fever - Jeff
    Kinney   *c, y* 248

Heffley, Roderick
Diary of a Wimpy Kid: Cabin Fever - Jeff
    Kinney   *c, y* 248

Henry
Pearl - Jo Knowles   *y* 882

Jack
Don't Want to Go! - Shirley Hughes   *p, c* 216

Jackson, Percy
The Lightning Thief: The Graphic Novel - Rick
    Riordan   *c, y* 416

Jeremiah
The Summer I Turned Pretty - Jenny Han   *y* 817

Joseph
Warriors in the Crossfire - Nancy Bo Flood   *y* 768

Kaufman, David
The Beginning of After - Jennifer Castle   *y* 681

Kento
Warriors in the Crossfire - Nancy Bo Flood   *y* 768

Lathem, Wyatt
Bullet Point - Peter Abrahams   *y* 597

Lucas
Legacy - Thomas Sniegoski   *y* 1093

Madison
*Jefferson's Sons: A Founding Father's Secret Chil-
dren* - Kimberly Brubaker Bradley   *c, y* 45

McDonald, Coke
Mission Unstoppable - Dan Gutman   *c, y* 183

Mehdi
Zahra's Paradise - Amir Amir   *y* 606

Musafa "Moses"
Never Forgotten - Patricia C. McKissack   *c, y* 319

Obie
The Space Between - Brenna Yovanoff   *y* 1193

Popovich, Troy
Pop - Gordon Korman   *y* 885

Prince Aleksander "Alek"
Leviathan - Scott Westerfeld   *y* 1153

Radley, Rowan
The Radleys: A Novel - Matt Haig   y 813

Reinstein, Felton
Stupid Fast: The Summer I Went from a Joke to a Jock - Geoff Herbach   y 836

Roland
I Shall Wear Midnight - Terry Pratchett   y 1021

Sam
Don't Want to Go! - Shirley Hughes   p, c 216

Samuel
Woods Runner - Gary Paulsen   c, y 382

Schneider, Louis
The Brooklyn Nine: A Novel in Nine Innings - Alan Gratz   c, y 171

Smithers, Lance
Burn My Heart - Beverley Naidoo   c, y 967

Telemachos
King of Ithaka - Tracy Barrett   y 621

Troy
Bronxwood - Coe Booth   y 648

Tyrell
Bronxwood - Coe Booth   y 648

Whitcomb, Jared
The House of Tomorrow - Peter Bognanni   y 646

SONGWRITER

Kate
The Kind of Friends We Used to Be - Frances O'Roark Dowell   c, y 116

SORCERER

Aspeling
Lost - Sarah Prineas   c, y 399

Douglas
Hold Me Closer, Necromancer - Lish McBride   y 928

Sam
Hold Me Closer, Necromancer - Lish McBride   y 928

SPIRIT

Berg, Alex
Between - Jessica Warman   y 1150

Cassie
Wintergirls - Laurie Halse Anderson   y 608

Crutchfield, Sophia
The Ghost of Crutchfield Hall - Mary Downing Hahn   c, y 186

Daisy
Andromeda Klein - Frank Portman   y 1019

Emily
Anya's Ghost - Vera Brosgol   y 662

Jessie
Tighter - Adele Griffin   y 807

Korlov, Anna "Anna Dressed in Blood"
Anna Dressed in Blood - Kendare Blake   y 640

Lisette
Ruined: A Ghost Story - Paula Morris   y 955

Olive
Dying to Meet You - Kate Klise   c, y 254

Peterson, Henry
Through Her Eyes - Jennifer Archer   y 610

Valchar, Liz
Between - Jessica Warman   y 1150

SPOUSE

Clive
The Mostly True Story of Jack - Kelly Barnhill   c, y 23

Dad
Mission Unstoppable - Dan Gutman   c, y 183

Darwin, Charles
Charles and Emma: The Darwins' Leap of Faith - Deborah Heiligman   y 833

Darwin, Emma
Charles and Emma: The Darwins' Leap of Faith - Deborah Heiligman   y 833

Hayden
The Six Rules of Maybe - Deb Caletti   y 672

Heffley, Frank
Diary of a Wimpy Kid: Cabin Fever - Jeff Kinney   c, y 248

Heffley, Susan
Diary of a Wimpy Kid: Cabin Fever - Jeff Kinney   c, y 248

Juliet
The Six Rules of Maybe - Deb Caletti   y 672

June
A Month of Sundays - Ruth White   y 558

Kahlo, Frida
Me, Frida - Amy Novesky   c 360

Miss Latah
Carolina Harmony - Marilyn Taylor McDowell   c, y 315

Lilith
The Space Between - Brenna Yovanoff   y 1193

Linden
Wither - Lauren DeStefano   y 731

Lucifer
The Space Between - Brenna Yovanoff   y 1193

Mabel
The Mostly True Story of Jack - Kelly Barnhill   c, y 23

Mama
Waiting for the Magic - Patricia MacLachlan   c 293

Mom
Mission Unstoppable - Dan Gutman   c, y 183

Naamah
Naamah and the Ark at Night - Susan Campbell Bartoletti   p, c 24

Noah
Naamah and the Ark at Night - Susan Campbell Bartoletti   p, c 24

Nutmeg
Tumtum and Nutmeg: Adventures beyond Nutmouse Hall - Emily Bearn   c, y 29

Papa
Waiting for the Magic - Patricia MacLachlan   c 293

Penelopeia
King of Ithaka - Tracy Barrett   y 621

Radley, Helen
The Radleys: A Novel - Matt Haig   y 813

Radley, Peter
The Radleys: A Novel - Matt Haig   y 813

Rhine
Wither - Lauren DeStefano   y 731

Rivera, Diego
Me, Frida - Amy Novesky   c 360

Rose, Betty
A Month of Sundays - Ruth White   y 558

Tumtum
Tumtum and Nutmeg: Adventures beyond Nutmouse Hall - Emily Bearn   c, y 29

SPY

Mr. E.
The Case of the Case of Mistaken Identity - Mac Barnett   c, y 22

Fleabottom, Fenton J.
The Mostly True Adventures of Homer P. Figg - Rodman Philbrick   c, y 389

Quinn, Mary
A Spy in the House - Y.S. Lee   y 895

SQUIRREL

Squirrel
Waiting for Winter - Sebastian Meschenmoser   p, c 326

STEPBROTHER

Hunter, Leigh
After the Moment - Garret Freymann-Weyr   y 776

STEPMOTHER

Lisa
This World We Live In - Susan Beth Pfeffer   y 1012

STEPSISTER

Diribani
Toads and Diamonds - Heather Tomlinson   y 1132

Pike, Lainey
The Snowball Effect - Holly Nicole Hoxter   y 846

Tana
Toads and Diamonds - Heather Tomlinson   y 1132

Vallery
The Snowball Effect - Holly Nicole Hoxter   y 846

STORE OWNER

Dog
Dog Loves Books - Louise Yates   p, c 586

Mrs. Proust
I Shall Wear Midnight - Terry Pratchett   y 1021

Mr. Venezi
Hamster and Cheese - Colleen A.F. Venable   c 541

STREETPERSON

Hooper
First Day on Earth - Cecil Castellucci   y 680

Kid
Brooklyn, Burning - Steve Brezenoff   y 658

No
No and Me - Delphine De Vigan   y 726

Scout
Brooklyn, Burning - Steve Brezenoff   y 658

Willa
City of Orphans - Avi   c, y 15

STUDENT

Adrian
Same Difference - Siobhan Vivian   y 1140

Auden
Along for the Ride - Sarah Dessen   y 729

Audrey
Crash into Me - Albert Borris   y 649

Bettina
Miss Lina's Ballerinas - Grace Maccarone   c 292

Billy
When I Grow Up - Al Yankovic   c 585

Breen, Winston
The Potato Chip Puzzles: The Puzzling World of Winston Breen - Eric Berlin   c, y 33

Carver Ellis-Chan, Robert "Bobby"
Bobby versus Girls (Accidentally) - Lisa Yee   c, y 587

Casey
The DUFF: Designated Ugly Fat Friend - Kody Keplinger   y 871

Chen, Rebecca
The Red Blazer Girls: The Ring of Rocamadour - Michael D. Beil   y 629

Cheslav
No Safe Place - Deborah Ellis   y 757

Christina
Miss Lina's Ballerinas - Grace Maccarone   c 292

Cissy
The Glorious Adventures of the Sunshine Queen - Geraldine McCaughrean   c, y 312
The Glorious Adventures of the Sunshine Queen - Geraldine McCaughrean   c, y 312

Dominique
Jumped - Rita Williams-Garcia   y 1170

Edwina
Miss Lina's Ballerinas - Grace Maccarone   c 292

Einstein
The Dunderheads - Paul Fleischman   c, y 138

Everstar, Chrysanthemum "Chrissy"
My Fair Godmother - Janette Rallison   y 1029

Fiona
Same Difference - Siobhan Vivian   y 1140

Frank
Crash into Me - Albert Borris   y 649

Gemz, Carli
Dirty Laundry - Daniel Ehrenhaft   y 754

Jaimes, Lee Ann
The Red Blazer Girls: The Ring of Rocamadour - Michael D. Beil   y 629

Jake
The Potato Chip Puzzles: The Puzzling World of Winston Breen - Eric Berlin   c, y 33

Jessica
The DUFF: Designated Ugly Fat Friend - Kody Keplinger   y 871

Jin-Ae
Crash into Me - Albert Borris   y 649

Junkyard
The Dunderheads - Paul Fleischman   c, y 138

Justina
Miss Lina's Ballerinas - Grace Maccarone   c 292

Katrina
Miss Lina's Ballerinas - Grace Maccarone   c 292

Kookie
The Glorious Adventures of the Sunshine Queen - Geraldine McCaughrean   c, y 312
The Glorious Adventures of the Sunshine Queen - Geraldine McCaughrean   c, y 312

Leticia
Jumped - Rita Williams-Garcia   y 1170

Mal
The Potato Chip Puzzles: The Puzzling World of Winston Breen - Eric Berlin   c, y 33

Marina
Miss Lina's Ballerinas - Grace Maccarone   c 292

Mia
Where She Went - Gayle Forman   y 771

Mina
My Name Is Mina - David Almond   y 603

Molly
Season of Secrets - Sally Nicholls   c, y 357

Newport, Fellini "Fun" Udall
Dirty Laundry - Daniel Ehrenhaft   y 754

Nina
Miss Lina's Ballerinas - Grace Maccarone   c 292

Novak, Darcy
Dirty Laundry - Daniel Ehrenhaft   y 754

Pearl
Pearl verses the World - Sally Murphy   c 338

Pencil
The Dunderheads - Paul Fleischman   c, y 138

Piper, Bianca
The DUFF: Designated Ugly Fat Friend - Kody Keplinger   y 871

Preston
I Shall Wear Midnight - Terry Pratchett   y 1021

Regina
Miss Lina's Ballerinas - Grace Maccarone   c 292

Robyn
Same Difference - Siobhan Vivian   y 1140

Rush, Wesley
The DUFF: Designated Ugly Fat Friend - Kody Keplinger   y 871

Sabrina
Miss Lina's Ballerinas - Grace Maccarone   c 292

Spencer, Kevin
Liar, Liar: The Theory, Practice and Destructive Properties of Deception - Gary Paulsen   c, y 999

Spicer, Lil
Okay for Now - Gary D. Schmidt   c, y 451

Spider
The Dunderheads - Paul Fleischman   c, y 138

St. Pierre, Sophie
The Red Blazer Girls: The Ring of Rocamadour - Michael D. Beil   y 629

Stern, Karl
The Berlin Boxing Club - Robert Sharenow   y 1073

Swieteck, Doug
Okay for Now - Gary D. Schmidt   c, y 451

Trina
Jumped - Rita Williams-Garcia   y 1170

Tristan
My Fair Godmother - Janette Rallison   y 1029

Violet
Luv Ya Bunches - Lauren Myracle   c, y 343

Wheels
The Dunderheads - Paul Fleischman   c, y 138

Wrobel, Margaret
The Red Blazer Girls: The Ring of Rocamadour - Michael D. Beil   y 629

Zulaikha
Words in the Dust - Trent Reedy   y 1033

STUDENT—BOARDING SCHOOL

Alex
The Mockingbirds - Daisy Whitney   y 1158
Paper Covers Rock - Jenny Hubbard   y 848

Amiq
My Name Is Not Easy - Debby Dahl Edwardson   y 749

Bunna
My Name Is Not Easy - Debby Dahl Edwardson   y 749

Chickie
My Name Is Not Easy - Debby Dahl Edwardson   y 749

Clea
Reality Check - Peter Abrahams   y 596

Deveaux, Rory
The Name of the Star - Maureen Johnson   y 862

Donna
My Name Is Not Easy - Debby Dahl Edwardson   y 749

Faraday, Destiny
The Miles Between - Mary E. Pearson   y 1001

Fisher, Benson
Variant - Robison Wells   y 1151

Glenn
Paper Covers Rock - Jenny Hubbard   y 848

Holmes, Sherlock
Death Cloud - Andrew Lane   y 890

Ingrid
Dreams of Significant Girls - Cristina Garcia   y 779

Jacklin
Out of Shadows - Jason Wallace   y 1146

Karou
Daughter of Smoke and Bone - Laini Taylor   y 1120

Kitrell, Katie
Breathless - Jessica Warman   y 1149

Luke
My Name Is Not Easy - Debby Dahl Edwardson   y 749

Shirin
Dreams of Significant Girls - Cristina Garcia   y 779

Sonny
My Name Is Not Easy - Debby Dahl Edwardson   y 749

Viola
Viola in Reel Life - Adriana Trigiani   y 1133

Vivien
Dreams of Significant Girls - Cristina Garcia   y 779

STUDENT—COLLEGE

Alexander "Xan"
Angry Young Man - Chris Lynch   y 912

Barbra
Angel in My Pocket - Ilene Cooper   c, y 82

Clayborne, Eldric
Chime - Franny Billingsley   y 634

Jasper
Love Is the Higher Law - David Levithan   y 899

Luks, Jonah
The Space between Trees - Katie Williams   y 1167

Nolan, Mark
Guardian of the Dead - Karen Healey   y 831

Parker, Tom
You Against Me - Jenny Downham   y 743

Quinn, Maggie
Highway to Hell - Rosemary
Clement-Moore   y 694

Robert
Angry Young Man - Chris Lynch   y 912

Shapiro, Mimi
The Uninvited - Tim Wynne-Jones   y 1179

STUDENT—ELEMENTARY SCHOOL

Breen, Mattie
Hound Dog True - Linda Urban   c, y 529

Deja
Nikki and Deja: Birthday Blues - Karen
English   c 131

Lee, Clara
Clara Lee and the Apple Pie Dream - Jenny
Han   c 189

Lynwood
Squish: Super Amoeba - Jennifer L. Holm   c 208

Nate
Big Nate: In a Class by Himself - Lincoln
Peirce   c, y 385

Nikki
Nikki and Deja: Birthday Blues - Karen
English   c 131

Peggy
Squish: Super Amoeba - Jennifer L. Holm   c 208

Pod
Squish: Super Amoeba - Jennifer L. Holm   c 208

Squish
Squish: Super Amoeba - Jennifer L. Holm   c 208

STUDENT—EXCHANGE

Vladescu, Lucius
Jessica's Guide to Dating on the Dark Side - Beth
Fantaskey   y 763

Zaksauskas, Gobija
Au Revoir, Crazy European Chick - Joe
Schreiber   y 1063

STUDENT—HIGH SCHOOL

Afton, Regina
Some Girls Are - Courtney Summers   y 1114

Aleah
*Stupid Fast: The Summer I Went from a Joke to a
Jock* - Geoff Herbach   y 836

Alex
Bitter End - Jennifer Brown   y 663

Ambrose, Violet
The Body Finder - Kimberly Derting   y 728

Amelia
The Ghosts of Ashbury High - Jaclyn
Moriarty   y 954

Angel
Payback Time - Carl Deuker   y 732

Annaleah
You Are Not Here - Samantha Schutz   y 1064

Archer, Madison
Wish You Were Dead - Todd Strasser   y 1107

Arielle
Just Another Hero - Sharon M. Draper   y 745

Armstrong, Will
Will - Maria Boyd   y 652

Ava
Pink - Lili Wilkinson   y 1161

Barton, Neal
Americus - M.K. Reed   y 1032

Baumgarten, Mary Ashley
Sister Mischief - Laura Goode   y 797

Bianchi, Carmen
Virtuosity - Jessica Martinez   y 925

Bizza
Into the Wild Nerd Yonder - Julie Halpern   y 815

Bones
Gentlemen - Michael Northrop   y 981

Carlos
No More Us for You - David Hernandez   y 837

Char
Into the Wild Nerd Yonder - Julie Halpern   y 815

Charlie
Please Ignore Vera Dietz - A.S. King   y 876

Chase, Kyle
You - Charles Benoit   y 630

Chloe
Accomplice - Eireann Corrigan   y 708

Claire
Love Is the Higher Law - David Levithan   y 899

Cole
Bitter End - Jennifer Brown   y 663

Cooper, Tiny
Will Grayson, Will Grayson - David
Levithan   y 898

Corazon, Eddie
Muchacho - LouAnne Johnson   y 860

Devon
The Dark Days of Hamburger Halpin - Josh
Berk   y 632

Dietz, Vera
Please Ignore Vera Dietz - A.S. King   y 876

Drea
Harmonic Feedback - Tara Kelly   y 868

Emily
Same Difference - Siobhan Vivian   y 1140

Evan
Every You, Every Me - David Levithan   y 897

Fehey, Jonny
Over the End Line - Alfred C. Martino   y 926

Fei Ting "Frances"
Bitter Melon - Cara Chow   y 688

Finn
Accomplice - Eireann Corrigan   y 708

Fletcher, Kendall
Cryer's Cross - Lisa McMann   y 942

Flick, Jenny
Please Ignore Vera Dietz - A.S. King   y 876

Fraser, Tara
Mercury - Hope Larson   y 892

Gallagher, Shawna
Say the Word - Jeannine Garsee   y 781

Gellar, Liam
King of the Screwups - K.L. Going   y 794

Gorman, Janie
Ten Miles Past Normal - Frances O'Roark
Dowell   y 742

Grayson, Davis
With or Without You - Brian Farrey   y 764

Grayson, Will
Will Grayson, Will Grayson - David
Levithan   y 898
Will Grayson, Will Grayson - David
Levithan   y 898

Green, Min
Why We Broke Up - Daniel Handler   y 821

Grey, Nora
Hush, Hush - Becca Fitzpatrick   y 767

Griswold, Sean
Sean Griswold's Head - Lindsey Leavitt   y 894

Gritas, Payton
Sean Griswold's Head - Lindsey Leavitt   y 894

Halpin, Will
The Dark Days of Hamburger Halpin - Josh
Berk   y 632

Happyface
Happyface - Stephen Emond   y 759

Hendricks, Sage
Almost Perfect - Brian Katcher   y 865

Herold, Katherine "Kat"
Center Field - Robert Lipsyte   y 900

Hunter, Leigh
After the Moment - Garret Freymann-Weyr   y 776

Hutchinson, Scott "Bright Boy"
Sidekicks - Jack D. Ferraiolo   y 765

Isabel
No More Us for You - David Hernandez   y 837

Jac
Sean Griswold's Head - Lindsey Leavitt   y 894

Jericho
Just Another Hero - Sharon M. Draper   y 745

Jess
Into the Wild Nerd Yonder - Julie Halpern   y 815

Kate
Exposed - Kimberly Marcus   y 923

Khalid
Guantanamo Boy - Anna Perera   y 1004

Khan, Nina
Skunk Girl - Sheba Karim   y 864

Kingston, Samantha
Before I Fall - Lauren Oliver   y 990

Kofi
Just Another Hero - Sharon M. Draper   y 745

Kurt
Leverage - Joshua Cohen   y 697

LaVaughn
This Full House - Virginia Euwer Wolff   y 1172

Lia
Wintergirls - Laurie Halse Anderson   y 608

Liz
Exposed - Kimberly Marcus   y 923

Lloyd, Henriette "Henry"
Jersey Tomatoes Are the Best - Maria
Padian   y 997

Locke, Cat
Fat Cat - Robin Brande   y 654

Lupita
Under the Mesquite - Guadalupe Garcia
McCall   y 929

Madeline
Recovery Road - Blake Nelson   y 969

Marcy
Sister Mischief - Laura Goode   y 797

Character Description Index

Madame Lucille
Brontorina - James Howe   *p, c* 213

March, Miss May
The Glorious Adventures of the Sunshine Queen - Geraldine McCaughrean   *c, y* 312

Mr. McQueen
Bluefish - Pat Schmatz   *y* 1060

Meena
Words in the Dust - Trent Reedy   *y* 1033

Mr. Mixler
Julia Gillian (and the Quest for Joy) - Alison McGhee   *c* 317

Dr. Moore
This Full House - Virginia Euwer Wolff   *y* 1172

Mr. Mymer
Bad Apple - Laura Ruby   *y* 1048

Ms. O'Reilly
In Memory of Gorfman T. Frog - Gail Donovan   *c* 113

Papa
Waiting for the Magic - Patricia MacLachlan   *c* 293

Mrs. Peterson
Junkyard Wonders - Patricia Polacco   *c, y* 396

Mr. Purdy
Calvin Coconut: Trouble Magnet - Graham Salisbury   *c* 438

Quinn, Mary
A Spy in the House - Y.S. Lee   *y* 895

Schmidt, Herr
After the Train - Gloria Whelan   *y* 557

Starch, Mrs. Bunny
Scat - Carl Hiaasen   *c, y* 203

Yates
Same Difference - Siobhan Vivian   *y* 1140

TEENAGER

A.J.
Now Playing: Stoner & Spaz II - Ron Koertge   *y* 883

Abramson, Ari
So Punk Rock (and Other Ways to Disappoint Your Mother) - Micol Ostow   *y* 995

Adams, Saffron
The Dust of 100 Dogs - A.S. King   *y* 874

Alex
Ashfall - Mike Mullin   *y* 958
Bitter End - Jennifer Brown   *y* 663

Allie
Boyfriends with Girlfriends - Alex Sanchez   *y* 1056

Amy
Love You Hate You Miss You - Elizabeth Scott   *y* 1067

Andersson, Sig
Revolver - Marcus Sedgwick   *y* 1068

Anetta
Hidden Voices: The Orphan Musicians of Venice - Pat Lowery Collins   *y* 698

Angie
Putting Makeup on the Fat Boy - Bil Wright   *y* 1177

Anke
Because I Am Furniture - Thalia Chaltas   *y* 682

Anna
Moonglass - Jessi Kirby   *y* 877

Annaleah
You Are Not Here - Samantha Schutz   *y* 1064

Anya
Anya's Ghost - Vera Brosgol   *y* 662

April
Ten Things We Did (and Probably Shouldn't Have) - Sarah Mlynowski   *y* 951

Araene
The Floating Islands - Rachel Neumeier   *y* 978

Audrey
Crash into Me - Albert Borris   *y* 649

Bancroft, Ben
Now Playing: Stoner & Spaz II - Ron Koertge   *y* 883

Bartolomeo
Winter's End - Jean-Claude Mourlevat   *y* 956

Barton, Neal
Americus - M.K. Reed   *y* 1032

Baumgarten, Mary Ashley
Sister Mischief - Laura Goode   *y* 797

Ben
Lexie - Audrey Couloumbis   *c, y* 87

Birnbaum, Henry "Hen"
Friend Is Not a Verb - Daniel Ehrenhaft   *y* 753

Bishop, Katarina
Heist Society - Ally Carter   *y* 678

Bizza
Into the Wild Nerd Yonder - Julie Halpern   *y* 815

Blackstone, Ginny
The Last Little Blue Envelope - Maureen Johnson   *y* 861

Blake
Ostrich Boys - Keith Gray   *y* 804

Blue, Sophie
Fade to Blue - Sean Beaudoin   *y* 626

Book, Eli
Eli the Good - Silas House   *y* 844

Brennan, Tory
Virals - Kathy Reichs   *y* 1035

Burrows, Benjamin
The Apothecary - Maile Meloy   *y* 945

Caitlin
Hold Still - Nina LaCour   *y* 887

Caldwell, Jayson
Shooting Star - Fredrick McKissack Jr.   *y* 941

Caleb
Jumping Off Swings - Jo Knowles   *y* 881

Cannon, Jimmy
When the Whistle Blows - Fran Cannon Slayton   *y* 1082

Casey
The DUFF: Designated Ugly Fat Friend - Kody Keplinger   *y* 871

Castenada, Toni
The Cardturner: A Novel about a King, a Queen, and a Joker - Louis Sachar   *y* 1053

Char
Into the Wild Nerd Yonder - Julie Halpern   *y* 815

Charlie
The Storm before Atlanta - Karen Schwabach   *c, y* 454

Charlotte
A Need So Beautiful - Suzanne Young   *y* 1192

Cheslav
No Safe Place - Deborah Ellis   *y* 757

Chiko
Bamboo People - Mitali Perkins   *y* 1006

Christopher
Clean - Amy Reed   *y* 1031

Claire, Marie
Queen of Hearts - Martha Brooks   *y* 661

Cody
Tricks - Ellen Hopkins   *y* 843

Cole
Bitter End - Jennifer Brown   *y* 663

Connolly, Puck
The Scorpio Races - Maggie Stiefvater   *y* 1099

Cooper, Tiny
Will Grayson, Will Grayson - David Levithan   *y* 898

Corinne
Jumping Off Swings - Jo Knowles   *y* 881

Crane, Emmett
The Summer I Learned to Fly - Dana Reinhardt   *y* 1037

Crepsley, Larten
Birth of a Killer - Darren Shan   *y* 1072

Critter
Jump - Elisa Carbone   *y* 673

Curry, Amy
Amy and Roger's Epic Detour - Morgan Matson   *y* 927

D'Arcy
Five Minutes More - Darlene Ryan   *y* 1052

Dade
The Vast Fields of Ordinary - Nick Burd   *y* 667

Daiyu
Gateway - Sharon Shinn   *y* 1076

Dakota
Tangled - Carolyn Mackler   *y* 916

Dan
Past Perfect - Leila Sales   *y* 1055

de Boncouer, Eugenie
The Pale Assassin - Patricia Elliott   *y* 756

Devon
The Dark Days of Hamburger Halpin - Josh Berk   *y* 632

DJ
Hothouse - Chris Lynch   *y* 911

Duchannes, Lena
Beautiful Creatures - Kami Garcia   *y* 780

Eden
Tricks - Ellen Hopkins   *y* 843

Edie
Eli the Good - Silas House   *y* 844

Eli
Along for the Ride - Sarah Dessen   *y* 729

Emaline
The Blood Lie - Shirley Reva Vernick   *y* 1139

Emma
The Future of Us - Jay Asher   *y* 613

Erik
With or Without You - Brian Farrey   *y* 764

Escobar, Edilio
Hunger - Michael Grant   *y* 803

Eva
Clean - Amy Reed   *y* 1031

Evan
Every You, Every Me - David Levithan   *y* 897

Evans, Miranda
This World We Live In - Susan Beth
Pfeffer   y 1012

Ewing, Ella Kate
Stand Straight, Ella Kate - Kate Klise   c 252

Ezra
Past Perfect - Leila Sales   y 1055

Fade
Enclave - Ann Aguirre   y 599

Fade, Kenny
Fade to Blue - Sean Beaudoin   y 626

Fiona
Past Perfect - Leila Sales   y 1055

Fletcher, Kendall
Cryer's Cross - Lisa McMann   y 942

Flynn, Truman
The Space Between - Brenna Yovanoff   y 1193

Fox
Zenith - Julie Bertagna   y 633

Frank
Crash into Me - Albert Borris   y 649

Frankenstein, Konrad
*This Dark Endeavor: The Apprenticeship of Victor
Frankenstein* - Kenneth Oppel   y 993

Frankenstein, Victor
*This Dark Endeavor: The Apprenticeship of Victor
Frankenstein* - Kenneth Oppel   y 993

Gabriel
Clarity - Kim Harrington   y 825

Gershwin, David
How I Stole Johnny Depp's Alien Girlfriend - Gary
Ghislain   y 786

Giambanco, Gaston
Homestretch - Paul Volponi   y 1142

Ginger
Tricks - Ellen Hopkins   y 843

Goodwin, Abby
The Deadly Sister - Eliot Schrefer   y 1062

Goodwin, Maya
The Deadly Sister - Eliot Schrefer   y 1062

Grayson, Will
Will Grayson, Will Grayson - David
Levithan   y 898
Will Grayson, Will Grayson - David
Levithan   y 898

Griffin
Girl, Stolen - April Henry   y 835

Haloway, Lena
Delirium - Lauren Oliver   y 989

Halpin, Will
The Dark Days of Hamburger Halpin - Josh
Berk   y 632

Happyface
Happyface - Stephen Emond   y 759

Hari
Salt - Maurice Gee   y 783

Hawthorne, Gale
Catching Fire - Suzanne Collins   y 699
Mockingjay - Suzanne Collins   y 700

Helen
Winter's End - Jean-Claude Mourlevat   y 956

Igwash, Janine
Tilt - Alan Cumyn   y 716

Innocent
Now Is the Time for Running - Michael
Williams   y 1168

Jacob
North of Beautiful - Justina Chen Headley   y 830

Jamie
The Lighter Side of Life and Death - C.K. Kelly
Martin   y 924

Jarrah
The Call - Michael Grant   c, y 170

Jason
Clean - Amy Reed   y 1031

Jena
Tangled - Carolyn Mackler   y 916

Jenna
Boys, Bears, and a Serious Pair of Hiking Boots -
Abby McDonald   y 935
Brain Camp - Susan Kim   y 873

Jess
Into the Wild Nerd Yonder - Julie Halpern   y 815

Jessica
The DUFF: Designated Ugly Fat Friend - Kody
Keplinger   y 871

Jill
Knifepoint - Alex Van Tol   y 1131

Jin-Ae
Crash into Me - Albert Borris   y 649

John Joseph
Keep Sweet - Michele Dominguez Greene   y 805

Josh
The Future of Us - Jay Asher   y 613
Jumping Off Swings - Jo Knowles   y 881

Jumar
Dragons of Darkness - Antonia Michaelis   y 947

Kaede
Huntress - Malinda Lo   y 903

Kalinowski, Mandy
How to Save a Life - Sara Zarr   y 1197

Kane, Carter
The Red Pyramid - Rick Riordan   c, y 418

Kane, Sadie
The Red Pyramid - Rick Riordan   c, y 418

Kat
The Lighter Side of Life and Death - C.K. Kelly
Martin   y 924

Kelly
Clean - Amy Reed   y 1031

Kelly, Jenna
Gifted: Better Late than Never - Marilyn
Kaye   y 866

Kenny
Ostrich Boys - Keith Gray   y 804

Kimiko
Boyfriends with Girlfriends - Alex
Sanchez   y 1056

King, Jeremy
Virtuosity - Jessica Martinez   y 925

Klein, Andromeda
Andromeda Klein - Frank Portman   y 1019

Lana
Hunger - Michael Grant   y 803

Lance
Boyfriends with Girlfriends - Alex
Sanchez   y 1056

Lena
The Mermaid's Mirror - L.K. Madigan   y 918

Lend
Paranormalcy - Kiersten White   y 1156

Leonard "Wei Dong"
For the Win - Cory Doctorow   y 737

Lewis, Mercy
Wicked Girls: A Novel of the Salem Witch Trials -
Stephanie Hemphill   y 834

Linderman, Lucky
Everybody Sees the Ants - A.S. King   y 875

Lisa
Funny How Things Change - Melissa
Wyatt   y 1178

Liu, Ray
Money Boy - Paul Yee   y 1188

Lloyd, Henriette "Henry"
Jersey Tomatoes Are the Best - Maria
Padian   y 997

Lou
No and Me - Delphine De Vigan   y 726

Lucas
Brain Camp - Susan Kim   y 873
Surface Tension: A Novel in Four Summers - Brent
Runyon   y 1049

Luisa
Hidden Voices: The Orphan Musicians of Venice -
Pat Lowery Collins   y 698

Lupita
Under the Mesquite - Guadalupe Garcia
McCall   y 929

MacAvoy, Mack
The Call - Michael Grant   c, y 170

Mackee, Thomas
The Piper's Son - Melina Marchetta   y 922

Maddy
Illyria - Elizabeth Hand   y 820

Madeline
Recovery Road - Blake Nelson   y 969

Mal
First Day on Earth - Cecil Castellucci   y 680

Mala
For the Win - Cory Doctorow   y 737

Marcus
Pop - Gordon Korman   y 885

Marcy
Sister Mischief - Laura Goode   y 797

Mason
The Lighter Side of Life and Death - C.K. Kelly
Martin   y 924

Matthew
For the Win - Cory Doctorow   y 737

McCartney, Destiny
Beatle Meets Destiny - Gabrielle Williams   y 1166

Mellark, Peeta
Catching Fire - Suzanne Collins   y 699
Mockingjay - Suzanne Collins   y 700

Mercier, Kate
Die for Me - Amy Plum   y 1016

Miguel
We Were Here - Matt de la Pena   y 725

Milena
Winter's End - Jean-Claude Mourlevat   y 956

Milos
Winter's End - Jean-Claude Mourlevat   y 956

Minou, Colleen
Now Playing: Stoner & Spaz II - Ron
Koertge   y 883

Morland, Maia
After the Moment - Garret Freymann-Weyr   y 776

Morrison, Travis
Breathless - Lurlene McDaniel   y 934

Nailer
Ship Breaker: A Novel - Paolo Bacigalupi   y 618

Nick
Once Was Lost - Sara Zarr   y 1196

Nico
Cryer's Cross - Lisa McMann   y 942

Niya
Dragons of Darkness - Antonia Michaelis   y 947

No
No and Me - Delphine De Vigan   y 726

Noah
Response - Paul Volponi   y 1141

Nolan, Lola
Lola and the Boy Next Door - Stephanie Perkins   1007

Oliphant, Anna
Anna and the French Kiss - Stephanie Perkins   y 1008

Ouyang, Dennis
Level Up - Gene Luen Yang   y 1184

Owen
Crash into Me - Albert Borris   y 649
Tangled - Carolyn Mackler   y 916

Pearl
Salt - Maurice Gee   y 783

Piper, Bianca
The DUFF: Designated Ugly Fat Friend - Kody Keplinger   y 871

Popovich, Troy
Pop - Gordon Korman   y 885

Quinn
Hunger - Michael Grant   y 803

Rachel
A World without Heroes - Brandon Mull   c, y 335

Radley, Clara
The Radleys: A Novel - Matt Haig   y 813

Reaves, Wyatt
Why I Fight - J. Adams Oaks   y 987

Rebecca
White Crow - Marcus Sedgwick   y 1069

Reese
Bad Island - Doug TenNapel   y 1123

Regina
The Girl Who Became a Beatle - Greg Taylor   y 1117

Rew, Elizabeth
The Grimm Legacy - Polly Shulman   y 1078

Rockett, Esme
Sister Mischief - Laura Goode   y 797

Rodgers, Jomo
Shooting Star - Fredrick McKissack Jr.   y 941

Rogan
Illyria - Elizabeth Hand   y 820

Rosalba
Hidden Voices: The Orphan Musicians of Venice - Pat Lowery Collins   y 698

Rosalia
No Safe Place - Deborah Ellis   y 757

Rose
The Survival Kit - Donna Freitas   y 775

Rowie
Sister Mischief - Laura Goode   y 797

Ruka
Children of the Sea, Volume 1 - Daisuke Igarashi   y 853

Rush, Wesley
The DUFF: Designated Ugly Fat Friend - Kody Keplinger   y 871

Russell
Hothouse - Chris Lynch   y 911

Ry
As Easy as Falling off the Face of the Earth - Lynne Rae Perkins   c, y 386

Ryoko
Mangaman - Barry Lyga   y 909

Sam
Ostrich Boys - Keith Gray   y 804

Seeger, Jimmy
LIE - Caroline Bock   y 644

Sellers, Kyra "Goth Girl"
Goth Girl Rising - Barry Lyga   y 910

Sergio
Boyfriends with Girlfriends - Alex Sanchez   y 1056

Seth
Tricks - Ellen Hopkins   y 843

Sharpe, Cassel
Red Glove - Holly Black   y 636
White Cat - Holly Black   y 639

Silas
Sisters Red - Jackson Pearce   y 1000

Sinda/Nalia
The False Princess - Ellis O'Neal   y 986

Skye
Tangled - Carolyn Mackler   y 916

Smith, Eva
Jersey Tomatoes Are the Best - Maria Padian   y 997

Sophos
A Conspiracy of Kings - Megan Whalen Turner   y 1134

Stephanie
Taken - Norah McClintock   y 932

Stewart
Recovery Road - Blake Nelson   y 969

Taisin
Huntress - Malinda Lo   y 903

Taylor, Samara "Sam"
Once Was Lost - Sara Zarr   y 1196

Tegan
She Said/She Saw - Norah McClintock   y 931

Temple, Sam
Hunger - Michael Grant   y 803

Tess
Sister Mischief - Laura Goode   y 797

Thompson, Skylar
LIE - Caroline Bock   y 644

Tu Reh
Bamboo People - Mitali Perkins   y 1006

Tuck
Zenith - Julie Bertagna   y 633

Tyler
Moonglass - Jessi Kirby   y 877

Tyrell
Bronxwood - Coe Booth   y 648

Unnamed Character
The Gardener - S.A. Bodeen   y 645

Vi
Ten Things We Did (and Probably Shouldn't Have) - Sarah Mlynowski   y 951

Walcott, Margaret
Wicked Girls: A Novel of the Salem Witch Trials - Stephanie Hemphill   y 834

Walker, Remy
Funny How Things Change - Melissa Wyatt   y 1178

Wate, Ethan
Beautiful Creatures - Kami Garcia   y 780

Whitney
Tricks - Ellen Hopkins   y 843

Wood, Emma
Friend Is Not a Verb - Daniel Ehrenhaft   y 753

Zaksauskas, Gobija
Au Revoir, Crazy European Chick - Joe Schreiber   y 1063

TELEPATH

Kelly, Jenna
Gifted: Better Late than Never - Marilyn Kaye   y 866

TENNIS PLAYER

Lloyd, Henriette "Henry"
Jersey Tomatoes Are the Best - Maria Padian   y 997

TERRORIST

Coyle, Mistress
Monsters of Men - Patrick Ness   y 974

THIEF

Allister, Han
The Demon King - Cinda Williams Chima   y 687

Bishop, Katarina
Heist Society - Ally Carter   y 678

Digger
Liar's Moon - Elizabeth C. Bunce   y 666
Star Crossed - Elizabeth C. Bunce   y 665

Froi
Finnikin of the Rock - Melina Marchetta   y 921

Griffin
Girl, Stolen - April Henry   y 835

Harnett, Ken
Rotters - Daniel Kraus   y 886

McCartney, Destiny
Beatle Meets Destiny - Gabrielle Williams   y 1166

Monahan, Kelleigh
How to Steal a Car - Pete Hautman   y 829

Oliver
The Last Little Blue Envelope - Maureen Johnson   y 861

TIME TRAVELER

Aurora
Gateway - Sharon Shinn   y 1076

Gideon
Ruby Red - Kerstin Gier   y 787

Ogilvie, Oscar
On the Blue Comet - Rosemary Wells   c, y 554

Ombri
Gateway - Sharon Shinn   y 1076

Shepherd, Gwyneth
Ruby Red - Kerstin Gier   y 787

TOURIST

Sione
The Shattering - Karen Healey   *y* 832

TOY

Alligator
Hooray for Amanda and Her Alligator! - Mo Willems   *p, c* 566

Bobo
I Must Have Bobo! - Eileen Rosenthal   *p, c* 427

Jubilee
Me . . . Jane - Patrick McDonnell   *p, c* 314

Knuffle Bunny
Knuffle Bunny Free: An Unexpected Diversion - Mo Willems   *p, c* 563

Panda
Hooray for Amanda and Her Alligator! - Mo Willems   *p, c* 566

TRAINER

Gallagher, Eli
Not That Kind of Girl - Susan Donovan   *y* 740

Schmeling, Max
The Berlin Boxing Club - Robert Sharenow   *y* 1073

TRAVELER

Allbright, Billy
You Don't Know About Me - Brian Meehl   *y* 944

Blackstone, Ginny
The Last Little Blue Envelope - Maureen Johnson   *y* 861

Bly, Nellie
Around the World - Matt Phelan   *c, y* 388

Mac Cumhaill, Finn
Tyger Tyger - Kersten Hamilton   *y* 816

Minli
Where the Mountain Meets the Moon - Grace Lin   *c, y* 281

Slocum, Joshua
Around the World - Matt Phelan   *c, y* 388

Stevens, Thomas
Around the World - Matt Phelan   *c, y* 388

TRICKSTER

Mrs. Pepper
Tricking the Tallyman - Jacqueline Davies   *c* 101

TURTLE

Unnamed Character
The Voyage of Turtle Rex - Kurt Cyrus   *c* 98

TUTOR

Andrews, Jefferson
The Deadly Sister - Eliot Schrefer   *y* 1062

Crowe, Amyus
Death Cloud - Andrew Lane   *y* 890

TWIN

Aaron
The Unwanteds - Lisa McMann   *c, y* 320

Alex
The Unwanteds - Lisa McMann   *c, y* 320

Anna
Dangerous Neighbors - Beth Kephart   *y* 870

Bell, Cricket
Lola and the Boy Next Door - Stephanie Perkins   1007

Christy
The Brothers Story - Katherine Sturtevant   *y* 1112

Dryden, Jane
Dreamland Social Club - Tara Altebrando   605

Dryden, Marcus
Dreamland Social Club - Tara Altebrando   605

Eff
Thirteenth Child - Patricia C. Wrede   *y* 1176

Frankenstein, Konrad
This Dark Endeavor: The Apprenticeship of Victor Frankenstein - Kenneth Oppel   *y* 993

Frankenstein, Victor
This Dark Endeavor: The Apprenticeship of Victor Frankenstein - Kenneth Oppel   *y* 993

Frankie
The Mostly True Story of Jack - Kelly Barnhill   *c, y* 23

Jonathan
Adios, Nirvana - Conrad Wesselhoeft   *y* 1152

Katherine
Dangerous Neighbors - Beth Kephart   *y* 870

Lan
Thirteenth Child - Patricia C. Wrede   *y* 1176

Larkin, Briony
Chime - Franny Billingsley   *y* 634

Lennon, John "Beatle"
Beatle Meets Destiny - Gabrielle Williams   *y* 1166

Ling
Ling and Ting: Not Exactly the Same! - Grace Lin   *p, c* 280

Lugh
Blood Red Road - Moira Young   *y* 1191

McDonald, Coke
Mission Unstoppable - Dan Gutman   *c, y* 183

McDonald, Pepsi
Mission Unstoppable - Dan Gutman   *c, y* 183

Milthorpe, Alice
Prophecy of the Sisters - Michelle Zink   *y* 1199

Milthorpe, Lia
Prophecy of the Sisters - Michelle Zink   *y* 1199

Minkus, Andy
Angel in My Pocket - Ilene Cooper   *c, y* 82

Minkus, Vivi
Angel in My Pocket - Ilene Cooper   *c, y* 82

Miriam
Kindred - Tammar Stein   *y* 1098

Mo
Kindred - Tammar Stein   *y* 1098

Rose
Chime - Franny Billingsley   *y* 634

Saba
Blood Red Road - Moira Young   *y* 1191

Ting
Ling and Ting: Not Exactly the Same! - Grace Lin   *p, c* 280

Tucker
Unearthly - Cynthia Hand   *y* 819

Wendy
The Mostly True Story of Jack - Kelly Barnhill   *c, y* 23

Unearthly - Cynthia Hand   *y* 819

UNCLE

"Aunt" Pete
King of the Screwups - K.L. Going   *y* 794

Blair, Hugh
The Betrayal of Maggie Blair - Elizabeth Laird   *y* 889

Clive
The Mostly True Story of Jack - Kelly Barnhill   *c, y* 23

Gideon
The Romeo and Juliet Code - Phoebe Stone   *c, y* 496

Henry
Wild Things - Clay Carmichael   *c, y* 60

Jacob
Is It Night or Day? - Fern Schumer Chapman   *y* 683

Leach, Squinton
The Mostly True Adventures of Homer P. Figg - Rodman Philbrick   *c, y* 389

Trapp, Lester
The Cardturner: A Novel about a King, a Queen, and a Joker - Louis Sachar   *y* 1053

Uncle Bud
The Doom Machine - Mark Teague   *c, y* 510

Uncle Spade
Why I Fight - J. Adams Oaks   *y* 987

Victor
Emily's Fortune - Phyllis Reynolds Naylor   *c, y* 346

UNEMPLOYED

Richards, Alton
The Cardturner: A Novel about a King, a Queen, and a Joker - Louis Sachar   *y* 1053

VAGRANT

Applegate, Harold
On the Blue Comet - Rosemary Wells   *c, y* 554

Billy
A Small Free Kiss in the Dark - Glenda Millard   *y* 948

Jex
Blood - K.J. Wignall   *y* 1160

VAMPIRE

Crepsley, Larten
Birth of a Killer - Darren Shan   *y* 1072

Dave
The Reformed Vampire Support Group - Catherine Jinks   *y* 859

Eliot, William Stone
Pretty Dead - Francesca Lia Block   *y* 641

Emerson, Charlotte
Pretty Dead - Francesca Lia Block   *y* 641

Nile, Seba
Birth of a Killer - Darren Shan   *y* 1072

Nina
The Reformed Vampire Support Group - Catherine Jinks   *y* 859

Radley, Clara
The Radleys: A Novel - Matt Haig   *y* 813

Radley, Helen
The Radleys: A Novel - Matt Haig   *y* 813

Radley, Peter
The Radleys: A Novel - Matt Haig   *y* 813

Radley, Rowan
The Radleys: A Novel - Matt Haig   y 813
Will
Blood - K.J. Wignall   y 1160

VETERAN

McDermott, Bobby
Badd - Tim Tharp   y 1125
Sixes, Jimmi
The Orange Houses - Paul Griffin   y 810

VILLAIN

Dr. Chaotic
Sidekicks - Jack D. Ferraiolo   y 765
Creep, The
Happenstance Found - P. W. Catanese   c, y 63
Ereskigal
The Call - Michael Grant   c, y 170
Mr. Glueskin
Half World - Hiromi Goto   y 799
Dr. Havoc
Sidekicks - Dan Santat   c, y 441
Kalliovski, Count
The Silver Blade - Sally Gardner   y 158
Loompski, Lenny
The Secret of Zoom - Lynne Jonell   c, y 228
Pale Queen, The
The Call - Michael Grant   c, y 170
Dr. Phoenix
The Dragon's Tooth - N.D. Wilson   c, y 571
Snow, President Coriolanus
Catching Fire - Suzanne Collins   y 699
Mockingjay - Suzanne Collins   y 700

WAITER/WAITRESS

Alyssa
She Loves You, She Loves You Not... - Julie Anne Peters   1011
Katrina
Coffeehouse Angel - Suzanne Selfors   y 1070
Lexie
Pearl - Jo Knowles   y 882

WALRUS

Unnamed Character
Where's Walrus? - Stephen Savage   p, c 444

WARRIOR

Balsa
Moribito II: Guardian of the Darkness - Nahoko Uehashi   c, y 527
Darri
Nightspell - Leah Cypess   y 717
Jack
Blood Red Road - Moira Young   y 1191
Kaede
Huntress - Malinda Lo   y 903
Odysseus
The Odyssey - Gareth Hinds   y 839
Thorson, Barbara
I Kill Giants - Joe Kelly   y 867

WEALTHY

A.J.
Now Playing: Stoner & Spaz II - Ron Koertge   y 883

Astor, John Jacob
The Watch That Ends the Night: Voices from the Titanic - Allan Wolf   y 1171
Elena
The Firefly Letters: A Suffragette's Journey to Cuba - Margarita Engle   y 762
Gray, Penelope
Penny Dreadful - Laurel Snyder   c, y 477
Hartwell, Clayton "The Raptor"
Legacy - Thomas Sniegoski   y 1093
Morrow, Iain
The Eternal Ones - Kirsten Miller   y 949
Mortimer, Frankie
Life: An Exploded Diagram - Mal Peet   y 1003
Ojisan
Tsunami! - Kimiko Kajikawa   p, c 236
Olivia
Clean - Amy Reed   y 1031
Mr. Ozu
The Boy in the Garden - Allen Say   c 446
Spree, Twilly
Scat - Carl Hiaasen   c, y 203
Trapp, Lester
The Cardturner: A Novel about a King, a Queen, and a Joker - Louis Sachar   y 1053

WEREWOLF

Dusic, Ben
Low Red Moon - Ivy Devlin   y 733
Sam
Shiver - Maggie Stiefvater   y 1100
Uberwald, Angua von
I Shall Wear Midnight - Terry Pratchett   y 1021

WIDOW(ER)

Mam
The Christmas Eve Ghost - Shirley Hughes   c 217
Reinstein, Jerri
Stupid Fast: The Summer I Went from a Joke to a Jock - Geoff Herbach   y 836
Mrs. Roux
Stones for My Father - Trilby Kent   y 869

WITCH

Aching, Tiffany
I Shall Wear Midnight - Terry Pratchett   y 1021
Gray Lily
Warped - Maurissa Guibord   y 812
Greene, Rowena
Once a Witch - Carolyn MacCullough   y 915
Greene, Tamsin
Once a Witch - Carolyn MacCullough   y 915
Kate
Plain Kate - Erin Bow   y 650
Mabis
Witchlanders - Lena Coakley   y 695
Mrs. Proust
I Shall Wear Midnight - Terry Pratchett   y 1021
Ogg, Nanny
I Shall Wear Midnight - Terry Pratchett   y 1021
Otokoto, Black Hat
Akata Witch - Nnedi Okorafor   y 988
Smith, Eskarina
I Shall Wear Midnight - Terry Pratchett   y 1021

Weatherwax, Granny
I Shall Wear Midnight - Terry Pratchett   y 1021

WITNESS

James, Gabriel
The Interrogation of Gabriel James - Charlie Price   y 1024
Tegan
She Said/She Saw - Norah McClintock   y 931
Ty
When I Was Joe - Keren David   y 719

WIZARD

Harandron, Melaina
The False Princess - Ellis O'Neal   y 986
Jack
The Familiars - Adam Jay Epstein   c, y 132
Lex
The Runaway Dragon - Kate Coombs   c, y 79
Nevery
Lost - Sarah Prineas   c, y 399
Ostralis, Neomar
The False Princess - Ellis O'Neal   y 986

WOLF

Wilkins, Micah
Liar - Justine Larbalestier   y 891
Wolf, Big
Big Wolf and Little Wolf - Sharon Phillips Denslow   c 108
Wolf, Little
Big Wolf and Little Wolf - Sharon Phillips Denslow   c 108
Wolf, Mama
Big Wolf and Little Wolf - Sharon Phillips Denslow   c 108

WOMAN

Gabby
Angel in My Pocket - Ilene Cooper   c, y 82

WOODSMAN

Angel, Swamp
Dust Devil - Anne Isaacs   c 219

WORKER

Ackroyd, Clem
Life: An Exploded Diagram - Mal Peet   y 1003
Angie
Putting Makeup on the Fat Boy - Bil Wright   y 1177
Annabel
Killer Pizza - Greg Taylor   y 1118
Bump, Phineus
Tricking the Tallyman - Jacqueline Davies   c 101
Cinna
Catching Fire - Suzanne Collins   y 699
Dan
Past Perfect - Leila Sales   y 1055
Duarte, Carlos
Putting Makeup on the Fat Boy - Bil Wright   y 1177
Eli
Between Here and Forever - Elizabeth Scott   y 1065

Ezra
Past Perfect - Leila Sales   y 1055

Fiona
Past Perfect - Leila Sales   y 1055

Gallows, Frank
Ghostopolis - Doug TenNapel   y 1122

Ginger
Vintage Veronica - Erica S. Perl   y 1009

Glaser, Chelsea
Past Perfect - Leila Sales   y 1055

Grel
The Blue Shoe: A Tale of Thievery, Villainy, Sorcery, and Shoes - Roderick Townley   c, y 520

Lacey
Miles from Ordinary - Carol Lynch Williams   y 1164

Lenny
Vintage Veronica - Erica S. Perl   y 1009

Lunch Lady
Lunch Lady and the League of Librarians - Jarrett J. Krosoczka   c 260

O'Rourke, Molly
Sparrow Road - Sheila O'Connor   c, y 985

Otis
Otis - Loren Long   p, c 284

Papa
A New Year's Reunion - Yu Li-Qiong   c 276

Peter
Three Rivers Rising: A Novel of the Johnstown Flood - Jame Richards   y 1040

Sandoval, Marcelo
Marcelo in the Real World - Francisco X. Stork   y 1103

Smoot, Eunice "Bug"
Soul Enchilada - David Macinnis Gill   y 790

Strobe
Killer Pizza - Greg Taylor   y 1118

Tavo
Riding Invisible - Sandra Alonzo   y 604

Walsh, Veronica
Vintage Veronica - Erica S. Perl   y 1009

Zoe
Vintage Veronica - Erica S. Perl   y 1009

WRESTLER

Guardian Angel
Maximilian and the Mystery of the Guardian Angel: A Bilingual Lucha Libre Thriller - Xavier Garza   y 782

WRITER

Bloom, Roxanne "Roxie"
Not That Kind of Girl - Susan Donovan   y 740

Brown, Laura
The Carbon Diaries 2015 - Saci Lloyd   y 901

Calpurnia
The Secret River - Marjorie Kinnan Rawlings   c 407

Dickens, Charles
The Cheshire Cheese Cat: A Dickens of a Tale - Carmen Agra Deedy   c, y 105

Grumply, Ignatius B.
Dying to Meet You - Kate Klise   c, y 254

Hassan
Zahra's Paradise - Amir Amir   y 606

Jonathan
Adios, Nirvana - Conrad Wesselhoeft   y 1152

Mina
My Name Is Mina - David Almond   y 603

Moon, Millicent
Through Her Eyes - Jennifer Archer   y 610

Neruda, Pablo
The Dreamer - Pam Munoz Ryan   c, y 434

Oates, Bobby
Stay - Deb Caletti   y 671

Papa
Waiting for the Magic - Patricia MacLachlan   c 293

Pearl
Pearl verses the World - Sally Murphy   c 338

Perry, Pingpong
Pingpong Perry Experiences How a Book Is Made - Sandy Donovan   c 114

St. Pierre, Sophie
The Red Blazer Girls: The Ring of Rocamadour - Michael D. Beil   y 629

Miss Volker
Dead End in Norvelt - Jack Gantos   c, y 157

YOUNG MAN

Chen Yong
Silver Phoenix: Beyond the Kingdom of Xia - Cindy Pon   y 1017

Dominguez, Bras de Olivias
Daytripper - Fabio Moon   y 952

Ellijah
Wintergirls - Laurie Halse Anderson   y 608

Fossett, Peter
Jefferson's Sons: A Founding Father's Secret Children - Kimberly Brubaker Bradley   c, y 45

Gillen, Ned
Moon over Manifest - Clare Vanderpool   c, y 538

Jack
Calamity Jack - Shannon Hale   c, y 187

Jinx
Moon over Manifest - Clare Vanderpool   c, y 538

Lex
The Runaway Dragon - Kate Coombs   c, y 79

McClellan, Bosten
Stick - Andrew Smith   y 1088

Mizuno
Ooku: The Inner Chambers, Volume 1 - Fumi Yoshinaga   y 1189

Roth
The Knife That Killed Me - Anthony McGowan   c, y 936

Todd
Monsters of Men - Patrick Ness   y 974

Xander
Matched - Ally Condie   y 703

YOUNG WOMAN

Anning, Mary
Remarkable Creatures - Tracy Chevalier   y 686

Cassia
Matched - Ally Condie   y 703

Cranston, Olive
Secrets at Sea - Richard Peck   c, y 383

Crumb, Fever
A Web of Air - Philip Reeve   y 1034

Diido
The Returning - Christine Hinwood   y 840

Fire
Fire - Kristin Cashore   y 679

Fraser, Josey
Mercury - Hope Larson   y 892

Goldberg, Kana
Orchards - Holly Thompson   1127

Grace
Shiver - Maggie Stiefvater   y 1100

Jones, Ida Mae
Flygirl - Sherri L. Smith   y 1090

Jorgensen, Muriel
Crossing Stones - Helen Frost   y 777

McDermott, Ceejay
Badd - Tim Tharp   y 1125

Philpot, Elizabeth
Remarkable Creatures - Tracy Chevalier   y 686

Polydora
King of Ithaka - Tracy Barrett   y 621

Rapunzel
Calamity Jack - Shannon Hale   c, y 187

Rosa
The Running Dream - Wendelin Van Draanen   y 744

Sampson, Deborah
Soldier's Secret: The Story of Deborah Sampson - Sheila Solomon Klass   y 880

Smoot, Eunice "Bug"
Soul Enchilada - David Macinnis Gill   y 790

Viola
Monsters of Men - Patrick Ness   y 974

Virginia
The Queen of Water - Laura Resau   y 1038

ZOO KEEPER

McGee, Amos
A Sick Day for Amos McGee - Philip C. Stead   p, c 489

Unnamed Character
Where's Walrus? - Stephen Savage   p, c 444

Author Index

This index is an alphabetical listing of the authors of books featured in entries and those listed under "Other books by the author" and "Other books you might like." Editors and co-authors are interfiled with author names. For each author, the titles of books written and entry numbers are also provided. Bold numbers indicate a featured main entry; light-face numbers refer to books recommended for further reading.

The Red Blazer Girls: The Vanishing Violin 629

Beitia, Sara
The Last Good Place of Lily Odilon 721

Bell, Anthea
Dragons of Darkness **947**
Ruby Red **787**

Bell, Cece
Bee Wigged 30
Itty Bitty **30** , 55

Bell, Hilari
The Farsala Trilogy 796
The Goblin Gate 816
Shield of Stars 666

Bell, Joanne
Breaking Trail 863

Bell, Julia
Dirty Work 843

Bell, Ted
Nick of Time 185, 311, 493

Belloc, Hilaire
Jim, Who Ran Away from His Nurse, and Was Eaten by a Lion 237

Belton, Robyn
Herbert: The Brave Sea Dog 349

Belton, Sandra
Pictures for Miss Josie 396

Bemis, John Claude
The Nine Pound Hammer 554

Benduhn, Tea
Gravel Queen 902

Bennett, Anina
Boilerplate: History's Mechanical Marvel 1153

Bennett, Kelly
Your Daddy Was Just Like You 231

Benoit, Charles
Relative Danger 630
You **630**

Benson, Amber
Among the Ghosts 186

Bently, Peter
King Jack and the Dragon **31**
A Lark in the Ark 31
Shark in the Dark 31

Benway, Robin
Audrey, Wait! 631, 771
The Extraordinary Secrets of April, May and June **631** , 730

Berenzy, Alix
Sammy: The Classroom Guinea Pig 541

Berger, Carin
Forever Friends 269, 562
The Green Mother Goose 32
The Little Yellow Leaf 528
OK Go **32**

Berger, Samantha
Martha Doesn't Share 95, 563

Bergreen, Laurence
Columbus: The Four Voyages 296

Berk, Josh
The Dark Days of Hamburger Halpin 12, 258, 627, **632** , 810
Guy Langman, Crime Scene Procrastinator 632

Berkeley, Jon
The Hidden Boy 325
Underpants On My Head **192**

Berlin, Eric
The Potato Chip Puzzles: The Puzzling World of Winston Breen 33 , 629
The Puzzling World of Winston Breen 33, 136

Bernatene, Poly
The Shadows **555**

Berne, Jennifer
Manfish 53, 225, 584

Bernier-Grand, Carmen T.
Frida: Viva la Vida! Long Live Life! 360

Berry, Julie
The Amaranth Enchantment 902, 1029

Bertagna, Julie
Exodus 633, 734, 901
Zenith 633

Best, Cari
Goose's Story 447

Bial, Raymond
Cow Towns 370
Rescuing Rover: Saving America's Dogs 352
Tenement: Immigrant Life on the Lower East Side 15

Bickel, Cindy
Chimp Math: Learning about Time from a Baby Chimp 314

Biedrzycki, David
Ace Lacewing, Bug Detective: The Big Swat 544

Biesty, Stephen
Into the Unknown: How Great Explorers Found Their Way by Land, Sea, and Air **428**

Biggs, Brian
Everything Goes: On Land **34** , 492

Billerbeck, Kristin
Perfectly Dateless: A Universally Misunderstood Novel 740

Billingsley, Franny
Chime **634** , 832
The Folk Keeper 634
Well Wished 634

Binding, Tim
Sylvie and the Songman 112

Bingham, Kelly
Shark Girl 744

Birch, Beverly
Rift 950

Birdsall, Jeanne
Flora's Very Windy Day 35 , 94, 150, 244
The Penderwicks: A Summer Tale of Four Sisters, Two Rabbits, and a Very Interesting Boy 205, 317, 422, 477

Birdseye, Tom
Storm Mountain 36 , 841
A Tough Nut to Crack 36

Birney, Betty G.
The Seven Wonders of Sassafras Springs 365

Birney, Betty G.
The World According to Humphrey 545

Birtha, Becky
Lucky Beans 407

Bisaillon, Josee
Benno and the Night of Broken Glass 576

Bishop, Claire Huchet
Twenty and Ten 854

Bishop, Nic
Kakapo Rescue: Saving the World's Strangest Parrot 332
Nic Bishop Frogs 37, 38, 130, 247, 300, 1135
Nic Bishop Lizards 38
Nic Bishop Marsupials 37, 38
Nic Bishop Spiders 37, 38
Nic Bishop: Butterflies and Moths 38 , 130
Nic Bishop: Lizards 37
Nick Bishop: Butterflies and Moths 37

Bjorkman, Lauren
My Invented Life 887, 1161

Black, Holly
Black Heart 636
Curse Workers Series 832
Geektastic: Stories from the Nerd Herd **637**
The Good Neighbors: Kin 639, 909
Ironside 639
Ironside: A Modern Faery's Tale 636, 799
Kith 1100
The Poison Eaters: And Other Stories 639
Red Glove 639, **636**
Tithe 639
Valiant: A Modern Tale of Faerie 636, 639, 1015
Welcome to Bordertown: New Stories and Poems of the Borderlands 635
White Cat 639 , 788, 1148, 636
Zombies vs. Unicorns **638**

Black, Michael Ian
Chicken Cheeks 39
A Pig Parade Is a Terrible Idea 39 , 465, 483
The Purple Kangaroo 39

Blackaby, Susan
Brownie and Groundhog and the February Fox 326
Nest, Nook and Cranny 577

Blackall, Sophie
Are You Awake? **40**
Big Red Lollipop 244
Edwin Speaks Up 40, **495**
Pecan Pie Baby **580**
Spinster Goose: Twisted Rhymes for Naughty Children **556**

Blackman, Malorie
Naughts and Crosses 1002, 1003, 1076

Blackstone, Matt
A Scary Scene in a Scary Movie 897

Blackwood, Gary L.
Around the World in 100 Days 388

Mysterious Messages: A History of Codes and Ciphers 496

Blake, Kendare
Anna Dressed in Blood **640** , 693
Girl of Nightmares 640

Blake, Robert J.
Swift 288
Togo 308

Blank, Jessica
Almost Home 616, 726, 1188

Blazanin, Jan
A and L Do Summer 951

Block, Francesca Lia
Blood Roses 641, 842
The Frenzy 641
House of Dolls 115
I Was a Teenage Fairy 641
Pretty Dead **641**
The Waters and the Wild 641

Block, Francesca Lia
Wasteland 820, 1116

Bloom, Suzanne
A Splendid Friend, Indeed 202, 362
What about Bear? 457

Bloor, Thomas
The Memory Prisoner 723

Blubaugh, Penny
Serendipity Market 842

Blumberg, Rhoda
Shipwrecked!: The True Adventures of a Japanese Boy 1023

Blume, Judy
Are You There God? It's Me, Margaret 511
Soupy Saturdays with the Pain and the Great One 14, 35, 189
Starring Sally J. Freedman as Herself 206
Tales of a Fourth Grade Nothing 285, 298, 531

Blumenthal, Karen
Bootleg: Murder, Moonshine, and the Lawless Years of Prohibition **642**
Let Me Play: The Story of Title IX: The Law That Changed the Future of Girls in America 642
Mr. Sam: How Sam Walton Built Wal-Mart and Became America's Richest Man 642
Six Days in October: The Stock Market Crash of 1929 642

Blundell, Judy
Strings Attached **643**
What I Saw and How I Lied 643, 708, 814

Bluthenthal, Diana Cain
I'm Not Invited? 419

Bo, Ben
The Edge 794
Skullcrack 998

Bock, Caroline
LIE **644**

Bodeen, S.A.
The Compound 645, 708
The Gardener **645**

Boelts, Maribeth
The PS Brothers 507

Author Index

Job Site **71**

Clement-Moore, Rosemary
Hell Week 693, 694
Highway to Hell 693, 657, **694** , 790, 1118
Prom Dates from Hell 693, 694
The Splendor Falls 693, 694
Texas Gothic 694, 640, **693** , 717, 862

Clements, Andrew
Dogku 401
Extra Credit 72, 581, 587
Fear Itself 72
Frindle 72, 113, 138
The Landry News 83
No Talking 587
Things Not Seen 945
Things That Are 835
Troublemaker 72
We the Children 47, **72**
The Whites of Their Eyes 72

Clements, Jonathan
Darwin's Notebook: The Life, Times and Discoveries of Charles Robert Darwin 833

Cline-Ransome, Lesa
Major Taylor, Champion Cyclist 472
Satchel Paige 574
Young Pele: Soccer's First Star 222, 508

Clinton, Catherine
When Harriet Met Sourjourner 390

Clinton, Cathryn
The Calling 972

Club, AV
Inventory: 16 Films Featuring Manic Pixie Dream Girls, 10 Great Songs Nearly Ruined by Saxophone, and 100 More Obsessively Specific Pop-Culture Lists 1200

Clutton-Brock, Juliet
Horse 471

Coakley, Lena
Witchlanders **695**

Cobb, Vicki
I Face the Wind 35, 119

Coben, Harlan
Shelter 814

Coburn, Ann
Glint 816, 947

Cocks, Heather
Spoiled **953**

Coe, Jonathan
The Rotters' Club 646

Coerr, Eleanor
Buffalo Bill and the Pony Express 212

Cofer, Judith Ortiz
Call Me Maria 696
If I Could Fly **696**
An Island Like You: Stories of the Barrio 696

Coffelt, Nancy
Listen 1087

Cohen, Joshua
Leverage **697** , 824

Cohn, Amy
Abraham Lincoln 17

Cohn, Rachel
Nick and Norah's Infinite Playlist 771, 868
You Know Where to Find Me 692, 1010

Colasanti, Susane
Something Like Fate 904, 1066
Waiting for You 624
When It Happens 758

Cole, Babette
Prince Cinders 6, 590

Cole, Brock
Buttons 73
Good Enough to Eat 73, 514
Larky Mavis 73
The Money We'll Save **73**

Cole, Henry
Boycott Blues: How Rosa Parks Inspired a Nation 74
Dear Benjamin Banneker 74
Hold Fast to Dreams 74
Let It Shine: Stories of Black Women Freedom Fighters 74
A Nest for Celeste: A Story about Art, Inspiration, and the Meaning of Home 74 , 383
Sojourner Truth's Step-Stomp Stride 74

Cole, Joanna
Bony-Legs 110
The Magic School Bus and the Climate Challenge 119, 182
The Magic School Bus: Inside a Beehive 345, 480

Colebank, Susan
Black Tuesday 681

Coleman, Michael
On the Run 835

Colfer, Eoin
Airman 1034
Artemis Fowl 1013
Artemis Fowl Series 639

Collard, Sneed B.
The Deep-Sea Floor 225

Collard, Sneed B. III
Flash Point 935

Collier, Bryan
Dave the Potter, Artist, Poet, Slave **204**
Uptown 342

Collier, James Lincoln
My Brother Sam Is Dead 382, 389

Collier, Kristi
Jericho Walls 943

Collins, Pat Lowery
Daughter of Winter 698
The Fattening Hut 698
Hidden Voices: The Orphan Musicians of Venice **698**

Collins, Ross
Doodleday 515
Emily's Fortune **346**

Collins, Suzanne
Catching Fire **699** , 700
Gregor the Overlander 699, 18, 63, 548, 1017
The Hunger Games 418, 527, 599, 699, 700, 908, 956, 968, 1042
Hunger Games Trilogy 1191

Mockingjay 679, 699, **700**

Collins, Yvonne
Love, Inc. 595

Colon, Raul
Once upon a Time: Traditional Latin American Tales/Habia una vez: Cuentos tradicionales latinoamericanos **303**

Coman, Carolyn
The Big House 75, 346
The Memory Bank **75** , 162
Sneaking Suspicions 75
What Jamie Saw 551

Combres, Elisabeth
Broken Memory: A Novel of Rwanda **701**

Comins, Andy
The Frog Scientist **1135**

Compestine, Ying Chang
A Banquet for Hungry Ghosts **702**
Boy Dumplings 76
D Is for Dragon Dance 76
Revolution Is Not a Dinner Party 702
The Runaway Rice Cake 76
The Runaway Wok **76**

Compestine, Ying Chang
The Runaway Rice Cake 276, 340

Condie, Ally
Crossed 703, 1042
Matched **703** , 989

Conly, Jane Leslie
In the Night, on Lanvale Street 77
Murder Afloat **77**

Connelly, Neil
The Miracle Stealer **704**
St. Michael's Scales 704

Conner, Daniel
The Tempest (Graphic Shakespeare) 761

Connolly, John
The Book of Lost Things 1078

Connor, Leslie
Crunch 78 , 486
Waiting for Normal 78

Conrad, Lauren
Sweet Little Lies: An L.A. Candy Novel 953

Conrad, Pam
Call Me Ahnighito 458
Stonewords: A Ghost Story 115
Taking the Ferry Home 818

Cook, Kristi
Haven 825

Cook, Michelle
Our Children Can Soar: A Celebration of Rosa, Barack, and the Pioneers of Change 214

Cooke, Trish
So Much 272

Coombs, Kate
The Runaway Dragon **79**
The Runaway Princess 79

Cooney, Barbara
Eleanor 404

Cooney, Caroline B.
If the Witness Lied 1002

Cooney, Caroline B.
The Terrorist 899

Cooper, Elisha
Ballpark 81
Beach 81, 353, 568
Bear Dreams 80
Beaver Is Lost 80 , 159, 397
Building 81
Farm **81**
A Good Night Walk 80
Magic Thinks Big 80, 354

Cooper, Floyd
Back of the Bus **413**
A Beach Tail **568**
Coming Home: From the Life of Langston Hughes 215
Ruth and the Green Book **403**
These Hands **304**

Cooper, Ilene
Angel in My Pocket **82**
Jake's Best Thumb 128
Sam I Am 82

Cooper, Michelle
A Brief History of Montmaray 705, **706** , 741, 959, 1195
The FitzOsbornes in Exile 706, **705**

Cooper, Susan
King of Shadows 97, 185, 490
The Magician's Boy 281
Victory 267, 490, 554

Corbett, Sue
Free Baseball 83
The Last Newspaper Boy in America 78, **83**

Cordell, Matthew
Justin Case: School, Drool, and Other Daily Disasters **531**
Like Pickle Juice on a Cookie **494**

Cordova, Amy
Fiesta Babies **502**

Cormier, Robert
The Chocolate War 697
The Rag and Bone Shop 931, 1024
Tenderness: A Novel 932

Cornell, Kevin
The Trouble with Chickens **92**

Cornish, D.M.
Factotum **707**
Foundling 707, 1118, 1183
Lamplighter 657, 707, 1176
Monster Blood Tattoo series 838, 1181

Cornwell, Autumn
Carpe Diem 1096, 1140

Corrigan, Eireann
Accomplice 596, **708**
Ordinary Ghosts 708
Splintering 708
You Remind Me of You: A Poetry Memoir 708

Cortez, Sarah
Windows into My World: Latino Youths Write Their Lives 709
You Don't Have a Clue: Latino Mystery Stories for Teens **709**

Cotler, Steve
Cheesie Mack Is Not a Genius or Anything 47, 507

Author Index

Author Index

Q

R

Author Index

Author Index

Illustrator Index

This index lists the illustrators of the featured titles. Illustrators are listed alphabetically, followed by the title, with author names, age-level code(s) and entry numbers also included. The age-level codes are as follows: *p* : ages 1-4, *c* : ages 5-10, *y* : ages 11-18.

Illustrator Index

Uncover & Discover! - Roxie
Munro   *p, c* 256

Munsinger, Lynn
Tacky Goes to Camp - Helen
Lester   *c* 204

Muth, Jon J.
City Dog, Country Frog - Mo
Willems   *p, c* 415

Myers, Christopher
*We Are America: A Tribute from the
Heart* - Walter Dean
Myers   *c, y* 259

Myrick, Leland
Feynman - Jim Ottaviani   *y* 2

N

Neal, Christopher Silas
Over and Under the Snow - Kate
Messner   *c* 248

Niimura, J. M. Milliken
I Kill Giants - Joe Kelly   *y* 711

Nolan, Dennis
Sea of Dreams - Dennis
Nolan   *p, c* 271

Nyeu, Tao
Bunny Days - Tao Nyeu   *p, c* 274

O

O'Brien, Patrick
You Are the First Kid on Mars -
Patrick O'Brien   *c, y* 275

O'Malley, Kevin
Animal Crackers Fly the Coop -
Kevin O'Malley   *p, c* 279

Onoda, Yuta
Wild Wings - Gill Lewis   *c, y* 206

Ostow, David
*So Punk Rock (and Other Ways to
Disappoint Your Mother)* - Micol
Ostow   *y* 838

Oxenbury, Helen
King Jack and the Dragon - Peter
Bently   *p, c* 31
There's Going to Be a Baby - John
Burningham   *p, c* 51

P

Palacios, Sara
*Marisol McDonald Doesn't
Match/Marisol McDonald no com-
bina* - Monica Brown   *c* 44

Parker, Buzz
Emily the Strange: The Lost Days -
Jessica Gruner   *y* 656

Parra, John
Gracias Thanks - Pat
Mora   *p, c* 254

Paschkis, Julie
*Summer Birds: The Butterflies of
Maria Merian* - Margarita
Engle   *c* 101

Patricelli, Leslie
Higher! Higher! - Leslie
Patricelli   *p, c* 291

Pedersen, Janet
In Memory of Gorfman T. Frog -
Gail Donovan   *c* 91

Peirce, Lincoln
Big Nate: In a Class by Himself -
Lincoln Peirce   *c, y* 294

Persiani, Tony
*The Day-Glo Brothers: The True
Story of Bob and Joe Switzer's
Bright Ideas and Brand-New Col-
ors* - Chris Barton   *c, y* 26

Pham, LeUyen
*Alvin Ho: Allergic to Camping, Hik-
ing, and Other Natural Disasters*
- Lenore Look   *c* 215

Pham, Thien
Level Up - Gene Luen
Yang   *y* 1007

Phelan, Matt
Around the World - Matt
Phelan   *c, y* 297
*Big George: How a Shy Boy Became
President Washington* - Anne
Rockwell   *c* 320
Flora's Very Windy Day - Jeanne
Birdsall   *c* 34
The Storm in the Barn - Matt
Phelan   *c, y* 296
Two of a Kind - Jacqui
Robbins   *c* 318

Pinkney, Brian
*Sit-In: How Four Friends Stood Up
by Sitting Down* - Andrea Davis
Pinkney   *p, c* 299

Pinkney, Jerry
*Sweethearts of Rhythm: The Story of
the Greatest All-Girl Swing Band
in the World* - Marilyn
Nelson   *y* 814
Twinkle, Twinkle, Little Star - Jerry
Pinkney   *p, c* 300

Polacco, Patricia
Junkyard Wonders - Patricia
Polacco   *c, y* 301

Portis, Antoinette
A Penguin Story - Antoinette
Portis   *p, c* 302

Prange, Beckie
*Ubiquitous: Celebrating Nature's
Survivors* - Joyce
Sidman   *c, y* 347

Price, Nick
*Tumtum and Nutmeg: Adventures be-
yond Nutmouse Hall* - Emily
Bearn   *c, y* 29

Proch, Gregory
*How to Get Rich on a Texas Cattle
Drive* - Tod Olson   *c, y* 282
*How to Get Rich on a Texas Cattle
Drive: In Which I Tell the Honest
Truth about Rampaging Rustlers,
Stampeding Steers and Other
Fateful Hazards on the Wild Chi-
sholm Trail* - Tod
Olson   *c, y* 282

Prosek, James
Bird, Butterfly, Eel - James
Prosek   *c* 304

Purvis, Leland
Resistance: Book 1 - Carla
Jablonski   *y* 698

R

Raschka, Chris
A Foot In the Mouth - Paul B.
Janeczko   *c, y* 170
Little Black Crow - Chris
Raschka   *p, c* 307

Ray, Deborah Kogan
*Dinosaur Mountain: Digging into the
Jurassic Age* - Deborah Kogan
Ray   *c* 308

Rayner, Catherine
Posy - Linda Newbery   *p, c* 268

Rayyan, Omar
Nightshade City - Hilary
Wagner   *c, y* 403

Renier, Aaron
The Unsinkable Walker Bean -
Aaron Renier   *c, y* 311

Rex, Adam
*The Case of the Case of Mistaken
Identity* - Mac Barnett   *c, y* 24
*The Case of the Case of Mistaken
Identity: The Brixton Brothers,
Book 1* - Mac Barnett   *c, y* 24

Reynolds, Peter
Guyku: A Year of Haiku for Boys -
Bob Raczka   *c* 305

Roberts, David
The Dunderheads - Paul
Fleischman   *c, y* 108

Robinson, Tim
*Which Way to the Wild West?: Every-
thing Your Schoolbooks Didn't
Tell You about Westward Expansion* - Steve Sheinkin   *c, y* 345

Rodriguez, Beatrice
The Chicken Thief - Beatrice
Rodriguez   *p, c* 321

Rogers, Jacqueline
Calvin Coconut: Trouble Magnet -
Graham Salisbury   *c* 329

Roth, R.G.
Busing Brewster - Richard
Michelson   *c* 250

Roth, Susan L.
*The Mangrove Tree: Planting Trees
to Feed Families* - Cindy
Trumbore   *c* 389

Ruell, Karen Gray
*The Grand Mosque of Paris: A Story
of How Muslims Rescued Jews
During the Holocaust* - Karen
Gray Ruell   *c, y* 323

Rumford, James
Rain School - James
Rumford   *p, c* 324

Ruth, Greg
City of Orphans - Avi   *c, y* 17
The Wild - Christopher
Golden   *y* 639

S

Santat, Dan
The Adventures of Nanny Piggins -
R.A. Spratt   *c, y* 363
Bobby versus Girls (Accidentally) -
Lisa Yee   *c, y* 434

Sarcone-Roach, Julia
Subway Story - Julia
Sarcone-Roach   *c* 331

Sattler, Jennifer
Pig Kahuna - Jennifer
Sattler   *p, c* 332

Say, Allen
The Boy in the Garden - Allen
Say   *c* 334
Drawing from Memory - Allen
Say   *c, y* 333

Scharschmidt, Sherry
Tuck Me In - Dean
Hacohen   *p, c* 143

Schlossberg, Elisabeth
Adios, Tricycle - Susan Middleton
Elya   *p, c* 100

Schneider, Josh
Tales for Very Picky Eaters - Josh
Schneider   *c* 338

Schoenherr, Ian
The Apothecary - Maile
Meloy   *y* 788

Seeger, Laura Vaccaro
What If? - Laura Vaccaro
Seeger   *p, c* 342

Sendak, Maurice
Bumble-Ardy - Maurice
Sendak   *p, c* 343

Shepperson, Rob
The Memory Bank - Carolyn
Coman   *c, y* 65

Sis, Peter
The Dreamer - Pam Munoz
Ryan   *c, y* 326

Sisson, Stephanie Roth
*Princess Posey and the First Grade
Parade* - Stephanie
Greene   *c* 137

Small, David
Stitches: A Memoir - David
Small   *y* 917

Smith, Jeff
Little Mouse Gets Ready - Jeff
Smith   *p, c* 355

Smith, Lane
It's a Book - Lane Smith   *c* 356
Lulu and the Brontosaurus - Judith
Viorst   *p, c* 400

Soo, Kean
Jellaby: Monster in the City - Kean
Soo   *c, y* 359

Spires, Ashley
Binky the Space Cat - Ashley
Spires   *c* 362

Spivey Gilchrist, Jan
*The Great Migration: Journey to the
North* - Eloise
Greenfield   *c* 138

Stead, Erin E.
A Sick Day for Amos McGee -
Philip C. Stead   *p, c* 367

Stein, David Ezra
Interrupting Chicken - David Ezra Stein   *c* 368

Stower, Adam
We the Children - Andrew Clements   *c, y* 62

Studio, Red Nose
Here Comes the Garbage Barge - Jonah Winter   *c* 424

Sturm, James
Adventures in Cartooning: How to Turn Your Doodles into Comics - James Sturm   *c, y* 370

Sweet, Melissa
Balloons over Broadway: The True Story of the Puppeteer of Macy's Parade - Melissa Sweet   *p, c* 371
Rubia and the Three Osos - Susan Middleton Elya   *p, c* 99

T

Tafuri, Nancy
All Kinds of Kisses - Nancy Tafuri   *p, c* 373

Talbott, Hudson
River of Dreams: The Story of the Hudson River - Hudson Talbot   *c, y* 374

Tan, Shaun
Lost and Found - Shaun Tan   *c, y* 375

Tanaka, Yoko
The Magician's Elephant - Kate DiCamillo   *c, y* 90

Tashjian, Jake
My Life as a Book - Janet Tashjian   *c, y* 376

TenNapel, Doug
Ghostopolis - Doug TenNapel   *y* 956

Thompson, Carol
Mommy, Mama and Me - Leslea Newman   *p, c* 270
Thunder-Boomer! - Shutta Crum   *c* 79

Thompson, Craig
Habibi - Craig Thompson   *y* 960

Thompson, Keith
Behemoth - Scott Westerfeld   *y* 983
Leviathan - Scott Westerfeld   *y* 982

Thomson, Bill
Chalk - Bill Thomson   *c* 381

Tobia, Lauren
Anna Hibiscus - Atinuke   *c* 16

Tonatiuh, Duncan
Dear Primo: A Letter to My Cousin - Duncan Tonatiuh   *c* 383

Townsend, Michael
Kit Feeny: On the Move - Michael Townsend   *c* 386

V

Varon, Sara
Bake Sale - Sara Varon   *c, y* 397

Velasquez, Eric
Grandma's Gift - Eric Velasquez   *c* 398

Villarrubia, Jose
The Lightning Thief: The Graphic Novel - Rick Riordan   *c, y* 881

Vitale, Stefano
Pond Circle - Betsy Franco   *c* 116

Voake, Charlotte
Insect Detective - Steve Voake   *c* 401

W

Waber, Paulis
Lyle Walks the Dogs: A Counting Book - Bernard Waber   *p, c* 402

Weisner, David
Art and Max - David Wiesner   *c* 412

Wiesner, David
Art and Max - David Wiesner   *c* 412

Wildish, Lee
Thomas and the Dragon Queen - Shutta Crum   *c* 80

Willems, Mo
Hooray for Amanda and Her Alligator! - Mo Willems   *p, c* 417
I Broke My Trunk! - Mo Willems   *p, c* 418
Knuffle Bunny Free: An Unexpected Diversion - Mo Willems   *p, c* 414

Naked Mole Rat Gets Dressed - Mo Willems   *p, c* 416

Winter, Jeanette
Biblioburro: A True Story from Colombia - Jeanette Winter   *c* 423

Wright, Eric
Frankie Pickle and the Closet of Doom - Eric Wright   *c* 431

Y

Yang, Gene Luen
The Eternal Smile - Gene Luen Yang   *y* 1008

Yates, Louise
Dog Loves Books - Louise Yates   *p, c* 433

Yelchin, Eugene
Won-Ton: A Cat Tale Told in Haiku - Lee Wardlaw   *c* 405

Yoshinaga, Fumi
Ooku: The Inner Chambers, Volume 1 - Fumi Yoshinaga   *y* 1010
Ooku: The Inner Chambers, volumes 1 & 2 - Fumi Yoshinaga   *y* 1010

Young, Ed
Tsunami! - Kimiko Kajikawa   *p, c* 181

Yue, Stephanie
Hamster and Cheese - Colleen A.F. Venable   *c* 399

Z

Zelinsky, Paul O.
Dust Devil - Anne Isaacs   *c* 168

Title Index

This index alphabetically lists all titles featured in entries and those listed under "Other books by the author" and "Other books you might like." Each title is followed by the author's name and the number of the entry of that title. Bold numbers indicate featured main entries; light-face numbers refer to books recommended for further reading.

Title Index

Title Index

Title Index

I

Title Index

Title Index

Title Index

P

Title Index

Title Index

Title Index